GENESIS 1-11

GENESIS 1-11

A Commentary

Translated by
John J. Scullion S.J.

AUGSBURG PUBLISHING HOUSE
MINNEAPOLIS

GENESIS 1-11: A Commentary

First published 1974 by Neukirchener Verlag, Neukirchen-Vluyn
in the Biblischer Kommentar Series.

First published in English 1984 by Augsburg Publishing House in the USA
and in Great Britain by SPCK, Holy Trinity Church, Marylebone Road
London NW1 4DU

Printed in the United States of America

Reprinted, February 1987

British Library Cataloguing in Publication Data
Westermann, Claus
Genesis 1-11
1. Bible, O.T. Genesis I-XI — Commentaries
I. Title   II. Genesis (Kapitel 1-11). *English*
222'. 1107   BS1235.3
ISBN 0-281-04033-8 (SPCK)
ISBN 0-8066-1962-7 (Augsburg)
Library of Congress Catalog Card No. 82-072655

Contents

Contents

Preface

This first volume, which covers the primeval story, Genesis 1-11, is to be followed by a second covering the patriarchal story, Genesis 12-50. The very material itself, and not just technical reasons, requires that the commentary appear in two relatively independent parts. As I worked on Genesis 1-11 it became more and more evident that these chapters, the biblical entrance antiphon, have a significance for the Bible as a whole which can only be fully appreciated when the words "in the beginning" are allowed their proper resonance. What emerges is that the beginning of the Bible is concerned not just with "Creation and Fall"; Genesis 1-11 forms a whole in which each individual section has its own contribution to make to the unity.

I would add a further note to this bulky volume. No large scholarly commentary on Genesis has appeared in German since those of Hermann Gunkel (1922) and Otto Procksch (1924). There has however been a flood of literature on Genesis 1-11 and a number of important, though short, and popular expositions like those of G. von Rad and W. Zimmerli. The present situation however demands a thorough survey and account of all the literature on Genesis — of the works of Protestant, Catholic and Jewish scholars, as well as the contributions of the pertinent secular disciplines. The bibliographies, general and particular, present this.

It would have been impossible for me to carry out this vast survey alone. I thank all who have worked at the Genesis Research Seminar, in particular my present assistants, Dr. R. Albertz, Dr. E. Ruprecht, Mr. R. Ficker. I thank especially my wife who worked assiduously at my side from one fascicule to the next, shared many a lively discussion and made many helpful suggestions.

My colleague at Heidelberg, Professor H.W. Wolff, co-editor of the series, showed great concern and patience with my commentary and contributed corrections as well as much useful advice. A word of thanks is due also to the Neukirchen publishing house, first, for the invitation to take part in the annual working-group meetings of those engaged in contributing to the series, which were always stimulating; second, for the generous way in which the volume has been produced; it was a very demanding task.

Finally I would like to record the deep joy I have experienced in being able to devote part of my active life in peace and health to so important a part of the Bible, and in the company of so fine a working group. Genesis 1-11 has been a living word to me during these years. It is my wish that the contribution of this commentary be that the biblical story of primeval event with its comprehensive God-talk about the world and humankind may continue effectively into the future.

Heidelberg   CLAUS WESTERMANN

Translator's Preface

The translator performs for others, at the price of dispersal and relative devaluation, a task no longer necessary or immediate to himself. But there is also a proprietary impulse. It is only when he "brings home" the simulacrum of the original, when he recrosses the divide of language and community, that he feels himself in authentic possession of his source. Safely back he can, as an individual, discard his own translation. The original is now peculiarly his. . . . After completing his work, the genuine translator is *en fausse situation*. He is in part stranger to the original which his translation has, in varying degrees, adulterated, diminished, exploited or betrayed through improvement. . . .

George Steiner, *After Babel.*
Aspects of Language and Translation.
(Oxford University Press, 1975, p. 380).

Professor Claus Westermann of the University of Heidelberg is well known to Old Testament scholars and students in the English speaking world. A number of his important books have already been translated. He has visited the United States of America several times and was made an honorary member of the Society of Biblical Literature. In 1977 he was honoured by the British Academy with the Burkitt Medal for Biblical Studies.

For almost twenty-five years Professor Westermann has been engaged in a commentary on the book of Genesis. Under his direction a Genesis-Research Institute was set up within the Theological Faculty of the University of Heidelberg in which a comprehensive bibliography was assembled. He brought this monumental commentary to a conclusion with the publication of the last fascicle on the Joseph story in 1982. The work has been published in three volumes in *Biblischer Kommentar, Altes Testament,* by Neukirchen Verlag, Neukirchen-Vluyn: *Genesis 1-11* (1/1), *Genesis 12-36* (1/2), *Genesis 37-50* (1/3).

It has been my pleasure to spend two semesters at Heidelberg where I have profited from Professor Westermann's scholarship and discussed the translation with him.

The translation of *Genesis 1-11* (the translation of the other two volumes is in progress) was done in "spare time" over a period of three years in the midst of a busy and regular academic and administrative program. The following points should be noted:

1. the translation of the Hebrew text of Genesis is deliberately rather literal, but attempts in every case to convey Professor Westermann's nuances.

2. the spelling of all personal, proper and place names in the Bible follows the Revised Standard Version.

3. citations from other parts of the Bible follow the RSV unless otherwise indicated.

4. abbreviations of the biblical books are those of the RSV, Common Bible.

5. the German word *Sage* is regularly rendered by "story", not by "saga".

6. Professor Westermann often uses the word *Geschehensbogen* to describe the movement of a narrative. As he wrote to me, *ein Geschehensbogen* "is like the arch of a bridge which spans the whole from beginning to end. Likewise the narrative arch spans an event from beginning to end and makes it into a self-contained whole." (Letter, 23.1.80). My translation of *Geschehensbogen* varies; sometimes it is "narrative span (arch)", sometimes a paraphrase according to context.

As this translation is printed and published jointly in the United States of America, convention requires that the word "man" be restricted to the male of the species and that "mankind" yield to "humankind". (It is not the place here to argue my conviction that "man" without the article — not "men" — for the most part and "mankind" virtually always are neutral terms). This has entailed the frequent replacement of "man" and "mankind" by "human beings", "persons", "people", "humanity", "humankind", "human race", and so on. The editing has been well done.

I compliment the editors of Augsburg Publishing House on their presentation, co-operation and understanding.

I thank four of my younger Jesuit brethren, Chris Horvat, Dan Madigan, Stephen Astill and Robin Koning who prepared the Indexes. They gave of their time and talents with the greatest good will.

It remains to thank Mrs. Leonie Hudson, the incomparable secretary of Jesuit Theological College, Parkville, who typed the whole translation twice, including the lengthy bibliographies. With never failing good humour and a patience rivalling that of Job she produced a manuscript which drew the admiration of both of the joint publishers, Augsburg, Minneapolis, and S.P.C.K., London. I also thank Shirley Sullivan, formerly of the Library Staff of Ormond College, for her assistance in reading the galleys.

JOHN J. SCULLION S.J.,
Newman College
(University of Melbourne)
887 Swanston Street,
Parkville, Vic. 3052

Introduction to the Story
of the Primeval Events

1. The Story of Primeval Events in the Pentateuch and its Prehistory

The biblical story of the primeval events hands down what has been said about the beginnings of the world and of humanity in an unbroken line from antiquity to modern times. It is in this above all that its significance lies. The biblical accounts of creation have had an uninterrupted audience from the time when the Yahwist planned his work in the 10th-9th century B.C. until the present day. The circles which handed them down pondered on them again and again. Whenever a new world view was sketched, what was said about the beginning was almost always resumed: in Deutero-Isaiah, in the priestly syntheses, in Paul and John in the New Testament, in Marcion and in the great confessions of the universal Church in the anti-Marcionite campaign, in the scholastic systems of the Middle Ages and in the Reformation, in the philosophical system of the West right up to the radical attack on the creation story in the assertions of the champions of evolution. The debate about the beginnings of the world and of humankind has long since passed from the field of religion to the field of science, and the Christian Churches of the last generations have renounced their claims to enter the lists in the scientific controversies. Nevertheless, there has been no break in that line of tradition which stretches back to the early stages of the Old Testament. The Christian Churches throughout the world continue in their formal worship to acknowledge their belief in God, the creator of heaven and earth, and every attempt to detach faith in the creator from faith in Christ has miscarried.

The Christian faith does not take its stand on an event at the beginning, but on an event in the "middle of the time"; but because it looks to the whole, it must speak of the beginning. If Jesus Christ came as the savior of all humanity, then his coming in "the middle of the time" must have something to do with the beginning. The Pauline and Johannine theologies alike are at pains to relate the event "in the middle" with the event at the beginning.

The Yahwistic and Priestly syntheses of the Old Testament, both of which begin with an account of creation, have already done this. The intention of each of these works in setting the story of primeval events before the historical section proper was to relate an event "in the middle" with an event at the beginning.

1

There is a further parallel: just as the theological thinking of early Christianity had to rely on an already existing pre-Christian tradition, namely the Old Testament, so the theological thinking of Israel had to rely on traditions both older than Israel and from outside Israel to relate the beginnings with the event "in the middle." A pre-Christian tradition penetrates the Christian confession of faith in God the creator; traditions which preceded Israel and from outside Israel penetrate what Israel has to say about God the creator, Yahweh, the God of Israel.

The story of primeval events should be thought of primarily as an element in the structure of the Pentateuch. The central part of the Pentateuch tells the story of the rescue at the Reed Sea, Ex 1-18. This event was the basis of the history of a people. It gave both parts of the book of Genesis the character of an introduction. Both the story of primeval events, Gen 1-11, and the stories of the patriarchs, Gen 12-50, are placed before the central part like two concentric circles. The relation of each circle to the central part is different. Hence, their introductory functions are different. While the stories of the patriarchs, Gen 12-50, present the history of Israel before it became a people, the story of the primeval events has a far wider horizon. It gives the events which take place in the middle of the Pentateuch a much wider horizon, extending them to world events in the broadest sense of the word. The different functions of these introductory sections become very clear in the summary confessions of faith which draw together the tradition developed in the Pentateuch, Deut 26:5; Josh 24:2-4. The stories of the patriarchs play their introductory role, while there is no mention at all of the story of primeval events.

There are however other writings in the Old Testament which draw together God's activity as a whole, from his saving action in the middle of the Pentateuch to those distant beginnings of his work of which the story of primeval events speaks: these are the hymns of the praise of God which describe at once both God's action and what God is. The hymn, polarizing the praise of God in his majesty and God stooping to speak to his creation, sweeps across the whole order from creation to the rescue of Israel, e.g., Pss 33; 136. The hymn of descriptive praise, in contrast to the confessions of faith, does not intend to describe chronological sequence or historical succession, but rather the all-embracing richness of God's activity. The story of primeval events is related to the whole in a different way from the stories of the patriarchs.

Accordingly, chs. 1-11 of Genesis must be regarded as a separate element of the Pentateuch, that is, as a relatively self-contained unity, and not primarily as a part of "Genesis." It is a relatively late component. The point of departure of our exegesis then cannot be those literary types whose form and content have been discovered in Gen 12-50. Such cannot be imposed on chs. 1-11. Nor can we without more ado apply the theological plan which draws together the patriarchal cycle to the story of primeval events. We must recognize this story as a distinct unity, as a separate element of the Pentateuch, and take it as our starting point.

Furthermore, the approach to the problem of Gen 1-11 as a whole had been frustrated and shackled by two presuppositions which had been passed on uncritically from one generation to another. The first was the presumption that the two decisive passages which colored the whole of the primeval story were Gen 1 and 3. A tradition of more than a thousand years had imposed itself; under this influence, and for the most part quite unconsciously, one summed up the basic content of the primeval story under the heading "Creation and Fall." The main reason for this was that from the primeval story into the New Testament, and from the New Testament into the teachings of the Christian Churches, it was creation and fall that prevailed. This emphasis on Gen 1 and 3 or 1-3 shows itself in the titles of books, such as Dietrich Bonhoeffer's *Creation and Fall* (1937; new impression 1955) or of articles, "The Creation and Fall" (H. Richards, *Scripture* 8 [1956] 109-115), as well as in those parts of many larger treatises which deal with the primeval story, and whose theological understanding of it is determined entirely, or almost entirely, by Gen 1-3.

The immediate consequence of this limitation is a diminution, however unconscious, of the intrinsic value of Gen 4-11, whose function is reduced to filling out or intensifying what has been said already. When chs. 1-3 are isolated in this way there results an understanding of them which is quite different from the purpose of the primeval story as a whole. The title "The Fall" given to Gen 3 is an indication of this attitude. But more of this later.

The second presupposition is connected closely with the first. The one-sided emphasis on Gen 1-3 has already decided that the genealogies of chs. 1-11 can have no particular significance, in any case, no determining theological significance. The commentaries deal very thoroughly with the names listed in these genealogies; but there is scarcely ever any discussion of the meaning of the genealogies for the whole. To devalue implicitly the genealogies or to leave them aside must have far-reaching effects on one's final understanding of and judgment on the primeval story.

Leaving aside these two traditional presuppositions, one must take the text just as it stands as the starting point of one's enquiry into its meaning as a whole. Two different types of writing strike us immediately; we will call them provisionally narrative and numerative. They are almost equal in extent. This is the only place in the Old Testament where genealogies and narratives are put together in such a way. It is this that gives the primeval story its unique character.

The origin of the world and of humankind is presented in such a way that a succession of generations stretches from creation to Abraham. A series of happenings is set into these genealogies, sometimes being merely mentioned, sometimes being narrated in detail. The genealogies trace the long succession of centuries from Adam to Abraham as well as the gradual expansion over the surface of the earth. They move from the first human pair to the furthest boundaries of the inhabited world as it was known at the time. The narratives which have been inserted deal either with individual human beings, with groups or with the whole of humanity.

This description of the whole which is part of the primeval story is common to the two literary traditions in which Gen 1-11 has been handed down to us. The Redactor (R) has altered nothing. If we compare the contents of J (Yahwist) and P (Priestly Tradition), it appears at first glance that P has a preponderance of numerative and J of narrative material. The story of the Flood is the only narrative where J and P are mingled together. It is both significant and understandable that only in Gen 6-9 did R shape one narrative out of the two that lay before him. And so there arises a third form of tradition in which narrative and numerative elements balance each other. (I leave aside here R's other redactional interventions.)

The very content of the text then forces the exegete to devote proportionate attention to both constituent parts of the primeval story. We can say then that an exegesis which lays a one-sided emphasis on the narratives, (or which emphasizes one-sidedly Gen 1-3), does not do justice to all three forms of tradition. We will only understand what the primeval story has to say to us when we take as our starting point each constituent part in its entirety.

The Prehistory of the Reflection on Creation and Primeval Times. We have seen above that the story of primeval events, viewed from the middle of the Pentateuch, forms the outermost circle; this is extremely important for the exegesis. The account of the Exodus is the account of a happening that took place once only; there was a series of events which ran their own course over a definite period of time and which concerned a particular group of people. This "once and for all" is there too in Gen 12-50, but in a much looser way. In Gen 1-11 it has been completely resolved. These chapters look to the universal; they include all humanity; and primeval time in which all takes place cannot be fixed on the calendar. This is the reason why there is little room for comparing the unique happenings "in the middle" with similar traditions from elsewhere; there is more ground for comparing the stories of the patriarchs with such traditions. But when it comes to the universal happening, to the happening that includes all humankind, then a comparison with similar traditions is of great importance and is a necessary pre-requisite for exegesis.

It is no mere chance that there are so many parallels to Gen 1-11 in the history of religions — more or less similar descriptions of creation, of the flood, as well as of other events; it is rather because of the very content of this part of the Bible, which is so deeply imbedded in the history of religions or the world. All religions are concerned in some way or another with a primeval happening, like Gen 1-11.

When we turn to the prehistory of what the Bible has to say about creation and primeval time, we are struck by the vast richness of stories in this area. They all share a common interest in the origins of our present world. There are stories of creation of every kind, of sin or misdemeanor which have as their consequence deficiencies and limitations in human life; there are stories of the origin of death, of great universal catastrophies, of difference of languages and of the scattering of the nations; stories too of the most important cultural achievements, and of human alienation from God or the gods. Other motits could be added, others unravelled; there are so many links between them and they occur with the most diverse colorings. Nevertheless one can be certain that there was a definite circle of motifs at hand.

It is from what is common to all these stories that we recognize that all of them are concerned with the origin of the present state of the world. It is not enough to designate them as "story" or "myth", because the history of what is said about creation and primeval time covers such a long period and includes such a wide range of cultures which make use of such different forms of speech. They range from tales, or primitive stories, through myth to mythical epic, as in Babylon, and to many other forms. Our present very extensive knowledge of the literature and stories about creation and primeval time does not allow us to draw a sharp line of distinction between the high cultures and the primitive cultures and then to exclude the latter from the prehistory of the bibilical story of primeval events. The discovery of the Sumerian myths has made us familiar with a stage in the development of the great Babylonian epics when the individual episodes were still independent stories (e.g., the flood in the Gilgamesh epic). The Sumerian myths of primeval time show a great number of characteristics which point back to an earlier stage and which occur quite often in the corresponding stories of the primitive cultures. The biblical story, for example, allows the snake to speak and takes it for granted. This points clearly to a pre-mythical stage. When one reflects that these stories are spread over the whole world, and that they are one of the most important elements which link the primitive and the high cultures, then one cannot pass them over when surveying the material at hand in the biblical stories.

It is not without reason and not at all arbitrary that the stories of primeval time are arranged according to the themes of Gen 1-11 in the surveys of primitive religion. J. P. Frazer in his book, *Folklore in the Old Testament* (abridged edition, London 1923) has drawn together the stories of primeval time according to the main themes of Gen 1-11. W. Wundt in his *Völkerpsychologie* (VI. Band, Mythus und Religion, 1915, 5. Kosmogonishe und theogonische Mythen 268ff. und 6. Weltuntergangsmythen 290ff.), refers constantly to the primeval biblical themes. H. Baumann in *Schöpfung und Urzeit des Menschen im Mythus der afrikanischen Völker* (1936; new impression 1964) has demonstrated that all the themes in the biblical story of primeval events occur too in the myths of primeval time among the African peoples. Though only some of the most important have been mentioned, two conclusions impose themselves from a study of these collections and surveys: first, despite the vast number of stories, the themes are very limited in number, and so it is possible to compare them with or arrange them according to the motifs of Gen 1-11. The ways in which people of all places and at all times are going to present the origin of humanity and the universe or of the present state of the world are not without limit; they are relatively few. And so there will be many similarities even though direct influence is excluded.

The second conclusion is that there are very many signs that the stories of creation and primeval time belong together. The different themes and motifs of the primeval happening do not stand in isolation from each other; there are all sorts of links and points of contact between them. The creation and the flood have special significance in Gen 1-11 in that both are used by J and P and are resumed by R. A survey of the history of religions shows that the creation and the flood are the themes which occur most often in the stories of primeval time. The many links between these two principal themes are found too in Gen 1-11. There are other examples too where the themes cross each other. There are many links too between creation and the genealogies, between creation and achievement, between creation and the origin of evil, between achievement and the origin of evil.

It is imperative therefore to keep in view the primeval event as a whole when one is inquiring into the prehistory of a narrative or of a motif in Gen 1-11; for example, that the flood stands in relationship to creation, or, as W. Wundt (op. cit., 290) says, creation and flood complement each other. It was neither J nor P who brought these themes together, even though they made basic alterations to the material at hand. Not only individual pieces in Gen 1-11, as for example the flood story of chs. 6-9, but the whole plan of the story of primeval events, go back to a complex of traditions within which there is many a crisscross pattern.

One of the deficiencies in the exegesis of Gen 1-11 up to the present has been that the comparison with extra-biblical texts or motifs has for the most part been made piece by piece. One has begun from the individual biblical texts and looked for parallels which were examined and judged separated from their context. It should be evident that such piecemeal comparison is exposed to errors and misunderstandings. (Cf. C. Westermann, "Sinn und Grenze religionsgeschichtlicher Parallelen" ThLZ 90 [1965] 489-496; K. Koch, "Wort und Einheit des Schöpfergottes in Memphis und Jerusalem", ZThK [1965] 251-293, esp. 251-253.) Moreover, it is noticeable that the comparison is often very uneven; to one scholar the Mesopotamian texts seem to be particularly important, to another the Egyptian, to a third the Ugaritic. The dominant question is for the most part: Are the biblical texts dependent upon the extra-biblical texts? This question however is not as decisive and important as is often thought. It is much more to the point to research, as far as possible, the prehistory of the biblical story as a whole, and then to examine it in the context of its background. Only then is it possible to set in relief the utterly unique character of the biblical story.

The real question is this: Why has Israel's confession of the god who rescued Israel from Egypt been extended back into the primeval events? And why did Israel speak of its rescuer as the creator of heaven and earth in a way which has so many points of contact with what the surrounding world said of its gods in the same context? It is basically a theological question which arises from Israel's confession of Yahweh as the rescuer that requires the exegesis of Gen 1-11 to research the relationship of the biblical story of primeval events to the tradition of the primeval happening in the history of humankind. This question presupposes the biblical story as a whole and compares it with the whole complex of extra-biblical texts which speak of creation and primeval time. It is not the intention of this introduction to overemphasize the importance of the extra-biblical texts and motifs in order to explain the biblical story; it is rather to bring out more clearly than has been done the special nature of the biblical text. The introductory survey enables us to relieve ourselves of the burden of a special exegesis of the comparisons from the history of religions.

2. The Numerative Sections in Gen 1-11: The Genealogies as the Framework of the Story of Primeval Events

The genealogies are an essential constitutive part of the primeval story and form the framework of everything that is narrated in Gen 1-11. Gen 1 has run its course with the creation of humans; it halts, while Gen 2-3 take up the story. A succession of generations begins with Gen 4 and progresses from the first created pair to Abraham, who introduces the second part of Genesis, the patriarchal cycle. Everything that happens between these two points, that is, between Adam and Abraham, takes its origin from and comes back to these genealogies. They give that continuity to all that happens which makes the biblical account of the origins unique in its kind in the history of religions. A coherent and summary history is prefaced, by means of the genealogies, to the salvation history which begins in Gen 12.

Origin in Tribal Traditions. The family trees or genealogies in Gen 1-11 belong to a many-faceted genre that runs through the whole of the Old Testament. This genre is found in a highly developed form in the patriarchal cycle, Gen 12-50, and occurs again only with the kings, the priests and priestly circle, and with the chronicler. It continues into the New Testament in the family tree of Jesus.

Earlier interpreters explained the genealogies as relics of sagas which dealt with an individual; only the name remained, and it was at a later stage that the story relics were threaded into a collection. (So H. Gunkel, *Genesis*, 1922, 5th ed., 49f, 134; cf. J. Wellhausen, *Prolegomena to the History of Ancient Israel*, 1905, 6th ed., 330f, "It is the natural chain to link the different stories together.") On the contrary the genealogies form an independent genre which is very ancient and very significant, and which had its origin and fullest development among nomad tribes. The nomad Arabs provide plenty of evidence for this, cf. R. de Vaux, *Ancient Israel*, 1960, 12ff; L. Ramlot, "Les généalogies bibliques," *Bible et Vie chrétienne*, 60 (1964) 53-70: "The conclusion is that the tribe and the genealogy that explains its history, its cohesion and alliances, are essential to the structures of nomadic life, and gradually disappear among those who become sedentary. . . ."

The basic form of social life among nomads is the tribe or family. Accordingly the genealogy, inasmuch as it is both the basis and the sign of origin and belonging, has a significance which gives direction to life in common (cf. de Vaux, op. cit., 12ff). The genealogies then take on something of a historical presentation of a form of existence which precedes history, as Herder had thought (both Wellhausen and Gunkel disputed this). It is a way of presenting the history of a form of life in common in which chronological continuity as well as the community and contiguity of the groups follow naturally from the ties of blood, from the origin from one father and from brotherly relationship.

Common to the genealogies with their historical presentation is a continuous succession of events which reaches its goal in the present. These events however have a pre-historical character, that is, they depend exclusively on begetting and birth; continuous event is not possible except in a succession of generations. This is the only way that the boring and apparently uninformative genealogies make sense to us today: "When Seth had lived a hundred and five years, he became the father of Enosh. Seth lived after the birth of Enosh eight hundred and seven years, and had other sons and daughters. Thus all the days of Seth were nine hundred and twelve years; and he died" (Gen. 5:6-8).

These sentences are as monotonous and have the same effect as those of Gen 1, presenting as they do the steady, ongoing rhythm of events which stamp the course of human existence — birth, length of life, begetting, death; all that is essential. The real significance of what is happening lies in the continuity of successive generations.

Consequently, the significance of the succession of generations together with the form in which it is expressed must decline or disappear completely when the form of community life to which it belongs is replaced by another (see the citation from Ramlot). Other events become important: struggles, authority, forms of authority, the foundation of states, the forms of states, i.e., all properly political matters. The genealogies can no longer mean what they once meant.

The genealogies begin to disappear from the Book of Exodus on. When they occur again they have but a partial function, to demonstrate, for example, that the claim of a particular priestly family is legitimate. In the work of the chronicler, the genealogies are nothing more than a collection of abbreviated lists of names.

Application to the Story of Primeval Events. The patriarchal cycle is the real source of genealogies. They were carried over from there to the story of primeval events. It would scarcely be possible to extend the patriarchal cycle back to the beginning of humankind in any other way than by the use of the genealogy form; and the story from Adam to Abraham needs a succession of generations. But the use of the genealogy form in the primeval story is much more than the mere extension of the line backwards. The genealogies are far more important to Gen 1-11 than to Gen 12-50.

The reason for this is the important place that the genealogies have had prior to their appearance in the biblical story of primeval events. Creation or Origins occur occasionally in primitive cultures as a birth or a succession of births. The cosmogony appears in its most highly developed form in the theogony, that is, in a series of generations of gods, in the high cultures of the Mediterranean world, in Egypt, Mesopotamia and in Greece (Hesiod). These genealogies which explain the origin of the world — heaven and earth, sea and winds, plants and animals — from a succession of births of gods, are the forerunners of the genealogies in the primeval story.

The word which P uses, תּוֹלְדוֹת shows this clearly. The priestly writing understands the whole primeval story as a series of "generations" (תּוֹלְדוֹת), as the headings of the individual parts indicate. P includes the creation of "the heavens and the earth" under the תּוֹלְדוֹת, 2:4a, preserving a tradition that there was a time when all origins were thought of and described as "generations." P brought creation by the word of the creator under the rubric "generation of the heavens and the earth," thereby recalling the cosmogony of Memphis, where the commanding word of Ptah had replaced the succession of divine births of an older cosmogony.

It is only in the light of this history of the genealogies in the context of the creation of the world that it becomes clear how thorough-going a change has been made in the genealogies of the biblical primeval story. Anything like the genealogies of the gods is excluded from the very beginning. Genealogies can begin only after the creation of humankind. The form of presentation is preserved; the event which is presented is freed from myth and is an event which concerns human beings and their world. It is the clear line of distinction that the biblical story of primeval events draws between creation and the genealogy of the birth of the gods that gives the human genealogies their distinctive meaning. The biblical genealogies describe the history of humankind only and so acquire an importance that they could not have in the realm of myth. The uniqueness of what happened before history or in the primeval event has moved from the story of the gods to the story of human beings. This is the reason why in Egypt and Mesopotamia, after the genealogies of the gods, it is the genealogies of the kings that are of importance, that is, merit being part of tradition. After the origin, the only real history is the history of the kings.

The primeval story of the Old Testament, however, includes people,

God's creatures, in the succession of generations right from the very act of creation. The genealogies run from Adam to Abraham. The difference becomes clear in a comparison between Gen 5 and the Sumerian king-lists (ANET 265f). All of the more recent commentaries on Genesis have drawn attention to the similarity of names, numbers and ages. But not enough notice has been given to the very important difference; the succession of generations in Gen 5 is on the other side of history; in the Sumerian king-lists it is a part of history. It begins:

> When kingship was lowered from heaven,
> kingship was (first) in Eridu,
> A-lulim (became) king and ruled 28,800 years. . . .

History begins at Sumer with the descent of the kingship from heaven; the biblical genealogies from Adam to Abraham have no meaning as an actual succession of generations. The system is deliberately abstracted from the historical character of the peoples mentioned; it is the blessing of the creator, constant and effective, enabling humanity to continue and to expand over the face of the earth, that is essential for humankind in primeval time.

The genealogies of the primeval story belong to a context whose horizontal and linear ramifications are vast and which has not yet been adequately researched. A form-critical study of the genealogies is yet to be elaborated. The point of departure would have to be the many appropriate texts in the patriarchal cycle; then there would follow the study of the genealogies of the primeval story, their history outside Israel, and finally their revival throughout the Old Testament right up to the genealogies of Jesus in the gospels.

The Genealogies of J and P. This brief consideration of the genealogies of the primeval story is concerned primarily with their form, and not with the proper names. There is a profound difference between the genealogies of J and P: in J the form is quite free, adaptable and varied; in P it is highly stylized and for the most part stereotyped. The genealogies of J stand very close to the narratives, in fact so close that they very often pass over into narrative. In P the genealogy retains its straitened form and is quite different from the narrative.

The Genealogies in J:
It must be borne in mind that the genealogies of J have not been preserved in their entirety; parts have dropped out in favor of P.

4:1-2: Adam and Eve, Cain, Abel
4:17-24: from Cain to the children of Lamech
    (the family tree of the Cainites)
4:25-26: Adam-Seth-Enosh
5:29; 9:18-19; 10:1b: Noah and his sons
10:8-30: the descendants of the sons of Noah
    (J's table of the nations)
11:28-30: the death of Haran, the wives of
    Abraham and Nahor (transition to the Abraham cycle)

Though there are only two larger complexes, 4:7-26 and 10:8-30, and the rest are but small fragments, they display a great variety of forms. The latter appear only after the flood; they are formally introduced in 9:19. The following forms occur:

9

NN knew NN — (conceived) — bore NN 4:1, 17, 25
    conceived again — bore NN 4:2a
to NN were born NN   4:18, 26; 10:21, 25
NN begot NN 4:18b (3 times); 10:8-18; 10:24, 26-29 (13 names)
NN took two wives, NN and NN
    NN begot NN (occupation) and his brother NN (occupation)
    NN begot NN (occupation) and his sister NN
    (the song of Lamech)   4:19-24
The sons of NN were NN, NN, NN   9:18f.
    these were born sons. . . .   10:1b
NN died, time, place   11:28-30
    Then NN and NN took wives
    NN's wife was called NN
    NN's wife was called NN, the daughter of NN, the
    father of NN and NN.

These texts will be seen in their proper perspective if one takes the beginning and the end as the starting point, namely 4:1-2, 17 and 11:28-29. They are very close to narrative and actually introduce narrative. The formula "NN begot NN" is furthest removed from narrative and nearest to pure numeration. In 10:13f. and 15-18 the formula becomes a mere enumeration of names united simply by "and." Another formula which merely enumerates is "the sons of NN were NN, NN, NN," 9:18f. The forms which occur between these two extremes do not need any special explanation; they give a list of two lines, sons of two wives, 4:19-24; 11:28-30.

The juxtaposition of these forms tells us something of the history of the genealogies: they grew out of narratives, gradually freed themselves, became ever more formal, and survived finally as lists of names. This becomes clearer when we take note of a feature which has been left aside up to the present, namely the addenda.

First, there are the explanations of the meanings of names, 4:1b, 25b; 5:29; 10:25b. The first two explain the name as the praise of God for the gift of a son. They belong in the context of the blessing which is effective in the gift of heirs; the words of praise which the mother utters as she names the child which has been given to her corresponds to the cry of joy with which the man greets the woman whom God has given him as his companion, 2:23. Both explanations are closely connected with the creation of human beings. They are saying that the blessing which the creator bestowed on humanity remains effective after the expulsion from the garden.

The third and fourth explanations of names are attached to well-known narrative motifs. The name of Noah is explained in 5:29 with reference to the foundation of viticulture which brings refreshment to people. The verse is to be taken with 9:20, where Noah was the first to plant a vineyard. The explanation of a name, together with further observations, belongs to the group of narratives that deal with achievements; it is an additional narrative piece. The fourth explanation is the same, 10:25b. It explains the name Peleg with reference to an event which took place at that time, the division of humankind, the same event as is narrated in 11:1-9. The third and fourth explanations of names are typical examples of the growth of a narrative out of a genealogy. A striking example from the patriarchal cycle is Gen 38, where a genealogy, vv. 1-6, is the exposition of a narrative. Likewise 4:1-2 is the genealogical exposition of the narrative of Cain and Abel, 4:1-16.

A second group of texts carries information about professions and crafts, especially 4:17-22:

> 4:2: Abel was a keeper of sheep, and Cain a
>   tiller of the ground
> 17b: and he (Henoch) built a city
> 20b: he was the father of those who dwelled
>   in tents and have cattle
> 21: he was the father of all those who played
>   the lyre and pipe
> 22: he was the forger of all instruments of
>   bronze and iron
> 10:8: he was the first on earth to be a
>   mighty man (גִּבֹּר)
> 9: he was a mighty hunter before the Lord
> 9:20: Noah was the first tiller of the soil.
>   He planted a vineyard

The concern here is with human contributions to the progress of civilization; they will be considered later. All these short sentences point to the beginning, the founding, or the discovery of something new or to the realization of a new capacity in people; this is very clear in 9:20 and 10:8. This is the meaning of the phrase, "he was the father of those . . ."; because each case deals with the beginning, the founding, or the discovery of something, we can conclude that each of these was a special event and was at one time narrated as such. This is confirmed by parallels from other religions. These passages cannot be understood properly apart from their background in the history of religion where the emergence of culture and civilization as well as of human skill are a dominating motif that underwent a many-sided development.

The motif has all but disappeared in the biblical story (except for Gen 11:1-9) and has been preserved only in these brief additions. The reason for this is the mythical nature of the stories of the growth of civilization in the cultures that preceded Israel. The Sumerian myths show very clearly how the motifs grew out of the genealogies (in this case genealogy of the gods); the information about the beginnings of civilization in the biblical genealogies comes from an earlier stage of their development.

A third group of additions speaks of the spread of humankind over the earth:

> 9:19b: and from these the whole earth was peopled
> 10:25b: for in his days the earth was divided
> 10:18b: afterward the families of the Canaanites spread abroad

The first two passages describe a primeval event, the third gives political and geographical information. The two passages are saying something very different; 10:25b is the narrative motif that lies behind 11:1-9 and is widespread in pre-Israelite primeval stories, 9:19b on the contrary goes back to the blessing and commission of the priestly tradition, "fill the earth." A fourth group of additions is of a geographical and political kind; the primeval story passes into the framework of world history. There is the description of the Mesopotamian empire

11

and its main cities in 10:10-12, and the geographical information about the territories of the Canaanites in 10:19 and of the sons of Joktan in 10:30. These verses are different; they are not narratives which enclose an event in a brief remark, but pieces of information about peoples and territories. The story is no longer the primeval story in the strict sense; it has moved on to the stage of world history. This is important inasmuch as the transition was already there in J and was not primarily the work of P.

The fifth group of additions includes sayings of or about people mentioned in the genealogies. One can include here explanations of names, especially when the saying is introduced as in 5:29. In the case of Nimrod a proverb is quoted 10:9b: "Therefore it is said, like Nimrod a mighty hunter before the Lord." The proverb refers to Nimrod's reputation, and so points back to stories which gave rise to it. The song of Lamech is similar, 4:23-24; this "braggart song" also goes back to a narrative tradition, without which it would never have arisen. These two proverbs reveal a circle of narratives about the heroes of old which had had a remarkable development in Sumer and Babylon, and which in a much earlier stage must have been of great importance for the ancestors of Israel. A fragment is preserved in 6:1-4. The reason why this circle of narratives of the heroes of old was not continued in Israel is that it was too deeply rooted in the world of myth. This is clear from the Babylonian account of the Gilgamesh story with its earlier Sumerian stage, as well as from the fragment of 6:1-4.

There remains finally the lone sentence of 4:26, "At that time men began to call upon the name of the Lord." It is a loose addition and has no connection with any name in the genealogy. It is very unlikely that the verse is the remains of a narrative. I can only make a suggestion about its meaning here: there were among Israel's neighbors stories about the origin of the cult which belong to the stories about the primeval events. According to the different Sumerian and Babylonian stories of creation people were created to serve the gods, or better to dance attendance on them. One could scarcely forge a stronger bond between the creation of humans and the beginning of cult! Cult was there at the beginning; it must be included in the story of the beginnings. The Yahwist, or his predecessor, saw this and taking his stand against it, linked the invocation of Yahweh's name to the primeval story in a quite different way. The theological meaning of the verse will be considered in the exegesis.

We have seen that the genealogies of J show an amazing variety of motifs and contain traces and fragments of a whole series of narratives and narrative cycles. This recurring relationship between genealogy and narrative is nowhere as evident as it is in the Yahwistic genealogies of the primeval story.

The Genealogies of P:
The genealogies of P present a very different picture; they trace an uninterrupted line from Adam to Abraham.

> 5:1-32: From Adam through Seth to Noah
> 6:9-10; 9:28-29: Noah and his sons, the death
>   of Noah
> 10:1-7, 20, 22, 23, 31, 32: The generations of the
>   sons of Noah
> 10:1-5: The sons of Japheth

6, 7, 20: The sons of Ham
22, 23, 31: The sons of Shem
32: conclusion
11:10-26: The family tree of Shem. From Shem
    to Abraham
11:27, 31, 32: The family tree of Terah
27: The sons of Terah
31: The departure from Ur of the Chaldeans,
    arrival in Haran
32: The length of Terah's life; his death
    (continued in 12:4b, 5).

A comparison of the language and structure of the two groups of genealogies shows the extensive difference between them and throws into relief the peculiar character of each. The complete systematization of the genealogies of P is striking. If J is like an eccentric unmade track, P is like a paved road. P received a tradition which was very suited to its ordered, systematizing tendency, and which it could shape into its own language. The adaptations which the genealogies underwent at the hands of P are important; they are something quite different from J and have a different purpose.

The adaptation appears first in the headings. P used them to create a clearly articulated whole out of very disparate components. At the same time P linked the self-contained story of primeval events firmly with the patriarchal cycle:

2:4a: These are the *generations* of the heavens
    and the earth when they were created
5:1: This is a book of the *generations* of Adam
6:9: These are the *generations* of Noah
10:1: These are the *generations* of the sons
    of Noah
11:10: These are the *generations* of Shem
11:27: These are the *generations* of Terah

The word "generations," תּוֹלְדוֹת, has a very wide range of meanings. Its scope enables P to create a series of events out of very different components, all of which are gathered together in some way under תּוֹלְדוֹת. P has made the תּוֹלְדוֹת the basic framework of the primeval story by including everything, even creation, under that heading. We find the form of the genealogies, and the additions to them, in Gen 5:

When NN had lived x years, he begot NN.
After NN had begotten NN, he lived another
x years and begot sons and daughters.
The whole life-span of NN covered x years.
Then he died.

This scheme embraces the begetting of a son at a certain age, the life-span after the begetting of this son, the begetting of further sons and daughters (names not given), information about the whole life-span, and the death. If we leave aside the ages, we are left with a cycle in which three factors are named: birth — begetting — death. The parts of the series are fitted together in such a way that it is the begetting of any individual by his father, not his birth, that is mentioned in the previous part. The series contains ten members from Adam to Noah.

The same scheme lies behind the genealogy of Noah 6:9f.; 9:28f.; but with two adaptations: three sons are named, and an event is inserted into the genealogy: the flood.

The genealogy of the sons of Noah, Gen 10, is divided: 1: Introduction, 2-5: the sons of Japheth, 6, 7, 20: the sons of Ham, 22, 23, 31: the sons of Shem, 32: Conclusion. The plan of the individual parts is as follows:

> The sons of NN: NN and NN and NN and NN and
> NN and NN and NN.
> And the sons of NN: NN and NN and NN.
> And the sons of NN: NN and NN, the NN and the NN.
> (addition)
> These are the sons of NN,
> in their lands, each with his own language,
> by their families, in their nations.

This is a completely new scheme which has practically nothing in common with Gen 5. While ch. 5 is a genealogy in the proper sense of the word, the "table of the nations" of P in ch. 10 is nothing more than a mere list of names. Nothing is said of birth, begetting, and death; the "sons" are not sons in the real sense of the word; "son" has the meaning of "belonging to." The names are not the names of real persons, but the names of groups, partly in plural. The meaning of this is as follows: P has united under the heading תּוֹלְדֹת real genealogies with a list of names of three groups of peoples who are derived from the three sons of Noah.

The genealogies of Shem, 11:10-26:

> When NN was x years old, he begot NN (addition).
> After NN had begotten NN, he lived another x
> years and begot sons and daughters.

We meet the same scheme here as in Gen 5 with this difference, that the two last members of the latter are missing, namely the sentences: "the whole life-span of NN was x years. Then he died." In fact there is scarcely any difference because the whole life-span can be calculated from the dates that are given. However, because these two last sentences are omitted, the genealogy of Gen 11 takes on a somewhat different character from that of ch. 5, which lays far greater stress on each individual member of the series, so that the life-cycle of each of the fathers in the series stands out as a self-contained whole. P uses this device, together with the shorter life-span in ch. 11, to introduce a decrease in the succession of genealogies from the era before the flood to that after it. But apart from this the form of the genealogies in ch. 11 is linked directly to that of ch. 5; together, both of them form a steady, monotonous succession of generations that stretches from Adam, through Noah and one of his three sons to Terah and his three sons, 11:26, one of whom is the starting point of a new history.

The "generations" (תּוֹלְדֹת) of Terah, 11:27, 31, 32, form the transition from numeration to narrative. Vv. 27-31 carry the scheme of the genealogies a step further; information about a new event is included in v. 31, Terah's migration from Ur. This is the beginning of something new.

The Additions:

(1) The sentences that frame the genealogies seem to be additions. Gen 5

begins with the heading "This is the book of the generations of Adam." It is followed immediately in vv. 1b-2 by a brief summary of the creation of humanity. It is by means of this interesting repetition that P intends to make clear that the genealogies take their origin from creation; they emphasize the effectiveness of the blessing (v. 2 "and God blessed them"). So the link between creation and the genealogies is forged.

Similarly the addition at the end, 11:31, links the genealogies of the primeval story with the beginnings of the patriarchal story. The additions in the middle serve to link the genealogies with the flood narrative. They are fitted into the story in such a way that the sentence which follows the heading of 6:9a: "Noah was a righteous and blameless man. . . ." introduces the flood story, while the sentence at the end, 9:28f., flows on into the generations of Noah. Here, as again in 10:32 and 11:10, it is only the phrases "after the flood," "two years after the flood," that link the genealogies which follow chs. 6-9 with the flood. Such devices are a clear indication that P was in possession of self-contained genealogies; of themselves they had no connection with the narrative.

(2) Apart from the beginnings and the end, the long genealogy in Gen 5 has only one addition — v. 24, which speaks of Enoch's piety and removal from the earth. The sentence may well have originated from a narrative in the distant past. But P is not interested here in traces of the narrative growing out of a genealogy; his only concern is to point to Enoch as one man among those specially-favored ancestors who was particularly pleasing to God.

The sentence that stresses that Noah was a righteous and blameless man who "walked with God," 6:9, is very like that which describes Enoch. The similarity becomes even more striking when one thinks of the Sumerian-Babylonian story in which immortality was granted to the Ziusudra-Utnapishtim. This is clear proof that both sentences, 5:24 and 6:9, go back to an earlier motif that occurred elsewhere. It is very significant that P takes up this motif twice in the very few additions which he makes to the genealogies. It touches the priestly theology much more closely than, for example, the primeval motif of the heroes of old that J uses.

(3) Gen 10 is a mere enumeration of names, and so additions are not to be expected. The one sentence that stands out seems to be nothing more than an expansion of the enumeration. It occurs partially in 10:5a, "From these the coastland peoples spread," and completely in the concluding sentence of 10:32b, "and from these the nations spread abroad on the earth after the flood." The sentence is saying nothing more than that only the most important names of the three main lines have been mentioned. Other branches are indicated in summary fashion.

(4) There is not a single addition in the family tree of Shem, 11:10-26. The same regular monotonous sentences follow each other without interruption, only the names and the numbers changing. It is the perfect genealogy. Nothing happens but begetting and death.

If we draw together all the additions in P, and leave aside the link passages in chs. 5; 9; 11 and the expansion in ch. 10, we find that there is but a single addition in the genealogies proper, 5:24 and 6:9. The far-reaching difference between the genealogies of P and J becomes even clearer when we reflect that the genealogies of P are more than twice as long as those of J.

We can say in conclusion: In J, genealogy and narrative are reasonably close to each other; in P they stand far apart. In J they are varied and flexible; in P they are monotonous, uniform and systematized to the last detail. In J all sorts of narrative pieces, even afterthoughts or traces, appear constantly between two elements of a genealogy; in P there is quite deliberately no elaboration or dressing, and there remains but the sober recital of the succession of birth and death. But P has made a positive contribution to the genealogy form. With his highly abstract and highly systematized stylization, P has expounded with extraordinary power the real meaning of the genealogy, namely the continuous event of generation following generation.

One question remains: what does P mean by "the generations of the heaven and the earth," and what is his intention in including the creation of the world in the series of "generations"? He certainly means "the origins" of the heavens and of the earth; תּוֹלְדוֹת can have this broad meaning and such a description is very suitable when co-ordinating the creation of the world with the "story of origins."

But such an explanation is not sufficient. There can be no doubt that on every occasion P related the word תּוֹלְדוֹת to its basic meaning of "begetting," even when it had taken on the broader meaning of "origin." This is clear from chs. 5 and 11 where P has shaped the genealogy form in such a way as to emphasize the succession of generations as a succession of begettings. We can assume then that when P describes the events of Gen 1 as "the begettings of the heavens and the earth" he has not lost sight of the basic meaning of the word. We know that P was familiar with the Sumerian-Babylonian mythology; he must have known then that the creation of the world was described in a great variety of ways as a theogony along the lines of a genealogy of the gods. At the very beginning of Enuma Elish a hint is given of the origin of the world from the genealogy of the gods. It is not necessary then to describe the heading in 2:4a as secondary and as added "because of the need for system" (von Rad, *Genesis* 63), and one cannot say that "its application to heaven and earth goes beyond the original meaning of the word תּוֹלְדוֹת" (von Rad, loc. cit.). Rather, P preserves by means of this word the tradition that the origin of the heaven and the earth was at one time understood as a succession of begettings.

The peculiar style of Gen 1 favors this view. There is an unmistakable parallel between the solemn succession of generations in chs. 5 and 11 and the solemn succession of the events of creation in ch. 1, especially when one reads chs. 1 and 5 together.

S. Herrmann has made another suggestion to explain the peculiar style of Gen 1 in his essay, "Die Naturlehre des Schöpfungsberichtes, Erwägungen zur Vorgeschichte von Genesis 1," ThLZ 86 (1961), 413-424. Herrmann refers to "those encyclopaedic lists which, in the ancient east, had a sort of international claim on the oldest form of 'Wisdom'; their purpose was to arrange in order and as fully as possible all parts of the visible world. The Onomastikon of Amenemope . . . begins with the heavens, water and earth; then it adds a list of persons and their duties, proceeds through classes, branches and particular races to a detailed account of Egypt itself . . ." (416f.). After referring to similar lists from Mesopotamia Herrmann continues: "It should cause no surprise then if P, when enumerating the works of creation, makes use of this way of describing the world." Nevertheless Herrmann has to concede that "naturally these reflections remained very vague" (417).

The similarity lies only in the objects listed; it goes no further. We have shown when comparing the genealogies of J and P that the list-style is but marginal and a secondary development. The parts of Gen 10 that belong to P are no longer a genealogy, and of those that belong to J only vv. 13 and 16 are such. The real genealogies are not lists nor are they arranged in the form of lists. They are rather an independent genre, whose variety in both form and language can in no way be equated with the list-form. Nor can it be said in any way that Gen 1 is a list; it is much closer to chs. 5 and 11 than to ch. 10.

When P describes Gen 1 as a תּוֹלְדוֹת, then there is ground for similarity of style with the genealogies, however remote it may be. Such a comparison is based not only on the enumeration of the parts of the world in Genesis 1 and the theogonies, but on the way in which the origin of the world is presented both in Egypt and in Mesopotamia. P de-mythologizes the form; but echoes of it still remain in the monotonous succession of the works of creation which is certainly not narrative.

A relationship between Gen 1 and the genealogies was proposed very early. S. Landersdorfer, refers to it, *Die sumerischen Parallelen zur biblischen Urgeschichte: Alttest, Abhandlungen VII 5* (Münster 1917): "According to Radau (*The Creation-Story of Genesis 1, a Sumerian Theogony and Cosmogony,* Chicago 1902) the chapter contains an account of creation in the form of a genealogy, 'the generations of the heavens and the earth', which correspond to the Sumerian presentation."

Toward a Theology of the Genealogies. The genealogies do not speak of any special action of God; nor are they given any theological coloring or brought into any relationship with God's action. If this separation were significant then one would have to regard the genealogies as completely secular. Are they secular or religious?

P relates the genealogies very clearly to the work of God in the blessing and its commission: "Be fruitful and multiply," 1:28. The effect of the blessing is described in the genealogies. What is valid for P is valid also for J though no express blessing is found in his story. The creator made humans with the potentiality to increase their kind; this god-given dynamism is effective in the succession of new births which the genealogies report. It is the blessing that actualizes this potentiality, that makes possible the succession of births, and the names given to the two children in J, 4:1 and 25, point to God's power at work.

The effectiveness of God's blessing is the continuation of his creative power. It is to be distinguished clearly from God's saving action. The blessing is effective in the quiet, steady march of growth, expansion, prosperity and fertility. There are no particular accomplishments to be noted; when a child is born, grows, becomes an adult and in turn begets a child, the power is at work. Later we can deal with the varied and complicated history of the blessing; here it is sufficient to note how the basic structure of the genealogies in Gen 1-11 treats of the effectiveness of God's blessing. Von Rad writes in his introduction to Gen 5, "Now nothing more is said about . . . the blessing of man . . ." The contrary is the case. In 1:28 the first couple is told to "be fruitful and multiply. . . ." This blessing is effective as they increase and multiply through the genealogies of ch. 5. Nor can one say that "for J the primeval story is the story of disaster and curse" (R. Rendtorff, "Hermeneutische Probleme der Urgeschichte," *Festschr. F. Smend*, 1963, 22). J reports in the genealogies the continual effectiveness of the blessing after the man and the woman have been driven out of the garden, and this is expressed very clearly by the words of praise when names are given to the children in 4:1 and 25.

3. The Narrative Sections of Gen 1-11

Introduction: The Three Groups of Narratives. It is generally accepted that the narrative sections of Gen 1-11 are much more important than the numerative sections both in extent and in content; but it is not as simple as all that. It has been shown that Gen 1 is not simply narrative; it is very close to the genealogies; hence both sections are almost the same in extent:

Numerative Texts	Narrative Texts
(1:1-2:4a) (P)	(1:1-2:4a) (P)
4:1-2 (J)	2:4b-3:23 (J)
	4:3-16 (J)
4:17-26 (J)	
5 (P)	
	6:1-4 (J)
6:9-10 (P)	6:5-9:19 (J and P)
9:28-29 (P)	9:20-27 (J)
10 (J and P)	
	11:1-9 (J)
11:10-26 (P)	
11:27, 32 (P)	11:28-31 (J and P)

This table presents the content of the text in its final form; no account is taken of the division into sources. An analysis of the sources however shows an important difference between J and P; J is predominantly narrative, P numerative.

There are three groups of narratives: creation, achievements, crime and punishment. While it is easy to delineate clearly the first and third group, it is not easy to recognize the second. The only narrative which clearly belongs to it is the story of the Tower of Babel, 11:1-9; but it belongs too to the third group. And there is no detailed narrative of the achievements; they are indicated only by motifs or by additional notes. We will show later the reason why they are to be treated as a separate group. The division of these three groups is as follows:

Creation	Achievements	Crime & Punishment
1:1-2:4a (P)	(1:26b, 28b, 29) (P)	
2:4b-15; 18-24 (J)	(2:8, 15, 16, 20a	
	3:7, 21) (J)	2:16f; 3:1-24 (J)
		4:3-16 (J)
	4:17b, 20b, 21b, 22b,	
	(26b) (J)	
5:1b-2 (P)	5:28b (J)	6:1-4 (J)
9:1-7 (P)	9:2-3 (P), 20 (J)	6:5-9:17 (J and P)
	10:8f (J)	
	(11:1-9) (J)	11:1-9 (J)

The table shows that the entire narrative section of Gen 1-11 can be divided among these three groups, and that the groups are closely related to each other and to the genealogies. Creation is the subject of the story not only in Gen 1 and 2, but also in 5:1-2 where it is related to the genealogies, and in 9:1-7 where it is related to the flood story. Creation is related to crime and punishment in Gen 6-9 just as it is in chs. 2f. Reference to the achievements occurs in the genealogies, in the creation stories and in the stories of crime and punishment.

The question now arises whether these large blocks of material which are heaped together without any apparent connection are more closely united than it seems at first glance. If so, there is the futher question: is justice done to the text by an exegesis which only takes the primeval story as a whole as its starting point and never loses sight of it? In any case, this initial survey shows where the difference between the primeval story and the patriarchal cycle lies. The genealogies are the link between the two even though those of the primeval story are very different from those of the patriarchal cycle. As for the content of the narrative sections, the three groups described above belong exclusively to the primeval story; there is no sign of them in the patriarchal cycle, even though the story of Sodom and Gomorrah has something of crime and punishment about it.

Accordingly, the general conclusion of Gunkel, "Genesis is a collection of stories," is no longer adequate. Even if one describes the narratives of Gen 12-50 and Gen 1-11 as "stories," one must add straightaway that the narrative style of chs. 1-11 is basically different from that of chs. 12-50. They belong to two different forms and lines of tradition. It is better then to be very reserved about drawing any general conclusion and to determine and describe as clearly as possible what is proper to the narrative forms of the primeval story and the patriarchal cycle. The peculiar character of the narratives of Gen 1-11 and the interweaving of the genealogies with the narrative blocks make an important contribution to the theological message of the primeval story.

A. The Creation Narratives

Introduction: Creation in the History of Religions and in the Bible. Before we begin the exegesis of the creation narratives we must take a general look at the very broad context of Gen 1-3. But first of all a general reflection. The work of the theologians, the students of religion, and the ethnologists from the 17th century right up to the present has demonstrated that stories of the creation of the world and of mankind are spread over the whole earth and throughout the whole of humanity; they reach from the oldest, primitive cultures to the high cultures and beyond. No other statement about God or a god has such a broad geographical and chronological dissemination. Moreover, what they say about the creator and creation retains its own vital import even when all other statements about God fade or disappear. This is most striking in the western Enlightenment, where reflection on creator and creation outlasted all other theological themes.

When the parallels to Gen 1 were first made known, Christian theologians, almost without exception, regarded them as a threat to the revelation of the biblical story of creation. The interpreters of the Bible put themselves into a state of siege and took up an attitude which prejudged the question and which sought to demonstrate the unique character or the religious superiority of the biblical account. This apologetic mentality persists today among certain evangelical, Catholic, and Jewish interpreters.

We must ask if this apologetic attitude really does justice to the biblical texts. The question should rather be: Could not the agreement between the biblical and non-biblical accounts in this area make a positive contribution to our contemporary understanding of the biblical texts? So put, the question leaves us open to ask whether the Christian confession in God the Creator does not serve to link the Christian with so many other people both of today and of all stages in the history of humanity. Only then, as part of the confession of faith, does it fulfil its special function in coordination with the second and third articles of the Creed.

Before making any judgment on the content of the stories, it must be pointed out that what the Bible says about the creator and creation in Gen 1-3, in the praise of the creator in the Psalms, in Job, Deutero-Isaiah and in a number of other places, is related to what is said about the creator and creation not only in the neighboring religions but in most religions of the world anywhere and at any time. Only then can we discuss the question of the difference between the biblical and non-biblical accounts.

It is not possible to give here a comprehensive survey of reflection on the creator and creation in the whole of the history of religions. Attention must be drawn however to a change in attitude to this aspect of the history of religions which is of great importance for our understanding of the biblical creation stories. It becomes clear for example when one compares the articles on "creation" in the three editions of RGG. The article in the first edition, by Gunkel, begins: "The concept of creation. . . ." The approach here is essentially conceptual. It accepts the philosophical inquiry into the origin of the world and of humanity as the main motifs in the development of the creation myths. The article in the third edition by C.M. Edsman, begins: "Contrary to a purely intellectual interpretation of the belief in creation . . . it must be emphasized that these stories are real myth." And the myth has its meaning for the present life of the community. "The cosmogonies take on a vital function in these circumstances by means of recitation or dramatic presentation . . . they relate to every decisive moment in the life of the community and of the individual."

R. Pettazzoni provides a good insight into the change in the understanding of the creation myths in his essay "Myths of Beginning and Creation Myths," in *Essays on the History of Religion,* Leiden, 1954, 24-26. He understands these myths as follows: "The proper worth of myth consists in the necessary and sufficient justification which it gives to whatever is most essential to human life and to society, by relating it to a primordial act of foundation recorded by the myth," p. 26. This holds for the myth of the creation of humankind: "The existence of humanity depends in some sort on the myth which tells of the appearance of the first person on earth, for the recital of that myth has the power to establish and ensure the continuity of human life," p. 26. The same holds for the myth of the creation of the world: "The recital of the myth of the origin of the world makes real and guarantees the stability and duration of the universe," p. 26.

What holds in general for all the creation myths holds too for the recitation of the creation epic at the Babylonian New Year festival. It has long been recognized that the cultic representation of the myth serves to guarantee the stability of the world (e.g., V. Maag, "Sumerische und babylonische Mythen von der Erschaffung des Menschen," *Asiatische Studien* 1-4, 1954, 86-88).

Pettazzoni concludes from this that the difference between creation myths and myths of origin is secondary. What is decisive is that both have the same function. Bertholet has hinted at this in his article on creation in the second edition of RGG: "The main distinction is between creation as a personal act of the divinity and cosmogony as the spontaneous coming into being and growth of the world by virtue of an inherent dynamism. Practically, it is impossible to carry this distinction through" (V, 225). We see that the primary function of the myth is to maintain the stability of the present state; it is this that is common to the whole vast circle of stories about the creation or origin of the world and of human beings.

A most important conclusion has now been reached about the religious and theological significance of the "creation faith." It is not a stage in the religious development of the understanding of creation; it is not its spiritual high-point. Its importance lies in the relationship to the here and now of what is said about the origins. Pettazzoni sees it this way: "Whether the world was created by the will of God, or formed, by gradual accretions, from a seed or a speck of mud brought from the bottom of the sea, or by the cosmic growth of the different bodily parts of a gigantic primeval being, is all of no more than secondary importance in principle. What is of the greatest importance is that there should be a myth of beginnings, which may or may not be a myth of creation, but which cannot possibly be done without, for on this myth, be it what it may, the very existence of the universe and of humanity depend in any case" (27f.).

This brings a corrective to an attitude toward the stories of the origins which was prevalent until recently in the schools of the history of religions and which is still represented often enough, namely, that reflection on the creator and creation was primarily an answer of the human spirit to the question of the origin of the world. So, for example, S.G.F. Brandon, *Creation Legends of the Ancient Near East*, London 1963, p. 65: "The evidence that we have of ancient Egyptian cosmogonic speculation places it in a unique category in the history of human thought as one of the two earliest attempts by man to abstract himself from immersion in present experience, and to conceive of the world as having had a beginning, and to make a sustained intellectual effort to account for it." This attitude prejudges the situation completely and obscures the original meaning. The stories of the origin or of the creation of the world and humanity are not the result of an intellectual inquiry into the origin of the here and now. They stem from a concern for security in the face of the existing situation. The importance of the intellectual inquiry about the origins should not be disputed; but it is something which has been added later. The question of existence itself takes precedence.

It is worthy of note that the more the creation stories are detached from their original function, the more the intellectual question comes into the foreground. It is this function of relating to the present that links together all the early creation stories. We have here an independent genre of myths of creation and of origin which is known all over the world from the hunters and the food gatherers of the earliest stages of development right up to the beginning of antiquity. The various collections of stories are found in the works of J. Frazer, W. Wundt and H. Baumann mentioned above. For the Ancient Near East one should consult S.G.F. Brandon, *Creation Legends of the Ancient Near East,* London, 1963, as well as *Quellen des Alten Orients,* ed. M. Eliade, 1964. Further literature will be found in the articles "Creation, History of Religions" in the three editions of RGG, in EKL and BHH.

This type of myth had its original setting in a set of institutions aimed at securing the stability of the world, of life and its framework. This was done either by narrating the myth or by enacting it in some way. The epic Enuma Elish, which was recited at the Babylonian New Year Festival, is a very late stage in this process of development. A much earlier stage can be seen in the "Myth of an Old Babylonian Ritual to Assist Birth" in which the mother goddess is addressed in the following way:

> The goddess calls on them (that is, the gods),
> the mother,
> the helper of the gods, the wise Mami,
> thou are the mother womb,
> which is able to create man! (V. Maag p. 99).

This birth ritual invokes the mother goddess and refers to her action of creating a human being. It is quite common in primitive cultures to link a creation myth with an event in the present in which the myth is actualized. "The natives of Nias have a long poem descriptive of the creation, which they recite at the dances performed at the funeral of a chief . . ." (Frazer, op. cit., p. 7; the motif of the creation of the person in the image of God is very clear in this poem). The same is true for the flood story; it is actualized and linked with present events so as to prevent the repetition of the flood.

This original function of the myths of creation or of origin help us to understand why they are still widespread and subject to almost unlimited ramifications. All the motifs of the creation stories are distributed very widely; for example, the formation of the first man out of clay. We can understand then how the forms and motifs extend from the earliest and most primitive phases to the high religions and right up to the most recent stage. The example of the birth ritual given above in which the mother goddess is invoked as creator has its roots in primitive religious expression. It is not possible to draw a sharp line of distinction between the creation narratives of primitive and high cultures. On the contrary they have much in common. H. Baumann has shown how complex the relations are when he remarks that there are many African creation myths which contain ". . . ancient mythological material common to Semitic and Hamitic cultures alike and widespread among the east Hamitic cattle breeders of Africa" (op. cit., 242). This would indicate that there is a long history of contacts between the creation motifs of these cultures.

It is not a question of a literary dependence, direct or indirect, between these many and widespread stories or myths of creation. It is rather a matter of setting the biblical accounts of creation in the context of this massive complex of stories and genres so as to understand them better and to see how they differ.

We must now try to introduce some distinctions into this vast array of creation material so as to enable us to classify the various ways in which people have spoken of the creator and creation.

I. Creation of the Whole and Creation of the One. The question, what was created, precedes the question, how did creation take place. Two basic types may be distinguished: there are stories of the creation or origin of the whole and stories of the creation or origin of the one (i.e., of a particular thing). Generally speaking the creation of the whole (that is of the world and of humankind) is the later form, and creation of the one is the earlier form.

Pettazzoni says that it is easier for us today to recognize the existential function of the myths of creation or origin: "This explains for instance why the myth of the origin of certain animal species is told especially in order to ensure the capture of those species." Or: "The myth of the origin of corn will give to anyone who knows and tells it the power to exert a favourable influence on the growth of the corn" (op. cit., 29). The significance for the present moment of the myth of origin appears more clearly here than, for example, in the recitation of the Babylonian creation myth. We must be very careful not to pass a one-sided negative judgment on the creation of the one, the particular thing, in relation to the creation of the whole, inasmuch as we are accustomed to regard the creation of the whole as the only "real" creation.

As we survey the creation stories throughout the world we can draw some clear lines of distinction between the creation of the one and the creation of the whole. There are many more stories of the creation of the one, so that we can say in general that the creation of the one is an earlier type, and that the creation of the whole belongs to a later stage. The relationship of the great Babylonian epics to the Sumerian myths is important in this context for the biblical stories. Each story has its own individual history and we know now that individual myths lie behind the great Babylonian epics, especially the Gilgamesh story and the Enuma Elish. Sumerian mythology provides the greater part of what were once a number of independent stories. S.N. Kramer has presented the material: "The Epic of Gilgamesh and its Sumerian Sources, a Study in Literary Evolution" JAOS 64 (1944) 7-23. The creation of the world and the creation of human beings are described independently in separate stories. The creation of the one predominates. There is a text about the creation of humanity in S.N. Kramer's *Sumerian Mythology,* Philadelphia, 1944 pp. 68-71; it stands independently in the introduction to the myth of cattle breeding and grain (72f.), of the pickaxe (51f.), of plants for food and plants for healing (54-59). The creation of the world and the creation of humanity are mentioned together in the summary introduction, (37), which is clearly a literary construction. From a comparison of the Sumerian myths with the Babylonian epics it is concluded "that the myth of the creation of the world has prevailed over the myth of the creation of human beings, and drawn it into its own narrative framework" (V. Maag, op. cit., 102).

This picture becomes clearer when we go behind the Sumerian myths. The motif of the creation of humans is older than that of the creation of the world, and the creation of the one is older than the creation of the whole. H. Baumann says of the African myths: "It should be emphasized that . . . the idea of creation is concerned primarily with man and beast, much less frequently with the heavenly bodies and scarcely ever with the earth . . . the African story of creation is above all anthropogenesis" (op. cit., 163). The same is true of Frazer's collection which is drawn from the whole world. The title of his first chapter is "The Creation of Man"; there is practically no mention of the creation of the world.

The evidence shows that the theme of the creation of a particular object is older than that of the general creation, and in particular the creation of humans is older than the creation of the world. Baumann writes as follows: "There is little concern among the Africans for the origins of the inorganic world which surrounds them. The first human being is the focal point of their mythology. Whatever goes beyond this is a sign of something outside Africa, motifs, for example, such as the primeval sea, the primeval reptiles in the primeval sea, the eruption of things through God, the world egg; all these are unmistakable signs of the ancient high cultures of the lands of the Nile" (op. cit., 202).

It is not true that the theme of the creation of the particular thing has yielded completely to that of the general creation. Even in Babylon there are special stories of the creation of human beings, cf. A. Heidel, *The Babylonian Genesis,* 1951 2nd ed., 68-71. Alongside them stands the creation of the particular. What distinguishes the creation of humans from the creation of the world is either that the event is different or that the motivation is different or that the creator-god is different. These texts, so varied, so numerous and so different show clearly that the creation of humans is originally an event completely different from the creation of the world and is told in a different way. It is a late stage in tradition when in the Babylonian Epic Enuma Elish the creation of the world and the creation of human beings are drawn together and Marduk appears as the creator of the world and as the creator of humans (cf. the citation above from V. Maag). One can see from the way in which the strands of tradition are bound together how independent they once were: Marduk devises a plan to make a human being but Ea, the older god, either cooperates in the plan or is actually the creator (Tablet VI). In an older stage of the tradition the creation of humans was the work of another god.

The Egyptian cosmogonies are very instructive. Creation is almost always identified with the creation of the world; there is scarcely mention of the creation of humans. Brandon in *Creation Legends of the Ancient Near East,* remarks: "The most remarkable omission from this cosmogonic pattern is the creation of mankind . . ." (p. 56). He thinks that the reason for this is that the priestly circles had no interest in the origin of humanity. That may be. However, a more likely reason would be that the cult at the important shrines which gave rise to these cosmogonies was directed to guaranteeing the stability and order of the world. In any case the mythologies of Egypt show that the creation of the world and the creation of human beings were independent and were passed on in different traditions.

These reflections have direct bearing on the understanding of the biblical creation narratives. The Bible contains both basic types: universal creation in Gen 1 and the creation of the particular, namely humans, in Gen 2. Gen 2 gives the impression that the creation of human beings is an act in the scheme of universal creation as in Gen 1. We speak of two creation stories at the beginning of the Bible and ask why the order of acts of creation is different in each. The exegesis will show that a story of the creation of humans is the source of Gen 2. There are further indications in Gen 1-3 that the creation of the particular has its effects on the universal creation.

P presupposes a long history in which the traditions of the creation of the world and of humanity are joined together. Yet even here, in Gen 1:26-28, one can discern a variation from what has gone before in the account of the creation of human beings.

There are many other variations in the creation Psalms, e.g., Ps 104 which speaks of the creation of the world, and Ps 8 which speaks of the creation of people. The description of God as "creator of heaven and earth" goes back to a tradition of the world creator. The distinction can be traced right through the reflections on creation in Deutero-Isaiah and Job. It is important too for Christian theology. It is no accident that the creeds speak only of "the creator of heaven and earth." Luther on the other hand lays emphasis on the creation of humans in the Small Catechism: "I believe that God created me together with all creatures. . . ."

II. Creation and Beginning. There is a second difference — between myths of beginning and myths of creation. If we agree with Pettazzoni's thesis that the basic function of both myths is the same, then we can understand better why in theistic religions, where a personal god becomes the creator, the myth of beginning not only does not disappear, but even appears side by side with the creation story. They are often found together. Nevertheless, the transition from one to the other is the most far reaching adaptation in the history of creation accounts. The contrast between the two types can be best seen in the primitive cultures. One type does not simply succeed the other. The result of H. Baumann's inquiry into the powers of the creator is that there exists side by side the high god as creator and the simple beginning: ". . . the idea of the high god stands or falls with the description of the act of creation. . . . Finally there is found in a number of different places a type of creation which takes place of itself without any intervention by the divinity; sometimes men or objects 'come forth' without any command or action of being regarded as personal; sometimes the creation follows some sort of scientific process of development" (op. cit., p. 163). One must be very careful about passing judgment here. We prefer to leave open the question whether what is said about the creator and creation represents a higher or more intellectual stage of development than the story of the beginning; and the modern theory of evolution too belongs to this sort of talk about the beginning of the world and of humankind.

It is the personal element in talk about the creator and creation that introduces something completely new into the discussion of the beginnings. At the beginning a personal being acts; the beginning of the world and of humanity is as it were a "deed"; consequently there is made possible a personal relationship to this event and to the one who effected it, which is expressed in an address of praise to the creator. The praise of the creator becomes possible only with the transition from origin to creation. It should be noted that this is possible, not automatic! The primitive high god who is regarded as the creator is not generally the object of cult. Praise of the creator does not appear at this stage.

All of Israel's neighbors spoke of a personal creator-god when speaking of the beginnings of the world and of people; there was a personal relationship to the creator god; and this, be it noted, thousands of years before the beginning of Israel's history. It is no innovation in Israel when people invoke God as creator, give an account of his works of creation, praise him as creator. Israel shares this in common with people of many races and religions who have spoken and thought along these lines for generations. It is only when we see what they have in common that we can also see the decisive difference between them. Before Israel and outside Israel people spoke of the creation of the gods in the same way as they spoke of the creation of the world or of humanity. But this is not possible in Israel. Creation, therefore, be it simple creation or making or forming, has different overtones. The object of creation is without exception something outside the divine. The action of God as creator is directed exclusively to the world. God is outside creation; to be created means to be not-god.

Creation completely dominates origin in the Old Testament. Nevertheless, the latter has not completely disappeared. The plan of the works of creation is interrupted in Gen 1:24 by the words: "Let the earth bring forth. . . ." Origin is in a sense circumscribed by creation. This way of expressing the beginnings is part of the tradition history of the myths of origin which still leave their stamp on Gen 1. There are traces of the same in Ps 139:15 where the origin of human beings from the womb of mother-earth is the background (cf. V. Maag, op. cit., 93). These examples should be enough to show that the biblical narratives of creation should not be taken out of the general context of stories of creation and of origin. It is not without surprise that we affirm that very ancient motifs continue effectively even in the most recent stories.

III. The Types of Creation.

III. The Types of Creation. Some distinctions must now be made about the way in which creation is presented. It is not possible to give a comprehensive account; only the main lines which serve to understand Gen 1-3 will be sketched. If I understand it correctly, there are four main types of creation to be distinguished in the world outside Israel: (1) creation by birth or by a succession of births; (2) creation through struggle; (3) creation as fashioning, making or forming; (4) creation through utterance. This division makes no claim to be comprehensive; it merely outlines the main types. One can ask whether the four can be traced back to two basic types, creation as birth and creation as act where there would be some sort of parallel to the division between creation and origin. Number (1) would belong to the first type, numbers (2), (3) and (4) to the second.

(1) Creation by Birth, or by a Succession of Births. The successive acts of creation in Gen 1 are summed up in 2:4a under תּוֹלְדוֹת. This transferred meaning of the word is evidence of the recollection of a time when all origins were understood as birth. There are many examples in many languages of words meaning "birth" or "begetting," used in different contexts and combinations, all of which indicate how deeply embedded in the human spirit is the basic mystery of origin. The Egyptian and Mesopotamian cosmogonies, so different from each other in everything else, agree in a remarkable way when they describe the origins of the world as a succession of births. This goes back to the primitive cultures. What follows is a continuation of what was said above about the genealogies.

C.M. Edsman gives an example of origin by a succession of births in his article "Schöpfung und Weltentstehung, . . . religionsgeschichtlich" (RGG³ V, 1470): "When the genealogy of the head of a line is recited, and it often begins with creation, then the emphasis is not only on the relationship to primeval time but also on the significance of this relationship. It is said of Tongareva: 'The lineage goes back to the heaven as Father, the lineage goes back to Atea. Bind them so that they hold firm; let the link be strong . . . so that it holds.'"

An especially significant part of the Sumerian myths of origin is the coming into being of the world as the result of a succession of births (S.N.

Kramer, *Sumerian Mythology,* Philadelphia, 1944). This is the case in the myth "Enlil and Ninlil, The Begetting of Nanna," op. cit., 43-47; "Cattle and Grain," pp. 53-54; "Enki and Ninhursag," pp. 54-59; the framework of the narrative is a succession of births, the genealogy of the gods is the basis of the creation of the world. There are many other myths in which the origin from the birth of the gods is but one motif among others. The narrative generally begins with a birth of the gods, or with a series of births of the gods, followed by some other event as, for example, in the myth "Emesh and Enten," 49f.; or a list of the Sumerian gods begins with the goddess Nammu, "the mother who bore heaven and earth" p. 39. The myth "Cattle and Grain" 53f., which described the birth of the gods of cattle breeding and of grain, begins as follows (A. Falkenstein: Festschr. B. Landsberger, *Assyriological Studies* 16 [1965] 129):

> When An had begotten the Anunna gods
> in the mountains of heaven and earth. . .

The origins of cattle breeding and plant farming are described in terms of the birth of the gods; and the stories of the birth of the gods are found in the context of the origin of the world and its furniture. The myth of "Enki and Ninhursag" (op. cit., 54-59, ANET 37ff., cf. Brandon, *Creation Legends,* 74ff.) describes the cultivation of plants, both ordinary and medicinal, as taking their origin from the birth of the gods.

It is different in the Babylonian creation myths. Origin from the birth of the gods is in the background; instead we meet the formula, the god X created this and this, with no further description of the way in which the creation took place. This is illustrated by the collection of stories in A. Heidel, *The Babylonian Genesis,* ch. 2 "Related Babylonian Creation Stories," pp. 61-81, especially in the following excerpt:

> When Anu had created the heavens,
> (And) Nudimmud had built the *Apsû,* his dwelling
> Ea nipped off clay in the *Apsû;*
> He created Kulla for the restoration of
>   [the temples];
> He created the reed marsh and the forest for
>   the work of [their] construction;
> He created Ninildu, Ninsumug, and Arazu, to
>   complete the work of [their] con[struction];
> He created the mountains and the seas for
>   whatever [.......];
>
>   (6 Lines)
>
> He created the king, for the mainten[ance of
>   the temples];
> [He created] mankind for the doi[ng of the
>   service of the gods(?)];

It is even more important to note that the great epic Enuma Elish begins with a genealogy of the gods (ANET pp. 60-61):

> When on high the heaven had not been named,
> firm ground below had not been called by name,
> naught but primordial Apsu, their begetter,

27

(and) Mummu-Tiamat, she who bore them all,
their waters co-mingling as a single body. . .
(Lines 9-17: The Succession of Generations of other gods.)

A detailed genealogy of the gods resuming all the traditions precedes the drama of the disturbance of the older gods by the younger and the consequent decision to destroy the source of the trouble. The beginning is not an act of creation but a succession of births. Creation is but a consequence of the drama which is beginning. The older idea of creation from a succession of births is given precedence to the later idea of creation as a result of a struggle.

In Egypt creation as a succession of births is predominant. The cosmogonies of the different shrines consist of the genealogies of the gods. I refer to A. Erman, *Die Religion der Ägypter,* 1934, 88ff., and I cite the following from E. Otto, *Ägypten,* 1958 on the cosmogony of Heliopolis, 57f.:

Once more there is a bi-sexual primeval god at the beginning, Atum. . . . The pair begotten by Atum are called Shu and Tefnut, the air . . . and the dampness, which the god has vomitted forth. They are the elements from which the world is built. The heaven (the goddess Nut) and the earth (the god Geb) . . . were separated out by Shu. . . . These five formed the nucleus of the nine gods of Heliopolis.

The first five of the nine gods of Heliopolis are representatives of the cosmic elements and their story shows quite clearly how the origin of the world is presented as a succession of births of the gods. An important observation follows on the order of events in the cosmogonies of Hermopolis, Heliopolis and Memphis. E. Otto, p. 57, insists that the Hermopolis story is one of the earliest accounts of the origin of the world: "Four pre-existing primeval powers preside over chaos . . . They are described as serpents and frogs . . . They created the primeval egg on the primeval hill and from it there arose the primeval bird. These are all very ancient images which one can not very well describe as 'creation of the world'; it is a very simple explanation of the origin of the world." The cosmogony of Hermopolis then would recall the type of "world origin" treated in the previous passage.

This impression is confirmed by a comparison with similar motifs in African myths. The intermediary cosmogony of Heliopolis described the creation as a genealogy of the gods: "It is a later type which can be described as the classical form of Egyptian teaching on the origin of the world" (Otto, op. cit., 57). Then comes the cosmogony of Memphis where creation through the divine word takes the place of the genealogies of the gods. The great cosmogonies of the Egyptian centers of worship present us with an amazing succession of creation stories that offer us a profound insight into the history of reflection on creator and creation. There is much more to be said about creation in Egypt. We are dealing here only with the origins of the world from the birth of the gods. Reference should be made to the detailed account in Brandon, *Creation Legends,* 23ff., and to the essay of S. Herrmann referred to above. The theogony of Hesiod indicates the importance of the question for Greece, cf. Brandon, op. cit., 166ff.

(2) Creation as the Result of a Struggle or a Victory. The best known example of this type and the one nearest the Old Testament is that of the creation of the world by Marduk after the struggle with Tiamat in Enuma Elish. This epic not only links the genealogies of the gods with the struggle between the gods, but

is also familiar with two stages of this struggle. The first stage begins in Tablet I, 21 when the younger gods disturb the older gods and it ends with the victory of Ea over Apsu, Tablet I, 59-78. The consequence of this victory is not the creation of the world but the building of a house (temple) on the conquered foe; "On Apsu he established his dwelling place," I, 71. The first phase agrees generally with the struggle of Baal with Yam in the Anat texts from Ugarit (cf. L.R. Fisher, "Creation at Ugarit and in the Old Testament," VT 15 [1965] 313-324; Fisher is wrong, however, when he makes the struggle of Baal parallel to that of Marduk).

We find here the following elements: the struggle of the god with the primeval monster of the sea or with the god of the sea (Apsu corresponds to Yam), the acquisition of dominion through the struggle, the construction of the house (temple) because of the struggle. Fisher maintains that the temple is a microcosm and that the temple building corresponds to the creation. Certain aspects of the temple would seem to indicate this. Accordingly the house which Ea builds over the conquered Apsu would stand for the earth and would point to a creation. But that is very questionable. One would require a much broader comparative basis in order to equate creation with the construction of a house or temple.

It is the second stage of the struggle that leads to creation. The struggle of Marduk with Tiamat, Kingu and their helpers has been described often enough. Struggle and creation are closely linked here. Immediately after Marduk has killed Tiamat (IV, 129-132), he divides the corpse in two and creates the heavens by spreading out one half like a roof. It seems that he makes the earth from the other half, but the text is not clear about this. Then follows the creation of the heavenly bodies (V) and of humans (VI).

The article of R. Labat presents another view of the creation of the earth: "Les origines et la formation de la terre dans le poème babylonien de la création," *Studia Biblica et Orientalia* III, Rome (1959), pp. 205-215. He disagrees with the translation of Heidel in IV, 144-145 and refers to a group of newly discovered fragments which speak very clearly of the creation of the earth. "Marduk created the earth by applying to the surface and to the interior of a solid sub-stratum the dust which Anu had already created in the heavens" (211).

There can be no doubt that the description of creation as the consequence or effect of the victory of one god over another, the primeval monster of chaos, has found a clear echo in the Old Testament. True there is in Gen 1:2 but the faintest trace of the primeval struggle; nevertheless, the echo is clearly heard in a number of Psalms.

We must refer here to the pioneering work of H. Gunkel, *Schöpfung und Chaos in Urzeit und Endzeit,* Göttingen (1985). The subtitle is "Gen 1 and Rev 12 and the History of Religions: An Investigation." The inquiry goes far beyond these two texts. Gunkel's starting point is the thesis: "Gen 1 is not a free construction of the author" (4-16). "The very ancient elements handed down in Gen 1 demonstate . . . that Gen 1 goes back to a very ancient tradition" (6-14). "Certain elements (chaos, stars) point to the Babylonian origin of the tradition" (15f.). Gunkel pursues this Babylonian origin. He describes the Babylonian cosmogony according to the Greek accounts of Damascene and Berossos (17-21) and the cuneiform texts (21-27). But he does not stop with this comparison. Unlike so many of his predecessors Gunkel does not consider the cuneiform account to be the model in the literary sense. He looks to the pre-Israelite history of the traditions as a whole and asks what vestiges of it are embedded in the Old Testament. And so a long section has been added entitled "References to the Myth of the Struggle of Marduk with Tiamat in the Old Testament apart from Gen 1" (29-114). Gunkel examines the traditions of the dragon and of the primeval sea and compares the way in which it was handled in the Old Testament and in the Babylonian texts. It is only then that the inquiry reaches its goal, the thesis of the Babylonian origin of the story of creation in Gen 1. The concluding account of the relation of the biblical story of creation to the Babylonian creation myth is of particular importance (114-121).

Gunkel's study has its limitations inasmuch as it is restricted to individual elements of the traditions such as the dragon traditions or the traditions of the primeval sea and is little, if at all, concerned with the traditions and their history as a whole. Form criticism had not yet come to terms with tradition criticism. It is only in his commentary on Genesis that this is taken up. The creation episode is a part of the Enuma Elish; Gen 1 is part of Gen 1-11. Gunkel shows no interest in the unities to which these parts belong. The limitations of his study are clear not only here but also in a very hesitant approach to the definition of the various genres. Even if we go a long way in the direction in which Gunkel has pointed, we cannot accept without more ado the thesis of the Babylonian origin of the creation accounts of Gen 1. There is much evidence in favor of the view that the relationship between Gen 1 and the corresponding parts of Enuma Elish is far more complicated. And the literary criteria appear to be too sharply defined when Gunkel speaks of the Babylonian creation myth, the Babylonian original and the Hebrew recension. There are parts of the Psalms which cannot be described simply as recensions of a myth.

However, Gunkel's study marked a decisive turning point in the exegesis of Gen 1 beyond which there can be no return. "Gen 1 is not a free construction of the author"; "Gen 1 goes back to a very ancient tradition"; "Gen 1 is not an isolated unit . . . it is a link in a long chain" (p. 117). It is this last sentence that shows most clearly the perspective of the history of tradition.

If Gunkel's conclusion is valid then two questions must be asked: What is the significance of the three-fold context in which Gen 1 occurs: the context of the Pentateuch, of the Priestly writing and of the primeval story? At the same time one must ask: What is the significance of Gen 1 in the context of its pre-history? One cannot be dispensed from this second question by saying that P has put the account of creation into an entirely new context and consequently given it an entirely new meaning. What is new either in context or in meaning can only be thrown into relief by a thoroughgoing inquiry into the process of tradition which has led to Gen 1 as it stands. One could put it simply: what is important for the understanding of Gen 1 is not only the fact that P reworked thoroughly a tradition that came down to him, but also that he set himself in the line of that tradition which he accepted. Some half century after the appearance of Gunkel's study the situation is completely different, because there is a much deeper and broader appreciation of the religious background of Gen 1.

A further question now arises: What particular type of description of creation is it in which creation follows or results from a struggle? The Sumerian myths describe creation without any reference at all to a struggle. Brandon writes: "Another characteristic is the absence of any disposition to think that creation had been achieved by conflict" (op. cit., p. 86). Brandon refers to the motif of the struggle with the dragon which occurs in the Sumerian myths: "There are three fragmentary texts which tell of the overthrow of a dragon named Kur. . . . But, although this monster was associated with the primeval waters. . . .no clear cosmogonic theme is developed in the myths concerned" (cf. Kramer 76-83). However, Th. Jacobsen has contested that Kur always has the meaning of a monster and consequently of a mythological being, cf. "Sumerian Mythology — A Review Article," JNES 5 (1946), 128-152. Kramer's explanation rests on a series of conjectures which cannot be sustained. A motif of a struggle with Chaos or of a struggle with a dragon has not yet been attested in Sumerian mythology. Jacobsen's article must be quoted as a steadying corrective to Kramer's book.

We can conclude as follows: the motif of the struggle with the dragon or with Chaos did not belong originally to the creation theme. We can be certain of this because none of the Sumerian descriptions of creation know of a creation which had its origin in a struggle or which was based on a struggle. It was Babylon that first joined together the struggle of the gods (the struggle with Chaos) and creation. Neither in Ugarit is there any clear connection between the struggle with the dragon or with Chaos and creation, cf. A. Caquot "Schöpfungsmythen der Kanaanäer" *Quellen des Alten Orients, Die Schöpfungsmythen,* ed. M. Eliade, 1964, 175-182.

These findings have far-reaching consequences for the understanding of the Chaos struggle motif in the Old Testament. The mere occurrence of the motif does not allow one to conclude immediately that creation is meant. It is found in Enuma Elish but is excluded from Gen 1; (it leaves but the faintest echo in Gen 1:2); there has been an important accommodation; consciously or not there has been a return to the earlier stage of tradition when creation and struggle were not linked. Is this in harmony with P's understanding of creation as תּוֹלְדוֹת and with the language of a creation account which reflects the formulas of a genealogy? In any case we must establish a complete and deliberate separation of creation and struggle as was the case before Enuma Elish. Gunkel was quite certain that creation and struggle were bound together so as to make creation a result of the victory over the powers of Chaos. But this is only one way among many of presenting creation. It is not *the* mythical presentation.

If one pursues the chaos motif further one finds that it is only very rarely an action that precedes and conditions creation. Its meaning is found rather in the area of cosmogony; it "describes the clash between the autochthonos powers which represent the old order and the conquering aggressors who ultimately establish the new. . . . The victory over the autochthonos dragon signifies the victory over Chaos" (cf. M. Eliade, Article "Drache" in RGG³). There are many places then where the myth of the struggle with the dragon has no relationship at all with the myth of creation. In Egypt, for example, the myth of the struggle of the sun god Re with the dragon Apophis has no connection at all with creation; or as in the instruction for King Meri-Ka-Re. It belongs to the succession of primeval events together with creation:

> Well directed are men, the cattle of the god.
> He made heaven and earth according to their desire,
> and he repelled the water monster (ANET 417).

The killing of a god in the course of a cosmogony can have another meaning too where the idea of struggle disappears completely. A large group of primitive religions witness to this as A.E. Jensen points out in *Mythos und Kult bei den Naturvölkern*, 1951, 116f.:

The Marind-anim of New Guinea have a common name for the totality of the primeval beings and for the divine creative forms which are subject to them. They call them Dema. . . . The most striking characteristic consists . . . in the temporal activity of the divinities . . . their proper activity takes place in the primeval time. The creative process is likewise very different . . . the decisive event which gives rise to the important elements of the world is the killing of the Dema divinity by the Dema . . . the Dema-existence ceases with the end of primeval times; mortal, earthly life takes the place of immortality.

Here creation results from the killing of a god who is a primeval divinity. This motif has its role in Enuma Elish in the creation of human beings: Kingu, the leader of Tiamat's successors, is killed in order to create humans to serve the gods.

The Old Testament passages that take up the dragon or Chaos motifs must be studied anew in the light of these findings. Gunkel's study of these motifs is still the most thorough. Many later studies are limited because their discussion proceeds from a consideration of too few texts. We can no longer agree with Gunkel's final conclusion: "Both the Hebrew and the Babylonian myths agree in all their main points. Accordingly, we are dealing not with two myths but with one and the same myth which has been preserved in two different recensions . . . Israel took over the Tiamat-Marduk myth from Babylon and formed it into the Yahweh myth" (op. cit., p. 113f.). What is obscured here is the fact that the myth is not narrated in any of the passages alleged by Gunkel; all passages are found in a different context in which they either recall the myth or refer to it in passing. And even more importance is to be given to the fact that the names of the Chaos monster whom Yahweh conquers are so very different.

רַהַב: Is 51:9; 30:7; Ps 87:4; 89:11; Job 9:13; 26:12
לִוְיָתָן: Is 27:1; Ps 74:14; 104:26; Job 40:25
בְּהֵמוֹת: Job 40:15
תַּנִּין (dragon): Is 51:9; 27:1; Jer 51:34; Ezek 29:3; 32:2; Job 7:12
נָחָשׁ (serpent): Amos 9:3; Is 27:1; Job 26:13 (cf. Gunkel 82).

The name תְּהוֹם does not appear at all in any of these passages. This would indicate that there are references in the Old Testament to a number of different myths of different origin. This view is confirmed by the discovery of a whole series of Chaos myths especially at Ugarit. We can now arrive at certainty because some of the names about which Gunkel could not be sure occur in the Ugaritic texts: תַּנִּין, לִוְיָתָן and especially יָם, which Gunkel had not known as a proper name (Is 51:9f.; Ps 74:13f.; Job 3:8; 7:12; 26:12). Many more recent works have drawn attention to the similarity between the names in the Bible and those at Ugarit and have confirmed the Ugaritic tradition of these texts. We can now be certain that there were many different sources of different origin which influenced the Old Testament Chaos texts; together with Babylon and Canaan, there was also Egypt, as Gunkel had already indicated.

A further modification is now necessary. Gunkel took as his starting point the struggle of Marduk against Tiamat in Enuma Elish; consequently he took for granted that all texts which deal with the Chaos struggle are by that very fact concerned with creation. Since the discovery of the Sumerian and Canaanite texts which deal with the Chaos struggle without any apparent reference to creation, this presupposition must be abandoned (so also W.H. Schmidt, *Die Schöpfungsgeschichte der Priesterschrift*, WMANT 17, 1964).

There is a variety of passages in the Old Testament which speak of or refer to the Chaos struggle; the clearest and most striking of these belong to a group of laments of the people where they look back on God's earlier saving action: Is 51:9f.; Ps 89:10-15; Ps 74:12-17. God is reminded of what he has done earlier so as to move him to intervene in the present distress. The purpose of these texts is not to balance or to link creation and redemption (von Rad stresses this in his essay "The Theological Problem of the Old Testament Doctrine of Creation" in *The Problem of the Hexateuch and Other Essays*, Edinburgh/London: Oliver & Boyd, 1966, pp. 131-143), but to set side by side the wonderful interventions of God in the present and in the primeval period. What is determinative here is not reflection on creation as such but the peculiar way in which the tradition of the struggle has come down. The conclusion imposes itself that in Israel God's marvelous intervention on behalf of his people in the present corresponds to a primeval event in which God conquered the powers of Chaos; God's present action is thus brought into contact with an ancient and widely spread tradition from outside Israel, one strand of which linked the Chaos struggle with creation, the other did not. It is the struggle with Chaos and not creation that is common to all these passages.

The victory of Yahweh over a monster of Chaos has no fixed place apart from the passages in the laments of the community. The myth as such is rejected; and for this reason the absence of any fixed place for the motif in the Psalms of praise is especially important, notwithstanding Gunkel. The references to the myth and the contexts in which it appears are many and varied, showing that Israel was familiar with a variety of forms of the tradition of the Chaos struggle. It has been reworked thoroughly. The victor is Yahweh, the one God; the sphere of myth is abandoned. The motif is linked with creation in only a few passages; for the most part it is quite clear that the victory over the monster of Chaos has nothing to do with creation.

(3) Creation by an Action or Activity. Creation by action is expressed in many ways in primitive religions: the actual creation is often described as a sort of magic and often enough differs little from it. But apart from this the motifs that describe the creation of the world and of people by an act or activity are very infrequent. There is only one creation motif, be it of human beings or the world, which is widespread and occurs with any frequency — the creation of the world by separation or division, the creation of people by forming them out of clay.

(a) The act of separation occurs very frequently in the context of creation. In Enuma Elish it is the act that is the basis of creation: Marduk provides the corpse of Tiamat (Tablet V, 137ff.); out of one part he makes the heavens, out of the other the earth. The motif goes back to a Sumerian tradition. The introduction of the myth "Gilgamesh, Enkidu and the Underworld" begins:

> When heaven had been set at a distance from earth,
> When earth had been detached from heaven,

When the name of mankind had been fixed,
When Anu had taken away the heavens,
When Enlil had taken away the earth . . .
          (S.N. Kramer, op. cit., 37f.)

This is all that the introduction says about the creation of the world; the separation of heaven and earth represents the acts of creation. There is no mention of a struggle. It is the same in the introduction to the myth of the making of the pick-axe:

He resolved to separate heaven from earth,
He resolved to separate earth from heaven
          (Kramer, op. cit., 51f.)

This is the only action mentioned at the creation of the world. When one reflects that the introductions to the myths summarized briefly current traditions, then one concludes that the separation of heaven and earth must have been an early and widespread tradition. In neither case has this theme anything to do with a struggle; we can be certain therefore that the linking of the separation of heaven and earth with the Chaos motif is secondary. Consequently, the motif of separation which plays such an important role in Gen 1 belongs to the tradition in which the separation of heaven and earth, the basic action of world creation, has not yet been linked with the Chaos motif.

This conclusion is supported by similar descriptions of separation in Egypt. The god of the air Shu (Enlil too is the god of the air) separates the god of earth Geb from the goddess of heaven Nut, as the well-known bas-relief shows (cf. Erman, *Die Religion der Ägypter,* p. 62). Here too the separation of heaven and earth is the real act of creation, as Erman writes, p. 63: "That was the real origin of our present world; since heaven and earth were separated from each other in this way all things retain their present order. . . ." The separation has its place in the cosmogony of Heliopolis (E. Otto, *Ägypten,* 58); here the origin of the world as a theogony is joined with the origin of the world by separation.

We will give only one example of separation as a creation motif in other religions: "There is an Indian cosmogony which describes how the world egg which had its origin in the primeval water was split into two parts, the upper part which was of gold became heaven, the lower part which was of silver became earth" (Bertholet, "Schöpfung, rel. gesch" RGG[2]). The descriptions of the creation of the world by separation in Mesopotamia and Egypt are essentially the same; this suggests that in both cases the creation of the world was narrated as separation of heaven and earth; that is to say, the separation was not just a part of the narrative of the creation of the world, as in Enuma Elish and in its own way in Gen 1, but represented creation as a whole. This is characteristic too of primitive cultures (Wundt, op. cit., 270 and 273 e.g., in the Polynesian stories of creation), and is another example of the extraordinary vitality of the creation traditions. A way of describing creation in a much more primitive form of narrative was not lost with a refinement of technique, but became part of that series of acts which together make up world creation.

This background makes it worthwhile considering the thesis that the Hebrew word for creation by God, ברא, has the original basic meaning of "divide" or "separate," E. Dantinne, "Création et Séparation," *Le Muséon,* 74

(1961) 441-451. He begins with the passages Josh 17:15, 18; Ezek 23:47 (1 Sam 2:29, and Ezek 21:24, are not clear), where the verb means "cut off" or "cut in pieces." While the new lexicons recognize another root, Gesenius in the Thesaurus and in the dictionary of 1883 had proposed a development in meaning from the concrete "separate, divide" to the more abstract "create." "To express the idea of creating . . . the ancient Hebrews used a word associated with the idea of separation which is so often explicitly mentioned in the narrative of creation," p. 446.

(b) The Formation of Humanity. The creation of human beings was originally an independent motif and the subject of an independent narrative. The formation of humans from mud or clay is probably the most common and most widespread creation motif. It is found in primitive as well as in high cultures. The theme of the formation of humans out of mud or clay is found on almost every page of J.G. Frazer's collection of creation stories. The same is true of the examples given by H. Baumann. The result of the first part of his work is: "The high god in heaven 'shapes' the person. He forms the individual out of clay, splinters of wood, his own blood. . . ." (p. 164). Frazer writes: "Turning now to Africa we find the legend of the creation of humankind out of clay among the Shilluks of the White Nile who ingeniously explain the different complexions of the various races by the differently colored clays out of which they were fashioned"; Tucapacha first made man and woman out of clay. . . .", (*Folklore in the Old Testament,* pp. 10, 13). One could continue endlessly.

In the primitive culture, creation is limited by and large to human origins. In Egypt creation is essentially cosmogony while the creation of humanity is marginal. It could be said perhaps that in Egypt the divine descent of the kings took the place of the creation of humans (A. Erman, op. cit., 52). The passage in the instruction of Meri-Ka-Re which speaks of the creation of humans would be "a democratization" of the divine descent of the kings (E. Otto, *Ägypten,* p. 111):

> He has created the air so that their noses can live.
> They are images of him, they have come forth from his body.

Egypt is also familiar with the well-known theme of the creation of humans from clay. It is significant that the operation takes place on the potter's wheel. The potter god, Chnum, originally a god of fertility, is addressed as follows:

> Thou art the master of the wheel,
> who is pleased to model on the wheel,
> Thou art the Almighty . . .
> And thou hast made men on the wheel. . .
> (Brandon, op. cit., 61).

The formation of the person from clay is normal in Mesopotamia. One of the many Sumerian myths begins as follows:

> After Anu, Enlil, Enki and Ninhursag
> had fashioned the blackheaded people. . . (Brandon, p. 87).

It is the same in the myth "The creation of man" Kramer, 68f.; Maag (op. cit., 91) resumes the passage:

Nammu tells her sleeping son that he should get up and do something useful, namely create servants for the divinities . . . Enki takes up her request: the being which Nammu wanted took shape immediately . . . Enki's instruction to his mother serves this purpose: with the support of an army of divine kneaders of clay and especially with that of Ninmah, the goddess of birth and of motherhood, she is to form a person from the clay of primeval Chaos . . . humanity is made from earth, and this is basic (cf. also S. Landersdorfer, *Die sumerischen Parallelen zur biblischen Urgeschichte,* Münster 1917, p. 86).

Maag sees in the background an even more ancient theme: "The oldest form of this theme is that the divine mother earth gave birth to the first children of herself" (op. cit., 92). He refers to the old Babylonian birth ritual cited above, and recalls Ps 139:15: "When I was being made in secret, intricately wrought in the depths of the earth." The Yahwistic author of Gen 2 was not saying anything new to his listeners when he spoke of the creation of humanity from the earth; it was an ancient theme, well-known to the world in which Israel lived.

It remains to draw attention to two characteristics of the account of the creation of human beings in Gen 1 which have had a long pre-history: the first is that the creation of humans is the result of a particular decision. Such an apparently unimportant and marginal trait occurs in a number of passages; it has a history. The Sumerian Myth quoted above relates that the creator god Enki is "awakened" and urged by his mother to create a person. The narrative of the Shilluk of the While Nile relates: "He formed humans in the following way. He took a lump of earth and said to himself, 'I will make a person. . . .'" (there follow some reflections about what this person should be), Frazer, *Folklore in the Old Testament,* p. 10. The decision to create a human being is found in a number of primitive creation narratives. It is formulated in a very impressive way in the Enuma Elish Epic:

When Marduk hears the words of the gods,
his heart prompts (him) to fashion artful works.
Opening his mouth, he addresses Ea
to impart the plan he had conceived in his heart:
"Blood I will mass and cause bones to be.
I will establish a savage, 'man' shall be his name.
Verily, savage man I will create.
He shall be charged with the service of the gods
that they might be at ease." (ANET p. 68)

This element of the narrative always stresses the special place of humans in relation to the whole of creation. The capacity to reflect, which distinguishes a human from other living beings, is mirrored in the decision of the creator by which the creation of humanity is set apart from everything else. S. Landersdorfer who had drawn attention to this trait both in the Sumerian and Akkadian texts as well as in Gen 1 reflects that "it is not excluded that we have here a remnant of the common primeval tradition" (op. cit., 86f.). But we have no need of such a tradition when we realize that we have here one of those elements of primitive events which are found everywhere in creation narratives.

The second characteristic is the creation of humanity in the image of God. It is surprising how often it occurs. It was the theme which, according to the older commentaries on Genesis, was peculiar to the biblical story and which elevated it to a loftier level than all other accounts of creation. But this is so

36

widespread a characteristic, extending even to the primitive cultures, that such an opinion can no longer be sustained.

An impressive description is found in Frazer:

> The natives of Nias, an island to the south-west of Sumatra, have a long poem descriptive of the creation, which they recite at the dances performed at the funeral of a chief. In this poem, which is arranged in couplets after the style of Hebrew poetry, the second verse repeating the idea of the first in somewhat different language, we read how the supreme god, Luo Zaho, bathed at a celestial spring which reflected his figure in its clear water as in a mirror, and how, on seeing his image in the water, he took a handful of earth as large as an egg, and fashioned out of it a figure like one of those figures of ancestors which the people of Nias construct. Having made it, he put it in the scales and weighed it; he weighed also the wind, and having weighed it, he put it on the lips of the figure which he had made. . . .
>
> *(Folklore. . .* pp. 7-8).

The creation of humanity in the image of the god is attested in Egypt both in the passage already cited from the teaching of Meri-Ka-Re and in the image of the potter god, Chnum, where he sits at the potter's wheel and makes a person according to a model.

V. Maag speaks of this same characteristic in the Mesopotamian Myths as follows:

> The creation of humanity in the divine image is clear; the way in which the divine quality is passed on to the creature is described differently in different texts. When one looks carefully at these texts and their nuances, one asks whether they might not reflect something of primitive magic or a more spiritualizing trait. . . .
>
> (AsSt 1-4 [1954])

There is no need for further details here. It seems however that this trait has undergone a historical development inasmuch as it can be traced from the primitive to the high cultures. Landersdorfer notes its occurrence in the Sumerian Myths: "The opinion that humanity is created in the image and likeness of God is firmly grounded in Sumerian tradition," p. 87. Though it is not found in the creation of humans by Marduk in Enuma Elish, it does occur in the creation of the hero Enkidu by Aruru in the Gilgamesh Epic:

> When Aruru heard this,
> a double of Anu she conceived within her.
> Aruru washed her hands,
> pinched off clay and cast it on the steppe.
> (On the steppe) she created valiant Enkidu.
> (ANET p. 74)

An important conclusion follows from this for the interpretation of the stories of the creation of humanity in the Bible. The creation of people from clay occurs in the older account, the creation of people in the image of God occurs in the later account. The conclusion had long since been drawn that the former belonged of its very nature to a more primitive type of reflection, the latter to a more spiritualized type. But that cannot be when both occur in the same text as in the creation of the hero Enkidu in the Gilgamesh Epic. Each can belong to quite different stages or levels of development; they cannot be interpreted outside the context of the history of their traditions.

This holds too for the long drawn-out discussion about the meaning of "the image and likeness of God" in which attempts have been made to explain the text of Gen 1:28 in isolation. It is not possible to explain such a text without taking into account the history of its tradition. H. Wildberger has made an important contribution to the discussion in "Das Abbild Gottes," ThZ 21 (1965), 245-259, 481-501. After studying the history of the idea in Babylon and Egypt he comes to the conclusion "that Gen 1:26-30 is rooted ultimately in the royal ideology of the ancient near east" (p. 255). I think he has demonstrated that this is the background of the language of Ps 8. But I am not so certain that it is the sole explanation of Gen 1:26, especially when the motif occurs in the primitive accounts of creation. The reflections on the subsequent history of the idea in the New Testament are very helpful, as are the discussions of modern literature on the image and likeness of God.

(4) Creation Through the Word. Creation through the word belongs to the same context as creation through an event or an action. As the motif is of great theological importance in Gen 1, it is necessary to examine its historical background very carefully. This has been done by O. Grether, *Name und Wort Gottes im Alten Testament,* BZAW 64, 1934, especially in the section "Word and Nature," pp. 135-144. He considers that the reason why "the *dabar*-idea was applied to nature only at a relatively late stage," p. 135, was that Yahweh's relation to history took precedence. "It is only in Deut 8:3 that there first occurs an unambiguous reference to Yahweh's intervention by the word," p. 136. Besides Gen 1 other passages are Is 40:26; 44:24ff.; 48:13; 50:2; 55:10f., Ezek 37:4, and Pss 33:6, 9; 147:4; 104:7; 147:15-18; 148:3-5. Grether sees "the act of relating the word to nature as an ultimate outcome of typical Israelite thinking." Of special importance in this context is "the acknowledgement of the formative power in history of the prophetic word," p. 139.

One can agree so far, however questionable it may be whether so abstract an idea as the transference of the דָּבָר-idea from the realm of history to that of nature is appropriate to the texts. But Grether goes further; he quotes a whole series of parallels in which "the word appears as an effective element in the origin of the world and in events of nature." Grether concludes on this basis that "there is a profound difference between the Bible and non-biblical religions," p. 144. These latter "put the divinity into a relationship with the world that is partly magical, partly naturalistic, partly pantheistic or in some way distorted," p. 144. There is a corresponding distortion in what is said of the word of God. One wonders why so negative a verdict is still necessary when assurance has been given both at the beginning and the end that "there can be no question of the Bible taking over extra-biblical points of view," p. 144. The criticism of Grether by K. Koch takes the same direction, "Wort und Einheit des Schöpfergottes in Memphis und Jerusalem," ZThK 62 (1965) 251-293, especially 284f.

A. Heidel's view is basically the same in his brief treatment of the matter in *The Babylonian Genesis,* 1951², p. 126f. He refers only to the passage in Enuma Elish IV, 23-26, where Marduk at the request of the gods demonstrates his power by destroying and restoring a garment by his word. He then continues: "But this is the only manifestation of such power in all the Babylonian creation stories . . . the word of the Babylonian deities was not almighty." On the contrary, the word of the creator in Gen 1 is almighty: "He commands and the result is in perfect conformity with his command." It is the same in Ps 33:9. One could argue as follows: If this is the case, why does not Gen 1 consist only of the word of command and its fulfillment as in 1:3-5? Why do the following verses speak of making, dividing, initiating, and so on? Heidel had only to use the Babylonian hymns cited by Grether where it is beyond question that the creative word of the gods was thought to be almighty. And what would be Heidel's judgment on creation through the word in the theology of Memphis?

The same is to be said here as was said of creation in the image of God. It can have very different meanings in different contexts. Such differences, of course, are completely irrelevant when from the very start a completely negative judgment is passed on every occurrence of this theme outside the Bible. Something like creation through the word is found in primitive cultures, especially in the earlier levels. H. Baumann speaks of creation by "calling forth" which occurs among a group of chthonicmantic gods: "Mukuru of Herrero and Unkulunkulu are above all divine ancestors. Both have acquired something of the character of a high-god and have overthrown the older gods of the heaven. Both simply call the first beings out of the primeval tree or the primeval reed. . .", p. 171f. This passage shows that the word can occur even in a very primitive context to describe a calling-forth of the first beings. It is not really creation.

Creation through the word occurs often in the praise of God both in Mesopotamia and in Egypt. This has been described in a number of older and more recent studies; for example, W.H. Schmidt, *Die Schöpfungsgeschichte der Priesterschrift*, 1964, pp. 172-177, and the literature which is cited there. A few examples will be sufficient: "Everything that is has come to being through his words" (L. Dürr, *Die Wertung des göttlichen Wortes im Alten Testament und im antiken Orient*, Leipzig 1938, 28; from the period of Ptolemy IV). "What streams from his mouth, happens, and what he pronounces, takes place" (Dürr, p. 27f.).

Besides Gen 1, passages which speak of creation through the word are found in the context of the praise of God in the Psalms, e.g., Pss 33:6, 9; 148:5, as well as in Deutero-Isaiah, e.g., 48:13.

The succession of cosmogonies from the great Egyptian shrines teaches us how the description of creation through the word reached an advanced stage of theological development at Memphis; this itself was an advance on previous cosmogonies from other shrines. The reason for the development was to give a basis for and to assure the precedence of the god Ptah and his shrine at Memphis (cf. E. Otto, *Ägypten*, 1958[3], 60f.; S.G.F. Brandon, op. cit., 29-43: "The Cosmogony of Memphis"; H.A. Frankfort, *Kingship and the Gods*, Chicago 1948, 24ff.).

The relationship of creation through the word in the Old Testament to the theology of Memphis is presented in greater detail and with a broader background in the article of K. Koch, "Word und Einheit des Schöpfergottes in Memphis und Jerusalem," ZThK 62 (1965) 251-293. I refer to this article for further details and I agree with the main lines of argument. I received it only after the completion of my manuscript.

The genealogies of the gods and the cosmogonies of the older shrines were developed into a system at Memphis; on the one hand there was the very significant tendency to explain the gods of the early cosmogonies as manifestations of Ptah, the one god, embracing them all; on the other hand there was the daring attempt to present creation as coming from the heart and tongue of Ptah and so to outdo the origin of the world from the birth of the gods. Frankfort, op. cit., p. 28, speaks as follows:

And there we can watch how the ancient Egyptian language . . . is made the vehicle of some truly astonishing abstractions. The author expresses no less than the conviction that the basis of existence is spiritual: ideas conceived by the Creator and objectified by his utterances. The text expresses this by describing the "heart" and the "tongue" as the organs of creation. These terms are concrete enough. But we should misread our document completely if we took them at their face value. We know from numerous other texts that "heart" stands for "intellect," "mind," and even "spirit." The "tongue" is realizing thought; it translates concepts into actuality by means of "Hu," authoritative utterance.

It is very important for our purpose that this new description of creation is related expressly to an older description from Heliopolis where Atum was the creator. Brandon quotes the passage on p. 35:

His (Ptahs) Ennead is before him as teeth and lips (being) the semen and the hands of Atum. The Ennead of Atum indeed came into being through the semen and fingers of Atum. But the Ennead (of Ptah) is the teeth and the lips in his mouth which pronounced the name of all things, from whom came forth Shu and Tefnut who created the Ennead. . . So were all the gods created and his Ennead completed. Every utterance of the god truly came into being through that which was conceived by the heart and commanded by the tongue.

Not only is there a detailed correspondence between this passage and the creation account through the word in Gen 1, but the histories of the traditions also correspond. In both cases creation through the word is the final stage of a long process of development, replacing an older and well-established description and doing so in such a way that elements of this older description are subsumed into the later.

The work of creation in the Egyptian text concludes with the description of Ptah's judgment on his work which is parallel to the judgment of God in Gen 1: "Thus was Ptah satisfied, after he had made all things and every divine utterance." There is no need to look for a direct influence of one upon the other. The text demonstrates in a very impressive way that the creation narratives embrace a complex of traditions that give rise to many parallels even when there is no direct dependence.

A correspondence such as this may be regarded as the model for the possible relationship of a theological theme essential to the Bible to something similar in the non-Israelite world. It is foolish to deny or to minimize this. It is no less foolish to consider such a theme in isolation saying, for example, that the creative word in Gen 1 is almighty while in the other text it is not almighty. No definitive answer can be given to the question whether the description of creation by the word of God was taken over from outside or whether it is to be explained from within Israel. So Grether, op. cit., p. 52, and W.H. Schmidt, op. cit., in the excursus "creation through the word," pp. 173-177. I agree essentially with what Schmidt says and with his conclusion:

Though there are many points of comparison between the creative word of God in the ancient east and in the Old Testament, no historical dependence can be demonstrated.... . The priestly description of creation through the word is explained better from the prophetic tradition within Israel rather than from direct borrowing from ancient near eastern tradition.

Our present state of knowledge demands prudence and reserve. But would it make any real difference to our understanding of Gen 1 were it to be proved one day that there was direct dependence? I do not think so. The uniqueness of the biblical and priestly description of creation through the word does not depend on whether the author was or was not familiar with the Egyptian and Mesopotamian stories. It is based exclusively on its setting in the priestly work as a whole which is colored and determined by the words "and God spoke . . . and it was so," as W.H. Schmidt has observed: "It is characteristic of the priestly work throughout that there is correspondence between God's command and its fulfillment," p. 171, n. 2.

The correspondence between creation through the word in the theology of Memphis and Gen 1 is explained by the fact that both are concerned with the same subject matter, and each belongs to a relatively late stage in the history of its tradition. It is simply because the motifs and the way in which they are expressed are so limited that correspondences are to be expected without any dependence of one upon the other. It is exactly the same as in the case of the creation of humans from the earth (from mud or clay); the widespread occurrence of this motif does not call for any interdependence.

It is to be expected that there will be points of contact, similarities, and agreements in the stories of creation and of primeval events. The question of dependence therefore is of no real significance. Any motif or phrase, such as creation throught the word in Gen 1, can be explained in the sense intended only in its proper context, which alone allows us to see what is peculiar to the biblical account in comparison with the extra-biblical texts.

(5) The Rest of the Creator. Rest is associated with activity, and is not something that is simply suited to creation through the word. Gen 2:2b is clearly an older element to which P has given a new meaning by putting it into a new context. Behind this verse is a very ancient theme that occurs frequently in primitive creation stories. R. Pettazzoni cites examples from south-east Australia in "Myths of Beginning and Creation-Myths," op. cit., 32. The creator-god disappears after the completion of his work of creation; for example, he withdraws into heaven and is no longer concerned about his work. "The originator lives only in the past; it is always that he has done something, he will not intervene again."

The Sumerian and Babylonian Myths probably express this leisure of the creator-god when they describe him, as they do for the most part, as the ancient god, the god who never or scarcely ever is active in the present. This is clear in Enuma Elish; Apsu and Tiamat are the ancient gods; primeval creation took its origin from them. They must die so that a new creation can begin which is not simply creation, but an act of rescue that overthrows the enemy. Pettazzoni explains the leisure of the creator-god as follows:

It is possible that leisure belongs to the essence of the creator; it is in a certain sense the filling-out of his creative activity. The work of the creator is concluded when he has made the world and set it in order. Any further intervention on his part would not only be superfluous but possibly dangerous because any change in the cosmos could cause it to sink back into chaos . . . the leisure of the creator . . . what might be called this inactive present, is the condition which permits . . . the maintenance of the status quo'' (op. cit., p. 32).

If this is so, then we have a very important directive for the understanding of creator and creation. The act of creation is unique and independent; it stands separate and apart from every other event. The creation of the world and of humanity, God's creating action, is not the beginning of a series of acts; there can be no *creatio continua*. In other words, creation is a primeval event and not the beginning of history.

This being the case, we have the explanation of a matter to which reference has often been made, but which has not yet been explained adequately: what is said about God's creating action in Gen 1-3 is limited in a peculiar way to the primeval story. While God's acts in history, like the deliverance from Egypt, have been repeated through the centuries and appear again and again in very different contexts, neither Gen 1 nor Gen 2f. has been the point of departure of a history of tradition. The teaching about the person in the image and likeness of God from Gen 1 or about the fall from Gen 2-3 have played an important role in Christian tradition; they have no corresponding role in the Old Testament where they scarcely appear. This is the result of an awareness which was later lost namely that creation is a primeval event and not the beginning of history. It is of great significance then when P calls the creator-god by a name different from that which he uses when God begins to intervene in history, Ex 6; (for E, cf. Ex 3); here too is found the explanation of the combined name ''Yahweh Elohim'' in Gen 2-3 (J).

Something must be said now by way of conclusion about theological reflection on creation. The confession of faith of the Apostles' Creed has trained us to think of ''belief in God the creator'' as self-evident and to describe as equally self-evident the ''creation faith'' of the Old Testament as it appears in Gen 1-3. This is the case, to mention but two examples, with von Rad's essay ''The Theological Problem of the Old Testament Doctrine of Creation,'' in *The Problem of the Hexateuch and Other Essays*, 1966, pp. 131-143 (the essay first appeared in German in 1936), and with W. H. Schmidt's monograph cited above, (especially p. 180f.). We forget that our point of departure is a concept of belief which describes the total relationship of the person to God as faith, as in the New Testament, and which consequently embraces the relationship of the person to the creator, as in the Apostles' Creed.

This is not the case in the Old Testament where there is not a single passage where creation or the creator is brought into immediate contact with the concept of belief. Phrases such as ''belief in the creator'' or ''creation belief'' are not possible in the language of the Old Testament. When without more ado we speak of ''a creation faith'' in the Old Testament, associations are evoked which are quite foreign to it. This is the case when a salvation or redemption faith is set over against a creation faith or when one asks about a creation revelation in the Old Testament. What is said about creator and creation in the Old Testament has nothing at all to do with revelation. The question whether the first three chapters of the Bible testify to a creation faith or not can be answered neither positively nor negatively because the question cannot even be properly stated.

The idea of "belief in God the creator" presumes the possibility of an alternative, namely of non-belief, which was just not an option for the people of the Old Testament; and that is the reason why there is no mention of a belief in the creator. We have seen that Israel shares this with the whole of the ancient world, from the most ancient stages of primitive cultures right up to the high religions of the great empires of the ancient east. Nowhere and at no time in the vast and varied talk about creator and creation is there any serious and conscious questioning that humanity and the world were created. Even where it is a question of the origin of the world and of humankind rather than of creation there is no opposing thesis; rather, the gods take some part in the origin in the myths of beginning. Our conclusion must be that it was a presupposition or just taken for granted by the whole of the ancient world, including Israel, that the world and humanity had been created. There was no viable alternative. There was no understanding of existence or of the world which was not based on the conviction of creation. If we want to understand the Old Testament when it talks about creator and creation, then we should not associate it with or subject it to a concept of faith that presumes such an alternative.

(6) "When There Was Not Yet. . ." What was said above about the divine repose could be understood as contradicting the continuing present of the creation story. Why is the creation event continually being made present if the creator-god is "at rest"? if his intervention in creation could endanger the cosmos? What can be the significance of the continual realization of the creation event in the narrative of creation when the creator-god can no longer be active?

There is no easy answer to this question. We must begin from the fact that the presence of such an abundance of creation stories spread over the whole world leads inevitably to the existential necessity of the realization of the creation event. The purpose of this realization is to underscore the utter uniqueness of creation — it is as unique as a birth — and to contrast it with present reality, thereby preserving what is special to it. Every story of creation of whatever kind accomplishes anew the action of separation and thereby sets up a contrast to the present state of things. This state and all that is taken for granted with it is, as it were, abolished for a moment; the present and apparently permanent state of the world is taken back to a moment when an event is taking place in which the present state is in a process of becoming; the event starts from a "not yet," from a state of nothingness of chaos. This is expressed in the introductions which are so characteristic of so many creation stories: "When there was not yet. . ." Enuma Elish begins:

> When on high the heaven had not been made,
> firm ground below had not been called by name.

One version of the creation of the world by Marduk begins by enumerating in nine lines everything that was "not yet," and concludes in line 10 with the words: "all the lands were sea"; then in line 12 the work of creation begins: "Then Eridu was made, Esagila was built. . . ." The same type of introduction occurs in Gen 2:4b, and an earlier form of it is the background to Gen 1:1-2.

The same beginning occurs too in the pyramid text from Heliopolis from the old kingdom: "The god Pharao Pepi was engendered by the god Atum when

existed not the heaven, existed not the earth,
existed not men,
before the birth of gods, before the existence of death.

This opening can be traced back to the creation stories of primitive cultures. Frazer gives many examples (p. 11):

The Eskimo . . . tell of a time, when there was no man in the Land. The Diegueno Indians . . . say that in the beginning there was no earth nor solid land, nothing but salt water. . .

This formula, "when there was not yet. . ." perseveres as late as the pseudepigraphical book of Ezra:

In the beginning of the terrestrial world
before ever the heavenward portals were standing,
    or ever the wind-blasts blew;
before the rumblings of thunderings did sound,
    or ever the lightening flashes did shine;
when the foundations of paradise were not yet laid,
    nor the beauty of its flowers yet seen;
before ever the motive powers (of heaven) were established,
    or the numberless armies of angels were gathered;
before ever the heights of the air were uplifted,
    ere the spaces of the firmaments were named;
    ere the footstool of Sion was appointed.
Before the years of the present were reckoned,
    ere the councils of present-day sinners were spurned,
    or the gatherers of the treasures of faith were sealed —
even then I had all these things in mind;
and through me alone and none other were they created;
as also the End (shall come) through me alone and
none other. [2 (4) Esdras 6:1-6; trans. R.H. Charles].

A formula which is so widespread and of such long standing must say something very important about the idea of creation. The action of creation is understood as a transformation, as a changing of chaos or nothingness, however these are understood, into the world as it now is, that is, into the world which is destined for people to live in. This way of speaking about transformation prevents the world and its existence from being taken for granted; the world in its contingency is traced back to an event which transcends it, namely the act by which the creator brought about change. This way of speaking is of great significance because it is the place where talk about creation becomes narrative in the strict sense. It brings a flash point into the creation event. It is here that the question of *creatio ex nihilo* must be introduced. Can the phrase "when this and that was not yet" be replaced simply by "when as yet there was nothing" without altering the purpose of the narrative which is to describe creation as a change? We will return to this question. We wish to establish here only that the introductions to the creation stories known to us never make the step from "when this and that was not yet" to "when there was nothing."

H. Grapow has studied this way of describing the primeval event in Egypt in his essay "Die Welt vor der Schöpfung" ZÄS 67 (1931) 34-38. It occurs surprisingly often and with many variations, for example, in "the book of the destruction of Apophis":

> The heavens had not yet come forth,
> the earth had not yet come forth,
> the soil of the earth had not yet been created,
> and the worms in that place. . .(Pap. Brit. Mus. 10188,25,22).

The most common formula in these texts is: "when . . . had not yet come forth." What had not yet come forth could be the heavens and the earth, gods and people, flood and the underworld, and, in a whole series of texts, something quite negative: death ("the worms in that place," "when death had not yet come forth") or the limitations of existence:

> "When disturbance had not yet come forth"
> "When that fear had not yet come forth,
>   which comes because of Horus' eyes"
> "When rage . . . tumult . . . strife . . . disturbance
>   had not yet come forth,
> When the eye of Horus had not yet been wounded."

What preceded creation can also be included in these formulas:

> "When heaven and earth had not yet come forth
>   from Nun;"
> "When the two supports (that is Shu and Tefnet)
>   had not yet come forth"
> "When the elevation of Shu had not yet come forth"
> "When the gods had not yet been born"
> "When nothing at all had yet been given a name"
> "When I (the sun god) had not yet vomited forth
>   anything as Shu,
> Nor had I spat forth anything as Tefnet."

Many different creation events are included here in the formula "when not yet. . .", such as theology, the separation of heaven and earth, and others. Later texts show a tendency to be more abstract:

> "(Amun), who came forth first, when nothing had
>   yet come forth, which came forth," or
> "When nothing at all had come forth, because
>   the earth was still in the darkness of night."

Grapow refers to similar formulas in other places: in the Old Testament in Gen 2:4-7, in Babylonian, in Indian (Rigveda), in Old High German (the Wessobrunner Prayer), old Norse (the older Edda), he explains the similarity as "a sharing in something which is grounded in humankind itself — basic related ideas and their expression in words" (p. 35).

The texts Grapow has collected show the significance of this formula and demonstrate at the same time the different ways in which it can be used. Its basic function is always the same; to fix a point in the course of events when time and existence as experienced in the everyday world are marked off from a primeval state when all that conditions present existence had not yet come to be. One could describe the formula as the narrative trait that marks off primeval time. Its very general meaning would explain its worldwide use.

The Egyptian texts apply the formula in quite a variety of ways which determine it further and which remain always very concrete. Even where there may be a tendency to speak in more abstract terms, e.g., "when nothing at all

45

had yet come forth," there is always a concrete description, "because the earth was still in the darkness of night." The reason for this is that the formula "when there was not yet" is the narrative characteristic that marks off primeval time. Narrative must speak of something; it cannot tell of nothing.

This calls to mind Gen 1:2, for the explanation of which we have now an important insight. The survey shows that it is Gen 1:2 and not Gen 1:1 that corresponds to the formula. Consequently the argument for translating Gen 1:1 as a subordinate clause corresponding to the formula disappears. On the other hand Gen 1:2 corresponds exactly, the only adaptation being that the negative expression is changed into a positive one as with the example cited from the Egyptian texts. Gen 1:2 must be explained from the history of the tradition of this motif. This means that its intent is not to describe a state that preceded creation, but to mark off God's act of creation from a "before" which is beyond words and can only be described in negative terms.

The primary purpose of all these sentences is to delimit and not to describe, even where a positive expression such as "darkness and night" or וָבֹהוּ תֹהוּ has replaced the negative sentence. I cannot agree with E. Würthwein when, in an essay referring to Grapow's study, he begins: "Many myths of cosmogony speak about the world before creation," and continues: "When one wants to speak of the world before creation. . ." ("Chaos und Schöpfung im mythischen Denken und in der biblischen Urgeschichte," *Zeit und Geschichte, Festschr. R. Bultmann zum 80. Geburtstag,* 1964, 317-327, quotation from p. 138). However this is not the intent of the introductory formulas, "when this and that was not yet," which are not for all that an "expression of the mythical experience of the world." They occur in pre-mythical as well as in the biblical accounts of creation (Gen 2: 4-7; cf. Ps 90:2).

The formula "when there was not yet" makes it possible for the old creation narratives to describe creation as an event or as an act. Acts and events occur only in a series in any given narrative, linked in some way to what has gone before. Creation is narrated as the primal beginning which took place "when this and that was not yet there." The purpose of the formula is to give creation the character of an event.

Gen 1 has no option but to speak in concrete terms which mark off creation as an event from any "before" which can only be described negatively. If Gen 1:1-2 intended to describe *creatio ex nihilo,* then that would be a μετάβασις εἰς ἄλλο γένος, something that simply cannot be reported. One can teach *creatio ex nihilo;* but one cannot narrate it.

(7) Creation and the Praise of God. The motif "when not yet" can perhaps help to clarify the relationship between the creation narrative and the praise of the creator, though it is not possible to go into details here, nor to discuss the relationship in the Wisdom literature. (Some remarks on this will be found in W.H. Schmidt op. cit., part B, "Die hymnischweisheitliche Tradition," 32-48.)

The creation story in the Old Testament is not the beginning of any tradition-history. It is more or less independent of the theme of the praise of the creator in the Psalms and in the other places. The praise of God in Israel takes as its point of departure God's saving act at the beginning of Israel's history, Ex 15:21. The most obvious point of contact between the saving act as a turning point in distress and the activity of the creator is creation seen as a turning of chaos-nothingness into the ordered world of humankind. The Psalms of descriptive praise, the hymns, link the praise of the creator with the lord of history. The linchpin is God's transforming action, e.g., Ps 107:32-37, prominent also both in Deutero-Isaiah and in Job.

The drama of creation is expressed and experienced much more strongly in the more ancient accounts. Moreover, we observe that in some places the praise of the creator and the story of creation are side by side. The Enuma Elish epic is as a whole directed to the praise of Marduk, and its account of creation is set in this context. The Sumerian Myths are further evidence that the praise of God and the story of creation belong together. The myth of "the creation of the pick-axe" (Kramer, op. cit., p. 51f.) is introduced in the manner of a hymn to the god:

> The lord, that which is appropriate verily
>   he caused to appear;
> The lord whose decisions are unalterable. . .

The myth "Enlil and Ninlil, The Begetting of Nanna," p. 43ff., concludes with the praise of God: "Our myth then comes to a close with a brief hymnal passage in which Enlil is exalted as the lord of abundance and the king whose decrees are unalterable," p. 47. Several of these myths of creation conclude with a praise of god: ". . . O Father Enlil, praise," p. 51; "O Father Enki, praise," pp. 58, 63. In these examples the story of creation is clearly the praise of God. S. Herrmann, after a consideration of the hymn-like description of the works of creation in the teaching of Meri-Ka-Re and of a hymn to Amun, comes to the conclusion: "Knowledge . . . is subordinated to God's creative power and in the description of his work of creation is directed to his greater glory" ("Die Naturlehre des Schöpfungsberichtes. . ." ThLZ 86, 1961, 413-424). Pettazzoni also links both: ". . . for men are convinced that by telling of the great cosmic events and proclaiming the might of the creator they succeed in ensuring the stability of the universe and obtaining the protection of God" (*Myths of Beginnings and Creation Myths,* p. 29f.).

The Sumerian Myths as well as Enuma Elish are poetic in form; the narratives there use more or less the language of the Psalms; one has grounds then to see in them something of an early form of descriptive praise of the creator in which the praise of God and the story of creation are still one.

B. The Narratives of Crime and Punishment

Introduction. All the narrative passages of Gen 1-11 are concerned in some way with crime and punishment (cf. C. Westermann, Arten der Erzählung in der Genesis, ThB 24, 1964, 9-91; III, pp. 47-58).

Our starting point has been that the story of primeval events must be seen as a whole. The genealogies permeate and color this whole. They are closely linked to the creation story so that they themselves could have been at one time a sort of description of creation. What is their relationship to the group of narratives in Gen 1-11, all of which are concerned with crime and its expiation?

The first sign that we are dealing here with a special kind of primeval story is that, besides the creation stories and genealogies, there are only stories with this particular theme. One must distinguish between J and P. What has been said holds strictly only for J, because P contains only one story of crime and punishment, namely the story of the flood. The outline of the primeval story in P is much more simple and clear: creation-genealogy-flood-genealogy. The additional material in the J narrative deals almost exclusively with concrete examples of crime against which God has to intervene with punishment, 3; 4; 6:1-4; 11:1-9. Such examples are completely absent from P even in the flood story where specific crime is mentioned as the object of God's punishment.

I. The Flood, Gen 6-9. Gen 6-9 can be described as a narrative of crime and punishment only with certain reservations. The span of the narrative is not from a crime which people have committed to its discovery and its punishment: crime and punishment are rather the background which gives rise to another narrative scheme, namely the salvation of an individual from a flood that destroys all. Gen 6-9 is, strictly speaking, the story of an act of salvation that presumes the punishment of humanity by means of the flood. This is the reason why the flood story is to be given special consideration apart from the other stories of crime and punishment; it has had its own very extensive history.

The discovery of the flood story in the Gilgamesh epic has shown the biblical narrative stands in a well-established tradition. (A recent comprehensive presentation is that of A. Heidel, *The Gilgamesh Epic and Old Testament Parallels,* Chicago, 1946.) The stories show such similarities, even to agreement in details, that it is impossible to deny some sort of relationship. It was the Babylonian flood story that set in motion what has been called the Babel-Bible controversy (Friedrich Delitzsch, *Die grosse Täuschung,* 1920). It is regrettable that at the time too many were satisfied with an indignant rejection of extreme conclusions, and did not face the problem presented by the existence of a very similar extra-biblical flood story. Nor was it a proper handling of the problem to detach details of the Babylonian narrative and to pass negative judgment on them and use them to demonstrate the superiority of the biblical story. Careful consideration and judgment are required; and one must ask what are the reasons why and what is the significance of the fact that two stories of the flood so far apart in time and location have such striking similarities.

The situation today is very different from that at the time of the Babel-Bible controversy, and even from that which was the background of Gunkel's commentary on Genesis. The present discussion is no longer concerned with the relationship between the biblical and Babylonian flood stories, but with the relationship of these two to a stream of tradition in which other forms have been handed down, e.g., accounts which have been assumed into the Gilgamesh Epic and the Atrahasis Epic as episodes, and the Sumerian form which has come down as an individual narrative (cf. A. Heidel, op. cit., pp. 102-136). There is no longer a place for the earlier question whether J and P may have used a literary model from the Gilgamesh Epic in constructing their accounts of the flood. The flood narrative has made it abundantly clear that its background is a tradition of a thousand years or more which must be considered carefully before making comparisons or judgments.

S.N. Kramer in his essay "The Epic of Gilgamesh and Its Sumerian Sources, a Study in Literary Evolution," JAOS 64 (1944) 7-23, has demonstrated that almost every section of the Gilgamesh Epic exists as a separate entity in Sumerian — including the flood. This independent Sumerian form of the story of the flood has particular significance for Gen 6-9 inasmuch as in it creation precedes the flood. The conjunction of creation and flood in the biblical story has a precedent. Both are primeval events and so belong together. (Besides the work of A. Heidel mentioned above, see W.G. Lambert and A.R. Millard, *Atrahasis, the Babylonian Story of the Flood,* OUP, 1969.)

The flood as a primeval event is a motif found all over the world. Frazer surveys the scene in his work *Folklore in the Old Testament,* ch. 4 "The Great Flood," 46-143; W. Wundt, *Völkerpsychologie,* VI, Band 6, "Weltunter-gangsmythen"; J. Riem, *Die Sintflut in Sage und Wissenschaft,* Hamburg 1925. In part 2, "Die Berichte," Riem advances texts from the Indogermanic peoples, the near east, Europe, non-Indogermanic peoples, north, south and east Asia, Malaysia, Australia, the south sea islands, Africa, North America, Central America, and South America. H. Baumann has dealt with the African scene, *Schöpfung und Urzeit des Menschen im Mythus der afrikanischen Völker,* "Die Weltkatastrophe," 306-327.

In the exegesis of Gen 6-9 the pre-history of the flood story, with the exception of the Babylonian account, is almost completely neglected. At times it is explicitly stated that it has no relevance at all for the explanation of Gen 6-9. This is valid enough as long as one is considering only the literary aspects. But it is not so when one considers the story from the point of tradition-history. Two aspects of the flood story make this clear:

(a) If the flood story belongs to the primeval events, to the "myths of beginning," then one would expect that, just as with the creation story, there would be some sort of celebration which would actualize it and bring home its meaning for the well-being of the community. But no trace of a cultic commemoration of the flood has yet been found in Mesopotamia. On the other hand there are many examples in primitive cultures of the story of the flood being linked with a celebration. Frazer writes as follows:

> The legend of a great flood plays an important part in the traditionary lore of the Lolos, an aboriginal race who occupy the almost impregnable mountain vastnesses of Yunan and other provinces of Southwestern China. . . To this day the ancestral tablets, which the Lolos worship on set days of the year and on all the important occasions of life, are made out of the same sort of tree as that in which their great forefather found safety from the waters of the deluge. . .
>
> (*Folklore. . . .*p. 83).

Lucian describes the shrine of Hierapolis on the Euphrates. He tells the Greek story of the flood which ends with the earth opening and the water flowing away into the crevice. Lucian continues:

> I have seen the crevice; it was a very small one beneath the temple. . . The following ceremony commemorates the event: twice a year water is brought to the temple from the sea. It is fetched not only by the priests, but by the whole of Syria and Arabia; many go to the sea even from the far side of the Euphrates and they all bring water. The water is poured into the crevice and although the crevice is only small it takes in a tremendous amount of water. By doing so they believe that they are continuing the custom which Deucalion introduced into the shrine as a reminder of the event and as a sign of thanksgiving.

Frazer gives a very vivid account of one commemoration of the flood among a tribe of Indians:

> The Mandan Indians had a tradition of a great deluge in which the human race

perished except one man, who escaped in a large canoe to a mountain in the west. Hence the Mandans celebrated every year certain rites in memory of the subsidence of the flood which they called "the sinking down or settling of the waters" (p. 112f.).

These texts are sufficient witness that the flood as a primeval event is related to present existence, and that this relationship is expressed in a celebration. All explanations which understand the flood story as an echo of a historical event fall to the ground. Many stories of the flood may well contain a recollection of a great catastrophe; but the event narrated here is something more. It is a primeval story and as such a once and for all event. As primeval event it retains its significance for the present.

(b) It is only when one surveys the whole pre-history of the flood story that one is struck by the unique and many-sided relationship to the story of creation. At the beginning of his section about myths of world catastrophe, to which the flood myths belong, W. Wundt writes: "The story of world catastrophe is the mythological complement to the account of the creation of the world" (Vol. 6, 290). If this view is correct, and there are many texts which favor it, then we must regard these two narratives as complementary to each other, and not linked primarily by chronological succession. This, and Frazer's "before the flood," and "after the flood," as in the Sumerian king lists, would be no more than a rationalization. It has often been remarked that the flood story in both J and P contains many striking echoes of the creation stories; these are to be seen against the background of the history of the stories. One notable point of contact is that in the Sumerian texts the restoration of the world after the flood is described as a new creation (S.N. Kramer, *History Begins at Sumer,* Anchor Books, p. 154:

An and Enlil uttered "breath of heaven," "breath of earth," by their . . . it stretched itself, Vegetation, coming up out of the earth, rises up.

This indicates that the stories of creation and the flood are closely related. The relationship is very clear in a number of primitive stories. There are flood stories which are at the same time stories of creation; for example, among the Benua-Jakun, a tribe on the Malaysian peninsula (cf. Frazer, p. 82, and the collection of Riem no. 65, p. 56), or the Kato Indians (Riem no. 228, p. 126f.). A characteristic trait of the flood stories is that all humanity took its origin from those who were saved from the flood (Frazer, pp. 80, 83, 92); and there is the very sensitive story of the Shawnee Indians (Riem no. 22, p. 122) which relates both. Very often the flood which destroys is almost identical with the primeval flood, as for example in the stories of the Diegueno Indians and the Hopi- or Moqui Indians (Frazer, pp. 12 and 13); it is not without interest to note that here, as in many other stories, the birds of the creation narrative play a role very similar to that in the stories of the flood. It is important too to note that where polytheism prevails it is always the creator god who takes the decision to destroy humankind which he has created (S. Landersdorfer draws attention to this, op. cit., p. 97).

These examples are sufficient to demonstrate that there are many points of contact between creation and flood stories. We can note here that this is of great importance for the understanding of apocalyptic. Apocalyptic belongs basically to myths of world destruction of which the flood stories form an earlier group, as

W. Wundt has correctly seen. Apocalyptic is a projection of primeval events into the future as Gunkel has written in *Schöpfung und Chaos in Urzeit und Endzeit*. Sufficient attention has not yet been paid to the significance of this — apocalyptic, both in content and in intention, is subordinated not to salvation history but to primeval history, especially to the history of creation and of the flood.

(c) Part of the flood story is the resolution to destroy made by the assembly of the gods or the decision to destroy made by a single god. In the profusion of stories, no other motif is as closely linked with the flood event as this. It occurs in the biblical narrative; it is found in Egypt, even though there is no detailed account of the flood; for example, in the Book of the Dead, Atum says:

> I will destroy all that I have created.
> The earth will once again look like the
>   primeval ocean,
> like the mass of water at the very beginning.
>   [cf. Brandon, op. cit., 16f.].

There is often, as here, no reason given for the decision to destroy, or the reason given is utterly insignificant. The Gilgamesh Epic says simply: ". . . their heart led the great gods to produce the flood" (ANET 93). The passage is destroyed in the Sumerian account; Kramer assumes that there is a resolution to destroy that corresponds to that of the Gilgamesh Epic. The broader context of the latter shows that a revolt on the part of humanity is presumed, but that is not a matter which receives great prominence (Landersdorfer, p. 97: "The Sumerian tradition lays no particular stress on human culpability for the flood").

The history of the tradition of the flood story explains this. The complex of the flood stories divides into two main groups: in the first and structurally older group the flood is simply a disaster, a catastrophe that overwhelms the human race. In the second group the flood is a punishment, the reason it is sent is the revolt of humankind. W. Wundt had already noted this in 1915. And this observation was confirmed by the work of H. Baumann in Africa in 1936:

> Wundt . . . distinguishes quite correctly an older stage of the myth where the flood is portrayed simply as an extraordinary event or as magic, and a later stage which fashions the catastrophe into a primeval myth and understands it as a divine punishment. (p. 321)

A third stage in the tradition appears in the Gilgamesh Epic. The decision to destroy is not unanimous. Some of the gods either from the very beginning or at a later stage are not in agreement with the decision to destroy. Ea expresses reservations to Enlil:

> Thou wisest of gods, thou hero,
> how couldst thou, unreasoning, bring on the deluge?
> On the sinner imposed his sin,
> On the transgressor imposed his transgression?
> (Yet) be lenient, lest he be cut off,
> be patient, lest he be dis(lodged)!   ANET p. 95

Here the resolution to destroy is no longer taken for granted; the writer is rather reflecting on the resolution and is asking if the destruction of humanity is an appropriate action for the gods to take.

We find the same attitude, but in a different form, in Gen 18:17-33 when Abraham is faced with the destruction of Sodom. Here too is a decision on the part of God to destroy; here too an objection is raised: such a catastorphe would destroy the just together with the unjust. It is very like the objection which Ea puts to Enlil. It is clearly the same motif: in the one case the destruction is by a flood, in the other by a consuming fire. Both are found, often side-by-side, in myths of the destruction of the world, as W. Wundt has shown in general and H. Baumann has shown for Africa. The destruction of Sodom in Gen 19 belongs to the category of primeval stories; it corresponds to Gen 6-9 in that one person, a just man, is saved from the destruction. The story has been altered by its insertion into the circle of stories about the Patriarchs; nevertheless its essential lines are clear. One can see a connection between the two because there are some flood stories which are familiar with the motif of the violation of the law of hospitality in the context of a visit from a divine messenger. Frazer has drawn attention to this in the narrative of the Lolos of Southwest China mentioned above.

The story of Abraham's petition in Gen 18 takes on a new aspect with this background. A primeval event has been linked with the story of the Patriarchs in an extraordinary way. The divine resolution to destroy is the basis of Gen 18:17-33; the dialogue is not, as is often alleged, a later edition. It is a transition passage which links Gen 19 with the Abraham cycle. A comparison with the passages from the Gilgamesh Epic cited above shows in a very striking manner how in the biblical text the intercession of a human being takes the place of the difference of opinion among the gods. It is the same motif. But the person confronts God on behalf of the just of Sodom who would otherwise be involved in the general catastrophe. It is only by examining the history of this tradition that we can understand the significance of the adaptation of the ancient motif in the biblical narrative.

The point of departure of the flood stories is the decision of the gods or of a god to destroy. The decision to destroy is not necessarily identical with a decision to punish. The presupposition is that the creator god can make the decision to destroy humanity; that the decision to destroy humanity can be taken in the same circle of gods which decreed its creation. The flood is a primeval event, and this is its link with creation. The creation of humanity allows the possibility of its destruction. This means that creation and flood are complementary within the context of a primeval event. This complementarity and the almost equal distribution in cultures of creation and flood stories means that human consciousness of its own and of the world's created state goes hand in hand with a consciousness that there may be a total destruction which transcends both the death of the individual and the annihilation of the cosmos. The catastrophe of the flood concerns the whole as does the creation. It is something peculiar to human existence, which distinguishes human being from beast, that a person can conceive of the possibility of total destruction. And so a completely new dimension enters human existence: the continuation of existence because of a saving action. Salvation by an act of God, so important a religious phenomenon, is grounded in the primeval event of the flood story.

The motif of crime and punishment is secondary, however early it may have been added to the basic motif. And so the flood becomes a punishment for the corruption of humanity, and the one who is saved is exempted from this corruption. In explaining the flood story and its significance one will have to distinguish between the basic motif and any elaboration.

II. *Further Narratives of Crime and Punishment in J*. The two first stages in the tradition of the flood story show that the motif "destruction as punishment for revolt" has been added; that is, it was originally an independent motif. It is important for the understanding of the biblical account of primeval events to recognize this. It is the key to the understanding of the real difference between J and P in the primeval story. P, in accordance with the priestly theology, is interested only in the decision to destroy; (the cause of the decision, namely the corruption of humankind, comes as a surprise and without motif immediately on chapter 1, so R. Rendtorff, "Hermeneutische Probleme der biblischen Urges-chichte," *Festschrift F. Smend,* 1963, p. 23). The whole of J's interest is directed to the reason for the destruction, the capacity of God's creatures to turn against him. J, as always, is vitally interested in the person, in the individual's potential and limitations. Consequently his treatment of the material which belongs to the stories of the origins is concerned on the one hand with the person's capabilities and accomplishments, and on the other with the story of crime and punishment and the terrifying possibility that a human being, created free, can revolt against God the creator.

It is questionable, however, that, as so many modern interpreters think, J intends to present a crescendo of sin. In any case one should not speak of a "growth of sin to avalanche proportions" (Rendtorff, op. cit., p. 21); the text knows nothing of this. The intention of J in the main body of this early narrative is to use a series of stories of crime and punishment to illustrate the various ways in which the creature can revolt against the creator; direct disobedience to God, the extreme case of the murder of one's brother, impiety towards one's parents (Canaan). In addition there are the examples of the revolt of the community against God: general corruption (indicated in the flood story, but developed later in Gen 19), the arrogant overstepping of the limitations imposed by genealogy, 6:1-4, and the arrogant abuse of technology, 11:1-9. The intention of J becomes clear only in what is common to these narratives of crime and punishment; it is to expound the variety of ways which the creature can turn against the creator. I think that the current description of a crescendo of sin from Gen 3 to Gen 11 is due to an abstract theology of sin which has no foundation in J.

We can be certain that it was not J who first shaped these stories even though their history is nowhere near as clear as that of the flood story. The history of each of these stories must be examined individually and this can only be done in the exegesis of each passage. One can suspect that here too there was a fixed group of stories already in existence. The J stories have something further in common; all of them are etiological. That is, their intention is to explain something of the negative side of present human existence by means of a punishment caused by a revolt. The etiological motif is almost completely absent in P. This group of narratives has a history which is readily recognizable in the combination of these two basic motifs. Frazer entitles the second chapter of his *Folklore in the Old Testament,* "The Fall of Man." Baumann has a corresponding title: "The Fall (The Lost Paradise)." Without going into details I will limit myself to citing a summary passage from Baumann, p. 267:

The biblical account is not the basis of the whole complex of myths of the fall which we have to study. Nevertheless, the examples given above show that it is not only in Africa . . . that the origin of death is a central theme in the stories of the fall, or rather in the myths of the loss of a primeval Paradise. Everything that happened in primeval time was in the opinion of the natives something quite different from the present: people lived eternally and did not die; they understood the language of the animals and lived at peace with them; they did not have to work, there was plenty of food, they collected it without any effort and this guaranteed them a life without any anxiety; there was no sex or begetting of children — in short everything that preoccupied present-day folk was unknown to them. But one day these concerns appeared and they were due to some neglect or other, the overstepping of some command, curiosity, or some similar action which affronted God, who then punished them in some way or another. All these myths form the kernel of the African mythologies of the primeval state. . .

It is beyond dispute that the African myths about the primeval state and the biblical stories of crime and punishment in J correspond both in their leading motifs and in their structure. The main reason why the exegesis of the biblical primeval story has overlooked or rejected the parallels is that there is practically no connecting link between the primitive and Mediterranean high cultures. Up to the present, the main interest has been in direct dependence of biblical upon non-biblical texts, that is, in literary dependence; one agreed with or disputed the alleged dependence but showed no interest in texts where dependence was out of the question. But now W. Wundt (op. cit., pp. 275f.) has demonstrated with an abundance of examples that the great myths and epics of the high cultures have taken a considerable number of their motifs from what he calls "the myths and tales" of earlier primitive cultures.

H. Gunkel also noted this but had limited his consideration to individual motifs. H. Baumann too remarks at the beginning of the relevant chapter that "after all, the Genesis story, as well as the stories of the high cultures, depends on the general world view of the primitive myths of the fall." It is not easy to avoid this conclusion when in addition to the formal correspondence there is detailed agreement in the type of punishment inflicted. Baumann divides the punishments in the following way:

1. The origin of death (death as punishment)
2. The World Catastrophe
3. The withdrawal of God
4. Work and hunger as a punishment for the first created humans
5. Difficulty in birth and bride-price as punishment
6. The first humans become apes
7. The difference of races as punishment for the primeval sin

There occurs too the tower motif and the dispersal of the nations. And so the great majority of the punishments God inflicts on people for their revolt in Gen 1-11 are found also in the primitive cultures.

It is no accident that this group of stories about crime and punishment (apart from the flood story) has practically no pre-history in the myths of Egypt or Mesopotamia, but finds a striking counterpart in the stories of the primitive cultures. This J material of the biblical story presupposes a history which is relatively uninfluenced by the surrounding cultures. An indirect witness to this is, I think, that this group of stories is no longer found in the Sumerian-Babylonian myths, but only individual motifs which are fused into other narratives. I would allege as an example from the Sumerian myths the story of the land of Dilmun (Enki and Ninhursag, Kramer, *Sumerian Mythology,* pp. 54-62), that tells of a paradise in which the pain of childbirth does not exist, and from the Gilgamesh Epic the motif of the plant which preserves eternal life and which is snatched away by the serpent. This is a typical motif which belongs to "the myths and tales" and which has its counterpart in every detail in the primitive myths of the loss of paradise. The latter of these motifs shows clearly that the old motif was still there but had been changed radically through further reflection and transferred into a new setting.

On the other hand, the motif which dominates Gen 1-11, namely that of crime and punishment, of the revolt of humanity and of its punishment by God, and which has its many-sided counterparts in the primitive myths, is almost completely absent from the myths of the high cultures. I would like to make some observation on this.

A very common motif in the Sumerian, Babylonian and Canaanite myths is that of the revolt of a god or of a group of gods. It is often the young gods who revolt against the old gods. In many myths the one against whom they revolt is the creator god. The consequent war between the gods often takes on the character of a judgment against those who revolt. Now it is well known that the myths of the primitive cultures do not know of the war of the gods and its attendant drama. Though the myth of the war between the gods certainly has other roots, nevertheless it is quite possible that where it is the dominant motif, the revolt of humankind which is punished by the gods recedes into the background or passes over into the war motif. If this is correct, then one would readily understand how in Israel, where the motif of a war between the gods or of the revolt of one god against another was utterly out of place, humanity's revolt against God and its consequent punishment came to the fore.

The study of R. Pettazzoni, *The All-Knowing God. Researches into Early Religion and Culture,* London, 1956, has shown how significant a role is played in the history of religions by the creator god as one who punishes, although only in the very early stages. He demonstrates that many early forms of religion unite the idea of a supreme being who is omniscient, that is, who sees everything everywhere, with the punishment of all evil deeds of humanity by this same being. It is amazing how widespread is this series of motifs. One can only conclude then that, in the pre-history of Gen 1-11, the idea of a creator and that of an omniscient being who punishes the revolt of humankind belong together. This is an early and very remarkable stage in the history of religions.

The story of humanity's revolt and punishment by God stands in contrast to the story of the beginning of God's people in a minor detail which is nevertheless significant. There is no mention of God's anger in Gen 1-11. At the end of his explanation of the flood story von Rad writes, "The story of the flood . . . stands at the beginning of the Bible as the definitive word about God's lethal anger at sin." But it is not correct to dismiss the matter in so summary a manner when neither the flood narrative nor any other of the crime and punishment narratives so much as mention the anger of God. The reaction of God is so different for example in Ex 32:11 when the covenant is breached: "Now therefore let me alone, that my wrath may burn hot against them and I may consume them. . . ." One can sense clearly a distance between the creator and the creature in the primeval story of human revolt and punishment; correlative to this is the peculiar form of the decision to punish and to pardon which occur only here. Though one should not overemphasize this, nevertheless, it makes clear that God's judgment and punishment in the primeval story was seen by tradition in a different light from his action toward his people who were bound to him by covenant.

C. The Stories of Human Achievements

We come now to a section of the primeval story to which exegesis has scarcely given any attention or significance. Gunkel is an exception; but the directions in which he pointed have not been followed. Let us anticipate one aspect of the significance of this section: had the meaning of this motif been understood, then no one would ever have maintained that the J account of primeval events is exclusively the story of humanity and creation under a curse or of condemnation. (Cf. however J. Wellhausen, *Prolegomena to the History of Ancient Israel*, 6th ed., pp. 302-303.)

I. The Achievements in J and P. All texts that deal explicitly with human achievements occur in J. P's treatment of the question is exactly the same as in the case of humanity's revolt. Just as P is content with the general remark about human corruption, Gen 6:11ff., so too he anticipates human achievements in the commission given the man and the woman in creation, 1:26b, 28b. There can be no doubt that the commission to subdue the earth, exemplified in the commission to have dominion over the animals, points to human achievements which result in human domination of the earth. P's theological outlook permits no further interest in the details of human progress in civilization. All he has to say is included in the commission of God to his creatures; everything has its basis and legitimation there.

From the priestly point of view we can, in however grossly oversimplified a manner, discern three stages in tradition which indicate the shift in emphasis on human achievements in the story of primeval events.

The third and last stage is reached in the priestly narrative. P has no particular interest in human achievements, especially in human progress in civilization. The reason is that worship, which is the center of priestly concern, has no longer any direct relationship to a community way of life which is politically and materially orientated. Consequently all the more attention should be given to the fact that P too sees and acknowledges the significance of these achievements for the history of humankind, and hence they are expressly subordinated to the charge given by God at creation. P is aware that humanity's god-given destiny is to master the resources of the earth.

We recognize the second stage of tradition in J. He is clearly interested in human achievement as such. This is illustrated both by Gen 11 as well as by the Cainite genealogy. This interest corresponds to the attitude in the kingdom under David and Solomon, and is quite natural in the context of the political, economic, and cultural life of that era. However, it must not be overlooked that J's interest is somewhat muted. J sees a danger for his people in their great political successes and in the economic and cultural consequences. His only concern is to impress upon his people the action of their god. This becomes clear in the primeval story inasmuch as human achievements are often interwoven with the accounts of crime and punishment, e.g., in Gen 3 and 11, or, as in the case of the successors of Cain, are described between the story of fratricide and the song of Lamech. J's reservation is particularly effective in the way in which he curtails the motif. There are but brief references to human achievements in Gen 4, hints in ch. 3, while the story in ch. 11 shows how progress and crime can readily become enmeshed.

II. The Accomplishments in the Sumerian Myths. We cannot infer all that has just been said from the biblical story alone. This insight has only been made possible recently. It had long been recognized that there must be a long history behind the brief remarks and references of J in Gen 4. Gunkel's commentary shows that there was at least something in the nonbiblical texts. However, the significance of this motif for the story of primeval events became clear only with the discovery and the decipherment of the Sumerian mythological texts. A brief description of their content is indispensable. I am relying mainly on S.M. Kramer, *Sumerian Mythology,* Philadelphia, 1944. The Sumerian myths are for the most part myths about the origin. They do not deal with the origin of the world and of humanity, but with the origin of the gods, and with the origin of those things necessary for the life of the gods and of humanity. The genealogy of the gods and the origin of certain elements of civilization can so interpenetrate that the origin of certain plants is described as a birth of the gods. This illustrates how the origin of such things as trees, grain, tools etc., belong immediately to the realm of creation.

In the myth "Emesh and Enten," p. 49, Enlil decides to grow trees and grain and so to create a state of abundance and prosperity in the land. He creates the two gods Emesh and Enten, fertility gods, and assigns them their work.

In the myth "Cattle and Grain," p. 53, Lahar and Ashnan were created in the private room of the gods so that the gods might have food to eat and clothes to wear. But because the gods could not even begin to do this, human beings were created. Lahar and Ashnan then come down from heaven to earth bringing humans the gift of beasts of burden and of grain. In the myth "Enki and Ninhursag," pp. 54-59, fresh water is first brought to the land of Dilmun. The result is superabundance. Then at the end of a succession of births, Uttu, the goddess of plants, is born. As a result of the fertilization by Enki eight different types of plants spring up. Enki is cursed by Ninhursag for devouring the plants. As a result of the curse Enki is near death; to cure him Ninhursag causes one plant to spring up for each of Enki's maladies (the origin of medicinal plants).

In the myth "Enki and Sumer," pp. 59-62, Enki goes to the cities of Sumer, Ur, Meluhha and others and determines their fate and blesses trees and leaves, cattle and birds, silver and gold, bronze and copper, and humankind. He controls the plough and the yoke, grows seeds, charges the gods with the supervision of the canals and the ditches, and puts in office Ashnan the goddess of grain. He then turns to the pick-axe and the making of bricks and installs a god for this purpose, and likewise for the building of houses. Finally, Enki builds barns and corrals, fills them with milk and fat and puts them under the direction of Demuzi the god of the herds. The myth "The Creation of the Pick-axe," pp.

51-52, tells of the creation of the pick-axe and of other technical instruments. It begins with the creation of heaven, earth and growth. Then it continues:

> He brought the pickax into existence, the
>   "day" came forth,
> He introduced labor, decreed the fate,
> Upon the pickax and basket he directs the "power."
> Enlil made his pickax exalted. . . .
>
> The pickax and the basket build cities,
> The steadfast house the pickax builds,
> The steadfast house the pickax established,
> The steadfast house it causes to prosper. . .

Just as in the myth "Cattle and Grain," the pick-axe is created primarily for the gods and then is given to humanity:

> The Anunnaki who stood about him,
> He placed it (the pickax?) as a gift in their hands.
> They soothe Enlil with prayer,
> They give the pickax to the blackheaded people to hold.

The poem ends with the praise of the pick-axe. When considering these myths in relation to the biblical story the following should be borne in mind:

(1) The act of creation in the myths is not limited to heaven, earth, and humankind; creation is much more the established, ordered and cultivated world, including artificial irrigation, the cultivation of plants, cattle breeding and finally the most important farming implements (there is a complete absence of weapons). The earth in which people are to live is an earth which is already cultivated. There is no separation between nature and civilization. It is possible to present creation in this way because the products of civilization as well as the instruments that produce them are created by the gods, and take their origin either from the birth of the gods or from a special act of creation. The discoveries and achievements of humanity are elevated to the level of divine acts of creation.

(2) The tools and products of civilization take on a theological meaning which is quite different from our understanding of the scope of theology. The action of the gods is concerned not only with the world and people and their destiny; it includes civilization and technology.

(3) This divine action, affecting both civilization and technology, is closely linked with the blessing in all these myths. In fact the border between creation and blessing is often obscured. The blessing of fertility which Enlil and Enki bestow upon the land of Sumer is in the same order as the birth of the gods of cattle-breeding and agriculture and, therefore, of the origin of these occupations. The making of the pick-axe is told as the crown of the work of creation, which begins with the separation of heaven and earth and with the bestowal of fertility, "Enlil, who brings up the seed of the land from the earth." This blessing is understood as an act of creation which embraces fertility and the natural development of human work and which extends to everything that people do and to the tools they use.

Civilization is included in the work of creation in the Gilgamesh Epic. We are here at a very highly developed stage. The first tablet describes the creation of Enkidu. There is a vivid description of his development from the wild state to a civilized human being. Here too civilization is something planned and ordered by the gods, though at the same time human elements, above all the influence of woman, stand out clearly.

III. *The Stories of Achievements in Primitive Cultures.* The origin of the instruments and products of civilization plays a remarkable role in the Sumerian myths (see further S.G.F. Brandon, *Creation Legends of the Ancient Near East,* pp. 78ff.) The motif recedes into the background in the Babylonian myths and epics, and where it does occur, it is changed notably. The reason for this is most likely that the Sumerian myths lie closer to the myths of primitive cultures in which the origins of civilization play a dominant role. The unity of creator and founder of civilization goes back to primitive myths. The figure of the founder of civilization or of a civilization hero is widespread throughout the world (cf. J. Haekel, "Kulturbringer," RGG[3] IV 108; A. Metraux, "Culture Hero," *Dictionary of Folklore, Mythology and Legend,* New York 1949; W. Wundt, J. Frazer, H. Baumann, E. Jensen, *Mythos und Kult bei Naturvölkern*). He either takes his stand with the creator or is identified with him; in any case he belongs to the primeval period. I refer particularly to H. Baumann, *Schöpfung und Urzeit,* III, "Die Ursprünge der menschlichen Kultur im afrikanischen Mythus." There are many points of contact with the Sumerian myths.

The stories that trace the origins of civilization and the cultivation of the land to an intervention of God occur most frequently. The High God bestows on humanity the means of subsistence from the very beginning and teaches people to sow seed in the earth or to plant the bulbs. (p. 343)

There is a parallel to this in Is 28:23-26 where the prophet compares God's action with that of the farmer; he traces the action of the farmer back to instructions given by God. It is interesting to note that the motif of the discovery of fire occurs very often in the African myths of the origins of civilization while it is entirely lacking in the Sumerian myths. The discovery of fire of course is hidden too deeply in the distant past for anything to be said about it. However Greek mythology has preserved the motif. The Prometheus story also connects the creation of humankind with the hero who brings civilization and fire; the link goes back to the earliest stages of mythology.

The African myths include among the achievements of the primeval period the preparation of the means of subsistence, the art of the smith, the weaver, the potter (H. Baumann, p. 363ff.); the origin of customs and of religious practices is likewise set in the same period.

It is clear then that the Sumerian myths of the origins of civilization go back to the corresponding primitive myths and that there are many points of contact between them. What is common to both is that the origin of all instruments and benefits of civilization are traced back to the primeval periods and that they are closely linked with creation.

However, there is more to be said. The Sumerian myths also attribute many forms of evil to the gods. The deficiencies and evils in human existence are not regarded merely as punishments; they can also be created immediately by the gods. In the myth "Enki and Ninhursag" the illness of the god Enki is caused by a curse from the god Ninhursag; the curse is a punishment for Enki's having eaten the plants which the goddess had created. The illness is a punishment for a transgression. On the other hand in the myth "The Creation of Man," (Kramer, pp. 68-72), the person is created laden with all sorts of afflictions as a result of a bizarre competition between Enki and Ninma; e.g., the barren woman. "The Myth is basically etiological inasmuch as it gives the reasons both for the creation of the human race as well as for the many afflictions which surround it" (Brandon, p. 76). These myths show that not only all good, but also the deficiencies and burdens of human life are traced back to the action of the creator gods. It is important to note, however, that there is no sign of dualism here. The same gods are the source of the blessings which give growth to civilization as well as of illness and evil.

IV. The Nature of the Motif in Gen 1-11. Our starting point has been that the biblical primeval story has given very little attention to talk about human civilization, and even less to its theological significance. The survey of the mythological material has confirmed this so that it has become clear only now how much it has receded and how marginal a place it holds in Gen 1-11. This is the fact; it requires further explanation.

(1) The remarks about human achievements in Gen 4:17-26 occur in the context of the genealogy of the descendants of Cain. The Sumerian myths explain the connection inasmuch as they very often describe cosmogony as theogony. This process includes the origins of civilization. But there is a difference. In Sumer it is from the genealogy of the gods that civilization and its benefits take their origin; in the Bible it is from the genealogy of the human race. It is human endeavor and not "divine birth" that gives rise to civilization.

We can say moreover that the notes appended to the genealogies in Gen 4:17-26 are the relics of older stories which told of the origins of certain aspects of civilization. This is confirmed by analogy with the Sumerian myths. There are other indications in the Bible that such stories existed, and the remark in Is 28:26 that the farmer receives instructions from God as to how to cultivate his field goes back to one of these.

(2) The motif of the development of civilization has been heavily muted by J and even more so by the more abstract P; nevertheless it retains its importance in that it has been preserved and recognized as a constituent part of the primeval story. The biblical story is not restricted to the origin of the world and of humankind. It includes the origin of all aspects of civilization which are the basis of present day life. P says that God created people to master the earth and its resources. Human achievements in the area of civilization correspond not only to the will of the creator, but go back to his word of command. J says that the account of the origin of humankind as presented in the primeval story includes the origin of the more important aspects of civilization. The existence of humankind in the primeval period is colored not only by humanity's revolt and overstepping of limits, but also by human progress as people fulfil their destiny. The foundations of present-day civilization are, according to J, laid in the primeval period. But neither P nor J lays emphasis on the progress of civilization at this period, nor do they reveal its significance. The reasons for this will be discussed later.

(3) The motif of the progress of civilization has been changed radically in the biblical primeval story. There is no mention at all of a divine origin. It is impossible that civilization should take its origin from the birth of the gods; and

further, the discoveries and inventions of civilization are not first prepared by the gods and then given to man (there is a special reason for the incident in Gen 3:21). Faced with the mythology of the Ancient Near East, the Bible takes the same stand as does the modern secular historian: all progress in civilization is a human achievement. Cattle-breeding, horticulture, metal work and other arts and crafts are the work of human beings, not the outcome of the internal conflicts of the gods. This accords well with the description of the destiny of humanity in Gen 1-3 which is quite different from that found in Babylon and Egypt; people were not created to minister to the gods, but to master, cultivate and preserve the earth.

This difference has theological importance. The Sumerian myths extol and praise the gods because they are the creators of the pick-axe or the plough; but Israel takes nothing away from the majesty and might of God when human discoveries and inventions are seen as their own. This is reflected in Ps 8 for example where the praise of God in the first and last verses frames the reflection, "What is man that thou are mindful of him. . .", a reflection which is grounded in a following verse, "Thou hast given him dominion over the works of thy hands. . . ." Job says the same thing in a quite different way when he stands in amazement at humanity's mighty achievements in the field of mining engineering, ch. 28. Both texts are examples of the attitude of the Bible toward human achievements which are to be distinguished clearly from the creative action of God.

(4) However, Israel does see a divine activity behind human achievements. It is not God's creative action, but the blessing which God has bestowed on the person as his creature. P is quite clear: the command of Gen 1:26b, 28b is in the context of blessing, and is part of the blessing itself. It is not so obvious with J. It has often been remarked that the blessing in J first occurs in 12:1-3. But the texts do not permit us to explain this in such a way that J's primeval story is dominated completely by a curse while the story of the blessing only begins in Gen 12. Despite disobedience and punishment, humanity is left with life and its vital power, with the land and its fertility. Neither human dominion over the animals nor the command to increase and multiply are countermanded. This is the way in which J understands the blessing and its effects.

The story of humankind created by God, driven out of paradise, is resumed in the form of a genealogy, that is, as the story of a vitality which is continually active. Gen. 4:17-26 is part of this story: as generations pass and people develop they acquire new skills and achieve more. This is the effect of the blessing of God which continues to act in the man and the woman after they are driven out of the garden, and even in the posterity of the fratricide Cain. As the line moves to Cain to Lamech a shadow falls over the potentialities of people; but they are still there and they lead them further.

The same two effects, fertility and civilization, are the result of the creative activity of the gods in the Sumerian myths. They show that creation and blessing are much more closely connected and cover a far wider range than in the biblical texts. The Old Testament changes the idea of blessing when the products of civilization are no longer created and then bestowed on humanity. Blessing is concentrated on humanity in the Old Testament; the power and dynamism of the blessing enables people to "fill the earth and subdue it," and to make, discover, and invent. The blessing penetrates far more deeply into the story of humanity;

the creator does not bestow ready-made products on people, but gives them the capacity to acquire and to create.

The comparison shows how closely God's creative activity and his blessing belong together. Taking one's stand in the here and now in which the Sumerian myths are recited, one notices the point of contact between the creative activity of the gods and the present effect of their blessing. This is true also of the Old Testament: the activity of God who blesses is the activity of God who creates, as P has stated so clearly.

D. The Primeval Story as a Whole

I remarked at the beginning that the primeval story in both J and P takes its point of departure from an already existing whole. This is not to be understood in the literary sense; the whole did not exist in a self-contained or pre-literary block; nevertheless it was there in a clearly recognizable circle of stories which dealt with the primeval period or with the beginnings of the world and of humankind.

This whole has already appeared in many different ways: in the remarkable correspondence between the motifs of the primeval events and those of Gen 1-11, in the groupings of the primeval motifs such as creation and flood, creation and genealogy, creation and the origin of the limits and deficiencies of human existence, in the origin of death, crime and punishment. The correspondence is most striking in the cycles of stories circulating among Israel's immediate neighbors: the Sumerian myths for example are for the most part myths about the primeval period, differing in this from the mythical epic of the Babylonians. There are two additional pieces which occur in the introductions to Sumerian and Egyptian stories and which link the narrative with a primeval event.

In the Egyptian stories these pieces introduce the narrative with the formula, "When this and this had not yet come to be. . ." We have already encountered such sentences. They have been studied by H. Grapow. Their most striking characteristic is the way in which they put side-by-side the positive and the negative, the state of before and after, the limitations of existence:

> The heavens had not yet come to be,
> nor had the earth,
> The soil had not yet been created,
> nor the worms in it. . . .
> (Pap. Brit. Mus. 10188, 26. 22; H. Grapow, "Die Welt vor der Schöpfung,"
> ZÄS 67 [1931] 34.)

These introductory sentences are saying, when heaven, earth, and the surface of the earth came to be, then there came to be too "the worms that belong there." Death belongs as much to this primeval state as does the creation of the heaven and the earth. It could be simply stated, "When death had not yet come to be"; one could generally substitute "disorder" for death. Grapow quotes many texts of this kind. The great disorder, be it the consequence of death or of the revolt of humanity or of a catastrophe, is part of the account of the creation of heaven, earth and mankind. This corresponds to the biblical account. The idea "disorder" contains within itself the idea of a planned creation. There is another formula that corresponds to the biblical primitive story:

> When that fear had not yet come to be,
> which came to be through the eye of Horus.
> (Pyr. 1040, Grapow, op. cit., 35)

> When the eye of Horus had not yet been wounded
>> (Pyr. 1463, Grapow, op. cit., 35)

Part of the primeval event is the origin of fear "because of the eye of Horus," that is, the fear that comes from evil deeds, all of which are noticed by the all-seeing eye of Horus (the sun). R. Pettazzoni was the first to study the connection between omniscience and the punishment of evil which is described here: "Ra, the sun god of the old Egyptian religion, sees and knows everything that people do" (*The All-Knowing God* . . . [1956] pp. 49ff.). The origin of fear from the eye of Horus, or looked at from another point of view, the wounding of the eye of Horus (through the evil deeds of humanity), is correlated to the primeval event, that is, to the creation of the world and of humankind. The formula "When there was not yet. . ." is co-ordinated with the primeval event in the Egyptian texts:

> The creation of heaven, earth and humankind
>> (a series of different events in the process of creation)
> The origin of death or of disorder
> The origin of fear because of the eye of Horus
> or because of the wounding of the eye of Horus.

These motifs show a remarkable agreement with those of the biblical primeval story. The formulas, "when there was not yet. . .", have an introductory function, setting the stage. The point at which narrative begins has not yet arrived. The formula has become a literary expression for the positive and the negative of the primeval event. There is another introductory formula in the Sumerian Myths that link the narrative to the beginning, that is, to the creation, in a different way:

> When heaven had become distanced from the earth,
> When earth had dropped down from heaven,
> When the name of humanity had been set up. . . .
>> (S. Kramer, *Sumerian Mythology,* p. 37).

There follow six lines each beginning with "When. . . ." This sort of beginning occurs often. Kramer explains it as follows: "The Sumerian scribes were accustomed to begin their stories with several introductory lines dealing with creation," p. 38. There is no systematic attempt to describe the positive and negative aspects of the primeval events as there is in the Egyptian texts with their formula "When there was not yet. . . ." The intention of the introductory formula in Sumerian is simple, namely to link what is to be narrated with the beginning, that is, with the primeval event. The birth of the gods too can be described as primeval event in place of the separation of heaven and earth:

> After on the mountain of heaven and earth
> An had caused the Anunnaki to be born. . . .
>> (Kramer, op. cit., 39)

The introductory sentences "When. . ." mean that everything contained within them was the beginning of all that has happened, the simple outright beginning. What is now to be narrated is quite separate from the unique event of the beginning. This too is the function of the primeval story in the Old Testament: what is to be narrated is prefaced by Gen 1-11 which is the beginning of everything.

One cannot allege that the introductions in the Egyptian and Sumerian texts are merely single sentences while Gen 1-11 is a detailed narrative. Each of the introductory sentences stands for a narrative and contains an event which can be narrated in detail for itself. The constituent parts of the primeval story, creation, crime and punishment, catastrophe, formed a block and as such had been prefaced to the history (i.e., Gen 1-11 before Gen 12ff. and Ex 1ff.) before the formation of the P and J narratives as a whole.

It is only with this background that the peculiar nature of Gen 1-11 as a whole becomes clear. The primeval event has become a story. Everything in Egypt, Sumer, Babylon and the primitive cultures which can belong to the primeval event form a relatively closed circle of motifs which do not occur in a fixed order. In the sentences, "When there was not yet. . . ." and "after (when). . .", the motifs remain independent and completely free both in their order and manner of presentation. The motifs of the primeval event form a pool and they can be used arbitrarily in a quite kaleidoscopic manner. The biblical primeval story is arranged in a strict order; it is prefaced to a history, and in such a way that there is a succession of generations from a primeval pair leading up to the story of Abraham. Primeval history derives from primeval event.

4. The Theological Significance of the Primeval Story

The signpost to an understanding of the theological significance of the primeval story as a whole points in two directions: toward the center of the Old Testament itself and beyond, and toward the prehistory of the Old Testament and beyond to the beginning of the world and of the human race. The usual practice is to look only in the first direction and let it go at that. But the patent fact is that Gen 1-11 is linked at every step with what pre-Israelite tradition has said about the primeval events. There would be no point in drawing attention to this obvious link if J and P had merely intended to say that the savior of Israel is the creator of the world. If the Elohist had created a work of his own, complete in itself, and this must remain an open question, then the possibility would remain of a description of the growth of Israel without any primeval story. If E is nothing more than a development of J then it is not without significance that, in the opinion of the majority of scholars, he did not take up the question of the primeval story.

We cannot avoid the fact that both J and P in Gen 1-11 not only adapted and refashioned their material, but also were heirs of an already formed tradition. They indicate clearly that their purpose is to pass on something that they have received and that is not the result of but prior to their confession of Yahweh as the savior of Israel. The intention of J and P to accept traditions about the beginning of humankind, to adapt them and hand them on as part of the community of Yahweh, and to join them to Israel's own traditions which are the result of her confession of Yahweh as savior, must be understood and given its proper theological value. The confession gives the texts a peculiar limiting function; the intention of passing on what has been received gives them the function of connecting and bridging. It is difficult to reconcile them.

But the peculiar nature of the primeval story demands a special methodology for its exegesis. The primeval stories look in two directions; they look back into primeval times where the present world and everything in it had its origin. Israel shared this retrospective view with her neighbors and her predecessors, with all humanity and with every race. There are limits in practice to the way in which one can reflect on the relationship between primeval time and the present. The narrative motifs are very alike both in form and groupings. The biblical narratives are no exception. They must not be taken out of their broader context. In interpreting them, one must never lose sight of this aspect of retrospection which they share with so significant a circle of human traditions.

The stories also look forward to the history of Israel and of the people of God. This is realized when the primeval story is linked with the history of the nations. This connection is itself an exegesis of the primeval story; it gives it a new setting in life and a new meaning; it is accomplished on the one hand by the overall view of J and P and on the other by the transition from Gen 11 to Gen 12. When the primeval story is seen as a prologue to the history of God acting with Israel, then each narrative and each genealogy is affected, and each individual text takes a new direction. The texts no longer speak to Israel in the context of the action of the primeval period on the present — there is no cultic actualization — but through the medium of history. The created cosmos is not created and ordered anew in Israel with the recitation of the creation story; rather, God's action, which Israel has experienced in its history, is extended to the whole of history and to the whole world.

In the interpretation of the primeval story, one must be well aware that these two points of view cannot be fully harmonized. One must always be conscious that one is dealing with a tradition which has had a long and varied history, which grew and was adapted for hundreds of years in Israel before it took written form under J and P, and of which every single part had a prehistory outside Israel. One must be aware then that what J or P wanted to say to the Israel of their day through this or that story need not necessarily agree with the intention of the story in an earlier Israelite or pre-Israelite form. It would not be the mind of the narrators to give voice merely to the specifically Israelite adaptation and meaning of the primeval stories; they wanted more; they wanted their audience to hear something that belonged to the prehistory of Israel.

All parts of the biblical primeval story are concerned with experiences and attempts to understand which are common to the whole of humankind, and to which the widely dispersed basic motifs are a witness. J and P must have been conscious of what they shared in common with others because both readily resume the traditions about humanity which are at their disposal. All over the world people know that their existence and their relationship to the world goes back to a beginning and they try to relate this beginning in some way to the present; (they see themselves threatened by catastrophes [a flood], their very existence hemmed in by all sorts of evil and outrage, endangered by the possibility of revolt and punishment;) they trace back to its source the power which carries on their existence from generation to generation, which preserves life by conferring fertility and which gives them the potential to master the world.

What is peculiar to the biblical primeval story is that it links the account of the primeval period with history. Both J and P prefix the primeval story to a history which begins with the call of Abraham. The transition from one to the other is smooth, and herein lies the key to their meaning for Israel. The whole of the primeval story is thereby completely freed from the realm of myth. This process of liberation has its effect on each individual part of the biblical primeval story. On the other hand, Gen 1-11 acquires a certain self-contained unity through its role as a preface. Prior to J and P there was a whole complex of fixed motifs which were joined together in various ways. In Gen 1-11 all these motifs were woven into a continuous whole which stretched from Adam to Abraham in a succession of generations. Here is the basic difference between the biblical account and all that preceded it. Consequently the primeval story is transformed and takes on a resemblance to the history that begins with Abraham. The stories of a primeval event are taken out of their original setting in life: the primeval event loses its immediate and direct link with the present and resumes its connection with it through the medium of history.

We noted at the very beginning that the history of the patriarchs has a place in Israel's creeds, but that the primeval story does not. On the other hand, the story of creator and creation has a fixed place in hymns of the descriptive praise of God. God is praised both as creator and as Lord of history, e.g., Pss 33; 135, 136. The structure of the Psalms of descriptive praise corresponds to the way in which the Pentateuch as a whole links creation and history as well as to the transformation of primeval event into primeval history within Gen 1-11. The correlation of creation and history is clearest in Deutero-Isaiah and in Job. It is in the affirmation of the creator that humans realize the meaning of God; in distress and despair people look to the creator and find in him the god who saves. The deliberate union of creation and history in the primeval story reaches its ultimate conclusion here.

The other elements of the primeval story have the same relationship to history. The genealogies are part of the human condition and remain so in Gen 1-11. P states explicitly that they are the working out of the blessing given at creation and that it is this same blessing which is at work in the succession of generations leading up to Abraham as well as in the line which takes its beginning from him. The line of generations which leads from the birth of Abraham back to human beings who have not been born but have been created puts the birth of Abraham in a context analogous to the history of Israel as it moves from the beginning to its goal. In this way the genealogies that lead up to Abraham are brought into a relationship with history. Among Israel's neighbors, the genealogies of the kings occur only after the genealogies of the gods; in Israel the genealogies follow immediately on the creation of humankind. This illustrates further their connection with history. The theological significance of the genealogies in Israel is seen with the beginning of political history in the real sense. There is no sudden breaking off of interest in the succession of generations; the interest perseveres just below the surface, as the history of David's succession shows. Israel was always conscious of its origin from one father. This, side-by-side with Israel's beginnings as a people based on a covenant with God, remained an essential element of its historical consciousness and persevered through all vicissitudes and failures. This is the source of the importance of the family throughout the history of Israel.

The account of crime and punishment in the primeval story is depicted primarily as part of the human condition. Sin, guilt and revolt are not the results of a long encounter with God as are the sins of Israel which are condemned by the prophets. There is a conscious distinction. They belong to human existence as such and are common to all people in all places. The story of sin as part of the

66

history of the people of God, as for example in Ex 32-34, is set deliberately in the broader context of sin, guilt and punishment outside the history of Israel. The same is true for this aspect of the human condition, namely the potential to sin, as is true for creation — it has meaning for the present only through the medium of history. The Old Testament does not speak of a fallen creation or of humankind fallen from grace; rather as it narrates the history of God's dealing with his people it draws attention to the many points in common between what is happening in Israel and what has been said about human sin and revolt at the beginning.

The bias of this history shows that God's punishment and forgiveness cannot be restricted to Israel alone, but must extend in some way beyond these limits to the broader horizon of sin and revolt as part of the human condition. The effect of the disorder which the sin and revolt of humanity has brought into creation is such that Gen 12 is not the beginning of a course of salvation history which is played out and runs to its goal within the enclosed framework of a community chosen by God; rather, God's saving action is concerned with humanity and the world and must be bound up in some way with the sin and revolt of humankind. So sin as part of the human condition — and the primeval story is dealing with this — is linked with history; God's dealing with his people and his concern with human sin are brought into relationship. The extension of God's action to the whole of humankind, to its sin and revolt, in the later part of the Old Testament (e.g., Deutero-Isaiah), stands in immediate relationship with what the primeval story says about sin as part of the human condition. And the whole of the Apocalyptic Literature is intelligible only in this context.

The theological significance of what is said about human achievements in the primeval story is restricted to freeing them from the realm of mythology. What humans achieved was neither divine nor was it extolled as such. Human endeavor and cultural progress were desacralized in Israel from the very beginning. There could be a high level of technical achievement as Job 28 shows. Secularized human endeavor and cultural progress retained their link with divine activity because it was God alone who gave success to humankind, a success which is rooted in the blessing. It is the person who is blessed; the person does the work; but human achievements in civilization do not acquire a divine origin. So the person becomes particularly important; the creature is unique in its immediate relationship to God, just as God is unique as the one who creates.

This holds for the whole of the primeval story. It is there in the genealogies and stories of crime and punishment, but most clearly in the creation story. There is an inner connection between the uniqueness of the creator, the limitation of creation to humanity and the world, and the meaning that this gives to human beings and their history. Where gods are created, where they can be creatures, then the creature state cannot have the same meaning as when it is identified with the world and human existence. Where God is unique, (and all that is not God is but humanity and the world), where there is no place for excitement and drama in the realm of divine such as love and conflict, birth and death, rise and fall, then this unique being which is not God, namely the individual and his history in the world, becomes of great importance. The creation of human beings in the image of God, a common creation motif, acquires a special meaning in this context; a human being created in the image of God is the unique expression of the unique God. The biblical story does not destine humans to minister to the gods; people are orientated to the fields and to the world which has been given them. It is here that everything will take place concerning God's dealing with his people. One can understand then how this history leads ultimately to God becoming human.

Additional Note. (Translator's note: Professor Westermann wrote this additional note in 1966. Since then the Atraḫasis Epic has been published in English both in transliteration and translation: W.G. Lambert and A.R. Millard, *Atraḫasis: The Babylonian Story of the Flood,* OUP, 1969. Accordingly, the opening paragraph of this additional note has been modified.)

The newly discovered Atraḫasis Epic confirms in a surprising manner my thesis that the motifs of the primeval story belong together as a whole. The myth is preserved on three tablets, each of eight columns, though with large gaps and notable disorders. It deals not only with the creation and the flood, but also with a number of other motifs which, in part, occur in the same order in Gen 1-11. The following is a brief outline: part 1: the revolt of the Igigu (Tablet 1, cols 1-3); part 2: resolution of the conflict by the creation of human beings (cols 4-6); part 3: the achievements of humanity and its increase on the earth, the curse of Enlil and its consequences (cols 7-8); part 4: the second and third judgment of the god (Tablet 2); part 5: the flood and the saving of Atraḫasis (Tablet 3).

The course of events is as follows: while the gods were still human, the Igigu were conscripted into forced labor (it is here that the name Igigu is first explained: the Igigu are the lower class of gods, the Annunaki are the upper class). This took place under the rule of the king of the gods, An. The Igigu decided to ask for freedom from the forced labor or to extort it. During the night they encircled the house of the god Enlil. He sent a message to An which was delivered to him in the assembly of the gods. A decision was taken to negotiate with the revolutionaries. The ground of their complaint was that the forced labor was too difficult. An acknowledged the justice of their case. To relieve the burden Mami (the mother goddess, = Nintu) was to create humans to bear the burden of the gods. Mami agreed under the condition that Enki help her in the work of creating humans. Enki demanded that a god be killed; Nintu was to mix his flesh and blood with clay. The decision was carried out and the episode concludes with Nintu being rewarded and elevated to "Mistress of all gods." The creation of humanity is then described once more in greater detail with emphasis on the special creation of a man and a woman and their destiny to marriage. Mami is the obstetrician and conditions for the birth are laid down.

Humanity achieves technical success (the manufacture of new axes and spades; the building of the great canals); people multiply and Enlil is disturbed by the noise that is made. He pronounces an oath and brings fever and plague over humankind. Atraḫasis complains to the god Enki. The second judicial act follows the same pattern. Humanity increases and Enlil is annoyed by the noise they make. He decides to cut off supplies (there is a large gap here). The third judicial act is the decision to destroy humanity by the flood. The story of the flood follows the pattern of the Gilgamesh Epic.

There are the following parallels to the biblical story: the special creation of a man and a woman and their destiny to death is explained by the mingling of clay with the flesh and blood of the god who had been slain. The primeval couple then begins to increase and multiply and their achievements are narrated. They disturb the god of heaven by the noise they make. There follows the decision to destroy humanity in three acts, the third decision decreeing a flood.

The importance lies less in the parallels themselves than in the following: In the Atraḥasis Epic the primeval event is not a history of the gods nor an event in the realms of the gods to the same extent as it is in the Babylonian myths; the emphasis is rather on something that happens between God and his people. Consequently more importance is placed on human destiny than in the later myths, (the opening words of the Epic are, "When the god-like men bore the work and suffered the toil. . .''). This ancient myth makes clear that the great themes of the primeval story — creation, flood, the increase of humanity, human accomplishments, judgment — are concerned more with human beings before the gods than with happenings between the gods themselves.

There are many other points of contact with motifs in the Old Testament which cannot be discussed here.

5. Literature

1. History of Religion:

a) *General:* F. Lukas, *Die Grundbegriffe in den Kosmogonien der alten Völker* (1893). F. Delitzsch, *Das babylonische Weltschöpfungsepos,* AG Leipzig 17, 2 (1896). L.H. Gray, "Cosmogony and Cosmology"; J.F. Burns, "Cosmogony and Cosmology"; H. Jakobi, "Cosmogony and Cosmology"; ERE 4 (1911) 125-179, 145-151, 155-161. J.G. Frazer, *Folklore in the Old Testament,* (abridged ed. 1923). W. Wundt, *Völkerpsychologie VI,* Mythus und Religion 3 (1923³) 268-290. A.W. Nieuwenhuis, *Die Sintflutsagen als kausal-logische Natur-Schöpfungsmythen* (no date). A. Jirku, *Altorientalischer Kommentar zum Alten Testament* (1923). K. Seeliger, "Welfschöpfung, Weltbild," W.H. Roscher, ALGM IV (1924/1937) 430-505. K. Ziegler-S. Oppenheim, *Weltentstehung in Sage und Wissenschaft,* Aus Natur und Geisteswelt Bd. 719 (1925). A. Jeremias, *Das Alte Testament im Lichte des Alten Orients* (1904, 1930⁴). G. Mensching, *Die Idee der Sünde. Ihre Entwicklung in den Hochreligionen des Orients und Occidents* (1931). E. Meyer, *Geschichte des Altertums II 2* (= GA) (2nd fully rev. ed., 1931, 1953³). F. Strothmann, *Die Anschauungen von der Weltschöpfung im Alten Testament und in der ägyptischen, babylonisch-assyrischen und phönizischen Religion,* Diss. Münster (1933). H. Baumann, *Schöpfung und Urzeit des Menschen im Mythus der afrikanischen Völker* (1936, reprint 1964). W. Schmidt, "Die Schöpfungsgeschichte der biblischen und der ethnologischen Urzeit," StZ 68, 134 (1937/1938) 295-305. L. Dürr, *Die Wertung des göttlichen Wortes im Alten Testament und im antiken Orient,* MVÄG 42, 1 (1938). B. Bonkamp, *Die Bibel im Lichte der Keilschriftforschung* (1939). W. Staudacher, *Die Trennung von Himmel und Erde. Ein vorgriechischer Schöpfungsmythus bei Hesiod und den Orphikern* (1942). G. van der Leeuw, "Die Bedeutung der Mythen," *Festschr. A. Bertholet zum 80. Geb.* (1950) 287-293; "Urzeit und Endzeit," ErJb 17 (1950). S.G.F. Brandon, *Time and Mankind. An Historical and Philosophical Study of Mankind's Attitude to the Phenomena of Change* (1951). R. Pettazzoni, "Myths of Beginnings and Creation-Myths," *Essays on the History of Religions: Studies in the History of Religions,* Numen (Suppl) 1 (1954) 24-36. V. Maag, "Alttestamentliche Anthropogonie in ihrem Verhältnis zur altorientalischen Mythologie," AsSt 9 (1955) 15-44. R. B. Onians, *The Origins of European Thought about the Body, the Mind, the Soul, the World, Time and Fate* (1951, 1954²). A. Goetze, "Hittite Myths, Epics, and Legends," ANET (1950, 1955²˒³) 120-128. L. Woolley, "Stories of the Creation and the Flood," PEQ 88 (1956) 14-21. W.K.C. Guthrie, *In the Beginning. Some Greek Views on the Origins of Life and the Early State of Man* (1957). R. Hönigswald, *Vom erkenntnistheoretischen Gehalt alter Schöpfungserzählungen: Schriften aus dem Nachlass Bd. I* (1957). M. Eliade, "Structure et fonction du mythe cosmogonique," *Sources orientales I* (La naissance du monde) (1959) 469-495. M. Vieyra, "La naissance du monde chez les Hourrites et les Hittites," *Sources orientales I* (La naissance du monde) (1959) 153-174. S.G.F. Brandon, "In the Beginning: The Hebrew Story of the Creation in its Contemporary Setting," HT XI (1961)

380-387. S.N. Kramer (ed.), *Mythologies of the Ancient World,* Anchor Books A229 (1961). H.G. Güterbock, *Hittite Mythology: Mythologies of the Ancient World,* Anchor Books A229 (1961). F. Michaéli, "Textes de la Bible et de l'Ancien Orient," CAB 13 (1961). E. Fascher, *Vom Anfang der Welt und vom Ursprung des Menschengeschlechts. Eine Studie zur Religions- und Kulturgeschichte,* AWR NF 3 (1961). H. Schwabl, "Weltschöpfung," PRE Suppl IX (1962) 1433-1582. R.E. Whitson, "The Concept of Origins," *Thought* 37 (1962) 245-268. S.G.F. Brandon, *Man and his Destiny in the Great Religions* (1962); "The Propaganda Factor in Some Ancient Near Eastern Cosmogonies"; *Promise and Fulfilment. Essays Presented to S.H. Hooke* (1963) 20-35; *Creation Legends of the Ancient Near East* (1963). G.J. Botterweck, "Die Entstehung der Welt in den altorientalischen Kosmogonien," BiLe 6 (1965) 184-190.

b) *Egypt:* G. Roeder, *Urkunden zur Religion des alten Ägypten: Religiöse Stimmen der Völker* (1915, 1923²). K. Sethe, *Dramatische Texte zu altägyptischen Mysterienspielen:* Untersuchungen zur Geschichte und Altertumskunde Ägyptens 10 (1928, reprint 1964). A.S. Yahuda, *Die Sprache des Pentateuch in ihren Beziehungen zum Ägyptischen* I (1929). H. Kees, "Ägypten," HdA III 1, 3, 1 (1933). K. Sethe, *Amun und die acht Urgötter von Hermopolis,* AAB 1929, 4 (1929); Urgeschichte und älteste Religion der Ägypter, AKM 18, 4 (1930). H. Grapow, "Die Welt vor der Schöpfung," ZÄS 67 (1931) 34-38. A.H. Sayce, "The Egyptian Background of Genesis 1," *Studies presented to F. L. Griffith* (1932) 419-423. G. Roeder, "Die Kosmogonie von Hermopolis," *Egyptian Religion I* (1933) 1-27. H. Junker, *Die Götterlehre von Memphis (Schabaka-Inschrift),* AAB 1939, 23 (1940). H. Kees, *Der Götterglaube im alten Ägypten* (1956², previously MVÄG 45, 1941). S. Schott, *Mythe und Mythenbildung im alten Ägypten: Untersuchungen zur Geschichte und Altertumskunde Ägyptens* 15 (1945). S. Morenz, "Ägypten und die altorphische Kosmogonie," *Aus Antike und Orient. Festschr. W. Schubart* (1950) 64-111; "Der Gott auf der Blume. Eine ägyptische Kosmogonie und ihre weltweite Bildwirkung," ArtAs (Suppl) 12 (1954). H. Brunner, "Die Grenzen von Zeit und Raum bei den Ägyptern," AfO 17 (1954/1956) 141-145; "Zum Zeitbegriff der Ägypter," StGen 8 (1955) 584-590; "Zum Raumbegriff der Ägypter," StGen 10 (1957) 612-620. S. Sauneron-J. Yoyotte, "La naissance du monde selon l'Égypte ancienne," *Sources orientales I* (La naissance du monde) (1959) 17-91. C.J. Bleeker, "L'idée de l'ordre cosmique dans l'ancienne Égypte," RHPhR 42 (1962) 193-200. K. Koch, "Wort und Einheit des Schöpfergottes in Memphis und Jerusalem," ZThK 62 (1965) 251-293.

c) *Mesopotamia:* G. Smith, *The Chaldean Account of Genesis* (1876, rev. ed. 1880). A. Loisy, *Les Mythes babyloniens et les premiers chapitres de la Genèse* (1901). L.W. King, *The Seven Tablets of Creation I* (1902). J. Hehn, *Sünde und Erlösung nach biblischer und babylonischer Anschauung* (1903). A. Jeremias, *Hölle und Paradies bei den Babyloniern. Unter Berücksichtigung der biblischen Parallelen,* AO I 3 (1900, 1903²). H. Zimmern, *Biblische und babylonische Urgeschichte,* AO II 3 (1901, rev. 1903). F. Lukas, *Der babylonische und der biblische Weltentstehungsbericht* (1903²). J. Morgenstern, *The Doctrine of Sin in the Babylonian Religion,* MVG 10, 3 (1905). H. Winckler, *Die babylonische Weltschöpfung,* AO VIII 1 (1906). J. Hehn, *Siebenzahl und Sabbat bei den Babyloniern und im Alten Testament,* LSSt II 5 (1907); "Ein neugefundenes Sintflutfragment aus altbabylonischer Zeit," BZ 8 (1910) 225-227. A. Kirchner, *Die babylonische Kosmogonie und der biblische Schöpfungsbericht. Ein Beitrag zur Apologie des biblischen Gottesbegriffes,* ATA III 1 (1910). A. Deimel, *'Enuma Eliš' sive epos babylonicum de creatione mundi* (1912). S.H. Langdon, *Sumerian Epic of Paradise, the Flood, and the Fall of Man* (1915). H. Zimmern, "Marduks (Ellils, Aššurs) Geburt im babylonischen Weltschöpfungsepos," MVG 21 (1916) 213-225. A.J. Carnoy, "Iranian Views of Origins in Connection With Similar Babylonian Beliefs," JAOS 26 (1916) 300-320. L. W. King, *Legends of Babylon and Egypt in Relation to Hebrew Tradition,* Schweich Lectures 1916 (1918). S. Landersdorfer, *Die sumerischen Parallelen zur biblischen Urgeschichte,* ATA VII 5 (1917). S.H. Langdon, "Necessary Revisions of the Sumerian Epic of Paradise," AJSL 33 (1917) 245-249. A.J. Wensinck, *Tree and Bird as Cosmological Symbols in Western Asia: The Ideas of the Western Semites. . . ,* VAA NR XXII 1 (1921). A. Deimel, "De Cosmogonia Babylonica et Biblica," VD 3 (1923) 155-160. P. Schnabel, *Berossos und die babylonisch-hellenistische*

Literatur (1923). Ch.F. Jean, *Le péché chez les Babyloniens et les Assyriens* (1925). J. le Guen, *La création dans la Bible et les Inscriptions Akkadiennes et Sumériennes* (1925). S.H. Langdon, *The Babylonian Epic of Creation, restored from the recently recovered Tablets of Aššur* (1923). B. Meissner, *Babylonien und Assyrien II* (1925). L. Woolley, *Ur of the Chaldees: a Record of Seven Years of Excavation* (1929, 1938). S.H. Langdon, "Semitic," *The Mythology of all Races V* (1931, reprint 1964); "The Sumero-Babylonian Origin of the Legend of Adam," ET 43 (1931/1932) 45. Ch.F. Jean, *La Bible et les récits Babyloniens* (1933). R. Labat, *Le poème Babylonien de la création* (1935). E. Burrows, "Some Cosmological Patterns in Babylonian Religion," *The Labyrinth*, ed. S.H. Hooke (1935) 45-70. F.M.T. de LiagreBöhl, "Schets der Sumerische Wereldbeschouwing," NThS 19 (1936) 97-109 = *Opera Minora* (1953) 149-162, 488. S. Mowinckel, "The Babylonian Matter in the Predeuteronomic Primeval History (JE) in Gen 1-11," JBL 58 (1939) 87-91; Reply of W.F. Albright, ib. 91-103. S.N. Kramer, *Sumerian Mythology. A Study of Spiritual and Literary Achievement in the Third Millennium BC*, MemAmSoc. XXI (1944); *The Epic of Gilgameš and the Sumerian Sources* (1944); "Enki and Ninhursag. A Sumerian 'Paradise' Myth," BASOR 1 (1945). T. Jacobsen, "Sumerian Mythology. A Review Article," JNES 5 (1946) 128-152. R. Pettazzoni, "Der babylonische Ritus des Akītu und das Gedicht der Weltschöpfung," ErJb 19 (1950) 403-430. A. Heidel, *The Babylonian Genesis. The Story of Creation* (1942, 1951² = 1963). M.F. Unger, "The Babylonian and Biblical Accounts of Creation," BibSac 109 (1952) 304-317. V. Maag, "Sumerische und babylonische Mythen von der Erschaffung der Menschen," AsSt 8 (1954) 85-106. F.M.T. de LiagreBöhl, *Das Menschenbild in babylonischer Schau*, Numen Suppl 2 (1955). R. Labat, *Les origines et la formation de la terre dans le poème babylonien de la création*, SBO 3 (1959) 205-215. P. Garelli-M. Leibovici, "La naissance du monde selon Akkad," *Sources orientales I* (La naissance du monde) (1959) 116-152. M. Lambert, "La naissance du monde a Sumer," *Sources orientales I* (La naissance du monde) (1959) 93-113. S.N. Kramer, *Sumerian Literature and the Bible*, SBO 3 (AnBib 12) (1959) 185-204; *From the Tablets of Sumer* (1956) = *History Begins at Sumer* (1958, 1962²). W.G. Lambert, "New Light on the Babylonian Flood," JSSt 5 (1960) 113-123. B. Landsberger-J.V.K. Wilson, "The Fifth Tablet of Enuma Eliš," JNES 20 (1961) 154-179. J. Duchesne-Guillemin, "Weltschöpfung (Iranische Kosmogonien)," PRE Suppl IX (1962) 1582-1589. J. Albertson, "Genesis 1 and the Babylonian Myth," *Thought* 37 (1962) 226-244. A. Heidel, *The Gilgamesh Epic and Old Testament Parallels* (1946, 1949² = 1963). S.N. Kramer, *The Sumerians. Their History, Culture, and Character* (1963). W.G. Lambert, "A New Look at the Babylonian Background of Genesis," JThS NS 16 (1965) 287-300.

d) *Canaan, Phoenicia:* P. Leidecker, *Étude de mythologie orientale. Débris de mythes canaanéens dans les neuf premiers chapitres de la Genèse* (1921). C. Clemen, *Die phönikische Religion nach Philo von Byblos*, MVÄG 42, 3 (1939). O. Eissfeldt, *Das Chaos in der biblischen und in der phönizischen Kosmogonie*, FF 16 (1940) 1-3 = KS II (1963) 258-262. S. Moscati, "The Wind in the Biblical and Phoenician Cosmogony," JBL 66 (1947) 305-310. J.B. Bauer, "Die literarische Form des Heptaemeron," BZ NF 1 (1957) 273-277. O. Eissfeldt, "Phönikische und griechische Kosmogonie: Elements Orientaux dans la Religion Grecque Ancienne," Colloque de Strasbourge 22-24 mai 1958 (1960) 1-15 = KS III (1966) 501-512. F. Hvidberg, "The Canaanitic Background of Gen I-III," VT 10 (1960) 285-294. S.E. Loewenstamm, "The Climax of Seven Days in the Ugaritic Epos," Tarb 31 (1961/62) 227-235. L.R. Fisher, "Creation at Ugarit and in the Old Testament," VT 15 (1965) 313-324.

2. *Creation:*
a) *General:* W.C.L. Ziegler, "Kritik über den Artikel von der Schöpfung nach unserer gewöhnlichen Dogmatik," MRP 2 (1794) 1-113. J.P. Peters, "Cosmogony and Cosmology (Hebrew)," ERE 4 (1911) 151-155. G. von Rad, "The Theological Problem of the Old Testament Doctrine of Creation" (1936) in *The Problem of the Hexateuch and Other Essays* (1966) 131-143. W. Foerster, "Der Schöpfungsglaube im AT," ThW III (1938) 1004-1015. P. Denis, *Les origines du monde et de l'humanité* (1950). E. Brunner, *Dogmatik II. Die christliche Lehre von Schöpfung und Erlösung* (1950, 1960²). B. Bavink, *Weltschöpfung in Mythos und Religion, Philosophie und Naturwissenschaft*, GuW

4 (1950, 1951²).   G. Lindeskog, *Studien zum neutestamentlichen Schöpfungsgedanken I*, UUA 1952, 11 (1952).   G. Lambert, "La création dans la Bible," NRTh 75 (1953) 252-281.   R. Jolivet, *Essai sur les rapports entre la pensée grecque et la pensée chrétienne. Aristote et St. Thomas ou l'idée de création. Plotin et St. Augustin ou le problème du mal. Hellénisme et Christianisme,* (1931, new ed. 1956).   K. Barth, *Church Dogmatics* III, 1, (1958).   G. Widengren, "Early Hebrew Myths and Their Interpretation," *Myth, Ritual, and Kingship,* ed by S.H. Hooke (1958) 149-203.   J. Bottero, "La naissance du monde selon Israël," *Sources orientales I* (La naissance du monde) (1959) 185-234.   L. Lecrand, "La création, triomphe cosmique de Yahvé," NRTh 83 (1961) 449-470.   J. de Fraine, *The Bible and the Origin of Man* (1962).   C.M. Edsman, "Schöpfung," RGG³ V (1961) 1469-1473.   B.D. Napier, "On Creation-Faith in the Old Testament," Interp 16 (1962) 21-42.   R.W. Gleason, "Creation in the Old Testament," *Thought* 37 (1962) 527-542.   T. Boman, "The Biblical Doctrine of Creation," CQR 165 (1964) 140-151.   C. Westermann, "Das Reden von Schöpfer und Schöpfung im AT," *Festschr. L. Rost* (1967).

b) *Creation and Science:* R. Hönigswald, *Erkenntnistheoretisches zur Schöpfungsgeschichte der Genesis,* SGV 161 (1932).   O. Schüepp, *Schöpfungsbericht und Naturwissenschaft* (1945).   J. Bauer, *Kausalität und Schöpfung. Grundfragen der Ontologie und Metaphysik* (1947).   V. von Weizsäcker, *Am Angang schuf Gott Himmel und Erde,* KVR 37/37a 1954; 1963⁶.   R. Hönigswald, *Vom erkenntnistheoretischen Gehalt alter Schöpfungserzählungen: Schriften aus dem Nachlass Bd. I* (1957).   R. Hooykaas, *Natural Law and Divine Miracle. A Historical-critical Study of the Principle of Uniformity in Geology, Biology and Theology* (1959, 1963²).   S. du Toit, *Progressive Creation. An Attempt at a New Approach Towards the Problem Creation — Evolution* (1962).   G. Altner, *Schöpfungsglaube und Entwicklungsgedanke in der protestantischen Theologie zwischen Ernst Haeckel und Teilhard de Chardin* (1965).   S.M. Coder-G.F. Howe, *The Bible, Science and Creation* (1966).

3. *The Primeval Story (Genesis 1-11):*
J.G. Eichhorn-J.P. Gabler, *Urgeschichte I* (1790).   H. Ewald, "Erklärung der biblischen urgeschichte," JBW I 1848 (1849) 76-95; II 1849 (1850) 132-166; III 1850-1851 (1851) 108-115; VII 1854-1855 (1855) 1-28; IX 1857-1858 (1858) 1-26.   K. Budde, *Die Biblische Urgeschichte (Gen. 1-12, 5) untersucht* (1883).   J. Wellhausen, *Die Composition des Hexateuchs und der historischen Bücher des Alten Testaments* (1899³, 1963⁴).   A. Ehrenzweig, "Biblische und klassische Urgeschichte," ZAW 38 (1919/1920) 65-86.   D.B. MacDonald, "The Pre-Abrahamic Stories of Genesis, as a Part of the Wisdom Literature," *Studia Semitica et Orientalia (pres. to J. Robertson)* (1920) 115-125.   H. Junker, *Die biblische Urgeschichte in ihrer Bedeutung als Grundlage der alttestamentlichen Offenbarung* (1932).   F. Ceuppens, *De Historia Primaeva. Genesis c. 1 ad c. 11* (1934).   G. Kuhn, *Erklarungen zu Genesis, Kapitel 1-14: Studia Biblica. Ex Vetere Testamento I* (1937).   S. Mowinckel, *The Two Sources of the Predeuteronomic Primeval History (JE) in Genesis 1-11,* ANVAO 1937, 2 (1937).   P. Heinisch, *Probleme der biblischen Urgeschichte* (1947).   T. Schwegler, "Das Pentateuchproblem und die biblische Urgeschichte im Lichte der Kirchenlehre und der Wissenschaft," SKZ 116 (1948) 330-331, 340-341, 352-353.   R.A.F. MacKenzie, "Before Abraham was...!;" CBQ 15 (1953) 131-140.   F. Ceuppens, *Questiones selectae ex historia primaeva* (1953³).   T. Schwegler, *Die biblische Urgeschichte* (1962²).   L. Rost, "Theologische Grundgedanken der Urgeschichte," ThLZ 82 (1957) 321-326 = *Das kleine Credo* (1965) 36-44.   B. Hessler, "Die literarische Form der biblischen Urgeschichte," WiWie 21 (1958) 188-207; 22 (1959) 28-42.   K. Cramer, *Genesis 1-11 Urgeschichte? Zum Problem der Geschichte im Alten Testament* (1959).   T. Schwegler, *Die biblische Urgeschichte im Lichte der Forschung* (1960).   P. Morant, *Die Anfänge der Menschheit. Eine Auslegung der ersten elf Genesis-Kapitel* (1962²).   R. Rendtorff, "Hermeneutische Probleme der biblischen Urgeschichte," *Festschr. F. Smend* (1963) 19-29.   J. L. McKenzie, "Myth and the Old Testament," *Myths and Realities, Studies in Biblical Theology* (1963) 102-200.   C. Westermann, "Arten der Erzählung in der Genesis, Teil III: Erzählungen von Schuld und Strafe in Genesis 1-11," *Forschung am Alten Testament. Ges. St.,* TB 24 (1964) 47-58.   H.Gross, "Der Universalismus des Heils. A. Nach der Urgeschichte Gen 1-11," TThZ 73 (1964) 145-153.   J. Daniélou, *Au Commencement. Genese 1-11* (1963).

Literature

4. *Genesis 1-3:*
J.P. Gabler, *Neuer Versuch über die mosaische Schöpfungsgeschichte aus der höheren Kritik* (1795). F. Schwally, "Die biblischen Schöpfungsberichte," ARW 9 (1906) 159-175. G.C. Aalders, *De goddelijke openbaring in de eerste drie hoofdstukken van Genesis* (1932). A. Geddes, "Creation, and the Blessing or the Curse Upon Fruitfulness. An Anthropologeographical Interpretation of Genesis I-III," Man. 45 (1945) 123-128; "Creation. A Study of the Contrasted Accounts in Genesis," HibJ 44 (1945/1946) 22-25. F. Ceuppens, *Genèse I-III* (1946). C. Hauret, *Origine de l'univers et de l'homme d'après la Bible (Genèse I-III)* (1950, 1953⁴). G. Lambert, "L'encyclique 'Humani generis' et l'Écriture Sainte," NRTh 73 (1951) 225-243 (espec. 231-241). D.T. Asselin, "The Notion of Dominion in Genesis 1-3," CBQ 16 (1954) 277-294. G. von Rad, *Die biblische Schöpfungsgeschichte: Schöpfungsglaube und Evolutionstheorie* (1955) 25-37. D. Bonhoeffer, *Creation and Fall. A Theological Interpretation of Gen 1-3* (1962). E. Lussier, "'Adam' in Genesis 1, 1-4, 24," CBQ 18 (1956) 137-139. H.J. Richards, "The Creation and Fall," Scrip 8 (1956) 109-115. H. Renckens, *Israel's Concept of the Beginning. The Theology of Genesis 1-3* (1964). M. Bič, *Vom Geheimnis und Wunder der Schöpfung. Eine Auslegung von 1. Mose 1-3*, BSt 25 (1959). F. Hvidberg, "The Canaanitic Background of Gen. I-III," VT 10 (1960) 285-294. J. Hempel, "Gott, Mensch und Tier im Alten Testament, mit besonderer Berücksichtigung von Gen. 1-3," *APOXYSMATA. Festgabe J. Hempel*, ZAW 81 (1961) 198-229.

The Creation of
the World

Literature

Genesis 1:1-2:4a: H. Ewald, "Erklärung der biblischen urgeschichte I, 1. Die schöpfungsgeschichte nach dem B(uch) der ursprunge Gen. 1:1-2:4," JBW I 1848 (1849) 76-95. E. Schrader, *Studien zur Kritik und Erklärung der biblischen Urgeschichte Gen.* Cap. I-XI (1863), "Die Composition der biblischen Schöpfungsgeschichte Gen 1:1-2:4a," 1-57. H. Gunkel, *Schöpfung und Chaos in Urzeit und Endzeit. Eine religionsgeschichtliche Untersuchung über Gen 1 und Ap Joh 12* (1895, 1921). M.J. Lagrange, "Hexaémeron," RB 5 (1896) 381-407. V. Zapletal, *Der Schöpfungsbericht der Genesis (1:1-2:3) mit Berücksichtigung der neuesten Entdeckungen und Forschungen* (1911²). K. Budde, "Wortlaut und Werden der ersten Schöpfungsgeschichte," ZAW 35 (1915) 65-97. J. Morgenstern, "The Sources of the Creation Story — Gen 1:1-2:4," AJSL 36 (1919/1920) 169/212. G. Beer, "Zur Geschichte und Beurteilung des Schöpfungsberichtes Gen 1:1-2:4a nebst einem Exkurs über Gen 49:8-12 und 22-26," *Beiträge zur atl. Wissenschaft. K. Budde zum 70. Geb.*, BZAW 34 (1920) 20-30. W.E. Barnes, "Who Wrote the First Chapter of Genesis?," Exp. 22 (1921) 401-411. M. Lambert, "A Study of the First Chapter of Genesis," HUCA 1 (1924) 3-12. K. Holzhey, "Das Hexaémeron," ThGl 20 (1928) 473-475. T.A. Orbiso, "Narratio biblica creationis (Gen 1:1-2:3)." VD 11 (1931) 141-155. F. Ceuppens, *De Hexameron Gen c.1 v.1-c.2 v.3* (1931, 1934²). L. Rost, "Der Schöpfungsbericht der Priesterschrift," CuW 10 (1934) 172-178. A. Bertholet, "Zum Schöpfungsbericht in Genesis I," JBL 53 (1934) 237-240. P. Humbert, "La relation de Genèse 1 et du Psaume 104 avec la liturgie du Nouvel-An israélite," RHPhR 15 (1935) 1-27 = OH *Festgabe P. Humbert, Mémoires de l'Université de Neuchatel* 26 (1958) 60-82. H. Dumaine, "L'Heptaémeron biblique. Remarques sur le récit de la création (Gen 1:1-2:4a)," RB 46 (1937) 161-181. J.B. Lang, "Der Demiurg des Priesterkodex (Gen I-II, 4a) und seine Bedeutung für den Gnostizismus," Er 1941 (1943) 237-288. T. Maertens, *Les sept jours (Genèse I)* (1951). A. van der Voort, "Genèse I, 1 à II, 4a et le Psaume CIV," RB 58 (1951) 321-347. J. Schildenberger, "Der Eingang zur Heilsgeschichte. Eine Erklärung des Schöpfungsberichtes (Gen 1:1-2:4a)," BenM 28 (1952) 193-204, 371-388. L. Johnston, "Genesis Chapter I and the Creation Myth," Scrip 5 (1953) 142-148. J. Hempel, "Glaube, Mythos und Geschichte im Alten Testament," ZAW 65 (1953) 109-167. E. Beaucamp, "Dieu et l'univers et Dieu de l'histoire," SBFLA 4 (1954) 5-116. N.H. Ridderbos, *Beschouwingen over Genesis I* (1954). J. Hempel, "Priesterkodex," PRE XXII 2 (1954) 1943-1967. P. Humbert, "Trois notes sur Genèse I," *Interpretationes ad Vetus Testamentum pertinentes S. Mowinckel septuagenario missae*, NTT 56 (1955) 85-96 = OH (1958) 193-203. W.S. LaSor, "Notes on Gen 1:1-2:3," GordR 2 (1956) 177-189. C.A. Keller, "'Existentielle' und 'heilsgeschichtliche' Deutung der Schöpfungsgeschichte (Gen 1:1-2:4)," ThZ 12

(1956) 10/27.   J.B. Bauer, "Die literarische Form des Heptaemeron," BZ NF 1 (1957) 273-277.   C.F. Whitley, "The Pattern of Creation in Genesis, Chapter 1," JNES 17 (1958) 32-40.   A. Pohl, "Der Schöpfungshymnus der Bibel," StZ 163 Jg. 84 (1958/ 1959) 252-266.   H.J. Kraus, "Die Entstehungsgeschichte der priesterlichen Schöpfungslehre Genesis 1,' FuH 13 (1960) 76-94.   C. Westermann, *Der Schöpfungsbericht vom Anfang der Bibel;* CwH 30 (1960, 1966⁵).   S. Herrmann, "Die Naturlehre des Schöpfungsberichtes. Erwägungen zur Vorgeschichte von Genesis 1," ThLZ 86 (1961) 413-424.   J.H. Kroeze, "Remarks and Questions Regarding Some Creation Passages in the Old Testament," OTWSA.P 5 (1962) 15-26.   E.J. Young, *The Days of Genesis* (1962).   D.F.X. Connolly, "Genesis 1," *Thought* 37 (1962) 211-225.   J. Weingreen, "Exposition in the OT and in Rabbinic Literature," *Promise and Fulfilment: Festschr. S.H. Hooke* (1963) 182-201.   D.F. Payne, *Genesis One Reconsidered,* TOTL 1962 (1964).   J.B. Bauer, "Der priesterliche Schöpfungshymnus in Gen 1," ThZ 20 (1964) 1-9.   W.H. Schmidt, *Die Schöpfungsgeschichte der Priesterschrift,* WMANT 17 (1964).   D. Hermant, "Analyse littéraire du premier récit de la création," VT 15 (1965) 437-451.   H. Lubsczyk, "Wortschöpfung und Tatschöpfung. Zur Entwicklung der priesterlichen Schöpfungslehre in Gen 1:1-2:4a," BiLe 6 (1965) 191-208.

Genesis 1:1-3: T.K. Cheyne, "Notes on Genesis I, 1 and XXIV, 14," Hebr 2 (1885/1886) 49-50.   A. Dillmann, *Handbuch der alttestamentlichen Theologie,* ed. R. Kittel (1895) (*bara'* 286-288).   J.P. Peters, "The Wind of God," JBL 30 (1911) 44-54; 33 (1914) 81-86.   F.M.T. de LiagreBöhl, "ברא, bārā' als Terminus der Weltschöpfung im alttestamentlichen Sprachgebrauch," *Alttestamentliche Studien. R. Kittel zum 60. Geb.,* BWAT 13 (1913) 42-60.   W. Caspari, "Tohuwabohu: Orientalische Studien F. Hommel zum 60. Geb.," Bd. 2, MVG 22, 1917 (1918) 1-20.   A.J. Wensinck, *The Ocean in the Literature of the Western Semites* (1918).   W.F. Albright, "Contributions to Biblical Archaeology and Philology. 1. Chaos and the Origin of Light in Genesis I," JBL 43 (1924) 363-369.   K. Smoronski, "Et spiritus Dei ferebatur super aquas," Bib 6 (1925) 140-156, 275-293, 361-395.   P. Joüon, "Quelques remarques sur Genèse I, 2," RSR 16 (1926) 304-307.   L. Waterman, "Cosmogonic Affinities in Genesis I: 2," AJSL 43 (1926/1927) 177-184.   J.M.P. Smith, "The Syntax and Meaning of Genesis I:1-3," AJSL 44 (1927/1928) 108-115.   R. Dussaud, "Les trois premiers versets de la Genèse," RHR 100 (1929) 123-141.   E.F. Sutcliffe, "Primeval Chaos not Scriptural," *Miscallanea Biblica II, Scripta Pontifici Instituti Biblici* (1934) 203-215.   W.H. McClellan, "The Meaning of ruaḥ Elohim in Gen 1, 2," Bib 15 (1934) 517-527.   P. van Imschoot, "L'esprit de Jahvé, source de vie dans l'Ancien Testament," RB 44 (1935) 481-501.   H.G. May, "The Creation of Light in Genesis 1:3-5," JBL 58 (1939) 203-211.   O. Eissfeldt, "Das Chaos in der biblischen und phönizischen Kosmogonie," FF 16 (1940) 1-3 = KS II (1963) 258-262.   C.H. Ratschow, *Werden und Wirken. Eine Untersuchung des Wortes hajah als Beitrag zur Wirklichkeitserfassung des Alten Testamentes,* BZAW 70 (1941).   A. Vaccari, "In principio creavit Deus caelum et terram (Gen. 1:1)," VD 24 (1944) 161-168.   N.H. Snaith, *The Distinctive Ideas of the Old Testament* (1944; paperback 1964).   J. van der Ploeg, "Le sens du verbe bārā'. Étude sémasiologique," Muséon 59 (1946) 143-157.   S. Moscati, "The Wind in Biblical and Phoenician Cosmogony," JBL 66 (1947) 305-310.   A.R. Johnson, "Aspects of the Use of the Term פָּנִים in the Old Testament," *Festschr. O. Eissfeldt zum 60. Geb.* (1947) 155-159.   E.P. Arbez-J.P. Weisengoff, "Exegetical Notes on Genesis 1:1-2," CBQ 10 (1948) 140-150.   H. Ringgren, "Är den bibliska skappelseberättelsen en kulttext?," SEÅ 13 (1948) 9-21.   W. Eichrodt, *Theology of the Old Testament,* 2 Vols., 1961, 1967. K. Galling, "Der Charakter der Chaosschilderung in Gen 1, 2," ZThK 47 (1950) 145-157.   S. Aalen, *Die Begriffe 'Licht' und 'Finsternis' im Alten Testament, im Spätjudentum und im Rabbinismus,* SNVAO 1951, 1 (1951).   A. Ehrhardt, "Creatio ex Nihilo," StTh 4 (1950) 13-43.   G.M. Girardet, "Tohu Wabhohu," Protest 7 (1952) 19-22.   G. Lindeskog, *Studien zum neutestamentlichen Schöpfungsgedanken I,* UUÅ 1952, 11 (1952).   O. Eissfeldt, "Gott und das Meer in der Bibel," *Studia orientalia Iohanni Pedersen septuagenario* (1953) 76-84 = KS III (1966) 256-264.   H.G. May, "Some Cosmic Connotations of Mayim Rabbim, 'many Waters'," JBL 74 (1955) 9-21.   P. Humbert, "Trois notes sur Genèse I," *Interpretationes ad Vetus Testamentum pertinentes S. Mowinckel septuagenario missae,* NTT 56 (1955) 85-96 = OH (1958) 193-203.   E. Hornung, "Chaotische Bereiche in der geordneten Welt,'' ZÄS 81 (1956) 28-32.   H. Junker, ''Die theologische Behandlung der Chaosvorstellung in der biblischen Schöpfungsgeschichte,'' *Mélanges Bibliques, rédigés en l'honneur de A. Robert* (1957) 27-37.   A. Dussaud, ''Yahvé, fils de El,'' Syr. 34 (1957) 232-242.   N. Walker, ''Do Plural Nouns of Majesty exist in Hebrew?,'' VT 7 (1957) 208.   A. Massart, ''L'emploi, en égyptien, de deux terms opposés pour exprimer la totalité,'' *Mélanges Bibliques, A. Robert* (1957) 38-46.   G. Ryckmans, ''Le ciel et la terre dans les Inscriptions Safaïtiques. Baʿalsamin, 'le Maître des Cieux',''' *Mélanges Bibliques, A. Robert* (1957) 354-363.   H.M. Orlinsky, ''The Plain Meaning of Ruah in Gen 1:2,'' JQR 48 (1957/1958) 174-182.   P. Reymond, ''L'Eau, sa vie et sa signification dans l'Ancien Testament,'' VT.S 6 (1958).   N.H. Ridderbos, ''Genesis I 1 and 2,'' OTS 12 (1958) 214-260.   P. Humbert, ''Emploi et portée du verbe bârâ (créer) dans l'Ancien Testament,'' ThZ 3 (1947) 401-422 = OH (1958) 146-165.   E. Lipinski, ''Genesis 1:1-2,'' RBL 11 (1958) 177-189.   M. Miguens, ''Spiritus Domini ferebatur super aquas,'' SBFLA 9 (1959) 37-93. E.J. Young, ''The Relation of the First Verse of Genesis One to Verses Two and Three,'' WThJ 21 (1958/1959) 133-146.   O. Kaiser, *Die mythische Bedeutung des Meeres in Ägypten, Ugarit und Israel*, BZAW 78 (1959, 1962²).   B.S. Childs, *Myth and Reality in the Old Testament*, SBT 27 (1960).   J. Hempel, ''Die Lichtsymbolik im Alten Testament,'' StGen 13 (1960) 352-368; ''Licht, Heil und Heilung im biblischen Denken: Antaios 2 (1960/1961) 375-388.   J.H. Scheepers, *Die gees van God en die gees van die mens in die Oud Testament* (1960).   E.J. Young, ''The Interpretation of Gen 1:2,'' WThJ 23 (1960/1961) 151-178.   J.B. Schaller, *Gen 1:2 im antiken Judentum* (Diss. Göttingen 1961); Summary by author ThLZ 87 (1962) 784-786.   E. Dantinne, ''Création et séparation,'' Muséon 74 (1961) 441-451.   V. Hamp, ''Die zwei ersten Verse der Bibel,'' *Lex tua veritas. H. Junker zum 70. Geb.* (1961) 113-126.   S.E. Loewenstamm, ''The Climax of Seven Days in the Ugaritic Epos,'' Tarb. 31 (1961/1962) 227-235.   D. Lys, *'Rûach'. Le souffle dans l'Ancien Testament* EHPhR 56 (1962).   I. Blythin, ''A Note on Gen 1:2,'' VT 12 (1962) 120-121.   W. Eichrodt, ''In the Beginning. A Contribution to the Interpretation of the First Word of the Bible,'' *Israel's Prophetic Heritage. Essays in Honour of J. Muilenburg* (1962) 1-10.   W.R. Lane, ''The Initiation of Creation,'' VT 13 (1963) 63-73.   H.M. Orlinsky, ''The New Jewish Version of the Torah. Toward a New Philosophy of Bible Translation,'' JBL 82 (1963) 249-264.   A. Orbe, ''Spiritus Dei ferebatur super aquas. Exegesis gnóstica de Gen 1:2b,'' Gr. 44 (1963) 691-730.   E. Wurthwein, ''Chaos und Schöpfung im mythischen Denken und in der biblischen Urgeschichte,'' *Dankesgabe an R. Bultmann* (1964) 105-108.   P. Humbert, ''Encore le premier mot de la Bible,'' ZAW 76 (1964) 121-131.   R. Kilian, ''Gen. 1:2 und die Urgötter von Hermopolis,'' VT 16 (1966) 420-438.

Text

1:1 In the beginning God created[a] the heavens and the earth.

2 The earth was still a desert waste, and darkness lay upon the primeval deep and God's wind was moving to and fro over the surface of the waters.

3 And God said: Let there be light! And there was light.

4 And God saw how good the light was. And God separated the light from the darkness.

5 And God named the light day, but the darkness he named[a] night. And it was evening and it was morning, one day.

6 And God said: Let there be a solid vault in the middle of the waters, so as to form a division between water and water. (And it was so.)[a]

7 And God made the solid vault and created a division between the waters above the vault and under the vault.[a]

8 And God named the vault heaven. And it was evening and it was morning, a second day.[a]

9 And God said: Let the water beneath the heaven gather into one place[a], so that dry land may appear. And it was so.

10 And God named the dry land earth, but the gathering of the water he named sea. And God saw how good it was.

11 And God said: Let the earth sprout forth fresh greenery: plants which produce seed, (and)[a] fruit trees that bear fruit on the earth, each of its kind, (fruit) containing its own seed. And it was so.

12 And the earth sprouted forth fresh greenery: seed-bearing plants, each of its kind, and trees that produce fruit, containing its own seed, each of its kind. And God saw how good it was.

13 And it was evening and it was morning, a third day.

14 And God said: Let there be[a] lights in the vault of the heavens, to separate the day and the night; let them serve there as signs to determine the seasons, days, and years.

15 And let them serve as lights in the vault of the heavens, so that it may be light on the earth. And it was so.

16 And God made the two great lights: the greater[a] light to rule over the day, and the lesser light to rule over the night, and the stars too.

17 And God put them in the vault of the heavens to give light over the earth,

18 to rule over the day and the night and to separate light and darkness. And God saw how good it was.

19 And it was evening and it was morning, a fourth day.

20 And God said: Let the waters teem[a] with the living beings, and let birds[b] fly over the earth across the vault of the heavens.[c]

21 And God created the great sea monsters and every living being that moves, with which the waters teem, each of its kind, and every winged bird, each of its kind. And God saw how good it was.

22 And God blessed them saying: Be fruitful and increase and fill the waters in the seas, and let the birds increase on the earth.

23 And it was evening and it was morning, a fifth day.

24 And God said: Let the earth bring forth living beings, each of its kind: cattle and reptiles and wild animals, each of its kind. And it was so.

25 And God made the wild animals, each of its kind, and the cattle, each of its kind, and all animals that creep on the ground, each of its kind. And God saw how good it was.

26 And God said: Let us make human beings according[a] to our image, after our likeness, and let them rule over the fish in the sea and over the birds in the heavens and over the cattle and over all 'wild animals'[b] and over every crawling thing that moves on the earth.

27 And God created humanity according to his image, according to the image of God he created it, as male and female he[a] created them.

28 And God blessed them, (saying)[a]: Be fruitful and increase and fill the earth and make it subject to you! Rule over the fish in the sea and the birds in the heavens and over every living[b] that moves on earth!

29 And God said: And so I hand over to you every seed-bearing plant over the whole face of the earth and every tree with seed-bearing fruit[a]; they are to serve you for food.

30 While to every animal on earth and to every bird in the heavens and to every animal that creeps on the earth, (to everything) that has the breath of life in it, (I give)[a] every sort of grass and plant for food.

31 And God saw everything that he had made, how very good it was. And it was evening and it was morning, the sixth day.

2:1 And so the heavens and the earth with all their adornment were completed.[a]

2 And on the seventh[a] day God completed the work that he had done. And on the seventh day he rested[b] from all the work that he had done.

3 And God blessed the seventh day and made it holy; because on it he rested from all his work which God had created[a] by his action.

4 This[a] is the origin of the heavens and the earth, when they were created.[b]

1:1a Textual questions are one of the determining factors in the discussion of the relationship of the first three verses to each other, and so they must be treated first. Four possible interpretations have been proposed:

(1) The traditional interpretation is that vv. 1, 2 and 3 are each successive principal sentences and that בראשית is st.abs.

(2) בראשית is st.cons.; vv. 1 and 2 form one sentence. The *waw* at the beginning of v. 2 is the *waw apodosis* Ges-K §143d; 111h; 112oo; cf. Köhler, Lex. ו n. 24: "After statements of time ו introduces the verb." The ברא which belongs to the construct chain with בראשית can then be understood in different ways: (a) vocalize as בְּרֹא, because only the infinitive of the verb would provide a clear constructional link; the translation would be: "At the beginning of God's creating. . . .", or "At the beginning, when God created the heavens and the earth, the earth was. . . ."; (b) others maintain that it is not necessary to vocalize ברא as infinitive and understand that part of the sentence that follows בראשית as a genitive of elaboration (or relative sentence).

(3) V. 2 is a parenthesis and the principal sentence occurs only in v. 3: "In the beginning, when God created the heavens and the earth — now the earth was without form and void. . . . — then God said: Let there be light!" Or "When God began to create the heavens and the earth. . . ."

(4) The real action, i.e., the act of creation, begins in v. 2b, more precisely in the third of the three sentences of this verse. This interpretation is found with בראשית as st.abs. (Ridderbos) or as st.cons. (Humbert). However it is not possible syntactically because each of the three sentences in v. 2 are descriptive in style. Discussion hitherto has shown that the question of the relationship of the first sentences to each other cannot be solved by grammatical and syntactical considerations alone. Arguments from fact must decide the issue: the case for translating v. 1 as a principal sentence can only be argued in the context of the exegesis of the passage.

5a The sense of the perfect is to associate the naming of night with the naming of day; it is not a continuation of the work of creation. And so it is not a case of the imperfect consecutive but of the perfect, with the sentences reversed. For the explanation, cf. L. Köhler, *Deuterojesaja stilkritisch untersucht,* BAZW 37, 1923 and D. Michel, *Tempora und Satzstellung in den Psalmen,* 1960.

6a It is questionable whether the fulfillment report ויהי כן is in place at the end of v. 7 between the separation and the naming, because it never occurs in such a place elsewhere, but always belongs to the creation command. Gk puts it at the end of v. 6, immediately after the command to which it belongs. BHK and the majority of modern exegetes follow Gk here. But throughout Gen 1 one can discern clearly the tendency of LXX to schematize and to allow the same pattern of sentences to recur as regularly as possible. This harmonizing tendency could be at work here. In favor of the Gk here is the fact that in all other places, vv. 3, 9, 11, 15, 24, 30 (missing in v. 20) ויהי כן always follows immediately on the creation command.

7a cf. note on 6a.

8a Translate "a second day," in contrast to 1:31 where the article occurs, Ges-K §126w.

9a Gk reads συναγωγή, which could correspond to מקוה in v. 10. But Gk does not read συναγωγή in v. 10, but τὰ συστήματα τῶν ὑδάτων. In the sentence immediately following where Gk reports the fulfillment of the creation command (the sentence is lacking in MT) συναγωγή occurs again. Gk reads here: καὶ συνήχθη τὸ ὕδωρ τὸ ὑποκάτω τοῦ οὐρανοῦ εἰς τὰς συναγωγὰς αὐτῶν, καὶ ὤφθη ἡ ξηρά. This sentence is not to be inserted into MT (contrary to many exegetes) nor is מקוה to be read in v. 9 in place of מקום. U. Cassuto has justified correctly the retention of מקום: "The number *one* can readily be understood in connection with place. . . . but it is not appropriate to pool. . . ." Moreover the מקוה in v. 10 describes the result, the מקום in v. 9 the process of creation; the choice of different nouns is deliberate.

11a The question whether, with Sam and other versions, one should read ועץ instead of עץ depends on one's understanding of the sentence as a whole. If three species of plants are enumerated, then an asyndetic arrangement is possible; but if תדשא דשא ("Let the earth put forth vegetation") is the governing idea then the asyndetic succession of עשב and עץ would be harsh. The threefold division is supported by Dillmann, Driver, Budde and others, and twofold by Delitzsch, Holzinger, Skinner, Gunkel, Procksch, von Rad, Zimmerli, Cassuto, Speiser and the majority of modern exegetes. With the twofold division there are two possibilities: תדשא דשא can be understood as a construct chain (so Procksch, following the LXX βοτάνην χόρτου, "green of plants"). But תדשא דשא is for the most part considered to be the governing idea and עשב and עץ to be the two species. It is better then, with this almost unanimous interpretation, to read ועץ instead of עץ. This reading is attested by Sam, Gk, TgJ, Syr, Vg, and accords too with v. 12.

14a Divergences from the basic rule that the predicate conforms with the subject in number and gender are frequent when the predicate precedes the subject Ges-K §145o; BrSynt §50a.

16a cf. Ges-K §133f: "The correlative comparatives *greater-less*. . . . are expressed by the simple adjective with the article. . . . Gen 1:16, 19; 19:31, 34; 27:15; 29:16, 18, 26."

20a Object-accusative: "The addition of an object in the form of a noun derived from the same stem" Ges-K §117p. **b** In the second command in v. 20 the order of the words is reversed; however the jussive remains at the beginning of the sentence. The sense of the inversion here is to stress the balance between fish and birds in the work of creation as beings that inhabit the sea and the sky. One could render this by "as well. . . . as"; but this is not necessary. **c** One would expect to find the fulfillment command ויהי כן after the creation command; the LXX adds it, following its tendency to schematize.

26a Ges-K §119h: "Underlying the varying uses of this preposition (ב) is either the idea of being or moving. . . . or else the idea of *fastening on* something, *close connection with* something (also in a metaphorical sense. . . . or in a comparision. . . .)." **b** With Syr, add חית; this is indicated by vv. 24 and 25. This can only be explained as a scribal omission; so too Delitzsch, Lese- und Schreibfehler n. 92.

27a The twice repeated resumption of the imperf. consec. with the inverted perf. ברא is to be understood in an explicating sense.

28a The way in which the first two sentences in v. 28 are linked is stylistically improbable with P and syntactically harsh: אלהים is twice repeated as the subject and as the third word of each sentence: the imperf. consec. can scarcely be understood as a continuation of ויברך. And so with the Gk לאמר is to be read instead of the second sentence (so too BHK). **b** Sam adds the article to the MT חיה. However the MT is not to be emended, cf. Ges-K §117c, BrSynt §96. LXX and Sam insert ובבהמה; the harmonizing tendency is again at work; the addition is not required. The critical note to v. 28b in BHK is not accurate; Gk assimilates the text to the sequence in v. 26.

29a It is probable that the text at the end of v. 29 is disturbed; but a reconstruction is not necessary because the sense is clear. V. 29 confirms that the division of the plants in v. 11 is twofold, not threefold.

30a The verb נתתי from v. 29 completes the sense (cf. 9:3); it is not necessary to insert it into the text.

2:1a The imperf. consec. serves as the final summing up of the preceding narrative, Ges-K §111k.

2a Sam, Gk, Syr (and others) read הַשִּׁשִׁי "the 6th day"; even though this reading makes more sense, the MT should not be altered.   **b** A rather large number of Gk miniscules insert ὁ θεός here and Heb 4:4, Philo and Eusebius seem also to have read it. This would be more in accordance with P's style and it may well be that it preserves the original text. But as the attestation is so weak, the MT should remain.

3a The ל in לַעֲשׂוֹת is explained in bges-K §114o, cf. Köhler, Lex, ל, n. 25d. It is possible that in this closing sentence P has again deliberately put side-by-side the two different words for God's act of creation.

4a Instead of אֵלֶּה LXX has the beginning of 5:1, זֶה סֵפֶר.   **b** A number of manuscripts have the *littera minuscula* ה in the last word, cf. Ges-K §5n; it has been proposed therefore that the verb should be read as a qal infinitive; however there is no objection to the MT.

Literary Form

Gen 1:1-2:4a is a narrative. Even if this description needs to be modified quite a bit, it must nevertheless be the starting point. Every story of no matter what kind is planned as a whole and is to be grasped as a whole. We get this overall view when we look to the beginning, the end and the middle or the climax of what is narrated. In Gen 1 the beginning and the end are clearly defined and are closely related to each other; it is not so easy to recognize the central point or the climax of what is narrated. One could say that the creation of humanity is the climax, and this is true to a certain extent. But it is not true that Gen 1:26-28 is the high point of the story in the sense that the verses resolve a tension.

A story by its very nature tells of an event, complete in itself, which has a beginning and an end; it moves as it were in an arch *(Geschehensbogen)*; there is a tension in the arch as the story moves to its climax and then resolves itself. And so the description of Gen 1 as a story must be modified. The narrative of Gen 1 is characterized by its onward, irresistible and majestic flow that distinguishes it so clearly from the drama narrated in Gen 2-3. No tension is built up in Gen 1, and the steady, onward movement is effected by constantly recurring sentences which begin in 1:3 and end in 2:4a. If one were to look for any tension in 1:1-2:4a it would be in 1:2 and its link with the preceding or following verses, that is, either in the transition from 1:2 to 1:3 or from 1:1 to 1:2f. This is the only place in Gen 1 where there could be any sort of dramatic element.

If we examine the structure of the creation story in the epic Enuma Elish, we note something of which nothing but a suspicion remains in Gen 1: the element of tension dominates the struggle between Marduk and Tiamat; it unfolds and it is only because of the struggle that Marduk is able to create heaven and earth. There is a profound difference here between the Babylonian story and Gen 1. Nevertheless, the broad context of both accounts gives some clear pointers to the form of the narratives, and why Gen 1 has acquired this peculiar narrative-form which is really no narrative at all.

Since George Smith published the newly discovered Babylonian account of creation in the year 1876 *(The Chaldean Account of Creation)*, scholars have been concerned with the similarities with the biblical story (cf. A. Heidel, *Babylonian Genesis: The Story of the Creation,* 1963³, W.H. Schmidt, *Die Schöpfungsgeschichte der Priesterschrift* 1973³, pp. 2-24; W.G. Lambert, "A New Look at the Babylonian Background of Genesis," JThS 16 [1965], 287-300). It has been demonstrated in the meantime that Enuma Elish is not the only Babylonian account of creation, but one among many. It has been demonstrated too that Gen 1 might contain motifs from the Egyptian accounts of creation. Gen 1 must be seen in the context of a number of creation stories. Gen 1 took on its peculiar form in the course of the history of traditions in Israel; but the process was not only older than Israel, it extended far beyond her to a variety of peoples and cultures throughout the world. This has been pointed out in the introduction to the primeval story.

The decisive difference between Gen 1 and the Babylonian account of creation is that creation in Gen 1 is not the result of a struggle; the dramatic element is missing. This indicates broader contexts. Gen 1 has a language peculiar to itself which takes the place of dramatic action; a series of similar sentences is repeated throughout. This solemn monotony recalls the genealogies and their recurring phrases (cf. Introduction). The correspondence becomes very clear when one reads Gen 5 as the immediate continuation of Gen 1. The manner of speech which is characteristic of Gen 1 should be seen in the context of creation accounts that have preceded it.

P is following the example of presenting creation in a succession of generations, a device which is of great importance in Egypt, Sumer and Babylon as well as in the primitive cultures. But P has introduced a basic modification; there is no genealogy of the gods. Nothing remains but the succession of events continually repeated and described in the same words. The Priestly Tradition indicates its intention to recall the creation by means of the genealogies by retaining the term תולדות (generations) in 2:4a. What is described in 1:1-2:4a is the תולדות השמים והארץ, the generations of the heavens and the earth.

This explains for the most part the peculiar literary form of Gen 1. In fulfilling his task of proclaiming the creation to his own generation, P looked in two directions: he entered into dialogue and debate with a tradition which had come down to him and which was both older and broader than Israel, and he reflected on God's message which had been entrusted to Israel. Nevertheless, it is not a question of the simple alternative: is P dependent on creation accounts from outside Israel, be they Babylonian or Phoenician, or not? The question is much broader: P is heir to a complex of traditions that are varied and many-sided, widespread and with many branches; all leave their traces. In the introduction we divided the accounts of creation into four types. We saw that creation through struggle, which is quite a dramatic kind of story, has but the faintest echo in 1:2; P rejected such a description, though there are many similarities with the account in Enuma Elish. P also rejected the description of creation as a series of births of the gods, though it too has left some traces in the language and in the heading of Gen 1.

The third main type of creation story is creation by making or by effecting. P accepted this type as being much closer to his own view, and he blended it with his own account of creation through the word in such a way that the result was a completed whole, Gen 1 in its present form.

We have now entered the main stream of research into Gen 1. The enquiry into the nature and origin of Gen 1 which was begun in 1779 (or in 1754) has continued down to the present day; we must therefore now sketch its main lines in order to situate clearly the starting point of exegesis given here. This has

already been done by W.H. Schmidt, *Die Schöpfungsgeschichte der Pries-*
terschrift, 1973[3], pp. 9-20. I am relying on this survey of research for the brief
account which follows. J.G. Eichhorn discovered in his *Urgeschichte*, 1779, that
the succession of the works of creation was not coherent. According to W.C.L.
Ziegler, *Kritik über den Artikel von der Schöpfung nach unserer gewöhnlichen
Dogmatik*, 1794, the question of the temporal relationship between cosmogony
and the Sabbath (Gen 2:1-4 would be from another hand) allows for two possibilities, a later addition and the confluence of two accounts which were originally independent. Ziegler considers the possibility of the influence of older
non-Israelite traditions on the origin of Gen 1.

J.P. Gabler in his *Neuen Versuch über die Mosaische Schöpfungsgeschichte aus der höheren Kritik*, 1795, concludes to an inconsistency between the
eight works of creation and the six days. He draws attention to the constantly
recurring phrases. He is quite sure that "the creation account is pre-Mosaic and
very probably of Semitic origin" (op. cit., 28). "The analysis of the text of Gen 1
did not for a long time go beyond the work of Ziegler and Gabler" (W.H.
Schmidt, p. 13). A number of scholars drew attention to the discrepancy between
the eight works of creation and the six days, for example, H. Ewald and
E. Schrader.

The discovery of numerous cosmogonies among Israel's neighbors introduced an entirely new point of view. Gunkel's book, *Schöpfung und Chaos in
Urzeit und Endzeit*, 1895, in which he worked out their significance for the
understanding of Gen 1, was the most important work of that period of research.
He had now proved what Ziegler had already suspected, namely, that Gen 1 goes
back to very ancient traditions. In his commentary Gunkel comes to the conclusion "that P had before him an ancient narrative which itself would have had
behind it a very long history," p. 118f. Gunkel's work is the basis of the understanding of the history of the tradition of Gen 1: Gen 1 is "a quite peculiar
mixture of very ancient and very recent motifs which can only be explained by a
long history of tradition," p. 129. Gunkel thinks that P reworked his material so
thoroughly that the original wording is now completely lost.

It was only at the beginning of this century that the two different types of
creation were noticed: creation by making and creation by word stand side-by-
side (B. Stade and F. Schwally). F. Schwally, "Die biblischen Schop-
fungsberichte" ARW 9 (1906) 159-175, says "The formula 'and God said, let
there be,' and its complement, 'and it was so,' cannot be reconciled in any way
with the formula, 'and God made'; The conclusion must be that these two types
are of different origins" p. 164. R. Kittel, *Geschichte des Volkes Israel I*, 1932[7],
p. 246, n. 7 summarizes the situation as follows, "Creation through the
word. . . . presupposes a different origin from creation through action. . . . P
seems to have been the first to introduce this manner of speaking."

There were many attempts to separate the account of creation by word
from the account of creation by action. J. Morgenstern, "The Sources of the
Creation Story," AJSL 36 (1919/20) 169-212, distinguishes an older "divine
fiat" from a younger "making"-version. M. Lambert, "A Study of the First
Chapter of Genesis," HUCA 1 (1924) 3-12, wanted to reverse the order. G. von
Rad, *Die Priesterschrift im Hexateuch*, 1934, attempted a literary division of the
whole of the priestly writing and distinguished in Gen 1 an "action-account," A,

and a "command-account," B. P. Humbert rejected such a division in a very thorough enquiry, "Die literarische Zweiheit des Priester-Codex in der Genesis," ZAW 58 (1940/41) 30-57. Many other scholars took a positive or negative attitude. Von Rad did not pursue this division any further in his commentary.

W.H. Schmidt concludes his survey as follows: "Would not the command-account follow the action-account by way of interpretation? . . . . The failure of literary criticism. . . . has made it clear that the elements of tradition in Gen 1 cannot be split up. . . . The contradictions and inconsistencies have their origin in the pre-literary stage. If the division into sources does not solve the difficulty, then the question arises: What does tradition history tell us about the priestly creation story over and above oral tradition?" p. 19.

W.H. Schmidt reviews the pre-history of the material and then studies at length the relationship between the accounts of creation by word and by deed in the text of Gen 1. He draws together his conclusion in part IV, Tradition and Interpretation. The account of creation by action is shown to be original, everything else is additional. However, "there is no block of tradition that stands out clearly enough to be designated the primary material or the primary text;" in many places ". . . the theological intent of P shapes the material." This makes it "impossible to conclude to a primary text," pp. 160f. The oldest stage of the text which we can still recognize would be, according to Schmidt, vv. 2, 4b, 7, 9 Gk, 12, 16, 21, 25, 26-27a, 2:2f, p. 161. Nevertheless, "there is already at this stage a confluence of many streams of tradition,"

  (a) the water cosmogony,
  (b) the myth of separation,
  (c) the motif of emergence,
  (d) the theme of God at work, and
  (e) the theme of Mother Earth, p. 162.

"This block of tradition is now subjected to a gradual and thorough process of interpretation. . . . , the final result of which is the text as it now lies before us," p. 163. Here one must "distinguish a number of priestly interpretations," and the conclusion is that "the account of creation by word, which was responsible for the most thorough-going reshaping of the tradition . . . never had an independent existence of its own," p. 164. Nevertheless, "creation by word did not replace creation by action — the tradition was not erased, but interpreted anew," p. 171.

Schmidt's study is an important step forward. I agree in all essentials with the way in which he has advanced the question. He has established definitively that the first chapter of Genesis had its origin in the course of a history of tradition of which the written text of P is the last stage, and which stretches back beyond and outside Israel in a long and many-branched oral pre-history.

However, I would question whether one can reduce the tradition history of Gen 1 simply to the two elements of tradition and interpretation as does Schmidt. It is correct that interpretation is part of P's new arrangement of the creation event. However, P's intent is not mere interpretation. He wants to say something specific about God, about God's action; he is in a certain sense proclaiming. His real intent is to assert, not merely to explain. It is not possible simply to balance tradition and interpretation. What P by means of his "command-account" adds to the "action-account" which has come down to him, is not just interpretation or further theological reflection. There are in addition demonstrable elements of tradition. We cannot demonstrate with certainty that P was familiar with the cosmogony of the theology of Memphis or with the Babylonian hymns, where creation through the divine word occurs; nor can we exclude this possibility. On the other hand Schmidt himself says that in the "account of creation by action" tradition and interpretation are already merged together.

I think that one of Schmidt's presuppositions is an idea of tradition which puts too much emphasis on the *traditum;* the *traditum* which is there at hand is interpreted. If our starting point, as Schmidt himself says, is that the main stress is on the oral part of tradition, then the emphasis shifts to the *tradere* (the process of handing on). There is a double process in operation here; *tradere* is at the same time receiving and giving. The history of tradition then, inasmuch as it is essentially oral, must be seen as a procedure which embraces both receiving and giving; taking over and passing on is a function of the community in which the process takes place. The community must be integrated into the whole of this question. Why then does not P tell his hearers what he has to say about creation in his own words, in his own theological language? Why does he take his stand on the side of the receiver and pass on what he has received?

The first question is what are "P's own words," and therefore what is meant by the "command-account." I agree with Schmidt that it is not possible to define this with certainty. Nevertheless, there are a number of phrases in Gen 1 which recur with only slight alterations and which provide a good criterion to enable us to discern the substance of P's contribution.

ויאמר אלהים	3, 6, 9, 11, 14, 20, 24, 26
יהי יקוו	3, 6, 9, 11, 14f., 20, 24, (26)
ויהי כן אור	3, 7, 9, 11, 15, — 24, 30
וירא אלהים כי טוב	4, — 10, 12, 18, 25, 31, ( )
ויהי ערב	5, 8, — 13, 19, 23, — 31

These phrases are the framework of all the works of creation; they are saying as they are constantly repeated that each successive work of creation is essentially the same event. What sort of event is this, and how are its parts related to each other?

I. Introduction	And God said
II. Command (in the Jussive)	Let it be, let them be gathered
III. Completion	And it was so
IV. Judgment	And God saw that it was good
V. Time Sequence	And it was evening. . . .

These constantly recurring phrases have a function; they are part of a process and spell out the fulfillment of a command. The account is introduced with the words "And God said" (I), the command is formulated in the Jussive (II). The fulfillment of the command is then reported (III) in military-like language. Now a command only has meaning in a community and is always in some way related to it. The object and fulfillment of the command must be for the good of something or someone. At the creation itself, the object to which creation is directed is not yet there. The response of praise of the creation is contained in the divine judgment and approval because there is not yet anything there that can praise God (IV). This sentence gives expression to the profound reflection that the praise of God cannot be separated from his works; his works demand the response of praise. The fifth element is not of itself part of the account of the fulfillment of the command; but for P it is important; it is the time sequence (V).

All that takes place must follow a time sequence which is an essential part of the priestly narrative. Events must be fitted into the framework of the chronology which runs through the whole of the priestly work just as the fulfillment of the creation commands must be fitted into the basic framework of the seven days. By creating, God enters into time, and so time must be an expression of the action of God. From the very beginning creation is subordinated to an unbroken sequence of time which ultimately leads to God just as it took its beginning from his word: the succession of days leads finally to God's day.

One will misunderstand the purpose of P as long as one's starting-point is a general and abstract notion of "word." Creation through the word as such is not what P is about. P's purpose is to arrange God's work of creation into a network of sentences whose succession follows the pattern of the fulfillment of a command. The word of command has a special significance that colors the whole of P's theology. Everything that happens has its source in God's word of command. The only difference between God's action in history and his action in creation is that in the one case his command is directed to a person (Abraham) or a mediator (Moses), while in the other it is a command without an addressee, and hence a creation command. The precise significance of the structure of Gen 1 can only be grasped in the context of the overall theological outlook of the priestly writing. And this only becomes clear when it is recognized that the constantly recurring phrases of Gen 1, which give the passage its character, are part of a process, the fulfillment of a command.

We now come to another question: Why doesn't P use his own words and phrases when speaking of the action of the creator? Why doesn't P limit his account of the creation of the world and of people to the structure outlined above? Why does he take up and fit into this structure a completely different structure, that of creation by action? P is telling us that as a theologian he has something new to say at this stage; he is at the same time the receiver of a tradition and the one who has to pass on what he has received from his ancestors. P's presupposition is clearly that everything that is said about the creator and creation must be conscious of its limitations. P could not say that the only possible and correct way to describe creation is by means of a structure which presents the fulfillment of a command. He must, of course, speak of creation in this way. However, he lets other voices speak which have described creation differently. This decision is of great theological moment. The redactors of the Pentateuch and of the canon made a similar decision when they decided to leave side-by-side very different descriptions of creation. This means that when there is talk of creation there must be preserved a succession of very different voices which add their contribution to what is being said.

We will follow P in what he has taken up into his presentation of the creation. He is both concrete and many-sided in his peculiar approach. Very different and self-contained actions follow each other.

God divided	4	7	(9)			
God named	5	8	10			
God made		7		16		25
God put				17		
God created					21	27
God blessed					22	28

These verbs are distributed over the eight acts of creation in the following manner:

1.	Light 3-5	God divided		named
2.	Firmament 6-8	God made	divided	named
3.	Sea-Land 9-10	God (divided)		named
4.	Plants 11-13	(The Earth brought forth)		
5.	Heavenly bodies 14-19	God made	he put them	
6.	Beasts of the water and of the air 20-23	God created		blessed
7.	Land beasts 24-25	God made		
8.	Human beings 26-31	Let us make!	God created	blessed

The distribution of the verbs and their assignment to the various works of creation show that there is no fixed pattern. This series of verbs is very different from the other series not only in content but also in the way in which they are used. We must always remember that we are not dealing here with a literary stratum which could be reconstructed; it is rather that P has taken over an older description of creation which he has merged with his own in such a way that we have to take account of P's recasting at every stage. And so it only confuses the issue when one wants to divide Gen 1 into a "command-account" and an "action-account"; the former never existed as such, and the latter cannot be reconstructed.

The verbs "make" and "create" predominate. What is the relationship of עשׂה and ברא to each other? ברא is given prominence in the title to the chapter and in the concluding verses, 1:1; 2:3, 4, and in the creation of humans, 1:27 (3 times), cf. 5:1, 2. A preference is shown here for the verb ברא over the more manual עשׂה. The reason is theological, because the verb is only used with God as subject. It is all the more noteworthy then that P does not replace עשׂה with ברא on every occasion. This means that P, in his choice of words for God's creative action, is aware that he is at the same time a theologian of his age as well as one who receives a tradition which he has to pass on. And so it is just as important for P to retain עשׂה in certain places as it is to prefer ברא in others. This has not been noticed for the most part; consequently many exegetes have explained the variation by saying that P has replaced עשׂה by ברא in those places which are especially important for him. But such an explanation is not adequate. P's preference for ברא in the three places mentioned above is further defined when he introduces the creation of man with the words נעשׂה אדם. If P uses both verbs for the same act of creation then the conclusion must be that he understands them in essentially the same sense. When P says:

86

"God *created* the great sea monsters. . . . and every winged bird. . . .", he is not making any distinction between the verbs. One cannot explain the different use of the words as does W.H. Schmidt: "Where the creation story wants to say something really theological, it is obvious that עשׂה, 'make,' is replaced by ברא, 'create'," p. 164. The conclusion is otherwise: P certainly prefers ברא to עשׂה in certain places, but in others he uses both words without distinction.

"Make" or "create" are not used for all the works of creation. God made or created the firmament, the stars which he put into the firmament, the animals and people. That is, God made or created a world ruled by space and time, and living beings to inhabit it. These verbs indicate the creation of a world that is meant to be a living space for humankind, not the world in the sense of the universe. We recognize here an attitude toward creation which is very close to that of Gen 2: the world which God created is meant to be the world of people. There is in the tradition which P resumes a connecting link which goes back to an older conception of creation.

1. *God separated*. The verbs "created" or "made" occur in the second work of creation and then in the fifth to eighth works. In the first three works P says: God separated — God named. There are signs here that the creation tradition that came down to P had a history in which different ways of describing creation had gradually grown together. It has been shown in the Introduction that each of these could describe at one stage creation as a whole. To understand creation as a whole as separation is very ancient and widespread. It is clear what P is doing: he takes up this description and fits it into his work in such a way that the first three works of creation in which the world is ordered into its dimensions of time and space are described as a separation. Separation here is not concerned with the creation of the objective world, that is, of the sum total of what is; it looks to the creation of the world of time and space where people live out their lives.

2. *God named*. The naming is on all three occasions linked with the separation. God does not give a name to everything that he has created. He gives names only to what is the result of his act of separation, to those basic elements of space and time that determine human existence: day and night v. 5, heaven v. 8, land and sea v. 10. Naming has the sense of defining in this context. By naming them God destines space and time to be the world of humanity forever and in this very same action shows himself to be the master of the world so defined. In the traditions which P received, in Sumer and Babylon, naming is the finish of the act of creation. Talk about the creator therefore is talk about the master of creation.

3. *Let the earth bring forth*. After the first three works of separation and naming there comes the surprising sentence, "Let the earth put forth vegetation. . . ." This too has a deliberate purpose in the structure of the whole. Its background is the ancient idea of the origin of life from the earth. The earth, the mother of all life, brings forth what is living. P allows this ancient idea to continue to echo. He works this into his overall structure in such a way that after the creation of the earth by three works of separation and naming, life can come forth on it, but only if the creative word of God is at its origin. And so P allows yet another voice to speak, that of the origin of life from the earth. It is set apart quite clearly from the first three works.

4. *God made (created).* There begins now the series of works five to eight in which God makes or creates. There are two important additions here:

(a) everything that God makes or creates is given a destiny. For the earth or the world there is no need for this; but everything else, on the earth or in the world, is given a purpose; their significance is established with their creation (the purpose of plants and animals is only mentioned later). Creation is not just making something which is then there; it is an action which has a goal; it is an event whose aim is to give each object of creation a meaning and function.

(b) God creates living things according to species. And so there is yet another trait in P's creation account which does not belong either to theological or religious tradition but rather to the tradition of the natural sciences.

Both these additions show very clearly that P is concerned to relate his talk about creation to the world in a way that was intelligible and accessible to the people of his time. Gen 1 is not merely concerned with explaining that God created the world, but also that he created the world accessible to the state of contemporary understanding.

5. *God blessed.* P distinguishes between animate and inanimate creatures. The animate creatures are blessed by God. To bless means "to bestow with a dynamism to increase" (L. Köhler, *Lexikon*), and this is primarily the power of fertility given to humans and to beasts. It is this that makes it possible for living beings to exist; in the case of humanity the blessing itself works itself out in the series of the genealogies which form the framework of the primeval story. The blessing of animate creation binds creation with history.

By way of conclusion we may say that we have established the following concerning the various activities of God the creator: on the one hand there is a long history of creation accounts which are early Israelite or which are older than Israel; on the other, P uses them to describe in a succession of acts the anatomy of the world. The universe with all its parts is not suddenly established by one sweeping act; it is set into the categories of time and space. A distinction is made between the world as such (the first three works) and what is in the world and upon the earth (works three to eight), and again between animate and inanimate life. There is a gradual progression in this arrangement: everything that God has created has a destiny; this destiny reaches its goal in humanity which God created as his counterpart; with human beings creation points the way into history.

The Succession of Works and the Pattern of the Seven Days.

One of the first difficulties to which scholars drew attention in the course of the exegesis of Gen 1 was that the number of the works of creation did not agree with the number of days. Eight works are distributed over six days, with two on each of the third and sixth days. The many attempts to solve the problem are recorded in W.H. Schmidt's survey, pp. 9-20. The general opinion today is that "the framework of the seven days belongs to a later stage in the history of the text." The numbering of the days has a fixed place in the fifth part of the structure which delimits the creation command. It is part of an arrangement by which P preserves an older tradition; it extends from the work of the first day which makes it possible, right up to the seventh in which it reaches its goal. A systematization of the succession of the works of creation is already there in the numbering of the days; and this is something completely different from the succession of the works of creation determined by the object actually created.

All attempts to bring the works of creation into a systematic order must be given up. There was never any intention of doing this. As we have seen, the arrangement can be explained much better by the confluence of many strands of traditions and motifs from a variety of earlier creation stories. This too is the source of much of the unevenness in the narrative. There is no need to discuss the various attempts to redistribute the works. W.H. Schmidt has referred to a number of such attempts on p. 55, n. 1.

A glance at the order of events in Enuma Elish shows that the order in Gen 1 is to be explained from its pre-history and is not to be altered. The similarity is so striking that one can scarcely deny some sort of relationship. A. Heidel, *The Babylonian Genesis,* p. 129, sets the events of the two accounts side by side, and E.A. Speiser resumes the pattern in his commentary with the observation: "Except for incidental differences of opinion in regard to the exact meaning of the first entry in each column. . . . the validity of this listing is not open to question." I would add the further reservation that such a comparison has only a limited value. It is useful as a first step. There is a correspondence in the general succession of events: Chaos at the beginning, the creation of the firmament, of the dry land, of the heavenly bodies and of people. God's rest corresponds to the feast of the gods. Heidel sees further correspondence between the creation of light in Genesis and the light which emanates from the gods in Enuma Elish. But that is open to question.

Even if one leaves this aside, as well as the correspondence in the first line between the divine spirit and matter, there are enough points of contact that are certain. We do not conclude to a literary dependence (cf. Introduction). Even if P was familiar with Enuma Elish, there were many other creation accounts of which we know only a little. The explanation lies in the preliterary stage of history of tradition. We cannot accept a direct dependence any more than we can accept any alteration or reconstruction of the order of events in Gen 1 which does not take account of this pre-history (so too W.G. Lambert, "A New Look at the Babylonian Background of Genesis," JThS 16 [1965] 287-300).

What is the meaning then of this seven-day pattern, this "creation week" as some call it, which P has arranged? P has gone very deeply into the creation theology that has come down to him (cf. W.H. Schmidt, p. 70). P had no predecessor for his new arrangement. There is no creation story that is arranged in a succession of days. P wanted to say something that was in accordance with his own understanding of creation. The succession of the seven days becomes a self-contained unit by means of the seventh day. It is clear that there is a reference to the sabbath even though P does not name it (see commentary on 2:1-3). It is not the number 7 that links the seven-day pattern with the work of creation, but the meaning of the seventh day. The rest of creation does not belong to the tradition of creation by word, but rather to that of creation by making or acting. Rest has meaning only in this latter context. The point of contact lies in the rest of the creator which brings the work of creation to its conclusion. This was a tradition which came down to P and which is widely attested in creation stories previous to and beyond Israel. The rest of the creator had nothing to do with a day of rest in the earlier traditions. P takes over the rest of the creator from tradition and creates out of it something entirely new. He transforms it into a day of rest which concludes the "creation week." We can note here very clearly P's profound insight as he brings together what he has received and what he will contribute.

By fitting the motif of rest into the creation week, P has given creation the character of an event that moves through time toward its goal. P knew quite well that primeval events cannot be dated, that they are beyond the standpoint of history; by reflecting profoundly on the standard theology of creation he was able to alter this basic presupposition. Under P, creation was made to take after history in that he looked at creation in the context of continuous time and not merely in the context of unapproachable and intangible primeval time. There is a parallel then between fitting the creation event into the overall stream of time and setting a historical event into the realization of a divine command which is the result of God's overall plan in history. In both cases the event rests on God's command. The seven-day pattern corresponds to P's conception of the whole: in it he is saying that it is always the same God in action, that God is the god of history as well as of creation. God's action is directed toward a goal not only in history but also in creation; and the ultimate goal in creation is not the last work of creation, humanity, but what is hinted at in the description of the seventh day.

The seven-day pattern is in accord with P's overall view again in that P is concerned throughout his work with linear time and the celebration of the holy and the goal to which they are directed. "P wants to point to a course of history in which God's economy is revealed step-by-step and in which his dispositions gradually secure and assure the prosperity of his people" (G. von Rad, *Die Priesterschrift im Hexateuch*, 1934, p. 188). The week of creation is thus a deliberate counterpart to God's action in history to which P must have attached great importance. God's action takes place in carefully regulated periods of which the conclusion, the celebration of the holy, gives unity to the whole.

P introduced the seven-day pattern to reshape the tradition he received in accordance with his own overall view that linked God's action in creation and his action in history very closely. One must agree with W.H. Schmidt when he writes: "The seven-day scheme has a meaning of its own, and is not to be explained by the creation story," p. 68; but one must have reservations when he continues: "The words 'evening and morning' describe an actual day of 24 hours; otherwise the succession of six days ending with the sabbath loses its meaning." But P does not present "a succession of six days ending with the sabbath"; he presents a whole, an articulated chronological unity, which is a whole because of its goal. It is not a question of seven times 24 hours, but of the chronological unity which is the basis of all else and which is itself articulated in the same way. One does not just count up the seven days; they are rather like a parable. P wants to say that time, properly ordered and directed in carefully regulated periods toward its God-given goal, began with creation.

Gen 1 — Poetry and Prose.

Gen 1 contains a fusion of poetry and prose that is unique in the Old Testament. This is to be explained from the pre-history of Gen 1, especially from the union of what have been called the command-account and the action-account. While the latter is simply report or narrative, the former takes on something of a poetic form because of the constantly recurring phrases. The sentence that concludes each day of creation divides the whole as it were into strophes, and the individual sentences of the account of creation by the word have a definite rhythmic stamp. However, it is better not to try to fit it into any fixed metric pattern. It would be easy to arrange the text metrically in many places, but this should be avoided. The rhythm belongs to the overall account and should remain irregular. It is not the elevated rhythmic language itself that gives the chapter its peculiar character, but the unique union of disparate elements, which are so like the genealogies in the monotonous repetition of the same sentences, with something quite different, namely, an attention to the natural sciences as exemplified in the descriptions of the different species of plants. It has also been said that the language of Gen 1 is so colored mathematically that the number pattern is evident in the use of words, phrases, and the division of lines. Even if this is the case, the number pattern remains subordinate to the structure as a whole, which is determined by its object.

Setting in Life

There must be a thorough study of the question of "the setting in life." Strictly speaking this term of Gunkel's can only be used when a fixed, self-contained formula has a recognizable function in the life of a community, e.g., a community lament on an occasion that calls for it. It must be possible to recognize or conclude to such a function from the literary setting in which the formula has been handed down. Normally the setting in life means an occasion when something is said, e.g., the utterance of a prophetic oracle, the pronouncement of a blessing, the acclamation at an enthronement. When such a sentence is handed down in a literary context, the original life-setting is no longer there and the sentence appears in a different context. It is a matter of judgment whether this literary context is a setting in life; for the sake of clarity it would be better to limit the phrase "setting in life" to the original function and context. The phrase is given a new context in its literary setting and, almost always, must be seen in the stream of tradition history. Generally speaking then the question of the setting in life of a phrase must not be separated from the question of tradition history.

We meet Gen 1 as a part of the priestly work which in its turn is a part of the Pentateuch. Let it be said here once and for all that the interpretation of each individual part is concerned with the whole process of formation from the smallest unit and its setting in life right up to the final literary product that lies before us. The primeval story (Gen 1-11) stands out as a distinctive, relatively self-contained unit within the priestly writing, whose function is not only to be part of Genesis, but a part of the Pentateuch. The primeval story points to a very special tradition history as indicated in the general introduction. Within this context Gen 1 is part of a particular cycle of creation narratives or stories. It was demonstrated in the Introduction that the creation narratives had their own special independent setting in life, namely occasions when such narratives served to assure and stabilize the state of the world, of life, and of human existence. In the primitive cultures, one setting in life was the rites of passage. Another and later function was cultic when the story of creation was recited as part of the Enuma Elish epic at the Babylonian New Year festival.

One must be careful of any generalization. It cannot be proved that all creation narratives had such a setting in life any more than it can be proved when, how and under what circumstances the narratives were freed from this setting. All that can be presumed with certainty is that the creation narratives were not originally answers to the question about the origins of the world and of humanity; they arose from the everyday concern about the stability of the present state and of human existence.

It should not be presumed that the occasions in which the creation narratives had their original setting in life were governed by a notion of cult such as we are familiar with from the high cultures, especially in the orient; that is, a notion of cult which presumed a particular complex of cultic events. It was more a question here of what Martin Buber called "pan-sacralization," where the whole way of life of a group was informed by cult, or better, where there was not yet a separation of the cultic and the profane. It is this that substantiates that the creation narratives were freed from the celebrations at a very early stage and were handed down as such. It is already difficult to recognize in the Sumerian creation myths the cultic event and setting where they belonged.

The link with the cult which is still quite recognizable is the praise of God. This is precisely the case in the Babylonian epic, Enuma Elish, where the narrative of creation is found in the context of the praise of Marduk. It is the same in the Egyptian stories of creation. In the Koran the story of creation is taken up in the praise of the creator. The praise of God unites the creation narratives with the creation hymns or psalms which nevertheless have been handed down in separate streams of tradition. One can recognize in the peculiar, closely-knit language of Gen 1 an undercurrent of the praise of God; this is explained by a pre-history in which the creation narratives and the praise of the creator functioned together.

The original setting of the creation narratives is much older than P. "There is no sign at all in the biblical creation story that it was once recited at a festival and in some way 'happened' by being presented in dramatic form" (W.H. Schmidt, p. 73). P was not the first to free the creation story from its original setting; the separation preceded him. What follows from this?

When the creation narrative lost its setting in life, it also lost its original function which served to maintain and secure the present state of the world and of life. What then remained of its function and meaning? One must distinguish two stages. In the first stage, the creation narratives were freed from their original setting in cultic celebration and were narrated and handed down as individual stories; it is difficult to give a uniform description of their meaning and function at this stage; all that we can say for certain is that they acquired the function, which later controlled them, of explaining the origin of the world and of humanity. Other motifs could be added as, for example, the rival cosmogonies of the different shrines in Egypt show (cf. S.G.F. Brandon, "The Propaganda Factor in Some Ancient Near Eastern Cosmogonies," *Promise and Fulfilment. Essays presented to S.H. Hooke,* 1963, pp. 20-35).

In the second stage the creation narratives take on a new meaning and function from the new, broader context in which they are inserted. This occurs already in the Sumerian myths where an event which is to be narrated is introduced by a few lines which give an account of creation. This occurs on a different level in the Babylonian Enuma Elish, in the works of J and P in Israel, as well as in the prologue to the Gospel of John, though with more notable adaptations and in a shorter form.

The creation narrative handed down to us in Gen 1 finds a new setting as the beginning of the priestly work. It takes on the function and character of a solemn overture. It is the beginning of a series of events which starts with the creation of the world and spans *(ein Geschehensbogen)* the call of the Patriarchs, the revelation in act (Reed Sea) and word (Sinai) that is the basis of the covenant with Israel, the journey of the people through the desert, right up to the erection and dedication of the sanctuary which was to establish forever Israel's life as a life before God.

The overture and the events it introduces are not of the same kind. When one considers the very esoteric nature of the laws of cult which form the center of the priestly writing, one would scarcely expect to find such an entrance gate to the way that leads to such a legal code. The code that establishes Israel's liturgy once and for all and thereby sets apart the community which must worship in this way alone, is the code of the God who created not only Israel, but heaven and earth, and who blessed all creation and the whole of humanity.

One cannot overestimate the significance of preserving and passing on a tradition about humanity in which God's vis-a-vis is not Israel with its rubricized liturgy and law, but the cosmos, creation and people. Israel, with all its esoteric and exclusive traditions, never lost sight of what God was doing for the world and its inhabitants.

Commentary

[1:1] "In the beginning God created the heavens and the earth." The first sentence of the Bible is controversial. Is 1:1 a principal clause or is it a subordinate temporal clause? If v. 1 is a subordinate clause, is the principal clause to be found in v. 2 or v. 3? It is a question of syntax, of the relationship of the first three verses to each other. The discussion so far shows that the meaing of the first verse of the Bible is not to be separated from the question of syntax. It is often maintained that the solution of the question of syntax automatically solves other problems — is Gen 1 speaking of *creatio ex nihilo*? or does the narrative presume some sort of matter that provided the "raw material" for creation?

If Gen 1 is a self-contained whole and as such is part of P's primeval story, and if further it belongs to the broader context of creation narratives, then it is essential for the solution of the question to survey these broader contexts. Any attempt to solve the problem which leaves the first two or three verses in isolation and does not enquire into the function of these verses as part of a whole neglects a very important methodological approach. The creation narratives in general present a fixed, stereotyped introductory formula which can be compared readily with the opening of the book of Genesis. We have studied it in the Introduction. Its structure is: "When this and this was not yet. . . . then. . . .", and its function is to make the account of creation a story within the dimension of time. The formula is found in Gen 2:4bff., it forms the introduction of the Enuma Elish epic, and occurs often in Sumerian and Egyptian.

A comparison of these texts with Gen 1 shows that the antecedent clause of the formula corresponds to the content of Gen. 1:2, and the final clause to that of Gen 1:3. Gen 1:2, which is positive in its formulation, "The earth was without form and void," corresponds in content to the temporal clause, "When . . . was not yet," and the introduction to the creation command of v. 3, "And God said . . . ," corresponds to the final clauses where the work of creation begins. P alters the form of the introduction so that (a) the negative formulation becomes positive (this also occurs elsewhere), and (b) a sentence is prefixed to the whole which has no parallel in other creation stories, but is a construction of P himself (Gunkel had recognized this).

The sentence in 1:1 is not the beginning of an account of creation, but a heading that takes in everything in the narrative in one single sentence — and it is much more than a mere heading. It speaks of the creation of heaven and earth in the same way as do the hymns of the praise of God. One could say that the formula which is predicated of God, "Creator of heaven and earth," has been reshaped into a verbal sentence. It has often been said that Gen 1 has echoes of a hymn or that as a whole it is very like the praise of God. The reason for this is that the first sentence itself is really a cry of praise.

The explanation of v. 1 given here has two points of departure: its relationship to other creation stories and the position of P in the history of these stories. It is supported by two main arguments: (a) The content of Gen 1:2 corresponds to the sentences "When there was not yet" in the other creation narratives, and this is in direct opposition to any interpretation of v. 1 as a temporal subordinate clause; (b) There is no parallel at all to v. 1 in the other creation stories; this indicates that v. 1 is a creation of P and has been put at the beginning deliberately.

The discussion up to date has not taken sufficient account of these arguments. We will sum it up briefly.

(1) There is unanimity that both constructions are grammatically possible in vv. 1-3: one understands v. 1 as a main clause (A) and the other understands it as a temporal subordinate clause (B). Meaning A is found in the massoretic punctuation, which provides בראשית with a Tiphḥā (so F. Delitzsch: בראשית has tiphḥa, and is thereby separated from what follows as if it was being said: "In the beginning, then God created. . . ."; likewise König and Procksch. Meaning A is also implied in the old translations (so, e.g., N.H. Ridderbos, "Gen 1:2 and 2" OTS 12 [1958] 228: "This is the interpretation of the Massoretes and all of the old translations"); the Gr reads: Ἐν ἀρχῇ ἐποίησεν ὁ θεὸς τὸν οὐρανὸν καὶ τὴν γῆν. An indirect confirmation of this interpretation is seen in Jn 1:1; the sentence Ἐν ἀρχῇ ἦν ὁ λόγος, καὶ. . . reflects an interpretation which understands Gen 1:1 as a main clause. It has been asserted that the massoretic vocalization of the verb ברא as a perfect demonstrates that it is a main clause; but that is not correct or at any rate not certain, because the sentence from ברא to ארץ can be understood as what is known as a genitive clause in place of a noun in the genitive (e.g., W.H. Schmidt, p. 74, n. 2; see too n. 1 in the same place for a brief survey of scholars who see in Gen 1:1-3 a complex of sentences). One can say really no more than that the vocalization speaks as much in favor of a main clause as of a subordinate clause. The conclusion is that the text allows for both possibilities and that the oldest witnesses, namely the massoretic punctuation, the old translations and the New Testament speak in favor of a main clause. One can add that the Greek transcription presumes in many cases בְּרֵאשִׁית; "In the Greek transliterations of the Hebrew text. . . . . bereshith in the opening verse of Genesis appears as βαρησήθ, βαρησέθ, βρησίθ, βρισήθ, and βρησίδ" (A. Heidel, p. 93; see too the summary of arguments in favor of a main clause on p. 94).

(2) The Middle Ages saw the interpretation of v. 1 as a temporal subordinate clause. Rashi (Rabbi Solomon ben Isaac, d. 1105) was the first as far as is known to propose this view, but it is possible that it had already been proposed in Jewish tradition. It takes the following form (Ba):

1 protasis:	When God began . . .	
2 parenthesis:	the earth was . . .	
3 apodosis:	then God said . . .	

Another Jewish scholar, Abraham ibn Ezra, proposed another form of this interpretation (Bb):

1 protasis:	When God began . . .	
2 apodosis:	the earth was . . .	

This second interpretation was taken up by Hugo Grotius but only by a very few after him. The other interpretation (Ba) has found many adherents: H. Ewald, E. Schrader, K. Budde, P. Smith, W.F. Albright, O. Eissfeldt, R. Dussaud, P. Humbert (he proposes that the principal clause begins with the third clause of v. 2), S. Herrmann, H.M. Orlinsky, C.A. Simpson, E.A. Speiser.

Nevertheless, the interpretation of v. 1 as a main clause opens many possibilities. "Verse 1 narrates the creation of raw material of which v. 2 gives a description" (Ridderbos, p. 229). Ridderbos refers to other representatives of this view (Aa): J. Calvin, J. Wellhausen, E. König, G. Aalders, A. Heidel. J. Skinner writes: "that the verse asserts the creation (*creatio ex nihilo*) of the primaeval chaos described in V. 2" and thinks that this is the prevailing opinion in Jewish and Christian interpretation; in recent times it was supported by such important figures as Wellhausen. Two objections have been brought against this view: the object "heaven and earth" contradicts it, because these two words together always describe the world of order; the predicate also contradicts it because the creation of chaos is a contradiction in terms (so J. Skinner, N.H. Ridderbos, B.S. Childs, G. von Rad and many others). This explanation, in a somewhat different form, is the basis of the interpretation of Ridderbos.

According to the other opinion (Ab) v. 1 is as it were a heading, a finely chiselled independent main clause (this is the traditional understanding; in more recent times it has been supported by H. Strack, H. Gunkel, O. Procksch, W. Zimmerli, G. von Rad, W. Eichrodt, W.H. Schmidt, H.A. Brongers, U. Cassuto). It has often been objected that this opinion gives rise to an insuperable difficulty in the relationship of v. 2 to v. 1. Gunkel remarks: "It must be conceded that there is an internal contradiction here, but it is to be understood historically; the material of v. 2 is one of the elements which had been passed on to Judaism." This argument has been accepted by many scholars since Gunkel.

So much for the outline of the various opinions about Gen. 1:1. I will now draw together the most important arguments in this almost endless discussion:

(a) בְּרֵאשִׁית: It has been maintained constantly that this phrase without the article cannot be translated "in the beginning," but can only be treated as the first part of a construct chain. Consequently the remainder of the sentence is a genitive governed by בְּרֵאשִׁית. P. Humbert tried to demonstrate this by showing that רֵאשִׁית is never used in the absolute sense in any other place in the Old Testament (Knobel-Dillmann had already pointed this out). Humbert concludes that רֵאשִׁית, when temporal, always has a relative sense. And so, the argument goes, the phrase has a relative sense in Gen 1:1 and the syntax must be construct chain.

There are two flaws in this argument. First, it maintains that a word-count can solve the complex of Gen 1:1, and second, it does not see that the study of individual words must include a study of the vocabulary of the context. This is pointed out by N.H. Ridderbos (op. cit., p. 218) and W. Eichrodt, "In the beginning," *Israel's Prophetic*

Heritage, Essays in Honour of J. Muilenburg, ed. B.W. Anderson, 1962, pp. 1-10. Eichrodt cites Prov 8:23, "where mērōš is unequivocally determined by the preceding mēʿōlām," p. 4. And it can be said in addition: "The article is quite often missing in such indeterminate indications of time" (O. Procksch). Ridderbos and Eichrodt come to the same conclusion in their examination of Humbert's study: there is no convincing proof that the בראשית cannot be used in the absolute state at the beginning of a sentence to indicate time. No new arguments are brought forward in the subsequent discussion between Humbert, "Encore le premier mot de la Bible," ZAW 76 (1964) 121-131 and W. Eichrodt: ThZ 20 (1964) 161-163. The discussion has been bound up very much with the question of an absolute or construct state, of whether Gen 1:1 is speaking of an absolute beginning or not. One must be very cautious about using the words absolute and relative here; W.H. Schmidt, p. 75, asks justly "if this is really in accordance with the Old Testament way of thinking." In any case one should not give too much weight to these alternatives.

(b) Another argument is the syntactical construction of the first three verses. E.A. Speiser, who supports the interpretation, Ba, bases it on the conviction that בראשית must be part of a construct chain, without considering the arguments against this view. A more important argument for him is "the syntax of the entire first paragraph." What is decisive is the parenthetic nature of v. 2 which is shown by the form of the verb: "A normal consecutive statement would have begun with wattehi hāʾāreṣ." Speiser presupposes that v. 2 must be understood as a consecutive clause if v. 1 is a main clause. But that is not the case. A. Heidel, p. 93, takes up Speiser's argument. He refers to examples such as Gen 3:1 where there is inversion with the perfect in order to break the continuity of the narrative so as to draw attention to some characteristic; the subject of this characteristic becomes the focus of attention by its position at the beginning of the sentence. Note should be taken of the position of the subject in the first of the three sentences: the subject "the earth" in v. 2 must be separated carefully from the object "heaven and earth" in v. 1, because the predicates of the clauses in v. 2 are not the equivalent of "heaven and earth," but of "the earth." The series of attempts to explain the relationship between vv. 1 and 2 syntactically show clearly that grammar alone offers no solution; the relationship of these two verses can be explained only from the process of formation of Gen 1, as Gunkel had already recognized. The difficulty is compounded when U. Cassuto and E.A. Speiser in their recent commentaries use arguments from syntax to come to quite opposite conclusions.

(c) Can theological arguments solve the problem? They have always been used. G. von Rad notes in his introductory remarks to the first verses: "We do not follow the old conjecture that v. 1 is not to be understood as an independent sentence but as the introductory clause to v. 2 or even to v. 3. Syntactically perhaps both translations are possible, not theologically." The decisive argument for von Rad is that otherwise what is said of Chaos would precede what is said of creation both temporally and logically. W.R. Lane, VT 13 (1963) 64-66, has replied in detail to this sort of argument. He objects that we cannot know what P means if we have not already decided on objective grounds how Gen 1:1-3 is to be translated. Von Rad's method of argument puts us in too great a danger of determining the meaning of the text from convictions already held. One can maintain this objection even if one agrees with von Rad's conclusion. A purely theological argument is dubious because a different theological point of view could demand that a different explanation was equally necessary. Theological arguments alone cannot decide the problem.

(d) E.A. Speiser strengthens his argument from syntax by reference to parallels: "The analogous account (by J) in 2:4b-7 shows the identical construction. . . . The beginning of Enuma Elish exhibits exactly the same kind of structure." A number of other interpreters have referred to the same parallels. But the alleged correspondence is not the point. Enuma Elish begins: "When this and this was not yet, then. . . ." Lines 1-8 form the antecedent sentence, lines 9-10 the temporal statement:

> "When on high the heaven had not been named,
> firm ground below had not been called by name,
> . . . .
> Then it was that the gods were formed within them. . . ."

A comparison with the first verses of Gen 1 shows that lines 1-8 correspond to the three clauses in Gen 1:2; line 9 corresponds to Gen 1:3. Gen 1:1 is completely outside this structure; the sentence is much more like a prelude and has no equivalent in the opening lines of Enuma Elish. Heidel, p. 95, points this out; the *Babylonian Enuma* (Sumerian *udda*) corresponds to the Hebrew ביום as in Gen 2:4b, and not to בראשית. The beginning of Gen 2:4ff. differs from that of 1:1 inasmuch as 2:4b gives an indication of time and is saying something different from v. 7: "In the day that the Lord God made the earth and the heavens. . . .then the Lord God formed man. . . ." The relationship of 2:4b to 2:7 is different from that of 1:1 to 1:3. (Heidel points out a further difference, namely that an imperfect follows the words ביום עשות and not a perfect.) The function of 2:4b is to link the story of the creation of man with the summary statement about the creation of the world. The two parallels which Speiser uses to strengthen his thesis do not correspond exactly to 1:1-3 (see also W.H. Schmidt, p. 78).

(e) There is also the stylistic argument. "But this translation is desperate"; so Wellhausen remarks about the temporal subordination of v. 1 (*Prolegomena to the History of Ancient Israel*, N.Y., 1957, p. 387, n. 1). This judgment can be supported stylistically. What is peculiar to the language of P in Gen 1 is the continual repetition of the same short sentences: "And God saw that it was good." "And there was evening and there was morning, one day." If v. 1 is the work of P, and this can scarcely be disputed, it belongs to this same series. It would be completely out of harmony with P's style in Gen 1 to arrange the first three verses into one complete sentence. The style of the chapter leaves us to expect that v. 1 is a main sentence.

It is clear then that vv. 2 and 3ff. at the beginning of Gen 1 correspond to the traditional pattern "When not yet. . . . v. 2, then. . . ." v. 3ff. Verse 1 does not fit the pattern; it was prefixed later. A confirmation of this is that v. 1 has no parallel in the other creation stories, while all three sentences of v. 2 are based on traditional material. The tradition history of the creation stories provides us with an answer to the question about the inter-relationship of the first verses of Genesis which is certain.

The first verse then is to be understood as a principal sentence. The creation of the world by God is expressed in one sentence as in the praise of God. And because this sentence is prefixed to the actual account of creation it acquires monumental importance which distinguishes it from other creation stories. "There is nothing in the cosmogonies of other peoples which can compare with the first sentence of the Bible" (H. Gunkel). It has no precedent; it is a construction of P and has been prefixed by him to the account of creation. It corresponds to the phrase "Creator of heaven and earth," Gen 14:19. The narrative unfolds everything that it contains; when one has said that creation is the work of God, then one has said everything that there is to say about it. One can unfold what the verse contains, but one can say nothing further about creation.

בראשית: reference has been made above to Humbert's attempt to prove that ראשית is a temporal relative and consequently the first part of a construct chain. W. Eichrodt has objected that account must be taken of similar indications of time without the article which can have an absolute meaning, as for example, מראש, "from the very beginning," Is 40:21; 41:4; in Prov 8:23 מראש is parallel to מעולם. Such temporal expressions can be used in both an absolute and a relative sense. N.H. Ridderbos argues in a similar way and comes to the same conclusion. Likewise F. Vattioni, Aug. 4 (1964) 105-108, and A. Heidel, p. 92f., who discusses the contrary opinion advanced by W.F. Albright, JBL 62 (1943) 369-370. Eichrodt points out that it accords completely with P's overall view to speak of an absolute beginning and that there are similar phrases in Deutero-Isaiah who belongs to the same era as P (so too O. Procksch ad. loc., and B.S. Childs, p. 41). F. Delitzsch has understood the intention of P correctly: "His point is not that heaven and earth had a beginning, but that the creation of heaven and earth was the beginning of all history."

The sentence which P fashioned contains the word for creation for which he has a special preference, ברא. There have been many studies of this word. Before discussing it let us recall the warning sounded by J. Barr in *The Semantics of Biblical Language,* 1961, not to read too much into the word as such. One cannot draw theological conclusions about the idea of creation from the word itself but only from the contexts in which it is used. The discussion about the history and meaning of the word is very important: is it an ancient word to designate creation by God (so H. Gunkel and P. Humbert), or is it relatively late (so the majority of scholars)?

ברא: Literature: F.M.Th. Böhl, "bara' als Terminus der Weltschöpfung," BWAT 13 (1913) 42-46. W. Förster, κτίζω, ThWNT 3 (1938) 1004-1015. P. Humbert, "Emploi et portée du verbe bārā' (créer) dans l'A.T.," ThZ 3 (1947) 401-421, = OH 146-165. J. van der Ploeg, "Le sens du verbe hébreu bārā', Etude semiasologique," Muséon 59 (1946) 143-157. N.H. Ridderbos, "Genesis 1:1 and 2," OTS 12 (1958) §3, 219-223. É. Dantinne, "Création et séparation," Muséon 74 (1961) 441-451. W.H. Schmidt, op. cit., pp. 164-167. G.J. Botterweck-H. Ringgren, ברא ThWAT, 1 (1973) 769-777. E. Jenni-C. Westermann, ברא, THAT 1 (1971) 336-339. See also the commentaries and the theologies of the Old Testament.

Two peculiarities in the use of ברא were recognized early and have been repeated right up to the present: 1) Yahweh is always the subject of ברא, never humans or another deity; 2) ברא is never used with a preposition or an accusative of the material out of which God creates.

P. Humbert describes the history of the word as follows: In the earliest stage the word was used only in cosmogonies, specifically in the language of cult. It is because of this esoteric use that it occurs but rarely in the pre-exilic period, even in J. In a second stage the word took on a soteriological meaning, as in Jer 31:22 and a number of places in Deutero-Isaiah. This adaptation is only temporary and really goes back to Deutero-Isaiah's own personal rhetoric. The third stage is the use of the word by P. P takes up again the old sacral meaning and gives it a marked theological thrust, using it to express the transcendence of the creator.

Gunkel described the history of the word in a similar way. He writes in his commentary, "The word is used here as a narrative term and so according to the canons of the history of saga must be considered very old. . . . It was a later era that gave it a more sophisticated supernatural stamp." Gunkel based his opinion that ברא was very old on the thesis that certain words, especially those that occur but rarely, belong to definite stories and so go back a long way. This argument however is not to be used here because Gen 1 as a whole is not an old narrative, but has grown out of several layers, and it cannot be proved that ברא goes back to the oldest layer.

Wellhausen was of the contrary opinion: "Gen 1 has a special word used only to describe the divine activity and so to dissociate it completely from any analogy with human doing or shaping. . . . Such abstraction is unheard of in an underdeveloped people; it is only after the Exile that such words and ideas came more and more into common use among the Hebrews, parallel to the sudden appearance of Yahweh as the all-powerful creator in the Exilic Literature," (*Prolegomena . . . .* p. 305).

The basis on which Humbert builds his thesis of the early cultic use of ברא is very weak. He is of the opinion that the three pre-Exilic uses of ברא, (Deut 4:32; Jer 31:22; Amos 4:13), allow one to refer to a tradition in which the word was used with the same meaning as in the cosmogonies. But none of these three passages is certainly pre-Exilic. Apart from this it is unlikely that a specifically theological idea which deliberately separates God's action as creator from any human activity belongs to an earlier period. What was unique to the creative action of God, what set it apart, was that it was he, God, who created heaven and earth; there was no need for any further intellectual refinement. Everything favors the view that P's use of ברא is peculiar to him and does not belong to an earlier stage which has been reworked.

What conclusions can be drawn from the occurrence of the word in the Old Testament? Let us start with what is certain. There are two main areas where the verb is used, in Deutero-Isaiah, 11 times, and in P, 11 times. Each uses it differently; Deutero-Isaiah uses it of God's action in history and of his on-going action in creation, while P uses it of God's creative action at the beginning. The verb is used too in relation to God's action in history in Ex 34:10; Num 16:30; and Jer 31:22. There is unanimity that in these three places it means "to create something new or unheard of," as often in Deutero-Isaiah. The evidence allows us to conclude with certainty that the word was used of God's action in history as well as of his creative action at the beginning before P restricted it to the latter; by doing this P wanted to say how entirely different was God's creative action from anything that humans can do. The usage in Deutero-Isaiah and in the three other places cited is relatively late, about the time of the Exile. We can say nothing certain about an earlier usage.

It is possible that at an earlier stage ברא described creation by God in the same way as עשׂה or יצר, particularly if its basic meaning was "cut," or "separate," as F. Delitzsch thought. J. van der Ploeg writes: "En taillant la pierre, le bois, on lui donne une forme nouvelle, et d'une certaine façon un être nouveau. Il n'est donc point étonnant de voir se rejoindre en hébreu bārā' (Kal) × créer et bārā' (pi) = couper, découper. On peut en conclure que l'élément bar a primitivement signifié couper" (p. 151). So also F.M.Th. de Liagre Böhl: ". . . .en zijn woord voor scheppen betekent eigenlijk 'in tweeën houwen' of 'splijten'" (*Opera Minora*, 1953, 3). E. Dantinne has taken up this explanation of the word and has linked it with creation as separation. Dantinne starts from the five places where ברא does not mean to create; two of these are not clear, 1 Sam 2:23; Ezek 21:24. "Jos 17:15-18 le piel exprime l'action de défricher une forêt, de couper des arbres; Ez 23:47 de tailler en pièces par l'épée; dans les trois l'acte de couper, c'est à dire d'établir, au moyen d'un instrument tranchant, une séparation dans une matière ou un corps" (p. 446). He points out that the old dictionaries, in contrast to the new, acknowledge only one root not two, in which the meaning "cut," "separate" can develop logically into "create." "Pour exprimer l'idée de créer. . . .les anciens Hébreux ont employé un mot auquel s'associe la notion de séparer, si souvent formulée explicitement dans le récit de la création" (p. 446).

If this is correct — and there is no other convincing attempt to trace the derivation of ברא — then the Priestly ברא is based on a concrete idea, something like יצר. We do not know if the word was used of creation by God in this concrete sense before Deutero-Isaiah and P. One must be cautious about attributing too much to the word as if it could of itself say something about the uniqueness of the creative act of God. It is clear that it was P's intention to use a special theological word for creation by God. But it is not correct to regard this word as the only one and to neglect such words as עשה or יצר. Nor is it correct to read *creatio ex nihilo* out of the word as such as, for example, does P. Heinisch: "If not always, then for the most part, the word indicates *creatio ex nihilo.*" On the other hand A. Heidel is correct: "This concept *(creatio ex nihilo),* however, cannot be deduced from the Hebrew verb bārā', to create, as it has been done. . . . There is no conclusive evidence in the entire Old Testament that the verb itself ever expresses the idea of a creation out of nothing," p. 89.

It is instructive to compare the use of the word in the Gk (cf. W. Forster, ThWNT III, 1022-1027). Of the 46 times that the LXX encounters the Hebrew ברא = create, it renders it by κτίζω only 17 times; κτίζω is not found in Genesis; only ποιεῖν is used. κτίζω and ברא came to have the same meaning only after the Gr translation. The LXX translators had no Greek equivalent of the Hebrew ברא; ברא in Gen 1 together with עשה in Gen 2 is rendered by ποιεῖν. It is only later that κτίζω took on the special meaning of creation by God. Its original meaning was much more like that of the Hebrew קנה = to found, a word which is commonly used in Ugaritic for "to create." κτίζω took on this specialized meaning mainly through the foundation of Hellenistic cities; the founder (κτίστης) of a city is honored by the gods. There seems to be a distinct parallel to the development in the Old Testament; the limited, specialized meaning belongs to a later time. κτίζω too has a basic concrete meaning; it means originally to cultivate the land or to make it habitable.

אלהים: We must be clear that the word "God" at the beginning of Genesis did not evoke the same idea in the minds of the people in the Old Testament as it does in the modern western mind. We can put before ourselves the possibility, is there a god or is there not? We can also ask what the word god is meant to signify. Such questions do not arise here. When the writer of Gen 1 speaks of God, he speaks of a God who acts; he is not concerned with the existence of God. He is not speaking of a "first cause"; such thinking and language would be impossible. The God of Gen 1 is a God who acts and a God who speaks; it is that which makes him God. There is no question of an abstract existence behind this speaking and acting. God is real because he acts; he is not a reality behind his action. The reality of this one who acts is an unquestioned datum. There is no idea of reality which could abstract from God's action or stand apart from it. There is reality because God acts. When the Old Testament speaks of God it means the reality of one who acts, not one who is, who can be the object of human thought. When we talk about the idea of God we are not talking about what the Old Testament means by God. One cannot ask about the god of the Old Testament in such a way as to prescind from his word and act and try to catch a glimpse of who or what he is in himself apart from his word and act.

The description of God at the beginning of Genesis as אלהים cannot be separated from what is told about him. One can well say that P, by using this description of God, stands in a historical context and that to this extent there is a history of the idea of God. P neither invented this term for God nor was it revealed to him. He received it and is passing it on. There are many branches to the history of the description of God as אלהים; it is an extremely complicated process and cannot be gone into here. L. Köhler, *Old Testament Theology* (1957) has drawn the basic lines of development clearly: "God is called אלהים in Hebrew; but אלהים means not only God, it means also a God, the God, Gods and the Gods," p. 36. These several possible meanings point to a history which has many layers.

One must emphasize that all these meanings occur in the Canon of the Old Testament. The way in which P uses the word in Gen 1 belongs to the latest stage: "In Gen 1 God is the utterly unique one that exists, a proper name. . .", p. 18. But there are always echoes of the older use even in later times, as for example when God is related to a people; "the God of Israel," Ex 5:1, "the God of Jacob," Is 2:3; Ps 46. Both mean, "the God of the people Israel," just as one might say, the gods of Egypt, Ex 12:12, of the Amorites, Josh 24:15, of Aram, of Moab, of the Ammonites, of the Philistines. . . .all nations have gods, Deut 12:2; 13:8; . . . .every nation still made gods of its own, 2 Kgs. 17:29," p. 19. We must keep in mind this vast range of meanings if we want to hear clearly the echoes of אלהים in Gen 1:1. It is simply God, God "without any limiting point of reference," p. 21, who created heaven and earth; but it is the same god who can be spoken of quite ingeniously as the god of Israel in distinction to the gods of other nations. P understands the word only as a singular noun (N. Walker, "Do Plural Nouns of Majesty Exist in Hebrew?", VT 7 [1957] 208). For the history of the word it is useful to compare the commentary of O. Procksch and the article of G. Quell, "El and Elohim im AT," ThWNT III (1938) 79-90.

את השמים ואת הארץ: O. Procksch remarks that: "השמים and הארץ together mean the universe." But there can be an important difference when a given totality is described by one word or by two opposites. It is common to all languages to describe totality by two words. In a study of this phenomenon in Egyptian, A. Massart writes: "L'emploi de deux termes opposés pour exprimer la totalité est commun à toutes les langues" (*Mélanges bibliques,* 1957, pp. 38-46). Massart cites as an example a poem on the occasion of the enthronement of Ramses IV: "Quel heureux jour! Le ciel et la terre sont en joie, car tu es le seigneur de l'Egypte!" H. Frankfort, *Kingship and the Gods,* 1948, 1962⁴, p. 19, points out the importance of this for Egypt's understanding of the world: "This extraordinary conception expressed in political form the deeply rooted Egyptian tendency to understand the world in dualistic terms as a series of pairs of contrasts balanced in unchanging equilibrium. The universe as a whole was referred to as 'heaven and earth'." Parallel to this is the totality and the individuality of upper and lower Egypt: "The dualistic forms of Egyptian kingship. . . .embody the peculiarly Egyptian thought that a totality comprises opposites."

There is no need to presume an Egyptian setting and understanding of this pair of words for Gen 1:1; they occur together in the same sense in Mesopotamia and in many other places. A language which designated a totality by means of two opposites had no need to coin a new word. As confirmation we note that single words which occur in other languages at a later stage to designate "heaven and earth," such as cosmos, κόσμος, in Greek, *universum* in Latin, "All" in German, are only substitutes; they are abstract in kind and show thereby that there are limits to the human faculty of apprehension. Even today we think of the universe as "heaven and earth," despite our vastly extended picture of the world. Even though we know that our earth is but a tiny fraction of a myriad of systems, nevertheless it is only from our situation on earth that we are capable of grasping the limitless sweep of the universe. And this gives fresh significance to the fact that the compendium of the story of creation which describes the universe as heaven and earth has its effect right down to the present day when the Christian confession of faith speaks of *creator coeli et terrae.*

[**1:2**]   The relationship of the first verses to each other, as explained above, is:

1: Introductory Resume
2: The Situation into which God's creative action entered
3: The Beginning of Creation.

The three clauses of v. 2 correspond to the clause "When not yet" of the older creation narratives except that they are formulated positively. The language of the verses shows quite clearly that P is taking his stand here on the tradition that came down to him. It is much easier to exegete the verses when we can presume that the intention of the writer is not really to give a picture of the situation that preceded creation, but to present the act of creation as an event, corresponding to the "When not yet" of the older narratives (similar explanations are given by G. von Rad and K. Galling). We can leave aside then any attempt to draw up a coherent and complete picture of Chaos from these clauses. P is not concerned to portray Chaos as such, but the contrast between Chaos and its opposite.

F. Delitzsch explains the construction: "The perfect preceded by the subject is the normal way to reverse the progress of the story, 3:1; 4:1; 18:17-20. The היתה is not just the connecting link: the earth such as it exists, was a *Tohuwabohu.*" B.S. Childs writes: "We have a nominal clause of circumstantial force: the earth having been chaos."

R. Kilian has proposed a new explanation ("Gen 1:2 und die Urgötter von Hermopolis" VT 16 [1966] 420-438). He wants to show "that the clause 'and the earth was' at the beginning of v. 2a belongs to the same stage of tradition as the Israelite v. 1 . . . it serves clearly as a transition in that it presents the earth which was created by God in v. 1 as *Tohuwabohu* and so acts as a balance between v. 1 and v. 2ff." And so the translation of v. 2 would be: "*Tohuwabohu* and darkness were over the primaeval deep, and the spirit of God moved across the water." V. 2 then would be simpler and clearer because it would comprise two nominal sentences parallel in meaning. But it must be objected that it would be very difficult to understand תהו ובהו as being over the deep; v. 2 then must consist of three sentences standing side-by-side.

תהו occurs 20 times in the Old Testament, בהו three times, on each occasion with תהו. תהו is a well-defined word whose meaning has developed in a number of contexts, while בהו is only a word which accompanies תהו. Albright's view that תהו derives by assonance from בהו is to be rejected. Nor can I agree with Cassuto when he says: "It is profitless to compare passages in which either of the words occurs." He understands תהו ובהו as a poetic expression that goes back to an ancient Hebrew epic which he believes to have existed, and ultimately to ancient Canaanite poetry. The meaning of the expression, he continues, can only be determined from the context and the rest of v. 2 shows that the idea of the deep is already contained in תהו ובהו. This last sentence is pure supposition; the use of the word תהו in the Old Testament which must be the point of reference for any explanation, is clearly against it.

There is a group of passages among the 20 occurrences of תהו in the Old Testament in which it is used to describe the desert: Deut 32:10; Job 6:18; 12:24 = Ps 107:40. תהו is the grim desert waste that brings destruction; Deut 32:10 reads, "He found him in a desert land, and in the howling waste of the wilderness"; Job 6:18 speaks of the waste where man perishes; Job 12:24 = Ps 107:40 speaks of the trackless waste where people wander.

In a second group, especially in proclamations of judgment, תהו means a desert or devastation that is threatened: Is 24:10; 34:11; 40:23; Jer 4:23; (in Is 34:11 and Jer 4:23 it is used together with בהו). Both usages show clearly the echoes the work had for the people of Israel. We can understand then why the state which is opposed to and precedes creation is called תהו. Two passages, very like Gen. 1:2, confirm this: Is 45:18 says of the creator that "He did not create it a chaos." תהו here is the direct opposite of creation. This is also the case in Job 26:7: "He stretches out the north over the void, and hands the earth upon nothing." In this passage תהו is in parallelism with "nothing"; this accords with the third group of texts in which תהו means nothingness: 1 Sam 12:21 (twice); Is 29:21; 40:17; 41:23; 44:9; 45:19; 59:4; there are other words expressing nothingness which stand in parallelism to תהו in these passages, אפס Is 40:17 or הבל and ריק Is 49:4. It should be noted that in none of these passages does "nothing" or "nothingness" indicate the existence of a material "nothing"; it is contrasted rather with meaningful existence; it is "meaningless," "futile," or some such. The meaning of תהו in the first two groups of passages, desert, waste, devastation, is drawn from experience; its meaning in the third group becomes intelligible from the first two.

We have then the explanation of the meaning of תהו in Gen 1:2; בהו is added only by way of alliteration, as in the other two passages, Is 34:11 and Jer 4:23. There is no sign of either personification or mythological allusion in the biblical use of תהו. It is not a mythical idea but means desert, waste, devastation, nothingness. Nor can one say: "The word *Tohuwabohu* is the rationalization of a mythical idea" (H. Junker, 34). And when תהו and בהו occur together there is no real difference in meaning. Earlier the word had been connected with the Sumerian-Babylonian goddess Bau (consort of Ninib-Ninurta) or with the Phoenician goddess βααυ. W. Caspari has tried to demonstrate that תהו derives from תהום. (So too W.F. Albright, cf. U. Cassuto.) N.H. Ridderbos repeats the opinion which is still prevalent: "Any connection with the Sumerian goddess Bau is no longer accepted. A connection with the Phoenician goddess Baau is very dubious," p. 224. B.S. Childs says that "There is no evidence that either expression ever possessed a personal character in the Old Testament," p. 33. The course of the debate about the mythical explanation of תהו ובהו indicates clearly that the arguments for a mythical background are becoming weaker and weaker. The discussion can now be considered closed.

E.A. Speiser describes the phrase as "an excellent example of hendiadys"; it means the desert waste and is used as the opposite of creation (so too G.M. Girardet, *Tohuwabohu* and W.H. Schmidt, p. 78f.). The translations "formlessness" or "shapelessness" (O. Procksch, G. von Rad, O. Heinisch) are not quite accurate. Nor is K. Galling's explanation entirely suitable: "With *Tohuwabohu* P wants to describe absolute nothingness. Something like: 'And the earth had been in the state of non-existence'." It would be nearer to the sense if the nothingness, the non-existence, were understood as something gruesome. Ridderbos is right when he points out: "These notions are much more ominous for the Israelites than for us," p. 225; F. Delitzsch speaks even more strongly: "There is something fearful about this pair of words" and he cites a pair of words with similar alliteration from the old Norse: *gimminga gap,* literally "gaping of yawns," i.e., the gaping abyss. This too is the meaning of the Greek χάος: chasm, abyss, and also darkness. So Hesiod in his cosmogony (*Theogony* 5, 116): "First of all there arose chaos and later the earth."

H. Junker distinguishes an even later use of the word, "which described the confused mingling of the disordered and unformed elements before the cre-ation of the world" (some such adaptation of an older and more elementary idea of chaos seems to lie behind the LXX translation of תהו ובהו. It translates by "invisible and not yet in order." One notes a rationalizing tendency here; G.M. Girardet sees Platonic influence. Other translations sharpen the difficulty: the Vulgate rendered by "inanis et vacua," Aquila "a waste and a nothing," Theodotion "a nothing and an emptiness." These last two translations are closer to the Hebrew text than is that of the LXX.

וחשך על־פני תהום: חשך is the predicate of this second nominal sentence. The sentence is not describing anything objective but presenting an aspect of the situation which is the opposite of creation. Darkness is not to be understood as a phenomenon of nature but rather as something sinister. Darkness has different meanings and is related to different situations: animals panic when there is a darkening of the sun; but they are aware of the difference between a darkness which protects existence and a darkness which threatens it, between darkness which is part of the natural order and the darkness of chaos. It is the latter that is intended in Gen 1:2. And so it is not surprising that in many cosmogonies throughout the world darkness precedes creation.

Darkness is part of the oldest Greek concept of χάος; darkness or night is everywhere opposed to creation where the creator is the god of light or the sun god, as also in Mesopotamia and Egypt. In one of the Egyptian "When not yet" sentences we read: "When nothing at all had yet come forth, while the earth was still in night and darkness" (H. Grapow, p. 37). Darkness is also part of the Phoenician description of primeval chaos according to the quotation from San-chuniaton in Eusebius, *Präparatio evangelica:* "He thinks that at the beginning of everything there was darkness and a strong wind or darkness and a whining wind and a black slimy chaos. It was unordered and undefined and remained so for an age" (O. Eissfeldt, "Das Chaos in der biblischen und in der phönizischen Kosmogonie," KS II, 1963, pp. 258-262, esp. p. 259).

Gunkel writes: "We find the doctrine that the world came out of darkness among the Babylonians, the Egyptians, the Indians, the Phoenicians, the Greeks, the Chinese"; so too J. Skinner and S. Aalen, *Die Begriffe Licht und Finster-nis.* . . . 1951, pp. 10-20. He refers to passages in the Old Testament where darkness is used together with תהו, Is 45:19; Jer 4:23, with the primeval deep, Ps 88:7; Is 5:30, with the desert, Ps 44:20; Jer 4:23ff., and with שאול, Job 17:13, which indicates that the darkness of Gen 1:2 is to be understood in a mythical context. The opposition between darkness and creation, so widespread in the cosmogonies and creation stories of the world, shows that creation and the world are to be understood always from the viewpoint of or in the context of human existence. Darkness is always to be seen in the framework: what does it mean for people. We see then that the creation of the world is always related to humanity in some way or another and that the creation of human beings as distinct from the creation of the world is the primary way of talking about creation.

The word תהום could well have been part of the ancient mythology because it is a proper name (no article) or very close to it. This is quite inde-pendent of its relationship to the Babylonian Tiamat (cf. A.J. Wensinck, p. 36, or A. Heidel, p. 99). One should not make too much of the absence of the article; חשך too is without the article (W.H. Schmidt, p. 81). The function of the word in the present case is obviously to describe the situation which preceded creation, parallel to darkness as in the first sentence of the cosmogony of Berossus (quoted by Eusebius, H. Gressmann, AOT p. 137): "There was once a time, so he says, when everything was darkness and water." The phrase "over the face of the waters" at the end of the verse has the same meaning and shows that תהום in Gen 1:2 cannot be intended to signify a mythical person or even a personified power. The same parallelism occurs in Jon 2:6.

תהום occurs 35 times in the Old Testament, 21 times in the singular and 14 times in the plural. Apart from Is 63:16 and Ps 106:9 (plural) it is always used without the article. תהום always means a flood of water or the deep; there is no personification. The word occurs also in the context of the creation event in Ps 33:7; 104:6; Job 38:16; Prov 3:30; 8:24-27, each time without any mythical reference. Some passages speak of the water which brings blessing and fertility, Gen 49:25; Deut 8:7; 33:15; Ezek 31:4; Ps 78:15; Prov. 8:28; other passages speak of the flood which destroys or threatens, Gen 7:11; 8:2; Ex 15:8; Is 51:10; 63:16; Ezek 26:19; Amos 7:4; Jon 2:6; Ps 36:7; 71:20; 106:9; 107:26; the passages which describe the Reed Sea belong to this group, Ex 15:5, 8; Is 51:10; 63:16; Ps 106:9; the flood is used quite generally to describe a phenomenon of nature in Ps 135:6; Job 28:14; 38:30; 41:24; e.g., Job 38:30: "The waters become hard like stone, and the face of the deep is frozen"; the flood is a creature that praises God Pss 42:8; 148:7; the deep trembled at the approach of God, Ps 77:17; Hab 3:10; the deep mourns, Ezek 31:15.

The survey shows that תהום in the Old Testament has no other meaning than the deep or the waters of the deep. It can mean that which blesses or destroys just as can water. Even in Is 51:9 where תהום is used in the context of the chaos struggle it is of the drying up of the deep. תהום can be said to belong to God's creation inasmuch as it can be called upon to praise God; it can be a phenomenon of nature too and Job can speak of the freezing over of the deep. The evidence does not allow us to speak of a demythologizing of a mythical idea or name as do many commentaries. When P inherited the word תהום, it had long been used to describe a flood of water without any mythical echo.

The mythological explanation relies on the similarity between תהום, allegedly used as a proper name, and the Babylonian name Tiamat. The relationship between the two words is described by A. Heidel, pp. 98-101: Tiamat in Babylonian is almost always a proper name and is only rarely used for the ocean or the sea, which are regularly called *tamtu*. Tiamat is a mythical being and תהום never has this meaning in the Old Testament. The phrase "upon the face of the deep" shows that it is not a case of a mythological being but of a flood of water. It is impossible phonetically and grammatically to derive תהום from the Babylonian Tiamat; תהום has a masculine ending, Tiamat a feminine; the ה of the Hebrew תהום cannot be explained as deriving from Tiamat.

A. Heidel comes to the conclusion that both words go back to a common Semitic root. The same root is the basis of the Babylonian *tamtu* and occurs too in other Semitic languages. In Arabic Tihâmatu or Tihâma is used for the coastal strip in west Arabia (cf. U. Cassuto, commentary) and in Ugaritic t-h-m is the ocean or the deep. There is widespread agreement then that תהום and Tiamat go back to a common Semitic root; but the occurrence of תהום in Gen 1:2 is not an argument for the direct dependence of the creation account of Gen 1 on Enuma Elish.

When one has managed to break free from the question of direct dependence, then the occurrence of תהום, like to a proper name and related by root to the Babylonian Tiamat, shows that both belong in the broader context of the history of the creation narratives. All this is sufficient explanation of the striking similarities of the words used to describe the primeval flood. One is no longer obliged to accept the view that תהום in Gen 1:2 had originally a mythical and personal meaning which P had to demythologize. There is no sign at all of any struggle between God and תהום corresponding to the struggle between Marduk and Tiamat (so too Skinner, Ridderbos, Würthwein, Galling, W.H. Schmidt and others).

The similarity between תהום and Tiamat would go back to a stage in the history of the creation narrative when the story of the struggles between the gods had not yet been linked with creation. This is supported by the fact that in so many cosmogonies the sea or the deep or the primeval flood is there at the beginning. Franz Delitzsch writes in this context: "It was in this sense that antiquity spoke of Okeanos as the source of everything and of water as the mother of life — this attitude dominates the oldest cosmogonies." He alleges, among other examples, the Phoenician cosmogony and the Orphic which derives from it, the Aztec and the philosophical cosmogony of Thales. The primeval sea plays an important role in the Sumerian cosmogony: "Heaven and earth were . . . conceived by the Sumerians as the created products of the primeval sea," S.N. Kramer, *Sumerian Mythology,* p. 39.

The most notable common characteristic of the Egyptian cosmogonies is the flood of water at the beginning: ". . . .le Noun est le seul trait absolument commun à toutes les cosmogonies égyptiennes" (S. Sauneron and J. Yoyotte, "La Naissance du monde selon l'Egypte ancienne," *Sources orientales, La naissance du monde,* 1951, p. 22). The primeval sea and darkness are found together in the Egyptian and Phoenician cosmogonies just as in Gen 1:2. We can be certain then that Gen 1:2 belongs to a history of creation narratives in which the motif of the primeval deep, with or without darkness, very often represents the situation before creation, but that the link between creation and the struggle of the gods is not part of its pre-history.

ורוח אלהים מרחפת על־פני המים: The third clause of the second verse is both very difficult and very controversial. By way of introduction there are two stylistic observations: (1) The second verse consists of three nominal clauses which describe a situation. They form a series; the portrayal of the situation runs through all three clauses. There is no reason to separate the third of the nominal sentences from the first two on the ground that it reduces an intervention. (2) If the first work of creation were to begin with the last sentence of v. 2, then the structure of the narrative that introduces each section with the words "and God said" would be destroyed. Both of these stylistic remarks show clearly that the last sentence of the second verse belonged to the picture of chaos.

It has already been shown that the two phrases על־פני תהום and המים על־פני have the same meaning (so too J. Skinner, U. Cassuto). They are two expressions that describe what is over the surface of the deep: darkness and רוח אלהים (cf. B.S. Childs, p. 34). The participle does not describe an action of the רוח, but the way in which it moves across the surface of the deep; so there is not a contrast but a parallel between darkness and רוח. But if the phrase אלהים רוח is understood as referring to "the spirit of God" then it must be understood as a contrast. The question of the meaning of the sentence has often been raised; for the history of the exegesis cf. K. Smoronski, "Et spiritus Dei ferebatur supra aquas," Bib 6 (1925) 140-156, 275-293, 361-395.

One alleged meaning of the sentence can be rejected definitively: it is that which understands the verb as "brood" and refers to the world egg which was hatched and out of which the world arose. Jerome pointed out this meaning in the patristic period and it was supported in more recent times by Dillmann and Delitzsch and particularly by Gunkel from whom it was taken over by a number of others. There is, of course, a cosmogony of this kind; but its appearance in Gen 1:2 relies solely on the interpretation of רחף as "brood." This meaning is generally rejected today (L. Köhler, G. von Rad, K. Galling, E.A. Speiser, U. Cassuto, N.H. Ridderbos, B.S. Childs, W.H. Schmidt *et alii*). What is contested is whether the word רוח means wind or spirit; the discussion is important; if the meaning is "spirit", this would be an argument in favor of separating the third sentence of v. 2 from the other two and referring it to some positive intervention of God, and not to the description of chaos.

The starting point is the participle מרחפת. L. Köhler, *Lexikon,* renders it by "hover and flutter" in Gen 1:2 and Deut 32:1; in Jer 23:9 he renders the qal form by "shake." The same root is found in Ugaritic, and Gordon in UT 1947 no. 2327 renders it by "to soar"; E.A. Speiser writes: "The Ugaritic cognate describes a form of motion as opposed to a state of suspension or rest." This corresponds to the use of the verb in both of the Old Testament passages: Jer 23:9 (qal) "all my bones shake" and (piel) Deut 32:11: "Like an eagle that stirs up its nest that flutters over its young." One can conclude then with B.S. Childs that the word מרחפת no longer offers any problem: "The verb can best be rendered by some verb as 'hover,' 'flutter' or 'flap'." So the earlier translation "brood" no longer holds, nor does any reference to the world egg cosmogony. This conclusion is supported by the old translations, all of which render the verb by a word denoting movement: Gk 'επεφέρετο; Vulg *ferebatur,* see 'ΑΣΘ.

With the meaning of the verb settled it remains to examine the word רוח. If it means the spirit of God, then the verb can only be translated by "hover" or something like it; but if, as in the other two passages in the Bible, its meaning has something to do with "shaking" or "vibrating," then it can only be rendered by "wind." But it is difficult to understand רוח as wind and at the same time link it with אלהים. Consequently B.S. Childs, though he has understood מרחפת correctly and has seen that the three sentences are a description of chaos, has been led nevertheless to interpret רוח as the creative spirit of God in contrast to Chaos. The argument which is decisive for him is that רוח אלהים does not occur anywhere else in the Old Testament with the meaning "wind of God." But this argument loses its force inasmuch as "the spirit of God" is not found elsewhere in the Old Testament either with רחף or with any similar verb. We are dealing here with a traditional description and so must be ready to accept ideas which do not occur elsewhere in the Old Testament.

J.N.P. Smith in "The Use of Divine Names as Superlatives," AJSL 45 (1928-29) 212-220, has proposed that אלהים should be understood in an adjectival sense as a superlative; the meaning would be a mighty, a fearful wind. It is generally acknowledged that אלהים can have this superlative meaning. This meets the difficulty of understanding רוח as wind. This interpretation has been accepted by many modern scholars (W.F. Albright, J.P. Peters, H.G. May, W.H. McClellan, H.M. Orlinsky, K. Galling, G. von Rad, W.H. Schmidt, E.A. Speiser). The meaning, wind, is found at a very early stage: W.H. Schmidt writes: "The Targum Onkelos is probably the first to understand the word as 'wind'," p. 83; so too in the interpretation in the Talmud (U. Cassuto ad. loc., who decides however in favor of the meaning "spirit of God"). G. von Rad refers to a similar description in Dan 7:2. W.H. Schmidt pp. 81-84 discusses the phrase thoroughly and gives a full bibliography.

The wind plays a part in several cosmogonies, cf. S. Moscati, "The Wind in Biblical and Phoenician Cosmogony," JBL 66 (1947) 305-310. E. Lipinski explains the link with the verb r-h-p from the Sumerian description of the god of the storm in the form of a huge primeval bird. On the other hand R. Kilian prefers to explain all three sentences in Gen 1:2 from an Egyptian cosmogony, "Gen 1:2 und die Urgötter von Hermopolis," VT 16 (1966) 420-438. He explains the four primeval pairs of gods, Nun and Naunet, Huh and Hauket, Kuk and Kauket, Amun and Amaunet, as follows: because Nun alone is something concrete only he can represent the eight as a whole; the three other pairs are qualities of Nun. Nun is the world before creation; the three other pairs, all of which are negative in character, describe Nun, the primeval sea: the second pair describes its limitless extent, the third the darkness, and the fourth its invisible hidden nature.

This description of chaos corresponds to Gen 1:2 in that what characterizes it is the primeval flood of which darkness is a part. There would be a third point of contact because Amun, the god of the wind, has been closely related to the Eight of Hermopolis since the 18th dynasty. R. Kilian maintains that it has been demonstrated that Gen 1:2 "is based as a whole on the Egyptian description of chaos" (op. cit., p. 438). But this is not justified because on the one hand there are notable differences, and on the other the established point of contact, namely the link between the primeval flood and darkness, is by no means limited to the cosmogony of Hermopolis. However, this study does demonstrate that one cannot derive Gen 1:2 onesidedly from the Mesopotamian descriptions. Its pre-history is so broad and far-reaching that any direct derivation must remain questionable.

Kilian's comparison confirms that the third sentence of v. 2 is part of the description of the situation before creation. The verse and all its parts correspond to and have the same function as the "When not yet" of the older cosmogonies.

We are now in a position to answer the question whether Gen 1:1ff. is describing *creatio ex nihilo* or whether it presumes already preexisting material. The question has been asked from the earliest times whether the teaching of the church on *creatio ex nihilo* is explicit in the first verses of Genesis. Many interpreters presume that this is the teaching of Gen 1: Gen 1 must teach *creatio ex nihilo* because this is the only appropriate way in which to speak of creation. Others are of the opinion that it is not possible to derive *creatio ex nihilo* from these verses by purely exegetical methods. Others again would be more reserved. The text is not explicit, but it is the sort of thing that P is saying; or, this was never a question for P. However, had the question been put to him he must certainly have decided in favor of *creatio ex nihilo*. There are many other variants of this opinion which need not be listed here. There has been a growing number in recent times who maintain simply that P does not speak of *creatio ex nihilo,* or who state explicitly that the description of creation by P presumes already existing material.

However, the alternatives which this question raises come from a causal way of thinking which does not belong to Gen 1. It goes behind creation and asks, Where did it come from? The fact that the verb ברא is not used with any preposition with the meaning "out of" indicates that such a question was irrelevant for P. What is peculiar to biblical talk about the creation of the world is that it looks wholly and solely to the creator: God has created the world; and so everything has been said that one can say. If one wants to know more one must move outside this framework. The sentence, God created the world out of nothing, does not say more but rather less than the sentence, God created the world. The question, "Is it *creatio ex nihilo* or not?" is not relevant to the text.

We must now deal with the other aspect of this problem, namely whether or not there was matter at hand before creation. There is no point in giving a list of scholars who answer yes or no to the question. I refer to N.H. Ridderbos, p. 229, who classifies one group as follows: v. 1 narrates the creation of matter without order, which v. 2 goes on to describe. He lists as representatives of this view J. Calvin, J. Wellhausen, E. König, G.Ch. Aalders, A. Heidel. Two of the latest commentators who represent this point of view write as follows: "Just as the potter . . . . the Creator first prepared for himself the raw material of the universe. . . ." (U. Cassuto ad. loc.) and C.A. Simpson (IB, 1 1952 ad. loc.). "What P intended to imply was that the first step in the creation of the organized universe was the creation of chaos, which God then proceeded to reduce to order."

Many modern commentators however point out quite correctly that the creation of chaos is a contradiction in terms (e.g., B.S. Childs, G. von Rad). W.R. Lane, p. 72, is an example of the opposite opinion: "Both translations (whether v. 1 is a main clause or a subordinate clause) presuppose preexistent material which was transformed by creation." According to one opinion then God first creates matter, v. 1, and this is followed by a description of the state of chaos, v. 2. According to the other opinion matter, in the state of chaos described in v. 2, is there at hand in the very moment that the creation of the world begins.

Both alternatives presume a way of thinking that is foreign to Gen 1. Our idea of matter is abstract; one can speak of matter only insofar as one prescinds from the question whether what is meant by it is creation or something over and against creation. Such an abstract way of thinking was not part of the thought pattern of P; it was not possible to conceive of matter in our sense. What we mean by matter could only be for P either something created or the *Tohuwabohu*, but never something as neutral as matter. It is meaningless then to ask whether P thought if there was or was not matter before creation. F. Delitzsch sensed this when he wrote of *Tohuwabohu:* "Both the sound and the meaning of this combination of words are fearful." Delitzsch however does not draw the consequences, but argues from the Greek idea of matter in explaining the third sentence of v. 2: "The spirit of God hovers over the primeval matter in order to prepare it for order; he communicates life to it which comes from his own fulness of life and which develops gradually in many and varied ways to self-awareness. . . .the primeval matter has in itself the capacity of further progress. The pliable mass is now there and waits to be formed; the process begins in v. 3" (Comm. ad. loc.). This is clearly a very Greek way of thinking.

We know when the term matter passed from Greek philosophy into the language and thought of creation theology. We read in the Wisdom of Solomon, 11:17: οὐ γὰρ ἠπόρει ἡ παντοδύναμός σου χεὶρ καὶ κτίσασα τὸν κόσμον ἐξ ἀμόρφου ὕλης (*Septuaginta,* A. Rahlfs, Vol. 2, 361). A. Heidel comments, p. 94: "The wisdom of Solomon is a combination of Greek and Hebrew thought, and the expression 'formless matter,' as it stands, conveys a purely Greek philosophical conception." This idea of "formless matter" was taken up by Augustine and through him passed over into western theology: ". . . .the world structure which Augustine took over from Aristotelian physics, though in the context of Neo-Platonism, always remained important for him; it was a pyramid of existence with a matterless form at the summit and formless matter at the base" (D. Ritschl, "Die Last des augustinischen Erbes," *Parrhesia, K. Barth zum 80. Geburstag,* 1965, 470-490, p. 475).

It is no accident that the idea of *creatio ex nihilo* occurs in literature which is contemporary with the passage from the Wisdom of Solomon, namely 2 Macc 7:28: ὅτι οὐκ ἐξ ὄντων ἐποίησεν αὐτὰ ὁ θεός. Both formulations, that God created the world out of nothing and that there was a formless matter before creation, first occur where Judaism has come under the influence of Greek thought. The tenacity with which these ideas have persevered shows how significant they have been from the time when they encountered late Judaism right through the whole history of Western exegesis. But when we realize that the ideas are foreign both to the language and thought of P, then we can no longer put the question whether P imagined that some sort of pre-existent matter preceded creation or whether he wanted to describe creation out of nothing (so too S. Aalen, op. cit., p. 15, n. 2). The text of Gen 1 intended neither the one nor the other. It stands by the sentence, God created the heavens and the earth.

[1:3]   With the words: "And God said, let there be light . . ." the real process of creation begins. The first work of creation is so to speak coterminous with the first day of creation; however, it must be noted that it is the work of an instant and not the work of a day that is described. Creation through the word does not fit exactly into the pattern of the work of the six days. There is no need to go into details about the structure of vv. 3-5; each sentence of these verses describes a self-contained event; there is no subordination. Language and event correspond in monumental wise. There is every indication that the verses are a construction of P; there is only "command-account" and there is no sign at all of any older description of an action of God.

The words ויאמר אלהים introduce a command. It is not any sort of talk nor is it a question of the abstract idea of "word"; it is rather a definite, concrete happening — there is speech and its function is to command. It has been shown in the Introduction that the works of creation are described in the context of the "command-account" following the pattern of a command. This presumes that man has experienced that a word can set an event in motion as, for example, in Ps 33:9, cf. also Matt 8:9. However, we must remember that it is not quite exact to call the process "creation by the word" because the verb does not convey the same meaning as the noun; the verb אמר does not form a noun like דבר or like the English "word." It would be more correct to say: creation by speech; but even this is not a precise rendering because in the context the event which is the object of the command is known from the word; it is not just a general utterance.

The beginning of the Gospel of John echoes Gen 1:3: "In the beginning was the word." But the λόγος of John with all its associations in Greek tradition is far removed from Genesis, so far in fact that at the beginning of Goethe's Faust John 1:1 is misunderstood and is parodied by its opposite: "In the beginning was the deed." But there is a certain irony, because this apparently revolutionary variation comes rather close to the original meaning in Gen 1:3; what God says in Gen 1:3 is to be understood as a creative command, as a deed.

One must be careful not to be led astray by the formula "creation through the word." If one surveys the priestly writing as a whole, one notes that God's activity through the word is by no means limited to creation but also describes his action in history. The words "and God said," found in the form "and Yahweh said" after the revelation of the name of Yahweh, introduce the institution of the cult in Ex 25:1, the difference being that here Moses is addressed; but it is the same as in Gen 1:3 — God is acting through a command. So the first words of v. 3, which introduce all the other works of creation, can be understood correctly only in the context of the priestly writing as a whole, where the action which is the basis of every event in creation or in history is the command whose execution must necessarily follow.

The command "Let there be light" is followed by its execution, "and there was light," just as in the case of any potentate who issues a command; but there is this difference, there is nobody there to whom the command is directed, through whom the command can be executed. It is this that constitutes a creation command, that makes the word of command a creative word. It is here too that the creative word comes dangerously close to the magic word as, for example, when Marduk in Enuma Elish destroys and creates again a garment by magic:

> Say but to wreck or create; it shall be.
> Open thy mouth: the cloth will vanish!
> Speak again, and the cloth will be whole!
> At the word of his mouth the cloth vanished.
> He spoke again, and the cloth was restored.
> (Tablet 4, 22-26, ANET 66)

The episode and the language of the command are very close to Gen 1:3. Many commentators have seized the opportunity to understand the creative word of God in Gen 1:3 by analogy with the magical word. The wording itself is no guarantee against such a misunderstanding. In any case the episode from Enuma Elish is not from the immediate context of creation but is rather a demonstration of the power of Marduk which wins the applause of the other gods. The creation of the world by Marduk which then follows is not described as creation by a word of command. One can secure Gen 1:3 against misunderstanding only when one understands it in the context of God's creative action through his word in the priestly writing as a whole. Magic in word and action has no historical context: magical activity is of its nature not historical activity. God's creative action through the word in Gen 1:3 is a prelude to and directed toward his action in history.

The same is to be said in regard to the theology of Memphis where an Egyptian cosmogony describes the creation of the world by the word of a god. The content is very much closer to the Genesis account than the passage from Enuma Elish and shows that Israel was not the only place that knew of the creation of the world by the word of a god (K. Koch, "Word und Einheit des Schöpfergottes in Memphis und Jerusalem," ZThK 62 [1965] 251-253). The peculiar contribution of the biblical expression can be understood only from the broader context of the priestly writing as a whole: the creation command of the first chapter is the introduction to God's overall action in history which moves along its own peculiar way and to its own peculiar goal. A command without an object to be commanded is beyond description; but it is a necessary part of all formulations of creation, be they creation by word or by any other means.

The first thing that God created was light. If we take as our starting point that vv. 3-5 are a creation of P for which, as far as we know, he was not indebted to any tradition, then it is obvious that the creation of light should be understood in the context of P's overall view as seen in the framework of the six-day scheme with the conclusion on the seventh. It is only possible to describe the work of creation as a whole because of the creation of light at the beginning. And so those exegetes are correct who understand vv. 3-5 as a process which makes creation possible rather than as a single work of creation. But the point should not be pressed. In any case light is not meant to be "the most subtle of all elementary forces" or "a material full of mystery" (A. Dillmann), "the most sublime element," "a subsistent thing, a subtle material" (H. Gunkel). Such descriptions are impossible because for P the first three acts of creation are not as it were the manufacture of substances, but the basic divisions of the universe. The separation of light from darkness is temporal, not spatial. The creation of light is put before these divisions because it renders possible the temporal succession into which, according to P, the world is set. God creates brightness and thereby makes possible the basic cycle of time and order.

This is the explanation of the apparent contradiction of the creation of light before the creation of the heavenly bodies. That the creation of the heavenly bodies presupposes the creation of the heavens in which they are set is something which P received. But the idea that the creation of light is the beginning of the whole of the work of creation belongs to P, who puts the basis of the temporal order before the creation of the world of space. It remains an open question whether there is some faint echo, however distant, of the Egyptian cosmogony in P's introduction. In the cosmogony of Hermopolis the creation of light follows immediately on the description of chaos (the four pairs which form the eight); the rays of the sun stream over the primeval ocean: "Presque tous les textes sont formels sur un point: les Huit sont 'les couples créateurs de la lumière', 'les pères et mères de Rê', 'les dieux ancêtres, qui firent le dieu de l'horizon'; 'le soleil est leur héritier'" (S. Sauneron and J. Yoyotte, "La naissance du monde selon l'Egypte ancienne," *Sources orientales I, La naissance du monde*, 1959, p.54).

The commentary on v. 2 showed that there are certain points of correspondence between the description of chaos at Hermopolis and Gen 1:2. In both cases the creation of light follows the description of chaos; and so even though in 1:3-5 P is speaking very much in his own language, nevertheless the possibility of echoes of other cosmogonies remains. Light also appears as the first thing created in other cosmogonies. However, for P the creation of light is more than just the "condition of all order" in the cosmological sense; it makes the order possible and determines it; that is P's intention in providing the framework of the seven days and in directing this order from its beginning, the creation of light, to its goal, where time comes to its rest.

[1:4] It is not the creation of light but the separation of light and darkness that sets in motion the march and rhythm of time. What is reported in v. 4 then belongs to the first work of creation.

The first sentence of v. 4 has a structure peculiar in Hebrew which is difficult to translate adequately. W.F. Albright, "The Refrain 'And God Saw ki tôb' in Genesis," *Mélanges bibliques, en l'honneur de André Robert,* 1955, 22-26, translates: "And God saw, how good it was" or in other places, "And God saw, that it was very good." The procedure in itself is quite clear: a craftsman has completed a work, he looks at it and finds that it is a success or judges that it is good. The Hebrew sentence includes the "finding" or "judging" in the act of looking. He regards the work as good. The work was good "in the eyes of God," it exists as good in God's regard of acceptance. The light is good simply because God regards it as good; the light and its goodness cannot be separated from God's attentive regard. The constantly recurring sentence, "And God saw that it was good," is part of the structure of the narrative and is telling us that such recognition belongs to the very process of creation. During the process of creation it remains dependent on the regard of God, but with the completion of creation it becomes the praise of the creator which is echoed by all creatures, Job 38:7.

God's regard, which recognizes that what he has done is good, provides here the clearest link between the account of creation and the praise of the creator. The praise of the creator is a continuation of the recognition by the creator. The account of creation and the praise of the creator are even more closely linked in the early Sumerian cosmogonies. In the Koran, where one can recognize clearly the point of contact with the early Semitic religions, what is said of creation is almost completely subsumed in the praise of the creator: "Dans toutes ses parties, le Coran se présente à nous comme un hymne au Créateur" (Toufu Fahd, "La naissance du monde selon l'Islam," *Sources orientales I,* 1959, 239).

The judgment that in God's regard the light was good precedes the separation of light and darkness. Most commentators think that this is an indication of the divine "preference" for the light. It is not said that God saw that the darkness was good. Inequality is there from the very beginning. Even when God makes his final judgment over creation as a whole, "And God saw everything that he had made, and behold, it was very good" it does not mean that everything is equally good. Darkness is good insofar as it is a necessary part of God's creation, but it is not as good as the light which alone received God's approval. This inequality sets up a scale of values. Everything in creation is not exactly equal just because everything is the work of God; God's "preference" for the light shows that something is happening.

"And God separated the light from the darkness." We can see here what P has done with the material he received. Before him was the cosmogony of separation. There was a time in the history of the cosmogonies when the separation or the division of heaven and earth was the decisive event. It was one of the original motifs (many examples will be found in *Sources Orientales I, La naissance du monde* where M. Eliade sums it up on p. 480: "La séparation entre le ciel et la terre marque à la fois l'acte cosmogonique par excellence et la rupture de l'unité primordiale"). P dovetailed the traditional material with his own contribution; he joined the motif of separation with his own formulation of the creation of light and so succeeded in making the first work of creation the source of the time-cycle of night and day, which determines everything else. He put at the beginning of creation what J put at the end of the flood story when God promised to preserve what he has created and never again to destroy the world, 8:22, the basic rhythm of day and night. Everything that God creates, including human existence, is determined by this polarity: the beginning and the conclusion of creation, the preservation of what has been created, the story of nature, and the story of humanity. The separation of light and darkness sets in motion this rhythmic polarity which will always belong to creation. Time takes precedence over space in P's presentation of creation; creation does not begin with the division of space, but with the division of night and day as the basis of time.

An element of inequality, which does not accord with the rhythm of time, is built into time in its very creation; it is of light only that it is said that God created it and that it is good. There is something inexplicable in the relationship between light and darkness: God created the world in such a way that light has a priority. God created the world in such a way that darkness, which is described neither as created by God nor as good, is a necessary part of the created order. The priority given to light is clear because light can be used to describe salvation and is allied to life, while darkness is allied to death. The alternation between night and day brings a constant rhythm into creation; the priority of light introduces an element of movement which never dissipates as the rhythm goes on.

Gen 1:3-5 maintains very strongly that light is something created. P departs here from the Egyptian cosmogonies; light is created, it is not divine like Re who shines over the primeval chaos. P does not understand light as the sphere of God as in Ps 104:2, or in 1 Tim 6:16 or in Jas 1:17; nor could P say: ". . . God is light and in him is no darkness at all," 1 Jn 1:5. These passages do not preserve the boundary between creator and creature which for P was absolute. When light is equated with God then it can no longer be a creature of God. Persian religion on the other hand teaches the divinity and eternity of light: "In Persian cosmogony. . . .light, as the sphere in which Mazda dwells, is increated and eternal" (J. Skinner, Comm. ad. loc.). Cf. S. Aalen, *Die Begriffe Licht und Finsternis*. . . . 1951.

[1:5] *The Naming:* All subsequent namings name something that is already there and tangible; this first naming names the basic units of time. Naming, like the act of separating, is part of the tradition P received (were it only creation by the word naming would not be necessary). P joins the two motifs together to include the first work of creation with what follows. The work of the first day is not just an account of the creation of day and night, but of the creation of light, then of the separation of light and darkness, and then of the naming of all the elements concerned. Naming has been part of the creation since the very beginning; to "name" can often be a parallel to "create," as in the opening lines of Enuma Elish and in many other places.

The parallel is explained by the attitude that the name and what is named can be identical. Many commentators explain the naming as an act of dominion. Zimmerli, ad. loc., refers to 2 Kings 23:34 and 24:17 where Pharaoh and the king of Babylon respectively give new names to the kings they have appointed. This is correct, but there are two further considerations. Naming in the context of creation is not only an act of dominion, but also gives what is named its destiny. The creator gives the object its destiny with its name. Second, many cosmogonies show that the creator as such is the lord of what he has created. Naming is an exercise of this right of dominion.

God names not only the light which he has created but also the darkness of which it is not said that he created it. God takes dominion over the darkness by this act and so the darkness of which he is the lord is different from the darkness of v. 2. The darkness is called night and thereby temporal limitations are introduced which subject it to God's dominion. So darkness becomes part of the order of creation. The uncreated moves into the created in a way which is beyond the understanding of man. We experience here the limitations of all attempts to comprehend creation in language as well as the intangibility of the priority of light over darkness which is expressed in the structure of the sentences: "The antecedent sentence which names the light takes precedence over the sentence which names the darkness" (W.H. Schmidt, p. 99).

"And there was evening and there was morning, one day." The question has been raised whether the day begins in the evening or in the morning, cf. H.R. Stroes, "Does the day begin in the evening or morning," VT 16 [1966] 460-475 (an account of the discussion in the context of Gen 1:5 is found on p. 473f.). The question is irrelevant for the understanding of Gen 1. What is essential for P is only the chronological disposition of the works of creation. The alternation between night and day is not conceived as a period of 24 hours, as a unity with a precise beginning; the 24 hours comprise two parts. The constantly recurring sentence which concludes the work of each day plots the regular rhythm of the passage of time, and gives P's account of creation the character of an event in linear time which links it with history. P's own contribution to the presentation of creation is clearest here. It can be appreciated fully of course only in the context of the priestly writing as a whole; but it is this sentence which is the most obvious link between Gen 1 and the continuation in Gen 2; the monotony of constantly repeated sentences is continued in the genealogies.

There is one grammatical note: "One day" is the normal expression of order for the digit 1 which only took on the meaning of number later by analogy with the other ordinal numbers.

[1:6-8] Creation by word and creation by act come together first in the work of the second day. The account that P received began with the creation of the firmament, that is, the separation of the waters which followed immediately on the description of chaos. The waters that were separated were the waters of chaos, as in a number of cosmogonies.

In explaining the work of the second day we must remember that among the traditional material that came down to P was the idea of creation as separation or division and the image of the heavens as a solid vault over the earth, something like a bell or a tent or a roof. These descriptions have their roots in primitive cultures, and it is not possible to pinpoint their origin. Many modern commentators say that the way in which P describes the creation of the firmament gives us an idea of the world picture of the time, but that the world picture has changed in the meantime and no longer holds. This, however, is not entirely accurate. It is not really appropriate to speak of a world picture. P had no world picture as we understand it. It is not so much the contemporary description of the world which is the background of these verses but the description of the world that P received. When P speaks of the heavens as a solid partition or vault that separates the earth from the waters above, he is not giving a description of his own or of the contemporary world, but one which is part of the creation tradition that he received.

We cannot say for certain whether or not the priestly circle which gave the narrative its final form shared all these views. A solid partition that separates the waters above from the surface of the earth and the space between presumes that the rain comes down through openings in the partition, as several passages in the Old Testament indicate, Gen 7:11f.; 2 Kings 7:2, 19; Ps 104:13. The Old Testament writers are also familiar with the rain coming from the clouds: "Later the Hebrews developed a more realistic explanation of the formation of cloud and rain from the mists rising from the earth, Jer 10:13; Job 36:27; Ps 135:7; the older description yielded gradually to this or was left to the poets" (Dillmann, ad. loc.). We do not know for certain whether the authors of the priestly writings were aware of this. Even when ideas change, the old traditional ways of speaking retain their force and meaning and are not rendered obsolete. We must be careful then of imposing our rigid notion of a world view according to which one opinion is correct and the other is false.

There is yet a further consequence of P's acceptance and passing on of traditional material. The description of the heavens, presumed in Gen 1:6-8, as a solid substance and of the basic act of creation as a separation of the primeval waters by means of the solid, are not thought of by P and his predecessors as something revealed and to be handed on as such; P is neither saying nor intending to say anything new.

The description of the creation of the firmament given in v. 6, which is in line with P's theology, did not take the place of the older description which P received, v. 7, but was joined to the latter, despite the consequent difficulties. The descriptions do not harmonize; one can say either that God made the partition and then erected it so as to separate the upper and lower waters ("two acts of God which follow each other chronologically," W.H. Schmidt ad. loc.), or that God said: "Let there be a partition — and it was so. Those responsible for passing on the text saw the difficulty and hesitated as to where to put the sentence, "and it was so," the MT putting it at the end of v. 7, The Gr at the end of v. 6. In all other places it follows immediately on "let there be. . . ."; only in this position does it make sense. It is unnecessary, to say the least, after the sentence "and God made. . . ." The conclusion is that at one stage it stood at the end of v. 6. When it was displaced to the end of v. 7, where it now stands in the MT, this is evidence of the embarrassment the juxtaposition of vv. 6-7 caused to those handing on the text. It was put at the end of v. 7 in order to make clear that vv. 6 and 7 were dealing with one work.

This is a good example of P's method; he did not wish to absolutize his own way of describing creation through the word, nor did he wish to suppress the older description. P is not bound to any particular world picture and so is not bound to any particular description of creation. But he is bound to preserve the continuity of tradition. When he speaks to his contemporaries about creation, he can only do so by taking over what has already been said. It is clearly not P's intention to describe creation in such a way that we can imagine how it took place. Our way of looking at things is not adequate for what took place in the works of creation.

116

[1:6] This verse is different from the verse describing the creation of light; the chiselled brevity is lacking and a sentence of explanation has been added to "let there be. . .", further determining the object being created. We have here in process the blending of two different modes of creation: the command-account of creation has only to arrange in succession the parts of the world to be created, whereas the action-account constructs them. Division and separation are part of the action-account; the command-account transposes the act of separation into the nominal expression יהי מבדיל.

The background of all this is the very ancient description of creation as a division or separation (see Introduction). The early cosmogonies describe it for the most part as the separation of heaven from earth; the heaven is raised above the earth and then set firmly in position. Others, especially the Egyptian, describe it as the separation of firm land from the primeval deep. The two are combined in Gen 1 and that is the reason why the division of the waters is unspectacular.

P attaches great importance to the separation even though it does not fit in too well with creation through the word. Separation is part of the first three works of creation. P is saying by this that the world only became the world by separation and only remains the world as long as separation lasts. The whole order and structure of the world depends on it. This is part of the tradition that P received. It is only in the context of the priestly work as a whole that P's own contribution to these traditions becomes clear. There is a hint of this in the way in which the seventh day is set apart; it points in the direction of the cultic as distinct from the profane.

The Firmament: the verb רקע means "to stamp with the feet" in Ezek 6:11; 25:6 (W. Zimmerli, BK XIII, 145), and "to stamp down" in 2 Sam 22:43; in Ex 39:3, in Piel, it means "hammer out, flatten." רקיע then is that which has been hammered out; it is found with the same meaning in Ps 19:2, and in Job 37:18 as "hard as a molten mirror." O. Procksch writes ad. loc.: "מרקע is found in Phoenician for a hammered out bowl (Lidzbarski, *Epigraphik I* pp. 340, 471)".Greek usage is the same when Homer calls the heavens χάλκεος or σιδήρεος.

In earlier times the heavens were almost always regarded as solid: "The description of the solid vault of the heavens is very widespread among primitive peoples" (H. Gunkel ad. loc., quoting Tylor). The Gk translates by στερέωμα, the Vg by *firmamentum*, "One of the Bible's indirect contributions to Western lexicons" (E.A. Speiser ad. loc.). Language has retained something of the ancient description (Firmament, vault or dome of heaven, etc.). The heavens are also described as a tent which has been spread out, Ps 104:2; Is 40:22. The heavens remain solid and it is difficult to reconcile the waters above the earth with such a description (cf. H.N. Torczyner, "The Firmament and the Clouds, Raqia and Shehaqim," StTh 1 [1947] 188-196).

The Old Testament refers several times to the waters above the solid vault of heaven or to a heavenly ocean, Ps 104:3, 13; 148:4; 2 Kings 7:2, 19, and especially in the flood narrative, Gen 7:11ff. Water pours down upon the earth through openings in the vault of heaven, Gen 7:11; 2 Kings 7:2, 19. It is a widespread image (references in Gunkel ad. loc., who remarks "This heavenly sea is originally heaven itself which is described as a crystal-clear mass of water suspended above; the 'sea of glass' of Rev. 4:6").

[1:7]   We have now an account of two successive acts of God. Nothing more is said about the creation of the firmament, neither of the material out of which it is made, nor of its shape; there is concern only for the wonderful act of creation; everything else remains a mystery. Nor is there a word about the setting-up of the firmament; only its function is described.

W.H. Schmidt is of the opinion that the word הבדיל in v. 7 "would be a sign of the priestly language and could only be late"; that may be true for the lower limit because "it is an important concept in the priestly teaching and is often used (pp. 102 and 167, with reference to Begrich and Zimmerli; O. Procksch observes that the word does not occur before Deuteronomy). But it is certainly not true of the event described because the act of dividing or separating occurs all too frequently in the old cosmogonies. It is part of the action-account of creation.

U. Cassuto lays great emphasis on the difference between the biblical account and the mythical description of the dividing of the body of Tiamat. This is quite justified and is in contrast to the remark of Gunkel, "It is closely related to the Babylonian story where Marduk splits Tiamat, the primeval sea, into two parts." However, it is not to the point when Cassuto contrasts Gen 1:6-8 with the passage (ANET, p. 67, Tablet IV, 137-140) as liberation from the mythical: "Here we have neither war nor weapons; a body is not carved up, nor are its segments used for construction; a simple process of physical unfoldment takes the place of the mythical train of events described in the pagan legends." What Cassuto says of the biblical description could be said just as well of other "pagan" descriptions of creation where the separation of heaven and earth is narrated without any sign of struggle. The combination of the motif of dividing with a struggle between the gods is rare, and was not part of the tradition history of Gen 1:6-8. The situation is quite different: in the one case, separation by cutting in pieces, in the other, separation by interposing a partition.

[1:8]   *The Naming.* Only when the name is given does it become clear that the solid dividing wall created in vv. 6 and 7, the firmament, is the heavens. The heavens are featured again in vv. 14 and 17 when the stars are put there. "Heaven and earth" then comprise the earth together with the vault of heaven, but not the waters above the firmament. This is yet another indication that the creation of the world is being described as an event which can be grasped only in a limited way. In vv. 3-5 it is not said that God created darkness; yet darkness passes over into the framework of creation and enters into the limitations of night; in vv. 6-8 the waters above the firmament, which have been separated from the waters below, remain on the other side, apart from the heavens, as the "waters above the firmament."

So P in the work of the first two days repudiates any talk which simply equates what has been created with the universe and contrasts it with nothingness. The world which God created is not according to P identified with the All. This is to acknowledge that people are incapable of conceiving either the All or nothingness. To assent to God as the creator of the world is to acknowledge the limits of human thought. This holds quite independently of any speculation about how the world came about. P takes seriously the human capacity to think and to construct and points to human limitations by the very way in which he speaks of

God's activity. And so it is of little account if what we think of the origin of the world differs from what P thought.

שָׁמַיִם: Bibliography: G. von Rad, 'οὐρανός' B, Altes Testament: ThWAT, V 501-509. S. Morenz, "Himmel I Religionsgeschichtlich" and G. Gloege "II Biblisch und dogmatisch," RGG³, 328-332. L. Rost, "Himmel," BHH II 719. Th.H. Gaster, "Heaven," IDB II 551-552 with further bibliography.

Originally there was no distinction between heaven as a part of the world and heaven as the god of heaven or as the dwelling of a god or gods. Heaven is at the same time both a mythical and a scientific notion. This is quite independent of the fact that there is often a linguistic distinction between heaven as part of the world and heaven as a divinity, as in Egypt, and that just as often the same word is used for both, for example, the Sumerian An and the Chinese *t'ien*. The separation of heaven from earth at the beginning is described for the most part in mythical terms as the separation of the god of heaven from the earth goddess (only in Egypt is it the reverse); the heavenly divinity then is identical with the natural heaven.

Heaven in the Old Testament is simply something created; it has no divine character at all. The creation and naming of the firmament is affirming strictly that heaven is created; it is part of "not God." Heaven is not a different sort of creature from earth; it has not a closer relationship to God than earth (Deut 10:14); God is on the other side of heaven just as the earth is on this side. It does not accord with the evidence when G. Gloege writes in his article in RGG: "A distinction is to be made in the Old Testament between the cosmological and the theological heaven." One cannot establish such a distinction in the Old Testament. Heaven is simply something created. When the Old Testament speaks of heaven as a dwelling of God, as it rarely does, or of God acting from heaven, then this is either metaphorical or the language of tradition.

There is no indication at all in the Old Testament that God created heaven for himself to live in as happens, for example, in Egypt: "When heaven was separated from earth, when the gods climbed up to heaven" (S. Morenz, p. 331). One can say that where God is one, heaven loses its meaning as a dwelling of the gods. The Old Testament can speak of the destruction of heaven at the last judgment simply because heaven, like earth, is something created (Is 34:4; 51:6; cf. G. von Rad, p. 508f.). God's throne or dwelling in heaven has meaning only in the context of the heavenly court where he is surrounded by heavenly beings or servants as, for example, in 1 Kings 22. The heavenly court is an image which Israel received, it is not specifically Israelite (G. von Rad, p. 504). The mythical concept of heaven which ancient Israel rejected was taken up again only at a much later period when heaven was described as the abode of the dead, as in late Greek thought and the New Testament, Heb 12:22ff.; Acts 6:9ff.; 7:4ff. The idea of a heaven beyond had long since been established in Egypt (S. Morenz, p. 331).

[1:9-10] It is this third work of separation that puts all others in perspective. The three acts of separation are the source of the three basic categories in which creatures, and above all living beings, live out their existence — the category of time and the categories of space. The alternation of night and day is the basis of time, the creation of the firmament, the basis of the vertical dimension, the separation of the water and the land, the basis of the horizontal dimension. Let it be pointed out again that P gives precedence to the category of time over those of space; the older descriptions of creation which P received, creation by action, knew only of the two spacial divisions; P introduced the separation of light into the tradition he had received and gave it precedence.

We must put aside any idea that the author of the creation story wanted to present a "picture" of what happened at the moment of creation. Such a mentality betrays a basic misunderstanding of the meaning and purpose of the cosmogonies. Their object is not to communicate a description of the course of events of creation. It is much more: it is to establish the reality that conditions present existence; what is narrated in the cosmogony is not directed to the description of creation but to what exists as a result of creation (so M. Eliade, "Structure et fonction du mythe cosmogonique," *La Naissance du monde,* p. 471f.).

The exegete must be very cautious about attempts to explain the individual events of creation in a way that allows us to follow them with our imagination. F. Delitzsch does something like this in his commentary when he explains Gen 1:9 from Ps 104:3-8: "We must accept that while God's creative power set in motion the physical and chemical energies of the teeming mass swimming in the primeval waters, the dry land rose out of it. Ps 104 . . . confirms this in v. 8." There is the same attempt to present graphically the individual events of creation in the commentary of U. Cassuto one hundred years later: "Thus as soon as the firmament was established in the midst of the layer of water, it began to rise in the middle, arching like a vault, and in the course of its upward expansion it lifted at the same time the upper waters resting on top of it." It is a misunderstanding of the real meaning of the cosmogonies to go to such extremes to describe the various happenings. Explanations like this which strive after images strip the narrative of that reality which is completely beyond imagery and which is concerned with the state of the world as it is (cf. H. Gunkel ad. loc.).

[1:9]   There is no sign of a juxtaposition of "creation by act" and "creation by word" in the third work of creation. V. 9 is an account of creation by word: there is the introduction to the command, the command in the jussive, and the report of its fulfillment. However, it does not follow that P had no traditional material. W.H. Schmidt writes: "The action-account has disappeared in the third work," p. 51. One can say this, but can one prove it? Creation as separation of the land from the primeval deep or sea occurs often in the cosmogonies. I refer to the excursus in Cassuto's commentary ad. loc., about the battle of the gods with the primeval sea monster; the passages from the Rabbinic writings are particularly useful. However, it is very one-sided when Cassuto designates the struggle as the pagan description and contrasts it with the description in the Torah where the creator disperses the waters to their respective places.

The separation of the land and the water without any sign of a struggle is by far the most common description and is found in many forms in Egypt. The description of the primeval hill rising out of the deep predominates. It is never said that anything was made or formed or erected; there is simply the account of the separation of the land from the water. Perhaps the "action-account" which came down to P ran something as follows: "And God gathered the water beneath the heaven into one place so that the dry land became visible" (or something corresponding to Job 28:10f.). The creation command as formulated in v. 9 differs so little from this that it was not necessary to insert an action-account.

W.H. Schmidt wants to demonstrate that the MT originally contained an action-account which is still preserved in the Gk. But in the first place one cannot say: "It (the action-account) is nevertheless passed on by the Gk," p. 104; then the sentence quoted from the Gk is not an action-account, but the unfolding of the sentence "and it was so." It is therefore an account of the carrying out of the command of creation. Schmidt wants to conclude that the Gk is familiar with an action-account from the expression εἰς τὰς συναγωγὰς αὐτῶν (instead of מקום of the MT). This conclusion is improbable because the giving of the names in vv. 9 and 10 is quite comprehensible: in the creation command, the waters are ordered to gather into one place; only after this has happened can one speak of the place where the waters were gathered together. P then left aside the action-account which he received because his own formulation of the creation command was very like it.

It is worth noting that the command is addressed to the waters although the work of the third day is directed to setting up the dry land. The earth is not "made" by God as was the firmament; it is rather set free by being separated from the water. There is no creation command by which the earth comes into being. Separation then is not something added to creation, but is itself creation. It is clear here that there can be no question of a *creatio ex nihilo;* our query about the origin of matter is not answered. The account says nothing more than that the waters of chaos below the firmament were divided into land and sea.

The sentence "and it was so" follows the creation command in the MT. The Gk develops it: "And the water under heaven gathered together into its own place, and dry land became visible." Even if this development corresponds to the creation command which preceded it, nevertheless preference is to be given to the MT.

The separations end with v. 9 and do not occur in the subsequent acts of creation. P has described the basic works of creation as acts of separation. He is not talking about the component parts of matter but rather about the basic categories of existence, namely time and space (W.H. Schmidt relates the categories to space only, p. 103). These three basic works are concerned not with the mere existence of the world as such but with the world as related to human existence.

With the description of creation as a series of separations, P is part of a tradition that reaches back into the distant past and across the whole face of the earth. This has been shown in the Introduction. In this context, creation by separation is the correlative of a primeval chaos. They both go together. The older cosmogonies throughout the world describe creation by separation in very different ways — the primeval egg, the cutting-up of the primeval being, or some such; nevertheless, it is significant that P takes his stand here on this ancient and widespread tradition. Common to him and the tradition is an understanding of the world in which a state of separation and so of order are basic to its existence. The world is not conceived of primarily as that which is, that which is at hand, but rather as something divided and ordered and comprehensible only in this framework. P shares this understanding of the world with mythical and pre-mythical primitive thinking, inasmuch as the origin of the world by separation or division goes back so far.

A question arises here. The description of creation as separation reveals an understanding of the world that is concerned with human existence. Is this closer to the modern scientific understanding of the world than that which takes as its starting point the existence of matter, rendering intelligible its absolute and objective reality? An article by D. Sternberger, "Schöpfung und Scheidung": *Der Monat* 17, 201 (1965) 5-15, points in this direction: "Critical thought is as old as creation. Creation reaches its fulfilment in critical thought and is not to be separated from it. . . . Genesis is witness of this. Separation and distinction were as such the work of God in creation," p. 5. "In the whole of the creation story of Genesis, I can find nothing whatsoever of the *creatio ex nihilo* of speculative and dogmatic thought," p. 6f. "In any case there can be no question of a 'creation' in the traditional dogmatic sense. Or, to speak in the categories of Kantian logic, God's action here would be basically analytical, and in no wise synthetic," p. 10.

The meaning of the separations in the first three works is found in their differences. P is not describing a particular way in which separation takes place and then applying it to three successive cases. He is trying to show that separation as an act of separation has plenty of variety: "The separation of light and darkness, of the upper and the lower waters, of the earth and sea, all have their subtle differences. There is the separation which gives rise to something new, that which brings to light what was originally there, and that which divides the same primeval material and assigns it to different places. All belong to Genesis and Genesis is the critical point" (Sternberger, p. 10).

[1:10]   The giving of names by God belongs to the work of separation. This is important. Both come to an end with the third work. I hold that it is possible that this remarkable coincidence of separation and naming goes back to a tradition which P received and which saw creation only as separation and naming. But I cannot demonstrate this. It has already been noted that naming can be used as a description of creation.

The combination of separation and naming in the first three works is to be explained as follows: under certain circumstances a part of the world only exists when it has a name; we have an analogy in the case of a newly discovered star or island. Under these particular circumstances the naming has the function of separating; what is peculiar to the thing named is the name itself. To this extent separation and naming go together. But when in the first three works God is the one who gives the name, then what is said is that the basic categories of time and space are simply a prerequisite for man; their significance and function are determined by God. The works of creation that follow are not a presupposition for existence in the world in the same way.

How is God's act of naming related to his command? Both of these ways of speaking by God (one can add too his judgment) are drawn to each other clearly and deliberately. In the creation command "let there be . . . ," "let them gather . . . ," the word of command is identical with the creative word (Ps 33:9). By giving the name, God determines that what is created will remain such as its name describes it: day and night, heaven, land and sea (so too Dillmann ad. loc.). The word that determines and stipulates is co-ordinated with what is being created; and this is in accord with the two basic meanings of the word of God in history in P: God commands that something happen (as for example, the building of the Tabernacle); and he stipulates or determines what is to remain permanently. Naming in the sense of determining is related closely to the creation command as well as to creation by separation: "While God divides things, he thereby divides also ideas and names. That is what is meant when God gives a name. When man distinguishes he but echoes the distinction that God has impressed on things" (F. Delitzsch ad. loc.).

"And God saw that it was good": it is significant that this judgment is absent in v. 8; the disposition of space had not then been concluded. The sentence can only stand at the end of v. 10. This makes the connection between the second and the third works clear; in both, the world is created as ordered space. God's judgment that it was good rounds off the basic disposition of time, v. 4 and space, v. 10. It should be noted that this judgment is not just a summary applicable to all that has been created. In v. 4 it is the light that is good, not day and night; in v. 10 it is not the dry land that is good; the judgment is pronounced after the naming of the land and the sea (this is contrary to the explanation of K. Barth, CD, III/1, pp. 141ff., which is cited and accepted by W.H. Schmidt: "What is approved in the work of the third day is the earth and the earth only"). These fine distinctions are not without importance; they point out again that the judgment of God is not our judgment.

[1:11-13]   *The Creation of Plants.*

Literature: Text: L. Köhler-K.L. Schmidt-A. Debrunner, "Hebräisches jāṣā' und Mc 8:11," ThZ 3 (1947) 471-473.   D.N. Freedman, "Notes on Genesis 1," ZAW 64 (1972) 190-191.   S. Esh, "Note on אצי'," VT 4 (1954) 305-307.   P.A.H. de Boer, "Etude sur le sens de la racine QWH," OTS 10 (1954) 225-246.

A. Dieterich, *Mutter Erde. Ein Versuch über Volksreligion,* 1905, 1925³.   Th. Nöldeke, "Mutter Erde und Verwandtes bei den Semiten," ARW 8 (1905) 161-166.   L. Köhler, "Biblische Spuren des Glaubens an die Mutter Erde?" ZNW 9 (1908) 77-80.   E. König, "Die Bedeutung des hebräischen מין," ZAW 31 (1911) 133-146.   F. Schepens, "Le sens de מין dans le récit de la création," RSR 13 (1913) 161-164.   F. Altheim, "Terra mater," RVV 22, 2 (1931).   E.Fascher, "Vom Anfang der Welt und vom Ursprung des Menschengeschlechts," AWR n.f. 3 (1961) Kap. III 49-57.   H. Cazelles, "MYN = espèce, race ou ressemblance?" *Mémorial* 10 (1964) 105-108.   H. Schmid, "Die 'Mutter Erde' in der Schöpfungsgeschichte der Priesterschrift," Jud 22 (1966) 237-243.   M. Eliade, 'Erde,' RGG³ II, 548-550.

The division of works and their distribution into days is not clearly defined after the three works of separation. Something new is introduced with the creation of vegetation in v. 11 and the method of creation is different. It must be recalled that the earlier cosmogonies describe one single creation event — the creation of heaven and earth forms one narrative, that of humans another, that of vegetation a third — there is one narrative for each. An example is the Sumerian myth "Enki and Ninhursag," ANET 37-41; S.N. Kramer, *Sumerian Mythology,* 54-59. The story tells that the result of the union of the god Enki with the goddess of plants Utu, whom he had begotten, was eight ordinary plants and, later in the story, eight healing plants. The origin of the plants in this myth is part of a broader cycle of events; but it can still be seen that the origin of plants from a union of the gods was once a story in its own right.

When the creation of vegetation together with the creation of animals, people, the heavenly bodies and so on, form part of a creation narrative, we have a systematization which is foreign to the old creation stories. As the Sumerian myth quoted above shows, the original intention is not to tell the story of the origin of vegetation as part of the world, but rather to point to the meaning these plants have for people, be they edible or healing plants. This is the reason why the older creation narratives, especially the primitive, speak of the origin or the creation of individual plants or groups of plants, not of plants in general. This is the case, for example, in the Sumerian myth "Cattle and Grain" (S.N. Kramer, op. cit., p. 53f.) and in the African stories which are found in the chapter "Die Herkunft der Nutzpflanzen," in H. Baumann's *Schöpfung und Urzeit*. . . . pp. 343-352. It is very clear here that the stories are not interested in the origin of plants as such, but only of edible plants which provide the necessary means of life for the group. The creation of plants is never linked with the creation of the world. Enuma Elish shows indirectly that the creation of plants has its own line of tradition; when Marduk creates the world, there is no mention of plants (or of animals), but in Tablet VII 2 Marduk is called "The Creator of Grain and Vegetables."

This shows that two processes of systematization or abstraction have taken place before the description in Gen 1, one the generalization with regard to plants, the other its insertion into the account of the creation of the world. There is a large gap between Gen 1:11-12 and Enuma Elish. The description in Genesis is on the way to a scientific explanation of the origin of plants. The classification of the plants shows a scientific interest. An objective interest has taken the place of a purely functional interest in plants as nourishment for humans. The significance of the classification of the plants can only be understood in the background of the two processes of abstraction indicated above.

[1:11] "And God said 'Let the earth put forth vegetation'." The formulation of the fourth work of creation is very different from what has preceded. "God's word . . . now abdicates its creative power, i.e., the word now allows what has just been created to be the origin of something new" (W.H. Schmidt, *Die Schöpfungsgeschichte*. . . , p. 106). This does not accord with P's concept of creation; by analogy with the creation command which has preceded, the formula should be: "Let there be vegetation upon the earth, plants and fruit trees . . . and it was so." It is due to the tradition he has received that P diverges so markedly from his own way of describing creation, but not only to this. If it is correct that P is moving toward a scientific explanation, then he would find the traditional description of the origin of the plants from the earth quite suitable to this line of thinking (cf. Introduction).

P points out that the question of the origin of plants stands in no wise in contradiction to what is said of God as the creator of plants. God commands the earth to bring forth plants. It is just because God's creative action allows for "origin from" that there can be no basic opposition between the two. Even if the explanation of the origin of plants is very diversified, nevertheless one can hear the creation command behind every stage of each process. "דשא . . . generally describes budding plants" (W.H. Schmidt, p. 107). Ges-Buhl: "Young, fresh, green grass"; the verb occurs only here and in Joel 2:22 (Qal). The hi. form תדשא, "Let there green forth," which occurs only here, is probably a formation of P to embrace trees and plants as they come into being and shoot forth from the earth. As a matter of fact in the earliest stages of their growth all plants are more or less alike. This etymological formation (as also in v. 20) serves the steady monotonous style that characterizes the chapter. This form of speech shows that the division of plants is twofold, not threefold, and that דשא like שרץ in v. 20 must mean the whole (so most scholars, cf. W.H. Schmidt, p. 107, n. 3).

The division of plants after their kind is not made according to their relationship to humans, as many interpreters think. P differs here from the earlier creation accounts; he is not thinking of those plants which serve humans for food, but is concerned with the general division of all plants according to their kind. This is something very different. It is certainly correct that the species, particularly of animals, are very important for P in the division into clean and unclean (Lev 11:3ff.); however, one cannot say that this latter division is foreshadowed here. The division of plants into two main groups has nothing at all to do with clean and unclean; it shows P's systematic way of thinking. But the mentality goes far beyond the priestly-cultic mentality and tries to arrange creation analytically: "One is reminded unmistakably of the term *natura;* the term, however, is bounded by the term *creatura* " (von Rad ad. loc., p. 55).

All God's acts so far have been acts of separation. There is separation here too, but in a different way; it is no longer God who divides. The earth is called not only to bring forth, but to bring forth according to kind, and in two basic categories, each comprising those kinds of plants peculiar to it (the beginning of all separation and division is that one divides from one). By the command of the creator, vegetation is a subdivided whole, not an unorganized mass. Just as creation is a subdivided and circumscribed whole, so too are the plants that cover the earth. As long as the earth exists, every single one of the millions of plants must belong to its species as part of the organized whole. The most unprepossessing piece of grass or strip of moss is part of God's coordinated world; each in its own species fits into the ordered whole. It is in this way that vegetation is part of God's creation.

[1:12] "The earth brought forth." The effect of the command הארץ דשא תדשא, "Let the earth put forth vegetation," is described in detail in v. 12 with the word ותוצא, "the earth brought forth." The same verb is used again with the same subject in 1:24; the formula is: "And God said, let the earth bring forth living creatures." The meaning of "the bringing forth" is primarily: "Let something which is within come out." The plants are in the earth and the earth lets them come forth. It is the same in Is 61:11, "For as the earth brings forth its shoots" (parallel with, causes to spring up) or Hag. 1:11, "What the ground brings forth," cf. Num 17:23; Ps 104:14; Is 65:9. The background is the widespread image of Mother Earth, the earth as the bearer of all life and all the vegetation: "From the day they come forth from their mother's womb to the day they return to the mother of all," Sir 40:1. People too can be born from the earth "like grain spontaneously sprouting" (AOT 136, Line 1); Ps 139:15 makes reference to this. The matter has been treated fully by A. Dieterich, *Mutter Erde,* 1925[3], L. Köhler, and Th. Nöldeke and others. The terms "to bring forth from . . . or to come forth from . . ." are found especially in primitive creation narratives (H. Baumann, op. cit., pp. 202-242).

The combination of the phrase "let (something) come forth," used in its primitive sense, with the detailed classification of v. 11, which at least shows traces of scientific thinking, is saying something; it is tracing the line of development from the earliest descriptions of the earth as mother which brings forth plants, through creation by the word, to reflection on the ways in which the plants have had their origin. These two versions are a good example of how it is possible to talk about creation only within the tradition of a variety of descriptions; P's presentation of the creation of plants by the word of the creator excludes neither the primeval description of the origin of plants from the earth, nor the later question of how this took place. The old description is certainly modified. It is only God's creative word that enables the earth to bring forth the plants; it cannot do so of itself. But this happens in such a way that the older voice can still be heard. P knows and shows at every stage that he is heir to a tradition which he has to correct and pass on.

The word מִין is prominent and frequent in the creation narrative; it occurs however only in the context of plants and animals. Its meaning is precisely the same as that of the word used today in the natural sciences, namely species or genus. The word is used only in two contexts in the Old Testament: in Gen 1:11, 12, 21, 24, 25 (10 times in all); this usage is taken up again in the flood narrative, 6:20; 7:14, then in Lev 11:14, 22, 29 and in the corresponding passages in Deut 14:13-15, 18 in the context of the distinction between clean and unclean animals. (In Ezek 47:10 לְמִינָה occurs without any recognizable context; it is perhaps an addition. It occurs in Sir 43:25 "all kinds of living things" in the same sense as in Gen 1; cf. Sir 13:15f.). Even if its use is different in these two groups of texts, its general sense remains the same. Occasionally it is used in the context of knowledge. The wise or the clever man can distinguish and enumerate the different kinds of things. In the context of P's careful distinction of the species of plants and animals, one can speak of a scientific interest, provided one distinguishes it from our idea of "science." This distinction is not made for its own sake, out of some need to classify in order to take proper possession of the object, though this may have had some weight with P.

The function of the classification of the plants and animals lies in its significance for people. This is a reflection of the earlier stage when the creation of each lot of plants and animals was the subject of a creation story in itself and looked to the particular needs of humanity. The distinction between the two major groups, "plants" and "trees," is made primarily from the point of view of their meaning for people and for the animals (1:29f.; 9:3), as is the distinction between the various species of seeds and fruits. Clearly then, the way in which this distinction is formulated is the result of careful thought; one can see the transition to theoretical reflection on the basis of the distinctions. This is shown by a comparison with Ex 10:15 (J), where the same division into "plants" and "fruit-trees" occurs, but without the further interest shown in Gen 1.

[1:14-19]   The Creation of the Heavenly Bodies

Literature: P. Humbert, "Das fünfte Schöpfungswerk Genesis 1:14-19," ZAW 35 (1915) 137-141.   K. Budde, "Zum vierten Schöpfungstag (Genesis 1:14-19)," ZAW 36 (1916) 198-200.   O. Rühle, *Sonne und Mond im primitiven Mythus,* 1925.   J. Pedersen, *Israel, its Life and Culture* I-II, 1926, pp. 486-490.   S. Aalen, *Die Begriffe 'Licht' und 'Finsternis' im AT, im Spätjudentum und im Rabbinismus,* 1951, pp. 10-20.   J. Muilenburg, "The Biblical View of Time," HThR 54 (1961) 225-255.   W.H. Schmidt, *Die Schöpfungsgeschichte der Priesterschrift,* WMANT 17, 1964, Excursus: "Zur Verehrung der Gestirne," 117-120.   B. Landsberger-J.V.K. Wilson, "The Fifth Tablet of Enuma Elish," JNES 20 (1961) 154-179.

The account of the fourth day of creation is notably longer than the accounts of the other days. A closer examination of the text shows that this is due not to a more detailed description but to a succession of repetitions which are concerned wholly and exclusively with determining the function of the sun and the moon. This function, in terms of the reason why they were created, is presented in vv. 14-18 in seven sentences, some long, some short. There are four functions: to separate, to indicate, to give light, to rule; each is mentioned twice, with the exception of the second, to indicate, which is mentioned only once.

The reason for this unusual repetition is that of all the works of creation mentioned in Gen 1, only the sun and the moon were divinities in the world in which Israel lived, and divinities of the utmost importance. What distinguishes the priestly account of creation among the many creation stories of the Ancient Near East is that for P there can be only one creator and that all else that is or can be, can never be anything but a creature. P thereby contested a well-established point of view, taken for granted and beyond discussion in the world in which Israel lived. P is speaking polemically; he must establish in every way possible his thesis that the sun and the moon are creatures and nothing more. How difficult this was is demonstrated by one of the functions assigned to the sun and the moon: they are to rule, vv. 16 and 18. Man too is destined to rule, vv. 26 and 28 (different verbs are used). Ruling is a personal function; even in Gen 1 there persists an echo, however faint, of the divinity of the sun and the moon, so deeply ingrained in the Ancient Near East. P meets the problem in two ways. The function of ruling given to the sun and the moon is a derived function. They were made by God and set in the firmament of the heaven for that purpose. Further- more, this function is limited by its object; the sun and the moon are ''to rule'' day and night. This is not dominion in the full sense.

P's concern to describe as a mere creature something which was a divinity in the surrounding world shows clearly how he understood the distinction be- tween creator and creation, between God and creature. The distinction lies in their function, not in their nature and being. This is very important for P's theological understanding of creator and created. P makes no attempt to demon- strate a distinction in being or nature between God and the sun. The fact that the sun and the moon are created does not mean for P that they are different sorts of beings from God — some kind of matter over against God. This mode of thought has no place here. God differs from the sun and the moon solely in this, that he is the creator and consequently the lord of all that is created. The sun and the moon differ from God in that they have a limited function within creation. It is this function of service that distinguishes them from God. The function can be de- scribed in different ways as the text of vv. 14-18 shows. But however the function is understood, it is but an aspect of the creature state of sun and moon. Sun and moon belong to the order of creation in their function of service, and in no other way.

The structure of vv. 14-19 is clear. The first sentence, v. 14, introduces the creation of the heavenly bodies by the word of the creator, and the last sentence, v. 15, closes the account with ''and it was so.'' P's pattern demands now the formula of approval and the chronological framework, the last sentence of v. 18 and v. 19. The action-account is inserted here into P's pattern in vv. 16-18a: ''God made . . . and God set. . . .'' The action-account and the command- account can be clearly distinguished and separated here. The structure of vv. 14-18 is as follows:

    v.14   And God said: Let there be light,   to . . .
    15   And it was so.
    16   And God made the . . . lights . . .   to . . .

127

17   And God set them . . .   to . . .
18b And God saw that it was good.
19   And there was evening . . .

The action-account and the command-account are so clearly distinguished here that the question arises whether there are any signs that the action-account represents an older stage of tradition than the command-account. In vv. 16-17 the creation of the heavenly bodies takes place in two acts: God made — God set. This corresponds to the two acts in the creation of the firmament: God made — God separated, v. 7, except that the second act is not described in such concrete terms here. Such an account of setting something up in several (at least two) successive acts is the ordinary way to describe a process of manufacture.

There is a succession of different manipulations which constitute the essence of the operation. The onlooker who is witnessing the emergence of a piece of handiwork is held by the process; the process forms the basic framework of the verbal report which is given later. This structure is there in Jeremiah's account of the potter at work, Jer 18, in the ironic account of the craftsman making images of the gods in Is 40:19-20; 41:6-7; 44:12-15, and elsewhere. This sort of description is highly stylized in Gen 1, but nevertheless is clearly recognizable, especially in this particular work of creation. In vv. 16-17 a work of creation is described after the fashion of the making of handicrafts. It should not be forgotten that products of the hands were regarded as works of art in the ancient world; there was as yet no distinction between art and craft; it was the overall plan, the product of the hands as conceived by the spirit, that was held in esteem.

A further misunderstanding must be forestalled: the two verbs which describe God's actions, "made" - "set," are not meant to arouse in the listener an image of a course of events which he can follow (as, e.g., L. Rost CuW 10 [1934] 174: "One will have to imagine the heavenly bodies being formed on the earth"); the purpose is to point to the analogy between the creation of the heavenly bodies and the work of the craftsman. The work of creation differs from that of the craftsman precisely in that it is a primeval event and as such not accessible to human imagination. In any case we can be certain that the description in vv. 16-17 belongs to an older stage of tradition. The two successive acts are not present in P's own description of creation. The creation command: "Let there be lights in the firmament of the heavens . . ." unites the making and the disposition of the heavenly bodies. Creation by the word is the work of an instant: "And it was so."

Moreover the function of the sun and the moon "to rule" occurs only in vv. 16-17, the action-account and not the command-account. The older description could still speak of the rule of the sun and the moon without embarrassment; the later description omits this function because it does not seem to be sufficiently secured against mythical misunderstanding. Instead the later description, the command-account, describes the functions of the sun and the moon in terms of the calendar; they are to "be for signs and for seasons and for days and years. . . ." This is in accord with P's area of interest.

It is certain then that in vv. 14-19 P has inserted an older account, an action-account, vv. 16-18a, into his own command-account, vv. 14-15, 18b, 19. But it is not as simple as all that; one can not assign each sentence in vv. 14-19 either to the older or to the later stage of tradition. This is not enough. We have to do with a gradual blending, the result of which is the traditional text. W.H. Schmidt has made a careful and well-argued attempt to trace each step of this process, but his conclusions must remain hypothetical. I agree with him when he takes account of additions to the action-account and concludes: "Accordingly one can conclude that the oldest stage of vv. 14-18 was: "And God made the two great lights: the sun to rule by day and the moon to rule at night (and the stars). And God set them in the firmament of the heavens," p. 116.

[1:14] God orders that there be lights in the firmament of the heavens, that is, that they are to come into being. The verb is in the singular. According to Ges-K §145o there are many exceptions to the basic rule that the gender and number of the predicate should follow those of the subject, "when the predicate precedes the subject." When the stars are called lights at the beginning of the passage then their function is at one with their description. This description of the stars in terms of their function expresses clearly their state as creatures in accordance with the intention that dominates the whole pattern; the sun and the moon are creatures of God; it is in this that their dignity and their limitations lie.

This first sentence is a rejection of any trace of divinity in the sun. P is not thereby making a caricature of the stars as certain recent commentators would have it. He is not as it were degrading the stars to mere "lamps." One can only say this if one does not pay attention to the language and the traditions of which P is the heir. In Egypt, a "lamp" can also be a description of the sun god (H. Gunkel ad loc.: "the Egyptian calls the sun-god 'the living lamp'"); to describe them as מארת is not to degrade them, but to set their limits. To describe the sun and the moon constantly as lights or lamps is to put the heavenly bodies as a whole in the context of creation. This is so important theologically that it can scarcely be exaggerated.

The first duty of the lights is "to separate the day from the night." It includes everything else and provides the framework of P's scheme of creation of the heavenly bodies, vv. 14 and 18. P lays special stress on this duty by using the verb which was the key word in v. 3 and which covered the three basic works of separation which put order into the world, vv. 3-10. By emphasizing the function of separating given to the heavenly bodies P is saying that this is the same work of creation, based on and continuing the first works of separation, in however different a way. This is shown too by the formulation which labors under certain difficulties and which is somewhat abstract; the details of all other functions are more concrete. One must use circumlocutions to describe what is actually meant. For example, the alternation between sunlight and moonlight effects the separation of day from night — but that is not very exact. There is a difficulty in the wording of v. 18, "and to separate the light from the darkness," because that has already happened in v. 4. But the echo of v. 4 in v. 18 is intentional; separation colors the whole of God's work of creation.

The second function of the heavenly bodies is "to be for signs and for seasons and for days and years." This function is stated more simply in Ps 104:19. The significance of the heavenly bodies for the division of the seasons and the determination of the yearly feasts is well-known all over the world and at all levels of civilization accessible to us. One of humanity's earliest and most significant achievements was to derive chronological order from the course of the stars. We can see how deeply rooted this is in human history when we reflect that even today the festal calendar differs from the fixed calendar because the feasts are still calculated according to the heavenly bodies, though their content has no longer anything to do with it. This phenomenon is so well known that it is not necessary to allege parallels.

The fifth tablet of the epic Enuma Elish describes the creation of the heavenly bodies and their function:

> He determined the year by designating the zones:
> He set up three constellations for each of the 12 months.
> After defining the days of the year (by means) of (heavenly) figures . . .
> The moon he caused to shine, the night (to him) entrusting.
> He appointed him a creature of the night to signify the day. . . .
>   (ANET pp. 67-68, lines 3ff., line 12.)

W.H. Schmidt notes in this context: "This is related to what is said of the moon god Sin: 'He fixes day, month and year.' In the Sumerian version of 'The creation of the moon and the sun', the moon is 'the landmark of heaven and earth'" (p. 113, n. 4).

The construction of the four successive nouns is difficult. There is no doubt that "and for days and years" is one member of the series because the preposition ל is not repeated before שָׁנִים. The heavenly bodies were created to determine the days and the years, i.e., the calendar. A separate element is the determination of the feasts, מוֹעֲדִים. W.H. Schmidt, and many others, understand the distinction in this way: "The heavenly lights are to serve as signs, in particular to fix cultic observances and the calendar" (p. 114). I do not think that this covers exactly the distinction intended. The words themselves do not give sufficient grounds for a distinction between cultic and non-cultic dates, though they distinguish clearly continuous, extended time (days and years) and those fixed, determined times marked out within it.

This systematic distinction of two inter-related types of classification corresponds to P's thinking. In Gen 1, P distinguishes *genera* constantly: he spans wholes in such a way as to describe the whole in its basic divisions. Here he includes the two basic ways in which time is classified, the unchanging unities (days and years) and the sections marked out with special significance. This is supported by Ps 104:19 where the word has the same meaning in the same context: "Thou hast made the moon to mark the seasons." the word מוֹעֵד can designate the place appointed (the place that one has fixed, agreed upon) Josh 8:14 and the time appointed Ex 9:5; 10:13. It is this general meaning that predominates (e.g., the fixed time for the stork in the heavens, Jer 8:7); the word indicates a cultic festival in Num 10:10 and a simple feast in Is 33:20. The cultic festivals are certainly included in Gen 1:14, though the word is used in its most general sense, namely a fixed point designated within the stream of time (so too F. Delitzsch and A. Dillmann).

When this distinction and classification is understood correctly then the first of the four names, "for signs," takes on a broader meaning which embraces both: "Let them be for signs, and indeed for. . . ." The only meaning that אוֹת can have in this context is that given in the lexicon of L. Köhler under no. 1: "Distinguishing mark" (so too U. Cassuto) and not "an omen (an indication of something to come)" which occurs in the lexicon under no. 6. Here Köhler is following the interpretation of H. Gunkel who quotes Jer 10:2 and explains it as follows: "They announce the movements of the heavens and the things to come." The explanation of T. Boman is also misleading: "As the rainbow, when it appears occasionally, is the sign and guarantee of the covenant of grace with Noah, so are sun, moon, and stars the daily signs and guarantees of his mercy shown forth in the whole of creation" (*Hebrew Thought Compared with Greek,* 1960, p. 132).

[1:15]   The third duty of the two great heavenly bodies is indicated by the word מארת in v. 14. The same thing is repeated three times in one sentence: ". . . let them (= the lights) serve as lights . . . to give light. . . ." This awkward accumulation of phrases can be explained in part by assuming that the sun and the moon were the subjects of the sentence in the old formulation that was at hand to P. P carefully omits the concrete names so as to avoid any possible mythical association and their place as subject is taken by a word which indicates their function, מארת. The same occurs in the action-account in v. 17. W.H. Schmidt is of the opinion that this was their original place and that they were inserted in v. 15. But this, I think, is to make too much of the literary stage. P has described the purpose of the lights at the beginning of his account (and also at the end, v. 17). However, in the second part he has taken over a traditional piece of material which has been linked with the creation of the heavenly bodies. This tradition had been united with the third part and P retained the link. A Sumerian version of the creation of the moon demonstrates that these two functions of giving light and acting as signs had been brought together already (A. Heidel, *The Babylonian Genesis,* p. 74). P is also dependent upon tradition in vv. 14 and 15, the command-account.

[1:16-18]   *The action-account.* A notable difference between vv. 14-15 and vv. 16-18a is the addition of the words "and the stars" to v. 16. The addition is not necessary in vv. 14-15 because the word "lights" can include the stars too; it is necessary in v. 16 if the creation of the heavenly bodies is meant. It has been pointed out often that "and the stars" looks like an appendage and is not part of the whole. As far as I know a complete explanation of it has not yet been given. However, some light is given when one recalls that in the history of the creation narratives the creation of the individual precedes that of the whole. Before the narrative of the creation of the heavenly bodies as a whole, there is the story of the creation of the sun, the moon and the stars one by one (cf. A. Heidel, p. 73f.). The passage in Gen 1:16-18 is in the stream of a tradition that narrated the creation of the sun and the moon and was not part of the broader narrative of the creation of the universe. When the passage was assumed into the broad compass of Gen 1 it was necessary to add the stars.

The accumulation of functions and goals in vv. 14-18a is thereby explained better. They belonged originally to different accounts of the creation of the sun and the moon (separate and together) and were preserved when these became part of the story of the creation of the world. The variety of the individual narratives finds an echo in the variety of functions. (Cf. W.H. Schmidt, Excursus: Zur Verehrung der Gestirne, 117-120.)

[1:16]   One function is clearly dominant and original in vv. 16-18: "to rule. . . ." It may go back to the stage when it was part of an independent narrative of the creation of the sun and the moon in which it was quite comprehensible to speak concretely of the sun and the moon ruling the day and the night. Many commentators have pointed out that this function reflects a time when "the heavenly bodies were alive and regarded as lords or gods" (H. Gunkel). In Enuma Elish the creation of the moon is linked with its dominion over the night:

> The Moon he caused to shine, the night (to him)
> entrusting.   (ANET p. 68; Tablet V, line 12)

The moon is to rule and to give light. The association of these motifs could well be a further reason why they are linked again in Gen 1:16f. U. Cassuto draws attention to this. The personification of the heavenly bodies, in evidence here, is a pre-Israelite motif which is so persistent that it recurs later in Judaism when there is no longer any danger of it being understood mythologically: ". . . in the Rabbinic legends the heavenly bodies appear again as personalities, who hold intercourse with the creator" (U. Cassuto, ad. loc.).

The question still remains, what did P mean by "rule" and why did he retain the motif in spite of its mythological origin. There is nothing peculiar to P here. The expression is rather general and occurs in other places: "To him who made the great lights . . . the sun to rule over the day . . . the moon and stars to rule over the night . . . ,' Ps 136:7-9. The passage could be dependent on Gen 1, but not necessarily so. The phrases are somewhat different: Gen 1:16 היום למֶמְשֶׁלֶת, Gen 1:18 למשל ביום, Ps 136 לְמֶמְשֶׁלֶת בַּיּוֹם; actually they are saying exactly the same thing. We are dealing here with the more abstract notion of "rule, dominate" which we use to describe an elevation that dominates a landscape or of "predominating influences." Day and night are dependent on the sun and the moon inasmuch as they are dominated by them.

The repetition of the word גדל gives rise to a slight difficulty: "God made the two great lights; the greater light. . . ." In the first case the "two great lights" are opposed to the stars, as in Ps 136, and in the second case the "greater light" is the sun, and the lesser light is the moon. The description is repeated because the sun and the moon are not mentioned by name.

[1:17]   After the "making" of the sun and the moon there is the act of setting them in the firmament. We have discussed the order of events in the introduction to the exegesis.

In vv. 17b and 18a, when the sun and the moon are set in the firmament, they are given three further functions: to give light, to rule, to separate. These functions are, of course, not restricted to the second act but cover the whole presentation of the sun and the moon. This is obvious because none of the three functions is saying anything new: the first repeats the content of v. 15, the second that of v. 16, and the third that of v. 14. The accumulation of functions is clearest in this closing part. It must be emphasized again that the sun and the moon have been created solely to fulfill certain functions in respect to the universe and man, and that their state as creatures rests on these same functions.

A comparison with the description of the creation of the heavenly bodies in the Babylonian Enuma Elish (Tablet V, lines 1-22) shows both the originality of Gen 1:14-19 and its place in the stream of tradition (translation and references, ANET 67-68):

1-4   Marduk constructed stations for the great
        Gods, fixing their astral likenesses
        as constellations.
5-7   Marduk founded the station of Nibiru (i.e.,
        the planet Jupiter)
  8   Alongside it he set up the station of Enlil
        and Ea
9-10   Having opened up the gates on both sides,
        he strengthened the locks to the left
        and to the right
  11   In the belly of Tiamat he established the
        zenith
12-22   Marduk caused the moon to shine, the night
        (to him) entrusting
        15-22 He fixes the course of the moon.

Very different elements are assembled in the Babylonian description. It is clear
that they were once independent. Only line 11 links the creation of the heavenly bodies
with the creation of the world by the slaying of Tiamat, "In her belly he established the
zenith" (cf. Tablet IV, line 138). This line stands without any link between lines 9-10 (the
sun) and lines 12-22 (the moon). The three passages, 1-8 stars; 9-10 sun; 12-22 moon are
very different from each other. One can speak of a creation only in the case of the moon,
line 12: "The moon he caused to shine, the night (to him) entrusting." Nothing corresponding to the creation or positioning of the sun is described in lines 9-10; Marduk rather
arranges for the rising and the setting of the sun by opening certain doors and strengthening certain locks. (A. Heidel, p. 44, n. 103: "The gates refer to the mythological gates at
sunrise and sunset through which the sun-god was believed to come out in the morning
and leave in the evening.") Nor is there any account of the creation of the stars; Marduk's
action consists in constructing stations for the great gods and fixing their astral likenesses
as constellations. The reason for this is that the heavenly bodies are gods and the gods of
the Pantheon already exist in the plan of Enuma Elish. So there can be no account of their
creation. The beginning of Tablet V shows this clearly:

> He constructed stations for the great gods, fixing their
> astral likenesses as constellations.

There is here a very notable difference between the biblical and Babylonian accounts of
creation: in the biblical accounts everything created, whatever it may be, can never be
anything else than a creature; the state of being a creature is and remains decisive for
everything that is created. In the Babylonian Epic the gods are parts of what Marduk has
created; they are not to be separated from the stars and their astral likenesses which
represent them. As Tablet V shows, this means a notable break from the idea of creation
because we can no longer speak of the creation of the heavenly bodies.

The mythical talk about the heavenly bodies is even more impressive when in
lines 5-7 the station of Nibiru is set apart from the other constellations and given the
special function of ruling:

> After defining the days of the year (by means)
>   of (heavenly) figures,
> He founded the station of Nibiru to determine
>   their (heavenly) bands,
> That none might transgress or fall short.

Nibiru is Jupiter, the star of Marduk. The precedence and privileged place given to
Marduk in the Pantheon throughout the Epic is reflected here in the precedence given to

the star Nibiru: "His position in the middle of the heavens enables him to rule the movement of the heavens in such a way that any error in the course of the stars is avoided" (M. Eliade ed., *Quellen des AO 1:* "Die Schöpfungsmythen," 245 n. 61). The brief mention of the old high-gods Ea and Enlil in line 8 is an indication that their importance has grown less.

In Enuma Elish the star Jupiter (that is Marduk) stands in the center and rules over the other heavenly bodies; in the biblical account, the sun and the moon, creatures of God, rule over a limited area of creation, day and night.

Line 12 of the Babylonian Epic reads: "The moon he caused to shine, the night (to him) entrusting"; this is very like the biblical formulation, God created the moon to rule the night. The passage which deals with the moon, lines 12-22, differs markedly from what has preceded: here the moon is described as a heavenly body with a particular function; there is no mythical reference throughout the whole of this long passage of Tablet V. An earlier independent description of the creation of the moon has been worked into the Epic at this place. There are other passages too describing the functions of the heavenly bodies which are parallel to the biblical expressions:

L.12	The moon he caused to shine (cf. LL.15 and 16) The night to him entrusting	v.15	to be lights to give upon the earth
		v.16	to rule the night
L.13	to signify the days	v.14	to be for signs and for seasons and for days and years
L.14	Monthly without cease, form designs with a crown	v.14	to be for signs

When all the functions of the heavenly bodies in Gen 1:14-18, with one exception, occur also in the Babylonian description of creation, then this confirms that the only deliberate addition made by P is at the beginning and the end, in vv. 14 and 18, "to separate" (cf. above, exegesis of v. 14). P takes us a step further: the separation of light from darkness, which introduces and provides the foundation of the work of creation, is developed further in the creation of the heavenly bodies on the fourth day.

[1:20-23] Creation of the Water Animals and Birds

The structure of this part differs from the preceding by the introduction of a new element — the blessing. This is in accordance with the content: living beings are created. If we take as our starting point that in the history of creation stories the creation of the individual precedes that of the whole, it becomes clear that v. 20 is the beginning of something new. The creation of a living being is entirely different from the creation of everything mentioned so far, and so we can expect at once a different structure. God's creative action now takes place in two stages instead of one. A pronouncement, a word, is now added to the creative act, however this may be formulated. It is not just an address as W.H. Schmidt, p. 121, and most exegetes would have it, but a word pronounced over the beings created. The process of creation becomes thereby a different sort of event. The starting point is twofold: God created — and God blessed it. What is the relationship between what has come to P and what he himself has contributed, between the action-account and the command-account? W.H. Schmidt, pp. 120-124, wants to describe the relationship by analogy with what has preceded. The addition of the blessing has no significance at all for the structure and development of this part. He comes to the following conclusion: "Drawing together the reflections on Gen 1:20f., it is likely that the tradition behind v. 21, filled out later by the command of v. 20, was 'And God made the great sea monsters and the fish of the sea and all winged birds'" (p. 124).

Schmidt takes no account of the blessing and so involves himself in a number of difficulties in his attempt to show that v. 21 is an action-account and v. 20 a command-account, because v. 21 is for the most part formulated in the language of P (p. 123). The formulation demanded by an action-account must be very different from the wording given in v. 21.

I think that it is more in accordance with the text to renounce any attempt to set "word" and "action" accounts over against each other. The absence of the words "and it was so" (Gk's love of order has added them) would counsel against such a separation, and would indicate that P intended v. 21 to be the fulfillment of the command of v. 20 instead of the formula. The priestly language of the verse confirms this.

The structure of vv. 20-23 follows P's plan with the addition of the blessing:

   I. And God said
  II. Let the waters swarm
 III. And God created
 IV. And God saw
     And God blessed
  V. And it was so

There is no doubt that P, in contrast to vv. 3-5, has taken up an older tradition, but his wording does not allow us to separate it out. However it is certain, and in opposition to Schmidt, that this older tradition had two parts and spoke of both the creation and the blessing of the fish and the birds. This is not to be based on the wording of vv. 20-23 which, on the contrary, could well argue against it because there is no blessing in the formula of creation of the land animals. However the history of the accounts of the creation of the animals shows that the blessing is not a specifically theological idea added here with intent by P. The examples given below in the Excursus on v. 22 show that creation and blessing have a history together. But this does not always have to be expressly stated. The very creation of animals includes fertility.

It was noted long ago that the creation of the water animals and the birds is not reported in the same way; the creation of the birds seems to be attached to that of the fish. The sentences that refer to the water animals seem to hang together rather loosely and are obviously disturbed by those describing the birds:

V.20b   And let the birds fly above the earth
          across the firmament of the heavens
21bb   And every winged bird according to its
          kind
22bb   And let birds multiply upon the earth.

We can say with certainty that at one stage the creation of the water animals was a separate story and that the creation of the birds was grafted on to it. This took place at a rather early stage, because they were together in the tradition that came to P. The link between the fish and the birds is well founded in tradition and occurs in the praise of the creator in Ps 8:9a "The birds of the air, and the fish of the sea." W.H. Schmidt alleges a passage from the hymn to Amon-Re: "Who made that (on which) the fish in the river may live, and the birds soaring in the sky. . . ." (ANET, p. 366, (vi), L. 5 and 6). One should not give any particular significance to this grouping; it is just the simplest and most obvious way of distinguishing them from the land animals.

[1:20] "Let the waters swarm. . . ." The verb שׁרץ occurs in Ex 7:28, J, (RSV 8:3): "The Nile shall swarm with frogs," and is taken up again in Ps 105:30; otherwise it is restricted almost exclusively to P. It is used in the flood story of the animals, Gen 7:21; 8:17; of the multiplication of humankind upon the earth, Gen 9:7; Ex 1:7; of animals that creep along the ground and which are unclean, Lev 5:2; 11:10, 20f., 29, 41-44, 46; 22:5; Deut 4:16; Ezek 47:9. U. Cassuto writes: "The primary signification of the stem שׁרץ is, 'movement' with specific reference to the abundant, swift movement of many creatures." The etymological image of v. 11f., for example, is significant for the language of P in Gen 1. The abundance of life which is P's concern here is described in very striking terms. The expression נפשׁ חיה consists of two beats standing in apposition between two sentences each of three beats which explain it. נפשׁ חיה can have two meanings. In Gen 1:30 food is given to the animals; the different kinds of animals are named and then are described together: אשׁר בו נפשׁ חיה "Everything that has the breath of life" or "in which there is a living soul." In all other places it describes a living being: J uses it of humans Gen 2:7; and of the animals 2:19 (the latter is perhaps a gloss). Besides Gen 1:20, 21, 24 P uses the expression a number of times at the end of the flood story, 9:10, 12, 15, 16. In the first three passages it describes the animals, in the fourth both humans and the animals. In Lev 11:10, 46 it occurs in the same context as שׁרץ, likewise in Ezek 47:9. The expression נפשׁ חיה then can describe the animals in general, animals and humans together as living beings, and finally that which mades the animals and humans living beings, namely the breath of life.

All this is saying that the animals and people are what they are because of the breath that gives them life; they are living beings and this, or life as such, is the determining characteristic they have in common. (Cf. commentary on 2:7.)

The Gk, like other versions, understands the first sentence of v. 20 as a command directed to the waters to spawn fish (ἐξαγαγέτω), by analogy with v. 11. W.H. Schmidt, and many others, maintain that this interpretation is correct, while Karl Barth (C.D, III/1, pp. 171ff.) as well as A. Dillmann reject it. "Just as the waters and heaven were there before the dry land, so too the living creatures which fill it were created" (A. Dillmann, ad. loc.). V. 11 does not agree with the interpretation of the Gk; its purpose is to describe origin from the earth which can be understood also as generation by the earth. It is different in v. 20. W.H. Schmidt is correct when he writes, p. 121 n. 3: "V.20a is not stating that the sea is to generate the water animals, but merely that these animals are to swarm in the water, that is to be present there." Nothing more than this is intended.

Another argument against the Gk is its tendency to systematize: it deliberately assimilates v. 20a to v. 11. We must be on our guard against this and note that P was careful to preserve the unique character of each work of creation knowing full well that they were once independent. P is saying, guardedly, that the creation of plants was different from the creation of the living beings in the water and in the air. But v. 24, which states clearly that the earth is to generate the land animals, seems to be in contradiction because it is the earth itself which is to generate both land animals and plants. But this is clearly an analogical construction. One cannot say: "The place where the water and land animlas live is also the place of their origin — plants, v. 11, animals, vv. 21 and 24" (W.H. Schmidt, p. 121). P is stating clearly that the creation of the water animals and the birds is a different process from the creation of the plants, even though it is not explained any more clearly. This is confirmed by the fact that the earth had been known far and wide under the ancient title of "Mother Earth"; there is no analogy for the sea and the air.

Living space for the birds. A more accurate translation of עוֹף would be "winged creatures": that is all living beings that can fly, Lev 11:19f. P describes the living space by using the preposition עַל in two different ways: "Let birds fly above (עַל) the earth, across (עַל) the firmament of the heavens." It is very difficult for us to render the preposition here as it has such a broad scope; what is intended is, over the earth and under the vault of heaven. Hebrew had to use some such roundabout expression because it had no word for space or atmosphere, where the air was, but only for air in motion (L. Köhler, ZAW 32 [1912] 12).

[1:21]   Instead of the formalized "And it was so" there is a detailed sentence which takes up an older account, but retains the language of P. The word ברא occurs here for the first time since v. 1; it may have been chosen deliberately at the beginning of the creation of living beings (so G. von Rad and others). It is worth noting that the water animals are simply big and small and are not classified according to their species as are other plants and land animals, thus showing a more lively concern for the latter. The birds are created "according to their kind"; there is no further distinction.

The manuscripts vary between the singular and the plural in the first use of "according to their kind." It should be singular here because מִין occurs elsewhere only in the singular. The variation reflects an uncertainty whether the water animals as a whole are considered as a "kind" or whether it is a question of the different kinds of water animals. P cannot be restricted to the one or the other; all that matters to him is that God's creative act is according to kind.

תַנִּין sea-monster, sea-dragon, serpent or crocodile. Commenting on this passage in *Schöpfung und Chaos,* p. 120, H. Gunkel remarks: "The primeval monsters of Chaos have given rise to an extraordinary type of fish that take their place among the other created beings." There are two stages in the use of the word: an older stage where תַנִּין is the mythical monster of Chaos, and a later where תַנִּין is one creature among others. But the explanation is not as simple as all that.

First, there is the mythical use: תַנִּין occurs in the context of the struggle with Chaos in Is 51:9; Ps 74:13; Job 7:12 (on Ps 74:13 cf. the Ugaritic parallels, Ugarit *I* AB I, I;* ʿnt III 39; ANET 137, first column, 37-39; H. Donner, ZAW 79 [1967] 341); this mythical use is taken up again in the apocalyptic, Is 27:1.

Then there is a group of passages where תנין is a creature and is mentioned in the context of creation; beside Gen 1:21 it is addressed in the call to all creatures to praise God in Ps 148:7. If these were the only two contexts in which תנין occurs then one could agree with Gunkel's conclusion. However there is a third group of passages where תנין appears no longer simply as an animal. Ex 7:9, 12 speaks of a rod which was changed into a snake; Ps 91:13, speaking of God's providential hand, promises: "The young lion and the serpent you will trample under foot"; Deut 32:33 speaks of the poison of serpents. Ezek 29:3 and 32:2 compare Pharaoh with a mighty dragon; it is generally considered that תנין here means a crocodile. Jer 51:34 speaks of a monster that swallows.

There are other passages in the Old Testament where תנין occurs. For the most part תנין is simply an animal, serpent or crocodile or some such water beast without any mythological echo, but without any indication that it is "only" a creature. It is very unlikely that this use presumes or is necessarily later than the mythical use. There is no reason for thinking that the use of תנין simply to describe an animal, however monstrous and dangerous, could not go back to the earliest stages of the language (cf. G.R. Driver, "Mythical Monsters in the OT," *StudOr* I, 1956, 234-249).

The word תנין, used simply to describe an animal, acquired a mythical meaning only in one particular strand of tradition and in a definite context (Is 51:9; Ps 74:13; Job 7:12; Is 27:1); only here did it become personified as the monster of Chaos, and that under influence from outside Israel. It is possible that there is a mythical association in Gen 1:21, and that P has demythologized; but that is not necessary. One should not over stress P's antimythological tendency in the use of תנין (as, for example, U. Cassuto does). In any case it is certain that P was familiar with at least one usage of תנין in the sense of a huge water animal.

P's distinction between big and small water animals shows that he, like Ezekiel, means crocodiles and their like (so too A. Dillmann). There is an exact parallel in the creation Ps 104:25-26 where the same distinction is made; the big animal is called Leviathian (Luther translates as "whale"), the word used in some contexts for the primeval monster of Chaos, Ps 74:14; Is 27:1, and in others for the crocodile, Job 40:25 (RSV 41:1). The other water animals are not simply called fish; they are specified. For the grammatical contstruction cf. Ges-K §1 26x; the subject is determined by כל.

[1:22] "And God blessed them. . . ." First the construction: the words לאמר between the first two sentences means that the blessing acts when God says: "Be fruitful. . . ." There is one operation which is made effective by the pronouncement of the word. "Where God speaks a blessing, what he pronounces is at the same time effective in act" (F. Delitzsch, 1872[4], ad. loc.). The imperative then is not a command directed at the water animals; rather it has the effect of conferring something; Ges-K §1 10b: "To express permission"; it endows the animals with the power to reproduce their kind. The sentence referring to the words at the end of the verse is in the jussive; this corresponds to the normal sequence, imperative-jussive, in the call to praise in the Psalms, e.g., Ps 113:1 and 2. The jussive is used simply because the creation of the birds is appended to the creation of the sea animals, and, however much it may seem to lag, one should not conclude that the winged creatures have a lesser share in the blessing.

In introducing this section of the work of creation it was said that its structure differed from what went before inasmuch as it is in two parts: "God created — and blessed them. . . ." This means that the creation of living beings is a different process from the creation of the heavenly bodies. It is impossible to think of a living being otherwise than as a creative being that reproduces itself; the living being is by definition reproductive. One cannot say that the animals were created and then received a blessing over and above; the act of creating living beings includes endowing them with a capacity to reproduce themselves. A living being, נפשׁ חיה, would not be a living being if it did not have this capacity even when it is not mentioned expressly, for example, in the creation of the land animals, vv. 24-25. The living being, be it animal or person, has the capacity to reproduce simply because it is a living being. It is clear then why the blessing must be part of P's description of the process of the creation of living beings.

Excursus: *Blessing*

Literature: C. Westermann, *Der Segen in der Bibel und im Handeln der Kirche,* 1968.

It is not possible to give a detailed and comprehensive account of the concept of the blessing; we are concerned here only with its relation to creation.

The blessing in its latest stage is part of the institutionalized cult. It is imparted to the community by the duly commissioned president of the assembly and has retained this function through some thousands of years of constant worship.

Side-by-side with and even preceding this, there is mention of a blessing which is not part of the cultic action nor necessarily connected with it. Such blessings take very different forms and the two most important areas where they occur are marked out by their object, namely the people of Israel and the patriarchs to whom blessing is promised and given. The one is found in Gen 12-50, the other in Deuteronomy and in many other places, such as the Psalms. In both areas the blessing is God's and he alone imparts it; but parallel to this is another usage where the one who blesses is a man, a father who blesses his son or sons. Here too there is a variety of stages.

One must distinguish between the blessing in the areas just mentioned and the blessing in the primeval story, especially in the creation and flood narratives. One can talk of a blessing in general and of a blessing which is part of a narrative. They are very different. The primeval story can talk of blessing in the course of a narrative without even mentioning the idea. All narratives unlimited in scope and content in primeval time are narratives of blessing (S.N. Kramer, *Sumerian Mythology,* p. 107):

> In those days there was no snake, there was no scorpion,
>> there was no *hyena,*
> There was no lion, there was no *wild dog,* no wolf,
> There was no fear, no terror,
> The human being had no rival.
> In those days the land Shubur (East), the place of
>> plenty, of righteous decrees,
> *Harmony-tongued* Sumer (South), the great land of the
>> "decrees of princeship,"
> Uri (North), the land having all that is *needful,*
> The land Martu (West), resting in security,
> The whole universe, the people *in unison,*
> To Enlil in one tongue *gave praise.*

Side-by-side with this is the narrative of how a god blesses his land; here too blessing and increase are part of the creation (S.N. Kramer, op. cit., p. 49f.):

> Enten caused the ewe to give birth to the lamb, the
>> goat to give birth to the kid,

> Cow and calf he caused to multiply, much fat and
>   milk he caused to be produced,
> In the plain, the heart of the *wild goat,* the sheep,
>   and the donkey he made to rejoice,
> The birds of the heaven, in the wide earth he had
>   them set up their nests,
> The fish of the sea, in the swampland he had them
>   lay their eggs. . . .

There are many other myths in which creation and blessing are directly linked and whose effect is growth, increase and abundance.

"The narrated blessing" occurs in the Old Testament in J's account of the garden of God in Gen 2, and in the genealogies. The blessing of the living beings by the creator in Gen 1 is very different from the Sumerian narratives and is formulated theologically. The history of such narratives shows clearly that both the blessing of living beings by God and the image of a land or a garden of abundance originally belonged together. The opinion that it is only P who speaks of blessing in the primeval story and that J, on the contrary, has no knowledge of blessing is shown thereby to be incorrect.

Interpreters are unanimous about the meaning of the blessing in the primeval story: blessing is the power of fertility, i.e., the imperatives of 1:22 are explicative: the blessing which God confers on the creatures which he has created is the power to reproduce, multiply and fill the earth. The blessing is not something or other added to this power.

It can be taken as certain then that the verb "to bless" is used in its fundamental meaning in Gen 1:22. This meaning was later enlarged, modified and spiritualized, but persevered nevertheless right through to the latest stages. A typical and rather late use of the word which is characteristic of P is the cultic use, e.g., Lev 9:22f., and especially Num 6:22-24. When P uses the word in its original meaning in Gen 1:22 where it occurs for the first time, and in the context of the creation and blessing of the fish and the birds, he is showing very forcefully that its basic meaning is always there and that he is quite capable of controlling the full range of its use, from the power of fertility conferred in creation to the blessing of Yahweh bestowed on the worshiping community. Gen 1:22 shows P to be the heir of a tradition in which the blessing that confers the power of fertility is inseparable from creation where the creator is the one who blesses and the created living being has the power to reproduce itself because of the blessing.

The connection between blessing and creation remains basic to all further uses of the word. When God blesses, it is the creator who blesses and the blessing itself works itself out effectively in the life of what is blessed or of the one asking the blessing. Blessing implies creation and is effective as the work of the creator. To speak of life and its dynamism is to speak of the effective action of the creator.

פרו ורבו: "Be fruitful and multiply." The same pair of words in the imperative occurs again in Gen 1:28; 9:1, 2 (Noah and his sons); all passages belong to P; they are found in the perfect in Gen 8:17 (animals). The words occur together in the stories of the patriarchs Gen 35:11; 47:27; 28:3; 48:4; all passages belong to P and all are concerned with the promise of increase to the patriarchs. They occur again in Ex 1:7 (P) in the introduction to the story of the people of Israel. This is not a promise but a report: God's promise of increase to the patriarchs begins to be effective in Egypt. The formula serves P as a link between parts of his work: the blessing of living beings at the creation, the promise of increase to the patriarchs, the beginning of the story of the people. Lev 26:9 (P) belongs to the same context where P uses the formula again in the blessing and curse which seals the law; the permanence of the blessing is bound to the obedience of the people.

All these passages belong to P. Outside of P the formula occurs only in three exilic passages, Jer 3:16; 23:3; Ezek 36:11, which promise an increase to the people after their restoration and renewal. This is a deliberate addition to the function which the formula has in P.

The two verbs occur often in the context of blessing: פרה, e.g., Ps 128:3, רבה Ps 107:38: "By his blessing they multiply greatly," or Deut 30:16: ". . . then you shall live and multiply, and the lord your God will bless you in the land. . . ." The verbs occur often in the prophets in the context of the promise of a blessing.

The word "fill" מלאו is the third word that explains the blessing. All three occur in Gen 1:22, 28; 9:1. Fertility and increase point to abundance; abundance belongs to blessing; abundance, wealth and plenty are both signs and the effect of blessing. It is essential to the understanding of God's blessing and its effectiveness to recall that it is the experience of those who are speaking here that abundance, wealth and plenty are very positive; there is not as yet any indication that they can be dangerous. It is only later that the situation changes. Up to the time of P the blessing shows itself effective in growth, increase and plenty without any limitation, and such abundance can only be the effect of blessing. Finally abundance and plenty are part of the picture of the "end time."

[1:24-25] *The Creation of the Land Animals*

Literature: M.L. Henry, "Das Tier im religiösen Bewusstsein des Alttestamentlichen Menschen," SGV 220/1, 1958.

The Structure: It is easy to distinguish here an action-account v. 25 and command-account v. 24. The creation command of v. 24 "let the earth bring forth. . . ." concludes with the phrase "and it was so." V. 25 begins "and God made. . . ."; it is independent and does not presume v. 24. Vv. 24 and 25 then present two completely independent descriptions of the creation of the land animals. But "the slight differences in the command-account . . . and action-account . . . offer but little for purposes of comparison" (W.H. Schmidt, p. 125). When listening to them one scarcely notices that these two successive verses are saying exactly the same thing because P, with great stylistic skill, has been able to differentiate the two. V. 24 is comprehensive, inclusive and unifying. V. 25 subdivides and ennumerates. This is achieved by using on the one hand the general expression נפש חיה at the beginning of v. 24, as in v. 21, and including the three kinds of animals in the expression למינה, and on the other in v. 25 by subdividing the kinds of animals on each occasion by the words למינהו, למינה respectively. The listener has the impression that v. 24 is giving an account of the creation of the animals as a whole, and v. 25 of the different kinds of animals. The subtlety of the composition appears in the preservation of what has been handed down, and that of the style in the construction of a unity out of such diversity.

It is notable that there is no blessing. However it is not excluded as P has been forced for stylistic reasons to combine the creation of the land animals and of humans into one day. It is possible too that the text has been disturbed (H. Gunkel allows for both possibilities). The double introduction to v. 28 is stylistically awkward: "And God blessed them, and God said to them. . . ." It is possible that the introduction to the blessing over the animals which is missing here is contained in one of the two sentences. It is possible too that P has deliberately used the blessing formula "God blessed" only three times, 1:22, 28; 2:3: "The deliberate use of ויברך only three times sheds light on all sides" (F. Delitzsch, 1872[4], ad. loc.). "As the fish and the birds which were created on the same day received only one blessing, so too on the sixth day animals and humans received only one" (V. Zapletal, 1911, ad. loc.); likewise A. Dillmann, U. Cassuto; cf. also W.H. Schmidt 147. The only explanation that is excluded is that while the fish, the birds and people were blessed by God, the land animals were not because these are included in the blessing of 8:17.

[1:24] "Let the earth bring forth." The earth has part in the creation of the land animals just as it does in the creation of the plants. But the expressions used are different (v. 11: "Let the earth green forth fresh green"; v. 12: "And the earth greened forth"). One should not press these differences. When P says "Let the earth bring forth" in v. 24, then that cannot mean a direct participation of the earth in the creation of the animals — there is no sign of this in the action-account — but only that the animals belong to the earth. The earth with its variety of formations, surfaces and structures provides the living conditions for the different species of animals. We can say that certain formations bring forth certain fauna. The sentence means something like that (so too F. Delitzsch, 1872[4], ad. loc.). The mythical view that the earth gives birth to the animals, which occurs in a number of cosmogonies, is well in the background (cf. H. Gunkel ad. loc.).

[1:25] The kinds of animals are not described in exactly the same way in each verse; v. 24: 1. בהמה 2. רמש 3. חיתו־ארץ; v. 25: 1. חית הארץ 2. בהמה 3. כל־רמש האדמה. The differences in order and formulation are not important. One can conclude that a definite order was not part of the tradition that came down to P. There is a tendency to classify and order that runs through Gen 1 which did not belong to the original creation stories. It comes from a systematizing or even a scientific attitude which is concerned with ordering the parts of a whole. Gen 2:19 narrates the creation of the animals very differently. The land animals here are called simply כל־חית השדה, and the narrator is not interested in the animals themselves but in their significance for people. Moreover Gen 2:19 shows that the creation of the animals was not, in the earlier stages, part of a creation story where everything created was arranged systematically, as in Gen 1, but was either part of the story of the creation of humans or was an independent story. Systematization and classification belong to a later stage; the three different kinds of land animals do not represent a stereotyped grouping which was part of tradition, but rather a tentative attempt to divide the animals into their principal kinds. This is the only way to explain why J in 2:19 describes the land animals as חית השדה, while P uses חית הארץ for the same.

[1:26-28] The Creation of Human Beings

Literature: J. Boehmer, "Wieviel Menschen sind am letzten Tage des Hexaëmerons geschaffen worden?," ZAW 34 (1914) 31-35. F. Strothmann, *Die Anschauung von der Weltschöpfung im AT und in der ägyptischen, babylonisch-assyrischen und phönizischen Religion,* Kap. III: "Die Eigenart des alttestamentlichen Gedankens von der Erschaffung des Menschen, Diss. Münster, 1932. H. Junker, "Der Mensch im AT," *Festschrift*

Tillmann, 1934. D. Buzy, "Le concordisme prehistorique ou la fin du concordisme," *Melanges Podechard*, 1945, 17-26. Ch. Hauret, *Origine de l'univers et de l'homme d'apres la Bible* Genese I-III, 1950, 1953⁴. G. Pidoux, "L'homme dans l'AT Anthropologie religieuse," Numen Suppl 2 1955. P. Winter, "Ṣadoqite Fragments IV 20, 21 and the Exegesis of Genesis 1:27 in late Judaism," ZAW 68 (1956) 71-84. N. Walker, "Do Plural Nouns of Majesty Exist in Hebrew?," VT 7 (1957) 208. J. de Fraine, *The Bible and the Origin of Man*, 1962. W. Helck, "Urkunden der 18, Dynastie," UÄA 17-22, 1961. G. Cooke, "The Sons of (the) God(s) (Gen 1:26-27)," ZAW 76 (1964) 22-47. F. Vattioni, "La sapienza e la formazione del corpo umano (Gen 1:26)," Aug. 6 (1966) 317-323. For further Literature see excursus to exegesis of 1:26-27. For 1:28-29, J. Milgrom, "The Biblical Diet Laws as an Ethical System," Interp. 17 (1963) 288-301.

The second work of the sixth day stands apart from what has gone before both by its length and the solemn introduction "Let us make man. . . ." The reason for this is found in the history of tradition, as will be shown later. The creation of humans was once an independent narrative and became part of the story of the creation of the world only at a late stage. This independence has left its traces not only in the introduction but also in the structure: "By way of exception, the command-account is linked to the action-account as a critical interpretation of the latter and cannot be separated from it" (W.H. Schmidt, p. 128). The most striking feature of the creation of humans, and in this it differs markedly from the other works of creation, is that it is not described as creation by the word. A further difference is that the judgment expressed in v. 31 is not directed to the creation of people, but to everything. The pattern which frames the other works of creation is not to the fore here.

The structure is important. Vv. 29-30 add the provision of nourishment for humans with the same provision for the animals in v. 30. Vv. 26-29 are divided as follows:

26ai	Introduction (as in the preceding works)
26aiib	Decision to create people together with their determination
27	Creation of humans with two more detailed characteristics
28	Blessing of humans and the commission (28b corresponds to 26b)
29	Provision for the people

"Let us make . . . and God created" correspond to "God said — and it was so. . . ." of the other works of creation. However, the emphasis is not on this but on a number of details which are added both to the decision itself and to its execution. Attention is on the creation of people as such, on how and to what purpose God created them. The narrative gives the impression that it is not just a free flowing story but that it achieves its effect from juxtaposition. The manner and purpose of humanity's creation are relatively independent elements. This is highlighted by the repetitions: the details "in our image, after our likeness" v. 26 occur again when the decision is put into effect, "in his own image, in the image of God" v. 27. Dominion over the animals is part of the divine decree, v. 26, and also forms part of the blessing, v. 28. If the repetitions were omitted the text would read: let us make man in our image, like us! And God created humankind, he created it man and woman. And God blessed humanity and spoke to it: Be fruitful and multiply and fill the earth! And subdue it . . . and God said behold I have given you. . . . P goes to great pains here to repeat and to emphasize and thus gives us some insight into his attitude to the traditional material that has come to him as well as into his concern to underscore what he thinks to be theologically relevant.

[1:26-27] *The Decision.* "Then God said, let us make man. . . ." The new introduction is God's decision to create human beings and most interpreters understand the words as the expression of this decision. W.H. Schmidt understands them as an announcement: "V. 26 is the announcement of an action" p. 127. But an announcement would only have meaning if there were an audience present to which it could be made. Even if the plural is referred to the heavenly court, one could scarcely expect P to allow a group of minor gods to participate in such a way that the creation of humans had to be announced to them. Both of the Akkadian parallels which W.H. Schmidt quotes show clearly that it is a question of a decision. The creation of humanity begins with a decision in Enuma Elish (Tablet VI, 5-8, ANET 68). An Assyrian text reads:

> What are we to change, what are we to create?
> O Annunaki, you great gods,
> What are we to change, what are we to create?

And the answer comes:

> We will slay Lamga, the double (deity),
> We will create mankind from its blood. . . . AOT 135

Other examples have been given in the introduction, (3,A. Creation Narratives). The motif of a decision to create humans occurs also in the primitive creation narratives. Each context shows that the decision is concerned with the significance of the creation of humans (A. Heidel, *The Babylonian Genesis,* pp. 118-122). There is a fixed and widespread pattern behind this that refers to the special destiny of humanity (see below, Excursus). One could also say that there is here a distant, and probably older, parallel to the description of the creation of people by the word; people were not created by the word, but their creation stems from the decision of the creator; and so P could not use his formula, "God said: let there be. . . ." in Gen 1:26.

The explanations of the plural, "Let us make man," may be summarized as follows:

(1) It was often explained in the early church as an expression of the Trinity, the threefold God (G.T. Armstrong, *Die Genesis in der alten Kirche,* 1962, pp. 39, 69f., 132 n. 1); but that is a dogmatic judgment, which is echoed in Karl Barth, *Church Dogmatics,* III/1, pp. 191ff.

(2) It is God together with the heavenly court. This is suggested not only by the Babylonian parallels (cf. the dialogue in the texts already cited), but also in the description of a heavenly court in the Old Testament: 1 Kings 22:19; Job 1:6f.; 2:1f.; 38:7; etc. Is 6:8 is alleged as a parallel to Gen 1:26: "Whom shall I send, and who will go for us?" There may be a distant connection: so J.P. Gabler, *Neuer Versuch* 1795, 35-37; also *Urgeschichte I,* 1790, 217ff., n. 25 (quoted in W.H. Schmidt); then H. Gunkel, A. Alt, KS 1, 351ff., G. von Rad, W. Zimmerli and many other exegetes. But it is impossible that P should have

understood the plural in this way, not only because he was not familiar with the idea of a heavenly court, but also because of his insistence on the uniqueness of Yahweh, besides whom there could be no other heavenly being. Angels or any sort of intermediary beings are found nowhere in P.

(3) It is also highly questionable theologically that the plural is used so as to avoid the idea of any immediate resemblance of humans to God (W. Eichrodt, *Theology of the Old Testament*, 2, 1966, pp. 120ff.; H. Gross, *Festschrift H. Junker*, 1961, 94ff.; G. von Rad, *Old Testament Theology*, 2, 1965, pp. 67ff.), or because P wants to avoid the first person singular if God is not revealing himself (A. Dillmann, L. Köhler and others).

(4) The grammatical construction is a plural of deliberation, Ges-K §124f, n. 3; Joüon, §114e; E. König, Comm. ad. loc.; H. Junker, Comm.: "Typical of the deliberative style." The plural of majesty does not occur in Hebrew (cf. Joüon, §114e), so this older explanation has been completely abandoned today; it occurs only in Ezra 4:18. In favor of a plural of deliberation in 1:26 is the fact that in Is 6:8 the plural and the singular are used in the same sentence with the same meaning; similarly in 2 Sam 24:14 where it is a question of one and the same conclusion: ". . . Let us fall into the hand of the Lord . . . but let me not fall into the hand of man." C. Brockelmann describes the cohortative as "a form of speech which occurred primarily in self-deliberation" (*Grundriss der vergleichenden Grammatik der semitischen Sprachen II*, 24, 14a; W.H. Schmidt 130 n. 3; U. Cassuto p. 55: "Plural of exhortation"). A clear example of this type of deliberation occurs in Gen 11:7: "Come let us go down. . . ." (the continuation in v. 8 is in the singular). L. Köhler, ThZ 4 (1948) 21, has shown that this usage perseveres right down to the present day.

J.J. Stamm concludes in his account of the state of the question in 1956 (*Festschrift K. Barth*, 1956, 84-98) that there is unanimity that the plural of Gen 1:26 refers to the heavenly beings which surround God, p. 92. W.H. Schmidt however is of a different opinion in his survey, p. 128ff.; we agree with him substantially. The idea of a heavenly court may well be in the background; however it is not necessary for the explanation and P could not have intended it to be so. The plural of deliberation in the cohortative is an attested and sufficient explanation.

בצלמנו כדמותנו 1. *The Prepositions.* Early attempts to distinguish between ב and כ have been given up. K.L. Schmidt presents a good summary of the situation ("Homo Imago Dei im Alten und Neuen Testament," Er. 15 [1947] 165-169). He remarks, p. 168 n. 17: "W. Baumgartner. . . .is convinced that ב and כ have the same meaning in Gen 1:26" and refers to A. Kropat (BZAW 16, 1909, 39): "The preposition ב is often used in place of כ in the later period to mean 'according to' or 'like'." This is in accordance with the Gk and Vg which use only one preposition, κατά and *ad* respectively. The prepositions are freely interchanged in the passages in Genesis, 1:26, 27; 5:1, 3; 9:6. The preposition ב cannot be limited to ב-*essentiae;* the translation must use words very similar in meaning such as "after, according to." It is in accordance with the sense to render both prepositions in the same way. Both the nouns and the prepositions are interchangeable (cf. the table in W.H. Schmidt p. 165); one verb covers both phrases, כדמותנו and בצלמנו; we have not two but one expression. Even though צלם and דמות have each its own proper meaning, nevertheless the fact that they are interchangeable (both nouns are used, now the one and now the other) shows clearly that we have here one expression which further determines the creation of humans. There is widespread agreement about this today.

2. *The Nouns: a)* צלם. Cf. the detailed study of P. Humbert, *Études sur le récit. . . ,* 153ff. L. Köhler has extended this study by considering the roots in the different Semitic languages, "Die Grundstelle der Imago-Dei-Lehre, Gen 1:26," ThZ 4 (1948) 16-22. In most cases the word means "sculpture, plastic image, statue" (1 Sam 6:5, 11; 2 Kings 11:18; 2 Chron 23:17). It is used too to signify images of the gods (Ezek 7:20; Amos 5:26; Num 33:52 molten images). The meaning in Ezek 16:17 is an image of the gods made in a human likeness; the same is true of 1 Sam 6:5, 11 and Ezek 23:14, images of the Chaldeans. P. Humbert summarizes his findings as follows: "In conclusion all the Old Testament passages understand צלם solely in the sense of a material image, a concrete representation, without any spiritual or moral dimension," p. 157. But one can justly ask if the nuance contained in this conclusion is really in the text. I do not think that the text is concerned with the corporeal or spiritual aspects as such, but rather with the portrayal of something. I think it is dangerous to render צלם simply by "material image" (l'effigie extérieure). The meaning is more that of concrete representation. So too W.H. Schmidt: ". . . the word does not have to be restricted to 'material form,' but rather means a 'representation'," p. 133, n. 1. צלם is not the technical term for an image of god although it can have that meaning in some places.

If צלם is understood primarily as image or representation, then the two difficult passages Pss 39:7 and 73:20 (shade, outline) are accounted for and there is no need to derive the word from another root as does P. Humbert (W.H. Schmidt: ". . . as the shadow reflects an object"); so too M. Buber according to K.L. Schmidt: "If the basic meaning of *ṣelem* is reflection or representation, then there is no need to look for a second root," op. cit., p. 171, n. 19. The meaning "representation" holds for all places independent of the root, which remains uncertain. Most interpreters derive the word for a verb צלם, "cut, cut off"; but it does not occur in Hebrew. The earlier derivation, which had been rejected for the most part, from צל "shade," (with ם added to the stem) has been proposed again by A.S. Marmardji, *La lexicographie arabe à la lumière du bilittéralisme et de la philologie sémitique,* 1937, 193ff. (Arabic; Review F. Rosenthal, Or NS 8 [1939] 148-150); see also W. von Soden, "Grundriss der akkad, Grammatik," AnOr 33 (1952) 96, §73b.

b) דמות The derivation of this word is clear: it is an abstract formation from the verb דמה "to be like" (the verb and the noun occur side-by-side in Is 40:18) and means "that which is like something, likeness, representation" (in 2 Kings 16:10 it means the replica of an altar). It is often said that דמות is a weakening of the word צלם; but this cannot be demonstrated from the way in which the words are used. When the word is translated by "likeness," as is possible in some passages, it should not be understood as if the meaning were: not the same, but only like. The Hebrew word does not carry this attenuating sense. The word is used in Hebrew only when something is compared with something else. It can have the same meaning as צלם: 2 Chron 4:3, (representations of wild cucumbers), corresponds exactly to 1 Sam 6:5, 11; Ezek 23:14 describes the representations of the Babylonians by צלם, and v. 15 by דמות. The word can be used for a comparison as in Ps 58:5, "like the venom of a serpent."

146

Ezekiel finds the word particularly apt to explain his vision. Of the nineteen passages where it occurs, twelve are found in Ezekiel, seven elsewhere. Ezekiel uses the word with many shades of meaning which fluctuate between "representation" and "something which is like."

Excursus: *The History of the Exegesis of Gen 1:26-27.*

Literature: Th. Nöldeke, "צלמות and צלם," ZAW 17 (1897) 183-187. W. Riedel, "Die Gottesebenbildlichkeit des Menschen," *Alttestamentliche Untersuchungen I* (1902) 42-47. A. Struker, *Die Gottesebenbildlichkeit des Menschen in der christl. Literatur der ersten zwei Jahrhunderte. Ein Beitrag zur Geschichte u. Exegese von Gen 1:26* (1913). J. Hehn, "Zum Terminus 'Bild Gottes'," *Festschr E. Sachau* (1915) 36-52. F.K. Schumann, "Imago Dei," *Festschr G. Krüger "Imago Dei," Beitr. zur theol. Anthropologie* (1932) 167-180. B. Jacob, *Das erste Buch der Tora, Genesis* (1934). W. Vischer, *Das Christuszeugnis des AT,* I (1934; 1946[7]). J. Hempel, "Gott und Mensch im AT," BWANT III, 2 (1936[2]). F.K. Schumann, *Vom Geheimnis der Schöpfung (Creator spiritus und imago dei)* (1937). J. Hempel, *Das Ethos des AT,* BZAW 67 (1938; 1964[2]). E. Osterloh, *Die Gottesebenbildlichkeit des Menschen,* ThViat (1939) 9-32. P. Humbert, "Etudes sur le recit. . . , L'imago Dei dans l'AT," *Mémoires de l'Université de Neuchâtel* 14 (1940) 153-165. G. von Rad, "Vom Menschenbild des AT," *Der alte und der neue Mensch,* Evth Beitr. 8 (1942) 5-23. T.C. Vriezen, "La création de l'homme d'après l'image de Dieu," OTS 2 (1943) 87-105. K. Galling, "Das Bild vom Menschen in biblischer Sicht," Mainzer Univ. Reden 3 (1947) 11-12. L. Köhler, "Die Grundstelle der Imago-Dei-Lehre, Genesis 1:26," ThZ 4 (1948) 16-22. K.L. Schmidt, "Homo Imago Dei im AT," ErJb 15 (1947) 149-195. S. Mowinckel, "Urmensch und 'Königsideologie'," StTh 2 (1948) 71-89. J. Giblet, "L'homme image de Dieu dans les commentaires littéraires de Philon d'Alexandrie," StHell 5 (1948) 93-118. Hvd Bussche, "L'homme créé à l'image de Dieu (Gen 1:26-27)," CBrug 31 (1948) 185-195. W. Zimmerli, *Das Menschenbild des AT,* TEH NF 14 (1949). F. Horst, "Face to face. The Biblical Doctrine of the Image of God," Interp. 4 (1950). A Bentzen-E. Sjöberg, "'Adam' og 'Menneskenne'," SvTK 27 (1951) 166-168. P.N. Bratsiotis, "Genesis 1:26 in der orthodoxen Théologie," EvTh 11 (1951/52) 289-297. W. Rudolph, "Das Menschenbild des AT," *Festgabe H. Schreiner, "Dienst unter dem Wort,"* (1953) 238-251. V. Maag, "Sumerische und babylonische Mythen von der Erschaffung der Menschen," AsSt 8 (1954) 85-106; "Alttestamentliche Anthropologie in ihrem Verhältnis zur orientalischen Mythologie," AsSt 9 (1955) 15-44. M. Buber, *Der Mensch und sein Gebild* (1955). E. Lussier, "Adam in Genesis 1:1-4:24," CBQ 18 (1956) 137-139. K-H Bernhardt, *Gott und Bild,* ThA 2 (1956). J.J. Stamm, "Die Imago-Lehre von Karl Barth und die theologischen Wissenschaften," *Festschr. K. Barth* (1956) 84-98. E. Jacob, "Le thème de l'Imago Dei dans l'AT," *Congress of the Orientalists Bol. II* (1957) 583-585. S.E. Löwenstamm, "Man as Image and Son of God," Tarb 27 (1957) 1-2. I. Engnell, "Die Urmenschvorstellung und das AT," SEÅ 22-23 (1958) 265-269. P. Humbert, "Trois notes sur Genèse 1, Kap II: L'image de Dieu'," OH (1958) 196-198. B. Hessler, "Die literarische Form der biblischen Urgeschichte," WiWie 21 (1958) 188-207; 22 (1959) 28/42. J.J. Stamm, "Die Gottesebenbildlichkeit des Menschen im AT," ThSt 54 (1959) 81-90. A.M. Dubarle, "La conception de l'homme dans l'AT," *Sacra Pagina, Congress Vol. I* (1959) 583-585. P.G. Duncker, "L'imagine di Dio nell'uomo (Gen 1:26-27). Una somiglianza fissica?," Bib 40 (1959) 384-392. J. Jevell, *Imago Dei. Gen 1:26f. im Spätjudentum, in der Gnosis und in den paulinischen Briefen,* FRLANT 76 NF 58 (1960). C. Westermann, *Der Schöpfungsbericht vom Anfang der Bibel,* EwH 30 (1960; 1966[5]). H. Müller, "La creacion del hombre segun Gen 1:26-30 y 2:5-7, 9, 10, 15," RevBib 22 (1960) 121-127. H. Gross, "Die Gottesebenbildlichkeit des Menschen," *Festschr. H. Junker, "Lex tua veritas"* (1961) 89-100. A. Kruyswijk, *"Geen gesneden beeld. . . ." (1962).* W.H. Schmidt, *Die Schöpfungsgeschichte der Priesterschrift,* Kap. III B 9: "Das achte Schöpfungswerk: die Menschen. Gen 1:26-28," WMANT 17 (1964) 127-148. F. Festorazzi, "L'uomo immagine di Dio," BeO 6 (1964) 105-117. H. Wildberger, "Das Abbild Gottes, Gen 1:26-30," ThZ 21 (1965) 245-259, 481-501. P. Bordreuil, "'A l'ombre d'Elohim'. Le thème de l'ombre protectrice dans l'Ancien Orient et ses rapports avec 'L'Imago Dei'," RHPhR 46 (1966) 368-391. E. Brunner, *Der*

Mensch im Widerspruch (1937).   E. Schlink, *Gottes Ebenbild als Gesetz und Evangelium,* EvTh Beitr. 8 (1942) 68-87.   K. Barth, CD III/1 (1958).   P. Brunner, *Der Ersterschaffene als Gottes Ebenbild,* EvTh 11 (1951/52) 298-310 = GesAufs (1962) 85-95.   G.T. Armstrong, *Die Genesis in der alten Kirche. Die drei Kirchenväter* (1962).   E. Schlink, "Die biblische Lehre vom Ebenbilde Gottes," *Festgabe Erzbischof Jäger, Bischof Stählin, "Pro Veritate"* (1963) 1-23.   G. Söhngen, "Die biblische Lehre von der Gottesebenbildlichkeit des Menschen," *Festgabe Erzbischof Jäger, Bischof Stählin, "Pro Veritate"* (1963) 23-57.

The following remarks may serve as an introduction to this survey: 1. Since biblical interpretation came in contact with Greek thought and the modern understanding of humanity, scarcely any passage in the whole of the Old Testament has retained such interest as the verse which says that God created the person according to his image. The literature is limitless. The main interest has been on what is being said theologically about humankind: what is a human being? What is striking is that one verse about the person, almost unique in the Old Testament, has become the center of attention in modern exegesis, whereas it has no such significance in the rest of the Old Testament and, apart from Ps 8, does not occur again. This interest does not derive from the Bible itself but from certain presuppositions in the spiritual order which we cannot overlook.

2. There is another striking fact: this interest has been confined almost exclusively to the area of church doctrine from Irenaeus to Karl Barth. Specialists in Old Testament studies have taken up the discussion only since the end of the 19th century, and its effects for theology as a whole are not yet known. Though the way has been opened for dialogue between these two disciplines, New Testament research remains uninterested. And this is all the more surprising as one of the most notable characteristics of New Testament studies in recent decades has been its interest in anthropology. One point on which scholars are agreed is that according to the Old Testament the person's "likeness-to-God" was not lost with the "fall," but remained part of humanity. How does this relate to those passages in the New Testament that speak of the person before and apart from Christ? The neglect of this question by New Testament scholarship can be taken to indicate the state of theology as a whole. J.J. Stamm *(Festschrift Karl Barth),* and W.H. Schmidt have described the more recent history of research in this area. The former concentrates on the main lines of the discussion, while the latter is concerned more with compassing the literature. These surveys allow us to separate the following groups:

1. *A distinction is made between the natural and supernatural likeness to God,* based in part on the different names used in Gen 1:26: "Irenaeus was the first to distinguish clearly between *imago* and *similitudo*" (P. Bratsiotis, p. 290). This distinction goes right through the east and the west, perseveres throughout the whole of the Middle Ages, and occurs again in the Orthodox Church. It has scarcely left a trace in Protestant theology, apart from F. Delitzsch in the 19th century and its rather faint-hearted reintroduction by E. Osterloh in the 20th; it predominates in Catholic theology. Orthodox theology has tried to overcome the distinction: "Intellect and freedom (the main element in the image of God in man) have been brought together in this striving after God (Basil) and thereby the distinction between image and likeness has been overcome" (P. Bratsiotis, p. 297). Traces of the distinction are rare in Protestant theology (E. Schlink, p. 85); it has been widely rejected; the most radical is Karl Barth. Catholic theology (not Catholic exegesis) however has retained it but in a form that differs from the classical teaching which found the distinction in Gen 1:26f.: "Catholic teaching sees the person's natural likeness to God expressed in the Old Testament, one's supernatural likeness above all in the New Testament. . . . Catholic teaching refers Gen 1:26a and 27 to a person's natural likeness to God . . . it consists in the spiritual nature of the human being" (G. Söhngen, p. 23f.). The supernatural likeness of the person to God in the New Testament is based now on the sentence: "Christ is the image of God"; this refers to the Christ-image. So the classical

teaching of the natural and supernatural likeness of human beings to God, according to which humans were created in Gen 1:26f., is abandoned. It is generally acknowledged that Gen 1:26f. is not speaking of a distinction between the natural and the supernatural and that such talk about the person does not accord with the Old Testament. There is unanimity in the abandonment of the distinction.

2. The likeness to God consists in *spiritual qualities or capacities*. We have here a line of interpretation that distinguishes a natural from a supernatural likeness, insofar as the natural likeness consists in spiritual qualities or capacities. This interpretation appears first in its fully developed form in Philo: ἡ δὲ εἰκὼν λέλεκται κατὰ τὸν τῆς ψυχῆς ἡγεμόνα νοῦν (Opificium mundi 69); one can see here a very strong philosophical influence. The explanation given by Philo was taken up in the early church both in the east and in the west, again under the influence of the philosophers, as the "natural image of God." This explanation has appeared in very different forms right down to the present day and is most certainly the commonest explanation of the passage in question. For Augustine, this likeness consists in the power of the soul, in the memory, intellect and will, an explanation which is very like to that of the 19th century, and which is found in all theological schools which take up the text.

A Jewish writer understands the image and likeness of God as "spiritual capacities and a duly instituted ruler of noble qualities" (B. Jacob, p. 59); a Greek Orthodox theologian: "We understand the likeness to the divine in a person to consist mainly in human intellect and freedom" (P. Bratsiotis); a Roman Catholic dogmatic theologian: "It is the spiritual nature of human beings that really puts them in the image and likeness of God" (G. Söhngen, p. 26). For the Protestant Schleiermacher it is "a religious and moral personal life." More recent Old Testament interpreters find the likeness in personality, understanding, the will and its freedom, self-consciousness, intelligence, spiritual being, spiritual superiority, the immortality of the soul, e.g., A. Dillmann, E. König, O. Procksch, E. Sellin, W. Eichrodt, P. Heinisch, J. Junker, H. Gross and numerous others such as F. Ceuppens, H. Müller and G. Fohrer.

3. The image and likeness of God is seen *in the external form*. This interpretation occurs only occasionally among the older writers (Th. Nöldeke, ZAW 17 (1897) 186, to which W.H. Schmidt refers); A. Dillmann makes it dependent on the spiritual interpretation (cf. the citation above: "It is the very spiritual nature of this being that confers external nobility and dignity . . . the corporeal form is the expression and instrument of the spirit, and is not to be separated from the spiritual nature. . ."). H. Gunkel takes a quite different nature, basing his explanation on Gen 5:3, which can be understood of appearance or external form, and on the anthropomorphic way in which the Old Testament describes God when he is clearly presented in human guise. He says: "The first human being is like God in form and appearance." G. von Rad follows him: "The likeness of the person to God is to be understood in a predominantly corporeal sense," and W. Zimmerli: "There is no getting around the fact that this first expression intends a real external relationship. The human form is an image of the divine form."

The majority of those who hold this view do not hold it in an exclusive sense, as indicated by the cautious way in which von Rad speaks of the matter and by his later remark that one should not separate the spiritual and the corporeal. Gunkel too writes: "The image and likeness of God is concerned primarily with the human body but by no means in such a way as to exclude the spiritual." The study of P. Humbert however seemed to have come down definitively on the side of the external form. After a thorough study of the nouns used in Gen 1:26f., which L. Köhler extended later to other Semitic languages, he comes to the conclusion that the person is created "avec la même physique que la divinité, qu'il en est une effigie concrète et plastique, figurée et extérieure." This study has exercised a marked influence. L. Köhler, who in his *Old Testament Theology* (1957) p. 147 had earlier supported the view that the passage referred to human dominion over the animals, was convinced by Humbert's thesis, and took it further to refer to the person's upright carriage (this occurs too in the Rabbinic exegesis). J.J. Stamm considers that Humbert's study in 1940 was an important advance in the history of exegetical research. He writes: "Since 1940 there is substantial agreement among the great majority of exegetes that what is proper to the *Imago* is best described by the external likeness" p. 88.

Nevertheless there has been an increasing opposition to Humbert's onesided thesis similar to that which had been raised against Gunkel's thesis. K. Galling, e.g., rejects the isolation of the corporeal form; that would be "too great an assimilation of God to human categories" (p. 11). A.M. Dubarle, p. 526f., takes up an earlier thesis, proposed e.g., by W. Eichrodt in his *Theology of the Old Testament*, Vol. 2 (1965), pp. 118f., namely that an earlier stage of the tradition could well have intended a physical likeness, but that such would be too crass an anthropomorphism for P himself. G. Duncker sharply rejects any physical likeness for similar reasons. H. Wildberger, p. 248f., also advances a list of reasons why the external form alone could not have been intended. J.J. Stamm, who had given prominence to Humbert's thesis, concludes "that Gen 5:3 . . . intends something internal as well as external"; "The idea of relationship to God imposes itself on the phrase 'image and likeness of God', because it embraces at the same time an external dimension and, closely linked with it, an internal, spiritual dimension which says something about what it is," p. 98. All these objections or reservations are a clear sign that the last word has not yet been spoken.

4. The criticisms or reservations expressed above about Humbert's thesis have not led to any clear statement on the matter. However, T.C. Vriezen and others have raised a very telling objection: the Old Testament knows nothing at all of a separation of a person's spiritual and corporeal components; it sees the person as a whole. "It looks to the totality of the human being embracing not only its corporeal but also its spiritual capacities" (Vriezen, p. 99; A. Dillmann had come to the same conclusion by other means). G. von Rad too, despite his emphasis on the corporeal aspect, writes: "Therefore, one will do well to split the physical from the spiritual as little as possible: the whole person is created in God's image," p. 58. F.K. Schumann had written: "The *Imago Dei* does not consist in any particular detail of the person but describes the human being as a whole without limiting itself to anything taken in isolation." We are on firm ground here. The discussion whether the image and likeness of God referred to the corporeal or the spiritual aspect of the person has brought us to the conclusion that the question has been placed incorrectly. Gen 1:26f. is concerned neither with the corporeal nor with the spiritual qualities of people; it is concerned only with the person as a whole. And so the discussion among the Old Testament exegetes agrees with one of the main theses of the systematic theologian Karl Barth: "It does not consist in anything that man is or does. It consists as man himself consists as the creature of God. He would not be man if he were not the image of God. He is the image of God in the fact that he is man," CD III/1, 184).

If one agrees with this then the discussion is closed. The following have expressed agreement with this sentence of Barth's: J.J. Stamm, (even though somewhat hesitant), F. Horst and apparently K.L. Schmidt. W.H. Schmidt writes: "The most recent exegesis has managed to pry the phrase "in the image and likeness of God" free from an idea foreign to the Old Testament, namely the separation of the corporeal and the spiritual," p. 136. There can now be basic agreement that when Gen 1:26 talks of the image and likeness of God, it envisages the whole person, and not just the corporeal or the spiritual side.

5. *The person as God's counterpart*. The correction that Barth advanced is linked with an explanation of Gen 1:26f. already known but given thereby further support. "The image and likeness of God" describes the special nature of human existence by virtue of which the person can take a stand before God; . . . a human being is one whom God can address as "You" and an "I" who is responsible before God. Barth speaks too of "partnership" (CD III/1, 182ff.).

J.J. Stamm follows this line; he confirms that what the Old Testament in general says about humanity agrees with this: ". . . a human being is regarded as God's counterpart, as the 'You' who must listen to God, whom God questions and who must answer him . . . following the Old Testament one is correct in agreeing with Karl Barth that the basic meaning of the *Imago Dei* is that of partnership, of ability to enter into relationship" (1959, p. 19). The explanation which F. Horst gives is almost the same; he too is speaking in the context of agreement with Barth: "When he speaks of human existence he is not speaking of a quality in the person, or of something which the person, cut off from God, can dispose of, or of something or other which might be counted among one's possessions. He is speaking rather of human existence as blessed by God, who in his sovereign freedom has ruled that the human being alone out of all creatures is to be his counterpart and to correspond to him, and with whom he will speak and share and who in turn must talk to him and live 'in his presence' (lit: before his face)," p. 230f.

This conception of the image and likeness of God is not new. It is found in a study by W. Riedel, *Die Gottesebenbildlichkeit des Menschen,* 1902: "It consists in this, that God and human beings can have dealings with each other, that God can speak to humans and that they can understand him and answer him, in short in their disposition toward religion," p. 42. It occurs too in F.K. Schumann p. 177, W. Vischer, K. Galling, K. Krieger p. 265f., P. Brunner as a Systematic theologian p. 305f., W. Rudolph p. 248, C. Westermann p. 23, B. Hessler.

T.C. Vriezen supports the Barthian thesis that the text is concerned with the person as a whole. This is important for the history of the exegesis: "The human being stands apart from other living beings because of a special relationship to God . . . that of the child toward the father. . . .", "because it is with him alone that God has a direct and personal relationship. . . .this is to sum up in its noblest terms and briefest compass the Old Testament idea of the relationship between God and humanity," pp. 98f., 104.

There is another important voice to be heard which comes to the same conclusion by means of a completely different approach. V. Maag writes as the result of his study of the question in the context of the history of religion: "To say that a human being has been created as a being like God means that a person is capable of entering into a relationship with the creator" (AsSt 9 [1955] 34).

This survey shows that the explanation did not originate with Karl Barth but that it was supported long beforehand and from other points of view. The great influence that Barth's explanation has exercised is due first to the emphasis put on its presupposition, namely that the text was not concerned with something that belonged to humanity, but with humanity itself, and then to the far-reaching effects of the presupposition inasmuch as the history of the study of the text which Barth presented shows that scholars had not yet arrived at that point. Rather than speak of the explanation of Barth one should speak of the particular way in which he proposed his explanation.

6. *The person as representative of God on earth.* The study of H. Hehn, "Zum Terminus 'Bild Gottes'," *Festschrift E. Sachau,* 1915, was the starting-point of an explanation of "the image and likeness of God" that has gained an ever increasing influence in the latest stage of the history of the exegesis of the passage. Hehn studies "the meaning of images among the Babylonians." He showed that the image can stand in the place of the god, that it can even be divinized (the god *ṣalmu*), and that a particular image (*ṣalmu*) can represent some god or other. Accordingly the king can be described as an image of the god, and the images as the representatives and caretakers of the divinity. Hehn referred briefly to the Egyptian description of the king as "image of god." The image of god then is the representative or viceroy of the god.

G. von Rad is one who has taken up this explanation: "As earthly rulers . . . erect images of themselves in the provinces as signs of their presence, so too has God put human beings on earth in his image and likeness as a sign of his majesty" (EvTh Beitr. 8 [1942] 7). The same explanation is given by E. Jacob, p. 583f., and H. van der Bussche,

p. 195: "God created the person as his representative, his vizier, who in some way is like the master. . . ." "The person becomes God's attorney and administers his goods. . . ." So too J. de Fraine, 1959, A. Kruyswijk in his dissertation, 1962, and a number of other authors who mention it in passing. The two most recent studies of the question by H. Wildberger, TZ (1965) 245-259, 481-501, and W.H. Schmidt, WMANT 17, 1964, pp. 127-148, have confirmed this explanation and given it a new dimension by means of a number of Egyptian and Mesopotamian texts which speak of the king as the image of God. Both studies, which were made independently and almost simultaneously, derive the expression "image of God" from the royal ideology of the Ancient Near East: the background of Gen 1:26f. is what Egypt and Mesopotamia say about the king as the image of God. A person as the image of God corresponds to the king as the image of God; both are God's viceroy or representative. It is impressive that two scholars have studied the same comparative texts at almost the same time and have come to the same conclusion about their contribution to the explanation of the biblical texts.

For the sake of clarity we will present the comparative texts and the way in which the conclusion is argued.

The thesis that the description of a person as the "image of God" goes back to the Mesopotamian and Egyptian description of the king as the image of the god is not new. J. Hehn had mentioned a number of appropriate texts in the essay already cited. In his discussion, "Urmensch und 'Königsideologie'," StTh 2 (1948) 71-89, S. Mowinckel says that it is more likely that Gen 1 ". . . has taken this idea (that of the image and likeness of God) from the royal ideology," p. 83. I. Engnell says the same thing in passing. S.E. Löwenstamm, Tarb. 27 (1957) 1-2, developed this as an independent thesis: "This idea developed from the pattern of ancient Oriental thought, in which the king was likened to a god." He quotes a number of texts in which the king is spoken of as the image of God. His judgment on them is different from that of H. Wildberger and W.H. Schmidt: "In pointed contradiction (to the last mentioned evaluation of humanity) the biblical account of creation attributes godliness to the person as such."

Wildberger's starting-point is to note that *ṣelem* is not the usual word for an image of a deity in the Old Testament. The use of *ṣalmu* in Babylonian civilization is the closest non-Israelite source. He quotes a long series of texts in which the king is described as the image of God. He concludes, p. 255: ". . . the places where the king is spoken of as the *ṣalmu* or *muššulu* of his god . . . suggest that Gen 1:26-30 are rooted ultimately in the royal ideology of the Ancient Near East." The vocabulary too of Gen 1:26 reflects the royal tradition, especially the verb רדה. The parallel to Ps 8 shows this even more clearly. Egypt is even richer in texts that describe the king as the image of God. "On a stele of Amenophis II from Amada the Pharaoh is praised as 'the beloved son in bodily form of Re, ...the good god, the creature of Re, the ruler. . . .image of Horus on the throne of his father, mighty in power. . . .'", p. 485. "'Image'. . . .in a later period this was found to be an adequate expression of the relationship of the king and the god; it became very influential," p. 485. "This assures us that the context of Gen 1:26 is that of the royal ideology of the Ancient Near East," p. 488. Usage clarifies the meaning: "The image of God is always some sort of representation of the God himself." The divinity is present in the king. The explanation of Gen 1:26b is then: "A person is. . . .the representative of God."

W.H. Schmidt summarizes the present state of opinions, p. 134f., and underscores the "scandal" caused by Barth's view. He supports the intention to do away with the distinction corporal-spiritual. The difficulty remains however that the text presumes that the meaning of the expression "image of God" is well known. This is best explained if the "image of God" is already a fixed formula. Are there any parallels? Surely not in the Babylonian creation myths. "However the expression occurs often in the Egyptian court style . . . as a fixed formula," p. 137. It is found in the new kingdom particularly in the 18th dynasty: "Image of Re," "holy image of Re," "living image upon earth," "likeness of Re," etc. It is important to note the link between the image of God and creation. Pharaoh is "the glittering image of the Lord of all and a creature of the gods of Heliopolis. . . . Re begot him for himself. . . . : as his own living image," p. 138. Pharaoh says of himself: "I am his son (that is of Osiris), his defender, his likeness, who comes forth from him." The words of Amun to Amenophis III are preserved on a stele: "My living image, creation of my limbs, whom Mut . . . has born to me."

Pharaoh, as the representative of the god on earth, is called "his very image." So in an address of Amon Re to Amenophis III: "Thou art my beloved son, come forth from my limbs, my very own image, which I have put upon the earth. I have permitted thee to rule over the earth in peace," p. 139.

The description of a king as "the very image of the god" is attested also in Mesopotamia. The parallels to Ps 8 make it perfectly clear "that the expression about a person being in the image and likeness of God in Gen 1:26 has its roots in this royal tradition," p. 140.

Both H. Wildberger and W.H. Schmidt base a particular interpretation of the phrase "image and likeness of God" on its derivation from the royal ideology. H. Wildberger writes: "A person is . . . as such (God's image) God's representative. . . . There is only one proper image by means of which God shows himself in the world, and that is humanity." "It cannot be stressed enough that Israel . . . by a daring adaptation of the image theology of the surrounding world, proclaims that a human being is the form in which God himself is present," pp. 495f. W.H. Schmidt writes: "If the phrase means that the king is the living image or representative of God on earth, then wherever the king appears, the divinity appears. So in the Old Testament, wherever a human being is, God is proclaimed. The person represents, attests, God on earth. So the person as such, created by God, is God's witness . . . it is of the nature of an image to allow what it represents to appear; so where the person appears, God also appears," p. 144.

But the following objections may be raised against this view:

(a) It makes a lot of sense to speak of the king as taking the place of the deity on earth; the king is God's representative before other people. Representation in this context is concerned with an individual in relation to a community. But this is not possible in the case of "man." "Man" is not an individual, but a species. What can be meant by saying that "man" represents, takes the place of, God on earth? This could only make sense if "man" (i.e., humankind) were to represent God before the rest of creation. But that is certainly not the meaning here. In any case both Wildberger and Schmidt are right when they say that dominion over the rest of creation is the consequence of the image and likeness of God.

(b) Such an explanation scarcely accords with the theology of P. Schmidt writes: "According to the Old Testament wherever a human being is, God is proclaimed," p. 144. But such thinking is entirely foreign to P because his theology is dominated by God's holiness and his revelation of himself only at the holy place. Even if this theology of holiness can have developed only after the construction of the holy place, it is nevertheless inconceivable that P could have meant "wherever a human being appears, there God appears," when he is concerned with presenting a manifestation of the unique holiness of God. God appears in his *kabod,* and that is a manifestation before man, not in man. P could conceive of an appearance, manifestation, or representation of God only as a holy event, completely outside the range of ordinary events. He could not possibly think of a human being as standing in the place of God on earth.

(c) When dealing with the comparative material Wildberger and Schmidt are concerned with the idea "image of God" and not with the creation of humanity in the image of God. The Egyptian and Babylonian parallels are in the context of the former and of the latter. One may ask, should one not look for parallels that are speaking of the same thing, namely of the creation of humanity in the image of God? Wildberger quotes two parallel passages which deal with creation in the image of God, pp. 255 and 489; but he considers neither of them important to the tradition from which he derives the idea contained in Gen 1:26f. However he shows by means of the two passages that the creation of humans in the image of a god occurs in both Egypt and Mesopotamia, but in a context which has nothing to do with the description of the king as the image of God. When such parallels exist, one is obliged, methodologically, to take them as a starting-point.

The parallels from Babylon and Egypt have their limitations. Only the king is described as being in the likeness of God. Nothing at all can be said about humanity in this context (S.G. Löwenstamm among others has emphasized this). And, as Wildberger himself has pointed out, Egypt has not democratized this idea. The instruction of Meri-Ka-Re belongs to another tradition.

Both scholars have shown that the idea "likeness of God" has a fixed place among the predicates applied to the king in Mesopotamia and Egypt. It is possible that there is an echo of this in Gen 1:26f., perhaps in the verb "to exercise dominion" over the animals (it is clearer in Ps 8); but it has not been proved that these royal predicates are the source or the beginning of the tradition of the idea in Gen 1:26f. And so the same problem recurs: it is a question of talk about the creation of humanity in the image of God.

One can well understand why V. Maag, when studying the accounts of the creation of humanity, cites a very different set of texts (e.g., ANET pp. 100, 108), "Sumerische und babylonische Mythen von der Erschaffung des Menschen," AsSt 8 (1954) 85-106. He comes to the conclusion that "whatever the process involved in the application of the divine image to the creature, the human being has been formed in the likeness of a divinity." This is made very clear in the creation of Enkidu in the Gilgamesh Epic (ANET p. 74). And so it is no accident that Maag's study of the pre-history of Gen 1:26f. leads him to conclusions different from those of Wildberger and Schmidt. He writes that "the gods have created their counterpart"; "the deity had to . . . create a counterpart like itself," p. 97.

The whole history of talk about the creation of humanity in the image of a god forces us to look for the explanation of the phrase in this context, despite the many attestations that describe the king as the likeness of God. It is not a question of direct dependence. The same sort of talk about the creation of humans after the image of God in Egypt indicates the contrary (e.g., in the instruction of Meri-Ka-Re, see Introduction). I have pointed out in the Introduction that descriptions of this kind cannot be confined to the high cultures of the Ancient Near East; they occur also in primitive accounts of creation, though not very often. I would add another example to that already cited:

The Maoris of New Zealand say that a certain god, variously named Tu, Tiki, and Tane, took red riverside clay, kneaded it with his own blood into a likeness or image of himself, with eyes, legs, arms and all complete, in face, an exact copy of the deity; and having perfected the model, he animated it by breathing into its mouth and nostrils, whereupon the clay effigy at once came to life and sneezed. So like himself was the creature whom the Maori Creator Tiki fashioned that he called him *Tiki-ahua,* that is, Tiki's likeness. (J.G. Frazer, *Folklore* . . . , p. 5).

These examples of course cannot be used to prove with certainty that such descriptions were widespread in primitive religions (e.g., they do not occur at all in Africa). But they do show that talk about the creation of humans in the image of God has had a very varied history outside Israel. We must be very careful of speaking about a uniform derivation. In any case we will have to look for the pre-history of Gen 1:26f. in the context of talk about the creation of human beings, even though there are echoes of the Egyptian and Mesopotamian predicates of the king as the likeness of God.

7. *Other Explanations.* There are some other explanations that should be mentioned even though they have had little impact.

(a) Earlier the image and likeness of God was thought to consist in dominion over creation. It was often closely linked with one of the other explanations: e.g., the gift of spirit, intellect and will enabled people to dominate creation, or the office of God's viceroy was fulfilled in dominion over other creatures, or such like. More recently scholars like H. Holzinger, L. Köhler (who later abandoned the view), J. Hempel supported the opinion that the image and likeness of God referred to dominion over other creatures; H. Gross has written "that the image and likeness of God consists essentially in one's sharing in the dominion of God," p. 98; and G.P. Oberholzer has proposed that humanity's image and likeness to God is shown in its dominion over nature as well as in its ability to propagate the species (this latter is certainly incorrect, because the ability to propagate is common both to humans and to animals).

A whole series of studies has shown quite correctly that this opinion is wrong, and that according to the text dominion over other creatures is not an explanation, but a consequence of creation in the image of God.

(b) Since the era of the fathers of the church, the image and likeness of God has been understood as a command or an admonition to strive for something. Though this opinion fell out of fashion it does recur occasionally: e.g., A.M. Dubarle: "The image of God is not a static quality conferred once and for all, it is a call to imitate in action the one whose image is carried. It is a call to live a life of religion: 'Be holy, because I am holy'," *Sacra Pagina* I, p. 528.

(c) Mention must be made too of the attempt to give the creation of humanity in the image of God a christological meaning. The image of God would be Christ; the individual would be created in a Christ-image. This explanation is found among Catholic (G. Söhngen) as well as among Evangelical (E. Schlink) theologians. (Both contributions are found in *Festgabe Erzbischof Jäger, Bischof Stählin, "Pro Veritate,"* pp. 23-57 and 1-23 respectively.) E. Schlink begins with the sentence: "Christ is the image of God. God created human beings after the image and likeness of Christ," p. 78. Such an explanation however is forced to say that fallen humanity is not the image of God, (EvTh Beitr. 8 [1942] 84). But this is opposed to the unanimous opinion of all interpreters of the text.

B. Brinkmann has defended the Christological explanation in a recent study: the meaning of Gen 1:26 demands, together with God, an image which differs from him, and which serves him as a *causa exemplaris* of his creation. The God-man is the model after which God created humanity.

This survey of studies of Gen 1:26-28 reveals a common trait: all exegetes from the fathers of the church to the present begin with the presupposition that the text is saying something about people, namely that people bear God's image because they have been created in accordance with it. The whole question therefore centers around the image of God in the person: what is intended, in what does it consist, what does it mean. Scarcely one of the many studies of the text asks about the process that is going on. Nor do they try to isolate and understand it so as to distinguish between it and the conclusion, namely, that it is humanity created in this way by God that is the image of God. There can be no question that the text is describing an action, and not the nature of human beings.

Most interpretations presume without more ado that the verb "create" can be understood in itself and apart from the context in which it is set. But the text is speaking about an action of God, and not about the nature of humanity. A false start has been made here which could have been avoided. Gen 1:26f. is not making a general and universally valid statement about the nature of humankind; if it were, then the Old Testament would have much more to say about this image and likeness. The fact is that it does not, and this has been noted on a number of occasions (e.g., K.L. Schmidt, 1947, 178f.). In any case, what the Old Testament says about the creation of humanity in the image of god has meaning only in its context, namely that of the process of the creation of human beings.

There seems to be some confused thinking here. Without any proper methodological consideration, Gen 1:26f. has been subordinated to a teaching about humanity in the image of God that is taken for granted. The phrases are taken up into a biblical anthropology and used to construct an Old Testament image of humanity. The presupposition is always that something is being said about human beings which can be taken out of its context and assumed into the very different context of a systematic teaching on human nature. But when it is recognized that Gen 1:26f. is not primarily concerned with human nature, but with the process of the creation of human beings, then the discussion takes a new starting point. Talk about the process of the creation of humans means talk in the context of primeval event. Primeval event is not the beginning of history; it transcends the event of the moment. When it is said in the context of primeval event that "God created man. . . .", then something is being said about the beginning of humanity that is not accessible to our understanding. Our experience of the beginning of humankind is through conception and birth. We cannot imagine it otherwise. It is not possible to detach what is said about the image and likeness of God from this event. Any such further determination would deprive the process of the creation of human beings of its uniqueness.

But how does all this contribute to the understanding of the text? The explanation must come from the process of creation as such, and not from the question, How is humanity described? The question is, What can a narrative mean that wants to tell about the creation of humanity and which has as its kernel the creation of a human being in the image of God? What is the purpose of the creator God when he decides to create a person in his image? This way of putting the question links closely the two sentences that color the narrative, the creation of a human being in the image of God, and the decision, "let us make. . . ." Both were part of what P inherited. Both the decision and the specification indicate that the creator God decides to create something that is his own personal concern.

As far as I know there has been no attempt to derive the principles for the understanding of Gen 1:26f. from the passage as a whole. It is usually said: the immediate context says nothing about the meaning of the image and likeness; the text presumes it and the hearers knew what was meant (e.g., H. Gunkel). Form critical considerations must enter in here. They show that the phrases in Gen 1:26f. are part of a report or a narrative. The narrative deals with the creation of human beings; this, in Gen 1:26-30, is part of the creation as a whole. Many interpreters have drawn attention to the many ways in which this work of creation differs from those which precede it. W.H. Schmidt insists that Gen 1:26-30 has a different pre-history from the other works, p. 128.

The discussion so far has not considered the possibility that Gen 1:26-30 may go back to an independent narrative about the creation of humanity. It is certain that the creation of the world and the creation of human beings formed originally independent traditions; the creation of human beings is the older tradition and was joined to the creation of the world only at a later stage. None of the parallels alleged by V. Maag form part of a world creation; in all of them the creation of human beings is an independent theme. This would mean that the creation of human beings in the image of God belonged originally to this independent tradition.

If Gen 1:26-30 had its origin in an independent narrative about the creation of human beings which in its present form has been completely integrated into a narrative about the creation of the world, then the exegetical perspective has been altered.

The introductory sentence is the first sign of this: "Then God said, let us make man. . . ." The sentence preserves the beginning of a once independent narrative. It is similar in Enuma Elish (Tablet VI, 5-8, ANET 68). The sentence which begins the crowning work of creation in the present structure (and this can well be the reason why it was inserted) had once been a sentence which introduced a narrative: the way in which the creation of humanity is narrated is that a god decides to create human beings (plural of deliberation, see above). This decision, when one prescinds from the aspect of world creation, must have a definite purpose: the creation of human beings must have a meaning which is independent of the creation of the world. This is clear from the Babylonian texts: people were created to minister to the gods (cf. V. Maag, p. 97).

In Gen 1 humanity was created by God to rule over the rest of creation. It is probable however that the narrative of the creation of human beings took this direction only after it became part of the story of the creation of the world. While the narrative was still independent, this further determination must have had something to do with the decision to act. What God decides to create must be something that has a relationship to him just as in the Sumerian and Babylonian texts people are related to the creator god as servants of the gods.

There is a further argument that supports this. Gen 1:26-30, with its pre-history as an independent narrative, is a parallel to Gen 2. Gen 2 is also an independent narrative of the creation of human beings but with a completely different stamp. Its concern is the following: the creation of humanity has as its goal a happening between God and human beings; consequently it can achieve this goal even where the motif of creation in the image of God is absent.

Form critical considerations then support the opinion of W. Riedel (1902), K. Barth (1945), F. Horst (1950), J.J. Stamm (1959) and others, that the creator created a creature that corresponds to him, to whom he can speak, and who listens to him. The strength of this explanation is only seen when the question is put in another form. It is not one of many possible answers to the question: "What is the image and likeness of God or in what does it consist?," but an answer to the question: "What is the meaning of this further determination in the account of the creation of human beings?" It consists in determining further the nature of the act of creation which enables an event to take place between God and humans; it is not a question of a quality in human beings.

The reason why the examples given above are lacking in clarity or certainty is that the proper question has not been clearly put. This is true too of the explanation given by K. Barth, and it is possible that he was not conscious of the consequence of an important sentence which he wrote; "It (the image and likeness of God) consists as man himself consists as the creature of God" CD III/1, p. 184). This means that the creation of human beings in the image of God is not saying that something has been added to the created person, but is explaining what the person is. There is no essential difference between the creation of humans in 1:26 and Gen 2; the person is also created by God as his counterpart in Gen 2 so that something can happen between creator and creature. The difference is that Gen 2 expresses it in story form and not in conceptual terms.

157

The protest of Is 40:18f., that God is incomparable and that there is nothing like him, does not stand in contradiction to Gen 1:26f. The sentence in Gen 1:26f. which seems at first glance strange in context, nevertheless has its own proper meaning in the theology of P: it is humanity as a whole that is created as the counterpart of God; the intention is to render possible a happening between creator and creature. And this for P is directed toward the holy event in which history reaches its goal, as indicated in Gen 2:1-3.

There is an important theological consequence to this understanding of Gen 1:26. If it is a question of human existence as such and not of something over and above it then it is valid for all people. God has created all people "to correspond to him," that is so that something can happen between creator and creature. This holds despite all differences among people; it goes beyond all differences of religion, beyond belief and unbelief. Every human being of every religion and in every place, even where religions are no longer recognized, has been created in the image of God.

Seen from another point of view, the sentence means that the uniqueness of human beings consists in their being God's counterparts. The relationship to God is not something which is added to human existence; humans are created in such a way that their very existence is intended to be their relationship to God.

[1:26b]   "And let them have dominion over. . . ." What people will be, their destiny, is taken up into the decision of the creator to create. It is characteristic of the stories of the creation of human beings that they are there for a definite purpose or goal. And it is characteristic of living beings, both humans and animals, that they are blessed. The power of fertility that is bestowed on living beings, and on them alone enables them to continue their species through conception and birth. A further characteristic is that only among living beings is a hierarchy of order established; humans and the animals are put in relationship to each other in that humans are entrusted with dominion over animals.

The verb רדה means "to tread the wine press" in Joel 4:13; it means "to subdue" in Num 24:19 and Lev 26:17, and is used of the dominion of the king in 1 Kings 5:4; Pss 110:2; 72:8; Is 14:6; Ezek 34:4. Ps 8:6 is saying exactly the same but in different words: "Thou has given him dominion (משׁל) over the works of thy hands; thou has put all things under his feet," and in the following verses 7 and 8 the animals over whom he exercises dominion are listed.

H. Wildberger (ThZ 21 [1965] 481-483) and W.H. Schmidt (op. cit., 140f.), have pointed out that the expression has its origin in the language of the royal court in Babylon and Egypt, and have shown that what is said in Gen 1:26f. and in Ps 8 about human dominion over the animals comes from there. Wildberger writes: "The verb *rdh,* whose basic meaning is 'to tread down', is not the obvious expression for the dominion of humans over the animal world," p. 259. It occurs in the Old Testament especially in passages "in which . . . there are echoes of the Ancient Near Eastern royal ideology: Pss 110:2; 72:8; Is 14:6; Ezek 34:4." . . . . "The use of the verb in Gen 1 is a clear indication . . . of the perseverence of an old element of the royal ideology." Wildberger finds confirmation of this in Ps 8 (p. 482). Similar expressions are found in the description of the king in Egypt, p. 487: "The king, beloved (son of Re) . . . the good god, image of Re, son of Amun, the one who tramples under foot the foreigners" (W. Helck, *Urkunden der 18. Dynastie,* 17-22, 1961, with the further examples cited by W.H. Schmidt, pp. 137 and 141). In the birth story of Amenophis III from Luxor, the promise is made: "You will be king of Egypt and ruler of the desert. All lands are under your surveillance, the boundaries lie united under your sandals" (W. Helck).

The language certainly corresponds. The conclusion is that the expression רדה, describing dominion over the animals, is derived from the court language of the great empires. However the sentence acquires a different meaning because "tread down," used of dominion over the animals, now qualifies humankind as a whole. It replaces the destiny assigned to a person at creation in the Sumerian and Babylonian narratives. There the person is created "to bear the yoke of the gods," to minister to the gods, to relieve the gods of the burden of everyday work (cf. S.G.F. Brandon, *Creation Legends.* . . . 115). The creation of humans in this context is directed towards the cult, *colere,* in the sense of continually ministering to the gods. In Gen 1:26 the goal of humans is within this world — dominion over the animals. The creation of human beings introduces the possibility of a hierarchical order which is characteristic of "being in this world." The goal of the creation of humans is detached from the life of the gods and directed to the life of this world.

P's intention here only becomes clear when the verse is read in the context of both 1:16 and 1:29. The conclusion from the latter is that dominion over the animals cannot mean killing them for food. What then is meant? It is here that we must look to 1:16. We saw that there "to rule" can only have a non-literal meaning — the sun rules over the day, the moon over the night; the same meaning is appropriate to 1:26b; among living beings, humans rule over the animals without condition. It is quite possible that we have here an echo of the belief that the animal was the human's deadly enemy in the early stages of the human race, and that consequently the person's dominating role in relation to the animals is saying something that concerns our very existence. Dominion over the animals certainly does not mean their exploitation by humans. People would forfeit their kingly role among the living (that is what רדה refers to) were the animals to be made the object of their whim. The establishment of a hierarchical order between humans and the animals means that the animals are not there just "to vegetate"; the relationship set up between them is to be understood in a positive sense.

There is a further question: Why is there mention of the animals only? Are not humans to exercise dominion over the rest of creation as well? In the thinking and language of P and of the Old Testament dominion can be exercised only over what is a living being. The relationship to plant life is different as vv. 29-30 show; a relationship to metals or to chemical substances could not be called "dominion." The rest of creation is not withdrawn from the disposition of humans as 1:26b indicates; the suffix attached to כבש indicates that the earth is subject to humans. The second part of v. 26 gives us to understand that it is the attitude of humans toward other living beings that should characterize the human attitude to the world about them; and this means a markedly personal attitude. People can only remain human in their dominion over the animals: the shepherd speaks with a human voice which communicates with his fellow creatures (Jn 10:3); Something of this too belongs to the rider, the horse trainer and even the hunter. A person's "dominion over matter" is not excluded by Gen 1.28b; P indicates in unmistakeable terms that all human relationships with the rest of creation are to be determined by one's rule over the animal world. Language preserves something of this when it uses "dominion" in a transferred sense to describe mastery; one masters an art or a craft or a language. Strictly speaking what is meant is a relationship to a living being.

[1:27b] "Male and female he created them." This pair of words is typical of the language of P. It occurs with reference to humans in Lev 12:2-7; 15:33; 27:2-7; Num 5:3 (in Num 1:2, 20; 3:15ff. etc., only זכר occurs); with reference to animals Gen 6:19; 7:16; Lev 3:1, 6 etc. The pair is found in the J tradition in Gen 7:3, 9; H. Gunkel considers this latter to be due to the influence of P; also in the late chapter Deut 4:16. "The words זכר ונקבה are a legal expression, cf. the Aramaic זכר ונקבה in the Jewish-Aramaic papyri from Asswan G.17" (H. Gunkel).

The creation of the human race as two sexes has a pre-history in which the division of the sexes in the act of creation played an important part in the narrative. The creation of the man and the woman was each narrated separately, as is often the case in primitive creation stories, as well as in Gen 2. This short sentence of P prescinds from the narrative form and states in the briefest possible compass the creation of both man and woman. One should not attack it as does Karl Barth (cf. J.J. Stamm op. cit., 94, W.H. Schmidt op. cit., 146 n. 4); it is an important part of P's presentation that the division of the sexes belongs to the immediate creation of humanity. A consequence of this is that there can be no question of an "essence of man" apart from existence as two sexes. Humanity exists in community, as one beside the other, and there can only be anything like humanity and human relations where the human species exists in twos. W. Zimmerli is exaggerating when he writes in his commentary: "A human being in isolation is only half a human being." A lone human being remains a complete human being in his lonesomeness. What is being said here is that a human being must be seen as one whose destiny it is to live in community; people have been created to live with each other. This is what human existence means and what human institutions and structures show. Every theoretical and institutional separation of man and woman, every deliberate detachment of male from female, can endanger the very existence of humanity as determined by creation.

[1:28] We can refer back to v. 22 for the explanation of this verse. The only difference is that in v. 22 the blessing is introduced with לאמר, and in v. 28 with ויאמר להם. The difference is certainly intended; the two can be addressed with the blessing because God has created them as his counterpart with whom he can speak. W.H. Schmidt writes: "While the formula which introduces God's words in Gen 1 is always 'and God said', this verse alone, addressed to man, runs 'and God said to them'," p. 148. Apart from this difference however the same blessing is imparted both to humans and to animals. The blessing is effective for all living creatures, for everything that is נפש חיה (cf. Excursus above). This blessing does not give humans any advantage over the animals; it is the power of fertility that makes the continuance of the species possible, as the words of blessing say unequivocally.

This blessing works itself out in the succession of generations in the genealogies of Gen 5 which follow immediately on 1:1-2:4a. The blessing conferred on humanity at creation is effective in begetting, conception, and birth and the succession of generations. The continued effectiveness of the blessing is usually called "preservation": "Apparently the priestly writing intends the words added to the blessing to indicate the transition from creation to preservation" (W.H. Schmidt, p. 148). When we use the word "preservation" we must emphasize that the Hebrew word ברך does not describe the maintenance of a state, but a continuous, ever present power, effective into the future. The world in which Israel lived divinized the vital and explosive power of fertility and so gave birth to a whole range of myths and cultic practices, and of highly colored poetic, literary and ritual images.

It is of the greatest importance for its understanding of God that Israel completely subsumed and subordinated this power under the activity of Yahweh, the God of Israel. Yahweh alone is the master of this power, he alone as creator confers it on every living being, he alone remains lord of creation, he alone disposes of the power. That is what is meant by saying that he confers the blessing on every living thing. This vital, effective power that makes the future possible, is indeed something more than, something different from, mere preservation. The phraseology of the genealogies (cf. Introduction, 2, "The Numerative Passages. . . .") shows that, in primeval time and in the period of the patriarchs, the blessing which effected the succession of generations was understood as the basic power of "history." What is presupposed here is an idea of history that is completely different from ours; it is that the movement of history, the forces at work in history, are seen to consist in continuous growth and expansion.

One cannot then describe or understand the blessing which the creator god conferred on living creatures as God's bounteous or saving action. The blessing given to humanity in Gen 1:28 means that as long as humankind exists, God will remain effectively at work in them because of this action at creation. It is something essentially different from what we call God's saving action and never dissolves into it. It can never fail wherever there is talk of an action of God directed toward humans (cf. C. Westermann, *Der Segen in der Bibel und im Handeln der Kirche,* 1968, plus bibliography, and art. 'Segen' in EKL).

[1:28b]   The command to rule over the animals agrees with v. 26b, except that in the command given directly to humans an additional verb כבש is added to the verb רדה. This second verb, like רדה, belongs to the context of subordination or domination. In the Qal it is used of slaves: Jer 34:11, 16; Neh 5:5; 2 Chron 28:10; in the Niphal it is used of a land which has been brought into subjection: Num 32:22, 29; Josh 18:1; 1 Chron 22:18. It is possible that this verb too derives from the rule of the king (see above), even though it is not used in this context in the Old Testament. In practice it has the same meaning as רדה. I refer back to what was said in v. 26b; the point to be stressed is that here the earth is the object of כבש.

[1:29-30]   Provision for Living Beings

This section too begins "and God said. . . ." The man and the woman are addressed and the instructions for the nourishment of the animals are added only in v. 30. The animals are not addressed, and the verb of the instruction is not repeated. The instruction for the nourishment of humans takes precedence; it alone is a direct address of the creator to his creatures. There is a difference in the vegetarian food provided for humans and for the animals that echoes the classification in 1:11f.; to humans is assigned mainly grain and fruit, to the animals grass and plants. The instruction does not go into details, "it is a very broad distinction" (A. Dillmann).

The passage begins with the formula "behold I have given you. . . ." The same formula הנה נתתי occurs in Gen 20:16 (E), and also in P in Ex 31:6; Num 18:8, 21; where a portion is allotted to the priests: "And behold, I have given you whatever is kept of the offerings made to me. . . ." The formula occurs without הנה in the priestly passages Gen 9:3; 23:11, 13; 17:20; Lev 6:10; elsewhere it occurs only in Deut 11:14. Gen 9:3 corresponds exactly to 1:29. It is the allotment of food to humanity after the flood. The context in which it occurs does not allow one to be all that certain that it is a legal formula (W.H. Schmidt, p. 151); the formula describes rather an assignment or a conveyance as a public act which can occur in a number of different contexts. In any case it is not a question of a "food command" (H. Gunkel, W.H. Schmidt, p. 149) or of the "provision of a basic law for creation" (A. Dillmann). Nor does Karl Barth command agreement when he writes that "in fact a prohibition is implicitly pronounced" (CD III/1 pp. 207ff.; W.H. Schmidt quotes Barth with approval). An assignment or conveyance does not imply any prohibition; it is an action of the creator who is making provision for his creatures.

The perfect is used "to express *future* action, when the speaker intends by an express assurance to represent them as finished, or as the equivalent to accomplished facts" (Ges-K §106m). The words signify a definite arrangement. This however does not mean a command or a law, but an assurance or an allotment, just like the allotment of a part of the offering to the priests in Num 18:8, where the same formula is used. The purpose for which the allotment is made is expressed in a fixed formula: "To be to you for food." Apart from Jer 12:9 the word אכלה occurs only seven times in the priestly writing and ten times in Ezekiel, always with the preposition ל: to give for food Lev 25:6; Ex 16:15; Ezek 15:4, 6; 29:5; 35:12; 39:4, or to serve as food Gen 1:29; 6:21; 9:3; Lev 11:39; 25:6; Ezek 21:37; 34:5, 8, 10: "To serve for food is a fixed formula of the priestly language" (W.H. Schmidt, p. 152). These two standard formulas which occur elsewhere only in P, have been expanded by details about the different sorts of plants; this is a clear proof that v. 29f. is as a whole a formulation of P which shows no sign of an older tradition behind it.

This, among other reasons, leads W.H. Schmidt to the conclusion that "the priestly writing is not a re-working of traditional material as a unit, but has inserted into the creation story an element of tradition which was originally foreign to the context." He is then forced to say, "Nevertheless, Gen 1:29f. is not without tradition" (p. 153); and he looks for this tradition in certain Babylonian and Egyptian texts (see below). The difficulty that arises here, however, disappears when it is recognized that Gen 1:26-30 goes back to the originally independent tradition of the creation of humanity. The provision of food is an element often found in stories of the creation of humanity together with the role for which human beings were created, as also in Gen 2. These stories usually tell of the creation of the food given to humans; P therefore must establish independently that the plants have already been created. The allotment of food, as in

Ps 104:27f., has taken the place of the creation of the food, as has the garden in Gen 2. Schmidt quotes the hymn to Amon Re:

> Thou are the sole one, who made (all) that is,
> the solitary soul (one), who made what exists. . . .
> He who made herbage (for) the cattle,
> And the fruit tree for mankind,
> Who made that (on which) the fish in the river
>   may live,
> and the birds *soaring* in the sky.   (ANET, p. 366)

A Sumerian creation myth describes the creation of vegetation and the animals immediately after the creation of humans:

> After Anu, Enlil, Enki and Ninhursag
> Had fashioned the black-headed (people),
> Vegetation luxuriated from the earth,
> Animals, four-legged (creatures) of the plain,
> Were brought artfully into existence. . . .
>   (ANET, p. 43)

It is the allotment of vegetarian food to both humans and the animals that shows unmistakably that there is an originally independent tradition behind 1:29f. The tradition is well known and widespread and occurs in the Gilgamesh Epic:

> With the gazelles he (Enkidu) feeds on grass,
> With the wild beasts he drinks at the water-
>   ing place,
> With the creeping creatures his heart
>   delights in water. . . .   (ANET, p. 75).

Enkidu is described as a savage who lives with the animals and feeds on grass until the girl the gods send to him brings him into the human community. Another description of humans feeding on grass after their creation, and closer to Gen 1:29f., is a Sumerian creation story which W.H. Schmidt, p. 154, quotes from C.F. Jean, "L'origine des choses d'après une tradition sumérienne de Nippur," RA 26 (1929) 33-38 and R.M. Dussaud, RHR (1929) p. 124f. A number of Egyptian texts could be quoted that link the creation of humans and their nourishment, especially the instruction for Meri-Ka-Re, where both plants and animals are described as human food: "He made for them plants, animals, fowl, and fish to feed them" (ANET, p. 417). S. Herrmann draws attention to a series of parallels in the sarcophagus texts of the 11th to the 19th dynasties which refer to "nourishment of humans and of animals" ThLZ 86 (1961) 414-424, esp. pp. 418, 421).

The Mesopotamian tradition, in agreement with Gen 1:29f. is very different from this. And it is in nowise confined to Mesopotamia. A. Dillmann (comm. 6th ed., p. 36) quotes A. Knobel: "According to Plato, Laws 6p, 782 and Plutarch, Symp. 8,8,3 humans acquire their taste for meat only because they realize that killing the animals is unlawful. . . .; Ovid 2, Met. 15, 96f., and Fast. 4, 395f., when describing the golden age, allows humans to eat only fruit and vegetables, and no meat; and Vergil, Georg. 1,130, allows the wild beasts to live on vegetables only at the beginning." Once more it is a question of what we could call human traditions, because it is restricted neither to place nor to culture.

The allusion is to the paradise motif which will be taken up in the context of Gen 2. What is "common to humanity" is the awareness that the killing of living beings for food by other living beings is not right, and so not in accordance with the will of the creator at the beginning although it is necessary in the present world. A. Dillmann expresses it in this way: "It is partly the historical recollection of older conditions and customs like this, partly natural sympathy with a fellow creature, and the inner conviction that persecution and the use of force among creatures cannot be the original will of the creator," (comm., 6th ed., p. 36).

The same can be said of the other idea, namely that death was not in the original intention of the creator. It is a question here of understanding what talk about primeval time is. If we understand it as the beginning of history we become ensnared in inextricable difficulties. While F. Delitzsch makes every effort to make plausible an era in which there was no killing for food, A. Dillmann points the way out. He reflects that one could imagine an era when humans did not use animals for food, and then continues: "It is much more difficult to imagine such a situation with regard to the animals and their food," p. 36. Dillmann gains support by showing that the author had not been aware of this difficulty. But this is highly questionable. P, with his precise knowledge of nature which is everywhere in evidence, certainly knew that it was not possible to conceive of all animals as vegetarian. But P is speaking of primeval time which is not subject to the conditions of present experience.

The 19th century commentaries go to great pains to solve the problem whereas those of the 20th century do not. None of the commentaries accessible to me asks the question, "What is the tradition behind vv. 29-30 all about?" We described in the Introduction the peculiar character of the primeval events of Gen 1-11. In the light of this we must abandon the old explanation of vv. 29-30 which understood them as a description of an era of human history and of the history of non-human living beings which was accessible to us. We can never demonstrate that there was a period when neither humans nor animals ate meat. Nevertheless the primeval statement in vv. 29ff. is talking about reality. There are two aspects to the reality described: the first concerns the very existence of animals and humans. These words, which are in accordance with one of the traditions of humankind, express an awareness of a period in the history of humans and animals which was different from the present. We can say then that this tradition is aware that both animals and humans have undergone a process of development up to the present state even though there are no guidelines at our disposal to study the process carefully. What is essential is that this tradition understands both animals and humans as creatures that have gradually developed into what they now are. It is clear once more that reflection on creator and creation is completely compatible with a recognition of development.

The other aspect is concerned with the understanding of the nature of their existence. The human being in the world is acutely sensitive to a lack, to something wrong or contradictory; the killing of a living being touches the very existence of living beings. Such experience is linked with an awareness that the origin of all this must lie elsewhere, in a primeval period which is beyond the present. This is the source of the motif that P has taken up in Gen 1:29-30. And so it becomes clear how this motif of primeval time finds its counterpart in the motif of end time. There are a number of texts which speak of peace between the animals, Is 11:2-9; 65:25; Hos 2:10; Ezek 34:25; cf. H. Gross, "Die Idee des wiegen und allgemeinen Weltfriedens im alten Orient und im AT," TThSt 7 (1956) 83-93; J.J. Stamm, *Weltfrieden.* . . . esp. p. 18. Both factors are at work here: the lived experience of destruction and contradiction, and an awareness of the future that has grown up out of the history of God's people, above all out of prophecy.

Two more difficulties must be met: H. Gunkel takes up with approval a remark of R. Kraetzschmar (*Die Bundesvorstellung im AT,* 1896, p. 193f.), that v. 29f. contradicts v. 26b: "What is left of humanity's right to dispose of the animals, apart from domestic animals, if people have been forbidden to use them as food?" Kraetzschmar concludes that vv. 29f. are a secondary addition to the text. Gunkel rejects this conclusion and explains, "that there is here but a faint clue to what is immediately evident to one familiar with the history of story namely that the author himself, P, has united two originally disparate traditions" (comm. ad. loc.). W.H. Schmidt concludes from the same evidence that "the priestly writing in 1:29f. . . . has inserted what was originally a foreign element of tradition into the creation story," p. 152.

I think that Gunkel's explanation is more in accordance with the facts than Schmidt's. There are signs that there has been a long history of tradition in which motifs from different narratives of the creation of humans have merged together. One must express a reservation about Kraetzschmar's remark: human dominion over the animals in v. 26b cannot be described simply as "the free right of disposition." This dominion must be clearly distinguished from the "assignment" of v. 28a; a dominion in which the master merely enjoys the profits coming from his subjects is unthinkable in the Old Testament. It always includes some sort of independent existence for the subject so that dominion over the animals does not just mean that a person can kill and eat them.

There is a second difficulty. W.H. Schmidt affirms that "Gen 1:29f. is inconceivable without a continuation" (p. 153), because the limiting of food to vegetable life must of necessity be abrogated, as happens in Gen 9:3. So he puts the question: "Is it possible that vv. 29f. have been inserted into the creation only after it had been linked with the flood story?" (p. 152f.). The solution of the problem is given when one recognizes that the primeval event is a self-contained whole within which one cannot speak of before or after. It is not at all necessary in stories set in the primeval period that the assignment of vegetable food to humans and animals "be necessarily abrogated later." The listener knows the limits of the primeval event. One can add that it is typical of the studied pedantry with which P describes every succession of events, that he expressly and formally insists that the situation is different after the flood (that is, after the primeval period).

[**1:31**] "And God saw everything that he had made, and behold, it was very good." This formula of approval, as it is often called, is not the close of a particular work, but of the whole work of creation. We may add the following to what was said above about this formula under "form" and commentary on 1:4a: an event in the Old Testament, is always an event in the community; it has no meaning unless it happens for someone or something. It is proper therefore to

acknowledge anything that happens and to express thereby that the work is good
or not good for someone or something. Every work of humanity requires not only
reward, but also acknowledgement; so too with the works of God. What he does
for his people arouses praise and the Old Testament is full of praise of his mighty
acts. The same must be true for God's work of creation. It is above all in the
Psalms creatures are called to praise, as in Ps 148 where the whole of creation is
addressed. In Job 38:7 the praise of creatures is linked directly with creation.

The same also occurs outside Israel. The creation of the world by Marduk
in *Enuma Elish* is in the context of the praise of Marduk, and in the Sumerian
Myths the praise of the creator god occurs at the end of the description of
creation: "Our myth then comes to a close with a brief hymnal passage in which
Enlil is exalted as the Lord of abundance and the king whose decrees are unalterable," (S.N. Kramer, *Sumerian Mythology,* "Enlil and Ninlil, p. 47). But the
praise of God does not normally occur in the creation narratives. The priestly
writer switches the motif of acknowledgement, which consists in the praise of
God, to the judgment of the creator on his work: what will later be the praise of
the creatures is now in the creation story the reflection of God on his work. So the
"formula of approval" which recurs as a refrain after each work of creation and
then after the work of creation as a whole, bears a certain resemblance to the
structures in the Psalms.

The word טוב is strengthened by מאד in this concluding sentence. מאד is
really a noun and it means "power, ability, wealth" (e.g., in Deut 6:5; and
2 Kings 23:25); used as an adverb it gives a strengthening quality, "very, extremely." The word טוב itself has a broad range of meanings; "It is a word of
many facets: pleasant, practical, suitable, nice, friendly, just, morally good."
Though the nuance to be stressed in Gen 1 is that of "appropriate" (so too KBL),
the meaning of טוב should not be confined to it. In any case "good" is not to be
understood as indicating some fixed quality; the meaning is rather functional:
"good for. . . ." The world which God created and devised as good is the world
in which history can begin and reach its goal and so fulfill the purpose of
creation.

טוב is also used in the same way in which we use "beautiful, nice,"
though in a somewhat different sense to that usually given to this word. We use
the word "beautiful, nice" to describe the beauty of an object, of something
tangible; when we look back on a gathering or a celebration and say "that was
beautiful (nice)!," we are referring to an event. "Good, beautiful" as a description of an event is the predominant meaning in Hebrew, though at the same time
there are also objects that are beautiful (e.g., people, Ex 2:2; 1 Sam 16:12;
1 Kings 1:6). When the Psalmist sings, "It is good to give thanks to the Lord,"
Ps 92:1, it is a question of an event. טוב is used at times to describe an object in
Gen 1, and in 1:31 to describe "all that he had made"; however every use is
colored by the functional sense: "being good for. . . ." The beauty (the being
good) of what has been created is not something added to it after creation; being
good for, suited to, belong to the state of creation. In the context of the creation
of human beings, it means that human beauty, goodness, appropriateness, is
something given in the very act of creation. One can draw attention to the beauty
of a particular human being, but in effect this beauty is something that belongs to
humanity as a creation of God.

It is in complete accord with our way of thinking to refer the words, "And behold, it was very good (beautiful)" to the beauty of nature, with the reservation that this beauty has not yet been objectified nor experienced as a thing "in itself"; there is always some point of contact with the fact of being created, with existing "together with". . . , existing for. . . . When the Old Testament speaks of the *kābōd* of the forests of Lebanon, it means just what we mean by the beauty of the forest. But it is not merely the beauty of the spectacle; it is saying something about the meaning of the forest for people and for the land. The Hebrew does not contemplate the sheer beauty of what exists prescinding from the function of what is contemplated.

[2:1-3]   Conclusion of the Creation Narrative

Literature: J. Hehn, *Siebenzahl und Sabbat bei den Babyloniern und im AT*, II, 5 (1907);   R. Pettazzoni, *Essays on the History of Religions*, Numen Suppl. 1(1954) 32-34;   E. Jenni, *Die theologische Begründung des Sabbatgebotes im AT*, ThSt (B) 46 (1956);   J.B. Bauer, "Die literarische Form des Heptaemeron," BZ (1 (1957) 273-277;   W. Eichrodt, *The Theology of the Old Testament* I, (1961);   Z. Dus, "Die Heiligung des siebenten Tages (1. Mose 1:2-2:4a)," KrR 25 (1958);   A. Szabo, "Sabbat und Sonntag," Jud 15 (1959) 129/142;   H. Lubscik, "Wortschüng und Tatschöpfung, BiLe 6 (1965) 191-208;   J.H. Meesters, *Op zoek naar de oorsprong van de Sabbat*, SSN 7 (1966).

The concluding verses, Gen 2:1-3 are very different from what has gone before. They are not part of the day-by-day succession which forms the framework of the first chapter. They do not describe the work of a day and the former structure is no longer there. What do these closing verses mean, and have they any discernible structure?

(a) We must distinguish two stages in our enquiry: a tradition which came down to P, and the meaning given by P. In his study of the first question, W.H. Schmidt quotes "the theology of Memphis," following K. Sethe: "Ptah rested, after he had made everything, as well as all the divine order." But Schmidt also gives Sethe's older translation. S. Herrmann translates: "And so Ptah was satisfied, after he had made everything, as well as all the divine order" (op. cit., p. 422; see ANET, p. 5, line 59). The same translation appears in S.G.F. Brandon, *Creation Legends*, p. 41. The sentence then would be a parallel to Gen 1:31. If the meaning were "Ptah rested. . . ," it would indicate that the rest of the creator after the completion of his work did not in fact belong to the theology of creation by the word at Memphis, but was part of an older tradition.

The background to what is said about the rest of God at the end of his creative action is a motif which is widespread in the history of religions, the leisure *(otiositas)* of the creator God. R. Pettazzoni has drawn particular attention to it. The *otiositas* belongs to the very nature of the creator God, "It is in a certain sense the completion of his creative activity" (R. Pettazzoni, *Myths of Beginnings and Creation-Myths*, p. 32). It means that the creator god will not intervene any more in the work which he has completed so as to disturb his established order. Creation is thus set apart from all that follows as a unique, once and for all event. Creation then is primeval event, not the beginning of history.

The motif was at hand, having come down from primitive creation stories. Creation as an act of making presupposes an activity which the rest complements.

167

P has modified the motif by joining the rest of the creator with the work of the seventh day, that is with his overall plan of seven days into which he has fitted the work of creation. So the rest of God after the completion of the works of creation has become the rest on the seventh day. This shows the extraordinary power and depth of P's theological reflection. The transition from a very old creation motif to P's idea of the theology of history is made in such a way that no discontinuity appears in the text. The old motif is resumed, but the rest of God on the seventh day has become something entirely new. The language of these verses bears the seal of P. Every sentence is evidence of P's hand, especially the places where there is talk of the Sabbath. W.H. Schmidt has drawn attention to this in detail, pp. 155-158.

(b) Is there any structure recognizable in Gen 2:1-3? The difficulties, especially the repetitions, are such that the passage has become the starting point for the literary criticism of Gen 1 (W.H. Schmidt, p. 155, refers to J.G. Eichhorn, W.C.L. Ziegler, J.Ph. Gabler and others). The more recent commentaries scarcely touch on the difficulties of structure in Gen 2:1-3. Gunkel writes: "The presentation here has a special solemnity about it with many repetitions"; W.H. Schmidt remarks on "the care for details and the consequent density of the priestly writing," p. 155; U. Cassuto thinks that there is a conscious choice of words and sentence structure and that the repetition of "the seventh day" three times in vv. 2a, 2b, 3a is deliberate. That may well be true for the final form of the text, but it does not exclude a development of the passage through different stages.

Tradition history provides a firm basis for the explanation of the structure of 2:1-3.

1. The first verse, 2:1, an obvious ending, is a self-contained conclusion to the work of the creator which goes back to a stage in the tradition when the works were not yet part of the seven-day structure (so too L. Rost, "Der Schöpfungsbericht der Priesterschrift," CuW 10 [1934] 172-178; W.H. Schmidt, p. 155). P leaves the passage unaltered in accordance with his tendency to preserve what has been handed down.

2. What follows has been shaped by P so as to include the conclusion of the work of creation in the seven-day structure. The process has taken place in two stages: the first stage is v. 2a where P joins the completion of the works of creation with the seventh day. While the traditional piece, 2:1, is linked with Gen 1:1 and looks back to it, 2:2a is linked with the work of the first day, 1:3-5. The work of creation, begun on the first day, is described as completed on the seventh day. Understood in this way the sequence v. 1, v. 2a makes good sense. Verse 3a then is to be read immediately after v. 2a:

V.2a: And on the seventh day God finished his work which he had done.
V.3a: So God blessed the seventh day and hallowed it.

P has thus impressed on the text his own understanding of the conclusion of the creation.

Now there is a second step. V. 3a, which is of such importance for P, is framed between two verses which are verbally almost the same and which both comment on v. 3a and underscore it:

V.2b: And he rested on the seventh day from all his work which he had done,
V.3b: Because on it God rested from all his work which he had done in creation.

This framework introduces both the rest of God and the word שׁבת, and most certainly has been shaped to serve this purpose. Both sentences echo the Sabbath command; both serve to comment and to emphasize. Whether they were added later for this purpose or put there deliberately by P cannot be decided. Actually they do not add anything new. The mention of the seventh day in vv. 2a and 3a hints at the rest of God without saying so expressly. The two sentences which serve as a framework give the whole passage an almost liturgical flavor. However they cannot hide the fact that v. 3a is the real conclusion. It is this verse that brings new meaning to the old motif. The sanctifying and blessing of the seventh day is a result of the rest of the creator. It is a gift to humankind (a sort of demythologizing of the old creation motif), a gift that regulates human existence, inasmuch as the command to rule the remainder of creation by one's work is limited by what is implied in the sanctification and blessing of the seventh day. P's universal mentality is once more in evidence.

We have then an explanation of the structure of Gen 2:1-3. 2:1 is the traditional concluding piece without any interpretation. Interpretation begins with vv. 2a and 3a by joining them to the seven-day scheme; vv. 2b and 3b introduce expressly the rest of God with echoes of the Sabbath command. The conclusion of creation has its effect in the history of humankind because the rest of the creator has given rise to a day which has been sanctified and blessed.

[2:1]   The sentence refers back to 1:1. The final summing up calls what God has created "heaven and earth"; let us recall what was said about this phrase in 1:1. The concluding sentence adds "and all the host of them." This brings together what has been described in the individual works. The word צבא is usually referred to the heaven: "the host of the heavens"; it is extended here to the earth as in the hymn "the heaven and the earth with all their host. . . ." It could also be translated "with all their fullness"; however the translation "host" (army) gives greater precision. The stars are called צבא in Is 40:26; the heavenly hosts are called to praise God in Pss 103:21; 148:2.

The Gk probably read עֶדְיִ; it translates by κόσμος and the Vg by *ornatus*. This led the scholastics to divide the works of creation into *opus distinctionis* and *opus ornatus*, a division which has retained its influence right up to the present (cf. V. Zapletal, *Der Schöpfungsbericht der Genesis (1:1-2:3). . . .*, 1911[2], pp. 107ff.). The meaning is clear: "Everything that exists in heaven and in earth, even what is not expressly mentioned in Gen 1, is included here" (A. Dillmann). The meaning of צבא in Is 34:2 is practically the same where it is parallel to "all peoples." (For the history of the meaning of צבא cf. V. Maag, "Jahwäs Heerscharen," *Festschrift L. Köhler*, 1950, pp. 27-52.)

"The meaning is not that God completed his still unfinished work on the seventh day" (F. Delitzsch); some translators have understood it in this way and have altered the ordinal to "on the sixth day." But the sentence is saying that the work was by now completed. There could be forensic resonances here with something of a declarative sense; A. Heidel translates: "And on the seventh day God declared his work finished" (*The Babylonian Genesis*, p. 127). U. Cassuto provides a detailed explanation of this form of speech with examples (Gen 17:22;

24:19; 49:33; Ex 40:33): the verb "he finished it" is a statement that the work has been completed, not the act of bringing it to a completion.

[2:2a] The last example, Ex 40:33, shows at the same time that there was a fixed form of speech at hand to P. Chapter 40 closes the erection of "the tent of the meeting" which Moses had been ordered to erect in ch. 25 after the Sinai theophany. The ceremony is solemnly closed by the appearance of the כבוד יהוה in the cloud, 40:33. The sentence "so Moses finished the work" is a clear echo of Gen 2:2 (W.H. Schmidt points out that the preceding passage, Ex 39:32-43, offers some parallels to Gen 1: 39:32a to 2:1f.; 39:43a to 1:31; 39:43b to 2:3a). The same phrase "and he finished" occurs too in the priestly writing in Gen 49:33; 17:22; Lev 16:20; Num 4:15; 7:1; 16:31. The quite unnecessary relative sentence "which he had made," ". . . should evoke the recollection of the Sabbath command," W.H. Schmidt, p. 156. The phrase is rooted in the reason for the command, Ex 20:9; Deut 5:13f.; Ex 31:14; 35:2. It occurs in the priestly writings too in Ex 35:35; 36:1, 4, 7. The phrase occurs three times in the short passage Gen 2:1-3.

The word מלאכה is the normal word for ordinary work; e.g., ". . . Joseph went into the house to do his work," Gen 39:11. This word is used here three times for the creation of heaven and earth. This is all the more striking as P describes creation as effected by the commanding word of God. He must have been aware that this is not work in the ordinary sense of the word. The stress on the completion of the work in 2:1-3 is directed toward humans, and this is confirmed by the echoes of the language of the Sabbath command. The conclusion of creation creates a rhythm which will effect the whole of creation.

[2:3a] In order to understand properly the meaning of the sanctification and blessing of the seventh day, it is most important not to isolate it, but to see it as the conclusion of a whole. Special attention is given to the seventh day; it is holy and blessed precisely as the conclusion of the work of the previous six days and can only be understood in relation to them.

"Blessing and sanctification in relation to the Sabbath (Gen 2:3; Ex 20:11) appear . . . as two interrelated ideas"; this "terminological relationship" is found only here, F. Horst, Interp. 4 (1950).

There are two explanations which are sharply opposed to each other. The first refers the blessing and sanctification of the seventh day to God alone and to his work as creator; so W.H. Schmidt and many other exegetes: "The rest, like the whole of creation, remains simply a work of God." He quotes J.P. Gabler: "The explanation of Gen 2: 2-3 was already disputed in the 18th century. Gabler's reflections are instructive. First, in the introduction to Eichhorn's *Urgeschichte* (1790), he had written that the seventh day is not concerned with 'the solemn celebration of the Sabbath by the people', because this is a later institution of Moses; it is concerned with the rest of Yahweh. . . . Later he regarded this explanation as 'a necessary help' . . . ." (p. 157f. n. 6). What Gabler meant was that one's "exegetical instinct" senses that Gen 2:3 "does not simply constitute the seventh day of the week, following as it does six days of creation, a solemn day for God himself. . . ." This "instinct" rests on the fact that the verb "to sanctify" expresses a cultic idea and cannot be referred to a day destined for God himself, but must in some way or other signify something related to people.

God is holy; a holy period of any sort can only be concerned with the person who celebrates it (see the explanation proposed by W.H. Schmidt, "to arrange a cultic event," 2 Kings 10:20; Joel 1:14).

The other explanation understands Gen 2:3 as a sort of preparation of the Sabbath, and so a preparation of something holy. G. von Rad writes: "Even more, that God has 'blessed', 'sanctified' . . . this rest, means that P does not consider it as something for God alone but as a concern of the world, . . . The way is being prepared, therefore, for an exalted and saving good. Nothing of that is apparent to the people . . . but once a community and a tabernacle are present, they will be bound to observe this rest of God (Ex 31:12ff.) . . . . Thus at creation God prepared what will benefit his people in this life. . . ." (*Genesis,* 1972[2], p. 62). One must agree with von Rad's first sentence against Schmidt; likewise that it is not a question here of the institution of the Sabbath, but rather that there are echoes of the Sabbath (cf. K. Barth, CD III/1, p. 98, §41,2, "Creation as the External Basis of the Covenant"). But does P really mean "that the way is being prepared, therefore, for an exalted, even the ultimate saving good?" I do not think that this explanation takes sufficient account of the human orientation of creation. When P says that God blesses and sanctifies the seventh day, then first that must have something to do with humankind; only then can 2:3 really be the goal of the creation account of P.

We must take as our starting point that when P arranged the works of creation in a seven-day pattern he was not concerned merely with a succession of seven days, but with a whole, with a basic unit of time, which becomes a whole in the climax of the seventh day. It is only then, in the seven-day week as a whole and with the seventh day as the goal, that the importance of the seventh day is properly appreciated. This means that when he arranged the works of creation in the seven-day pattern, P intended to structure a unit of time which consists of two parts: it would not be a whole without the seventh day, which is something different from the six days. Creation is set out on a time scheme comprising days of work and of rest. This is stated explicitly in 2:3. The root קדשׁ has the meaning of separation. When God sanctifies the seventh day (i.e., declares it holy), he sets it aside from the works of the six days as something special. The sanctification of the seventh day determines the time which begins with creation as structured time, and within which one day is not just the same as another. The days each have their goal in a particular day which is different from the rest — a day which is holy and apart. Days of work are not the only days that God has created. The time which God created is structured; days of work have their goal in a day of rest.

There is here much more than a mere reference to the Sabbath in later Israel. The sanctification of the Sabbath institutes an order for humankind according to which time is divided into time and holy time, time for work and time for rest. The work of creation began with three acts of separation. The first was the separation of light and darkness. Its purpose was to determine what time was for humans; the existence of everything created is determined by the polarity of day and night. By sanctifying the seventh day God instituted a polarity between the everyday and the solemn, between days of work and days of rest, which was to be determinative for human existence. This is a gift of the creator to his people and is not merely an anticipation of the Israelite Sabbath. This becomes clear from the context of the Sabbath command where the person is the subject who is to sanctify the day (Ex 20:11; Ezek 20:20; Jer 17:22, 27; Neh 13:22). People "sanctify" the Sabbath by observing it; they desecrate it by doing forbidden work on that day.

In Gen 2:3 God sanctifies the seventh day and this means that it is God's sanctifying action alone that sets it apart. Human action, human observance or non-observance, can make no difference. So this special day, this solemn day, which has been set apart cannot be determined by or limited to Israel's Sabbath. There is more to it than the Sabbath. The story of humanity, which begins with the conclusion of the work of creation, is determined not merely by the power of the blessing which is common to all living beings; a new dimension is introduced with the sanctification of the seventh day: to give the holy a special place in the stream of events is to indicate the goal of creation, a goal which corresponds to that which God set for himself. This goal is not part of the six ordinary working days, but a holy day set apart.

I would draw attention to another passage of the priestly writing where there is a succession of six days concluded by a seventh without any mention of the Sabbath. In his description of the theophany at Sinai, Ex 24:16, P writes: "The glory of the Lord settled on Mount Sinai, and the cloud covered it six days; and on the seventh day he called to Moses out of the midst of the cloud."

The context here is very significant. Ex 24:15b-18, which is a continuation of the priestly description of Ex 19:1, 2a, is the basis of Israel's cult and worship. According to this passage the holy place, the holy period of time, the mediator of the holy are basic to the structure of the cultic event. Though it is only in this event that the holy place is founded (Sinai and the tent of the meeting which derives from it and which prefigures the temple in Jerusalem), the holy period is nevertheless already there ("six days . . . and on the seventh day"). P is pointing out here that the holy period of time as a basic part of the cult has a strongly universal character, while the holy place has a strongly particular character. While the holy period of time in Gen 2:1-3 is expressly a gift of the creator to his people, the holy place receives its function only with the beginning of the history of the people. This distinction of P has very probably a justification in the history of religions. It would have to be pursued further in a discussion of worship in the Bible and in Christianity.

This passage stands midway between the six days of creation with the concluding seventh and the Sabbath command, showing that the seven-day complex which takes its meaning from the seventh day was something that P took over.

But what is the meaning of the other sentence, that God blessed the seventh day? There can be no doubt that this third blessing in the course of the creation event is of the same kind as the blessing given to living creatures and to humans, 1:22, 28, where it meant the power of fertility. The meaning is essentially the same here though much more abstract. God's blessing bestows on this special, holy, solemn day a power which makes it fruitful for human existence. The blessing gives the day, which is a day of rest, the power to stimulate, animate, enrich and give fullness to life. It is not the day in itself that is blessed, but rather the day in its significance for the community. In the context of creation it is for the world and humankind. The power of the blessing, i.e., the power of enterprise and success, has its point of departure here.

A new catchword occurs in these two parallel sentences: God rested on the seventh day. The catchword goes a step further than what was said in vv. 2a and 3a: in 2a and 3a the seventh day is merely referred to; here in 2b and 3b the new catchword points to the concrete Sabbath day in Israel. It is not vv. 2a and 3a, but rather 2b and 3b, that have a clearly etiological character. It is a question neither of the institution of the Sabbath nor of its preparation. The verses however reflect the later founding of the Sabbath, Ex 31:12-17; 35:1-3, and also Ex 20:11.

This is true too even if, as a number of scholars think, the verb שבת is to be separated from the noun שַׁבָּת. The verb שבת means really not "to rest," but "to cease from"; e.g., Gen 8:22: "While the earth remains . . . shall not cease . . .", or Is 14:4: "How the oppressor has ceased"; Lam 5:15: "The joy of our hearts has ceased." U. Cassuto translates: "He abstained . . . from all his work." The meaning "to rest" derives from a particular use of the word: "to cease from work," e.g., Neh 6:3. This is the way in which the word is used in the context of the Sabbath command Ex 16:30; 23:12; 31:17; 34:21; the meaning is transferred to the land in Lev 26:34f.

It can remain an open question whether the verb שבת is to be linked with the noun שַׁבָּת; they already occur in the same context in J in Ex 16:29f., (cf. M. Noth, *Exodus*, 1962, p. 136). We cannot here enter into a discussion about the origin and history of the Sabbath; cf. E. Kutsch, 'Sabbat', RGG[3] with later bibliography: W. Rordorf, *Sunday. The History of the Day of Rest and Worship in the Earliest Centuries of the Christian Church*, 1968; J. Morgenstern, IDB 4, 135-141. E. Kutsch thinks it likely that the noun derives from שבת meaning to cease, whereas Noth would derive the meaning of Sabbath from שבע, meaning seven.

Purpose and Thrust

The interpretation of this chapter has shown that church teaching on creation and the Bible must be thoroughly rethought. It is a question of something which is of the utmost importance for the whole teaching on creation. Church teaching has tended always to speak of the creation of the world and of humanity in fixed formulas: "God created the world out of nothing," "God created the world in seven days"; "God created man in his own image," and so on; the biblical text shows everywhere the opposite tendency. Talk about creator and creation is everywhere colored by a reverent concern to guard the inaccessible mystery of creation from the human attempt to describe it. The attitude that one discerns behind all this is that of a speaker who praises the majesty of the creator god. Our first encounter with this attitude was in the very first sentence which embraced the whole work of creation, and also in the antiphon verse which closes the various works: "And God saw that it was good."

However these chords of the praise of God are not decisive. What is decisive is something that dominates the description and expresses at the same time the whole basic attitude: whoever asks about the beginning, the source, the origins, must remain outside the doors; they are not opened to them.

1. This becomes very clear inasmuch as P knows that he has neither the first nor the last word on creation, but that he is one of a choir; he stands in a line in which there are others in front of him, Israelites and non-Israelites, who have described creation. P does not say that all of these were wrong or inadequate and that he alone is right. As he speaks, he allows others to speak with him at the

173

same time. If recent exegesis of Gen 1 has demonstrated anything at all, it is that the author of Gen 1 is both a receiver and a giver. He does not claim that his description of creation by the word of command of the creator is absolute, but he takes up into it an older way of describing creation in which God makes, separates, sets up, puts. He shows preference for the specialized theological word ברא while allowing the traditional word עשׂה to remain and even using it himself. Any exegesis of Gen 1 must respect this; any exegesis that wants to absolutize P's manner of presentation and to insist that it is the only valid one and that all other presentations are wrong and are to be eradicated, will have misunderstood an essential aspect of P's intent.

We cannot of course know just how P's listeners reacted. But we can be pretty certain that they experienced the massive tradition behind P as he spoke as one amid so many other voices. When they heard the words, "Let the earth bring forth . . .", they knew that it was the language of a primeval cosmogony very different from that of P; when they heard, "God made the firmament. . . .", they knew that such talk was in polarity to "God said: Let there be. . . . and there was." It was precisely this massive historical dimension that implied both for P himself and for his listeners that talk about creation must be something unique. One can speak about creation only with the many voices of successive generations; there was nothing that was at the exclusive disposition of anyone.

2. This is clear too in the language P himself uses when he has something of his own to say about creation. P does not answer the question, "How did God make the world?" so as to explain the word "how"; such information was at the disposal of his hearers. He tells of the creation of the world and of humanity in such a way as to make them face how incomprehensible, inscrutable, indescribable is the subject of his story. We saw when explaining the chapter that P deliberately does not answer the questions we ask; while speaking about creation he preserves its secret. The creation of light as the first work is in opposition to the creation of the stars whose function it is to give light. P does not answer the question of how these two are related to each other. He does not give a clear answer to the question whether God created the night or the primeval deep. He does not say that God created the waters, but only that he separated the waters above and below the firmament. God separated the light from the darkness and made the darkness part of the created order known as night; it does not say that he created the darkness. It is quite inappropriate to ask if P's description of creation has anything to do with *creatio ex nihilo*. This is a complete distortion of the intention of P; he wants to guard with reverence the mystery of creation, not to explain it.

The second part of the story hints at an opposition between the world that God created and the world of our experience, and indicates the limitations of our understanding of creation. God created living beings in such a way that it was not necessary for them to stand in mortal opposition to each other so as to sustain themselves with food. Our experience of God's world, and this was also P's, is that mortal opposition is utterly unavoidable. Creation as we know it and creation as intended by God are in opposition to each other. We repeat, our understanding of creation comes up against unsurpassable limitations.

It was God's judgment that creation was good. It can never be our judgment, the fruit of our own experience. Our knowledge and experience are always limited by the unexplained and the incomprehensible. We can speak about creation then only with reference to the creator for whom it presents no riddle. Both human beings and the world are creatures and as such can only be understood in reference to the creator.

3. What Gen 1 says about the creator and creation cannot simply be integrated into and subordinated to what the Bible as a whole says about the action of God. The two are certainly related, but one is not the other. What P says about the creator and creation in Gen 1 is not the immediate result of Israel's encounter with God in the Exodus from Egypt and at Sinai. The "historical credo" (G. von Rad) contains no reference at all to the creator or creation. One cannot therefore refer what is said about God's saving act in history to God's creative action without more ado. The Old Testament does not speak of faith in the creator; there is no "creation faith." And more, the idea of revelation is not simply to be linked with God's creative action. One could not speak of a "creation revelation." The goal of creation is not a self-manifestation of God, so that God can be known from his work of creation *(revelatio generalis)*. Any opposition between the natural and the supernatural, between a knowledge of God derived from creation and a knowledge derived from his saving action, is foreign to the Old Testament. Here, there can be no "natural theology."

It is not possible to regard Gen 1 directly and without reservation as the beginning of salvation history or even as its preparation. The reason why this chapter is at the beginning of the Bible is so that all of God's subsequent actions — his dealings with humankind, the history of his people, the election and the covenant — may be seen against the broader canvas of his work in creation.

The creation of heaven and earth and of all creatures including humans has the appearance of a "once and for all" event. It cannot be repeated; it is not simply continued. It is not appropriate therefore to describe the further action of the creator either as *creatio continua* or a "preservation." One is saying too much, the other too little. It is the idea of blessing that intimates the further action of the creator. Blessing, the power of fertility, causes the permanence and the continuation of creation, causes "the history of nature" (C.F. von Weizsäcker). Blessing in the Old Testament is something peculiar to the work of creation. It is not taken over by God's saving activity, but remains always in some way related to what has been created.

4. The Old Testament has something of its very own to say about the creator and creation; this must be left intact, and must not be seen merely in its relationship to salvation history. Otherwise we will not perceive accurately what else is being said about another action of God which we find both in Gen 1 and in talk about creator and creation in the rest of the Old Testament. The result of this has been that God's action in history has taken on a dominating role and has come to be regarded almost exclusively as the only action proper to God. What is said about the creator and creation has been assimilated to or subordinated to God's action in history; consequently it has been taken up into a theology completely dominated by this theme.

New Testament theologians have gone a step further and have said that biblical expressions are only relevant for us when they are clearly related to human existence. But when existentialism becomes the only principle of interpretation, then biblical talk about the creation of the world loses its meaning.

It loses its meaning too when theology becomes so colored by soteriology that the two are practically identical. When God's saving intervention is absolutized, it is no longer possible to see what belongs to God as creator. If the whole of the Bible is the basis of biblical theology, then a theology which is completely soteriological or completely existential is not biblical. Both what is said about the beginning as well as what is said about the end loses its relevance; what is said about the end both in the Old Testament and in the New Testament is stamped with the language of creation.

The simple fact that the first page of the Bible speaks about heaven and earth, the sun, moon and stars, about plants and trees, about birds, fish and animals, is a certain sign that the God whom we acknowledge in the Creed as the Father of Jesus Christ is concerned with all of these creatures, and not merely with humans. A God who is understood only as the god of humankind is no longer the God of the Bible.

5. Since the Enlightenment, people in the west have lost their sense of the impact of the creation story because a scientific explanation of the origin of the world and of humanity has taken the place of the mythical and religious. The churches, which acknowledge in their Creed that God is the "creator of heaven and of earth," cannot deny that this change has taken place. And it is in no wise altered when one seriously questions both the fact and the results of scientific research into the beginnings and development of the world and of humankind.

In the light of all this, one may ask whether the outright rejection of the beginnings of science and its findings about the Bible in the 16th and 17th centuries was justified or necessary. Our present understanding of Gen 1 does not permit us to maintain this attitude. Our explanation has shown the reasons:

(a) P is not presenting his understanding of the beginning of creation as definitive and rejecting all other explanations. When he takes up older descriptions and lets them speak through his narrative there is no reason why more thorough research of the beginnings could not be seen from the perspective that colors his presentation.

(b) P tries to preserve the mystery of creation; he does not supply a ready answer to every question about creation, but deliberately leaves his hearers without an answer on many occasions.

(c) P is not aware of any opposition between a scientific and a theological explanation of the origin of the world and of humanity. This is true too for the whole tradition behind him. P's demythologizing tendency strips the heavens and the earth of any divinization. Heaven and earth are accessible to human research inasmuch as they have been denied any mythical-divine character. One can discern a scientific direction in P's thinking when he goes in for separations into categories, where he speaks of the heavenly bodies only in the context of their functions, where he understands the origins of plants and animals according to their species, and finally where he sees the world coming into being in stages This description of creation cannot be shown to be in complete contradiction to scientific research. Gen 1 does not exclude a scientific explanation of the origin of the world and of humanity, insofar as such an explanation remains open to the same reverent recognition of the creator that characterizes P.

6. There remains the question about the connection of Gen 1 with the Old Testament as a whole and with the Bible as a whole, especially with the Good

News of the New Testament. We may recall here what was said in the very first pages of the Introduction to the primeval story: the setting and meaning of Gen 1 consists in its being the beginning of the primeval story and so of a historical work that leads through the patriarchs and the exodus from Egypt to the erection of the holy place and the entrance into Canaan. This course of events, with its restrictions of time and place, finds in Gen 1 a limit that ties it to the beginning of time, the beginning of the world and the beginning of humankind as a whole.

The significance of Gen 1 in this broad context is that anything at all that takes place within this span is always related to that beginning. Nothing in the course of all these events, the liberation from Egypt, the theophany on God's mountain, the crossing of the Jordan, can be understood adequately if the point of reference is only God active in history; the God who is at work in all this is always the creator God. This is true too for what is narrated in the New Testament. There too the succession of events which brought salvation to humanity is always, both as a whole and in details, related to the beginning. God who sent the Savior remains the creator; the New Testament can only speak of a new creation because God remains the creator.

One can discern in Gen 1 a gradual ascent — toward the creation of human beings. It moves toward the decision to create humans and to the phrase that God created them in his image, to correspond to him, so that something can take place between God and his people. This is the basis of the history that the Old Testament narrates, the history of God with his people. When what is told about Jesus Christ in the New Testament is understood as the fulfillment of the Old Testament, the reason is that something decisive for humankind has taken place in him. When God created human beings so that something may happen between God and these humans, then what is told about Christ in the New Testament is the decisive middle point of this happening.

P's account of creation does not end with the creation of human beings. The sanctification and blessing of the day of rest indicates that the story of humankind is not exhausted by the increase that comes from the blessing, not by humanity's spreading over the earth, nor even by the exercise of dominion over the rest of creation; the holy day points toward a goal. Just as in Gen 1 God's work of creation does not come to an end with the creation of humans, so too in the Bible as a whole God's work does not come to an end with the saving action by which Christ redeemed humankind. The Bible is speaking of a definitive event which concerns not only humankind but the whole of creation. There will be more about the relationship between *Urzeit-Endseit* in the exegesis of Gen 6-9. It is important merely to point out here that in the apocalyptic texts the Bible speaks of a goal for the whole of creation, not merely for the history of humankind.

The Creation of Man and Woman and the Expulsion from Paradise

Literature

Survey of Exegesis: P. Humbert, "Die neuere Genesisforschung," ThR 6 (1934) 147-160, 207-228. O. Eissfeldt, "Neues und Altes zur Paradieserzählung," OLZ 43 (1940) 401-409. A. Bea, "Neuere Probleme und Arbeiten zur biblischen Urgeschichte," Bib 25 (1944) 70-87. Y. Laurent, "Le caractère historique de Genèse 2-3 dans l'exégèse française au tournant du XIXe siècle," EThL 23 (1947) 36-69. F. Hesse, "Die moderne Pentateuchforschung," ELKZ 7 (1953) 164-167. R. de Vaux, "A propos du second centenaire d'Astruc-réflexions sur l'état actuel de la critique du Pentateuque," VTS 1 (1953) 182-198. M. Metzger, *Die Paradieseserzählung (Gen 2:4b-3:24). Die Geschichte ihrer Auslegung von J. Clericus bis W.M.L. de Wette, Diss. Bonn.,* APPP 16 (1958/1959). W.F. Albright, *New Horizons in Biblical Research. The Whidden Lectures for 1961* (1966). K. Koch, "Altes Testament (Genesis)," PBC 106 (1966) 727-737. C. Westermann, "Neuere Arbeiten zur Schöpfung," VF 14 (1969) 11-28.

History of Research: K. Budde, *Die biblische Urgeschichte (Gen 1-12:5) untersucht* (1883) 46-88. A. Dillmann, *Genesis, 2-3; Die Schöpfung des Menschen, sein Urzustand und Fall,* KEH (1886⁵) 39-84. H. Holzinger, *Genesis, II. Das Paradies und der Sündenfall,* KHC (1898) 24-45. H. Gunkel, *Genesis übersetzt und erklärt.* Die Urgeschichte bei J, HK (1901; 1922⁵) 1-40 (1964⁶). B. Stade, "Der Mythus vom Paradies Genesis 2, 3 und die Zeit seiner Einwanderung in Israel," ZAW 23 (1903) 172-179. J. Wellhausen, *Prolegomena to the History of Ancient Israel,* (1905⁶, 1957 reprint) 297ff. R. Smend, *Die Erzählung des Hexateuch. Auf ihre Quellen untersucht* (1912). J. Meinhold, *Die Erzählung vom Paradies und Sündenfall,* BZAW 34, *Festschr. K. Budde* (1920) 122-131. H. Gressmann, "Die Paradiessage," *Festg. A von Harnack* (1921) 24-42. O. Eissfeldt, *Hexateuch-Synopse,* (1922). O. Procksch, *Die Genesis übersetzt und erklärt.* A. Die Jahvequelle (1924²⁻³) 15-44. H. Schmidt, *Die Geschichte von Paradies und Sündenfall,* SGV 154 (1931). K. Budde, *Die biblische Paradiesgeschichte,* BZAW 60 (1932) 1-91. J. Begrich, "Die Paradieserzählung. Eine literargeschichtliche Studie," ZAW 50 (1932) 93-116 = GesStud. ThB 21 (1964) 11-38. B. Jacob, Das Erste Buch der Tora, *Genesis übersetzt und erklärt* (1934). Die Toledot des Himmels und der Erde 71-134. P. Humbert, "Mythe de création et mythe paradisiaque dans le second chapitre de la Genèse," RHPhR 16 (1936) 445-461. S. Mowinckel, "The Two Sources of the Predeuteronomic Primeval History (JE) in Gen 1-11," ANVAO II (1937) 1-84. P. Humbert "Études sur le récit du paradis et de la chute dans la Genèse," *Mémoires de l'Univ. de Neuchâtel* 14 (1940) 1-193. W. Zimmerli, *1. Mose 1-11. Die Urgeschichte I. 2. Der jahwistische Bericht,* ZBK (1967³) 107-203. J. Coppens, "Miscellanées 18-23," EThL 24, II, 8 (1948). G. von Rad, *Genesis* (1972²). J.B. Pritchard, "Man's Predicament in Eden," RR 13 (1948/1949) 5-23. A.

Lefèvre, "Bulletin d'exégèse de l'AT," RSR 36 (1949) 455-480. J. Coppens, "Miscellanées 25, L'unité littéraire de Genèse II-III," EThL 27 (1951) 91-99. J. Schildenberger, "Die Erzählung vom Paradies und Sündenfall," BiKi 1, 2 (1951) 2-46. H.J. Stoeve, "Gut und Böse in der jahwistischen Quelle des Pentateuch," ZAW 65 (1953) 188-204. R.H. Pfeiffer, *Introduction to the OT* (1953). W.G. Lambert, "Le drame du jardin d'Eden," NRTh 76 (1954) 917-948, 1044-1072. J. Pedersen, "The Fall of Man (Gen 2:4b-3)," NTT 56 *Festschr. S. Mowinckel* (1955) 162-172. J. Dus, "Zwei Schichten der biblischen Paradiesgeschichte," ZAW 71 (1959) 97-114. U. Cassuto, *From Adam to Noah, I Genesis 1:1-6:8* (1961) 71-177. F. Hesse, Art. 'Paradieserzählung', RGG³ V (1961) 98-100. H.J. Stoebe, "Grenzen der Literarkritik im AT," ThZ 18 (1962) 385-400. J.L. McKenzie, *Myths and Realities*, "The Literary Characteristics of Gen 2-3" (1963²) 146-181. A.J. Bjørndalen, "Hvem er Adam?," TTK 34 (1963) 80-93. S.G.F. Brandon, *Creation Legends of the Ancient Near East* (1963) 122-140. E.A. Speiser, *Genesis*, AncB (1964) 14-28. H. Haag, "Die Komposition der Sündenfall-Erzählung," TThQ 146 (1966) 1-7. W.H. Schmidt, *Die Schöpfungsgeschichte der Priesterschrift*. Anhang: Die jahwistische Schöpfungs- und Paradiesgeschichte, WMANT 17 (1967²) 194-228. W. Fuss, Die sogenannte Paradieserzählung (1968). O. Loretz, *Schöpfung und Mythos. Mensch und Welt nach den Anfangskapiteln der Genesis*, SBS 32 (1968).

Introduction: J. Wellhausen, *Die Composition des Hexateuchs und der historischen Bücher des AT* (1899³; 1963⁴). B.D. Eerdmans, *ATliche Studien, I. Die Komposition der Genesis* (1908). H. Holzinger, "Nachprüfung von B.D. Eerdmans "Die Komposition der Genesis," ZAW 30 (1910) 245-258. A. von Hoonnacker, "The Literary Origin of the Narrative of the Fall," Exp 8 (1916) 259-299. D.B. Macdonald, "The Preabrahamic Stories of Genesis as a Part of the Wisdom Literature," SSO, *Festschr. J. Robertson* (1920) 115-125. U. Cassuto, *La questione della Genesi* (1934). A. Murtonen, "The Fixation in Writing of Various Parts of the Pentateuch," VT 3 (1953) 46-53. M.S. Seale, "The Glosses in the Book of Genesis and the JE Theory," ExpT 67 (1955/1956) 333-335. I. Lewy, "The Two Strata in the Eden Story," HUCA 27 (1956) 93-99. I. Engnell, "Genesis–dess litteräre och ideologiska problem," RoB 18 (1959/1960) 3-22. J.L. Koole, "Het litterair genre van Gen 1-3," GThT 63 (1963) 81-122.

Gen 2-3, as a whole: J.Ph. Gabler, *Neuer Versuch über die mosaische Schöpfungsgeschichte aus der höheren Kritik* (Nachtrag zum I. T. seiner Ausgabe der Eichhorn'schen "Urgeschichte") (1795). B. Studer, *Das Paradies und der Sündenfall*, Separ. aus "Die Reform" (1878). J. Meinhold, *Did biblische Urgeschichte, I* (1904). B.D. Eerdmans, *"De beteekenis van het Paradijsverhaal,"* ThT 39 (1905) 481-511. A. Wünsche, "Schöpfung und Sündenfall des ersten Menschenpaares," ExOrLux 2 (1906). A. van der Flier, "Het Paradijsverhaal," ThStU (1910) 300-348. E. Albert, "Ein neuer Erklärungsversuch," ZAW 39 (1921) 276-283. N. Rhodokanakis, "Genesis 2-4," ZAW 39 (1921) 76-83. A. Deimel, "Die biblische Paradieserzählung und ihre babylonischen Parallelen," Or 16 (1925) 90-100. S. Landersdorfer, "Der Sündenfall," ThGl 17 (1925) 38-60. K. Fruhstorfer, *Weltschöpfung und Paradies nach der Bibel* (1927). A.H. Krappe, "The Story of the Fall of Man," AJSL 43 (1926/1927) 236-239. H. Schmidt, "Noch einmal. Neuestes zur Paradiesgeschichte," ChW 46 (1932) 532-533. K. Budde, "Neuestes zur Paradiesgeschichte.–Noch einmal. Zur Paradiesgeschichte," ChW 46 (1932) 198-208, 719-720; "Ein Austausch zur Paradiesgeschichte mit A. Lods," ThBl 12 (1933) 1-10. H. Hellbardt, *Der Jahwist in der biblischen Urgeschichte. Diss. Bonn* (1935). A. Brock-Utne, "Der Gottesgarten, eine vergleichende religionsgeschichtliche Studie," ANVAO 2, 2 (1935/1936) 1-134. W. Staerk, "Hat sich der Paradiesemythos in Genesis 2f. in parsistischer Tradition erhalten?," BZAW 66 (1936) 225-232. A. Weiser, "Die biblische Geschichte von Paradies und Sündenfall," DTh (1937) 9-37. J. Hempel, *Gott und Mensch*, BWANT III, 2 (1936²). Th.C. Vriezen, *Onderzoek naar de Paradijsvoorstelling bij de oude semietische volken. Diss. Utrecht* (1937). E. Robertson, "The Paradise Narrative in Gen 2-3," JMUES 22 (1938) 21-35. J.J.M. de Groot, "Un Paradis Palestinien," *Mélanges R. Dussaud I* (1939) 65-72. P.A.H. de Boer, *Genesis II en III, het verhaal van den hof in Eden* (1941). M.A. van der Oudenrijn, *De zonde in den tuin. Een exegetische studië over Genesis 2:4b-3:24*, BijblMonogr (1941) 70-87. A. Geddes, "Creation. A Study of the Contrasted Accounts in Genesis.–The Origin of Sin in Genesis and a Missing Legend," HibJ 44 (1945/1946) 22-25, 248-253. P. Schempp, *Geschichte und Predigt vom Südenfall 1. Mose 3 aufs neue ausgelegt* (1946). J. Coppens, "Le sens de Genèse II-III," EThL 23 (1947) 179-182. A. Peter, *Das Echo von Paradieserzählung und Paradiesesmythen im AT unter besonderer Berücksichtigung der prophetischen Endzeitschilderungen, Diss. Würzburg* (1947). Review by H.G. May of P. Humbert, "Études sur le récit du paradis. . . . (1940)," JBL 66 (1947) 228-234. F.J. Leenhardt, "La situation de l'homme d'après la Genèse," *Festschr. E. Brunner* (1950) 1-29. H.W. Hertzberg, *Die Botschaft vom Anfang, Eine Auslegung der ersten Kapitel der Bibel* (1950). G.R. Castellino, "La storicità dei capi 2-3 del Genesi," Sal 13 (1951) 334-360. W.G. Lambert, "L'encyclique 'Humani generis' et l'Ecriture Sainte,"-"Les récits de création," NRTh 73 (1951) 225-243. Ch. Hauret, *Origines de l'univers et de l'homme d'après la Bible (Gen I-III)* (1953⁴). M.M. Labourdette, *Le péché originel et les origines de l'homme. Sag et Cult* (1953). I. Engnell, "'Knowledge' and 'Life' in the Creation Story," VT.S 3, *Festschr. H.H. Rowley* (1955) 103-119. M.M. Labourdette, *De erfzonde en de oorsprong van de mens* (1956). H. Renckens, *Israel's Concept of the Beginning* (1964). L.F. Hartman, "Sin in Paradise (Gen 2:4b-3)," CBQ 20 (1958) 26-40. H. Haag, "Die Themata der Sündenfall-Geschichte," *Festschr. H. Junker* (1961) 101-111. R. Rendtorff, "Gen 8:21 und die Urgeschichte des Jahwisten," KuD 7 (1961) 69-78. J.A. Soggin, "La caduta dell'uomo nel terzo capitolo della Genesi," SMSR 33 (1962) 227-256. N. Lohfink, "Genesis 2f. als 'geschichtliche Ätiologie'? Gedanken zu einem neuen hermeneutischen Begriff," Schol 38 (1963) 321-334. M. Bic, "The Theology of the Creation Epic," SEA 28-29 (1964) 9-38. L. Alonso-Schökel, "Sapiential and Covenant Themes in Gen 2-3," ThD 13 (1965) 3-10. W. Trilling, *Denn Staub bist du. . . Eine Einführung in den Bericht von Paradies und Sündenfall* (1965). W.H. Gispen, *Schepping en paradijs. Verklaring van Gen 1-3* (1966). F. Festorazzi, "La Bibbia e il problema della origine. L'inizio della storia della salvezza," Paideia, Esegesi bibl 3 (1966). L. Scheffczyk, *Von der Heilsmacht des Wortes. Kap 2* (1966). W. Richter, "Urgeschichte und Hoftheologie," BZ 10 (1966) 96-105. R. Lavocat, "Réflexions d'un paléontologiste sur l'état originel de l'homme et le péché originel," NRTh 89 (1967) 582-600. C. Westermann, "Der Mensch im Urgeschehen," KuD 13 (1967) 231-246.

History of Religions: P. Jensen, *Assyrisch-babylonische Mythen und Epen*, KB VI, 1 (1900). A. Loisy. *Les mythes babyloniens et les premiers chapitres de la Genèse* (1901). H. Zimmern, *Biblische und babylonische Urgeschichte*, AO II, 3 (1901; 1903³). J. Urquhart, *La haute critique, les découvertes archéologiques et les premiers récits de la Genèse* (1904). H. Gressmann, "Mythische Reste in der Paradieserzählung," ARW 10 (1907) 345-367. S.H. Langdon, *The Sumerian Epic of Paradise* (1915). A.H. Sayce, "The Garden of Eden and the Fall of Man According to the Sumerians," ExpT 27 (1915/1916) 88-93. F.M.Th Böhl, "Paradijs en Zondvloed in Sumer Studiën en Akkad," (1916) 433-449; *Het verhaal van het verloren Paradijs volgens de oude babylonische mythen* (1918). A. Lods, "Un poème babylonien sur l'age d'or, le deluge et la chute. Ses rapports avec la Genèse," RThPh 2, 3 (1916) 269-286. S. Landersdorfer, *Sumerisches Sprachgut im AT. Eine biblisch-lexikalische Studie,* BWANT 21 (1916). M. Jastrow, "The Sumerian View of Beginnings," JAOS 36 (1916) 122-135; "Sumerian and Akkadian Views of Beginnings," JAOS 36 (1916) 274-299; "Sumerian Myths of Beginnings," AJSL 33 (1916/1917) 91-144. H.Th Obbink, *Het bijbelsche Paradijsverhaal en de babylonische bronnen* (1917). S.H. Langdon, "The Sumero-babylonian Origin of the Legend of Adam," ExpT 43 (1931/1932). S. Thompson, "Motif-Index of Folk Literature. A: Creation and Ordering of Human Life," FFC Nos. 1200-1699 (1932; 19ff²-1958) 150-179. G.G. Scholem, *Geheimnisse der Schöpfung* (1935). A. Lods, "Quelques remarques sur les poèmes mythologiques de Ras Chamra et leurs rapports avec l'AT," RHPhR 16 (1936) 101-130. R. Gordis, "The Significance of the Paradise-Myth, I," AJSL 52 (1936) 86-94. E.F. Weidner, "Die Schöpfung des Menschen und die Einsetzung der Anunnaki," AfO 11 (1936/1937) 72-74. M. Witzel, "Eine weitere angebliche sumerische Parallele zum biblischen Sündenfall-Bericht," Anton 12 (1937) 237-250. B. Bonkamp, *Die Bibel im Lichte der Keilschriftforschung* (1939) 52-107. R. Pettazzoni, "Verità del Mito," SMSR 21 (1947/1948) 104-116. H.A. Frankfort, *The Intellectual Adventure of Ancient Man* (with J.A. Wilson, Th

Jacobsen, W.A. Irwin) (1946). V. Maag, (1954) AsSt 1-4 (1954) 86-88; 9 (1955) 15-44. J. Laessøe, "The Atrahasis Epic. A Babylonian History of Mankind," BibOr 13 (1956) 90-102. G.R. Castellino, "Les origines de la civilisation selon les textes Bibliques et les textes Cuneiformes," VT.S 4 (1957) 116-137. A. Pohl, "Das AT und die altorientalische Umwelt; Gedanken zum Paradiesesbericht," StZ 83 (1957/1958) 241-248. V. Soria, "Marduk y Elohim frente a la creacion del hombre," CuBi 15 (1958) 93-100. F. Festorazzi, "Il 'Mito' e l'AT," RivBib 9 (1961) 144-172. S.G.F. Brandon, *Creation Legends. . .* (1963). W.G. Lambert, JThS 16 (1965) 287-300. J.P. Lebeuf, "Un mythe de la création" (with B. Mambeke-Boucher), SMSR 35 (1964) 3-21. W.G. Lambert-A.R. Millard, *Atra-Hasis. The Babylonian Story of the Flood* (1969).

Dogmatic-Systematic: H. Bavinck, *Gereformeerde Dogmatiek, IV §11* (1928) 379-382. A. Kolping, "Inhalt und Form in dem Bericht über Urstand und Erbsünde. Methodisch-dogmatische Bemerkungen zu Gen 2-3," *ATliche Studien, Festschr. F. Nötscher* (1960) 137-151. E. Brandenburger, "Adam und Christus," WMANT 7 (1962) 45-47.

Text

2:4b When[a] Yahweh God[b] made earth and the heavens[c] —

5 there was not[a] yet[b] any plant of the field on the earth nor had any shrub yet sprung up for Yahweh God had not yet caused rain to fall upon the earth, nor was there any man to till the ground;

6 and a stream of water[a] used to rise[b] from the earth and water[c] the whole face of the ground, —

7 then[a] Yahweh God formed the man out of dust[b] from the ground and breathed into his nostrils the breath of life; so the man became a[c] living being.

8 And Yahweh God planted a garden in Eden, in the east[a], and put the man that he had formed in it.

9 And Yahweh God made all kinds[a] of trees grow out of the ground, pleasant[b] to look at and good to eat, and the tree of life in the middle of the garden, and the tree of the knowledge[c] of good and evil[d].

10 And there is a river going out from Eden to water the garden[a]. And from there it divides into branches and becomes four (separate) streams[b].

11 The name of the first[a] is Pishon[b]; it is the one that flows around the whole of the land of Havilah, where[c] there is gold[d],

12 and[a] the gold of this land is precious[b]. There is fine resin[c] there and onyx stone[d].

13 The name[a] of the second river is Gihon[b]; it is the one that flows around the whole of the land of Cush[c].

14 The name of the third river is Tigris[a], that is the one that flows across from Ashur. And the fourth river, that is the Euphrates[b].

15 And Yahweh God took[a] the man and put him in the garden Eden, to till and watch over it[b].

16 And Yahweh God commanded the man[a]: Of all the trees of the garden[b] you may eat[c];

17 but of the tree of the knowledge of good and evil[a] you may not eat; because on the day that you eat[b] of it you must die[c].

18 And Yahweh God reflected: It is not good that the man be[a] alone; I[b] will make a helper for him[c] that is fit for him.

19 And Yahweh God formed out of earth[a] every kind of animal of the

field and every kind of bird of the heavens, and he brought them to the man, to see how he would name them; and just as the man would name[c] the living beings[b] so was that to be their name.

20 And the man gave names to all cattle and to the birds[a] of the heavens and to all animals of the field, yet for man[b], he found[c] no helper fit for him.

21 Then Yahweh God caused a deep sleep to fall on the man, so that he fell asleep. And he took one of his ribs and closed up[a] its place with flesh.

22 And Yahweh God built the rib, which he had taken from the man, into a woman[a], and he brought her to the man.

23 Then the man said: This[a] at last bone of my bone and flesh of my flesh! This one[b] shall be called woman, because she is taken from man[c]!

24 And so a husband leaves[a] his father and mother and stays fast[b] by his wife, and they become[c] one flesh.

25 And the man and his wife were both naked, and they felt no shame before each other.

3:1 And the serpent[a] was more astute than[b] all the animals of the field which Yahweh God had made. And it said to the woman: Has[c] God really said: you may not eat of any of the trees of the garden[d]?

2 The woman answered the serpent: Of the fruit[a] of the trees of the garden we may[b] eat;

3 but of the fruit of the tree in the middle of the garden God said: you shall not eat of it, you shall not even touch it, otherwise you shall die[a].

4 And the serpent said to the woman: You will certainly not die[a]!

5 God knows well, that as soon as you eat of it, your eyes will be opened[a], and you will be like God, knowing what is good and evil.

6 Then the woman saw that it would be good to eat from the tree, that it was pleasant[a] to look at and that the tree[b] was desirable so as to become clever. So she took some of its fruit and ate, and she gave it to her husband with her[c], and he ate[d].

7 Then the eyes of both of them were opened, and they realized that they were naked, and they sewed fig-leaves together and made themselves aprons.

8 When then they heard Yahweh God moving about[a] in the garden at the time of the day breeze, the man and his wife hid themselves[b] from the presence of Yahweh God among the trees of the garden.

9 And Yahweh God called the man and said to him: Where are you?[a] He answered:

10 I heard you coming in the garden, and I was afraid because I am naked; so I hid myself.

11 He said: Who told you that you are naked? Is it that you have eaten from the tree from which I forbade you to eat?

12 The man said: The woman whom[a] you gave me as a companion, she it is who gave me of the tree, and so I ate[b].

13 And Yahweh God said to the woman: What is it[a] you have done! The woman answered: The serpent[b] induced me to eat.

14 And Yahweh God said to the serpent: Because you have done this, cursed are you among all cattle[a] and among[b] all animals of the

field; you shall crawlᶜ on your belly, and you shall eat dust your whole life long.

15 Enmityᵃ I am putting between you and the woman, between your seed and her seed; it will crush your headᵇ and you will snap at its heel.

16 To the woman he said: I will increase greatly your pains in childbearingᵃ, in pain you shall bear your children. Your longing shall be for your husband, but he shall rule over you.

17 And to the manᵃ he said: Because you have listened to the voice of your wife and have eaten of the tree of whichᵇ I had forbidden you to eat: cursed is the ground because of you; with toil you shall eatᶜ from it your whole life long;

18 Thorns and thistles it shall bear you, and you shall eat the plants of the field.

19 In the sweat of your face you shall eat your bread until you return to the ground again, because you were taken out of it. Yes, youᵃ are dust and to dust you shall return.

20 And the man named his wife Ḥawwah (Eve) because she became the mother of all living.

21 And Yahweh God made coats of skinsᵇ for the manᵃ and his wife and clothed them.

22 And Yahweh God said: Now man indeed has become like one of us, in knowingᵃ what is good and evil. However: that he may not now stretch outᵇ his hand, take from the tree of life, eat and live for ever!ᶜ

23 So Yahweh God sent him out of the garden to till the ground from which he was takenᵃ.

24 And God expelled the man and at the east of the garden of Eden he stationed cherubim and the flickering flaming swordᵃ, to guard the way to the tree of life.

2;4a ביום עשׂות: Ges-K §114e: "This use of the infinitive construct is especially frequent in connection with בְּ or כְּ to express time determinations." b יהוה אלהים: this description of God in Genesis is found only in chs. 2-3; Gk has ὁ θεός in 2:5, 7, 9, 19, 21. For explanation see commentary. c Sam and Syr have שׁמים וארץ instead of ארץ ושׁמים. This is by analogy with 2:4a; the usual sequence of MT is to be retained.

5a H. Gunkel understands v. 4b as antecedent, vv. 5, 6 as parenthesis, v. 7 as final sentence. So too Meyer, *Textbuch*. b טרם, actually "before," in the main sentence "not yet." As a rule it is used with the imperfect; כל . . . טרם "none . . . yet" Ges-K §152r; BrSynt §142a; L. Köhler, *Deutero-jesaja stilkritisch untersucht*, BZAW 37, 1923; D. Michel, *Tempora und Satzstellung in den Psalmen*, 1960; H.W. Kuhn, *Enderwartung und Gegenwärtiges Heil*, 1966, p. 21, n. 3.

6a The old versions (e.g., Gk πηγή) show that the meaning of the word אד was uncertain even then; the same accounts for the variants in the preposition in Tgᵐ (לֹ for מן). KBL renders the passage: "the sub-terrenean-sweet water stream, basic water(?)"; also bibliog. b The precedence of the subject makes this sentence too a circumstantial sentence; the imperf. יעלה describes continuous action in the past, Ges-K §107b.d; BrSynt §135d. c The perf. following the imperf. would, as in vv. 10, 24, be explanatory, cf. D. Michel, op. cit. §13; somewhat different Ges-K §112e.

7a The main sentence begins here, cf. Meyer, *Textbuch*. b עפר accus. of material out of which something is made; so too with יצר 1 Kings 7:15, Ges-K §117hh; Meyer,

Textbuch.   **c** ל describes the result or product of an action, so here and in v. 22, BrSynt § 107ig.

8a מקדם "The basic meaning (of the prep. מן) is 'part of. . . .'. Because a part of a thing can also be presented separated from the thing itself. . . . , מן can also express the location at a place different from the standpoint of the subject." Gen 21:16; Ex 2:4; 20:4 etc., BrSynt § 111a.c.d; Meyer, *Textbuch*.

9a The last eight words of the verse, "and the tree of life . . . and the tree of the knowledge. . . ." are uncertain and sound like a later addition. However the traditional text, constant in the whole textual tradition, is to be retained. The question is one of tradition history, not textual criticism.   **b** כל-עץ ". . . before an indeterminate genitive כל is used in the more indefinite . . . *sense of all kinds* . . . or distributively, *each, every*, e.g., *every* (kind of) tree, כל-עץ, Gen 2:9" Ges-K § 127b.   **c** נחמד:for the Gerundive meaning of the passive Ges-K § 116e.   **d** The infinitive as substantive has retained its verbal force, so as to govern the accus. object טוב ורע, Ges-K § 115d; BrSynt § 99b.

10a The series of imperf. consec. is interrupted by vv. 10-14. The first sentence is a nominal sentence describing a situation: "Driver . . . rightly lays stress upon the inherent distinction between the *participle* as expressing *mere* duration, and the imperfect as expressing *progressive* duration (in the present, past or future). Thus the words וְנָהָר יֹצֵא Gen 2:10 represent the river of Paradise as going out of Eden in a continuous, uninterrupted stream, but יִפָּרֵד, which immediately follows, describes how the parting of its waters is always taking place afresh." Ges-K § 107d, cf. BrSynt § 44c.   **b** ראשׁים can mean "departments" "detachments," e.g., Judg 7:16, 20; 1 Sam 13:18: division of an army into four; this is the meaning here.

11a שׁם האחד "The cardinals are determined by the article, when they refer back . . . to a number or list already mentioned, e.g., Gen 2:11" Ges-K § 134k.   **b** the name of the river פּישׁון occurs only here in the OT; חוילה as the name of a land only here, but as one of the sons of Cush in Gen 10:7; 1 Chron 1:9; cf. Gen 10:29; 1 Chron 1:23.   **c** אשׁר שׁם, cf. Ges-K § 141n and BrSynt § 152b: "In place of a preposition with dependence the adverb שׁם is found rather often."   **d** The article in הזהב describes the type, BrSynt § 21c.

12a וּזֲהַב ḥateph under initial sibilants after ו copulative, Ges-K § 10g.   **b** One Sam manuscript adds מאד to טוב; it is a secondary strengthening.   **c** בדלח, bdellium ". . . sweet-scented, golden, translucent resin from south Arabia. . ." KBL³; elsewhere only in Num 11:7: "The appearance of the manna was like that of bdellium-resin."   **d** אבן השׁהם onyx stone found in Yemen and India, 10 times in OT.

13a שֻׁם exception from the rule that closed unstressed syllables have only short vowels, Ges-K § 260n, n. 1.   **b** גיחון only here of a large river; as a spring in Jerusalem 1 Kings 1:33, 38, 45; 2 Chron 32:31; 33:14.   **c** ארץ כושׁ can describe different lands, see commentary.

14a חדקל old Persian, Tigra, Τίγρης, Tigris, elsewhere only in Dan 10:4.   **b** פרת Akk. Purattu, old Pers. Ufrātū; Euphrates 18 times in OT.

15a The narrative thread is resumed with the imperf. consec.   **b** "The masc. גן is in conjunction with the fem. עֵדֶן used as the name of a land" BrSynt § 16g.

16a צוה על as in Is 5:6 "I will command the clouds," also with accus., אל or ל of the person; KBL is incomplete here.   **b** עץ־הגן: the same as שֵׁם v. 13.   **c** "the inf. abs. is used to give emphasis to an antithesis . . . here it is permissive . . . so that v. 16 is in antithesis to v. 17." Ges-K § 113p.

17a The text-critical difficulty of the description of the forbidden tree is not to be set aside, cf. v. 9.   **b** vocalization of אכלך, Ges-K § 61d.   **c** The inf. abs. puts stronger stress on the idea contained in the verb; cf. the corresponding emphasis in the legal formulas.

18a The subject of the nominal sentence is a sentence, "that the man be alone"; in place of this sentence there is an inf., BrSynt § 15f.; cf. Beer-Meyer § 102, 2. The inf. is treated as masculine here, BrSynt § 16e.   **b** The Gk and Vg read the plural here: "We will make for him. . .'', by analogy with 1:26; MT is to be retained.   **c** לוֹ with *dageš forte* conjunct. (see also on v. 23), Beer-Meyer § 14, 2b and Meyer, *Textb*.

19a Sam and LXX insert an 'again'; this may be an attempt to adjust it to Gen 1; but it can also mean ''over and above.''   **b** A number of authors regard נפשׁ חיה as a later gloss (Ges-K § 131n, n.; H. Holzinger; Meyer, *Textb*.). This is possible, but by no means certain, because to summarize the species of animals already named in נפשׁ חיה can be deliberate.   **c** The singular suffix יקרא־לוֹ denotes the preceding collectivity, Ges-K § 145m.

20a BHK improves the text with the help of some Mss of the ancient versions to ''all birds.'' But this can be simply analogy. The more difficult reading of MT is to be retained.   **b** For וּלְאָדָם it has been proposed (e.g., Meyer, *Textb*.) that וְלָאָדָם be read, with the article. But this alteration is not necessary. H. Gunkel, referring to F. Delitzsch, says: ''no art., because meant qualitatively.''   **c** The proposed emendation of מצא to נמצא is not necessary; some want to understand the verb as qal passive.

21a תחתנה: ''It is but seldom that prepositions occur with verbal suffixes,'' Ges-K § 103d.

22a ל describes the result or product of an action, as in 2:7.

23a זאת with *dageš forte* conjunct. (see too v. 18): Ges-K § 20c; Beer-Meyer § 14, 2b; Meyer, *Textb*.   **b** No fore-tone *Qameṣ* because of the close link with the verb, Ges-K § 102g. No article as demonstrative pronouns are of themselves determinative, Ges-K § 125i.   **c** לְקֻחָה: *Ḥateph-Qameṣ* often stands under consonants which ought to have *dageš*, Ges-K § 10h. The *dageš forte* often drops out when the middle radical has *šewa*, Ges-K § 52d.

24a The imperf. to express actions which may be repeated at any time or on a given occasion, Ges-K § 107g, BrSynt § 135d.   **b** For the perf. ודבק and והיו, see v. 10.   **c** Sam Gk Syr Vg Tgʲ insert ''the two of them'' after והיו. Despite good attestation this would be due to analogy from the context.

3:1a Because of the inversion of the verb, v. 1a almost takes on the character of a nominal sentence, Ges-K § 142c; cf. D. Michel op. cit. ''The circumstantial sentence which precedes should give the reason for what follows,'' W.H. Schmidt op. cit. 211.   **b** מכל ''from among. . . .'', Ges-K § 119w.   **c** It is not necessary to add the interrogative particle to אף.   **d** ''In connexion with כל . . . לא is used to express an absolute negation. . . , e.g., Gen 3:1. . . ye shall not eat of any tree of the garden,'' Ges-K § 152b; cf. also Meyer § 98, 3a; Meyer, *Textb*.

2a מפרי: the versions add ''all'' (cf. BHK, but only some of the Greek); but the text is comprehensible without the addition.   **b** The imperf. has here a permissive sense, Ges-K § 107s.

3a תמתון, and in v. 4, full plural ending in ־וּן with the tone, Ges-K § 72u, not *nun* - paragogic, Meyer 63, 5a; Meyer, *Textb*.

4a An exception to the rule that the regular place of the negative is between the intensifying inf. abs. and the finite verb; cf. 2:17, Ges-K § 113v.

5a The perfect as announcing future actions or events after simple expressions of time, Ges-K § 112oo.

6a נחמד *desiderandus (desiderabilis)*, Ges-K § 116e.   **b** The versions smooth the text by omissions; the text should remain.   **c** עמה: closer definition of a noun by means of a preposition, Ges-K § 131t; cf. L. Köhler VT 3 (1953) 84-85.   **d** Sam and some Gk Mss read the plural; MT is to remain.

8a מתהלך: ''There can be added to a self-contained verbal sentence . . . an action or state . . . belonging to the object which is distinguished from an attribute by the absence of the determining article,'' BrSynt § 103a; cf. Ges-K § 118p; Meyer § 104, 2a; Meyer, *Textb*.   **b** ויתחבא: ''The verb with two subjects is generally in the singular and, where the genders are different, follows that of the first,'' BrSynt § 132; cf. Ges-K § 145f.; Meyer § 94, 7b.

9a איכה "To the interrogative particle is attached the subject as suffix," BrSynt §80e; cf. Meyer §31, 2c.

12a On אשר, cf. E. Schild, VT 4 (1954) 296-302. **b** ואכל (also v. 13), imperf. consec. in pause, Ges-K §68e; Meyer §77, 1c; *Textb*.

13a זאת sometimes used almost as enclitic to emphasize interrogative words, Ges-K §136c, 148b. **b** הנחש: the noun is at the beginning for emphasis, Ges-K §142a, BrSynt §48, Meyer §91, 2; *Textb*.

14a מכל הבהמה many regard these words as an addition. This is possible but has no support in the textual tradition; the MT therefore is to be retained. **b** מן as in v. 1. **c** תלך "Commands can be expressed by the short form of the imperf. used as jussive," BrSynt §5b; Meyer §100, 4e; *Textb*.

15a ואיבה the noun is at the beginning for emphasis. **b** ראש . . . עקב The second accus. determines the first more closely by indicating the part more closely affected, Ges-K §117ll, BrSynt §94c; Meyer §106, 2d; *Textb*.

16a The textual tradition of the two words והרנך and בעצב is uncertain. LXX has τὸν στεναγμόν σου (= הגינך?), Sam הרינך. Despite the uncertainty there is no need to alter the MT, cf. Ges-Buhl, Ges-K §154a, n.

17a לאדם: read לָאָדָם as in v. 21, cf. v. 20. **b** אשר: The retrospective pronoun is very often omitted where the predicate of the qualifying clause is a verb of saying *(verbum dicendi)*, Ges-K §136b. **c** תאכלנה for *hateph-patah* under כ cf. Ges-K §10g.

19a עפר אתה: Special emphasis is on the predicate and so it is at the beginning, BrSynt §27c, Ges-K §141l.

21a לאדם, cf. v. 17. **b** עור genit. of material Ges-K §128o.

22a לדעת: ל is to be turned by "that" or a gerund, Ges-K §114o. **b** פן־ישלח: ". . . the imperf. serves to express actions, events or states, the occurrence of which is to be represented as willed (or not willed) . . . in independent clauses after final conjunctions. . . ." Ges-K §107m, q; 112p; here "פֶּ is to be regarded as virtually dependent on a cohortative, which immediately afterwards (v. 23) is changed into an historic tense," Ges-K §152w. **c** וחי Ges-K §76i.

23a מֹשם: "In place of a preposition with dependence, there is often found the adverb שָׁם," BrSynt §152b.

24a . . . להט literally "the flame of the flickering sword," cf. Meyer, *Textb*.

The History of the Exegesis of Gen 2-3

Exegetes are constantly turning to Gen 2-3; they never cease proposing fresh interpretations. In fact there are so many that only the most important can be outlined here. The generally acknowledged conclusion that Gen 2-3 is to be attributed to a different literary source (J) from Gen 1 (P) is presupposed. All of the many studies of Gen 2-3 make this clear. Today there are only a very few exegetes who think that Gen 1-3 was from the beginning a unified account of creation, e.g., U. Cassuto and B. Jacob.

One of the most important and decisive results of literary criticism was the acknowledgement that Gen 2-3 was an independent and separate narrative. It is but logical to use this same method as a tool for a more exact interpretation of the passage. K. Budde was the first to attempt this in *Biblische Urgeschichte*, 1883. In Part II, "The Tree of Life," pp. 46-88, he takes as his point of departure what he considers to be the only real difficulty in the text, namely the presence side-by-side of the two trees in paradise. He removes as later additions all those verses or parts of verses that speak of the tree of life. He thinks that by doing so he has put aside all difficulties and has restored the original text of Gen 2-3, which now forms a unified self-contained narrative. This purely literary separation of additions from the basic text is bound up with an already formed theological view: the later addition, "The Tree of Life," represents the prevalent mythology of popular religion, while "the tree of the knowledge of good and evil" represents the superior spiritual-ethical religion which is characteristic of the school of J. This study of Budde's was the beginning of a series of works that followed the same or similar lines.

H. Holzinger (1898) took over both conclusions, a) that the narrative in Gen 2-3 is a unity, b) that the verses which speak of the tree of life are later additions.

H. Gunkel (1901; 1922[5]; 1964[6]) holds to two Yahwistic accounts; he refers to Budde, but sees in the version which deals with the tree of life (Jj) something independent and older side-by-side with the main thread (JE). R. Smend (1912) goes even further, speaking expressly of two sources: J[1] and J[2] (the earlier: Yahweh, tree of life, nomads; the later: Elohim, tree of knowledge, farmers). The attempt to find two sources or layers or narratives in Gen 2-3 has gone further and continues even today. J. Meinhold (1920) found two complete paradise narratives (J[1] and J[2]), and side-by-side fragments of a third; likewise H. Schmidt (1931). O. Eissfeldt (1922) discovered two sources of narratives (L and J); so too R.H. Pfeiffer (1953[2]), O. Procksch (1924[2,3]); W. Zimmerli (1943; 1967[3]), A. Lefèvre (1949); J. Dus (1959); S. Mowinckel (1937); H. Haag (1966); W. Fuss (1968).

The principles of literary criticism are determinative also for those scholars who on the contrary want to show that Gen 2-3 is a unity. Besides Budde and Holzinger these are in particular J. Coppens (1948 and 1951), J. Schildenberger (1951), H.J. Stoebe (1953 and 1962), G. Pidoux (1954), W.G. Lambert (1954), U. Cassuto (1961[2]), A.G. Bjørndalen (1963), E.A. Speiser (1964). This survey shows already that the method cannot lead us to any certain conclusion. "All attempts at an explanation by means of literary criticism are not really satisfying" (F. Hesse, RGG[3] V, 1961, 98-100). Likewise W.H. Schmidt (1967[2], Anhang), J.L. McKenzie (1963[2], 102-200), and even more pointedly, J.B. Pritchard: "Source analysis has led to almost complete anarchy" (1948/49, 5-23).

H. Gunkel adopts a new approach by looking to the pre-literary stage of the story. When dealing with oral tradition it is most important, methodologically, to recognize the line of demarcation and the unity of any individual narrative piece. Gunkel's first question was: Is Gen 2-3 a unified individual narrative, told as such before it was committed to writing? The answer is no. According to him Gen 2-3 "is woven together out of two traditions: 1. a story about paradise and expulsion from it; 2. a sort of story about creation" (*Komm*. 27). When Gunkel says that "the narrative is not an original unity," he uses the word "unity" in a different sense from the way it is used in literary criticism: he means that in the pre-literary stage, Gen 2 and 3, broadly speaking, were each narrated as independent stories. This basically new insight does not come through clearly enough in Gunkel's work because he was not able to explain and justify Gen 2 ("a sort of creation story") as an individual narrative unity, and was concerned almost exclusively with the paradise story. Hence this new approach of his is hardly ever mentioned by later exegetes.

This new approach was taken up by J. Begrich (1932). But here too the literary-critical attitude is so dominant that he calls his contribution "a literary-historical study." He begins like Gunkel with the separation into sources and their criteria, and his conclusion, it seems, is to reveal more literary layers. But it is a quite different approach that is decisive for him. He is impressed that the creation of the animals and of the woman are not essential to the story of the transgression: "They give the impression of a somewhat too long drawn out *exposé*," p. 103, and v. 24 sounds like the end of an etiological narrative. Thus Begrich has abandoned the literary-critical approach. He is talking about narratives as a whole, about exposition and conclusion, and so about the form of the narrative. These form-critical reflections lead to the conclusion that the creation narrative of Gen 2 was originally independent: "it was already there in fixed form," p. 108. He thinks too that the paradise narrative is composite; but we can leave this aside for the moment.

The form-critical approach is, for Begrich, very closely related to the tradition history approach. Apart from the question of unity, it was debatable whether Gen 2-3 was a conception of the Yahwist (emphasized by Budde), or whether it contained motifs from outside Israel (as maintained in an extreme degree by H. Gressmann, 1921). Begrich is of the opinion that it must be presumed that the paradise narrative had its origin outside

Israel. But these alternatives no longer hold when it is recognized that Gen 2-3 underwent a gradual growth in the oral stages of its formation. One can accept non-Israelite motifs for the early stages, but the narrative took its final form only in Israel.

Begrich's study with its method and orientation, just like Gunkel's new beginning, did not have any notable effect. There were reasons for this.

An unusual complicating factor now entered the discussion. Shortly after Begrich's contribution (1932), there appeared one of the most thorough and influential studies on Gen 2-3, P. Humbert's "Mythe de création et mythe paradisiaque dans le second chapitre de la Genèse," RHPhR 16 (1936) 445-461. Humbert reached the same conclusions as Begrich, but by a different way, namely that of literary criticism. However, one can only say this with reservation. He does not see the necessity of a new method of approach, like Gunkel and Begrich, even though his discussion of the results of the literary-historical method is predominantly critical. Humbert takes up a remark of A. Lods: "ce sont deux traditions primitivement indépendants," p. 445, and proves that in Gen 2 there is a creation myth independent of the paradise myth in Gen 3. He is of the opinion of course that it is preserved only in fragments because he, like most scholars before and after him, suspects a cosmogony in Gen 2.

Humbert cannot give a scholarly justification of his thesis because he, in contrast to Begrich, does not raise the question of the form of the narrative. He thinks that, instead of two sources, it is simpler and more natural to suppose that creation and paradise were originally two quite independent themes (so too G. von Rad, particularly his observation on 2:24). His thesis was not effective in the long run because there was insufficient scholarly justification for it. Also Humbert had not seen that Gunkel supported the same thesis. He quotes only Gunkel's literary separation into two sources, which he rejects, pp. 446f. In his subsequent larger work, "Études sur le récit du paradis et de la chute dans la Genèse" (1940), Humbert justifies the unity of the paradise narrative by means of a very thorough treatment of the recognized doublets in Gen 2-3 taking again a purely literary-critical approach and remaining thereby in this line of research.

It could be due to this unusual complicating factor that great confusion reigned in scholarly circles after Humbert's "Études." On the one hand the old literary criticism pursues its path and contests the unity of Gen 2-3 or its many sources. On the other, special emphasis is placed on the non-Israelite background and its influence (J.B. Pritchard, J. Pedersen, J. Dus, S.G.F. Brandon, E.A. Speiser) in contrast to a number of scholars to whom this is more or less irrelevant for the explanation of the narrative (K. Budde 1932, G. von Rad 1949, J. Schildenberger 1951, H.J. Stoebe 1953, G. Pidoux 1954, U. Cassuto 1961).

It is only quite recently that the methodological approach of Gunkel and Begrich has been taken up again. I would refer especially to the study of J.L. McKenzie, *Myths and Realities* (1963[2]) 146-181. In his survey of scholarship he takes Gunkel as his starting point and goes on to discuss the possibility of a non-Israelite background and history for Gen 2-3. He arrives in this way at a tradition-history approach. He distinguishes, like Begrich and others, the unified end product which is Gen 2-3 from an oral pre-history in which ch. 2 and ch. 3 were independent narratives: "The author has woven into a unified whole popular traditions and background-elements drawn from highly diversified sources," p. 169.

A position which is essentially the same is taken by F. Hesse in his article "Paradieserzählung," RGG[3], V, 1961, 98-100. The history of scholarship leads him to the conclusion that the endeavors of literary criticism are not at all satisfactory and that an approach like that of Gunkel and Begrich along the lines of tradition criticism is necessary. Its starting point is that the material has already been subject to many changes in the oral stage, particularly to embellishments. This means that Gen 2-3 as a whole can scarcely be pure Israelite material and that consequently one must look to the non-Israelite pre-history of individual motifs, even though the narrative was given its definitive form on Israelite soil.

The explanation of Gen 2-3 outlined by W.H. Schmidt in the Appendix to his study of Gen 1 (1967[2]) is basically the same. He comes to the conclusion that Gen 2-3 has a very tortuous and complicated pre-history which despite the efforts of scholarship remains difficult to explain. However, one thing can be said with certainty, namely that the creation and paradise narratives do not belong together originally, but that each was independent of the other. The most radical alteration in the tradition-history was the fusing together of these two originally independent traditions. But this is by no means a complete explanation of the pre-history; there are traces of a whole series of other independent motifs and elements which must be taken into account in the process of formation of the end product.

To summarize the result of this extremely concentrated outline of the history of scholarship, the following appears to be certain:

(1) A purely literary-critical or literary-historical method does not accord with the text of Gen 2-3. Consideration must be given to the pre-literary stage as well as to the literary. And so one possibility is excluded: Gen 2-3 did not come into being as a free creation of J.

(2) If many scholars advocate the method of tradition history, this is a sign that they wish to avoid extremes. Because the text of Gen 2-3 came into being gradually and bears signs of many stages of growth, the method of exegesis appropriate to these stages and layers must be many-sided and open. It must do justice to the many factors involved in the long process of growth. And so another possibility is excluded, namely that the text can be explained as it stands without worrying about the process of its formation.

(3) The history of the exegesis of the passage has shown that there are certain extremes which are to be avoided. Among these are approaches which are purely literary-historical or belong merely to the history of religions as well as those which begin from an already formulated ideology and from fixed dogmatic principles. The text of Gen 2-3 is complex and contains many different elements; account must be taken of this complexity.

(4) All attempts to explain Gen 2-3 which look for the key to the explanation in one motif or in a single detail of the text are of their very nature questionable. The history of exegesis has shown that the starting point must be the text as a whole and its structure, and that only exegesis based thereon leads anywhere.

The introductions to the more recent commentaries (E.A. Speiser 1964, U. Cassuto 1961), are restricted in their essentials to the question of sources (Cassuto) or to the historical and religious background (Speiser). Methodologically, both commentaries have adhered to the approaches which prevailed in the pre-Gunkel era, namely to literary criticism and to the method of the history of religions.

Speiser states first that it is a question of two sources, P and J; but he then notes that there is something common in the Babylonian background of both chs. 2-3 and ch. 1. All that he says about the narrative itself is that the central point is the tree of knowledge. He does not touch the question of the unity of Gen 2-3, the structure and nature of the narrative, its relation to already existing traditions, its final form, and so on.

Cassuto's starting point is that we have in Gen 2-3 teachings which are presented by means of narrative. Behind Gen 2-3 (as behind Gen 1) are poetic epics which existed in ancient Israel. This is shown by the use of poetic words and expressions, and particularly by the parallel passage in Ezek 28. The similarities and differences are presented in great detail in par. 3. Other near Eastern motifs are mentioned in par. 4 but the parallels affect only details. "But the Thora came and opposed all this." The rest of the introduction, par. 5-10, is taken up entirely with the question of literary criticism. Cassuto rejects the two sources P and J and proceeds to demonstrate the original unity of Gen 1-3. All other questions are left aside oee merely touched on in passing.

Comparing these two commentaries, we note that Speiser is so convinced that ch. 1 and chs. 2-3 belong to different sources, that he as it were presumes it, while Cassuto sees the question of sources as the decisive problem that takes up the major part of his introduction. Again, Speiser sees one of his most important tasks in elaborating the religious-historical background, while Cassuto stresses again and again how completely new and unique are Gen 2-3, and how they detached themselves from this background. One overestimates, the other underestimates. The new methodological approaches which Gunkel brought to the exegesis of these chapters are not taken into consideration in either of the two commentaries.

Literary Form

A basic presupposition for the interpretation of a narrative such as Gen 2-3 is to find out what it wants to say. The narrative is conceived as a whole and its interpretation is circumscribed strictly by the limits of the event that it spans. The starting point must be the whole as defined in the text. Gen 2-3 is a story which was originally told orally and which received its closer definition in the broader context of a number of other stories among which it was but one. Apart from the question whether or not there are direct parallels to Gen 2-3, we must begin with the fact that the subject of the story — the creation of humanity, its offense, the origin of hardship, pain and death — belongs to the context of primeval event about which there are stories the world over.

The subject matter of the narrative is of universal interest and extent, and so account must be taken of a great number of narrative additions and motifs belonging to the formative period which are now a prominent part of the literary product (cf. Introduction, 4, "The theological significance of the primeval story"). This is the reason why there are in Gen 2-3 repetitions, lack of agreement, lack of balance, gaps in the line of thought, contradictions. One could not expect anything else. The interpreter therefore has to come to grips with two factors: first there is the text as we have it extending 2:4b-3:24; then there is the many-sided process of the formation of this text. This tradition-history approach enables us on the one hand to give proper significance to the final written text as it has come down to us, and on the other hand to be conscious of a great number of older narratives, narrative additions, motifs and motif-links, which are all concerned with the creation of humanity and the basic question of human existence and its limitations, and all of which lead ultimately to the final product which is the text of the narrative as preserved for us in Gen 2-3 (see C. Westermann, "Der Mensch im Urgeschehen," KuD 13 [1967] 231-246).

Gen 2-3, differing from Gen 1, is, as it lies before us, a narrative in the strict sense where an event is portrayed within defined limits (H. Gunkel, *Komm.* XLVII). When one speaks about the structure of a narrative text, one must begin from the whole; the narrative moves up to a climax and then tapers down to a conclusion; the event as a whole corresponds to the narrative as a whole (E. Lämmert, *Bauformen des Erzählens,* 1955, 24-26).

The whole event described in Gen 2-3 reveals a carefully constructed arch which begins with the command that God gives to his human creatures, and ascends to a climax with the transgression of the command. It then descends from the climax to the consequences of the transgression — the discovery, the trial and the punishment. The conclusion, the expulsion from the garden where God has put the man and woman, calls to mind again the beginning. There is a well-rounded, clear and polished chain of events.

[Translator's note: here and elsewhere Westermann used the word *Geschehensbogen* to describe a narrative; it means literally an arch which spans an event. The image is a good one. The arch has a definite beginning, moves to its apex, and then descends to a definite point. The narrative spans an event in the same way. No attempt has been made to give an English equivalent of *Geschehensbogen;* nor has it been paraphrased consistently.]

Parts of the narrative which are not essential to this structure have not been mentioned in the exposition given. First there is the rather lengthy introduction; then there is an intermediary passage, 2:18-24, which separates the giving of the command, v. 16f., from the temptation in 3:1 that leads to the transgression. The last verses of the intermediary passage have the character of a conclusion to a narrative, as has been recognized by H. Gunkel, J. Begrich, G. von Rad, J.L. McKenzie, W.H. Schmidt and others. In any case v. 24 is clearly the etiological conclusion of a narrative, similar examples of which are frequent. V. 25 is a transition piece which can only be understood from what follows; there is nothing in what has preceded to give occasion for it (likewise Gen 11:30).

The question now arises whether the narrative which concludes in v. 24 is preserved intact or whether there remain only motifs or fragments. What is the nature of this narrative? The etiological conclusion in v. 24 is preceded by the "jubilant welcome" in v. 23 where the narrative reaches its climax. The creation of the man, v. 7 (vv. 4-6b are introduction), is already there as a successfully completed work. But the man, made by God as a living being, had not as yet that sort of existence that God really intended. A first attempt is not successful, v. 20b. It is only with the creation of a female companion that the earlier unsuccessful work of creation is completed, and it is this which evokes the joyful cry of welcome. This is a complete self-contained narrative with the exposition in 2:4b-6, the beginning of the action in v. 7, the course of the action in vv. 8 and 18-22 leading to the climax in v. 23a, and the conclusion in vv. 23b and 24. Moreover, the structure of the narrative is shaped by the course of the event described. If one wants to present the act of making or constructing in narrative form, then one must conclude with the completed work. But the process contains an inherent tension; it can succeed or not succeed, and so the narrator is able to divide it into several acts.

This is the case with the potter whom Jeremiah watches at work, Jer 18. The narrative structure therefore corresponds to the event. The individual acts are divided according to the action and its success (or lack of it). Introduction, 4b-6; I. 7a and b: the formation of the man in two stages; 7c: the result, "and the man became a living being." II. 8a and b: God plants a garden and puts the man in it; the result, "something is not good"; this is expressed in the reflection of v. 18, and with it the tension begins. III. 19-20a: God creates the animals and leads them to the man; the result, 20b, the man finds nothing that corresponds to him. IV. 21-23: the whole process comes to a successful conclusion. Gen 2:4b-24, without vv. 9-17, is clearly a self-contained narrative with a narrative structure that corresponds to the course of the event.

There is a tremendous difference in style between the two narratives. God is the dominating character in Gen 2 from beginning to end. Very few sentences in the whole narrative have any other as subject. On the other hand the paradise narrative describes something happening between God and his human creatures;

the dialogue takes up most of the space, whereas it is completely absent from Gen 2. Here the man is the object, while throughout Gen 3 the man and the woman form the subject. This stylistic difference is quite enough to demonstrate the original independence of the two narratives.

There are two main reasons why the nature and structure of this originally independent narrative had not been recognized:

(a) The whole history of the exegesis of this passage shows that almost all scholars maintained that Gen 2 was a parallel to Gen 1 (one spoke of the older and later accounts of creation) and consequently saw in Gen 2 only traces or fragments of a creation narrative (particularly P. Humbert). It is impossible to find a self-contained narrative in Gen 2 in this way. One can do so only in the previous knowledge that Gen 2 belongs to that group of stories about the creation of humanity which forms one stream of tradition parallel to those about the creation of the world (cf. Introduction. A. The Creation Narratives. I. Creation of the Whole and Creation of the One).

(b) The other reason for the misunderstanding was that the peculiar nature of the narrative was not recognized. The goal of the narrative was thought to be the creation of woman, the origin of love between the sexes (H. Schmidt) or the first consummation of marriage (which was detached when the paradise story was added, J.L. McKenzie). Such a view does not take account of the compass of the narrative as a whole *(Geschehensbogen)* which thereby loses its real meaning. From beginning to end it is a question of the creation of humankind which is only complete when the man is given a companion who corresponds to him in the woman. The creation of woman completes the creation of humankind.

The old presentation of the creation of humanity does not do justice to the peculiar nature of the narrative. It is no longer enough to say that God created people out of clay and breathed life into them. A person, created as a being whose existence derives from God, can no longer be described as the mere adaptation of something already there. The problem that arises here was transposed into an act of creation that was either incomplete or that misfired. The traditional description, v. 7, does not really cover what human existence is. The purpose of the narrative is to lead a new understanding of the creation of humanity. God's creature is humankind only in community, only when human beings interact with each other.

It is only in this way that we can understand why J joined this narrative to the paradise story. The former can serve very well as an *exposé* for the latter because in it (the latter) something happens between God on the one side and humans in community on the other, that is, man together with woman. It is certain that J was familiar with a whole series of descriptions of the creation of humans; he chose the one which corresponded as exactly as possible to the paradise story.

The course of events in the paradise story has already been briefly outlined. The structure is clear when it is recognized that the story of the creation of human beings acts as an *exposé* to the paradise story. The beginning of the action in 3:1 is prepared by the prohibition in 2:16-17 which has been neatly worked into the *exposé* (link with v. 9). Events move to a climax with the transgression of the command, 3:6-7. Then follows the punishment which is described in great detail in vv. 8-24 (8-13: exposure and trial; 14-19: verdict; 20-24: expulsion from the garden). There are two main parts, the prohibition and its transgression, and the punishment. Every single sentence takes on meaning according to its position in these parts. It is clear what the whole is all about: it is a story of the breaking of a law and punishment. There are countless stories, epics and dramas that deal with this theme. In the Old Testament, e.g., there is the story of the sin of Achan, Josh 7.

What distinguishes the story in Gen 2-3 from Josh 7 or from Dostoyevsky's *Crime and Punishment* is that everything takes place in a direct confrontation between humans and God: God addresses the prohibition directly to the man. God himself discovers the transgression, conducts the trial and pronounces judgment. Such directness is not found anywhere else. When the Old Testament speaks of God's judgment on human sin later, this can only be something indirect. The narrative of Gen 2-3 does not describe an event such as we experience in the course of our lives, but an event that is beyond our experience of history (in the broadest sense of the word); that is, primeval event. This is its distinguishing mark. It is only in the perspective of primeval event that the offense is a transgression aimed directly at God's express prohibition. Only there is the punishment an event which takes place in a direct confrontation between God who speaks and the people who listen. There is only one other passage in the Bible which is parallel to Gen 2-3 and where God passes judgment directly on human sin by trial and sentence. It is the world judgment scene in Matt 25. The parallel is possible because of the correspondence between *Urzeit* and *Endzeit*.

The paradise story then is a primeval narrative of crime and punishment. All narratives in Gen 1-11 (4:1-6; 6:1-4; 6-9; 11:1-10) belong directly or indirectly to this broad category (C. Westermann, *Arten der Erzählung in der Genesis; Erzählungen von Schuld und Strafe in Genesis 1-11*, ThB 24, 1964, 47-58). When we classify Gen 2-3 under this heading, we gain insights which are essential for the exegesis:

(a) The structure of a Crime-Punishment narrative is not as such primeval; each individual sentence corresponds to something experienced in the present. We are dealing with a legal process and so the vocabulary and the forms of speech of the court are used (see H.J. Boecker, *Redeformen des israelitischen Rechtslebens*, WMANT 14, 1964). The question is, how does something that is unique, such as is narrated here, differ from something that is happening constantly and can recur as a legal process.

(b) The question of unity, doubling, breaks, contradictions and so on can only be explained from this structure. Does each part, each sentence of Gen 2-3 belong to this span of action *(Geschehensbogen)* formed by sin and punishment. And how does each belong?

(c) Likewise the question of possible parallels can only be answered from this structure taken as a whole. A direct parallel would have to contain the two main parts, sin and punishment, as primeval event. Questions about parallels in details would have to begin with the place of the detail in the whole.

The fusion of these two narratives into one is an ingenious piece of work. Though W.H. Schmidt is of the opinion that is is difficult to decide what precisely is due to the Yahwist, nevertheless one can certainly recognize his hand in the way in which the narratives are fitted together. His method is clearest in the way in which he links and unifies the traditions that have come down to him. It must be emphasized that the unified narrative which appears in the final literary product presents a new, independent story; and that is because J has not just put the narratives at hand side-by-side, but has woven them together by anchoring the beginning of narrative B, Gen 3, in the beginning of the course of events of narrative A, Gen 2; and this gives rise to a new unified narrative. The structure demonstrates J's technique and intention in fitting the narratives together.

In narrative A, the sentence, 2:8, that God planted a garden and put the man in it (perhaps too v. 15aii), is closely associated with the beginning of the action in v. 7. To this J links the beginning of narrative B, vv. 9 and 15. While B was still a separate, independent narrative, two circumstantial sentences portrayed paradise. A certain perceptiveness is needed here: the garden that God planted for his creature in v. 8 has nothing to do with paradise. It serves to provide nourishment for the creature and nothing more. The two sentences, vv. 9 and 15, however portray a particular garden, behind which stands the very ancient and widespread description of a paradise. In this particular garden are particular trees; and so the theme of narrative B is sounded. The *exposé* of narrative B, now built into the action of narrative A, has achieved its purpose.

Vv. 9 and 15 were circumstantial sentences which originally portrayed paradise. One can understand then why vv. 10-14, describing the rivers of paradise, were inserted here. What has been done here is typical of ancient historical works, and particularly of J. A piece of "information" is inserted into the action or narrative at a suitable place; here it is a geographical piece. The passage 2:10-14, as information, belongs to a different form of speech than the narrative. It is enumeration (like the genealogies) and belongs as such to another line of tradition. That the piece was inserted here by J is clear from the framework into which it is set, vv. 9 and 15, which also are from J.

The action in narrative B is prepared by the prohibition in vv. 16-17. The prohibition was linked with the temptation while B was still an independent narrative.

The main part of narrative A, 2:18-24, lies in between. This gives rise to a slight difficulty, namely that it is only the man who heard the prohibition in 2:16f., while in 3:1 the woman knows of it. The seams of the joint are not well trimmed. But this difficulty is insignificant with what is achieved. By means of the inset, 2:18-24, J enables the action of Gen 3 to presuppose the community of man and woman as partners before God. This is the origin of the deep polarity between the positive and negative potential of this community.

A real difficulty arose because the inset, 2:18-24, with its definitive conclusion in v. 24, seriously disturbed the flow of the narrative from 2:17 to 3:1. J, with great ingenuity and simplicity, constructed a bridge passage, 2:25, which joined the narratives firmly together. Actually it belongs to the picture of the situation in paradise, vv. 9 and 15, i.e., to the *exposé*. And so 3:1ff., is linked directly to what precedes.

J's purpose in joining the two narratives was to present the primeval event of crime and punishment as one which involved humankind in community. A comparison with the only other parallel in the Old Testament, Ezek 28, shows that this was J's intention. This narrative too is concerned with sin and the expulsion of someone. It is a question of an individual, as in the alleged non-Israelite parallels. It is possible to discern behind certain parts of Gen 2-3 a still older form in which the narrative speaks of one person (J. Begrich, p. 108). The narrative readily divides into two parts which articulate the twofold nature of human existence: the temptation 3:1-7, and the trial and sentence vv. 11-19. The structure of the narrative shows that both are elaborations of the simple process of offense and punishment (both parts are lacking in Ezek 28). The story of the transgression is elaborated by the scene which describes how it came about; the story of the punishment by a detailed account of a legal process consisting of exposition, trial and sentence.

These two elaborations, which are a particular demonstration of J's art, are not constructions of his imagination. J's art consists rather in this: he made a selection from the many traditional stories about humanity in primeval time, chose those passages that suited his story, and fitted them together in such a way as to give the impression of a perfect whole. This view of the origin of Gen 2-3 gives a simple and a natural answer to the difficulties exegetes have found there.

Many scholars acknowledge the peculiar nature of the temptation scene, but explain it in different ways. One must accept that behind 3:1-7 there is a once independent narrative element which was concerned with a primeval sin of the woman and in which the serpent played a defined role. Reconstruction is not possible because it is so firmly fixed in J's narrative that we cannot say what he may have altered. One can still recognize clearly enough that the lengthy narrative of the trial and sentence is an elaboration. It has long since been observed that the man (and the woman?) receives a double punishment: expulsion together with what is pronounced in the sentence. W.H. Schmidt has emphasized that there is a lack of proportion between the sin and the numerous penalties. It is not in accordance with the one-stranded nature of the narrative to present the act of punishment in two sets of sentences side-by-side. It can be shown with certainty that the expulsion from the garden was the original punishment. This accords with the beginning of the narrative, and the same is true of Ezek 28.

The trial and sentence then are elaborations of J in which he makes explicit his intention of referring the primeval event of crime and punishment to humankind in community. J, with surprising readiness, fits into his narrative traditional primeval motifs which are recognizable from their etiological character. There is a whole series of parallels that show that an important function of primeval narratives was to explain present day limitations and deficiencies from primeval events, particularly from punishment and sin (cf. Introduction). Each individual sentence in 3:14-17 is to be explained from already existing motifs which once formed individual narratives. By combining all these individual elements which were trying to say something about human existence, J has succeeded in giving a convincing explanation of human existence as a whole and in its all-embracing ramifications, as having its origin from God, though disturbed by sin. The individual sentences passed in 3:14-19 lead to the expulsion from the garden. This means that every human limitation is in the context of alienation from God.

It is precisely the composite character of Gen 2-3 that throws into relief J's impressive theological plan. It was possible to fuse the two narratives together only because their contents were so similar; both deal with humanity in primeval event. A narrates the creation of human beings, B their alienation from their creator. If one looks at the two narratives in the context of their formation one

195

notes that the both motifs, which characterize the whole cycle of narratives about the creation of human beings, have been brought together (see Introduction, 3, A, "The Narratives of Crime and Punishment"; D, "The Primeval Story as a Whole").

Setting in Life

The original setting in life of each of these independent narratives in Gen 2 and 3 lies in the remote past. They belong to a cycle of narratives about the creation of the human race which at one time must have been of greatest significance for the community. We can draw this conclusion from the variety and number of creation motifs which are still preserved as fragments or reminiscences. As for the oral tradition, its length and its stages, we can only make conjectures. What is certain is that the creation of humanity was once an independent stream of tradition with a great number of variations and motifs distinct from the creation of the world, and that it must have had a different setting in life from the latter. It might have been connected with definite events in the life of people in the distant past, with the birth of a child for example, or with puberty rites. But these are only conjectures.

We can draw a further conclusion about the development of the oral tradition. The two parts of Gen 2-3 which were once independent narratives are representative of the two main groups of narratives about the creation of humanity in the oral stage; one group was concerned with the actual creation of human beings, the other with the meaning of human existence, what characterizes it, the fact that it is a created state, and consequently with its limitations.

J chose these two narratives out of the many that were known to him and formed them into a unity because the final product seemed to him particularly suited to serve as introduction to the first part of his work, the primeval story. Fitted into a larger work the narrative of Gen 2-3 acquires a new setting and function. What is said of the creation of the man and the woman, of their fall and expulsion from paradise, is taken up into a conception of history whose central part describes God's dealing with Israel and its ancestors. Gen 2-3, as part of the primeval story, now acquires a new function: it presents God's dealings with Israel against a background of his more universal activity toward the human race as a whole. The human being who takes part in the particular story of the people of God and on whom God works, is a limited being created as such by God.

The history of Israel together with everything that happened in it, is part of the history of humankind and cannot be set apart from it or put in a different order. One cannot say then that salvation history begins in Gen 2-3, but in such a way that the "fall" introduces a story of curse which is followed by a story of blessing beginning in Gen 12. The express function of the primeval story in the whole plàn of the work of the Yahwist is much more, namely to give meaning to God's action toward humankind as a whole; this colors the whole work. God's action toward his human creatures and the goal he has set for them, Gen 12:3, remains always the background to what is said about his special action toward his people. This accords with the lively interest which J shows in human beings, their potential and their limits, in his presentation of the patriarchal history.

Gen 2-3 provides an overture to the Yahwistic work as a whole — primeval story, history of the patriarchs, history of the people — and its themes recur again and again throughout: the many-sided aspects of the human community, the riddle of human sin and defections, human speech in all its ramifications. The patriarchal history recalls Gen 2-3 — people are destined to live in community of which the family is the basic unit. The heart of the Pentateuch, the exodus tradition, shows God's attention to a limited group of people and immediately afterwards the disobedience and revolt of those who have been the object of his favor. The promise of the land as the living space which God has given his people recalls the garden where God put a man and a woman. The Yahwistic work wants to tell us that the holy community, the restoration to life after failure, the living space and the means of livelihood, are all gifts from the hand of God, that they constitute a history with God, and that God is more than them all.

Commentary

Literature 2:4b-25: P. Humbert, "Mythe . . .", RHPhR (1936) 445-461. B. Kipper, "Genesis 2:4b-25, una segunda narrativa de criaçao?," RCB 4 (1960) 101-105. A. Vaccari, "In Gen 2:4-17 c'è un secondo racconto della creazione del mondo?," BeO 5 (1963) 9-10.

[2:4b-8] The structure of this first part is quite clear and easy to explain: vv. 4b-6 comprise the antecedent, v. 7 is the main statement, which is continued in v. 8. V. 7 tells us what the story is all about; what precedes, vv. 4b-6, tells us something about the situation in which what is narrated in v. 7 takes place. It can only be described as a "not yet," because such it was when humans were created. The stylistic form "when . . . not yet" has been dealt with in the commentary on 1:1-3 and in the Introduction. There is only a hint of it in 1:2, and it has been much changed. It appears in 2:4b-6 in something like its original form; nevertheless it seems at first glance that vv. 4b-6 is composite. Vv. 4b and 6 do not belong to the form "when . . . not yet"; both are positive sentences. Since v. 4b clearly refers to Gen 1 and is similar to the introduction, 1:1, it can be understood as a prefix which makes it easier to join Gen 2-3 to Gen 1: "It forms the transition from the priestly to the Yahwistic story of creation" (W.H. Schmidt, p. 196). V. 6, on the contrary, is an elaboration which introduces a notable break in the movement and which must come from a very different context. It is necessary neither for what goes before nor for what follows and so we cannot know the reason why it was put in nor its meaning. V. 5 would have made up the early form of the introduction with v. 7 added later. This makes it even clearer that it is the creation of humanity and not the creation of the world that is introduced by the formula. The sentence "when . . . not yet" presumes a situation where the world already exists (this is generally the case in stories of the creation of human beings, cf. H. Baumann, op. cit., 163); the description of humanity follows immediately on this introduction. What is then created is referred directly to people; it provides them with nourishment, and so belongs indirectly to the creation of humans.

    Most commentaries compare the order of the works of creation in Gen 1 and Gen 2-3. For example, H. Gunkel writes at this point: "The earth is originally dry; then there is water, man, trees, animals and woman. The order is very different from P." Assigning trees and animals to man is completely different from setting up the constituent parts of the world.

[2:4b] The ביום at the beginning of the introduction serves as a temporal conjunction: "At the time when. . . ." (Ex 6:28; Num 3:1; Is 11:16; Ezek 28:13). It corresponds exactly to the opening words of Enuma Elish: "When on high the heaven had not been named. . . ." This explanation of the origin of the introductory ביום renders otiose the question whether it means the first day of creation or the undetermined time of the beginning or whether according to J the world and humans might have been created on the same day.

Literature: Name of God: J. Skinner, *The Divine Names in Genesis* (1914). A. Jirku, "Der Gottesname in Genesis 2:4b-3:24," NKZ 27 (1916) 457-465. Ed. Naville, *Les deux noms de Dieu dans la Genése* (1917). H. Renckens, "De naam Javeh als sammenvatting van Israëls godsbesef," Bijdr 19 (1958) 117-136. K.H. Bernhardt, "Zur Bedeutung der Schöpfungsvorstellung für die Religion Israels in vorexilischer Zeit," ThLZ 85 (1960) 821-824. H.N. Tur-Sinai (Torczyner), "JHWH Elohim in der Paradies-Erzählung Gen II:4b-III:24," VT 11 (1961) 94-99. S.B. Gurewicz, "Some Examples of Modern Hebrew Exegeses of the OT," ABR 11 (1963) 15-23. S. Herrmann, "Der alttestamentliche Gottesname," EvTh 26 (1966) 281-293.

The description of God as יהוה אלהים presents formidable difficulties beginning from how the combination is to be understood grammatically to the question of its author. If 2:4b is the beginning of the Yahwistic narrative, as most scholars agree, then one expects the designation, Yahweh. How then is Yahweh-Elohim to be explained? First of all let us look at the facts. The combination occurs only once outside Gen 2:4b-3:24, and that is in Ex 9:30, where the text is not certain and the versions and the Samaritan differ. As the combination for all practical purposes does not occur outside Gen 2-3 the suggestion presents itself that it is an *ad hoc* formation. In any case it is certain that Yahweh-Elohim was not a usual way of describing God (contrary, H. Renckens, Bijdr. 19 [1958] 117-136). It must be explained from the special nature of the subject — talk about creation. The action of the creator God is underscored by this special way of describing him. This explanation does not exclude redaction, as F. Delitzsch indicates: ". . . the author makes the transition from אלהים to יהוה (c. 4) by means of יהוה אלהים. . . ." p. 113; but we ascribe it to a redactor rather than to the author. This explanation seems to be confirmed by the Gk which takes the process of assimilation further inasmuch as it reads ὁ θεός in 2:4, 5, 7, 9, 19, 21. This tendency to assimilation shows itself too in the story of the flood where it reads κύριος ὁ θεός in 7:1; 8:11; 9:12. A further indication that the combination of יהוה and אלהים is not a normal description of God comes from the dialogue between the woman and the snake in 3:1-5 where only אלהים appears.

Other attempts to explain the double name can only be mentioned in passing. B. Jacob and U. Cassuto understand v. 4 as a unity, maintaining the same author for Gen 1 and for Gen 2 and 3 and explaining each of the descriptions of God according to its particular function. The author varies the name with full deliberation and intent. B.D. Eerdmans (*Die Komposition der Genesis*, 1908) sees in the double name a sign that what was originally a polytheistic story has been applied to Yahweh. K. Budde, H. Gunkel and many others explain it as a result of the working together of two sources of the paradise story. H. Renckens understands it as a real name which came into use at the time of the Babylonian captivity. O. Procksch holds that אלהים was originally in the narrative, others that it was יהוה. E.A. Speiser, Tur-Sinai and others reckon with the possibility that, in accordance with Mesopotamian practice, the determinative "god" has been added to the proper name of the god. It is really impossible to translate Yahweh-Elohim (O. Procksch) and so for want of anything better it is turned by "the Lord God" (so too Gunkel).

The usual succession "the earth and the heavens" (cf. Is 45:12; 48:13) is likewise an *ad hoc* formation, in distinction from 1:1, so as to point out that what follows is very different. It has been shown that v. 4b is a transition piece. The combination Yahweh-Elohim, which occurs here for the first time, serves, as does the whole sentence, to clamp together the two creation narratives in c. 1 and c. 2.

[2:5] The sentence v. 5 contains two pieces of information about what was not yet there, and two reasons for it, each applicable to one part of the data. The only function of the information in v. 5 is to introduce the main sentence in v. 7 in such a way as to qualify it chronologically. The four negative sentences taken together determine the time of the creation of humanity as primeval time. It is not so important to say what it was that did not yet exist, but only to express clearly that reality as we know it was not yet.

What was "not yet" was "no plant of the field" and "no herb of the field"; this is a reference to what is basic for every living being. It does not mean, as W. Zimmerli and others explain it, that J is trying in his own way to describe "nothing," as if "the arid, lifeless earth of the desert" were an image of nothingness; or G. von Rad, "like P, so J tries to communicate an idea of chaos." But if, as we have seen, the narrative has as its goal the creation of man and woman and with them the creation of life, then the "not yet" sentence describes "what was not living." It is this that is the arid, lifeless earth of the desert (cf. Is 45:18).

The two words shrubs, שׂיח, and herbs, עשׂב, include the plants so that שׂיח describes mainly but not exclusively shrubs or the wild shrubs of the steppe (Gen 21:15; Job 30:4, 7), and עשׂב plants that serve for food or domestic plants. The word כל, used with both sorts, means that there were no plants at all, neither the one nor the other. The word שׂדה has the broad meaning of the plain or an empty tract of land. The first word then refers rather to wild plants or plants of the steppe; they need only rain for their growth; the second to cultivated plants which need man's care.

Gunkel draws attention to the difference between this division and that in 1:11-12. The wordplay that concludes the sentence, אדמה—אדם, points to the basic relationship between the soil and the person which in reality characterizes agricultural life. Basically soil and people are related to each other inasmuch as they are assigned to each other. Just as the cultivation of the land, which is more than simply the acquisition of food, is part of human existence, so too the אדמה is what it is because of the attention that people give it. Soil and people are associated with each other in agricultural life in such a way that each is determined by this mutual association.

A necessary pre-condition for agriculture is the rain that makes the seed grow and the fruit ripen. Rain is obviously considered to be the work of God: Yahweh-Elohim had not yet caused it to rain. It is presumed that it is Yahweh who gives the rain and the consequent prosperity, the blessing of growth. These few sentences of the *exposé* which sketch with negative data the setting in which the creation of humanity took place give us an outline of the world in which the narrative was conceived. It is a world where people cultivate the soil surrounded by steppe and desert, where life depends on the rain that gives growth to the shrubs of the steppe and to the seed of the cultivated land. It is a world which corresponds to that of the Palestinian farmer. However it is not the intention of the introduction to say merely that, but rather: when all this was not yet there, then. . . . It is here that v. 7 can join v. 5.

[2:6] *Literature:* 2:6 אֵד: E. Dhorme, *Recueil Dhorme* (1907). H. Zimmern, *Akkadische Fremdwörter als Beweis für babylonischen Kultureinfluss* (1917²). F.M.Th. Böhl, "Volkethymologie en woordspeling in de Genesisverhaalen," MAB.L 59 A 3 (1925) 49-79. E.F. Sutcliffe, "The Clouds as Water-Carriers in Hebrew Thought," VT 3 (1953) 99-103. W.L. Holladay, "EREṢ — 'Underworld'. Two More Suggestions," VT 19 (1969) 123-124. M. Saebö, "Die hebräischen Nomina 'ed und 'ēd — sumerisch-akkadische Fremdwörter?," StTh 24 (1970) 130-141.

V. 6 does not belong to the syntactical construction. If vv. 4b-6 are taken as a description of the situation, the question can be asked, how are vv. 5 and 6 related to each other as parts of this description. P. Humbert raised this question (*Etudes*. . . . pp. 10-14) and came to the conclusion that vv. 5 and 6 harmonize very well when one adverts that the rain is meant to be the natural way of watering the earth and the אֵד the supernatural. He understands אֵד as an extraordinary means by which God intervenes once and for all. Humbert concludes then that vv. 5 and 6 are not doublets. He has not noticed however that v. 6 on its own is part of a description of a situation, whereas v. 5 is part of the "when . . . not yet" construction. V. 6 does not fit into the construction because it is a positive description of a circumstance. For this reason and others W.H. Schmidt concludes: "It is probable that two originally different presentations are joined in vv. 5 and 6; with v. 6 another tradition has broken into the course of the narrative of Gen 2:5-2:7," p. 197. (So too H. Gunkel and others.) We observe that from the great number of motifs and narrative phrases in the creation narratives one motif or phrase from one narrative is very often assumed into another narrative.

If this explanation is correct, then we can take as our starting point in this much-discussed question of the meaning of אֵד, that we do not know the original context in which it was narrated that an אֵד went up from the earth and watered the whole face of the ground; in any case, the context was not 2:4b-6. This explains the uncertainty about the meaning of the word. We can divide the explanations of the meaning אֵד into three groups:

(a) A comparison is made with the only other place in the Old Testament where אֵד occurs, Job 36:27, where it is translated by G. Fohrer as a stream of water coming down through the clouds. The verb עלה shows clearly that this cannot be the meaning in Gen 2:6. The explanation of the word as vapor or mist seems to have been influenced by this (Luther, F. Delitzsch, K. Budde and many others; for the rabbinic explanation cf. E.F. Sutcliffe, VT 3 [1953] 99-103). The meaning "clouds" is the result of a deliberate attempt at harmonization (Targum).

(b) Another explanation begins with the verb עלה which is used e.g., in Num 21:17 to describe the springing up of a well: hence well or spring. So H. Holzinger: "Num 21:17 used עלה of springs; this suggests that אֵד should be understood as a spring, with Gk, Aq, Pesh, Vg."

(c) A third explanation is based on Mesopotamian equivalents. A. Dillmann had already referred to the Babylonian *edû*, flood. This explanation has been taken up again and supported by E.A. Speiser who made a closer study of the occurrence of *edû*, a Sumerian loanword in Akkadian: "The sense would be that of an underground swell, a common motif in Akkadian literary compositions" (BASOR 140 [1955] 9-11). This one word, he finds, covers different ways in which water comes forth: *edû* is explained as the waters "that water the fields." A verb similar to that in Gen 2:6 is used.

Together with these word groups, "to water" and "to go up" are found in similar contexts, and this leads Speiser to the conclusion, "The biblical verse might have been lifted out verbatim from an Accadian lexical work." W.F. Albright (JBL 57 [1938] 231 and 58 [1939] 102-103) derives אד from the Akkadian *id*, streams of sweet water beneath the earth or water from the ground (E. Dhorme had already referred to *id* in RB 4 [1907] 274). U. Cassuto follows this explanation: "The best explanation is the one based on the Mesopotamian name Id, . . . the guardian deity of the waters of the deep" (likewise W.G. Lambert, H. Renckens). M. Saebö has supported the derivation from the Akkadian *id* with new and forceful arguments. More important however is that a presentation similar to that in Gen 2:6 occurs in the Sumerian myths of primeval time. The myth "Enki and Ninhursag, a Paradise Myth" runs: "From the . . . of Nanna, from the mouth where issues the water of the earth . . . brought her sweet water from the earth; . . . makes her city drink from it the waters of abundance . . . he furrowed fields (and) farms bore her grain" (S.N. Kramer, *Sumerian Mythology*). This distant parallel shows that Gen 2:6 is concerned with something different from the "when . . . not yet" construction, namely a positive aspect of creation of which the watering of the land is part.

Excursus: *Adam (2:7)*

Literature: Adam: E. Brockelmann, *Grundriss I* (1908) 166. E. Nestle, "Adam," ExpT 21 (1909) 139; "Adam bei Symmachus," ZAW 30 (1910) 153. A. Christensen, *Les types du premier homme et du premier roi dans l'histoire légendaire des Iraniens*, Archives d'Etudes Orientales, 14, 12, 2 (1917, 1934). E.G. Kraeling, "Anthropos and Son of Man. A Study in the Religious Syncretism of the Hellenistic World," OSCU 25 (1927) 128-130. B. Murmelstein, "Adam, ein Beitrag zur Messiaslehre," WZKM 35 (1928) 242-275; 36 (1929) 51-86. S. Mowinckel, "Urmensch und 'Königsideologie'," StTh 2 (1948/1949) 71-89. A. Bentzen, "King Ideology - 'Urmensch' - 'Troonsbestijgingsfeest'," StTh 3 (1949) 143-157. E. Sjöberg, SvTk 27 (1951) 166-168. I. Engnell, "Die Urmenschvorstellung und das AT," SEÅ 22-23 (1957/1958) 265-289. H.G. May, "The King in the Garden of Eden," *Israel's Prophetic Heritage, Essays in Honor of J. Muilenburg* (1962) 166-176. A.J. Bjorndalen, "Hvem er Adam?," TTK 34 (1963) 80-93. C. Westermann, Art. "אדם," THAT, 1 41-57, (1971, 1975²). F. Maass, "אדם," ThWAT 1, 81-94 (1973).

The word occurs in other Semitic languages with the same meaning. Th.C. Vriezen follows H. Bauer in deriving אדם from a corresponding Arabic word meaning "skin," "surface." Used as *pars pro toto* in South Arabic and Hebrew it took on the meaning "human being," "man." אדם and אדמה derive then from the same word, meaning primarily the surface of the earth and only secondarily the cultivated land.

Of the 555 occurrences of the word 136 are in Ezekiel and of these 95 occur in the formula בן־אדם which God addresses to the prophet. Apart from this the greatest number of occurences is in Gen 1-11 (46 times) and Qohelet (48 times). There is no regularity about its occurrence elsewhere though it is frequent in the Psalms and the Proverbs. The word is not used indiscriminately when speaking of humans, nor has it anything specifically to do with God's saving action. There are no fixed literary complexes or forms of speech in the historical books or prophets where אדם has a fixed place.

The following are the main groups where it occurs:

(1) The concentration of the word in Gen 1-11 is in marked contrast to Gen 12-50 where it occurs only in 16:12. This indicates that אדם in the Old Testament describes a human being without any further qualification. The passages in Gen 1-11 deal with the creation of humanity and the limitations of the human state.

(2) There are a series of passages outside Gen 1-11 where the creation of human-kind is recalled or hinted at, e.g., Ex 4:11; Deut. 4:32; Ps 8, and elsewhere. Many of these references are to the person's position before God, as Gen 9:5f.; Lev 24:17; Ps 8, and negatively Ps 22:7; and Is 52:14. A number of passages speak of a person's preservation by God, Job 7:20; Ps 36:8, and elsewhere.

(3) There are some 60 passages where a human is contrasted with God: אדם means human existence in relation to God. The person often contrasted with God, Is 2:9, 11; 31:3, 8; the same holds for the way in which God addresses the prophet Ezekiel.

(4) The creation of the man and the woman is the basis for grouping humans and the animals together as living beings, Gen 1:22, 28; 2:7, 18-24; so too in the fixed formula מאדם עד בהמה, Gen 6:7; 7:23; Ex 9:25, and elsewhere. There are many other contexts where humans and the animals are named together.

(5) It belongs to the human state that the person is perishable Num 16:29; Ps 49:13, and particularly the Psalms which lament this Pss 49, 90. The contingent nature of human beings is closely linked with their fallibility and their capacity for wrong, Num 5:6; Ps 140:2; Prov 6:12, and elsewhere.

(6) The perishable nature of humanity is the special theme of Qohelet. Basic to the preacher's conception of humanity is a realization of its nothingness.

(7) The first six groups speak of the person's state as creature. There is a further group in which אדם simply means human as a species, quite neutrally and without further qualification as in modern speech. Other usages belong to this context such as the land of peoples, the voice of the people, etc. So the word אדם can be used simply for "anyone" or negatively for "no one." It must be said in conclusion that אדם is only a partial equivalent of our term human being. אדם does not mean a person as the exemplar of all, nor primarily the individual, but the species, humankind. The word is colored by its origin; it looks to the created state of a person, a meaning that runs through most of its usages. The use of Adam in the New Testament, especially in Paul, with its distinctive meaning in the story of salvation, is not Old Testament usage.

Literature (The Creation of Man): H. Bauer, "Kanaanäische Miszellan," ZDMG 71 (1917) 410-413. W.F. Albright, "The Goddess of Life and Wisdom," AJSL 36 (1919/1920) 258-294. H.W. Robinson, *The People and the Book. Hebrew Psychology* (1925) esp. 357-360. B. Attout, *Les premiers pages de la Bible* (1933). L. Köhler, *Die Theologie des AT* (1936) 116, 136, 139 (1966⁴). K. Adam, "Der erste Mensch im Lichte der Bibel und der Naturwissenschaft," ThQ 123 (1942) 1-20. P. von Imschoot, "De creatione hominis in Gen 2:7," CBG 30 (1947) 223-227. V. Marcozzi, "Poligenesi ed evoluzione nella origine dell'uomo," Gr 29 (1948) 343-391. D. Zähringer, "Besinnung und Umschau, I, Herkunft des Menschen," BenM 27 (1951) 250-258, 513-521. J. Schildenberger, "Die Erschaffung des Menschen nach der Paradieseserzählung," BenM 27 (1951) 276-290. J. de Fraine, "Jeux de mots dans le récit de la chute," *Mélanges Bibliques* (1957) 47-59. E. Amsler, "Adam le terreux dans Genèse 2-4," RThPh 3 Ser 8 (1958) 107-112. H. Müller, "La creacion del hombre. . . ," RevBib 20 (1960) 121-127. J. de Fraine, *The Bible and the Origin of Man* (1962). K. Rahner, *Das Problem der Hominisation. Über den biologischen Ursprung des Menschen* (mit P. Over-hage), Quaestiones disputatae 12/13 (1961) 34-42. A. Diez Macho, "El origen del hombre segun la Bibbia," EstB 21 (1962) 213-272. R. Amiran, "Myths of the Creation of Man and the Jericho Statues," BASOR 167 (1962) 23-25. J. de Fraine, *Adam and the*

Family of Man (1965).   F. Vattioni, "La spaienza e la formazione del corpo umano (Gen 1:26)," Aug. 6 (1966) 317-323.   N.P. Bratsiotis, "Ἀνθροπολογία τῆς Παλαίας Διαθήκης. I. Ὁ ἄνθρωπος ὡς θεῖον δημιούργημα" (1967), Review ZAW 80 (1968) 270-271.   J.V. Roslon, "Creatio protoparentum (Gen 1:26; 2:7) unicus hymnus?," VD 45 (1967) 139-149, 281-290.   F. Vattioni, "La creazione dell'uomo nella Bibbia," Aug. 8 (1968) 114-139.

יצר: P. Humbert, "Emploi et portée bibliques du verbe yāṣar et de ses dérivés substantifs," *Festschr. O. Eissfeldt,* BZAW 77 (1958) 82-88 (1961²).

[**2:7**] V. 7 is the main sentence, the statement, to which the introduction in v. 4b is directed: the creation of a human being. The event consists of two acts and their outcome. The creation of a human being as such is limited to this verse.

The verb used at the beginning of v. 7, יצר, is characteristic of the creation of a human being. P. Humbert has studied its usage (BZAW 77 [1958] 82-88). In 42 out of 63 occurrences, God is the subject. The object can vary: God forms humans, the animals, the dry land, the mountains, summer and winter, light. The verb describes God's creative work at the beginning as well as in history and in the present. The use of the word is not limited to the early period, though it is lacking in the vocabulary of P as well as in Deuteronomy and in Deutero-Isaiah. The verb has the concrete meaning of "to shape" or "to form" out of some material; in particular it is used to describe the work of the potter, 2 Sam 17:28; Is 29:16; Jer 18:2, 3, 4. After studying the use of the substantive as well, P. Humbert formulates his conclusion as follows: "In brief, the use of the substantive *yeṣer,* like that of the verb, begins with the potter's craft; i.e., its primary and basic meaning is concrete, plastic and technical. . . ." p. 88. It should be added that יצר is the verb used specifically for the creation of humans (and of the animals); its use for the rest of creation is secondary.

It is not at all certain, as P. Humbert's study would have it, that the verb יצר can be referred so one-sidedly to the potter's craft. Th.C. Vriezen, among others, has raised objections: "יצר does not evoke any special memory of the potter's craft, as it is often said to. . . . The use of the word עפר scarcely allows it because the specific word for clay or potter's earth is חמר. . . ," p. 129. When we think of the potter, we think of something mechanical, studied and constantly repeated; such is certainly not the meaning here, but rather a simple once-and-for-all event that we associate with the formation of a work of art. The use of יצר in Gen 2:7 can be compared with the fashioning of a figure out of clay (so S.G.F. Brandon, who thinks that the first human figures shaped in the Stone Age gave rise to the idea of creation, pp. 7f., 123), but that must be clearly distinguished from the potter's craft (so H. Baumann: "There was no need for the potter's craft to have existed in order to form the idea of a figure out of clay," p. 203).

The formation of human beings from the dust of the earth in Gen 2:7 is often explained with reference to the potter's craft. The reason for this is the many parallels which exist, especially those from Egypt, where the creator god, Khnum, is portrayed as fashioning the king's son, Amenhotep, and his *ka* on the potter's wheel. We are dealing here with an unusually common motif:

1. The creation of human beings from the earth or from clay or from dust occurs not infrequently in the Old Testament itself. "Remember that thou hast made me of (like?) clay," Job 10:9; and further "Thy hands fashioned and made me," Job 10:8; see Ps 119:73. This is hinted at in Job 4:19, "Those who dwell in

houses of clay''; cf. Is 29:16. The same idea is referred to indirectly when it is said that all people will return to the earth or dust from which they came, Gen 3:19, 23; 18:27; Pss 90:3; 103:14; 104:29; 146:4, and elsewhere. We can infer from the many occurrences and references that the idea of the creation of human beings from the earth or from clay was widespread and known at all times.

It has been mentioned already in the Introduction that in the background or side-by-side with it there is another description, that of man rising out of the earth. When Gunkel writes of 2:7 that ''the earth, mother of all that lives, has brought him forth like the plants and the rest of created things,'' then this is to be carefully distinguished from the creation of humans out of earth. It is yet another well-known way of describing human origins (A. Dietrich, *Mutter Erde,* 1925[3], pp. 170-171); it finds echoes in the Old Testament only in Ps 139:15. Its relation to the creation of human beings out of earth has not yet been clarified. It is likely that those oft-recurring passages which say that all people will return again to the earth have more to do with the description of their coming out of the earth than with the creation of humankind out of earth. In any case one cannot say with Gunkel ''The idea has been changed here to suit monotheism.'' The description of human beings created out of earth reaches back into the primitive cultures. What is new in J is that he speaks of the god of Israel as the creator of all people.

2. We know for certain that descriptions of creation of this kind occur in primitive cultures. I refer to the collection of stories from Africa in H. Baumann's work, pp. 203-205, and in J.G. Frazer's works (e.g., *Folklore. . . .* [1923], pp. 14-15). Frazer has no doubt that the raw material for the descriptions of creation in Greece, Israel, Babylon and Egypt has come down from their less cultivated primitive ancestors.

3. If the description of the creation of human beings out of earth or clay can be traced back to the primitive cultures, then Gen 2:7 (and the other occurrences in the Old Testament) have a long pre-history, reaching far into the past, and cannot be derived from similar descriptions in the immediate environment. The Mesopotamian and Egyptian texts too that deal with the creation of human beings out of earth and clay have their own long pre-history. It must be admitted therefore that the description of the Egyptian creator god, Khnum, mentioned above, is a late and a rationalized form which retains but echoes of the original story of the creation of human beings and which uses it as a means of describing the birth and coming into being of the royal child.

4. The frequent occurrence of the motif in Mesopotamian culture allows us to outline the history of the tradition; V. Maag has traced this in his essay ''Sumerische und babylonische Mythen von der Erschaffung des Menschen'' AsSt 8 (1954) 85-106. A form of the story, older than the Egyptian one, occurs in a description of the creation of Enkidu (the verb used is the same as in Job 33:6);

> When Aruru heard this,
> A double of Anu she conceived within her.
> Aruru washed her hands,
> Pinched off clay and cast it on the steppe.
> (On the step(pe) she created valiant Enkidu.)
>   (ANET p. 74)

Here too there are signs of secondary re-working of an older motif so that it has again become a means of presenting the ''creation'' of a human being in the course of human history. The other passages show variations of the motif which exhibit ever new adaptations and developments (see V. Maag, S.G.F. Brandon, *Creation Stories. . . ,* pp. 60, 77, 88-89, 123).

5. A constant in this tradition of creation seems to be that it takes place in two acts; the formation out of earth is followed by the giving of life (S.G.F. Brandon: "The formation of man is conceived as a twofold process"). In the Egyptian presentation the goddess Hat-Hor holds the symbol of life, the *ank,* to the mouth and nose of the form created by Khnum (S.G.F. Brandon, 61, 124). This is clearly a very abstract adaptation of the older form where the creator breathes the breath of life into what he has shaped. This older form appears in the primitive descriptions, as well as in the account of a Babylonian story of the creation given in Berossos (S.G.F. Brandon, p. 107), and in Gen 2:7. The creation of humanity through Prometheus also takes place in two acts: J.Ch.F. Tuch (quoted by A. Dillmann, ad. loc.): "The closest parallel is the story of Prometheus who fashions the body of a man out of clay and gives it life by means of a spark stolen from the gods."

The result of such a survey, which could only be given here in outline, is that the description of the creation of human beings out of earth or clay together with the breath of life was at hand to J. It can no longer be said, as it has been in the past, that this is J's own older and more primitive description over against P's. It is not original to J, but something that he had taken over and passed on. J's own description consists not in the actual description of the creation of humans as such, but in the way he takes it up and passes it on. One cannot agree with H. Gunkel when he wants to create a graphic connection between vv. 4b-6 and v. 7: "The whole hangs together in this way: originally the earth was dry, then it is moistened, and finally God creates his creatures out of moist earth, humans and animals alike, just as the potter . . . shapes his wares out of moist earth" (similarly O. Procksch). There is no sign of such a process in the text. 2:4b-6 is an independent piece of tradition; its function is not to prepare for vv. 7ff. It merely describes the situation: "When . . . there was not yet, then. . . ." The sentence in v. 6, that Gunkel wants to use as a link, probably stems from another tradition, and so its function is uncertain. But apart from all this, the creation of humans from the dust of the earth is independent. No attempt should be made to picture the event in such a way that the אד of v. 6 moistens the dust and makes it suitable for moulding. The creation of human beings out of dust (and so correctly H. Holzinger, ad. loc.) is presented as an inexplicable, indescribable and wonderful process. It is primeval event, and as such not accessible to our understanding, just like creation. This description of the creation of human beings out of earth has come down to the Yahwist through the millennia, and his intention is simply to point out how inaccessible to us is the event.

Attention is often drawn to two features of the narrative:

(a) Yahweh formed the person out of dust. If Th.C. Vriezen is correct in his determination of the relation between אדם and אדמה, then special emphasis falls on the word עפר (acc. of material, Ges-K §117hh). It is not simply dispensable, as many writers think, nor is it just a supplementary addition (H. Gunkel, O. Procksch); rather the word "has been obviously chosen . . . to point to the perishable material from which human beings are made (Vriezen, p. 130; Th. Boman, *Hebrew Thought Compared with Greek,* 1960[2], pp. 91-92); 3:19 also uses the same word in the same sense. J's choice of this word in the whole context and history of the motif makes it clear that for him, the idea which is immediately suggested by the use of "pinching off" and shaping out of clay or earth, is not the main one. Many interpreters have noted that the word עפר is not at all suited to kneading or shaping (W.H. Schmidt, "Dust is not the potter's material"); by using it J intends to say something about the nature of what is created, something about human existence. The act of creation as such, as an event that can be observed or described, is in the background. What is at the center here is something that J wants to say about humanity and its state in the context of the whole.

(b) The עפר is taken from the אדמה; dust from the face of the earth. Exegesis for the most part has laid great emphasis on the interrelation between אדם and אדמה, and many have seen in it the main theme of the narrative. However, a distinction is to be made between the demonstrable linguistic relationship and the word-play as intended by the narrator. The former has been discussed in the excursus to אדם. אדמה means primarily the surface of the earth and then the arable land. One can derive neither the person from earth (= the earthly one; see S. Amsler, RThPh 3 Ser 8 [1958] 107-112), nor earth from the person (= land of man); rather the same word is at the root of both, a word originally meaning skin or surface. One cannot ascribe עפר and אדמה in 2:7 to different traditions (to an agricultural and a desert tradition, like J. Begrich). Nor can one simply explain the relation of אדם to אדמה by saying that the person must be thought of as a farmer and that consequently the narrative must have had its origin in an agricultural community. The words do not allow this. The relationship attests that human beings and earth belong together, that the earth is there for humanity and human beings are there to populate it, Is 45:18.

The meaning of the wordplay for J and what he wanted to say with it is another matter (J. de Fraine, *Mélanges Bibliques* [1957] pp. 47-59). There are a number of possibilities. The wordplay can indicate what עפר says more clearly, namely that the person with its limitations is a creature belonging to the earth. 3:19 says both: "You are dust and to dust you shall return" and "Till you return to the ground, for out of it you were taken"; so we can take it as certain that both words in 3:19 and 2:7 refer to the limitations of the person's earthly existence. It is probable too that besides this primary meaning, another is intended, namely, human beings are directed to the earth in their work and that the earth is directed to the work of humans (H. Gunkel ad. loc.: "Man is created from the ground and he is called to till the ground; his dwelling is on the ground and he returns to the ground when he dies"). Even though this is the meaning, 2:7 should not be so constricted as to give the impression that it was speaking only about the creation of the farmer. This is certainly not the intention. The passage deals with the creation of humanity and all that it is capable of, not just with the farmer.

The second act in the creation of human beings was also part of the tradition that came down to J. It points to an understanding of humanity or of human nature that had clearly prevailed for thousands of years: a human being does not consist of a number of parts (like body and soul and so on), but rather is "something" that comes into being as a human person by a quickening into life. Behind this understanding lies the experience that a human being "is" in this twofold way: as just something (the mere body) and as something quickened into life. To exist as a human being then is to exist in undivided unity, as expressed in the last sentence of 2:7. And so it is not at all permissible either to read into the sentence that something of the divine was given to humans at creation (so Gunkel: "Going deeper: a person is related to God, his breath an outpouring of the divine. . . ."), or to explain רוח from the Greek or contemporary idea of spirit.

This explanation received great support from Philo and has had its effect right down to the present day, e.g., A. Dillmann: "And so we find here the specific difference between humans and the animals, i.e., when the breath of life is breathed into humans it means that what is communicated to them personally is not merely physical life but the life of the spirit." H. Holzinger, referring to Gen 7:22, and Th.C. Vriezen, referring to Gen 1:20, 21, 24, 30, rightly take issue with this: "Humans do not receive the breath of God as such, but God breathes into them the breath of life." Vriezen refers to the occurrence of "the breath of life" *(šaru balāṭi)* in the Amarna letters. In letter no. 143 Ammuniri of Beirut presents himself as "dust" before the Egyptian king who is "the breath of life." "This could be a reference to a typical Canaanite connection between the breath of life and dust," p. 132.

The breath of life then means simply being alive, and the breathing in of this breath, the giving of life to humans, nothing more (cf. Ps 104:28f.; Gen 7:22). And so there are no grounds for the opinion that God created humans immortal, as A. Dillmann has noted correctly. This view received strong support from K. Budde, and Th.C. Vriezen has noted that it colors the whole of Budde's interpretation of Gen 2-3, p. 132; this meaning is not in the text. There is another view, that the blood is the seat of life, cf. Gen 9:6, P.

Literature: Living Being: R. Dussaud, "La notion d'âme chez les Israélites et les Phéniciens," Syr 16 (1935) 267-277.   A. Laurentin, "Le Pneuma dans la doctrine de Philon," EThL 27 (1951) espec. 390-437.   M. Seligson, *The Meaning of* נפש מת *in the OT*, StOr 16, 2 (1951).   D. Lys, "A la recherche d'une méthode pour l'exégèse de l'AT. (Chapitre d'introduction d'une thèse en préparation sur 'emploi, portée et signification du terme Nephesh dans l'AT')," ETR 30 (1955) 1-72; *Nephesh. Histoire de l'ame dans la revelation d'Israel au sein des religions proche-orientales*, EHPhR 50 (1959).   G.E. Whitlock, *The Structure of Personality in Hebrew Psychology* (נפש;רוח;בשׂר) (1960).   W.H. Schmidt, "Anthropologische Begriffe im AT. Anmerkungen zum hebräischen Denken," EvTh 24 (1964) 374-388.   J. Scharbert, *Fleisch, Geist und Seele im Pentateuch. Ein Beitrag zur Anthropologie der Pentateuchquellen*, SBS 19 (1966).   H.J. Schultz, (ed.) *Was weiss man von der Seele?* (1967). On OT: C. Westermann 167-176.

"And man became a living being." The final result is set apart from the two stages of the act of creation. The person created by God is a living person. This sentence is very important for the biblical understanding of humanity: a person is created as a נפש חיה; a "living soul" is not put into one's body. The person as a living being is to be understood as a whole and any idea that one is made up of body and soul is ruled out. A person created as a living being means that one is a person only in one's living state. A person cannot be made into an object of study apart from the living state in which that person exists. An "image of humanity" or a doctrine about humanity cannot comprehend human existence as it is.

[2:8] Part of the story of the creation of human beings is concerned with providing for them. The fact that they have been created as living beings means that they must be provided with the means to live. This too is a tradition already at hand and, as we have seen, is found in the primitive creation stories. It is enough however to refer to the parallels in Gen 1:26-30. Here too provision of the means of life is part of the process of creation. Likewise both passages agree that the creator has provided his creatures with a vegetarian diet. (An ancient "piece of information" is assimilated here: the Greek and Roman classics also mention that at an earlier stage a person's principal means of nourishment was fruit; cf. A. Dillmann's commentary for details.) There can be no doubt then that v. 8 belongs in vv. 4b-7. V. 8 is the continuation of v. 7 that one expects.

The parallels to which we have pointed (2:8 is parallel to 1:29, not to 1:11-12) show that 2:8 is not a narrative about the creation of plants, but about the provision of nourishment for the human creatures; this is a very important difference. The narrator is not interested in plant life and vegetation in general because he is talking about the creation of humans. God plants a garden to provide for his human creatures, not as part of the creation of plants. So any exegetical reflections which begin with a parallel between 2:8 and 1:11-12 are void. The garden God planted to provide for his people has nothing to do with a garden of God (or of the gods) or with what is popularly called paradise. As Vriezen has remarked there can be no question of a garden of God because this garden was planted by God only after the creation of human beings and is meant for them alone.

The garden takes on a further significance of its own only because something is said about it or happens in it as in vv. 9, 15-17. The Gk renders the word גן by παράδεισος and it is this that first gives the garden a significance which it does not have in the narrative. The idea of a paradise therefore only comes up for discussion with vv. 9 and 15-17. The present verse, v. 8, is to be explained independently — it is "a garden in Eden in the east." Prescinding first from the meaning of the words, the grammatical construction shows that the garden which God planted is localized by two further qualifications: the garden is in Eden, and Eden is in the east, i.e., to the east of the speaker; there is both limitation and distance. "Eden" then is used to describe a land in the east.

The two narratives about the creation of humans and expulsion from the garden meet or overlap in the garden motif. However it must not be concluded that the idea of a garden in each of them is the same. There were many descriptions of paradise among Israel's neighbors and her predecessors, and the garden motif (or the garden of the gods or paradise) is found in many kinds of narratives; this plurality must be our starting point. The garden has a very different function in each narrative. And so we must assume that each is dealing with something different and has a different history. The garden in narrative A can mean nothing more than just an orchard planted in Eden in the east. The garden in narrative B on the contrary has quite another function. It is the garden from which the people were driven out because of their sin. It is here and here only that the garden stands for the "lost paradise." It is also possible that there is an echo of the garden of God. It is important for the understanding of these two originally independent narratives, as well as for the final form in which they are joined, to be aware that two different descriptions of a primeval garden are brought together which once presented two different motifs.

Excursus: *"Eden."*

Literature: A. Jeremias, "Hölle und Paradies bei den Babyloniern," ATAO 4 (1900) 81-83. F. Hommel, *Die Insel der Seligen in Mythe und Sage der Vorzeit* (1901). A.

Bertholet, *Die Gefilde der Seligen,* SGV 33 (1903). P. Capelle, "Elysium und Inseln der Seligen," ARW 25 (1927) 245-364. E. Burrows, "Tilmun, Bahrain, Paradise," Or 30 (1928). J. Theis, *Das Land des Paradieses* (1928). A. Schulz, "Eden (עֵדֶן) Genesis 2:(8)," ZAW 51 (1933) 222-226. J. de Fraine, "Paradisus apud Sumeros?," VD 25 (1947) 161-171. A.G. von Hamel, *De tuin der goden, I. Mythen der Egyptenaren, volken van Voor-Asië, Indiërs, Grieken, Skandinaviërs en Kelten,* with H.Th. Obbink (ed.) (1947²). A. Auer, "Vom Paradies," Gl Dei 3 (1948/1949) 68-76. J. Kroll, "Elysium," AFLNW 2 (1952) 7-35. A. Jepsen, Art. "'Paradies' II. Im AT," RGG³ V (1961) 96-98. F.M.Th. Böhl, Art. "'Paradies' I. Religionsgeschichtlich," RGG³ V (1961) 95-96.

The word Eden occurs in the Old Testament 14 times in the singular and three times in the plural;

(1) Garden in Eden: Gen 2:8, 10 (?)
Garden Eden: Gen 2:10 (?), 15; 3:23, 24; Ezek 36:35; Joel 2:3
Eden: Gen 4:16; Is 51:3; Ezek 31:9, 16, 18 (twice)
Eden, the garden of God: Ezek 28:13; trees of Eden in the garden of God: Ezek 31:9
Eden parallel to the garden of Yahweh: Is 51:3.

Eden is a name in all these passages of the Old Testament where it occurs in the singular; the picture is the same; it is presumed that it is an area (or region or garden) that is well known, that it is a well-watered, beautiful and fruitful area, a land of plenty, the "land of bliss." This is shown by the sharp contrasts as in Is 51:3: "For the Lord . . . will make her wilderness like Eden"; also Ezek 36:35; Joel 2:3. The region was known for its beautiful lofty trees, Ezek 31:9, 16, 18.

(2) Some passages put this area (or garden) on a par with the garden of Yahweh (God): Is 51:3; Ezek 28:13; 31:9; cf. Gen 13:10, "The garden of Yahweh" (without 'Eden'). We can be certain that these passages presume narratives about the garden of God and that they were set in primeval time.

(3) This is confirmed by Ezek 28:13 which deals with the expulsion of a primeval (?) person out of Eden, the garden of God. We have here an exact parallel to the Eden of Gen 2:3. The same name occurs in the context of the same event. However, in Ezekiel Eden is described as the garden of God: "You were in Eden, the garden of God."

(4) Th.C. Vriezen argues that the passage cannot be referring to the garden of God because the garden is planted expressly by God as a place where humans are to live and to find the means of life. This opinion, which is held by many others, seems to be in contradiction to the conclusion that derives from Ezek 28:13, where Eden is described as the garden of God.

(5) The only solution to the problem is that the many stories about Eden reflect not one but a whole cycle of narratives. This is confirmed by the different ways in which the name is used, in particular that now it is the garden (of Eden), now the garden in Eden. This variation occurs only in Gen 2-3. The description "a garden in Eden" is found only in 2:8 (2:10 is uncertain); the "garden (of) Eden" in (2:10?); 2:15; 3:23-24. This means that "a garden in Eden" occurs in the story of the creation of human beings, and the "garden (of) Eden" in the story of the expulsion from the garden. Vriezen's thesis that 2:8 could not refer to the garden of God is to the point, but only for 2:8, i.e., only for narrative A. The thesis is not to be extended to Gen 2:15; 3:23-24. The "garden (of) Eden" in these passages belongs to another narrative and stream of tradition, the same stream that lies behind Ezek 28:13ff. It has often been noted that "the sound of the Lord God walking in the garden," 3:8, points to the garden of God. It is very probable that the older presentation of the garden of God is the background of the "garden (of) Eden" in narrative B, as in Ezek 28.

(6) We come to the conclusion then that any attempt to derive the word Eden in Gen 2-3 from one presentation or tradition must be given up. Instead, one must start with the presupposition that a whole cycle of narratives from different streams of tradition and with different presentations lies behind both the Old Testament and other writings. We have then the following results:

(a) All interpreters agree that Eden in Gen 2:8 is a geographical description referring to the land or region where Eden lies (this can be said with certainty only of 2:8, but not of the other passages).

(b) Some interpreters are of the opinion that this land or region can be given further precision from place names that occur outside Gen 2-3: עֵדֶן = Akkad. bīt adīni, an area lying on both sides of the Euphrates, 2 Kings 19:12; Is 37:12; Ezek 27:23; in Amos 1:5 we read בֵית עֵדֶן (so e.g., Th. Schwegler).

(c) Others (KBL, E.A. Speiser, O. Loretz) relate עֵדֶן to the Akkad. ādinu, steppe, desert, and explain the garden of Eden as an oasis in the steppes (H. Gunkel, W. Zimmerli, W.F. Albright, W.B. Kristensen, W. Caspari and others). Against this however is the fact that the first letter of the Akkad. edinu does not correspond to the Hebrew עֵדֶן, whereas Ugaritic has a word which corresponds exactly to the Hebrew and has a similar meaning, "delight" (U. Cassuto, Th.C. Vriezen); also, that the derivation of the word from the Hebrew name in the plural suggests itself and explains it adequately (Jer 51:34; 2 Sam 1:24; Ps 36:8: "And thou givest them drink from the river of thy delights"). So too U. Cassuto. For further discussion, see Th.C. Vriezen and A. Brock-Utne, AN-VAQ, 2, 2 (1935-1936) 1-134.

(d) Eden then means an actual land (or region); the name "intends to describe definite land" (F. Delitzsch ad. loc.). But this land cannot be located geographically, it "cannot be shown to exist outside the Bible" (A. Dillmann ad. loc.). "The author uses Eden in Gen 2 as an old name; he presumes that it rings a bell in the mind of the reader" (Th.C. Vriezen ad.loc.). "Names in ancient stories are always tradition" (H. Gunkel and others). The narrative wants to set the land far, far away; and so it has echoes of "land of good fortune," "land of delight," (so F. Delitzsch, A. Dillmann, Th.C. Vriezen and others).

(e) One must distinguish from this the use of the name as a direct description of the garden, גַן־עֵדֶן (so O. Procksch, W. Zimmerli,Th.C. Vriezen and others). Vriezen's triple distinction of the meaning into geographical, symbolical and mythical, does not seem necessary. It is likely that the name of the area where the garden lay has been transferred to the garden, and that this happened because the distant land already had overtones of the land of bliss. This explains all occurrences in the Old Testament. The reverse position that Vriezen presents, namely that the author of Gen 2 first constructed a definite locality out of the mythical name Eden and thereby removed it from the sphere of myth, is not convincing because he had already spoken of a "garden in Eden" in 2:15; 3:23-24, and so made it quite clear that he was giving the garden a definite locality.

(7) The Gk translates גַן of 2:8 by παράδεισος; the Vg turns a "garden in Eden" into paradisus voluptatis. The loan word פַּרְדֵּס which occurs in the Old Testament in Song 4:13; Neh 2:8; Eccles 2:5, comes from the Persian, or more precisely from old Bactrian. It is an Avesta word (H. Gunkel) whose primary meaning is "a walling," "a hedging around," and so it means "a pleasure garden surrounded by a stone or earthen wall" (F. Delitzsch). The word has the same meaning as גַן; as a loan word it is impressed with distinct associations, such as we attach to the word paradise. But this is not the meaning in Gen 2:8. It is rather a fertile, beautiful and well-watered garden with trees.

מִקֶּדֶם means "in the east," i.e., to the east of the narrator, not to the east of Eden, which would be possible grammatically. When Th.C. Vriezen writes of this detail that "it does not make the location of paradise much clearer," then it seems that he has missed the point. The intention is not to fix the area geographically but to push the scene of the event into the far, unknown distance (similarly A. Brock-Utne ad. loc.). This is a fixed stylistic trait of narratives of this kind and it occurs elsewhere, cf. A. Jolles, *Einfache Formen,* 1958². The expression מקדם has the same meaning in Gen 11:2, and one cannot be all that sure that it is meant to indicate that "humankind migrated from East to West" (A. Dillmann; B. Jacob); Brock-Utne, e.g., disputes it. If it is not easy to reconcile the geographical detail of 3:24, "he made them dwell to the east of the garden of Eden," with 2:8, then this is due once more to the fact that narratives A and B were originally independent.

The relative clause at the end of the verse, אשר יצר, closes the cycle of events begun in v. 7a. This unobtrusive detail brings together once more the two acts, the creation of and the provision for human beings. One expects now the beginning of a new act. But this comes only in v. 18 which is to be read immediately after v. 8.

[**2:9**] The lengthy discussion of the question of doublets in Gen 2-3 (especially by J. Begrich and P. Humbert) has led to one certain result, namely that vv. 8 and 9 of Gen 2 are doublets. The planting of the garden and the giving of growth to the trees describe one and the same thing; there is no avoiding this. Here narrative B moves into narrative A; they can be joined together because of their common motif of the garden. Nevertheless, there is in v. 9 a slight shifting of emphasis over against v. 8; the garden now becomes the object of interest. This is clear from the description of the beauty of the trees which only has meaning in narrative B. Gunkel is of the opinion that ויצמח is less anthropomorphic than ויטע of v. 8. This would accord with the different character of narratives A and B which shows out in such details.

In addition, the "planting" of the garden expresses more smoothly the concern of the creator for his creature, while the "made to grow" indicates a change of interest in favor of the garden. Two further qualifications show this much more clearly; they are part of the *exposé* of an event which has to do with these trees and their fruit; "to look at" and "to eat" anticipate the climax of the narrative in 3:6. It is perfectly clear then that 2:9 belongs to narrative B; it presents part of the *exposé* which is continued in vv. 15-17. There must have been one or more sentences preceding 2:9 in the original independent narrative B which have been left out when it was joined to A. A reconstruction is neither possible nor necessary. (For 2:9 cf. W. Caspari, "Gottespflanzen und Gartenwärter," AfO 3 (1926) 57-64.

The Trees in the Garden

The two trees in the middle of the garden have produced not only beautiful fruit but also a vast assortment of literature.

The Tree of Life

Literature (2:9 and 3:22-24): K. Budde, *Die biblische Urgeschichte,* II. Der Baum des Lebens (1883) 46-86.   J. Nikel, *Genesis und Keilschriftforschung. Ein Beitrag zum Verständnis der biblischen Ur- und Patriarchengeschichte* (1903) 133-134.   E. Dhorme, "L'arbre de la vie et l'arbre de la verité," RB 4 (1907) = *Recueil E. Dhorme* (1951).   W.B. Kristensen, "Een of twee Boomen in 't Paradijsverhaal?," ThT 42/43 (1908) 215-233.   T. Barns, Art. 'The Tree of Life', ERE (1908).   A.J. Wensinck, VAA NR XXII 1 (1921) 'Tree and Sun' I-34.   W. Holmberg, *Der Baum des Lebens* (1922/ 1923).   A. Ungnad, "Die Paradiesbaume," ZDMG 79 (1925) 111-118; 80 (1926)

201.   F. Nötscher, *Altorientalischer und alttestamentlicher Auferstehungsglaube* (1926) esp. 316-318.   H.Th. Obbink, "The Tree of Life in Eden," ZAW 46 (1928) 105-112.   W. Staerk, "L'arbre de la vie el l'arbre de la science du bien et du mal," RHPhR 8 (1928) 66-69.   K. Budde, "Zu Th. Obbinks Aufsatz 'The Tree of Life in Eden'," ZAW 47 (1929) 54-62;   "Der Baum der Erkenntnis in der Paradiesesgeschichte," ZDMG 86 (1933) 101-110.   N. Perrot, "Les représentations de l'arbre sacré sur les monuments de Mesopotamie et d'Elam," Bab 17 (1937) 1-144.   H. Bergema, *De boom des leven in Schrift en historie. Bijdrage tot een onderzoek naar de verhouding van Schriftopenbaring en traditie betreffende den boom des levens binnen het kader der OT-wetenschap. Diss. Amsterdam* (1938).   H.G. May, "The Sacred Tree on Palestine Painted Pottery," JAOS 59 (1939) 251-259.   R. Marcus, "The Tree of Life in Proverbs," JBL 62 (1943) 117-120.   I. Engnell, *Studies in Divine Kingship in the Ancient Near East* (1943) esp. 25-27.   G. Widengren, "The King and the Tree of Life in Ancient Near Eastern Religion. King and Saviour IV," UUA 4 (1951).   G. Pidoux, *L'homme dans l'AT,* CTh 32 (1953);   "Encore les deux arbres de Genese 3," ZAW 66 (1954) 37-43.   F. Schmidtke, Art. 'Baum,' RAC II (1954) 1-34.   J. Dus, "Der Baum des lebens," DrR 24 (1957) 103-108.   S. Moscati, *Le antiche civiltà semitiche* (1958) 73-75.   R.L. Cleveland, "Cherubs and the 'Tree of Life' in Ancient South Arabia," BASOR 172 (1963) 55-60.   E.O. James, *The Tree of Life. An Archaeological Study,* NumenSuppl 11 (1966). A.G. Levin, *The Tree of Life. Genesis 2:9 and 3:22-24 in Jewish, Gnostic and Early Christian Texts. Diss. Harvard* synops. HThR 59 (1966) 449-450.   F. Vattioni, "L'albero della vita," Aug. 7 (1967) 133-144.

The following may serve as a preface to the protracted and endless discussion about the two trees in Paradise: To ask whether there were two trees in the middle of the garden or only one is to put the question incorrectly. It is impossible to answer such a question. We have only this narrative before us, and it is there that our enquiry must begin. Does it deal with one tree or with two? A proper answer can be given only by looking at the narrative as a whole; it is concerned with one tree only. K. Budde has demonstrated this convincingly (we can leave aside the conclusions he draws) and nothing has been advanced yet to refute him. He has shown that there is only one tree in the body of the narrative, 3:2, 3, 5, 11, 12, and that it is qualified in two ways — the tree in the middle of the garden, 3:3, and the forbidden tree, 3:11.

Budde's argument is basically literary-critical, to which must be added the argument which derives from the structure of the narrative. The tree of life appears only in the introduction, 2:9, and in the conclusion, 3:22-24. We can draw from this fact the certain conclusion that a narrative which was concerned with one tree in the middle of the garden has been expanded both at the beginning and at the end by the addition of a motif that belonged to an independent narrative.

This conclusion is supported by 3:22; God's reflection is independent of the narrative in which expulsion is a punishment. It introduces a point of view which is foreign to the movement of the narrative. The "tree of life" has its roots in an elaboration of a narrative which originally had one thread. The divine reflection is a sign of the principal motif of another narrative which is concerned with the tree of life. Here, the man is in search of the fruit of the tree of life so as to preserve life; he is looking for eternal youth or a guarantee against death, but God prevents him by guarding the tree of life against any assault, v. 24. We are familiar with this motif, though in a modified form, from the Gilgamesh Epic; it occurs elsewhere too.

The tree of life in 2:9 is to be explained from 3:22-24. The person who attached the motif of the tree of life to the end of the narrative and at the same time set it in the introduction, 2:9, intended it to be part of the whole span of events (i.e., part of the *Geschehensbogen*). He wanted to say that a similar event was linked with the tree of life as with the tree of the narrative. If we presume a variety of narratives about the primeval event from which one type was chosen, then this procedure of allowing the narrative of the tree of life to speak through that of the tree of knowledge — a second voice as it were together with the melody — is an ingenious and intelligent resolution. We can take it that we are not dealing with a secondary addition; the whole has been deliberately shaped by J himself so that the final product appears as a unified composition.

This explanation makes it clear why the two trees are mentioned at the beginning, 2:9, whereas the tree of life disappears as the course of the action begins in 2:16f. The tree of life and the tree of knowledge come together only in the *exposé* and the conclusion.

If this explanation is correct then we have the solution of yet another difficulty. The description "tree of life" is attached to this tree in each place that it is mentioned, 2:9; 3:22, 24. This is not the case with the other tree. The description "tree of the knowledge of good and evil" is found only in 2:9 and 17. The tree is mentioned in the main part of the narrative, 3:2, 3, 5, 6, 11, 12, 17, but is never described by this title. It is either "the tree" or "the tree in the middle of the garden" or "the tree from which I forbade you to eat." This is a striking difference; and there is another. Only the description "tree of life" is a fixed formula which occurs elsewhere both in and outside the Old Testament. This suggests that the formula "the tree of life" was at hand to the author, whereas he fashioned the title of the other tree out of the narrative itself, 3:5b. He was obliged to do this only after he added the motif of the tree of life to the Introduction; the other tree then had to have a name. However, he used this name only in the beginning of the narrative. In Gen 3 he left the description of the tree as it was before it was linked with the tree of life. The conclusion is that before this the tree was called "the tree in the middle of the garden" in 2:9 and 17 also.

There is no question of altering the text in 3:5 and 2:17. The process of the history of tradition which we have just described is only intelligible when we leave the text in its present state. This is the only way to arrive at the various stages of the formation of the text. The oft-raised objection that if "the tree of life" in 2:9 is an addition, then it would be natural to mention it after the tree of knowledge, collapses because the whole of v. 9b is a new formation and the formula "tree of the knowledge . . ." is an imitation of the formula "tree of life."

If the formula "tree of the knowledge . . ." has grown out of the narrative itself, namely out of 3:5b, then it will be appropriate to explain it there.

The "tree of life" is mentioned several times in Proverbs, e.g., 11:30, "the fruit of the righteous is a tree of life"; see also 3:18; 13:12; 15:4. F. Vattioni, "L'albero della vita," Aug. 7 (1967) 133-144, remarks that whereas these passages do not presume Gen 2-3, those in later Judaism, Test-Levi 18:10-11; 4 Esr 8:52; 4 Macc 16:18, and in the New Testament, Rev 2:7; 22:1-2, 14, 19, are clearly connected with it. The tree of life was well known in ancient Israel, even apart from Gen 2-3. It is not peculiar to Israel but belongs to ancient near east. The best known example is the plant of life in the Gilgamesh Epic, XI, 266-295:

266 I will disclose, O Gilgamesh, a hidden thing,
267 And [*a secret of the gods* I will] tell thee:

268 This plant, like the buckthorn is [its . . .].
269 Its thorns will pr[ick thy hands] just as does the *rose*.
270 If thy hands obtain the plant, [thou wilt find new life].
281 Its name shall be 'Man Becomes Young in Old Age';
282 I myself shall eat (it), and thus return to the state of my youth.
(ANET p. 96)

The story then tells how the serpent took the plant from him, 285-289: "Going back it shed its slough" (i.e., by virtue of the plant, it renewed its youth).

This passage is decisive for the motif. The plant has two effects: the return to youth and the preservation of life (278f.: ". . . this plant is a plant *apart*, whereby a person may regain one's *life's breath*").

The meaning of the plant is obscured when it is understood from the effect that it produces. Its real meaning is found in the phrase: "a plant apart." Because of the death of his companion Enkidu, Gilgamesh is obsessed with the horror of the inexorable fate of death and goes in search of life that is not subject to death. He finds it in two forms: Utnapishtim has been elevated to the gods; but this is not open to ordinary mortals. Utnapishtim shows him the other possibility: the plant of life. But he loses it. He is back where he was when the "ale-wife" spoke to him at the beginning of the journey, X, 3, 1-5.

"Gilgamesh, whither rovest thou?
The life thou pursuest thou shalt not find.
When the gods created mankind,
Death for mankind they set aside,
Life in their own hands retaining."
(ANET, p. 90).

The Gilgamesh Epic shows that the motif of the plant of life is in the context of the horror and dread of death. The plant is magical. Tales in general speak positively of such things as waken the dead or prolong life or preserve youth. There are examples the world over. In the mythical stage, as in the Gilgamesh Epic, a magical means like the plant of life can only be regarded negatively because someone has lost it. The fruit of the tree of life in Gen 2:9; 3:22 derives from a magical (and hence non-mythical) understanding of existence. Its origin is to be looked for not in the high cultures of the Mediterranean but in primitive cultures (J.G. Frazer, *Folklore*. . . , p. 26f., gives a number of examples). The brief reference to the tree of life in Gen 2:9; 3:22-24 agrees with that in the Gilgamesh Epic in that both conclude that eternal life is inaccessible. Humans have nothing that can save them from death.

The lengthy discussion about the relationship of the tree of life to the tree of knowledge, whether both trees stood in the middle of the garden, whether the man in 3:22 had eaten the fruit of the tree of life, whether it was enough to eat once of the tree to eternal life or whether one had to eat of it continually — all these questions and many others disappear in the light of the explanation given. All that we know of the tree of life which J introduces into the narrative at the beginning and at the end is the motif and the negative conclusion; we must be content with this. The tree of life has no part in the main section which begins in 2:16f.

[2:10-14] *Literature:* E. Bertheau, *Die der Beschreibung der Lage des Paradieses Genesis 2:10-14 zu Grunde liegenden geographischen Anschauungen. Ein Beitrag zur Geschichte der Geographie. Gött. Stud.* (1847). F. Delitzsch, *Wo lag das Paradies?* (1881). P. Jensen, *Kosmologie der Babylonier* (1890). W. Engelkemper, *Die Paradiesesflüsse* (1901). F. Hommel, "Vier neue arabische Landschaftsnamen im AT. - Die vier Paradiesesflüsse in altbabylonischer und altarabischer Uberlieferung," Augs. u. Abhdlg. III, 1 (1901) 273-343. A.H. Sayce, "The Rivers of Paradise," ExpT 17 (1905) 469-471; "A Babylonian Tourist of the Abrahamic Age and his Map of the World,"

ExpT 18 (1905/1906) 68-71. E. Robertson, "Where was Eden?," AJSL 28 (1911) 254-273. A.H. Sayce, *The Land of Nod,* PSBA 38 (1916). A. Boissier, "La situation du paradis terrestre," Le Globe t. 55, Mémoires (1916) 1-26. P. Riessler, "Zur Lage des Gottesgartens bei den Alten," ThQ (1916) 273-319. Th.G. Pinches, "The Babylonian Paradise and its Rivers," ExpT 29 (1918) 181-184. W.F. Albright, "The Mouth of the Rivers," AJSL 35 (1919) 161-193. - "The Location of the Garden Eden," AJSL 39 (1922/1923) 15-19. A. Ungnad, "Das wiedergefundene Paradies," Kulturfragen 3 (1923) 3-11. E.F. Weidner, "Das Paradies am Sternenhimmel," Archiv für Keilschriftforschung 2 (AfO) (1924/1925) 124-130. A. Deimel, "Wo lag das Paradies?," Or 15 (1925) 44-54. H. Gressmann, "Der Eingang zum Paradies," AfO 3 (1926) 12. A. Herrmann, *Die Erdkarte der Urbibel* (1931). K. Jensen, "Kennen wir die altmesopotamische Elementargeographie?," ZAW 49 (1931) 274-279. S. Mowinckel, "De fire Paradiselvene," NTT 39 (1938) 47-64. G. Hölscher, "Drei Erdkarten," SAH 3, 1944/1948 (1949) 35-44. J. Rammer, "Ethnologische Parallelen zur Bibel," BiLi 24 (1956/1957) 205-206. L.I. Ringbom, *Paradisus terrestris. Myt, Bild och Verklighet,* Acta Societatis Scientiarum Fennicae NS C, I No. 1 (1958). J. Simons, *The Geographical and Topographical Texts of the OT* (1959) #58. H. Müller, "Donde estuvo el Paraiso?," RivBib 23 (1961) 169-173. S.N. Kramer, "Die Suche nach dem Paradies. Dilmun und die Indus-Zivilisation," W.Z. Halle 12 (1963) 311-317. W.H. Gispen, "Genesis 2:10-14," *Festschr. Th.C. Vriezen* (1966) 115-124. E.A. Speiser, "The Rivers of Paradise," *Festschr. J. Friedrich* (1959) 473-485 = *Oriental and Biblical Studies,* ed. J.J. Finkelstein-M. Greenberg (1967) 23-34.

The problem about the passage 2:10-14 has not yet been clarified. Is it originally part of the narrative 2:4b-3:24, or is it a secondary insertion? The passage was recognized early (J. Wellhausen, K. Budde) as a secondary addition (Th.C. Vriezen, "almost unanimously"); nevertheless some scholars have reconsidered it and regarded it as part of the original narrative. The question has been discussed mainly from the viewpoint of literary criticism. But more important than this is the difference in the form of speech between 2:10-14 and its immediate context. We have distinguished in the Introduction two basic forms of speech in the primeval story: the narrative and the numerative. It is primarily the genealogies that belong to the numerative class. There is also numeration in Gen 2:10-14; it is geographical numeration as distinct from the spatial numeration of the genealogies, and its purpose is to provide geographical information (so W.H. Schmidt), whereas the genealogies are concerned with information about past generations, and the tables of the nations with information about peoples. The passing on of knowledge about distant lands and peoples by means of numeration is very different from narrative; it was originally part of oral tradition which was reduced later to written tradition. A numerative, descriptive *genre* like this has its own independent purpose and significance side-by-side with narrative.

Gen 2:10-14 belongs to this tradition. It originated there and was taken up into the narrative of Gen 2-3 by the author. This presumes of course that the passage was at hand to the author and was an older piece of information (so too Th.C. Vriezen and many others).

The beginning of the passage, v. 10a, is to be distinguished from what follows. It provides the link with the paradise narrative; the information is in vv. 10b-14. V. 10a presumes a story of the Garden of Eden in a version which tells of the fertility of the garden brought about by a river which waters it. It is something like the description of the city of God in Ps 46:5: "There is a river whose streams make glad the city of God. . . ." The river that waters the garden becomes subsequently the source of the rivers that water the world. Its division into four branches or, more accurately, into four sources, is not the result of observation or information, but a (theoretical) attempt to link the "information" about paradise with geography. The purpose is to state that the rivers which bring fertility (= blessing) to the world have their origin in the river which brings fertility (= blessing) to the garden of God.

This being the case, all attempts to explain or locate the sources of the four rivers geographically are ruled out. We have in 2:10-14 a spatial parallel to the time structure. Everything that happens has its origin in a primeval happening; e.g., the succession of generations in Gen 5 derives from the creation of human beings. The intention of the author in inserting 2:10-14 was not to determine where paradise lay, as the majority of interpreters hold, but rather to point out — by way of parenthesis and at the place where a land (Eden) with its garden is first mentioned — that the "life-arteries" of all lands of the earth have their source in the river that watered paradise.

We can understand then why the names and description of the four rivers are so vague and in part so incomprehensible. The main theme of 2:10-14 links a statement about the primeval land with information about the known world, indicating the great age of the tradition behind 2:10-14 with its hazy and primitive notions of geography.

One must ask if the extraordinary labor that exegetes have expended to establish the geographical details does not begin from a false presupposition. It does more justice to the text to distinguish clearly what is significant and what is not and to set aside hypotheses that are not soundly based.

[2:10] The participle יֹצֵא is to be translated as a present. Only in this way does it become clear that vv. 10-14 describe a situation which is quite separate from the narrative which has gone before. The objection of F. Delitzsch, H.L. Strack, Th.C. Vriezen, W.H. Gispen and others, that the passage is part of the narrative in the text as it stands and must be translated: "A river went out from . . .", misconstrues its deliberately parenthetic nature. The question whether the river takes its source from inside or outside the garden cannot be answered. It is natural to suppose that it began in Eden and passed through the garden watering it in its course (so W.H. Gispen, K. Budde); but the author is not all that precise. Nor does the text say whether the river divided into branches immediately on leaving the garden or later on in its course. In any case it does not mean that the river divided while still in the garden (so H. Renckens); the river in the garden must be marked off clearly from the four rivers of the world.

The verb decides the meaning of the sentence; the river divides itself (niph. פרד). We can only translate what follows by "into four branches." The Hebrew text, "And it became to four sources (heads)" has been understood in various ways: beginning, sources, river sources, outlets, upper course, main current. . . . F. Delitzsch has rendered it correctly: "The beginnings of the rivers that branched from it"; he refers to a corresponding Arabic expression. Similarly O. Loretz: "The place where the great river divides," corresponding to a Sumerian expression. Th.C. Vriezen discusses other explanations on p. 154f. However, the difficulties that arise here disappear when one realizes that the author does not want to describe in detail any geographical area, but the transition from the river of paradise to the four rivers of the world; they begin at the point where the river of paradise divides itself.

216

The word ראשים is saying that the four rivers which take their source where the river of paradise divides are not rivers of paradise. In fact, it is a misunderstanding of the text to speak of the "four rivers of Paradise" as H. Holzinger does. The number 4 stands for completeness; H. Gunkel notes that "the ancients speak of the four corners of the world, the four directions of the heavens, the four parts of the earth . . . each Continent has its river." W.H. Gispen is of the opinion that one is not justified in attributing a symbolic meaning to the number 4 in this case. But there is no need to describe it as symbolic. The structure of 2:10-14 shows that the 4 indicates completeness. Their origin from the garden sets them over against the world. It is the world which receives life and fertility from the four rivers that flow from the river of paradise. It would not fit the structure if the four rivers were just any four and the lands just any lands.

The most important parallel which indicates the meaning of the number 4 occurs in the Apocalyptic writings where the world is often described as consisting of four parts or four regions. A striking example is the first night vision of Zechariah: the four horses, 1:8, that patrol the earth (1:11 "the whole earth"). S. Mowinckel has advanced further parallels, "De fire Paradiselvene," NTT 1 (1938); cf. too G. Hölscher, *Drei Erdkarten,* 1949, 39, n. 1. If the intention of vv. 11-14 is to describe the four rivers as belonging to the four regions of the world, then one cannot expect precise details and descriptions of definite circumscribed areas.

[2:11-14]   The four rivers form two pairs. The Tigris and the Euphrates are well known names; Pishon and Gihon are descriptive names which do not occur elsewhere, nor are there any rivers with such names. This shows that the description has grown out of disparate elements. We cannot know what rivers are meant by the first two names in v. 11. For further discussion see the studies of Th.C. Vriezen and W.H. Gispen.

[2:11]   פישון is probably from פוש = to spring up fitfully (KBL) and גיחון from גיח = to burst forth, to bubble (Köhler); for the philology see W.F. Albright, AJSL 39 (1922) 23, n. 2. Neither description is particularly suited to great rivers, but rather to springs like the spring of Gihon in Jerusalem, 1 Kings 1:33, 38, 45; 2 Chron 32:30; 33:14. It is almost universally accepted today that the names derive from the verbs given above. Pishon has been identified as the Indus (A. Dillmann, F. Delitzsch, K. Budde, F.M.Th. Böhl, C.A. Simpson) or the Ganges (Josephus) or the Nile (Rashi), the Kercha (and the Gichon Karun, G. Hölscher), and about half a dozen other rivers. H. Holzinger said rightly in 1898 "nothing can be concluded from the name of the river," and W.H. Gispen repeated these words almost verbatim in 1966.

The land Havilah is mentioned in Gen 10:7, 29; 25:18; 1 Sam 15:7; they are areas in South and North-East Arabia. In Gen 10:7 it is in the land of the Cushites. Many exegetes accept its derivation from the root חול (West Semitic) which means "sand" and hence "the land of sand" (so Ges-Buhl, L. Köhler, F. Delitzsch, O. Procksch, J. Skinner, W.H. Gispen, Th.C. Vriezen). The word is used here (and here only) with the article, החוילה, and so the meaning that would echo through would be "the land of sand." One can well understand that a number of areas in different places could be called by this name. The three places where the name occurs are in Arabia. Now Arabia was well-known as the land of gold; so one would be thinking of Arabia in general without limiting the name to any particular area (such as North-West, South-East, South Arabia and other areas). J. Simons and W.H. Gispen think that the whole of Arabia is meant.

[2:12]   Three products are often mentioned in the context of Arabia: "Gold, Incense and Myrrh," Mt 2; "Gum, Balm and Myrrh," Gen 37:25. Here it is gold, bdellium and onyx stone. (Gold and land of gold in the Old Testament cf. Th.C. Vriezen, ad. loc.)

בדלח is a sort of resin, *budulhu* in Assyrian (cf. W. von Soden, AHW), and is mentioned by ancient writers like Pliny; they ascribe its origin to many countries; in Greek it is βδέλλιον. O. Procksch quotes Galen: "bedellio lacrimum est arboris, quae in Arabia nascitur." A. Dillmann describes it as "a transparent gum like wax"; H. Gunkel as an aromatic resin. U. Cassuto thinks that it could be a precious stone.

Onyx *(shoham)* stone is a type of gem, mentioned several times in the Old Testament. It is not possible to be more precise.

[2:13]   The word Gihon means "the turbulent one," "the bursting or bubbling forth one." The verb is used in Job 38:8; 40:23 of the sea and of the Jordan. It is the name of a fountain in Jerusalem (today, Mary's fountain) 1 Kings 1:33; 38:45; 2 Chron 32:30; 33:14. Many scholars identify the river Gihon with the Nile — F. Delitzsch, A. Dillmann, F.M.Th. Böhl, H. Holzinger, H. Gunkel (cautiously, "later identified with the Nile"), K. Budde ("necessary assumption"). The two studies of Th.C. Vriezen (with hesitation) and W.H. Gispen agree. Gispen says correctly that the strongest support for this hypothesis comes from the information about the land around which the river flows — Cush.

What is Cush and where is it? In the Old Testament, Cush is mainly Ethiopia or Nubia, the land to the south of Egypt, or more exactly the area between the first and fourth cataracts of the Nile. The classical writers call this area Ethiopia. F. Delitzsch conjectures that Cush was the land of the Kassites in Upper or Central Babylonia, and this has been taken up by others (M.-J. Lagrange, A. Clamer, E. Meyer, *Israeliten,* 209). But this is scarcely tenable because Gen 2:11-14 is talking about divisions of the world, and hence very large areas. Since the Old Testament for the most part uses Cush to designate the area south of Egypt, this should be its meaning here. However, Cush should not be limited to fixed borders. It means the southland in a broad and vague sense (so F.M.Th. Böhl). H. Gunkel writes; "South Arabia together with Nubia, thought to be linked with it." A number of interpreters hold that Egypt can be included (H. Grapow, W.F. Albright). But it does not necessarily follow that Gihon means the Nile. The question remains open because the name is not used and because one cannot say that the Nile flows around this area. If one can conclude from v. 10b that the source of the four rivers is the same, then the Nile would be ruled out. We cannot then identify the first two rivers with any rivers known to us.

[2:14]   The word חדקל means the Tigris here and in Dan 10:4. The word corresponds to the old Persian *tigra,* the Sumerian *(i)digna,* the Akk. *indiqlat,* the Aram. *deglat,* the Arab. *diglat,* and the Greek Τιγρις or Τιγρης. The further detail, i.e., the river which flows east of Ashur, cannot be elucidated any further.

The view of F. Delitzsch and O. Procksch, that Ashur must mean the country here (and not the city) because vv. 11 and 12 also speak of countries, is only relevant if the same preposition were to be used; the preposition קדמת is not very suited to a country. It should be kept in mind that the details about the Euphrates and the Tigris and the Pishon and the Gihon are probably of different origins.

It is probable that the city of Ashur is meant because of the preposition "east of" or "opposite" (so many interpreters). The precise meaning of the preposition here cannot be decided, but that is not important. H. Gunkel (among others) has pointed out that the oldest capital, Ashur, the center of the oldest kingdom of Ashur (until about 1300 B.C.), lay west of the Tigris. If the city is meant, then there must be a very ancient tradition here which goes back to a time before Nineveh became the capital of the Assyrian kingdom.

The Euphrates, Akk. *pūrattu,* old Persian *ūfratūs,* Greek Ευφράτης, Sum. *buranun* = the great river, as in Gen 15:18. It is presumed that the river is well known and so no further details are given.

Both the Tigris and the Euphrates are mentioned at the beginning of the Atrahasis Myth in the context of primeval event. The text is poorly preserved. The following is proposed by W.G. Lambert and A.R. Millard, Atrahasis, *The Babylonian Story of the Flood,* Oxford, 1969, pp. 42-43:

> The Tigris river. . . . the Euphrates after it
> . . . .from the deep
> there (. . . .)they set up.

[2:15-17]   The first sentence of v. 15 belongs to one of the demonstrable doublets in Gen 2-3 (P. Humbert, *Études.* . . , p. 15). It resumes v. 2:8b:

> 8b: and there he put (שׂים) the man
> whom he had formed
> 15a: and the Lord God took the man and
> put him (hiph. נוח) in
> the Garden of Eden.

This resumption of v. 8b was occasioned not merely by the insertion of vv. 10-14 but also by the addition of v. 9 to v. 8. V. 8b spoke of the man, v. 9 of the garden, doubling v. 8a, and vv. 10-14 of the four rivers. If the narrative is to resume its account of the man (the prohibition in v. 16f.), it must take up the previous action of v. 8b. V. 15 then is a necessary link with vv. 16-17 and the prohibition. Vv. 9:15-17 introduce narrative B and are continued in 3:1 after the transition verse in 2:25. But the narrator not only repeats v. 8b and v. 15; he adds the purpose for which the creator put his creature in the garden, "to till it and keep it." It is not certain whether this latter detail belongs to narrative A or B. It is probable that it belonged to v. 8b and was taken up deliberately by J, who joined the narratives, only when he resumed this half-verse in v. 15.

This suggestion is confirmed in that the purpose has no apparent function in narrative B, whereas it fits in well with God's reflection in v. 18, "I will make him a helper fit for him''; and more, if it once belonged to v. 8b, then it immediately precedes the divine reflection. Another detail in favor of this is that the cultivation of the earth is part of the introduction to the narrative, v. 6bii. Finally, this explanation offers a solution to the difficulty of the feminine suffixes to the two infinitives in v. 15: if J took the statement of intent from v. 8 when he resumed it, then the object of the verbs can be אדמה as in v. 5bii. It is more likely then that the statement of intent really belongs to narrative A, though the other possibility is not excluded.

[2:15] *Literature* (Work): S.H. Langdon, "The Gardener in the Epic of Paradise," ExpT 29 (1918) 218-222. G.H. Dalman, *Arbeit und Sitte in Palästina, II Der Ackerbau* (1932). I. Engnell, "Work in the OT," SEÅ 26 (1961) 5-12. W. von Soden, "'Als die Götter (auch noch) Mensch waren.' Einige Grundgedanken des altbabylonischen Atramhasis-Mythus," Or. 38 (1969) 415-432.

All interpreters agree that v. 15a repeats v. 8a with minor modifications. Most explain it as a resumption of what was said there after the long parenthesis. But another voice is speaking here, the same as that which makes the transition from v. 15 to the prohibition in vv. 16-17, because v. 8a speaks of a "garden in Eden" and v. 15 of a "garden of Eden" (see above). There is added: "to till it and keep (or guard) it." This is a decisive verse for the whole understanding of Gen 2-3. K. Budde struck out v. 15 (later only the last two words); the logic of this is that he must regard v. 5bii as an addition also. He writes: "Nowhere does the second hand betray itself as clearly as here. The man is in paradise for blissful enjoyment, not to work and guard it." It is only when God passes judgment in 3:17 that work is imposed on people, and if the text of 2:15 stands then "serious damage is done to 3:17ff." (Budde, *Urgeschichte,* p. 83; this is acknowledged too by H. Holzinger ad. loc.). H. Gunkel too writes: "This detail shows that the author does not conceive of paradise as a place of complete perfection, but as a wonderful place of sojourn."

But what is the source of Budde's idea that the man in paradise is destined to "blissful enjoyment"? There is here quite clearly a notion of paradise that is completely foreign to the text of the Old Testament. Hesiod describes the golden age in this way as does the Koran (Sure 38:49ff.; texts in W. Zimmerli, Comm. ad. loc.). This is called the starting point for the current idea of paradise (G. von Rad notes correctly that it depends on the loan word "paradise"). It is of the utmost significance that the Old Testament knows nothing of such an idea of paradise. It is no mere chance that Budde's interpretation, especially in the *Urgeschichte* of 1883, is influenced very strongly by an ethical idealism that shows itself above all in his explanation and appraisal of the two trees. The "blissful enjoyment" in paradise comes from an understanding of humanity which undervalues manual work over against the activities of the spirit and mind, because it is too closely bound to material objects. But this is completely foreign to Gen 2-3.

The story of the creation of human beings in Gen 2 makes quite clear the essential components of human existence. Human beings are created by God, and so from the very beginning they stand in a relationship to their creator, 2:7. A human being as a complete person is a living being because God has breathed life into him, 2:7. Human existence includes occupation or work, v. 15b, and, most important of all, community with other human beings, vv. 18-24. Work is regarded here as an essential part of human existence. Life without work would not be worthy of human beings. Just as in Gen 1:1-2:4a the activity of the creator follows the rhythm of work and rest (as F. Delitzsch has noted), so too God-given human existence follows a pattern of duty. Human existence cannot have meaning or fulfillment without such obligation.

It is to misconceive the meaning of the passage to ask if it refers to the occupation of the farmer or the gardener, or if the relatively easy occupation of the gardener is being contrasted with the more difficult one of the farmer. Because it is a question of the creation of human beings, it is only the work of humans that can be intended. It is quite correct that the narrator in using the words "to till and keep" has in mind the work of the Palestinian farmer. However, it would be wrong to restrict his intention to this work; he is concerned with the duty which God has laid upon and entrusted to his people in the living space assigned to them. B. Jacob (Comm. ad. loc.) has noted this "עבד and שׁמר are complementary; they refer in a positive way to vocational activity — creating the maintaining, working and keeping." It can be said that every human occupation shares in some way in this "tilling and keeping." The narrator, in using these two verbs, has given a basic definition of human activity. At the same time he wanted to say that work and all that a person is capable of was the intention of the creator for this his creature.

We must look now at the relationship of the biblical destiny of humanity to its destiny as presented in the Sumerian and Babylonian creation myths. According to these myths, people were created to carry out the work of the gods or to relieve them of the heavy burden of work:

> At that time the gods had to provide
>> their own sustenance by the drudgery
>> to which they were bound;
> The higher gods supervised the work, the
>> lower gods carried the panniers. . . .

The narrative then tells how Nammu, the mother of the gods, rouses the god Enki from sleep and says to him:

> Make a substitute for the gods,
> that they may throw off their burden.

This leads to the creation of human beings. Further texts are given by G. Pettinato in his inaugural lecture at Heidelberg, *Das altorientalische Menschenbild und die sumerischen und akkadischen Schöpfungsmythen,* Heidelberg: Carl Winter, 1971. People were created to relieve the gods of their burdens and the Sumerian text, KAR-4-Mythus, describes their obligations:

> That they dig permanent borders,
> take the pickaxe and pannier in their hands,
> for the temple of the great gods,
> which is appropriate (as) a lofty dwelling place,
> to set the fields in order,
> to dig permanent borders,
> to get ready the dyke,
> . . . .
> to make all sorts of plants grow,
> . . . .
> that they bring increase to the grain fields,
> bring abundance to the land,
> celebrate becomingly the feasts of the gods,
> pour out cold water.   (Pettinato, p. 78, lines 29-50)

[Translator's note: Professor Westermann was using Pettinato's manuscript here; the translation above is based on the slightly revised text which appeared in the published lecture.]

According to this text human beings were created to perform primarily the duties of agriculture. In contrast to Gen 2:15 they are to cultivate the "field of the gods" and their work is linked immediately with the cult, with the temples which they are to build, and with festivals.

In the Enuma Elish epic too, people were created to lift the drudgery from the shoulders of the gods. The beginning of the Atrahasis Myth treats this in great detail. In the first stage, the drudgery was borne by the higher gods; however, they soon imposed "their drudgery on the Igigi gods, a group of lower divinities" (Pettinato, p. 27). There follows then a description of the revolution which the Igigi gods plan. Enki solves the problem by creating humans and laying the work upon them. The goddess Mami proclaims the creation of humans to the gods:

> I have removed your heavy work,
> I have imposed your toil on man.
> You raised a cry for mankind,
> I have loosed the yoke, I have established freedom.
> (Translation: W.G. Lambert and A.R. Millard, *Atrahasis,* pp. 60-61, lines 240-243; cf. Pettinato, p. 28).

But the people soon rebel against the heavy work; the gods react with a series of punishments which recall the plagues of Egypt; finally they decide to eliminate the people by means of the flood.

This is very different from Gen 2:15. The Sumerian and Akkadian Myths refer human work to the world of the gods from the very beginning; this is typical of myth: the gods need people for the heavy work. These myths differ basically from the primitive creation stories where the motif is entirely absent.

Gen 2:15 strips work of any mythical connection with the world of the gods. The work that human beings are to carry is a mandate from God; but the creator is one and there is no world of the gods to which the work of humans is directed. Work is part of human existence because the living space which the creator has assigned to his people demands this work. Human work is demythologized; civilization, of which agriculture is a constitutive part, acquires thereby its own independent significance.

Human work then, as a mandate from God to his creatures, is a necessary part of the exchange between God and his people. Work is a determining factor in a God-created person. The dignity which belongs to civilization rests on the mandate of God to his creatures.

[2:16-17] *Literature* (Commandment): E. Gerstenberger, *Wesen und Herkunft des "apodiktischen Rechts,"* WMANT 20, 1965.   G. Liedke, *Gestalt und Bezeichnung alttestamentlicher Rechtssatze,* WMANT 39, 1971.

With regard to the form of the prohibition, it is to be noted in the first place that the actual restriction occurs only in v. 17; v. 16 is not a restriction, but a release; "God begins with a great release," G. von Rad. The release of all other trees in the garden means that the man need suffer no deprivation; there is plenty of food there. The restriction cannot mean that the man is going to lack anything.

What then is the meaning of the prohibition which forbids the man to eat of the fruit of one tree? G. von Rad writes: "To seek a purpose in the divine prohibition is in our opinion not permissible." This is correct insofar as it concerns the object of the prohibition. The text as we read it can only mean that

God forbids the man the fruit of a tree which gives knowledge of good and evil; he forbids the man the acquisition of this knowledge. But this is not the intention of the old narrative. Exegetes have long since recognized the difficulty in the description of the tree. G. von Rad formulates it: "If God here reveals the mystery, what sense has the snake's explanation?" A similar judgment has been given by K. Budde, H. Holzinger, H. Gunkel, J. Begrich, W.H. Schmidt. It is not a literary difficulty but one which has to do with the disruption of the course of the narrative which is not to be attributed to the original author.

Our explanation (see above on 2:9) is that because of the addition of the motif of the tree of life, the other tree, which has no name in Gen 3, receives a name in vv. 9 and 17 which has been shaped by the narrative. Before the addition of the motif, the tree of whose fruit the man had been forbidden to eat could only be described as the tree in the middle of the garden. There is no ground then for any explanation which relates the prohibition in v. 17 directly to the acquisition of knowledge. It is a misunderstanding of the meaning of the text to ask why God wanted to withhold from the man the knowledge of good and evil. But if one takes as one's starting point that the prohibition in the old narrative is not now being explained by the name of the tree, then all that is being said is that the prohibition is to protect the man from death, v. 17b.

In order to understand the meaning of these two verses we must first of all be aware that J has linked the narrative of the expulsion from the garden (B) with that of the creation of humanity (A). Whoever joined the narratives together, and we think it was J, added something more by inserting vv. 16-17: a relationship of the human creatures to their creator which arises from the command which their creator gives them. This particular aspect of human existence really belongs to the narrative of the transgression of the command and its consequences. But the composer intended to give it a special meaning when he inserted it into narrative A at this point: the relationship of a human being to God which arises from the command is associated with those elements which determine one's existence as a creature. And so it takes on a more general and fundamental significance than when it was merely a part of the *exposé* of narrative B. This coheres particularly well with the Old Testament understanding of humanity: such a personal relationship to God is part of human existence as a whole, and it only becomes possible through a commandment of God: Deut 8:2.

The form of both sentences in v. 17 confirms that this is what is meant. They are the two basic forms of command and law. The prohibition (= command) has the form of the commandments of the Decalogue (see E. Gesternberger, G. Liedke), and the second sentence that of apodictic law consisting of condition (case) and consequence (punishment). The authoritative form of the command as direct address in the second person has been of the utmost importance for the relationship to God in Israel since the earliest times. It presumes a situation which is unique to Gen 2:17, namely that God is within call, and so the address "Thou shalt not eat" is without mediator, spoken and direct. For that very reason the command of Gen 2:17 belongs to primeval time; there can be no such directness in historical times.

The meaning of the command becomes clearer when it is compared with the duty imposed on the man in v. 15b. The duty of tilling and keeping the garden is something comprehensible; the command need not be comprehensible, and such is the case here. The meaning is this: the command remains the word of the one who commands. One can only hear it while one hears in it the one who commands and is obedient to him. The command then opens up the possibility of a relationship to the one who commands. By the command something is entrusted to the man; he is given an area of freedom which the animals do not possess; it is not a limitation but an enlargement of his potential (so too W. Zimmerli).

Where there is the capacity to decide there is at the same time a limit. Every command sets limits. And so the original form of the command is the prohibition. The prohibition which restricts the man hems him in with threat. This limitation is expressed in the law, and here in the sentence, "In the day that you eat of it you shall die." This is not in fact a threat of death, but rather the clear expression of the limit which is the necessary accompaniment of the freedom entrusted to humanity in the command. To say no to God — and this is what freedom allows — is ultimately to say no to life; for life comes from God.

The primeval nature of the prohibition shows itself in that it transcends the divisions into areas of cult and ethic. One could even say that there are echoes of the basic primitive form of the prohibition, the taboo. It is not some way of conducting oneself that is forbidden, but a "something"; one tree is singled out from the others as taboo. This aspect of the taboo appears clearly in 3:3: "Neither shall you touch it." It is part of the taboo that there is no rational basis for it. The motif of a prohibition that is transgressed is not a motif of the myth, but of the tale (forbidden fruit, forbidden area, forbidden to touch; H. Grimm, *Hausmärchen,* notes to nos. 3 and 46). H. Gunkel noted this. The primeval prohibition which, without any further refinement, recalls a taboo, indicates that neither community among humans nor any sort of relationship with God can exist without such limits. Where human freedom means utter lack of restraint and hence complete arbitrariness, then human community and relationship with God are no longer possible.

The meaning of the death penalty for transgressing the command is still a matter of debate. U. Cassuto discusses some five possibilities. The many explanations all end up with the one alternative which matters: Was the punishment imposed when the command was transgressed or not? To answer this question it is important to understand the phrase ביום. Th.C. Vriezen has treated the problem in detail. He demonstrates from the use of the expression ביום in the Old Testament that the opinion (B.D. Eerdmans, E. Albert, J. Skinner, H. Gressmann and others) that it must be understood literally, i.e.: "On the same day on which the command is transgressed," is untenable. He established that ביום can have a very different meaning ("at the time when," "at that time when," "if"), and that in a number of places its meaning is general: Gen 2:4; 5:1f.; Ex 6:28; 10:28; 32:34 and elsewhere; e.g., Ex 10:28: "If you see my face again, you must die." The meaning cannot be that death is a direct consequence of eating; moreover the formula clearly describes a penalty. The meaning is not that death must intervene on the same day. The other extreme explanation is that the words מות תמות mean that man has become mortal, that he has been condemned to die: "you shall be doomed to death" (E.A. Speiser) or "you will be unable to achieve eternal life, you will be compelled one day to succumb to death" (U. Cassuto).

Behind this explanation there is clearly a concern to avoid the necessary consequence, namely that no announcement of the death penalty follows. But this explanation is excluded because the oft used formula for the death penalty, מות תמות, has a fixed meaning. The meanings "you will become mortal" or "you will die sometime later," are quite impossible. The majority of exegetes have rejected this explanation. One must agree then with H. Gunkel, and many others: "This threat is not fulfilled subsequently: they do not die immediately; this fact is not to be explained away, but simply acknowledged" (so too W.H. Schmidt). Gunkel says that our difficulty with this was not felt so strongly by the ancient narrator, who would reply that God is and remains master of what he says. One must agree. But the narrative itself can throw further light on the difficulty: the death penalty, as shown above, is not really a threat; it is, in the context, much more a warning. After the man and the woman have eaten from the tree, a new situation arises in which God acts differently from the way he had indicated. This "inconsequence" is essential to the narrative; it shows that God's dealing with his creatures cannot be pinned down, not even by what God has said previously. And so even God's acts and words are open to misinterpretation and the serpent makes use of this.

[2:18-24]   *Literature* (the Giving of the Name): F. Schwally, "Die biblischen schöp-fungsberichte," ARW 9 (1906) 159-275, esp. p. 170f.   H.Th. Obbink, *Die magische betekenis van den naam, inzonderheid in het oude Egypte,* Diss. Amsterdam (1925).   A. Menes, "Die sozialpolitische Analyse der Urgeschichte," ZAW 43 (1925) 33-62.   L. Kopf, "Arabische Etymologien und Parallelen zum Bibelwörterbuch," VT 8 (1958) 161-215, esp. p. 184f.

When narrative A was still independent, v. 18 followed directly on v. 8. We have seen that in the narrative of the creation of human beings the creator is the one who acts from beginning to end; the narrative then divides itself accordingly. The introduction 4b-6 is followed by the creation of a man v. 7; God gives him living space and provides him with food, v. 8. Then the tension begins: the man is not yet the creature that God planned; there is something that is still "not good," namely that the man is alone, v. 18a. To meet this lack, God makes a new decision (like the decision in 1:26 "let us make man"); "I will make him a helper fit for him (or: corresponding to him)." The details of this decision are told in two acts: the creation of the animals does not really meet the lack, but the creation of the woman does. So the goal of the creation of human beings is achieved. Humankind is now man and woman as the creator wanted it. V. 23 forms the real conclusion of the narrative; the etiological reflection in v. 24 is not necessarily part of it.

H. Gunkel writes in this context: "The scene presumes a very naive notion of God. God makes an experiment that is futile. The Melanesians too tell of a number of attempts to create humans which misfire" (similarly A. Menes, F. Schwally, G.J. Thierry, K. Budde, L. Köhler). This explanation has been contested especially by Th. C. Vriezen. But he too emphasizes that it is here if anywhere that there is a mythical background. It has to be proved nevertheless that the unsuccessful attempt is a widespread motif in primitive stories about the creation of human beings; here are a few examples:

The Dyaks of Sakarran in British Borneo say that the first man was made by two large birds. At first they tried to make men out of trees, but in vain. Then they hewed them out of rocks, but the figures could not speak. Then they moulded a man out of damp earth and infused into his veins the red gum of the kumpang-tree. After that they called to him and he answered. They cut him and blood flowed from his wounds, so they gave him the name of Tannah Kumpok or "moulded earth." (J.G. Frazer, *Folklore* . . . , p. 7).

The narratives often tell of the creator god reflecting as to how he can repair his creatures (Frazer, p. 8f.). An echo of the same motif occurs in the Sumerian Myth "the creation of man" in S.N. Kramer, *Sumerian Mythology*, pp. 68-72:

"Then the poem describes a feast arranged by Enki for the gods. At this feast Enki and Ninmah drink much wine. . . . Ninmah takes some clay and fashions six different types of individuals, while Enki decrees their fate and gives them bread to eat. The last two types, the barren woman and the eunuch. Then Enki makes some creations . . . a failure, it is weak in spirit and body. . . . Finally Ninmah seems to utter a curse against Enki because of the sick, lifeless creature which he produces" (p. 70).

Finally we can note that in the Gilgamesh Epic Enkidu becomes a real man in two stages or acts; when he lived with the animals, he was not really a man; he becomes so only by means of the woman whom the gods send to him.

But both of these bear only remote traces of the older motif which is preserved much more clearly in Gen 2. What is the meaning of this experiment in the creation of human beings? To describe the creation of a human being as the work of an artist or a sculptor is to introduce *eo ipso* the possibility of success or failure, or the way to ultimate success through failure. The former is no less anthropomorphic than the latter. If this step from initial failure, or better from initial inadequacy, ("it is not good"), to ultimate success is required only for the creation of humans, and nowhere else, then it is acknowledging that there is something special about human beings. Gen 2 acknowledges that people do not find the true meaning of human life in the mere fact of existence; if this were the case, then community with the animals would be enough. But people find the meaning of life only in human community; it is only this that makes true humanity.

The same is said about Enkidu in the Gilgamesh Epic. At the beginning Enkidu lives with the animals (this corresponds to the possibility, presumed in Gen 2:19-20, that the man might find a helper fit for him among the animals). It is told of Enkidu too that he was formed out of earth, that he was led astray by a woman and came thereby to experience human community. These similarities are striking. Behind the Enkidu scene then there is an old tradition that has certain characteristics in common with Gen 2-3. But there is an important difference; in the Enkidu scene the woman is the means by which Enkidu really becomes a human being. However, the meeting with the woman is only an episode; the goal is friendship with Gilgamesh. In Gen 2 on the contrary the goal is the community of man and woman as such.

The old tradition that lies behind the Enkidu scene agrees with Gen 2:19-20 in that there is a background echo of a distant past when humans and beasts were closer to each other: "Shaggy with hair is his whole body, he is endowed with head hair like a woman" ANET, p. 74; I, 36f.). When Gen 2:19-20 raises the mere possibility that the animals could be the man's helper, it recalls this however faintly. But Gen 2:19-20, in contrast to the Enkidu scene, says emphatically that the animals cannot be a helper corresponding to the man: "The animals are not the man's counterpart" (Vriezen).

[2:18] The reflection of the creator points back to a deficiency: "The man is alone"; it looks to a form of human existence where the man is living in a state in which he has no proper counterpart.

The creator considers the-being-alone quite negatively: it is not good. Ecclesiastes says the same, 4:9-12 (cf. J. Pedersen, *Israel*, I 263). When the prophet Jeremiah is bidden to remain alone 16:1-9, then this is meant to be a sign that God's judgment upon his people is near. God can bid one to be alone in such extreme and circumscribed situations; but this in itself remains a negative way to the full life which is found in community.

All human community is centered around the community of man and woman. This is described in two phrases which look first only to the community of man and woman, and then in a broader sense to all human community.

עֵזֶר means support or help. In Is 30:5 it describes a people, in Hos 13:9 and Ps 121:1 it is asked for. God is עזר in Ex 18:4; Deut 33:7; Ps 20:3, and elsewhere. The usual word for help is עֶזרה; here the neutral form עֹזר (masc.) is used deliberately. The majority of interpreters (so F. Delitzsch, A. Dillmann, Th.C. Vriezen) have stressed correctly that the meaning is not just help at work (with reference to 2:5 so W.H. Schmidt, p. 200) nor is it concerned merely with the begetting of descendants (Augustine and the older interpreters, H. Böhmer); it means support in a broad sense. F. Delitzsch writes: "Human beings cannot fulfil their destiny in any other way than in mutual assistance." Ecclesiastes explains well what is meant: "For if they fall, one will lift up his fellow; but woe to him who is alone when he falls and has not another to lift him up," 4:10. The man is created by God in such a way that he needs the help of a partner; hence mutual help is an essential part of human existence (Tob 8:6, "a helper and support," βοηθὸν στήριγμα).

כנגדו L. Köhler, *Old Testament Theology* (1957) 248, "נגד is literally that which is over against, counterpart." E.A. Speiser renders "corresponding to him"; H. Gunkel "corresponding to him, his counterpart" (so too Th.C. Vriezen). Together with the mutual help is the mutual correspondence, the mutual understanding in word and answer as well as in silence, which constitutes life in common. These two phrases describe in an extraordinary way what human community is; it has to do primarily with man and woman, and determines human existence for all times.

[2:19] The verb ויצר is a continuation of v. 7 where the same word occurs at the beginning of the sentence. The long interpolation of vv. 9, 15-17 and 10-14 have separated vv. 7a and 19a in such a way that their sequence can no longer be followed. While the narrative was still independent it was given direction by the three verbs: God formed, v. 7; God formed, v. 19; God made, v. 22. This framework, still clearly recognizable, shows that the narrative was once independent.

The descriptions of the animals in vv. 19a and 20a are different. 19a: "Every beast of the field and every bird of the air"; 20a cattle, birds of the air, every beast of the field. The descriptions here, in contrast to Gen 1, are not expressed in formulas and can vary, even in their order. When H. Gunkel writes that "the narrator overlooks the fish" — and a number of interpreters say something similar — then the presupposition is that the narrator is concerned with the creation of the animals in general, as was P. But that is not the case. He is thinking of the animals from the viewpoint of human beings. Can animals be their helpers or companions? And so the fish do not come into consideration (so too H. Gunkel).

The animals are formed from the earth, like the humans. It is not said that they are given life by God breathing into them. But this need not necessarily indicate a deliberate variation from the account of the creation of humans (against W.H. Schmidt 199); it can be conditioned simply by the narrative technique. In any case the animals too are created as living beings.

God brings the animals to the man: this procession gives expression to the intention of God in making the animals; it implies that it is the man who finds out and decides what sort of helper corresponds to him.

This passage can serve as a good example of how exegesis must adhere strictly to what the narrative says. J. Hempel, BZAW 81 (1961) 198-229, exaggerates when he says that God really meant the animals to be human companions; however, the man misused them and so God gave him as a punishment the woman who brought distress. This interpretation misunderstands the whole thrust of the narrative which leads from the divine reflection, v. 18, to the accomplishment of the intent, v. 22, and its acknowledgment by the man, v. 23. Th.C. Vriezen opposes this and tries to understand the creation of the animals as an attempt which is not successful. He finds a way out because in vv. 19-20 God is only concerned to see how the man reacts face to face with the animals. But the author is showing with all the emphasis he can that the animals are not the man's counterpart. He wants, if only polemically, to stress the difference between a human being and a beast. While Hempel sees too much in the creation of the animals, Vriezen sees too little; he sees only the negative presuppositions of vv. 21-22.

The narrative stands between these two extremes; it tells of the possibility that the creation of the animals may offer the man the help which is suited to him, no more and no less. It is the man who decides whether this is so or not, and he decides against it. Nevertheless, the animals retain a positive meaning for the man which is described when he names them.

The creator wants the man to name the animals. This means first and foremost that the man is autonomous within a certain limited area. The creator has formed the animals; the man can do nothing about this, but must accept them as God presents them to him. This is the point where the man begins to exercise his capabilities. He names the animals and with the name determines the relationship they have to him. P says this in a more abstract way, namely that the creator has appointed the man to be master of the animals, 1:26, 28; J tells how this came about. The exercise of dominion does not begin with the use or exploitation of the animals for human ends. The meaning is not, as most interpreters think, that the man acquires power over the animals by naming them. (This is quite a different notion; the one who knows the name of a being can by this knowledge dispose of it.) But rather that the man gives the animals their names and thereby puts them into a place in his world.

This is not a question of magic, but basically a rational procedure. Animals simply as creatures have no name. It is only the giving of the name that creates the world of humankind. "This naming is thus both an act of copying and an act of appropriative ordering" (G. von Rad ad. loc.). By naming the animals the man opens up, determines and orders his world and incorporates them into his life. The world becomes human only through language. The act of naming is directed not to things but to the animals, to living beings (against F. Delitzsch, A. Dillmann, O. Procksch who think that things are named here). Names are given first to living beings because they are closest to humans (in the primeval event the *nomen generis* and the *nomen proprium* are not yet differentiated, as becomes clearer in v. 23). This accords with what is known from the history of language, namely that the appellative (das *Nomen*) includes originally the name in the real sense as well as the general descriptive sense; but the personal naming is primary. What is named is not the thing but the agent.

[2:20] Instead of ולאדם many exegetes read the וְלְאָדָם (H. Holzinger, O. Procksch). אדם is certainly not meant to be a proper name. One can leave the Massoretic pointing as do F. Delitzsch and H. Gunkel ("no article, because meaning is qualitative"); F. Delitzsch renders "for a human being such as he is," and Th.C. Vriezen understands it in a reflexive sense. There is no longer any ground then for Holzinger's hesitation; the "for one man" does not enter into the discussion. In any case the subject of מצא must be the man, and it is not necessary to change the word into a niphal as many have proposed.

The first act of the decision taken in v. 18b is concluded in v. 20b. The creator has not yet achieved what he wanted; the state of "not good" has not been altered. The tension which began in v. 18a is intensified. The sentence is at the same time preparatory; the key word of v. 18, עזר כנגדו, is resumed, but negatively. And so it prepares vv. 21-23; it need not be expressed further. A. Dillmann has described the anticipatory function of v. 20b with reference to 1:26: "The dignity of human nature cannot be portrayed better than in this brief phrase."

[2:21-24] *Literature* (The Creation of Woman): W.R. Smith, *Kinship and Marriage in Early Arabia* (1903[2]). M. Löhr, *Die Stellung des Weibes zu Jahwe-Religion und -Kult*, BWANT 4 (1908). S. Reinach, "La naissance d'Eve," RHR 78 (1918) 185-206. J. Döller, *Das Weib im AT. Biblische Zeitfragen III*, 7/9 (1920[2]). J. Böhmer, "Die geschlechtliche Stellung des Weibes in Genesis 2 und 3," MGWJ 79 (1935) 281-302. J.G. Thomson, "Sleep. An Aspect of Jewish Anthropology," VT 5 (1955) 421-433. S. Thompson, *Motif-Index of Folk-Literature. A* (1955[2]-1958) Nr. 1241-1243. J.L. Helberg, "A Communication on the Semasiological Meaning of Basar," OTWSA.P 2 (1959) 23-28. L. Arnaldich, "La création de Eva. Genèse 1:26-27; 2:18-25," *Sacra Pagina I* (1959) 346-357. W. Reiser, "Die Verwandtschaftsformel in Genesis 2:23," ThZ 16 (1960) 1-4. M.R. Lehmann, "Genesis 2:24 as the Basis for Divorce in Halakhah and NT," ZAW 72 (1960) 263-267. W. Plautz, "Zur Frage des Mutterrechts im AT," ZAW 74 (1962) 9-30 (with Literature); "Monagamie und Polygynie im AT," ZAW 75 (1963) 3-27. O. Schilling, *Das Mysterium Lunae und die Erschaffung der Frau* (1963). P. Grelot, *Mann und Frau nach der heiligen Schrift* (1964). D. Lys, *La chair dans l'AT. "Bâsâr"* (1967). C.J. Vos, *Woman in OT Worship*. Diss. Amsterdam (1968). G. Molan, "Towards a Biblical Understanding of Womanhood," *Ministry* 8 (1968) 3-9.

The creation of the woman. It is here that the creation of humankind achieves the goal intended by God; his work has now succeeded. V. 23 here corresponds to God's judgment over the individual works of creation in Gen 1: now it is good. This section is constructed in the following way: there is a series of five sentences in narrative form in vv. 21-22 with God as subject, broken only by the single verb with the man as subject וייש; there follows in v. 23 the cry of the man; this brings to conclusion not only vv. 21-23, but the whole action begun in v. 18.

[2:21-22]   The creation of woman from the rib of the man should not be understood as a description of an actual event accessible to us. It is a misunderstanding of the narrative to say with U. Cassuto that God not only took out the rib but also took some flesh, or with P. Humbert that the operation left behind a scar, or with others that it is the first anesthetic. The event described in primeval event and the creation of the woman out of the rib of the man can no more be presented than the creation of the man out of earth or dust. One cannot say that J, who passes on these narratives, imagines the creation of man and woman in this way. He presumes that his hearers know that he did not shape the imagery himself, but is passing on very ancient traditions formed long ago.

Besides the creation of the man out of earth or clay there were other narratives in which a human being was created out of other materials (the materials in the Sumerian-Akkadian Myths is different), particularly in the African narratives. For example, a person is formed out of wood and H. Baumann writes in this context: "The motif is concerned mainly with the origin of woman," p. 242. Behind the description of the creation of the man out of earth, there lies the ancient technique of producing human figures out of clay. The artist uses "two materials, clay and reeds, fashioning the clay on the bone. . . ." R. Amiran ("Myths of Creation of Man and the Jericho Statues," BASOR 167 [1962] 23-25) compares this with the creation of woman in Gen 2:21f.: "The creation of Eve was accomplished by building or fashioning clay around the rib of Adam, . . . its counterpart has been uncovered in natura at Jericho."

These references indicate that a very old tradition or description of the creation of humankind lies behind 2:21f., and that it has been inserted into the narrative very artistically. The intention is clear: the process of creation itself explains how man and woman belong together (it is possible that there is yet another creation motif at work here: creation out of a part of an already existing man; e.g., the Eskimos have a story about woman created out of man's thumb; or the origin of a god from a bodily part of another god; for examples, see F. Delitzsch ad. loc.).

One will be rather reserved then when it is suggested that there are etiological traits in vv. 21-22. P. Humbert sees in v. 21b a naive attempt to explain the existence of the navel; others, e.g., G. von Rad, the absence of a rib; or a reference to the dispensability of a rib (O. Procksch). Such explanations deviate from the main thrust of the narrative which aims at explaining what man himself is, not something that just belongs to him. The rib probably has its basis in a Sumerian word play (cf. J.B. Pritchard, 1948/1949, p. 15: ". . . in Sumerian there is established through a play upon words, a definite connection between the rib and 'the lady who makes live'").

The deep sleep (1 Sam 26:12; Is 29:10; H. Gunkel accepts the motif of the magic spell in the fairy tale) is explained in an interesting manner in the view that the man ought not be a witness of the work of creation (J.G. Herder, A. Dillmann, and recent interpreters; J.G. Thomson, VT 5 (1955) 21f.). But this is probably too rational an explanation for this ancient motif. We can only be certain that the way in which the narrative describes the creation requires such a sleep. The word בנה is part of the creation terminology: "The verb bānu ('to build') is the regular term employed in Akkadian literature to describe the creation of human beings by the gods; so, too, in Ugaritic, one of the titles of the deity who is the father of the gods and of humans *('b'dm)* is *bny bnwt,* i.e., creator of creatures'' (U. Cassuto, p. 134). In contrast to this בנה only occurs again in Am 9:6 to describe the work of creation.

[**2:23**]   The man reacts with a ''jubilant welcome'' (J.G. Herder) to the new creature that God leads to him. He has now found the helper that is fit for him. It has long been recognized that the words follow a rhythmic pattern; the first line consists of three colons of two stresses each and the second of two colons of three stresses each (so, e.g., P. Humbert and H. Gunkel, and the disposition of the verses in BHK). The only other occurrence of a rhythmic pattern is in Gen 2-3 in the pronouncement of the punishments, 3:14ff. Gunkel writes: ''The words have a marked rhythmic form as is often the case at the climax of a story or of a tale.'' That may well be the case, but it does not touch what is essential, namely that the ancient narratives which arose in the period of oral tradition distinguish even more clearly the two basic forms of speech, ordinary language and the cry.

Here an exclamation is put into rhythmic form; language becomes a poetic explanation. In a cry, language is compressed and the result of such concentration is a rhythmic pattern. The rhythm is not something superimposed later on the language, as is the case with meter, but belongs to the very form of the cry. It is a misunderstanding of the cry in Gen 2:23 when W.H. Schmidt writes: ''When God . . . leads the woman to the man, he expressly establishes . . . . intimate community.'' If it were only a question of establishing something, there would be no need for a rhythmic form. It is no chance that the two basic rhythmic forms occur precisely at this place, the double (3 x 2) and the triple (2 x 3). They are perceptively different: the double beat in the first line forms the purely emotional, joyful cry, the triple beat in the second the announcement and fulfillment which require the broader rhythm of the triple beat. P. Humbert has explained the difference accurately: the first verse ''finds its meter in the joyful surprise and has an almost explosive meter, while in the second the grouping of 3:3 broadens the rhythm and gives the thought solemnity and harmony.'' Two of the basic functions of human speech are taken up into this narrative of the creation of humans; the naming and the cry.

The word זאת occurs three times, at the beginning of the first line and at the beginning and at the end of the second. It refers to the woman in each case and is the feminine demonstrative pronoun, ''this,'' ''the one here.'' This pronoun has greater force in Hebrew than in our modern languages; it is much more vital in its point of reference and much more existential, as well illustrated here. The word הפעם too has the article with demonstrative force (A. Dillmann) as in Gen 29:34, 35 where it is used in a similar way; see too Gen 30:20; 46:30; Ex 9:27.

There is a deliberate subtlety in the giving of the name, which is the goal of v. 23; it is in the third person and is meant to be a direct continuation of the naming of the animals in v. 20. The three-fold ''this'' is at the same time a ''jubilant welcome'' and a cry of joy to the creator that he has given the man a helper fit for him. This use of the third person does not mean that there is some sort of gap, as is shown in the descriptive praise of God where he is praised in the third person.

"Bone of my bones and flesh of my flesh": the author uses what is known as "the formula of relationship" (W. Reiser), as in Gen 29:14; Judg 9:2, 3; 2 Sam 5:1; 19:13, 14; in each case it is a permanent relationship. The formula is altered slightly by the plural מעצמי and the preposition מן, and so adapted to the situation.

The word play is an essential part of the second half of the verse. In English, "woman, derived from 'wife of man', would offer a better linguistic foyle than the Hebrew noun" (E.A. Speiser). It is an open question whether the assonance in the Hebrew has an etymological basis (F. Delitzsch, A. Dillmann, O. Procksch) or not (E.A. Speiser).

We have in v. 23b a name etiology in the purest form. It is firmly fixed in the narrative and has been prepared by vv. 19-20. There, God wanted the man to name the animals which were led before him and to express by the name the significance that each had for him. The same occurs in the naming in v. 23, though the man does not need to be asked to do it; it happens spontaneously. The naming of the woman is an essential part of the narrative which ends in v. 23. V. 24, in contrast to v. 23b, is an etiological addition, without which the narrative would be quite complete.

Even though there is a name etiology in v. 23b, it does not make 2:4b-24 an etiological narrative which would answer questions implied in v. 23b (or in 24) or explain the meaning of אישה. The suspense that begins in v. 18 is conditioned by vv. 7 and 8 which it presumes. The narrative then is not concerned with the creation of woman, nor with the origin of the mutual attraction of the sexes. It is concerned with the creation of humankind which reaches its goal in the complementary society of man and woman. The name etiology of v. 23b, though certainly belonging to the narrative and firmly fixed in it, is a secondary trait, not a goal.

What then is said about the relationship of man and woman? The narrative in Gen 2 reflects a stage in civilization which was aware of the great importance of the role of woman in the existence of humankind. Gen 2 is unique among the creation myths of the whole of the Ancient Near East in its appreciation of the meaning of woman, i.e., that human existence is a partnership of man and woman. A trace of this motif occurs in some primitive creation stories, e.g., the Ewe-speaking tribes of Togo in West Africa tell that "in the beginning God fashioned a man and set him on the earth; after that he fashioned a woman. The two looked at each other and began to laugh, where upon God sent them into the world" (J.G. Frazer, *Folklore.* . . . p. 11). It is significant that we in our present stage of civilization agree with what Genesis 2 says about the relationship of man and woman.

The words "a helper fit for him" refers neither to the sexual nature of woman (so Augustine) nor to the help which she could offer to the farmer. Any such limitation destroys the meaning of the passage. What is meant is the personal community of man and woman in the broadest sense — bodily and spiritual community, mutual help and understanding, joy and contentment in each other.

It has been said that the narrative is the foundation of monogomy (F. Delitzsch, A. Dillmann and others). However, it is not concerned with the foundation of any sort of institution, but with primeval event.

[2:24] There is a change of speaker between vv. 23 and 24. It is not the man who is speaking now but the narrator (so A. Dillmann and O. Procksch against F. Delitzsch and most moderns). It is clear then that v. 24 is but an addition to the narrative which is complete without it, ending with v. 23; it is "a short epilogue, as it were, after the curtain has fallen" (G. von Rad). However, one cannot say that "in this statement the entire narrative so far arrives at the primary purpose toward which it was oriented from the beginning" (G. von Rad, similarly H. Gunkel). The narrative 2:4b-8, 18-24 belongs to the cycle of narratives about the creation of humankind (it is not therefore "a myth about the origin of the wife," H. Gunkel). This is a narrative cycle that is completely *sui generis* in that its goal is always the same: the existence of humankind as it is today. The etiological motif of v. 24 is then an addition, an explanation of "the basic drive of the sexes to each other." It can be shown clearly that v. 24 has been added; whereas v. 23 remains within the action of the narrative, v. 24 steps outside it. "It is not possible for the couple which has just discovered that they belong together to leave father and mother" (similarly B. Jacob). It has been pointed out correctly (W.H. Schmidt, p. 202) that in the foregoing narrative it is always האדם; איש is first used in v. 23 for the word play; v. 24 resumes איש, but from v. 25 on it is אדם again.

The two verbs "he leaves" and "he cleaves to" should not be understood in any way as descriptions of an institution (so too H. Gunkel). It is a misunderstanding of the purpose of the verse to suppose that there echoes here a memory of the matriarchal state of society (R. Smith and many others; for literature see Th.C. Vriezen). It should be stressed that the drive of the sexes toward each other is not the only element in the institution of marriage as we meet it in the Old Testament, be it monogamy or polygamy. Often it is not even the decisive element. In general, family, social and economic elements are decisive. This is shown by the important part that parents play in the arrangement of the marriage of their children from the patriarchal stories right up to the book of Tobit.

The significance of the verse lies in this that in contrast to the established institutions and partly in opposition to them, it points to the basic power of love between man and woman. It has been asked whether "they became one flesh" refers to sexual intercourse or to the child in which man and woman become one flesh. Neither is correct. The latter explanation (O. Procksch, G. von Rad) cannot hold because v. 24, like v. 23, is not talking about marriage as an insitution for the begetting of descendants, but of the community of man and woman as such. The former explanation (H. Gunkel) is too one-sided, because the Hebrew בשר does not stand in opposition to spirit or soul, like the Greek σάρξ, but describes human existence as a whole under the aspect of corporality. F. Delitzsch saw this when he understood the phrase "one flesh" as "spiritual unity, the most complete personal community."

On the two verbs: the man leaves his parents (it is important that it does not say "parent's house"), i.e., those people who have hitherto been closest to him, so as to start his own household (so too Th.C. Vriezen following K. Budde, and E. Meyer): he "cleaves to" his wife, i.e., he enters into lasting community of life with her because of his love for her. This does not mean a social state, but a situation of very personal concern, fidelity and involvement. B. Jacob grasps the meaning: "Father and mother are the natural roots of the child; together with brothers and sisters it has grown on the same stem; but man and wife each come from a different family and up to that point have not even known each other. Nevertheless for the sake of the wife he has chosen, the man leaves father and mother, loosing the strongest bodily and spiritual bonds." It is amazing that this one word presents the basic involvement of man and woman as something given with and rooted in the very act of creation. The primary place is not given to propagation or to the institution of marriage as such. The love of man and woman receives here a unique evaluation.

The narrative 2:4b-8, 18-24 is brought to a conclusion in v. 24.

[2:25]   This is the only verse in Gen 2-3 which portrays human existence in the garden as a state. H. Gunkel expresses it in the heading to v. 25: "The primeval state." With it are linked a number of attempts to explain the primeval state, the nature of human existence "before the fall." Much depends on the meaning of the verse.

The function of the verse is to form a bridge from the creation narrative to the narrative of the expulsion from the garden. It can only be explained from what follows, particularly from 3:7. The intention of the author then is not to portray a state; 2:25 is rather a preparation for 3:7.

The verse is taken up into the stylistic device that we have already met a number of times in the description of the primeval event, especially into the pattern: "when . . . there was not yet. . . ." While this pattern describes in narrative form in Gen 2:4b-6 what was before creation, 2:25 describes what was before the sin of man, the "fall." The Egyptian "when there was not yet" sentences offer quite striking parallels (H. Grapow, "Die Welt vor der Schöpfung," ZÄS 67 [1931] 34-38) one text reads

> When not yet heaven had come to be
> When not yet earth had come to be
> When not yet the two supports (Shu and
>   Tefnet) had come to be
> When not yet disorder had come to be
> When not yet that fear had come to be
> Which came to be because of Horus' eye.
>   (Pyr. 1040, Grapow)

These texts bring together by means of the "when there was not yet" sentences two different elements, cosmic and those relating to humans: the "disorder" which is not described further and then the fear because of Horus' eye which sees everything that happens on earth; the fear of a bad conscience therefore or fear before the judge. It can also be: "When the eye of Horus was not yet wounded" (Pyr. 1463). And instead of "disorder" we find, "when death had not yet come to be" (Pry. 1466). In later texts only the first element occurs.

It is the same basic presentation that occurs all over the world. The creation of the world as it now is together with the great disorder in it are traced back to that primeval time which is on the other side of the here and now. This can be described in very different ways, but it always looks to the existence of human limitation, that limitation that comes through death and sin.

234

It is this "when there was not yet" in the bridge passage of v. 25 that prepares the narrative of Gen 3; it introduces a suspense that is resolved in 3:7.

We noted when commenting on 1:2 that this pattern serves to bring the primeval event into narrative form. Creation, insofar as it is narrated, must begin somewhere at that point "when there was not yet." One would be in error if one wanted to conclude to two different epochs or situations or periods, to a protracted state of chaos followed by a state of creation. There is something similar here. To put what is intended in Gen 3 into narrative form, there must be a before and after. But one should not conclude from this that the narrator wanted to contrast the two states, one before and one after the fall. When H. Gunkel asks, "how long was man in paradise?" and replies that the myth of its nature cannot give such details, the question is not pertinent to the purpose of the narrative.

The expulsion from the garden presumes logically a period during which the man and the woman sojourned in the garden. However, the narrator's intention is not to describe two successive phases or situations, but to present an event which caused the present state of human reality to be what it is. To narrate this, one must present it in terms of before and after. Both "points of time" belong to the primeval event, i.e., the putting of the man into the garden, 2:15, and driving him and the woman out, 3:22-24. Both instants are on the other side of historical time. The narrative does not intend to present a chronological separation between "primeval state" and the "state" after the expulsion. There are important consequences here for those who construct a teaching on the basis of two chronologically successive states of humanity before and after "the fall."

"And the man and his wife were both naked." It is told of Enkidu too that he was naked at the beginning and that the whole of his body was covered with hair. We can recognize in both cases a piece of information behind the statement. It was narrated that in the distant past people did not wear clothes (so too Th.C. Vriezen). Recollections of various stages in the history of civilization are reflected in the narrative even though they remain well in the background. It is no chance that the three stages indicated in Gen 3 "naked—clothed with leaves — clothed with skins" correspond to a demonstrable development. But these are only echoes; they do not belong to the main thrust of the narrative. H. Gunkel takes a different line: "The first picture is of the state of children," and he elaborates this (so too others). But the change from 2:25 to 3:7 is only intelligible if it is a question of adults in both places.

"And they were not ashamed." Much depends on the understanding of these words which introduce the suspense. O. Procksch says that the sentence shows "how far removed from the human community of man and wife was any consciousness of sensuality. The discovery of the secret of sex in the sense of shame is a consequence of sin." This explanation is in accordance with a very traditional Christian conception of the story of the "fall." It is a telling example of how fixed and firm ideas can influence the understanding of the text. There is nothing in the text to support Procksch's explanations. That the sense of shame is a consequence of sin is excluded from 3:7 as is the proposition that the secret of sex was discovered in the sense of shame.

This understanding of the narrative Gen 2-3 is largely responsible for the identification of sexuality, consciousness of sexuality and sin which has colored so strongly the whole Christian era. Is there really foundation for this in the text?

I quote the definition of F. Delitzsch, cited by G. von Rad: "Shame is the overpowering sense of a disordered inner harmony and peace within oneself. They were not ashamed of their nakedness, and why not? Shame is the co-relative of sin and guilt." This explanation of Delitzsch contains two errors. Shame originally is not something that takes place in the individual, but in relationship with others. Secondly, to limit shame to a "co-relative of sin and guilt" is disastrous. Being ashamed is rather a reaction to being discovered unmasked. It is a reaction of the whole person as the blushing which accompanies it indicates. It is an extremely puzzling phenomenon, such as the absence of shame can indicate on the one hand lack of self-consciousness or innocence, as in 2:25, or on the other hand the way to being inhuman.

A person who is without shame is no longer completely human. Shame is ethically an ambivalent phenomenon. As a reaction to a mistake, shame can be very positive; in itself it is effective in turning one away from the mistake. Here, the sense of shame should not be restricted to a reaction to sin or sensuality. This does not mean that the people in the garden were still guiltless nor that they experienced no "sensuality." The sentence is rather a preparation for the change in 3:7, in that it says that shame does not yet exist for those who are living together in the garden. In the background is the human awareness that shame can come and go without any explanation. One can suddenly feel ashamed where one previously experienced no shame, and vice versa, an indication of certain important variations in human existence.

[3:1-7] *Literature:* O. Holmberg, *Das Motiv der Neugier im Paradiesmythus. Eine literargeschichtlich Parallele,* 1933. K. Koch, "Die Hebräer vom Auszug aus Ägypten bis zum Grossreich Davids," VT 19 (1969) 37-81, esp. 72f.

C. 3, together with 2:9, 15-17, is a narrative of crime and punishment (see Introduction); it tells of a transgression and its penalty. It is constructed in two parts, the transgression 3:1-7, and the punishment 3:8-24. The transgression is brought about by a temptation, though temptation does not necessarily belong to the course of events *(Geschehensbogen)* of crime and punishment; motivation was necessarily not required. One could cut out the temptation of vv. 1-5 and read vv. 6-7 immediately after the prohibition in 2:17. The temptation then is an elaboration of the narrative; the narrator wanted to use it to explain how the transgression came about.

3:1-7 consists of three parts: 1-5, the temptation, 6, the transgression, 7 the change brought about by the transgression. The temptation consists of the introduction 1a, and the dialogue, 1b-5, in which the serpent speaks first, 1b, then the woman, 2-3, then the serpent again, 4-5. Interpreters have often underlined the great skill with which the narrative has been shaped; I refer particularly to H. Gunkel and G. von Rad. The exegesis has concerned itself primarily with the function of the serpent. Before going into this discussion we must ask what the author intended with this scene. The narrator tells us that the woman was tempted to eat the fruit of the forbidden tree. The serpent that tempts the woman appears only in this context and its meaning can only be explained out of it. The tempter cannot be a person because the story is about the first human couple; it must be one of the other creatures. This is sufficient reason for the introduction of the serpent as tempter, and all attempts to explain its appearance in 3:1-7 from other contexts are from the very beginning questionable.

[3:1-5] *Literature* (The Serpent): W.W. Graf Baudissin, *Studien zur semitischen Religionsgeschichte I* (1876) 286-291; "Esmun-Asklepios," *Festschr. Th. Nöldeke* (1906) 325-327, 729-731. A.H. Sayce, "The Serpent in Genesis," ExpT 20 (1909) 562. H. Schmerber, *Die Schlange des Paradieses. Religionsgeschichtlich-kunsthistorische Studie* (1915). J. Hehn, "Zur Paradieses-schlange," *Festschr. S. Merckel* (1922) 137-151. P. Thomsen, RLV XI (1927/1928) 264-265. S.A. Cook, *The Religion of Ancient Palestine in the Light of Archaeology. Schweich Lectures* 1925 (1930) 54, 98. A. Brock-Utne, " 'Der Feind'. Die alttestamentliche Satansgestalt im Lichte der sozialen Verhältnesse des Nahen Orients," Klio 28 (1935) 219-237. K. Galling, BRL 225-227. 458-460. A.S. Yahuda, "The symbolism and Worship of the serpent," Lecture Nov. (1938). B. Renz, "Die kluge Schlange," BZ 24 (1938/1939) 236-241. J. Hofbauer, "Die Paradieses-schlange (Gen 3)," ZKTh .59 (1947) 228-231. P. von Imschoot, "De serpente tentatore," CBrug 31 (1948) 5-10. H.N. Tur-Sinai, *Vom Unsinn der Bibel*, Wiss. d. Judentums 49 (1949). B.S. Childs, *Myth and Reality in the OT*, SBT 27 (1960) 43-50 (1962²). L. Randellini, "Satana nell' AT," BibOr 5 (1963) 127-132.

The Serpent

For the form and function of the serpent I refer to the detailed presentation given by Th.C. Vriezen, pp. 103-133. He synthesizes the various opinions into groups which are reproduced here, but in a somewhat different order:

(a) The serpent is Satan in disguise. Satan is the real tempter; it is Satan then who is cursed in 3:15. This is an old and long-standing Christian explanation, especially in dogmatics, but it has been abandoned in modern exegesis. It is surprising then that it crops up again in the context of an interpretation which sees Baal, the Canaanite god of fertility, behind the form of the serpent. Baal is the great opponent of Yahweh (so in far less subtle form, F. Hvidberg).

(b) The serpent is purely symbolical; it symbolizes human curiosity (Talmud, B. Jacob), or "intellectual curiosity" (N.P. Williams).

(c) The serpent is a mythological form which was first reduced to an animal in Israelite tradition (so H. Gunkel and others). Within this mythological context there is a whole series of modifications and refinements: I. The serpent brings prosperity; this is the case in many religions. It is the animal that brings wisdom and life and advances knowledge in a number of ways. The magic element can also be included here: the serpent is a magical animal and the prototype of the one who brings prosperity. II. The serpent has a dualistic character. It is the animal of life and death; it is a deity of the underworld. The serpent is a mythological being belonging to Chaos and opposed to God, or a demon and God's enemy.

(d) The serpent is an animal that is particularly clever. Its ability to speak is a characteristic of the tale.

Vriezen, after his synthetic presentation and rejection of other explanations, comes to the conclusion that the serpent in Gen 3 belongs to the realm of magic and is meant to be an animal of life and wisdom. Now this explanation agrees with the data of the narrative. 2 Kings 18:4 together with Num 21 refer to a cult of the serpent in Israel which presumes such an explanation. This serpent cult was very probably taken over from Canaan (W.F. Albright, K. Galling, and others). The role of the serpent then would be positive. It was the Yahwist who made it a tempter. What is condemned then in 3:15 is the "oriental-heathen pattern of thought that claims to have a higher knowledge of life by means of the magic and divination associated with the serpent." This polemic forms the real background of the narrative.

This explanation has predominated in recent years. It has been worked out particularly by J.A. Soggin, 1962 and is supported by J.L. McKenzie, J. Daniélou, J. Coppens, O. Loretz. The last named writes: "It (the serpent) in Gen 3 is the symbol of the Canaanite fertility cult and as such promises life (Soggin)"

p. 117. But this explanation, so widespread and dominant today, runs up against a difficulty in the text that, remarkably, has scarcely been adverted to: the relative sentence in 3:1, "that the Lord God had made," describes the serpent expressly as a creature of God; it refers back to 2:19. How then can it be said that the serpent, a creature of God, incorporates "the oriental-heathen pattern of thought" or the Canaanite fertility cult? This seems to me to be excluded. If J wanted to say that the serpent was really the incorporation of something opposed to Yahweh, then he could not say in the same breath that Yahweh created it.

The function of the serpent derives from the structure of the narrative. The couple's transgression in the garden where God put them is elaborated by the temptation motif portrayed in an action. It could have been presented as something that took place in the person, but that would not suit the character of the narrative. It is described as a personal event spelled out in a dialogue. Besides the two people, there are only animals in the garden. The serpent is a candidate for the role inasmuch as it is the cleverest of the animals, and is introduced as such. The animal that talks is characteristic of the tale or fable. By resuming this fairy tale trait the narrator points the way into the realm of primeval event, beyond the here and now, and so into the cycle of narratives about the creation of humanity. This cycle, like the tale, has its roots in primitive cultures, in marked contrast to the cosmogonies which belong to the high cultures. H. Gunkel finds a whole series of fairy tale motifs in Gen 2-3 which correspond to primitive narrative.

One cannot allege in favor of the mythical explanation the extraordinary capabilities of the snake shown by its speech and knowledge of divine secrets. The African narratives often speak of the clever animal in just this way. An animal (that can also talk) has almost always a role to play in the narrative cycle of "how death came into the world." It is the bearer of a message that promises humankind (eternal) life, but which is always delayed or does not come at all (J.G. Frazer, H. Baumann). One should not compare the function of a trickster of this sort with that of the serpent. These stories of the loss of immortality, which are found in the broader context of the creation of human beings, show the role of the serpent in what is clearly a pre-mythical character. The serpent can also slough off its skin and renew its life; and so it knows what life and death are all about.

Again, one cannot allege for the mythical explanation the enmity of the serpent toward God and conclude from it that the serpent is a demon or divine being opposed to God. The text says nothing about such enmity toward God. The serpent has its place only in the incident of the temptation and is introduced only for this. One must agree with G. von Rad when he writes: "The mention of the snake here is almost incidental; at any rate, in the 'temptation' by it the concern is with a completely unmythical process . . . we are not to be concerned with what the snake is but rather with what it says." The words of the serpent are certainly directed against God, but this does not become the theme of the narrative. We are not justified by the text in seeing behind these words a complete orientation of the serpent against God or a being at enmity with God.

What is the significance of the serpent for the question of the origin of evil? Any basically dualistic notion according to which the serpent is seen as the embodiment of evil, as Satan who leads people to evil and sets them apart from God, is excluded for J. As a consequence, the mythical explanation of the serpent is questionable. Such an explanation would clearly establish its origin: the source of evil is religion opposed to Israel. But that cannot be the meaning of Gen 3. Evil, or the power of temptation, of which Gen 3 speaks, must be a human phenomenon, just like human sin, the transgression. Adam does not stand for Israel, but represents humankind.

When J allows the man and the woman to be led astray by the clever snake, creature of God, he is saying that it is not possible to know the origin of evil. We are at a complete loss in face of the fact that God has created a being that can lead people to disobedience. The origin of evil remains a complete mystery. The most important thing that J has to say here is that there is no etiology for the origin of evil; a mythical explanation which pinpoints the origin would destroy this. I agree then with W. Zimmerli when he says: "The temptation . . . stands as something absolutely inexplicable; it appears suddenly amid the good that God has created. It will remain there as a riddle."

[3:1a]   The amazing skill of the narrator shows itself first in that he does not really introduce the snake; he draws attention to one of its qualities that colors the following scene. J often uses this narrative device, namely beginning with a sentence that describes a circumstance. ערום, astute, clever, cunning, occurs in Job 5:12; 15:5 and often in Proverbs. The cunning of the serpent is proverbial (Mt 10:16); it is associated with its ability to produce poison or to change its skin. The association of a particular quality with an animal in tales and fables that derive from them is common. The narrator emphasizes explicitly by means of the relative clause that the serpent is not outside the circle of those already mentioned in the narrative; it is one among the animals created by God, 2:19.

[3:1b]   The masterly dialogue holds the center of the scene. The serpent and the woman are the sole actors, the passage having been originally independent. In addition, conversation in ancient narratives are always conducted by two people only. The serpent begins with an enquiry, seeming to speak sympathetically. "It opens the conversation . . . in a cautious way with an . . . interested question" (G. von Rad; cf. too H. Gunkel). By exaggerating the command "it gives the woman the opportunity to justify herself and put up a defence on God's behalf" (W. Zimmerli). אף כי often introduces a statement: "Well now" or "look here," 1 Sam 21:6; 2 Sam 16:11. The purpose is clear from the very first sentence of the question; it is God's command and this is put into question. The serpent speaks only of אלהים and a sufficient reason for this is that the name יהוה belongs only to the context of the relation of humans to God.

[3:2-3]   The woman counters the serpent by stating correctly the command of God. The command is not harsh; they can eat from all the trees in the garden, with one exception, so that they do not die. They are provided for and at the same time protected from danger. But while the command of God is being discussed, it is altered in the very act of defending it. The narrator makes this known by means of the slight refinement that the woman introduces: "Neither shall you touch it." God had not said that. G. von Rad explains: "It is as though she wanted to set a law for herself by means of this exaggeration." This sentence makes it clear that a command that is questioned is no longer the original command, as the continuation of the narrative makes even clearer. One who defends a command can already be on the way to breaking it. V. 3 describes the forbidden tree only as "the tree in the middle of the garden." This sentence shows that the tree cannot yet be described as "the tree of the knowledge of good and evil" (so H. Gunkel).

[3:4-5] The serpent's counter to this is to dispute the consequence of the eating of the fruit, v. 4, and to justify its position, v. 5. The serpent's reply can be made in a way that is quite friendly to the woman, like the enquiry in v. 1a. It is a real temptation, and only recognized as such in its consequences. One can scarcely say: ". . . the serpent can now drop the mask. . . ." (G. von Rad). The serpent enlightens the people about God's real intention: "God's jealousy is the reason for the command" (W. Zimmerli).

The explanation can go so far; it can trace the dialogue in thrust and counterthrust. It should not go further. It is to exceed the limits when, e.g., O. Procksch says: "The serpent . . . makes God a liar by mocking his command as difficult," or when interpreters argue whether God actually lied or not. The one is of the opinion that no one can whitewash God from being a liar, the other retorts that no one could possibly think of God having lied. Both sides however misunderstand the text. One must bear in mind what the basic situation is, as J. Pedersen has described it. The narratives that want to present the origin of death are dealing with a phenomenon that is intangible. God intends with this warning to bring knowledge and death together in a way that is very mysterious. It is something like the Gilgamesh Epic where the dying Enkidu curses the woman who has seduced him to knowledge. The serpent proposes to give another dimension to life which is linked with knowledge, somewhat as in the epic.

It is the same with the explanation that proposes that the serpent wanted to say God is jealous, he begrudges man knowledge. One can of course say that, and this motif plays an important role in the Adapa myth. However, one must note here that such "jealousy of God" which the serpent is implying, can only be understood from the matters that are at issue. The possibility of a higher dimension to life which this knowledge offers is ambivalent; it can elevate life or put it in danger. This is what is meant, even if the command can be understood in such different ways. For the motif of "the envy of the gods," see comments on 3:22.

"Your eyes will be opened." The same expression occurs in Gen 21:19. "Then God opened her eyes and she saw. . . ." It is an extraordinary "opening of the eyes" that enabled someone to see what was up to then not there. Whereas in Gen 21:19 it is God who opens Hagar's eyes, here it is the eating of the fruit of the tree. This is characteristic of the tale; what happens here is a sort of magic. At the basis of this lies that understanding of existence portrayed above, where animals speak, humans, animals, and God live side-by-side, and eating of a fruit can bring about a change in a person. This must be distinguished from what is properly mythical thinking or presentation. For "opening of the eyes" cf. G. Pidoux, 1954.

[3:5] *Literature* (Knowledge of Good and Evil): J.J.P. Valeton, *De hof van Eden. Studiën* (1881) 363-373. H.D. Major, "The Tree of the Knowledge of Good and Evil," ExpT 20 (1908/1909) 427-428. J. Fischer, "טוב ורע in der Erzählung von Paradies und Sündenfall," BZ 22 (1934) 323-331. F. Dornseiff, "Antikes zum AT, I. Genesis," ZAW 52 (1934) 57-75 = Antike und Alter Orient, KS I (1956) 203-246. G. Lambert, "'Lier - délier', l'expression de la totalité par l'opposition de deux contraires," *Vivre et penser*, 3 = RB 52 (1945) esp. 91-93. B. Bavink, *Das Ubel in der Welt* (1947¹). J. Coppens, *La connaissance du bien et du mal et le peché du paradis. Contribution à l'interpretation de Genèse II-III*, ALBO Ser II 3 (1948).   G. Mensching, *Gut und Böse im Glauben der Völker* (1950²).   K.A. Hidding, "Tweerlei kennis in het paradijsverhaal," *Festschr. G. van der Leeuw* (1950) 233-240   W. Russer, "Gott und das Übel in der Welt," GenM 27 (1951) 367-375, 461-470.   P. Boccacio, "I termini contrari come espressioni della totalità in ebraico," Bib 33 (1952) 173-190.   M. Buber, *Bilder von Gut und Böse* (1953²) 15-31.   C.H. Gordon, *Introduction to OT Times* (1953) 19-37, 97.   H.J. Stoebe, "Gut und Böse in der jahwistischen Quelle des Pentateuch," ZAW 65 (1953) 188-204.   G. Bouwman, "De kennis van goed en kwaad en de compositie van Gen 2-3," Bijdr 15 (1954) 162-171.   J. Bottéro, "L'Ecclésiastique et le problème du mal," NC 8 (1956) 133-159.   G.W. Buchanan, "The OT Meaning of the Knowledge of Good and Evil," JBL 75 (1956) 114-120.   B. Reicke, "The Knowledge hidden in the Tree of Paradise," JSSt 1 (1956) 193-201.   R. Jolivet, *Plotin et St. Augustin ou le problème du mal. Hellénisme et Christianisme* (new ed. 1956).   R. Gordis, "The Knowledge of Good and Evil in the OT and the Qumran Scrolls," JBL 76 (1957) 123-138.   A. Massart, "L'emploi . . . de termes opposés. . . ," MelBib. A. Robert (1957) esp. 42-43.   H.S. Stern, "The Knowledge of Good and Evil," VT 8 (1958) 405-418.   H.W. Huppenbauer, *Der Mensch zwischen zwei Welten. Der Dualismus der Texte von Qumran (Höhle I) und der Damaskus Fragmente* (1959).   J. Barr, "Theophany and Anthropomorphism in the OT," VT.S 7 (1960) 31-38.   J.J. Scullion, "An Approach to the Understanding of Isaiah 7:10-17," JBL 87 (1968) 297-299 esp. n. 53.   W.M. Clark, "A Legal Background to the Yahwist's Use of 'Good and Evil' in Genesis 2-3," JBL 88 (1969) 266-278.

ידע, to know: E. Baumann, "ידע und seine Derivate. Eine sprachlich-exegetische Studie," ZAW 28 (1908) 22-41, 110-143.   H.W. Wolff, "'Wissen um Gott' bei Hosea als Urform von Theologie," EvTh 12 (1952/1953) 533-554 = ThB 22 (1964) 182-205; "Erkenntnis Gottes im AT," EvTh 15 (1955) 426-431.   F. Gaboriau, "Enquête sur la signification biblique de connaître," Ang 45 (1968) 1-43.

"And you will be like God, knowing good and evil." The protracted discussion about the meaning of the knowledge of good and evil has not given sufficient attention to two presuppositons which enable us to determine more clearly the meaning:

1. The expression "to know good and evil" is to be understood as a whole. It would be misunderstanding to divide it into a verb "to know" with an object "good and evil." It is a whole and as such describes a particular way of knowing. This way of knowing is not a knowledge of some thing, of an object, as it is very often explained; it is rather a functional knowledge. "Good and evil" does not mean something that is good or evil in itself, but what is good or evil for humans, i.e., what is useful or harmful. Knowledge that is related to what is useful or injurious is to be thought of in the context of the struggle for existence. The person, by knowing and distinguishing the useful and the injurious, masters one's obligations and brings them to fruition. This is just what the woman says as she reflects in v. 6: ". . . to be desired to make one wise"; the verb here השכיל can also be translated "succeed." Success is made possible by distinguishing between good and evil.

If "the knowledge" is functional and concerned with mastering one's existence, then the meaning of "good and evil" is explained. There is no question of an isolated object which is good or evil in itself.

2. Traditional Western thought, without any further ado or reflection, has, in its exegesis of the expression "to know what is good and evil," taken as its starting point that the subject of the knowledge is an individual. This presupposition is not in accordance with the meaning and intention of the text. It should not be forgotten that אדם is collective. The man and the woman are not individuals in our sense but represent humankind in its origin. The "knowledge of good

and evil'' therefore should not be understood — or at least not merely understood — as the function of an individual or something that happens to an individual. The subject of the knowledge of what is useful or injurious in the context of mastering life is really humankind in its origin, not a first individual (or two individuals). The mastery of life (הַשְׂכִּיל) which is meant here is not limited to the life of the individual, nor is it concerned either with moral knowledge (K. Budde) or with material knowledge of the individual (J. Hempel). It is a knowledge which is directed to the life of the community and which reaches its fulfillment in it. The knowledge is concerned above all with the life of the group, with existence in community. This explanation is supported not merely by the collective understanding of אָדָם, and so with humankind in its origin. It is supported too by the fact that J in joining 2:4b-24 with Gen 3 wanted to say that the man is what God intended him to be only as a man in community, and that its basic form is the community of man and woman.

To Know Good and Evil

1. The expression is a *leitmotif* in the narrative; it occurs 4 times, 2:9, 17; 3:5, 22. From the point of view of construction it occurs in the exposè, 2:9, 17; at the climax, 3:5, and in the final survey, 3:22. Its meaning then must color the whole narrative, i.e., the narrative in its final form. If we look at the growth of the narrative, we must say that the tree whose fruit was forbidden is called the ''tree of the knowledge of good and evil'' only in 3:5, not in the introductory passages (see analysis above), and that 3:22 serves to join the motif of the tree of life to the narrative about the other tree. We conclude then that 3:5 is the central passage, and that we must take it as the starting point of our explanation.

2. The verses in which the expression occurs are saying: a) 3:5: the effects of eating of the fruit of the tree are, I. you will not die, II. your eyes will be opened, III. you will be like God knowing good and evil. b) 2:17: I. the fruit is forbidden, II. the fruit brings death. c) 3:22: the man has become like one of us knowing good and evil.

The conclusions from this are: (1) All passages, including 2:9, 17 agree that the effect of the fruit is the knowledge of good and evil. (2) The other effect is disputed: you will die — you will not die. (3) The sentence ''your eyes will be opened'' describes the process of how they come to the knowledge of good and evil. (4) The sentence ''you will be like God'' describes not an effect of the fruit over and above that of knowledge, but the ability to know good and evil (so the grammatical construction in 3:15 and 3:22). The eating of the fruit then does not cause them simply to be like God, but brings about a mode of being (''to be as God'') which makes the knowledge of good and evil possible.

The four passages together describe only two effects of eating the fruit, one beyond dispute, the other disputed. Now the text contains yet a third remark about the effect of the fruit and that is in 3:6 when the woman looks at the tree and desires it: ''to be desired to make one wise.'' There can be no question that the words refer to the ''knowledge of good and evil'' which the serpent has proposed to her. The narrator is telling us here what constituted the desire or temptation of the woman; it was the הַשְׂכִּיל. He then makes a decisive comment on the meaning of ''knowledge of good and evil.'' The woman oversteps the command and risks punishment (which the serpent has questioned) so as ''to become wise''; for her, this is ''knowing good and evil.''

Explanations of ''the knowledge of good and evil''

(1) The knowledge is completely subordinated to the command, ''through which any further determination of the knowledge of good and evil as good as disappears'' (Th.C. Vriezen, p. 142); so the explanation traditional in Christianity; e.g., F. Delitzsch: ''The emphasis is more on the knowledge than on the objects. Good: obedience with its happy consequences; evil: disobedience with its evil consequences.'' Similarly L. Köhler and B. Jacob.

(2) The knowledge of good and evil does not mean moral knowledge. K. Budde had defended this position vigorously (against J. Wellhausen and A. Lods).

(3) Knowledge is a broader and general sense: J. Wellhausen, *Composition*, p. 301: "In Hebrew good and evil always have the primary meanings of helpful and harmful . . . there is no intention of opposing actions because of their moral difference, but rather of bringing things together by virtue of their polarities according to which they are helpful or harmful to people." Two aspects of Wellhausen's explanation must be distinguished: (a) Good and evil are to be understood as meaning helpful or harmful or useful or injurious, i.e., it is to be understood functionally, and not in accordance with an objective standard. What is its meaning for human beings? Does it help or harm them? This functional meaning of "good and evil" has been taken up by a number of commentators (A. Dillmann, H.J. Stoebe, E.A. Speiser, J. Pedersen, A. Lods, P. Humbert, H. Schmidt). (b) "Bringing things together by virtue of their polarities." The function of the object of "to know" is not to separate, but to bring together: a whole is described by the two extremes. This explanation of Wellhausen has also been taken up by a number of scholars and clarified further, especially by G. Pidoux, "a means of expressing totality"; he also gives a bibliography. A. Massart notes the same in Egyptian: "To say you have not written to me at all, one says: you have written me neither good nor evil." Also W.G. Lambert, G. von Rad ("means predominantly one 'all'" in general); likewise P. Humbert, H.A. Brongers.

These explanations of Wellhausen that "good and evil" have (a) a functional and (b) an all-embracing sense can be presumed. They accord with the meaning of the text. Decisive objections are no longer raised against them. The translation of טוב ורע then must be "good and bad," because "good and evil" could be misunderstood as limiting the phrase to the moral field. E.A. Speiser in particular emphasizes this. One must agree: one can retain the traditional translation "good and evil" only with the reservation that "bad" in the general sense is meant.

While there is agreement about the general meaning, opinions diverge notably in explaining the details.

(4) The knowledge is restricted yet again to sexual knowledge; knowledge of the difference between the sexes or of the ability to beget and give birth. So H. Gressmann: "Now, conscious of their sex, they begin to beget and create life. That is the knowledge that the deity wanted to withhold from them because it makes them like God; begetting and sparking life is a divine craft." Similarly H. Schmidt: "Knowledge of what is special to sex, the awakening of the sense of sex. Knowledge of the secret of begetting and bearing is something divine," p. 22. So also H. Gunkel, but more reservedly: "The knowledge or ignorance that is in question here is primarily about the difference of the sexes . . . cf. Deut 1:39. But this . . . is not the whole, rather only a particularly notable example. . . ."

I. Engnell has recently proposed this explanation again: "The expression undoubtedly refers to the sexual sphere. Adam is now like the 'gods' in that respect too, that he is now capable of begetting. The whole stress is laid on the ability to procreate" p. 115. In a somewhat different form too, J. Coppens, J.A Soggin, J.L. McKenzie, and O. Loretz.

In favor of this explanation is that it seems to explain the whole sentence "you will be like God, knowing good and evil": the ability to beget makes one like God. The decisive objection to it is that it restricts the "knowledge of good and evil" to one area, sexual knowledge. Another objection is raised by scholars (e.g., J. Pedersen, H. Renckens): consciousness of sexuality and the ability to propagate is given in 1:26-29 as well as in 2:4bff. with the creation of the man. This explanation then is quite untenable.

(5) The emphasis is on the words "you will be like God" and the knowledge of good and evil is understood as divine knowledge, i.e., knowledge proper to God. A. Dillmann: "To know good and evil is a divine prerogative." Th.C. Vriezen, p. 146: "This knowledge then is a sharing with a higher being, God or an angel . . . an expression for a higher knowledge, the absolute numinous knowledge. The tree is a forbidden,

numinous tree'' (cf. 2 Sam 14:17; following O. Procksch). G. Pidoux: "The tree . . . is that which gives strength, complete power . . . a mark of the divinity," p. 41. W.G. Lambert: "The expression describes that which is required to gain something beyond what is human." G. von Rad: "The knowledge of good and evil means a knowledge of everything in the broadest sense of the word." Many scholars lay emphasis on the personal autonomy which would result from this knowledge: F. Delitzsch, J. Daniélou, J. Coppens, J.L. McKenzie, G. von Rad, W. Zimmerli. This is particularly so with H.J. Stoebe: "Man, by eating the fruit, wants to win the power to decide for himself what is and what is not suitable for him. . . ." "Man has really become like God when he can decide between good and evil and shape his life independently," pp. 397-398. This view of the knowledge of good and evil is closely connected with the view that understands the sin of man as ὕβϱις, so H. Renckens, G. von Rad, P. Humbert; contrary O. Loretz, 111f.

(6) "The claim to divine knowledge and power is hidden in the 'science' of magic"; the phrase can be understood then as a promise by the serpent of magical knowledge and powers. This explanation has been defended by Th.C. Vriezen after synthesizing other opinions: "The tree is the Israelite counterpart to magical power . . . the narrative is a polemic against the attitude represented by magic. It seems to us beyond dispute that the point of the story is directed against the polytheistic-magical attitude of the world of the Ancient Near East . . . to know good and evil like God means to want to dispose of good and evil. This religious and pedagogical intention of the narrative includes the dispute with magical thinking," p. 147.

G. Bouwman has a variation of this opinion, namely that the author of Gen 2-3 had at hand an old narrative with magical traits which he altered by giving it a moralistic direction. W.G. Lambert too sees in the superhuman faculties gained by eating the fruit "the power exercised by all types of magicians, a power stolen from an unwilling God."

(7) The interpreters who see in the snake a phallic symbol and so a symbol of the Canaanite fertility cult (F. Hvidberg, J.A. Soggin, O. Loretz) have to put the "knowledge of good and evil" into this same context. O. Loretz, agreeing with Soggin, writes "that the serpent in Gen 3 is one of those mythical serpents that represents life and death together. It stands . . . as a symbol of the Canaanite fertility cult and as such promises life" p. 117. . . . "It embodies the great temptation to which Israel had been exposed since entering the land of Canaan". . . . "Israel's sin was to prefer the serpent to the service of Yahweh," p. 121. This explanation would be possible if the serpent were connected with the tree of life. But this is not the case. It is not explained how the Canaanite fertility cult, to which the serpent will seduce the couple, is to bring the knowledge of good and evil.

The explanations given in 6) and 7) must face the question whether the text really admits of a polemic either against magic or "the polytheistic-magical attitude" or against the fertility cult. This seems to me to be a misunderstanding of the intention and nature of primeval narratives. Such a polemic has its place after the human race has divided itself into peoples and religions; this makes opposition possible. But the uniqueness of the primeval narratives consists in this, that they are concerned with the world and its inhabitants before and beyond such divisions. The parallels to be discussed below show the same.

(8) Th.C. Vriezen notes in his synthesis that each of the explanations given can find some support in one or other element of the text. This tells us something very important about the methodology. No explanation will be convincing that does not take proper account of all elements in the text. One does not do this by giving "the knowledge of good and evil" one of the many possible meanings. One must ask if the phrase can be explained out of the context of the narrative as a whole.

J. Pedersen opens the way to such an explanation in *Wisdom and Immortality*, 1955. His starting point is that the creation of human beings introduces an element of suspense: "a dramatic element in the relation between gods and human beings which is on the one hand due to man's craving for more, on the other hand to the god's zealous maintenance of their absolute superiority." Human beings are created in such a way that they are capable of advancing their life and of advancing their knowledge. This leads to conflict with God or the gods. There is a difference between these two human aspirations. To aspire after life comes in conflict with the inexorable barrier of death; to strive for wisdom or knowledge meets no such barrier. People have within themselves the potential "to become like God."

Starting from this basis it is possible to arrive at a non-Israelite pre-history to Gen 2-3 and to recognize the specific characteristics that set it apart from its background. It is only the broader view that gives us sound criteria for understanding the meaning of "the knowledge of good and evil" in Gen 2-3.

Literature (Parallels in the Old Testament): J.L. McKenzie, "Mythological Allusions in Ezek 28:12-18," JBL 75 (1956) 322-327.   H.G. May, "The King in the Garden of Eden: A Study of Ezekiel 28:12-19," *Festschr. J. Muilenburg* (1962) 166-176.   Th. Lescow, "Micha 6:6-8. Studien zur Sprache, Form und Auslegung," AzTh I 25 (1966) esp. 34-39.   N.C. Habel, "Ezechiel 28 and the Fall of the First Man," CTM 38 (1967) 516-524.

The Old Testament itself shows that Gen 2-3 stands in the line of a tradition history. Signs of a narrative similar to it are found in Job 15:7f., and another which is essentially the same in outline lies behind Ezek 28.

Many interpreters have long since drawn attention to narratives outside Israel which occur in the same context, the Adapa Myth and the Enkidu Episode in the Gilgamesh Epic.

One can recognize the basic motif which J. Pedersen underscored in all these narratives and fragments. This is the proper point of departure for understanding all of them — the situation which is consequent on the person's created state. We are faced with a set of circumstances which are very similar to many other narratives of the primeval event: a quite simple state of affairs arising out of this event which allows any number of variations. Only a brief outline can be given here:

    1. Job 15:7-8:   Are you the first man ever born,
                         were you brought forth before the hills?
                         Do you eavesdrop on the divine council
                         do you hold a monopoly on wisdom? (Trans. Marvin H. Pope, AncB)

These verses are a part of Eliphaz's second intervention. He exaggerates and distorts what Job has just said as if Job were claiming a monopoly on wisdom. "Eliphaz is clearly making use of what was originally a mythical presentation of primeval humanity which occurs also in Ezek 28:11-19 and Sir 49:16. The narrative told how the primeval persons . . . belonged to the heavenly council and in this way appropriated to themselves divine wisdom" (G. Fohrer, Comm. ad. loc.). This passage with its poetic language and Gen 2-3 both link the creation of human beings with a grasping after wisdom to which the creature has no right. The way in which the "adam" of this text acquires wisdom is quite different.

    2. Ezek 28:11-19: This is a prophetic lamentation over the king of Tyre whose fall is seen as the fall of the primeval person from the mountain of God which is equated with Eden. The text is extremely difficult and uncertain, but the following parallels are clear enough (translation RSV; explanations following G. Fohrer and W. Zimmerli, Comm.);

a) the creation of human beings
   "on the day that you were created" 28:14, 15
b) the place is the mountain of God, equated with the
   Garden of Eden vv. 13, 14
c) "You were blameless in your ways" v. 15
d) You were filled with crime (RSV, violence) and
   you sinned, v. 16
So I cast you as a profane thing from the
   mountain of God. . . . I cast you to the ground
By the multitude of your iniquities . . . I turned
   you to ashes upon the earth v. 16f.

Despite the uncertainty of the text, five stages in the event are clear, all having parallels in Gen 2-3. Apart from the application to the King of Tyre, the most important differences from Gen 2-3 are: the being in paradise is not just a human, but a divine or semi-divine being (in v. 14 it is likened to a cherub); "a signet of perfection," "full of wisdom and perfect in beauty . . . every precious stone was your covering . . . wrought in gold were your settings. . . ." In this tradition the primeval person is a superterrestrial being.

b): The outrage is ὕβρις: "Your heart was proud because of your beauty. . . ." (v. 17, cf. v. 6 in the previous passage: "Because you consider yourself wise as a god.")

d): The punishment is that he is cast down from the mountain of God; it differs from Gen 2-3 in that a "fall" is narrated; this is conditioned by the fact that the primeval creature is a higher being who was one among other such on the mountain of God.

The narrative that is the background of Ezek 28:11-19 is clearly Babylonian in character (G. Fohrer) and is expressly mythical. A comparison with Gen 3 shows that the latter is not presented in the same mythical fashion.

3. The Adapa Myth (ANET 101-103). It is not possible here to go into the various explanations that have been given (that of J. Pedersen is the more perceptive). The following are the most important points of comparison: "To him he had given wisdom; eternal life he had not given him." Ea had created him as a model of man. — Ea instructs Adapa: "As thou standest before Anu when they offer thee bread of death, thou shalt not eat (it). When they offer thee water of death, thou shalt not drink (it)." Adapa follows this instruction. Whereupon Anu says: "Come now, Adapa! Why didst thou neither eat nor drink? Thou shalt not have (eternal) life! . . . Take him away and return him to his earth." Anu looked at him and laughed at him, because of Ea's command, and said: "Of the gods of heaven and earth, as many as there be, whoever gave such a command, so as to make his own command exceed the command of Anu!" The following are the points in common: it is a question of wisdom (knowledge) and life, and that for the man created by the deity (Ea); he is called here the "model of man"; he is intended to be man. The result is that man acquired wisdom but not life.

What is behind the loss of life is the rivalry between the two Gods Ea and Anu. A prohibition to eat and drink given by one god plays the decisive role; Adapa loses life by obeying the command, contrary to what happens in Gen 3.

There are echoes of similar motifs in both. The narrative as such, inasmuch as it is mythical in character, cannot be alleged as a parallel to Gen 3. The

Adapa Myth, like Ezek 28, shows how varied a pre-history there is to Gen 3.

What Gen 3 calls "knowledge of good and evil," the Adapa Myth calls wisdom, and so wisdom is equated with ability and unfolds itself in the many activities that Adapa exercises and masters.

4. The Enkidu Episode (Tablet I, ANET 73f.). The whole of the episode is in the context of the creation of human beings. Just as in Enuma Elish the creation of the world is central, so in the Gilgamesh Epic it is the creation of humans. Gilgamesh was created as a superman or semi-god (I, ii, 3f.). He becomes a tyrant and complaints about him reach the gods. Aruru is commanded to "create his double." She creates Enkidu.

Enkidu is a wild man; he goes about naked and lives with the animals: "With the gazelles he feeds on grass, with the wild beasts he jostles at the watering-place." (S.G.F. Brandon, "Enkidu represents mankind before civilization" 127). — Anu sends a cult prostitute who entices him to sexual intercourse and thereby tames his wildness. The animals flee from him. And so Enkidu has become another man: Startled was Enkidu, as his body became taught, his knees were motionless — for his wild beasts had gone. Enkidu had to slacken his pace — it was not as before; but he now had wisdom, broader understanding. Returning he sits at the feet of the harlot. He looks up at the face of the harlot, his ears attentive as the harlot speaks; the harlot says to him, to Enkidu: "Thou art wise, Enkidu, art become like a god! . . ." (Tab. I, iv 26-34, ANET 75). Finally, in the face of death, Enkidu curses the cult prostitute who has brought him to life which can only end in death (Tab. VII, II, 5-37, cf. S.G.F. Brandon 132).

Neither can this episode be described as a parallel to Gen 2-3. Nevertheless there are not only single motifs that are similar, but a series of motifs. There is the creation of a man followed by seduction by a woman which gives rise to a state of existence different from the original, natural state and which is described by, among other things, the provision of clothing. The similarity of the words which the woman uses to describe the change is very striking: "Thou art wise, Enkidu, art become like a god!" There is an indication here of a link between this change and death to which man is destined.

This text shows that it is certain that Gen 2-3 had a pre-history both in Israel and in the Ancient Near East. Though the thesis of many interpreters that there is no direct parallel to Gen 2-3 still holds, it must nevertheless be modified. It is not merely a case of single motifs, but of the same succession of similar motifs which occurs in several other texts.

The comparison with other religions has provided an important orientation for the understanding of "the knowledge of good and evil." As J. Pedersen has shown, these narratives are concerned with a conflict between God and his creatures which derives from the fact that people are created with a strong aspiration after life and knowledge. Both occur in a number of narratives with some sort of connection with each other, as in Gen 3. The motif of knowledge for itself occurs in Job 15:7f., where the first man sets himself up as wise in an unauthorized manner. All passages are concerned with knowledge (or wisdom) in the general, comprehensive sense. Any limitation of the meaning of "the knowledge of good and evil" is thereby excluded. It can mean neither moral nor sexual nor any other partial knowledge, but only that knowledge which includes and determines human existence as a whole. The word "wisdom" in both Babylonian myths and in Job 15:7f. means mastery of one's own existence, just as in Gen 3:5.

This broader context also establishes the meaning of the other sentence which the serpent utters: "You will be like God." There is a direct parallel in the Gilgamesh story as we have seen above where the woman says: "Thou art wise, Enkidu, art like a god." Both here and in Gen 3:5 the two sentences complement each other; they are not saying two different things. The promise "to be like God" is not something over and above knowledge, but describes it and all that it is capable of. It is concerned with a divine and unbridled ability to master one's existence. This excludes the common explanation which understands "to be like God" in an ontological sense and the transgression as ὕβρις.

[3:6-7] *Literature* (Sin): F.R. Tennant, *The Sources of the Doctrine of the Fall and Original Sin* (1903). F. Bennewitz, *Die Sünde im alten Israel* (1907). H.L. Jansen, *Het verband van zonde en dood in het OT,* Diss Amsterdam (1911). F.R. Tennant, *The Concept of Sin* (1912). H. Gressmann, "Paradies und Sünde (Kritik an E. Brunner)," CLW 40 (1926) 842-846. N.P. Williams, *The Idea of the Fall and of Original Sin* (1927). K. Fruhstorfer, *Die Paradieses-Sünde* (1929). G. Quell, Art. "ἁμαρτάνω' A. Die Sünde im AT," ThWNT (1933) 267-288. L. Housman, "Sin and Herdinstinct," HibJ 44 (1945/1946) 97-105. J. Coppens, "Miscellanees 18-23," EThL 24 (1948) 395-439. F. Ascensio, "Tradición sobre un pecado sexual en el paraiso?," Gr 30 (1949) 490-520; 31 (1950) 35-62, 162-191. C.R. Smith, *The Bible Doctrine of Sin* (1951). G. Morelli, *Paradiso terrestre e peccato originale: Secoli sul mondo,* ed. G. Rinaldi (1955). H.S. Smith, *Changing Conceptions of Original Sin. A Study in American Theology Since 1750* (1955). P.E. Miras, "El pecado original en el Genesis," CiFe XII 47 (1956) 7-68. A.M. Dubarle, "Le péché originel dans la Genèse," RB 64 (1957) 5-34. S. Lyonnet, "Quid de natura peccati doceat narratio Gen 3," VD 35 (1957) 34-42; "De natura peccati quid doceat VT," VD 35 (1957) 75-88. L. Hartman, "Sin in Paradise," CBQ 20 (1958) 26-40. A.M. Dubarle, *Le péché originel dans l'Ecriture: Lectio Divina* 20 (1958). J.E. Bruns, "Depth-Psychology and the Fall," CBQ 21 (1959) 78-82. P. Humbert, "Démesure et chute dans l'AT," *Hommage à W. Vischer* (1960) 63-82. A. Maillot, "Un peu de Gnose sur Genèse 3," *Hommage à W. Vischer* (1960) 127-136. L. Ligier, *Péché d'Adam et péché du monde, I: L'AT,* CT 43 (1960). J. Gross, *Entstehungsgeschichte des Erbsündendogmas. Ein Beitrag zur Geschichte des Problems vom Ursprung des Übels. Von der Bibel bis Augustinus* (1960). G.E. Wright, *The Rule of God,* (1960) 21-43. St. Porubcan, *Sin in the OT. A Soteriological Study* (1963) 401-585. S. Lyonnet, "Péché d'Adam et péché du monde," Bib 45 (1964) 95-98. A. Gelin-A. Descamps, *Sin in the Bible* (1965). R. Knierim, *Die Hauptbegriffe für Sünde im AT* (1965; 1967²). D. Ritschl, "Die Last des augustinischen Erbes" in *Parrhesia: Karl Barth zum 80. Geburtstag* (1966) 470-490. H. Ringgren, "Literarkritik, Formgeschichte, Überlieferungsgeschichte," ThLZ 91 (1966) 641-660. M.G. Gomez, "La narración del pecado original, un mito etiologico y parenético," Burg 8 (1967) 9-64. U. Bianchi, "Sul pecatto originale in prospettiva storico-religiosa," RivBib 15 (1967) 131-149. A. Safran, "La conception juive de l'homme," AStE 2 1964/65 (1967) 39-58. K. Condon, "The Biblical Doctrine of Original Sin," IThQ 34 (1967) 20-36. P. Grelot, "Réflexions sur le problème du péché originel," NRTh 89 (1967) 337-375, 449-484.

[3:6] "So when the woman saw. . . ." This sentence can be linked immediately with the prohibition. The temptation scene is self-contained; it is an independent element in the narrative. The woman acts independently in transgressing the command and so is fully responsible. One could also say that the woman is led astray by her desire, depicted in three steps in v. 3. The narrator, with economy of detail, manages to describe the woman as she allows herself to be led astray by simply gazing at the fruit side-by-side with the temptation by the serpent. It is a case of the general human phenomenon of the attraction of what is forbidden. The prohibition itself fixes attention on what is forbidden, making it in a mysterious way seductively and irresistably attractive.

Two motifs are at work in this seduction. The first has nothing to do with the temptation by the serpent; it is simply the fruit which is attractive and entices her to eat: "Good to eat and pleasant to look at" (Luther). What is meant here is desire (covetousness) as formulated in the Decalogue, Ex 20:17; it belongs to the very nature of the human state. The senses of sight and taste work together to arouse this desire. But the desire as such is neither bad nor suspect nor sinful (this is the beginning of the complete misunderstanding of the passage by Augustine). It is rather the completely natural, normal and God-given reaction to the fruit of the trees in the garden: the woman and the man ought to find it pleasing, and it ought to taste good. The desire of the sense is part of God's gift.

But the text will say more. The desire of the senses finds itself restricted at one point — at the forbidden tree. The narrator is speaking of the well-known phenomenon of the hightening of desire when faced with a prohibition. H. Gunkel's remarks (and what he writes here does not accord with the rest of his interpretation): "With a desire that is innocent and child-like she does something which has the most serious consequences for her life," or those of G. von Rad "the unthinkable and terrible is described as simply and unsensationally as possible," show the effect of the traditional explanation of the "fall," from which they cannot shake themselves free. What is described is not the extraordinary, the shocking, the "unthinkable and terrible," but the completely natural and perfectly human.

But now comes the second motif, "to be desired to make one wise." The desire is directed not merely to what is forbidden (as in Ex 20:17), because as such it attracts the senses, but also to acquiring wisdom, as the serpent had said. This motif joins the attraction to what is forbidden with something else that is attractive and which no longer has anything to do with the desire of the senses, namely the capacity to strive which enabled one to rise above oneself.

The delightful, attractive fruit that draws one to bite it does not as such contain temptation. There had to be one who said it, who disclosed the connection between the satisfaction that comes from the enjoyment and that constituted the transgression of a limit, and the longing for a new and hitherto excluded dimension to life. With the greatest restraint and reserve J is saying here that at bottom what entices a person to transgress a limit is not the sensual pleasure heightened even more by the prohibition, but the new possibilities of life that are apparently opened by the transgression. The narrator wants to point to the inscrutable riddle which is always part of human existence wherever and as long as it is lived, namely, that people have the urge to transcend themselves by overstepping the limits set for them.

This explains why v. 6 does not need to say, nor can it say, that the woman wants to become "like God"; that is not the intention, though it is generally interpreted this way. It is implied in the "becoming wise," the "achieving success," inasmuch as it means a transcendence of herself by the woman in overstepping the limits set for her.

"She also gave some to her husband and he ate." H. Gunkel comments: "The temptation of the man by the woman is a common motif." But it is not a temptation that is narrated here. The sentence functions rather like an appendage. It is the tradition history that allows us to say this inasmuch as the temptation scene in 3:1-5 is relatively independent and goes back to a narrative which told of the sin of one person only (as in Ezek 28). J wants to say by means of this addition that no temptation was needed in the case of the man; he simply fell into line. Beside one way that leads to transgression, namely temptation vv. 1-5, he puts another which is equally characteristic of humans, namely conformity.

He shows thereby the other side of the community of man and woman expressed in the "jubilant welcome." Because people are subject to error, mutual support in community can also be mutual support in sin. It is very important for J that human community in its basic form as community between man and woman in ambivalent; it can lead to fulfillment together and to sin together. It is not likely that J wanted to characterize the relationship between the sexes by saying that the woman is more susceptible to temptation than the man, and that after being tempted she became man's temptress (so, in a surprisingly gross way, J. Hempel). S.G.F. Brandon alleges the Greek myth of Pandora and the Enkidu episode where the woman is the temptress. There is certainly a primeval motif behind the Pandora myth, but it is far from Gen 3.

[3:7] The conclusion of this part of the narrative portrays three events: the opening of their eyes, the awareness, the covering. What the serpent had announced now takes its effect. The fruit begins its really extraordinary work: they are changed, they see what they had not seen before. But that is only one side. The other side is what they became aware of: "They knew (became aware) that they were naked." The awareness indicates a lack, something in them that was not right. They can make up for this lack by making themselves aprons. But it becomes clear at once that what they have done is no real help. When God approaches, the man says: "I was afraid, because I was naked," (v. 10).

The conclusion of 3:1-7 had already been foreshadowed in 2:25, "the man and his wife were both naked, and were not ashamed." Nothing more needed to be spelled out in v. 7: now they are ashamed. What has changed?

Opinions differ sharply here. One group of scholars sees the change as an awakening of sexual consciousness, in particular K. Budde: "The eating from the tree brings with it the first consequence of the knowledge gained; the man and the woman were ashamed because of their nakedness"; similarly O. Procksch: "The awareness in people proceeds from knowledge to conscience, to consciousness of guilt before God,". . . "the tree of knowledge is shown to be the tree of conscience."

A second group understands the change as the acquisition of the consciousness of sexuality, so in particular H. Schmidt (see above).

A third group understands the knowledge gained in the context of a change from a primitive to a civilized state. First among these is J. Wellhausen. Somewhat differently, but in the same direction, H. Gunkel writes: "The first humans experienced the passage from ignorance to knowledge just as each of us does." The narrator "has some hazy notion that enlightenment, maturity, is acquired only through sin."

Th.C. Vriezen, in his detailed account of the interpretations of 3:7, points out that all opinions come up against difficulties in the text. The great variety of possible opinions rests above all on the enigmatic nature of the text which is deliberately only suggestive.

It was remarked when commenting on 2:25 that shame is a reaction to being unmasked or exposed. If this is correct, then each of the three explanations outlined can reflect part of the meaning of v. 7, though neither of them compasses the meaning of the text as a whole. When the two people, on eating the fruit, notice that they are naked (i.e., according to 2:25, that they experience shame in each others presence) then the text is simply saying: they feel that they are exposed, and this is a new experience for them.

In the discovery of the mutual shame, the narrator brings together very skillfully two threads which up to that moment had traced their own separate ways. The one, the giving of the command — the transgression — the consequence; the other, the way open to the possibility of a new dimension to or level of existence — the actualization of this possibility. It follows necessarily from these two threads that the situation that comes about from eating the fruit must be ambivalent; the narrator intends this. The three explanations outlined above can now be resumed and set in place: the two people suddenly experience shame. It does not mean that they become conscious of sexuality (this is already presumed in 2:23); however this consciousness is something different from what it was before; it is something new, something strange, and it causes them embarrassment.

Something has been lost by the transgression which cannot be replaced, the state of unaffected innocence in which people were not yet conscious of their nakedness. What was right beforehand is now wrong. But the fact that they now know, are now aware, that is not merely "consciousness of sin" or the "twinge of conscience," but undeniably something positive as well.

This is the correct aspect of the approach begun by Wellhausen and supported by Gunkel: that the man and the woman now know that it is not right for them to continue naked. And when this knowledge gives the man the ability to make something to cover himself, the narrator intends this to indicate progress; they have also become clever (הַשְׂכִּיל). God's reflection in 3:22, "the man has become like one of us," shows that this is the meaning and says that the couple, by eating the fruit, have become more than they were before, know now what they did not know before.

The text gives but an indication of how the man and the woman have progressed by eating the fruit. It recalls, e.g., that the change in a person bears a distant resemblance to the change from childhood to the adult state, because it is in this process that shame is awakened in both its positive and negative aspects, as one progresses to maturity and to a realization of responsibility (so H. Gunkel). A further point is that it is not the individual but the species, humankind, that is the subject. When people come to know what it means to be masters of their existence, they can then make progress in civilization. When people have learned that it is not right for them to be naked before others and make aprons to protect themselves, this is to be understood against the background of the great social significance which clothing had both in antiquity and in the Old Testament. Clothing is not, as it is with us, an individual phenomenon but a social phenomenon and hence is of great significance in the history of civilization. That this is what the narrative of Gen 3 is thinking of is demonstrated by the order of the three stages described in the text: naked — clothing with foliage — clothing with skins, which corresponds with the development known to have taken place in the course of civilization.

When God concedes in 3:22 that the man "has become like one of us, knowing good and evil," the author is expressing conceptually what 3:5 tells in story: what the man and the woman do here corresponds externally to what God does in 2:8f. Both God in 2:8f. and the couple in 3:7f. know that something is not good; both "create" something to help the situation. But there is the widest gulf between what is actually done in each case. The words "like God" include the following correspondence: a knowledge that something is right or not right (good or evil), and the creation of something to meet the situation.

It is only the encounter with God that shows that the couple's efforts to make something to counter their nakedness has not been successful, and that ultimately the serpent is not justified. The aprons that man and woman made do not hide them from God.

Literature: 3:7: B. Pipal, "Und sie machten sich Schurze. Gen 3:7," *Křestanská Revue* 29 (1962) 38-39. J.K. Zink, "Uncleanness and Sin. A Study of Job XIV 4 and Psalm LI 7," VT 17 (1967) 354-361.

[3:8-24]   The Penalty

The narrative 3:1-24 consists of two parts, one dealing with the crime, 3:1-7, and the other with the penalty for it, 3:8-24. The second part follows step for step the prodecure of a legal action:

8-10:   Hiding and discovery
11-13:   Interrogation and defense
14-19:   The three sentences of punishment

The narrative is tightly knit up to this point; the conclusion, vv. 20-24, is not a unity but clearly a compilation. Vv. 23 and 24 narrate a punishment which is independent of the three sentences passed in vv. 14-19. The same punishment, the expulsion from the garden, is narrated twice, vv. 22 and 23. The expulsion from the garden in v. 22 is linked with a reflection of God which joins together the tree of knowledge and the tree of life. This verse, 22, together with v. 24, belongs to a later stage in the development of the narrative.

Vv. 20 and 21 are independent of each other and are inserted loosely before the conclusion: the naming of the woman, v. 20, and the clothing with garments of skin, v. 21.

[3:8-13]   The transition from 3:1-7 to 3:8ff. indicates too that the narrative has advanced from a mere succession of facts, with something of the magical still at work underneath, to an event that is personal. It is only this personal event that can have the structure of a legal process (K. Koch, "Gibt es ein Vergeltungsdogma im Alten Testament?," ZTK 52 [1955] 1-42). The transition is completed with the entrance of God. The narrative points to the two stages in the understanding of the effect of a crime. In the earlier stage of human history the crime of its very self was the source of the harmful consequences to the one who perpetrated it. This was succeeded by another stage in which there was a personal judicial process between two people or between God and the people (J. Skinner notes this, Comm. ad. loc.).

If interpreters are aware of this transition when considering the text of 3:8ff., they must conclude that what is described here cannot be intended as a merely "religious" event. A legal process is described, even if the judge is God; and more, it is a primeval event, before the separation of law and religion. One must then be very reserved and cautious in attributing a moral and religious value to what is said and to the way in which the people conduct themselves. K. Budde says: "The process uncovers the cowardice of the two people"; W. Zimmerli: "Man appears before God with the mask of piety"; K. Budde and O. Procksch insist that the first words that come from the man's lips when he encounters God are a lie; G. von Rad comments on 3:10: "He admits that fear had driven him into flight from God," and "Fear before God was the sign of a disorder in his relation to his creator." One must ask if the narrative is really saying this.

The narrator is talking about people who have committed a crime and are not threatened with punishment. A man in this situation conducts himself as portrayed here. His reactions are in accord with this situation. Gen 3 does not narrate such an event as one among many, but as a beginning. The common opinion that the passage describes "the fall" reads into the narrative its own understanding of sin and then finds it there step-by-step. If one follows what is happening here word-for-word as it is portrayed, then one cannot interpret human conduct and what the people say from v. 8 on as belonging to repentent sinners caught in the act. The structure of vv. 8-13 shows that it is only when God questions the man in v. 11, "have you eaten of the tree. . . ?" that the crime comes to light. It is not the man conscious of his guilt who exposes the crime, but the judge with the accusation implied in the question and the three times repeated, "you have done," vv. 11, 13, 14. The man must first be told that he is guilty and has committed a crime. If the goal of the event narrated in vv. 8-13 is the threefold "you have done," then one must recognize a gradual movement; the verdict of guilty cannot as yet be presumed in v. 8. What the man says and does before the sentence is not the action of one who has been found guilty. This is confirmed if one attends to the words of the text.

It is said twice that the man and his wife hid themselves from God. And the man explains this: "I was afraid, because I was naked." First, it must be stated that these words express directly neither a consciousness of guilt nor a fear that results from it. Had J wanted to say that, he would have said it clearly and unequivocally. But he is saying something else: something has happened, something is different. What is different cannot be comprehended in the words: the man and the woman have sinned against God, now they hide themselves from him and are afraid. The text is not saying that. What is different can only be expressed by J as: "I was afraid, because I was naked." These words encompass something much broader and much more basic than what we call sin or guilt, consciousness of sin or consciousness of guilt. It is the couple's fear of being naked before God, of being unmasked before God, in spite of their self-made protective covering. The profound insight of the narrative is this, that the couple's nakedness, their exposure before God, is represented as something that is new, as that which is different.

[3:8-10]   The following scene presumes that God and human beings are on the same level. This is not to be explained as an anthropological presentation of God (e.g., F. Michaeli, *Dieu à l'image de l'homme*, 1950; Th.C. Vriezen, ad. loc.), but by the primeval nature of the narrative; the man and his wife have not yet been expelled from the garden where they are together with God. It is only in this way — being ashamed, fear, hiding oneself — that the disruption of the partnership can be clearly expressed.

Literature: Gen 3:8: T.J. Meek, "Old Testament Notes," JBL 67 (1948) 233-239. K. Koch, "Gibt es ein Vergeltungsdogma im AT?," ZTK 52 (1955) 1-42. F. Michaeli, *Dieu à l'image de l'homme*, 1950. P. Wernberg-Møller, "A Note on לְשׂוּחַ בַּשָּׂדֶה in Genesis XXIV 63," VT 7 (1957) 414-416. R.A. Carlson, "Élie à l'Horeb," VT 19 (1969) 416-439.

[3:8] קוֹל is here, clang, noise; the noise of footsteps in 2 Sam 5:24; 1 Kings 14:6; 2 Kings 6:32. R.A. Carlson, p. 436, refers the passage to the rustling of the tree at a cultic place; but that is not in accordance with the character of the narrative. The preposition לְ has a temporal sense: at the time when. . . . "the time involved is towards sundown, when fresh breezes bring welcome relief from the heat" (E.A. Speiser, AncB, ad. loc.; so too most commentators). For a different view T.J. Meek (ZAW 62 [1950] 298). See also Song 2:1-7; 4:6. The sound of footsteps causes the man and his wife to hide themselves. By eating the forbidden fruit they have become different. The two are now ashamed in each others presence and cover themselves. The disruption is now heightened: the garments of fig leaves are ineffective at the sound of God's footsteps. They now realize that despite the covering they are exposed before God; they are afraid and hide.

[3:9] It is crucial to the understanding of the narrative that God's call introduces what follows. The call alone articulates the disruption that has entered into an offense against God; at the same time it makes clear that the succession of events which follows, leading finally to punishment and expusion from the garden, comes from God's concern for his people. God takes the initiative to the couple in hiding (R. Bultmann, "Adam, wo bist du?," *Glauben und Verstehen*, II, 1952, 105-116). The God who punishes people is the God who cares for people.

[3:10] What is new is the fear in the man's reply. "I was afraid because I was naked." It is correct indeed to say: "Man now betrays himself by defending himself" (O. Procksch), or "Man betrays himself by excusing himself" (H. Gunkel); but this does not go to the core of J's intent. The sentence makes two statements: I heard you coming, then I became afraid; I was ashamed because I was naked. Because both are brought together in one sentence, the shame becomes the ground for the fear. And so the new state of affairs, fear, becomes the formal expression of shame before God, which is different from shame before other people. This fear should not be understood one-sidedly as anguish arising from sin. It is ambivalent, as is the Old Testament phrase יראת יהוה (cf. S. Plath, "Furcht Gottes," AzTh 2, 1962): the man and woman who are no longer in the garden, who are no longer with God, are now possessed by "the fear of God."

Literature: Gen 3:11-13. D. Daube, "Direct and Indirect Causation in Biblical Law," VT 11 (1961) 246-269.

[3:11-13] *Interrogation and Defense.*

The purpose of the trial scene is to make clear to the man and the woman what they have done. It is only God's question "have you eaten. . . ?" that establishes what has actually happened. The series of questions and answers uncovers how this took place. What is said does not imply any judgment; it is merely to establish the facts. The succession of events is important: in 3:1-7 it leads from the serpent to the woman and to the man; in 3:8-13 the questions are addressed to the man and then to the woman; the serpent does not appear. The sentences again follow the course of events: serpent, woman, man. The interrogation comes between the action and the sentence, but is directed only to the man and to the woman. By making this distinction between the people and the serpent, J is simply pointing out the basic meaning of human responsibility, namely, that people have to answer for what they do.

The same distinction occurs in the sentences of punishment in 14-19. Only the serpent is cursed; the people are punished and their punishment is to be understood on the basis of interrogation in vv. 11-15. There is a logical clarity both here and in the Prophetic Literature in God's judgment and punishment. But at the same time there are limits. The crime began with the serpent, a creature of God; there is no explanation why the serpent did this and so there is no explanation of the origin of evil. The serpent is not interrogated; it is cursed.

The purpose of God's question is to make the man aware of the new element that has entered his life with shame before God: how do you know this, how did it come about? It is only the second question: "Have you eaten. . . ." that reveals the connection. It is essential for J that the question put to the man makes the connection. The implication, "you have done it" (see vv. 13 and 14) makes the man's action a crime against God, a sin. It is not important whether and to what extent the man was conscious that what he had done was a sin. J is saying much more: what constitutes a crime against God, a sin against God, is what people do in defiance of God and nothing else, not a consciousness of sin nor a bad conscience.

[3:12] The answer that the man gives to God's question is implicitly, Yes: ". . . I have eaten." But this is not the whole answer. The man who is now confronted with his crime by God has still an area of freedom in which to move where he can defend himself against a sentence of punishment. This is essential: the man can defend himself against God. Interpreters are unanimous in describing his defense as an attempt to shift the blame. The man tries "to clear himself of guilt and to place it . . . on God" (G. von Rad, ad. loc.). O. Procksch sees in it "a good example of human sinfulness which brings remorse in thought and word." Such remarks are typical of the traditional understanding of the passage which starts from a preconceived idea of sin. The text says nothing about this.

What the man alleges in his defense is quite in order. If the man has this area of freedom in which to defend himself, then what he says cannot be a mere confession of guilt. J is saying much more here, namely that the crime against God that he is describing is very complex. This does not in any way lighten the guilt; but it makes clear that an action of a person directed against God, what we call sin, is, from the person's point of view many-sided, but from God's point of view single and clear cut. Commenting on "the woman whom you gave to be with me" H. Gunkel writes: "Insincere, he dares to reproach God." G. von Rad says the same in the citation given above. But what J wants to say is this: Inasmuch as people are given freedom to defend themselves, so too is it possible for them to turn against God. We have here a first indication of the charge that

God can bring against Israel in her dialogue with God. But the sentence remains inevitable as does the imposition of the punishment: both leave intact man's freedom even before God.

What Gen 3 presents is as far from a fatalistic and basically magical understanding of guilt as found in classical antiquity, as it is from a static teaching on sin as found in Christian tradition.

Literature: Gen 3 "Original Sin": H.W. Bartsch, *Schöpfung und Schuld vor Gott* (1948). P. Ricoeur, "Culpabilité tragique et culpabilité biblique," RHPhR 33 (1953) 285-307. G. Lambert, "Le drame du jardin e'Eden, II," NRTh 76 (1954) 1033-1072. R. Prenter, *Schöpfung und Erlösung* (1958). C. Reilly, "Adam and Primitive Man," IThQ 26 (1959) 331-345. W.B. Neenan, "Doctrine of Original Sin in Scripture," IThQ 28 (1961) 54-64. A. Weiser, *Die biblische Geschichte vom Paradies und Südenfall. Glaube und Geschichte im AT und andere ausgewählte Schriften* (1961) 228-257. J.A. Soggin, "Osservazioni filologico-linguistiche al secondo capitolo della Genesi," Bib 44 (1963) 521-530. H. Rondet, *Original Sin. The Patristic and Theological Background* (1972). H. Haag, "Der 'Urstand' nach dem Zeugnis der Bibel," ThQ 148 (1968) 385-404. J. Scharbert, *Prolegomena eines Alttestamentlers zur Erbsündenlehre. Quaestiones disputatae 37* (1968). H. Haag, "Zur Diskussion um das Problem der 'Erbsünde'," ThQ 149 (1969) 86-94.

[3:13] The woman's defense is more straightforward and naive; but she too is justified in what she says. What is valid for the man, v. 12, is valid for her too. By making the barest use of the motif of "interrogation and defense" the author reconstructs the crime nicely but in reverse order. H. Gunkel is not correct when he says "so the whole event is laid out clearly before God"; the reconstruction breaks off just where one would expect to find the reason for what had happened. The man refers to the woman and the woman to the serpent. The serpent should now say why it led the woman to eat the fruit. But that does not happen. The serpent is not interrogated. The intention of the narrator is clear: the origin of evil cannot be explained. The sentences of punishment which follow immediately are ultimately inexplicable, thus plumbing the depths of human responsibility.

Literature: Gen 3:14-19; Dictionary Articles: S. Gevirtz, 'Curse', IDB I, 749b-750b. W.J. Harrelson, 'Blessing and Curses', IDB I, 446a-448a. F. Horst, 'Segen und Fluch', II. im AT, RGG³, 1343-1346. C. Westermann, 'Fluch und Segenssprüche', BHH I, 489-490.
L. Waterman, "The Curse in the 'Paradise Epic'," JAOS 39 (1919) 322-328. S.H. Blank, "The Curse, Blasphemy, the Spell and the Oath," HUCA 23 (1950-1951) 73-95. J. Scharbert, "'Fluchen' und 'Segnen' im AT," Bib 39 (1958) 1-25. S. Gevirtz, "West-Semitic Curses and the Problem of the Origins of Hebrew Law," VT 11 (1961) 137-158. H.C. Brichto, *The Problem of 'Curse' in the Hebrew Bible,* JBL Monograph Series 13 (1963). P. Buis, "Deuteronome XXVII 15-26. Malédictions ou Exigences de l'Alliance?," VT 17 (1967) 478-479. W. Schottroff, *Der altisraelitische Fluchspruch,* WMANT 30 (1969).

[3:14-19]   The Sentences of Punishment.

In an older form of the narrative the expulsion from the garden followed immediately on the discovery and the trial, vv. 8-13; the expulsion was the only penalty. This conclusion derives from the parallel that lies behind Ezek 28. The unusual accumulation of punishments in vv. 14-19 also points in this direction as W.H. Schmidt has remarked. He concludes his explanation of 3:14-19 as follows: "In the story before us guilt and punishment do not stand in direct proportion to each other," p. 218. In particular, there is a remarkable difference in content between the punishment of expulsion and the punishments enumerated in vv. 14-19. The former is firmly fixed in the structure of the narrative inasmuch as God put people in the garden — God drove people out of the garden. The punishments in vv. 14-19 on the contrary have no direct relationship with the offense: they describe factually the present state of existence of serpent, woman and man which by way of after-thought are explained as punishments. W. Schottroff has demonstrated in detail that the pronouncements of condemnation in 3:14-19 do not belong to the original plan of the narrative (see above, pp. 87-91, 142-147).

It is important to establish this for the explanation of the narrative as a whole. The original and the only punishment was the expulsion from the garden and alienation from God. The narrative had reached its goal without the elaboration of 3:14-19; people were expelled from the garden for disobedience and were alienated from God. The pronouncements of punishment have been added as a further elaboration. Exclusion from the garden and from proximity to God denotes humanity's present state of existence with its variety of limitations. It cannot be said then that "the curses . . . form the goal and high-point of the whole story" (H. Gunkel ad. loc.; also G. von Rad).

It should be underlined that the form of the sentences in vv. 14-19 is poetic. The address to the serpent consists in three stichs each with two stresses, twice repeated. The introductory sentence which gives the reason, "because you have done this," does not belong to the pattern. As W.H. Schmidt has observed, it is, from the point of view of the history of tradition, secondary. The curse stands without this introduction (for further details cf. W. Schottroff, p. 91); v. 15 is very different from v. 14 in its metre: 3 (or 4?) stichs of two beats and 2 of 3. The rhythmic, poetic form is to be explained from the function of the pronouncements; they declare a punishment; they portray an event which corresponds to the ancient legal pronouncements which are also presented in rhythmic and poetic form.

Is it a question of the pronouncement of punishment or a curse? The question cannot be answered disjunctively. In the context of the narrative they are clearly pronouncements of punishment and as such part of a legal process in which, after the discovery of the crime, interrogation, defense and judgment follow each other, the latter being pronounced by the judge. But that does not fit the ארור-formula. Cursing is a different procedure from punishing. Gen 3:14-19 indicates that the cursing once preceded the punishing. The cursing is replaced by the punishing, but the earlier stage of the cursing is preserved in the text. A further indication of an earlier stage is that the man and the woman are not cursed, but the serpent and the ground are (the latter because of the man)

The curse comes from the period of magical thinking when there was not yet a sharp distinction between thing, animal and person (cf. Jer 20:14f.). Only humans can be punished through a legal process (the Book of the Covenant still knows of the punishment of animals); only a person is the subject of a right (O. Procksch). This intertwining of curse and punishment in 3:14-19, which nevertheless distinguishes both clearly, is yet another indication of J's narrative method. With a minimum of devices he allows a traditio-historical background to define itself clearly. W.H. Schottroff demonstrates in detail that in 3:14-19 it was originally a question of curses whose form and content can be traced in the history of the curse formula (142-147).

Literature: Gen 3:14-15: L. Dürr, *Ursprung und Ausbau der israelitischjüdischen Heilandserwartung* (1925). A. Schulz, "Nachlese zu Genesis 3:15," BZ 24 (1939) 349. J.M. Vosté, "Le Proto-Évangile selon l'exégèse de Mar Iš᷾ odad de Merw (c. 850) (Gen 3:15)," Bib 29 (1948) 313-320. E. Zolli, "Il verbo 'shuf' nella letteratura antico testamentaria," Mar 10 (1948) 282-287. T. Gallus, *Interpretatio Mariologica Protoevangelii (Gen 3:15) a tempore postpatristico usque ad Concilium Tridentinum* (1949). A. Miller, "Zur Typologie des Alten Testaments," BenM 27 (1951) 12-19. A.M. Dubarle, "On the Biblical Sources of Mary's Title as the Second Eve," *Mélanges J. Lebreton.* (1951). J. Michl, "Der Weibessame (Gen 3:15) in spätjüdischer und frühchristlicher Auffassung, I-II," Bib 33 (1952) 371-401, 476-505. T. Gallus, "Principia exegetica S. Augustini ad Gen 3:15 applicata," VD 32 (1954) 129-141. B. Rigaux, "La femme et son lignage dans Genèse III 14-15," RB 61 (1954) 321-348 (Engl. Tr.: ThD 6, 1958). S. Grill, "Die Schlange Schlangentreterin. Gen 3:15," BiLi 23 (1955-1956) 292-294. H.W. Wolff, "Jahwe als Bundesvermittler," VT 6 (1956) 316-320. G. Bertram, "Praeparatio Evangelica in der Septuaginta," VT 7 (1957) 225-249. J. Knackstedt, "Das Protoevangelium im ordentlichen Lehramt der Kirche in den letzten hundert Jahren," ThPQ 109 (1961) 277-291. N. Lohfink-J. Haspecker, "Genesis 3:15: 'weil du ihm nach der Ferse schnappst'," Schol 36 (1961) 357-372. P.P. Saydon, "The Conative Imperfect in Hebrew," VT 12 (1962) 124-126. J. Dheilly, 'Protévangile', *Dictionaire Biblique* (1964). T. Gallus, *Der Nachkomme der Frau in der altlutherischen Schriftauslegung, I. 'Der Nachkomme der Frau' (Gen 3:15) in der Schriftauslegung von Luther, Zwingli und Calvin* (1964). R.A. Martin "The Earliest Messianic Interpretation of Genesis 3:15," JBL 84 (1965) 425-427. B. Rinaldi, *Mary of Nazaret, Myth or History?* (1966). P.R. Ackroyd, "Meaning and Exegesis," *Words and Meanings. Essays presented to D. Winton Thomas* (1958) 1-14.

[3:14-15]   The Serpent.

A distinction is to be made between the two metrical pronouncements in v. 14 and v. 15; they are relatively independent of each other, v. 15 being connected directly with the preceding narrative, and v. 14 connected only by the reason alleged. A very old curse formula is present in v. 14 (i.e., v. 14 minus the reason). Cursing is formulated originally in direct speech, as here too; the curse as a pronouncement which is effective demands this. It is presumed that the curse comes into effect as it is pronounced. When a curse is formulated in this ancient pattern there is no need to give any reason for it because, arising as it does out of the situation, it is pronounced in direct speech. This explains why the reason in v. 14 is a subsequent addition (so too W. Schottroff). The ancient curse formula is retained only in the address to the serpent, and the fact that it is found in the Old Testament as a direct address coming from God only in 3:14 and 4:11 (v. 17b is already modified) shows its primeval character. God blesses in a variety of ways in the Old Testament; he curses only in the primeval story, and never outside it.

The curse in v. 14 is constructed in three parts: (1) the formula of cursing ארור אתה; (2) a further qualification by means of מן; (3) the explication: what this curse means for the serpent. The formula ארור אתה occurs only here and in 4:11 with God as speaker; elsewhere (not with God as speaker) Deut 28:16-19; plur. Josh 9:23 (in all other places it is used in the third person). The further qualification by means of מן, used here in the original sense of "apart . . . from," shows that the curse intends a setting apart. Accordingly E.A. Speiser translates it by "bann." This setting apart can have different meanings in different stages and situations, from setting apart from the community to setting apart from humanity (J. Pedersen, *Israel, its Life and Culture II*, 451-452; J. Scharbart, TWAT, I, 437-451; C. Westermann, BHH, I, 487; C.A. Keller, THWAT, I, 235-240; S. Gevirts, IDB, I, 749f.).

The meaning of the curse over the serpent is that it is being separated from the rest of the animal kingdom because of its form and way of living. This is how W. Schottroff explains מן, p. 58f. Here as in 4:11 it has the sense of separation: "As J. Pedersen first underlined, the curse is in both cases an ex-communication, its effects fall into social categories; according to v. 14a the serpent is taken from the community of animals by the curse and set aside" (J. Scharbart: "Cursed and so banished"). The curse explains the extraordinary way in which the serpent moves and feeds itself. There is clearly an etiological motif here. As in 2:24 this etiological motif has been grafted on to the narrative, i.e., it did not originate when the narrative was being composed, but is the result of an observation independent of it. When one observes what is peculiar to the serpent, the question arises, "Why is that so?" The answer is given by telling the story that led up to this; the serpent's peculiar way of life is traced back to a curse pronounced over it. The motif, which may once have shaped a separate narrative, belongs, as H. Gunkel remarks, "to the very common myths and stories which tell how certain animals acquired their peculiar characteristics."

It is a misunderstanding of the etiological motif to conclude from 3:14f. that the serpent must have had before this another shape and another way of life (e.g., O. Procksch: "Its earlier way of life appears to have been different"; or Th.C. Vriezen, "The presumption clearly is that in primeval time the serpent walked upright on paws"). H. Gunkel is correct with his contrary view: "The myth is concerned with the snake's present way of life and finds the reason for it in the curse; the thinking does not go further." So too W. Schottroff with further details, p. 145f. The etiological explanation is not interested in an earlier state of affairs in contrast to the present, but only in explaining the present.

[3:15] The same holds too for v. 15. A new etiological motif enters in here which forms a link with the foregoing narrative. The sentence is only very loosely joined with the curse formula in v. 14; it could be quite independent of it. Enmity is introduced in v. 15; v. 15b tells what it consists in. Apart from the present passage the noun איבה occurs only in Num 35:21, 22 and Ezek 25:15; 35:5. The two Ezekiel passages use the word with the same meaning as here: never-ending or perpetul enmity from long ago. The purpose is to describe the phenomenon that enmity exists not merely in a determined situation but has grown to a continual state, something like an institution. This is an indirect way of saying something important about the relationship of humans to the animals. Such enmity as a state or institution does not exist between humans and the animals, not even the wild animals; it exists only between humans and the serpent; this goes back to a curse (W. Schottroff offers examples from ancient oriental curse formulas).

The meaning of "all the days of your life" in v. 14 (i.e., as long as there are serpents) is given in 15ai with the mention of the descendants of both parties. The parallelism makes it clear that "seed" refers to a line of descendants and not to an individual.

The enmity will work itself out by humans and the serpent continually (the imperf. in 15b is to be understood iteratively) trying to kill each other; the person by crushing the head of the serpent, the serpent by biting the person on the foot from behind. This two-sided approach is expressed in Hebrew by a word-play in which both actions are expressed by the same word שׁוף. The verb occurs only once more, in Job 9:17 (the text of Ps 139:11 is uncertain); it has the same meaning as in Gen 3:15, "He would crush me with a tempest," M. Pope, AncB; or "in the storm he snaps after me" G. Fohrer. In both places the word is to be understood as a by-form of שָׁאַף (so KBL and the majority of interpreters). For the other side of the word-play, "It will crush your head," a verb שׁוּף meaning "crush, trample under foot," is used; it occurs only here in the Old Testament, but has an equivalent with the same meaning in Akkadian, *šâpu* (KBL). Other scholars understand it in the same sense in all four places. Th.C. Vriezen: "The general meaning 'to overpower' suits all four places"; P.P. Saydon ("The Conative Imperfect in Hebrew," VT 12 [1962] 124-126): "The correct translation is, 'He will attack you in the head, and you will try to attack him in the heel'," (similarly G.R. Driver). This explanation is improbable because, in spite of the external similarity of the constructions, the two actions are different, corresponding to the different bodily forms of the parties.

3:15 as Protoevangelium.

From the time of Irenaeus, Christian tradition has understood the passage as a prophecy about Christ (and Mary). The "seed of the woman" was referred to one individual descendant who crushed the head of the serpent, whose seed was also an individual in the person of the devil (Satan), who is locked in deadly struggle with "the seed of the woman," and who eventually succumbs to it. This explanation runs from Irenaeus right through the history of exegesis in both Catholic and evangelical tradition. It has also had a profound influence on the proclamation of the Gospel as shown by Christian art and hymnology, e.g., the ancient Christmas hymn, still sung today, *Quem pastores laudavere:* "The star of Jacob now is risen, stills the longing heart's desire, breaks the ancient serpents head, shatters hell's dark reign."

There are two main reasons that do not allow such an interpretation: First, it is beyond doubt that זֶרַע is to be understood collectively. The text is speaking of the line of descendants of the woman as well as of the serpent. The second reason is form-critical. The word occurs in the context of a pronouncement of punishment (or of a curse). It is not possible that such a form has either promise or prophecy as its primary or even as its secondary meaning.

The explanation of 3:15 as a promise has been abandoned almost without exception. G. von Rad says: "The exegesis of the early church which found a messianic prophecy here, a reference to a final victory of the woman's seed (Protoevangelium) does not agree with the sense of the passage." O. Loretz in his Excursus on the question of the Protoevangelium writes: "If theology really wants to free itself from the charge of distorting the meaning of Gen 3:15 . . . then it will be forced to leave aside the allegorical-typological interpretation of this passage and not to attribute any absolute theological meaning to the time-conditioned patristic and medieval tradition. It would be advisable not to use the concept of a Protoevangelium in the context of Gen 3:15." It is not necessary to give an account of the whole discussion of the exegesis of Gen 3:15. The evangelical tradition follows on from the Reformers (Calvin was most reserved); it holds out for orthodoxy and continues right up to the end of the nineteenth and even with a few into the twentieth century.

The last weighty exegesis of Gen 3:15 as Protoevangelium is that of F. Delitzsch, *Messianische Weissagungen* 1890, 23-28. J. Michl has provided a thorough account of the history of exegesis for Catholic tradition. It should be pointed out that suggestions of a messianic interpretation are found in late Judaism, but not in the New Testament. After some pointers in Justin, it is first attested in Irenaeus: "In the course of the Middle Ages Irenaeus' interpretation of the Protoevangelium found a firm place in theology. It won its final victory at the beginning of the modern era when it was acknowledged in dogmatic encyclicals of the highest church authority" (J.M. Vosté, p. 501).

Side-by-side with the messianic (or mariological) explanation of Gen 3:15 is the "ethical" which understands the snake as the embodiment of a demonic power of evil and explains the enmity as the struggle between humanity and this power. This explanation goes back to Philo and occurs in the commentary of Mar Isodad of Merv, c. 850, (J.M. Vosté Bib 29 [1948] 313-320); in modern times it is found in A. Dillmann (with whom H. Holzinger and J. Skinner disagree), O. Procksch, Th.C. Vriezen, G. von Rad and others. Holzinger is justified in his objection to this explanation: "When the text speaks of the descendants of the serpent, this shows that it is a question of an animal and that the animal is being punished and not some demonic power behind it." Even apart from this, such an interpretation misunderstands the intention of J who describes the serpent expressly as a creature of God and wants to point out that the temptation to disobedience remains unexplained and inexplicable.

Literature: Gen 3:16, 17-19: E. Albert, "Zu Genesis 3:17-19," ZAW 33 (1913) 1-19. E. Ebeling, *Tod und Leben nach den Vorstellungen der Babylonier* (1931) (esp. 11-12). J. Hempel, "Wort Gottes und Schicksal," *Festschr. A. Bertholet* (1950) 222-233. C. Lattey, "Vicarious Solidarity in the Old Testament," VT 1 (1951) 267-274. D.N. Freedman, "Notes on Genesis," ZAW 64 (1952) 190-194. W. Vollborn, "Das Problem des Todes in Genesis 2 und 3," ThLZ 77 (1952) 709-714. H. Rondet, "Élements pour une théologie du travail," NRTh 77 (1955) 27-48, 123-143. R. Martin-Achard, *De la mort à la resurrection d'après l'Ancien Testament: Bibliothèque Théol* (1956). J.B. Curtis, "A Suggested Interpretation of the Biblical Philosophy of History," HUCA 34 (1963) 115-123. J. Schreiner, "Geburt und Tod in biblischer Sicht," BiLe 7 (1966) 127-150. R. Bergmeier, "Zur Septuagintaübersetzung von Genesis 3:16," ZAW 79 (1967) 77-79. A. Chazelle, "Mortalité ou immortalité corporelle du prémier homme crée par Dieu?," NRTh 89 (1967) 1043-1068. H. Dee, "Zur Frage nach dem Sinn von Sterben und Tod," PTh 56 (1967) 489-500. N.J. Tromp, *Primitive Conceptions of Death and the Nether World in the Old Testament*, BibOr 21 (1969).

[3:16] *The Sentence of Punishment on the Woman.*

The punishment inflicted on the woman and the man have not the character of a direct curse. The verse is again metrical: one line of 7 beats and one 4 (or two twos). V. 16a, in two parallel sentences, assigns to the woman pain in bearing children and in giving birth; v. 16b extends this to her relationship to her husband — she is bound to him, but subordinate to him. These are not "three facts" as von Rad says, but one: woman's existence is described from two points of view, that of a wife and a mother.

V. 16a is a typical Hebrew sentence. The line of 7 beats expresses rhythmically the heaviness of the punishment. The description takes the form of parallelism, one arm pronouncing the sentence, the other spelling it out. And it is underscored by the same root עצב in both parts with the weighty infinitive absolute construct at the beginning. This construction is found with this verb only in Gen 16:10; 22:17. According to O. Procksch עצבון is a '*fa 'alān* form with a duplicated second radical," a form which occurs again only in 3:17 and 5:29, all three being in the same context. The contruction ''I will greatly multiply your pain and your childbearing'' is a typical hendiadys; it means: the pains that childbearing will bring you. The noun for childbearing occurs only here; the Samaritan reads הרינך, the Gk τὸν στεναγμόν σου, which could reflect הגינך, (BHK). But no emendation is necessary.

Again, there is an etiological motif behind the sentence of punishment on the woman. Something worthy of remark in the present state of reality is explained by a primeval happening, in this case as punishment for a crime. One must be on one's guard against two false leads when taking account of the etiology. First, one cannot reconstruct a state which preceded the present state as, e.g., H. Holzinger does: ''The punishment of the woman is twofold; her situation is altered to her disadvantage; her relationship to her husband is different; originally they were equal, now she is subject to him.'' The passage is not explaining a change in state, but rather the burdensome, painful state of woman here and now. Many interpreters point to the incongruity between 3:16 and 2:18, as if the position of the woman in 2:18, ''a helper fit for him,'' were a description of the relationship between man and woman ''before the fall,'' and the state in 3:16 were that of ''fallen humanity.'' However, both descriptions are concerned with woman as she is here and now, though there is a profound tension between them. 2:18 is looking to the mutuality of the relationship, the complementarity of the companionship. This does not exclude a relationship of subordination: one could not say in 2:18 that man is created as a helper for the woman.

Another misunderstanding is to equate the punishment imposed in 3:16 with the existence of the woman as such. U. Cassuto rightly draws attention to the lack of proper proportion between punishment and crime in the common interpretation: ''The decrees pronounced by the Lord God appear unduly severe: because Adam and his wife sinned, was it right that their children and children's children should be punished for all time?'' (so too W.H. Schmidt). One cannot agree with him however when he sees nothing but a promise behind 3:16, a promise of descendants. Nevertheless he is right when he understands the punishment as touching what is unique and inscrutable in the life of woman. The punishment does not in any way alter the fact that woman achieves the fulfillment of her being and her honored place in the community by belonging to her husband and being a mother. The pains of pregnancy and birth in no way diminish the dignity of womanhood and motherhood, as 3:20 expressly confirms.

Despite this, the domination of the husband and the consequent subordination of the wife is seen as something which is not normal (hence as punishment). It is not a description of ''the fixed state of the wife in antiquity'' (A. Dillmann), but a phenomenon of the human race which goes with the bodily constitution of man and woman. Zimmerli is too brusque when he says: ''The biblical witness speaks of the degrading servitude of woman under her husband.'' The situation of the woman cannot be called ''degrading'' because of the domination of the husband, but only when she has no children or when she does not belong to any husband. The explanation of W. Vischer, quoted by G. von Rad, is a distortion of the text: ''In the bondage of compulsive drive and yet most immediately involved in the wonder of creation; groaning in pain, cramped in travail, humiliated, overburdened, careworn, and tearstained. . . .'' This is to read too much into the text as the result of an already fixed understanding of it.

What he really wants to say is much more sober: just where the woman finds her fulfillment in life, her honor and her joy, namely in her relationship to her husband and as mother of her children, there too she finds that it is not pure bliss, but pain, burden, humiliation and subordination. The positive undertone here would receive further support if the surmise of L. Rost were to be found pertinent. He sees behind 3:16 a "formula of conferring" from the ritual of the initiation ceremony: "Punishment is suggested only by the emphasis put on the labor and effort; the remaining statements on the contrary express in part a blessing. . . ." (op. cit., 1965, 62 n. 34; for the variant Gk translation of 3:16, see R. Bergmeier, ZAW 79 [1967] 77-79).

[3:17-19] The Sentence of Punishment on the Man.

This sentence clearly carries the most weight; it is the most detailed and the crime is mentioned yet again at the beginning, 17a; it is a compilation (so too W. Schottroff, p. 153). Behind the different parts of vv. 17-19 are different answers to the same question — why is man's work, and in particular the work of the farmer, so difficult and so full of obstacles. These different answers, once independent, go right back to the stage of oral tradition. It is unlikely that vv. 17-19 can be separated into literary sources. One can only try to find out the origin of the motifs and how they hang together.

The reason given in 17a is due to the process of the composition of the narrative, as in 14; it is a link with the curse. The curse formula has the same structure as that over the serpent: it consists in the cursing (here in the third person) and its explication, i.e., the explanation of the way in which the curse will work itself out. The explication however follows not in v. 17bii, but only in v. 18a. We can take the structure of the curse formula as a certain starting point. Consequently we can say that v. 17bii and 18a belonged together in an early layer of tradition. The curse is not directed precisely at the man, but at the ground because of the man. It must follow the man then, and it does in v. 19a,b; the theme word אדמה, repeated in the first and last sentences, emphasizes that the pronouncement is self-contained:

> Cursed is the ground because of you . . . ,
> Thorns and thistles it shall bring
>   forth to you.
> In the sweat of your face
>   you shall eat bread,
> till you return to the ground;
> for out of it you were taken.

The sentence in v. 17bii: "In toil you shall eat of it all the days of your life" is clearly an insertion in order to link the pronouncement over the man with that over the woman by means of the catchword עצבון. The sentence in v. 18b: "And you shall eat the plants of the field" falls quite outside of the curse formula and has been regarded as an addition by many interpreters (e.g., H. Holzinger). Its purpose is to stress the contrast between the food provided for the man in paradise and that which he extracts from the ground. It is an addition then that must be late because it presumes the compilation of Gen 2 and 3. The sentence in v. 19c "You are dust and to dust you shall return" is a variant of what has preceded. It is a proverbial saying which is widespread and differs from 19b in being independent and self-contained and having no connection either with the curse or the narrative. Similarly proverbial sayings have been added to many of Jesus' words in the Synoptic Gospels. This addition describes the man as dust taken from the dust and so articulates his contingency, as do a number of similar formulas.

There have been many attempts to explain how 3:17-19 was put together; I will go into only one of these. R. Smend was the first to divide it into two sources; this division was taken up by O. Procksch and J. Begrich (with variations), W. Zimmerli, G. von Rad, W.H. Schmidt (cautiously and with question marks). Two parallel strands were seen in 17b, 19a and in 18, 19b (or 17, 19a and 18, 19c, or other divisions). ". . . there is reference to two different ways of life: the first to the difficulties of the work of the farmer, the second to those of nomad life in the desert" (W.H. Schmidt). P. Humbert (*Études*. . . . 1940) has shown that such a division based on vocabulary is uncertain, if not impossible. The division comes to grief if one takes the structure of the pronouncement as a starting point, because it separates 17bii and 18a into two sources. This is impossible because 18a is the necessary explication of 17bii. A further argument is that the catchword in the first and last sentences shows that the sentence of punishment is self-contained. W. Schottroff, p. 143f., gives a convincing refutation of a division into a "nomadic version" and an "agricultural version." We can be certain then that the sentence of punishment on the man is a complete unity, that it has been elaborated by three additional sentences, and that the motif of each of these is recognizable. A citation confirms the position we have taken: "In Jub III 25 the passage is quoted in an abridged form, the line 'Cursed . . . sake' being immediately followed by 'Thorns . . . to thee', and 18b being omitted. . . ." (J. Skinner).

[**3:17a**]   Read וּלְאָדָם. U. Cassuto gives a detailed explanation of why the MT is vocalized without the article; but he cannot explain why this deviant vocalization occurs only three times, 2:20; 3:17, 21. The detailed reasons given underline the significance of the sentence of punishment on the man and link it with the core of the narrative. The sentence shows that the narrator sees the real crime in the transgression of the command.

[**3:17b**]   The curse cannot be pronounced in direct speech here as it was in v. 14; there is no direct cursing. From the point of view of the ancients, a curse can be directed at humans, animals and objects alike, the earth or the land, e.g., Is 24:6; Jer 23:10. The Gk has read the third radical of בעבורך as ד, and renders ἐν τοῖς ἔργοις σου; Σ ἐν τῇ ἐργασίᾳ σου; Θ ἐν τῇ παραβάσει σου. Aquila and the Syriac follow the MT. The MT is supported by Gen 8:21. The purpose of the last sentence is to link the pronouncement of punishment with what has preceded: the בעצבון corresponds to the same word in v. 14, and כל ימי חייך occurs in v. 14. The suffix to אכל is rather difficult; the meaning is: you shall eat from the produce of the earth.

The curse on the ground in 17bii will be effective in the thorns and thistles that will grow and diminish the output and make the harvest difficult. The meaning is not that the ground will only bear weeds, but something like what we read in the parable of the weeds among the grain in Mt. 13:24-30. The word pair קוץ ודרדר occurs again only in Hos 10:8, with the same meaning, overgrowth.

קוץ occurs by itself in Ex 22:6; Judg 8:7, 16; Is 33:12; Jer 4:3; 12:13; Ezek 28:24; Ps 118:12. Jer 4:3 and 12:13 speak of thorns among the grain. In Ex 22:6 the concern is for thorns among the standing corn or the stacks. When W.H. Schmidt assigns v. 18a to the nomad version and remarks: "Thorns and brushwood, v. 18a, do not mean weeds (instead of grain) but what grows on the steppes (Judg. 8:7, 16; Is 32:13; Jer 4:3; Hos 10:8)," this holds only for Judg 8:7, 16, while Jer 4:3; 12:13; Ex 22:6 use קוץ only with grain. This is confirmed by the parallel curses from Israel's neighbors that W. Schottroff assembles, p. 153. An Akkadian curse reads (CH XXVIIb, 7-13): "May Adad, the ruler of heaven and earth overwhelm his fields, so that there may spring up abundantly weeds in place of green herbs and thorns in place of grain!" (L.W. King, *Boundary-Stones*, 41).

[**3:18b**]   The sentence in 18b is independent and easily recognizable as an addition. H. Holzinger draws attention to the successive repetition of "eat" which is stylistically disturbing, vv. 17bii, 18b, 19a. עשב means the growth of the field (including the grain) as distinct from the trees (so U. Cassuto). The purpose of this half-verse is to draw attention to the change in the sort of food. H. Holzinger writes: "The half-verse clearly points back to 2:16." The sentence of punishment in its earlier form, without the additions, was not concerned about a change in the sort of food; in v. 19 too לחם is not used in contrast to fruit trees.

[**3:19**]   "In the sweat of your face you shall eat bread." This is saying exactly the same as the last part of v. 17. A stylistic comparison shows that 19a belongs originally to the sentence of punishment and that 17bii has been added (against H. Gunkel). 19a and b belong together and Dillmann turns them correctly: "You will labor to feed yourself until you die." H. Gunkel explains: "The myth expresses an extremely pessimistic view of human life and of agriculture; the view current at the time that agriculture is a blessing bestowed by the divinity is now opposed by an opinion which regards the earth as cursed, and introduces a note of pessimism from the primeval period. . . ." But the etiological motif that lies behind the statement is speaking neither of human life nor of agriculture. It is speaking about a singularly extraordinary phenomenon which requires explanation: the remarkable fact that a person's work is always joined in some way with toil, trouble, even with sweat and thorns. There are thorns and thistles in every field of work; every harvest demands sweat.

To acknowledge this fact and to reflect upon it has nothing to do with pessimism. It is sober realism which excludes any idealization of human work. People can do nothing to get rid of the difficulty of work, toil and sweat accentuated by "thorns and thistles"; it belongs and will always belong to the human state. If this is what is meant, and not the work itself, then the curse is in no wise altered by the fact that work brings human life to fulfillment. Nor does it alter the fact that God's commission to the man to work, 2:15, was received as and remains a gift. The ground is burdened with the curse; but it will still give people bread (cf. H. Rondet, NRT 77 [1955] 27-48, 123-143).

[**3:19b**]   "Till you return to the ground." The toil which is joined with work will accompany one through the whole of one's life right up to death. This is saying that toil is not something that can be overcome by a person's industry. It is not over and done with when the house is built, the ground prepared, the institution founded. This toil cannot be confined to one period of life only; it is part of human existence and is with us to the end. 19b is understood correctly only in close association with 19a; it is not an independent statement but a subordinate sentence which further qualifies the main sentence of 19a. Death here is not meant as a punishment nor can the intention be to say that this is humanity's first experience that its fate is death; "the fact is referred to as part of the natural order of things" (J. Skinner). Only with death will there be an end to toil. When death is described as "a return to the אדמה," the cycle of the sentence of punishment begun in v. 17 is concluded. At the same time the words "for out of it you were taken" recall the creation of human beings.

[**3:19c**]   This is a repetition of 19b; it is a wisdom saying. W.H. Schmidt writes: "It is probable that . . . v. 19b does not come from the story of creation in Gen 2 but from the widespread description of human beings as 'dust' in Gen 18:27 (J); Ps 103:14; the parallel expression of 'return to dust' is common, Ps 104:29; Job 34:15." One can add Job 10:9; Ps 90:3; 146:3, 4; Sir 40:11; compare Cicero: *reddenda est terrae terra*. This sentence, which is so like a wisdom saying, is a fitting conclusion to the sentence of punishment in vv. 14-19. The statement itself does not qualify the punishment, but says something about human existence now affected by the preceding pronouncements. In their origin and in their destiny human beings belong to the dust. Everything noble and great that can be said of a person and of one's capabilities must be circumscribed by this limit which has been set to all that is human.

Is death meant to be a punishment? The majority of exegetes hold that there are two aspects to the punishment; e.g., H. Holzinger: "This (punishment) also is twofold; the relationship to the אדמה on which he lives is changed, and then he is under sentence of death." However it cannot be said that the latter is explicitly stated in vv. 19b and c. The exegesis has oscillated back and forth. A. Dillmann saw no difficulty in saying both things together: "It is presumed that death is a natural consequence of one's origin from the earth. Likewise it is a punishment." Exegetes who followed him have found themselves able to decide only for the one or for the other, and some of them have not found the decision easy.

O. Procksch and G. von Rad have looked for a middle way: the death sentence was not pronounced on the man in 3:19; here however he has his first experience of his fate. O. Procksch: "He now experiences the grim connection between *'adam* and *'adamah* from which he can never break free." G. von Rad: ". . . man now learns something of his end; it is forced into his consciousness. . . ." But both can still point out that death has something of punishment about it: ". . . thematically it belongs with special emphasis to the penalty" (G. von Rad; similarly O. Procksch). W. Zimmerli is quite clear that death is a punishment: "The return to dust goes with the disobedience and is part of the penalty imposed on humanity . . . the wages of sin is death, Rom 6:23." Th.C. Vriezen holds a very detailed debate with other opinions and concludes decisively that the words imposed death on humanity and hence that death is a punishment. But one senses that he is in difficulties with his arguments.

J. Skinner, H. Gunkel (without expressly saying so) and L. Köhler maintain that death is not meant to be a punishment in this passage. Köhler emphasizes in his *Theology of the Old Testament* that "the Old Testament . . . knows nothing of death as a punishment for humanity. . . ." W. Schottroff too writes: "3:19 does not speak of death as a punishment but presents it as an established fact rooted in humanity's origin"; so too W. Vollborn, E. Brandenburger.

Our point of departure then is that the penalties are an addition to the narrative and that the motifs lying behind them are independent of it. The pronouncement in 3:17-19 (without the additions) is answering one question: Why is work so full of toil and so burdensome? The question about the origin of death is not presumed in this sentence of punishment (against H. Gunkel). The words of 19b, "till you return to the ground, for out of it you were taken," have one function, to underline that the man's work will be full of toil right up to his death; his whole existence will be stamped with it. The sentence that gives the reason, "for out of it you were taken," introduces a further nuance; the man's return to the earth will close the lifespan *(Daseinsbogen)* begun with creation. There is something positive here, namely that the return to the earth at the end of a life of hard work can be good — at death he was "old and full of days." And so death (and J. Skinner notes that the word is not used here) in 3:19 is not a punishment for the man's transgression, but the term of his toilsome work.

Literature: Gen 3:20-24: F. Baethgen, *Beiträge zur semitischen Religionsgeschichte.Der Gott Israels und die Götter der Heiden,* 1888. H.S. Gehman, "Hebraisms of the Old Greek Version of Genesis," VT 3 (1953) 141-148. J. Heller, "Der Name Eva," ArOr 26 (1958) 636-656. W. Eichrodt, *Der Heilige in Israel,* 1960. N. Walker, "'Adam' and 'Eve' and 'Adon'," ZAW 74 (1962) 66-68. A.F. Key, "The Giving of Proper Names in the OT," JBL 83 (1964) 55-59. J. Heller, "Namengebung und Namendeutung. Grundzüge der alttestamentlichen Onomatologie und ihre Folgen für die biblische Hermeneutik," EvTh 27 (1967) 255-266.

[**3:20-24**] The close of the narrative is not a unity. A number of sentences which are not in the direct line of the narrative have been loosely attached to the real ending, the expulsion from the garden, which is narrated twice, in vv. 23 and 24. The peculiar way in which the ending has been constructed shows yet again that the narrative of Gen 2-3 has grown out of a variety of stories and motifs. One has the impression that there have been gathered together in the conclusion all sorts of end pieces which happen to have been lying about and which could not be fully integrated. The starting point of the explanation will be that the conclusion must be in line with what has already been narrated. This could only be v. 23 which reports the expulsion alone. The variants of the conclusion in v. 24 go with v. 22; both are concerned with the tree of life. V. 20 must be an elaboration; it presumes that the woman has already given birth to a child. There must have been some event that gave occasion for the naming of the woman, and this can hardly have been anything else than the birth of a child.

Must v. 21 also be an elaboration? Most interpreters take it as such. But when one assumes that the penalties in 14-19 were only gathered together in the course of the formation of the narrative, then one can admit that in an earlier stage, 3:21 followed a pronouncement which proclaimed the expulsion from the garden in one sentence in place of these penalties. V. 21 followed the proclamation of expulsion as a sign of the "merciful punishment," and it too was followed by the execution of the punishment in v. 23. So the original conclusion, 3:21 and 23, underwent two elaborations: the naming of the woman, v. 20, and the prohibition of the tree of life, vv. 22 and 24.

[**3:20**] "This verse is almost unanimously regarded as an insertion" (Th.C. Vriezen, *Onderzoek naar de Paradijsvoorstelling.* . . . 1937). Two questions then must be asked:

(1) If the sentence is an insertion, where can it have come from? H. Gunkel says: "The verse comes from another context and from another source." W.H. Schmidt: 'It is a lone tradition that does not belong to a narrative." The majority of exegetes wonder whether the sentence should precede or follow 4:1 because it presumes the birth of a child. But one cannot concede that it belonged originally to a narrative (or to another version of this narrative). The verse is very like a piece of information from a family tree and it is quite conceivable that the woman receives her proper name in this new context of the genealogy; the appropriate occasion for this is the birth of a child.

(2) What is the meaning of the insertion of this piece of information from a family tree in 3:20? It can be that it is only to preserve information which otherwise would have been lost. In that case it would be traced back not to J but to a later redactor. But if it was inserted by J, and this is not to be excluded, then his intention would be to say that the blessing conferred on humans, namely the power of procreation, has not been lost by the crime and the punishment.

The name echoes the word "life," however it is to be explained (Gk, ζωή); the man names the woman saying by means of the name what she means for him, namely life — she is the bearer of life. The name is really the husband's response to the first birth; it is to be understood as the result of reflection on the event of the birth. It is an explanation which cannot be part of the name-giving itself, and as a reflection of the husband who gives his wife the name 'life" it is not possible (so correctly U. Cassuto). It is rather a subsequent explanation from a distance of the name *Ḥawwā* which is in place in a genealogy in which *Ḥawwā* stands at the beginning followed by a line of descendants.

But this is not the end of the explanation; both parts of the verse, namely 20a and 20b, together with the name *Ḥawwā* and the phrase "mother of all living," were at hand to form it; both belong to ancient tradition. "Mother of all living" is called "mother earth" in Sir 40:1 ("till the day they return to the mother of all"). This goes back to a traditional description. It is implied in the very old description of the earth as mother (see Intro. A. III. "the types of creation"). One need not conclude that *Ḥawwā* is to be equated with Mother Earth. One can however concede that the title "mother of all living," which was once the title of the primeval mother, whether known as Mother Earth or by some other descriptive mother title, has become free standing and continues on to find an echo here. There could be something similar behind the name *Ḥawwā* (so e.g., J. Skinner, S.G.F. Brandon). That would mean that the title "Mother of all living" and the name *Ḥawwā* could have the same origin. This allows us to see the unity of the verse in its present context without difficulty. The presentation here, which at one time was joined with the name as well as with the title, has lost its concrete mythological meaning both for the author and for the listeners. The purpose of the name and the title, and so of the naming and its explanation, is to express joy over motherhood whereby life is protracted into the future.

One should check Th.C. Vriezen's compilation for the many attempts to explain the meaning of the name חוה; he lists and discusses eight. Special place is given to the meaning "serpent goddess" who as such is the goddess of life (earlier, reference was to the Aram. חויה = serpent; so Wellhausen); so in particular H. Gressmann referring to *Lidzbarski, Ephemeris I*, p. 39ff., who concludes from a Phoenician inscription to a Phoenician serpent goddess or goddess of the underworld חות. This is taken up by a number of commentators. I. Eitan (JAOS 49 [1929] 30ff.) explains the name in the Phoenician inscription with reference to *genetrix* or *magna mater* and is of the opinion that such a meaning can be demonstrated philologically for חוה too. Th.C. Vriezen also inclines to this explanation. Others explain חוה as woman, H. Bauer, ZDMG 71 (1917) 413, or as Mother, N. Walker, ZAW 74 (1962) 66ff.; cf. also J. Heller EvTh 27 (1967) 255-266.

Literature: Gen 3:21, 23: E.Richter, "Kannte die Priesterschrift eine Geschichte vom Sündenfall? Ein Wort zu Genesis 3:21," ZAW 57 (1939) 285-287. M. Gertner, "The Masorah and the Levites. An Essay in the History of a Concept," VT 10 (1960) 241-284. B. Murmelstein, "Spuren altorientalischer Einflüsse im rabbinischen Schrifttum. Die Spinnerinnen des Schicksals," ZAW 81 (1969) 215-232.

[3:21]   Scarcely any attention has been paid so far to the fact that the verb עשה, which hitherto had been used only of the creative action of God, is used here — and only here in the Old Testament — of "manual work" on God's part; he fabricates something out of material at hand to him. This is very remarkable (H. Gunkel, "very anthropomorphic") and can only be explained if one sees behind it an independent primeval tradition according to which God and his people not only occupy the same living space, but where one also spoke of God's action in the same way as of human work. If this verse belongs to the J narrative, as acknowledged above, and took its place in an earlier form of it between the proclamation of the punishment, which stood in place of vv. 14-19, and its execution, v. 23, then this anthropomorphic talk is saying that here God and his people are still side-by-side. The statement retains its meaning in the context; the last action of the creator toward his creature before expelling him from the garden is an action of care and concern. It is just this primitive anthropomorphic language that is such a wonderful expression of this concern: the creator "protects" his creatures while putting them at a distance, and the protective action accompanies them on their way.

J has taken up here an older presentation which belonged in a different context. It is a very widespread presentation in which the possessions, instruments and institutions that form the basis of civilization are not human achievements but gifts of the gods. There are countless examples of this in primitive and higher civilizations. It is enough to recall the Sumerian myths which narrate how the pickaxe, the basket, the baked brick and many other things were created by the gods and then given to people (S.N. Kramer, *Sumerian Mythology,* 1944). The basic idea is always the same and is preserved in Gen 3:21: God makes the appropriate object and hands it on to humans for their use. But this is not typical of the Old Testament; what is typical is that the creator gives people the ability to make the cultural advances themselves (see Intro. C. III. The Stories of Human Achievements).

3:21 forms a conscious exception to this. A comparison between 3:21 and 3:7, where the two make themselves aprons out of leaves, makes this clearer. There is no contradiction here nor are the passages variants, belonging to different sources. They are in deliberate tension with each other. The provision of clothing continues the line of 2:25 and 3:7 and as a gift of God acquires a special value. There is no distinction between the cultural and religio-cultic meaning of clothing (see Robertson Smith, *The Religion of the Semites*, 1894², 437; 1927³). Clothing, as something which is part of this life, belongs to human existence in the world in which people live. It seems to me that H. Gunkel misses the point of the text when he writes that clothing "is to be understood as a last, meager alms, an endowment in distress."

The connection of clothing made out of skins with the killing of animals and so with sacrifice can well operate in the ancient pattern which lies behind 3:21, but it plays no role in the present context. (J. Skinner: "In the Phoenician legend of Usöos, the invention is connected with the hunting of wild animals, and this again with the institution of sacrifice"). However, clothing occurs in a similar context in the Enkidu episode in the Gilgamesh Epic where the acquisition of knowledge, clothing and the taking of food suited to humans are all found together. (Tablets II, iii; III; ANET 77f.). A presentation similar to Gen 3:21 is found in "a song of praise to Gula-Baba from the late Assyrian period," line 13 (E. Ebeling, Or NS 23 [1954] 345-350): "Who covers shame with clothes, who gives the power of life (to God and to humanity). . . ."

[**3:23**]   (V. 23 which closes the narrative is taken up before vv. 22 and 24 which deal with the motif of the tree of life.)

"Therefore the Lord God sent him forth from the garden. . . ." This is the proper and the original punishment for the transgression of God's command. It touches human existence as a whole, and indeed the life of the man as well as of the woman, and as such is different from the punishments in vv. 16-19 which are directed to particular, limited aspects of the existence of the man and the woman separately. Here it is a question of existence as such. It is in this verse that the narrative really reaches its goal, as becomes clear from the structure: it begins, the man created by God is put into the garden, 2:8; it ends, he and his wife are driven out of the garden 3:23. The purpose of the narrative is to explain the present state of human existence as an existence on earth which is limited by earth, i.e., as an existence which is at the same time a state of alienation from God. The division that people experience as they live out an existence that they are aware is created, and at the same time their experience of their limitation as fallible and destined to death, is narrated here as a state. Human existence in history begins with this, that the person is where God is not.

"To till the ground from which he was taken." The sentence rounds off the narrative. The duty of the man, now separated from God and driven out of the garden, is to cultivate the ground. He is there to labor in and for the world. The introduction to the creation narrative tells that there was no plant or grass because the land had not yet been watered and there was no one to cultivate it. This closing sentence gives the cultivation of the ground — and so the civilizing work of humans in general — a further positive value. The man is destined to work on and for the earth. His created state ("for out of it you were taken") simply corresponds to his duty, and the commission given to the man serves the earth.

Literature: Gen 3:22, 24: W. Collins, "Genesis 3:22," ET 28 (1916²), H.Th. Obbink, "The Explanation of Gen 3:22," ET 28 (1916-1917); 44 (1932-1933), 475; 45 (1933-1934) 236-237. L.J. Kuyper, "To Know Good and Evil. Gen 3:22a," Interp I (1947). J. Coppens, "A propos d'une nouvelle version de Genèse III 22," EThL 24 (1948) 413-429. H.S. Gehman, "The Hebraic Character of Septuagint Greek," VT 1 (1951) 81-90. F. Sierksma, "Quelques remarques sur la circoncision en Israél," OTS 9 (1951) 136-169. H. Schmid, "Jahwe und die Kulttraditionen von Jerusalem," ZAW 67

(1955) 168-197.   R. Largement, "L'arbre de vie dans la religion Sumérienne," *Akten d. 24. Internationalen Orientalisten-Kongresses,* 1957, 188-190.   G. Vermes, "Haggadah in the Onkelos Targum," JSSt 8 (1963) 159-169.   G. Cooke, "The Sons of (the) God(s)," ZAW 76 (1964) 22-47.   A.G. Levin, *The Tree of Life. Genesis 2:9 and 3:22-24 in Jewish, Gnostic and Early Christian Texts,* HThR 59 (1966) 449 (summary of diss.).   F. Vattioni, "L'albero della vita," Aug 7 (1967) 133-144.

[3:22, 24] The state of scholarship with regard to the three last verses of Gen 3 is very confused and we can only sketch here the most important lines. We can take as certain that vv. 22 and 24 belong together and form a single conclusion that is independent of v. 23. This was first noted by B. Stade (1903) and the otherwise very different interpretations of Stade and Budde agree here. This conclusion was taken up by H. Gunkel. All subsequent explanations that diverge from this conclusion have not led to any convincing alternative. Three arguments are alleged to show that vv. 22 and 24 belong together and form a separate conclusion:

(1) *Content:* Both these verses deal with the tree of life which is not mentioned in the rest of the narrative apart from 2:9.

(2) *Style:* This new motif, which has not appeared in the narrative so far, is introduced by a reflection of God which takes up literally the motifs of 3:5 and draws a conclusion from them which leads into the new motif. The execution of the sentence in v. 24 is the outcome of the conclusion. This is not in accord with the narrative method of the rest of the passage, but illustrates clearly how in the course of composition reflection introduces a new motif into the narrative.

(3) *Composition:* The reason for the expulsion of the couple from the garden is, according to what has preceded, their disobedience. The unity and directness of the narrative is destroyed inasmuch as another reason is given in v. 22: the man and the woman must be prevented from taking from the tree of life; and so they must be expelled from the garden and the way to the tree of life must be guarded. The difficulty that exegesis has experienced up to the present is due partly to a failure to recognize that the insertion of the motif of the tree of life in this place is part of the process of composition. The mention of the tree of life in 2:9 has meaning only in the context of 3:22, 24, but not in the narrative of the tree in the middle of the garden.

Reflections as to whether the fruit of the tree of life was also forbidden, or whether the two had eaten of it or not, can be left aside. The constantly repeated attempts to find a logical balance for the juxtaposition of the two trees start from a false presupposition. The narrative of the expulsion from the garden which reaches its goal in 3:23 is concerned with one tree. Only vv. (2:9); 3:22, 24 are concerned with the tree of life. These two narratives have two points in common which the author makes use of to join them together: both trees are planted in the garden of God, and both narratives end with expulsion of the man and the woman from the garden. Contemporary listeners who were familiar with the motif and narrative of the tree of life could recognize clearly enough what the narrator was saying. He was telling the story of one tree in such a way as to allow for echoes of the story of another tree. The interpreter must keep the two narratives separate; only 3:22, 24 allow us to draw any conclusion about the narrative of the tree of life.

B. Stade (1903) had already seen the basic lines of this explanation: "3:22, 24 derive from a parallel narrative. . . ." He notes that "the body of the narrative . . . knows of only one tree'' and says "that the introduction of the tree of life in 2:9 as a balance to 3:22, 24 should be regarded as proven," p. 172. H. Holzinger's explanation follows the same line. A number of scholars see v. 23 as the conclusion of the main narrative, B. Stade, K. Budde, H. Holzinger, J. Skinner, H. Gunkel, O. Procksch, W. Zimmerli; these same also hold that vv. 22 and 24 belong together as a variant of the conclusion, or something similar; so too S.G.F. Brandon, W.H. Schmidt,, J. Dus, W. Schottroff. Some interpreters lay greater emphasis on the mythological character of vv. 22 and 23 (so H. Holzinger, J. Skinner and others.)

[3:22]   What can we conclude from the two verses? V. 22 contains only one clearly new element; everything else in it makes use of what has already been said. What is new is the last phrase: וחי לעלם = "and live forever." The new motif is best comprehended in these two words: God will prevent his creatures from living forever. There is a difference in acquiring the fruit of the two trees. There is no sign at all that an express prohibition surrounds the tree of life. What is emphasized is that the fruit is unattainable. This corresponds to the motif of the tree of life in the Gilgamesh Epic, and is the point of the guard that bars the way to the tree of life. We have here the situation of a man setting out to acquire the fruit of the tree of life exactly as in the Gilgamesh Epic.

The two elements already mentioned from v. 22 and v. 24, which belong to the separate tradition of the tree of life and which occur only in these two verses, are linked in the first sentences of v. 22 with elements from the story of the tree of knowledge. God's reflection which gives the reason for barring access to the tree of life is but a consequence of what has already been narrated, resuming as it does its very words. The words resumed are clear evidence that the traditions have been brought together at a secondary stage. Now that the man and the woman by eating of the tree of knowledge have become God-like in their ability to know good and evil, it is necessary to withhold from them the fruit of the tree of life.

The reason belongs to neither of the two narratives; it is merely the result of their being joined. It is easy to see why they have been brought together: wisdom and eternal life are the two qualities that are peculiar to the Divinity and it is conceivable that by means of them human beings can come near to God or the gods. The difference between humans and God cannot be shown more clearly than by the limitation of these two qualities. Human beings can acquire the "knowledge of good and evil" even when it does not bring them advancement but loss; "life forever" is forbidden them. By linking these two motifs the author of Gen 2-3 stands in a line of tradition in which what defines human existence is seen to consist in the distinction between these two possibilities. It is enough to refer to the Adapa Myth and the Gilgamesh Epic.

Th.C. Vriezen has gone into the structure of the sentence, particularly into the meaning and function of הן, ועתה, and פן. H. Holzinger has drawn attention to the grammatical difficulties: "The verse gives the impression that the conclusion is missing"; "ועתה hangs in the air." Vriezen discusses these difficulties in detail, taking as his starting point the unity of vv. 22-24. The difficulties find their solution when it is recognized that vv. 22 and 24 join a new motif to the narrative in the way shown above. And so another question cancels itself out, namely whether the phrase "like one of us" means "the higher spiritual beings" (A. Dillmann), or the heavenly court (H. Gunkel and the majority of recent interpreters), or whether God includes the other gods with himself, the phrase being actually polytheistic in intent. The expression is to be understood from the history of the motif which was concerned with the point of contact between the divine and the human in the area of wisdom and knowledge. There is no thought of any sort of rank in the realm of the divine.

"And life forever"; for the form וחי, see Ges-K §76i. The meaning of the לעלם is not to be taken from the Greek idea of immortality (H. Gunkel renders "and become immortal"); there is no thought of endless, unlimited extension, but rather of "living on" in the sense of overcoming the boundary of death.

The Motif of the Envy of the Gods. The motif is very widespread; it plays a role in events involving the gods themselves as well as the gods and humans. The motif of the "jealous god," אל קנה, is to be carefully distinguished from it. F.R. Walton (Hybris, RGG³ III 407f.) describes the motif thus: "Closely linked with the whole idea of *Hybris* is the not so noble ethical notion of the envy of the gods (φθόνος θεῶν), which begrudges creatures their too great success and so lures them either directly or indirectly through *Hybris* to destruction. This teaching reflects the deeply-felt uncertainty of human beings and, as the word "envy" shows, presents the gods as completely amoral beings who . . . carefully guard their pre-eminence."

The motif has a faint echo in 3:22. It could be that it was more prominent in the prehistory of vv. 22 and 24. Even fainter is the echo in the words of the serpent in 3:4. The basis of the motif is a recognition that the relationship between God and his people is full of tension. The gods have created people as their servants and as such they must stand in a definite relationship to the gods; the animals cannot be the servants of the gods in the same way. But this relationship hides the possibility of a rivalry as is shown very markedly in the Prometheus motif.

All narratives in which the motif of "the envy of the gods" occurs are concerned with the relationship of tension which accompanies the fact of being created by the gods: one is granted the power of life in being created. This driving power in a person moves in two directions: there is the drive after life and the drive after knowledge, the latter being directed to the mastery of existence. It is possible then for the person to overstep the limit and this involves the motif of "the envy of the gods." It remains however very much in the background in Gen 2-3. It undergoes a very important alteration: the moment of rivalry which could arouse envy is eliminated. What remains is only the possibility of overstepping the border which is protected by God. But there is a difference. The motif in 3:4f stands under a negative signature inasmuch as the serpent wants to suggest to the woman the envy of God; the divine reflection in 3:22 parries any approach to God by humans. 3:22 and 24 together with 2:9 are closer to a mythical presentation than is the narrative of the tree of knowledge. But even in 3:22 one can only speak of an echo of the motif of "the envy of the gods"; also the divine reflection is not concerned with God and his being but with people who must be prevented from overstepping their limits.

Literature: Gen 3:24: Dictionary Articles: K.H. Bernhardt, 'Cherub', BHH I, 298-299.   T.H. Gaster, 'Angel', IDB I, 128-134.

L. Dürr, *Ezechiels Vision von der Erscheinung Gottes (Ez 1 und 10) im Lichte der vorderasiatischen Altertumskunde,* Diss. (1917), (esp. 21-31).   G. Jacoby, "Zur Erklärung der Cherube," ARW 22 (1923) 257-265.   Hans Schmidt, "Kerubenthron und Lade," *Festschr. H. Gunkel, I,* (1923) (esp. 120-122).   P. Dhorme-L.H. Vincent, "Les Chérubins," RB 35 (1926) 328-358; "Les Chérubins Bibliques," 481-495.   H. Gressmann, "Der Eingang zum Paradies," AfO 3 (1926) 12.   A.S. Kapelrud, "The Gates of Hell and the Guardian Angels of Paradise," JAOS 70 (1950) 151-156.   E. Kutsch, "Die Wurzel עצר im Hebräischen," VT 2 (1952) 57-69.   E.F. Sutcliffe, "A Note on 'AL, Lᵉ and FROM," VT 5 (1955) 436-439.   R. de Vaux, "Les Chérubins et l'Arche d'Alliance," *Mélanges R. Moutarde,* 37 (1960-61).   R.L. Cleveland, "Cherubs and the 'Tree of Life' in Ancient South Arabia," BASOR 172 (1963) 55-60.   E. Tsoref, "Die Keruben in der Altertumskunde und nach Y. Kaufmann," BctM 11 (1965-66)

59-88. R. de Vaux, *The Bible and the Ancient Near East*, 1972, ch. 3.   N.J. Tromp, *Primitive Conceptions of Death and the Nether World in the Old Testament*, BibOr 21, 1969.

[3:24] A. Dillmann, presuming the unity of vv. 22-24, had explained the relationship of the two verbs in 23 and 24 in this way: "After God had sent the man and his wife out of the garden, that is, told them to go out, he drives them, still hesitating, out. . . ." This explanation was taken up by G. Lambert, P. Humbert, A. Lefèvre, U. Cassuto (without reference to Dillmann). It can remain an open question whether the narrative in its final form has a heightening effect; but this cannot be an argument for its unity. According to the rules of ancient narrative art it is a pretty certain sign that two originally independent accounts of the expulsion have come together.

"East of Eden": The many attempts to balance the information about the place, which corresponds to 4:16 (Th.C. Vriezen against H. Gunkel), with 2:8 collapse when vv. 22 and 24 are a motif added to the narrative. On the preposition see E.F. Sutcliffe.

The description of the guardians who protect the access to the tree of life brings together two traditions. According to one they are the cherubim, according to the other "the flickering flame of a sword"; this is generally acknowledged. It is likewise acknowledged that the narrator is relying on non-Israelite traditions. The discussion about the origin and the meaning of the cherubim has been extensive. The conclusions can be summed up briefly: Th.C. Vriezen divides the occurrences of the cherubim in the Old Testament into groups — (a) guardians of God's garden, Gen 3:24; Ezek 18:14, 16; (b) bearers of Yahweh in the Epiphanies, Ps 18:10f. used in parallelism with wind and clouds; (c) figures in the temple; (d) bearers of Yahweh's throne, Ezek 9:3; 10:1-22; Ps 80:1. Similar groupings are found in IDB and BHH. One concludes from the variety of contexts in which they appear that the different presentations have different origins. Mythical guardians who protect access to a place forbidden to humans, guardians at the door to the underworld, guardians of a sanctuary — all these are widespread. But the word itself and the presentation indicate Mesopotamia; one can refer here to the extensive study of P. Dhorme-L.H. Vincent.

The word in Hebrew is a descriptive term which is not to be derived from the root כרב. The closest cognate is the Akkadian *kâribu* or *kârubi* which is also a being at the entrance to the sanctuary. Its original meaning is that of an intercessor corresponding to the primary meaning in Akkadian of a mediator of prayers; *kâribu* or *kârubi* is, according to P. Dhorme "the one who prays par excellence." The history has been studied by L.H. Vincent with the discoveries in Mesopotamia as a basis. The ways in which this form is presented are so different and have changed so much in the different periods that it is not possible to derive the cherubim of Gen 3:24 from any definite one. The writer most likely had in mind some composite being as in Ezekiel or the Apocalypse. See BHH I, 298f. for composite beings in the ivory carvings from Calah and Megiddo.

"The flashing flaming sword." This is an independent image stemming from a different tradition (so H. Gunkel ad. loc.; also N.J. Tromp, *Primitive Conceptions*. . . .). The Sumerian myths speak of the weapons as often as they do of independent beings. The personification of a weapon is common, and even the Old Testament speaks of "the avenging sword of God" Jer 46:10; Is 34:5;

Zeph 2:12. The Hebrew expression "the flashing flaming sword" recalls the lightning flash which often occurs as a weapon of God's; both coalesce here. F. Thureau-Dangin (*La glaive tournoyant* I, 1896, 147ff.) quotes an example from an inscription from Tiglath-pileser I in which a description of the king as an avenging lightning flash "takes the place of a *laḥmu* or some other 'guardian'" (see P. Dhorme-L.H. Vincent, 482, A. 4). It is indeed no accident that these two expressly mythical forms do not appear in the basic narrative of the expulsion of the man and the woman from God's garden, but rather in the parallel motif of the tree of life, vv. 22, 24 which we know to be a mythical motif from the world around Israel. It is not without importance that the basic narrative of which v. 23 is the conclusion tells of the expulsion from the garden without mentioning any mythical being as guardian. It is to be noted further that the function of these guardian beings in the text is not really to guard the garden so that no one can go in — this is the way in which it is usually understood, and this conclusion is drawn from the geographical note "East of the Garden of Eden." These guardian beings are not required in the basic narrative; the expulsion of the man and the woman from the garden by God is in itself definitive.

Purpose and Thrust

The narrative of Gen 2-3 concerns the human race. It is one of the few biblical stories that is known to the whole world even to this day. General talk about Adam and Eve, paradise, the serpent and so on shows that the narrative still lives even outside the Christian ecclesiastical tradition. This in turn accords with the fact that the basic motifs of the narrative did not begin in Israel, but belong to the traditions of the human race which stretch both geographically and chronologically into the far distance and whose origins cannot be determined. But there is the widest of chasms between the broad sweep of the original meaning of these narratives and the restricted dogmatic meaning given them in their traditional Christian explanation. This is illustrated by the description "the fall" which has become the title of the story in all Western languages. When this description occurs today in scholarly works, and it often does, it is usually written in quotation marks. It has rarely been contested up to the present, so deeply is it rooted in Western tradition. The description implies that the narrative has a definite meaning, the meaning which has become established in the Christian dogmatic teaching on the Primeval State, Fall and Original Sin.

The description and the meaning inherent in it has a history of which the main line can be easily traced. Its origins lie not in Christian tradition, but in the tradition of late Judaism. They are found in 2 (4) Esd 7:118 (48):

> O Adam, what have you done?
> For though it was you who sinned,
> the Fall was not yours alone,
> but ours also who are your descendants. (RSV)

The Esdras passage expounds Gen 2-3 as a story of Adam's sin which was passed on to his descendants (cf. W. Harnisch, *Verhängnis und Verheissung der Geschichte*, 1969, esp. 106-120. The second stage is in the Pauline theology, particularly in the Adam-Christ typology, but not only there. Paul's explanation of Gen 2-3, as often stated, is in the context of the explanation given in late Judaism, cf. the Esdras passage. It did not arise out of his encounter with Christ, but is rooted in late Judaism. The third stage is the full development on the teaching of Original Sin in Augustine. D. Ritschl quotes a passage from Augustine that is typical: ''The fall of man must be understood as a slide down into a lower level of existence, so that sin must be understood not as a lack but as a degradation of being'' (''Die Last des augustinischen Erbes,'' *Parrhesia, Festschr. Karl Barth,* Zürich, 1966). Augustine's teaching on sin determined later Christian tradition in the West (see also O. Loretz, *Schöpfung und Mythus,* SBS 22, pp. 20-30).

Quite apart from any theological judgment one may pass on this line of tradition from late Judaism through Paul to Augustine, one can no longer say that it accords with the intention of Gen 2-3. As for the description ''the fall,'' it is an entirely possible way of describing a primeval event which corresponds to Gen 2-3, and which occurs in the narrative behind Ezek 28. But it is no accident that the narrative that shows through Ezekiel has an expressly mythological character which is avoided in Gen 2-3. ''The fall'' is saying something passive, fateful, such as formulated in the Esdras passage. The narrative of Gen 2-3 does not speak of a fall. One should avoid therefore a description which differs so much from the text and is so inaccurate and deceptive.

But the real misunderstanding that is hidden under the title ''fall'' lies deeper. It is that the intention of the narrative is to say that our present history begins with the fall, the ''original state'' before the fall being a state of innocence and sinlessness in paradise beyond the present. But this is to misunderstand the narrative of Gen 2-3 as primeval event. The whole course of the event, from the moment that the man was put into the garden up to his expulsion from it, is primeval, i.e., an event on the other side of our historical experience. One cannot cut it down the middle and say that the first part, before the eating of the fruit, is the *status integritatis* beyond our historical experience, but with the eating of the fruit the *status corruptionis* began. The whole event described is, from beginning to end, primeval event and belongs to an aspect of reality in which what happens is described differently from what we understand by history. This does not mean any lessening of reality, rather it is only when the narrative is understood as primeval event that it is properly related to reality.

The narrative explains human existence in its essential elements as something which came about in primeval time, and indeed the created state in contrast to the state of humanity limited by death, suffering and sin. It is a misunderstanding of the narrative as a whole to explain it as a succession of historical or quasi-historical incidents. I quote here the Catholic exegete H. Haag who has written: ''The current view in Catholic and Evangelical dogmatics that the primeval state was a chronological period at the beginning of human history . . . does not accord with the Bible. It knows no 'man before sin' and so no primeval state.'' (''Der 'Urstand' nach dem Zeugnis der Bibel,'' ThQ 148 [1968] 385-404; discussion ZAW 8a [1969] 267.) There is no tradition of the narrative of Gen 2-3 throughout the whole of the Old Testament, and this has impressed a number of scholars in recent times. It is not quoted and is never mentioned. It is never included in the syntheses of the acts of God (Credo). The reason for this is that Israel never considered it to be a historical incident side-by-side with other historical incidents. The Israelites did not think of it as a definite event to be dated at the beginning of human history, even though it remained eminently real to them. It was only in late Judaism, when the perception of the difference between historical reality and primeval reality was lost, that the ''fall'' of humanity was leveled off to a historical or quasi-historical incident and the explanation outlined above became possible.

The goal of the narrative of Gen 2-3 is not a state which is to be opposed to an earlier state, but the expulsion of the man and the woman from the garden and the consequent separation from God. The question behind the narrative is not primarily, how did death come into the world? or what is the origin of sin? even though these questions contributed to its formation. The real question which determines the whole narrative is: Why is a person who is created by God limited by death, suffering, toil and sin? But this question is not primarily causal, an objective search for the primeval cause. It is the question of human beings affected by their limited state. It is this existential question that the narrative is really about.

The answer which the narrative gives then is not a piece of objective information which answers directly the question about the cause. The answer is found in the connection shown between one's guilt and one's limitation by suffering, death and toil. But the narrative does not say the last word here: the death sentence which was announced is not carried out. The curse does not touch the couple directly, but only in passing. The alienation of the man and the woman from God does not mean a definitive separation. God drives them out of the garden, but leaves them life, and by giving them a commission outside the garden, God gives meaning to their alienated existence. Guilt and death are now stark realities that keep them shackled, but even so they remain creatures of God.

The narrative of Gen 2-3 will always retain its meaning for humankind. Something basic is said about humanity which no religious or ideological, no scientific, technical or medical development or change can or will in any way alter. It is part of human existence that a person is fallible. One cannot be a human being other than a fallible human being. This is the context of the limitation of human existence; not indeed that death is the penalty for the offense committed by a first man, but rather that fallible, sinful, disobedient humanity is humanity separated from God. A person separated from God is a person limited by death, suffering and toil. It is completely compatible with the sense of the narrative of Gen 2-3 to find there the representative event of "original sin" which as such is an actuality for the whole human race. But one must avoid the mistake of viewing this "original sin" in terms of a universal and abstract notion of sin. Such a concept is not found in the OT. K. Condon also comes to this conclusion: ". . . one does not find in the Old Testament any word that means precisely what we mean by 'to sin'. There was breach of law, and consequent fear before God, there was guilt and a sense of liability to punishment, there was consciousness of evil and suffering and a linking of suffering and the misery of the human condition with sin, but all this was not absolutized into SIN" (IThQ 34 [1967] 20-36; discussion, ZAW 79 [1967] 380f.).

A careful distinction must be made between the event described in Gen 2-3 and what can only take place in a history between God and his people: the disobedience, apostasy, disloyalty of this people which presumes a meeting in history. The basis of the difference is the universal character of Gen 2-3; what is said here holds for all people. From J's point of view it is as valid for Egyptians, Edomites, and Philistines as it is for Israelites; from ours, for Christian and non-Christian, for believers and atheists. J saw the offense which he describes as "primeval sin" as disobedience to God; and so he points to a connection between this "primeval sin" and the offense of the people of Israel which was decisive before God. We have an indication then that Israel's own history with her God, her disloyalty to this God which determines her history, must be seen in the broader context of the history of God with humankind which is alienated from him.

Paul in the idea of history which he outlines in Rom 1:18-3:20 takes as his starting point that Jews and pagans are equally sinners and under wrath of God. Paul prescinds here from the difference between the "primeval sin" and the disloyalty of Israel to her God; he is only concerned to stress that Jews and pagans alike are sinners. The sense of his argument can only be understood in the context of a preparation for Rom 3:21-31, outside of which it is unintelligible. The "sin" of the pagans and the "sin" of the Jews are essentially very different. From the perspective of Gen 2-3 the equation cannot be made to coincide. It is not possible by using Gen 2-3 to present the history of humankind from Adam to the coming of Christ as negatively as Paul does in Rom 1:18-32. The "primeval sin," inasmuch as it is a reality for the whole of humanity, does not mean that everything one does is sinful or offensive before God. But if the idea of history which Paul develops in Rom 1-3 cannot be based on Gen 2-3, then a further reflection is necessary which takes as its starting point that Gen 2-3 cannot be understood from the perspective of a general and abstract notion of sin.

The universal meaning of Gen 2-3 consists in this, that a person's state as a creature is seen together with one's limitation through fallibility, suffering, toil and death. This makes it possible to bridge the gap which had opened between church teaching on Original Sin based on Gen 2-3 and scientific research into the beginnings of the human race. If Gen 2-3 is not concerned with two individuals but with the primeval representatives of the human race, if the disobedience and crime are not moments that can be fixed in history, but primeval event, if there can be no talk of a hereditary state of sin or of death as a penalty, then there is no longer any need for an insuperable opposition between what the narrative wanted to say and research into the origins of the human race.

It need no longer be contested that the phenomenon of sin or evil is a phenomenon belonging to the human race which has been in process for thousands of years, and that there are various aspects to it, anthropological, sociological and psychological. I refer to the study of L. Housman, "Sin and Herdinstinct," HibJ 44 (1945-46) 97-105, to S. Freud and the direction he gave to the study of depth psychology, and to K. Lorenz, *Das sogenannte Böse. Zur Naturgeschichte der Aggression,* 1964[3], (see O. Loretz *Schöpfung und Mythos* . . . , SBS 32, 1968, c. 1). It is only when it is acknowledged that sin or evil as a phenomenon of the early history of humankind are open to scientific research without any restriction, that the meaning proper to Gen 2-3 emerges: what this sin or this evil is which constitutes one's opposition to God and what does it mean. On the other side, one can expect that scientific research into the beginnings of humankind will see the significance of the fact that the phenomenon of sin or evil in the early period of the human race cannot be separated from one's understanding of oneself as a person in opposition to a divine power. It is only in this way that the meaning of Gen 2-3 for humankind is preserved; only thus does it retain its validity as a starting point for the history of God with his people.

Genesis 4:1-16

Cain and Abel

Literature

Introduction: J. Wellhausen, *Die Composition des Hexateuchs.* . . . (1899³, 1963⁴). W. Moser, "Die Kainssage in ihrer ursprünglichen Gestalt," Nord u. Süd 104 (1903) 54-66. A. Ehrlich, *Randglossen zur hebräischen Bibel,* I, Kap. IV (1908) 17-26. B.D. Eerdmans, *Alttestamentliche Studien,* I-IV (1908-1912). W. Eichrodt, *Die Quellen der Genesis, von neuem untersucht,* BZAW 31 (1916). W. Staerk, "Zur alttestamentlichen Literarkritik. Grundsätzliches und Methodisches," ZAW 42 (1924) 34-74. S. Mowinckel, *The Two Sources* . . . , ANVA II (1937) 25-43. C.A. Simpson, *The Early Traditions of Israel. A Critical Analysis of the Pre-Deuteronomic Narrative of the Hexateuch* (1948) 57-60, 451-498. O. Eissfeldt, *Die ältesten Traditionen Israels. Ein kritischer Bericht über C.A. Simpson's The Early Traditions of Israel,* BZAW 71 (1950); "Erwägungen zur Pentateuchquellenfrage," OLZ 61 (1966) 213-218. E. Testa, "Il genere letterario della disputa e il racconto di Caino ed Abele," BeO 8 (1966) 157-166.

Text: R. Lepsius, "Verbalinspiration und Textkritik," Reich Christi 6 (1903) 168-180. V. Aptowitzer, *Kain und Abel in der Agada, den Apokryphen, der hellenistischen, christlichen und mohammedanischen Literatur* (1922). L. Koehler, "Syntactica IV," VT 3 (1953) 299-305. A Murtonen, "The Fixation in Writing of Various Parts of the Pentateuch," VT 3 (1953) 46-53. P. Grelot, "Les Targums du Pentateuque. Étude comparative d'après Genèse IV, 3-16," Sem. 9 (1959) 59-88. A. Diez Macho, "Un manuscrito babilonico de Onqelos en el que se confunden los timbres vocalicos Pataḥ y Qamez (MsT - SB 10, 5)," Sef. 19 (1959) 273-282. G. Vermès, "The Targumic Versions of Genesis IV 3-16," ALUOS 3 (1963) 81-114. O.L. Barnes, *A New Approach to the Problem of the Hebrew Tenses and its Solution without Recourse to Waw-Consecutive* (1965). R. le Déaut, "Lévitique XXII 26-XXIII 44 dans le Targum Palestinien. De l'importance des gloses du Codex Neofiti 1," VT 18 (1968) 458-471.

Narrative: H. Ewald, "Erklärung der biblischen Urgeschichte. I, 4 Die geschlechter des ersten Weltalters," JBW VI (1853-1854) 1-19. H. Lüken, *Die Traditionen des Menschengeschlechts.* §35: Kain und Abel (1869²) 162-179. F. Lenormant, *Les origines de l'histoire d'apres la Bible et les traditions des peuples orientaux,* I (1880) 140-143. K. Budde, *Die biblische Urgeschichte (Gen 1-12:5) untersucht* (1883) 183-204. B. Stade, "Beiträge zur Pentateuchkritik. 1. Das Kainszeichen," ZAW 14 (1894) 250-318 = Ausgewählte akad. Reden u. Abhandlungen (1899; 1907²) 229-273. H. Zeydner, "Kainszeichen, Keniter und Beschneidung," ZAW 18 (1898) 120-125. H. Guthe, Kain, RE³ IX (1901) 698-701. E. Böklen, "Adam und Quain im Lichte der vergleichenden Mythenforschung," MythBibl I (1907). H. Gressmann, "Sage und Geschichte in den Patriarchenerzählungen," ZAW 30 (1910) 1-36. H. Weinheimer, "Zu Genesis Kapitel 2 und Kapitel 4," ZAW 32 (1912) 33-40. A. Ehrenzweig, "Kain und Lamech," ZAW 35 (1915) 1-11; "Biblische und klassische Urgeschichte, II. Die Ermordung des Stadtgründers," ZAW 38 (1919-1920) 65-86. O. Gruppe, "Kain," ZAW 39 (1921) 67-76. N. Rhodokanakis," Genesis 2-4," ZAW 39 (1921) 76-83. A. Sanda, "Moses und der Pentateuch," ATA 9 (1924) 157-159. J.G. Bellet, *Die Welt vor der Flut und die Patriarchen* (1925). A. Menes, "Die sozialpolitische Analyse der Urgeschichte," ZAW 43 (1925) 33-62. R. Eisler, "Das Qainszeichen und die Qeniter," MO 23 (1929) 48-112. H. Gunkel, 'Kain und Abel', RGG² III (1929) 584-585. W. Stoderl, "Der Brudermörder Kain," Zeitenwächter 24 (1930) 132-139. K. Fruhstorfer, *Der ersten Menschen erste Nachkommen (Kapitel 4 der Genesis)* (1932). G. Kuhn, *Studia Biblica ed Irenicus Audax ex Vetere Testamento I. Erklärungen zu Genesis Kapitel 1-14* (1937). S.H. Hooke, "Cain and Abel," Folkl. 1 (1939) 58-65. P.A.H. de Boer, "Kain en Abel. Genesis IV 1-16," NTT 31 (1942) 197-212. C.A. Keller, *Das Wort OTH als 'Offenbarungszeichen Gottes'. II. Die Geschichte des Begriffes, Kap. 9. Das Kains-zeichen* (1946) 69-78. I. Engnell, "Kain och Abel. En rituell interpretation (1. Mose4)", Svensk Jerusalems Föreningens Tijdskr 46 (1947) 92-102. P. Heinisch, *Probleme der biblischen Urgeschichte* (1947). H.H. Schrey, "Die alttestamentliche Forschung der sogenannten Uppsala-Schule," ThZ 7 (1951) 327. O.R. Sellers, "Problems in the Story of Cain," *'To Do and to Teach' Essays in Honor of Ch.L. Pyatt* (1953) 53-64. J.B. Bauer, "Kain und Abel," ThPQ 103 (1955) 126-133. N. Strosetzki, "Kain und Romulus als Stadtgründer," FF 28 (1955) 184-188. J. Klug, "Pastoral und Exegese," ThPQ 104 (1956) 235-238. B. Otte, "Cain y Abel (Gen 4:1-17)," RevBib 19 (1957) 61-62. C.A. Keller, 'Kain und Abel', RGG³ III (1959) 1089-1090. P. Humbert, "Démesure et chute dans l'Ancien Testament," *maqqél shâqédh, la branche d'amandier, Hommage à W. Vischer* (1960) 63-82. St. Lach, "Problemy w relacji biblijnej o Kainie i Ablu," RTK 7 (1960) 13-38. P. Morant, *Die Anfänge der Menschheit. Eine Auslegung der ersten elf Genesis-Kapitel* (1960; 1962²). M.A. Beek, *Auf den Wegen und Spuren des Alten Testaments. A. Urgeschichte, §4. Kain und Abel* (1961) 13-15. D. Barthélemy, *Dieu et son image. Ebauche d'une theologie biblique* (1963). A. Ibanez Arana, "La narración de Cain y Abel en Gen 4:2-16," ScrVic 11 (1964) 1-39, 281-319. C.J. de Catanzaro, "The Early Chapters of Genesis - A History of Salvation," ACQ 4 (1964) 175-181. H. Heyde, "Kain, der erste Jahwe-Verehrer. Die ursprüngliche Bedeutung der Sage von Kain und ihre Auswirkungen in Israel," AzTh I 23 (1965). L.M. Hoppe, *A History of the Interpretation of Genesis 4:1-16 and its Relevance for Biblical Hermeneutics,* (Diss, Boston) DissAbs 26 (1965-1966) 2893. K.A. Deurloo, *Kain en Abel* (1967). M.S. Enslin, "Cain and Prometheus," JBL 86 (1967) 88-90. W. Zimmerli, "Zur Exegese von Genesis 4:1-16," EvErz 20 (1968) 200-203.

History of Religion: Ph. Buttmann, "Über die mythische Periode von Kain bis zur Sündflut," Mythologus I (1828) 152-179. J.G. Frazer, *Anthropological Essays, presented to E.B. Tylor* (1907) 101-174. A Boissier, *Les élements babyloniens de la légende de Cain et Abel* (1909). A.H. Sayce, "The Archaeology of the Book of Genesis," ET 21 (1910); 22 (1911) 426-430. A. Eberharter, "Der Brudermord Kains im Lichte der ethnologischen und religionsgeschichtlichen Forschung (Gen 4:8-16)," ThQ 98 (1916) 67-76, 355-365. J.G. Frazer, *Folk-Lore in the OT. Studies in Comparative Religion, Legend and Law.* (1919); 1923²) 33-45. E.B. Cross, "An Answer to J.G. Frazer anent Cain and Abel," JBL 54 (1935) XII. H. Baumann, *Schöpfung und Urzeit des Menschen im Mythus der afrikanischen Völker* (1936; 1964) 253-256. A. Brock-Utne, "Die religions-historischen Voraussetzungen der Kain-Abel-Geschichte," ZAW 54 (1936) 202-239. H.A. Frankfort, *The Intellectual Adventure....* (1946; 1950³; 1967⁶). J. Laessøe, "The Atrahasis Epic. A Babylonian History of Mankind," BibOr 13 (1956) 90-102. G.R. Castellino, "Les origines de la civilisation selon les Textes Bibliques et les Textes Cunéiformes," VT.S 4 (1957) 116-137. S.N. Kramer, *Sumerian Literature and the Bible,* AnBib 12 = SBO III. Oriens Antiquus (1959) 185-204.

Kenite Hypothesis: B. Stade, *Geschichte des Volkes Israel, I* (1887). G.A.Barton, "A Sketch of Semitic Origins and Language," *Etudes sur les Religions Sémitiques* (1902). E. Meyer, *Die Israeliten und ihre Nachbarstämme,* (1906) 389-399. B.D. Eerdmans, "De Kenieten en het Jahwisme," ThT 41 (1907) 492-507. H. Gressmann, *Mose und seine Zeit,* FRLANT NF 1 (1913). H.P. Smith, *The Religion of Israel* (1914). E. Naville, *Les deux noms de Dieu dans la Genèse* (1917). J. Morgenstern,

"The Oldest Documents of the Hexateuch," HUCA 4 (1927) 1-138. W. Vischer, *Jahwe der Gott Kains* (1929). A. Lods, *Israel des origines au milieu du VIIIe. siècle* (1930). W.O.E. Oesterley-Th. Robinson, *Hebrew Religion, its Origin and Development* (1930; 1955[3]). H. Schmökel, "Jahwe und die Keniter," JBL 52 (1933) 212-229. E.A. Leslie, *Old Testament Religion in the Light of its Canaanite Background* (1936; 1947[2]). E. Dhorme, *L'evolution religieuse d'Israel. I. La Religion des Hebreux nomades,* Ser. de l'Or aux Bruxelles (1937). J. Coppens, *Histoire critique des livres de l'Ancien Testament* (1942[3]). H.H. Rowley, *The Missionary Message of the Old Testament* (1945). M. Burrows, *An Outline of Biblical Theology* (1946). S. Nyström, *Beduinentum und Jahwismus* (1946). B.D. Eerdmans, *The Religion of Israel* (1947). H.H. Rowley, *From Joseph to Joshua. Biblical Traditions in the Light of Archaeology* (1950). S. Abramski, *The Qenites,* Eretz-Israel Annual 3 (1954). Ch.H.W. Brekelmans, "Exodus XVIII and the Origin of Yahwism in Israel," OTS 10 (1954) 215-224. J.P. Hyatt, "Yahweh as 'the God of My Father'," VT 5 (1955) 130-136. H.H. Rowley, "Mose und der Monotheismus," ZAW 69 (1957) 1-21. G.M. Landes, 'Kenites', IDB III (1962) 6-7. W.F. Albright, "Jethro, Hobab and Reuel in Early Hebrew Tradition," CBQ 25 (1963) 1-11. J.P. Hyatt, "The Origin of Mosaic Yahwism," *Biblical Studies: The Teacher's Yoke, Studies in Mem. of H. Trantham* (1964) 85-93. S. Herrmann, "Der alttestamentliche Gottesname," EvTh 26 (1966) 281-293. Th.C. Vriezen, *The Religion of Ancient Israel,* (1967). H. Gese, "Bemerkungen zur Sinaitradition," ZAW 79 (1967) 137-154.

Text

4:1 Now the man[a] knew his wife Eve, and she became pregnant and bore Cain. And she said: I have acquired a man, with[b] Yahweh!

2 And she bore again (a son), Abel, his[a] brother. Abel became a keeper of small cattle and Cain[b] a farmer.

3 After some time Cain presented[a] an offering to Yahweh from the produce of the field.

4 And Abel too presented an offering from the first-born of his flocks, that is from the fat portions[a], and Yahweh directed his gaze on Abel and his offering,

5 but not on Cain and his offering. So Cain was very[a] angry and his face fell.

6 Then Yahweh said to Cain: Why are you angry?[a][b] and why has your face fallen?

7 Surely, if you do good, is there not a lifting up, and if you do not do good, sin is there[a] lying in wait[b] at the door, it is greedy for you, but you must master it.

8 And Cain said to his brother Abel. . . .[a] And when they were in the field, Cain rose up against his brother Abel and killed him.

9 And Yahweh said to Cain: Where is your brother Abel? And he said: I do not know. Am I my brother's guardian?

10 And he said: What have you done? The voice[a] of your brother's blood is crying to me from the ground.

11 But now: cursed are you away from[a] the ground, which has opened itself to receive your brother's blood, shed by your hand.

12 When you till the ground, it will no longer[a] give you of its vitality. A vagrant and fugitive[b] you shall be in the land.

13 And Cain said to Yahweh: My punishment is too heavy to bear[a].

14 See, you have now driven me from the ground. And I must hide myself from you. And I must be a vagrant and fugitive in the land. Anyone who meets me can kill me!

15 And Yahweh said to him: Not so[a]. Anyone who kills Cain, ven-

geance shall be taken on him seven-fold [b]. And Yahweh put a mark on Cain, so that anyone who might meet him might not [c] kill him.

16 And Cain went away from the face of Yahweh and lived in the land of Nod, to the east of Eden [a].

4:1a A. Dillmann: "The new beginning, without imperf. consec., shows that there is no immediate connection with the preceding." **b** את־: Gk reads διὰ τοῦ θεοῦ, Vg *per dominum*, Tg° מאת יהוה. את(?) "the man of Yahweh's sign." See Commentary.

2a For the repetition of את, BrSynt §65a. **b** וקין "by means of ו a new subject is introduced in express antithesis to one just mentioned" Ges-K §142d; likewise v. 4.

3a "In 1 Kings 1:41 as in Gen 1:5; 4:3f.; 7:11; 9:23f. . . . simultaneity of two events is expressed by an imperf. consec. followed by a perfect separated from the copula by the insertion of a word between them," E.F. Sutcliffe, JSSt 3 (1958) 80-81.

4a ומחלבהן Ges-K §91c, emendation not necessary. For the ו, Ges-K §154a, n. 16: "Frequently *wāw copulativum* is also explanatory . . . e.g., Gen 4:4 *and* (i.e., *namely*) *of the fat thereof*." For the suffixes, cf. commentaries, esp. H. Holzinger. הביא; for the perf. cf. E.F. Sutcliffe, v. 3a.

5a ויחר לקין מאד: the subject אפו is missing, cf. Gen 39:19; BrSynt §35b.

6a F. Delitzsch: "חרה לך with recessive accent, but, as always, without Dagesh after the verb alone." **b** "The third person singular is often used impersonally, e.g., . . . חרה followed by לו . . . he became angry Gen 4:6" Ges-K § 144b.

7 The whole verse is textually uncertain; see commentary. **a** לפתח BrSynt §107a: "ל . . . has generally preserved its original meaning of direction towards a goal . . . , 'sin lurks at the door' Gen 4:7." On Gk. M.S. Enslin, "Cain and Prometheus," JBL 86 (1967) 88, thinks it possible that the Gk, which translates by διέλης (presuming probably לנתח for לפתח), saw Cain's sin in the improper carving of the sacrificial animal as in Hesiod's story of Prometheus. **b** רבץ: "In Gen 4:7 רֹבֵץ is a substantival participle (a lurker, a croucher)" Ges-K §145u.

8a What is missing after אחיו is supplied by the versions Sam, Gk, Syr, Old Lat השדה נלכה; Vg *egrediamur foras*.

10a "קוֹל . . . is to be taken as an exclamation, and the supposed predicate as in apposition to the genitive, e.g., Gen 4:10 . . . 'hark! thy brother's blood is crying'," Ges-K §146b. Against, BrSynt §14c translates: "the voice of your brother's blood is crying to me." In § 124a: ". . . the predicate to a construct chain often refers back to the *regens* rather than to the *rectum*."

11a N. Glueck, JPOS 12 (1932) 101f. holds מן־האדמה to be dittog. of the same words in v. 10; but that is improbable.

12a לא־תסף "The short form of the imperf. with the negatives לא and אל serves to express prohibition . . . later used without distinction," BrSynt §5a. **b** נע ונד only here and v. 14.

13a מנשא too heavy to . . . , Ges-K §133c. Word order BrSynt §27d; Ges-K §141m.

15a Instead of לכן, Gk, Syr, Symm, Theod, Vg read לא כן certainly correctly; F. Nötscher, VT 3 (1953) 372-380, renders לכן by "indeed." **b** שבעתים, 7-fold, Ges-K §97h, BrSynt §88 and 101. **c** לבלתי: construction Ges-K §114s, 116w, 117e.

16a קדמת: opposite to, BrSynt § 116a.

History of Interpretation

The interpretation of the passage divides itself into two main lines: A. the individual-primeval, B. the collective. Type A ruled almost undisputed until about the end of the 19th century. From the time of J. Wellhausen and B. Stade to the present, type B has ruled in Protestant exegesis while in Jewish and Catholic scholarship type A has held its place. Critical reviews of type B can be found in J. Skinner, R. Eisler, U. Cassuto, K.A. Deurloo. H. Ewald (1853-1854) had already pointed to the collective interpretation while holding to type A as did the two commentaries of F. Delitzsch (1872) and A. Dillmann (1875³: 1886⁵) which were determinative for exegesis for a long time.

J. Wellhausen builds on the results of Ewald's work. He sees in Cain, the Kenites, and in the desert to which Cain was banished, the desert in the south of Judah. This is the switch-point for the whole of the new exegesis; it made the story of Cain and Abel and its origin intelligible and could find support in the name of the leading figure. K. Budde accepts what is essential to Wellhausen's thesis of the two opposing presentations of Cain in 4:17f. and 4:2-16 and thereby the opposition between an older nomadic story and a later one in which the determining factor is the opposition between arable land and the desert.

B. Stade laid the basis for the collective interpretation in the sense of an ethnological etiology. His study *Das Kainszeichen,* 1894, has been extremely influential right up to the present day. He bases his interpretation on Wellhausen's argument that the narrative intends to contrast the arable land of Palestine with the desert to the south of Judah. He sees the key to the understanding of 4:2-16 in Wellhausen's view. The narrative is for him an "ethnological etiology" (H. Gunkel). Before this terminology was hammered out, Stade had given the classical example of it in his explanation of Gen 4:2-16. What is typical of this etiological story is, he thinks, the following: "Only those characteristics are of significance for the story and its meaning which have their background in the life and activity of the Kenites." Everything else is by the way, "indifferent aids." He explains the sign of Cain as the sign of the tribe of the Kenites.

It is precisely the unilateral direction of the explanation that has brought conviction. It has the advantage over Budde's explanation in that it is not a construction that has been thought out, but "in all its details a natural product of the popular way of looking at things." H. Holzinger (1898) stresses this, as do H. Guthe (1901) and E. Meyer (1906); H. Gunkel (1910) accepts Stade's explanation in the 3rd ed. of his commentary. Stade's explanation differs from that of Gunkel's 3rd ed., only in this that Gunkel, as in the 1st ed., distinguishes an older and a later form of the story. What for Stade are "unimportant aids," are for Gunkel a later version in which the author presents "great primeval truths about the human race." O. Procksch, W. Zimmerli, G. von Rad follow him.

In the period following there has been a whole series of variants of the collective explanation: E. Meyer (1906), B.D. Eerdmans (1908-1912), J. Skinner (1910; 1912²), W. Weinheimer (1912), O. Procksch (1924), A. Menes (1925) and W. Staerk (1924). A. Ehrenzweig (1915) understands Gen 4:1-26 as a parallel to the story of Romulus and Remus (so already F. Lenormant 1880). He sees Abel's murder as a "building sacrifice." The explanation given by A. Brock-Utne (1936) is somewhat different: the farmer and the shepherd wanted to obtain a blessing by means of the sacrifice. The farmer who was not successful tries to win the blessing by human sacrifice. In the second part Brock-Utne works out another Kenite hypothesis according to which Cain is the tribal ancestor of the lower cult officials. H. Schmökel (1933), who understands Gen 4:2-16 as an "anti-Kenite flyleaf" which attests the later change of view about the Kenites, thinks that 4:17f. presents Cain positively.

S. Mowinckel (1937) undertook a thorough revision of Stade's opinion. He follows Stade and Gunkel inasmuch as he sees the original intention of the story to explain the life and culture of the tribe of which the eponymous hero is Cain. The narrative handed down in 4:2-16 belongs, according to Mowinckel, to the E tradition, while only a fragment of the older J tradition, 4:17b, has been preserved. It originates from the tribe of Cain and commemorates the first ancestor. Like A. Ehrenzweig, Mowinckel sees a parallel to the Romulus and Remus story in the older form. C.A. Keller (1946) follows Stade's explanation in the form presented by Mowinckel. He sees in the "mark of Cain" a "mark guarding revelation." H. Heyde (1965) sees in the Cain story the "primeval story of Yahweh worship" in which "the Kenites living in Midian traced their faith, cult and destiny back to Cain," p. 33.

W. Zimmerli and G. von Rad in their commentaries appeal for detailed exegesis and theological conclusions, to a narrative set in primeval time which concerns an individual. (So too Zimmerli in a later work, "Zur Exegese von Genesis 4:1-16," EvErz 20 [1968] 200-203.) He refers to an earlier form of the narrative in an appendix in which the history of the tribe is presented in the way Stade had explained it, and where Zimmerli sees the pre-history in two phases (like Mowinckel), one of which spoke of Cain cursed by God, the other of a special nearness of Cain to God. One continues to find brief references to the collective meaning right up to the present; e.g., G. Sauer ("Die Tafeln von Deir 'Allā," ZAW 81 [1969] 145-156), who says that Gen 4 reflects the opposition between sedentary life and life in the desert.

Gen 4:2-16 plays an important role in what is known as the Kenite hypothesis which looks into the pre-history of the worship of Yahweh among the Kenites (Midianites). H.H. Rowley gives a thorough presentation of the hypothesis with all the pertinent literature in "Mose und der Monotheismus," ZAW 69 (1957) 1-21.

One simple observation throws considerable light on the history of the exegesis of the passage: the radical and one-sided collective explanation of Gen 4:2-16 is found almost exclusively in monographs, i.e., in studies which proceed thematically. In the commentaries on the other hand the narrative is explained either as consisting of two layers of which only one is collective (H. Gunkel, H. Holzinger, J. Skinner, O. Procksch, W. Zimmerli, G. von Rad) or as the story of an individual in the primeval period (H. Ewald, F. Delitzsch, A. Dillmann, A. Ehrlich, P. Heinisch, B. Jacob, U. Cassuto, K.A. Deurloo). It seems clear to me that the conclusion from this striking fact is that a sentence-for-sentence exegesis of the text which would explain the whole succession of episodes as tribal history or history of a people is extremely difficult, if not impossible.

The individual, primeval explanation which had generally prevailed up to J. Wellhausen and B. Stade remained the ecclesiastical and conservative explanation even after them, and prevailed on the popular level. The collective explanation found practically no entrance in Jewish and Catholic exegesis. As indicated above, it had a certain internal dynamism and was always open to development and variation, while the individual explanation remained generally static; it gave no overall convincing explanation of the text. I see the way to a new and convincing explanation in U. Cassuto (1961 English ed.) and K.A. Deurloo (1967). Cassuto begins with the decisive argument which J. Skinner had already brought against the collective explanation; none of the collective explanations pays sufficient attention to the order in which the events are narrated. The solution which requires an older form of the text (as with S. Mowinckel) is attenuated by the fact that the text does not offer any convincing clues for it. Cassuto therefore returns to an individual primeval explanation; "Cain, who killed his brother, is the prototype of the murderer. All human beings are brothers and whoever sheds human blood sheds the blood of his brother." Being brothers is understood in the sense of being members of the human race and so with the possibility of taking a brother's life. The explanation of K.A. Deurloo (1967) is similar in many points and is taken up by M. Buber who also understands Cain in the individual primeval sense. He thinks that 4:2-16 is closely connected to Gen 2-3. Both passages are concerned with human beings; 2-3 with the person as God's creature and with the community between man and woman, 4:1-16 with the person in one's relationship to other people.

The history of the exegesis of the passage has been outlined only from the point of view of the individual or collective explanation. Further important aspects, the question of the origin and growth of the text, of the Israelite and non-Israelite background, of the theological meaning, must be left aside here.

Literary Form

The question of the form of the text of Gen 4:2-16 begins with the fact that it is part of a greater whole, the primeval story. Genealogies follow immediately on the creation story in both J and P; in P, 5:1f. follows 1:1-2:4a; in J, 4:1f. follows Gen 2-3. In both cases the genealogy begins with the birth of the child from the couple created by God; in both cases the birth is brought into relation with the creation of human beings which has preceded it. The consequence of this for the structure of Gen 4 is that vv. 1-2 and vv. 17-26 belong together and form the genealogy which follows the creation (J. Wellhausen had already indicated this). Gen 4 then consists of a genealogy, vv. 1-2, 17-26, and a narrative which has been fitted into it, vv. 3-16 (v. 2 serves at the same time as the *exposé* of the narrative). Accordingly the narrative of 4:2-16 is an elaboration of a genealogical table. An observation is made or an episode reported about one person named in the genealogy.

There are many different examples of the way in which such an elaboration takes place. It is clear from Gen 4 that the narrative has grown out of a genealogical table:

(a) The narrative is not concerned with two brothers, but with Cain. Abel plays only a passive role. Cain's name is explained in the genealogy in v. 2, whereas Abel's is not. He is constantly described as Cain's brother 2a, 8a, 8b, 9a, 9b, 10, 11a (so H. Gunkel). For the narrator Abel is only Cain's brother, more specifically, the brother whom Cain murdered. Here we have the explanation of Abel's name. It is not really the name of a person but an appellative, constructed out of the story.

(b) The murder of Abel in v. 8 is striking in its brevity and abruptness. This verse is meant to be the climax of the narrative; it is not something mentioned in passing, but rather like a news report.

(c) U. Cassuto and others have noted that the whole weight of the narrative rests on the dialogue, while the events are described very briefly and concisely.

One can conclude then that in 4:2-16 a short genealogical note about Cain has been developed into a narrative (K. Budde had suggested something similar). Besides information about the conception, birth and naming of Cain the note refers only to Cain's profession and remarks that he killed his brother (who had no name here) and was banished by Yahweh from the arable land. The information which elaborates the genealogical note has been constructed into a narrative. The two sentences which provide this information have become the two parts of the narrative which describe the crime and its punishment.

Gen 3 also deals with crime and its punishment; and there is every sign that the course of the narrative in 4:2-16 follows closely the pattern of Gen 3. Just as in Gen 3, so too here, the trial takes place face to face, vv. 9-10, and punishment is expressed in the form of a curse, vv. 11-12. Again, as in Gen 3, the punishment is tempered, vv. 13-15, and it is God himself who is responsible for the action which protects the transgressor from the full consequences of his crime 4:15b and 4:21; as in Gen 3, the punishment consists in alienation — expulsion.

The parallels between Gen 4 and 3 are so striking and thorough as to make the intention of J unmistakable, namely to construct in ch. 4 a narrative of crime and punishment corresponding to that in ch. 3. H. Ewald and J. Wellhausen, and later H. Gunkel, had pointed out a number of parallels, and in particular J. Skinner: "The literary form of 4:1-16 contains striking reminiscences of that of ch. 3 . . . there are several . . . turns of expression which recall the language of the earlier narrative. . . . In both we have the same sequence of sin, investigation and punishment. . . ." If this is so, we should be able to discern the specific points in which J intended the narrative to differ. And we can do this: Cain's crime is the murder of a brother. In J's primeval story a narrative of two brothers at enmity follows the narrative of the creation and expulsion of the first human couple. This can only mean in the context that on the primal relationship between man and woman there follows the primal relationship of brothers living together. As the patriarchal history later shows, this means for J the basic potential of people to coexist in community with its consequences of subordination of the sexes and the relationship between parents and children.

While J describes the relationship of man and woman to each other as mutual help in Gen 2, he wants to point out the other possibility in Gen 4, namely that of enmity and opposition between brothers which can only arise out of life together and of God's reaction to it. Brothers are naturally rivals, as the patriarchal history shows; rivalry, competition, quarrels, enmity are rooted in being brothers. This does not normally grow out of the partnership of man and woman, nor out of the relationship between parent and child, though it is a possibility. But it does normally grow out of the mutual coexistence of equals because the possibility of conflict is there. J is not describing a conflict between brothers in 4:2-16 but the final result of it. Every murder, J is saying, is really the murder of a brother.

S. Mowinckel writes: "the Cain-Abel legend is a variant of a very common type of folklore motif, which is called 'the hostile brothers', the same type of legend to which also the Romulus-Remus legend belongs," p. 27. One must agree with this starting point. But when he continues: "the primitive Cain legend intended to explain why and how the tribe of Cain had become what it was, viz., a proud revengeful nomadic Bedouin tribe, protected by Yahweh . . . ," then this is but one way of interpreting the basic motif of the enmity, and not the only one. Mowinckel interprets the motif without any discussion as belonging to tribal history, just as Wellhausen, Budde, Stade and many others, and with them seems to think that it is the only possible explanation. But, as we have shown above, J has structured Gen 4:2-16 so as to correspond unmistakably to Gen 3. He has distinguished ch. 4 from ch. 3 by adding the relationship between the two brothers to the relationship between man and woman. He thus introduces the possibility of conflict that can lead to murder. His intention then can only be to portray a primeval event in which the parties are two brothers, unless compelling reasons to the contrary can be alleged.

This primeval, individual explanation of the passage would be further strengthened if we could show that there are narratives in which the motif of brothers at enmity is developed simultaneously as individual (rivalry between two brothers) and primeval (sons of the first couple). Such a demonstration is possible (see Excursus below); the individual, primeval explanation however is not dependent on such a proof. What speaks decisively in its favor is the fact that Gen 4:2-16 is not only a part of the Yahwistic primeval story, but also that of parallelism to and the difference from Gen 3 can only be meant in this sense. The comment that has been made since the time of H. Gunkel: an etiological narrative of the origin of a tribe has been subsequently recast into a primeval narrative of a fratricide is quite incredible, because no scholar who supports such an opinion can give a good and clear reason for such recasting.

In the light of this analysis how is the structure of 4:2-16 to be understood in detail? The two parts of the narrative which correspond to the two pieces of information about the family tree are 2-8 and 9-16. The first part consists of three members: the *exposé* (v. 2 merges into the genealogy so that it belongs to the genealogy, 1-2, 17-26, as well as to the narrative), the occasion of the action, 3-5, and the action, 8. An address by Yahweh to Cain, 6-7, is inserted into the narrative; it is a warning in the text as we have it and acts as a brake on the movement of the narrative itself. However this address is not absolutely necessary for the progress of the event and could well be omitted. The first part contains two difficulties apart from vv. 6-7: the beginning of v. 3 ויהי מקץ ימים presumes that something has already taken place; it does not follow smoothly on the bare information about the birth and occupation of Cain and Abel. The other difficulty is the absence of what Cain said to his brother in v. 8 (the words are supplied in the translations). Both difficulties indicate that the narrative has not been preserved in its original form. It seems too that the description of the occasion of the action in vv. 3-5 leaves questions open and that the action, even apart from the absence of what Cain said to his brother, is strangely sparse.

But apart from these difficulties the narrative proceeds logically and consistently. This part does not contain the slightest hint that anything else could be meant than an incident between the two brothers. There is no sign of anything that could be taken as referring to an incident between two tribes.

In the second part the pronouncement of the penalty, 11-12, follows the trial, 9-10. The conclusion, v. 16, could well follow immediately. The narrative would then be complete. However Cain's objection, 13-14, and God's reply, 15, are a necessary part of the narrative as a whole because they include the mitigation of the penalty which is characteristic of the crime-punishment narratives of the primeval story. The second part is very different from the first. The first part (apart from 6-7) contains almost exclusively action, the second is predominantly talk; the second part does not give the impression of being abrupt and brief. It is only the second part that contains elements which gave occasion for a collective explanation (arable land and desert — it should be noted in any case that the text does not speak directly of the "desert" — "whoever finds me," sevenfold vengeance).

These differences between the first and second part of the narrative have been pointed out often; but they should not be exaggerated. The narrative has unity and forms a whole. One can only say that the narrator lays special emphasis on the second part (similarly U. Cassuto). Besides, it is to be insisted that what has given occasion for a collective interpretation is contained only in vv. 12-15 (so J. Skinner); vv. 9-12 and 16 contain nothing of this kind. It is only the detailed exegesis that will expound the proper meaning of vv. 13-16. Otherwise the second part corresponds completely with the first; the crime occasions the penalty and it is in accordance with primeval event that the one who imposes the punishment is God himself without any human or institutional intermediary, and that God too conducts the trial and sets a limit to the punishment in response to an objection. But there is one question which cannot be avoided in this first general survey: Why is Cain, who has killed his brother, not to die? What is the meaning of Cain being allowed to live? The answer can only be given in the exegesis.

Commentary

[4:1-2] *Literature:* 4:1-2, V. 1: F. Field, *Origenis Hexaplorum quae supersunt; sive veterum interpretum Graecorum in totum Vetus Testamentum fragmenta. I: Prolegomena. Genesis-Esther* (1875; 1964). I. Goldziher, *Der Mythus bei den Hebräern und seine geschichtliche Entwicklung: Untersuchungen zur Mythologie u. Religionswissenschaft* (1876). J. Halévy, *Recherches bibliques, I* (1895). E. Nestle, "The Septuagint rendering of Gen 4:1," *AJT* 9 (1905) 519. E. Baumann, "ידע und seine Derivate. Eine sprachlichexegetische Studie," *ZAW* 28 (1908) 22-41, 110-143. L.H.K. Bleeker, "Genesis 4:1b," *ThSt(U)* 27 (1909) 289-292. F. Hommel, "Zur semitischen Altertumskunde," *Florilegium de Vogüe* (1909). Th. Nöldeke, *Neue Beiträge zur semitischen Sprachwissenschaft* (1910). K. Budde, "Die Erklärung des Namens Kajin in Gen 4:1," *ZAW* 31 (1911) 147-151. W. Bacher, "Die alten jüdischen Erklärungen zu Gen 4:1b," *ZAW* 32 (1912) 117-119. K. Budde-D. von Doorninck, "Noch einmal zu Gen 4:1," *ZAW* 32 (1912) 120-122. E. König, "Der Evaspruch in Genesis 4:1," *ZAW* 32 (1912) 22-32; "Jahwes Funktion in Genesis 4:1b," *ZAW* 32 (1912) 232-237. C.F. Burney, "Christ as the APXH of Creation," *JThS* 27 (1926) 160-177. J.J. Stamm, "Die akkadische Namengebung," *MVÄG* 44 (1939) 325-353 (also WO 2, 1955, 111-112). H. Otten, "Mythen vom Gotte Kumarbi," *AAB* (1950-1951). M. Black, "The Origin of the Name Metatron," *VT* 1 (1951) 217-219. J. de Savignac, "Note sur le sens du verset VIII 22 des Proverbes," *VT* 4 (1954) 429-432. I. Engnell, "'Knowledge' and 'Life' in the Creation Story," *VT.S* 3, (1955) 103-119. H. Schmid, "Jahwe und die Kulttraditionen von Jerusalem," *ZAW* 67 (1955) 168-197. F. Vattioni, "Il significato della radice qanah," *RivBib* 3 (1955) 220-228. G.R. Driver, *Canaanite Myths and Legends,* OTSt 3 (1956). J. Fichtner, "Die etymologische Ätiologie in den Namengebungen der geschichtlichen Bücher des AT," *VT* 6 (1956) 372-396. Ch. Hauret, "Notes d'exégèse. Genèse 4:1. 'Possedi hominem per Deum'," *RSR* 32 (1958) 358-367. P. Humbert, "Qânâ en hebreu biblique," *Festschr. A. Bertholet* (1950) 259-261. R. Borger, "Genesis IV 1," *VT* 9 (1959) 85-86. F. Vattioni, "A proposito di Genesi 4:1," *RivBib* 7 (1959) 180-181. C.H. Gordon, *Introduction to Old Testament Times* (1959). W.A. Irwin, "Where shall Wisdom be Found?," *JBL* 80 (1961) 133-142. M. Walker, "'Adam' and 'Eve' and 'Adon'," *ZAW* 74 (1962) 66-68.

V. 2: J. Wellhausen, *Reste arabischen Heidentums* (1887; 1961³) 17. C.H. Gordon, "Fratriarchy in the Old Testament," *JBL* 54 (1935) 223-231. H.S. Gehman, "The Hebraic Character of Septuagint Greek," *VT* 1 (1951) 81-90. A. Gelin, "Abel," *D'ThC* I (1951) 5. H.S. Gehman, "Hebraisms of the Old Greek Version of Genesis," *VT* 3 (1953) 141-148. L. Koehler, "Syntactica IV," *VT* 3 (1953) 299-305. C.Rabin, "Etymological Notes," (in Hebr.): Tarb. 33 (1963) 109-117.

[4:1a]   *Beginning of the Genealogy.*

The construction at the beginning shows that there is a new introduction; 4:1 does not continue the preceding narrative; it introduces a new event, a genealogy starting with "the man." The purpose of the word order is to draw special attention to "the man" at the beginning (K.A. Deurloo). Gen 2 and 3 deal with the man; Cain now takes on the role of Adam. The first sentence has three parts, conception, pregnancy, birth. The second sentence describes the naming of the child. Comparing it with the continuation of the genealogy in v. 17, the emphasis is on the woman. The man knows his wife, the wife becomes pregnant, bears the son and names him. The same event is described in 5:3 but in a different way. There Adam begot a son, here the mother has a greater significance. This can reflect an older attitude to the birth of a child. Perhaps too it is a sign of the high estimation in which the mother is held as in 3:20.

ידע often means the sexual act in the Old Testament. The verb does not mean a recognizing or a knowing in the objective sense, recognizing or knowing something, but recognizing as the result of an encounter (so correctly A. Dillmann ad. loc.: "to come to know, to make acquaintance with"; E.A.

Speiser, somewhat different, but similar, "to experience"). This makes the thrust of the meaning of Gen 4:1 intelligible. It shows that the bodily relationship of man and woman is not thought of primarily as physiological, but as personal. It is not the generation of a child that is primarily in mind but rather an event between husband and wife which has its real meaning in community. F. Delitzsch points out that ידע is used in this sense only of humans in the Old Testament, not of animals. K. Budde had maintained that ידע was used in the Old Testament of the first act of co-habitation; but this is not the case and many scholars have rejected the proposal.

קין: Besides Gen 4, where it is clearly a personal name, the name Cain occurs in Num 24:22 (קיני is in parallelism in 24:21) and Judg 4:11 where it is clearly a gentilic name describing the tribe of Kenites. It occurs as a place name in Josh 15:57. The name is not simply univocal in Hebrew: קין occurs in 2 Sam 21:16 meaning a "spear"; but no scholar understands it in this sense in Gen 4. In a number of Semitic languages the same or a similar word means a smith or a worker in metal (O. Procksch: "the name occurs in Nabatean and Sinaitic inscriptions"; cf. KBL, and B. Jacob). According to U. Cassuto (ad. loc.) the meaning of the root קין in Arabic is "to fashion, shape, form," and the noun derived from it describes not only the smith but in general one who works with his hands. He explains in this way both the meaning "spear" (weapon) and the proper name: a creature, literally, "a formed being." Even if this has not enough support to make it certain nevertheless an explanation which sets it in the context of metal working is certain. There occurs in Gen 5:9-14 the name קינן and in Gen 4:22 (twice) תובל קין, to both of which metal working can be traced back. The conclusion from this word study is: 1. The name Cain goes back to a root which has to do with the working of metals (the craft of the smith). 2. Because Hebrew has another word to describe the smith, קין does not mean simply smith. This holds both for the personal and the tribal name. 3. The name occurs in different contexts and forms in the Old Testament, but only in a few places. Its meaning must be determined from the context in each case; it is not possible to give it a meaning that covers all cases. The consequence for Gen 4 is that Cain in 4:2-16 is not the same Cain as in 4:17f., nor is Cain *eo ipso* identical with the Kenites, nor does it *eo ipso* mean a smith. We are dealing with a personal name in 4:2-16 the immediate meaning of which is no longer accessible to us. What is said of this Cain can be derived only from the narrative of 4:2-16.

[4:1b]   The explanation of the name by the mother. The sentence which explains the name Cain is a cry of triumph or praise. The name is a name of praise, like the name שת in 4:25. This triumphant cry at the birth of the child corresponds, in the structure of J's primeval story, to the "jubilant cry of welcome" of the woman by the man in 2:23. This joy of the mother at the birth of the child, expressed in words and often retained in the name of the child, and following the pains of pregnancy and birth, 3:16, is characteristic of the Old Testament and constantly recurs (e.g., Ps 113:9). H. Ewald writes: "The words of the mother after the pains of motherhood explain the name in an outburst of joy: I have created a man (i.e., a male child) . . . it is as the first child also an image of every individual (male particularly) child that it is welcomed by the mother" p. 10; so too E. König p. 32. The explanation of the name presents difficulties. However one should not lose sight of the fact that the meaning of the name-giving as a whole is clear. The creator with his blessing has bestowed on his people the power of fertility; the mother who bore the child responds to the gift with a cry of triumph (similarly K. Fruhstorfer).

The verb קנה occurs rather often (KBL 72 times) with the meaning "acquire," and in a few places with the meaning "create," Gen 14:19, 22; Ex 15:16; Deut 32:6; Ps 78:54; 139:13; Prov 8:22. This latter corresponds to the Ugaritic term to create, *qnj;* this is particularly clear in Gen 14:19, 22 (see P. Humbert, *Festschr. A. Bertholet,* 1950 = OH 1958). G. Driver (*OT Studies,* 1956) explains it as meaning creation through procreation or birth and refers to Gen 4:1 and Prov 8:22 (and this not only in Ugaritic, but also among the Hittites, as Otten has shown). P. Humbert contests the meaning "create" for Gen 4:1 because in all other passages where it means "create," God is the subject. J. de Savignac, VT 4 (1954), opposes Humbert and accepts a common meaning which embraces both "acquire" and "beget/create." R. Vattioni, RevBib 3 (1955) and 7 (1959), like P. Humbert, traces both meanings back to two different roots. He decides in favor of "acquire, buy" and is supported by Ch. Hauret, RSR 32 (1958) and R. Borger VT 9 (1959), who refers to a corresponding personal name in Assryian: *itti-ili-ašāmšu* "I-have-bought-him-from-God." Borger wants to explain the את as equivalent to the Assyrian *itti,* meaning "with." These studies show that it is necessary to distinguish the two meanings, and Borger's study in particular shows that according to the Assyrian parallel the meaning "acquire" is certainly possible. However, it must be said that in Gen 4, following as it does Gen 2-3, the meaning "create" is preferable. U. Cassuto supports this; after a detailed discussion of the Ugaritic parallels he explains: "the first woman, in her joy at giving birth to her first son, boasts of her generative power, which approximates in her estimation to the Divine creative power," p. 201. Likewise K.A. Deurloo, and similarly I. Engnell.

This explanation solves automatically the second difficulty in v. 1b, namely that the word איש cannot mean the newly born child and that it never occurs with the meaning "male child." But this is not the purpose of the mother's cry. Rather she sees in the child she has borne the (future) man; she boasts therefore that she has brought forth a man in a way that corresponds to the creation of the man by the creator. "The very use of the word איש vests Eve's words with the character of the earliest primeval time," K. Fruhstorfer. The last sentence gives a paraphrase of what את יהוה can mean. The third difficulty in the sentence, if not solved, is at least diminished by this. It has long been noted that the phrase את יהוה is difficult because the preposition את meaning "with the help of" is never used elsewhere in this sense; the word used is עם (A. Dillmann, O. Procksch, H. Holzinger, point this out). A number of interpreters have disregarded this and have understood את in the sense of "with the help of." So e.g., F. Delitzsch: "when one uses אֶת as a preposition referring to God's cooperation (he refers to Hannah's vow in 1 Sam 1:11) . . . then one understands Yahweh as the co-subject who brings forth the child. . . ."

The majority of more recent interpreters and most early Jewish interpreters proceed along similar lines (W. Bacher, ZAW 32 [1912]). A. Dillmann decides in favor of the meaning "with the help of" and looks for support in this, that "in the phrase which says that someone assists another, עם (e.g., 26:3; 28:15; 31:3) and את (e.g., 21:20; 26:24; 39:2) are mutually interchangeable." But in the passages to which he refers the word "with" is used always of God assisting man, never the reverse. The fact remains then that את in the sense of "with the help of" is never applied to God. E. König also is of this opinion and holds that it is supported by the ancient translations: "The Targum Onqelos, the LXX (διὰ τοῦ θεοῦ), and the Vg(*per deum*) are correct in interpreting את־ of Gen 4:1 in the sense of mutual help." But this conclusion is questionable. It is to be noted that none of the ancient versions uses the simple equivalent את = with; they must have sensed the difficulty.

Many other solutions have been proposed:

1. את instead of אֶת, K. Marti (1897) and H. Zeydner (1898). This has been taken up again by P.A.H. de Boer (1942), who gives as a reason that the description "man of the sign of Yahweh" is something like a heading which points forward to the climax in v. 15. D. van Doorninck (1912) sees את־יהוה as a gloss, and likewise R. Eisler (1929). De Boer's reason has no substance because the narrative 4:2-16 is independent in its origins of the genealogies vv. 1, (2), 17-24.

2. אִתִּי יהוה: A. Ehrlich (1908) divides the verse into two sentences: "I will win my husband again. Yahweh is with me." This is very like the still more unusual explanation of J. Meinhold (1904): (see below under 5). L.H.K. Bleeker (1909) gives an explanation similar to Ehrlich's; O. Procksch considers it.

3. M. Luther: "Est vir Dei, a Deo promissus et exhibitus"; E. König comments: "Luther interpreted איש את יהוה in the sense of a man bound to God."

4. את־ as the particle indicating the accusative: M. Luther in the last revision of his translation: "I have the man, the LORD. . . ." So too A. Vilmar, J. Döderlein and others. For the proofs and a detailed rejection of Döderlein, see E. König p. 25f. K. Budde (1911) likewise understands את־ as the particle of the accusative and translates: "I have got Yahweh as a man"; to the contrary E. König 27f., A. Ehrenzweig understands it in a mythological sense: ". . . the background to the Hebrew showed Cain as a son of God — like Romulus," p. 3f.

5. מאת יהוה: the Tg° may have understood it in this way: K. Budde (1883), and later J. Meinhold: "the man (Adam) knew his wife, and she bore him a son. Then the wife named the child (man) 'Cain' and said: I have received a man, that is a husband from God. The man has shown himself a husband by begetting a son, and so the strange remark is applied to a husband just as it is to a new born baby."

6. H. Gunkel proposes אתאוה = "whom I wanted for myself." This proposal which he made in the first edition is not retained in the third. L. Dürr and H. Schmidt propose other verbs.

7. O. Procksch understands את as "in the sight of"; but it is only one suggestion among others; he makes no decision.

8. את in the sense of "together with"; P. Riessler (1911): "I gave, like the Lord, life to a man." P. Haupt "as well as," "in the class of." This explanation has been taken up again by O.R. Sellers (1953) p. 55: "I, as well as Yahweh, have produced a man." J. Skinner concludes to the meaning "together with" from a Babylonian parallel: "A strikingly similar phrase in the bilingual Babylonian account of Creation . . . 'Aruru, together with him (Marduk), created (the) seed of mankind'. . . . The exclamation certainly gains significance if we suppose it to have survived from a more mythological phase of tradition, in which Hawwāh was not a mortal wife . . . but a creative deity taking part with the supreme god in the production of man" (ICC, p. 102f.). U. Cassuto understands 4:1b in the same sense: "I have created a man equally with the Lord," p. 198f.

The last explanation accords best with the context. The very nature of the proud and joyful cry "I have created (or brought forth) a man" sets the birth of a son side-by-side with the creation of the race. This meaning would be expressed if כ were used instead of את. A definitive conclusion is not possible. One cannot exclude the possibility that the text is not intact. It is possible that in an earlier form of the text the naming of the woman in 3:20 followed 4:1; this would presume that 3:20, like 4:1, also belonged to the genealogy which is then continued in 4:17ff.

[4:2] One difficulty with the explanation of this verse is that on the one hand it belongs to the genealogy and continues v. 1, while on the other the two sentences which comprise it, though belonging to a genealogy, can also stand as the introduction to a narrative. One cannot do away with this difficulty by trying to fix definite lines of division between genealogy and narrative. One can neither say that the narrative begins with v. 1, nor that it begins with v. 2a (or 2b or even with v. 3). Rather the *exposé* of the narrative is contained in the genealogical information of 4:1-2. The *exposé* tells of the birth of two sons one of whom became a breeder of sheep, the other a tiller of the ground. This overlapping has induced an alteration: the genealogical note told of the birth of one son and his naming; the narrative deals with two brothers, as shown in the unusual formulation of v. 2a "and again she bore. . . ." The continuation of the genealogy in v. 17 knows of only one son, Cain. Abel is not mentioned; he belonged to the narrative, not to the genealogy. The sentence "and again she bore" served only to introduce Cain's brother. The question whether Cain and Abel are to be regarded as twins can be left aside (H. Holzinger, e.g., correctly leaves it undecided).

The name of the second brother, הבל, is not explained. The brother acquires further definition from the fact that here, where he is first mentioned, and on several other occasions, he is described as Cain's brother. This makes it even clearer that it is only Cain who is named in the genealogy; the name הבל belongs to the narrative only. Everything points to this name having been formed in the context and course of the narrative: he is the one who was murdered by his brother and so is called הבל = breath, nothingness (so K.A. Deurloo and others, against KBL). Further, the name does not occur again outside this chapter; it is an appellative rather than a proper name (הבל with this meaning Ps 39:6; 144:4; Job 7:16). The name does not then derive from the Assyrian *ablu [hablu],* Sumerian *ibila* (A. Dillmann), nor is it a variant of יבל v. 20, as H. Ewald and J. Wellhausen hold. If this is correct, then the name has a special significance in the structure of J's primeval story. One of J's basic intentions in Gen 2-3 was to show the person in the polarity between his state as a creature and his limitation. Gen 3 describes one's state as a creature or a human being as "dust"; Gen 4 adds another aspect by using the name הבל. It looks to a person's contingency and nothingness and also to what can happen to those who live together in the human state. Nothing much more is said about Abel in the narrative other than that he was born and murdered. This is expressed in the name and the name is saying something which is essential to the very existence of humanity.

The second part of the second verse, which tells of the occupations of the brothers, also belonged to the *exposé*. We meet here a well-known narrative prologue which occurs very often and opens a whole variety of patterns. It occurs again in the Old Testament at the birth of Jacob and Esau. Both narrative prologues run parallel:

Birth of two sons	4:1, 2a	25:24-26
Naming of both sons		25:15b, 26b
Naming of one son	4:1b	
Occupation of both sons	4:2b	25:27

There is a further parallel in that both are preceded by genealogical information. The narratives which accompany this prologue can be very different, as in this case; the prologue is in itself a relatively independent narrative element. For the most part it introduces a conflict between the occupations, as in a group of Babylonian texts where such conflict is a popular theme; the details have been provided by G. Castellino, VT.S 4 (1957) 116-137, and P.E. Testa, *Il genere letterario della disputa e il racconto di Caino e Abele*, 1966, 157-166. However, one must be cautious in drawing conclusions: Testa wants to fit Gen 4:2-16 into the narrative genre of conflict of occupations and is of the opinion that he can demonstrate this from the structure. But that is not possible because conflict of occupations is not the real thing; it plays a role only at the beginning. The information about the occupations of the brothers in the prologue must be explained from the narrative prologue as such. Gen 25 describes the occupations of Jacob and Esau as occupations which they themselves have chosen; it is explained that the choice is in accordance with the temperament of each brother. Likewise the Babylonian texts alleged by Testa are concerned with the competition between two occupations which are two possible occupations among many. It is different in Gen 4:2-16, and this difference is most important. The occupations of Cain and Abel are those two occupations into which the brothers divide themselves, the two basic occupations of that particular time (so U. Cassuto), which are in fact the basic occupations of an epoch in the story of humankind.

After the birth of the first children the first remark about them concerns their occupations; the purpose of this must be particularly significant. It is saying that the division of labor has its origin in the variety in humankind that is there at the beginning and is described as two brothers living side-by-side. The creator gave the man the commission to work, 2:15; the natural consequence of the multiplication and division of humankind is the division of labor. Human existence in variety demands variety in work and occupation. Existence side-by-side demands work side-by-side. Christian tradition has not taken note of this, that is of the significance of the divine command to work and the necessary division of labor that accompanies it. The history of exegesis shows scarcely any awareness of it (e.g., in W. Schmidt). If work as a mandate of God is to have theological relevance, then part of this relevance is the ordered division of labor by God and the problems which it raises. Karl Marx was the first to recognize that the division of labor stands at the beginning of the history of civilization and is of fundamental importance for the development of humankind, and to describe all the consequences (see F. Stern, *Geschichte und Geschichtsschreibung*, 1956, 149-173).

Literature: Gen 4:3-4a: S.I. Curtiss, *Ursemitische Religion im Volksleben des heutigen Orients: Forschungen und Funde aus Syrien und Palastina*, 1903. E.W. Altvater, "Cain and Abel: Gen 4:3-8," BW 32 (1909) 277-280. G.B. Gray, "Cain's Sacrifice. A New Theory," Exp. 8 (1913) 21, 161-180. "The Sacrifices of Cain and Abel," Exp. 10 (1915) 1-23. A. Lods, "Examen de quelques hypothèses modernes sur les origines du sacrifice," RHPR (1921) 483-485. K.G. Kuhn, Ἀβελ-Κάϊν. A; Die Tradition des Judentums, B. Kain und Abel im NT, ThWNT I (1933) 6-7.   W. Schmidt, *Die Schöpfungsgeschichte der biblischen und der ethnologischen Urzeit*, StZ 134 (1937-1938) 295-305.   H.L. Ginsberg, "The Composition of the Book of Daniel," VT 4 (1954) 246-275.   P. Grelot, "Etudes sur le 'Papyrus Pascal' d'Eléphantine," VT 4 (1954) 349-384.   J. Aistleitner, "Ein Opfertext aus Ugarit (No. 53) mit Exkurs über kosmologische Beziehungen der urgaritischen Mythologie," AOH 5 (1955).   N.H. Snaith, "Sacrifices in the OT," VT 7 (1957) 308-317.   E.F. Sutcliffe, "Simultaneity in Hebrew. A Note on I Kings 1:41," JSSt 3 (1958) 80-81.   R. Rendtorff, *Studien zur Geschichte des Opfers im alten Israel*, WMANT 24, 1967.

[4:3-4a]   The division of labor, i.e., the different directions of the two different occupations, is not really the subject of the narrative; it is rather taken for granted. The conflict does not arise from the difference between the occupations and the narrative does not set them in opposition. The conflict arises from the acceptance and nonacceptance of the offerings of the produce. It is most unlikely that the question of acceptance is based on the difference of occupations so that Cain's offering is rejected because it consists of the produce of the field (some interpreters propose this, e.g., Julian, Weinheimer); it is equally unlikely that Cain murdered Abel because he was a shepherd. This means then that the real critical area of the narrative does not lie in the conflict of occupations, but somewhere else, namely in God's decision in favor of Abel and against Cain manifested in the acceptance and rejection of the offerings. The consequence of the decision is the "darkening" of Cain's countenance which leads to the murder of his brother. The God who took this decision against Cain is also the God who punishes him, vv. 9-16. What is narrated in vv. 3-6 is determinative for the whole narrative. The event is narrated tautly and clearly in three acts: (1) the presentation of the offerings, vv. 3, 4a, begins with a new introductory sentence; (2) then follows God's regard or disregard for the offerings, vv. 4b, 5a, and (3) Cain's reaction to it, v. 5b.

[4:3]   The introduction to the narrative presents a difficulty. It is to be translated: "And it happened after some time." Now such an introduction presumes that something has already happened beforehand. The phrase ויהי מקץ usually indicates a passage of time, and so we read in Gen 8:6 "and it happened after the course of 40 days. . . ."; also 18:3; 41:1; Ex 12:41; Num 13:25; Deut 9:11; 15:1; 31:10; Judg 11:39; 2 Sam 15:7; 1 Kings 2:39; Is 23:15, 17; Jer 34:14; 42:7; or with an indefinite indication of time, 2 Sam 14:28. The sentence ויהי מקץ ימים of Gen 4:3 occurs elsewhere only in 1 Kings 17:7, "it happened after some time." In all places without exception the sentence describes a continuation of the event, never a beginning. At the beginning of v. 3 the sentence indicates clearly how closely genealogy and narrative are related. The narrative of the sacrifice of the two brothers was preceded by some other event before it was linked with the genealogy. We cannot reconstruct it, but we can imagine that the beginning was something like that in 25:24ff. or 37:3ff. Attention has often been drawn to the chiastic ordering of the names.

The Sacrifice: Cain and Abel offer sacrifice from the produce of their work. The verb and the noun which are used here have no specifically cultic meaning or echo: "to bring" (hiph. of בוא) is used of the presentation of offerings (often in Lev.), but just as often in non-cultic contexts; מנחה became a technical word for sacrifice (later mostly for a meal offering) but can be used equally as well in a noncultic context, so e.g., Gen 43:11. According to J.

Pedersen, *Israel . . . III-IV*, p. 330, the word comes from נחה, to lead, to bring, to derive. K.A. Deurloo writes: ''The word מנחה is not used here in its cultic, but in its general sense.'' The words then point to an earlier understanding of sacrifice according to which it was part of daily life and not yet something restricted to the area of cult.

It is a question here of the first fruits of the flock or of the field (so too J. Skinner). This sort of sacrifice is found both among the primitives as well as in the high cultures; it has a very significant place in the primitive cultures. It is the only sacrifice in many places and in others the most important (W. Schmidt, *Ursprung der Gottesidee*, IV, 1933: ''Das Erstlingsopfer,'' 61-77; J. Pedersen, *Israel . . . III-IV*, 300-307; S. Mowinckel, *Religion und Kultus*, 1953, 102-108; H.J. Kraus, *Gottesdienst in Israel*, 1962², 135-140; R. Rendtorff, *Studien zur Geschichte des Opfers im Alten Israel*, 1967, 169-198). Several characteristics which are important for Gen 4 emerge: (a) It is directly connected with obtaining the means of subsistence in all forms (food gathering, fishing, hunting) and so varies a great deal. (b) It is not bound to any place of cult, but occurs where the means of subsistence are obtained. (c) The presentation takes place in very different ways: laying out, throwing down, burning, leaving over. (d) The meaning of the presentation is primarily an act of acknowledgement of the giver of the means of subsistence, secondarily an act of thanksgiving for the gifts and an assurance for the future. (e) With the sacrifice of the first fruits there is the possibility of error; it can be neglected, the gift can be inappropriate, the manner of presentation can be incorrect. G. van der Leeuw writes about this type of sacrifice: ''The sacrifice, in the first place the offering of a gift . . . is to make accessible a blessed source of the gifts . . . the center of the act of sacrifice, the power source, is the gift itself. It must be given, i.e., set in motion . . . the main thing is not that someone or other gets something, but that the stream of life continues to flow.'' (*Phänomenologie*, 1933, pp. 331f.).

There can be no question here in Gen 4 of the institution of sacrifice. The narrative presumes that there cannot be human life in common without sacrifice. B. Jacob (*Komm.* ad. loc.) writes: ''There is no divine institution of sacrifice; it grew and continues to grow out of human labor in which the people themselves create, but the utterly amazing growth and blessing of which they must ascribe to a higher power. They feel themselves under pressure to express this in the offering of sacrifice.'' It is certainly full of meaning when sacrifice is first mentioned in the context of the naming of the two basic occupations, agriculture and cattle breeding.They are both intimately connected. The produce of the field and of the flock is, as presumed here, the produce of blessing. There is a power at work in the produce as it comes to fruition that must be acknowledged and respected as something natural and normal. It is quite unthinkable to accept the produce without some such gift or acknowledgement. The economy in both its forms of agriculture and cattle breeding stands in an indissoluble relationship to sacrifice. There cannot be the one without the other. (This is to be maintained in opposition to Karl Marx in the work mentioned above).

When therefore Gen 4:3-5 gives an account of a sacrifice which the two brothers offer in the context of their occupations, then this has nothing to do with the matter of the sacrifice, but with the meaning and function of this sacrifice in the immediate context of their work (cf. J. Pedersen, Vol II, sacrifice of first fruits, pp. 299-307). Most interpretations presume that these sacrifices were presented on an altar (e.g., J. Meinhold: "Naturally a place of sacrifice and an altar are presumed"). Other questions about the altar are raised (e.g., O. Procksch) and G. von Rad says: "Thus there was more than one altar." But the text does not mention a number of altars or even one altar. It remains an open question how the gifts were presented. It should be remembered what was said about the sacrifice of first fruits in the primitive religions. R. Kittel had already suspected that neither sacrifice by fire nor altar was to be presupposed for Gen 4.

Literature: Gen 4:4b-5: W. Robertson Smith, *Lectures on the Religion of the Semites. First Series: The Fundamental Institutions,* 1894, 1927³, (esp. 178, 307, 462). E. Nestle, "Miscellen 2: Luther über Symmachus zu Gen 4:4," ZAW 26 (1906) 162-163. K. Barth, *Church Dogmatics* II/2: *'Erwählung' Kains und Abels,* (1946²) 376, 391. H.S. Gehman, "Hebraisms of the Old Greek Version of Genesis," VT 3 (1953) 141-148. A. Scheiber, "A Remark on the Legend of the Sacrificial Smoke of Cain and Abel," VigChr 10 (1956) 194-195. A.W. Argyle, "Outward and Inward in Biblical Thought," ET 68 (1957) 196-199. T. Canaan, "Das Blut in den Sitten und im Aberglauben des palästinischen Arabers," ZDPV 79 (1963) 8-23. Ch. Hartlich, "Warum verwirft Gott das Opfer Kains? (Genesis 4:1-6)," EvErz 20 (1968) 190-200. J. Heller, "Die Symbolik des Fettes im AT," VT 20 (1970) 106-108.

[**4:4b-5a**] שׁעה: to gaze, direct one's gaze to, to attend to, occurs 15 times in the Old Testament with God as subject, e.g., Job 7:19; 14:6; Ps 39:14. Throughout the whole history of exegesis these questions are persistently asked, "Why did God have regard for Abel's sacrifice and not for Cain's?" and "How did Cain know this?" These questions start from a false presupposition. We have seen that the sacrifice of the first fruits, which is meant here, is indissolubly linked with work and its produce. If the sacrifice is "regarded" by God, then that tells us something about the produce, likewise if it is not "regarded"; because prosperity is possible only with the balance of receiving and giving. When it is narrated that God regarded the sacrifice of one brother and not of the other, then it is saying that one experienced commendation from God and the other rejection. When such an experience as the brothers had is traced back to a divine action, then this is a sign that it is something immutable. It is fated by God to be so. God's disregard for Cain's sacrifice does not go back to Cain's attitude nor to a sacrifice that was not right nor to an incorrect way of offering the sacrifice. It is saying something about the immutable; it happens so.

Many interpreters understand the text of vv. 3-4 in such a way as if it intended to express a difference in quality between the sacrifices. If Cain's sacrifice were of lesser worth then one could draw conclusions about his attitude. U. Cassuto writes: "While Abel took pains to choose the best from what he had, Cain was indifferent. In other words, Abel endeavored to fulfil his religious obligation perfectly, while Cain on the contrary was satisfied merely to get by." But the text does not say this. It is only with Abel's offering that a futher qualification is given. At the time when the text received its present form the word מנחה was no longer the usual term for animal sacrifice (Old Testament usage shows this). And so an explanation is given in 4a that it was a question of an offering of the first fruits and that the fat portions were offered. The words cited from Cassuto are misleading, especially when he speaks of the "religious obligation." This does not accord with the event described in Gen 4. The presentation of the gift is something which pertains to existence itself. It is just as much a part of self-preservation as the work connected with field or flock. The gift belongs to the personal self-interest of the giver. This has nothing to do with religious obligation; the distinction between a better and worse attitude on the part of the one offering is a modern intrusion. It is also an intrusion when many interpreters speak of election and rejection; this is particularly the case among those of a reformed tradition like W. Vischer, K. Barth CD II/2, p. 340ff., P.A.H. de Boer. In Christian dogmatics, election and rejection refer to salvation and judgment. The regard or non-regard of God in Gen 4 refers to the sacrifice and with it to the advancement or hindrance of the potential of this life.

The other question, "How did Cain know this?" is otiose (some sort of visible sign at the sacrifice has been suggested, e.g., A. Bertholet, the different ways in which the smoke went up). One can say that he knew it because the blessing was absent (so A. Brock-Utne, U. Cassuto and earlier A. Ehrlich); but the experience of God's attention or its absence goes together with the experience of commendation and chastisement. What is meant is the experience of being rejected by God however it may be conceived. Cain experiences this rejection in the presence of his brother whose offering God regards and who is confirmed and commended in his work by God. We see here the basic motif of the narrative of Gen 4:2-16. It speaks of the existence of human beings as brothers (so too K.A. Deurloo), of the life in common of those who have equal rights. There come to the surface here those difficulties that endanger community, when one has more than the other, when one is successful and the other not. Inequality enters where there should be equality. This is what the story is all about.

The point of departure is equality; both have the means of subsistence in the division of labor. Both recognize the giver in their gifts and therefore both are linked with the power which is the source of blessing. Now inequality enters in; it has its origin in the regard of God. Blessing or its absence depends on the regard of God. It is a misunderstanding of the real meaning to look for the reason for the inequality of God's regard. The narrator wants to say that in the last analysis there is something inexplicable in the origin of this inequality. It does not consist in application, in attitude or in any circumstance that one can control. When such inequality between equals arises, it rests on a decision that is beyond human manipulation. The reason why God regards Abel's sacrifice and not Cain's must remain without explanation. And the narrator wants to make clear that this is one of the decisive motifs for conflict wherever there are brothers.

[4:5b] "From v. 5b Abel recedes into the shadows, he says and does nothing more and Cain is the center of the narrative" (K.A. Deurloo). Cain's reaction is an outburst of envy. J with his extraordinary interest in the individual as such continually brings these human phenomena to the fore in the course of the event. In Gen 2-3 it is shame; here it is envy. On both occasions J understands the phenomenon correctly as psychosomatic, taking hold of the whole person and showing itself in bodily transformation. Cain's reaction is twofold: Cain "flew into a passion" (A. Dillmann), he became inflamed. We can speak of "burning envy." His face fell, he became solemn (the "lifting up of the countenance" means, e.g., in Num 6:26, friendly approval, the falling of the countenance means alienation). "Cain in his anger breaks off community relationships; he will no longer look at him" (K.A. Deurloo).

The meaning of Cain's reaction is clear; it does not seem to require any explanation. Nevertheless this sentence, which is a climactic point in the narrative, is generally misunderstood. Typical is a remark of A. Dillmann: "(Cain) shows by means of his countenance that his spirit hitherto had not been in the

297

right direction." Cain then, according to this interpretation, must have been resentful beforehand; the murder of his brother shows how resentful a man he was. But this is to put the event described in the narrative completely out of focus. Cain's reaction is normal and justified; without reason he is disadvantaged and rejected. His outburst and his sullenness are the corresponding reactions. One must be clear that the narrator is not thinking of an individual or in terms of individual ethic but is concerned with human existence in common. It is only thus that one really comes to terms with the conflict which is rooted in the rejection and the reaction to it. When we speak here of "envy" then we must modify our understanding of this word; it once had a positive meaning. The reaction to the rejection and disadvantage gives rise to a power which as such is primarily positive, and at least ethically neutral. The narrator, who is describing a primeval event, wants to point to this power (a similar situation in Gen 37). He points to it as one of the most important conflict-motifs in the history of humanity.

It is not then the always resentful Cain whose anger bursts forth and whose countenance falls; it is the rejected, disadvantaged brother who is concerned with justifying himself. How can this tension be resolved?

Literature: Gen 4:6-7: E. Reuss, *Das Alte Testament, III. Der Pentateuch und Josua,* 1899. H. Duhm, *Die bösen Geister im Alten Testament,* (1904). E. Nestle, "Genesis IV 7," ExpT 19 (1907/1908) 139. A. Schulz, "Genesis 4:7," Kath. 39 (1909) 380-384. P. Riessler, "Das Alte Testament und die babylonische Keilschrift," ThQ 93 (1911) 493-504. C. Caverno, "The Rule in Cain's Case: A Study in Ethics," BSt 72 (1915) 235-245. A. van Hoonacker, "Expository Notes (Gen IV 7; XLIV 5; 1 Sam X 12)," exp. 10 (1915) 452-459. M.E. Canney, "Ḥattā't (Gen 4:7)," ExpT 36 (1924/1925) 525-526. I.W. Slotki, "Genesis IV 7 and a Form of Hebrew Poetry," ExpT 38 (1926/1927) 329-330. T. Canaan, *Dämonenglaube im Lande der Bibel,* 1929, pp. 36-39. H. Kaupel, *Die Dämonen im Alten Testament,* 1930, p. 77. A. Schulz, "Zu Genesis 4:7, 8," ThGl 22 (1930) 502-506. G.E. Closen, "Der 'Dämon Sünde,' ein Deutungsversuch des massoretischen Textes von Gen 4:7," Bib 16 (1935) 431-442. C.F. Jean, "Le Démon de la parte dans un verset de la Genèse," RA 63 (1936) 113-117. F. Salvoni, "Il monito del Signore a Caino (Gen 4:7)," ScC 72 (1941) 23-39. E.A. Mangan, "A Discussion of Genesis 4:7," CBQ 6 (1944) 91-93. N.H. Tur-Sinai (Torczyner), "לפתח חטאת רבץ (Gen 4:7)," Tarb. 16 (1944) 8-10. G.R. Driver, "Cain's Warning (Gen 4:7)," JThS 47 (1946) 157-160. J.O. Smith, "Serpens aut daemonium? (Gen IV 7)," *Miscellanea A. Miller, Stud. Ass* 27 (1951) 94-97. G.R. Castellino, "Les origines de la civilisation selon les Textes Bibliques et les Textes Cunéiformes," VT.S 4 (1957) 116-137. T. Jansma, "Vijf teksten in de Tora met een dubieuze constructie," NTT 12 (1957/1958) 161-179. G.D. Maeso, "Una nueva solución exégetica de Gén 4:7b (glosa á Gén 3:16!)," CTom 84 (1958) 53-58. G.R. Castellino, "Genesis 4:7," VT 10 (1960) 442-445. E.F. Sutcliffe, "The Translation of CDC 5:5-6," VT 11 (1961) 91-94. H.P. Rüger, "Ein neues Genesis-Fragment mit komplizierter babylonischer Punktation aus der Kairo-Geniza," VT 13 (1963) 235-237. G. Vermes, "Haggadah in the Onkelos Targum," JSSt 8 (1963) 159-169. J. Vella, "Il demonio a riposo. Nota al Gen 4:7," RivBib 12 (1964) 187-193. M.C. Doubles, "Toward the Publication of the Extant Texts of the Palestinian Targum(s)," VT 15 (1965) 16-26. R. Bergmeier, "Zur Septuagintaübersetzung von Genesis 3:16," ZAW 79 (1967) 77-79. L. Ramarason, "A propos de Gen 4:7," Bib 49 (1968) 233-237.

[4:6-7] No satisfactory explanation of these two verses has been proposed as yet; however a solution of the problem is not absolutely necessary for an understanding of the narrative as a whole. In v. 6 God puts a question to Cain, and in v. 7 he adds an explanation. The structure of the verses has the effect of a foreign body on the context. One must reckon with the possibility that this piece does not belong to the original. It is notable that the sentences in vv. 6-7 consist for the most part of repetitions, resuming words and phrases from elsewhere: v. 6 repeats 5b, turning the same word into a question. The second part of v. 7 resumes a phrase from 3:16 word for word but gives it a different meaning. All that is original is the first part of v. 7 which seems to consist of two separate sentences which have subsequently joined together. Faced with this situation one can scarcely go beyond conjectures. F. Delitzsch, and many others, sees in the question a "divine warning which tries to bring him to reflection and self-examination." This explanation, despite many others, is still the most probable. But it presumes an understanding of what has preceded which passes a moral condemnation on Cain; the question implies a reproach and does not see that Cain's resentment is justified. This confirms that the question in v. 7 presupposes an explanation of the narrative and of the figure of Cain; the repetition of the phrase from 5b falls in with this.

[**4:7**]   The warning and reproach in v. 6 imply that Cain's conduct is incorrect. V. 7a reads: if you conduct yourself correctly (if you do well), then there is "lifting up" (of the countenance). The sentence is out of shape; as נְשָׂא פָנִים is commonly used in contrast to נָפַל פָּנִים, 5b, and as v. 6 also resumes phrases from 5b, then שְׂאֵת is very probably to be expanded by פָּנִים (so F. Delitzsch, A. Dillmann and others). The meaning is then: all depends on Cain's attitude. He can lift up his face (again) if he does well. The note of warning will therefore make clear to Cain that it depends on him. The warning points to the alternative: "If you do not do well. . . ." One expects here something to balance שְׂאֵת, but it is lacking. Instead there follows a sentence which is incomprehensible: "At the door (lit. towards the door) a crouching one, (the) sin." All explanations or attempts at emendation of the text have failed. It must be admitted that the text is very corrupt (so already A. Dillmann). A particular difficulty is that רֹבֵץ is masculine, while חַטָּאת is feminine.

I propose an explanation which however is no more than a conjecture. Its starting point is the traditional text as it stands. As vv. 6-7 consist for the most part of material which has been resumed, the expression "one crouching at the door" is very striking. It lies completely outside the admonitory or warning style of the two verses. It has the effect of a foreign body too inasmuch as there is no similar expression anywhere in the Old Testament. The suggestion is that this expression is the remains of a text that has been completely displaced by vv. 6 and 7. G. von Rad writes that "one suspects that the meaning of the passage was once quite different." The moral warning which admonishes Cain to do good, 7a, and avoid sin, 7b, is, apart from all other difficulties, unlikely in the old narrative. But a warning to Cain about the consequences of his action would be quite conceivable and significant here between v. 5b and v. 8. It could well have included the words רֹבֵץ לַפֶּתַח. H. Duhm had already referred to רֹבֵץ in this sense in 1904 in his study *Die bösen Geister im Alten Testament,* pp. 8-10. So too H. Kaupel, *Die Dämonen im Alten Testament,* 1930, p. 77: "God's address to Cain in Gen 4:7 is an indication of a belief in doorstep demons." Cf. also G.E. Closen, Bib 16 (1935) 431-442; C.F. Jean, RA 63 (1936) 113-117; N.H. Tur-Sinai, Tarb. 16 (1944) 8-10; B. Hessler, WuW 22 (1959) 38-39 and E.A. Speiser, *Comm.,* all of whom refer to an Assyrian description of a demon *rabiṣum.* It can be taken as probable that רֹבֵץ is connected with the Assyrian *rabiṣum* and describes a demon.

All explanations mentioned take it that Gen 4:7 describes sin as a demon — one that lies in wait at the door. But this is very unlikely, first, because it is difficult to imagine such personification (demonizing) of sin in so early a text and, second, there is nothing like it anywhere in the Old Testament. On the other hand it is possible that in the text which has been overlaid by vv. 6-7, Cain is warned by the ghost of the one who was murdered that it will haunt him. This notion occurs very often and in the context of doorposts which give security against the invasion of the ghost (see the example in J.G. Frazer, *Folklore . . . ,* p. 39). It is understandable that this was eliminated; it is also understandable how it could be used in an adapted form when "sin" was made the subject. By way of conclusion let it be stressed once more that this can be no more than conjecture.

The closing words are taken from 3:16: "Its desire is for you, but you must master it." H. Ewald has already observed correctly that the quotation of the words from 3:16 in 4:7 is artificial and mechanical whereas the trial and the sentence of Gen 4 echo Gen 3 naturally and organically. This mechanical citation which gives the words a quite different meaning in the new context (so e.g., H. Holzinger) is the surest sign that 4:6-7 must be a subsequent addition or modification. It has even been suggested that the sentence is really a gloss to 3:16 which has found its way into the text in the wrong place (D.G. Maeso, CTom 85 (1958) 53-58). But this is not necessary as the sentence accords well with the style of vv. 6-7. With sin crouching at the door, a verb once more borrowed from 3:16 says: "its desire is for you." Perhaps the second verb: "you must master it," is added only because it seems to fit in well with what has already been said: Cain is warned not to let sin become his master. One can also interpret the sentence as a question (the absence of the particle introducing a question would be grammatically possible): "But you, will you be its master?" The sentence would then have echoes of a warning; but there is not a great difference.

The conclusion is that God's address in vv. 6-7 is to be understood as an addition, the purpose of which is to ascribe full responsibility to Cain for what he then does. God has warned him and has shown him how to avoid it. How can one explain this addition from the point of view of tradition history? It probably arose from some sort of theological scandal at the Cain and Abel narrative. Its author was aware of the understanding of the passage proposed here, namely that Cain is regarded positively and is justified in resenting his rejection and deprivation. Taking his stand against this, he explains by means of God's address that Cain alone is guilty and that he went on with his deed against God's warning.

The attempts to explain vv. 6-7 up to 1932 are synthesized by K. Fruhstorfer, *Der ersten Menschen erste Nachkommen (Kapitel 4 der Genesis)* 1932, pp. 31-42. The difficulty is acknowledged by most interpreters, and not a few of them (e.g., J. Skinner) come to the conclusion that no explanation is as yet satisfactory (O. Procksch: "The most difficult verse in Genesis"). The controversy is limited to v. 7, because v. 6 apart from the introduction is merely a repetition of v. 5b. (Cf. Literature to Gen 4:1-16 and 4:6-7.)

אם־תיטיב refers to the sacrifice: "if your offering is a good one," Arnheim, von Kamphausen, K. Budde.

שאת is interpreted as a pardon, H. Holzinger, Targum Onkelos, L. Ramarason, E.F. Sutcliffe, Jerome: Nonne si bene feceris, dimittatur tibi omne delictum tuum (PL 23, 993), or as retribution, or payment according to Vg, or as acceptance of the sacrifice, E.

König, Theodotion: acceptabile erit; or "to bear the rejection suffered," A. Ehrlich, P.A.H. de Boer; or as elevation over the brother, A. Ehrenzweig, O.R. Sellers; or "sin (demon) stands on its legs," J. Vella.

לפתח "doors of the soul," i.e., the countenance," K. Fruhstorfer, A. Schulz, with emendation of text. Adverbial, "clearly perceptible," K. Fruhstorfer; "door of the heart," P. Heinisch; "close at hand," P. Heinisch; door of a sanctuary, R. Eisler; at the parting of the ways, V. Aptowitzer; "out!," R. Eisler; Theiss, following Gk, alters to לנתח, H. Gunkel to תפל; "opportunity," A. Ehrlich.

חטאת is struck out by many, H. Duhm; A. Ehrlich, G. von Rad alter to חטא because of רבץ; some alter it to "serpent," E. Böklen, N. Rhodokanakis; a demon, M.E. Canney.

רבץ: Hummelauer reads רְבַץ (imper.) = be quiet; many as a demon corresponding to the Akk. *rabiṣu,* e.g., H. Duhm, G.E. Closen, E.A. Speiser, U. Cassuto. For A. Ehrenzweig it is the demon at the city gate. Some, A. Ehrlich, G. von Rad, alter it to תרבץ.

ואליך תשוקתו Kraemer: "and his feet (שׁוּק) are raised ready to trample on you"; the suffix refers to Abel, A. Ehrlich, E. Nestle, P.A.H. de Boer, O. Sellers.

ואתה תמשׁל-בו: "over him" refers to Abel, A. Ehrlich, Hummelauer, A. Ehrenzweig, P.A.H. de Boer, O. Sellers, K.A. Deurloo. The sentence is understood as a question by H. Ewald, G.R. Castellino. It is emended by P. Riessler: "You will fall prey to him."

The survey shows that the varied attempts have not led to a solution of the difficulty (so too R. de Vaux). It can be taken as certain, (a) that vv. 6-7 in their present form did not belong to the ancient narrative of Cain and Abel, (b) that in their present form they express a warning of God to Cain, (c) that the text in its present form is not intact. One can conjecture that the corruption of the text goes back to the time when an older text was overlaid. This suggests the conclusion that vv. 6-7 can only be made use of with caution to explain the Cain and Abel narrative, if used at all; they probably belong to a later stage in the transmission of the narrative.

Literature: Gen 4:8: W.H. McClellan, "The Original Text of Gen 4:8a," JBL 56 (1937) XII.   E. Zolli, "Notas filológicas a una serie de versiones biblicas," Sef. 10 (1950) 20; Sef. 20 (1960) 297.   H.S. Gehman, "The Hebraic Character of Septuagint Greek," VT 1 (1951) 81-90.   H.L. Hempel, "Zum Problem der Anfänge der alttestamentlichen Illustration," ZAW 69 (1957) 103-131.   S.E. Loewenstamm-J. Blau, *Thesaurus of the Language of the Bible,* 1957, XXX.   J.R. Diaz, "Dos notas sobre el Targum palestinense. B. El Altercado de Cain y Abel sobre la justification, en el mismo Targum," Sef. 19 (1959) 133-136.   Th. Jacobsen, "An Ancient Mesopotamian Trial for Homicide," AnBib 12 (1959) 130-150.   M. Greenberg, "Some Postulates of Biblical Criminal," *Y. Kaufmann Jubilee,* 1960, 5-28.   S. Zeitlin, "Some Reflections on the Text of the Pentateuch," JQR 51 (1960/1961) 321-331.   A. Ehrman, "What Did Cain Say to Abel?," JQR 53 (1962/1963) 164-167.   T. Canaan, "Der Mord in Sitten und Gebräuchen bei den Arabern Palästinas," ZDPV 80 (1964) 85-98.

[4:8]   According to our explanation the climax of the narrative follows either directly on the reaction of Cain in v. 5b or on the warning of God to Cain about the consequences of carrying out his intent, which has been overlaid by vv. 6 and 7. In any case the deed follows at once and is described abruptly and starkly. One concludes that it was the narrator's purpose to put before his listeners the bare fact of the murder of a brother prescinding completely from any circumstance, drama or emotion. One should note this intention and ask the reason for it.

At the beginning of v. 8 something that Cain said to his brother is introduced, but does not appear. We must reckon here with an omission in the text.

Because of the univocal way in which ויאמר is used it is impossible that אמר can mean: "Cain spoke to his brother Abel," (= conversed with him; so too A. Ehrlich, S.E. Loewenstamm, J. Blau). The old versions have filled in the gap, Sam, Gk, Syr, Vg נלכה השדה = "let us go out to the field." We cannot decide whether the versions found this text before them or filled in the gap. So too S. Zeitlin, JQR 51 (1960/61) 327: "This problem must remain unsolved for lack of evidence." If they filled it out, then they did so in accordance with the meaning of the text (so the majority of interpreters, e.g., F. Delitzsch, A. Dillmann). The abrupt description of the murder of the brother is not disturbed by this sentence which only provides the opportunity for the deed. Modern attempts to amend the texts are not convincing.

וישמר = "he watched out for Abel" (Böttcher, A. Knobel, A. Kuenen, Ol-shausen); an alteration of the meaning of ויאמר to "he made an attack," J. Boehmer; an equation of the meaning with וידבר, S.E. Loewenstamm-J. Blau; "And Cain told this (what preceded) to Abel," Jerome, Tuch; "fixing a place for meeting," U. Cassuto; said in a friendly way, K. Fruhstorfer. A. Ehrenzweig supplies what Cain said to his brother from the Romulus Story. "And Cain despised Abel his brother," A. Ehrman. According to Philo Cain summons his brother to the field of philosophical-theological disputation; Cain began to quarrel or became bitter (from מרה or מרר), H. Gunkel.

But when B. Stade, H. Holzinger and many others explain the words supplied by the ancient versions in such a way that Cain excludes his brother from access to God in the holy place, then they are going beyond the evidence; the offering of the first fruits does not require a holy place. What is meant is simply "outside," where there are no witnesses (so, many interpreters). The deed is reported in two acts: Cain rose up against his brother and killed him. This stylistic device, common in Hebrew, intends to describe the course of an action in two stages. The text is saying here that the "rising up" preceded the deed. In the "rising up" decision flows into act which is presented as conscious and deliberate (K.A. Deurloo). The terrible thing that took place is put before the listeners with sparse brevity as stark fact. There is no appeal to emotion (as perhaps there is in the description of the murder of Jezebel in 2 Kings 9). His intention is merely to state what happened. Man kills man, a brother kills a brother.

And this happens because the reaction of the one against the incomprehensible and unjust disadvantage he has suffered in relation to the other, can lead to the worst, to murder. J wants to say: such is humankind. It is not in any way to be understood in the sense: such is Cain, such is the angry man κατ' ἐξοχήν. When we listen to vv. 6-7 we hear, however reluctantly: Cain who would not heed the warning, is condemned even before the deed. But that is not what is meant. What is so shocking about the whole event is that a man like him, who does his work and presents his offering to God, is capable of this. It is not Cain, but everyone who can become the murderer of one's brother. The fact that the narrative is about Cain, not about Cain and Abel, confirms this interpretation. Abel is completely in the background; he is the victim of murder, and no more. His role is passive; he has nothing to say in the narrative. Only his blood cries out after he is murdered.

It is not really a dispute between the two brothers; that would require a completely different narrative structure. It is a question of preference which belongs to God; that alone arouses the envy that leads to murder. When brothers live side-by-side, equal and with equal rights, then inequality is a possibility. The one is accepted, the other is not. Because this inequality is conditioned by God's regard, then humankind must live with it and also with the possibility of the murder of a brother.

[4:9-16]   The second part of the narrative adds the punishment to the crime. The punishment is a primeval event because, as in Gen 3, God himself conducts directly and face to face the two acts of trial and punishment. This fact alone is sufficient proof that we have here primeval event; it is only in Gen 1-11 in the whole of the Old Testament that God acts directly as judge in this way. This is the basis of the striking parallel to Gen 3. This same procedure takes place only in these two places.

The Trial	4:9-10	3:9-13
The Pronouncement of Punishment (Curse)	11-12	14-19
Mitigation of the Punishment	13-15	21
Expulsion (Alienation)	16	23, 24

The parallelism can be seen moreover in the details; what is essential is that both have the same structure. Much of what holds for the narrative of 3:9-24 holds too for 4:9-16. The subject is a man created by God: he is capable of revolt and crime even as far as murder; but even though a criminal and a murderer he is still God's creature and deserving that his deed be expiated. While the crime is punished it remains a human crime. The criminal is acknowledged to be a human being in the punishment. W. Zimmerli writes: "The dignity of human beings is disclosed in that they are called to answer for what they have done."

W. Schottroff explains that the legal process in 4:9-16 is not a judicial action ruled by procedures; the curse is a means of imposing punishment privately and outside the forum of the court. Yahweh does not play the part of the judge, as most interpreters say, but that of the avenger of blood. To set outside the pale and to reject are to be understood as a special form of blood vengeance. He refers to F. Horst who says that an expiation like this would be regarded as equivalent to death and sees in the rejection of Absalom in 2 Sam 14:13f. the same form of punishment. One would agree with this insofar as the events of Gen 4, as of Gen 3, cannot presuppose a "regular judicial procedure before a court" but correspond rather to the "private punishment of a crime." But when Yahweh takes the part of an avenger of blood, that is, when he appears in the place of the avenger who is not at hand, then he acts not as a member of the clan, but as a court of higher authority. In order to express this, it is justified both here and in Gen 3 to speak of Yahweh's judicial action.

Literature: Gen 4:9-10: L. Morris, "The Biblical Use of the Term 'Blood'," JThS, NS 6 (1955/1956) 77-82. V. Maag, "Erwägungen zur deuteronomischen Kultzentralisation," VT 6 (1956) 10-18. J.E. Steinmueller, "Sacrificial Blood in the Bible," Bib 40 (1959) 556-567. H. Reventlow, "Sein Blut komme über sein Haupt," VT 10 (1960) 311-327. K. Koch, "Der Spruch 'Sein Blut bleibe auf seinem Haupt' und die israelitische Auffassung vom vergossenen Blut," VT 12 (1962) 396-416. H. A. Brongers, "Der Eifer des Herrn Zebaoth," VT 13 (1963) 269-284. J.C.H. Lebram, "Nachbiblische Weisheitstraditionen," VT 15 (1965) 167-237) esp. 187, 199) J.R.

Porter, "The Legal Aspects of the Concept of 'Corporative Personality' in the OT," VT 15 (1965) 361-380.

[4:9-10]   The Trial:

The question addressed to Cain "Where is Abel your brother?" corresponds to the question to Adam: "Where are you?" It serves to indicate participation. "The man" does not exist as a human being on his own; there is one there who questions him. Neither does the brother as brother exist alone. The question, "Where is your brother?" presumes that the brother knows where his brother is; the two are linked together be it in friendship or in enmity. Cain betrays this in his answer, as did Adam, by rejecting gruffly this quite normal familiarity with his brother. The answer "is as it were clothed in a blasphemous joke" (W. Zimmerli). Does the keeper need a keeper? "Am I my brother's keeper?" There is a subtlety in Cain's retort that can only be grasped from the whole context of the J work. Gen 37-50 of the patriarchal history deals with fraternal responsibility. What is said here is: surely a brother should not normally be the keeper of his brothers. However a situation can arise where a brother must be his brother's keeper and where he is responsible for his brother's fate. Gen 37 portrays such a situation.

Cain then is correct in his retort inasmuch as it is not really his job to be looking after his brother constantly. He is incorrect when he obscures the situation where he should have been his brother's keeper. K.A. Deurloo writes: "It is the question about responsibility that Cain rejects." This "disdainful witticism" (H. Gunkel) is joined to a direct lie: "I do not know." Many interpreters draw attention to the intensification of sin in this passage. A. Dillmann for example: ". . . this very different answer . . . shows the terrible progress of the power of sin" (likewise J. Skinner). This passage is used as one of the arguments for the thesis that J wants to describe in his primeval story the gradual intensification of sin, the deepening of the power of sin, and the growth of the curse among fallen humanity — or the like. It is certainly possible that J has this intensification in mind (compare 4:9-10 with 3:9); but it is not certain. In any case these formulations presume the Christian notion of sin which cannot without more ado be imposed on the text of the primeval story.

A. Dillmann says that Cain's answer shows "the terrible progress of the power of sin." This is questionable because the narratives 2-3 and 4:2-16 have grown up independently of each other. The question is what is the meaning of the lie in the narrative while still independent. The explanation is self-evident. When there is a murder there is usually a lie which serves to cover it up. Actually one of the most important settings of the lie as a cover-up for a fact is the context of murder and its consequences. J, who is interested in all that concerns human existence, is showing in Cain's reaction to the question "Where is you brother?" that the deed has brought about an alteration; the murder is followed by the lie which covers up the deed, and so Cain is now a different person even before God.

[4:10] Humanity is changed because of the murder; this is the reality; it is brought face to face with another reality in God's answer in v. 10: "The voice of your brother's blood is crying to me from the ground." This verse is the high point of the narrative. Externally the climax of the course of events is the execution of the murder in v. 8. But the narrator has portrayed the deed so tersely that he has succeeded in shifting the real weight of the action to the sentence: the blood of your brother is crying out. It is this sentence that really gives the narrative its dramatic character. (B. Jacob: ''The speech is highly poetic and prophetic in its feeling.'') God answers by confronting Cain and his cantankerous lie and saying to him face to face: ''What have you done!'' (as in 3:13). This does not evoke a retort from Cain which could pin him down on his lie; instead it expresses the perplexity which the deed must arouse in everyone. This summons says that it is no longer only Cain's deed (for the ''summons'' cf. W. Schottroff, p. 78; and H.J. Boecker, p. 29f.). It is not a deed that can be covered up. Cain wanted to be done with Abel. But he is not to be done with; the life that has been stilled cries out.

This is one of the monumental sentences in the Bible. It needs no explanation and retains its validity through the centuries for each generation. The most important word in the sentence is אֵלַי, ''to me.'' It is no empty sentence that the blood of the victim cries out; there is someone there to whom it cries out. Cain cannot hide his deed. This is but the other side of the situation which he cannot avoid when faced with the question ''What have you done?'' The murderer has no escape when faced with this question because there is someone who hears the victim's blood crying out. These words, valid for the whole history of humankind, protect the person as a creature of God from other people. Murder is and remains a possibility; the possibility of its success (''the perfect murder'') in the sense of eliminating a human being, is thereby definitively excluded.

It is the cry of the blood that overcomes Cain. Something like this is necessary here (other than in Gen 3) because Cain denies the deed. The accusation cries out from the blood, it is like the ''cry of murder'' which is raised when violence is committed and which demands expiation (see passages in B. Jacob). But even if no human ear hears this cry, God hears it. We see here the difference between the historical and the primeval: the same situation as here occurs in 2 Sam 12 and 1 Kings 21 in the murder of Uriah which is concealed and in the judicial murder of Naboth. God intervenes. In the realm of history this can only be done by a mediator. God sends a messenger who faces the king as accuser and who announces the punishment. But in Gen 4:2-16 God intervenes directly, without a mediator; the blood cries to God and God himself confronts the doer. There could not be any clearer way of saying that Gen 4:2-16 is presenting primeval event.

For the plural of blood, דמים, see H. Gunkel, J. Skinner and especially K. Koch, VT 12 (1962) 396-416; ''It is to be noted that דם is constantly in the plural as long as it refers to the blood of another shed violently which is upon the murderer's head.''

Literature: Gen 4:11-12: G. Locher, *Strafe, II, Dogmatisch-ethisch*, EKL III, 1160. G. Förster, *Das mosaische Strafrecht in seiner geschichtlichen Entwicklung*, 1900, 19-30. J. Slaby, ''Sünde und Sündenstrafe sowie deren Nachlass im alten Babylonien-Assyrien, I,'' BZ 3 (1910) 236-247. N. Glueck, ''A Note to Gen 4:11,'' JPOS 12 (1932) 101-102. P. Koschaker, ''Randnotizen zu neuen keilschriftlichen Rechtsurkunden,'' ZA 43 (1936) 206-207. S.H. Blank, ''The Curse, Blasphemy, the Spell, and the Oath,'' HUCA 23 (1950/1951) 73-95. P.P. Saydon, ''The Meaning of the Expression וְעָזוּב עָצוּר,'' VT 2 (1952) 371-374. J. Scharbert, '' 'Fluchen' und 'Segnen' im Alten Testament,'' Bib 39 (1958) 1-26. J.J. Rabinowitz, ''The Susa Tablets, the Bible, and the

Aramaic Papyri, Ib," VT 11 (1961) 56-76.   H.W. Wolff, "Das Kerygma des Jahwisten," EvTh 24 (1964) 73-98.   G. Wallis, "Die Stadt in den Überlieferungen der Genesis," ZAW 78 (1966) 133-148.   N.J. Tromp, *Primitive Conceptions of Death and the Nether World in the Old Testament*, 1969.

[4:11-12]   The Pronouncement of Punishment (Curse).

When one compares this sentence of punishment with that pronounced on the serpent in 3:14-15, one finds that there is an exact correspondence in 4:11a, 12b, while 11b, 12a, have no counterpart. Parallel to 3:14-15, the curse would run: and now, you are cursed from the ground, you shall be a fugitive and wanderer on the earth! The cursing, or the punishment, would be fully expressed in this way. (The ועתה belongs to the framework and is not part of the curse.) The verses 11b and 12a are an explanation or elaboration which on closer examination are seen to be saying something other than the curse. (W. Schottroff too has suggested that vv. 11-12 are not a unity.) These verses are not really a curse or a sentence but are saying something about the consequence of the deed. The same link between the punishment and the consequence of the deed is found in Gen 3. It points to an earlier stage of the story in which the murder had been covered up by the murderer burying the corpse.

The ground then appears as a being which as it were gulps the blood of the victim down its throat. It reacts to the blood by denying the arable soil its "power," i.e., the power of fertility and so its produce. We are here in the realm of magic. The magical element is neutralized in the present context because the event is taken up into God's address and so becomes an elaboration of the sentence of punishment. If one frees it from the context of the sentence and fits it into narrative it becomes obvious that 11b, 12a was an earlier version in which the punishment consisted in the consequence of the deed. The earth's jaws gaped open to swallow the blood of the one murdered by his brother and denied the farmer its produce.

The two versions coalesce in their conclusion: the farmer must abandon the field, he must sink into misery. The composite character of vv. 11-12 explains why the curse here, in contrast to that in Gen 3, is not rhythmic; its rhythm has been lost in the process of compilation. This can be seen yet again when 11a, 12b are read as an independent unit. By acknowledging that 4:11b, 12a comprise an originally independent motif, one can see the main reason for the elaboration. As with the motif of the tree of life in Gen 3, so here J has inserted another account of a murder with its consequences, and by means of the elaboration has underlined the totally human quality of the event described (two stages in the story of the punishment of the murderer have been fitted together). He talks of the crime of fratricide as something that can happen between human beings.

The Curse 11a, 12b:

In Gen 3 neither the man nor the woman are cursed but only the serpent. In Gen 4 however the man, Cain, is cursed. This difference is of utmost importance. A dogmatic presupposition which had constructed "fallen man" out of Adam must necessarily obliterate this difference. The punishment which Cain receives could well be seen as an intensification (e.g., J. Wellhausen "cursed from the arable land into the desert . . . and there he leads the wild life of the nomad. . . ." *Composition*. . . . 8); but this is precisely to miss the deliberate and very significant difference, namely that Adam was not cursed, but Cain was.

I think that the discrepancy here is the main reason why the collective meaning has found such ready entrance. It is not Adam but Cain who is cursed; that is, among those people who live alienated from God and limited by mortality and fallibility there is the exceptional possibility of life under the curse. This is embodied in Cain, the murderer of his brother.

The curse affects the individual. Its effect is to separate or cut off: ארור מן (so too W. Schottroff; the formula with ארור pp. 25, 53, 207). An individual is set apart from the community. W. Speyer in the main part of the article "Fluch," b. Fluch und Verfluchter, RAC, 1164-1165 speaks only of the individual as cursed. There is no case attested where a collective is cursed; this is always a secondary usage. It can only be an individual who is cursed in 4:2-16. The one who is cut off by the curse becomes taboo. "Usages in the ancient languages show how closely the ideas of holiness and curse were originally connected; they designate the one cursed as 'holy', i.e., taboo, handed over to the holy power" (1164). "The accursed and his possessions are bodily unclean, and so taboo . . . anyone who has dealings with the accursed becomes infected and himself accursed" (1165). This makes the sign of Cain comprehensible; so too the punishment that Cain receives and his complaint about its severity. He is expelled from the community of other people.

The same is true of the curse of Shimei against David, 2 Sam 16:7f.: "Begone, begone, you man of blood . . . the Lord has avenged upon you all the blood of the house of Saul . . . you are a man of blood!" One must be cautious then about concluding that expulsion is a lesser or milder punishment than the death penalty. It can be demonstrated that in earlier times it was the punishment for the murder of a member of the clan. K. Koch, VT 12 (1962) 409: "The only exceptions were in the case of the murder of a member of one's own clan which was punished by expulsion beyond the pale: cf. Gen 4." W. Schottroff, following Musil, O. Procksch, J. Scharbert and others, points out "that it is the practice among the Arab Bedouin even to the present day to punish one who sheds the blood of a member of the family by outlawing him." This punishment could be regarded as the equivalent of the death penalty. J. Pedersen, *Israel . . . II,* 451f.: "When Cain was cursed from the cultivated land, it means that all links with him were severed (Gen 4:11); . . . To be cursed is as good as losing one's life (Job 3:3)." This points to the distinction that the Old Testament makes between the curse "which affects the cursed in his own personal life" (W. Schottroff, p. 62), as in Deut 28:16-19, and the curse "which excludes a person from the community and the land" (ibid.); the former is partial, the latter total. One can compare the curse that bans someone with the curse of Ninmah against Enki: "Henceforth thou shalt not dwell in heaven, thou shalt not dwell on earth," in H. Frankfort, *The Intellectual Adventure. . . .* (1946, 1967[6]) p. 164.

Cain's Lament:

"Whoever finds me will slay me," means that Cain inasmuch as he is cursed is "infectious," and so a danger to the community. However he is also taboo in the sense that he is untouchable; he is protected by the curse. The mark indicates that he is cursed and so protects him: "Cain, made taboo by God's mark, is driven from the ground (Gen 4:12)" (RAC, 'Fluch', 1234).

"You shall be a fugitive and a wanderer on the earth": the unusual combination נע ונד occurs only in Gen 4:12, 14 in the Old Testament. We have no proof therefore that it has any fixed setting, though there is nothing against a setting in a curse formula as in the present text.

The verb נוד (28 times) means "to move hither and thither." It can have the meaning "to flee," Jer 4:1, in the qal, and "to drive out" in the hiphil, Ps 36:12.

The verb נוע has almost the same concrete meaning; e.g., to move the lips, 1 Sam 1:13; of the movement of the threshhold, Is 6:4; in the Niphal it means to be shaken, Amos 9:9; the people tremble faced with the theophany, Ex 20:18. The verb is used of the blind and of those looking for help, Ps 107:27; Amos 4:8; 8:12; particularly significant is Lam 4:14, 15: "They wandered, blind, through the streets. . . ." The meaning of the words נע ונד is quite clear in these places — an existence that is hunted and hounded. Both verbs express well the "hither and thither," the displaced wanderer. This is in complete agreement with the way in which the phrase is used in the pronouncement of a curse; the meaning is absolutely clear. The article "Fluch" already cited gives the following parallel: "The Hittites have the curse for the perjurers, 'and the oaths are to hound you unceasingly'."

Neither of the two verbs ever describes the way of life of the nomads. J. Wellhausen was the first to propose that the expression נע ונד referred to the nomad life after it had been hinted at by H. Ewald; B. Stade took it up and since then it has been repeated continually. A few exegetes have rightly sensed that the expression is not at all suited to the nomadic way of life. J. Skinner wrote: "The ordinary Bedouin could not be described as 'fugitives and vagabonds on the earth'." A. Dillmann: "There is no question of banishment to nomadic life or of a curse upon it." More recently too U. Cassuto, B. Jacob, K.A. Deurloo. They refer to the following examples, Ps 109:1-10; Job 15:22, 23; Is 21:14; Amos 9:4; Ps 59:16.

Literature: Gen 4:13-15; E. Schrader, *Studien zur Kritik und Erklärung der biblischen Urgeschichte Gen I-XI,* 1863, 1921². L. Günther, *Die Idee der Wiedervergeltung in der Geschichte und Philosophie des Strafrechts, I,* 1889. H. Schultz, *Alttestamentliche Theologie,* 1896⁵, 542-548. F. Bennewitz, *Die Sünde im AT,* 1907. E. Merz, *Die Blutrache bei den Israeliten,* BWAT 20, 1916. H.C. Vogel, *Kain ging von dem Angesicht des Herrn,* 1930. F. Nötscher, "Zum emphatischen Lamech," VT 3 (1953) 372-380. R. Haase, "Zum Tatbestand der vorsätzlichen Tötung eines Menschen in der hethitischen Rechtssammlung," BibOr 18 (1961) 14-16. W. Preiser, "Vergeltung und Sühne im altisraelitischen Strafrecht," *Festschr. Ed. Schmid* (1961) 7-38. J.G. Williams, "Concerning one of the Apodictic Formulas," VT 14 (1964) 484-489. R. Knierim, "Das erste Gebot," ZAW 77 (1965) 20-39. J.G. Williams, "Addenda to 'Concerning one of the Apodictic formulas' VT 14 (1964) 484-489," VT 15 (1965) 113-115. J.H. Tullock, *Blood Vengeance Among the Israelites in the Light of its Near Eastern Background,* (Diss. Vanderbilt 1966), Diss. Abs. 27 (1966-1967) 821A.

[4:13-15] The sentence is countered by a cry of lament from Cain; he parries the punishment which seems too heavy for him to bear. V. 13 states the counter, v. 14 unfolds it. God's answer in v. 15 mitigates the sentence without altering it substantially; the mitigation is at the same time a confirmation of the punishment. It has been said: the narrative would be complete even if v. 16 followed v. 12. However, vv. 13-15 belong to the original plan of the narrative. Their theme is the mitigation of the punishment threatened; and this is significant for the narrative of crime and punishment in the primeval story. Even so, the passage vv. 13-15 has a certain independence. It develops a motif independent in itself, the mark apparently, that God puts on Cain. But immediately there arises a methodological objection: the passage is concerned not merely with the mark put on Cain. If one takes in the whole context, there is a counter cry of lament from

Cain against the punishment and God's answer to it. What is the meaning and function of this whole? The narrative of Cain contains the cry of the blood of the victim and the lament of the murderer condemned for life. The cry and the lament are part of human existence; they are a defensive reaction to life threatened. Just as in v. 10 the blood of the one murdered does not cry in the void, so too the defensive lament of the murderer is heard. The person as a creature, and no matter what one's situation, remains within earshot of the creator; that is the meaning of the cry and the lament. The mark put on Cain is to be seen in this context: the murderer condemned for life receives the mark, and the mark put on him is in the context of his lament which is heard.

[**4:13**] H. Ewald had already translated the sentence: "My punishment is too great to bear," and this translation has gradually prevailed though some, particularly Catholic exegetes, have continued to stand by Luther's version: "My sin is too great for me to be forgiven." H. Schulz, (*AT-Theologie,* 1896, 543), repeats the prevalent interpretation: "Cain does not lament that the greatness of his sin excludes forgiveness, but that the punishment is harsh. . . ."; so too A. Dillmann. On the other hand A. Eberharter, 1916, set out to prove in his very detailed, but methodologically highly contestable study, that עָוֹן must be understood as "sin, guilt" in Gen 4:13. This interpretation is heard right up to the present, e.g., B. Jacob, U. Cassuto. But the question is not settled when one says, this interpretation is correct, that is wrong. The dispute starts from the false presupposition that we are dealing with one word which has two different and self-contained meanings. A concept of sin is presumed which sees "sin" as an isolated phenomenon. It is characteristic of the Hebrew עָוֹן that it describes an event which can include "sin" and "punishment." The word עָוֹן describes this complexity in which the stress is, according to the context, now on the one aspect, now on the other. When therefore Gen 4:13 is translated: "My punishment is too great . . . ," the meaning "sin" is included, not excluded; so already A. Dillmann. R. Knierim, 1965, p. 193, says of the passage: "The confession of Gen 4:13 — really it is more a cry of lament than a confession — is the consequence of the curse which has been pronounced. . . . What is decisive for Cain's fate is that Yahweh does not take away his *'awon,* but lays the full burden of it upon him." For the notion of "punishment" in this context, cf. K. Koch, VT 12 (1962) 401. It is important for J's theological plan that here, where the word עָוֹן occurs for the first time, it describes a crime which demands punishment. The narrative of Cain is saying that God has to do with the criminal and that the criminal has to do with God: the appeal of the condemned murderer who is weighed down with the burden of his עָוֹן, is to be understood in this way.

[**4:14**] The defense is articulated in a lament. It can be recognized as a real lament in that it contains, even if only by way of hint, all three elements of the lament (God-lament, I-lament, enemy-lament; see my essay, ThB 24, 1964, 266-305). The lament directed to God: "Thou hast driven me this day. . . ." only repeats the judgment expressed in the curse, vv. 11a, 12b, and so is identical with it in meaning. B. Jacob writes: "These first two elements are a highly emotional application of God's own words. What you are saying is: I am utterly banished!" In earlier times to be cursed is often the same as to be banished. "From the face of the ground" must have the same meaning as "cursed from the ground" in v. 11. What is meant in both places is simply the geographical area

where Cain and Abel lived their lives and which at the same time provided the
means for life to be lived, for nourishment, prosperity, security, protection.
Banishment meant the confiscation of the whole basis of life and with it exposure
to such danger of death as to be equivalent to surrender to death or worse (so J.
Pedersen, *Israel . . . II* 545; P. de Boer: "It is a question whether ancient man
saw any distinction at all between banishment and death").

"And from thy face I shall be hidden" (I-lament). This sentence, together with what goes before it, has been understood by B. Stade and those who
follow him to mean that being far from one's own land and culture (= Palestine)
includes being far from the place of the cult of Yahweh; for one sees the face of
Yahweh in the cult. To look for the face of Yahweh is to look for the place of cult
(so already H. Ewald, ad. loc.). This is the note sounded, but it presupposes that
the narrative takes place in the land of Palestine at the time when Israel was
settled there and worshiped as a sedentary people. We saw step-by-step that this
presupposition is misplaced. B. Jacob objects: "The ever present activity of God
is one of the firmest convictions of the Hebrew Bible." What does the sentence
mean then? It is exactly the same idea as in Ps 139:7-12; Amos 9:3-4. To hide
oneself, to cover oneself before God (before his face) refers to the anger of God
(so too U. Cassuto, A. Ehrlich). The burden of Cain's עֲוֹן is certainly not lifted
from him; he remains under it, even though it is lightened. And that means in Old
Testament thinking that his very existence remains exposed to the anger of God.
This is but another way of describing the state of restless anxiety into which Cain
is banished. J.J. Rabinowitz, *The Susa Tablets* . . . , 1961, 56: "The phrase . . .
('and from Thy face shall I be hid') is probably to be interpreted as meaning, 'I
shall be a fugitive and a wanderer in the earth', i.e., 'an outlaw'. . . ." But this
very basic notion is not peculiar to the Old Testament. It accords with the idea,
widespread throughout the world, of the "seeing" God, i.e., of the God who
sees crime and sin even when he remains hidden from man, cf. R. Pettazzoni,
The All-Knowing God, 1956, 1978. Cain laments that he must hide himself from
God who sees, who has intervened as his brother's avenger and whose anger he
must now fear.

The second sentence of the I-lament resumes the second sentence of the
curse, v. 12b, which described the consequences of the ban. It becomes even
clearer in this process that the intention of the passage is the personal fate of
Cain, banished by God, and not the nomadic way of life (cf. Prov 28:17). When
the narrator makes Cain repeat the sentence, he is saying that Cain has no way of
avoiding the fate destined for him. The mitigation, or limitation, of the punishment in v. 15 is not really modifying what was pronounced in vv. 11-12, but
parries the consequences of the life of an outcast which Cain feared. The last
section of v. 14 declares the consequence; it is like the lament about one's
enemies in the Psalms where the complaint that one is powerless and exposed to
one's foes is common. The outcast is without protection; this theme recurs
wherever his fate is described.

The sentence: "Whoever finds me will slay me" has from earliest time
onward given rise to the question which A. Dillmann formulates as follows:
"How can Cain presume that there are executors of vengeance present on
earth?" He synthesizes the various answers: one could think of wild animals, of
"Pre-adamites," of east asiatic peoples independent of Adam, of Adam's al-

ready existing or future descendants. He is inclined to think that the narrative was designed originally for another context. Most supporters of the collective interpretation are of the same opinion. S. Mowinckel has gone to great pains to demonstrate it. B. Stade's comment, that this sentence is completely outside the context of the beginnings of humankind, has been constantly repeated. But such a view does not accord with the character of the narrative. Gen 4:2-16 did not originate as a continuation of Gen 2-3 but as an independent narrative dealing with the primeval event. Even if Cain is described as the son of the first couple (and this information belongs to the genealogy, not the narrative) then the conclusion does not necessarily follow that at that time there could not have been other human beings. One should not apply criteria belonging to historical thought patterns to the presentation of the primeval events. When Cain presumes that there are other people "out there," he is speaking in an utterly unreflective manner. One should not forget that "Adam" is not meant to be an individual in our sense and that the creation of the first human pair does not admit of the mathematical consequences such as we draw. It is of the very nature of the presentation of the primeval event that questions of this kind, where could Cain's avenger have come from, where did Cain get his wife, cannot be put.

[**4:15**] The "No!" (= 'not so': read לא כן), with which God's answer begins, refers only to the consequence that Cain draws from the fate that is his lot, not to the expulsion as such that was imposed by the curse. It is an error therefore to conclude, as do some exegetes, that there is a contradiction between Cain the cursed and Cain the protegé of Yahweh, the one set apart by Yahweh's mark. The statement and the action which form God's reply to Cain's lament protect him from being open game to any assassin; Cain, who from now on is an outcast because of the curse, is protected. God's statement is an ordinance or regulation whose form corresponds exactly to that of the apodictic laws: "If anyone slays Cain, vengeance shall be taken on him sevenfold!" For this form see G. Liedke, Diss. Heidelberg, 1968, 107-167; he gives the following definition on p. 150: "At the beginning of the history of apodictic law there stands the single statement promulgated by the supreme legal authority in a concrete situation. It can be constructed either as a participial or relative sentence. Its function is to draw those limits to which subjects may go or aspire. It fulfils this function by the antecedent clause naming the limit and the subsidiary clause laying down the legal consequence which follows the overstepping or reaching of the limit." (Examples: Gen 26:11; 31:33; 44:9-10; Ex 19:17b. . . .)

What is the significance of this form of speech in this context? It can only mean that here, where Cain is cast out into a world where he is an outlaw, he is protected by a legal ordinance. U. Cassuto writes ad. loc.: "נקם is used here in its juridical sense," not as in v. 24. S. Gevirtz, VT 11 (1961) 154, writes: "'Any man who shall draw near'. Compare . . . Gen 4:15 . . . 'any one who . . . shall be cut off'. . . ."; so too J.G. Williams, VT 14 (1964) 488: ". . . Yahweh's response to Cain in Gen IV 15, which in the context seems to be an extremely emphatic apodictic statement: . . . 'Whoever slays Cain, sevenfold he shall be avenged'. . . ." This legal ordinance is to prevent a person, even a murderer, from becoming a prey for other people. The sentence is meant to forestall blood vengeance; the "sevenfold" is to act as a deterrent. The pronouncement presumes blood vengeance among men where fratricide is possible; but God intervenes and forbids it. Cain, who is his brother's murderer, stands under God's curse; but no human being has the right to step in and execute God's decision.

To prevent anyone from stepping in and carrying out God's sentence on Cain, God "puts" a mark on him. It is stated expressly that this is the meaning of the mark. And so it cannot be a tribal mark (B.Stade) or a general protecting mark or a general mark that indicates that one belongs to Yahweh. It is clearly stated and leaves no ground for misunderstanding that the mark is to protect Cain the cursed and the outcast from being a prey to other people. The mark is linked indissolubly with the legal ordinance whose function is just this. The conclusion is that the mark can only have an individual meaning and not a collective one.

Excursus: *The Mark of Cain.*

Literature: Gen 4:15: A. Jeremias, *Das AT im Lichte des Alten Orients. Handbuch zur biblisch-orientalischen Altertumskude,* 1904, 1930[4]. N. Schlögl, *Die heiligen Schriften des Alten Bundes,* 1922. J.A. Maynard, "The Mark of Cain," AThR 2 (1924) 325-326. T.E. Bird, "And the Lord Set a Mark upon Cain," CleR 8 (1934) 104-112. W. Michaelis, "Zeichen, Siegel, Kreuz. Ein Ausschnitt aus der Bedeutungsgeschichte biblischer Begriffe," ThZ 12 (1956) 505-525 (esp. 506-509). E.A. Speiser, "ṬWṬPT," JQR 48 (1957) 208-217. O. Sauermann, "Bemerkungen zum Kainszeichen Genesis 4:15b," Anton. 33 (1958) 45-56. S. Gevirtz, "West-Semitic Curses and the Problem of the Origins of Hebrew Law," VT 11 (1961) 137-158. P. Middlekoop, "The Significance of the Story of the 'Bloody Husband' (Ex 4:24-26)," SEAJT, 8 (1966/1967) 17-28.

The explanations of the mark of Cain in the history of exegesis can be divided: (a) according to the understanding of the sentence "the Lord put a mark on Cain"; (b) according to the object: is Cain, who receives the mark, meant to signify an individual person or a collectivity? (c) according to the function: a protecting mark or a mark of authentication; (d) according to the form of the mark: what did it consist in? (e) a textual emendation.

To (a) and (e): The sentence can be understood: God gave Cain a sign (mark), i.e., he effected some sort of sign in action. This can mean in turn that Cain received a sign from God (a thunder clap or something similar) which would confirm what had just been said (= a sign of authentication: Ibn Esra in the 12th century, J. von Hummelauer, J. Döller, E. König and others). But it can also mean that God gave the sign every time that Cain's life was threatened so that the attacker was deterred (= a sign of protection: A. Knobel). This explanation is found only rarely today. However it is supported by linking the אות with שׂים. O. Sauermann draws attention to this: "*Sym* is used for a sign (with *ōt* as object) which will only be given or instituted in the future or of a sign that God . . . has instituted. This use of the verb appears almost exclusively in poetic texts. *ʿaśah* on the other hand is used of a sign that is effected in the present. . . . This verb is used almost exclusively in prose passages. Besides, *sym* is never used elsewhere with the dative of the person." The expression is striking and does not occur elsewhere with the same meaning. In the other places where שׂים is linked with אות (Ex 10:2; Pss 74:4; 78:43; 105:21; Is 66:19; Jer 32:20; Ezek 14:8), אות is for the most part an event; in particular the signs God did in Egypt. In Ezek 14:9 a man becomes a sign, and in Ps 74:4 it means military colors; here שׂים has the meaning of to set up. The unusual usage is no reason at all for emending the text (as does O. Sauermann, who wants to alter אות into נואת: a place, in the sense of an asylum). The usual meaning of שׂים is "to put"; it is adapted here to mean "to make," "to fix to"; and this is quite justified (so F. Delitzsch). I suspect that this unusual usage of שׂים is due to the legal ordinance in v. 15a.

(b): The resolution of this alternative is most important. Is the mark meant for a single person or for a group? There can be no question that in the present context a single person is set apart. If one takes as one's starting point that this single person is meant to be the ancestor of a group, then it follows that the mark proper to this group is meant and that the narrative gives an explanation of the origin of the mark. Marks like this, signs, tatoos, which characterize a group, are well known throughout the world. This has been the dominant explanation since B. Stade (it had already found support from Robertson Smith, *The Religion of the Semites,* 1894; J.G. Frazer had taken issue with it). B. Stade wrote: "If Cain is the representative of the tribe of the Kenites . . . then we shall have to recognize in the mark of Cain a mark which was proper to the Kenite nomads and which distinguished them as such," p. 299. "The formulation of vv. 14-15 leaves no room for misunderstanding the meaning of the mark for Cain . . . the mark is a protecting mark." Subsequent scholarship has been able to add nothing of importance to this. The explanation of the mark of Cain as a tribal mark has remained the most generally accepted and clearest; there are no new arguments in favor of it. There are however a series of variants of the collective explanation: the mark is the distinguishing mark of a profession, that of the smith (B.D. Eerdmans, R. Eisler, P.A.H. de Boer; see K.A. Deurloo pp.28-30) or it is the mark of a cast of lesser cult officials (A Brock-Utne, p. 230).

Against the collective meaning of the mark is an argument deriving from the narrative (supported e.g., by K. Fruhstorfer): it is inconceivable that a sign given by Yahweh, which means that one belongs to Yahweh and to his cult, can be based on a narrative which reports fratricide where the murderer receives the mark.

The context favors the individual explanation of the mark. God's answer to Cain's lament consists in a statement and an action both of which have the same goal. It forestalls what Cain had feared in the third sentence of his lament, namely that whoever finds him will kill him. This is prevented by (a) the specification of the punishment, and (b) the mark. The statement and the sign then must be understood in the same way: both mean that Cain remains under the condemnation of God (i.e., under the curse pronounced over him), and that no one may intervene in carrying it out. The mark therefore designates Cain as the one who stands under God's curse and protects him as such, i.e., protects him against the intervention of anyone else.

The next question concerns the function of a mark which is linked with the execution of a punishment. B. Stade points out at the very beginning of his study that there are such marks, p. 250f.; he shows that they are world-wide and that they designate law breakers as such. He rejects the parallel however because he thinks that the mark of Cain is presented as a protecting mark and not as a stigma. This is correct; but it overlooks something — the text does not speak of protection as such, of a general sort of protection by a divinity, but of protection in the context of a cursing.

What could well be a direct parallel is found in Nuzi Tablets. J.J. Rabinowitz sees a connection between the banishment and a sign, VT 11 (1961) 55-59; Nuzi IV 369, 42 speaks of a condemnation: "It means banishment, excommunication." An outline of the fate of the condemned is then given: "The procedure described in *ana ittišū* sounds very much like excommunication and the shaving (of the head) there like a sign of excommunication. There is perhaps an allusion to the sign of excommunication in Cain's sign (Gen 4:15)," p. 59. P. Middlekoop thinks that one of the functions of the mark is to protect the person responsible from the consequences of the murder; he links it with Ex 4:24-26 (SEAJT, 8 [1966-67] 17-28).

It can be said in conclusion: there is no direct parallel which can clearly prove the individual or collective explanation. There are distinguishing marks like this both for individuals and for groups. One comes to a decision by looking at the content and meaning of the narrative as a whole — and the context points clearly to an individual mark.

(c): The question of the function of the mark. Is it a protecting mark of authentication? This question can only be raised on the presupposition of the individual explanation and has come up for discussion only in confrontation with the collective explanation which has held the field. K. Fruhstorfer has collected opinions for and against. The context shows clearly that the mark can only be meant as a protecting mark.

(d): In what form did the mark appear? Imagination has been unbridled here. Bühlau has collected the older opinions, *De signo Cain posito,* 1713, K. Fruhstorfer the more recent. The most common is that it was a tatoo mark or an incision on the face, a different way of arranging the hair, circumcision etc. One may mention as one among many, a Rabbinic suggestion: *Berakhot rabba* 22:12: God gave him a dog as his companion.

I agree with those scholars who refuse to give any answer to this question. This refusal can be justified; we are dealing here with a primeval narrative. This means in the present case that the narrator is dealing with an event that is beyond the present, where things happen differently from the world of time with which we are familiar. He did not mean a mark familiar and demonstrable to his contemporaries; he had no interest at all how this mark was to be presented. It has meaning only in the context which the narrative intends to describe. We must acknowledge that even the narrator himself had no definite idea of the form of the sign.

[**4:16**]   F. Delitzsch understands the first sentence thus: "Cain went away, away from the place of the divine revelation (like Jon 1:3)." This is to misunderstand the nature of the narrative (something similar is found in the very different interpretations of B. Stade and H. Gunkel). Cain cannot go away "from the place of the divine revelation" because in the primeval event there is no divine revelation. There is no indication of any divine revelation in Gen 4:2-16. What is characteristic of the primeval event is that God and a human being speak to each other directly, without any mediation or revelation; this is one of its distinguishing marks. It is significant too that the primeval event gives the reason for our alienation from God which begins there. This happens both in Gen 2-3 and in 4:2-16; at the end of each there is the alienation from God which is significant for the world of today.

But one should not set off against each other the conclusions to which the two passages move and should not say that Gen 4:2-16 takes place outside paradise or that (like J. Wellhausen) in Gen 4 Cain becomes even more alienated from God. It is rather a question of the same motif in two variants. Perhaps the word יצא has a particular meaning here. J.J. Rabinowitz writes: "The Accadian *wasu* (= Hebrew יצא)meaning 'to go out' is used in the technical sense of 'to be banished'. A similar usage of the Hebrew יצא occurs once in the Bible, in Gen 4:16, in the story of Cain and Abel. . . . Cain was banished from the presence of the Lord and he dwelt in the land of Nod (Wandering)," p. 56. The name of the land of Nod where Cain now lives is to be understood from this context. It is not a geographical name; the description "Land of the Restless Life" or "Land of Misery" (A. Dillmann) is much more in accordance with the primeval character of the narrative. It has often been observed that ישב can be understood as "he dwelt on," and so it is not in contradiction with the life to which Cain was condemned.

"East of Eden" is also to be understood in this sense. It is not a piece of geographical information but a reference to life "outside," in a state of alienation from God. It has been understood in this way in the novel *East of Eden* by John Steinbeck, where the motifs of the Cain and Abel narrative become as it were the leitmotif.

The way in which the narrative ends is to be noted. It concludes with a note of stability. It then moves back into the genealogical details out of which it had grown. And so we have a smooth transition to the genealogy that follows.

For this reason some scholars, e.g., J. Wellhausen, consider that v. 16 belongs to what follows.

Excursus: *The Background of Gen 4:2-16 in the History of Religions*

No direct parallel to Gen 4:2-16 has yet been discovered. However, it cannot be said that the motifs do not occur anywhere else. As a matter of fact many attempts have been made to look for an explanation of Gen 4:2-16 from non-Israelite material. However, the question of such a background has always been governed by a particular understanding of the Cain and Abel narrative.

It is quite natural that the collective and individual interpretations each looks to a different background. This is evident from a comparison of the parallels before Wellhausen and Stade with those which have been alleged by Stade and his followers. If one starts with the structure of the narrative as it has come down to us, then one looks for narratives which correspond to the three stages of Gen 4:2-16: the occasion of the conflict between the two brothers, the resolution of the conflict in fratricide, the divine punishment of banishment, and the whole conceived as a primeval event. It would seem that the most widespread parallel was the introduction: an opposition or conflict between two brothers in the primeval period, characterized as primeval for the most part because the two brothers are sons of the first human couple.

H. Ewald (1853-1854) alleged a parallel from the Old Persian in which the narrative of a fratricide is likewise presented as a primeval event. It is an old Persian story of three brothers who go their ways in the world. The youngest, who is favored by his father, arouses the envy of the other two and is eventually murdered by them. H. Lüken (1869[2]) produces on pp. 162-179 a number of narratives and narrative motifs from the ancient world which correspond to those of Gen 4:2-16: "Almost universally where we meet the first woman we find her as the mother of two sons who are unlike each other." Fratricide occurs often in these narratives. Leaving aside the details which recall the Cain and Abel story, there remains a narrative type which tells of two brothers in the primeval period, sons of the first couple, who are opposites or come into conflict which results in fratricide.

H. Lüken also gives two examples from Israel's neighbors. From Egypt there is the story of the two brothers Seth and Osiris; Osiris is murdered by his brother Seth. There is a story in Phoenician mythology of the two brothers of the first man Aeon: Usoos is killed by Hypsuranios. Both are also quoted by H. Gunkel who despite the collective meaning he gives to 4:8 says: "The motif of fratricide is repeated many times in the literature of the world: Osiris and Seth . . . Hypsuranios and Usoos, Romulus and Remus, Eteocles and Polyneices." J. Skinner commenting on v. 8 points out that in Philo of Byblos the institution of animal sacrifice takes place in the context of the conflict of the brothers. Later it is mainly Catholic authors (A. Eberharter, J. Feldmann, A. Sanda, K. Fruhstorfer) who refer to parallels from primitive cultures where the first woman has two sons who are opposed to each other, the result of which is fratricide.

H. Baumann, in the African context, speaks of a widespread and very striking "mythology of fratricide which not infrequently is very like the Cain and Abel story." He reckons with the possibility that it may have been passed on through Hamitic civilization. One narrative from the Dschagga bears striking similarities to Gen 4: "The Dschagga narrate that after the death of the primeval ancestor the first son got two sons. The father gave goats to each of them. Those of the younger son always produced double, those of the elder nothing at all. The father rejected a proposal for an exchange. On one occasion when they were together again with their goats in the field, the elder killed the younger. But the minister of God heard his cry and imposed upon the elder a very heavy penance in expiation of the blood," p. 255. In another narrative the first man had five sons. One of them, Kitwa, murdered one of his brothers out of envy, whereupon the father expelled him as a pariah.

These examples, which could be multiplied considerably, show that in primitive cultures particularly there were many narratives which corresponded to the basic motif of Gen 4:2-16, namely the conflict between the two sons of the primeval couple which leads to murder. This is proof that there is a background which allows us to see Gen 4:2-16 as a particular event in primeval time. It is a question of the basic motif only; one should not build too much on the frequent striking agreement in details.

It is remarkable that the narratives that correspond to this basic motif are centered in the primitive cultures, whereas in the higher cultures of Egypt and Greece they occur only in an adapted form. One can understand better then why one does not find a parallel in Israel's immediate environment. A subordinate or partial motif, highly developed, is found in Mesopotamia: the motif of rivalry linked with the diversification of occupations. S.N. Kramer, *Sumerian Literature and the Bible,* 1959, p. 192, writes: "The rivalry motif in the undoubtedly much abbreviated Cain-Abel episode was a high favorite with the Sumerian writers and poets." G.R. Castellino, VT.S 4 (1957) 133-137, refers to it: "The two brothers Cain and Abel are engaged in two different occupations which have formed the basis of all social life from the neolithic age on. They are the two established ways of life in the south of Babylonia . . . it is quite natural that they are documented . . . especially in the category of "Myths of Organization' . . . e.g., in the Myth of Laḥar and Asnan . . . of 'Enki and the ordering of the world'. . . ."

Th. Jacobsen goes into this dispute between the two (divine brothers) who represent the farmer and the shepherd in *The Intellectual Adventure*. . . , 1967[6], 166 (= *Before Philosophy,* pp. 180f.): the myth is "the wooing of Inanna." The divine farmer Enkimdu and the divine shepherd Dumuzi sued for the hand of the goddess Inanna; she gave her preference to the farmer. All these disputes end with a reconciliation. But the motif of the necessary division of labor between the two brothers has become so dominant here that the older motif of the conflict that leads to fratricide disintegrates. When E. Testa, *Il Genere litterario*. . . , 1966, 157-166, wants to draw an exact structural parallel between these disputes and Gen 4, he is going too far (Introduction, disputation, which can lead to mortal injuries, judgment by a god, reconciliation). Gen 4 lacks what is essential, the disputation (Testa looks for signs of this in 4:8a). It is a question of a subordinate motif only: the different occupations of the two brothers which gives occasion for Cain's hate for Abel. There are echoes of the motif of diversification of occupations which make possible the conflict, but it is not the main motif.

A group of scholars goes into details about the background of the last part of the narrative, the punishment of Cain. The result is a long series of proofs that among many peoples and civilizations of the early period the punishment for homicide — and in many cases for murder too — was not execution but banishment or expulsion or life outside the pale. A. Eberharter gives a number of examples from ethnologists where the homicide is punished by being put outside the pale or ostracized. O. Gruppe, *Kain,* 1921, refers to ordinances from a pre-Greek stage. One who has killed a member of the community is expelled to live with the wild animals. He was an outcast; he became "wolf," and anyone who killed him was exempt from punishment. O. Gruppe adds that Cain is described as "wolf" by J. All three elements of Cain's punishment occur here: (a) banishment as punishment for the homicide, (b) whoever killed him was exempt from punishment, (c) mitigation of the punishment by asylum. In asylum the homicide is under divine aegis and whoever lays hand on him there is punished severely.

The crucial point that the fratricide or murderer of a relative is not to be put to death but expelled has been established by Musil. In *Arabia Petraea III,* 360 he writes of the Arabs: "If anyone kills his own father or brother, he is not to be killed but is to be excluded from the tribal circle and no strange tribe, or even enemy tribe, is to receive him. By his crime he has lost the right to be a member of the human community." J.G. Frazer likewise gives examples of the banishment or expulsion of a murderer (*Folklore in the Old Testament*, pp. 33-45): "The murderer is thought to have poisoned the sources of life. . . . On this view it is intelligible that a homicide should be shunned and banished from the country to which his presence is a continuous menace. He is surrounded by a poisonous atmosphere," p. 34. There are echoes of this in 4:10b-11a. Frazer also gives a number of examples where the earth which has taken in the blood of the murdered one is regarded as contaminated. The mark of Cain too can be explained in this context (see Excursus immediately above).

It can be said in conclusion that the history of religions alone cannot decide the question whether Gen 4:2-16 is to be understood in a collective or an individual sense. There are no clear parallels which support the collective explanation. The background in the history of religions of a narrative about a conflict between two different sons of the primeval couple, a fratricide, the banishment of the murderer and the protection given him from lethal attack, can be recognized in the individual motifs; it favors an individual explanation.

Purpose and Thrust

It is crucial for the explanation of the Cain and Abel narrative whether or not J. Wellhausen's starting point is correct, namely that the opposition in the narrative between desert and arable land is related to Palestine where the Israelites lived their sedentary life. If the desert means the desert that borders on the southern part of Palestine (the word desert does not appear in the text), then the equation of Cain with the Kenites would be convincing, and so the explanation of Wellhausen and Stade.

The narrative is a constituent part of the primeval story whose object is not peoples and their divisions but humankind. Gen 1-3; 6-9 and 11 all deal with humankind. Apart from the context, there are three reasons why Gen 4 also deals with humankind: (1) the structure of the narrative in 4:2-16 is like that of Gen 3; both deal with a crime and its punishment; (2) the difference between Gen 2-3 and 4 is that chs. 2-3 deal with people before God in the community of husband and wife, while ch. 4 deals with the individual before God in brotherly relationship. These passages describe two basic relationships in the human community. (3) The occupations of the two brothers are in accord with this. G.R. Castellino, VT.S 4 (1957) 133, writes: "The two brothers Cain and Abel are engaged in different occupations: from the neolithic age on these have formed the basis of all social life." W. Schmidt says the same from the viewpoint of the ethnologist. Both therefore belong together: the brotherly relationship which includes the possibility of rivalry between the brothers, and the difference of occupation which "formed the basis of all social life."

These three reasons clearly support the primeval-individual explanation which has been proposed and developed in the previous paragraphs. The narrative of Cain and Abel is not merely a modification of a story which was originally a tribal history, as H. Gunkel and others thought, but belonged from the very beginning to that cycle of narratives where it had been set by those servants of tradition from whose hands we have received the first chapters of the Bible. This has a significance which reaches far beyond the explanation of the individual passage 4:2-16. H. Gunkel's statement, "Genesis is a collection of stories" which encapsulated in a thesis, supported with a wealth of detail, what the majority of interpreters had long since been thinking, had led many to regard the texts of Gen 1-11 and 12-50 as similar in many aspects: they were "stories" and agreed very much in character and process of formation. Both of the ruling explanations of Gen 4:2-16 relied on this: the text was explained as "ethnological etiology" or as "cult etiology." But both these types of story are a result of the study of the texts of Gen 12-50; exegetes wanted to explain Gen 4:2-16 by analogy with them.

This way not being accessible, the recovery of the text of Gen 4:2-16 has this to say for the cycle of narratives which comprise the primeval story: (1) the parallel between 4:2-16; and 2-3 can be taken up again. J deliberately attaches one narrative to the other. The narrative of Cain and Abel, explained in this way, not only looks backward to chs. 2-3 but also forward to 11:1-9. Gen 4:2-16 is concerned with the division of humanity into occupations, 11:1-9 looks to the division into peoples. The narrative of Cain and Abel has been set deliberately and for a definite purpose in a context where J deals with human existence before the diversification which determines man's historical existence. This is of decisive importance for the general plan of the Yahwistic work. If the explanation given of 4:2-16 is correct then J's intention is to describe the existence of a human being created by God with both its negative and positive potential; in other words, to describe ultimately what it means to be a created and limited being, i.e., to have one's origin from God. This means that Gen 2-3 has not yet said the last word about what ultimately constitutes created and limited humans; basic to this are the negative and positive aspects of existence together as brothers. "Man" is not just Adam and Eve, but also Cain and Abel.

(2) Now this has profound consequences for the theological meaning of Gen 4:2-16. According to the traditional interpretation the relationship between 4:2-16 and 2-3 consists in a far-reaching agreement in their presentation of an intensification of sin. One need not exclude this utterly; the motif of an intensification of sin may well find echoes as an element arising from the process of composition. But it is not relevant to the real relationship between the passages. "Man" in Gen 2-3 is not just simply the same subject as "man" in 4:2-16. The "man" meant in the latter is the brother. It is "man" who stands in a community relationship which is completely different from that of husband and wife. With the revolt of Cain, with the fratricide, J does not really intend an intensification of the "sin" of Adam and Eve; he is looking to another sin. Gen 2-3 has not yet said enough about it, and has not really been comprehensive about what man is with his positive and negative potential. This aspect of human existence could not be included in Gen 2-3. Gen 4:2-16 supplements Gen 2-3 so as to describe the person as a creature as one stands before God. Society is there only when people are together in community. Gen 4:2-16 shows the two basic social elements: the positive — the division of labor, the negative — the conflicts that spring from rivalry and can lead even to extermination.

(3) It is endemic to the Christian explanation of the "Fall" that it has given practically no significance at all to the social aspect. What was really decisive for one's historical existence took place with the fall. Cain's fratricide therefore meant only an intensification, it had only a quantitative not a qualitative meaning. The explanation of this fact is that the individual sin in Gen 2-3 was severely restricted to sin in the area of sex, while sin in the area of social conduct retreated frighteningly into the background.

318

(4) What does this mean for the exegesis of Gen 4:2-16 in the Christian community where the text is read as a part of the Bible consisting of the Old and New Testaments? The following passages in the New Testament speak of Cain and Abel: Mt 23:35: "That upon you may come all the righteous blood shed on earth, from the innocent Abel to the blood of Zechariah . . . whom you murdered between the sanctuary and the altar." 1 John 3:12: "For this is the message which you have heard from the beginning, that we should love one another, and not be like Cain who was of the evil one and murdered his brother. And why did he murder him? Because his own deeds were evil and his brother's righteous." Heb 11:4: "By faith Abel offered to God a more acceptable sacrifice than Cain, through which he received approval as righteous, God bearing witness by accepting his gifts; he died, but through his faith he is still speaking." Heb 12:24: "(But you have come) . . . and to Jesus, the mediator of the new Covenant, and to the sprinkled blood that speaks more graciously than the blood of Abel." All four passages go back to the same tradition, namely to the Rabbinic interpretation in late Judaism of the Cain and Abel narrative according to which the narrative was set into the theological contrast-scheme of the righteous one and the malefactor. Cf. V. Aptowitzer, *Kain und Abel in der Agada.* . . , 1922). Abel is the just one. Cain therefore can only be the opposite, the evil one, the one who "was of the evil one" and "whose deeds were evil" (1 John 3:12). Because Abel is "the just one" his sacrifice is offered "out of faith." So Abel is admitted to the ranks of the martyrs.

This New Testament interpretation of the narrative of Cain and Abel has been taken up often in the history of the Christian exegesis of Gen 4:2-16. The tradition begins with the fathers of the Church (C.G.T. Armstrong, *Die Genesis in der Alten Kirche. Die drei Kirchenväter,* 1962), passes through the reformers to the exegetes of the present day as, e.g., W. Vischer. Two remarks are in order here. First, more recent exegesis is sure that the New Testament interpretation of Gen 4:2-16 cannot be described as a specifically Christian interpretation; it has been taken over from late Judaism without any alteration. Its presuppositon that fits Cain and Abel into the contrast-pattern of the just one and the malefactor is not derived from the text; the exegesis proposed here has shown that we cannot support it.

In contrast to the traditional explanation, the narrative sounds a quite different note when Cain is not presumed to be the villain, the malefactor "whose works are evil," but is regarded positively right up to the sacrifice. Cain's crime is his decision to do away with his brother and his execution of it. And so Abel is no longer to be described as the just one. As his very name indicates, he is no more than the victim of rivalry in a competition which belongs to human existence as a community of brothers. The Bible at the very beginning includes crime under human existence, and so the possibility of murder. Cain became the outcast, Abel the victim. Before that they were both men like anybody else.

But there is something further to be added: the exegesis of Cain and Abel in late Judaism, as well as in the New Testament passages which have taken it over, understands the two brothers as individual people and the narrative as taking place in the primeval period. Our interpretation and that of the New Testament are at one here. But what does the narrative mean for the Christian who hears it as part of his Bible? One cannot avoid a choice between the interpretation of late Judaism, assumed into the New Testament, and the sense intended in the context of Gen 1-11. The latter is opposed to the individual passages of the New Testament where Gen 4 is quoted, but not to the message of the New Testament as a whole. The work of Christ which was done for humankind was directed as much to the person as a social being as to the person as an individual. As Christians listen to the text of Gen 4:2-16 it is important that they perceive that the tradition of the church has been concerned predominantly or even exclusively with "man" as Adam and Eve, but scarcely ever with "man" as Cain and Abel. It is important too, when they have recognized once more the proper meaning of the text, that they see it in the context of the social accusations of the prophets and, following this same path, in the context of the social aspect of the proclamation of Jesus, thus opening it anew.

The Cainites

Literature

"Genealogies" in Gen 4-5: Lexicons: R.A. Bowman, "Genealogy," II: IDB (1962) 362-365. H. Cazelles, "Généalogie," Cath IV (1948ff.) 1811. F. Prat, "Généalogies," DB (V) III, 163. P. Schmitt, "Frühe Menschheit," Die Urkulturen: *Historia Mundi* (1933ff.) Bd. I: 468-501.

A. Neubauer, *El Tholedoth (I. Mose)*, JA (1869). E. Sellin, *Die biblische Urgeschichte* (1905; 1912²) esp. 22-23. J.R. Fox, "Cain-Abel-Seth," ExpT 18 (1906/1907) 522-524. F. Hommel, "Die babylonischen Planetenlisten," *Assyr. u. arch. Studien* (1909) 170-188. J. Lieblein, *Recherches sur l'histoire et la civilisation de l'ancienne Égypte* (1910). S. Landersdorfer, *Die sumerischen Parallelen zur biblischen Urgeschichte* (1917) 4-6. A. Bertholet, *Kulturgeschichte Israels.* (1919; 1920²). H.H. Gowen, "The Cainite and Sethite Genealogies of Gen 4 and 5," AThR 2 (1924) 326-327. W.F. Albright, "The Babylonian Antediluvian Kings," JAOS 43 (1924) 323-329. Th. Jacobsen, "The Sumerian Kinglist," AsSt 11 (1930) 54-77. H.M. de Villard, *Storia della Nubia cristiana* (1938). A. Poebel, "The Assyrian King List from Khorsabad," JNES 1 (1942) 247-306; 2 (1943) 56-90. D. Buzy, "Le concordisme pré-historique ou la fin du concordisme," *Mélanges É. Podechard* (1945) 17-26. U. Cassuto, "The ten Generations from Adam to Noah," *L Ginsberg Jubilee Vol.* (1945) 381-400. M. Noth, *A History of Pentateuchal Traditions,* (1948, 1966²; Eng. tr. 1972). J.R. Garcia, "Las genealogías genesíacas y la cronologia. Introducción. Se encuadra el problema," EstB 8 (1949) 327-355. C. Jakubiec, "Prehistorija biblijna (Gen 1-11). Jej pochodzenie i rodzaj literacki," CT 21 (1949 & 1950) 259-283, 533-554. J. Renié, *Les origines de l'humanité d'après la Bible. Mythe ou histoire?* (1950). C. Schedl, *Geschichte des AT. I. Urgeschichte und Alter Orient* (1956) 121-123. E. Lussier, "Adam in Genesis 1:1-4:24," CBQ 18 (1956) 137-139. L. Arnaldich, *El origen del mundo y del hombre según la Biblia* (1957). A.I. Arana, "La edad del género humano y las genealogias del Gén. (4s.)," Lum. 8 (1957) 193-216. F. Jacoby, *Die Fragmente der griechischen Historiker,* III, C 1, Cap. V (1958). J. Gabriel, "Die Kainitengenealogie Gen 4:17-24," Bib 40 (1959) 409-427. A. Pohl, "Babylonische Urkönige und biblische Erzväter," StZ 85 (1959/1960) 412-422. M.B. Rowton, "The Date of the Sumerian Kinglist," JNES 19 (1960) 156-162. D.N. Freedman, "The Chronology of Israel," *The Bible and the Ancient Near East, Essay in Honor of W.F. Albright* (1961) 206-207. J.J.A. von Dijk, "Die Inschriftenfunde. II Die Tontafeln aus dem res-Heiligtum," UVB 18 (1962) 43-61. H. Haag, "Die biblischen Wurzeln des Minjan," *Festschr. O. Michel* (1963) 235-241. L. Ramlot, "Les généalogies bibliques," BVCr 60 (1964) 53-70. F. Festorazzi, *La Bibbia e il problema della origine* (1966). H.A. Brongers, "Die Zehnzahl in der Bibel und in ihrer Umwelt," *Studia Biblica et Semitica, Festschr. Th.C. Vriezen* (1966) 30-45. A. Malamat, "King Lists of the Old Babylonian Period and Biblical Genealogics," JAOS 88 (1968) 163-173. W. Röllig, "Zur Typologie und Entstehung der babylonischen und assyrischen Königslisten,'' *Festschr. W. von Soden, Alter Orient und AT 1* (1969) 265-277. M. D. Johnson, *The Purpose of the Biblical Genealogies with Special Reference to the Setting of the Genealogies of Jesus* (1969).

Text

4:17 And Cain knew his wife, and she became pregnant and bore Enoch, who became the builder of a city, and he called it Enoch, after his own name[a].

18 To Enoch was born[a] Irad, And Irad begot Mehujael, and Mehijael[b] begot Methushael, and Methushael begot Lamech.

19 Lamech took two wives. The name of the one[a] was Ada, the name of the other Zillah[b].

20 Ada bore Jabal, who became the father of those who live in tents[a] and with cattle[b].

21 The name of his brother was Jubal, who became the father of all those who play the zither and flute.

22 But Zillah too bore, Tubal-cain, (the father)[a] of all those who forge bronze and iron, and the sister of Tubal-cain was called Naamah.

23 And Lamech said to his wives: Ada and Zillah, hear[a] my voice, Wives of Lamech, listen to my word! A man I killed because of my wound, a boy because of my weal.

24 If Cain is avenged[a] seven times, then Lamech seventy-seven times[bc]!

25 And Adam knew his wife again, and she[a] bore a son and called him Seth[b], because God has set[c] for me another seed, in place of Abel, because[d] Cain killed him.

26 And to Seth too[a] a son was born, and he called him Enosh. It was then that men began[b] to call on[c] the name of Yahweh.

17a כשמו is to be read instead of כשם בנו; the justification of this is given in the comm.
18a ''Verbs which in the active take *one* accusative . . . may in the passive . . . be construed *personally,* the object of the active sentence now becoming the subject. . . .'' Ges-K §121ab; BrSynt §35d; cf. P.P. Saydon ''Meaning and Use of the Particle את,'' VT 14 (1964) 192-210. For the difference between ילד and הולוד, cf. U. Cassuto, *The Documentary Hypothesis,* 45-47. **b** מחייאל: the י is not to be changed to ו as in KBH; two variants are preserved in the text.
19a For אחד, BrSynt §21. **b** For the construction, cf. L. Köhler, VT 3 (1953) 299-305.
20a The verbs of ''dwelling'' are used transitively, Ges-K §117bb. Instead of Jabal Gk reads Ἰωβελ, Tgᴶ adds כל; neither is necessary. **b** The syntax of the last word is uncertain.
22a The text of the second part is disturbed; add אב before לטש; see comm.
23a On שמען, Ges-K §46f.
24a יקם Ges-K §29g. **b** For the number, Ges-K §134r. **c** For the abbreviated main sentence, Ges-K §159dd.
25a The Sam reads the masc., probably by analogy with 26a. **b** At the end of 25a Gk and Vg add לאמר. **c** ''In exceptions such as שת-לי Gn 4:25 (where šāt is required by the character of the form, although the closed syllable has lost the tone swing to the following Maqqeph), Metheg is used to guard against a wrong pronunciation. . . .'' Ges-K §26o, n.; B. Jacob, Comm. ad. loc.; J. Hoftijzer, VT 13 (1963) 337-339: ''The root sjt, constructed with ל *commodi,* has almost the meaning of 'give' 'procure'. . . .'' **d** כי, Ges-K §157b.
26a גם-הוא (not גם-לי) according to Ges-K §121g. **b** ''The perfect is used after אז

when stress is to be laid on the fact that the action has really taken place. . . .'' Ges-K §107c. The indefinite personal subject is expressed by the passive, Ges-K §144k. **c** "The LXX renders by οὗτος ἤλπισεν ἐπικαλεῖσθαι . . . as if the text read הוחיל זה, and the Targums understand the hoph. in the opposite sense of *profanari,* so giving an account of the beginning of idolatry," F. Delitzsch. "The older Jewish interpretation understands the passage as a description of the beginning of worship," B. Jacob, also A. Ehrlich.

Literature: Gen 4:17-26: W. Lotz, *Die Biblische Urgeschichte in Ihrem Verhältnis zu den Urzeitsagen anderer Völker, zu den israelitischen Volkserzählungen und zum Ganzen der Heiligen Schrift* (1897). M.J. Lagrange, *Études sur les religions Sémitiques* (1905²). G. Hoberg, *Die Genesis nach dem Literalsinn erklärt,* I-II (1908²). H. Guthe, 'Kain', RE XXIII³ (1913) 720. A Deimel, "Der Verfasser von Genesis 4:17-24 und die moderne Pentateuchkritik," Bib 3 (1922) 438-440. H. Obermaier, *Urgeschichte der Menschheit* (1931). A. Bea, *Institutiones Biblicae. II, 1 De Pentateucho* (1933²). J.A. Montgomery, *Arabia and the Bible* (1934). A. Bea, "Praehistoria et Exegesis libri Genesis. III. De exegesi Gen 4-11," VD 18 (1938) 14-20. B. Bonkamp, *Die Bibel im Lichte der Keilschriftforschung* (1939). Th. Jacobsen, "Sumerian Mythology: A Review Article," JNES 6 (1946) 128-152. J.M. Vosté, "Lettre de la Commission Biblique," Ang. 25 (1948). J. Schildenberger, *Vom Geheimnis des Gotteswortes* (1950) esp. 264-277. O. Eissfeldt, "Taautos und Sanchunjaton," SAB 1 (1952). A. Richardson, *Genesis I-XI.* Chap. IV. Canaanite Civilization, 4:17-24; J (1953; 1964²). G.R. Castellino, "Les origines de la civilisation selon les Textes Bibliques et les Textes Cunéiformes," VT.S 4 (1957) 133-137. Ch. Hauret, "Réflexions pessimistes et optimistes sur Gen IV:17-24," BEThL 22-23 (1959) 358-365. Th. Schwegler, *Die biblische Urgeschichte,* C. 3, (1960; 1962²) 129-150. R. North, "The Cain Music," JBL 83 (1964) 373-389. J.P. Audet, "La revanche de Prométhée ou le drame de la religion et de la culture," RB 73 (1966) 5-29.

Literary Form

Gen 4:1, 17-26 is to be interpreted in the context of the genealogies. A distinction was made in the Introduction between genealogies that arose from the community structure of the tribe and had their setting in the life of the tribe, and genealogies that present primeval events in the form of a succession of generations. The first difference is that the tribal genealogy deals only with a part; it is concerned with the pre-history of a group within other groups. The primeval genealogies on the other hand are concerned with the common origins of humanity and it is characteristic of them that the separation of humankind into peoples and tribes occurs only at the end. The tribal genealogy presupposes that this separation has already taken place. One can easily recognize the primeval trait in the genealogy of 4:1, 17-26; it deals with the founders of some important forms of human civilization.

The family tree in v. 25 begins again with Adam and presents a new genealogical line of Adam-Seth-Enosh. This demonstrates that vv. 25-26 are a separate genealogy, independent of 4:1, 17-24, and have been joined to the latter by the secondary addition of "again" in v. 25. However, the two genealogies 4:1, 17-24 and 4:25-26 each have an independent origin and are to be understood independently of each other.

The family tree 4:1, 17-24 has two distinct branches. 4:1, 17-18 is the direct line, 4:19-24 is the collateral line. A genealogy of course can present the mere succession of generations; but in such a case it restricts itself to only one line, as in Gen 5. It can also put its main emphasis on the collateral line, mentioning the different sons (and daughters) of one father, as in Gen 10. Both types are united in Gen 4:1, 17-24. If the genealogy can be described as a type of presentation of history in pre-historical form, then these two different sorts of genealogies foreshadow two basic procedures of all historical presentation: the presentation of an event in the direct and the collateral line whereby each has its point of departure in the context of the one event. Origin from the father in the present case becomes historical causality in the writing of history. Both are combined in the ramification of one line into three sons at the end of a genealogy.

The first part of the genealogy extends over seven generations: Adam-Cain-Enoch-Irad-Mehujael-Methushael-Lamech. The number 7 obviously describes a totality; these 7 designate the generations of the primeval period. There are only two elaborations: the explanation of the name of the first man born of a woman 4:1 (perhaps one might add, and quite appropriately, the naming of the first woman as "mother of all living," 3:20), and the building of the first city in 4:17b, i.e., the beginning of urban civilization. Both precisions are essential for the generations of the primeval period: the power of reproduction and the founding of a city, so determinative for the life of humankind together.

The second part of the genealogy, vv. 19-24, extends over one generation only, that of Lamech, where the succession of generations terminates, vv. 1, 17, 18: his two wives Ada and Zillah v. 19, the two sons of Ada, Jabal and Jubal, the son and daughter of Zillah, Tubal-cain and Naamah. The elaborations are obvious here. They all describe, by means of the sons of Lamech, the foundation of different ways of life: Jabal — the father of the nomads, and of different areas of civilization; Jubal — music; Tubal-cain — the forging of metals. A very different elaboration of the genealogy is the song of Lamech vv. 23-24, which clearly closes the section begun in v. 19.

When the elaborations in the genealogies are drawn together they make a rather striking impression. It is different however if we can assume that v. 2, which now serves as the exposé of the narrative in vv. 2-16, was also part of the genealogy, though in a somewhat different form. If Cain's occupation as well as his name was part of the genealogy, then we have a rational arrangement of the elaborations. The first part, 4:1 (2), 17, 18, described primeval civilization using the occupation of the farmer and the foundation of a city. The second part, vv. 19-24, put the life of the nomad side-by-side with this, v. 20, and related to it the primeval arts and the work of the smith, v. 22. The result is a rational whole. It is being said that the two forms of life, those of the farmer and the nomad, basic to human history, had their origin in the primeval generations. The foundation of a city is part of the sedentary life of the farmer, the arts and crafts of instrumental music and metallurgy are part of the life of the nomad. The genealogy reflects a view of the history of civilization in which the life of the farmer with its sedentary existence, given expression in the building of a city, takes precedence over the life of the nomad. On the other hand esteem is shown for the nomadic way of life by linking it with the arts of instrumental music and the craft of the smith.

It is only with the exegesis that the meaning of the song of Lamech as a conclusion of this genealogy can be explained.

Many interpreters describe 4:17-26 as "story." This goes back to H. Gunkel who used this passage to develop his theory that the family trees arose from defunct stories: "We have not here stories complete in themselves, but the final echo of stories." He refers to J. Wellhausen: "Collectors . . . include such family trees to bridge the time gaps. . . ." I have shown in the Introduction that this thesis is not tenable. The family tree or the genealogy is rather an independent genre whose specific function and history can be proved. A family tree is never used in the ancient texts merely to bridge a time gap. Its function is rather to present history, but in the manner of a succession of generations characteristic of the period before history. Once again there are different ways of doing this. The mere succession of generations, each with a definite name affixed, can describe the history of a family or of the larger community to which this family has given rise. At the same time the succession of families can be linked with particular works or accomplishments on the part of those named. In this case it is more a question of the history of the thing that is the object of these works or accomplishments; in 4:17-26 it is the history of cultural achievements. This shows an awareness of the development or of the history of civilization that goes far beyond the origin of individual aspects or achievements.

The additions which link genealogy and development are already manifest in the Sumerian texts. There are some very close points of contact with 4:17-22 in the newly discovered lists of the 7 *apkallu,* the "7 wise ones," (E. Reiner, "The Etiological Myth of the 'Seven Sages'," OrNS 30 [1961] 1-11). The *apkallu* teach humankind the pursuits of civilization, not in individual narratives, but by presenting the 7 wise ones one after the other. According to J. van Dijk, this could be intended as a genealogy (UVB 18 [1962] 43-61). There are points of contact even in details; van Dijk says of one of these *apkallu:* "Nungalpiriggal is apparently the inventor of the lyre (or harp) in this passage" p. 49.

The strongly-developed historical sense of the Israelites seized on this addition and fashioned the seminal notion of a history of civilization. It is to be noted that this family tree reflects a knowledge of the very great age of the inventions and discoveries that are the basis of civilization. However, there was no attempt to make Israel itself or its ancestors sharers in this history. The author of this passage makes it clear that the basic achievements of civilization belong to the primeval period and that in this area Israel is an heir to the common patrimony of humankind, as is expressed clearly in Deut 6:10-12.

Earlier it had often been maintained (e.g., by K. Budde, J. Wellhausen, J. Dillmann) that the author of 4:17-24 could not have known the flood because it would be meaningless to speak of the origin of civilization before it. A. Deimel has answered this well: "All these (Babylonian) texts lead . . . to the conclusion that the Babylonians traced all culture and civilization to the primeval period before the flood. They did not therefore regard the great flood as a break in the "continuity of human history" (Dillmann) although all humankind perished in it with the exception of Ziusudra and his family. One can allow to the author of the first chapters of Genesis . . . a view that was current among the Babylonians" p. 440. One can give a reason why this is so in both cases: the primeval narratives were independent in an earlier stage. The narratives of the great flood and of the origins of civilization existed side-by-side without impinging upon each other. The difficulty only arose when the primeval events were brought into a chronological sequence. But that is by and large only a secondary stage of the tradition. This holds too for the king lists where the flood becomes a dividing line and kings are classified as those before and those after the flood (this is by analogy with a later method of dating according to remarkable natural phenomena, e.g., "after the earthquake").

Setting in Life

1. The question of the setting of this passage should begin from the final stage of the text, the work of J. Gen 4:17-26 follows the Cain and Abel narrative in J's primeval story. It is followed by the narrative of the flood to which the "marriage of the angels," 6:1-4, is prefixed. J, by means of this framework, gives Gen 4:17-26 a significance which points in two directions — backward to the creation of humankind and forward to the flood narrative. It is the first that plays the dominant role. In the structure of the primeval story the passage serves to present the growth of a human being created by God, together with the growth and ramifications of civilization stemming from the duty laid upon that person, 2:15. The story of civilization is in J's understanding of history a necessary part of the story of humankind, formerly set in the divine commission and ennobled by the fact that it is a human being, God's creature, who leads the way along the path of progress, invention and discovery. By pointing to the primeval origin of human achievements in civilization, J makes clear — and this is important for him — that Israel here is but an heir, a receiver. J points in the other direction by putting the song of Lamech immediately after the beginnings of civilization and by having it echo the Cain and Abel narrative. It is precisely human achievements and the realization of human potential that hide the danger of an ever-growing consciousness of power and its effects. And so the text looks forward to Gen 6-8.

2. Many different ancient traditions are worked together in J's text: vv. 1, 17-18; 19-22; 23-24; 25-26. Vv. 23-24 belong to a cycle of secular songs from oral traditions; they are often found in story books. More accurately it is a "braggart song" used to frighten off enemies. There are no means of discovering its precise origin. The other three passages are genealogies of different kinds and origins. More precision will be given in the exegesis.

Literature: Gen 4:17: B. Gray, *Studies in Hebrew Proper Names* (1896). H. Kesteven, "Who was Cain's Wife?" NCent (1903) 330-336. R. Smend, *Die Erzählung des Hexateuch. Auf ihre Quellen untersucht* (1912). M. Weber, *Gesammelte Aufsätze zur Religionssoziologie. III. Das antike Judentum* (1923). A.S. Yahuda, *Die Sprache des Pentateuch in ihren Beziehungen zum Aegyptischen.* "I, 2 Sumerisch-akkadische Reminiszenzen als zeitbegrenzende Merkmale," (1929) 278-279. A. Duhm, "Kains Weib," ZEvRU 44 (1933) 219-224. H. Ranke, *Die ägyptischen Personennamen. I* (1935) 398 No. 25. J.J.A. von Dijk, *La sagesse Suméro-accadienne. Recherches sur les genres littéraires de textes sapientiaux avec choix de textes* (1953) 31-81. O. Eissfeldt, "Recht und Grenze archäologischer Betrachtung des AT," OLZ 49 (1954) 101-108. J. Fichtner, "Die etymologische Ätiologie in den Namengebungen der geschichtlichen Bücher des AT," VT 6 (1956) 372-396. Th.C. Vriezen, *Jahwe en zijn Stad* (1962). M.C. Astour, "Sabtah and Sabteca. Ethiopian Pharaoh Names in Genesis 10," JBL 84 (1965) 422-425.

Commentary

[4:17] The verse is in every way typical of a genealogy. The first part reports the birth of Enoch in the three acts characteristic of the genealogy: conception, pregnancy, birth. It would be possible to continue the verse with: "And he called his son Enoch," or something similar. Instead the two sentences are combined into one: "And she bore Enoch." If one imagines the first part of the verse to be expanded by the sentence "And he called his son Enoch," then the subsequent ויהי could only have Enoch as subject because קין would be too far away to fulfil this function. But even without this addition it is natural to refer the section "And he became the builder of a city'' to Enoch. It is only with the words כשם בנו at the end of the sentence that the reader becomes aware that the MT intended Cain as the builder. K. Budde refers to vv. 21 and 22: "The sentence stands immediately after the birth of the son and on each occasion the son is the subject." He adds: "Further, when the birth of the son is announced, it is not the practice to say anything more about the father, but about the son and what he has done." "Finally it is quite remarkable that Cain names the city after his son." (So too H. Holzinger.)

The reasons advanced by Budde receive strong support from the fact that the language of the genealogies, including the succession of the sentences, follows a fixed pattern. There is also a form critical consideration: when the genealogy 4:1, (2), 127-24, before being linked with the Cain and Abel narrative, says that Cain was a farmer, then it is scarcely possible to say that he was at the same time the builder of a city, v. 17 (so too J. Skinner). It is characteristic of a genealogy that describes the development of civilization to trace the path from agriculture to city life. This can only be done by a succession of births presented in such a way that the builder of the city must emerge as one of Cain's posterity. Budde's supposition that the text of v. 17 read originally כשמו instead of כשם בנו becomes very probable. Many exegetes have accepted it. However, as far as I know, no attempt has been made to explain the present text. If, as has been shown, the first part of the sentence could have read: ". . . and she bore a son and he called his son Enoch," then the שם בנו in the second part could be a fragment left over from the first. Even if this is no more than a suggestion, we can be certain that the founding of the first city was ascribed originally to Enoch.

There are a number of different explanations of the name חנך: L. Köhler, *Lexikon,* while referring to the Caan. *ḥanaku* = vassal, retainer, holds that a derivation from the verb חנך = *dedicate,* is also possible. F. Delitzsch, B. Jacob, U. Cassuto and others also make the connection. F. Schwally moreover (*Der heilige Krieg im alten Israel,* 1901, 91, in L. Köhler, *Lexikon*) refers to the Egyptian *ḥnk.t* = *offering* on the occasion of the laying of a foundation stone; this suggests that the name Enoch be explained from the verb חנך = *to dedicate.* The derivation of the name is important insofar as the agreement of the personal and the place name is an ad hoc formation. Cain's son like the city named after him would mean something like "founder" or "foundation." It would be the name neither of a specific person nor place, and no city of that name is to be traced anywhere on the map. This derivation then can only be a conjecture because the name חנך occurs as a personal name not only in the parallel genealogy 5:18, 19, 21, 24, but also as that of the firstborn of Ruben Gen 46:9; Ex 6:14; Num 26:5; 1 Chron 5:3; and as a son of Midian Gen 25:4; 1 Chron 1:33. In all these cases חנך is the name of a definite person.

The founding of the first city is reported in the genealogy 4:1, 17-24 as the first achievement of civilization. When this is ascribed to the son of Cain, it can only mean in the context that the founding of the city is considered part of sedentary civilization, the basis of which was agriculture (Cain, the farmer). The passage shows that Israel preserved the memory that the building of cities was something that happened prior to and outside its own history. The foundation of the first city is part of the primeval story, and neither Israel nor its ancestors had any part in it. Israel only advanced to urban civilization with the acquisition of the land and Israel was urged expressly to remember that it is but an heir. The cities are the gift of the God who saved Israel out of Egypt, and are not Israel's own work: "Great and goodly cities, which you did not build," Deut 6:10. This passage shows at the same time that Israel did not regard the foundation of cities and urban civilization as something a priori negative (a number of older exegetes like F. Delitzsch understood it in this way); rather progress in civilization is considered as a very positive part of the history of humankind. (Cf. G. Wallis, ZAW 78 [1966] 133-148; he puts the passage in the context of the culture myths of the ancient near east and lists the most important of the literature).

Literature: Gen 4:18: T. Worden, "The Literary Influence of the Ugaritic Fertility Myth on the OT," VT 3 (1953) 273-297. P.P. Saydon, "Meanings and Uses of the Particle את," VT 14 (1964) 192-210. P. Humbert, "Yahvé Dieu Géniteur? (Les verbes yālad et ḥil avec Yahvé comme sujet. Image ou réalité?)," AsSt 18/19 (1965) 247-251.

[**4:18**]   V. 18 differs from the preceding and the following by merely enumerating the descendants of Enoch down to Lamech without any further addition. This can scarcely be understood to mean that there was no progress in civilization in that period. The verse belongs rather to a different sort of tradition, that of a mere sequence of descendants, more like Gen 5 than 4:1, 17, 19-24. It is a sequence of five successive generations, each represented by one name: Enoch - Irad - Mehujael (Mehijael) - Methushael - Lamech. It is possible that the sequence once began with Adam (or Enosh?) and Cain and formed a series of 7. Such a sequence, which is but a succession of names, is on the border line between a genealogy and a list. Nothing more is known about those who bear these names and in one case the name itself is dubious; both versions of it have been set side-by-side. Accordingly the names are as good as beyond explanation. Most exegetes agree that the names are not Hebrew, and the majority incline to a Babylonian origin.

עירד: The meaning of this name is very uncertain; J. Gabriel makes a synthesis of the explanations, Bib 40 (1959) 412-413. A number of different derivations from Arabic are proposed and it is linked with place-names like Arad, Eridu and others. U. Cassuto suggests a link between the LXX reading Γαιδαδ and the Arabic *ghardūn* = reed hut, others a connection with עיר = city. But these are no more than conjectures and no satisfactory explanation of עירד has been given as yet.

(מחייאל) מחויאל: This and the following name are theophoric. אל is a common Semitic word and gives no clue to the origin of the name. Both forms with י and ו respectively are variants of the same name which have been preserved in the tradition (so B. Jacob, E. Speiser and U. Cassuto, like Pnuēl and Pniēl). So the attempt to read them as two names with different meanings comes to nothing (so O. Schedl and J. Schildenberger). Some exegetes see the verb מחא = "to strike" in the first part, others hiph. of חיה; hence the meanings "God strikes" or "God gives life." U. Cassuto understands it as *maḥḥu,* a class of priests or seers. But there is no certain explanation of the name.

מתושאל: There has been a certain unanimity about the meaning of this name. A number of exegetes have been accustomed to explain it as "man of God," understanding the ש in the middle as a genitive particle. But there was uncertainty because some wanted to derive it from Akkadian, others from the South Arabic (J. Gray, O. Procksch). Yet another group explained the second part as שָׁאֵל. M. Tsvat gives sounder reasons for this explanation when, following J. Lewy, he understands it as a composite of מתו and שָׁאֵל: "Man of the nether world"; he supports the explanation with the corresponding name in Gen 5 מתושלח which has almost the same meaning, because *Shalah* can be shown to be a god of the underworld. Even though this explanation is more probable, no certainty has yet been reached.

למך: (actually Lemech; the rendering Lamech is due to the pausal form at the end of v. 18). The name cannot be explained from the Hebrew; that at least is certain. It is usually explained from the Sumerian *lumga,* the title of the sky god Ea as patron of song and music. This is possible philologically and would suit well the present context. The older explanations from the Arabic are less probable. U. Cassuto wants to connect it with the Akkadian *lumakku,* the designation of a class of priests; S. Gevirtz (according to I.J. Gelb) with the early Akkadian name *Lam-ki-um* and *Lam-ki-mari.*

Literature: Gen 4:19-22: M. Grünbaum, *Neue Beiträge zur semitischen Sagenkunde* (1893). P. Koschaker, "Fratriarchat, Hausgemeinschaft und Mutterrecht in Keilschriftrechten," ZA NF 7 (1933) 1-89. C.H. Gordon, "Fratriarchy in the OT," JBL 54 (1935) 223-231. L. Koehler, "Syntactica IV," VT 3 (1953) 299-305. G. Fohrer, "Tradition und Interpretation im AT," ZAW 73 (1961) 1-30. C.H. Gordon, *Before the Bible: the Common Background of Greek and Hebrew Civilization* (1962). W.A. Irwin, "Where shall Wisdom be found?," JBL 80 (1961) 133-142. L. Hicks "Cain," IDB I, 482. G.M. Landes, "Kain," IDB III, 2. W. Plautz, "Monogamie und Polygynie im AT," ZAW 75 (1963) 3-26. E. Robertson, "The URIM and TUMMIM. What were they?," VT 14 (1964) 67-74. B. Margulis, "A Ugaritic Psalm (RS 24.252)," JBL 89 (1970) 292-204.

[4:19-22] Vv. 19-22 form a unity of their own within 4:1, 17-24. It happens often in the genealogies that there is expansion with the last member. While the preceding members describe each generation with one name only, the last member, i.e., the last generation, gives the name of a number of sons and daughters. The bracket of three in the last member corresponds to the style of the genealogy, e.g., the three sons of Noah in Gen 5:22. One can conclude with certainty from this trait that the original function of a genealogy was to present the early history of a group, of a community of some sort. If on the contrary it is a question of legitimatizing the claim of origin of a single person (as with the priestly family trees or the family tree of Jesus), then it can only conclude with the birth of a son.

4:19-22 is therefore the end piece of a genealogy which looks to a group, a community. The family tree does not in this case end up with an ethnic group. As it divides into branches it presents the corresponding division of human labor and creative cultural progress. Behind this is the awareness that the increase and growth of human endeavor and creativity is coterminus with the increase and growth of the human race. Increase and reticulation is part of the development of human creativity; this is why the genealogy is so adapted to describing it. The Sumerian myths already describe the origin and progress of civilization by means of genealogies (G.R. Castellino, VT.S 4 [1957] 133-137). The connection is not so clear here because it is a matter of the genealogies of the gods who are brought into relationship with the origin of civilization. Humans have received the material of civilization as a gift from the gods. The connection is clearer in the Phoenician myths which Eusebius (Praep. ev. I, 10), following Sanchuniathon, repeats from Philo of Byblos:

There descended from the first pair Αἰών and Πρωτογόνος three mortal children, Φῶς, Πῦρ, and Φλόξ, who invented fire by rubbing pieces of wood together and learnt how to use it. Then followed a generation of giants from whom [Σα]μημοῦμος (= שמי מרום) ὁ καὶ Ὑψουράνιος descended and founded Tyre. He invented huts of cane, rushes and reeds. . . . The brothers Ἀγρεὺς and Ἁλιεὺς are the inventors of the hunt and of fishing, two others the inventors of iron and its forging, one, Χρυσώρ, invented speech, conjuration and prophecy, Τεχνίτης and Γήϊνος Αὐτοχθών invented the tile by mixing clay with straw and drying it in the sun, and so arose the building of houses where Ἀγρός and Ἀρούηρος made further progress; the descendants of these were the people of the land and hunters. . . . (B. Jacob, *Comm.* 154).

It is probable that two different traditions are combined here. The text shows that the union of genealogy and the origin of civilization must have had a rich and many-sided history from which Gen 4:17-24 preserved just a few significant excerpts. However, it is important that almost every sentence in Gen 1-11 which has anything to do with the origin of civilization has counterparts in the text of Sanchuniathon.

The fact that passages that refer to the beginning of human civilization are assumed into J's primeval story shows a definite conception of the history of humankind: people's work is combined with the growth, increase and multiplication of the human race in such a way that obligation (to till and guard the earth), creativity and progress in this area are regarded as basic to human history and are seen as preparatory to political structures. In Egypt and the Sumerian king lists, the beginning of the history of humankind is at the same time the beginning of the kingship. Such structures have no part in the primeval story of Gen 1-11, while cultural creativity and progress belong to its essential elements. I think that this is of great significance for the concept of history in the Old Testament. Civilizing activity is a necessary and inseparable part of human history. Political structures take on meaning in history only with the separation of humanity into peoples, at the point where primeval event moves into national history.

Cain as the father and Enoch as the city builder stand for sedentary civilization. The group that is associated with Lamech as father stands for the nomads. A distinction is made here as the latter are descended from two mothers. The children of Ada lived in tents, were cattle breeders and musicians; the children of Zillah were smiths, workers of metal, singers and dancers (?). J.A. Montgomery, *Arabia and the Bible* (1934) 6, notes: "In 20-22 we have the three classes that appear all through Arabian history . . . i.e., the flock-grazer, the minstrel, and the artisan," and A. Pohl, StZ 85 (1959/60) 412-422: "The remarks about the working of metal and music are appropriate to . . . the occupation of small, often subordinated, nomad tribes who at the same time served the larger group as metal workers and as minstrels and rhapsodists."

The older view that the story of Lamech portrays the introduction of polygamy and is a sign of the moral corruption of Canaanites misunderstands the function of the genealogy; the mention of the two wives of Lamech serves to subdivide his children into two groups. Moreover it would be difficult to understand why polygamy should be a sign of corruption here and not in the case of the patriarchs. It could be that the polygamy of Lamech points to a growing state of material well-being (so H.J.T. Johnson, *The Bible and Early Man,* 1943), but this is not necessary. In any case the sentence implies no negative judgment on Lamech: "It is only with Deuteronomy that polygamy is criticized and circumscribed," W. Plautz, ZAW 75 (1963) 7. The names of Lamech's two wives, like the other names in this genealogy, cannot be explained with certainty. The name עדה is usually linked with עֲדִי "ornament," while the name צלה is linked with צֵל, "shade"; some interpreters understand shade negatively, others positively. Both are unlikely. Cassuto's conjecture is attractive, linking the name with צלצול, "cymbal," "an allusion to the sweetness of the female voice." This explanation raises the possibility that the two names form a meaningful word pair, suggested by their sound, as in Song 2:14, where voice and face are in parallel in praise of the girl's beauty.

Literature: Gen 4:20: J. Kennedy, "Genesis 4:20," ExpT 28 (1916/1917) 189-190.   F. Nötscher, "Entbehrliche Hapaxlegomena in Jesaia," VT 1 (1951) 299-302.

[4:20-21]   The Children of Adah – Jabal and Jubal.

The similarity in sound of the three names indicates that they arose in the context of the genealogies whose intention was to present the origin of the occupations they describe. It is possible that all three derive in some way from the verb יבל, "bring" (cf. יבול = "product," U. Cassuto), though it would not be possible to explain each immediately out of the context of its particular function. The similarity in sound could be due to the adaptation of very different names.

The text is uncertain in both vv. 20 and 22b where the occupations are described. This is due to the age of the tradition, and there should be no attempt to emend the text. Those who live in tents are traced back to Jabal, and it is said at the same time that they had herds of cattle. The same precision and detail occurs in the Assyrian king list A, where 17 "kings who lived in tents" are mentioned (W. Röllig, 1969, 266). A verb "to keep" is lacking; but it is obvious that this is what is meant. Some exegetes describe the linking of the two as "Zeugma," but J. Skinner says correctly: "The Zeugma is somewhat hard." In any case both designations describe unambiguously the life of the nomad or the bedouin, neither of whom, it is clear, falls under the curse upon Cain in 4:11-12. The nomad life is simply described here and no judgment is passed or implied — contrary to the earlier interpretation.

Literature: Gen 4:21: D. Wohlenberg, Kultmusik in Israel, Diss Hamburg (1967)

[4:21]   Musicians are derived from Jubal, the second son of Adah. The verb תפש means "to manipulate"; it describes the dexterity or art of the one who manipulates the instruments. The two mentioned here are meant to be "the oldest and simplest musical instruments" (J. Skinner). It may well be that there is a genuine piece of information in the background when the art of playing musical instruments is ascribed to the brother of Jabal, the father of nomadic life, namely that it was the wandering herdsmen, the nomads, who invented them. Everywhere in the world herdsmen are found in the context of music and musical instruments; "in Greek mythology the shepherd god Pan is the inventor of the σύριγξ" (B. Jacob). The σύριγξ is the equivalent of עוגב which occurs elsewhere in the Old Testament only Ps 150:4 and Job 21:12; 30:31. כנור and עוגב (there is in addition in 21:12, תף) are together in both the Job passages, each of which is concerned with secular music. כנור is in any case a stringed instrument, the lyre. The כנור became an instrument used in worship and is found often in this context in the Old Testament, whereas עוגב was never admitted to worship and occurs but rarely. The mention of the two instruments together both here and in the Job passages is a sign of an old tradition according to which they were part of secular usage (cf. K. Galling, BRL "Musik"; E. Werner, "Musical Instrument," IDB III 469-476).

Music is named as one of the arts. The reason for this is that music, both vocal and instrumental, always had great significance for Israel because it was so close to human speech and because art was all but identical with the art of speech and sound. So we hear much about music both secular and sacred in the Old Testament. The explanation is that the art of music is rooted in the primeval event (C. Westermann, "Musik III, Instrumentale Musik, Gesand und Dichtung in Israel," RGG³ IV). In Gen 4:21 instrumental music does not as yet know of any division into secular and sacred. It belongs to the basic potential which the creator gave to his creatures and which they are obliged to advance and cultivate. cultivate.

Literature: Gen 4:22: J. Goettsberger, "Eine Transkription aus Gk in MT? (Zu Gn 4:22)," BZ 17 (1926) 50. A. Bea, *De Pentateucho: Institutiones Biblicae II, 1* (1933²). J.M. Vosté, "Lettre de la Commission Biblique," Ang 25 (1948). M. Delcor, "Deux passages difficiles: Zach XII 11 et XI 13," VT 3 (1953) 67-77. S.E. Loewenstamm, "The Hebrew Root חרשׁ in the Light of the Ugaritic Texts," JJS 10 (1959) 63-65.

[4:22] The branch that produced the nomad herdsmen and music is distinguished from that which produced technology. Zillah, Lamech's second wife, gave birth to Tubal-cain to whom the craft of working metal is traced. The text has been disturbed here even more than in v. 20. One expects after Tubal-cain's name the word אבי, which follows the two names in v. 21. Its absence is an indication of the disturbance. But the text, even as it now stands, is scarcely possible. Some exegetes try to translate it literally, e.g., B. Jacob: ". . . Tubal-cain a sharpener of everyone who works in bronze and iron" (similarly U. Cassuto). But this translation shows that here, as in very many other passages in the Old Testament, a word has been appended to a verb in the course of the textual tradition to complement or elaborate it. It seems that this addition is also responsible for the disappearance of אבי.

M. Delcor (VT 3 [1953] 67ff.) has shown that the specifically technical term for "sculptor" is חרשׁ. We must admit then that the verb לטשׁ = to sharpen (elsewhere in the OT only in 1 Sam 13:20; Pss 7:13; 52:4; see Sir 34:26), has been added in the transferred sense of "to moisten" (the eyes), Job 16:9, either in the general sense of "hammer" or the specific sense of "sharpen," which envisages weapons. For the verbs לטשׁ and חרשׁ see J. Gabriel, Bib 40 (1959) 411, n. 1; for חרשׁ see S.E. Loewenstamm (JSS 10 [1959] 63ff.): "The Ugaritic word-combination *ḥrš a'nyt* = shipbuilder, *ḥrš mrkbt* = chariotbuilder provides an entirely new proof that the Hebrew word for craftsman is derived from an independent proto-Semitic root, not identical with *ḥrt*." נחשׁת Akk. *nuḥuštum,* copper or bronze, occurs 136 times in the OT. ברזל, iron, is a Hittite word *barzillu,* which has come across into the Semitic languages, Akk. *parzillu,* Ug. *brśl.*

There are different explanations of the name Tubal-cain. It is usually said that because the Gk here has only θόβελ, the original was תובל and that Cain was a later addition (e.g., O. Procksch). K. Budde takes Lamech as the original subject of this sentence because of v. 23. D.N. Freedman says that it is generally accepted that only the word Tubal is original, ZAW 64 (1952) 190-191. But the acceptance is not all that general and Gunkel leaves the double name, as do B. Jacob and U. Cassuto: "Qayin may be an allusion . . . to Tubal's craft, and signifies: 'Tubal the smith, Tubal the artificer'." It would be difficult to explain the subsequent addition of קין, and so the double name would be the original. One must however agree with H. Gunkel: "The double name seems to be due to the identification of two persons." J. Wellhausen identifies Tubal with the Tibarenoi, south-east of the Black Sea, "renowned as workers in bronze" (H. Gunkel). The reason for the identification, accepted by many, is given in Ezek 27:13, which reads: "Jaban, Tubal, and Mesech traded with you; they exchanged the persons of men and vessels of bronze for your merchandise." W. Zimmerli says of Tubal: "Thubal is to be linked with the Akk. *tabal* and the Gk. Τιβαρηνοί . . . Tubal lived in the region of Cilicia. . . . The mention of vessels of bronze as merchandise can be understood in the context of a report about Sargon II that he "plundered from the land of *tabal* bowls with golden ears" (ARAB II 95), and one about Assurnasirpal II that he "plundered objects of copper, oars, sheep and wine in *musku*." U. Cassuto rightly rejects this: "In Ezekiel XXVII 13, the vessels of bronze constitute only one of the articles of merchandise, and Tubal is but one of the peoples engaged in this trade." One might add that the similarity in sound of the three names could hardly be harmonized with such an explanation. The identification of Tubal with the Tibarenoi fails. An explanation of the name has been given above.

Cain, the second part of the composite name, indicates the craft of the smith; cf. comm. on v. 1. Cain has no connection with the family tree of the Kenites nor is he their primal ancestor. Inasmuch as it is part of a composite name in 4:22, Cain is neither univocal in meaning nor to be applied to any definite person or group. It is only in v. 22 and nowhere else, that there is any connection between the name and the craft of the smith. The origin of instruments of bronze or iron is traced back to Tubal-cain. E. Speiser remarks that the mention of iron is an anachronism (on this cf. A. Bea, *Institutiones*. . . . II p. 176; J.M. Voste, Ang. 25 [1948]). It is certainly true that the history of Israel begins at the period of the transition of the bronze to the iron age and that metallurgy cannot be set in the primeval period; but one cannot really speak of an anachronism.

The purpose of this note on the progress of civilization is to treat together the origins of metallurgy. These two widely-separated stages are seen together. The note in v. 22 is concerned with metallurgy as such as one of the decisive steps forward in the history of civilization (so too F.V. Winnett, "Metallurgy," IDB III, 366: "we are faced with a telescoping of two different traditions"). The significance of metallurgy for the history of Israel is reflected in other places in the Old Testament, e.g., 1 Sam 13:20; 1 Kings 9:26-28; 10:22. The beginnings of metallurgy is regarded in many places throughout the world as of the utmost importance in the history of humankind. It plays a basic role in the Sumerian myths, and it is well known in the myths of Greece and Rome. The intention of Gen 4:22 is that progress in technology as such, as illustrated by the possibilities which metallurgy opens up, facilitates progress in human living and life in community. As primeval time corresponds to eschatological time the facility acquired in primeval time is important once more in eschatological time: "And they shall beat their swords into plowshares, and their spears into pruning hooks," Is 2:4 = Mic 4:3. The conversion of instruments of destruction into instruments of human progress would not be possible without their discovery at the beginning of the history of humankind. The eschatological promise showed that no misuse of technology throughout human history can alter this in any way. Technology as such is regarded positively; it retains its function of furthering human existence.

Literature: Gen 4:23-24: J.G. Herder, *Vom Geist der ebräischen Poesie, I* (1782; 1825³) 302-309. G. Jacob, *Das Leben der vorislamischen Beduinen* (1895) 144-146. I. Goldziher, *Abhandlungen zur arabischen Philologie. I* (1896) 1-105. S. Daiches, "Balaam a Babylonian bārū," *Hilprecht Anniversary Vol.* (1909) 60-70. G.A. Smith, *The Early Poetry of Israel in its Physical and Social Origins: Schweich Lectures on Bible Archaeology 3* (1910³). J. Morgenstern, "A Note on Genesis 5:29," JBL 49 (1930) 306-309. H. Rongy, "Cain et Lamech," REcL 27 (1935/1936) 209-222. E. Dhorme, *L'évolution religieuse d'Israél. I,* (1937) 29-32. T. Wilhelm, "El Cantico de Lamec (Gen 4:23-24)," Rev Bib 10 (1948) 64-67. B. Gemser, "The *rîb-* or controversy-pattern in Hebrew mentality," VT.S 3 (1955) 120-137. L. Wächter, "Gemeinschaft und Einzelner im Judentum," AVTRW 16 (1959) 7-35. S. Gevirtz, "Patterns in the Early Poetry of Israel. Study II. Lamech's Song to his Wives (Gen 4:23-25)," SAOC 32 (1963) 25-34. H.G. Jefferson, "Psalm LXXVII," VT 13 (1963) 87-91. A. Malamat, "Kingship and Council in Israel and Sumer: A Parallel," JNES 22 (1963) 247-253. G. Sauer, *Die Sprüche Agurs. Untersuchungen zur Herkunft, Verbreitung und Bedeutung einer biblischen Stilform unter besonderer Berücksichtigung von Proverbia c. 30* (1963) 73, 77. P.D. Miller, Jr., "Yeled in the Song of Lamech," JBL 85 (1966) 477-478.

[4:23-24] The song of Lamech is loosely linked with what precedes. It is an independent self-contained elaboration of the genealogy; but it is joined to what has been said of the wives and children of Lamech in apparently narrative form (ויאמר). There is the introduction followed by the call to the wives of Lamech in rhythmic pattern (2:2:2:2). What they are to listen to follows in a sentence introduced by כִּי (3:2), which contains the braggart song itself. There is another כִּי sentence in v. 24 which sets the intensified retribution of v. 23b over against that threatened for the murder of Cain in v. 15. The song resembles in form those short songs of one or two verses which have been handed down from the early period: Ex 15:21; 1 Sam 18:7; Judg 15:16. . . . S. Gevirtz has pointed out that a critical appreciation of the verses shows that they are not the same: "Following the initial couplet, each of whose three component pairs of parallel terms has been structured entirely in accordance with the Syro-Palestinian poetic tradition, there ensues a rapid and continued disintegration to the tradition of fixed pairs, climaxed in the final couplet . . . which the poet has fashioned by the formulation of a deliberately nontraditional and even outlandish parallelism," p. 25 (see above). This raises the question whether the third line of the song originally belonged to it.

[4:23] The verbs "hear - harken" occur 18 times in parallelism in the Old Testament; קוֹל and אמרה are in parallelism even more often (U. Cassuto and S. Gevirtz treat the passages in detail). The summons to listen as the introduction of a saying or a song is not confined to any particular form of speech. It occurs often in prophecy, Is 32:9, as introduction to a wisdom saying Is 28:23, and, as here, as the introduction to a saying which is bound to a particular situation within a small circle. The circle is that of the family as the address shows. Such a lapidary summons to the wives is only possible when the audience that the speaker addresses is still one with the family circle. This shows that it must be a very early song.

The כִּי "gives the reason for the call to attention" (so S. Gevirtz). Even if in the context it indicates a reason, nevertheless its purpose here is to command attention (like הִנֵּה); and so the sentence that forms the body of the song must be a principal sentence. The object, אִישׁ and יֶלֶד, can be regarded as synonymous parallelism (so U. Cassuto: the same person is meant by both), or as a kind of mounting parallelism, which describes the murder of a youth as deserving more severe retribution (so P.D. Miller). The verb הָרַגְתִּי can be understood in different ways — either as perfect, and so Lamech's boast would refer to an accomplished fact (so H. Gunkel, who describes it very graphically, U. Cassuto, and others), or as present, in which case no particular occasion is called for (J. Wellhausen and others). One can only decide in the context of the meaning of the song as a whole.

[**4:24**]   It is rather clumsy to begin the third line too with כִּי. S. Gevirtz draws attention to the unusual parallelism of the verse. But one could go further: if v. 24 were not handed down as the third line of a song, one could just as easily read it as prose. It could well be that this verse is a later addition which links the old song with the Cain and Abel narrative. This is confirmed by the rather notable lack of cohesion between the second and third lines of the song. It is only v. 24, not v. 23b, that speaks of revenge in the specific sense (נקם). The mounting comparison with Cain in v. 24 presumes that the retribution is the consequence of a killing (that is all that is meant in 4:12); v. 23b on the other hand speaks only of wounding. This being the case we can be more precise about the original meaning of the song of Lamech. Commenting on the numbers G. Sauer writes: "Completion is expressed in the words of Lamech that he will be avenged seventy-seven fold. This should indicate that the ultimate has been achieved. . . ." *Die Sprüche Agurs. . . .* (1963) 73.

There are two reasons why it is difficult to explain the passage: first, the song is firmly fitted into the context of 4:1, 17-22 by its two parts, the three names in v. 23 and the name of Cain and the reference to 4:15 in v. 24; second, despite this connection, the meaning of the passage as a conclusion of 4:1, 17-22 is not immediately clear. In any case there can be no doubt that the song has been fitted into its present context with the precise purpose of forming a conclusion to the genealogy (so B. Jacob, W. Zimmerli, and others). It is possible that the meaning of the song here is not the same as it was outside this context. Further, the reference to 4:15 in v. 24 indicates that the song is meant to conclude not merely the genealogy but the whole of Gen 4.

The link with the Cain and Abel narrative is obvious; this is saying that when people live together there arises the possibility of the murder of a brother, while the song of Lamech sees this possibility aggravated and underscores it in hyperbole in v. 24. The song is addressed to Adah and Zillah, the mothers of the founders who are the subject of vv. 20-22. It must be supposed then that the mounting likelihood of killing, of the destruction of human life by another human, is to be seen in the context of the growing complexity of human existence represented by all the progeny of this father and this mother, and not merely in the context of metallurgy represented by Tubal-cain. The song of Lamech thereby takes on a meaning different from that usually ascribed to it.

The first stage in the explanation of the song is represented by J.G. Herder (*Vom Geist der ebräischen Poesie*, I, 1782; 1825³, 309): "The song has only one concern, it is

Lamech's response to the invention of the sword (when understood soberly in context, it is no senseless song of exultation over Cain's murder). The lines are measured and in assonance; the parallelism . . . lyric poetry and music are found within the one circle at the one time; the former was the daughter of the latter, and they have always been united together. Lamech became aware of the superior power of iron and the sword against other instruments of aggression.'' This explanation of the song of Lamech as ''the song of the sword'' which was in accordance with the meaning of the text insofar as it adapted an ancient song to the process of human development and brought it into relationship with the preceding inventions (though only with one of them) was replaced by Wellhausen's explanation (*Composition*[2]) p. 305: ''The boasting of the father of one branch of the family tree over against the others does not need any particular audience. And just as the Arabs are accustomed to preen themselves and boast in the presence of their wives, so too does Lamech.'' Wellhausen's explanation has been accepted by the majority of exegetes; e.g., O. Procksch writes: ''An uncouth Bedouin song which, because of the mention of Cain, must have its origin from the neighborhood of the Caanites.''

Wellhausen's explanation presumes that the song is not to be explained out of its present context. Gunkel also emphasizes this: ''The song of Lamech is in nowise connected with the inventions of the house of Lamech.'' He sees in it ''a genuine song of the desert: blood vengeance is at home in the desert. . . .'' He underlines the positive significance of the song: ''Those who sang the song of Lamech in the distant past did not feel terror at its savage cruelty but rather fascination at the mighty power of the hero.'' (To the contrary J. Pedersen: ''The reactions of J . . . are certainly more like terror and amazement at his braggart hero.'') A number of exegetes have noted that the song of Lamech is not concerned with blood vengeance in the strict institutional sense. J. Pedersen writes: ''The words of Lamech show that the essential feature of vengeance is not to kill life, because life has been killed. He also avenges slight hurts. Every breach of honor requires restoration through vengeance'' (*Israel* II, p. 380). So too K. Koch: ''When Lamech boasts, Gen 4:22ff. he will kill a man for his wound, and a youth for his scar, he is not speaking as an avenger of blood,'' VT 12 (1962) 409. So too J.R. Porter, VT 15 (1965) 375, who refers to Pedersen and Koch.

If this song is not particularly concerned with blood vengeance but rather with boasting about grossly exaggerated retribution for injuries which, though not lethal, were nevertheless a violation of honor, then it cannot be the intention to restrict it to a particular people (J. Wellhausen and others). Even if v. 20 suggests nomads — and Lamech is not the father of the nomads only — the intent of the song should not be restricted to them. If J has deliberately used the song as the conclusion of 4:1, 17-24 then it must be saying something about the growth of this branch of civilization. One will have to distinguish then between the meaning which the song once had in its original life-setting as the braggart song of a man of might in the presence of his wives, and the meaning it has acquired in the intent of J as the conclusion of a genealogy which describes the origin of civilization. It was in its original setting, as H. Gunkel describes it, a straight-out expression of a self-conscious and arrogant claim to power concerned with nothing else but the assertion of one's own Ego (S. Gevirtz: ''The song expresses Lamech's overwhelming pride, his refusal to suffer any hurt without a sevenfold and dire revenge'' p. 25).

The question has been raised whether the boasting is that of one who has just executed such a deed (H. Gunkel and U. Cassuto), or whether it is to be translated by a present tense and not related to a particular event. If one assumes that in the region in which the song originated the spoken word was still understood as effective in itself and that the song was to effect something, then it is most likely to be a threat; the horrific retribution is meant to terrify. The song as such is an intimidatory utterance, casting a spell, cf. 1 Sam 17:44; Judg 15:16. J.A. Montgomery explains it in this way, using Arabic parallels: "Lamech's taunt-song vv. 23-24 is our earliest example of the Arabian Hija or battle satire," *Arabia and the Bible* (1934). It can be understood then as a braggart song; but the bragging must not be understood as the self-inflated assertion of an individual. It is rather bragging in the face of one's enemies, and its function is to strike terror.

J has taken it over as such; but he wants to say more. The song is the conclusion of a genealogy which unfolds the advance of human potential and development. The genealogy of civilization in Gen 4 without the song of Lamech corresponds to ch. 2; the song of Lamech corresponds to the Cain and Abel narrative, as v. 24 suggests. The Cain and Abel narrative says that when people created by God live side-by-side in brotherhood there is at the same time the possibility of killing. The song of Lamech indicates that the increased progress activated by the human potential increases the possibility of mutual destruction. With the growth of one's capacities there is a growth of self-assertion and amour-propre that demands retribution without limit for even the smallest injury.

If this explanation is correct, then J has at the same time sensed both aspects of the progress of civilization: the mounting of openings to life which accompany it and the consequent mounting of "claims" which lead to overweaning self-assertion.

Literature: Gen 4:25-26: F. Schwally, "Zu hizkir besēm Jahwe," ZAW 11 (1891) 176-180. A. Lang, *The Making of Religion* (1898). R. Kittel, "Zum Jahvenamen," RE³ VIII; XXIII (1900) 529-531, 665. F. Giesebrecht, *Die alttestamentliche Schätzung des Gottesnamens und ihre religionsgeschichtliche Grundlage* (1901). C.F. Burney, "A Theory of the Development of Israelite Religion in Early Times," JThS 9 (1908) 321-352. J.I. Munro, "Genesis IV 26," ExpT 20 (1908/1909) 563. J. Skinner, *The Divine Names in Genesis* (1914) 188-200. N. Söderblom, *Das Werden des Gottesglaubens. Untersuchungen über die Anfänge der Religion* (1914; 1926²) 93-156. D. Völter, "Die Herkunft Jahwes," ZAW 37 (1917/1918) 126-133. A. Jirku, *Die Wanderungen der Hebräer im 3, und 2, Jahrtausend v. Chr.*, AO 24 (1924). W. Vischer, *Jahwe der Gott Kains* (1929). C. Toussaint, *Les origines de la religion d'Israel, I. L'ancien Jahvisme* (1931). E. König, "Einige Streiflichter auf die biblischen Gottesnamen," CuW 8 (1932) 94-97. A. Vaccari, "Jahve e i nomi divini nelle religioni semitiche," Bib 17 (1936) 1-10. O.E. James, *The Beginnings of Religion. An Introductory and Scientific Study* (1948). E. Dhorme, "Le nom de Dieu d'Israél," Lecture . . . 1951, *Institut de France* (1951) 1-3. A.M. Dubarle, "La signification du nom de Jahveh," RSPhTh 34 (1951) 3-21. G. Lambert, "Que signifie le nom divin YHWH?," NRTh 84 A (1952) 897-915. S. Mowinckel, *Religion und Kultus* (1953). P. Rohrbach, *Aufgang der Menschheit. Der Gottesgedanke in der Welt* (1953). S. Sandmel, "Interpretations of Genesis 4:26b," JBL 72 (1953) XVIII. E. Galbiati, *La struttura letteraria dell' Esodo; contributo allo studio dei criteri stilistici dell' AT e della composizione del Pentateuco* (1956). I. Lewy, "The Beginnings of the Worship of Yahweh, Conflicting Biblical Views," VT 6 (1956) 429-435. R.B.Y. Scott, *The Service of God:* "The Stubborn Faith," to Honor of W.A. Irwin (1956) 132-143. H.A. Brongers, "BᵉSĒM JHWH," NTT 11 (1956/1957) 401-416. F. Horst, "Die Notiz vom Anfang des Jahwekultes in Genesis 4:26," BEvTh 26 (1957) 68-74. N. Walker, 'Yahwism and the Divine Name 'Yhwh'," ZAW 70 (1958) 262-264. E.C.B. Maclaurin, "YHWH. The Origin of the Tetragrammation," VT 12 (1962) 439-463. S. Sandmel, "Genesis 4:26b," HUCA 32 (1961) 19-29. O. Eissfeldt, "Jahwe, der Gott der Väter," ThLZ 88 (1963) 481-490. G.T. Manley, "The God of Abraham," TynB 14 (1964) 3-7. H.A. Brongers, "Die Wendung besēm jhwh im AT," ZAW 77 (1965) 1-20. R. de Vaux, "The Revelation of the Divine Name," OT Essays in Honour of G.H. Davies (1970) 48-75.

[4:25-26]   The Sethites.

Vv. 25-26 are an independent genealogy which present a single self-contained tradition. It moves from Adam through Seth to Enosh and went perhaps even as far as Noah, as 5:29 indicates. The general opinion holds that this belongs to J. It is preserved only in a fragmentary state and has been notably altered. It is worthy of special note that the first and third names have practically the same meaning "so that both the father and the son of Seth have basically the same name" (B. Jacob). Jacob's explanation that Enosh is the first "real" man because he is the first begotten by one who was himself begotten, sounds somewhat contrived. Nevertheless one must concede that the genealogy contains elements of different origin. An older exegesis understood the purpose of the series to contrast a succession of generations pleasing to God with the Cainite genealogy which followed the path to destruction. For example, A. Dillmann writes "that it (Sethite) is conceived of as in moral and religious opposition to the Cainite line, corresponding to the opposition between the paths of good and evil that run through the whole history of humankind." K. Budde writes somewhat differently: "The Kenite family tree speaks of progress in civilization . . . the Sethite of a moral development of humankind. . . ." There is not enough support in the text for such an interpretation by way of contrasts. The purpose probably evolved in the process of composition (K. Budde: "J too must have narrated Noah's descent from the first man").

Literature: 4:25: J.R. Kupper, *Les nomades en Mésopotamie au temps des rois de Mari* (1957).   J. Hoftijzer, "Deux vases à inscription identique," VT 13 (1963) 337-339.   E. Lipinski, "Peninna, Iti'el et l'Athlète," VT 17 (1967) 68-75).

[4:25]   The text shows clearly that these verses have been linked subsequently to what precedes; a variant has been appended to the succession of generations that began with Adam by means of "again" in v. 25a and "an other" in v. 25b ("an addition scarcely feasible in the logic of language," H. Holzinger). Even more remarkable is the subsequent linking with the Cain and Abel narrative in the last sentence: "Instead of Abel, for Cain slew him," which is scarcely conceivable as part of the explanation of the name by the mother. J. Skinner remarks that this addition destroys the meaning of the name-giving because the verb שִׁית cannot have such a meaning as "substitute." Without the additions the sentence would run: "Adam knew his wife and she bore a son and called him Seth, because (so she said): God has set me seed!" The giving of the name in v. 25 then corresponds to that in v. 1. Its tone too is that of a jubilant cry which expresses joy over the son and with the son over the descendants. The name Seth then does not mean "substitute" or "one put in." The meaning as spoken by the mother is independent of the original meaning of the name Seth which is no longer known (so too B. Jacob and J. Skinner). It is very unlikely that the name Seth can be linked with the Aramean nomads, the Guti (so O. Procksch, G. von Rad), Num 24:17, because the story of primeval events is not concerned with relationships among peoples.

It is to be noted that אדם appears here as a proper name without the article, differing from 4:1. K. Budde, H. Gunkel and others assume that the article was originally present here as in v. 1. Perhaps the redactor was forced to leave it out for reasons of style: in the genealogy "the man" had to be changed to a name, inasmuch as אנוש too is possible here only without the article.

[4:26a]   For the first time the father gives the name. One cannot attribute any great significance to the difference between this and v. 25a where the mother gives the name. It can be conditioned by the composite nature of the genealogy. In any case there is not good reason why the mother gives the name in one case and the father in the other.

אנוש is really a collective noun like אדם; here it is used as a name. Some exegetes, like J. Skinner and W. Zimmerli, consider the possibility that it was once the first member of an older genealogy. J. Skinner suggests moreover that the genealogy may have arisen in a people in which אנוש was the usual word for man as is the case in other Semitic languages (Ar., Aram., Nabat., Sab., Ass.,). According to Wellhausen, Enosh was a doublet of Adam and once the primal ancestor of all humankind.

אנוש occurs 42 times in the Old Testament; 18 in Job, 13 in Pss., 8 in Is and once in each of Jer., Deut., 2 Chron. The word never has the article and is found only in poetic texts. In 32 of the passages it is used of humans in their mortality, contingency, limitation, or of a human being in contrast to God. The other 10 passages speak of humanity in a general or neutral way. They are fixed formulas or phrases where the general usage alone is retained. The passages where Enosh is a proper name belong to this general or neutral context: Gen 4:26; 5:6, 7, 9, 10, 11; 1 Chron 1:1 (see Articles אנוש־אדם in THAT).

[4:26b]   The last sentence of Gen 4: "At that time men began to call upon the name of the Lord" has given rise to much discussion, which has revolved predominantly around the question of the beginning of the worship of Yahweh. The problem is that in the book of Exodus the beginning of the worship of Yahweh occurs in the context of the origins of the people of Israel.

But it can be shown that it is not in accordance with the text to state the question in this way. The sentence is not meant to be a statement about the beginning of the worship of Yahweh in the sense in which this question understands it. The text indeed seems to say this, and to say it very clearly. But this is to overlook the context. J can have seen no contradiction between Gen 4:26 and Ex 3 because he is talking of something very different in the Exodus passage. There he is concerned with the beginning of the history of the people, whereas here he makes a primeval statement in which there is really no point of contact with the Exodus. The error in the discussion hitherto has been the starting point, namely to identify the descriptive term Yahweh יהוה in the two cases. As a consequence the whole discussion of the sentence has revolved about the name. But the sentence is saying something quite different, namely that the cult began in the primeval period. And so J was able to express this in the words "Man began to call on the name of Yahweh."

The whole emphasis must be put on the verb in order to understand the sentence properly. The meaning can be very general: at that time, in the primeval period, the cult began. J could not mean, "a very definite Yahweh cult began." It is only now that the real meaning of the statement comes to light. J has made a clear distinction between the worship of Yahweh in Israel and what we call "religion." He knows that religion is something that belongs to all peoples and to every epoch known to him. It is part of "being human" and as such is rooted in the primeval period. J. Skinner says correctly: "This conception is more ingenious that that of R (Ex 3) or P (Ex 6). . . ." (for the contrary A. Dillmann, who sees in Ex 6 "the more subtle distinction"); more ingenious, because J distinguishes between God's history in Israel and a relationship of God to humanity that embraces the whole of humankind and goes right back to its beginnings; it is what we call religion. J of course is aware that the religions of humankind had many other gods with many other names. When he uses "Yahweh" here, he is saying that, despite the variety of religions, the creator of humankind can only be one. He could not say אלהים, which would be clearer for the modern reader, because he is speaking of the very same God who has already been mentioned in 4:1, 6.

As F. Delitzsch and A. Dillmann had already seen, 4:26 is not referring to the worship of Yahweh properly so called, but to worship or cult in the most general sense. This is supported by the fact that in the description of the primeval event outside Israel, the beginnings of the cult are often found together with the achievements of civilization. H. Gunkel writes: "The foundation of religion in the view of the ancients goes right back into primeval time; the same occurs too in the Phoenician saga." But the sentence with which Gunkel continues does not agree with this: "We have here the oldest reflection on the antiquity of the worship of Yahweh and the impression that the verse reflects, that the name of Yahweh goes back into primeval time and is older than Moses and the people of Israel, is correct" (likewise O. Procksch and others; the protracted discussion about a pre-Israelite Yahweh religion by G. Lambert, I. Levy, E.C.B. McLaurin, J.P. Hyatt, C.F. Burney and others, synthesized by S. Sandmel, contributes nothing to the explanation of 4:26). J speaks of the primeval time and says that the invocation of God belongs to human existence from that time on. "J wants to say: the period before the meeting between God and his people Israel . . . was not simply a time bereft of God. It is not as if people cried out into the void and God never answered or acted. Here too it is a question of Yahweh, the *one* God" (W. Zimmerli).

The Invocation of God.

J. Skinner writes: "It rests on the primitive idea that a real bond exists between the person and his name." But this is not to be understood in the sense that one can exert some magical pressure on the person whose name is pronounced. It is rather that in the invocation a real contact with the one invoked is realized (the ב means: by means of the name; so F. Delitzsch, J. Skinner and others). It is not the name itself that brings about the contact but the invocation by meanings of the name.

The invocation of the name of God then is the action which is the foundation of every act of divine service. Neither sacrifice nor oracle nor solemn divine service nor any other cultic act is conceivable or possible without the contact point which is effected by the invocation of the name. It is the beginning of everything — of lament and praise, jubilation and entreaty, refuge and trust. It can embrace all and so stands above all and is independent, sufficient in itself. (Cf. J. Grether, *Name und Wort Gottes im AT,* BZAW 64, 1934.)

4:26b is decisive for the direction it gives to worship. Cult is here neither a recitation (which expresses a religious consciousness or mood) nor mere drama. Cult is of its very essence a happening between God and the worshiper which only comes about by means of the contact point, the invocation of the name of God. This attitude has prevailed in an adapted form right through the

Christian liturgy which always begins with "In nomine patris. . . ." There is another interpretation of קרא. Luther translated: "Then one began to preach in the name of the Lord." Some exegetes have taken this up, e.g., F. Delitzsch: "worshiping and proclaiming," justifying this interpretation with reference to Ex 33:19. Many exegetes also understand the verb in Gen 12:7-8 as "call out." קרא can certainly mean "call out"; however, there is no certain proof that the fixed phrase קרא בשם יהוה must be translated "to call out (proclaim) the name of Yahweh." Ex 33:19 is generally understood in this way, but the passage is too uncertain to be by itself the basis of such an explanation. On the contrary, passages such as Jer 10:25; Zeph 3:9 show that the rendering here has the general sense of the worship of God. This general meaning accords best with Gen 4:26. So too H.A. Brongers: " 'To worship in cult' in a general sense (e.g., Gen 4:26; 12:8; 13:4. . . .)."

G. von Rad closes his interpretation of the passage with the sentence: "Our notice (intends) . . . to indicate generally Yahweh-worship as the primeval religion of humankind in general." Taking this up, F. Horst tries to answer the question, "Why is it that this primeval religion, which goes back beyond Israel's first fathers, only appears with Enosh?" This can only be explained when one makes use of the construct "originator (creator)-faith" (N. Söderblom, *Das Werden des Gottesglaubens*, 1926², 93-156): "The only relationship of the created person (i.e., humankind before Gen 4:26b) to God is that of the thing made to its originator. It is only the historical person (from Gen 4:26b on) who has a real religious relationship, since that person calls on God's name." Horst sees behind this a state of affairs belonging to the history of the religions of the world in which Israel lived. The cult of Yahweh sloughs off a disintegrating, colorless relationship to Elohim, just as did the cult of Baal, the El-religion of Canaan. This interesting attempt to explain Gen 4:26b presumes that J intends here to mark a chronological transition from "created being" to "historical being." But there is no evidence for this in the text. The אז = *at that time*, means "in the primeval period," not "at the beginning of a new epoch in the primeval period." It does not accord with the character of the primeval event to distinguish within it distinct epochs in the history of religion. The positive contribution of Horst is that he gives the remark in Gen 4:26b a significance for humankind.

Excursus: *The Background in the History of Religions.*

A passage in Berossos deals with the origin and growth of civilization. After describing the land of Babylon, he goes on to say that at the beginning humankind multipled greatly and lived unstructured like cattle. Then in the first year (?) an animal rose out of the Red Sea that was half fish and half human and spoke with a human voice. During the day it went around among the people and taught them the practical matters of civilization, but at night it went back again into the sea. Later there appeared seven more animals like the original one: four were named, first being Oannes at the time of the first king Aloros. This report of Berossos has been confirmed and explained recently by cuneiform discoveries (text edited by O.R. Gurney, JRAS, 1935, 459ff.; see E. Reiner, "The Etiological Myth of the 'Seven Sages'," Or n.s. 30 [1961] 1-11; see above under "FORM"). The text deals with the seven sages called *apkallu;* it was used in an apotropaic rite of which the image of fish figures was part. This confirms the theory, already proposed by H. Zimmern, that the seven *apkallu* represent Oannes and the other fish-like beings which, according to Berossos, taught humans the practical matters of civilization.

A further text, J. van Dijk UVB 18 (1962) 43-61, offers a complete list of the sages in the period before the flood. The text is similar in structure to the king lists (KAV 182 and KAV 216 in which, together with the kings, the *ummanu* — learned men whom they employed — are listed. While this is merely by the way, the intent of text 200, 30, 7 is to present a series, perhaps even a genealogy. "These *apkallu* are the sages known from mythology who in a previous era came up out of the sea to reveal to man science, forms of community life and art" (p. 46). The first in the series is *u-an*, the Oannes of Berrosos, probably an abbreviation for *uan-adapa*. The mythical hero Adapa, who went up to An in the heavens, would be then the same as the *apkallu u-an*, the first of the seven sages. This is what is said of Enoch in Gen 5:24.

More certain is the agreement that occurs in text 200, 30, 7. It is said of one of the sages:

> Nun gal pi riggar. . . . The lyre out of bronze,
> (of which. . . .) — were of lapis lazuli,
> with the forge work of Ningal,
> (he made. In the. . . .) . . .-ku, the dwelling of. . . .
> one put the lyre of An. (J. van Dijk, p. 45).

J. van Dijk comments: "Ningalpiriggar appears in this passage as the inventor of the lyre (or harp)" p. 49. This obviously corresponds to Gen 4:21 and so J.J. Finkelstein concludes that one can see in the list of the Cainites an echo of the tradition of the seven sages *(apkallu)*, p. 50, n. 41. One must be content with this cautious formulation. There is a parallel in that in both cases the origin and growth of civilization is set in the primeval period and is linked with a succession of names, and musical instruments are mentioned. The correspondence goes no further. There is no real correspondence in the number seven; the seven is firmly fixed in Babylonian tradition. But one cannot say that all the seven names in the list 4:17-26 are linked with progress in civilization in the same way. The link in the strict sense holds only for those mentioned in vv. 19-22. But there is a difference. The seven *apkallu* are men in the later traditions. Behind these however one can recognize a prehistory in which they were mythical beings.

Another description of the origin and growth of civilization both in the primitive and in the high cultures is well attested and is the most widespread of all: the gods give the people the essentials of civilization, or the gods or intermediary beings or culture heroes teach people the basic arts and crafts and skills. Osiris in the Egyptian myth teaches the people how to till the ground and a great number of Sumerian myths deal with the origin and growth of civilization, as e.g., the myth of the creation of the pick-axe (S.N. Kramer, *Sumerian Mythology* 1944; G.R. Castellino, VT.S 4 [1957] 116-137). H.J.T. Johnson quotes myths of the origin and growth of civilization among the peoples of Central America in *The Bible and the Early History of Mankind* (1948): "The Caril Indians had a . . . myth of a culture hero, who came from the east, taught the Carils agriculture and the primitive arts, and then disappeared in the direction whence he came" p. 135. It is common to all these myths and to the Prometheus myth that the works of civilization are to be traced back to gods or semi-gods in every case.

Purpose and Thrust

When one builds into a genealogy the origin and growth of civilization one presupposes a development in its achievements; so, e.g., J.P. Audet: "Behind the genealogical sequence there is first of all a sense of development. . . ," RB 73 (1966) 19. But the development can be regarded in very different ways. J.P. Audet contrasts the promethean view of the origin of civilization with the biblical in Gen 4:17-26. The myth of Prometheus presumes that fire was originally reserved to the gods alone. Prometheus in an act of revolt steals it to give it to humans. As a result one can view the development in this way: the significance of religion has continually and irreversibly receded in the course of the millennia of human history, while the development of civilization made possible by stealing the fire has become determinative for humankind in an ever increasing degree. Advances in science and technology have step-by-step rendered the hypotheses of religion otiose. "The real revenge for Prometheus' act . . . is a promethean culture and civilization which, by its victories over the 'secrets' of our world, leads men gradually to despise and forget Zeus." In contrast the Old Testament is remarkable for the quiet matter of fact way in which it speaks of the basic achievements of civilization. No robbery is needed, no culture hero to rise in revolt against the gods and snatch from them the fire that makes civilization possible. It is a function of the blessing God bestows on his creatures to enable the creatures themselves to make the basic discoveries. Civilization and its effects then have a positive emphasis in Israel from the very beginning; it is founded in God's will for his creatures.

The mythological explanation of the origin of civilization fell by the way because for Israel God was one. Israel could indeed say on one occasion that Yahweh taught his people agriculture, Is 28:26. But when actually explaining the origins, Israel turned completely to humans; the basic achievements are human work. There is an obvious connection between the oneness of God and the this-worldliness of the beginnings of civilization. It is to human beings that one must trace agriculture, the founding of cities, nomadic and sedentary life, the arts. This is the reason why civilization and art could never have a divine or sacral character in Israel.

The history of the exegesis of 4:17-24 as a whole shows that by far the most frequent pronouncement is a negative judgment on the line of Cain in contrast to the line of Seth. The Sethites are the pious and god-fearing, the Cainites the godless and wicked. This view has prevailed right down to the present, as can be shown by the study of J. Gabriel, "Die Kainitengenealogie Gen 4:17-24," Bib 40 (1959) 409-427. The reason for Gabriel's opinion that "the function of the Cainite genealogy is to give an account of the moral decline and the alienation from God of this section of mankind" is, against K. Budde, the following: "It is certainly not the intention of holy writ to describe the progress of human civilization." This is a typical example of a prejudice which subjects the text of the Bible to itself. If this view were true, then a notable part of the text of the Old Testament would have to be struck from the canon. The Old Testament knows nothing of such a pre-judged and constricted concept of religion. Applied to Gen 4:17-26 the "progress of human civilization" is most certainly part of that which happens between God and his people. If God has given people the commission to work, 2:15; 3:23, then one cannot deny a connection between what is said in 4:17-26 and this commission.

If the Old Testament, in distinction to the mythical and the promethean explanation of the origin of civilization, sees progress and development in the meaning of the commission that God gave his people to work on earth and bases it on the effectiveness of God's blessing, then the consequence is not simply that the Old Testament gives a blanket approval to all forms of progress. There follows an orientation for theology which must take this approval into account. The question arises then whether the one-sided attitude of western theology in favor of intellectual pursuits and the ever-increasing alienation of theology from the natural sciences, technology, and the social sciences represents a false development that has contributed to the decline of the significance of theology today. One must concede that it is only in a few places that the Bible says expressly that God is concerned with a person's work and the life-styles that result from it. But when the Yahwist arranges that the passage dealing with the origin of civilization follows immediately on the creation of human beings, the crime against God, Gen 3, and the crime against the brother, 4:2-16, then he is saying something of fundamental significance for a person as a creature of God.

One can agree then with Descartes when, as one of the first, he speaks of the coming importance of the natural sciences in his *Discourse on Method,* Part 6: "For I thus saw that one may reach conclusions of great usefulness in life, and discover a practical philosophy in the place of the speculative philosophy taught by the Schoolmen; one which would show us the energy and action of fire, air, and stars, the heavens, and all other bodies in our environment, as distinctly as we know the various crafts of our artisans, and could apply them in the same way to all appropriate uses and thus make ourselves masters and owners of nature." (Descartes: *Philosophical Writings* trans. by Elizabeth Anscombe and P.T. Geach, Nelson, 1964, p. 46). It is only when theology makes this positive acknowledgement that it can enter the lists properly equipped to take issue with a technology that is overgrown and endangers humankind and that serves the brutal self-assertion of an individual or a group (4:23-24). The protests of theology and church against misdirected developments will remain ineffective as long as the balance is not restored and the hitherto one-sided orientation of the development of human civilization is not corrected.

There is a complete absence of political structures in the genealogies of the primeval story. Basic to the history of humankind is that effectiveness and progress in civilization which is not subordinated to but rather directed to the state. The pre-political aspects are here brought into relationship with the history of humankind; the outlook is rather broad. The medieval teaching of the two sovereignties (the two swords) and the Reformation teaching of the two kingdoms look only to a section of human history and take their stand on it. This can have no validity for the history of humankind as a whole. The primeval story of the Old Testament shows that the basic forms of community as well as the efficacy of civilization are determinative for the whole history of humankind and so are directed to political structures.

When J in the same context also associates the beginning of the worship of God with primeval time, he is pointing out that worship is as determinative for the whole history of humankind as is the work of civilization and that its universal aspect should not be lost sight of by way of the partial.

The Succession of Generations in the Primeval Period

Literature

H. Zimmern, *Urkönige und Uroffenbarung,* KAT³ (1902) 530-543. S. Euringer, *Die Chronologie der biblischen Urgeschichte (Gen 5 und 11),* BZfr 2 (1909). O. Fisher, "Die Chronologie des Priesterkodex und ihre Umgestaltung," ZAW 31 (1911) 241-255. E. Burrows, "Notes on the Antediluvian Kings," Or 7 (1923) 50-58. S. Langdon, "The Chaldean Kings before the Flood," (The Weld-Blundell Collection, II Historical Inscriptions, Containing Principally the Chronological Prisma, W-B 444, = OECT II), JAOS 42 (1923) 251-259. E. Dhorme, "L'aurore de l'histoire babylonienne," RB 33 (1924) 532-556; RB 35 (1926) 66-82, 223-239, 532-556. H. Zimmern, "Die altbabylonischen vor- (und nach-) sintflutlichen Könige nach neuen Quellen," ZDMG 78 (1924) 19-35. A. Deimel, "Die babylonische und biblische Überlieferung bezüglich der vorsintflutlichen Urväter," Or 17 (1925) 33-47. A. Jepsen, "Zur Chronologie des Priesterkodex," ZAW 47 (1929) 251-255. A. Deimel, "Die altbabylonische Königsliste und ihre Bedeutung für die Chronologie," *Sacra Scriptura antiquitatibus orientalibus illustrata* 6 (1935) 29-37. W. Moock, "Genesis 5 and Jo 16:16," ThGl 31 (1939) 435-440. U. Cassuto, *The Documentary Hypothesis and the Composition of the Pentateuch* (1942; 1961²) 17-26, 51-53. F.R. Kraus, "Zur Liste der älteren Könige von Babylonien," ZA 50 (1952) 29-60. M. Tsevat, "The Canaanite God Sälah," VT 4 (1954) 41-49. S. Makloet, "Zur Zahlensymmetrie in der Adamiten- und Semitenliste (Gen 5 und 11:10-26)," BiLi 24 (1956/57) 234-236. R. Borchert, *Stil und Aufbau der priesterlichen Erzählung,* Diss Heidelberg (1957). E. Reiner, "The Etiological Myth of the 'Seven Sages'," Or NS 30 (1961) 1-11. J. Meysing, "The Biblical Chronologies of the Patriarchs," CNFI 13 (1962) 3-12. J.J. Finkelstein, "The Antediluvian Kings: A University of California Tablet," JCS 17 (1963) 39-51. W.W. Hallo, "Beginning and End of the Sumerian King List in the Nippur Recension," JCS 17 (1963) 52-57. J.B. Bauer, *Die biblische Urgeschichte, Vorgeschichte des Heils,* Gen 1-11 (1964). J.C.H. Lebram, "Nachbiblische Weisheitstraditionem," VT 15 (1965) 167-237. J. Meysing, "Contribution à l'étude des généalogies bibliques," RSR 39 (1965) 209-229. F.N. Jasper, "Early Israelite Traditions and the Psalter," VT 17 (1967) 50-59. J.T. Milik, "Les papyrus Araméens d'Hermoupolis et les cultes Syrophéniciens en Égypte perse," Bib 48 (1967) 546-622. Cf. Literature to 4:17-26, Genealogies.

Text

5:1 This is the list of the genealogies of Adam[a]:

When God created humankind, he created[b] it in the image of God,

2 male and female he created them, and he blessed them and called them human beings when they were created[a].

3 When Adam was 130[d] years old, he[ab] begot (a son) in his own image, corresponding[c] to him, and named him Seth.
4 Adam's[a] life-span, after he begot Seth, came to 800 years. And he begot sons and daughters.
5 The total life-span of Adam came to 930 years. Then he died.
6 When Seth was 105 years old, he begot Enosh.
7 After Seth begot Enosh he lived another 807 years and begot sons and daughters.
8 The total life-span of Seth came to 912 years. Then he died.
9 When Enosh was 90 years old, he begot Kenan.
10 After Enosh begot Kenan he lived another 815 years and begot sons and daughters.
11 The total life-span of Enosh came to 905 years. Then he died.
12 When Kenan was 70 years old, he begot Mahalalel[a].
13 After Kenan begot Mahalalel he lived another 840 years and begot sons and daughters.
14 The total life-span of Kenan came to 910 years. Then he died.
15 When Mahalalel was 65 years old, he begot Jared[a].
16 After Mahalalel begot Jared he lived another 830 years and begot sons and daughters.
17 The total life-span of Mahalalel came to 895 years. Then he died.
18 When Jared was 162[a] years old, he begot Enoch.
19 After Jared begot Enoch he lived another 800 years and begot sons and daughters.
20 The total life-span of Jared came to 962 years. Then he died.
21 When Enoch was 65 years old, he begot Methuselah.
22 And Enoch walked[a] with God. After Enoch begot Methuselah "he lived another"[b] 300 years and begot sons and daughters.
23 The total life-span of Enoch came to[a] 365 years.
24 And Enoch walked with God. And he was no longer there, because God took him.
25 When Methuselah was 187 years old, he begot Lamech.
26 After Methuselah begot Lamech he lived another 782 years and begot sons and daughters.
27 The total life-span of Methuselah came to 969 years. Then he died.
28 When Lamech was 182 years old, he begot a son.
29 And[a] he named him Noah, saying: This one will create[b] relief for us from our work and from the toil of our hands from the ground which God has cursed.
30 After Lamech begot Noah, he lived another 595 years and begot sons and daughters.
31 The total life-span of Lamech came to[a] 777 years. Then he died.
32 When Noah was 500 years old he begot Shem, Ham[a], and Japheth.

1a Vg presumes הָאָדָם, correctly according to sense; but MT is to be retained. **b** For construction (the inf. governs subj. as well as obj.) Ges-K §115i.
2a For בְּיוֹם־הִבָּרְאָם, cf. text. note to 2:4a.
3a וַיּוֹלֶד E. Speiser: "Here the usage is absolute, since an immediate object would have been stylistically awkward; the implied object is *yeled* "child," so that "a son" may be supplied in translation without presupposing accidental omission of בֵּן." **b** The hiph. הוֹלִיד is restricted to P in Pentateuch (contrary E. Jacob). **c** The prepositions are reversed in some Mss to accord with 1:26, but MT should not be altered. **d** The form שְׁנָה מֵאת is peculiar to P, Ges-K §134d.

4a The Peshitta, harmonizing, reads at the beginning "And Adam lived. . . ."

12a Gk has Μαλελεηλ; it is not certain if this represents another Hebrew form of the name.

15a The usual transcription Jared is pausal, as with 'Lamech'; it would be correct to transcribe as Jered.

18a Sam omits ומאת שנה; also other numbers in 19, 20, 25, 26, 27, 28, 30, 31.

22a For the durative form, cf. JAOS 75 (1955) 117ff. **b** Insert ויחי חנוך with BHS, Gk and other versions. The omission in MT can only be an oversight.

23a Instead of ויהי, the plural, as regularly elsewhere, should be read; so too some Mss.

29a The verse is unanimously ascribed to J. But P too must have had the first sentence ויקרא את־שמו נח. **b** Gk reads διαναπαύσει ἡμᾶς, which presupposes יניחנו. This would be a better etymology for נח; one suspects then a later improvement.

31a ויהי cf. note on 2:3.

32a 17 Mss of Sam read ואת־חם for את־חם.

Literary Form

Gen 5 is the immediate continuation of the priestly account of creation in 1:1-2:4a. It is a genealogy that leads from Adam through ten generations to Noah and his sons. Each succession follows a fixed form, the same sentences with the same wording following each other and giving rise to a unique linguistic pattern so as to present in a remarkable way the stream of generations between creation and flood, the very beginning of the history of humankind.

It is most important for the understanding of this remarkable chapter to appreciate and evaluate properly its two basic elements: the one is the constant — the same sentences constantly recurring throughout, forming the successive links in the chain of generations: begetting, the length of the life-span before and after the birth of a son who is named, the begetting of further sons and daughters, death. The other is the variable — the series of names and the numbers. By presenting the very beginning of the history of humankind within this framework, P is pointing out that at its roots and in all its phases and forms the constant and the variable are there and intermeshed. The person's state as a creature and its consequences form the constant, the names and the numbers the variable.

This is basic and decisive for the understanding of history. The western view of history considers only the variables to be constitutive; this is the presupposition in the concept of historical development as well as in the underscoring of the historically unique. When P introduces his historical work with the genealogy of Gen 5 he is saying that history never consists merely in historically demonstrable processes, developments and an apparently unique course of events. Rather, there are at work in every event elements of the stable, always and everywhere the same, which are common to all humankind at all times and which render questionable a science of history that prescinds from these constants. The intention of Gen 5 is to set a limit to the application of this sort of historical science to what is intended in the biblical texts.

The history of exegesis has scarcely paid any attention to the first of these basic elements; it has been concerned almost exclusively with the names and numbers. This one-sided approach had to lead to errors. But the imbalance could have been put right by a single glance at the form of the chapter. The first member of the genealogy, vv. 1-5, differs from all the following in a remarkable way by the elaboration added to it. Its function is to link the genealogy of the ten generations from Adam to Noah with the creation of human beings. It is this elaboration that gives the genealogy of Gen 5 its peculiar character. Any other genealogical texts which are alleged by way of comparison show only a remote parallel or none at all. One can say further that this elaboration of the first member of the genealogy provides the key to its explanation. P is saying here that the plan of God in creating human beings is spelling itself out. The blessing and its power have been bestowed on the creature. The imperative, "be fruitful and multiply and fill the earth," is being carried out in Gen 5. The power of the blessing shows itself effective in the relentless rhythm and steady succession of generations that stretch out across time. The real meaning of the creation of a man and a woman in Gen 1:26-31 can only become clear when generation follows generation according to the rhythm of begetting and birth, life-span and death, as presented in Gen 5. P wants to say that a person created by God is not something that is just put there and continues to be around. A human being is the creature that extends out across time by virtue of the blessing. The history of humankind becomes a reality with the creation of the man and the woman. Part of this history is a succession of names in a succession of eras; this distinguishes humans from the animals who also receive the blessing of fertility at creation.

The second basic element in Gen 5 is the sequence of these names and the span of years linked with them. Both have provided occasion for a comparison with the Babylonian king list. There are the ten generations, the extraordinary numbers and the fact that both end in the same way: Gen 5 ends with Noah, and the king list with Ziusudra, who was saved in the great flood.

Before going into further detail, some very obvious differences should be pointed out. The most crucial is that the texts belong to different genres (cf. ANET, p. 265f. = Weld-Blundell Collection No. 1923, 444; Gen 5). Gen 5 is a genealogy, the old Babylonian king list is the arrangement of the succession of dynasties of a series of cities with the succession of kings and the length of their reigns. Further differences follow from this: the numbers in one case represent the life-span, in the other the length of the reign; one enumerates ancestors, the other kings; the context of one is that of the history of a people, of the other of the story of humankind before it separated into peoples. Gen 5 has its own peculiar way of expressing this in the constantly repeated appendage after the birth of the specific son: "And he begot other sons and daughters." As humankind increases and expands only one person is mentioned by name in each generation. The account is concerned with the growth of humankind from generation to generation, extending nameless and without limit. What is the meaning of the names that stretch from Adam to Noah? This question is to be pursued first by a comparison of the names with those in Gen 4, then with those in the old Babylonian king list.

The Names in the Genealogies of Gen 4:17-26 and Gen 5

The first three names in Gen 5 correspond to the last three names in Gen 4 — Adam, Seth, Enosh (4:25-26). There is agreement in the interpretation of Gen 4 that vv. 25-26 are a tradition which is independent of vv. 17-24. It is common to distinguish a Sethite genealogy (the description is erroneous) from a Cainite genealogy (the description is correct). What is peculiar to the sequence of names in Gen 5 in contrast to Gen 4 is that it begins as a "Sethite genealogy" with the three names from Gen 4:25-26, (1) Adam, (2) Seth, (3) Enosh, and continues with a sequence that corresponds clearly with 4:17-18; (4) Kenan corresponds to Cain, (5) Mahalalel corresponds to Mehujael, (6) Jared corresponds to Irad, (7) Enoch = Enoch, (8) Methuselah corresponds to Methusael, (9) Lamech = Lamech. Of these last six names, two are identical, Enoch and Lamech, two differ only phonetically, Jared-Irad, Kenan-Cain, and one is similar Mahalalel-Mehujael. The sequence is similar but not exactly the same. It is to be noted that the points of correspondence do not, as is usually said, extend across the "Cain-ite genealogy" as a whole, but only across 4:17-18; all corresponding names are restricted to these two verses. The correspondence does not extend to 4:19-22 which speak of the achievements of civilization; the sequence (4) to (9) in Gen 5 presents names which, just as in 4:17-18, are handed down merely as a sequence.

The conclusion is that there was a tradition which was taken up by both J and P. From this follows the composite character of Gen 5. The sequence of ten names has been constructed out of different parts which had been handed down independently. One part is found also in 4:25-26, another in 4:17-18. I will return to the tenth name, Noah, later. It is possible that P has taken over both sequences (1) to (3) and (4) to (9) from J (Gen 4); he could have received them too in a different way which is unknown to us. In favor of this are the differences in the sequence (4) to (9). The conclusion is that P did not have at hand a tradition of a sequence of ten names, and that both parts had had a history in Israel.

Genealogies of Genesis and the Old Babylonian King List

Gen 5		Gen 4		Berossos	Weld-Blundell 62
1	Adam	25	Adam	Ἄλωρος	Alulim
2	Seth	25	Seth	Ἀάπαρος	Alalgar
9	Enosh	26	Enosh	Ἀμήλων	[. . .]Kidunnu
12	Kenan	17	Cain	Ἀμμένων	[. . .]-alimma
15	Mahalalel	18	Mehi(u)jael	Ἀμεγάλαρον	[Dumu]zi, the shepherd
18	Jared	18	Irad	Δάωνος ποιμήν	[Enm]en-tuanna
21	Enoch	17	Enoch	Εὐεδωράγχος	[E]sipa-zianna
25	Methuselah	18	Methushael	Ἀμεψινός	Enmeduranna
28	Lamech	18	Lamech	Ὠτιάρτης	Uburtutu
32	Noah	—		Ξισούθρος	Ziusudra

This list serves as a classical parallel; it was known to interpreters from the beginning through Berossos (cf. *Die Fragmente der griechischen Historiker III C 1,* 1958) as a list of ten kings before the flood, the cities where they ruled and the years of their rule. The historians who quote from Berossos were resumed in the chronicle of Eusebius. Eusebius draws attention to the context (*Eusebius von Caesarea, Die Chronik, aus dem Armenischen übersetzt,* ed. J. Karst, GCS Bd. 20, 1911, 35): "On the other hand (contrary to the Greek tradition) the Hebrew writings have a not insignificant relationship with the Assyrian historical writings and with the narrative of the flood which is handed down in them. They tell that before the flood there was a succession of generations extending as far as the 10th." When the earlier exegesis alleged this parallel the presumption was that the biblical list was older than the Babylonian and that the latter confirmed it (cf. G. Hoberg, *Die Genesis nach dem Literalsinn erklärt,* 1908[2]). The commentaries of the 19th century held firmly that the Babylonian list was at least some hundreds of years older than the list of P in Gen 5 (e.g., E. Sellin, *Die biblische Urgeschichte,* 1905, 22-23). Consequently the biblical text must be dependent on the Babylonian. But scholarship up to 1923 had only the Greek text of Berossos as its point of reference. This text shows a striking agreement with the biblical text in the number ten, the remarkably high numbers and the flood as the final act in the sequence. Further, attempts were made to find names in the Greek text that corresponded to the biblical names by tracing the Greek names back to Akkadian from which the Hebrew names were thought to be translated. H. Zimmern (1902) was able to conclude: "There can scarcely be any doubt now that the biblical tradition Gen 5 (P) of the ante-diluvial primeval ancestors is basically identical with the Babylonian tradition of the ten ante-deluvian primeval kings" p. 539.

The cuneiform discoveries since 1923 (cf. S. Langdon, JAOS 42 [1923] 251-254; further finds are considered in the literature cited above; the lists are now attested in 6 cuneiform texts) have confirmed the broad lines of Berossos's picture in a remarkable way while at the same time making notable corrections. As a result of a whole series of studies (see Bibliog. above) three conclusions emerge which can be regarded as certain and which have important effects on the comparison.

(1) It had been established that in the old Babylonian king list (Text, ANET 265ff.), the part that enumerates the kings before the flood did not originally form a unity with the list of kings after the flood, but represented an independent tradition and was subsequently joined to the latter; see Th. Jacobsen, AsSt 11 (1930) 54-77.

(2) It has been established likewise that the number of kings before the flood in the older lists is eight, not ten. The dominance of the number ten in Weld-Blundell 62 (S. Langdon, 1923) goes back to the insertion into second place in this list of the city of Larsa with two kings, which does not occur in any other list. The list of Berossos comes to ten by means of two demonstrable elaborations. Later the number ten became as it were a norm for genealogies of kings; A. Malamat demonstrates this, JAOS 88 (1968) 163-173. But not even the number eight is certain. Though the great majority of lists contain the name Ziusudra as the king at the time of the flood, it is lacking in some, e.g., WB 444, and there is an older tradition according to which Ziusudra is not king but citizen of the city of Shuruppak, as also in the Gilgamesh epic. The very old tradition of the seven sages, the *apkallu,* which refers to the seven kings of primeval time, also favors the number seven. At the same time it is uncertain whether the old Babylonian king list in its oldest form ended with the king at the time of the flood.

(3) The most far-reaching result of the discovery of the cuneiform king lists was that the names of the kings turn out to be Sumerian. And so the whole theory of correspondence to the biblical names collapsed. This is the most thorough revision of conclusions hitherto held as certain that the newly discovered texts have provided. H. Zimmern, who had to correct his opinion, writes: "And so . . . practically all the earlier attempts to trace the first eight names of Berossos back to Babylonian models . . . are shown to be untenable. . . . All the fine combinations then (the comparison with the names of Gen 5) . . . disappear

beyond recall'' (1924, 24). Something similar can be found in S. Langdon 257, W.F. Albright 329, J.J. Finkelstein 50, n. 41. This thorough-going revision was made necessary because a group of six cuneiform texts became the point of reference in place of the single Greek translation of Berossos. When these versions were compared it became possible to trace some of the threads of the tradition history of the old Babylonian king list. Only then was a firmer basis for the comparison achieved.

Excursus: *The Genealogies and the King Lists*

A glance at Gunkel's commentary shows how much the situation has changed. He saw agreement (1) in the period before the flood, (2) in the number ten, (3) in the extraordinary numbers, (4) in the correspondence between the names in positions 3, 4, 7, 8, 9, 10 (order following Berossos).

The first point can stand insofar as it is only saying that the kings belong to the primeval period. It is subject to correction however since it has been proved that the list of primeval kings was once independent, that the datings "before the flood" and "after the flood" were only prefixed to the king lists after the flood, and that Ziusudra was not the last king on the list from the beginning.

To the second point it is to be said that the agreement in the number ten, apart from Berossos, occurs in only one text (WB 62), where it is clearly a locally conditioned elaboration. Otherwise the list contains eight, or seven, names of kings. And so there is no comparison of the individual names in the sequence from one to ten.

The third point, the extraordinary numbers, remains insofar as both in the king list before the flood as well as in Gen 5 it is a sign of talk of the primeval period. The agreement between the two texts here calls for no special comment. The practice of attributing extraordinarily long life-spans to primeval ancestors (or primeval kings) was widespread and had long been known. "Josephus can call on Egyptian, Chaldean, Phoenician and other ancient witnesses for the remarkable, and gradually receding, life-span of people" (F. Delitzsch). The systematic dating of the periods during which the kings and their dynasties reigned is then but a secondary stage. It can only be understood as a projection back into the pre-historical period of the dating of historical kings. (Cf. J. Meysing, RSR 39 [1965] 209-229.) Meysing says of the numbers: "The sum total of the chronologies is fixed in advance" p. 227. The addition of the life-span is secondary in Gen 5 too; the same names occur without the number of years in the genealogies 4:25-26, 17-18 (J). The dating in P too is a subsequent work of systematization. It is P's own work and is a basic characteristic of his whole plan. It is probable that P was familiar with the Babylonian king list and its high numbers; but it is not necessary to admit a dependence.

Gunkel's fourth point of agreement, the correspondence of the individual names, has collapsed completely (so e.g., E.A. Speiser, *Comm.*). This error could have been avoided had it been noticed that the sequence of names in P is a combination of two parts that are still handed down separately in J.

The old Babylonian list of primeval kings can no longer then be regarded as a parallel to Gen 5. This has been expressed in a radical way by A. Deimel: "It would be better to admit honestly that up to the present no connection whatever has been proved between the Babylonian and biblical traditions of the primeval ancestors before the flood," Or 17 (1925) 43. The relationship can now be formulated more cautiously and precisely: the agreements that had been accepted are for the most part not valid. Whatever parallels remain, such as the remarkable numbers, the number ten, the last name on the list, are to be explained from later stages of the tradition history, and exclude one from regarding the old Babylonian king list in its original form as the basis of Gen 5.

The comparison of Gen 5 and 4 with the Babylonian king list completed, the question arises about the significance of the names and numbers for P. It can be taken as certain that P is not dependent on this old Babylonian king list for the series of names. The list is *eo ipso* in the context of political-historical tradition (in ANET it stands under the heading: "Babylonian and Assyrian historical texts"), while the genealogy of P in Gen 5 is in a deliberately pre-political context; it belongs in the strictest sense to the genre of genealogies. P had at hand the number ten which was typical and normal for genealogies (A. Malamat, JAOS 88 [1968] 163-173), as well as two series of names of primeval ancestors, one of which was identical with that in 4:25-26, the other closely resembling that in 4:17-18. P made one series out of them and inserted them into the genealogical framework, which was wholly his own work, even though the elements throughout it had come down to him.

The greatest alteration that P made in the material he inherited was to add the life-spans. These are part of the genre of chronicle, which was current at the royal court, and of the list giving the succession of kings with the length of their reigns which is preserved in the court archives. Numbers are not part of the genre of genealogies in family and tribal circles. It is this that gave rise to the form of the genealogy in Gen 5 which suggested comparison with the king list. By fixing the year of the birth of each son who is specifically named, P succeeded in creating a chronological succession of primeval ancestors which bears an external resemblance to the succession of reigns. No one would ever have thought of the possibility of such a comparison had there not been this succession marked out by the year of the birth of the son.

The Numbers in Gen 5.

Two things are certain: First, the numbers in Gen 5 do not belong originally to the names with which they stand. The series of names came down to P without any life-span attached to them. The number scheme had an independent origin from the series of names. Second, the numbers in Gen 5 have an independent origin from those in the king list. Similarly the series of names and the number scheme in the Babylonian lists each had an independent origin. There follows an interesting point of correspondence. In both cases the tradition of the series of names is relatively fixed, while that of the numbers is remarkably fluid. One can speak of a number scheme in both cases because the point of departure is the sum total. In P the sum total is meant to fix the period from the flood back to the creation of humans. The individual names are inserted into this time-span in such a way as to add up to an already determined total. Accordingly it is certain that this number system is a subsequent construction. The system indeed had a meaning which explained the distribution of the numbers over the individual names. But the meaning was no longer known to those who handed down the text, or it was contested.

This is clear from the very different traditions in the MT, Gk, and Sam. There are tables that list these differences in many of the commentaries, e.g., J. Skinner p. 134. The total number of years, and so the date of the flood, is 1656 in MT, 1307 in Sam, 2242 in Gk. How the differences in the three traditions are to be explained, which is the original, and how did the variations come about — all this has been discussed thoroughly. U. Cassuto deals with differences in dating in great detail in his commentary. But because it is a question of constructions in all three traditions, and this is clear and undisputed, such a discussion is not profitable. I leave it aside and refer to Cassuto's commentary. However, the fact of three different number schemes side-by-side in three different traditions has significance for the exegesis, namely that those who passed on the tradition have made known the limit of their knowledge of the primeval period. When all three schemes coalesce in Noah and the date of the flood, then this reveals their point of departure. All three are attempts to reconstruct a period of time backwards with the flood as the terminal point. Neither of the three schemes is the correct one or the original one, because such is no longer possible here. Each wants to be recognized and so they are put side-by-side; they are indications of the limit of all knowledge about the primeval period.

What of the extraordinarily long life-spans? Most are up in the 900s, the longest, that of Methuselah, is 969 years, and the shortest, that of Enoch, 365 years. The numbers of the primeval kings in the Babylonian lists are very much higher. Instead of 1656, there are 432,000 years from the creation to the flood. (The length of the reign of Alalgar is given as 72,000 years in WB 62.) It is clear that the number schemes are not open to comparison. Both however are a reference to the generally widespread view that the life-span of the primeval ancestors was longer than the present life-span. This is often explained by the greater vitality of people in the primeval period, and the reduction of the life-span by the diminution of vitality. This may well have been a generally known motif. However it is not sufficient to explain the numbers either in Babylon or in the Bible. It is absurd to say that the life-span of the primeval Babylonian kings is an expression of their great vitality.

E. Dhorme (see bibliog. above) refers to the difference in the regal span of the kings in the historical lists after the flood. They are so far apart that the numbers attached to the primeval kings before the flood cannot belong to the same (historical) category. They are mythical numbers whose excess points to the realm of mythical event beyond history. Dhorme draws attention correctly to the parallels to the Egyptian presentation of the beginnings of the kingdom; the kings of the primeval period are described as gods. These descriptions are essentially at one. The institution of the kingship transcends history. In its beginnings it stretches back into a mythical realm beyond history which uses astronomical numbers to express the mythical character of the early era of the kingship (the subtle difference here between the Egyptian and the Sumerian-Babylonian presentation points to a further difference which shows itself elsewhere in the conception of the kingship; cf. H.A. Frankfort, *Kingship and the Gods,* 1948; 1962[2]).

The basically different function and meaning of the numbers in Gen 5 thereby becomes clear. This was a mistake because, in the points enumerated above, one had allowed oneself to be deceived by the apparent agreement between Gen 5 and the list of the primeval kings. The numbers in Gen 5 have no connection whatsoever with the political institution of the kingship. They describe the generations of humankind as they stretch back into remote antiquity. P is using here a way of describing the course of time in the period before history in order to say that the history of humankind stretches back so far into the past that it cannot be measured by the standards of present-day history.

The great ages in Gen 5 are not, or in any case not merely, an expression of greater vitality. There may be echoes of this motif. For P as for the Old

Testament as a whole the life-span of a person is fixed within the limits of childhood, youth, maturity and old age. Ages of some 900 years burst this limit. There is something like this in Is 65:20 where a hundred years is the upper limit in the period of salvation at the end-time. If the large numbers in Gen 5 do not serve the mythical transcendence of the institution of the kingship, as in the list of the primeval Sumerian kings, then they can only refer to the human race as it stretches far back into the distant past.

It is only now that we can see the relationship between the two basic elements out of which Gen 5 is composed. As the genealogical framework with its monotonous, constantly recurring sentences portrays the rhythm of ongoing generations, so the series of names with their astronomical numbers points to the extension of ancient time into an unimaginably distant past. P's purpose is thus revealed. He wants to initiate with a genealogy the course of ordered, subdivided time, the second part of which, the patriarchs, introduces God's dealing with his people. The genealogy sets in motion and puts into the length and breadth of human history the power of the blessing which God bestowed on his people.

Setting in Life

Three stages must be distinguished from the original setting in life of Gen 5 up to its insertion into the priestly work. The first is the early stage of the genealogy. This is a sort of pre-historical presentation of history in which the "where from" was preserved in family and tribe. The mention or recitation of the list of forefathers must have had a fixed place in the life of the tribe, earlier in the veneration of the ancestors, then in the tribal feasts, as mentioned in 1 Sam 6:25 (this interesting suggestion comes from A. Malamat, "King Lists. . . ." 173, n. 29).

The second stage is the transfer of the genealogy to the primeval event, thereby loosing it from its original setting in life. It now serves to present the history or origin of humankind or events related to humankind such as advances in civilization. In this second stage, when used as a means of answering the question about the origin and early period of humanity, the genealogy had great significance; the texts as preserved indicate a many-sided history. The primeval genealogies already had their beginning in the oral stage. It is not possible to know what their setting in life was.

The third stage is the resumption of the genealogy into the work of P. Here it takes on a new setting in life because of the strong link with P's creation story forged by the introductory passage, 5:1-3. P succeeds thereby in making the genealogy the linch-pin between creation and the history of humankind and at the same time marking this history as having its source in the blessing of the creator. The whole conception of P's work is thus stamped with a universal outlook. It spans the whole period from the creation of human beings, across the generations of human history, right up to the separate institution of the temple cult in Jerusalem, which is thereby set in a universal context. All *tōledōt* that follow Gen 5 stand in the perspective of the *tōledōt* of *'ādām*, of the history of humankind.

Literature: Gen 5:1-5: J. Wellhausen, *Prolegomena* ed. 1957, 316-317. K. Budde, "Ellä tōledōth," ZAW 34 (1914) 241-253; 35 (1915) 67-97; 36 (1916) 1-7. G.

von Rad, *Die Priesterschrift* (1934). H.L. Ginsberg, "The Composition of the Book of Daniel," VT 4 (1954) 246-275. P. Winter, "Sadoqite Fragments. . . ," ZAW 68 (1956) 71-84. O. Eissfeldt, "Biblos geneseōs," *Festschr. E. Fascher* (1958) 31-40 = KS III 458-470. A. Murtonen, "The Use and Meaning of the Words L^ebårek and B^eråkå^h in the OT," VT 9 (1959) 158-177. A. Kruyswijk, *Geen gesneden beeld. . . .* (1962). R.N. Whybray, "Proverbs VIII 22-31 and its Supposed Prototypes," VT 15 (1965) 504-514.

Commentary

[5:1-5] The special character of the first member, vv. 1-5, has already been pointed out. It consists of the regular pattern, vv. 3-5, expanded by בדמותו כצלמו in v. 3, and the link with the creation of man and woman in 1:26-31 by vv. 1-2. It is preceded by a title. It is underscored by means of a framework of two sentences whose wording is almost the same: "When God created man — when they were created." Four details have been inserted into the framework. The first three have been taken over from 1:26-31: 1. God made humankind in his image, 2. God made it male and female, 3. God blessed them. The fourth detail, that God named them "man," is missing in Gen 1; it must have a special meaning.

[5:1] The title, "This is the list of the family tree of Adam" is part of the genealogy and so is to be regarded as independent of vv. 1b-2. And so Adam is here a proper name as it is from v. 3 onwards. But if תולדת אדם belongs to Gen 5, then this must hold too for ספר. It can only refer to the unity of the genealogy of Gen 5, and so must be translated by "list" (or "document," H. Gunkel). H. Holzinger and B.D. Eerdmans had concluded from the fuller expression ספר תולדת in contrast to the shorter (2:4a; 6:9; 10:1; 11:10, 27; 25:12, 19; 36:1, 9; 37:2; Num 3:1) תולדות, with a name, that the priestly document began here. G. von Rad developed this further with his thesis of a Tōledōt-book, which would have contained only genealogies and have been the model for P. He assumes that the heading of this book still remains. But that would only be possible if תולדות were used in this title in a general, all-embracing sense. However, the title in the first sentence says clearly that it is giving the genealogy of Adam (proper name) in what follows. One must agree with H. Gunkel when he refers ספר alone to this chapter.

O. Eissfeldt *(Biblos geneseōs)* has dealt thoroughly with von Rad's thesis. He proves from the occurrence and meaning of *tōledōt* in P, that in 5:1-2 it can only be the introduction of this chapter and not of a *tōledōt*-book. It is to be understood then as a "piece of primeval information, title or list." This study also synthesizes the present discussion on *tōledōt* and concludes "that this series forms a meaningful whole which . . . must go back to a written plan which has been carefully worked out. The formula always occurs at those points in the presentation which are drawing attention to a restriction of the broader realm hitherto in question. It ceases just when the narrative has advanced to the domain which is really authoritative and the fulfillment of all the preceding development, namely the people of Israel or its cultic representatives, the priests and Levites," p. 461.

The reason why the designation ספר stands here is that in all other passages the title תולדות refers to narratives, but here merely to a genealogy, i.e. to a list or a document (so O. Eissfeldt and others).

"When God created man" — By introducing the genealogy of Adam with the creation of humankind and so presenting it as an independent event, P is linking it to the creation of humans that is carried on in the genealogy of Adam. And so he lay stress on the creation of the first man in the image of God by repeating the image formula at the begetting of the first human being by a human being, v. 3a. If the expression, as shown in the commentary on 1:26-31, means that God created humans corresponding to him, as his counterpart, so that something can happen between him and these creatures (see comm. ad. loc.), then the emphatic resumption of the phrase can only mean that the whole of humankind is God's counterpart and corresponds to him. It is something given to humans by the very fact of existence.

[5:2] The second characteristic of humans that is repeated here is that humankind consists of male and female. Even if P names only one male in each generation in the genealogy which he thus introduces, nevertheless this initial allusion to the complementarity of man and woman shows that the stream of generations through the ages presupposes they belong in community. This is what is meant by the birth of each child as the genealogy steadily progresses. The third characteristic, "And he blessed them," states expressly that the blessing of God becomes effective in the succession of generations that follows v. 3. So P underscores yet again that the blessing that God bestowed on the man and the woman in creation holds for the whole of humankind. God's blessing is at work as humankind grows, spreads and advances on its way. The fourth characteristic is the name that God gives. This sentence is new and is not found in 1:26-31, and this is important. It is beyond doubt that אדם is used collectively in this sentence, whereas in the title in v. 1a and from v. 3 on Adam is a proper name. The name "human," common to all, is expressly set over against the proper name. The naming of this creature by God here and not in 1:26-31 is deliberate. The name of the individual arises out of the name of the species, human, as the genealogy extends into history. P is saying at this point that the name of the species, human, is the name bestowed by the creator. The name preserves within it what God the creator wanted a human being to be. The history of humankind from its creation to its end is enclosed within this name.

[5:3] The pattern that determines the whole genealogy begins in v. 3 — apart from the addition which we have already discussed. The first two words of v. 3, ויחי אדם "and Adam lived," are meant to convey the outcome of the transition from the creation of the first couple to the continuation of human existence through time that now begins. This can only be expressed in the words "and Adam lived. . . ." It means exactly the same as what King Hezekiah said in the psalm of praise after he was cured from his illness: "The living, the living, he thanks you, as I do this day," Is 38:19. The beginning of the first genealogy points to an affirmation of life which is based on the affirmation of the creature state.

[5:6-8] It is this very affirmation of the creature state that is expressed in the genealogical pattern. The life of the human being is reduced to a series of external factors: he is begotten and born, he begets a child (marriage is presumed), there is his life-span and his death (cf. tombstone inscriptions); thereby is expressed the human condition everywhere and for all time. When we speak of a full and significant human life, we can never alter, overlook or erase these factors. The potential and limitation of human existence lies enclosed within them.

For the names Seth and Enosh, cf. comm. on 4:25-16.

Literature: Gen 5:9: A.C. Graham, "Adam and Enosh," ExpT 51 (1939/1940) 205.

[5:9-11] קֵינָן: The name occurs only here and is generally regarded as a by-form of קַיִן. Among the Sabaeans Kenan is the name of a god.

[5:12-14] מַהֲלַלְאֵל is clearly a Hebrew name. It can mean "praise of God" or "one who praises God." It occurs again as a proper name in Neh 11:4.

Literature: Gen 5:15-17: G.R. Driver, "On עלה 'went up country' and ירד 'went down country'," ZAW 69 (1957) 74-77.

[5:15-17] יֶרֶד corresponds to עִירָד in 4:18. Corresponding to the verb ירד the name would mean "descend," but that is not certain. L. Koehler links it with the Akk. *(w)ardu* = "servant," according to W.F. Albright; so too U. Cassuto.

Literature: Gen 5:18: J. Lindblom, "Die Vorstellung vom Sprechen Jahwes zu den Menschen im AT," ZAW 75 (1963) 263-288.

[5:18-20] On חֲנוֹךְ cf. the explanation of 4:17. It occurs also as the name of one of the sons of Midian in Gen 25:4 and as a son of Ruben in Gen 46:9. The name is usually derived from חָנַךְ = "to dedicate"; W.F. Albright would explain it from the Can. *ḥanaku* = "retainer," JBL 58 (1939) 62.

Literature: Gen 5:21-23: E.G. Kraeling, "Terach. - Methuselach," ZAW 40 (1922) 153-155. J. Salguero, "El dolor es meritorio y será recompensado en la vida futura," CuBi 22 (1965) 131-141. N. Tromp, *Primitive Conceptions*. . . . (1969) 149.

[5:21-23] מְתוּשֶׁלַח in place of the מְתוּשָׁאֵל of 4:18. The first part corresponds to the Akk. *mutu* = man. The second part שֶׁלַח occurs also independently as a name in Gen 10:24; 11:12-15. It has been understood as the name of a place or the name of a god derived from the verb שָׁלַח (missile?). The study of M. Tsevat "The Canaanite God SÄLAH," VT 4 (1954) 41-49 has made it probable that it is the name of a Canaanite god of the underworld. It would correspond to מְתוּשָׁאֵל even more clearly if it were to be read as מְתוּשָׁאֵל. The Gk has Μαθουσαλα both in 4:18 and 5:21-23; this has become our proverbial Methuselah, the oldest man to live, 969 years.

Literature: Gen 5:24: J. Kroon, "De Hemelvaart van Henoch," Studiën 131 (1939) 397-403. H.H. Rowley, "The Future Life in the OT," ConQ 33 (1955) 116-132. P. Grelot, "La légende d'Hénoch dans les Apocryphes et dans la Bible. Origine et signification," RSR 46 (1958) 5-26, 181-210. E. Osswald, "Beobachtungen zur Erzählung von Abrahams Aufenthalt in Ägypten im 'Genesis-Apokryphon'," ZAW 72 (1960) 7-25. E. Kutsch, "Sein Leiden und Tod — unser Heil. Eine Exegese von Jesaja 52:13-53:12," BSt 52 (1967). G. Fohrer, "Das Geschick des Menschen nach dem Tode im AT," KuD 14 (1968) 249-262. M. Gil, "Enoch in the Land of Eternal Life," Tarb. 38 (1968/1969) 322-337.

[5:24] This verse falls outside the genealogical pattern, indicating that it echoes a special tradition about Enoch. The repetition of the sentence "and Enoch walked with God" in 22a and 24a is to be noted. There is a further doublet in the second part of v. 24: the וְאֵינֶנּוּ, "and he was there no more," is subsequently explained by the sentence "for God had taken him away." We have here a combination of different traditional elements which are themselves but echoes of the traditions from which they originate. One must be careful therefore in explaining these fragments of tradition and pay attention to their fragmentary character.

(1) The short life-span, 365 years, is now regarded as interpretation; it is the latest of the three characteristic elements. The number, an expression of fullness borrowed from the calendar year, is certainly not meant to be mythical, referring to a solar deity, as many had earlier assumed; rather it tells us something about Enoch being taken away to God. His life-span was a full rounded whole that could be short because it did not end with death.

(2) "Enoch walked with God." The same sort of phrase occurs with לפני 17:1 (Abraham) and אחר Deut 13:5 (the people). Some interpreters emphasize the fact that the phrase "to walk with God" only occurs with reference to Enoch and Noah, 6:9, and see in it a closer relationship with God. Even if J. Skinner's warning about making too much of the difference in the prepositions is justified, nevertheless one can concede that P has deliberately restricted the preposition "with" to the two primeval figures. The phrase is usually explained with J. Skinner as "a fellowship with God morally and religiously perfect" or with B. Jacob, "It describes a way of life morally pleasing to God resulting from an obedient attitude to God." P can have given this meaning to the old tradition as the sentence explaining "to walk with God" in 6:9 shows. But the meaning of the phrase in the old tradition that resumes is obvious from 1 Sam 25:15f., where it describes friendly everyday conduct with regard to one's neighbors. The old tradition understood the words in the sense that Enoch stood in a direct and immediate relationship to God, (F. Delitzsch refers correctly to 3:8), and so was entrusted with God's plans and intentions. This is the starting point for the significance that the figure of Enoch had in a tradition that began early and reached its fullness only in the Apocalyptic literature.

Before the discovery of the cuneiform texts, one had seen the prototype of Enoch in the seventh king of the list of Berossos, Evedoranchos = Enmeduranki. It was said of him that he was taken up into the company of Shamash and Ramman and was inducted into the secrets of heaven and earth. Since the new discoveries have shown that the parallel between the series of ten in Berossos and Gen 5 is no longer tenable, one can no longer maintain a dependence of what is said of Enoch in Gen 5 on the seventh king in Berossos (nevertheless U. Cassuto still does). One can only point in general to a theme that occurs often in the myths of Israel's neighbors, that a certain person is especially near to God or is taken up to God or the gods. One would be more inclined to admit a parallel to Adapa, the first of "the seven sages," of whom it is said that he was taken away and given wisdom, being entrusted with the divine secrets.

(3) Enoch's removal is described in two different ways which belong to different traditions. The first: "He was gone," 1 Kings 20:40 and elsewhere, does not reflect on where he had gone to. What is amazing and unheard of and so deserving of being handed down is the fact that Enoch disappeared and no one knew where. All attention is focused here on the unexplained fact. The other expression: "God took him away," presupposes a different attitude. It wants to explain, to make the thing comprehensible. It is certainly a later statement, an attempt to "rationalize."

In Berossos's account of the flood it is narrated that Xisouthros disappeared suddenly after leaving the ship and that those remaining behind looked for him and called after him. Then a voice came out of the air saying that he had been taken away to live with the gods because of his piety (A. Heidel, *The Gilgamesh Epic. . .*, 1949, 117). The disappearance of Xisouthros is explained subsequently as removal to the gods. It has nothing to do with a notion of the beyond, but is an expression of the extraordinary impression made by this particular man; he did not die like an ordinary mortal, but one day he was no longer there. It is only the secondary explanation, i.e., that he disappeared because he was taken away to God or the gods, that brings in the idea of removal to a place beyond. But a comparison with Berossos shows that there is a still more important difference here: his language is expressly mythical when it is said that Xisouthros now dwells with the gods. In Gen 5:24 the expression "because God took him away" leaves his destiny open. There is no sign of a mythical notion of the beyond.

The explanatory addition lays stress on the extraordinary element in Enoch's disappearance, but says nothing about a place beyond whither Enoch was taken (so too H. Gunkel). Only gradually did the notion of removal as a state enter into the narrative of removal as an event. The language of Lk 16:22, "Abraham's bosom," shows this. It is presumed here that Abraham is "taken away," as already in Judaism in 4 Macc 13:17; 18:23. The notion does not require a narrative of removal; it is the expression of the exaltation of the figure of Abraham in the later Abraham tradition, and only here is found the notion, bordering on the mythical, that the one who was taken away dwells in a place beyond.

On the name Lamech, cf. 4:18.

Literature: Gen 5:29: I. Goldziher, "Zur Geschichte der Etymologie des Namens Noah," ZDMG 24 (1870) 207-208. P. Schwen, "Noah und Lot," ZAW 33 (1913) 314-315. F. Martin, "A Famine Element in the Flood Story," JBL 45 (1926) 129-133. E.G. Kraeling, "The Interpretation of the Name Noah in Genesis V 29," JBL 48 (1929) 138-143. J. Morgenstern, "A Note on Genesis V 29," JBL 49 (1930) 306-309. R.H. Mottram, *Noah* (1937). J. Lewy, "Nāh et Ruspān," *Mélanges Syriens offerts à M.R. Dussaud, I* (1939) 273-275. J.J. Stamm, "Die akkadische Namengebung," MVAG 44 (1939; 1968²) 79, 168-169. H.L. Ginsberg, "Essays über Noah, Daniel, Hiob," *Ginsberg Jubilee Vol.* (1945). N.H. Snaith, "The Meaning of 'The Paraclete'," ExpT 57 (1945/1946) 48-49. C.F. Jean, "Les noms propres de personnes dans les lettres de Mari," *Studia Mariana* (1950) 63-98. M. Noth, "Noah, Daniel und Hiob in Ezechiel XIV," VT 1 (1951) 251-260. J. Hempel, "Glaube, Schöpfung u. Mythos im AT," ZAW 65 (1953) 135-136. H.W. Wolff, "Zur Hermeneutik des AT," EvTh 16 (1956) 337-370.

[5:29] This verse is almost unaminously ascribed to J. The reasons are convincing: the use of the name יהוה, especially in a context where אלהים predominates; the clear reference to Gen 3, especially 3:17-19, and the fact that such explanations of names do not occur anywhere else in P. What is not so certain is the source whence this passage was taken. A redactor has inserted it into the P genealogy, attaching it to the name Noah. Since K. Budde, it has been almost universally agreed that it belonged originally to Gen 4:25-26 (e.g., H. Gunkel, J. Skinner and others). But that is unlikely because the sequence Adam-Seth-Enosh in 4:25-26 agrees with that in 5:3-8, and the sequence in 5:9-32 agrees very closely with that in 4:17-18. The appearance of Noah at the end of Gen 5 gives reason to presume a previous stage of the sequence in 4:17-18 that included Noah. One can more readily accept this because with Lamech in 4:19 there begins another tradition that did not originally belong in the sequence 4:17-18 (see comm. ad loc.). In support of this is that the explanation of the name belongs to the passage about Noah and the vine, 9:20-27; the relief that Noah brought cannot be anything else than the beginning of viticulture, inasmuch as it is so closely connected with the cursing of the ground and the burden of work which is its consequence. This explanation of the name is, in content, very much in accord with the description of the achievements of civilization in 4:17-22; there is no "trace of a mythological figure who brings prosperity" (J. Hempel).

The name נוח has not been explained. The explanation by means of ינחמנו is so far removed from the real name that the reading of the Gk διαναπαύσει, which presupposes יניחנו from נוח ("he will give us rest"), can only be an improvement as it is closer to the name itself. If the author is thinking of the significance of wine, then "comfort" is much better. The explanation of a name is usually given in one simple sentence. One can presume then an older form that lay behind 5:29: "Who will bring us comfort in (from) our work." This simple and quite sufficient explanation of the name has been elaborated by a recollection of Gen 3:17, "and from the toil of our hands from the earth that Yahweh has cursed." The elaboration sounds awkward; it seems to be the work of someone in the tradition who wanted to establish a connection with Gen 3:17. The explanation of the name then must be understood without the elaboration. It is to be seen in the context in which the Old Testament speaks of wine in the other places: "Wine to gladden the heart of man" Ps 104:15 (likewise Judg 9:13); cf. Sir 35:27f.; especially Prov 31:6f.: ". . . let them drink . . . and remember their misery no more." H. Gunkel refers to the custom of offering a cup of consolation to a mourner when someone has died, Jer 16:7. What is in mind here is the rhythm of work and celebration; and the discovery of the vine has provided hard-working people with a bringer of joy. This explanation is supported further by the addition that refers to Gen 3:17: it is the earth cursed by God that makes daily work a burden. But this same earth by producing the vine provides for relaxation, relief and refreshment.

Literature: Gen 5:31, 32: G. Kuhn, "Die Lebenszahl Lemechs (Gen 5:31)," ZAW 54 (1936) 309-310. F.C. Fensham, "The Son of a Handmaid in North-west Semitic," VT 19 (1969) 312-321.

[5:32]   The pattern that has dominated the whole chapter falls apart here; the other basic form of genealogy appears (cf. Intro.): the division into branches. This means a transition to another type. To the succession of generations is added the contiguity of "brothers." The very different genealogy of Gen 10 is now introduced; but between them comes the story of the flood.

Purpose and Thrust

The significance of Gen 5 is not that it bridges the time span from the creation to the flood but that it leads from the creation of humans into the history of humankind. Gen 5 of course does not present history in the strict sense, but the primeval event, the extension of humankind into time before the separations which render history possible. However, it presents the basic movement of all history. The human person, by virtue of the blessing, is the creature that extends into time.

The meaning of the creation of humanity can be misunderstood without the supplement of the genealogy in Gen 5. The person from the very outset is not a being that exists merely as an individual; the person exists only as a link in a chain, only as belonging to a part that comes out of the past and stretches on into the future. Humankind (אדם in vv. 1b-2) is there before the person (Adam in vv. 3-5); and humankind is not the sum total of people that exist here and now, but that humankind which extends through history and develops within history.

In the introductory verses, P sharpens the idea that a person is a creature that extends into time by virtue of the blessing. A person is human only in the community of man and woman. The name "human being" is bestowed on the person by God and with it goes the meaning of human existence. In the succession of generations, the person remains the creature that God has created as the one corresponding to him. A human being as a creature created in the image of God continues as such in the succession of generations, 5:3. P is saying that what happens in all epochs, in all races, religions and peoples is from the very outset and before everything else, a happening between God and his people. This is not based on a special act of God for a special group of people, but on the effectiveness of God's blessing that embraces all that lives. This presupposes a relationship of a person to God that is given by the very fact of human existence and is independent of any individual decision for or against any person or thing, or of any faith or of any religious allegiance. Something happens between God and his human creatures in the mere fact of the continuance of human history.

The understanding of humanity in Gen 5 (together with 1:26-31) stands in opposition to any understanding that thinks it can trace out an "ontology of human beings" or an "image of the person" apart from the history and the development of the human race. It is in harmony however with any understanding according to which one can talk meaningfully of humans only on the basis of human history seen as a whole.

This chapter is of fundamental importance for the priestly work as a whole. The goal of P's work is the erection of the sanctuary in Jerusalem and the establishment of worship there. But this very circumscribed role stands in a universal perspective. This means an understanding of God which sees the God who was worshiped in Jerusalem, and whose worshiping community is a group that is very confined racially and in cult, as the creator of the world and of humankind. This is what God is and must remain, otherwise what happens between the creator and humankind from the creation right up to the present, as well as the Jerusalem liturgy, would be hollow and meaningless. If P's path, which led to the founding of the sanctuary, also leads back into the immeasurable past (the high numbers) of a historical but remote and inaccessible antiquity, then this is his acknowledgement of the enduring significance of what happens between God and humankind, which remains utterly outside and beyond what happens in the Jerusalem liturgy. The priestly document has preserved here a universalism that has but seldom shown such breadth and openness.

One of the most remarkable parallels between the Old Testament and the New Testament is that in each case a genealogy is prefaced to the story of salvation. In the New Testament these are the genealogies in Mt 1:1-17 and Lk 3:23-38. Mt goes back to Abraham, Lk to Adam (in 3:36-38 the sequence of names is taken from Gen 5). It is of the utmost importance that Jesus of Nazareth is set in the context of the working out of God's blessing. The blessing starts with the creation of humankind, it is the source of the birth of Jesus, and it embraces the whole of humanity in the whole extent of its history. The theological significance of these genealogies at the beginning of the gospels is the declaration that God's saving action, which makes its beginning in this Jesus of Nazareth, is unthinkable apart from the functioning of his blessing, which embraces the whole of humankind, and that we cannot expunge it from our consideration of any one of his words, deeds, or stages on the way. The human existence of Jesus belongs not only to his work of salvation; it is just as much a constituent part of the history of humankind. To understand the work of Jesus of Nazareth purely "soteriologically" is to misunderstand one essential aspect of the gospels which appears in the genealogies of the Old Testament and can only be seen in the context of these right back to Gen 5.

Genesis 6:1-4

The Sons of the Gods
and the Giants

Literature

On the passage as a whole: J.J. Astruc, *Conjectures sur les mémoires originaux dont-il paroît que Moyse s'est servi pour composer le livre de la Genèse* (1753). J.H. Kurtz, *Die Ehen der Söhne Gottes mit den Töchtern der Menschen; eine theologische Untersuchung zur exegetischen, historischen, dogmatischen und praktischen Würdigung des biblischen Berichtes Genesis 6:1-4* (1857). L. Reinke, "Die Ehen der Söhne Gottes mit den Töchtern der Menschen; eine exegetisch-kritische und historische Abhandlung über 1. Mose 6:1-4," *Beiträge zur Erklärung des AT 5,* V (1863) 91-186. P. Scholz, *Die Ehen der Söhne Gottes mit den Töchtern der Menschen. Eine exegetisch-kritische, historische und dogmatische Abhandlung über den Bericht Genesis 6:1-4* (1865). I. Goldziher, *Der Mythus bei den Hebräern* (1876). K. Budde, *Die biblische Urgeschichte (Gen 1-12:5) untersucht,* (1883) 1-44. O. Gruppe, "War Genesis 6:1-4 ursprünglich mit der Sintflut verbunden?," ZAW 9 (1889) 134-155. H. Winckler, *Alttestamentliche Untersuchungen* (1892). Ch. Robert, "Les fils de Dieu et les filles de l'homme," RB 4 (1895) 340-373, 525-552; "A propos des fils de Dieu et des filles des hommes," RB 6 (1897) 264-271. J.W. Rothstein, *Die Bedeutung von Genesis 6:1-4 in der gegenwärtigen Genesis,* BZAW 34 (1920) 150-157. A. Lods, "La chute des anges," RHPhR 7 (1927) 295-315. K. Fruhstorfer, "Die Perikope von den Ehen der Gottessöhne — kein Mythus," ThPQ 84 (1931) 64-72. W. Stoderl, "Nochmals die Ehen der Gottessöhne," *Kathol. Korrespondenz* 25 (1931) 59-64. A. Bea, *Institutiones Biblicae. II* (1933²). G.M. Perella, "I figli di Dio e le figlie del uomo (Gen 6:2-4)," DTh 36 (1933) 435-450. A. Bea, *De Scripturae Sacrae Inspiratione* (1935²). H. Junker, "Zur Erklärung von Genesis 6:1-4," Bib 16 (1935) 205-212. A. Brock-Utne, "Regenzeit und Sintflutzeit. Eine Studie zu der Heroenschilderung Gen 6:1-4 und ihr Verhältnis zu dem jahwistischen Sintflutbericht," MO 30 (1936) 27-42. G.E. Closen, *Die Sünde der 'Söhne Gottes' (Gen 6:1-4). Ein Beitrag zur Theologie der Genesis* (1937). P. Joüon, "Les unions entre les 'Fils de Dieu' et les 'Filles des Hommes' (Gen 6:1-4)," RSR 29 (1939) 108-112. G. Philips, "De spiritualite angelorum et matrimonio 'filiorum Dei' (Gen 6:1-4)," REcL 31 (1941) 290-300. A. Johnson, *The One and the Many in the Israelite Conception of God* (1942). U. Cassuto, in: *Essays presented to J.H. Hertz, Chief Rabbi* (1943) 35-44. J. Enciso, "Los 'hijos de Dios' en Gen 6:1-4," EstB 3 (1944) 189-277. C. Goma, "La causa del diluvio en los libros apócrifos judios," EstB 3 (1944) 25-54. W.F. Albright, *From the Stone Age to Christianity, Monotheism and the Historical Process* (1940; 1957³) 199, 266. E.G. Kraeling, "The Significance and Origin of Gen 6:1-4," JNES 6 (1947) 193-208. M. Noth, *A History of Pentateuchal Traditions* (1972). M. Eliade, *Traité d'histoire des religions* (1949). J. Fischer, "Deutung und literarische Art von Gen 6:1-4," BBB 1 (1950) 74-85. O. Koch, *Engel und Dämonen in der Heiligen Schrift* (1951). J. Bamberger, *Fallen Angels* (1952). J. Heuschen, "De 'zonen Gods' in Gen

6:1-4," REcL 39 (1952) 90-95.   J. Hempel, ZAW 65 (1953) 114.   A. Kolaska, *Gottessöhne und Engel in den vorexilischen Büchern des AT und in der Ras Schamramythologie im Lichte des biblischen Monotheismus* (1953).   B.S. Childs, *A Study of Myth in Genesis I-XI:* Diss Basel 1954 (1955).   J. Murray, *Principles of Conduct. Aspects of Biblical Ethics,* Appendix (1957).   G. Mensching, *Die Söhne Gottes* (1958).   F.D. Weiss, "Die 'Söhne Gottes' in Gen 6:1-4," HTS 14 (1959) 53-67.   N.H. Tur-Sinai, "The Riddle of Genesis VI:1-4," ExpT 71 (1959/1960) 348-350.   B.S. Childs, *Myth and Reality in the Bible,* SBT 27, 1962².   W. Herrmann, "Die Göttersöhne," ZRGG 12 (1960) 242-251.   C.H. Gordon, *Before the Bible. . . . (1962).*   M. Ellenbogen, *Foreign Words in the OT* (1962).   G.E. Wright, "The Lawsuit of God," *Festschr. J. Muilenburg* (1962) 26-67.   G. Cooke, ZAW 76 (1964) 22-47.   F. Dexinger, *Sturz der Göttersöhne oder Engel vor der Sintflut? Versuch eines Neuverständnisses von Gen 6:2-4 unter Berücksichtigung der religionsvergleichenden und exegesegeschichtlichen Methode: Wiener Beiträge zur Theologie 13* (1966).   Y. Janssens, "Le thème de la fornication des anges," *Le origini della gnosticismo* (1967) 488-494.   O. Loretz, "Götter und Frauen (Gen 6:1-4). Ein Paradigma zu AT — Ugarit," BiLe 8 (1967) 120-127.   J. Scharbert, "Traditions- und Redaktionsgeschichte von Gen 6:1-4," BZ NF 11 (1967) 66-78.   W.H. Schmidt, "Mythos im AT, Kap. IIa, Gen 6:1-4," EvTh 27 (1967) 237-254.   C. Westermann, KuD 13 (1967) 231f.   O. Loretz, *Schöpfung u. Mythos,* SBS 32 (1968).   J.L.C. Ylarri, "Los bene ha 'elohim en Gen 6:1-4," EstB 28 (1969) 5-31.

Parallels to Gen 6:1-4 in OT, Apocrypha, NT. I: A. Dillmann, *Das Buch Henoch* (1853).   H. Kaupel, "Die Strafengel im Buche Henoch: ein Beitrag zur Angelologie der alttestamentlichen Apokryphen," ThGl 27 (1935) 146-195.   J. Morgenstern, "The Mythological Background of Psalm LXXXII," HUCA 14 (1939) 76-114.   P. Winter, "Der Begriff 'Söhne Gottes' im Moselied Dtn 32:1-43," ZAW 67 (1955) 40-48.   P. Grelot, "La géographie mythique d'Hénoch," RB 65 (1958) 33-69.   W.F. Albright, "Some Remarks on the Song of Moses in Deuteronomy XXXII," VT 9 (1959) 339-346.   L. Dequeker, "Les qedôšîm du Ps LXXXIX à la lumière des croyances sémitiques," EThL 39 (1963) 469-484.   A. Gonzales, "Le Psaume LXXXII," VT 13 (1963) 293-309.   M. Naor, "Hännepilîm hajû ba- 'araeṣ (Gen 6:1-4)," BetM 11 (1965/ 1966) 26-33.   B. Margulis, "Psalm LXVIII 18-19 and the Tradition of Divine Rebelion," Tarb 39 (1969/1970) 1-8.   J.A. Sanders, "Dissenting Deities and Philippians 2:1-11," JBL 88 (1969) 279-290.   B. Margulis, JBL 89 (1970) 292f.   H. Strauss, "Zur Auslegung von Ps 29 auf dem Hintergrund seiner kanaanäischen Bezüge," ZAW 82 (1970) 91-102.

Parallels II: W. Bousset, *Die Religionen des Judentums im neutestamentlichen Zeitalter* (1906).   J.M. bin Gorion, *Die Sagen der Juden,* I (1913).   F. Andres, *Die Engellehre der griechischen Apologeten des 2.Jh. und ihr Verhältnis zur griechisch-römischen Dämonologie* (1914).   PRE III (1918) 656.   W. Bousset-H. Gressmann, *Die Religion des Judentums im späthellenistischen Zeitalter* (1926).   L. Jung, *Fallen Angels in Jewish, Christian, and Mohammedan Literature* (1926).   PRE XII (1937) 1496.   W. Baumgartner, "Israelitisch-griechische Sagenbeziehungen," SAVK 41 (1941) 1-29.   P. Krüger, "Das älteste syrisch-nestorianische Dokument über die Engel," OstKSt 1 (1952) 173-321, esp. 283-296.   F. Nötscher, "Geist und Geister in den Texten von Qumran," *Mélanges Bibliques rédigés en l'honneur de A. Robert* (1955) 305-315.   P. Walcot, "The Text of Hesiod's Theogony and the Hittite Epic of Kumarbi," CQ 6 (1956) 198-200.   J.P. Lewis, *A Study of the Interpretation of Noah and the Flood in Jewish and Christian Literature* (1968) esp. 105-109, 122-123.

Text

6:1 And then, when humankind began to increase on the face of the earth and daughters were born to them,

2 then the sons of the gods saw that the daughters of humankind were beautiful[a]; and so they took wives for themselves from among them all[b], just as their fancy chose.

3 And Yahweh[a] said: My spirit shall not remain[b] for ever in humankind, because indeed[c] they are flesh. Its life-span shall cover 120 years.

4 The giants [nᵉpilim] were in the land in those days, and afterwards too, when the sons of the gods came to the daughters of humankind, and they bore (children) to them[a]; these are the heroes, the men of renown[b], who were there of old.

2a The second object of a verb is expressed by a separate clause, Ges-K §117h. **b** on the partitive meaning of מִן with verbs of choosing, Ges-K §119w, n. 1.
3a The balancing tendency of Gk appears where it presumes here and in 6:5 יהוה אלהים instead of יהוה. **b** ידון remains unexplained. Gk renders by οὐ μὴ καταμείνῃ; other versions are similar. On the form, Ges-K §72r; see further in Comm. **c** The variation in the Mss between בְשַׁגָם and בְשַׁגָם (cf. BH) shows uncertainty as to whether a verb or a combination of particles is intended. The Gk understands it in the latter sense: διὰ τὸ εἶναι αὐτοὺς σάρκας. Other versions are similar; Ges-K §67p suggests the possibility of a verbal form "in their error"; see further in Comm.
4a וילדו as a continuation of יבאו Ges-K §112e. **b** genitive construction to express a quality, Ges-K §128t.

History of Interpretation

The first chapter of G.E. Closen's book *Die Sünde der 'Söhne Gottes'* (1937) — 259 pages on 4 verses — is entitled "The Angel Theory"; the current title of the passage is "The Angel Marriages." Be the description popular or scholarly, the presumption is that the "sons of God" with whom the verses deal can be called angels.

This description was the beginning of a confusion which has not been eradicated even today. It goes back to the book of Enoch (c. 150 B.C.) where Gen 6:1-4 is rendered καὶ ἐθάσαντο αὐτὰς οἱ ἄγγελοι υἱοὶ οὐρανοῦ καὶ ἐπεθύμησαν αὐτάς . . . G.E. Closen, n. 1, remarks: "Enoch therefore read 'sons of God' in Gen 6:2 and added ἄγγελοι by way of interpretation and paraphrase." This equation has persevered right up to the present. The importance of this for the history of interpretation is that it is the reason why the "angel explanation" was at all possible in the Christian churches. The doctrine of angels was an important part of Enoch's thinking; accordingly it was developed in the Christian church and became part of the official teaching. The problem then was whether the angels, of whose existence there could be no doubt, could really be spoken of as in Gen 6:1-4, especially in the light of Mt 22:30. Without the identification of the sons of God with angels, exegesis could never have taken this turn. A dispute lasting hundreds of years between the "angels explanation" and the "Sethite explanation," whether the phrase בני אלהים in Gen 6:2 meant "gods" or "men," would never have been possible. With this in mind it becomes clear that today, when the true meaning of the Hebrew word can no longer be contested (as e.g., the Catholic exegete O. Loretz has shown), the passage is to be discussed in a completely new context. The history of the interpretation has been described in detail by G.E. Closen (1937), A. Clamer, *La Genèse:* LSB I, 1 (1953) 175-177 and F. Dexinger (1966). The main lines are found too in the commentary of B. Jacob (1934) 170-172; see too C. Westermann, *Genesis 1-11. Erträge der Forschung,* Wissenschaftliche Buchgemeinschaft 1972.

Literary Form

The narrative reaches its goal in v. 4; the event described culminates in the origin of the גברים, *gibbōrim*. The purpose of the narrative then would be to describe the origin of these *gibbōrim*. It begins by saying that the sons of the gods saw that the daughters of humankind were beautiful, v. 2a. This is the beginning of the action and is preceded by the exposé, v. 1, which reports that humankind began to increase on the earth. The subject here is humanity; the narrative is dealing with humankind. It is a primeval story of the origin of the *gibbōrim*. The explanation of the narrative form is on firm ground so far. One would expect that the action, having begun, would now move to a climax or that there would be a dramatic development. But there is no climax. The action simply continues:

> The sons of the gods saw. . . .
> they took wives for themselves. . . .
> and they bore (children) to them. . . .

The succession of events which these three sentences, considered in themselves, describe remains within the framework of a genealogical item or communication. Nothing more actually happens than that men take wives for themselves and that these bear them children. This is completely in accord with the goal of the narrative already indicated: the origin of the גברים.

However, it would be incorrect to conclude from this that Gen 6:1-4 was dealing only with a somewhat expanded genealogical item with an etiological goal. There is more to it. Stylistically, vv. 1-2 form a pure narrative introduction. They differ in content from a genealogical note; they do not speak of a particular marriage and of the child or children that result from it, but of two groups that come together and between which the subsequent event is played out. The flash point comes when these two groups are joined in marriage. The narrative introduced in vv. 1-2 is not continued in v. 3, which belongs to it neither in content nor in style. Nor is v. 4 a continuation of v. 2 in the form in which it has been handed down. The first sentence, "The giants were in the land in those days," has no context either before or after. The sentence that follows, "The sons of the gods came to the daughters of humankind," could follow directly on v. 2. But the fact that it is introduced by אשר and so made into a subordinate sentence indicates a break. Instead of the climax which one would expect after the introduction in vv. 1-2 there is only a conclusion that describes a situation; the result of the sons of the gods coming to the daughters of humankind is the גברים The relationship of these גברים to the נפלים of v. 4a remains unexplained because v. 4a is a note taken out of its context. While the course of the story has remained intact in vv. 1-2, the conclusion in v. 4a has been notably disturbed. However, its main thrust can be inferred.

The most serious disruption in the narrative is due to the insertion of v. 3 which has no relationship at all to the original course of the story. This verse is, in the form in which it is handed down, secondary and interpretative; the proposed rearrangements do not alter this in any way. Consequently any attempt to explain the passage must first of all stand by the introduction in vv. 1-2 which has been preserved intact (K. Budde had already written: "Everything is clear in vv. 1 and 2").

The main sentence in the introduction consists of a sequence of two verbs: "they saw," "they took." The "sons of God" observed the beauty of the "daughters of men." Many possibilities then are opened. One is perhaps the meeting of Jacob and Rachel: Jacob observed Rachel's beauty and is prepared to serve her father for her; hence the complicated situation. Another, and very different, is the story of the "ancestress in danger," Gen 12:10-20. The introduction of this narrative can be compared with that of 6:1-4. Common to both is the sequence "they saw — they took." The action in both begins with the discovery of the beauty of the woman (women). On both occasions the one who observes the beauty of a woman is the one who has the power, and so the opportunity, to take as a wife whom his fancy chooses. The world in which these stories arose obviously considered such a situation likely to cause strife — the perplexity arising from the beauty of a woman together with the more powerful position of the man who wanted her.

This motif is found in the primeval story, Gen 6:1-4, in the patriarchal story, 12:10-20 (and parallels), and in the political history, 2 Sam 11f. It is said of the sons of the gods that "they took wives for themselves . . . just as their fancy chose." The same is said of Pharoah in Gen 12 and of David in 2 Sam 11f. The difference is that the setting varies in each case: political history, family history, primeval event. It is this and this only that makes the introduction of the אלהים בני into Gen 6:1-4 comprehensible. When J has to introduce a class of beings utterly superior to humans so as to present the event he has in mind then, given the context of primeval event, he can do nothing else. "Humankind" is still a unity here; it has not yet been divided into social and political classes. By using בני אלהים the narrator wants to introduce a class that is utterly superior; persons who are so powerful that, when they desire a woman because of her beauty, they are not confined by the limits that restrain ordinary mortals.

Now if the introduction of "the sons of the gods" is conditioned by the event that the narrator wants to describe, then the question that has dominated the discussion up to the present, namely, Who are the "sons of the gods" and the "daughters of men"? is irrelevant. The starting point is rather: What are the functions of these two parties in the event? The narrative is dealing with a human phenomenon. The desire of beauty is part of the human condition; but when it oversteps certain bounds then it endangers a person in one's limited state. The really human event with which the narrator is concerned — as such it is certainly not mythical — is the critical moment when human existence is put in danger, and this can be the result of the desire of the beauty of a woman on the part of the man affected. It is not the desire as such that has anything to do with the offense. This is rather seen and confirmed as one of the great driving forces of the human state. But the capacity to burst the bounds that are a necessary part of human existence can lead to offense and so to divine intervention.

There is a distinction that admits of two stages in this motif which plays such a universal role in human history and is the occasion of stories. It is only in a later stage that the emphasis is on the individual aspect. The sequence of events begins when the individual encounters and desires a beautiful woman. The drama is then played out between these two; this is the love story or romance. There is a romance, too, in the earlier stage described here. The interest however is not in the personal fate of the man or of the woman or of both, but in the groups or levels that they represent; communities with their laws and destinies still had such a strong hold on people. This is the concern of all three examples cited. The question each time is: What happens when an encounter with beauty goes beyond the bounds which ought not be overstepped?

The conflict begins when the bounds are overstepped, not with the drama of the individual romance. The conflict requires some sort of solution; it cannot rest with the overstepping of the bounds. In all three examples therefore the first two stages, seeing and taking, are followed by a third — the intervention of God. This is clear in Gen 12:10-20 and 2 Sam 11f. But the course of events has been disturbed in Gen 6:1-4; there is no sign of any direct punishment of those who have transgressed. However, the parallel courses of events in 12:10-20 and 2 Sam 11f. have proved with certainty that there was once in place of v. 3 a direct intervention of God which punished the transgressors. We have then the basic framework of the original course of events in Gen 6:1-4. There ought to be a corresponding action in v. 3, an intervention of God that brought the sons of the gods back within their bounds. This has been altered considerably in the present text of v. 3.

How is the etiological conclusion of v. 4 related to this? Such a conclusion is not part of the sequence of events hitherto in motion. However it does belong to the sequence set in motion at the beginning. The sons of the gods saw — they took wives for themselves — these bore children to them. The statement that these children were the famous גברים belongs naturally here. So 6:1-4 contains two narratives of different origin. One is purely etiological and is really an elaborated genealogical note explaining the origin of the giants. But the other, connected with it, is a mythical story that told of a dangerous transgression of the bounds of the human state by the sons of God that caused God to intervene. The latter is preserved only in fragments and hints; the climax in v. 3 has been altered considerably. V. 4, in which two conclusions (נפלים and גברים) are woven together, shows further that two very different narrative threads have been intertwined in 6:1-4.

Setting in Life

If one begins with the last stage, it is clear that J put the narrative immediately after 4:17-26 and before the beginning of the flood narrative. Earlier explanations had understood 6:1-4 to be really part of the flood story, in fact its introduction; it would give the reason for God's judgment. F. Dexinger (1966), e.g., is so sure of this that he does not think it necessary to support it in detail. However, other reasons apart, this explanation collapses when one takes the primeval story as a whole. The common opinion, e.g., B.S. Childs (1960), is that the text, which was completely independent of the flood narrative in origin, has been put here by J to give the reason for the flood, and indeed as an example of the increase of sin: "It serves as a plastic illustration of the increasing sinfulness of man before God" (B.S. Childs, p. 58).

But neither does this explanation make clear J's intention in the composition of Gen 2-11. He does not want to describe the snow-balling of sin, but the variety of ways in which sin is actualized. He shows this clearly when he relates the two individual transgressions in Gen 3 and 4 to each other. J's two other narratives of transgressions, 6:1-4 and 11:1-9 have as subject not the individual but an undefined multiplicity. This difference is certainly deliberate; J wants to show that human offenses against the creator can take these two forms. One can truly say that the way in which these four narratives are placed, with 6:1-4 immediately preceding the flood, explain the corruption which is described in general terms in 6:5. But 6:1-4 can be no more than an example of this; of itself it cannot be the reason for the punishment of the flood either in the intention of J or of the final redactor of 1-11.

However, the position of 6:1-4 in J's plan as one of four examples of offenses and the corruption of humanity (3; 4:2-16; 11:1-9) can help us to understand the passage as a whole. In 3 and 4:2-16 J has set together two offenses by individual persons: disobedience to a command of God and enmity toward a brother that leads to murder. In 11:1-9 it is "men" who go beyond the prescribed limits by means of their technology; in 6:1-2 the only reason for God's intervention in v. 3 can be that limits are set to humans. Even if, apart from v. 3, the protagonists are the "sons of the gods" and what they do is not described as a revolt, the result, from the human part, can only be meant as a transgression. So God drives people back within the bounds prescribed to them. This explanation of 6:1-4 in its final form between Gen 4 and 6:5ff. suggests itself because it belongs to the pattern of the three other narratives of revolt and punishment in Gen 3-11.

If one starts from this last stage, which is clear enough, and proceeds backwards, one arrives at the stage where J took over the underlying myth; he presupposes that myth has found its way into Israel. For the present, we will say only this: the passage 6:1-4 shows incontestably that ancient Israel became familiar with the myths of the surrounding world in the course of its development and took notice of them. Israel itself could not of course be fertile ground for myth and, as far as we know, was the source of no myths at all; but it certainly became familiar with myths from the surrounding world. It is certainly not true, as has often been said, that when an Israelite encountered a myth he proceeded at once to demythologize it. When some myth or other from the surrounding world became known in Israel and was recounted, orally at first, there must have been some point of interest in it.

It is easy to recognize this point in the myth that underlies 6:1-4: it is a myth concerned expressly with primeval time and its leading motif was the elevation of the *genus humanum* as a group by super-men or semi-gods who were the fruit of the union of gods and women. This motif suited what J had in mind. It must be admitted that even before J inserted 6:1-4 into his work, myths of this kind were narrated in Israel. It is indeed possible to indicate the setting where such a myth was repeated — in an etiological narrative explaining the origin of the giants. It must be stressed that the thrust of such a narrative is very different from that of J. The broader context to which a narrative explaining the origin of the giants belongs cannot really be called mythical; and it is a question more of mythical remains which are set in the new context of information about distant lands and people.

The original setting of the narrative that lies behind 6:1-4 is the setting where it began and was handed down as myth. One can take as certain that it did not originate in Israel. It is very likely a Canaanite myth because the בני אלהים are known from Canaanite mythology where they are found often and clearly play an important role. One can say further that this myth belongs to a distinct cycle of mythical narratives that deal with one of two basic motifs: love or sexual union, and in particular union between gods and humans which occurs very often. One can conjecture further still that the main emphasis of the original myth lay in the dramatic development which resulted from the union of the sons of the gods and the daughters of men; the purely etiological aspect, the explanation of the origin of the giants, represents only a secondary stage.

Literature: Gen 6: E. Lussier, CBQ 18 (1956) 137-139.   H. Schwarzbaum, "The Overcrowded Earth," Numen 4 (1957) 59-74.   R. Knierim, ZAW 77 (1965) 20-39.

Commentary

[**6:1**] ויהי כי (26:8; 27:1; 43:21; 44:23; Ex 1:21; 13:17; see too Josh 17:13) describes mostly an action that takes its beginning in an event or process that is continuously and constantly going on: here it is the expansion of humankind. The sentence is the exposé; the action really begins in v. 2. This exposé, the beginning of the expansion of humankind, occurs in other primeval narratives, e.g., in the Atraḥasis epic: "The land became great, the people multiplied. . . ." This sentence introduces an event that leads to the decision to destroy by means of the flood. Even if one does not agree with E.G. Kraeling, JNES 6 (1947) 193ff. who concludes from this that 6:1-4 and the flood narrative belong together, nevertheless one cannot say that this agreement is mere chance nor can one reject out of hand some indirect contact. If we take as the starting point J's deliberate division of the crime-punishment narrative (3:1-24 and 4:2-16: the offense of an individual; 6:1-4; 6-9 and 11:1-9: the offense of people as a group), we find that 6:1-4 and 11:1-9 are in agreement in that the expansion of humankind, which is in fact a consequence of the creation blessing, begins to take on a negative side. The very first sentence, v. 1a, is a primeval motif that stands in the same context as the beginning of the Atraḥasis epic: the multiplication of humankind appears as an event that can jeopardize the relationship between the creator and his creatures (cf. H. Schwarzbaum, see above). (On אדם E. Lussier, above; C. Westermann, THAT 1, 41-57.)

The accumulation of the verb "to begin," חלל hiph., in Gen 1-11 is striking: 4:26; 6:1; 9:20; 10:8; 11:6. On the rendering "over the face of the ground," cf. R. Knierim, above, p. 24. W.H. Schmidt observes: "It can remain an open question whether v. 1 . . . is part of the tradition . . . or a later addition to link the narrative with the whole primeval event," EvTh 17 (1967) 243, n. 12. The way in which the narrative is constructed shows that the circumstantial statement of v. 1, as the exposé, is a necessary part. The beginning of the action in v. 2 presupposes that, as humankind begins to multiply, there comes too a danger point for the relationship of God (or the gods) to humans. A key moment in the origins of humankind is its expansion into a multitude, and this can become a threat, just as in the Atraḥasis epic.

Literature: Gen 6:2: A.H. Krappe, "Bene Elohim (Gen 6:2)," SMSR 9 (1933) 157-172.   J.E. Coleran, "The Sons of God in Genesis 6:2," TS 2 (1941) 488-509.   J. Renié, *Les origines de l'humanité d'après la Bible* (1950).   O. Eissfeldt, "El im ugaritischen Pantheon," BAL 98, 4 (1951).   J.B. Bauer, "Videntes filii Dei filias hominum (Gen 6:2)," VD 31 (1953) 95-110.   M.D. Goldman, "The Root ידע and the Verb 'to know' in Hebrew," ABR 3 (1953) 46-47.   J. Weingreen, "The Construct-Genitive Relation in Hebrew Syntax," VT 4 (1954) 50-59.   G.M. Girardet, "Noterella filologica: Il verbo piacere in ebraico e Genesi 6:2," Protest. 12 (1957) 168-169.   P.A.H. de Boer, *De Zoon van God in het Oude Testament: Leidse Voordrachten* 29 (1958).   H.S. Stern, VT 8 (1958) 407-408, 416.   H.A. Brongers, VT 13 (1963) 269ff.   R. Rendtorff, "El, Ba'al und Jahwe," ZAW 78 (1966) 277-292.

[6:2] The sons of God (or of the gods) observed the beauty of the daughters of men. Talk about beauty or being beautiful requires a point of reference. Beauty does not exist in the abstract, but exists insofar as it is observed or discovered. Being beautiful then is something that happens; it speaks when it sets an event in motion. A particular example of this is the case where a man who observes the beauty of a woman is set apart from her by some sort of barrier, but because of his position of superior power he breaks through it. This motif is common to Gen 6:1-4, Gen 12:10-20, and 2 Sam 11f. When the beginning of the action here is seen in the context of J's primeval story as a whole, it appears as a deliberate though polarized parallel to 2:18-24. The intention of 2:23 is something like the discovery of beauty, but in the sense of the discovery of a counterpart, which leads to living as one in marriage, 2:24. 6:1-2 introduces the other pole: the potentate can chooose among the many beauties who take his fancy; he can do this even where there are barriers, simply because he is powerful. The event in 2:18-24 is one way in which the sexes meet. This event is another, and it is seen primarily as a phenomenon belonging to the human condition. In the primeval context it can only be described in mythical language because the only beings there that are distinctly superior to humans are the divine beings. The event is meant to be typical and it is only in this sense that it can be understood correctly; the narrator has in mind a human phenomenon which he describes in mythical language.

Excursus: *The Sons of the Gods (or of God)*

A survey of the history of interpretation reveals several lines of enquiry that lead to conclusions which are certain:

(1) The chapter that asked, are the בני אלהים to be regarded as human or as non-human beings, can be considered closed. The number of voices supporting the view that they are human has diminished. One senses among the few who still adhere to this view a defensive attitude conditioned consciously or unconsciously by a mentality that demands that the explanation that it is a simple matter-of-fact reference to non-humans must be rejected unconditionally. B. Jacob in his commentary is a typical representative of Jewish exegesis, maintaining the traditional explanation, G.E. Closen (1937) and F. Dexinger (1966) of Catholic exegesis. The Catholic exegete O. Loretz (1968) has abandoned it.

(2) There is an opposite view, much more discriminating and more difficult to grasp, that presumes that the בני (ה)אלהים cannot be humans; it describes itself traditionally as the "angels-explanation." It retains the description "angels" which comes from the Gk version (and others) and is backed up by the belief in angels which is part of Jewish and Christian tradition alike. F. Delitzsch in his commentary takes as his point of departure that "everywhere else the benē haelohim means angels" and goes on to explain that the phrase "describes their nature, as mal'akim describes their function." So too A. Dillmann. It is surprising that both these scholars, who otherwise are so careful and precise, have not noticed that the two words are concerned with very different phenomena and occur in completely different contexts (cf. C. Westermann, "Engel," EKL I, 1021). The presumption without more ado, is that "angel" is a generally accepted and valid universal concept. And so K. Budde writes: "I agree with the opinion that designates spiritual beings by the word 'angels', in the category of 'sons of God'." One notes the beginnings of a difference in H. Holzinger's commentary, though he retains "angels": "The benē haelohim are angels, though originally they may have been gods." J. Skinner hesitates: "members (inferior) of the divine order or (using the word with some freedom) angels."

(3) The scandal of the angels-explanation, which led to the Sethite-explanation, and to others, appears among the defenders of the opinion themselves. This is particularly true of F. Delitzsch who is forced to accept the explanation because of linguistic usage, but with great reluctance. He asks: "Did angels mingle in the flesh with women of the human race?" He tries to explain and then says: "We must therefore, at least as exegetes, accept this paradoxical and scandalous idea." U. Cassuto, who surprisingly enough still equates the benē haelohim with angels, is also conscious of the scandal. He explains: "The angels are divided into different ranks, there are higher and lower angels. In 6:1-4 not angels

sublime and pure, but those of a degraded type are referred to." Perhaps he is not conscious of how deeply he has plunged into mythological thinking. F. Delitzsch takes the fact more seriously. This scandal in the text shows that the "angels-explanation" too is not readily reconcilable with what the rest of the Old Testament says.

(4) It was H. Gunkel who, as far as I know, first said clearly that the text could not mean angels. "The phrase benē elohim would have been understood in Hebrew usage as 'beings belonging to the category of elohim'." He notes at the same time: "Belief in such beings had originally nothing to do with the Yahweh religion" *(Komm.)*. So too A. Lods, review of L. Jung, *Fallen Angels,* (1926), AfO 5 (1928) 170-178: "The bene ha'elohim of Gen 6:4 were neither 'sons of might' nor (originally) angels, but divine beings," p. 177. If further confirmation were needed, there are the Canaanite parallels: W.F. Albright, *From the Stone Age. . . .* 1946, 1957[2] wrote: "This meant simply gods in Canaanite" p. 226. W. Herrmann, ZRGG 12 (1960) comes to the conclusion: "The Ugaritic expression *bn il* describes a group of genuine but second rank gods. . . ." He understands the Hebrew phrase בני (ה)אלהים (or אלים), in Gen 6:1-4 in an analogous sense. Likewise G. Cooke, ZAW 76 (1964) 368: "The 'Sons of (the) God(s)' are those who are of the realm of the gods, who partake of divinity"; see too R. Rendtorff, ZAW 78 (1966) 277f. who confirms this conclusion.

This explanation has been taken over in three new studies on Gen 6:1-4: B.S. Childs (1962[2]), W.H. Schmidt (1967), and O. Loretz (1967, 1968), all of whom agree completely on this point. This explanation occurs so frequently now that one can speak of a broad agreement. It is supported by G.E. Wright, A.H. de Boer, E.A. Speiser, J. de Fraine, G. von Rad, J. Weingreen, J. Gray, H. Strauss, J.L. Ylarri, W. Zimmerli and others (cf. Literature above). J. Morgenstern (1939), O. Eissfeldt, *Israels Religion* (1967) and A. Gonzales (1963) draw attention to Ps 82 where gods are reduced to humans in the heavenly council. "One can suppose that the fault in question was of the same sort as that of Gen 6:1-4" (Gonzales). E. Dhorme, *La démonologie* (1960), refers to a similarity with the demon in the Book of Tobit.

B.S. Childs formulates the conclusion: "The text speaks of a plurality of divine beings belonging to the class of god," or O. Loretz: "The sons of God are real gods. They are in no wise to be equated with angels." And so the interpreters of Gen 6:1-4 have the difficult task of explaining how these gods or divine beings took human women as wives and begot children through them; one cannot avoid the difficulty by simply saying that it is the language of myth, as H. Holzinger had already laconically said: "Sexual intercourse between angels and human beings is pagan mythology." H. Gunkel: "V. 2 is really mythological"; likewise the majority of modern interpreters. It must be stated first that the narrative in v. 2 is simply a report, containing no judgment on the event. 'They took wives" (cf. H.A. Brongers, 1963, 283; U. Cassuto, *Comm.:* "Simply the usual expression for legal marriage").

The narrative begins with the statement that the beauty of the young women or girls was noticed. This is implicit praise of their beauty, and it is the beauty, not the sons of the gods and their action, that sets events in motion. When this basic motif is recognized in Gen 12:10-20 and 2 Sam 11f. it becomes clear that the mythical clothing is but serving a function. The sons of the gods were required here because they were the only beings who could be considered to have power superior to humans and so to be capable of taking the "daughters of men." Looking at the story more closely and asking what they were required for, it would have been clear to both the narrator and the listeners in the period of the monarchy that they were not acting at all like gods. The only really divine thing about them is the superior power that enables them to take whichever woman they like, just as in the parallel stories of the Pharaoh and David. What is decisive for the older form of the story is the infringement that superior power makes possible.

Literature: Gen 6:3: A. Socin, "Exkurs über יָדֹון in Gen 6:3," Stud. u. Krit. 67 (1894) 211-212.   K. Vollers, "Zur Erklärung von ידון Gen 6:3," ZA 14 (1899) 349-356.   G.R. Berry, "The Interpretation of Gen 6:3," AJSL 16 (1899/1900) 47-49.   M.L. Margolis, "Miscellen: Genesis 6:3," ZAW 31 (1911) 313-315.   P. Karge, *Rephaim* (1917).   W.F. Otto, *Die Manen oder von den Urformen des Totenglaubens* (1923; 1958²) esp. 48-49.   A. Guillaume, "A Note on the Meaning of Gen VI 3," AJSL 56 (1939) 415-416.   C.A. Ben-Mordecai, "B'shaggam: an Obscure Phrase in Gen VI 3: Reply to A. Guillaume," AJSL 57 (1940) 306-307.   E. Jenni, "Das Wort ʿōlām im AT," ZAW 65 (1953) 1-25.   E.A. Speiser, "YDWN, Gen 6:3," JBL 75 (1956) 126-129 = *Festschr. E.A. Speiser* (1967).   P. Morant, *Die Anfänge der Menschheit. . . .* (1960; 1962²) 285.   Ch. Rabin, "Etymological Miscellanea," ScrHie 8 (1961) 384-400.   G.R. Driver, "Once Again Abbreviations," Textus 4 (1964) 76-94.

[6:3]   V. 3 is concerned with this infringement. Indeed, the verse in its present form still shows signs that it contains a punishment pronounced by God. But it does not read as a suitable continuation of vv. 1-2. One cannot therefore agree with those interpreters who assume that v. 4 originally stood after v. 3. The etiological conclusion would be meaningless before the sentence of punishment. V. 4 must stay at the end. The difficulty lies not in the position of v. 3 but in its content.

The verse is introduced by "And Yahweh said." It may be compared with 3:22 which also begins with a divine reflection and not with part of a dialogue. The reflection describes a decision; Yahweh has come to a settlement about what is to hold for the future. The decision consists of a negative part, "my spirit shall not remain. . . ," and a positive part, "its life-span shall. . . ."; the reason for the negative part is "because indeed they. . . ." Because the verse bristles with difficulties, we must take as our starting point what is unequivocally clear. It is generally said that the words are a sentence of punishment by God; it would be more accurate to say, a sentence imposing limits. Both the negative and positive parts express this limitation clearly. There is a further parallel to 3:22 (so too W.H. Schmidt): Yahweh prevents the man from approaching the tree of life so that he may not live forever; here too there is a limitation of the life-span. But this is where the difficulties begin.

1. First of all the parallel to 3:22 leads to the conclusion that only humanity can be the object of God's limiting judgment — as in 3:22. In both cases we have a primeval statement about humanity. But this does not fit the context; the sons of the gods are the guilty party, and nothing is said of their punishment. "There is no sign of guilt on the part of humans" (A. Dillmann ad loc. and others). Some interpreters try to smooth over the difficulty by suggesting that אדם in v. 3 carries a different meaning from the same word in v. 1. In v. 1 it means humankind, in v. 3 it could mean the new generation begotten of these strange marriages (e.g., E.G. Kraeling, 1956). But it is highly unlikely that in so short a text אדם carries different meanings in vv. 1 and 3; and more, a decisive reason to the contrary is that the language of the stories of the primeval event is already too firmly fashioned. אדם can only mean humanity here. The difficulty must remain therefore; the conclusion is unavoidable — the narrative here cannot be intact.

H. Gunkel asks: "Is it perhaps that too much of the mythological has been eliminated?" Likewise other interpreters. A comparison with 3:22 can point the way. O. Loretz is of the opinion that "the attempt at sexual union between humans and God . . . serves to prolong and secure life," op. cit., p. 43; he refers to the episode of the plant of life in the Gilgamesh epic. If 6:3 and 3:22, 24 are read together, then something becomes clear which does not when 6:1-4 is read by itself, namely that the limiting sentence in 6:3 must presuppose an attempt on the part of man to prolong life. (If this is the case, then K. Budde's insight is correct in his carefully constructed attempt to transpose 6:3 to 3:22; however, a literary-critical solution is not possible and no one has taken it up. Nevertheless it is acknowledged that from the point of view of tradition history 6:3 is parallel to 3:22.)

We might suggest then that there lay behind 6:3 a version of the story that has been deliberately obscured, according to which the sons of the gods, like Prometheus, took the part of humankind by marrying the daughters of men, aspired to raise the status of the human race and so forced the creator to intervene. The parallel to 3:22, also to 11:1-9, becomes clear; the clue lies in the thrust of the introductory sentence: "When humankind began to increase on the face of the earth"; something very similar follows this in the Atraḥasis epic. This explanation agrees too with the interpretation of the beginning of the action given above, namely that 6:1-4 is concerned with a human phenomenon. So the most formidable difficulty in v. 3 is overcome; the others are easily solved.

2. "My Spirit": The comparison with 3:22 makes it clear that the restraining judgment of God is aimed at an intolerable attempt to prolong life. The meaning therefore is clear: "What is meant is the breath of life that makes one a living being 2:7" (F. Delitzsch, Comm., and others). What is in mind is man, the living being, made such at the creation by the creator breathing into him the breath of life (cf. Ps 104:29f.). J. Wellhausen (*Composition* 307-310), from the context of vv. 1-2, had concluded: "רוחי then is to be referred to the angels, to the spiritual material of which they as well as Yahweh himself consist, while humans are flesh." He sees the contradiction to v. 4a and solves it by explaining the sentence "its life-span shall cover 120 years" as a gloss which has misunderstood v. 3a. J. Skinner follows this interpretation which still continues to crop up often in the course of exegesis. But this is quite incomprehensible because the explanation of רוחי which is Wellhausen's starting point is quite impossible in the Old Testament and no attestation at all has been discovered for such linguistic usage. The severe inroads on the text that follow from it are not justified.

Besides Wellhausen's explanation, with which he agrees, J.Skinner mentions three others: spirit as an ethical principle, the divine feeling that has been aroused (A. Klostermann, *Der Pentateuch,* 1907), the divine principle of life shared with humans at creation. B. Jacob in his commentary understands it as a charismatic gift by which the "sons of God" (= men) become prophets, poets, heroes. G.E. Closen, while recognizing the physical sense, lays emphasis on the ethical meaning; he understands it as the "principle of one's moral life" (pp. 40-50 with bibliog.). A survey of the explanations of "my spirit" leaves the marked impression that the root of the problem is the difficulty of the passage as a whole. The negative sentence of v. 3a and the positive sentence of v. 3b leads to the conclusion that "my spirit" can only mean "the power that bestows life" (B.S. Childs, *Myth and Reality. . . ,* 1962[2]).

3. לְעֹלָם . . . לֹא could mean "never more," as some interpreters understand it (e.g., G.E. Closen). In the context it can only mean "not for ever," as H. Gunkel and many others interpret it; cf. esp. E. Jenni, "Das Wort ʿōlām im AT," ZAW 65 (1953) 11.

4. יָדוֹן. H. Gunkel's survey of explanations in 1910 does not differ notably from those of G.E. Closen (1937) and O. Loretz (1968).

(a) The old translation of this hapax legomenon presumes the meaning "to remain, to last." A. Dillmann writes: "It is possible that they knew another reading, but also that they guessed the meaning." The traditional meaning predominates in more recent translations and explanations. More recently still it has received a more solid philological base (cf. Lit. on 6:3).

(b) Derivation from דִּין "to judge," O. Procksch, *Komm.;* H. Gunkel mentions it with the remark that it does not fit the context. And so a number want to derive it from the same stem and render it by "rule," e.g., K. Budde; F. Delitzsch links the rendering "rule" with אָדוֹן.

(c) דּוּן following the Arabic *dâna* "to humble oneself," Gesenius, A. Dillmann, similarly E. König; J. Scharbert: "to suffer a loss of esteem."

(d) Following the Akk. *danânu* "to be strong, powerful" K. Vollers, B. Jacob, G. von Rad.

(e) דּוּן following Akk. *dinānu* "to shield, to substitute," E.A. Speiser, see above.

(f) Following Ug. *dnt-* "to be oppressed, humbled," O. Loretz, *Schöpfung und Mythos* (1968).

None of these explanations goes beyond conjecture. The most likely meaning from the context is "remain," and this has the support of the old translations, Gk οὐ μὴ καταμείνῃ, Vg. *permanebit*. This is a conclusive argument too for H. Gunkel. The only philological support that G.E. Closen can offer, and he decides in favor of this meaning, is that of A. Socin (see above) "who refers to *dán, jidán,* in the Egyptian dialect of Arabic," p. 37 (cf. too M.L. Margolis, above, "to abide"). U. Cassuto offers a sounder basis. He refers to A. Guillaume (see above), who recalls the Arabic *danna* which means "to remain, to exist" in the fourth form, and fills this out with (a) a second root *danānu* in Akk. with the substantives *dinnu, dinnutu, madnanu,* bed or couch, (b) the word *dan,* jug with a sharp edge, which can be stuck into the ground (so as to make it stand still) and (c) the verb in the sense of remain or to be at a certain place (also in Qal) in the Talmud, in Aramaic and eventually in Hebrew. Cassuto translates "to abide permanently" (cf. E.A. Speiser and C.A. Ben-Mordecai above). The translation "remain" seems to have sufficient basis.

5. בְּשַׁגַּם: J. Wellhausen (*Composition* 309) gives a detailed rejection of the attempt to read the word as an infinitive with suffix "because of their aberration" (e.g., A. Dillmann). The only possibility is to understand it as the juxtaposition of the preposition בְּ, the relative שׁ and גַּם (also). This is what the Gk has done, διὰ τὸ εἶναι αὐτούς. This is difficult because it occurs nowhere else and שׁ is not found elsewhere in the Pentateuch as a relative particle; the גם too is difficult in the context. Wellhausen assumes therefore that the text is corrupt, while maintaining that the meaning of the sentence is quite clear. Most interpreters understand the word as a composite of this kind; so e.g., F. Delitzsch, "next

to הוא it gives the impression of proposing a reason, *quoniam,*" H. Gunkel, and others.

There are further reflections; H. Holzinger holds it to be purely logical for "a completely meaningless reason." But the real difficulty is that the reason for Yahweh's judgment must be an action, not a state. The judgment would be better in content and style were no reason given. If it is the later addition of some reader, גם too would be explained: "yes he too is flesh!"

בשר means in any case a person in one's limitation and fallibility, "a helpless earthly being" H. Gunkel; cf. W.H. Schmidt "Anthropologische Begriffe im AT," EvTh 24 (1964) 374-388.

6. "Its life-span shall cover 120 years": F. Delitzsch understood this precision of time as a period of grace given to the human race until the flood: "The words are not saying that henceforth human life is to be restricted to a span of 120. . . . All the post-diluvial patriarchs from Shem to Terah 11:10f. reach a much higher age . . . but . . . that a further period of grace lasting 120 years is to be given to people." He refers to his predecessors who held this opinion — Jerome, Augustine, Luther, and moderns. According to Delitzsch, O. Gruppe (1889 see above) supported this view with new evidence from the history of religions (for a critical appraisal, see J. Skinner and B.S. Childs); it is further supported by C. Kuhl, G.E. Closen, E.A. Speiser and others. But this explanation falls together with its presupposition, namely that 6:1-4 is a constitutive part of the primeval story of the flood.

B.S. Childs puts the question: Does the sentence refer to humankind or only to the new generation? Different answers are given. But there can be no question but that humankind as a whole is meant, since it is clear that the narrative of 6:1-4 is concerned with humankind as a whole from beginning to end; cf. the explanation of v. 2. Behind the union of the sons of God and daughters of men there is the instinct to prolong and secure life. And so both the negative and the positive parts of the divine judgment have the same meaning: a person is thrown back within the bounds that one has overstepped and one's life-span is limited. This is parallel to 3:22, 24 where the person is excluded from the tree of life.

So the drama moves through its climax to resolution *(Geschehensbogen)*. It begins in v. 2 with the desire of the sons of the gods for the daughters of men which led them to overstep the boundaries, and arches to the judgment of God which fixes the boundaries for ever. It is only natural to say something further about the fruit of such strange unions. But the narrative has reached its proper goal in the pronouncement of judgment in v. 3.

Literature: Gen 6:4: F. Schwally, "Über einige palästinische Völkernamen. V. Die Nephilim," ZAW 18 (1898) 142-148.   W.H. Bohanan, *Nephilim* (1908).   A. Boissier, "À propos de Nephilim," OLZ 13 (1910) 196-197; "Nimrod et les Nephilim," ZAW 30 (1910) 35-36.   K. Fruhstorfer, "Gigantes erant super terram (Gen 6:4). Ein biblisches Referat," KKZ 66 (1926) 383-385.   E.G. Wright, "Troglodytes and Giants in Palestine," JBL 57 (1938) 305-309.   M. Jouhandeau, *Annotations en marge de la Genèse* (1947).   W.F. Albright, *Recent Discoveries in Bible Lands* (1955).   J.G. Raposo, "Os Nephilîm de Gên 6:4," RCB 2 (1958) 158-166.   J. Blau, "Adverbia als psychologische und grammatische Subjekte/Praedikate im Bibelhebräisch," VT 9 (1959) 130-137.   S. Gevirtz, VT 11 (1961) 141-142.   A. Bustanoby, "The Giants and the Sons of God," Eternity 15 (1964) 19-20.

[6:4]   The structure of this verse presents yet again formidable difficulties. The first sentence stands by itself without any grammatical link either before or after; it is simply a piece of information: "The giants were in the land in those days." Then what is obviously a later correction has been inserted: "And afterwards too." It is not clear what the following אֲשֶׁר refers to; it is best understood temporally: "when. . . ." is obviously a subsequent attempt to link the two sentences and indicate a disruption of the text. It is only now that we have the continuation of v. 2: that children were the fruit of the union of the sons of the gods with the daughters of men and what these children became.

It has already been said that the text must be disrupted. How does one explain the constituent parts of v. 4 each in itself and in their relationship to one another? One must attend first of all to the type of sentence. V. 4a and v. 4c are circumstantial sentences; v. 4b reports a sequence of two actions. The sentence that reports an action belongs of its nature to the movement of the narrative, while the circumstantial sentences, seen from the point of view of the structure of the narrative, can be either incidental remarks or a conclusion of a narrative in which the action reaches its term in a particular state. This means that v. 4b, now reduced to the state of a subordinate sentence by אֲשֶׁר, belongs to the movement of the narrative. If, as is generally admitted (e.g., by F. Delitzsch), v. 4a cannot be original, then the אֲשֶׁר will only have been introduced into the text when the shape of the sentence was changed by v. 4a.

V. 4b was a principal sentence in the original narrative context and began with וַיָּבֹאוּ. It does not really matter whether אֲשֶׁר is understood as temporal (with most interpreters) or iterative (so E. König, W.H. Schmidt and others) or as causal (e.g., B.S. Childs; against, and correctly, W.H. Schmidt); אֲשֶׁר is an afterthought, its function being in fact only to link and so to subordinate. If this is correct, then the explanation of the majority of interpreters is not relevant, namely that one "expects first of all to find out about the fruit of the union" (O. Procksch; P. Karge, 1917, see above). This must be read out of v. 4a; it is said much more clearly in v. 4b if it is read as a principal sentence. It is not necessary then to alter v. 4a so that what is expected may emerge (K. Budde proposes an impressive reconstruction); v. 4a is to be regarded as parallel to v. 4c in the disposition of the narrative: it says who the children are who were born from these marriages.

This simplifies the understanding of v. 4: the action advances in 4b, 4c is a circumstantial conclusion, 4a is a modified variant of 4c. Gunkel's explanation of the juxtaposition of נְפִלִים in 4a and גִּבֹּרִים in 4c, which has prevailed almost without exception, is no longer tenable, namely that the word נְפִלִים, which was outmoded at the time of the writer, was explained in 4c by a less mythological word, גִּבֹּרִים. It is a question rather of two variants, two narrative conclusions quite distinct from each other, as is often the case with etiological conclusions (cf. Gen 11:9). Only in this case one of them, 4a, has been modified to an incidental remark. The relationship of the variants to each other only becomes clear when the words themselves are explained.

The explanation given of 4a confirms that the interchange of v. 3 and v. 4, which many scholars require, is not necessary. The overstepping of the bounds, introduced in vv. 1-2 but not narrated further, is parried by the judgment of God in v. 3. This judgment consists not in annihilation but only in setting a limit to the life-span. Consequently the narrative can now say that children were the fruit of these marriages. This sequence of events is confirmed by something similar in Gen 3 and 4:2-16. In neither case does God annihilate the guilty party; in each case the story tells immediately of the birth of children. Nothing should be altered in the sequence of 6:1-4.

[6:4a[1]] The sentence in its present form is an "antiquarian gloss" (J. Skinner) communicating an ancient piece of information. It does not tell us who or what the *nephilim* were. In any case they were inhabitants of the earth or land. The only other place where the *nephilim* occurs is Num 13:33 where they are described as "giants." The scouts' report: "And there we saw the Nephilim (the sons of Anak who come from the Nephilim); and we seemed to ourselves like grasshoppers, and so we seemed to them." One could be satisfied with this explanation; but the later gloss "and afterwards too" has sensed correctly that the chronological distance between Num 13:33 and Gen 6:4 is too great, because 6:1-4 is talking of the primeval event. However the adaptation of the originally mythical statement into an antiquarian gloss is saying the same thing. Only later, in the context of history, was Nephilim used to designate the giants, a group of people particularly tall, wherever they happened to be.

However, it must have been originally a term to describe mythical beings, semi-gods, like Gilgamesh who was said to be two-thirds god and one-third human. It is precisely this that is the reason for the alteration of the original sentence. U. Cassuto points out that נפל is used in Ezek 32 as a key-word; it occurs in 32:20, 22, 23, 24, 27: "They all fell by the sword and descended to Sheol." נפלים in v. 27 could refer to the Nephilim (so E.G. Kraeling and others). According to P. Humbert (Démesure. . . , 1960) the word is to be understood as the "deposed" (this is more likely than the "attackers," i.e., "violent," F. Delitzsch, M. Naor, 1965/66, and others). W. Zimmerli, with many others, sees here a reference to the narrative of 6:1-4. He translates: "And they do not lie with the mighty men who fell 'in remote antiquity', who went down to the underworld with all their weapons of war, whose swords were laid under their heads and whose 'shields' lie upon their bones." Zimmerli refers to the form of the semi-gods in Babylonian and Greek myths and says: "There is an ingenuous reference here to these beings of times immemorial . . . as if they were part of humankind's distant memory" (BK XIII, 789). There is every reason to think that the Nephilim in 4a refers to mythical semi-divine beings, the fruit of the marriages of the gods with humans, who are connected with the overstepping of the bound presumed in the divine judgment of v. 3.

[6:4a[2]] "They came to (them)'': " 'to come to' refers in this connection only to the male who visits a woman's quarters, 30:16; 38:16" (E.A. Speiser, AncB). This sentence states expressly that children were the fruit of the union of the sons of the gods with the daughters of men, and clearly, they must be something special; they could not be just plain ordinary mortals.

[6:4b] Three statements are made about them: they are described as הגברים, as men of renown, and as heroes of old. There is obviously a fixed pattern of three members (clearly rhythmic, 3 x 2) which shows that there is a tradition behind it and that it is not just an explanation of the little-known Nephilim. There is nothing mythical here. It is quite possible that when the two terms were brought together in 6:1-4 the Nephilim were identified with the גברים. Originally they did not designate the same object, because Nephilim is a name whereas גברים describes a group. While the Nephilim of 4a, in the light of Ezek 32:27, are clearly mythical, 4b makes no reference to mythical figures. All three statements describe human beings; the אנשי השם are real men. This only confirms that two narrative conclusions are brought together in v. 4, one following a mythical line and the other simply an etiological line. Both coalesce in vv. 1-2, and so the narrative there is smooth and intact. V. 4a^1 and 4a^2 are a direct continuation of the etiological line, the purpose of which is simply to explain the origin of the famous heroes of old. It makes no comment on the marriage between the sons of the gods and the daughters of men in remote antiquity. This is just a piece of information that is to be handed down; a merely etiological line is not interested in passing judgment.

The mythological line is narrating the story of the overstepping of a limit due to the marriage of the sons of the gods with the daughters of men. It is preserved only in fragments. We must now ask if these fragments can be completed from Israel's neighbors.

Literature: History of Religion I: J. Köberle, *Babylonische Kultur und biblische Religion* (1903). M.J. Lagrange, "La Paternité de Dieu dans l'Ancien Testament," RB NS 5 (1908) 481-499. W. Wundt, *Völkerpsychologie,* VI (1923³) 290-292. B. Bonkamp, *Die Bibel im Lichte der Keilschriftforschung* (1939). C. Clemen, "Die phönikische Religion nach Philo von Byblos," MVÄG 42, 3 (1939). H.G. Güterbock, "Oriental Forerunners of Hesiod," AJA 52 (1948) 123-125. H. Otten, *Mythen vom Gotte Kumarbi, Neue Fragmente* (1950/1951). J. Aistleitner, "Götterzeugung in Ugarit und Dilmun," AO 3 (1953) 285-312. F.M.Th. Böhl, "Mythos und Geschichte in der altbabylonischen Dichtung," *Opera Minora* (1953) 217-233. H.M. Pope, *El in the Ugaritic Texts* (1955). A.E. Draffkorn, "ilani/elohim," JBL 76 (1957) 216-224. G.E. Wright, *Biblical Archaeology* (1957) 29-37, 104. J. Aistleitner, *Die mythologischen und kultischen Texte aus Ras Shamra* (1959). E. Dhorme, "La démonologie biblique," *Hommage à W. Vischer* (1960) 46-54. M.G. Kline, "Divine Kingship and Genesis 6:1-4," WThJ 24 (1961/1962) 187-204. O. Betz-O. Michel, "Von Gott gezeugt," BZNW 26 (1960) 3-23. J. Gray, *The Krt Text in the Literature of Ras Shamra* (1964²). O. Eissfeldt, "Israels Religion und die Religionen seiner Umwelt," NZSTh 9 (1967).

II: C. Bezold, *Die Schatzhöhle* (1883). J.A. Bogorodskij, *Beginn der Geschichte der Welt und des Menschen nach den ersten Seiten der Bibel* (1906). E.H. Foschiani, "De gigantibus in sacris libris," VD 3 (1923) 340-343. J.R. Broderius, *The Giant in Germanic Tradition:* Diss Chicago (1932). F.L. Ceuppens, *De historia primaeva. Genesis c. 1 ad c. 11* (1934). J. Enciso, "Los gigantes de la narración de diluvio," EstB 1 (1942) 543-557, 647-667. A.G. Barrois, *Manuel d'Archéologie Biblique, II* (1953). F.L. Ceuppens, *Quaestiones selectae ex historia primaeva* (1953). C. Lanczkowski, "Die Geschichte vom Riesen Goliath und der Kampf Sinuhes mit dem Starken von Retenu," MDAI 2 (1958) 214-218. F.M. Bergounioux-J. Götz, *Die Religionen der vorgeschichtlichen und primitiven Völker* (1960). J. Hasenfuss, "Heros," LThK 5 (1960) 268-269. 269.

Background in the History of Religions

1. The introductory motif is "the theme, widespread in Greek antiquity, of the union of a god with a woman of the human race" (W.H. Schmidt, *Mythos,* 1967, 243, who refers to the texts collected by H. Braun, ZThK 54 [1957] 354f.; see also O. Betz-O. Michel, "Von Gott gezeugt," BZNW 26 [1960] quoted by O. Loretz). The Egyptian account which describes how the god begets the Pharaoh with the queen mother is of special importance (H. Brunner, *Die Geburt*

des Gottkönigs, 1964, mentioned by W.H. Schmidt). It is in the context of the elevation of a person beyond the limits of human existence. U. Cassuto writes of the motif in Ugaritic: "Although the Ugaritic poems on 'the pleasant and beautiful gods' are not clear in detail, yet this at least is certain, that they refer to El as having married two daughters of man and begotten from them two sons: šḥr and šlm."

The introductory motif of Gen 6:1-4 is developed particularly in Phoenician mythology (Philo of Byblos). E.G. Kraeling discusses the matter in detail and sees in the background "the mythology of goddesses consorting with men," 207. The same occurs in Hesiod's theogony. Here the Titans and the giants are described as the sons of Ouranos and Gaia. It is to be noted that they too are the fruit of the marriage of two opposite partners.

H.G. Güterbock (see above) has referred to Hurrian myths in Hittite texts which are like the Ouranos cycle in Hesiod. They go back to the middle of the second millenium, indicating how widespread was the tradition history of this sort of myth. One can say then that the motif with which Gen 6:1-4 begins, the union in marriage of gods and humans which gives rise to a particular kind of being, was known among Israel's neighbors.

2. There are many stories of the generations of the heroes of primeval time or of the giants of antiquity — they are mentioned in Gen 10:8-11 and Ezek 32:27. H. Gunkel writes of "stories of giants among the Arabs, Phoenicians, Greeks, Germans." It is often said that giants were the original inhabitants of a land. To be distinguished from giants or generations of heroes are individual figures like Gilgamesh who was partly divine and partly human (cf. F. Dexinger, *Sturz der Göttersöhne. . . ,* pp. 46-53, and O. Loretz, *Schöpfung und Mythos,* pp. 40-42). J. Skinner quotes an example from the Koran: "The Koran has frequent references to the peoples of 'Ad Thamad' primeval races noted for their giant stature and their daring impiety . . . destroyed by a divine judgment." A.G. Barrois refers to megalithic monuments and the situations in which they are found as the source of legends about the size and strength of ancestors, so too A. Morant, J. Bauer, K. Rabast.

3. In a series of examples of the judgment of God, Sir 16:7 says: "He was not propitiated for the ancient giants who revolted in their might" (E. Kautzsch, commenting on the verse in *Apokryphen.* . . . 308: and n. i: "cf. Gen 6:1-4 and for the later embellishment Bar 3:26; Wis 14:6; 3 Macc 2:4; also the book of Enoch and the book of Jubilees; cf. Dillmann on Gen 6:1-4"). There seem to be here echoes of a tradition according to which "the giants of old" revolted against God. Some scholars agree that the real reason for the sentence of punishment in v. 3 was a revolt of this kind and that it is concealed under the present form of the story (e.g., E.G. Kraeling: "attempts to storm the heavens or other actions are in the background here"). One might think of the story of the battle of the Titans in Greek mythology and of something similar in Phoenician; also of the tradition from the Koran referred to by J. Skinner. A revolt of potentates against God could also be behind the tradition in Ezek 32:27. The most notable occurrence of the motif is in the Atraḥasis epic which begins, like Gen 6:1-4, with the multiplication of humankind on earth; a group of gods revolts against the ruling gods and the revolt is continued by a person on whose shoulders has been laid the burden which had been carried by the gods who revolted. There follows a series of

punishments culminating in the flood. There is a striking parallel of three motifs: multiplication of humankind (a threat) — revolt — punishment by the flood. However, all this must remain conjecture; all that the text shows is that there was once something following vv. 1-2 which continued the mythical event introduced there. In conclusion it must be stated emphatically that, though any number of comparative motifs can be alleged from outside Israel, there is, up to the present, no narrative known which corresponds to 6:1-4.

Purpose and Thrust

The aim of the earlier exegesis of Gen 6:1-4 was broadly to work out a contrast between the "pagan myth" (H. Holzinger) underlying the text and the completely new interpretation given it by Israel. J. Skinner is a typical representative of this attitude: "The few passages where a trace of polytheism still appears (1:26; 3:22, 24; 6:1ff.; 11:1ff.) only serve to show how completely the faith of Israel has transformed and purified the crude ideas of pagan mythology and made them the vehicle of the highest religious teaching" pp. X-XI. One may compare with this the judgment of F. Delitzsch: "Schelling rightly sees in 6:1-6 a highly colored and characteristically mythological passage. . . . We stand here . . . at the source of pagan mythology and saga which are concerned with that race of demons and heroes that stands between the gods and humans whom paganism revered as ἡμίθεοι. . . . This page of biblical history, if it is not to be distorted . . . must at least be allowed to stand on its own merits." Has not Delitzsch seen the point at issue more correctly and with clearer insight than Skinner?

The effect of the text on Delitzsch was to leave him at a loss and scandalized. Hence one can understand how exegetes have gone to such great pains to bypass the mythical talk and to disclaim it by giving a new interpretation. This is now by and large at an end. The most recent exegesis in Jewish, Catholic and Evangelical traditions concedes that the text actually says that gods united with women and that children were born to them.

At the same time however it seems that the scandal that the text caused Delitzsch is no more. One comes to terms with it somewhat too readily. One no longer uses Skinner's words, but insists as he did that all is thereby in order. One says that the myth has been interpreted in Israelite fashion in v. 3: "There is no longer any real myth there; it has been overlaid with historical self-understanding" (W.H. Schmidt p. 246; similarly O. Loretz and B.S. Childs). According to these interpreters the decisive Israelite contribution to the interpretation of the myth is that Israel has converted it to history. One may agree with the direction of this interpretation; but one may ask if the opposition between myth and history expresses clearly enough what is going on. It is not J's intention to write history but to tell the story of a primeval event which is as much beyond history as is creation. It is precisely this that is the reason for the mythical language, which has a definite and deliberate function. The purpose is to describe the overpowering force of human passion that brings people to overstep the limits set for them.

In the realm of primeval event this could not be described in any other way than by the interplay of passion between the sons of the gods and the daughters of men. One must not lose sight of the fact that the "interpretatio Israelitica" (O. Loretz), the decisive adaptation, has left the gross mythical event of vv. 1-2 intact and run the risk of the terrible scandal which the contemporary listeners must have experienced. No exegesis will succeed in removing this scandal. One cannot simply maintain that the event in vv. 1-2 has been turned into a historical event by the interpretation given in v. 3. This verse is certainly a judgment; but even so the event is confirmed precisely as an event in itself. F. Delitzsch perceived this: "It is not to be distorted." There is only the question whether we draw the same conclusion as he, namely to allow the text to stand on its own feet.

The exegetical situation today is very different from what it was a hundred years ago. We no longer understand myth as "pagan mythology," as a lie opposed to the truth, but as a way of presenting reality which has its proper place in the history of humankind. (Cf. W.H. Schmidt, *Das Verständnis des Mythos*, 237-242.) Even the radical criticism of myth in the Old Testament and the fact that no myths originated in Israel does not alter the situation. In J's view, mythical events had an undeniable significance for humankind both before and beyond the history of Israel. There are times then when he too can present the primeval event in mythical form.

It is clear from the very start that J does not intend myth insofar as it stands opposed to Israel's belief in God, but myth insofar as it can say something about humankind as a whole. Here there is a story that tells how the sons of the gods do something that is typical of humankind. They do not comport themselves according to what they are, but do what is transparently human.

A comparison of Gen 6:1-4 with 11:1-9 makes clear J's purpose in using mythological talk. In 11:1-9 he presents people's attempt to transcend the human by means of technology (in fact, the people wanted in this way to achieve union with heaven), in 6:1-4 by means of raising humanity's status, by union with the divine power of life. When one reflects on the extent and significance of this elevation of a person's status by means of union with the divine and the many forms in which it appeared among Israel's neighbors, one can understand why J introduces the mythical motif in its human dimension just at this point.

His own contribution is clear in any case. Simply by introducing the name of Yahweh in v. 3 a limit is set to the level to which humans can rise, "by subordinating their activity to a direct judgment of Yahweh" (B.S. Childs, p. 57). One cannot say that Yahweh's judgment in v. 3, which limits the life-span of humans, cancels the mythological talk of vv. 1-2. Rather by acknowledging the reality that the mythical talk reflects, Yahweh's action of restraining humanity within limits is set supremely and unconditionally above any effort on the individual's part to raise one's state and overstep the limits set for human beings.

One can see then a connection between the real intent of 6:1-4 and a particular motif in prophecy. The proclamation of the supreme dominion of Yahweh over the enemies of Israel where there is any sign that people are raising themselves beyond their station, the outstanding example is the song of the downfall of the king of Babylon into the underworld in Is 14.

This explanation of Gen 6:1-4, the mythical presentation of reality which denies mythical content, opens the possibility of a positive explanation of the presentation of the primeval event. The question can be asked whether 6:1-4 shows any signs of an older layer, of premythical language and motifs. The inquiry can begin with v. 1: "When humankind began to increase on the face of the earth." This part of the exposé is not taken further; one has the impression of an already fixed formula which could be a fragment of an earlier layer. H. Schwarzbaum, *The Overcrowded Earth* (1957) wants to explain the passage from this sentence. He proves first that the motif of the overpopulated earth occurs all over the world in the narratives of primitive peoples, and always in connection with the origin of death; i.e., in myths of primeval time where it is explained how death came to humanity. In the case of Gen 6:1-4 he concludes: "We may say that this Genesis myth is nothing else than an origin of death, explained in terms of over-population," p. 73. He thinks that he can be certain of this because two of the constituent motifs of this myth occur in Gen 6:1-4: the beginning, the over-population of the earth, and the end, the shortening of the life-span of humans.

But one cannot draw such a conclusion so easily because too many motifs and connections are overlooked. The study certainly shows that the sentence about the multiplication of humankind, which also stands at the beginning of the Atraḥasis epic, has its original setting and meaning in the myths of the origin of death where it forms a constitutive part of the course of events; but one cannot be so certain about this either in Gen 6:1-4 or in Atraḥasis. Likewise the shortening of the life-span has its origin at least in the myths of the origin of death where it is also a constitutive part.

One must be cautious about the conclusions drawn. The points of agreement allow the possibility that in 6:1-4 traces of an earlier layer are recognizable where the multiplication of humankind (whereas yet there was no death) and the limitation of the life-span were motifs that colored the whole. But these are no more than traces, because both motifs in 6:1-4 are in a completely different context and so have a different meaning. Nevertheless it is important that there is here yet again the trace of a pre-history of the narratives of primeval time that goes right back to the primitive cultures.

The Flood

Literature

General: H. Drexelius, *Noë, architectus arcae in diluvio navarchus descriptus et morali doctrina illustratus* (1644). J.G. Eichhorn, "Über Mosis Nachrichten von der noachischen Fluth," *Repertorium für biblische und morgenländische Literatur* 5 (1779; 1799²) 185-216. H. Hupfeld, *Die Quellen der Genesis und die Art ihrer Zusammensetzung von neuem untersucht* (1853). Th. Nöldeke, *Untersuchungen zur Kritik des AT:* Die sogenannte Grundschrift des Pentateuch (1869) 1-144. F.F. Woods, "Flood," DBH II (1893) 16-23. A. Stenzel, *Weltschöpfung, Sintflut und Gott* (1894). T.K. Cheyne, "Deluge," EBrit I (1902). G. Jakova-Mertury, *Il diluvio biblico: esame critico del testo scritturale* (1903). W.J. Beecher, "Is the Deluge Story in Genesis Self-contradictory?," HomR 46 (1905) 258-262. H. Lesètre, "Les récits de l'histoire Sainte. Le Déluge," RPA 16 (1906) 212-217. G.L. Young, "The Intrinsic Value of the Deluge Story," BSt 7 (1907) 32-37. E. Trenkle, "Ist die Sündflutgeschichte aus zwei Quellen zusammengearbeitet oder ist sie ein geschlossener einheitlicher Bericht?," ORPB 10 (1908) 225-238, 361-363. H.C. Thomson, "The Assured Results of Modern Criticism tested by the Flood Narrative," BSt 10 (1909) 178-183, 245-254. M. Maurenbrecher, *Biblische Geschichten. Beiträge zum geschichtlichen Verständnis der Religion.* Kap II: Sintflutgeschichten (1909-1910). K. Marti, "Das neue Fragment einer Sintfluterzählung und der Priesterkodex," ZAW 30 (1910) 298-303. A. Schulz, "Die Ausdehnung der Sündflut nach der Hlg. Schrift," BZ 8 (1910) 1-6. J. Happel, "Weltgericht, Weltbegnadigung und Neuordnung der Welt nach dem 1. Buch Mosis," ZMR 25 (1911) 332-348, 354-361. E. König, "Die alttestamentliche Flutgeschichte und die moderne Entlehnungstheorie," Refor 37 (1914) 434-437. A. Brassac, "Les documents dans le récit du déluge," RPA 30 (1920) 5-17. G. Lamerant, *Twee Bijbelstudien: 1. De Zondvloed* (1921). M. Löhr, *Untersuchungen zum Hexateuchproblem. I. Der Priesterkodex in der Genesis,* BZAW 38 (1924). G. Hilion, *Le Déluge dans la Bible et les inscriptions akkadiennes et sumériennes:* Thèse Angers (1925). J. Kroeker, *Noah und das damalige Weltgericht: Das lebendige Wort 2* (1925²). F. Martin, "A Famine Element in the Flood Story," JBL 45 (1926) 129-133. A.W. Nieuwenhuis, *Die Sintflutsagen als kausallogische Natur-Schöpfungsmythen,* (1928). B. Jacob, *Die biblische Sintfluterzählung. Ihre literarische Einheit* (1930). P. Romanoff, "A Third Version of the Flood Narrative (Quellen JPM)," JBL 50 (1931) 304-307. J. Boehmer, "Tellurische Trümmerstücke im Flutbericht der Genesis," ZAW 50 (1932) 117-124. J. Enciso, *El duplicado de la narración del diluvio* (1935). S. Mowinckel, ANVAO 11 (1937) 1-84. A.C. Custance, "The Flood Traditions and the Bible," BibSac 96 (1939) 412-427. D. Poulet, "The Moral Causes of the Flood," CBQ 4 (1942) 293-303. F. Ceuppens, "Le déluge biblique, Genèse 6:1-9:17," PenCath 16 (1945). K. Fruhstorfer, *Die noachische Sintflut (Gen 6-9)* (1945). J. Daniélou, "Déluge, baptême, jugement," DViv 8 (1947) 97-111. E.L.

Dietrich, "Die Religion Noah's; ihre Herkunft und ihre Bedeutung," ZRGG 1 (1948) 301-315. D.C. Allen, *The Legend of Noah. Renaissance Rationalism in Art, Science, and Letters,* Illinois Studies in Language and Literature 33 (1949). K. Elliger, "Entdeckung der Arche Noah?," Für Arbeit und Besinnung 3 (1949) 605-611. J. Daniélou, *Sacramentum Futuri* (1950). J. Heuschen, "Le déluge biblique," REcL 39 (1952) 193-207, 227-232. E. Nielsen, *Oral Tradition,* SBT 2 (1954) 93-103. E. Bettencourt, "O Diluvio Biblico," REB 13 (1953) 351-378. G. Lambert, "Il n'y aura plus jamais de déluge (Genese IX, 11)," NRTh 77 (1955) 581-601, 693-724. K. Koch, *Die israelitische Sühneanschauung und ihre Wandlungen,* Habil Erlangen (1956). L. Arnaldich, "El diluvio," VyV 15 (1957) 145-182. W.J. Dalton, "The Background and Meaning of the Biblical Flood Narrative," ACR 34 (1957) 292-304; 35 (1958) 23-39. R. Bultmann, *Geschichte und Eschatologie* (1958). H. Gese, "Geschichtliches Denken im Alten Orient und im AT," ZThK 55 (1958) 127-145. P. vd Eynde, "Reflexions sur le Deluge," BVC 25 (1959) 49-59. R.P.C. Hanson, *Allegory and Event* (1959). O. Eissfeldt, "Die älteste Erzählung vom Sinaibund," ZAW 73 (1961) 137-146. C.H. Gordon, *Before the Bible* (1960). S. Lach, *Die biblische Sintflut in der gegenwärtigen Exegese* (1961) 5-60. M. Wittenberg, "Gotteszorn und Menschensünde in alttestamentlicher Sicht," ELKZ 15 (1961) 250-255. K. Rahner, "Die Arche Noe als Schiff des Heils," ZKTh 86 (1964) 137-179. B. Celada, "El diluvio. Sentido religioso y fondo histórico," CuBí 22 (1965) 206-217. J. Hempel, "Gottes Selbstbeherrschung als Problem des Monotheismus und der Eschatologie," *Festschr. H.W. Hertzberg* (1965) 56-66. H. Cazelles, "Pentateuque," (1966) 736-738. K. Koch, "Sühne und Sündenvergebung um die Wende von der exilischen zur nachexilischen Zeit," EvTh 26 (1966) 217-239. W. Brueggemann, "David and his Theologian," CBQ 30 (1968) 156-181. J.P. Lewis, *A Study of the Interpretation of Noah and the Flood in Jewish and Christian Literature* (1968). W. v Schöfer, *Was geht uns Noah an? Aus dem Unbewussten der Sprache* (1968). L. vd Wijngaert, "Die Sünde in der priesterschriftlichen Urgeschichte," ThPh 43 (1968) 35-50. F.C. Fensham, "The Obliteration of the Family as Motif in the Near Eastern Literature," AION NS 19 (1969) 191-199. O. Loretz, "Die Vertrauenswürdigkeit der Welt als Schöpfung: 'Die Frage nach dem Sinn der Evolution'," Weltgespräch 9 (1969) 55-74. M. Smith, "The Present State of Old Testament Studies," JBL 88 (1969) 19-35. F.A. Filby, *The Flood Reconsidered* (1970). W. Herrmann, "Das Todesgeschick als Problem in Altisrael," MIOF 16 (1970) 14-32. W.M. Clark, "The Flood and the Structure of Pre-patriarchal History," ZAW 83 (1971) 184-211. S. McEvenue, *The Narrative Style of the Priestly Writer,* AnBib 50 (1971).

History of Religions: G.L Bauer, *Hebräische Mythologie des alten und des neuen Testaments.* I (1802). F. Lenormant, *Le déluge et l'Epopée Babylonienne* (1873). G. Smith, *The Chaldean Account of Genesis* (1873; 1880²) 213-234. A. Jeremias, *Izdubar-Nimrod, eine altbabylonische Heldensage* (1891). M. Jastrow, *The Religion of Babylonia and Assyria* (1898). H. Usener, *Religionsgeschichtliche Untersuchungen III. Die Sintflutsagen untersucht* (1899). M. Winternitz, "Die Flutsagen des Altertums und der Naturvölker," MAGW 31 (1901) 305-333. T. Schneider, *Was ist's mit der Sintflut? Die Versuche ihrer Deutung als Geschichte, Sage und Mythus. Zugleich ein Beitrag zur Babel- und Bibelfrage* (1903). M. Henning, "Der biblisch-babylonische Sintflutmythos," Das freie Wort 2 (1905) 16-23. W. Lotz, *Das AT und die Wissenschaft* (1905) 189-195. E. Naville, "A Mention of the Flood in the Book of the Dead," PSBA 26 (1905) 251-257, 287-294. P. Jensen, "Der babylonische Sintflutheld und sein Schiff in der israelitischen Gilgamesch-Sage," *Festschr. F. Nöldeke, Orientalische Studien* 2 (1906) 983-996. J. Hehn, "Ein neugefundenes Sintflutfragment aus altbabylonischer Zeit," BZ 8 (1910) 225-227. F.M.Th. Böhl, "Sumerische Mythen von Sintflut und Sündenfall," ThT (1914) 470-472. S.H. Langdon, *The Sumerian Epic of Paradise* (1915). F.M.Th. Böhl, *Paradijs en Zondvloed. . . ,* (1916). A. Lods, "Un poème babylonien sur l'âge d'or, le déluge," RThPh 2, 3 (1916) 269-286. S. Landersdorfer, *Die Sumerischen Parallelen. . . ,* (1917) 96-101. N.D. v Leeuwen, *Het bijbelsch-akkadisch-schumerisch zondvloedverhaal:* Diss Amsterdam (1920). F. Leidecker, Lit §5.1, (d). A.T. Clay, "A Hebrew Deluge Story in Cuneiform and other Epic Fragments in the Pierpont Morgan Library," YOS 5 (1922) 58-69, 81-82; *The Origin of Biblical Traditions* (1923) 173-186. E.A.W. Budge, *The Babylonian Story of the Deluge and the Epic of Gilgamesh. With*

Account of the Royal Libraries of Niniveh (1924; 1929²). E. Daque, *Urwelt, Sage und Menschheit* (1924; 1928⁵). A. Deimel, "Der biblische Sündflutbericht und die Keilschriften," Or 20 (1926) 69-79; "Diluvium in traditione Babylonorum." "Biblica diluvii traditio cum traditione babylonica comparata." "Diluvii traditio et critica 'scientifica' recentiorum," VD 7 (1927) 186-191, 248-251, 336-342. H. Plessis, "Babylone et la Bible. Le Déluge," DB (1928) 754-764. E. Dhorme, "Le déluge babylonien," RB 39 (1930) 481-502. J.H. Schoneveld, *De oorsprong van het bijbelsche zondvloedverhaal*, Diss Groningen (1938). S.N. Kramer, Lit. §5.1 (c) (1944). W.F. Albright, *From the Stone Age. . .* , (1946; 1957²) 128, 146, 180-181, 201. A. Heidel, *The Gilgamesh Epic and Old Testament Parallels* (1946; 1963⁴) 224-289. W.B. Kristensen, *Verzamelde Bijdragen tot kennis der antieke godsdiensten* (1947) 5-14. A.L. Oppenheim, "The Sumerian Kinglist," Or 16 (1947) 209-211; Or 17 (1948) 39-40 (ANET, 265-266). G. Contenau, *Le déluge babylonien* (1941; 1952²). A.S. Kapelrud, "God as Destroyer in the Preaching of Amos and the Ancient Near East," JBL 71 (1952) 33-38. F.M.Th. Böhl, "Das Problem des ewigen Lebens in Zyklus und Epos des Gilgamesch," *Opera Minora* (1953) 234-262, 498-502. M. Eliade, *Die Religion und das Heilige.* Kap. V/72 (1954) 244-248. R. Pettazzoni, "Myths of Beginnings and Creation-Myths," *Essays on the History of Religions:* NumenSuppl 1 (1954) 24-36. J. Laessøe, BibOr 13 (1956) 90-102. L. Woolley, "Stories of the Creation and the Flood," PEQ 88 (1956) 14-21. M. Eliade, *Patterns in Comparative Religion* (1958; 1971²). W.G. Lambert, "New Light on the Babylonian Flood," JSSt 5 (1960) 113-123. F. Heiler, "Erscheinungsformen und Wesen der Religion," *Die Religionen der Menschheit,* Bd. I (1961) 284-285. J.H. Marks, "Flood," IDB 2 (1962) 278-284. E. Sollberger, *The Babylonian Legend of the Flood* (1962; 1966²). L.G. Nielsen, "Syndflod og Kaos," DTT 28 (1965) 206-240. F.C. Fensham, "The Destruction of Mankind in the Near East," AION NS 15 (1966) 31-37. L. Matous, "Zur neueren epischen Literatur im Alten Mesopotamien," ArOr 35 (1967) 1-25. A.R. Millard, "A New Babylonian 'Genesis' Story," TynB 18 (1967) 3-18. V. Schneider, *Gilgamesch* (1967) 187-207. D. Hämmerly-Dupuy, "Some Observations on the Assyro-Babylonian and Sumerian Flood-Stories," AUSS 6 (1968) 1-18. G. Pettinato, "Die Bestrafung des Menschengeschlechts durch die Sintflut," Or 37 (1966) 165-200. W.G. Lambert-A.R. Millard, *Atra-Ḥasis. The Babylonian Story of the Flood with the Sumerian Flood Story, by M. Civil* (1969). L. Matous, "Die Urgeschichte der Menschheit im Atraḥasis-Epos und in der Genesis," ArOr 37 (1969) 1-7. A. Ohler, *Mythologische Elemente im AT. Eine motivgeschichtliche Untersuchung* (1969) 85-101. G. Pettinato, "Die Flutberichte in keilschriftlicher Überlieferung," BeO 11 (1969) 109-123, 159-173. Th.C. Vriezen, "The Study of the OT and the History of Religion," VT.S 1968 (1969) 1-24. E. Fisher, "Gilgamesh and Genesis: The Flood Story in Context," CBQ 32 (1970) 392-402. W. v Soden, "Grundsätzliches zur Interpretation des Atramḥasis Mythos," Or 39 (1970) 311-314.

Ethnology: Ph. Buttmann, *Mythologus* I, 7, (1828) 180-214. F. Creuzer, *Symbolik und Mythologie der alten Volker* (1819). H. Lüken, *Die Traditionen des Menschengeschlechts* (1869²) 189-287. O. Zöckler, "Die Sintflutsagen des Altertums nach ihrem Verhältnis zur biblischen Sintflutgeschichte," JDTh 2 (1870). L. Diestel, *Die Sintflut und die Flutsagen des Altertums* (1871). R. Andree, *Die Flutsagen ethnographisch betrachtet* (1891). E. Böklen, "Die Sintflutsage. Ein Versuch einer neuen Erklärung," ARW 6 (1903) 1-61, 97-150. H. Winckler, "Himmels- und Weltbild der Babylonier als Grundlage der Weltanschauung und Mythologie alter Völker," AO 3, 2-6 (1903²). J. Riem, *Die Sintflut in Sage und Wissenschaft* (1906; 1925²) "Die Sintflut, eine ethnographisch-naturwissenschaftliche Untersuchung," Christentum u. Zeitgeist 9 (1906) 1-54. W. Restelle, "Traditions of the Deluge," BibSac 64 (1907) 148-167. G. Gerland, *Der Mythus von der Sintflut* (1912). H. Schneider, *Die Wanderungen und Wandlungen der Sündflutsage* (1913). C. Nimuendaju-Unkel, "Der Sagen von der Erschaffung und Vernichtung der Welt als Grundlage der Religion der Apapocuva-Guarani," ZE 46 (1914). A. Reinach, "Noé Sangarion. Étude sur le déluge en Phrygie et le syncrétisme judéo-phrygien," REJ 67 (1914) 212-245. W. Wundt, *Völkerpsychologie, VI, 6.* "Die Weltuntergangsmythen" (1915) 290-309. H. Stieglecker, "Zur indischen Flutsage," KKZ 59, 9 (1918). K. Ziegler, *Weltuntergang in Sage und*

Wissenschaft "Aus Natur und Geisteswelt" Bd. 718 (1921). W. Anderson, *Nordasiatische Flutsagen* (1923). J.G. Frazer, *Folklore.* . . , 46-143. A. Seitz, "Geschichtliche Menschheitsüberlieferung der Sündflut," ThGl 18 (1926) 236-257. W. Müller, *Die ältesten amerikanischen Sintfluterzählungen,* Diss Bonn (1930). H. Baumann, *Schöpfung und Urzeit.* . . , 306-327. A.R. Herrmann, "Die Sintflut im Völkerleben," BenM 27 (1951) 153-155. P. Grimal, *Mythen der Völker:* Fischer Bücherei 1 (1967).

Texts: History of Religions: A. Schoene (ed.), Eusebii chronicorum libri duo. I. Die Sintflut nach Berossos (1879). P. Haupt, *Der keilinschriftliche Sintflutbericht. Eine Episode des babylonischen Nimrodepos* (1881). A. Köhler, *Der Flutbericht des Berosus in Excerpten erhalten bei Eusebius' chron. armen:* ed. J.B. Ancher. I, 3 (1894) 31-37, 48-50. P. Haupt, "The Introductory Lines of the Cuneiform Account of the Deluge," JAOS 25 (1904) 68-75. Th.G. Pinches, "Gilgameš and the Hero of the Flood," PSBA 25 (1903/1904) 113-122, 195-201. L. Delaporte, "Le premier fragment d'une nouvelle version du déluge babylonien," RHR 61 (1910) 343-348. H.V. Hilprecht, *Der neue Fund zur Sintflutgeschichte aus der Tempelbibliothek von Nippur* (1910). P. Haupt, "Some Difficult Passages in the Cuneiform Account of the Deluge," JAOS 32 (1912) 1-16. L. Waterman, "The Date of the Deluge," AJSL 39 (1923) 233-247. W.F. Albright, "The Babylonian Matter in the Pre-Deuteronomic Primeval History," JBL 58 (1939) 91-103. F. Michaeli, "Textes de la Bible et de l'Ancien Orient," CAB 13 (1961). E.G. Kraeling, "Xisouthros, Deucalion and the Flood Traditions,' JAOS 67 (1944) 177-182. A.Schott-W. v Soden, *Das Gilgamesch-Epos* (1958) 86-99. D.W. Thomas, *Documents from OT Times,* (1958). J. Aistleitner, *Die mythologischen u. kultischen Texten aus Ras Shamra* (1959). L. Cagni, "L'epopea di Erra," SS 34 (1969).

Archaeology – Geology: A. Bosicio, *Die Geologie und die Sündfluth. Studie über die Urgeschichte der Erde* (1877). E. Suess, *Das Antlitz der Erde,* I, 1 Die Sintfluth (1883) 25-98. G.A. Adams, "Where was the Flood?," BibSac 59 (1902) 579-583. G.F. Wright, "Geological Confirmations of the Noachian Deluge," BibSac 59 (1902) 282-293, 537-556, 695-716. D.G. Whitley, "Noah's Flood in the Light of Modern Science," BibSac 64 (1907) 519-551. H.W. Magoun, "The Glacial Epoch and the Noachian Deluge," BibSac 66 (1909) 217-242, 431-457; 67 (1910) 105-119, 204-229. B. Mendelsohn, "Die Erdbeben und Fluterzählungen des AT in geologischer Beleuchtung," Deutsche Rundschau 148 (1911) 241-258. H. Hörbiger, *Glazialkosmogonie* (1913). J.M. Schneider, "Die Geologie der Sündflut und Chronologie," ThPQ 77 (1924) 50-61. H. Fischer, *Weltwenden. Die grossen Fluten in Sage und Wirklichkeit* (1926³). P.J. le Riche, "Scientific Proofs of a Universal Deluge," Journal of the Transactions of the Victoria Institute 61 (1929) 86-117. E.T. Brewster, "Genesis and Flood Theories in the Light of their History," BibSac 90 (1933) 220-227. D.J. Whitney, "The Problem of the Flood," BibSac 90 (1933) 469-478. J. Fischer, *Die Sintflut und Hörbigers Welteislehre* (1937⁶). J. Bright, "Has Archaeology found Evidence of the Flood?," BA 5 (1942) 55-62. H. Quiring, "Sintflut, Stufenturm und erstes Gotteshaus," Saec 1 (1950) 397-404. C.C. Gillispie, *Genesis and Geology, A Study in the Relations of Scientific Thought, Natural Theology, and 1790-1851 Social Opinions in Great Britain* (1951). A.M. Rehwinkel, *The Flood in the Light of the Bible, Geology and Archaeology* (1951). N.L. Falcon-J.M. Lees, "The Geological History of the Mesopotamian Plaines," Geographical Journal 118 (1952) 24-39. A. Parrot, "Déluge et arche de Noé," CAB 1 (1952). L. Woolley, *Excavations at Ur* (1954). A. Parrot, *The Flood and Noah's Ark - Nineveh and the OT. - The Tower of Babel.* G.E. Wright, *Biblical Archeology* (1956). H.M. Morris-C.J. Whitcomb, *The Genesis Flood - The Biblical Record and its Scientific Implications* (1961). A. Barrois, *Manuel d'archéologie biblique* 3 (1964) 52-64. M.E.L. Mallowan, "Noah's Flood Reconsidered," Iraq 26 (1964) 62-82. R.L. Raikes, "The Physical Evidence for Noah's Flood," Iraq 28 (1966) 52-63.

Text

6:5 When Yahweh[a] saw, that the wickedness of humankind was great on earth, and every planning[b] and striving of its heart was always wicked,

6 he was sorry that he had made humankind on earth, and he was grieved at heart[a].

7 And Yahweh said: I will wipe out humankind whom I have created[a] from the face of the earth, from humans to beasts, reptiles and birds of heaven[a], because I am sorry that I have made them.

8 But Noah had found favor in the eyes of Yahweh[a].

9 This is the story of Noah: Noah was a just man. He was blameless[a] among his contemporaries[b]; Noah walked[c] with God.

10 And Noah had three sons: Shem, Ham and Japheth.

11 But the earth was corrupt in God's eyes[ab], the earth was full of violence.

12 God looked at the earth and it was certainly corrupt, because all flesh had corrupted its way of life on earth.

13 And God said to Noah: I have decided[a] to put an end[b] to all flesh, because the earth is full of violence because of it[c]. And so I will wipe it "from"[d] the earth.

14 Make an ark[a] for yourself out of teak-wood[b], make it with rooms[c], and cover it with reeds and coat it inside and outside with pitch[d];

15 you are to make it in this way: its length is to be 300 cubits[a], its width 50 cubits, and its height 30 cubits.

16 You are to make a window[a] in the ark at the top, [you are to set it one cubit (from the top)][b], and you are to put the door in the side of the ark, and you are to make three decks, lower, middle and upper.

17 I am going to unleash the flood upon the earth[a] so as to destroy all flesh under heaven that has in it the breath of life; everything that is on the earth shall perish[b].

18 But I am setting up a covenant with you: You are to go into the ark, you and your sons, and your wife and the wives of your sons with you.

19 And from all that lives[a], from all flesh, you are to bring two of each[b] (kind) with you into the ark, to keep them alive with you; there is to be a male and a female of each.

20 Two of every kind of bird, two of every kind of animal, of every[a] reptile that crawls on the ground; two of all these are to come to you to be kept alive with you[b].

21 You are to take every sort of food that is eaten, and store it up; this is to serve as food for you and them.

22 And Noah did everything just as God had commanded him[a].

7:1 And Yahweh said to Noah: Go into the ark, you and your whole household, because you[a] I have found[b] just among your contemporaries.

2 Take seven pairs of every clean animal, male and female, and one 'pair'[a] of every unclean animal, male and female,

3 [and seven pairs of every bird of the air, male and female][a] to keep their kind alive on earth.

4 Because in seven days from now[a] I will bring rain[b] upon the earth for 40 days and 40 nights, and I will wipe from the earth every existing thing[c] that I have made.

5 And Noah did everything that Yahweh commanded him.

6 Noah was 600 years old when the flood (water) came upon the earth[a].

7 And Noah and his sons and his wife and his sons' wives[a] went into the ark to escape the waters of the flood.

8 Of clean and unclean animals, of birds and of all[a] that crawls on the earth,

9 two of each, male and female[a], went into the ark with Noah, as God had commanded him.

10 And after seven days the waters of the flood came[a] upon the earth.

11 In the 600th year[a] of Noah's life, in the 2nd month, on the 17th day[b] of the month, on this day all the fountains of the great deep[c] burst forth, and the windows of heaven were opened[d].

12 And rain[a] poured upon the earth for 40 days and 40 nights.

13 On this very day[a] Noah went into the ark with his sons, Shem, Ham and Japheth, with[c] his wife and the three[b] wives of his sons;

14 they[a] and wild animals of every kind, and cattle of every kind, and all that crawls on the earth of every kind, and birds of every kind, every winged bird[b].

15 They all went into the ark, to Noah, two and two of all flesh that had life in them[a].

16 And those that went in were male and female of all flesh, and they went in as God had commanded him. And Yahweh shut the door behind him[a].

17 The flood continued [40 days][a] over the earth, and the waters increased and lifted up the ark so that it was high above the earth.

18 And the waters mounted and increased greatly upon the earth, and the ark floated upon the surface of the waters.

19 And the waters mounted greatly[a] upon the earth, and all the high mountains under heaven's expanse were covered.

20 The waters[a] mounted and rose 15 cubits above the mountain[b] tops.

21 All flesh[a], all that moved upon the earth, perished, birds[b] and cattle and wild animals, and all that swarmed upon the earth, and all humankind.

22 Everything that had the breath of life[a] in its nostrils[b], everything that[c] lived on the dry land, all died.

23 So he[a] wiped out every existing thing on the face of the earth, man and beast and crawling thing and bird of heaven[b] — all of them were wiped from the earth. Only Noah was left and what was with him in the ark.

24 And the waters mounted over the earth for 150 days.

8:1 Then God thought of Noah and of all the wild animals and cattle that were with him in the ark[a]. And God made a wind blow over the earth so that the waters subsided.

2 And the fountains of the deep and the windows of heaven[a] were closed, and the rain from heaven was stopped[b],

3 and the waters receded gradually[a] from the earth; at the end of 150 days[b] they had disappeared.

4 On the 17th[a-b] day of the 7th month the ark came to rest on the mountains of Ararat[c].

5 The waters continued to recede until the 10th month; on the 1st day of the 10th month[a] the tops of the mountains became visible.

6 At the end of 40 days[a] Noah opened the window that he had made in the ark

7 and he sent[a] the raven[b] out and it flew to and fro[c] until the water on the earth had dried up[d].

8 Then he sent out the dove to see if the waters on the earth had subsided further.

9 But the dove did not find any place where it could rest the sole of its foot, so it came back to him in the ark because there was still water over the whole earth. He put out his hand and caught it and brought it back[a] into the ark.

10 He waited[a] another 7 days; then he sent the dove out of the ark again.

11 And the dove returned to him in the evening, and it had a fresh olive leaf in its beak. So Noah knew that the waters had subsided from the earth.

12 He waited yet another 7 days and sent the dove out again; this time it did not come back to him.

13 In the 601st year of Noah's life[a], on the 1st day of the month, the waters on the earth had dried up[b]. Noah removed the hatch from the ark, and he saw that the surface of the earth was dry.

14 On the 27th day of the 2nd month, the earth was completely dry.

15 Then God spoke to Noah. He said:

16 Go out of the ark, you and your wife and your sons and your sons' wives with you.

17 And[a] all the animals that are with you, all creatures, birds and cattle and all crawling things that spawn upon the earth bring them out with you[b], that they may breed upon the earth[c], and increase and multiply upon the earth.

18 And Noah and his sons and his wife and his sons' wives went out together

19 And[a] all the wild animals and all the cattle, and all the birds and everything that crawls on the earth[b], all of them went out of the ark by families[c].

20 And Noah built an altar to Yahweh. He took clean[a] animals and birds of every kind and offered whole-burnt offerings[b] upon the altar.

21 And Yahweh smelled[a] the sweet odor and reflected: "Never again will I curse the ground because of people[b]; indeed the inclination of the human heart is evil[c] from its youth; And never again will I slay every living creature, as I have done.

22 While earth lasts, there shall never cease[a] seedtime and harvest, frost and heat, summer and winter, night and day."

6:5a Gk κύριος ὁ θεός, likewise in 6 & 7.   **b** יצר ''un terme de métier'' (P. Humbert).
6a ויתעצב cf. Gen 34:7.

7a The enumeration ''from humans to . . . of heaven'' is a redactional addition, also perhaps אשר בראתי.

8a Many interpreters agree that there is a gap in J's text after v. 8 which contained the commission to build the ark.

9a Sam and Vg read ותמים; C.J. Ball (SB 1896) and others hold that צדיק has been inserted here from 7:1 (J); H. Gunkel, J. Skinner, E.A. Speiser concede two sentences; U. Cassuto "A wholly righteous man, cp. Prv 11:5."   **b** E.A. Speiser: ''in his time''; U Cassuto: "the plural seems to glorify Noah"; J. Skinner: "the successive generations covered by his lifetime."   **c** התהלך ''an old Semitic form which is durative or iterative in connotation and has formally coalesced with the hithpael'' (E.A. Speiser).

11a האלהים ''one of the few instances of P's use of the article with אלהים'' (J. Skinner).   **b** לפני ''according to God's (regretful) conclusion'' (E.A. Speiser).

13a לפני E.A. Speiser: ''I have decided''; U. Cassuto: as in Esther 9:11 ''was brought before the king"; J. Skinner: "has entered into my purpose." **b** "the hour of doom" (H.L. Ginsburg, "The Composition of the Book of Daniel," VT 4 [1954] 272; M. Wallenstein, "Some Lexical Material in the Judean Scroll," VT 4 [1954] 212). **c** מפניהם through them, cf. Ex 8:20; 9:11; Judg 6:6 and elsewhere. **d** Read מאת (haplog.); very many emendations or explanations of את have been proposed.

14a תבה only here and Ex 2:3-5; U. Cassuto: "a loan word, e.g., tb.t chest or box" (so too J. Skinner and others). **b** תעשה juss. Ges-K §76t; double accus. with עשה (also in vv. 15, 16b) Ges-K §117ii. G.R. Driver ("Problems and Solutions," VT 4 [1954] 243) reads קנים = "woven with reeds" and understands the second עשה as "cover": "make yourself an ark of teak-wood and cover the ark with reeds"; likewise others. **c** P. de Lagarde (Or2) (Philo too) has proposed the reading קנים קנים, accepted by H. Holzinger, J. Skinner, O. Procksch, H. Gunkel. U. Cassuto and E.A. Speiser hold the emendation unnecessary. H. Gunkel accepts H. Winckler's proposal (A. Tilche, *Untersuchungen*, 1892) to read 14b before 16b. **d** כפר only here in OT; the corresponding word for the same material *kupru*, pitch, is used in the same context in the Gilgamesh epic.

15a "The usual Hebrew cubit is estimated at 45-49 cm. (ca. 18in.), the cubit of Ezekiel at 52-55 cm. (ca. 21 in.)" (H. Holzinger).

16a צהר only here in OT; meaning uncertain; Gk ἐπισυνάγων, Vg *fenestram* (also Sam). "The meaning 'back' is supported by ar. *zahr*" (J. Skinner). **b** The following sentence ואל־אמה תכלנה is not clear; probably the text has been disturbed.

17a An explanatory addition. **b** Sam has hiph. instead of לשחת. — יגוע only in P in the Pentateuch, e.g., 7:21; 25:8, 17; 35:29; 49:33; twelve times in all; otherwise only poetically (J. Skinner).

19a Instead of החי Sam reads החיה (as 8:17); so too Gk which adds two other species of animals, as in 7:14, 21; 8:19. **b** שנים, to be repeated with Gk and Sam, as in 7:9, 15.

20a Some ancient versions read ומכל and some exegetes follow this (C.J. Ball, O. Procksch et al.); this is not necessary if רמש is used here in a broader sense. Gk has inserted כל before all groups so as to harmonize. **b** להחיות intrans. hiph., whereas it is better to translate it transitively in v. 20 (against Speiser).

22a "The object is expressed by the separate pronoun . . . compare Gen VI 22 . . . VII 5 . . . ," (S. Talmon, "Double Readings in the Massoretic Text," Textus 1, 1960, 183).

7:1a אתך emphasized by position in sense of "you alone." **b** ראיתי in the same sense Ps 22:12 (H. Gunkel).

2a Read שנים שנים with the versions corresponding to the previous "seven of each."

3a The first sentence is probably a redactional complement (Gk adds further "clean").

4a ל indicates a time terminus, more precisely the end of a period of time. **b** The participle in the nominal sentence with a future meaning Ges-K §116p. **c** היקום again only in 7:23 and Deut 11:6, from root קום; for the formation Ges-K §85d; Gk ἀνάστεμα, Vg *substantia*, the subsisting.

6a "The simultaneity of two facts is expressed through coordination of two nominal sentences" (H. Holzinger), Ges-K §164a.

7-10a belong substantially to J, but are heavily glossed (so H. Holzinger, H. Gunkel et al.). The addition of אתו and the enumeration which it concludes is characteristic of P; likewise the enumeration in v. 8. Many interpreters make cancellations and inversions in vv. 7-10 on the grounds that R has accommodated the passage to P.

8a read ומכל with Sam and the versions.

9a זכר ונקבה, priestly language, so too אלהים. V. 9 is a clear example of the redactional work.

10a For sentence construction, Ges-K §164a.

11a For the additional שנה, Ges-K §134o. **b** Gk reads 27th day instead of 17th. **c** תהום רבה without article, poetic; so too Amos 7:4; Is 51:10; Ezek 31:7; Ps 36:7. **d** v. 11b (after the date) can be read rhythmically, 7-beats.

12a   "Hebr. גשם unlike מטר signifies abnormal rainfall" (E.A. Speiser).
13a   בעצם היום always P; H. Holzinger, *Einleitung* 346.   **b** On שלשת Ges-K §97c.   **c** Gk and Sam have אתו instead of אתם, as 8:16, 18.
14a   המה is missing in Gk.   **b** The last four words do not appear in Gk and some Mss. They may be an addition. U.Cassuto explains them: "Every bird of every sort."
15a   Gk adds "male and female."
16a   Most interpreters agree that the verse stood between vv. 10 & 12 in J.
17a   "40 days," to which the "40 nights" of Gk would be an addition, has been appended by R for balance.
19a   BrSynt §93k, 129b; Ges-K §133k.
20a   Ges-K §118h; BrSynt §101.   **b** Gk "the high mountains."
21a   For the absence of the article before בשר BrSynt §60a.   **b** J is specific, Ges-K §119i.
22a   A composite expression out of נשמת חיים (J, as in 2:7) and רוח חיים (P as in v. 17). One can see again in vv. 22-23 the redactional work that joins J and P; this explains the addition of רוח.   **b** For construction BrSynt §152a.   **c** For this usage of מן, Ges-K §119w. U. Cassuto: explicative, "that is to say."
23a   On the form וימח Ges-K §75o, shortened form of imperf. qal. E.A. Speiser: "Hebrew often employs actives in an impersonal sense." It is not necessary then to insert the subject after the verb (so O. Procksch, H. Gunkel et al.).   **b** The enumeration is a redactional link.

8:1a   Gk adds the birds; J. Skinner observes: "The addition of Gk . . . is here very much in place."
2a   H. Gunkel draws attention to the parallel to 7:11b; 2a could also be rhythmic, and he asks whether a verb is missing at the end.   **b** The last sentence of v. 2 belongs to J.
3a   On the construction, Ges-K §113u; BrSynt §93a.   **b** Read מקץ, with Strack and most modern interpreters; קצה mainly locative.
4a   Gk has 27 days.   **b** "Ordinals are replaced by cardinals when giving dates by the day." BrSynt §86.   **c** "The Ararat range, not a particular peak" (E.A. Speiser, also U. Cassuto) Ges-K §124o. R. Gordis "Job XL 29," VT 14 (1964) 492f. speaks of a "distributive use of the plural." "Pesh. and Tg translate Ararat by *Qardu* (= Kordyene)" H. Gunkel.
5a   Ges-K §129f, 134p.
6a   BrSynt §123h.
7a   "The" raven Ges-K §126r.   **b** Gk adds after v. 8. לראת הקלו המים.   **c** Ges-K §113s; Gk and others add ולא שב.   **d** Ges-K §70a, n. 2.
9a   BrSynt §80c.
10a   O. Procksch, H. Holzinger, J. Skinner and others propose here and in v. 12 the reading וייחל; cf. Ges-K §69t.
13a   Gk inserts לחיי נח (cf. 7:11).   **b** E.A. Speiser: "חרב denotes 'to be or to become free of moisture'; complete dryness is signified by יבש, v. 14."
17a   Gk, Sam, Syr read וכל (v. 19 also).   **b** The Qerē היצא cannot be explained. I.L. Seeligmann, "Indications of Editorial Alternation and Adaptation in the Massoretic Text and the Septuagint," VT 11 (1961) 201: "It is difficult to explain the form of the Qerē היצא (Gen VIII 17) except as a result of a tendency to preserve in their original form all the elements that reached the editors of the Massorah." On the form U. Cassuto: The פ"ו verb is treated as if it were פ"י; Ges-K §69v, 70b.   **c** The words וישרצו בארץ are missing in Gk; in Vg all verbs are in the imperf.
19a   cf. 17a.   **b** Gk adds the enumeration.   **c** משפחת, because the plural of מין is not usual (J. Skinner).
20a   "and clean birds of every kind" is missing in Gk and Vg.   **b** Gk and Syr read עלה.
21a   On the form, Ges-K §72aa.   **b** Gk διὰ τὰ ἔργα.   **c** Gk adds "only."
22a   On the word order, Ges-K §146d, BrSynt §122s.

Literary Form

The Structure of the Flood Narrative

1. The structure of the flood narrative is cyclic: it begins with the decision of God to destroy humankind and reaches its goal in the decision of God to preserve humankind from now on and never to destroy it again.

The basic structure, comprising the decision of God and its consequences, finds a parallel in the creation narratives showing that the flood narrative is really an appendage to the creation narrative, in particular to the creation of humans. The parallel goes further still: there is a moment of crisis in the story of the creation of humans in Gen 2 because the first attempt miscarries, 2:18. What is created is "not good"; it is not humankind as God intended to create it. The introduction to the flood narrative says that humankind whom God has created has failed: humankind is wicked, 6:5-6, the earth is corrupt, 6:11-12 P.

There is a far-reaching parallel between the creation of humans and the flood narrative. Both begin with a decision of God about humanity; both envisage the possibility of the failure of humanity as God's creation; both are concerned with the existence or non-existence of humanity. Flood narrative and creation narrative (of humans) are from the very start obviously interrelated; they complement each other (W. Wundt). Humankind as God's creation cannot take for granted its own existence in the world; its existence is problematic and remains such in the presence of its creator. The creation decision can be revoked. The pre-history of the biblical flood narrative makes it even clearer that it is directed to the narrative of the creation of humans. A great number of flood narratives show many points of contact with the creation of human beings (see below).

2. The decision to destroy humanity and the reversal of it does not build and resolve a tension. The extinction of humanity cannot really be the subject of a narrative because with it all tradition would be at an end. The decision therefore must find its complement in another decision to preserve an individual. It is only through the one saved that the account of the flood can be passed on. This is just what happens in the Gilgamesh epic where the story is narrated by the one who was saved. And it is precisely here that the difference between the flood story and the story of the creation of people reveals itself. The flood, though primeval event, is a happening in time, something that can be attested. Consequently it stands in the middle, between creation and history. This is the reason why the flood has come to mark a division of eras: "Before the flood" — "after the flood."

The decision to preserve the individual makes an event possible; a drama can develop. A flood narrative only becomes possible by the confrontation of destruction and preservation — humankind to be destroyed, an individual to be preserved. The narrative proceeds along two lines from this double-pronged beginning. That is what gives it its character: it tells of the implementation of the twofold decision.

(a) The implementation of the decision to destroy humankind, 7:10-24, is divided into:

> the coming of the flood
> the effect of the flood.

This division is parallel to that of one part of the prophetic announcement of judgment, the intervention of God and its consequence. The actual description of the flood, which is really the main part, is relatively short. The reason for this brevity is that the coming and the effect of the flood are presented without comment or dialogue. There is no reaction from those involved; no lament, cry, death agony — nothing at all of this sort. There is absolute silence; herein lies much of the effect. In the midst of this awful silence the whole drama consists in the story of salvation. The narrative would have to be called "Noah's salvation from the flood" were not the framework: God's decision to destroy — to preserve humankind.

There is yet another aspect to the wordless action of this part. In the prophetic proclamation of judgment the drama lies in the tension between the announcement and its realization: those to whom the judgment is announced can react to it. In the flood narrative no announcement is made to those involved in God's judgment. The judgment is like a sudden disaster, a pitiless fate that bursts over humankind.

(b) The judgment is announced only to the one whom God intends to save! There is communication with him alone. And so the structure of the execution of the decision to preserve Noah is different and carefully articulated. It consists of two parts centered about the middle part, the destruction of humankind.

The commission to Noah and its execution;
The end of the flood, exit from the ark, reaction of those saved.
These two sections are closely connected and actually form a single part. So two themes run through the flood narrative corresponding to the double thrust of the introduction. The second part, the preservation of Noah, is constructed in such a way that everything begins from and is determined by a single sentence: the announcement of the flood. The commission to build the ark stems from the announcement and provides the means of preservation. Noah's reaction is to carry out the commission. But the action cannot stop here. If the commission means an offer of salvation, then there are two consequences: the experience of salvation (Noah treads again the high ground) and the response of the one saved to the savior (the sacrifice). The essential difference between the two parts consists in this: one line traces the execution of the decision of God to destroy humankind as a brute fact, the other the execution of the decision to preserve Noah narrated as a personal encounter in words.

Everything said so far about the structure holds for the composite J and P narrative as a whole. This composition offers the very rare case where two literary narrative threads (J and P) have been preserved with all parts intact, both containing the same event with the same divisions and only the slightest variations. The conclusion therefore is that the narrative was already well fixed in form before it came to J and P.

The study of the structure of the narrative consisting of two common literary threads has yielded so far the following results: the biblical flood narrative does not show the characteristics of an event which took place on this earth. The beginning and the goal of the event lie with God. The span of the event moves from a decision of God to a modified decision of God. This framework spans yet another framework *(Geschehensbogen)* which is fitted into it — the announcement of the flood to its conclusion. This being the structure that lies behind both the J and P narratives, the question arises: Does the history of the narrative allow us to come to any conclusion as to how these two frameworks, the exterior and the interior, are related to each other? Was there a stage in the history of the flood narrative when it consisted only of the interior framework, which moved from the announcement to its conclusion? We can now say that the destruction of humanity and the preservation of the individual belonged to the flood narrative from the very beginning. We have established therefore that we are dealing with a narrative of primeval time that is in the context of the story of the creation of humans. Side-by-side with the creation of humanity there is now the possibility of its destruction; this leads to the preservation of humankind by saving the one. The creation of humans and their preservation involve a catastrophe; but the saving action does not take place in the realm of the history of humanity. It is an event that precedes history.

Setting in Life

The flood narrative is widespread throughout the world. Only a survey of its occurrence in all places and in the most diverse civilizations can enable us to answer the question of its origin. We can say at once that the flood narrative like the creation narrative is part of the common property of humanity. It is humankind's basic expression of its being-in-the-world, of the threat to human existence and at the same time of its permanence.

The history of the flood narrative reveals that at one time — at any rate in many places — it was situated in a celebration which was intended to serve to ward off a recurrence of the world catastrophe. Traces of this are apparent only in primitive cultures, not in the high cultures. For the most part the flood narrative occurs as an independent, self-contained story with no sign of the event or occasion that gave rise to it. However, it is certain that everywhere it was narrated and handed down by word of mouth. The narrative found a different situation in the high cultures when it became part of larger words in written form, as in the Atraḥasis epic and, in a completely different way, in the Gilgamesh epic. It was taken up in a similar way into the historical works of J and P.

The Flood Narrative According to J and P — Gen 6:5-9:17

	J	P	
1. God's decision to destroy humanity and to preserve Noah	6:5-8		
a) Decision		6:9-22	Genealogy of Noah (+ 7:6), decision to destroy, address to Noah
b) Reason			
2. Execution of decision to preserve Noah (I)			
a) Commission to build Ark			
b) Reason: announcement of flood	7:1-5		
c) Execution by Noah	7, 10	7:11, 13-16a	

3. Execution of decision to destroy humanity		
a) Coming of flood	12, 16b 17b	17a
b) Effect of flood	22, 23a, 23c	18-21, 24
4. Execution of decision to preserve Noah (II)		
a) end of flood	8:2b, 3a, (6)	8:1-2a, 3b-5
sending out of birds	6-12, 13b	
b) exit from Ark		14-19
5. Response to the preservation: sacrifice	20-22	
6. God's decision to preserve humanity		9:1-17 Blessing and covenant with Noah
		18-19 Genealogy of Noah, Noah's life span and death

The first step in the inquiry into the tradition of the flood narrative must be a comparison of the two accounts contained in Gen 6-9 and an explanation of the way in which they are put together; the comparison must then be extended to the extra-biblical parallels. When we inquire into the way in which J and P are put together we depart from the literary-critical method because we are concerned with the whole and not with the individual sentences piece-by-piece. We can accept therefore the present results of source criticism. The narrative has 6 parts (see above), five of which are common to J and P; only Part 5, Noah's sacrifice after the flood, is missing in P, because in P sacrifice begins only with Sinai. Consequently Part 6 is very much more detailed in P. Apart from this all that is missing in P is the sending out of the birds.

If we compare the structure in J and P and the process involved in putting them together, we notice first that P has taken precedence and J has been worked into P's basic material. P is preserved in large coherent blocks; only rarely is an individual sentence from P fitted into a J-context or sentences from J fitted into a P-context. It is very difficult with J; J comprises only rather small units, passages are often chopped up and parts have dropped out, whereas the P narrative is preserved intact. The broad lines of the process of composition are clear enough: Parts 1 and 2 form the P block 6:9-22; it is self-contained P material, undisturbed by words or sentences from J. J was joined with this block in such a way that Part 1, 6:5-8, preceded it and Part 2, 7:1-5 followed it. This large block at the beginning of P is balanced by a large block at the end: Part 6, 9:1-17, again self-contained and undisturbed by J. It is here that P differs most markedly from J. The very short Part 6 of J, 8:20-22, precedes it containing, apart from Noah's sacrifice, what is missing in P. The marked difference in Part 6 shows how very differently J and P conceived the flood. The P narrative is heavily loaded towards

396

the stern. The narrator puts all his emphasis on the closing passage in such a way as to color the whole narrative; blessing, 9:1-7, and covenant, 9:8-17, show that P's real intent lay in theologizing the flood narrative. A comparison of J with P shows clearly the transition from narrating an event to static, conceptual thinking.

      J and P are worked together more firmly in Parts 3 and 4. But here too P is preserved mainly in fixed blocks, J in additions and insertions. Part 3, the coming and effect of the flood, is narrated in P in 7:11, 13-21, 24; there is a verse from the J narrative at the beginning, v. 12, in the middle, vv. 16b, 17b, and an insertion toward the end, vv. 22-23. Again the central passage of P is virtually self-contained. Sentences from J are scattered through Part 3 and the short passage 22-23 (the effect of the flood) inserted just before the end. Part 4 is yet another clear example of the technique of composition. P narrates the end of the flood in two self-contained blocks, 8:1-5 and 8:13a, 14-19. Noah leaves the ark and treads the earth (2b and 13b are insertions from J). The reconstruction of the method of composition is simple. The composite narrative allows the certain conclusion that J and P rely on a common tradition in which the lines of the flood narrative, as contained in J and P, had already been firmly drawn. By establishing that P can have known J, one cannot conclude that J was the material at hand to P; in any case J is not the only tradition that was at P's disposal.

Differences in the Flood Narratives of J and P

J	P
The name of God יהוה (further linguistic differences). Seven pairs of all clean animals, one pair of all unclean animals, 7:2f.	The name of God אלהים (further linguistic differences). One pair of all animals 6:19f., 7:15f.
Rain for 40 days, 7:12	The waters above and the waters below 7:11.
Only approximate indications of time. After 7 days, rain for 40 days, 7:4 (also 7:10, 12; 8:6-12, 13b).	Precise dating. The waters rose for 150 days, 7:24, and took 150 days to abate, 8:3.
	Beginning of the flood, 7:11; in the 600th year of Noah's life, the second month, the 17th day. End of the flood, in the 601st year of Noah's life, the first month, the first day, 8:5. Precise details for individual stages of the flood.
	Details of the dates in Noah's life.
Sending out of birds, 8:6-12. Sacrifice by the one saved, 8:20f.	

Details narrated twice:	J	P
The destruction of humanity	6:5	6:11-12
The decision to destroy	7	13

Commission to enter the Ark	7:1-3	18-21
Entering of the Ark	7	7:13
Coming of the flood	10	11
Death of all creatures	22f.	20f.
End of the flood	8:2b,3a	8:3b-5
Promise that the flood will not recur	21b-22	9:17

There is missing in J the announcement of the flood, the commission to build the ark, and the leaving of the ark.

The separation of J and P yields two flood narratives which represent two stages in the tradition history of the story. The question must now be asked: What are the consequences of this for the comparison of J and P and for the broader history of the extra-Israelite parallels?

The Flood in the History of Religions

There is no passage in the Old Testament which has such a background in the history of religion as the flood narrative of Gen 6-9. On the one hand there is the flood story in Tablet XI of the Gilgamesh epic about whose close resemblance to Gen 6-9 there can be no doubt. On the other hand there are narratives of a great primeval flood the world over. Hitherto biblical scholarship has for the most part expressly denied that flood stories outside the immediate environment of Israel had any significance for the interpretation of Gen 6-9. For example, H.P. Smith wrote in the review of J. Frazer's *Folklore in the OT:* "The 250 flood sagas scattered across the world are worthless as regards the Old Testament; the Babylonian texts are enough. . . ." (1924, 63-82). Most interpreters of Gen 6-9 consider only the Babylonian parallels.

But the judgment just noted must be supported by reasons. Earlier, the reason for leaving aside the remote parallels was the presupposition that demonstrable dependence was required in order to show significance. Apart from methodological considerations which render such a procedure questionable, it is no longer adequate to the state of the question as we know it. Besides the single Gilgamesh text there is now available a series of Sumerian, Babylonian and Assyrian versions of the flood. When a comparison is made with Gen 6-9 there is no longer just a single text, but a whole history of flood traditions within a single area. The situation has altered even further because the Greek texts of the flood show dependence on the Mesopotamian (Sumerian rather than Babylonian) texts, as well as elements of tradition that cannot be explained from Mesopotamia. E.G. Kraeling in particular has demonstrated this in *Xisouthros, Deucalion and the Flood-Traditions,* 1947, 177-183. The flood stories of the high cultures of the Mediterranean contain elements of stories from early cultures so that it is no longer possible to draw a sharp line of demarcation.

There is in addition a further general consideration: all flood stories that have been narrated or written down are stories of primeval time. One of their peculiarities is that motifs are so few. The little that is narrated about the primeval event is the same the world over. The experience common to all humankind is more impressive than the experience of isolated groups. This is the explanation of the astounding similarity of the individual motifs of the flood stories throughout the world. We are dealing here with a particular sort of tradition. It is not the result of an individual event, but of a series of identical or similar events which have been fashioned into a type. The flood is the archetype of human catastrophe, and as such has been formed into narrative. What the flood narrative aims at expressing is derivation as a result of the preservation of the one amidst the demise of all others. It is precisely this that is the goal of the flood narrative.

Both the early and the high cultures had common basic material at hand for their actualization of primeval time in narrative. Because of the vast collection of flood narratives a very abbreviated outline must take the place of the necessary detailed comparison.

Excursus: *Other Ancient Flood Narratives*

1. (a) The main lines of the structure of the flood narrative in Gilgamesh XI and in the Old Testament are the same (apart from the external framework due to the insertion of the narrative into the Gilgamesh epic). In both cases it is a narrative within a framework. In Gilgamesh XI the decision of the gods, 11.8-112 (ANET) and the modification of the decision, 11.164-186, form the framework, in the Old Testament the decision of God and the modified decision. The decisive difference is that a multitude of gods makes the decision in Gilgamesh while in the Old Testament it is the one God. In Gilgamesh the decision of a god (Ea-Enki) is opposed to the decision of the gods in council, in the Old Testament one God decides at the same time to destroy humankind and to save one person. This is a classical example of polytheistic and monotheistic narrative style side-by-side. This difference elucidates further differences while the basic structure remains the same.

Only an explanation which takes into account the framework can explain the narrative as a whole in both cases. This contradicts any attempt to explain the narrative merely as the recollection of a definite event. The flood narrative does not reach its goal with the end of the flood, but with the affirmation that humanity is never to be destroyed again.

(b) An essential difference is the form of the narratives. Gilgamesh XI is part of an epic, Gen 6-9 is a narrative that stands on its own. Gen 6-9 is a simple prose narrative; Gilgamesh XI is in epic verse with the accompanying epic sweep which goes into detailed description (cf. A.B. Lord, *The Singer of Tales*, 1960). The Old Testament narrates only what is necessary for the movement of the narrative. The Gilgamesh epic presumes a highly developed epic style in an urban civilization, while the narrative of the Old Testament is still within the framework of simple, popular narrative style. The background of urban civilization shows itself at every step in Gilgamesh XI; e.g., in Utnapishtim's dialogue with Ea, 11.32-48, where he asks: "[but what] shall I answer the city, the people and the elders?" or in the description of the building of the ship which is to take not only people, animals and food, but in addition silver and gold, 11.80-82, and "all the craftsmen." All this is, and must be, missing in the Old Testament; the cultural difference is clear.

(c) *The Reason for the Flood*. No reason for the destruction of humankind is given at the beginning of the narrative of Gilgamesh XI, only: "When their heart led the great gods to produce the flood." The absence of any reason here, in contrast to J and P who both give the corruption of humankind as the reason, has often been the grounds for censure: "Here the flood is presented as a sentence of God upon simple humanity (6:7 J, 6:13 P); in the extrabiblical parallels it arises from the capricious council of the great gods" (G. Wallis, "Sintflut," BHH III, 1966, 1805-1807). When one views Gilgamesh XI as a whole, one cannot say this. The speech that Ea makes to Enlil, 11.177-188, clearly presupposes that the flood is meant to be a punishment for humanity's revolt. Ea objects to Enlil that complete destruction was not appropriate to the crime; a mitigated punishment would have been more sensible. The version of the flood in the Atraḥasis epic has shown that the flood is meant to be a punishment of the guilty (cf. W.G. Lambert-A. Millard, 1969). This motif is developed extensively there (cf. G. Pettinato, Or 37 [1968] 165-200).

In Gilgamesh XI Ea proposes to Enlil a number of other mitigated punishments that would have been appropriate (wild animals, famine, plague); in the Atraḥasis epic a series of such calamities precedes the flood. It is only when they have no effect that Enlil sends the flood. And so the reason for the flood in the Babylonian version is humanity's crime. There is further reflection in the versions about the appropriateness of the punishment. When Ea says: "On the sinner impose his sin," it is a sign of real concern about the problem of the reason for the flood.

(d) *The Opposition Between the Gods*. The narrative of Gilgamesh XI is more vivid and picturesque as it develops the decision of the gods to destroy and the contrary decision of the god Ea to preserve. Such dramatic conflict is not possible in the Old Testament because the subject is One. The opposition is developed in two stages: the first stage, 11.96-126, is the different effects of the flood on the earth, 11.105-112, and on the gods, 11.113-126. The gods were frightened and, shrinking back, they ascended to the heaven of Anu, 11:113-115; Ishtar's lament gives expression to anguish and pity at the destruction of humanity: "Would that I had never decided on the flood." The gods join her in the lament, 11.124-126. The rupture of the common decision to destroy humanity becomes very clear when the other gods want to prevent Enlil having access to the sacrifice of Utnapishtim, 11.115-161, because he wanted to destroy humanity completely.

The second stage results in the confrontation with Enlil, now isolated from the other gods, in Ea's address to him; this closes the narrative, 11.170-188. Ea has to defend himself against the charge of not executing the common decision of the gods. He prefaces his defense with a counter-charge that Enlil has brought the flood upon humanity unreasonably. Enlil yields; he himself assumes Utnapishtim among the gods, 11.189-196. So the unity of the council of the gods is restored. But the council does not end with the solemn promise never again to send a flood. It is Ishtar who pronounces the oath: "I shall be mindful of these days, forgetting (them) never," 11.162-165. Anger and pity do not come to a definitive settlement, for the gods are many.

Those parts of the story in which the specifically mythical character is particularly prominent, that is where something is happening between the gods only, stand out from the movement of the events of the flood in the structure of Gilgamesh XI. They are merely the external framework, the question of Gilgamesh to Utnapishtim: ". . . how joinedst thou the assembly of the gods?," 11.1-7, and the conclusion, 11.189-196: Enlil takes Utnapishtim among the gods. The elaborations can be readily recognized as additions or insertions; the main line of the action is quite complete without them.

It is just these parts that are missing in Gen 6-9. Agreement is possible because the mythical, polytheistic character is scarcely noticeable in the main line. A careful examination of these mythical parts shows that they are a reflection on and a reaction to what is described in the basic narrative; they do not stem from ancient tradition, but from a rationalizing tendency. They are still missing in the Sumerian version, insofar as it is known to us. What lies behind this mythical elaboration are questions about the effect of the flood, the reason for it, its meaning for the relationship of the gods to his people.

2. The flood narrative in the Atraḥasis epic diverges from Gilgamesh XI in two points: (a) the goal of Atraḥasis is the new creation of the human race. Though missing in Gilgamesh XI, it is also the goal in the Sumerian version. This original conclusion has been suppressed in Gilgamesh XI by Utnapishtim's assumption among the gods.

(b) What is peculiar to the Atraḥasis epic is the lengthy elaboration in the introduction. The flood is the third in a series of punishments and intervenes only after the first two have failed to reach their goal. There is a prelude to the series: the crime that gives rise to the punishment is a single, concrete event. The guilty parties are not humans, but a group of subordinate gods (Igigi) who revolt against the heavy toil imposed on them. The council of the gods acknowledges that the revolt is justified; humans are created to bear the heavy yoke of the gods. The next motif is the "noise" (revolt?) of humanity which introduces the series of punishments that lead to the flood. There was at hand to the Atraḥasis epic a sequence of motifs of primeval events: the creation of humans (to minister to the gods), the gift of the instruments of civilization, the revolt of humanity (the same introduction as Gen 6:1-4, "when humankind began to increase. . . ."), the flood. The description of the flood in Atraḥasis is somewhere between the Sumerian version and Gilgamesh XI, though rather closer to the latter.

3. *The Sumerian Flood Narrative* (cf. A. Heidel, 1963⁴, 102-105; W.G. Lambert-A. Millard 138-145). It is difficult to compare it with the other versions because the Sumerian account of the flood is only preserved in fragments. The course of events is all but identical; the narrative itself is essentially the same.

The external framework into which the flood narrative is set in the Gilgamesh epic must of course be missing in the Sumerian version. The internal framework, the decision of the gods and the ultimate modification of the decision, is the same, as is the opposition of the goddess Nintu (Ishtar) and the god Enki (Ea) to Enlil's decision to destroy. On the other hand the Sumerian version diverges from Gilgamesh XI in that a short introductory account of the creation and the founding of five Babylonian cities precedes the flood narrative (A. Heidel p. 102); there is a parallel here to the Atraḥasis epic. Those parts of Gilgamesh XI which interpret the flood in markedly mythological terms, 11.113-126 and 170-188, seem to be completely absent from the Sumerian version. In any case no sign of them has been preserved. Ishtar's (Nintu) lament certainly occurs in the Sumerian version, but immediately after the decision of the gods. The absence of the parts is decisive for the tradition history: the narrative of the flood has remained unchanged from the Sumerian version to Atraḥasis and Gilgamesh XI; the mythical interpretation has grown considerably.

The original conclusion of the flood narrative in the Sumerian version, which has been suppressed in Gilgamesh XI by the detailed exultation of Utnapishtim, is still extant. Ziusudra, who has been saved and elevated to the divine, gives one of the gods the honorific title: "Preserver of the seed of humanity." This name is saying that the real goal of the flood narrative is the preservation of humanity, as also in the biblical accounts.

4. *The Flood Narratives of Apollodorus and Ovid*. The Mesopotamian flood narratives show a steady progression towards a marked mythological shaping. The story in Apollodorus gives an important clue to their pre-mythical form (W.H. Roscher, *Lexikon der Mythologie,* Deucalion). According to W. von Soden ("Sintflut," RGG³VI) this is a modified continuation of the Sumerian narrative. There are ten points of agreement in the unfolding of the event. However, it is not possible to conclude to derivation from this line alone. The story of Deucalion and Pyrrha diverges from the Mesopotamian tradition in one very important point. There is not yet any confrontation between the god who destroys and the god who preserves. It is the decision of Zeus to wipe out humanity. After the exit from the ark Deucalion offers sacrifice to Zeus as the savior god. The Greek narrative has preserved here a pre-mythical trait and so agrees with the biblical account against the Mesopotamian.

Another pre-mythical trait is the new creation of humans after the flood. By order of the god, Deucalion and Pyrrha throw stones behind them from which humankind, a male and a female, comes into being. This is a magical motif which occurs in identical or similar form in the flood stories of early cultures. A primitive motif occurs too in Ovid's *Metamorphoses,* Book I, namely that the reason for sending the flood was a breach of hospitality. The rest of Ovid's flood story is a bin of the most diverse elements whose only significance is to show that the narrative of the great primeval flood remained alive in the classical Roman period.

5. *The Flood Narrative in Early Civilizations*. If one does not reject completely the use of the flood narratives from early civilizations, then there is no Old Testament

passage that has so many parallels as the flood. The collection of R. Andrée (1891) contains 88 texts; J.G. Frazer (1919; 1923²) has assembled 250 texts covering almost 100 pages; J. Riem's collection (1906; 1925²) offers 302 texts. M. Winternitz (1901) distinguishes 73 flood stories proper from a countless number that are not. It makes little sense to stress a number; what is important is that it has now become questionable to limit the comparison to certain areas, as was done earlier, because flood stories have come to light in so many disparate places as to make it probable that it is a worldwide phenomenon.

The most important traits can be synthesized here. The significance of these texts is that they present a pre-history of the biblical story in which the mythical procedure of the Mesopotamian narratives forms but a small segment. There is no question of direct dependence. The most important stages in this history, apart from any direct connection of influence, must be clarified.

(a) The first surprising result of a survey of all the known flood narratives throughout the world is that the whole complex of motifs of primeval event occurs in the narratives themselves or in the immediate context. The most common link is with the creation of humans as in the Atraḥasis epic. There is also the creation of humans out of clay and the breathing in of the breath of life; the creation of man and woman each individually, the creation of the woman from the rib of the man, of humans in the image of God, and the blessing on creation. Other primeval motifs in the flood narratives are the origin of civilization, the genealogy of the ancestors, the motif of the sons of the gods and the giants, the building of the tower, the division or dispersion of the peoples, the multiplicity of languages, as well as many primeval etiologies.

It is clear that the flood narrative is so central to the primeval event that each of the remaining primeval motifs can look to it as the focal point. This becomes even clearer when in a number of cases the flood narrative is identical with the creation narrative, the primeval flood with the destructive flood and the one who is saved with the first human being. This fact demonstrates that the flood narrative in the whole of its tradition history is describing a primeval happening, not a historical event.

(b) There are two basic types in this collection of flood narratives: one begins with the decision of the god or gods to destroy humanity by a flood and ends with a modification of this decision. The biblical, Mesopotamian, Egyptian (only the decision to destroy, ANET 10-11), and Greek texts belong to this type. On the other hand the decision to destroy at the beginning and its modification at the end is almost completely absent across the whole spectrum of primitive flood stories. The narratives of the high cultures, be they polytheistic or monotheistic, are in agreement here against those of the early cultures. The difference has nothing to do with any sort of deliberate adaptation of the event and its consequences, but represents a further reflective stage: the event is set into the context of the mutual relationship with God(s). The emphasis is shifted from the stark event of the flood to its theological significance. It could be called a theologizing of the flood narrative.

(c) An important difference within the primitive flood narratives is that in one group the coming of the flood is due to a revolt of humankind (in about one third of the texts) while in the other group any such reason is absent. This too must be seen as a reflective stage; it is something that transcends what is happening, an answer to the question, why has the flood come. It follows from this that the flood narrative even in the primitive cultures was much more than a mere report of an event.

(d) It is to be noted that sacrifice by the one saved is not part of the conclusion of the primitive narratives; it occurs only in a few texts, less than one percent. A clue to the explanation of this omission is that the motifs of sacrifice and the modification of the decision of the god or gods are closely linked in the Babylonian, Greek and biblical flood narratives. The offering of sacrifice and the existence of humanity stand together (the same link as at the basis of the creation of humanity). The addition of sacrifice in the narratives of the high cultures is a sign of a modification of the understanding of civilization.

(e) The announcement of the flood is missing in about one half of the primitive narratives. The reason is obvious: the announcement is almost always linked with the commission to construct the means of salvation (box, raft, ship, etc.). The announcement is necessary where salvation is effected by some technological means. In one group of narratives salvation is not achieved by technological means. People take refuge on a high place, usually a mountain peak, not reached by the flood; an announcement is not absolutely necessary here. In this earlier stage life alone is the object of salvation; there is salvation unaided by technology. In a later stage salvation is linked with human technological advance. Here it is not only the life of an individual that is saved, but also that of the family and the animals by means of the food taken on board. One can see here how the narrative art is developing: the motif of the announcement introduces the element of crisis (in about fifty percent of texts). Narrative refinement is accompanied by theological refinement: the announcement aims at the salvation of the one whom it concerns. It is something like a promise, but not entirely in the context of the creation event. One can believe the announcement or not, as narrated expressly in some variants. The announcement of salvation (promise) can be part of the salvation event in the primitive forms of the flood narrative; the one addressed can respond by believing or not believing.

One can discern yet again a gradation in the means which effect salvation. It can be an object that can be used just as it is, a large pumpkin, a sack, the bark of a tree. For the most part however it is a means of transportation that is to be constructed, a tree trunk to be hollowed out, a raft, a ship, a box (ark). We see then that the tradition history of the story of the flood has passed through a massive time span.

(f) The motif of fitting out the ship also shows that the story has passed through several stages. There is the commission to build a ship that is to be the means of salvation. To this there is often added the commission to bring the family (or wife), animals and food into the ship, e.g., "He is to build an ark out of wood, then take into it a pair of every species of bird and animal as well as a little maize and water" (J. Reim, p. 145). There are many variants of this; but that the one to be saved is to take his wife (family), animals and food with him on the journey is so fixed and constant a theme that it can be regarded as something especially typical of the flood story. There is a convincing explanation of this in Gen 2(J). The story of the creation of humanity includes the provision of food, relationship with the animals, and the creation of woman. If one is to describe the preservation of humankind, then one must include the family, animals and food.

(g) The most amazing of all motifs is that of the birds; it is utterly decisive for the tradition history of the story. It is almost incredible how widespread this motif is and how similar the most widely separated texts are. The addition which concludes the motif in one case leaves no option about the explanation: "The old man was happy because he then knew that the waters had disappeared." This joy resolves the tension; the process of salvation is over. This longing for life in the midst of the destruction of all life by the flood is described in the bird motif. The sending out of birds presented itself readily because it was well known in many places as a means by which a ship took direction (so H. Gunkel, C.H. Gordon and others).

This however is but an explanation of the form of the motif, not of its function in the flood narrative, which is complete without it as many examples show; in the Bible, P, side-by-side with J, has no bird motif. There is a variant however in which the motif is a necessary part of the story. The tradition passed on by Berossus says of the second flight of the birds: "These again returned to the ship, but with their feet muddy." This is but an echo of the motif which is fully developed in many primitive narratives: ". . . he made the beaver, the otter, the musk-rat and the norse duck dive one after the other to look for the earth. Only the latter came back with some mud on its webbed feet. The old man threw the mud on the surface of the water where it spread under the force of his breath so that gradually he was able to put all the animals on it and finally land himself'' (J. Riem, p. 97, No. 175).

The idea here is that the earth, destroyed by the flood, has disappeared and must be restored again. This is only possible by bringing up some earth from under the water. The motif in this shape must be the older because it is indispensable for the course of events. It presents an early form of the creation of the earth as the living space for animals and people. This then has its original setting in the context of the flood narrative while the independent creation narratives speak only of the creation of humans (and animals). One notes further that the creation of the earth is narrated here in a way analogous to the creation of humans. The mere material, part of the earth brought up out of the deep, must be given life by the breath of the creator in order to expand in such a way as to provide living space for animals and people.

(h) The goal of the flood narrative is the restoration of humankind. This can be described in a number of ways. When those who are saved are husband and wife, humanity can be restored by their having children: ''. . . and they begot children and from these came all people who now live on earth'' (J. Riem, p. 32). If only one male is saved then a woman must be created. In the Greek story of Deucalion and Pyrrha, they both throw stones behind them from which people come into being; similarly in Pindar. This motif comes from primitive flood stories: ''Those saved throw fruit from a palm back over their heads and men and women come from the stones'' (J. Riem, p. 108; cf. 151, 153). Or the gods create people anew after the flood: ''Meanwhile the great spirit with the help of Montezuma had furnished the earth anew with humans and animals'' (J. Riem, p. 109; cf. 120, 122).

''The restoration of humankind'' (new creation) is of special significance for the history of the narrative. It is the clearest sign of progress from the mere report of an event (coming of the flood — end of the flood) to a narrative with a specific goal. The natural conclusion of a mere report would be that the survivors lived on as before. But the narrative underlines the significance and uniqueness of the event by replacing mere survival with a new beginning, something like the creation. The narrative then reaches its climax with the end of the flood conceived as the beginning of humankind as it now exists. A primeval event has been constructed out of an event in the past.

(i) An etiological conclusion is often linked with the restoration of humanity; it can take very different forms. The present inhabitants of the land take their origin from those saved from the flood, or two peoples from two couples who were saved; all people of earth, yellow, white, brown and red, originate from this couple (J. Riem, p. 103; 44, 56). The motif is often developed by the scattering of the nations: ''At that time urban dwellers in the plain were scattered over the whole earth,'' or ''they were scattered round about. At that time their languages were multiplied,'' ''they were divided and acquired different languages''; ''then those saved separated'' (H. Lüken, p. 229). There are many ways then in which the motifs can be joined together and the same motifs of the primeval event occur again and again throughout the world.

A present day place or a particular mountain can be linked with the flood; so many places in Greece, a crevice in the ground of a temple area (J.G. Frazer, *The Golden Bough*). Deucalion founded a sanctuary, Apamea Kibotos is named after the ark which is impressed on a coin. The origin of mountains and valleys is traced back to the flood (M. Winternitz 3104). There is a narrative of a monument to recall the flood: ''A stone pillar stands there for all time as a memorial of the danger.'' The pyramids in Mexico are understood as ''artificial mountains'' erected to commemorate salvation from the flood. This motif is developed by that of the tower (Gen 11:1-9): ''When the flood waters abated, . . . (they began) to erect an artificial mountain as a memorial to Tleloc, who protected them when the flood covered the whole land. When the artificial mountain threatened to reach the clouds the gods sent fire and destroyed many of the builders. Hence the pyramids of Cholula remain today only half finished" (J. Riem, p. 144).

The flood lives on in a rite. There are rites in a Greek temple in connection with the crevice in the ground of the temple area where the waters of the flood are said to have flowed away (J.G. Frazer, *The Golden Bough*). "To this day the ancestral tablets, which the Lolos worship on set days of the year and on all important occasions of life, are made out of the same sort of tree as that in which their great forefather found safety from the waters of the deluge. . . ." (J.G. Frazer, *Folklore.* . . . p. 83). "To commemorate their salvation they erect in each of their villages a model of the building (a wooden tower) which is . . . still there" (J. Riem, p. 114).

The rainbow too occurs in primitive narratives at the same place and with the same function as in P. "The Peruvians venerate the rainbow as the sign which calls to mind the cessation of the world flood" (J. Riem 150). "When the rainbow appears in the heavens, it is the boy who emerges from the water and hunts away the rain." "Then he showed the men the rainbow and said to them: this is the sign that the earth will never again be covered with water: . . . and when you see it, it means that the rain is over."

As a result of this study, we will now try to sketch in broad lines the stages in the history of the flood story:

1. The structure of the flood narrative in its simplest form:
   The coming of the flood
   Salvation from the flood
   The end of the flood

2. The most widespread form of the primitive flood narrative:
   Announcement of the flood with the commission to construct the means of salvation
   The coming of the flood (with reason)
   The effect of the flood
   Saving (preservation) of one by the means at hand
   The end of the flood (testing, birds)
   The restoration of humanity

3. The structure of the flood narrative in the high cultures:
   Decision of God (the gods) to destroy humanity
   Contrary decision to preserve humanity
   Execution of the contrary decision: announcement of the flood with the commission to construct the means of salvation
   Execution of the decision to destroy: the coming of the flood
   The effect of the flood
   Execution of the contrary decision: the end of the flood (testing by means of birds to see if the flood has abated)
   Leaving of the ship, stepping upon the earth
   The response of the one preserved: sacrifice
   The decision of God (the gods) to preserve humanity
   (Restoration of humanity)
   (Divinization of the one saved from the flood).

This very rough outline can only be a direction-finder amid the several texts (the parts in parentheses are not necessarily parts of the outline). It is the theologizing of the flood that marks the sharpest line of division between the primitive and the high cultures. The real drama is no longer a course of events which leads from the coming or announcement of the flood to its conclusion and the restoration of humanity; it is a drama that is played out between God (the gods) and humans leading from the decision to destroy to its abbrogation. This is the dividing line that reveals one of the most important differences between the "theology" of the early and the high cultures. The theologizing of the flood narrative, common to polytheism and monotheism alike, shows a basic orientation to theological abstraction which presupposes as necessary a theological grasp of reality, of human existence as lived in the world. It is only when the flood story is re-shaped into an event that involves the gods, i.e., an event that starts from, is the result of a decision of the gods, that there is anything like the beginnings of theology (or religion). It is only when the coming of the flood is referred back to a decision of the gods (or God) that they receive their self-authentication. Only with this does religion and (or) theology begin. Polytheism and monotheism are at one here. What they have in common over against the primitive religions is more important than what separates them from each other.

But more: it is not possible to understand the flood narrative in the high cultures either in its polytheistic or monotheistic forms apart from its pre-history in the early cultures.

Commentary

Literature: 6:5-8: A. Jirku, *Altorientalischer Kommentar zum AT* (1923). A. Murtonen, VT 3 (1953) 46-53. E. Galbiati, *La struttura litteraria dell' Esodo.* . . . (1956). A.M. Dubarle, *The Biblical Doctrine of Original Sin* (1964). G. Fohrer, ZAW 73 (1961) 1-30. H.W. Wolff, EvTh 24 (1964) 73-98. W.H. Schmidt, *Das erste Gebot,* TEH 165 (1969).

[6:5-8] Tracing the articulation of the sentences in J's introduction one finds striking repetitions, 6a and 7c, and accumulations. The most notable is that the reason for the decision in v. 6: "And Yahweh was sorry. . . ," is continued further and taken up again after the decision by way of supplement: "For I am sorry. . . ." And so the same sentence is repeated almost word for word before and after the decision, and in neither place is it necessary. This is not a more original narrative style: an attempt to interpret the event has obviously affected the shape of the introduction. The nucleus is contained in the two sentences 5a and 7a:

And Yahweh saw,
that the wickedness of humankind was great on earth.
And Yahweh said:
I will wipe out humankind from the face of the earth.

The reason for the decision and the decision itself are thus adequately expressed; everything else continues, explains and underlines the reason. The separation of the narrative nucleus from the elaborations is important here because it brings us face to face with the particular emphases that the narrator wants to give it in the form in which it lies before us. It is J who gave the introduction 6:5-8 its present form. In doing this he elaborated what came down to him in such a way as to emphasize and articulate his own understanding of the story.

One must distinguish this elaboration of J himself from the redactional elaboration of v. 7 which consists in the catalogue "from man to beast, reptiles and birds of heaven" and the relative sentence "whom I have created." The catalogue is redactional; most interpreters have seen that R has resumed the language of P here as in 6:20; 7:14, 21; 8:17, 19; 9:2, e.g., H. Holzinger "a catalogue in the style of P." The argument that the catalogue does not suit the word את־האדם which it is meant to qualify is given by H. Holzinger, H. Gunkel, J. Skinner and others. The usual reason advanced to show that the relative sentence אשר בראתי was redactional was the word ברא, which follows priestly usage, over against עשה in vv. 6a and 7c; a reason from form. A reason from content may now be advanced: vv. 6a and 7c with עשה are part of J's interpretative elaboration. Reference to the creation of humans has its proper meaning here while in 7b, where ברא is used, it has the character of a complement. The redactional elaboration then can be distinguished from the thematic elaboration intended by J.

A similar intention lies behind J's elaboration of this ancient introduction as behind the arrangement of 12:1-3 at the beginning of the patriarchal story, except that here the theological accent is linked to a single narrative. It consists of a supplement, vv. 6 and 7c and an underscoring, v. 5b. The supplement is an appendix to and a continuation of the reason for the decision, v. 5a. Between the two steps in the ancient narrative: "God saw . . . and God said. . . ." he inserts a further step: "God saw . . . God was sorry . . . God said." He thus links the flood narrative with the creation of humans in such a way that Yahweh, confronted with the present situation ("the wickedness of humankind was great on earth"), looks back and regrets what he had then done. Yahweh's regret is so important for J that he puts it before the decision to destroy and repeats it again after it. He considered it decisive for the understanding of the event which these verses introduce. What is underscored in v. 5b is linked directly with this. Every inclination and thought was always wicked; this explains why God regretted having created people. J is saying one thing, not many, with this supplement. How is it to be understood?

J's elaboration of the introduction to the flood narrative is a valuable witness to his theology and his understanding of the relationship between God and his human creatures. It is a witness to theological reflection and to his attempt to come to terms with the reason for the divine decision that has come down to him. There are still signs of J's struggle with the decision which show that he shrank back with horror at it. This is the reason why he underscores so heavily: "Every . . . always . . . only." The wickedness of people had risen to such an intolerable degree as to threaten their very existence. This is why the supplement says that God regretted that he had created people.

Interpreters speak here of anthropomorphisms. "A very human way of speaking of God, characteristic as it is of the author's very lively descriptive power" (A. Dillmann). H. Holzinger writes: "This anthropo-pathetic way of speaking hovers on the boundaries of a spiritual concept of God." There is here a concept of God which was formed in a world which thought very differently from that of J. J's God is not one who exists for himself with this or that sort of essence and whom one can conceive of in this or that way, spiritually, anthropomorphically, anthropo-pathetically, so long as one remains within the framework of a spiritual conception. J cannot disassociate his God from his position vis-a-vis humans. What interpreters call "anthropomorphic" picks up something of what this God is (so too B. Jacob in a detailed excursus — ad loc.). He is the one who acts on and reacts to people. Both action and reaction are never anything else but anthropomorphic. Even when it is said of God: "I am not a human," the thinking is still anthropomorphic. The reason why the anthropomorphism is so striking here is obviously the "anthropomorphic" presentation of a contradiction in his dealing with people: first he creates people — then destroys them. It is precisely here that we encounter J's intention in elaborating the introduction to the flood narrative. He confronts the inexplicable contradiction. He expresses the incomprehensible in his "anthropomorphic talk" about God's regret. J can only speak of this meaningfully and of necessity when he puts God's decision to destroy all people over against the creation of human beings. He himself introduced the inexplicable contradiction which made the explanation by mcans of God's regret necessary.

J's intention to point expressly to the contradiction is a direct parallel to those parts of the Gilgamesh epic Tablet XI where the god who preserves, Ea-Enki, rises up in opposition to the god who destroys. The question in the background in both cases is the incomprehensible contradiction in the conduct of the god who created people and the god who destroyed them. The polytheistic and the mythical is replaced in J by an answer which presumes that there is but one God: *dissention between the gods becomes dissention within God*. When dissention is transferred to God himself, he thereby becomes human, v. 6b: "And he was deeply concerned" (H. Gunkel). God is affected by the destruction of his creature: "It is the simple truth that God experiences regret when he sees his original loving plan frustrated, that he experiences pain when his holy love is rejected, and that he does not decide on the extinction of the world with cold indifference. The divine judgment and the divine pain are but two sides the external and the internal of one and the same reality. . . ." (F. Delitzsch).

Now there is an important distinction to be made here. Is God's pain to be related directly to the decision to destroy (so F. Delitzsch) or to a general and rather abstract notion of the sinfulness of humankind? H. Gunkel explains v. 5b: "At base, there is a deeply pessimistic reflection on human sinfulness." He explains in detail that laments like this over the general sinfulness of people do not appear for the first time in the Prophets or Psalms, but can already be found in ancient times. H. Gunkel alleges, among other things, the Egyptian and Babylonian narratives of the severe punishments which the gods brought upon sinful people. J. Skinner regards the whole course of events that has gone before as reason for the "pessimistic appraisal of human nature." It goes back to the fall and includes 4:2-16, 23-24; 6:1-4, which show "the gloomy view of early history," W. Zimmerli also refers to these four texts and continues: "No new story of humanity's defection is narrated here; it is simply brought to a synthesis."

G. von Rad starts from the old division (F. Delitzsch, A. Dillmann) according to which the flood narrative only begins in 6:9; 6:5-8 belong to 6:1-4. However, he modifies this view. 6:5-8 belong neither to 6:1-4 nor to 6:9ff.; they are a prologue to the story, fashioned completely by J without any foregoing tradition. But this is not correct. The many extra-Israelite flood stories show that the destruction of humanity together with the decision of God have a fixed place in the flood tradition. Von Rad has seen correctly that 6:5-8 is a construction of J. However J's own words are not the whole text of 6:5-8, but the elaboration presented above. Von Rad too relates 6:5-8 to the preceding narratives: "From the first fall sin has grown like an avalanche. . . ." Whereas up to now only the fact of the spread of sin was reported (B. Jacob), 6:5-8 contains "a reflection, a judgment upon it," "a meditation on the magnitude of sin now erupting over humanity." This meditation is to be detached from the disruption of order introduced by the angels in the passage immediately preceding.

The following comments may be made: 1. The sentence 5b is not to be considered in isolation as if it were a general statement about human sinfulness. As we have seen, it is rather an interpretation by J where he is wrestling with the incomprehensibility of the decision to destroy over against the creation of humanity and trying to give a reason for it. This is the only context in which it is to be understood. 2. It is not true that, without more ado, the words are "simply a synthesis" (W. Zimmerli), or that the pessimistic appraisal of human nature is based on the fall, the consequences of which appear in the passages cited (J. Skinner), or that they are "a reflection about the extent of sin which has overtaken people" (G. von Rad). The history of the flood narrative shows that a series of individual crimes is not required as the reason for it. It could be objected of course that it was J who set the narrative in such a context. But this is unlikely if J's intention in the construction of his primeval story is not to present the increase and growth of sin, but the different ways in which God's human creatures can defect.

The statement of v. 5a, "the wickedness of humankind was great on earth," is something else; it is something new in contrast to what has preceded. There is a wickedness of such magnitude as to lead to the decision to destroy. Any sober judgment would see that it would be absurd to use something like the murder of a brother, 4:2-16, as the reason for the destruction of humanity. The opinion that sees v. 5b as a general, timeless judgment about human nature and that explains this general sinfulness by means of the examples that precede, betrays a concept of sin that is unknown to the Old Testament, as has been shown in the commentary in Gen 3. The wickedness envisaged in giving the reason for the decision to destroy must correspond to the decision. It must be the wholesale corruption of a generation of a large group; a phenomenon that has occurred again and again in human history and has been experienced again and again as leading to condemnation to destruction. It is a corruption summed up in the realization "après nous le déluge."

The difference between this understanding of the passage and the traditional one is important. It is only thus that it becomes clear that J understood the defection of humans, God's creatures, differently from what is presumed in the interpretations outlined. He does not intend in his explanatory sentence v. 5b to describe a general sinfulness which is concretized in individual acts, but that God-created people are capable of the utterly horrifying. Under certain convergences of circumstances human wickedness can become so intense and erupt to such an extent as to involve and corrupt a whole generation or even several generations of a large group of people. It is clear then that one cannot presume in J an understanding of humanity and of sin that is in essence timeless and without history; an understanding according to which what is essential is the general sinfulness which is the result of the fall, and where the sinful acts are but concrete examples of this sinfulness. J's understanding of man is in essence historical. Accordingly he puts the emphasis on the different ways in which a person can defect. J is in a position therefore to put into perspective and to see the meaning for humankind of the extraordinary phenomenon of evil concentrated in and corrupting a whole group in a whole generation. Only something such as this requires the divine decision to destroy; only something such as this is meant by 6:5b.

Literature: Gen 6:5: P. Humbert, BZAW 77 (1958) 82-88. F.H. von Meyenfeldt, *Het hart (leb, lebab) in het Oude Testament* (with a summary in English) Diss Leiden (1950). R.E. Murphy, "Yeser in the Qumran Literature," Bib 39 (1958) 334-344.

[6:5] A narrative often begins by saying that God saw; i.e., that he discovered what the situation really was. The phrase does not mean that God merely noticed something, but serves always to introduce an action of God; this is its function. God sees "the wickedness of humankind on earth." The verb רעע means "to be bad." רע describes a state; it is not talking about a wicked action, but about a state of wickedness that is humanity's. This is rather difficult to express exactly. The adjective "wicked" catches the intent. One must distinguish between רע and "sin" (and the different ways in which Hebrew expresses this idea). All words for "sin" mean an action within certain defined areas. רע on the contrary describes a situation, a state. A state of corruption of massive proportions has come about (רבה רעת), and this is the reason why God has decided on destruction.

On יצר P. Humbert, BZAW 77 (1958) 82-88 and R.E. Murphy, Bib 39 (1958) 334-344. P. Humbert says that the verb "was a term to describe a profession" and J. Skinner: "The later Jewish theologoumenon of the יצר הרע . . . is based on this passage." Apart from the resumption of this passage in Gen 8:21 the word occurs only in Deut 31:21 in the Pentateuch where its meaning is similar: "I know which way their thoughts incline already" (NEB). One can read the following words "the thoughts of his heart" together with יצר and render "the imagination of the thoughts of his heart." But that is a very unwieldy expression, and in fact יצר and מחשבה have almost the same meaning. Luther's translation has rendered it correctly, "planning and striving" *(Dichten und Trachten)*. The meaning then is not so much "what is within, hidden. . . ." (W. Zimmerli and others following Dillmann), but what humanity is striving after. . . , the planning and devising. The מחשבת לב are human plans and intentions which are directed towards some action. Humanity's wicked state consists in striving after what is wicked. This is intensified further by the last words of the verse. The striving after evil determines a person's whole existence "always." The phrase כל־היום "occurs only in elevated, emotional speech" (B. Jacob).

Literature: Gen 6:6: R. Loewe, "Jerome's Treatment of an Anthropopathism," VT 2 (1952) 261-272. M. Treves, "Two Acrostic Psalms," VT 15 (1965) 81-90. O.B. Long, "The Divine Funeral Lament," JBL 85 (1966) 85-86.

[6:6] "God was sorry." B. Jacob deals with this in detail in his commentary pp. 180f. The same expression occurs in Ex 32:14; Jer 18:7, 8; 26:3, 13; Joel 2:13; Jonah 3:10. The present passage is very like 1 Sam 15:11: "I repent that I have made Saul king." On the contrary 1 Sam 15:29: "For he is not a man, that he should repent"; so too Num 23:19; Is 35:6f. The reason for this seemingly conflicting way of speaking is that God is experienced by humans as God in contradictions. Such talk is an attempt to interpret and explain the contrast between the creation of people and their destruction. It is when the sentence, God was sorry that he had created humans, is continued with: "And he was grieved at heart," that the real intent of the passage is explained. It is painful for God to be the judge of his people. The parallel between אל־לבו of v. 6 and the לבו of v. 5 shows that this human way of speaking is used deliberately of God.

This is expressed even more strongly in Gen 3:16, 17 where עצב is used to describe the painful punishment imposed on man and woman which now shackles the existence of humankind alienated from God. Here the verb from the same root is used to describe the pain of God in his decision to destroy his creatures. The same motif occurs in the prophetic pronouncements of judgment when God laments that he must intervene against his people, e.g. Is 2:2-3; Jer 12:7-13. This self-contradictory motif, that God suffers in the judgment that he himself brings, is the motif that leads to the positive significance of suffering for God's work of salvation in the story of Israel's relations with its God. (A Jewish interpreter, B. Jacob, sees the contradiction, *Comm.* ad loc.: "You say that God sees what is to come; why did he create people at all when he already must have known that people would cause him trouble?")

Literature: Gen 6:7: P. Humbert, "Emploi et portée du verbe bârâ (créer) dans l'Ancien Testament," ThZ 3 (1947) 401-422 = P. Humbert, *Opuscules,* (1958) 146-165. R. Mackenzie, "The Divine Soliloquies in Genesis," CBQ 17 (1955) 157-166. N.P. Bratsiotis, "Der Monolog im AT," ZAW 73 (1961) 30-70. D. Hermant, "Analyse littéraire du premier récit de la création," VT 15 (1965) 437-451, esp. 442, 449-450. J.L. Crenshaw, "YHWH Seba'ôt Šemô: A Form-Critical Analysis," ZAW 81 (1969) 156-175 (n. 66 on bara). J. Körner, "Die Bedeutung der Wurzel bārā im AT," OLZ 64 (1969) 533-540. R. Lapointe, "The Divine Monologue as a Channel of Revelation," CBQ 32 (1970) 161-181.

[6:7] On the composite character of this verse see above on 6:5-8. This verse pronounces God's decision to destroy which occurs in so many flood stories. The verb מחה, "to wipe out, obliterate" (also in 7:23), is used in Judg 21:17 of obliterating a tribe from Israel. It is a particularly severe way of describing the destruction and anticipates the utter horror of the decision. It is because of this very horror that the reason given in v. 6a is repeated in v. 7c, a stylistic device of inclusion rare in J but common in P. The use of the device shows that the passage ends with v. 7.

Literature: Gen 6:8: K. Fahlgren, *Sedākā* (1932). C.F. Jean, *Studia Mariana* (1950). G. von Rad, "Faith Reckoned as Righteousness" in *The Problem of the Hexateuch and Other Essays* (1966) 125-130. W. Zimmerli, "Erkenntnis Gottes nach dem Buche Ezechiel," (1954) in *Gottes Offenbarung* (1963) 41-119. J. Fink, *Noe der Gerechte in der fruhchristlichen Kunst* (1955). D.E. Ap-Thomas, "Some Aspects on the Root HNN in the OT," JSSt 2 (1957) 128-148. G.W. Coats, "Despoiling the Egyptians," VT 18 (1968) 450-457. H.H. Schmid, *Gerechtigkeit als Weltordnung* (1968) esp. 106-107. W.M. Clark, "The Righteousness of Noah," VT 21 (1971) 261-280.

[6:8] This verse introduces a new succession of events which is continued in 7:1ff. The decision to preserve Noah follows closely on the decision to destroy humanity. Most interpreters say that Noah must have been introduced already and the passage must have dropped out. But there is no need to presume this. Noah is a well-known figure as is shown by the way he is mentioned in a number of places (5:29; 1 Chron 1:4; Is 54:9; Ezek 14:14, 20); he could well have been mentioned in an earlier form of the genealogy in 4:17-26. The abrupt mention of him in 6:8 is meant to show that, in contrast to P's presentation, the motive for Noah's preservation lies with God and not in Noah's piety. The waw-adversative at the beginning clearly refers this sentence to vv. 6-7; the decision which God has been forced to take has not made him a pitiless destroyer. The one who is grieved at heart before the inevitable obliteration is the one with whom the single human being finds favor. There is an element of contradiction here. The corruption of humankind is portrayed in v. 5 as radical and all-embracing; in v. 8 however one among humankind can find favor with God. P on the contrary is rationalistic. He begins with Noah's righteousness in 6:9 so as to set in relief from the very beginning the reason for the exception. This is a typical difference between J and P.

[**6:9-22**]   The structure of P's introduction to the flood narrative is characteristically different from J's. The framework of the event is the same at certain points, due to the tradition that both received.

	J	P
The corruption of humanity	6:5	6:11, 12(13b)
The decision to destroy	7	(17)
The decision to save Noah	8, 7:1	(9) (18)
Announcement of the flood to Noah	7:4	13
Commission to Noah to build the Ark	—	14-16
Commission to Noah to take with him . . .	2-3	18-21
Account of carrying out of commission	5, 9b	22

The only clear elaboration by J is God's sorrow in vv. 6 and 7b; a comparison with P confirms that this is the work of J. On the other hand P's introduction is detailed and stamped with his style. There are two places where P's hand is most clearly at work.

1. P introduces the flood narrative with the genealogy of Noah, thereby making his most notable impression on the material that came down to him. The whole narrative now stands under the heading אלה תולדת נח. This constitutes a shift of emphasis. P balances it with his important and quite independent conclusion, 9:1-17, which consists entirely of a long speech by God to Noah; the genealogy begun in 6:9 is concluded in 9:28-29. This shift of emphasis converts the narrative of the flood into a narrative about Noah. It begins with Noah and ends with him; there is a long speech to Noah at the beginning, 6:13-22, and at the end, 9:1-17.

We have here a definite parallel to the Gilgamesh epic. The figure of the one saved from the flood is well in the foreground. The narrative begins and ends with Utnapishtim. Over and above this, Utnapishtim himself tells the story. Together with this parallel there is also an important difference: Utnapishtim is assumed among the gods. Noah remains a human being, and this is stressed in the genealogy that frames the narrative. The final sentence says that Noah died.

What then is P saying by this shift of emphasis? This becomes clear when we note that Noah's piety forms the introductory motif. The story is to tell of this pious man and of his significance for humanity in the great catastrophe. It is because of him that the story of humanity survives the flood; humankind is preserved in him. P is obviously addressing his contemporaries. Noah becomes the type of the pious man who remains blameless amidst the corruption of his world and walks his way with God. This one pious man becomes a sign of preservation for corrupt humanity. B. Jacob: "The kernel of the narrative is that the world is preserved because of one pious man."

2. The other peculiarity of P's arrangement in 6:9-22 is that God's long speech to Noah, vv. 13-21, dominates the introduction. This has its roots in the emphasis put on Noah and his significance which we have just been talking about. There is in addition a stylistic device that colors the whole of P's work. What is essential to the presentation as a whole is brought forward into the speeches, here, in Gen 17 and again in Ex 25ff. But this stylistic device has a

412

theological meaning. For P there is only one reason why an event takes place, that is, because God has given a command and this command is then carried out (Gen 1; 6; 17; Ex 25ff.). P has shaped the introduction to the flood narrative so that the event, in the form of God's command to Noah, vv. 13-21, and its execution, v. 22, follows the two-fold exposé (6.9f., Noah; 11f., the earth). He is thereby declaiming that the invasion of chaos, now to be reported, is framed in and controlled by another event: God's word of command goes out and its execution follows.

And so it becomes even clearer why P had to begin by describing the pious man, Noah. Here is pious Noah, there is the corrupt world; the command that goes out to Noah is what really sets the event in motion. The decision to destroy is set into the speech to Noah, v. 17, to make it clear that the sequence of command and execution that governs every event is not interrupted even by the catastrophe of the flood. This is far removed from J's presentation. In 6:5-8 (J) the focus is entirely on the effect on God of the decision to destroy — God is sorry and grieved at heart. There is no sign of this in P. Humanity is corrupt and must perish. But it is Noah, the pious man, who represents humanity. The word of command that preserves him goes out to him; the word is carried out. With this P has said all that he has to say.

The Structure in Detail

The twofold exposé 6:9-10. God's speech to Noah follows vv. 11-12 in two stages (this too is typical of the priestly style). The announcement of the destruction in vv. 13 and 17 divides the command to Noah into the commission to build the ark, vv. 14-16, and the commission to take into the ark with him his relatives, the animals and food. A brief sentence suffices to report that Noah carried out the commission, v. 22. The same theologizing that determines the structure of the whole is there too in the textual relationship of the commission, 13-21, and the execution, 22. The ancient storyteller is interested in presenting events, what is actually going on. A comparison with the corresponding passages in Gilgamesh XI and Atraḥasis makes this clear, where the building of the vessel is portrayed in epic dimensions and colorful imagery. The actual building of the ark has fallen out in P; it is brought forward and included in God's commission to build. The commission, i.e., "the word of God," has become the central theme; its implementation can drop out. All that really matters now is the mere fact that Noah implemented the commission obediently.

S.E. McEvenue presents a further list of stylistic observations on 6:9-22 in *The Narrative Style of the Priestly Writer,* AnBib 50 (1971) 36-54. This is a careful verse by verse study of the stylistic forms used by P. But one may ask whether questions of style in a work like P can be so isolated as they are in this study. Moreover a text cannot be divided on stylistic grounds alone. McEvenue separates the text: 6:9-10, 11-13, 14-16, 17-18a, 18b-20, 21, 22; 7:6. But this does not make clear that P has stylized the key event into a speech, 13-21, nor that P is presenting the introduction of the flood narrative as commission, 13-21, and execution, 22. One can comprehend the style of P only when one takes totalities as one's starting point and raises the question of division. But the totalities are not primarily literary combinations of words or sentences; they are events which are described, here events between God and people.

413

Literature: Gen 6:9: W.E. Read, "Further Observations on Ṣāḏaq," AUSS 4 (1966) 29-36.

[6:9] נח איש צדיק תמים: We can note here how P makes use of a very ancient narrative technique, that of a narrative growing out of a genealogy (Intro. §2). This is the first time that it occurs in P because up to now all that we have of P after the creation account is the genealogical succession in Gen 5. A first indication of it is found in 5:22-24, but the expansion of the genealogy is restricted to a brief note. The narrative about Noah emerges again into the genealogy at the end 9:28-29; and so the intention of the writer becomes clearer, namely to have the succession of events told about Noah framed by the genealogy.

There must be a pause to enable an event to emerge from the constant flow of generations. Something must be said about a person named in the genealogy, something descriptive over and above mere genealogical information which then becomes the basis of the event to be narrated (e.g., the fact that Sarah had no children in 11:30). Both passages in the primeval story, 5:22, 24 and 6:9, where this descriptive note emerges from the stream of generations and so becomes the point of departure of an event, describe the particular attitude of a particular person, to which corresponds a particular attitude of God to this person. This is characteristic of P. There could be no clearer way of showing that the goal of the work as a whole, the setting apart of the sanctuary, determines everything in it and is at work here shaping the narrative.

P uses the words צדיק and תמים to describe Noah's attitude or way of life. The words stand side-by-side without any linking particle; the likely explanation is that the tradition that lay before P had צדיק only, as in J too 7:1, and that P appended תמים to elaborate and clarify. Both words are in process from a specific to a more general meaning. צדיק is a social concept, used particularly in the legal context. A person is described as צדיק when one conducts oneself in accordance with the ordinances of a community, S.A. Cook. "What was due among a definite social group" (J. Skinner, p. 158). תמים is a cultic concept and describes a sacrificial animal that is without blemish, "free from defect" (J. Skinner). It is used in a general and transferred sense of humans (probably because of their affinity with the cult) and occurs frequently in P and in Ezek.

Literature: Gen 6:11 and 12: A.R. Hulst, OTS 12 (1958) 28-68. R. Knierim, "The Problem of an OT Hamartiology. Considerations to the Book of Stefan Porúb-čan. . . ," VT 16 (1966) 366-385, esp. 381-382.

[6:11 + 12] Vv. 11 and 12 form the second part of the exposé. This too is a descriptive statement like that about Noah in v. 9. It sets up a contrast — the waw at the beginning of v. 11 being adversative. The corruption of the rest of the world is contrasted with the piety of Noah. The statement is heavily underscored by means of repetitions, typical of the style of P. The four half verses of 11-12 repeat the same statement four times. V. 11 consists of two sentences parallel to each other with the same subject (earth) and different predicates: "Was corrupt in God's eyes" — "was full of violence." V. 12a repeats v. 11a almost word for word, but as a verbal sentence: "God saw. . . ." (cf. 1:31). V. 12b gives the reason for v. 12a; a new subject is introduced here: "all flesh," and the verb שחת is in the hiph., so the reason is really another repetition. Moreover, the same statement is repeated yet again in v. 13b.

What is the explanation of this peculiar composition with its many repetitions? It is certainly not a simple narrative of a course of events, but is permeated with reflection. We find an indication in the almost complete agreement between 11a and 12a:

> But the earth was corrupt in God's eyes
> God looked at the earth and it was certainly corrupt.

"In God's eyes" in 11a corresponds to "God looked at" in 12a. But the sequence requires as its continuation a consequence of "God looked at." This can only be the decision to destroy which P has left out because he has put it into the speech to Noah, v. 13b. The two parts that were in the tradition that came to P can still be discerned in v. 13:

> The establishment of the corruption of humanity
> The decision to destroy humanity.

P has put the decision to destroy into the address to Noah and thereby isolated the first part, setting it in contrast to the piety of Noah, a descriptive note in the genealogy and the basis of his overall plan. P was able then to underscore heavily the corruption of humankind by means of the numerous repetitions. We can discern in all this a theological intent: J's main concern is to express the reaction of God, "I am sorry. . . ."; P proclaims side-by-side the corruption of the world and the destruction that necessarily follows. The four or five-fold repetition underscores the fact and its gravity; the gravity of the judgment corresponds to the gravity of the fact: "the end . . . has come," v. 13a.

[**6:11**]   One can see the tendency to *magnificare peccatum* in P's insistence that corruption was widespread on "the earth." In vv. 11-12 "the earth" is the subject three times and once again in v. 13b. The corruption of humanity was, in P's priestly and cultic mentality, something massive, contagious, poisonous; it affected whatever place a person lived in. The subject, "the earth," is saying that the whole of people's area of operation was corrupted with them. On חמס, H.J. Stoebe writes in THAT 1, 585: "חמס would have meant originally the crime that lies like a pall over the land."

P says nothing about how this corruption came about. The assumption that P is referring to the paradise myth of Ezek 28 (L. van der Wijngaert, 1968, 35-50) has no support in the text. Nor can one say with H. Gunkel that P's view is "that the earth fell gradually into sin" (*Comm.* ad loc.), nor that "according to P too one should look for the source of sin in the first human being" (O. Procksch, *Comm.*). J. Skinner is correct: "The narrative of P contains no explanation of the change." The corruption of humankind is expressed in both a verbal (שחת) and a nominal (חמס) sentence; the latter describes rather the acts, the former the result. P uses neither of the words again to describe sin (Wijngaert). One can conclude with certainty then that the words here do not stand for some general notion of sin but are meant to describe something extraordinary and unique. Revolt and corruption have gone beyond all bounds and have reached a climax which demands a decree of destruction.

This is just what is being said when the same verb שחת is used in vv. 13 and 17 for God's decree of destruction. In vv. 11b, 12a, 12b שחת can only mean corrupt in the sense of destroy: the violent acts (חמס) of humanity had taken on such proportions that they had corrupted, destroyed the earth, the human world.

The earth as it should be, with the purpose for which God had created it, was destroyed (the same meaning as in Jer 18:3-4). חמס is not used in a general sense meaning sin or wrong (so U. Cassuto; H.J. Stoebe writes: "חמס becomes the comprehensive, general expression for sin"); it is used in the original sense of violence, crime, which consists in bloodshed, criminal oppression and force (so correctly H.J. Stoebe). This is what the earth is full of: and so it is corrupt, perverted in its proper function. W. Thomas would understand לפני האלהים in a superlative sense: "Anything that is great even in God's estimation must of necessity be of extraordinary dimensions," VT 3 (1953) 216. This is possible here, but not necessary.

[6:12] Many interpreters point out that 6:12 is formulated in parallel to 1:31 (e.g., A. Dillmann, O. Procksch, W. Zimmerli, U. Cassuto). The unexplained contrast between "very good" and "utterly corrupt" comes thereby into sharper relief. The writers of Greece and Rome are thinking abstractly and are systematizing what is meant here when they tell of the loss of the golden age and the invasion of general corruption (Pophyry, Vergil, Ovid, Lucian; cf. A. Dillmann, *Comm.*). Apollodorus describes the corruption before the flood of Deucalion in detail. The background of all these, as well as of P, is the experience of such an invasion of general corruption as has always been the case in the course of human history. The contrast between 1:31 and 6:12 is deliberate — humankind created by God can plunge into such corruption; this is left utterly unexplained (so too W. Zimmerli). It is no longer possible to subjugate Gen 6:11-12 (P) and Gen 3 (J) to the same concept of sin (e.g., O. Procksch writes: "Perhaps P is thinking of concupiscentia," and concludes "the primary elements of Paul's theology are already there in P"). Each passage is dealing with basically different phenomena which cannot be brought under the same concept of "sin": Gen 3 with the transgression of a command of God by an individual in the smallest of communities, Gen 6:11-12 with the corruption of a large group which has led to the destruction of the community and is the reason for the decision to destroy.

The subject in v. 12b is כל־בשר. Many interpreters have concluded from this that the animals too shared in the guilt that led to the pronouncement of destruction because כל־בשר includes all living beings. W. Zimmerli in particular says expressly that the animals shared in the guilt and sees in this a difference between J and P — as do others too. In his essay "Kol Basar in der priesterlichen Fluterzählung" OTS 12 (1958) 28-68, A.R. Hulst cites the overwhelming majority of interpreters who include humans and animals under כל־בשר in 6:12 and the few who differ. He then goes on to study the use of the phrase in P and the rest of the Old Testament. He comes to the cautiously phrased conclusion that the survey does not allow us to be certain at any rate that the animals share in the guilt. His weightiest argument is that in prophecy כל־בשר means only humans where it occurs in the context of guilt and judgment. One can come to no conclusion at all from P's usage alone because he uses it in different ways: humans in 6:12, 13; humans and animals in 6:17; 9:11, 16, 17; animals in 9:15. In any case after this searching study one can no longer be so sure that P differs from J because he has the animals share in the guilt that led to God's sentence of condemnation. I agree with Hulst that very probably 6:11-12 refers only to humans. I would add that the subject of חמס in the Old Testament is always humans, never animals. The rather broad notion of כל־בשר in 6:12 and 13 is to be explained in a similar way to the equally broad notion of "the earth" in vv. 11 and 12.

[6:13-21]   The structure of God's speech to Noah is fourfold: commission to Noah to build the ark (14-17) and to fit it out (17-21), the reason being given in the announcement of the flood which precedes each of the two parts (13 and 17). The two traditional elements, the decision to destroy and the announcement with the commission to construct the means of salvation, P has fashioned into a speech to Noah. The emphasis is on what is happening between God and Noah, the pious man. The spotlight is on the more important element, the promise (covenant) to save Noah; the decision to destroy is in the ever murky background.

Literature: Gen 6:13: H.L. Ginsberg, VT 4 (1954) 246-275.   C.A. Keller, "Die Gefährdung der Ahnfrau." Ein Beitrag zur gattungs- und motivgeschichtlichen Erforschung alttestamentlicher Erzählungen," ZAW 66 (1954) 181-191.   M. Wallenstein, "Some Lexical Material in the Judean Scrolls," VT 4 (1954) 211-214.   A.L. Oppenheim, *The Interpretation of Dreams in the Ancient Near East* (1956) 217-220, 246-249.

[6:13]   The second of the three sentences in this verse is a repetition of 11b, thus confirming that the decision to destroy must follow what is said in vv. 11-12. The מפניהם (the violence exercised through them) at the end of this sentence is an indication that it is a reflective construction. The third sentence is the real announcement of destruction. It stands naturally in 17b where it is repeated: what God actually announces is that he will unleash a flood of waters, 17b, and its purpose is to destroy every living being (17b = 13c). The את־הארץ at the end of 13c is difficult. It cannot be an accusative particle following immediately on the third person plural suffix. Many interpreters understand it as a preposition: "I will destroy them with the earth" (U. Cassuto and others). But that is not possible because in P too the whole earth is not destroyed. Nothing is said at the end about a new creation of the earth. The text must be corrupt. Perhaps one should amend את to מאת; for other proposed emendations see BHK, H. Gunkel, U. Cassuto (summary of proposals). What emerges then is that the real intent of v. 13 is in the first sentence, the other two being repetitions and belonging elsewhere.

"I have decided to put an end to all flesh." Two different sentences are condensed into one, "the end of all flesh has come" and "I have seen the corruption of the earth." The latter follows from 12a; what is said in 12a is taken up into the speech to Noah. The former is really out of place in the context; P has resumed a sentence from another tradition that has come to him. The same sentence occurs in Amos 8:2: "The end has come upon my people Israel," and is used as a theme-word in Ezek 7 (2f., 6f., 10, 12). It is a phrase which has its proper setting in the prophetic announcement of judgment where it concerns those who are directly addressed. It is out of place in the context of the flood narrative. By resuming a prophetic phrase of this kind, P is pointing to the connection between God's judgment on all humanity and his judgment on his people announced by the prophets. It is an important sign of P's systematic thinking which links history and primeval story.

There could be a further allusion to the prophetic announcement of judgment in the verbal parallel of guilt and punishment. They have (were) destroyed — I am destroying them; this is a fixed stylistic device with the prophets. It is no mere chance that in Ezek 7, dominated by the word קץ, there are other words from P's announcement of the flood: חמס 7:11; מלאה 7:23. By putting 13a at the beginning of the announcement of the flood to Noah, P is deliberately interpreting the ancient tradition which recalled the pre-exilic announcement of judgment by the prophets that used primeval motifs to portray the end of the world. In the Apocalyptic too the proclamation of the end of the world is addressed to the believers.

Literature: Gen 6:14-16: J. Halévy, "Le nom du matelot du Noé babylonien," JA 10 (1911) XVI, 627-628.   J. Döller, "Zu Genesis 6:16a," BZ 11 (1913) 5-9.   J.N. Epstein, "קינים קינים," MGWJ 69 (1926) 248-249.   C.C.R. Murphy, "What is Gopher Wood?," AsR NS 42 (1946) 79-81.   H.S. Gehman, "Hebraisms of the Old Greek Versions of Genesis," VT 3 (1953) 141-148.   G.R. Driver, "Problems and Solutions," VT 4 (1954) 225-245, esp. 243.   E. Ullendorff, "The Construction of Noah's Ark," VT 4 (1954) 95-96.   R. Largement, "Le thème de l'arche dans les traditions Suméro-Sémitiques," *Mélanges Bibliques rédigés en l'honneur de A. Robert* 1957, 60-65.   L. Knothe, "Zur Frage des hebräischen Denkens," ZAW 70 (1958) 175-181.   R.B.Y. Scott, "The Hebrew Cubit," JBL 77 (1958) 205-214; "Weights and Measures of the Bible," BA 22 (1959) 22-40.   J.F. Armstrong, "A Critical Note on Gen 6:16a," VT 10 (1960) 328-334.

[6:14-16]   Commission to Build the Ark.

This consists of the instruction to construct an ark (תבה) out of wood, with rooms, covered with pitch inside and out (14), with futher detailed instructions: the dimensions (15), with roof, door and three decks (16). The commission is extremely brief, a mere enumeration, distributed under the verb "make" (four times), and some details (use pitch, apply it, complete it?). The details may be tabulated:

1. An ark of teak-wood,
2. with rooms,
3. with pitch inside and out,
4. 300 cubits long, 50 wide, 30 high,
5. Roof,
6. . . .
7. Door in the side,
8. three decks.

The eight pieces of information, one of which, n. 6, is incomprehensible, are not sufficient to permit a detailed reconstruction, which is often attempted; not even the number of rooms is given. However, we have a general idea of the ark: a huge, rectangular box with a roof, divided into rooms. Vv. 14-16 are not based on any systematic plan of construction, as has been proposed (cf. S. McEvenue); any such would be unusable (so too B. Jacob). The details of the commission to build the ark develop out of the unique function it is meant to fulfil; they are to be understood only in this context. Each particular detail serves to emphasize the uniqueness of the construction. A comparison with Gilgamesh XI is useful at this stage.

XI	24	Tear down (this) house, build a ship,	cf. Gen 6:14a
	25	Give up possessions, seek thou life!	
	26	Forswear (worldly) goods and keep the soul alive!	
	27	Aboard the ship take thou the seed of all living things!	6:18-19
	28	The ship that thou shalt build —	15a

29	Her dimensions shall be to measure	15b
30	Equal shall her width and her length;	16b
31	Like the apsu thou shalt ceil her.	
32	I understood, and I said to Ea, my Lord:	22
33	[Behold], my Lord, what thou hast ordered,	
34	I will be honored to carry out.	
35-47	[But what] shall I answer the city . . .?	
48-74	The building of the ship	
76-86	The loading and fitting out of the ship.	

The main difference between Gilg. XI and Gen 6:14-22 is that the commission and its execution are narrated, the commission but briefly (XI 24-31), the execution in detail (XI 48-74 and 76-86). The texts of the commission and its resumption are very close to each other. The god, Ea, who had sat in the council of the gods and had heard there the decision to destroy (11.14-19), addresses a reed-hut (11.20-22), because he may not betray the secret of the gods; actually he is addressing Utnapishtim (23). He commands him to construct a ship. The tabulation above shows this to be an almost exact parallel to Gen 6:14-22. The Genesis passage differs from Gilg. XI only in the following: the elaboration in 11.25-26 is missing, the taking in of all the "seed of all living things" follows in P in vv. 17-21, and because P does not narrate the execution, the commission has a second part, vv. 18-21, which resumes the fitting out of the ark. There follows in P therefore the report that Noah did what God commanded him, v. 22; in Gilg. XI 32-34 Utnapishtim undertakes to carry out the commission. The reason for these minor differences is that P does not narrate the execution of the commission. With this reservation, the agreement is almost complete. The only explanation is that P and Gilg. XI were heirs to a common tradition. Nowhere in J is there such far reaching agreement with Gilg. XI.

If one compares the information about the ark with Gen 6, there is further far-reaching agreement. The eight pieces of data in Gen 6 correspond to 6 in Gilg. XI; the sixth (the incomprehensible detail) and the seventh (the door) are missing, though the latter is mentioned in Gilg. XI, 11.88. Gilg. XI has some more precise details, the division into rooms, the water-plugs and the punting-poles. The most significant difference is that the dimensions in Gilg. XI are much greater. The ark is cubic in shape, the length of the sides being 120 cubits (60 meters according to von Soden). The dimensions are even larger in Berossus. It is important from the standpoint of tradition history that this is the case too with Gen 5 and its Mesopotamian parallels: despite the similarities the numbers are different.

The comparison permits certain definite conclusions. There are so many points of agreement that there must be a common tradition behind both texts. This striking agreement is found precisely in the elaboration of the simple narrative which is lacking in J. The main difference between Gen 6 and Gilg. XI is that Genesis is shorter and the numbers much lower. There is at the same time a link with tradition and a distance from it.

The Details. 1. A box out of teak-wood. What is striking about the description of the ark is that in vv. 14-16 alone there are a number of words that do not, or scarcely ever, occur again in the Old Testament. תבה (only in Ex 2:3, 5 of the small basket in which Moses was found), גפר, כפר, צהר. We can be sure that these unusual words belonged to an earlier stage of the narrative and were taken over as an integral part of it. תבה is a loan word from Egyptian where *ṭb. t* means a box or chest (so U. Cassuto and others). The Gk turns it with κιβωτός, the Vg with *arca*, hence ark. In Sumerian the vessel is designated *magurgur* = a very large ship, in Babylonian *elippu rabitu* = a large ship, in Gilg. XI simply *elippu*. It is worthy of note in Gilg. XI a huge cubic box is called a "ship," while in Gen 6 the ark, which is much more like a ship, is described as a chest. This shows that the descriptions and designations each have their own history.

The material is given as גפר-wood. This detail can only have had its origin in an environment where this was a well-known tree. The tree is not mentioned elsewhere in the Old Testament. It is generally understood as a cone-bearing tree; some interpreters connect it with κυπαρίσσος, cypress. Cf. C.C.R. Murphy, Asiatic Review NS 42 (1946) 79-81. G.R. Driver calls it teak-wood, VT 4 (1954).

2. קנים, Rooms. The proposal of de Lagarde, together with A. Dillmann, O. Procksch and others, that קנים is to be read twice is very probable (Nestle found this reading in Philo). But attempts to vocalize the words as קָנִים and to render "woven out of reeds" (B. Jacob following Y. Yahuda, G.R. Driver and others), has no foundations, as the parallels in Gilg. XI show clearly. The remarkable agreement in the succession of motifs between Gilg. XI and Gen 6 dissuades any rearrangement of the text, as has often been suggested (H. Gunkel and others).

3. "Coat it inside and outside with pitch." In Gilg. XI the same word *kūprū* occurs in the same context which is all the more striking because it is found only here. This ends the general commission to Noah. The three details determine adequately the function of the construction and are to be distinguished clearly from the particular instructions that follow.

4. The special details begin with the dimensions: see R.B.Y. Scott, BA 22 (1959) 22-40; JBL 77 (1958) 205-214: ". . . there remains then some uncertainty in determining the length of the pre-exilic cubit (אמה). It was probably a somewhat shorter form of the Egyptian cubit, about 444.5 mm. long." The length would be reckoned at between 130 and 150m., the breadth about 22m., and the height some 12m. F. Delitzsch compares the shape to that of a prostrate man; B. Jacob: "Six times as long and more that twice as wide as the temple of Solomon." Utnapishtim's construction in Gilg. XI is very much larger.

[6:16] 5. צהר, following the old translations (Vg *fenestra*) used generally can be understood as a window or skylight (so too A. Dillmann and still U. Cassuto). Most moderns (already A. Ehrlich) understand it as a roof; J.F. Armstrong VT 10 (1960) 328-334, has furnished a detailed proof: "The Arabic term means 'back'.

.. (of a hand), (human) 'back' (later) the top of a ship . . . ṣōhar . . . became the logical word by which to speak of the top of Noah's ark.''

6. The following sentence is incomprehensible (J. Skinner and others); A. Dillmann: "You are to finish it up to one cubit from above." B. Jacob translates: "You are to end it up to one cubit," and asks: "Why is this expressed in so complicated a fashion?" J. Döller, BZ 11 (1913) 5-9, gives a detailed synthesis of interpretations up to that time and explains: the roof should extend about one cubit, so as to prevent the rain coming in through the window and the openings under the roof. But these are only conjectures.

7. "And you are to put the door in the side of the ark." This sentence tells us very clearly that the ark that Noah is to construct is not a ship. The door is mentioned here because the entrance into and exit from the ark form important stages in the narrative.

8. The ark is to have three decks (7 in Gilg. XI). This explains more precisely the general instruction of v. 14. The three decks make it possible to construct a large number of rooms. B. Jacob concludes his remarks on vv. 14-16: "The ark and the Tabernacle are the only buildings that the Torah describes" (cf. D.W. Gooding, VT 17 [1967] 143-172 on 1 Kings 6:1-38; 7:13-51). P looks to the Tabernacle, the place where Yahweh meets his people, as the goal of the history which begins with the covenant with Abraham and extends to the erection of the sanctuary in Jerusalem. The place where God allows his glory to appear is the place whence the life of the people is preserved. The ark corresponds to this in the primeval event where the concern is for the preservation of humanity and what is saved is natural creation. Such is the significance of the construction of the ark because by means of it God preserved humanity from destruction. The parallel between the ark and the tabernacle has a profound meaning. The people of Israel which alone has in its midst the place where God reveals his glory is part of the human race which exists now because it has been preserved by this same God.

Literature: Gen 6:17: J. Begrich, "Mabbul. Eine exegetisch-lexikalische Studie," ThB 21 (1964) 39-54.   M. Fishbane, "The Treaty Background of Amos 1:11 and Related Matters," JBL 89 (1970) 313-318.   J. Hoftijzer, "David and the Tekoite Woman," VT 20 (1970) 419-444, esp. 429.   H. Strauss, ZAW 82 (1970) 96.

[6:17a]   One would expect the fitting out of the ark to follow immediately; it comes only in v. 18. The announcement of the destruction is continued from v. 13. Only the first sentence is new in v. 17: "I am going to unleash the flood upon the earth." The second and third (to destroy every living creature) sentences are only a repetition of 13c (and 13a). The first sentence, 17a, is really part of the announcement in v. 13; God intends to destroy humanity by means of the flood and this is reason for the building of the ark. P first introduces the key word מבול immediately before the sentence: "You are to go into the ark." His purpose in composing the story in this way is to indicate in advance the establishment of a "covenant" by God with Noah. He thereby constructs a highpoint wherein he lets us know where he sees the real meaning of what is being narrated. The command to go into the ark introduces the salvation of Noah and with it the salvation of all that lives. It is here that we find God's real purpose in the whole event. The word ברית which indicates what is going on anticipates the unfolding of God's purpose in the ברית which is determinative for the era after the flood, 9:9.

מבול is really the heavenly ocean. J. Begrich has shown this clearly (see above). It occurs with this meaning in Ps 29:10; Gen 7:7, 10. It is used with the article in Gen 7:10 and 6:17, where it is first found, thus showing that it is a well-known term. This is confirmed by J who uses it only at the beginning of his narrative. The word acquires the specific meaning, the flood, in P; so 9:11, 15, 28; 10:1, 32; 11:10; also Sir 44:17. J. Begrich concludes from this fact that it is no longer necessary to look to the Akkadian for the derivation of the word, as is generally done (he and U. Cassuto gather together the various derivations); closest is the Hebrew יבל, to flow, to stream (יבלי־מים Is 30:25; 44:4, so too U. Cassuto and A. Dillmann).

[6:17b] כל בשׂר (see on v. 12) means here every living creature, humans and animals, as is confirmed by the addition which is an obvious echo of the creation. Once more there is reference to the contrast: God gave life — now he takes it away. The parallelism, "under heaven — on the earth" includes destruction embracing every living creature. It is only here that the consequence of this destruction is expressed in a single phrase: "Everything shall die." The verb גוע is peculiar to P in the Pentateuch (7:21; 25:8, 17; 35:29; 49:23; 12 times in all); elsewhere it is found only in poetry. Its specific meaning is "to pine away, to languish."

> *Literature:* Gen 6:18: W. Plautz, ZAW 75 (1963) 3-26.   E. Kutsch, "Gesetz und Gnade. Probleme des alttestamentlichen Bundesbegriffs," ZAW 79 (1967) 18-35; "Von ברית zu 'Bund'," KuD 14 (1968) 159-182.

[6:18-21]   The second part of the commission says who and what is to be taken into the ark: people (18), animals (19-20), food (21). The whole is introduced by the sentence: "I am setting up a covenant with you." We have explained above the meaning of the sentence in the composition of the speech vv. 13-21; for the idea ברית, see commentary on 9:9. It is enough here to explain the word from its context. The following sentence explains what the ברית consists in: the command to Noah to go into the ark (together with 18b-21). Noah is saved by entering the ark; the command implies salvation just as in 1:28, "be fruitful and multiply" implies blessing. God's word of command in the primeval event is not for P something added to his action of salvation and blessing; both are completely intertwined with each other. God saves in commanding; God blesses in commanding. It is this very action of salvation which reaches its consummation in the command to Noah that is called ברית. By bringing the flood (מבול) over the earth to destroy every living creature, God at the same time promises salvation to Noah by ordering him to enter the ark which saves. That is the meaning of ברית. The word is a solemn underscoring of the theological meaning of God's saving action toward Noah. It is not at all a special act by which the covenant is sealed, but only a theological explanation of what is happening. If 18a were struck out, there would be nothing missing in the course of the action.

F. Delitzsch explains: "God brings about a covenant relationship by saving him through the judgment while expecting obedience to his ordinances." H. Gunkel accepts this explanation. J. Skinner has objected that this does not accord with the use of ברית in P: it is always "a solemn and permanent embodiment of the divine will," and never a designation for a particular situation; he referred to Kraetzschmar. One must agree with Skinner inasmuch as there is not a real sealing of a covenant with the two elements of promise and command (as in Gen 17). One must agree further when he sees in the sentence a relationship to 9:9. He is subject to correction however in that even with P ברית can be a solemn promise related to a situation as is the case in 6:18. It is not really an "anticipation" of 9:9, but a relationship that is intended; the act of salvation which is initiated by the command to Noah makes possible what is said in 9:9. The explanation of U. Cassuto, that God promises in 6:18 the fulfillment of what was assured to the first man, is a misunderstanding; 6:18 is concerned with salvation, not with blessing.

[**6:18b**]   Noah's family, his wife, their sons and their wives, are to go into the ark to be saved with him. We learn here what the idea of family meant from patriarchal times and long before right down to P and long afterwards; not, as with us, parents with their children, but parents with their married sons. A family is fully there when the life that begins with the parents is carried on through the (married) sons. If all other life is destroyed, as by the flood, then there can only be salvation by means of a family that consists of two generations; otherwise continuation would only be possible through incest, as in Gen 19:30-38. By naming the people in v. 18b P means those who belong necessarily to the family. However, he does not intend to state that Noah and his sons were monogamous nor that Noah's sons did not have any children at that time (W. Plautz, ZAW 75 [1963] introduces a restriction: "Strictly speaking, the only conclusion one can draw from 7:13 is that the Old Testament considers the marriage of Noah's sons to be monogamous").

[**6:19-20**]   Noah is ordered to take a pair, one male and one female, of every kind of animal into the ark with him. This is the only way the life of the animals can be preserved: "To keep them alive with you" (cf. Gen 45:7; 50:20). The number of animals is one of the most notable differences between J (7:2) and P. This is conditioned by P's overall plan; in P there is no sacrifice after the exit from the ark. Nevertheless 1:29f. still holds: it is forbidden to humans and animals to eat flesh. A pair of each kind therefore is enough to preserve the species. The significance of the number is underlined by the repetition. The precise enumeration of the species not only accords with the style of P; it is a deliberate evocation of Gen 1: the creator of the animals preserves his creation despite the decision to destroy. The animals perish together with corrupt humanity (יגוע, v. 13) — the animals are saved with one person who is favored. If one asks how Noah carried out the command one becomes involved in inextricable difficulties. The commentary of F. Delitzsch shows this: "One can have some idea of how Noah was able to gather together . . . the many animals; the awareness of the imminent catastrophe came over the animal kingdom and drove them to him . . . but how was it that he did not miss any of them. . . ?" Delitzsch is concerned at every stage of his interpretation to explain the primeval event as an actual event analogous to what is attested historically. However, he capitulates here and ends by saying that "land animals" must have also been preserved outside the ark — the flood must have only been partial.

But if one understands the flood as primeval event, the anxious questioning, how did Noah get hold of all the animals, how did he accommodate them in the ark, is seen to be otiose and outside the scope of the narrative. The story is talking about another sort of reality: humans and the animals stand together in face of catastrophes that threaten life, just as they do at creation. The reality is twofold — the animals perish with people and people and animals are saved together. This is of the utmost significance for the history of humans and animals. The attitude is not found first in P and J; the salvation of animals and humans together had been a motif of flood stories for thousands of years beforehand.

[6:21]   We do not have to come to terms with the commission to Noah to take food for all into the ark; P has already indicated that it is a question of vegetarian food only. Animal life that is completely vegetarian is beyond our ken.

When one surveys vv. 18-21, it becomes clear what was the significance of the preservation of humanity for P and the tradition behind him. The understanding of humanity is not the same as in western thought where it is encountered objectively and independently, a thing defined according to its physical and psychic qualities, a being that is a rational animal. The narrative is not concerned with such a being. The people who are saved from the great world catastrophe are people who exist only with the relations which are included in the action of salvation. They are beings in community, i.e., they are members of a family, have relationships with the animals and must provide food. This is the way in which people have been created. J and P agree here; it is only a person with these relationships that is God's creature. The creation of humans and their salvation from the world catastrophe are at one here, and this forms a sound basis for the concept of humanity in the Old Testament: it is only with these relationships that a person is the creature that God intended.

[6:22]   Many extra-biblical flood narratives, especially those from Mesopotamia, describe now the carrying out of the commission. Gilg. XI is particularly lively and colorful: it begins with the offering of sacrifice for the success of the work, 11.50-51, and continues up to the enumeration of the varieties of wine and oil which the builder provides for the workmen on the feast day, 11.70-73. All this is missing in P; only one thing is important, Noah did what God commanded him. This sentence is pronounced with the greatest solemnity; it is like a musical pause. We have here for the first time something that runs through the whole of the priestly work like a regular beat: God commands and the one who is commanded carries out the command. It is the same with Abraham, Gen 17, Moses, Ex 24:25ff., and in many other places. Every event that determines the course of history is set in motion because God commands and is obeyed. This basic understanding of the movement of history has its foundation in the creation story: he spoke and it came to be.

Literature: Gen 7:1: J. Muilenburg, "The Linguistic Usages of the Particle כי in the OT," HUCA 32 (1961) 135-160.   H. Donner, "Israel unter den Völkern," VT.S 11 (1964) esp. 128.   J. Hoftijzer, "Remarks Concerning the Use of the Particle 't in Classical Hebrew," OTS 14 (1965) 1-99, esp. 33.   H.H. Schmid, *Gerechtigkeit als Weltordnung*, (1968) 106-108.

[7:1-5]   7:1-5 are still part of the introduction, the continuation of J which had begun with 6:5-8. J, 6:5-8 with 7:1-9, corresponds to P, 6:9-22. The redactor, R, wove together only the central section of the J and P flood narratives, i.e., the actual course of the catastrophe, leaving both introductions, P 6:9-22; J 6:5-8 and 7:1-9, and conclusions, P 9:1-17; J 8:20-22, intact and unaltered. We suggest that this was deliberate. The redactor realized that the meaning of the narratives lay mainly in the introductory and concluding parts where he must let each voice speak for itself. This was not so necessary as the event ran its course.

The result of the redactor's method is that the parallels stand out much more clearly in the unaltered introductions than in the part that narrates the event itself. It is this above all that demonstrates the thesis that the flood narrative is the result of the working together of two sources. There are some exegetes who contest this even today (E. Nielsen, U. Cassuto). Hence we must demonstrate yet again that the complete parallelism of the two introductory parts allows of no other explanation.

The core of the introduction consists of God's speech to Noah where he announces the flood and promises to save Noah, and Noah's reaction: P 6:13-21 and 22; J 7:1-4 and 5. Before this, God sees the corruption of humanity and decides to destroy it: P 6:11-12 and 13, J 6:5 and 6-7. The constructions of the introductions are completely parallel:

	P	J
God sees the corruption of humanity	6:11-12	6:5
and decides to destroy it.	13	6-7
God's speech to Noah,	13-21	7:1-4
Noah's reaction	22	5

In addition, there is wide agreement in content and almost every sentence in J corresponds to one in P. This then is one of the passages of the Old Testament which we can demonstrate with certainty to be a literary composition out of two originally independent sources. A check test of the contrary view confirms this result: the explanation of the parallelism or doubling both by Nielsen and Cassuto is very contrived. What is decisive is that neither of them can explain the complete parallelism in structure, as we have shown it above. The structure of 7:1-5 is to be seen in the immediate context of 6:5-8 of which it is a continuation. God's decision to destroy humanity, 6:5-7, limited by 6:8 ("but Noah. . . .") is followed by the commission to Noah to go into the ark, vv. 1-3, because God is to wipe everything from the earth, v. 4. V. 5 reports Noah's reaction: he obeyed.

The commission, "Go into the ark," v. 1, presumes that J too must also have spoken of the building of the ark. It is impossible that "the ark" should suddenly be there without anything having been said about it and its purpose and how it came to be. The account of the building of the ark must have fallen out in favor of P. There is a further indication that J must have at one time contained a commission to build the ark; it is v. 5: "And Noah did everything that Yahweh commanded him," which must have been connected originally with the commission to build, because it is only reported later that everybody went into the ark, v. 7.

[7:1] Gunkel comments on the introductory sentence, "And Yahweh said to Noah," that the appearance of God is not portrayed and so the narrative loses something in color, as in 4:6. But Gunkel misses the point here. There neither is nor can be any appearance of God in primeval narratives; God speaks with people and there is no need to bridge any gap (see above, 2:4b-3:24, Form). The commission to Noah to go into the ark is addressed to him and his whole house.

J. Skinner explains this: "The principle involved is the religious solidarity of the families; its members are saved for the righteousness of its head," so too J. Scharbert and others. But one must be cautious about such conclusions. All that is said is that humanity is preserved as a family because it is the only way that people can continue to exist.

The basis of the commission is that Noah has been found righteous. W.M. Clark has studied this recently, VT 21 (1971) 261-280. He takes as his starting point three traditional explanations which he finds inadequate and which are mainly concerned with the relationship of "found favor" in 6:8 to "was found righteous" in 7:1b. One view, e.g., J. Skinner, considers 7:1b as the basis of 6:8; Noah found favor because he was righteous; another, e.g., G. von Rad, considers that Noah is declared just as a consequence of having found favor. The building of the ark is a test of Noah's faith or obedience (as in Heb 11:7); God knows Noah's righteousness by it (cf. Gen 22:12). According to a third opinion (H.H. Schmid, *Gerechtigkeit. . . ,* 106-107) 7:1b is a resumption of 6:8; the finding of grace is the gift of righteousness. Clark thinks that the attitude of P to the righteousness of Noah is the same as in the Mesopotamian flood stories: Noah was already righteous in his way of life before the flood. According to J 6:5-7 on the other hand Noah is not an exception from the general corruption, but is exempted from God's judgment, v. 8.

After a careful study of the linguistic usage and a comparison with Gen 15 and 22, Clark rejects the explanation of the building of the ark as a test of obedience. Similar uses of ראה show that the sentence cannot be translated: "I have seen that you are just," and that it is not an expression of recognition as W. Zimmerli understood it (cf. Lit. on 6:8). If one understands ראה in the context of the election of a king as it is used in 1 Sam 16:1 and 2 Kings 8:13, one sees that צדיק acquires a meaning that looks to the future: "Noah is chosen that he may be Yahweh's ṣaddiq in the realization of Yahweh's purpose," Clark, p. 277. Just as David was not chosen because of his particular merits in 1 Sam 16, neither was Noah. The question here is rather about God's intention for humanity. Two further precisions are pertinent: the לפני means not so much "in my judgment" as "for me," and the בדור הזה "from these people": "you I have chosen king (ṣaddiq) to me (before me) from these people (in this generation)" p. 278.

This study introduces a completely new point of view into the discussion of which note must be taken. I would agree with Clark in his rejection of the current explanation because each is in its own way too onesided. The attention to the use of ראה in the election of a king is also, I think, a worthwhile contribution, especially 1 Sam 16:1: כי ראיתי בבניו לי מלך. It is certainly correct that ראה is directed primarily to the future; nevertheless there is a clear distinction: the one of Jesse's sons whom God has marked out is not yet king, but is to become so. One cannot say in the same way: Noah, whom God has chosen "in this genera-tion" is not yet ṣaddiq, but is to become so. I think that Clark goes beyond the evidence here. He admits himself: "while Noah's righteousness as a present reality is not entirely absent in 7:1. . . ." The thesis would only be convincing if Clark could prove a meaning that looks to the future from usages of the word צדיק.

One can say as a result of Clark's study that the ראיתי צדיק in 7:1b cannot be restricted to qualities already there in Noah, nor can they mean that God has seen that Noah is "just" from the test of obedience, nor that Noah found favor with God because he was already just. However, the words contain some orientation to the future because God has regarded Noah as suitable for the preservation of humanity. This of course does not exclude that Noah be judged "just" ("in my eyes").

Clark likewise wants to explain the relationship of 7:1b to 6:8 from the choice of the king. 6:8 would correspond to the decision of God to choose this king, 7:1b to the public proclamation of the choice. This is possible, but not necessary. If one reflects that in J's introduction 7:1-5 follows immediately on 6:5-8, then the two sentences are very close to each other and are to be explained from their proximity in the context. The transition from the decision to destroy, 6:5-7, to the speech to Noah needs a reason; it is given in 6:8. What 6:8 says by way of report, 7:1b says again in the speech to Noah.

Finally, à further word about the relationship of 7:1b (J) to 6:9 (P). The important difference is that the sentence in 6:9, "Noah was a just man" is part of the genealogy and so is a human judgment on Noah's conduct as a whole. It is a judgment that stands independently of what happens to Noah in the flood. The sentence assigns Noah to a definite category of people, the "just" or the "pious," as in Ezek 14:20. It is different with J; both 6:8 and 7:1b say something about Noah which has meaning only in the context of the narrative of the flood. Noah found favor in God's eyes despite the decision to destroy, and God saw him as "suitable" in this generation to be the instrument for the preservation of humanity. The same word צדיק is merely functional in J, whereas in P it describes more a state. The tradition history of the passage is not to be understood in the way Clark takes it. He is of the opinion that P and the Mesopotamian tradition are in agreement here; J received it and reshaped it. This is unlikely. If one takes 6:9 together with Ezek 14:20, then this is clearly a later formation in Israel. One must take as one's starting point the broader perspective of the history of the flood narrative. In an earlier form the choice of someone to be preserved in the flood was grounded simply in God's intention to have that person survive, not in some quality that the person had. J was relatively close to this earlier form, but P far away from it.

Literature: Gen 7:2: T. Worden, "The Story of the Flood," Scrip 13 (1961) 57-60. L.E. Toombs, "Clean and Unclean," IDB I (1962) 643. M.R. Lehmann, "Biblical Oaths," ZAW 81 (1969) 74-92. W. Paschen, *Rein und Unrein,* StANT 24 (1970).

[7:2-3] The context of vv. 1-3 is that of the commission: "Go . . . and take with you. . . !" The second part of this commission in vv. 2-3 is subdivided: "of every clean . . . of every unclean . . . to keep their kind alive." We see here the difference in the narrative styles of J and P. P is at pains to record everything in minute detail, here everything that is to go into the ark. J on the contrary is only concerned to present what happened; he only says what is absolutely necessary so that Noah can carry out the commission that is communicated to him. J fits the sentences in vv. 1-3 together with a chain of verbs: "Go . . . take . . . to keep. . . ," while P uses mainly numerative substantives. This difference in style is the most telling argument that v. 3a "and seven pairs of every bird of the air, male and female" is a secondary supplement (so F. Delitzsch, K. Budde, O. Eissfeldt, H. Gunkel, H. Holzinger and others); this is supported by an argument from language (זכר ונקבה).

J uses בהמה here in a general, comprehensive sense. A distinction is made only between clean and unclean animals, the higher number of clean animals indicating their greater significance for humans. The numbers — to the

שבעה שבעה for the clean there should be a corresponding שנים שנים for the unclean — suggest that the versions have preserved the better text. It is not certain whether "seven of each" and "two of each" mean individual animals (so F. Delitzsch, H.L. Strack, J. Skinner and others; contrary A. Dillmann, H. Gunkel and others).

J, differing from P, presumes the distinction between clean and unclean animals for the whole of the history of humankind down to his time. "This accords better with the facts of the history of religions than P's theory that the distinction derives only from the time of Moses" (H. Gunkel, similarly J. Skinner. U. Cassuto is different, and A. Dillmann still more so: "The author presumes the mosaic distinctions, and projects something which is later back into the primeval period"). This shows again the universal perspective of J. He starts from the state of knowledge of his own time; he knows that certain phenomena such as sacrifice, punishment, distinction between clean and unclean animals were not peculiar to Israelite religion but were very widespread and so were there long before Israel came into existence. H. Gunkel says rightly: "The original meaning of such customs is no longer known in antiquity." Nevertheless we know from the way in which antiquity understood it that the distinction between clean and unclean animals, i.e., among other things, their suitability or otherwise for sacrifice and food, was set in the context of securing the existence of primitive groups: "Since the nonhuman powers may be hostile to man, any object — a rock, a stream, a tree, or an animal — may be dangerous to human life, and the survival of the group demands exclusion from it of the potentially destructive elements in the world about it. This is done by a system of taboos" (L.E. Toombs, "Clean and Unclean," IDB I 643). The distinction that J makes between the clean and unclean animals which Noah is to take into the ark is a distinction based on their utility for humans, not on later legal ideas. It only becomes clear now that unclean animals are included among the living beings to be preserved; they have the same right to life as the clean animals.

The subsequent elaboration of v. 3a has misunderstood the comprehensive sense of בהמה in v. 2; the birds are added, quite unnecessarily: "seven of each, male and female." J's important distinction between clean and unclean is missing here (U. Cassuto has drawn attention to this difficulty). The Gk adds "of clean birds"; this does not help because the absence of the unclean is even more noticeable.

V. 3b follows directly on v. 2; the rhythm of the text is also better when v. 3a drops out. The sentence synthesizes the meaning of the whole of God's commission to Noah. There was no need to say that the "seed" of the human race is preserved in Noah; this is implied in 6:8 and 7:1. The sentence that concludes the commission expresses for the first time the meaning behind it: the preservation of life, and this includes every living being. The combination "to keep alive their seed" (חיה in Piel with זרע as object) occurs elsewhere only in Gen 19:32, 34 in the narrative of Lot's daughters. It is a question here of the continuation of a family or a tribe, and is certainly the older usage. The extension of the phrase in 7:3 to include all living beings, humans and animals, gives some indication of the breadth of view that lies behind the Yahwistic flood narrative. The sentence: "To keep their kind alive over the whole of the earth," expresses one of its basic motifs.

Literature: Gen 7:4: H.S. Gehman, VT 1 (1951) 88. R.B.Y. Scott, "Meteorological Phenomena and Terminology in the Old Testament," ZAW 64 (1952) 11-25. S. McEvenue, "A Source-Critical Problem in Nm 14:26-38," Bib 50 (1969) 453-465.

[7:4] The commission to Noah, concluded in v. 3b, is now justified by the announcement of the flood. There are three parts to the sentence: the deadline for the beginning of the flood, the announcement of God's intervention, and its effect. The two verbs form the framework of the sentence: "I will bring rain . . . I will wipe from the earth (everything I have made)." It is important for J's narrative that the event is described as due entirely to God's action; it is not "event" in our sense, but rather "action," the work of a person. "It" does not rain, but God rains (or brings rain); the flood does not cause destruction, but God destroys. This is reinforced further by the relative clause "which I have made." It says that God is acting with the same directness in the flood as in the creation. The narrative is about an action of God who destroys his own work.

The period of seven days to the beginning of the flood is a traditional number for a unit of time. It occurs also in Gilg. XI 76 though in a somewhat different context: "The ship was completed at sundown on the seventh day." (The ל to indicate a period of time, see Ges-Buhl, Lex., ל 2b. The participle with a future meaning, Ges-K §116p.) The cause of the flood in J is forty days of rain; this is one of the most notable differences from P. The rain lasting forty days and forty nights is meant to be a natural phenomenon but of catastrophic dimensions, such as never before experienced. One should not focus on the extraordinary numbers given by P. J's description is limited locally. The number 40 is a traditional one as, e.g., the forty years wandering in the desert. The effect of the flood too is a direct action of God: "Everything that exists . . . I will wipe from the earth." One must realize the enormity of this sentence which runs as a leitmotif through J's narrative: 7:4 resumes 6:7, and what is announced here is described in 7:23 as accomplished. מחה means "wipe out" (e.g., Num 5:23: wipe out what is written), then "annihilate." It can have a number of objects in this sense (e.g., a tribe in Judg 21:17), but only in these three places is the object every living being or all that exists. J underlines the contrast further when he resumes 6:5-7 by adding "that I have made" to the object that came to him in the traditions. היקום, that which exists, is a rare word, occurring only here, 7:23 and Deut 11:6, where it is also a question of the destruction of a whole (a clan). This points to a fixed phrase that was part of the tradition. For the Greek translation ἀνάστεμα, cf. H.S. Gehman, VT 1 (1951) 88.

Literature: Gen 7:5: C. Kuhl, "Die 'Wiederaufnahme' — ein literarkritisches Prinzip?," ZAW 64 (1952) 1-11.

[7:5] It must now be said that Noah does as God had commanded him; but that is said in v. 7, following directly the commission: "And Noah went into the ark. . . ." Further, it is very unlike the style of J to repeat the carrying out of the command twice in quick succession (vv. 5 and 7); one supposes then that v. 5 was originally J's account of the carrying out of the command to build the ark which P has suppressed. This becomes all the more likely because 7:5 is a direct parallel to 6:22 which has the same place in P.

The Coming of the Flood and Its Effect

[7:6-24]   This section forms the center of the flood narrative: the catastrophe is portrayed following the two parts of the announcement of the flood to Noah in 7:4 (J). Both here and in what follows the two sources have been worked together so as to present one event. The coming of the flood begins in v. 7 with a sentence from P, recognizable by the exact chronological details. This is followed in P by v. 11 which gives further precision to the dates and tells how the coming of the flood took place. There follows, almost without interruption, P's portrayal of the flood, 7:13-21 (omit 16b, 17b), ending with the high point in 7:24.

J's beginning, "and after seven days the waters of the flood came upon the earth," corresponds exactly to P's 7:6. But J's account of the flood, corresponding to P in 7:11, 13-21 does not follow; there are only individual sentences which are inserted into P's narrative at different places: 7, 10, 12, 16b. Only vv. 22-23, the conclusion of this part, form a continuity. We can see here just how the redactor went about his work. The beginning, 7:10, and the end, 7:22-23, of this part of J's work are retained. Only a few sentences from what lies between have been worked into the P narrative. The conjecture of many exegetes is thereby justified, that the redactor inserted the few sentences from J into the narrative of P where they are suited; and so one can ask, what was their original order in J. K. Budde, H. Gunkel, J. Skinner and others have answered the question with such unanimity that the few sentences of J that have remained can be ordered in the following way:

7:5	:	
10	:	And after 7 days the waters of the flood came upon the earth
7	:	And Noah. . . . went into the ark to escape the waters of the flood
16b	:	And Yahweh shut the door behind him (8-9)
12	:	And rain poured upon the earth for 40 days and 40 nights
17b	:	And the waters increased and lifted up the ark so that it was high above the earth
22-23	:	The effect of the flood

If one accepts this order, then it is possible that these sentences retain substantially that part of J which tells of the coming of the flood. What P has over and above is by way of amplification, intensification, underlining; but it remains the same event. Presuming this, it is the text in the order in which it has been handed down to us that is the object of exegesis; only then can it be explained in its present composite state.

[7:6]   "Noah was 600 years old when. . . ." This is the first time in the presentation of the primeval story that an event is dated. Certainly P has already given the works of creation some sort of dating, but only by a succession of days. The birth of sons is given a date in Gen 5, but it serves only the numerical structure of the list of patriarchs. God's speech to Noah, 6:13, is not dated. It is only here, in the middle of the narrative, that we have the first dating of an actual event — the beginning of the flood. This is only possible by fixing a point in the life of Noah. U. Cassuto explains this aptly by analogy with the dating of events by reference to the reign of kings, suggesting the Babylonian King lists, which document the event of the flood. Perhaps the Babylonian influence appears too in that the number 600 corresponds to a Babylonian *ner,* or that the age of Ziusudra before the flood is 36,000 years in the King lists, 600 units of 60 years (U. Cassuto).

"When the flood (water) came upon the earth": the verb היה means here "to happen, to take place."

Literature: Gen 7:9: E.F. Sutcliffe, VT 11 (1961) 91-94.

Gen 7:10: L. Loewenstamm, "The Ugaritic Myth of the Sea and its Biblical Counterparts," Erls 9 (1969) 96-101.

[7:7-10] The redactor has put a few sentences from J between vv. 6 and 11, which belong to P. V. 10, which is parallel to v. 6, has been put before v. 11, and v. 7 has been elaborated by enumeration after the style of P. The result is the following complex:

J	P
	6: the flood comes (with date)
7: Noah (with elaboration) goes into the ark (elab: the animals)	
10: the flood comes	
	11: How the flood comes (with exact date)
12: how the flood comes	
	13-16: Noah and. . . . go into the ark.

The outline shows how carefully planned the redactor's work is. He takes the same order of three motifs in both J and P (1. the flood comes, 2. how it comes. 3. Noah goes into the ark) and brings them into a narrative sequence in such a way that the result is a self-contained succession of events. One aspect of R's procedure however is very unusual and puzzling. He elaborates the persons who go into the ark in v. 7 and the animals in vv. 8-9. The usual explanation is that R intends to give balance (so A. Dillmann and W. Zimmerli). But this is not convincing here, because R himself introduces into the text a doublet not dependent on the sources: because of this elaboration vv. 7-9 become an almost verbal parallel to vv. 13-16 (P). R has thereby succeeded in giving a dominating role to the entrance into the ark with all the people and the animals. Noah's leaving the ark and treading the earth at the end of the flood has a parallel in the entrance into the ark. By this studied solemnity R lays greater emphasis on God's saving action over against his sentence of destruction. This shift of emphasis is already there in P, but R augments it notably.

When commentators exegete the flood narratives of J and P separately, as they generally do, there is danger that justice will not be done to the individual narrative form as it has come down to us. One cannot avoid the fact that R's composite narrative has something important of its own to say, and that the scope of its effect belongs neither to J nor to P but to R. One can see the direction of R's work in 7:7-10 where he has left his strongest impression.

[7:7] In J, v. 10 stood before v. 7. The entrance into the ark is part of the traditional material of the flood narrative, e.g., Gilg. XI 93: "I boarded the ship and battened up the entrance." The sentence contains two words that are characteristic of the flood narrative: תבה (see on 6:14) and מבול (see on 6:17). The elaboration agrees with v. 13b (P) in content, but not literally. In J v. 16b followed v. 7; cf. Gilg. XI 93.

431

[7:8-9]   The same holds for the enumeration of the animals after the style of P which is part of the elaboration according to A. Dillmann, K. Budde, H. Gunkel, J. Skinner, O. Eissfeldt and others.

[7:10]   This sentence is parallel to 7:6 (P). The beginning of the flood is described with the same verb היה in the sense of "to take place, happen." One can assume that the formulation was part of the tradition. For the Hebraism in the Gk version see H.S. Gehman, VT 3 (1953) 141-142.

Literature: Gen 7:11: K.D. Ilgen, *Die Urkunden des jerusalemischen Tempelarchives*, Bd.I (1798), esp. 390.   E. Bertheau, "Die Zahlen der Genesis in Cap. 5 und Cap. 11," JDTh 23 (1878) 657-682.   W. Bousset, "Die chronologischen Systeme der biblischen Geschichtsbücher," ZAW 20 (1900) 136-147. K.Sethe, "Der Name der Überschwemmungsjahreszeit," ZÄS 38 (1900) 103-106.   A. Bosse, "Die chronologischen Systeme im AT und bei Josephus," MVG 13 (1908) 101-176.   O. Goldberg, *Die fünf Bücher Mosis ein Zahlengebäude* (1908).   F.A. Jones, *The Dates of Genesis* (1909).   J. Dahse, "Zu Gen 7:11," ZAW 30 (1910) 68.   R. Smend, *Die Erzählung des Hexateuch auf ihre Quellen untersucht* (1912).   O. Fischer, ZAW 31 (1911) 241-255.   A.J. Wensinck, *The Ocean in the Literature of the Western Semites* (1918).   F.Bork, "Zur Chronologie der biblischen Urgeschichte," ZAW 47 (1929) 206-222.   A. Jepsen, ZAW 47 (1929) 251-255.   A. Ungnad, "Datenlisten," RLA II (1938) 131-194; 132.   E. Auerbach, "Die babylonische Datierung im Pentateuch und das Alter des Priester-Kodex," VT 2 (1952) 334-342.   A.M. Honeyman, "The Occasion of Joseph's Temptation," VT 2 (1952) 85-87.   A. Jaubert, "Le Calendrier des Jubilés et de la Secte de Qumrân. Ses origines bibliques," VT 3 (1953) 250-264.   E.F. Sutcliffe, VT 3 (1953) 99-103.   T. Worden, VT 3 (1953) 281.   A. Jaubert, "Le calendrier des Jubilés et les jours liturgiques de la semaine," VT 7 (1957) 35-61.   J.B. Segal, "Intercalation and the Hebrew Calendar," VT 7 (1957) 250-307.   E.F. Sutcliffe, JSSt 3 (1958) 80-81.   E. Kutsch, "Der Kalender des Jubiläenbuches und das Alte und das Neue Testament," VT 11 (1961) 39-47.   J. Meysing, "The Biblical Chronology of the Patriarchs," CNFI 14 (1963) 22-25.   J. Finegan, *Handbook of Biblical Chronology* (1964).   J. Meysing, "Contribution à l'étude des Chronologies Bibliques. Technique de la composition des Chronologies Babyloniennes du déluge," RSR 39 (1965) 209-255.   C. Schedl, "Worte und Zahlen. Neuer Zugang zu den Genesisquellen," ZAW 77 (1965) 259-267.   F. Weinreb, *Der göttliche Bauplan der Welt. Der Sinn der Bibel nach der ältesten jüdischen Überlieferung* (1966).   J. Meysing, *La triple Chronologie diluvienne en fonction du symbolisme cosmique de la Bible:* Diss. Strassburg (1967).   N.J. Tromp, *Primitive Conceptions. . . ,* Bib Or 21 (1969) 60.   M.K. Wakeman, "The Biblical Earth Monster in the Cosmogonic Combat Myth," JBL 88 (1969) 313-320.   B.S. Childs, "A Traditiohistorical Study of the Reed Sea Tradition," VT 20 (1970) 406-418.   G. Morawe, "Erwägungen zu Gen 7:11 und 8:2. Ein Beitrag zur Überlieferungsgeschichte des priesterlichen Flutberichtes," *Theologische Versuche* III (1971) 31-52.

[7:11a]   7:6 (P) gives merely the six hundredth year of Noah's life as the date of the beginning of the flood. 7:11a (P) however introduces the precise dating of each stage of the flood even to the very day, and this is continued in 7:23; 8:3b, 4, 5, 13, 14. It is quite surprising that the stages are given with such precision for an event like the flood. The only other place in the Old Testament where something similar occurs is in the prophecy of Ezekiel which is chronologically close to the beginnings of the priestly writing. It is certain therefore that this must be a contribution of P himself and that it could not have been in the tradition he received. Moreover "the numbering can only be understood in the light of the Babylonian calendar"; "for the ancient Israelite calendar did not reckon the months by ordinals but gave each month its specific name" E. Auerbach, VT 2 (1952) 340-341.

The system of numbering has been widely discussed, and S. McEvenue has presented its main lines in *The Narrative Style of the Priestly Writer,* 1971, 54-59. His starting point is that K.D. Ilgen (1798) had already regarded the system of dating as an obvious characteristic of the priestly writing as have most exegetes down to the present. He takes issue with and rejects the thesis of R. Smend (*Die Erzählung des Hexateuch* 1912) that the chronology is the work of the final revision of the Pentateuch because "these dates are a structural feature in the priestly document," from the seven days of the creation of the world through the various eras which P describes right up to the death of Moses. McEvenue finds a similar chronological structure in Ezekiel and reckons that the sense of order, regularity and legality suggested by such a structure had a peculiar power of attraction among the exiles. McEvenue mentions the many attempts to explain the system of dating only in a survey of the literature from E. Bertheau (1878) through O. Fischer (1911) and A. Jepsen (1929) to J. Finegan (1964), J. Meysing (1967) and "a more fanciful investigation" by C. Schedl (1965) and F. Weinreb (1966).

A. Jaubert (1953) and E. Kutsch (1961) have studied the relationship of the dates to those in the book of Jubilees. Kutsch's point of departure is that "the chronological limits 17.II.600-27.II.601 mark the period of a year, as is generally acknowledged" p. 42. The Gk and Jubilees, despite their different dates, also want to indicate the period of a year (the Ethiopian Enoch does so explicitly). "P calculates . . . a year of $354 + 11 = 365$ days, i.e., P reckons the length of the flood as exactly a solar year" (E. Kutsch, p. 43). The months indicated by the numbers are for P lunar months. A. Jaubert's thesis that the solar calendar of the book of Jubilees is found also in the Old Testament is not relevant.

It is not possible to record and discuss here the many different theses on the chronology of the flood. A final word remains to be said on 8:13, 14, because the dates of the flood only acquire their real meaning from the conclusion, as we found too with the numerical system of Gen 5.

[**7:11b**] ביום הזה is a necessary transition because of the lengthy details in 11a; it is missing in the Vg. Similarly Gen 39:11, see A.M. Honeyman "The Occasion of Joseph's Temptation," VT 2 (1952) 85-87. The words are outside the rhythmic pattern which H. Gunkel established in 11b.

"All the fountains of the great deep burst forth." The verb is linked with "the waters" in many Old Testament passages: Hab 3:9; Ps 74:15; Is 48:21; also in Ex 14:16, 21; Is 63:12 at the dividing of the waters of the Reed Sea; cf. M.K. Wakeman JBL 88 (1969) 315. The concrete image is that of the bursting of a skin, Job 32:19. תהום רבה is a fixed phrase that occurs only in poetry: Is 51:10; Amos 7:4; Ps 78:15 (in this verse בקע occurs too). U. Cassuto notes that in classical Hebrew גדלה is used instead; this is a certain indication that תהום רבה is an ancient lapidary phrase bearing a definite sense such that it occurs only in poetic texts. (The noun מעין source, fountain is used with בקע also in Ps 74:15.) For תהום as a description of the subterranean waters cf. note on Gen 1:2; also N.J. Tromp, *Primitive Conceptions. . . ,* 1969. He insists that the ideas for "the deep" and its environment in the Old Testament had a qualitative rather than a local character. The waters of the deep are a negative element, shapelessness. "It is there before creation, and swallows it up again, never abandoning its own peculiar mode of existence, i.e., its inability to take any shape," M. Eliade (1954) 248.

". . . and the windows of heaven were opened." ארבות is also used of openings in the vault of heaven in 8:2; 2 Kings 7:2, 19; Is 24:18; Mal 3:10, and in all cases with the same verb פתח. The same description is found in the Ugaritic texts in the context of the construction of the palace of Baal: "The very verb *pth* and the nouns *hln* and *'urbt* are found in Tablet IIAB col VII lines 17f" (U. Cassuto ad loc.; cf. T. Worden VT 3 [1953] 281). What was catastrophic about the opening of the windows of the heavens was, as E. Sutcliffe shows (VT 3 [1953] 99ff.), that the waters flowed down without the intermediary function of the clouds. This, together with the eruption of the waters of the deep, meant an invasion of chaos into the created order; the flood assumed cosmic proportions. The destructive might of the flood waters is a frequent theme in the Psalms, especially Ps 93, cf. 18:16; 65:5-8; 69:1; 89:9. The cosmic dimensions of the flood do not occur again until the Apocalyptic: Is 24:19 uses the same words, Dan 9:26 suggests the same (J.P. Lewis, *A Study of the Interpretation of Noah*. . . . 1969, 8-9) and there is mention of it in the texts of Qumran (G. Vermès, *The Dead Sea Scrolls in English*, 1962, 73, The War Rule, col.x). It is significant that the Apocalyptic announcement of the end catastrophe is linked with a sentence like 7:11b of which the language is expressly mythical.

Excursus: *What Lay Before the Priestly Writer? (7:11b)*

P's method and intention in the flood narrative emerges very clearly in this verse. H. Gunkel had already noted the marked contrast between 11a and 11b (U. Cassuto has followed him here. . . .). "V. 11b stands in striking contrast to this very prosaic dating. . . . These words present the very ancient and highly poetic description of a primeval ocean which is situated in the deep beneath the earth. . . . In form, the words make a verse of seven beats . . . from the tradition that P used" (H. Gunkel ad loc.). Gunkel proposes the same for 8:2a, perhaps also 1b. If one takes 7:6b also (and this is but conjecture; it stands in a similar relation to 6a as does 11b to 11a), one has the following text that was at hand to P:

7:6b	:	And the flood (water) came upon the earth (water: the word which appears as a gloss could be the remainder of the second half verse)
11b	:	Then all the fountains of the great deep burst forth and the windows of heaven were opened
18a	:	And the waters swelled and increased greatly upon the earth
19b	:	and all the high mountains under heaven's expanse were covered
21	:	Then all flesh, all that moved upon the earth, and all humanity, perished
18b	:	but the ark floated upon the surface of the waters
8:1b	:	Then God made a wind blow over the earth so that the waters subsided
2a	:	And the fountains of the deep and the windows of heaven were closed. . . .

I have put between 7:11b and 8:2a those sentences which show no sign of the language or thought of P so as to give an idea of what was at hand to P. It does not matter whether one of these sentences may not belong there while another does. What really matters is to be well aware that P had a set piece before him which he reworked (as in Gen 1).

We can now determine more clearly the difference between what lay before P and the form which he gave it. H. Gunkel and U. Cassuto have seen correctly that what lay before P was in verse, i.e., it had been arranged in *parallelismus membrorum;* it was a poem. One can add further that it was a narrative poem; P made a detailed report out of it. H. Gunkel is correct when he says that 11a (in contrast to 11b) speaks like a chronicle, and that the pedantic precision that dates every step creates another genre. It is no longer a narrative of an event, but a process that has been put on record. P has constructed a report which is concerned only with giving a factual account of an event. It is significant that in the adaptation of the material the dating, which produces the new genre, is fixed within the life-span of Noah. It is the story of Noah that is told in such a way that what is peculiar to it (i.e., what makes it worth passing on) rests on what is peculiar to this man. He alone was the just one in a corrupt generation; with him alone was the covenant sealed that was to be the foundation of a new humanity. There is a purpose behind the dating of every stage of the flood. P wants to make out of the unified drama of the great flood, with its climax and resolution, a succession of events which are datable and which lead necessarily from the decision to destroy to the renewal of humanity on the day when the decision is changed, the new year, the day on which the covenant is sealed with humanity descended from Noah.

It is only now that we can see clearly that we have in the dating, which is directed to a goal and so has reshaped the material, a parallel to Gen 1. There we have the course of events from the 1st to the 7th day; here the course of a year, ending with the new year (see further on 8:13a).

The material at hand simply narrated the event of the flood and is close to J. We can easily review what P has added. First there is the dating 7:6, 11, 24; 8:3b, 4, 5a, 5b, 13a, 14, together with the details of measurement 7:20; then there is the precise record of animals and people in the ark 7:13-16, 21b (outside the ark); 8:1b, 16b, 18, 19. The large block 7:13-16 is particularly striking, consisting solely of an enumeration of the beings that go into the ark. P shows here what he is about. Third, there are the verbal sentences which are in fact simply repetitions of verbal sentences from the material at hand: "went into the ark" 8:13, 15, 16; 17a repeats 6b; 19a and 24 (the waters swelled) repeat 18a; 20b repeats 19b (the mountains were covered); 8:5 repeats 3b (the waters subsided). The only independent verbal sentence in the P account says that God remembered Noah (8:1). It acquires thereby a deeper meaning; the turning point of the flood lies with God. H. Gunkel conjectured that this sentence was part of the traditional material.

It must be emphasized yet again that there can be no question of a thorough reconstruction of the material at hand to P, not to speak of working out two literary layers. P has integrated the material in such a way as to render any such reconstruction impossible. I agree with H. Gunkel and U. Cassuto that one can recognize clearly the material at hand only in 7:11b and 8:2a. But that is sufficient basis for admitting a *Vorlage* and one can be reasonably certain of P's own contribution as distinct from what was at hand to him. This consists principally in a) the dating of the stages of the flood and b) the record of the animals and people preserved in the ark. One can be certain too about P's technique; the dating and recording have been inserted into the many repetitions of the verbal sentences (describing an action) from the *Vorlage*. But this is done with such skill and stylistic assurance that the account of the flood which P has given us has the effect of a complete unity.

[7:12]   In J, 12 followed by 16b so that 16b ". . . and Yahweh shut the door behind him" concludes the part "the coming of the flood" and 12 is the transition to the part "the effect of the flood": the effect on the ark, 17b, 23c, and all living beings outside the ark. The 40 days and nights of rain in v. 12 are, as has often been noted, in sharp contrast to the portrayal of the flood in 11b; the difference between the two descriptions is very noticeable here. This becomes even clearer when one takes into account the description in Gilg. XI: storm and hurricane rage for six days and six nights and drive the waters of the sea over the land in a gigantic flood. W. Zimmerli comments: "This description is not all that different from the Mesopotamian." This means that the description of the flood in Gilg. XI is closer to J's here than to P's. Both Gilg. XI and J describe natural phenomena, however different, which caused the flood because of their enormous dimensions; P describes a supra-natural, mythical-cosmic event. The comparison shows that there were obviously a number of variants about the immediate causes of the flood.

Literature: Gen 7:13-14: W. Baumgartner, *Ein Kapitel vom hebräischen Erzählungsstil,* FRLANT 19 (1932) 147-157.

[7:13-16a]   *The Entrance into the Ark According to P.*

P has obviously put special emphasis on this part; the entrance into the ark is portrayed with a fulness of detail and a studied solemnity of tone. One can understand this if one actualizes the beginning and the close of the priestly flood narrative. It begins with the genealogy where prominence is given to Noah's piety. It ends with the covenant which God seals with Noah and which is the basis of the world order in the era after the flood. From that beginning the drama rises to its climax in 7:13-16a, and descends to its conclusion: Noah, by entering the ark, obeys God's word of command, accomplishes thereby his own salvation or preservation, and renders possible the covenant which is the basis of the new order.

One can understand too the studied solemnity. P portrays here the entrance of the obedient, pious man into the place of salvation or preservation, a very reserved and distant hint of the entrance into the sanctuary, the place of salvation and preservation. The participation of every species of animal in this solemn procession reflects the same attitude that we have seen in Gen 1: all living beings belong together and the blessing holds for all.

The text of 13-16a is constructed with the utmost care. The sentence structure is dominated by a single verb that occurs four times: "They went in" 13, 15, 16. Apart from this, there is only one other finite verb, in the last sentence: God has "commanded" it. This structure reveals the purpose of the description. The entrance into the ark is portrayed as a great procession; the movement echoes out from the repetition of the verbs. Every living being, 15b, takes part in it, yet the movement is orderly, "two by two," 15a, and behind it is the word of God that orders it, 6:18. The text reports in solemn form the carrying out of a command of God, as the structure shows. This is a basic characteristic of the whole of the priestly work; cf. Comm. on 1:3, also K. Elliger, "Sinn und Ursprung der priesterlichen Geschichtserzählung," ZThK 49 (1952) 121-143 = ThB 32 (1966) 174-198 and S.E. McEvenue, op. cit., 61, n. 54. Peculiar to P in Gen 6-9 is that the command of God to enter the ark is at the same time that which effects salvation. Command and promise are bound together in 6:18-20, which corresponds to 7:13-16a, and so the entrance into the ark is continued in the exit from it which is followed by blessing and covenant. It is clear from the structure of the narrative as a whole that 7:13-16a forms the climax of the whole event.

[7:13] "On this very day." The study of S.E. McEvenue pp. 61-62 has thrown much light on the meaning of the entrance: בעצם היום הזה occurs only in priestly writing. It is used four times in P[G], each time for a day on which a divine command is carried out, Gen 7:13; 17:23, 26; Ex 12:41. P[S] uses the phrase three times of the feast of the Pasch, Ex 12:17, 51; Josh 5:11, in dependence on Ex 12:41. It seems to refer to a day of remembrance or a feast day; the Holiness Code also uses it for a feast day Lev 23:21, 28, 29, 30. The phrase ביום הזה

occurs only seven times in the Old Testament, four times in P, only in Gen 7:11 and Ex 19:1 in P[G], i.e., only at the beginning of the flood and at the arrival of Israel at Sinai. S. McEvenue explains the relationship of "on this day" in vv. 11 and 13 as follows: "both the flood and the entry took place on that solemn date . . . on this day of condemnation, on this same very day a festive salvation by entry" p. 62. U. Cassuto gives a very enlightening explanation of the irregular feminine of the number in combination with a feminine noun in the phrase "and the three wives of his sons": as in Job 1:4 (it is different in Job 1:2) it is a question of a definite group, not of three individuals.

Literature: Gen 7:14: W.M. Clark, "The Animal Series in the Primeval History," VT 18 (1968) 433-449. E. Kutsch, "Sehen und Bestimmen. Die Etymologie von בְּרִית," *Festschr. K. Galling* (1970) 165-178.

[7:14] H. Gunkel thinks that "the description of all living beings entering the ark on the same day is utterly unreal." For J. Skinner, it is "an example of P's love of the marvellous"; likewise many others. But such judgment is misplaced. P does not intend to give a realistic picture but to present an event which he can only describe as a self-contained unit like a procession; P is speaking theologically.

The detailed list of all the animals occurs at the three key points of P's flood narrative: the entry into the ark, 7:14, the death of all living beings outside the ark, 7:21, and the exit from the ark, 8:19; cf. W.M. Clark op. cit.

The last words of v. 14 are omitted in the Gk, and many exegetes follow it. But the MT is to be retained with U. Cassuto, W.M. Clark, S.E. McEvenue, and others. E. Kutsch comments on צפור that it is one of those substantives in the Old Testament for which no corresponding verb is attested; cf. Akk. *ṣaparu,* to be pointed, to have a high-pitched voice, to chirp (cf. *Festschr. K. Galling* 173).

[7:15] The emphatic שְׁנַיִם שְׁנַיִם in the middle of the verse excludes the number seven which occurs in J. Not only is the number of animals different in P, but also the description of the entrance into the ark. The second part of the verse "that had life in them" is a conscious echo of the creation of the animals.

Literature: Gen 7:16a: S.E. McEvenue, "Word and Fulfilment: A Stylistic Feature of the Priestly Writer," *Semitics* I (1970) 104-110.

[7:16a] There is a subtlety here. The suffix does not agree in number with the noun: "they went in as God had commanded him." The command was issued to one person only; the huge procession into the ark was the result of the command to one.

[7:16b] (J) The short sentence "and Yahweh shut the door behind him" was part of v. 7 in J and is parallel to 13-16 in P. Gilg. XI reads: "I boarded the ship and battened up the entrance." There is a great difference between these two descriptions. J can preserve the naive and primitive description that God himself shut the door from outside the ark; it is more important for him to mention God's care than to give a spiritual description of God which could run into difficulties.

[7:17a] The first sentence of v. 17 is the same as v. 6, apart from the addition "40 days." This sentence too has been resumed again by P (so H. Gunkel) after v. 6 has been complemented by the more precise dating in v. 11, and after the episode of the entrance 13-16. "40 days" is an addition in P from J showing that

R can understand the 40 days only as an episode within the longer time span of the flood in P (so J. Skinner). The Gk adds "and 40 nights," correcting the addition.

[7:17b]   (J) V. 17b continues v. 12. The description of the flood itself in J is very meager. After the entrance into the ark, 7:7, 16b, and the beginning of the flood, v. 12, there is mention only of the two effects, on the ark, v. 17b, and on the living beings outside the ark, vv. 22-23; then follows immediately the end of the flood, 8:6a, 2b, 3a. The effect of this one sentence, that the waters lifted up the ark so that it was high above the earth, is all the stronger. "The picture is simple, majestic" (F. Delitzsch). J's style is in evidence here; he limits himself to episodes. 17b consists of three very short verbal sentences, each of which brings further precision: "and the waters increased — and lifted up the ark — so that it was high above the earth." It is a scene in three parts; there are three pictures. Nothing more needs to be said.

[7:18-21]   P's portrayal of the flood is markedly different from J's. P dramatizes the event by repetitions and verbal emphasis; the description is voluble. This does not mean however that the flood is described in a succession of individual episodes; it is portrayed as a single event — the mounting of the waters. This is repeated four times in 7:18a, 19a, 20a, 24, and by its very monotony gives dramatic effect to the whole. There is another detail that enhances even further the effect of the mounting of the waters, namely that all the mountain peaks were covered, 19b and 20b. There follows in v. 21 the effect of the flood: all animals, listed according to their main groups, perish and at the end, in two words, "all humankind." The intention is unmistakable: P puts the whole emphasis on the majesty of God's judgment. The pervading sense is not one of horror but of awe. One thinks at once of the word כבוד and its associations, but P only uses it from the Exodus event on. The majesty of God who judges is described in a similar way in Ex 14; P says here that God is "glorified" in his work of judgment.

[7:18]   The association of the verbs גבר and רבה (actually "to become strong" and "to become great") is a sign of P's thought pattern. Just as God, by the power of his blessing, can make a person grow and become strong, so too can he make the flood grow and become strong so as to destroy life. All power of increase and strength is for P the power of God. The parallel is attested to by the occurrence of the progressive מאד מאד both here and in the blessing in 17:2, 6, 20.

    While J describes the event, 17b, P portrays the state, 18b, a typical difference. The phrase "upon the surface of the waters" echoes Gen 1:2; and there is many an echo of Gen 1:1-2:4a in the passage 7:17a, 18-21, 24 (cf. S.E. McEvenue).

[7:19]   The theme of 18a is repeated and developed with little variation by what follows: all the mountains were covered. This has occasioned the following, rather restrictive, remark from F. Delitzsch: "It seems here that we are to imagine that the summits of the Himalayas and the Cordilleras were covered. But the statement is to be understood according to the limited geographical perspective of the time." J. Skinner objects: "P not only asserts the universality of the flood, but so to speak proves it by giving the exact height of the waters above the highest mountains." P's intention however is only to be understood in the context of the general thrust of the passage 7:17a, 18-21, 24; he is concerned only with the majesty of God's action. This is what is presented with the rising of the flood over the highest mountains.

[7:20]   "Fifteen cubits above"; an abstract reckoning. The concrete would be, "Fifteen cubits above the highest mountain." H. Gunkel commands agreement when he reads the verse together with 8:4: the ark drew fifteen cubits of water and so comes to rest at once as the waters subside. The Gk saw the difficulty and added הגבהים to ההרים, as in v. 19; this could then be understood in a superlative sense. Likewise the Gk alters גברו to גבהו, which suit better. The alterations in the Gk indicate that the dimension in v. 20 is probably a subsequent addition in the MT; it is stylistically out of harmony with what has preceded, and belongs to a later layer in P.

[7:21]   For the numbering of the animals, see 7:14. The verb ויגוע at the beginning of this verse echoes the same verb at the end of 6:17; what was announced there is accomplished here. A. Dillmann comments that כל־בשׂר is restricted to the animals; so too most interpreters. But if 7:21 is a deliberate echo of 6:17, and the same verb has "all flesh" as its object, then one must concede that the phrase has the same meaning as in 6:17, where it embraces both humans and the animals (so too A.R. Hulst). The participle הרמשׂ, which is striking as an attribute of כל־בשׂר, would deliberately include humans too: every living being that moves on the earth perishes.

[7:24]   The theme of the increasing might of the flood is there again at the end of the passage. It is enhanced by the statement of time — one hundred and fifty days long. In a flood of such monstrous proportion the subsiding of the waters follows immediately on their mounting; this is a further sign that the statement of time is contrived.

   Literature: Gen 7:22: J. Hoftijzer, "Notae Aramaicae, II," VT 9 (1959) 312-318.   T.C. Mitchell, "The OT Usage of Nešāmâ," VT 11 (1961) 177-187.

[7:22-23]   (J) One of the effects of the flood in J is reported in 7:17b (parallel to 18b in P), the other in 22-23: the destruction of every living being. A comparison with P reveals a very striking difference here; P puts the emphasis on the mounting of the flood (he takes seven lines, J takes one), J on the destruction of every living being, in accord with the introduction, 6:5-8. P, in his description of this human catastrophe, is concerned essentially with the majesty of God who destroys (cf. Comm. on 7:17-21, 24), J much more with humanity and its fate. Accordingly, J is more detailed than P here (R has also preserved this). P is content to report the demise of humans and the animals neutrally, J adds the scandalous, personal phrase: "so he wiped out. . . ."

[7:22]   E. Speiser turns the phrase which consists of three nouns side-by-side by: "the faintest breath of life." This would have to be supported by parallels, and there are none (A. Dillmann). Gunkel's explanation still holds: "the surprising phrase is a composition of נשמת חיים (J, 2:7) and רוח חיים (P, 7:15)." The sentence belongs clearly to J; רוח is a subsequent addition, even though we can no longer see the reason for it (harmonizing?). Its omission in the Gk and the Vg confirms this. The מן in מכל is explicative, to be turned by something like "that is," so U. Cassuto ad loc. and J. Hoftijzer, who points out that the same form occurs often in Arabic. The two parts of the sentence determine further "every living being": all that breathes — all that lives on the dry land. Perhaps the second qualification is meant to limit the first, with the exception of the water animals.

[7:23] The verb at the beginning is still usually understood as an abbreviated imperfect qal, different from 23b, where niphal is used (U. Cassuto); cf. Comm. on 6:4 and 7:4. The difference is deliberate; v. 22 reports the death of every living being, v. 23a speaks of the one who destroyed them. The natural sequence would be the reverse; H. Gunkel proposes to reconstruct the original text of J: 23a, 22, 23c. J. Skinner and others agree.

The enumeration in 23b, which corresponds word for word to 6:7, is, like the latter addition, in conflict with v. 22. The passage ends: "only Noah was left and what was with him in the ark." H. Gunkel comments: "The fearful catastrophe is reported with great composure: no horror at the demise of the whole of humankind." But that is not so certain when one compares J and P. J, in his short account of the flood itself, puts the emphasis on vv. 22-23, and, in contrast to P, uses the phrase, "he wiped out." One can sense here, in however reserved a way, the horror at the work of destruction. The last sentence wants to say that only this tiny remnant survived. The word "remnant," as in the announcement of the judgment in Amos 3:12, points to the gigantic scale of the destruction: "only a tiny point appears on the face of the terrible waters" (U. Cassuto).

Literature: Gen 8:1-22: J. Dahse, "Textkritische Studien, I. 3. Die Dauer der Sintflut," ZAW 28 (1908) 7-10. J.R. Porter, "The Pentateuch and the Triennial Lectionary Cycle: An Examination of a Recent Theory," *Essays presented to Prof. S.H. Hooke* (1963) 163-174.

[8:1-22]   The End of the Flood.

P describes the conclusion of the flood in detail 8:1-5 (less 2b, 3a) 13a, 14, while J takes only one verse, 2b, 3a. J adds the episode of the birds which concludes by confirming that the earth is dry once more, 13b. Parallel to this are vv. 13a, 14 (P), the command to leave the ark followed by its execution, 8:15-19 (P). J concludes the flood narrative with the sacrifice of Noah and the promise of God, 8:20-22; P's parallel is the detailed conclusion of blessing and covenant, 9:1-17.

[8:1-5; 13-14] P describes the end of the flood in three scenes: the cessation of the flood, the command to leave and its execution, and the long speech of God to Noah in Gen 9. The first scene begins with God's merciful remembrance of Noah, 8:1 and ends by stating that the earth is dry again 13a, 14. R has inserted the episode of the birds from J, vv. 6-12, before the conclusion (the drying up of the earth). The only other verses from J are at the beginning (2b) and at the end (13b).

The scene 8:1-5, 13-14 in P is the counterpart to 7:17-21, 24; a decrescendo balances the crescendo. The mounting of the flood is the theme of 7:17-21, 24, its subsiding the theme of 8:1-5, 13-14. J's division is: the coming of the flood — the length and effect of the flood — the cessation of the flood. P on the other hand divides: the coming of the flood — the mounting and effect of the flood — the subsiding of the flood — the cessation of the flood. P builds a tension into the course of the flood by means of the mounting and subsiding of the waters. The climax occurs with 8:1: "Then God thought of Noah. . . ." There is a tension in J too, but of a different kind. It is the experiment with the birds which describes the tension in those who are waiting to be liberated. The difference is very significant for the different conceptions of the flood event in J and P.

It is significant for P too that the mounting of the flood in 7:17-21, 24 is described objectively as a natural phenomenon: "Then the flood came . . . the waters mounted. . . ." The subsiding of the waters on the other hand is an act of God: "Then God thought of Noah . . . and God made a wind blow. . . ." There is theological reflection here which makes a deliberate distinction between the indirect action of God in the catastrophe and his direct action in saving; it is the work of God who is both distant and near. Another notable characteristic is the accumulation of dates in 8:1-5, 13-14. There are chronological details in 8:3b, 4, 5a, 5b, 13a, 14. There is no other place in the description of the flood where they occur in such immediate succession as here. The accumulation of dates in 8:1-5, 13-14 leads to the goal at which the system of dating aimed — the smooth, round number in 8:13a, not that in 8:14 (see below).

Literature: Gen 8:1: D. Lys, "Alchimie du verbe et démythisation. (Note sur l'humour biblique)," *Hommage à W. Vischer* (1960) 114-126. P.A.H. de Boer, "Gedenken und Gedächtnis in der Welt des Alten Testaments," *Franz Delitzsch-Vorlesung* 1960 (1962) 5-76 esp. 37-38. B.S. Childs, *Memory and Tradition in Israel,* SBT 37 (1962). O. Haggenmüller, "Erinnern und Vergessen Gottes und der Menschen (zkr - škh)," BiLe 3 (1962) 1-15. W. Schottroff, *'Gedenken' im Alten Orient und im Alten Testament,* WMANT 15 (1964). Th.C. Vriezen, "Enkele Opmerkingen over het Woordonderzoek," *Schrift en Uitleg* (1970) 237-247.

[8:1] "Then God thought of Noah." The Hebrew is one of those verbs typical of this context, זכר, which describes a process of thought and action, bridging the internal and external (see the studies of P.A.H. de Boer, W. Schottroff, B.S. Childs, and the comments by Th.C. Vriezen and O Haggenmüller). The meaning intended here becomes clear from Gen 30:22: "Then God remembered Rachel and listened to her prayer." There is an exact parallel in P in Gen 19:29 where the verb זכר is used to describe the saving of one person from the destruction of Sodom. "Remember" in this context implies mercy toward the one threatened with death. At the same time it introduces the saving action (so too Ex 2:24). God's merciful remembrance "extends in a touching way even to the animals in the ark" (H. Holzinger); some interpreters refer to Jonah 4:11.

The remembrance takes effect in an action; God made a wind blow over the earth so that the waters subsided. It is common experience that the wind dries moist or wet earth quickly; but it is not particularly apt here. "It is very naive to suppose that the wind dries out the whole earth in five months" (O. Procksch). But a remark like this does not do justice to the text. It is to be noted that the numbers and measures are the work of P, while the sentence that describes the drying out of the earth by the wind was part of the traditional material where it had a meaning appropriate to the context (so too H. Gunkel). The verb שכך, "subside," also accords with this in that it does not say that the waters all disappear; it is rare, only in Num 17:20 (P) and Esther 2:1; 7:10 (the text of Jer 5:26 is uncertain), and probably belongs to the tradition at hand.

Literature: Gen 8:2: T.J. Jones, *Quelle, Brunnen und Zisterne im Alten Testament* (1928). R. Kilian, "Gen I,2. . . ," VT (1966) 430. G. Morawe, *Theologische Versuche III* (1971) 31-52.

[8:2a] H. Holzinger comments: "Actually the order 2a, 1b would be more correct'' (so too A. Dillmann, J. Skinner, H. Gunkel and others). H. Gunkel has noted that 8:2a, corresponding to the rhythmic 7:11b, is also rhythmic; a verb has probably fallen out at the end. So the explanation which would put 2a before 1b is misleading. It is improbable too because the order of the verses in P is not disturbed anywhere else (in contrast to J). It is more likely that vv. 1b and 2a belong originally to two different traditions about the way in which the flood waters abated and have been joined together here. On the words used, see Comm. on 7:11.

[8:2b] J sums up the end of the flood very briefly. One must allow for the possibility of inversions because these two sentences have been inserted into the P account by R. Many commentators have observed that 8:2b does not follow smoothly on 7:22-23. A number (A. Dillmann, K. Budde, H. Gunkel, J. Skinner, O. Procksch) solved the difficulty by proposing that the chronological detail of v. 6: "at the end of 40 days Noah. . . ." be read before 2b. But the proposal is countered because 8:2b is the parallel to 7:11 (beginning of the rain — end of the rain) and the same detail is found there.

Literature: Gen 8:3: W.R. Smith, *Lectures on the Religion of the Semites. 1st Series* (1894; 1927³) 417.

[8:3a] J is content with the brief detail of cause and effect; the rain from heaven was stopped and the waters gradually receded. Once again the difference from P is unmistakable; here there is narrative, while the chronological details at each stage as the flood recedes sound a contrived note.

[8:3b] The intention can only be to link v. 3b with the one hundred and fifty days of 7:24; but in that case one expects the article before the number. Because מקצה refers for the most part to place whilst מקץ is always temporal (H. Holzinger) — Jer 50:26 is an exception — and the Sam reads מקץ, the text is certainly to be read as מקץ החמשים (J. Skinner and others). On the day that the causes cease, the waters abate.

Literature: Gen 8:4: A. Sanda, "Untersuchungen zur Kunde des Alten Orients: Ararat," MVG 7 (1902) 14-38. J. Döller, "Ararat und Urartu," BZ 1 (1903) 349-350. A. Sanda, "Nochmals Ararat und Urartu," BZ 2 (1904) 113-121. E. Nestle, "Die Auffindung der Arche Noä durch Jakob von Nisibis," ZKG 30 (1906) 241-243. A. Heidel, *The Gilgamesh Epic.* . . . (1946); 1963⁴) esp. 250-251. A. Parrot, *The Flood and Noah's Ark* (1955). J. van Ooteghem, "Le Déluge d'après Ovid," EtCl 25 (1957) 444-448. L. Delekat, "Die syropalästinische Jesaja-Übersetzung," ZAW 71 (1959) 165-201, esp. 188. R. Gordis, "Job XL 29 - An Additional Note," VT 14 (1964) 491-494. J.P. Lewis, *A Study of the Interpretation of Noah.* . . . (1968) 94. J.P. Brown, "The Mediterranean Vocabulary of the Vine," VT 19 (1969) 146-170; 148. A.R. Hulst, "De betekenis van het woord menūḥā," *Schrift en Uitleg* (1970) 62-78.

[8:4] The text gives the impression that the ark came to rest on Mt Ararat immediately as the flood waters began to recede. This conforms with the detail in 7:20 that the waters rose fifteen cubits above the highest peak. If the ark, thirty cubits high, drew fifteen cubits of water and was immediately above the highest peak at this moment, then this was possible. It becomes very clear here how contrived are the numbers: "a very ingenious theory" (H. Gunkel). Before P put the story at hand to him into the numerical framework, it simply said that the ark came to rest on Mt Ararat after the waters receded (on the verb cf. A.R. Hulst, op. cit.). J. Skinner wants to ascribe v. 4, minus the date, to J; the reason which he alleges can well be relevant if one presumes that here P is taking his stand on older material.

Excursus: *The Landing of the Ark on Ararat*

The landing on a mountain is one of the oldest and most widespread elements of the universal flood story. The words of 8:4: "on the mountains (of the land) of Ararat" show that the tradition had traveled a long way. A first sign of this is the vague indication of place which refers not to a particular mountain but to the country where this mountain lies (Ararat is described as a country in 2 Kings 19:37; Is 37:38; as a kingdom in Is 51:27; Akk. Urartu, Bab. Urashtu, mountain country to the west of the Tigris. H. Gunkel: "the country of Armenia between Lakes Van and Urmia"). A second sign is that the place of landing has no point of contact with the group of people where the story was told. "In the old traditions it is naturally a particular mountain and area, a place which was holy to those living round about" H. Gunkel ad loc.

In primitive flood stories the mountain is very often the place where the survivors were saved without any technical means; they fled to the mountain peak which the waters had not reached. It was only at a later stage of development that the story tells of a vessel that lands on a mountain. The narrative often has an etiological conclusion in this context. Either the mountain peak becomes a holy place or the narrative says that the remains of the ship are still to be found there, or there are traces of the footprints of those who were saved from the flood. All these elements are gathered together in the account of Nicholas of Damascus: "There is above Minyas in Armenia a great mountain called Baris, to which, as the story goes, many people fled for refuge in the flood and were saved. They say too that a certain man, floating in an ark, grounded on the summit, and that remains of the timbers were preserved for a long time" (A. Parrot, p. 62). The formulation of 8:4 is one of the most certain signs that the tradition of the flood narrative in P has long since been detached from the place where it was originally told, and has taken the final form in which we now have it only after a long journey. The name Ararat is in a very different frame of reference when, in the Israelite story, it is the name of the mountains where the vessel landed which saved Noah and his family: at the time when the story took shape, the mountains of the country of Ararat must have been considered the highest mountains then known in the area (J. Skinner). This is an exact parallel to the Indian flood stories where the place of landing is the Himalayas.

Traditions About the Place of the Landing.

This is treated in detail in the commentaries of F. Delitzsch, A. Dillmann, J. Skinner, U. Cassuto; see also A. Heidel, and A. Parrot. At the end of his excursus U. Cassuto says: "None of the identifications of the biblical Ararat with a specific mountain has any basis in the scriptural text." Gilg. XI gives Niṣir as the mountain of the landing, mentioned also in the annals of Ashurnasirpal II of Assyria, "about 450km north of Shuruppka in modern Kurdistan" (A. Schott-von Soden, 91). This is probably the mountain Pir Oman Gudrun, south of the lower Zab, and much further south than the biblical place. Berossos repeats another Babylonian tradition, the mountains of Kurds. So too the Peshitta and the Targum Onkelos: "On the mountains of Qardu"; Targum ps-Jonathan: "On the mountains of Qardun." (See for details J.P. Lewis op. cit. p. 94.) These mountains probably correspond to Jebel-Iudi, south of Lake Van, which the inhabitants of the area regard as the landing place of Noah's ark; it is also mentioned as such in the Koran. The book of Jubilees mentions Mt Lubar, 5:28; 7:1, and this has been taken up by others; Nicholas of Damascus: Baris.

This tendency to name a particular mountain has led to reading the distributive plural in 8:4 (cf. R. Gordis VT 14 [1964] 492f.) as a singular, designating it as the highest mountain in Armenia, and transferring to it the biblical name of Ararat: great Ararat

(Turkish büyük Agri Dag, Persian Kuh-i-nuḥ, Noah's mountain), 5156 m., and small Ararat, 3914 m. high. One may refer here to the detailed explanation of F. Delitzsch who describes the mountains precisely and adds: "No place in the old continent is . . . so centrally situated . . . in the middle of the longest line of distribution of the Caucasian race, in the middle of the great land lines of old, between the Cape of Good Hope and the Bering Straits."

One can read in A. Parrot, pp. 61-67, how, despite the biblical account which does not mention any particular mountain, there is no end to enterprises to find the ark or its remains, and how such enterprises always find credibility.

[8:5] V. 4, which speaks of the ark, is set between two verses, both of which speak of the receding of the flood. 5a says the same as 3b, apart from the details of time, 5b notes that the flood continues to recede: the tops of the mountains become visible. J. Skinner remarks correctly that the statement of v. 5 is really incompatible with v. 4. According to v. 4, on the 17th day of the 7th month, at least one mountain peak was visible, while according to v. 5 "the peaks of the mountains" only became visible on the first day of the 10th month. H. Holzinger's explanation does not help much: "The mountain where the ark landed is thought of as incomparably higher than the others." If that were meant, then there should be some indication of it in v. 5: the other mountains, or such like. The only possible explanation is from the history of the tradition. It was P who first impressed the system of numbers on the text; the sentence in v. 4 has been taken over from the tradition without alteration. It becomes even clearer now that the mounting tension of the narrative and its resolution — the rising of the waters and their recession — in Gen 7 and 8 together with the numbers which describe the stages, is the work of P. This was not in the traditional material which was much simpler. For the construction, cf. Ges-K § 113c.u. The reappearance of the mountain peaks recalls again the creation, especially 1:9.

Literature: Gen 8:6-12: W.O.E. Oesterley, "The Dove with the Olive-leaf (Gen VIII 8-11)," ExpT 18 (1906/1907) 377-378.   J. Dahse, "Die Aussendung der Vögel Gen 8:6-12," ZAW 28 (1908) 5-7.   K. Knortz, *Die Vögel in Geschichte, Sage, Brauch und Literatur* (1913).   A. Schulz, "Drei Anmerkungen zur Genesis (8:7-12; 23:3ss; 50:26)," ZAW 59 (1943) 184-188.   H. Heras, "The 'Crow' of Noe," CBQ 10 (1948) 131-139.   M.V. David, "L'épisode des oiseaux dans les récits du déluge," VT 7 (1957) 189-190.   C.H. Gordon, *Introduction to OT Times* (1953).

[8:6-12] The Sending Out of the Birds.

The determination of time: It has already been said on 8:2b (J) that the first words of v. 6: "At the end of 40 days. . . ." originally preceded v. 2b in J and so fixed the time when the rain stopped. There is place then for another indication of time in v. 6 to which one concludes from the "another seven days" in v. 10. The beginning of v. 6 therefore must have said that Noah waited seven days. Many conjecture that the settling of the ark on the mountain between 2b and 6 has yielded to P. The meaning would be that he waited seven days after the ark had settled. Gilg. XI 141-145 has a period of seven days before the sending out of the birds in the same place, following the landing on Mt Nisir: "When the 7th day arrived, I sent forth and set free a dove," 1.145.

The Structure of the Episode of the Birds in J.

It has often been noted (J. Wellhausen, H. Gunkel) that the sending out of the raven in v. 7 disturbs the balance of the scene in J: the dove is sent out three times, and on the third occasion achieves the goal of v. 8b. The conclusion is drawn that v. 7 belongs to P (F. Delitzsch, O. Procksch and G. von Rad following him), or that it is a later addition (A. Dillmann, W. Zimmerli) or a variant of J (H. Holzinger). "The verse must belong to another recension" (H. Gunkel). A comparison with the many variants of the motif in the pre-history of the flood narrative shows that the sequence of three is part of the structure of the episode; either one bird (or animal) is sent out three times, or three different animals are sent out (in Gilg. a dove, a swallow, a raven). The stylistic device of the mounting of tension is also part of the episode (H. Gunkel); it is only the third attempt that succeeds. One can be certain then with regard to the text of 8:6-12, that (a) there were only three experiments by Noah, each with the dove, in an older form of the episode, (b) v. 7 is the fragment of a variant. We have already noted on a number of occasions that J tends to preserve narrative variants in such a way as to resume them into the version he has adopted by way of hint or allusion (e.g., the variant of the tree of life in 3:22-23). The older form of the episode has the following structure:

(the Ark comes to rest)

I.

8:6, 8a:	After 7 days Noah opens a window and sends out a dove
8b:	The purpose of sending out the dove
9a:	The dove finds no resting place and returns to the ark
9b:	The water still covers the earth
9c:	The dove is taken back into the ark

II.

8:6, 10:	After waiting another 7 days Noah sends the dove out again
11a:	The dove returns at evening with a fresh olive leaf
11b:	So Noah knew. . . .

III.

12a:	He waited yet another 7 days. . . . and again he sent out. . . .
12b:	The dove does not come back
13b:	Noah removes the hatch from the ark. . . .

The three attempts (6-9: 10-11: 12, 13b) are each divided into three acts: the sending out — what the dove does — the consequence. The first act is the same in all three attempts. The mounting of the tension is made possible by the span of seven days which spaces the attempts chronologically. The second act introduces variation: the dove does something different each time. The difference in what the bird does entails different conclusions. In the first act it is simply that the water still covers the earth, in the second Noah "knows" something, in the third Noah acts. Corresponding to לראות in v. 8 there is now a וידע: the goal of the experiment has been reached.

This is a standard example of early narrative art. An event is described in such a way that, grammatically, each of its elements is covered by a self-contained sentence; narrative and the event narrated are in complete parallelism. The structure of the narrative corresponds to the structure of buildings in earlier times when the stones were heaped on each other without any joining so as to form a whole. The scene is describing an attempt or experiment. Throughout the whole of the narrative P is emphasizing the two sides of God's majestic action. Noah is always and at every step the obedient one. In P it is a word of God (8:15) that reveals to Noah what in J he discovers by experiment; this is a very significant difference. In J, Noah is the obedient one and at the same time the one who waits and longs for salvation and liberation from the ark; he is more human than the Noah of P. The episode of the birds then is a description of what is typically human; this way of acting is basic to human beings. The experiment or trial has its proper or original setting in a situation such as this, where a person is in danger, threatened, in a crisis, not in a situation where existence is assured and investigation can be carried out.

It is no chance either that the experiment is carried out with a living being and not with dead matter. The first great achievements in human civilization are those which are the result of experiments with plants and animals. Noah's experiment with the dove is in the broad context of making use of the animals. There is a parallel which many interpreters quote: Pliny says of the inhabitants of India: "... but they carry birds with them, sending them out quite often, and following the course of their flight as they make for land" (quoted by F. Tuch, A. Dillmann). "It was an old maritime custom, indispensable to an age that did not have the compass, to bring birds and let them loose on the high seas so as to be able to follow the course of their flight to land" (H. Usener, *Sintflutsagen* 254, quoted by H. Gunkel). Commentators often say or presume that this practice was the basis of Gen 8:6-12 or explains it. The history of civilization reverses the position: the maritime custom is a result of a crisis situation. The episode of the birds in the flood narrative therefore explains the origin of the maritime custom.

The Episode of the Birds: the Pre-History of the Motif.

We have referred above to the extraordinarily rich and widespread pre-history of the motif and have sketched its main lines. The following are the conclusions: (1) the sending out of animals is part of the pattern of many forms of the flood narrative both in primitive and high cultures; (2) the purpose is for the most part the same as in Gen 8:6-12, and the animals mentioned most often are the dove and the raven (crow); (3) the experiment often runs to three acts.

There were other, and probably earlier, variants in which an animal brought up some of the surface of the earth from below the flood so that the ship could land. Magic is here side-by-side with rational experiment. The rich pre-history of the motif necessitates a revision of the common opinion that the event narrated in Gen 8:6-12 is in itself the work of J. It is fairly certain that the event was part of the tradition at hand to J and that he only gave it the present narrative form. However, it is questionable whether one can agree with the explanation of H. Gunkel which many have accepted: "The purpose of the episode is to describe Noah's great wisdom." "Noah," who bears another name in other flood narratives, is rather the human being who longs for the firm land and liberation from confinement and who turns to experiment so as to be free. The episode in 8:6-12 is to be seen in close relationship to 4:17-25: humans, created by God,

446

have received a dynamic power which makes progress and new achievements possible. Something further can be done here: people can try to put animals and their instincts at their service in a crisis situation. One recalls Gen 2:19-20. One can of course describe the experiment as wisdom; but it is not the wisdom of a historical person. It is the wisdom of human beings as God created them who, when threatened, can always discover and put to use something new.

It should be noted that the sending out of the birds both in J and in the whole pre-history of the motif does not bring about salvation; it only indicates the moment when the ark can be left. Salvation is not effected by the knowledge acquired but only by the mighty one who made the flood come and who makes it end. Human potential is circumscribed within a limit where God alone is the savior.

[8:6] It has been shown that originally v. 6a preceded 2b in J. The work of R has caused the coming to rest of the ark to drop out as well as the detail to be inferred from v. 10, which is in the same place in Gilg. XI, namely that Noah waited seven days after the ark had come to rest before sending out the dove. The אשר עמה at the end of the sentence is perhaps an indication that J too had described briefly the building of the ark and had mentioned the "window" (H. Gunkel). Gilg. XI 135 reads: "I opened a hatch, and light fell upon my face."

Literature: Gen 8:7: O. Keller, "Rabe und Krähe im Altertum: 1. *Jahrbericht des wissenschaftlichen Vereins für Volkskunde und Linguistik in Prag* (1893). J. Goettsberger, "יצוא ושוב in Genesis 8:7," BZ 6 (1908) 113-116. J.A. Loader. "Die Vorstellung der Dunkelheit in der Wurzel 'rb/'rp: POS 9, VIII," *Essays in Honour of A. van Selms* (1971).

The Sending Out of the Raven

[8:7] The Gk provides v. 7 with an obelisk, indicating that it has been noted that the verse has dropped out in the history of the text. J. Dahse, op. cit., deals with the question in detail and concludes properly to a variant in which three different birds were sent out, as in Gilg. XI (what is said about the raven in Gilg. XI 153-154 is similar to 8:7). The definite article with the raven is an indication of the species, like "the" fox or "the" hare in the tale; other examples in the Old Testament are 1 Sam 17:35; 1 Kings 20:36; Amos 5:19. For the construction cf. J. Goettsberger. The Gk adds: "and did not come back" after v. 8. U. Cassuto makes much of the contrast between the raven and the dove, quoting the rabbinic literature; it is of special importance for him that the dove was a clean bird and the raven unclean. But it is questionable if this is the intention of the text, particularly if v. 7 is part of a variant of 8:6-12. F. Delitzsch comments on the result of the sending out of the raven: "It was a good sign that it did not come back." This holds also for Gilg. XI 153-154 where the raven is the third bird that is sent out, and the disembarkation from the ship follows at once. It can only be meant as an attempt which did not succeed in the present state of the text of 8:6-12: "It told him (Noah) nothing," U. Cassuto.

Literature: Gen 8:8: R. Bach, "Bauen und Pflanzen," *Festschr. G. von Rad* (1961) 7-32.

[8:8] This verse gives the purpose of the sending out; it shows that this was originally the account of the first sending. The bird which is set free can see whereas the man shut up in the ark cannot. The object of the experiment is to say that the bird can communicate in some way to the man what it has seen. It is not clear at the start how this happens; it can only be the result of several experiments.

[8:9] The first sentence of v. 9 is almost a verbal parallel to Gilg. XI 151: "Since no resting place for her was visible, she turned round." It is possible that מנוח is a play on נח, though the echo need not be deliberate. O. Procksch writes: "כף is the crooked hand or the surface of the foot." The addition "for the sole of its foot," over against Gilg. XI 151, means: not even the tiniest resting place.

The reason why the dove returned: "because there was still water over the whole earth," is at the same time the result of the first experiment.

The last part of the verse, which describes how Noah took the dove back into the ark, 9c, is the only deliberate development of the otherwise fixed pattern of the three stages of the experiment. There must be a special reason for this. Reference is often made to the charm of the picture, e.g., J. Skinner: "The description of the return and admission of the dove is unsurpassed even in the Yahwistic document for tenderness and beauty of imagination." But the aesthetic aspect is not enough. The particular reason for this delightful addition lies in what the narrator wants to say here: the pre-supposition for the success of the experiment, to put the vision of the bird at the service of the vision of humans, is a relationship of trust between animals and humans. The bird comes back to the place where it knows that it is safe. This little note confirms what was said of the relationship between humans and the animals in the comments on 1:26-28 and 2:19-20; it rests on the fact that both are creatures of God. This beautiful and tender description reflects the experience of this mutual relationship.

On the "stretching out of the hand" cf. P. Humbert, "Étendre la main" (Note de lexicographie hébraique)," VT 12 (1962) 383-395.

[8:10] The verb ויחל is to be understood either as the hiph. of חול, or as the piel of יחל (H. Gunkel); or one should read וייחל as in v. 12 (J. Skinner, O. Procksch and others). In any case the meaning is clear.

Literature: Gen 8:11: S. Speier, "Alttestamentliche Wortforschung: Tārāf, Gen 8:11," ThZ 2 (1946) 153-154. K. Galling, "Zur Deutung des Ortsnamens טרפל = Tripolis in Syrien," VT 4 (1954) 418-422, esp. 420. F. Heiler, *Erscheinungsformen...*, (1961) 168-170. J.J. Scullion, JBL 87 (1968) 297-298. J.R. Wilch, *Time and Event. An Exegetical Study of the Use of ʿēth in the OT in Comparison to Other Temporal Expressions in Clarification to the Concept of Time* (1969).

[8:11] The episode of the dove reaches its climax here; the first two sentences are the lead up, the third is the culmination. The scene is portrayed in almost rhythmic language (as is so often the case in Genesis at the climax of a narrative). The first two sentences have four syllabic stresses, the third sentence three lots of two.

The dove came back to Noah in the evening; "to him," once more as in v. 9 — at the time therefore when birds are making for their nests. This little note speaks for itself (on the temporal use of ל see J.J. Scullion, above; on עֵת, J.R. Wilch). "And see: a fresh olive leaf (or twig from an olive tree) in its beak!" Deliberately and adroitly the narrative tells how the "dumb creature" can bring a message: "a harbinger of peace" (U. Cassuto), as if it understood how much this message meant. Once again this would be impossible unless one presumed a relationship of trust between human and animal. טרף "freshly plucked," from Arabic *ṭaruta;* see L. Köhler, *Lexikon,* and K. Galling: "The word *ṭārāf* = fresh should exclude the possibility that this leaf had survived the flood'' (see above); also S. Speier. The last sentence gives the conclusion: Noah knew. . . .: "For the Hebrew knowledge was above all empirical and experiential," J. Scullion, p. 297. The experiment has been successful; Noah now knows what he had to know.

[8:12] The dove is sent out a third time; this only confirms and assures the result and the conclusion drawn in v. 11. The dove does not come back to Noah; it has a resting place on earth once more and enjoys freedom. By not returning it proclaims this freedom to those who are still shut up in the ark. They can now follow it.

Literature: Gen 8:13-19: W.B. Kristensen, *De Rijkdom der Aarche in Mythe en Kultus: Meddedeelingen der Nederlandsche Akademie van Wetenschappen Afd Letterkunde* (1942). H. Cazelles, "Sur les origines du calendrier du Jubilés," Bib 43 (1962) 202-216, Note by E. Vogt. G. Vajda, "Fragments d'un Commentaire Judéo-Arabe sur le livre d'Isaïe," VT 13 (1963) 208-224, 212. B. Porten-U. Rappaport, "Poetic Structure in Genesis IX 7," VT 21 (1971) 363-369.

[8:13b] V. 13b follows immediately on v. 12 in J: Noah has found out what he wanted; now he can act on it. The sentence is typical of J's narrative style; he often uses the phrase וירא והנה. It describes here the moment which resolves the tension built into the self-contained episode of the birds. When Noah removes the hatch from the ark (it will have been mentioned in J's description of the building of the ark which has not been preserved) a further tension is resolved. Noah looks out, and behold — the surface of the earth is dry! These simple words describe how Noah realized how he was saved or liberated. Noah looks out and finds the earth safe again. The way is opened to new life.

But it is not only the episode of the birds that is closed; this is part of the larger whole. The course of events which began in 7:10 with the coming of the flood and spans everything in between is also closed: the flood is over. The structure of the narrative now requires something further, corresponding to what went before 7:10, the decision of God to destroy humanity. The appropriate conclusion follows in 8:20-22 in J. It is probable that J contained a short account of Noah and the others leaving the ark which has been left out in favor of P, 8:14-19.

[8:13a, 14-19] The End of the Flood in P.

The difference between v. 13a (P) and v. 13b (J) is most significant: one narrates that the earth is now dry, the other reports it. J tells how Noah looks out and is amazed and thankful that the earth is dry; it is human experience. P reports and documents it as a fixed date.

The Structure of 13a, 14-19. There is again P's typical division into commission and execution of the commission; it is the same as at the beginning in 6:13-21. The event of the flood begins and ends with a commission to Noah which he carries out. The date on which Noah stepped on to the earth, 13-14, precedes the command to leave the ark, 15-17, and the exit follows, 18-19. It is to be noted that vv. 13a and 14 give two very different dates.

[8:13a, 14] How are the statements in vv. 13a and 14 related? To begin with, they seem to be a logical consequence of two stages. The statement in 13a חרבו המים describes the first stage: "the waters had dried up from the earth," corresponding to J's statement in 13b. The statement in v. 14 יבשה הארץ, "the earth was dry" (for the Targum version, see G. Vajda, above, p. 212), describes a second stage: only now is the earth completely dry. But the statement in v. 14 really requires that v. 13a be interpreted in the sense that the waters had run off, but that the earth was not yet completely dry. If v. 14 did not follow v. 13a, then one would not think of understanding v. 13 in this way; one would understand it analogously to v. 13b (J). This demonstrates that the dates in vv. 13a and 14 did not arise at the same time, but that they represent two stages of the dating of the flood in P.

U. Cassuto understands the statement in v. 14a as "one year and eleven days after the beginning of the flood: a complete solar year of 365 days." The two statements then would represent two different systems of calculation, the lunar year and the solar year. In any case we must recognize that the priestly school had worked on the dating of the flood a long time and that we can discern a number of layers of such work in the text that lies before us. The same holds for the beginning of the flood where two dates are given, 7:6 and 7:11. The sense of v. 13a allows further precision. It is introduced by ויהי, which marks the sentence off, and is to be understood from v. 5 which describes the gradual recession of the waters. ויהי indicates that the recession has now reached its goal, the earth is dry. This is the explanation of the precision of time where the number *one* is repeated three times: "in the 601st year . . . on the first day of the first month." There can be no mistaking the emphasis on the number *one*. This is in accordance with P's style which emphasizes and underscores by means of repetition. What is meant is the 601st year of Noah's life, as the Gk reads, corresponding to 7:11. However, it is possible that the MT has left out the name deliberately so as to give simply the numbers.

The new world era, the post-diluvial age, begins on this day. It is consecrated in Gen 9 and received its basic orientation in the laws that determine it. We encounter here the real thrust of the dating which frames the flood story and divides it into its individual phases. The dating fixes it within the stream of history that reaches right down to P and his community. The day on which the waters of the flood disappeared from the earth, the day of the end of the flood, becomes New Year's day. The cosmos is renewed in the cultic celebration of this day. It is the conclusion of the flood narrative that later, in muted and covert ways, provides the rationale for the annual cultic renewal of the cosmos at the New Year's feast.

It is only here that one becomes aware of P's intended parallel between the end of the creation and the end of the flood; it is deliberately concealed and only hinted at. In the former it is the 7th day, which God blessed and made holy, because on that day he rested from all the work he had created. In the latter it is the day on which the earth is restored and renewed because it has been liberated from the flood: the first day of the first month in the first (= 601) year. One cannot say that the Sabbath was instituted in Gen 2:1-3 or the New Year feast in Gen 8-9 (P); but both these sections in the primeval event lay a foundation. When the Sabbath and the New Year are set up in the history of God's people and become fixed institutions, they can be referred to the primeval event. So they take on a universal significance, at least potentially.

It is only here too that it becomes clear that there is a parallel between J and P in their conclusions to the flood story which is important for their relationship to each other. P, too, concludes the flood by establishing a fixed temporal cycle which is to persevere until the end of time. J describes it simply as the natural cycle of the seasons, 8:22. P only hints that it is the cycle from New Year to New Year with the indication that this will become in time the liturgical celebration of the turn of the year.

[8:15-17] The command to Noah to leave the ark is introduced in v. 15; it is extended to all who are in the ark in vv. 16-17b, and is elaborated in v. 17c by a renewed blessing of fertility which the animals receive.

[8:15] P uses the same formula word for word in Ex 25:1f. in the speech to Moses which introduces the command to build the Tabernacle.

Literature: Gen 8:16-17: I.L. Seeligmann, "Indications of Editorial Alteration and Adaptation in the Massoretic Text and the Septuagint," VT 11 (1961) 201-221; 201. A. Lancellotti, "I 'rettili' acquatici di Gen 1, 20s," SBFLA 21 (1971) 331-337.

[8:16] "Go out!" "The divine command stands over everything that happens here like a protecting roof," W. Zimmerli ad loc. The purpose of enumerating the members of Noah's family and the species of animals here is to describe the event in its fulness. P thereby expresses more forcefully that the command of God to go out, bestowing freedom and new life, holds for all who are in the ark; it is P's preferred way of making something concrete: he makes the exit into a solemn procession which is articulated by a fine, rhythmic language:

> Go out of the ark you,
> and . . . and . . . and . . . with you!
> all animals with you,
> all . . . all . . . bring out with you!

"His command envisages each individual group of creatures" (W. Zimmerli). On the two enumerations in vv. 17 and 18 and their relationship to other such, cf. W.M. Clark VT 18 (1968) 433-449. U. Cassuto remarks on the different reading of the hiph. of יצא that the Qerē understands יצא as a פ"י verb. I.L. Seeligmann understands the form as the result of a tendency on the part of the Masoretes to preserve all forms that have come down to them.

Literature: Gen 8:17: A. Murtonen, VT 9 (1959) 177. Th.C. Vriezen, "Exodus-studien, Exodus I," VT 17 (1967) 334-353; 346.

[8:17a] "Let them spawn" is missing in the Gk; the Vg has the imperative in place of the jussive. Such minor variants occur often in expressions that are frequently used. Most explanations say that the creation blessing over the animals (all animals, cf. Comm. on Gen 1:22) is renewed here. This is correct, but is not the most important. The blessing is renewed over the animals that have been saved from the flood and preserved from destruction. A new aspect of the blessing enters in here. The animals that are destined to live, to be fruitful and to multiply are, like humans, exposed to catastrophes; mass destruction is part of the existence of animals too. The animals that are saved are blessed with a view to this contingency, and no mass destruction or catastrophe in the animal kingdom can abolish this blessing.

[8:18-19] In obedience to the command Noah and his family step on to the earth, once more accessible, and all living beings go out of the ark "by families" to new life. For P, this is a classical example that the command of God means life and that following the command means possession of life. When H. Gunkel and J. Skinner say that the reason for the addition "according to their families" (the plural of מִין is not in use) is due to P's love for order, they may well be correct. However, what is important is that P, in the very place where the creatures created by God step into a new life as those saved from the catastrophe, has to say again that it is life in its entirety, life in community. Some Mss read וְכָל instead of כָל at the beginning of v. 19, and the Gk is a smoother text in what follows. S.E. McEvenue discusses the reason for retaining the MT, op. cit. p. 66, n. 56. One should note again the nicely formed rhythmic language which shapes the exit from the ark into a solemn procession; cf. S.E. McEvenue ad loc.

Literature: Gen 8:20-22: S. Makloet, BiLi 24 (1956/1957) 234.   J. Hempel, "Review of the article 'Sintflut' in RGG³ V/VI," ZAW 74 (1962) 236-237.

[8:20-22]   The Conclusion of J's Flood Narrative

This is as important for understanding J's flood narrative as is the introduction 6:5-8 to which it refers back. It is constructed in two parts; Noah's action, 20, and a statement by God referring to it, 21a, 21-22. As was shown in the introduction, the narrative as a whole reaches its goal with God's concluding statement.

Literature: Gen 8:20: R.M. Dussaud, *Les origines Cananéennes du sacrifice Israélite* (1921; 1941²).   G.B. Gray, *Sacrifice in the Old Testament. Its Theory and Practice* (1925; 1971²).   M. Löhr, "Das Räucheropfer im Alten Testament, eine archäologische Untersuchung," SKG 4 (1927) 155-191.   A. Wendel, *Das Opfer in der altisraelitischen Religion* (1927).   G. van der Leeuw, *Phänomenologie der Religion* (1933; 1956²) 328-338.   W.B. Stevenson, "Hebrew ʿolah and zebach Sacrifices," *Festschr. A. Bertholet* (1950) 488-497.   J. Morgenstern, "The Calendar of the Book of Jubilees. Its Origin and its Character," VT 5 (1955) 34-76; 36-37.   S. Makloet, BiLi 24 (1956/1957) 234.   R. Rendtorff, "Opfer" EKL (1958).   J. Henninger, *La religion bédouine préislamique* (1959).   R. Rendtorff, *Studien zur Geschichte des Opfers im alten Israel,* WMANT 24 (1967) 41, 110, 113, 117.

[8:20]   The Sacrifice of Noah.

The sacrifice of Noah is one of those elements which occurs very often in the flood narratives, e.g., in the Babylonian, Greek, Phoenician, Indian stories. Ziusudra, Utnapishtim, Deucalion, Demarius, Manu, all offer sacrifice after they have been saved. It should be noted however that the motif occurs particularly in the flood narratives of the high cultures (cf. Intro. to 6:5-8:22, Excursus 4[b]). The reason why P does not mention sacrifice is that for him it can only begin with Sinai.

One would think that the function of sacrifice would be clear when it occurs so often in the same context and situation. However, the commentators give very different explanations. H. Gunkel: "He offers sacrifice because God, who hitherto has been so terribly angry with hmanity, is still at enmity with it; he wants to silence what remains of the anger." A. Dillmann: "A sacrifice of thanksgiving or petition is in place anywhere after a severe judgment and at the beginning of a new course of events." O. Procksch: "The earth is now freed from the burden of the curse by means of the ʿōlōt . . . the sacrifice of Noah is a means of propitiation." J. Skinner: "A sacrifice of propitiation." G. von Rad: "A confession by a person of the need of propitiation."

The explanation of U. Cassuto is quite different: "When a person has been saved from a terrible danger, . . . his first reaction is to give thanks to him who saved him or helped him to escape." This corresponds best to the situation. The sacrifice is the response of the one saved. Those who come out of the ark must first of all do something special that articulates their awareness of the mortal danger from which they have been rescued and their entrance into the new life that has been bestowed on them. When there has been an extraordinary act of salvation, consciously experienced as such, the implication is that it must be celebrated. The celebration of the act of salvation by a sacrifice offered to the one who saved and which at the same time secures the new life so that a new beginning is assured, is one of the basic motifs of worship.

A comparison with the sacrifice of Cain and Abel reveals the two primal motifs: it has to do with the produce of labor; there is blessing where God regards the sacrifice. This sacrifice, in accord with the blessing of fertility, has the element of something constant, something that regularly recurs. The sacrifice of Noah has to do with one who has been in danger and preserved; it has something contingent about it. The sacrifice is celebrated in response to the action of salvation or liberation. These two motifs are constants in the whole history of worship (and of sacrifice). A spontaneous celebration, the result of salvation experienced, is just as much a part of the necessary life of worship as the permanent, regularly-organized service.

The details: The old commentaries remark that this is the first mention of an altar in Genesis. The qualification is important. Noah builds the altar for Yahweh. The first work in the new life is a work dedicated to Yahweh; the first building is an altar built to Yahweh. The author is drawing attention to a characteristic trait of sacrifice when he says that Noah takes some of the animals preserved from the flood. The valuable and precious is to be offered to God, thereby acknowledging him as the one to whom such is due. Only clean animals of course can be offered. The עלה is that form of sacrifice in which the whole animal is burnt; see above G. van der Leeuw, M. Löhr, J. Morgenstern, 36, 56-62; J. Pedersen, *Israel, its Life and Culture*, IV (1926; 1946) 330; R. Rendtorff, WMANT 24 (1967) 41-42, 113, 117; and the dictionary articles.

Literature: Gen 8:21: G. Baur, *Geschichte der alttestamentlichen Weissagung* (1861) 171-173. L. Reinke, *Beiträge zur Erklärung des Alten Testaments*, IV (1863) 1-3. J. Halévy, "Recherches bibliques, VIII," REJ 13 (1896) 170-172. B. Luther, "Die israelitischen Stämme," ZAW 21 (1901) 1-76. G.L. Young, "The Smelling of the Sweet Savor of Noah's Sacrifice," BSt NS 3 (1905) 64-67. P. Dhorme, "L'emploi métaphorique des noms de parties du corps en hébreu et en accadien," RB 4 (1922) 489-517; 492-508. S. Rappaport, *Agada und Exegese bei Flavius Josephus* (1930). C. Kaplan, "The Flood in the Book of Enoch and Rabbinics," JSOR 15 (1931) 22-24. J. Hempel, *Festschr. A. Bertholet* (1950). F.H. von Meyenfeldt, *Het hart . . .*, Diss. Leiden, (1950). S. Mowinckel, *Religion und Kultus* (1953) 70-72. B. Gemser, "God in Genesis," OTS 12 (1958) 1-21. = POS 7 (1968). A.R. Hulst, OTS 12 (1958) 28ff. R.E. Murphy, Bib 39 (1958) 334ff. A. Murtonen, VT 9 (1959) 158f. M. Haran, "The Uses of Incense in the Ancient Israelite Ritual," VT 10 (1960) 113-129. W. Zimmerli, "Sinaibund und Abrahambund. Ein Beitrag zum Verständnis der Priesterschrift," ThZ 16 (1960) 268-280 = *Gottes Offenbarung. Gesammelte Aufsätze zum Alten Testament*, ThB 19 (1963) 205-216. R. Rendtorff, "Genesis 8:21 und die Urgeschichte des Jahwisten," KuD 7 (1961) 69-78. J. Scharbert, "Verheissung," Handbuch Theologischer Grundbegriffe II (1963) 752-759. E. Wolf, "Über 'Klarheit der Heiligen Schrift' nach Luthers 'De servo arbitrio'," ThLZ 92 (1967) 721-730. H. Cazelles, "Israël du Nord et Arche d'Alliance," VT 18 (1968) 147-158. W.M. Clark, JBL 88

(1969) 266-278. K. Koch, VT 19 (1969) 37-81. E. Kutsch, "Die Etymologie von Berit," ZDMGSuppl 1 (1969) 356-361; *Festschr. K. Galling* (1970) 165- 178. R. Lapointe, CBQ 32 (1970) 161-181. O.H. Steck, "Genesis 12:1-3 und die Urgeschichte des Jahwisten," *Festschr. G. von Rad* (1971) 525-554.

[**8:21a**] "And Yahweh smelled the sweet odor." The scandal at this anthropomorphism is very old (examples from the Fathers in J.P. Lewis, *A Study of the Interpretation of Noah. . .*, 1968, p. 40) and continues even to the present (e.g., H. Holzinger: ". . . scarcely reconcilable with a spiritual idea of God, . . . a God who takes pleasure in drawing the κνίση into his nostrils has always something of the pagan about him"). It does not help much when it is suggested that the words be understood spiritually and not corporally (cf. G.L. Young, above). On the one hand the same image occurs in the same context in Gilg. XI 159-161: "The gods smelled the savor, the gods smelled the sweet savor, the gods crowded like flies about the sacrificer" (compare too 11.162-165 with 8:21b-22); on the other hand the phrase ריח הניחח remains part of the language of sacrifice right down to the latest period in Israel, Ex 29:18, 25, 41; Lev 1:9; it is very frequent in Lev and Num; Ezek 6:13, and elsewhere; Sir 45:16. These many examples show that the expression has become formalized. A. Dillmann: "A standard expression for the gracious acceptance of an offering of sacrifice"; U. Cassuto: " 'He smelt an odour' had already lost in Hebrew its original and literal signification and acquired a figurative connotation, such as 'he received favourably'." For the term itself, cf. R. Rendtorff, *Studien. . .*, WMANT 24 (1958) 253. J's scandalous use of this sacrificial terminology, unique in the Old Testament, is in accord with the primeval way of describing things, as the parallel in Gilg. XI shows. All that is meant is that God has graciously acknowledged Noah's sacrifice. It introduces God's address to Noah in the following verses.

[**8:21b-22**] The formulation of this divine address is the work of J and it refers clearly to the introduction, 6:5-8; however, one cannot say that J did not make use of material at hand to him (G. von Rad: "And as in the prologue, so here we are faced with the Yahwist's very own words"; R. Rendtorff and O.H. Steck follow him here). As in the prologue, it must be conceded that J is here working over material. The same decision by God in P 9:15 and by Ishtar in Gilg. XI 162-165 demonstrate this clearly. It is not possible to separate with certainty the traditional material from J's formulation. However, the last sentence of v. 21 gives grounds for conjecture as the two preceding sentences are clear echoes of the prologue 6:5-8 and Gen 3. The positive formulation in v. 22 of the abrogation of the decision to destroy is also to be regarded as a construction of J. He gives here what he considers to be the essential and definitive meaning of the flood story within the primeval event.

R. Rendtorff saw in 8:21 the key passage for a new understanding of the biblical primeval story. This verse is not only the conclusion of the flood narrative, but the conclusion of the primeval story which J has arranged thematically (KuD 7 [1961] 69-78; "Hermeneutische Probleme der biblischen Urgeschichte," *Festschr. F. Smend*, 1963, 19-29; K. Koch, "Die Hebräer. . .," VT 19 [1969] 72, agrees with Rendtorff here). Rendtorff bases his opinion on a new explanation of the second sentence of the decision of God. This is the result of a study of the verb קלל in piel; he translates: "I will never again declare the earth to be cursed (as I have done hitherto) on account of humanity, because the imagination of the heart is evil from one's youth. . . ." pp. 73-74. The text understood in this way obviously follows 3:17; according to Rendtorff 8:21 is linked with 3:17. The curse laid upon the earth there is cancelled in 8:21.

The passage 8:20-22 denotes the point of demarcation between the story of curse introduced in 3:17 and the story of blessing introduced here: "From now on it is no longer the curse, but the blessing, that rules the world. The era of the curse is at an end, the era of blessing dawns," p. 74. O.H. Steck has taken issue with this explanation. He objects: there is no doubt that 8:21a as well as 8:22 refer to the flood narrative; they conclude it. It is probable that the same holds for 21a² which belongs in the same context. The verb קלל does not stand in contradiction if it is not declarative in sense (declare to be cursed) but is understood with W. Schottroff, WMANT 30 (1969), as "shameful degradation." The verb is certainly not declarative in Gen 12:3, the only other passage in J where it occurs. The weightier objection refers to the reality: namely, that the circumstances which are the result of the pronouncement of the curse, the thorns and thistles, the burden of work, the pains of child bearing, and so on, continue beyond the flood. The citation above from Rendtorff is not to the point here.

There is no way out of these arguments which O.H. Steck develops. But there is a further question to be addressed to Rendtorff's explanation. Did J really conceive the primeval story as a story of curse, which is detached from a story of blessing? Rendtorff shares this conception with G. von Rad and others. He differs from them only by putting the line of demarcation between the story of curse and the story of blessing in another place. For the justification of this conception, see Introduction 3D. One can agree with Rendtorff: "that the flood in J is not described as an act of cursing" (so O.H. Steck *Festschr. G. von Rad* [1971] 529); but this does not require the conclusion that he draws. One can agree with him further that the conclusion of the Yahwistic flood narrative is a transition from primeval event to history (this is the case, analogously, with each of the primeval narratives), and consequently that Gen 11:1-9 is not to be regarded as an intensification of Gen 6-8. However, it can be taken as certain that 8:20-22 is to be understood as a unity and as the conclusion of J's flood narrative. We will consider further the direct reference to Gen 3 in 8:21a² in the exegesis of the individual verse.

The speech of God that concludes the flood is not to be understood as a promise; it is not directed to anyone (on אל־לבו see above H. Cazelles, 1969, P. Dhorme, 1922, F.H. von Meyenfeld, 1950). It is the abrogation of the decision to destroy. This is the reason why it is to be explained from the whole context of the flood narrative. It contains two parts; the decision of God is described in its negative and positive aspects. It looks backward and forward; the retrospect is formulated personally, "I will . . . ," the prospect impersonally, ". . . there shall. . . ." The retrospective decision is expressed in two sentences that have the same meaning. The second is clearer: "Never again will I slay every living creature, as I have done," a formulation in accord with the flood narrative, cf. 6:7. It is probable that this sentence or something like it was part of the tradition where it would have followed immediately on 21a.

The other sentence, which includes the reason for the decision, is an addition of J by way of interpretation (K. Budde had already pointed in this direction). The words אדם and אדמה obviously recall Gen 2-3. R. Rendtorff is correct when he sees here a deliberate reference to Gen 2-3, just as in J's prologue, 6:5-8, vv. 6 and 7 are an insertion referring to the same. This is probably the reason why J chose the verb קלל, even though it has the same meaning as נכה hiph. in the parallel sentence. The meaning corresponds to the definition that W. Schottroff gives, "קלל in the piel means the disdainful treatment and the shameful degradation that belittles another's own worth and self-esteem and paralyzes his growth and potential," WMANT 30 (1969) 29-30. O.H. Steck proposes the following translation: "Never again will I treat the earth with disdain" op. cit. 531. This is in accord with the meaning of קלל piel. However, because of the deliberate allusion to 3:17, one can retain the rendering "curse," provided it is understood in the broader sense.

R. Rendtorff however has not noticed that the sentence which alludes to 3:17 is followed immediately by a sentence giving the reason and is introduced by the particle כי. This resumes 6:5b almost literally; it cannot therefore refer to the matter in 3:17. It only resumes the reason which motivated the decision to destroy every living creature. The sentence 8:21a[2] which interprets, certainly alludes to 3:17, but here forms a bridge to the prologue to the flood narrative. It is here that one sees the scope of J's interpretative addition. There was a time when Yahweh cursed the אדמה because of אדם. It occurred because of a transgression of a command of God. This is never to happen again.

The reason for the judgment that brought the flood was different: a tendency to evil in people which belongs to them in such a way that they grow up with it. On יצר, see bibliog. on 8:21, R.E. Murphy; M. Luther, WA (1883ff.) 348, 31, comments on 8:21: ". . . quod sit animal rationale, habens cor fingens." The divine judgment of the flood does not alter this in any way. God decides to leave to אדם his אדמה despite this tendency to evil. God decides to put up with this state of evil. It is this that is the basis of the saying of Jesus given in Mt 5:45: "for he makes his sun rise on the evil and on the good, and sends rain on the just and on the unjust." J. Skinner: "The pledge of Yahweh's patience with humanity is the regularity of the course of nature, in which good and bad people are treated alike, (Mt. 5:45)." It is only here then that the real meaning of the conclusion of the flood narrative in the whole context of J's primeval story emerges. Humans, created by God, can be disobedient to God (Gen 3), a man can commit a crime against his brother (4:2-16), humans have an inclination to evil (from their youth). Not every expression of evil is reason for a fixed succession of events: sin — discovery — punishment and (or) forgiveness. God does not react in a uniform way, intervening with punishment on each occasion. He can simply let things be, putting up patiently with people just as they are with their inclination to evil. This inclination, growing stronger and stronger 6:5-7, is always capable of putting human existence in danger. But God promises that he will never again allow humanity to be destroyed. F. Delitzsch: "The era of patience is to begin now (ἀνοχή Rom 3:26)."

If one acknowledges that the reason, "because the imagination . . ." is part of J's interpretation, it becomes clear that the sentence which is part of the tradition, "I will never again slay every living creature, as I have done," needs no reason; it is a simple decision of God. A dispute among the gods is the background of the change of decision in the polytheistic description; in Israel the change belongs to One. There is no power that can shake this promise.

Literature: Gen 8:22: J. Hempel, ZAW 65 (1953) 114.   H. Cazelles, "Rezension E. Jacob, Théologie de l'Ancien Testament," VT 6 (1956) 326-330.   G. von Rad, "Les idées sur le temps et l'histoire en Israël et l'eschatologie des Prophètes," *Hommage à W. Vischer* (1960) 198-209; 200.   F.S. North, "Four-Month Seasons of the Hebrew Bible," VT 11 (1961) 446-448.   J.B. Curtin, HUCA 34 (1963) 115-123.   J.B. Segal, *The Hebrew Passover from the Earliest Times to A.D. 70,* London Oriental Series 12 (1963) (review H. Kosmala: VT 14 [1964] 504-509).   N.H. Snaith, "Time in the Old Testament," *Essays presented to S.H. Hooke* (1963) 175-186.   D. Hermant, VT 15 (1965) 449-450. S. Hermann, *Die prophetischen Heilserwartung im Alten Testament, Ursprung und Gestaltwandel,* BWANT 5, 5 (1965) (review H. Cazelles: VT 17 [1967] 244-248).   H.R. Stroes, VT 16 (1966) 466.   H.A. Frankfort, *The Intellectual Adventure. . . ,* (1946; 1967[6]) 23.   L. Ramlot, *Histoire et mentalité symbolique: Exégèse et Théologie* (1968) esp. 185.   W. Thiel, "Hēfēr Berit. Zum Bundbrechen im Alten Testament," VT 20 (1970) 214-229.   W. Brueggemann, "Kingship and Chaos (A Study in Tenth Century Theology)," CBQ 33 (1971) 317-332.   M. Saebø, "Creator et Redemptor. Om skapelsens teologiske plass og funksjon i det gamle testamente," *Festschr. I.P. Seierstad* (1971) 1-28.   G. Wallis, "Die Sesshaftwerdung Alt-Israels und das Gottesdienstverständnis des Jahwisten im Lichte der elohistischen Kritik," ZAW 83 (1971) 1-15.

[8:22]   The positive formulation of the promise now balances the negative. The positive עד (written defectively), which together with כל־ימי הארץ expresses the permanent state of terrestrial chronology, stands over against the negative עוד of v. 21. U. Cassuto comments correctly that the introductory phrase is not saying that the earth will remain forever or such like: "The earth is not eternal, only the creator is eternal. Since the earth had a beginning, it stands to reason that it will also have an end." The expression is very peculiar and, as far as I know, does not occur elsewhere: כל־ימי in other places always includes the totality of living beings, humans or animals. It describes here the permanence of the earth. It is probably a construction of J. For the first time in the story of humanity the cosmic event is seen as a whole in its extension in time. The sentence that closes J's flood narrative not only says that the rhythm expressed by the pairs of words will not be disturbed or broken again; it says more. It looks to "the history of nature" (F.C. von Weizsäcker, 1948; 1954[2]) as a whole, which is determined by this constant rhythm.

J's creation narrative in Gen 2 had said nothing of a self-consistent world. It looked at the world in its relationship to humans, at the trees, plants and animals insofar as they were there for humans. There was nothing about the existence of the world, about its own life and order. The world acquires a life of its own only when the flood story reaches its goal in 8:20-22. This is the way in which J's interpreting sentence is to be understood: ". . . never again the אדמה because of אדם." 8:22 is a creation statement which takes its place between the creation of humans in Gen 2 and the creation of the world in Gen 1. It is a creation statement with the qualification that it is not describing the institution of the world but its stabilization. The world is not primarily something that is there in space; it stands and subsists in time, in the steady, mighty rhythm portrayed in v. 22. The existing world is to be understood as that which subsists and has achieved permanence through catastrophe; the world that subsists is the world that has been preserved.

Humans became living beings because God breathed into them the breath of life. God's breath made the person a being that lives by the rhythm of respiration. Here the world subsists in the rhythm of day and night, summer and winter.

The meaning of these four pairs of words, which give expression to this rhythm, is not as obvious as it first seems. It is clear that the rhythm is of two beats and that each pair describes a whole. It is clear too that the pair "seed time and harvest" as well as "summer and winter" describe the year as a whole, just as "day and night" describe the day of 24 hours. But "cold and heat" pose a problem. They are almost always understood as another description of the year, e.g., F. Delitzsch: "The first three pairs divide the year into its two halves." O. Procksch: ". . . the first and third refer to agriculture and fruit farming, the second and fourth to the seasons and the division of the day." U. Cassuto: "Summer and winter are essentially the same as heat and cold." But it is to be noted that of the four pairs three describe the course of the year and one the course of the day. The question arises whether the second and fourth pairs do not stand in some sort of relationship to each other, cold and heat also referring to the course of the day, especially when one reflects that in the east cold and heat describe the alternation between day and night just as they do that between summer and winter. It is scarcely possible to restrict the pair to the alternation between day and night. It occurs nowhere else in the Old Testament. קר and חם are used very rarely in isolation and refer more to the seasons than to the divisions of the day (cf. F.S. North, VT 11 [1961] 447).

It is quite independent of this question that the two basic rhythms of the year and the day which these four pairs indicate describe the subsistence of the world. They are closely related to the subsistence of life: every living creature exists in and requires the alternation of day and night; humans, animals and plants require the alternation of the seasons to provide nourishment. The conclusion of J's flood narrative then provides the basis for an understanding of time that is rhythmically determined, what is called "cyclic" time (see bibliog. on Gen 8:21 and 22; also R.E. Murphy, "History, Eschatology, and the Old Testament," *Continuum* 7 [1970] 583-593). It is in any case insufficient to insist that the understanding of time in the Old Testament is exclusively linear. It cannot be denied that in the epilogue to the flood narrative J sets time and its subsistence in a decision of God, "while earth lasts"; time consists in a constantly recurring rhythm. From Abraham on and then from the Exodus on, time is presented in a succession of contingent historical events which reach out in linear fashion toward a goal. But this in no way abrogates the course of cyclic time established in 8:20-22. Rather it retains its significance for everything that happens. A substantial part of the working out of God's blessing takes place within the cycle established here; the working out of God's saving action takes place in contingent events (cf. C. Westermann, *Der Segen.* . . , 1968).

Blessing and Covenant (P)

Literature

J. Hamburger, "Noachiden," *Real-Encyclopädie für Bibel und Talmud,* II (1883) 663-866.   J.J.P. Valeton Jr., "Bedeutung und Stellung des Wortes berît (בְּרִית) im Priester-codex," ZAW 12 (1892) 1-22.   A. Wiener, *Die jüdischen Speisegesetze* (1895).   S.R. Driver, *An Introduction to the Literature of the Old Testament: The Priestly Narrative of the Hexateuch* (1897[6]; 1929[9]) 126.   R. Kraetzschmar, *Die Bundesvorstellung im Alten Testament in ihrer geschichtlichen Entwicklung* (1896).   V. Zapletal, *Der Totemismus und die Religion Israels* (1901).   P. Karge, "Geschichte des Bundesgedankens im Alten Testament, I," ATA 2 (1910) 228-229.   K. Wigand, "Die altisraelitische Vorstellung von unreinen Tieren," ARW 17 (1914) 413-436.   J. Döller, "Die Reinheits- und Speisegesetze des Alten Testaments in religionsgeschichtlicher Beleuchtung," ATA 7 (1917).   W.W. Petersen, *Das Tier im Alten Testament* (1928).   A. Bentzen, *Introduction to the Old Testament, I-II* (1948/1949; 1952[2]), I 232-234.   W.F. Albright, "The Hebrew Expression for 'Making a Covenant' in Pre-Israelite Documents," BASOR 121 (1951) 21-22.   O. Eissfeldt, *The Old Testament. An Introduction* (1966) 185.   H.W. Wolff, VT 6 (1956) 316-320 = ThB 22 (1973[2]) 387-391.   W. Zimmerli, "Die Weisung des Alten Testaments zum Geschäft der Sprache," *Das Problem der Sprache in Theologie und Kirche* (1959) 1-20.   ThZ 16 (1960) 268, 272.   D.J. McCarthy, "Covenant in the Old Testament: The Present State of Inquiry," CBQ 27 (1965) 217-240.   E. Kutsch, KuD 14 (1968) 159-182.   D.R. Hillers, *Covenant: The History of a Biblical Idea* (1969).   C.D. Jathanna, "The Covenant and Covenant-Making in the Pentateuch," *Bangalore Theological Forum* 3 (1969) 27-54.   R. Martin-Achard, "Remarques sur la signification théologique de la création selon l'Ancien Testament," RHPhR 1 (1972) 3-11.

Text

9:1 And God blessed Noah and his sons and said to them: Be fruitful and increase and fill the earth![a]

2 Fear and dread of you[a] shall come over all birds under heaven and over all[b] that creeps on the earth and over all fish in the sea; they are given into your hand[c].

3 All that moves and lives[a] shall serve you for food, as I have given you the green plants, so I give you all[b].

4 Only flesh with[a] its life, its blood[b], you shall not eat.

5 But[a] your own blood will I demand; from all animals will I demand it, and from humans in turn[b] will I demand the life of a human being.

6 Whoever[a] pours out human blood, by a human[b] shall his blood be poured out; because in the image of God have humans been made.

459

7 But you, be fruitful and increase, spread over the earth and rule over it![a]

8 And God said to Noah and to his sons with him:

9 Now I[a], I am setting up my covenant with you, and with your descendants after you

10 and with every living being that is with you, with the birds, with the cattle, and with all wild animals with you, with all that have come[a] out of the ark with you( )[b].

11 I am setting up my covenant with you that never again[a] shall all flesh be wiped out by[b] the waters of the flood, and that never again shall a flood come to destroy the earth.

12 And God said: This is the sign of the covenant that I am establishing between myself and you and every living being that is with you for all future generations[a].

13 My bow I am putting in the clouds[a], which shall be the sign of the covenant between me and the earth.

14 When I now form clouds over the earth, and the bow becomes visible in the clouds[a],

15 then I will remember my covenant which exists between me and you and all living beings, and never again shall[a] the waters become a flood so as to destroy all flesh( )[b].

16 And when the bow is there in the clouds, I will look at it so as to recall[a] the everlasting covenant, between[bc] God and all living beings, all flesh that is on the earth.

17 And God said to Noah: This is the sign of the covenant, which I am setting up between myself and all flesh that is on the earth.

28 And Noah lived another 350 years after the flood.
29 The whole of Noah's life-span was 950 years. Then he died.

1a   Gk adds וכבשה following 1:28.
2a   Ges-K §135m.   **b** ב "together with," some mss have ובכל.   **c** Sam, Gk נתתיו.
3a   On the construction Ges-K §138b, BrSynt §152a.   **b** Ges-K §117c, BrSynt §96.
4a   ב meaning "with" Ges-K §119n; construction Ges-K §131k.   **b** דמו "an explanatory apposition (if not a gloss) to בנפשו" J. Skinner.
5a   ואך suspect after preceding אך (J. Skinner).   **b** מיד איש אחיו "at the hand of the brother of every man" Ges-K §139c, H. Gunkel: "from you in turn"; J. Skinner comments: "All languages use breviloquence in the expression of reciprocity; cp. Zech 7:10."
6a   Construction Ges-K §116w, 143b.   **b** באדם missing in Vg. On the use of ב BrSynt §106e.
7a   Read ורדו following 1:28; so most exegetes.
9a   Juxtaposed nominal sentence, Ges-K §143a, BrSynt §121a.
10a   The verbs בוא and יצא meaning to go in, to go out, can be used with a direct accus., Ges-K §116h.   **b** The last three words are missing in the Gk; J. Skinner comments: "The sense of 'animal' in general immediately after the same expression in the sense of 'wild animals' makes the phrase suspicious."
11a   On construction Ges-K §152b.   **b** מן indicates the efficient cause, U. Cassuto, Ges-K §121f, BrSynt §111h.
12a   Tg has עולם לברית for לדרת עולם; this could be so, but is not sufficiently attested.
13a   For word order BrSynt §122i.
14a   Construction BrSynt §123h; Ges-K §112y, 117r. On the sequence v. 15 after v. 14, Ges-K §159g.

15a The verb is in the sing. because it precedes the subject. **b** בכל בשׂר an addition, see preceding words and same words in v. 16.

16a Construction Ges-K §131t. **b** Gk has ''between me''; but the אלהים accords with the style of proclamation. **c** On the use of the ב Ges-K §119i.

The Structure of 9:1-17.

P puts special emphasis on the conclusion of the flood narrative. One can rightly speak of a stylized, cumulative emphasis [Westermann uses here a technical narrative term, *Achtergewicht*]. P tends constantly to interpret in the body of the narrative; the same tendency appears in the closing address which is still concerned with the meaning of what has happened and puts the whole emphasis there. It is deliberately divided into two parts, each self-contained and each beginning and ending with virtually the same sentence (inclusion): 9:1 = 9:7; 9:9 = 9:17b. The parts, 9:1-7 and 9:8-17, have each their own message, but belong together as the divine address that concludes the flood. One cannot say that there are ''two addresses of God to Noah'' (Gunkel). How then are the parts linked? Why does P bring blessing, 1-7, and covenant, 8-17, together in the conclusion of the flood event? The answer is found in a comparison with the conclusion in J, 8:20-22. God's address in 8:21-22 consists of the promise that there shall never again be a flood, 21, and that the rhythm of life shall never again be interrupted as long as the earth lasts, 22. 8:21 corresponds to 9:8-17, and 8:22 to 9:1-7. However, it does not necessarily follow that 8:21-22 is the basis of the priestly conclusion. The comparison shows rather that the twofold division of God's concluding address in P was part of the tradition that came to him.

At the same time the stylistic form of the inclusion in both parts becomes clear. The two parts really contain only one message — the first renews the blessing over the living beings saved from the flood, the second promises that there shall never again be a flood. Everything else is subordinated to this.

There is a particular stylistic refinement. The closing sentence of each part goes beyond the introductory sentence by resuming the elaboration that follows it. V. 7 ends with the words ''and rule over it'' (see note on text) and thereby includes what vv. 2 and 3 say; v. 17 resumes the sign which is the subject of vv. 12-16. The device is carefully thought out and shows even more clearly that each part is self-contained.

These are the essentials of the structure of 9:1-17. One may add further that the complement to the blessing in 9:1-7, which grants the use of meat for food, contains two restrictions in vv. 4 and 5-6, each introduced by אך. God's promise in vv. 8-17 that there shall never again be a flood, vv. 9-11, is described as ברית, and so is complemented by a sign of the covenant, vv. 12-16.

Commentary

Literature: Gen 9:1-7: H. Revel, ''Noahide Laws,'' UJE VIII, 227-228. E.L. Dietrich, ZRGG 1 (1948) 301-315. P. Grelot, ''Le Papyrus Pascal d'Eléphantine et le problème du Pentateuque,'' VT 5 (1955) 250-265. J.E. Steinmüller, Bib 40 (1959) 556-567. K. Koch, ''Der Spruch 'Sein Blut bleibe auf seinem Haupt' und die israelitische Auffassung vom vergossenen Blut,'' VT 12 (1962) 396-416; 409-410. J. Milgrom, ''A Prolegomenon to Leviticus 17:11,'' JBL 90 (1971) 149-156. W.L. Moran, ''Atrahasis: The Babylonian Story of the Flood,'' Bib 52 (1971) 51-61.

[9:1-7] *The renewal of the blessing over all living beings.* The first sentence repeats 1:28 word for word; the two verbs וכבשה ורדו, 1:28, with the subsequent enumeration of the species of animals, corresponds to 9:2 in content, except that in the latter the exercise of dominion is expressed in stronger and more concrete terms. Also 9:3 corresponds to 1:29 by providing the people with food, but differs in content by allowing them a meat diet in addition to a vegetarian. The allotment of the meat diet contains two restrictions in vv. 4 and 5-6; 9:7 then turns back to 9:1.

Many commentaries stress that with the end of the flood a new era has dawned which receives its new order in Gen 9 (especially F. Delitzsch, G. von Rad and others). This agrees with the conception of the flood as a line of demarcation between two epochs in the Babylonian king lists (see Comm. c. 5). In particular 9:3 indicates a new epoch; it has its parallel in Hesiod's "Works and Days" 109ff. where the meat diet follows the vegetarian diet in the sequence of the five world epochs. Besides this, a like sequence occurs in the primeval period. It must be noted however that such epochs in the primeval period are always the result of later systematization. One must be cautious then about concluding to two epochs from Gen 9:3. To say that "the state of peace among creatures is gone" (G. von Rad) is not consistent with the reason given for the flood in 6:11-13. To harmonize the two F. Delitzsch goes so far as to propose that Gen 9 sanctions what living beings had already usurped. It would be more prudent to say that the blessing over creatures takes on a new aspect in Gen 9:1-7 in view of the preservation from destruction — human existence is now confronted with the necessity of killing.

It has been shown above (Intro. 3,B,I) that creation and flood do not stand primarily in a chronological but in a complementary relationship to each other. It is clear then that the question of the killing of living beings by living beings is to be dealt with in the context of the great destruction of life in the flood.

[9:1]   The repetition of the creator's blessing here shows that, despite the life-destroying catastrophe, life created and preserved by God is as such life that extends in a linear time. There is no other life but that which continues generation after generation and expands over the earth. Gen 10, The Table of the Nations, unfolds this: humanity, preserved from the flood, increases into the future and expands over the earth.

[9:2]   Dominion over the animals had already been given to humans at creation, 1:28. The verbs used there can also describe the dominion of the king (see Comm. 1:26-27, Excursus). One cannot say then: "The relationship of humans to the animals no longer resembles that which was decreed in Gen 1" (G. von Rad), though the negative side of this dominion is presented in 9:2. The same pair, "fear and dread," is used in Deut 11:25 in the promise of the occupation of the land of Canaan: "The Lord your God will lay the fear of you and the dread of you upon all the land that you shall tread. . . ," cf. also Deut 1:21; 3:8. The phrase at the end of v. 2 "into your hand they are delivered" is the same as is used in the language of the Holy War (S.E. McEvenue). Human dominion over the animals is determined further here. The human can kill them for food; the creator has expressly allowed this. Humans acquire power over the life of animals (Lev 26:25). The language of this verse, in contrast to what was said about the dominion of humans over the animals in 1:28, is meant to express the tension that now exists. On the one hand the animals are delivered into the hands of humans with the consequent "fear and dread," on the other there is the good will of the creator toward every living being. This is evident too in the description of peace among the animals in the end-time.

[**9:3**]   Attention is centered on the animals in v. 2; in v. 3 it is on humans who now receive the concession to eat meat. J. Milgrom remarks: "Wherever (in P) the subject of נתן is God, it means 'bestow, appoint, assign' (e.g., Num 8:10 . . . 18:8; 19; cf. also Gen 1:29; 9:3; Lev 6:10; 7:34; 10:17). . . ," JBL 90 (1971) 150. It should be added that where God is the subject of the verb "give," the context is always that of God effectively bestowing blessing. We confront then even more harshly the dilemma that the gift of the blessing also implies the possibility of taking life. Again the tension is evident: the blessing that God grants to all living beings includes the concession to kill. It is this tension that calls for the restriction that is now to follow.

> *Literature:* Gen 9:4: A.R. Johnson, *The Vitality of the Individual in the Thought of Ancient Israel* (1949; 1964²). E. Jensen, "Über das Töten als kulturgeschichtliche Erscheinung," Paid. 4 (1950) 23-38. L. Koehler, "Vier Marginalien, 2)," ZAW 64 (1952) 195-196. G. Widengren, "נפש" (Review M. Seligson, "The Meaning of נפש מת. . . ," StOr 16, 2 [1951]): VT 4 (1954) 97-102. L. Kopf, VT 8 (1958) 183-184. T. Canaan, "Das Opfer in palästinischen Sitten und Gebräuchen," ZAW 74 (1962) 31-44. E. Gerstenberger, "Covenant and Commandment," JBL 84 (1965) 38-51. *Wesen. . .* , WMANT 20 (1965) 110-111. N.P. Bratsiotis, "נפש-ΨΥΧΗ. Ein Beitrag zur Erforschung der Sprache und der Theologie der Septuaginta," VT.S 15 (1966) 58-89; 64-66. A. Charbel, זבח שלמים, *Il sacrificio pacifico nei suoi riti e nel suo significato religioso e figurativo* (1967). Y.M. Grintz, "Studies in Early Biblical Ethnology and History" (hebr.) (1969) 201-221. D.J. McCarthy, "The Symbolism of Blood and Sacrifice," JBL 88 (1969) 166-176.
> Gen 9:5, 6: G. van der Leeuw, *Phänomenologie der Religion* (1933; 1956²) 228-229. L. Nemoy, "A Tenth Century Disquisition on Suicide According to Old Testament Law," JBL 57 (1938) 411-420. C.L. Dewar, "The Biblical Use of the Term 'Blood'," JThSt NS 4 (1953) 204-208. B. Gemser, "The Importance of the Motive Clause in the Old Testament Law," VT.S 1 (1953) 50-66. A.M. Dubarle, *Sacra Pagina* 1 (1959) 583ff. M. Greenberg, "Some Postulates of Biblical Criminal Law," *Y. Kaufmann Jubilee Vol.* (1960) 5-28. A. Jepsen, "Was kann das AT zum Gespräch über die Zweireichelehre beitragen?," LR 15 (1965) 427-440. J. Barr, "The Image of God in the Book of Genesis - A Study of Terminology," BJRL 51 (1968/1969) 11-26. T. Lescow, "Redaktionsgeschichtliche Analyse von Micha 6-7," ZAW 84 (1972) 182-212. C. Westermann, "נפש," THAT II (1973). [See also Lit., Excursus to 1:26-27, W. Riedl (1902), W. Rudolph (1953), P. Humbert (1955); also Lit. 4:9-10.]

[**9:4-6**]   R. Smend and H. Holzinger expressed doubts whether vv. 4-6 belonged originally to this setting; all modern exegetes however regard them as original to P. Most recently S.E. McEvenue (op. cit.), referring to Smend and Holzinger, has qualified these verses as a later insertion. His reason is the context, which is that of blessing, not of law. There is no parallel either in Gen 1 or in the broader context. Moreover there are general stylistic observations. McEvenue's arguments certainly deserve attention; but when he alleges as the reason why vv. 4-6 are a subsequent insertion that a redactor misunderstood v. 3 as law, one can have doubts. The concession of meat as food in v. 3, understood as P must have intended it, does not exclude some sort of limitation. It is exactly the same case as in Gen 2:16-17 (J). This limitation implies no restriction of the bounty of the giver (H. Holzinger considers it a trifling restriction); it serves rather to preserve what has been conceded. Were there no limitation, what was conceded would no longer come under the blessing. This is based here (it is different in 2:16-17) on the tension that exists between the granting of the meat diet and the killing. McEvenue has not seen this. P has an important theological reason for adding a rider to the concession of the meat diet. So the contextual reason no longer holds and the stylistic grounds are not sufficient to strike out the verses.

It is essential for the interrelationship of vv. 4-6, and this is underscored further by the twice repeated אַךְ at the beginning of vv. 4 and 5, that the whole passage is intended as a restriction of the concession in v. 3. The two consequences of this are that vv. 4-6 are to be understood only as a self-contained entity, and that what is commanded in vv. 4 and 5 is to be understood in relationship to v. 3. It is not a question of independent commands or qualifications.

[9:4]   The First Restriction: "Only flesh with its life, its blood, you shall not eat." The translation of the sentence raises difficulties: 1. בָּשָׂר refers to the animals named in v. 3. B. Jacob explains correctly: "It is not a piece of flesh, but the animal as a complete being that consists of flesh." 2. One can understand בְּ in the sense of "with," e.g., B. Jacob: "Flesh with its life." It is of course quite possible to read בְּ in its usual local sense. נֶפֶשׁ then means the being that is alive — in its being alive. 3. דָּמוֹ: Most exegetes interpret it as an apposition of explanation: "In its life, i.e., in its blood," as Deut 12:23 says explicitly: "The blood is the life." Many conclude from this that דָּמוֹ is an addition, C.J. Ball (1896), H. Holzinger (1898; 1922), Ed. Sievers (1904), "perhaps" an addition, O. Procksch (1923), W. Zimmerli (1943) and others. But if P is resuming an already formulated phrase, then one had better concede that the phrase contained the addition because the interpretation seemed necessary. 4. L. Koehler understands the sentence quite differently. בָּשָׂר is a noun to which a relative clause has been appended: "Flesh, in whose life is its blood." But what does "flesh, in whose life . . ." mean? This translation does not seem possible.

The Form of the Sentence. The sentence is a prohibition like the commandments of the Decalogue and Jer 35:6f. E. Gerstenberger has explained them as originating from the clan ethos (*Wesen und Herkunft*. . . , 1965). Ex 23:18 and 19b are similar in form and content. These verses of the book of the covenant are reckoned among its oldest; the same is to be said of 9:4 (P). A distinction is to be made between the meaning that this ancient prohibition had in a series of prohibitions like those just mentioned, and the meaning that J gives it in the present context.

The Original Meaning of the Prohibition. B. Jacob paraphrases: "You may eat all flesh, but not flesh with its life." The commonly accepted explanation, that the sentence forbids the partaking of blood, is not correct, though one can certainly say that it follows; however it is not stated expressly. The sentence is stating rather that the eating of animal flesh is limited to such flesh as no longer has its life in it. It follows therefore that one must pour out the life beforehand. This rules out all explanations whose starting point is that the sentence is making a statement about the substance of blood. H. von Reventlow, for example, writes: "Blood belongs to the divinity and one must treat it with very special care," VT 10 (1960) 311-327; but this is not to the point. Likewise the dispute between C.L. Dewar and L. Morris (see Lit. on 4:9-10) whether blood is a symbol of life or of death is irrelevant. The history of religions shows the same:

D.J. McCarthy, JBL 88 (1969) 166-176, concludes, contrary to J. Wellhausen and W.R. Smith, that the data from the ancient Semitic and Aegean worlds does not witness to a widespread and general belief outside Israel that blood is a divine element which served as the basis or the explanation of sacrifice. 9:4 is not concerned with the partaking of blood or with blood as such. It is concerned with blood insofar as and as long as it is the life of "flesh," i.e., of an animal. The original object in the prohibition then is נפש, and דם is merely added by way of explanation.

B. Jacob has noted correctly: "It is therefore the pulsating . . . life-blood of which it is forbidden to partake, immediately after wounding or killing." A Jewish poet can write: "Our lives flew out on the edge of the swords" (above: L. Kopf, 1938, p. 183f.). It is only now that the reason for the juxtaposition of נפש and דם here and in Deut 12:23 becomes clear: נפש is not identical with the substance of blood, but only with the rhythmic, pulsating blood. Blood is understood here not in its objective but in its functional meaning (J. Milgrom, JBL 90 [1971] 149ff.). This is obscured when some interpreters speak of blood as the seat of life (O. Procksch). It is a misunderstanding too when it is said that v. 4 presumes that sacrifice has been secularized and reduced to killing, and so we have here a late reflection. V. 4, as such, reflects rather a specifically primitive notion that the life of every living being is identical with the pulsation of the blood. The meaning of the prohibition is clear then: you may eat the flesh of animals; but you may not eat the life of the animal together with its flesh (cf. R. Rendtorff, WMANT 24 [1967] 160).

The Meaning of the Sentence in P. P has set the prohibition to eat the "life" of an animal with its flesh in the context of the concession of meat for food. It is an extension of human dominion over the animals after the flood which in turn is in the context of the blessing bestowed on the living beings that survived. The prohibition thus acquires a new and extended meaning: the blessing is preserved by the restriction of dominion over the animals. The killing of animals carries within it the danger of blood-lust (Num 23:24; Deut 32:42; Jer 46:10), of killing for the sake of killing, of blood-thirstiness. The two restrictions in vv. 4 and 5 stand close together here: "The reasons for the prohibition with regard to blood are in the area of behavior and morality" (B. Jacob); and so they are "constantly classed with the moral laws (Ezek 33:25f.)" J. Skinner.

F. Delitzsch and A. Dillmann explain the prohibition about shedding blood as a preventative means against brutality. B. Jacob says it led to a horror of blood and forestalled barbarity: "They are the two elementary demands of humanity in the literal sense of the word." This is extremely important because barbarism and brutality, which are apparently unavoidable concomitants of certain phases of political and social history, cannot for the most part be regulated by law. It is a recognition of the connection between murder and brutality that has brought these two restrictions together. P shows great wisdom in illustrating the phenomenon of brutality by resuming the old prohibition and relating it to human conduct toward animals. One's conduct toward other people is not to be separated from one's conduct toward animals.

[9:5] V. 5 is introduced by the same restrictive particle, אך, as v. 4. One expects a parallel formulation: ". . . you shall not. . . ," a prohibition. K. Koch paraphrases: "After the flood God directs that the blood of animals may be shed but not partaken of, whereas the blood of humans may never be shed. . . ." (VT 12 [1962] 409-410). The content of the prohibition that one expects here is found in v. 6a, but in the form of an apodictic law. V. 5 on the contrary is P's own formulation. It corresponds to an official explanation: it says how God will carry out his lordship over the life of every living being. The verse is governed by the three times repeated אדרש:

But: Your own blood	will I demand,
from all animals	will I demand it,
and from human in turn	
the life of a person	will I demand.

This is one of P's very characteristic stylistic devices: the whole emphasis is put on the verb by the threefold repetition. The second and third sentences are but expansions of part of a sentence into complete sentences. The intention is clear: the command behind vv. 5-6: "thou shalt not kill" is deliberately and emphatically reformulated so as to express God's unconditional lordship over the life of his people. In the context of the blessing bestowed on those saved from the flood, this can only mean that the command "thou shalt not kill" holds for the whole of humanity unconditionally and without restriction. K. Koch explains the use of דרש here in this way: "A member of the community injured by the loss of the deceased prepares to 'look for' the blood of his fellow in the person of the murderer" p. 409. It means: "to demand account for it, to revenge," F. Delitzsch; so Ezek 33:6; Ps 9:13; 2 Chron 24:22. For the לנפשתיכם, U. Cassuto alleges the explanation of Ibn Esra: "of your souls that is your own blood." The proposition ל indicates the dative of possession, the blood of you yourself, as opposed to that of the animals.

The second sentence emphasizes that God also demands blood when it is a question of an animal that sheds the blood; this is prescribed in Ex 21:28-32. F. Delitzsch notes: "There is something similar in the code of Dracon and Solon as well as in Plato." But as far as I know no commentary says that a prescription to take vengeance on animals for the death of a human is only intelligible after the domestication of animals (the Exodus passage shows this). The prescription is only meaningful because the human has cared, provided for and protected the animal so that it becomes part of one's community.

It is only the third sentence that describes specifically the murder of one person by another, and this is expressly called fratricide. F. Delitzsch writes: "אחיו here is not just the colorless 'another'; it carries the full meaning of brother. Murder is the ultimate violation of the brotherly relationship of humankind." B. Jacob: "The relationship of murderer and murdered is that of איש ואחיו." U. Cassuto links the sentence with Gen 4:2-16: "Whoever takes human life is like Cain" (so too B. Jacob). Again we meet the difference: P expounds in principles what J tells in story.

Literature: Gen 9:6a: W. Richter, *Recht und Ethos. Versuch einer Ortung des weisheitlichen Mahnspruchs,* StANT 15 (1966). G. Liedke, *Gestalt und Bezeichnung alttestamentlicher Rechtssätze,* WMANT 39 (1971) 101-153.

[9:6] V. 6 adds nothing new to the two restrictions that vv. 4 and 5 brought to the concession of v. 3. The sentence only underscores what was said in v. 5. The prohibition of homicide is repeated not, as we would expect from v. 4, in the form of a prohibition, but in a prescription in two parts determining the punishment for the person who sheds human blood.

It is to be noted, as H. Gunkel first saw, that the words form a metric verse, 3:3. As is so often the case the narrative moves into rhythmic speech at the high points, e.g., the conclusion of the J flood narrative in 8:22. Many interpreters have observed that the sentence has been deliberately fashioned to an existing form, as shown too by the chiastic structure. 6a: "Whoever pours out human blood, by a human shall his blood be poured out." The variations in the interpretation of the verse are striking. H. Gunkel suggests: "it could be an old legal saying." J. Skinner: "possibly an ancient judicial formula which had become proverbial"; G. von Rad: "an extremely ancient sentence from sacral legal terminology." B. Jacob on the contrary says: "It is not a formal legal pronouncement; a threat, a prophetic admonition." S. McEvenue sees it quite differently: "The chiastic form and rhyming quality lean . . . toward proverb style" p. 70 (referring to E. Gerstenberger and W. Richter). He sees the clearest parallel in Mt 26:52: ". . . all who take the sword will perish by the sword." It can also be compared with the participial laws. McEvenue comes to the conclusion that it has been demonstrated neither that the sentence 9:6a is very old, nor that it is a law, nor that it belongs to P[G]. He argues against the conjecture or proposal of H. Gunkel and G. von Rad that the sentence is very old. It is closer to the formulation of the later *lex talionis* of Lev 24:19-20 than to the earlier Ex 21:23-25 and Deut. 19:21. It is most important in McEvenue's thesis that only an exact comparison of texts can lead to a precise determination of Gen 9:6a. Important too is the reference to the parallel in Mt. 26:52. The embarrassment remains that the interpreters vary between judicial formula, proverb and prophetic admonition.

G. Liedke concludes to a clear association of v. 6a with the "apodictic law," while distinguishing it from casuistic law on the one hand and prohibitions on the other. It consists of a "determination of fact and a specification of the legal consequence" p. 117; it is essential for its operation that "the apodictic law be fixed by the supreme legal authority" p. 125. "By means of the apodictic law the one in authority limits the area of action of the subordinate. The law defines these boundaries and determines the consequences of its transgression" p. 125. An apodictic law then is both possible and meaningful on the lips of God, e.g., Gen 4:15 (J) or Ex 19:12b: "Whoever touches the mountain shall be put to death." The clearest indication that Gen 9:6a belongs to the genre of apodictic law, apart from the form, is that in the majority of cases this form specifies the penalty as death.

The question of the genre to which Gen 9:6a belongs can be considered closed. But this does not answer all the questions that it raises. The stylistic form, with the rhythm and the chiastic parallelism in the three members of each half-verse, is not the equivalent of the apodictic law as such. There is no clear parallel in the many texts that G. Liedke alleges. Moreover the second half-verse: "by man shall his blood be poured out," does not correspond to the style of apodictic law. The specification of the legal consequence is too general and imprecise; juridically one cannot even begin. This half-verse takes its meaning from its context in P, in that sentence is to be pronounced unconditionally on murder. The solution of the differences of opinion about the verse is as follows: there is behind 9:6a an apodictic law which was simple and non-poetic in form, something like the מות ימות. P has shaped this into its present form. It is possible too that the law was the occasion of the formation of a proverb which functioned as a warning, as Mt 26:52 (cf. B. Jacob).

If v. 6a is to underscore the restriction of v. 5 and if there is a law as its background, then its purpose cannot be to transfer God's lordship over human life ("I will demand") to humanity as its executor. F. Delitzsch understood it in this way: "The authority to exact punishment, the prerogative of God alone, is here put into human hands"; similarly A. Dillmann; G. von Rad: "Humanity has been authorized to punish this crime. . . ." But the text has nothing to say about authorization. It is the form of the law underlying the verse that postulates that God's "demand" in v. 6 be executed by humans. The two stand side-by-side without logical link. V. 6 however points out that the demand made by the life taken is in reality resolved in a human encounter, namely in the process of law. The presupposition of this illogical yet quite obvious juxtaposition is that in antiquity the process of law was based on a commission of God or of the gods. The laws were instituted by God, and the execution of judgment took place in the name of God.

F. Delitzsch draws a far-reaching consequence from his view that it is a question here of the transference of authority to punish: "That is the first aspect of the institution of the authorities as executors of the order established by God and so as representatives of God" (quoted with approval by von Rad). A foreign, western understanding of authority is thereby put on the text. This is certainly not the intention in Gen 9:6a. To call the "authorities" executors and representatives in this context is to make them a center of attention of which there is no trace in the text. The presupposition of what is said in v. 6 about the execution of the death penalty by humans is something else. Whoever executes it and whatever form it takes, the demand for life taken is a demand made by God. The explanation of Delitzsch has a limited scope: the authorities of a particular people and land. But 9:6a is expressly universal. The execution of the death penalty by humans is the carrying out of the command of God. It is only this universal scope that gives meaning to what follows: "Because in the image of God have humans been made." W. Zimmerli: "Because the murder of a person strikes at the image of God, it is forbidden unconditionally."

The explanation given of Gen 1:26-28 shows that it is not a question of a quality in people but of the fact that God has created people as his counterpart and that human beings can have a history with God. The image and likeness of God is only there in the relationship between God and the individual. Murder then is a direct attack on God's right of dominion. Every murderer confronts God; murder is direct and unbridled revolt against God. In the later series of prohibitions in the Decalogue, the command לא תרצח is one among several. Here in Gen 9 murder is something utterly on its own; nothing can be compared with it. Throughout the whole sweep of human history, the murderer by his action despoils God. We have here the expression of a statement rather than a command: God will make demands for the many unexpiated crimes against humans as the image of God. This is in the immediate context of the scientific proof that the killing of one's kind (which P expresses by מיד איש אחיו) is a definite possibility and danger among people.

The passage indicates a limit that is set for humans in all places and at all times. When in the created world of humanity it is required that one person be killed by another (the second part of 6a), then the reason for this is that in this very world there is the possibility — exceptional — of murder among one's kind. A community is only justified in executing the death penalty insofar as it respects the unique right of God over life and death and insofar as it respects the inviolability of human life that follows therefrom. The death penalty carried out by the organs of state can also be murder. Every single violation of this limit, be it based on national, racial, or ideological grounds is here condemned.

The 'Noah commandments'

See Literature on Gen 9:1-17 and Gen 9:1-7 above; also J.P. Lewis, *A Study of the Interpretation of Noah and the Flood in Jewish and Christian Literature* (1968); and especially the commentaries of B. Jacob and U. Cassuto. "The 'Noah commandments' are a series of laws thought to be binding upon both Israelite and non-Israelite as the basic requirements of social progress," J.P. Lewis p. 186. The seven Noah commandments are the prohibition of the flesh of animals that are still living, of murder, idolatry, blasphemy, incest, theft, the acknowledgement of authority. This canon took shape in Judaism; they are minimal requirements demanded also of the Noachites. B. Jacob however contests that it is the purpose of Gen 9:4-6 to lay the foundation of the discipline for proselytes, as H. Holzinger supposes. J. Skinner is of the opinion that the rabbinic theologians remained true to the passage when they formulated the Noah commandments. This however is not relevant to the purpose of P: the two restrictions of the human right of dominion in 9:5-6 are not part of some series of commandments. They describe a basic demand which holds for the whole of humankind and which cannot have its like in other commandments. P is not concerned with naming one commandment among others, but with showing that human dominion, which has been broadened as a result of the concession of meat for food, can only exist within the restrictions specified here in the blessing of the creator.

The prohibition of the blood of living creatures has had such influence as a Noah commandment that it has been taken over in Islam as well as at the beginning of Christianity (Acts 15:29).

Literature: Gen 9:7: H.A. Sanders-C. Schmidt, *The Minor Prophets in the Freer Collection and the Berlin Fragment of Genesis* (1927) 288-289.   B. Porten-U. Rappaport, VT 21 (1971) 363-369.

[**9:7**] The passage 9:1-7 returns to its starting point in v. 7. The reason for this is to make clear that the restriction in vv. 4-6 is no "minor clausal limitation" (H. Holzinger) but is made so as to preserve the dominion granted to humans as something that has grown out of the blessing of the creator. The growth and spread of humankind, as it will be unfolded in Gen 10, needs this restriction. It is only then that human dominion becomes really human. The relationship of v. 7 to what precedes requires that the second רבו in the MT be read as רדו, following 1:28 and the Gk (contrary U. Cassuto and others).

Literature: Gen 9:8-17: H. Schultz, *Alttestamentliche Theologie* (1896⁵).   T. Vargha, "De foedere dei cum Noe (Gen 9:9-17)," Ant. 10 (1935) 165-172.   J. Morgenstern, VT 5 (1955) 56-57.   A.R. Hulst, OTS 12 (1958) 64-68.   N. Lade, "The Concept of Sin in the Law," BR 7 (1959) 54-57.   S. Grill, "Die religionsgeschichtliche Bedeutung der vormosaischen Bündnisse (Gen 9:9-17; 17:9-14)," Kairos (1960) 17-22.   F. Nötscher, "Bundesformular und 'Amtsschimmel'," BZ NF 9 (1965) 181-214.   P. Buis, "Les formulaires d'Alliance," VT 16 (1966) 396-411.   D. Lys, "The Israelite Soul According to the LXX," VT 16 (1966) 181-228.   E. Kutsch, KuD 14 (1968) 159-182.   H. Schmid, "JHWH, der Gott der Hebräer," *Missionsbote* 46 (1970) 10-17.   H.P. Müller, "Mythos und Transzendenz. Paradigmen aus dem Alten Testament," EvTh 32 (1972) 97-118.

[**9:8-17**]   The starting point of the explanations of this passage is for the most part the word ברית; how does P use it here? But this is to take too little account of the fact that in the whole length and breadth of the pre-history of the flood narrative nothing like the making of a covenant occurs. It is obvious right from the start that the word ברית can only be understood as an attempt at interpretation. It is a theological explanation whose purpose is to fit the flood narrative into the context of the priestly theology as a whole. Consequently 9:8-17 is not to be understood primarily from P's understanding of ברית elsewhere, but from the context of the flood story of which 9:8-17 is the conclusion.

The number of repetitions in 9:8-17 is striking. G. von Rad writes: "The passage is full of doublets so that two complete recensions can be distinguished readily." In his study *Die Priesterschrift im Hexateuch* (1934) von Rad in fact used this passage as the starting point to separate two literary layers in P. S.E. McEvenue comes to another conclusion on the basis of the same material: "There is no element of this unit which is not repeated twice or three times." And the reason for it: "it must be called simply love of detail and of complete enumeration." The question can only be decided by the exegesis.

The passage is divided by P himself when he introduces a new element in v. 12: 8-11 covenant, 12-17 the sign of the covenant. Vv. 8-11, after the introduction in v. 8, consists of two sentences: God's explanation in v. 9 that he is setting up a covenant with Noah (developed by the enumeration in v. 10), and the assurance in v. 11, after resuming v. 9a, that there will never again be a flood (with its consequences).

Literature: Gen 9:9: G.E. Mendenhall, "Covenant Forms in Israelite Tradition," BA 17 (1954) 50-76.

[**9:9**]   With a renewed and emphatic introduction ואני הנני P throws into relief the "setting up of the covenant" which dominates the whole passage (vv. 11, 12, 13, 15, 16, 17). There is no need to enter here into an extensive and many-sided discussion of the word ברית. I refer to the comprehensive article by E. Kutsch in THAT I (1971) 339-352, where he comments on the present passage: "The Old Testament speaks in different situations of Yahweh's *berit* as his 'self-obligation, promise'. . . . P also designates Yahweh's assurance to Noah that the earth will never again be visited by a flood as *berit* (Gen 9:8-17; cf. the simple promise in J, Gen 8:21, and the oath, Is 54:9). The rainbow as sign of the covenant is to remind Yahweh of this promise (Gen 9:12-17)." The meaning of the word ברית for the structure of the priestly work was recognized early. The thesis of J. Wellhausen of the four covenants has been constantly taken up, corrected and developed. G. von Rad writes: "Wellhausen could not win any acceptance for the thesis of the book of four covenants. Only gradually and with difficulty was it realized that P was not even a book of three covenants; it knew only of the solemn covenants with Noah and Abraham" (*Die Priesterschrift.* . . . p. 175). W. Zimmerli says: ". . . Gen 9:1-17 speaks of a covenant with Noah in the immediate context of the account of the flood and then in Gen 17 of a covenant of God with Abraham" (ThZ 16 [1960] 268-280 = ThB 19 [1963] 205-216). It is questionable whether there is a parallel between the covenant with Noah and that with Abraham — something happens between God and Abraham in Gen 17. Abraham responds in word and action. But nothing happens between God and Noah (and his family and the animals) in Gen 9. There is an address by God to Noah, and no reaction at all on Noah's part. It becomes even clearer that there is action on one side only when one recalls that the ברית expressly includes the animals (this is the reason why H. Gunkel sees this as part of the material at hand to P).

The agreement between Gen 9 and 17 is limited to the word; there is no agreement in what happens. The situation is only obscured when the covenants with Noah and Abraham are set in parallelism without reservation. The word does not describe an event between two or more persons in Gen 9, but what God says or prescribes or lays down. It is not in accord with the texts to put both together under the heading "sealing a covenant." The two texts have in common the address of God that prescribes and gives assurance as long as time lasts. It is this element contained in the word ברית that links the texts. Even if one retains the word "covenant" in translation, then in Gen 9 it means nothing more than "self-obligation, promise" (cf. E. Kutsch). Gen 9:8-17 is saying that God makes a promise to Noah and all living beings that came out of the ark with him, and not that he seals a covenant with them.

[9:10] The assurance is extended expressly and in detail to all species of animals which are once more bracketed with humans in the concluding words: "all that have come out of the ark." It is as if the author wanted to underscore yet again that those saved from destruction have the same destiny and that the same assurance stands as guarantee for all. It is this very verse, which extends the "covenant" to all species of animals, that makes clear that there can be no question of what is usually understood by covenant or of what is later called the promise. This assurance requires no acceptance or approval of any kind. It is there in effect in the mere existence of animals in their species "as long as the earth lasts." That is what is being said. God's word, God's assurance guarantees the continuation of the world and of every living creature, and takes precedence over all theology: it is the simple confirmation of what is.

Literature: Gen 9:11: G. Lambert, "Il n'y aura plus jamais de déluge (Genese IX, 11)," NRTh 77 (1955) 581-601, 693-724.   E. Jenni, *Die theologische Begründung des Sabbathgebotes im Alten Testament,* ThSt (B) 46 (1956).

[9:11] The verse, after resuming v. 9a, consists of two sentences that say the same thing: (1) Never again shall all flesh be wiped out by the waters of the flood, and (2) Never again shall a flood come to destroy the earth.

One can be certain that there is a doublet in the background here. As in 8:21 (J), so here, it is question of the material at hand to P. The simplest explanation is that P wanted to preserve the two versions of God's assurance, so important to him, that had come down. What we have already said about the idea of ברית is confirmed here: 8:21 is a simple assurance by God; Is 54:9 describes this as an oath (cf. E. Kutsch). A further sign that v. 11b belongs to the material that came down to P is that the word כרת occurs only here in the flood narrative, just as הכה only in 8:21 (B. Jacob).

Literature: Gen 9:12-17: A. Pavlica, "Der Regenbogen als Zeichen des Bundes," BZ 13 (1913) 289-291. J. Begrich, "Berit, ein Beitrag zur Erfassung einer alttestamentlichen Denkform,'' ZAW 60 (1944) 1-11 = Gesammelte Studien zum Alten Testament, ThB 21 (1964) 55-66. C.A. Keller, *Das Kainszeichen* (1946). W. Zimmerli, ThZ 5, 1949, 374-375. N.H. Tur-Sinai, ''Othoth ('signs') in the Bible and in the Lachish Letters,'' Tarb. 20 (1949) = Jubilee Vol. presented to J.N. Epstein (1950) 49-57. E. Jenni, ZAW 65 (1953) 1-25; 64 (1952) 197-248; 240f. M. Greenberg, *Y. Kaufmann Jubilee Vol.* (1960) 5-28. A. Jepsen, ''Berith. Ein Beitrag zur Theologie der Exilszeit,'' *Festschr. W. Rudolph* (1961) 161-179. M. Delcor, ''Les attaches littéraires, l'origine et la signification de l'expression biblique 'Prendre à témoin le ciel et la terre','' VT 16 (1966) 8-25; 18. P. Buis, ''La nouvelle alliance,'' VT 18 (1968) 1-15. M. Fishbane, JBL 89 (1970) 316-317. K. Kutsch, '''Bund' und Fest. Zu Gegenstand und Terminologie einer Forschungsrichtung,'' ThQ 150 (1970) 299-320. S.M. Paul, ''Amos 1:3-2:3. A Concatenous Literary Pattern,'' JBL 90 (1971) 397-403. M.W. Shaw, ''Studies in Revelation and the Bible,'' *Covenant Revelation in the Old Testament:* Catholic Seminary Foundation of Indianapolis (1971) 23-32.

[**9:12-17**] *The Sign of the Covenant*. The introduction in v. 12, ''this is the sign of the covenant. . . ,'' is elaborated by the preposition ''between,'' thus naming the parties, and by telling how long the covenant is to last. V. 13 states what the sign consists in and repeats briefly v. 12, describing differently the partners ''between'' whom it exists. The way in which the sign is to function is then described twice, in vv. 14, 15 and v. 16. Vv. 14, 15: when the bow becomes visible in the clouds then I will remember my covenant; v. 16: when the bow is there in the clouds, I will look at it so as to recall. V. 17: by repeating v. 12 and v. 9, it ties both parts together. One must distinguish in the many repetitions in vv. 12-17 between different repetitions of the same thing and repetitions stylistically conditioned. Vv. 14, 15 and v. 16 are genuine doublets: one aspect of what is happening is described twice in successive verses. They are parallel to the doublet in v. 11 in the previous parts, and are to be explained as follows. Two formulations were at hand to P and he wanted to preserve both. The other repetitions on the contrary are stylistic and are the creative work of P. It suffices to show this by one example:

    v.13:   as the sign of the covenant between me and the earth
      15:    between me and you and all living beings
      16:    between God and all living beings, flesh of every kind, that are on the earth
      17:    between myself and all flesh that is on the earth.

It is not really possible to separate the four-fold repetitions in this brief text into different layers. The slight variations which avoid mere mechanical repetition indicate that P has a purpose. He wants to hammer home the goal of the narrative as he sees it and, as it were by successive strokes, allow it to reverberate like the chimes of a tower clock as they continue to echo and re-echo. (Cf. H. Gunkel ad loc.) G. von Rad and S.E. McEvenue have given contrary explanations of the repetitions, as we have outlined above. Nevertheless one can say that both of them, though each only in part, have correctly seen that the text contains a doublet (14, 15 and 16), and that the other repetitions are deliberate stylistic devices of P. However, the stylistic explanation is of itself not enough; the repetitions are constructs and theological in intent.

[**9:12**] It becomes clear how this solemn conclusion was formed and what its purpose is when one takes as one's starting point that P introduced the word ברית into vv. 8-11 by way of interpretation; it is not part of the old flood narrative. This includes אות־הברית "the sign of the covenant," also no part of the old narrative but serving P theologically. It is P who describes the rainbow, already there in the old narrative, as "sign of the covenant." He introduces it then in v. 12 in typically solemn language. The sign that is often linked with the covenant in other places (Gen 21:30; 38:17) serves him as a pledge of the assurance and stresses that it is God alone who is active in this "covenant," and God alone who puts himself under obligation ("self-obligation"). The preposition "between" carries special weight (Hebrew always repeats it before each member; English does not). It describes a relationship between God and humanity in which the initiative is all on one side. This is further underscored when the function of the sign is explained; it reminds God of his solemn assurance. The word "between" is almost paradoxical, and that is just what P intends: God binds himself unilaterally and without reservation to the assurance that results from the end of the flood and includes humankind and all other living beings as well. The unconditional approval that God gives to his creation is the basis of the history of nature and of humanity. It is the basis of all life which can be shaken neither by natural catastrophes of any sort nor — and this is most important for P — by the transgressions, corruption or revolt of human beings. God's assurance remains firm "as long as the earth lasts."

[9:13] "My bow I am putting in the clouds." There was mention of the rainbow at the end of the flood narrative as it came down to P (this is the most convincing proof that P was familiar with other flood narratives than J). A survey of the many flood narratives throughout the world allows us to conclude with certainty that P found himself in the context of a concluding etiological remark; the flood narrative served to explain the phenomenon of the rainbow. This deals the definitive blow to the explanation fashionable since J. Wellhausen that the bow was the warrior's bow which Yahweh, the warrior, was laying aside or hanging on the clouds. Almost all exegetes since then have taken up this very misleading explanation. H. Gunkel, e.g., writes: "The original meaning of the sign derives from the word קשׁת which is the bow that takes aim. . . . Yahweh therefore is a mighty warrior who carries the bow and arrow. . . . When Yahweh has become tired of shooting arrows . . . he lays his bow aside: and so the rainbow appears in the sky after the storm." There can be no contesting that this image existed in Israel (Hab 3:9-11; Ps 7:13f.), Babylon, among the Indians, the Arabs and others. The rainbow can have many explanations; but the bow in the clouds at the end of the flood narrative has nothing to do with the image of God as a warrior carrying a bow.

As far as I know only B. Jacob has rejected this explanation definitively: "There was no trace in the flood of a fight with a mythical background." Opposing H. Gunkel's argument, קשׁת means a warrior's bow elsewhere in the Old Testament, B. Jacob says correctly that even so, where the word means "rainbow," בענן is always added (also Ezek 1:28). Before P explained it as a "sign of the covenant," the rainbow at the end of a flood narrative had the simple and obvious meaning of a natural phenomenon after rain or a thunderstorm. This was quite enough for P to describe it as the "sign of the covenant." F. Delitzsch derives the word קשׁת from an Arabic verb meaning "to bow," "to bend."

[9:14-15] The two parts of v. 14 form the antecedent, v. 15 the apodosis. An explanation is given of how the rainbow functions as a sign. The rainbow is not seen often, but only on special occasions. It is this that gives it its function of confirming God's assurance: it evokes surprise and joy when it appears at the end of a storm "and so in the Jewish blessing God is praised as 'he who remembers the covenant' when the rainbow is seen" (B. Jacob). The cognate accusative construction formed from ענן as well as the verb derived from it occurs only here in the Old Testament. It is part of the vocabulary of the narrative and so belongs to what came down to P. This is further attestation of the language of an earlier stage in which the natural phenomena like rain, thunderstorms, the gathering of the clouds were understood and described as a direct action of God. The next stage: "and the bow becomes visible in the clouds," sees the scene from the point of view of one who looks up to the sky. These different aspects are not at odds.

There follows in 15a the real function of the rainbow as sign: "then I will remember my covenant. . . ." W. Zimmerli remarks: "Here, where it is a question of God's fidelity to his covenant promise, P does not shy away from crass anthropomorphism." He takes to the limit what he wants to say throughout the whole of this concluding passage — the preservation of humanity and of life is completely and unreservedly in God's hands: he remembers it.

V. 15c follows awkwardly on v. 15b. The simple statement that there shall never be another flood to destroy the earth followed immediately on the appearance of the rainbow in the story that came down to P. This slight unevenness in style shows what lies behind P's theological explanation. It has been shown above that a doublet gave rise to vv. 14-15. The function of the sign of the covenant is explained again and the explanation is practically the same. P probably had two versions and wanted to preserve both. We have already found on occasions that the close of a narrative is preserved in a number of variants (e.g., in J, Gen 3:21-24). The same event is described less colorfully and more smoothly here than in vv. 14-15. The difference is that it is not the appearance of the bow (14b), but the fact that it is there in the clouds, that forms the antecedent. Then God looks at the rainbow so as to recall the ברית, which is described here as ברית עולם. Finally, the covenant is further specified as between "God" (not "me" as one would expect in a divine address) and all living beings. These last two details show that the divine address becomes at the end a solemn proclamation. The "eternal covenant" is a phrase typical of P, Gen 17:7, 13, 19; Ex 31:16; Lev 24:8; Num 18:19; 25:13.

[9:17]   The final verse links vv. 12-17 with vv. 8-11, and the last phrase is the same as in v. 16: "all flesh that is on the earth." This again shows the meaning of the many repetitions in P's conclusion. F. Delitzsch writes: "They are hammer blows that fix more firmly and drive home more deeply." All flesh, all life on the earth, every living being in the millennia of the history of nature and of humanity is preserved in God's affirmation of his creation.

[9:28-29]   These two verses form at the same time the conclusion of the flood narrative in P and the conclusion of the genealogy in 5:1-32 which remained unfinished. It is taken up again in 6:9-10; 7:6 is also part of it, and 9:28-29 bring the genealogy to a conclusion without so much as a single sentence missing. When these verses are seen in the context of the genealogy then it becomes obvious that for P the flood is "the great line of demarcation of the eras" (B.

Jacob) as in the Sumerian-Babylonian king lists. Nowhere else in the Old Testament are the years numbered according to a historical event (B. Jacob). Noah's death brings to an end the tenth part of the genealogy of Gen 5. In the Babylonian flood narrative the one saved from the flood is divinized. P, by inserting his flood narrative into the genealogy of Noah, has succeeded in ending it with the death of the one preserved: "He dies like all other humans" (U. Cassuto).

9:28-29 agree in form with the corresponding sentences in the genealogy in 5:1-32 with the exception of the insertion of the events of the flood and of the phrase "he begot more sons and daughters." The reason for this is that post-diluvial humanity is to take its origin from the three sons saved from the flood with Noah (so B. Jacob and U. Cassuto). The verb at the beginning of v. 29 has come down both in the singular and the plural; both are possible.

Purpose and Thrust

The starting point of the flood narrative is God's decision to destroy humanity and its goal is God's decision never to destroy humanity again "as long as the earth lasts." Gen 6-9 shares this theological framework with many flood narratives, especially with those of the high cultures. The significance of the introduction, the decision to destroy, is shown by the fact that it is attested even in Egypt where there is no detailed flood narrative at all. In the Book of the Dead, Atum proclaims: "I shall destroy all that I have made, and this land will return to Nun, under the flood waters, as (in) its first state," (S.G.F. Brandon, *Creation Legends. . . ,* [1963] 16f.; see also F.C. Fensham AION 15 [1966] 31-37). The Old Testament, as well as the New Testament, shares with the whole of antiquity the ability to speak of a destructive action of God or a god or gods. It is not part of the thought pattern to speak of God without speaking of his action of judgment or destruction. The reason for this is that talk about reality and talk about God's action (or the action of a god or gods) coincided at that time. There was no reality without catastrophes — all experience of reality was polarized. A consequence of this was that one could speak of God and gods only if one included the destructive action. A god who was only "good," only love, did not belong to the thought pattern. There is nothing specifically biblical in introducing the flood narrative with God's decision to destroy; the background is an idea of the action of God or the gods that was shared by the whole of antiquity.

What is specifically biblical about the flood narrative can only be seen when we ask about the connections between it and the rest of the Old Testament or the Bible as a whole. The implementation of the decision to destroy humanity is divided into the coming of the flood and its effect. Similarly, the prophetic announcement of judgment is divided into the intervention of God and its consequence (cf. C. Westermann, *Grundformen prophetischer Rede,* BEvTh 31, 1964[2], 122). The reason for the announcement is in fact an accusation; the reason for God's decision to destroy humankind, J 6:5-6, P 6:11-12, corresponds to this. What is peculiar to the prophetic announcement of judgment is that the destructive action of God — which belongs to the God-talk of the whole of antiquity — is focused in a special way on his own people. The Old Testament is certainly well aware of God's destructive action toward the enemies of his people. However the drama between God and his people reaches its climax in his judgment upon them. When the Torah and the Prophetic Books were put together there resulted a contrasting parallelism between the narrative of the destruction of corrupt humanity and the prophetic announcement of destruction that God will bring upon his own corrupt people, i.e., his people who had defected from him.

The story of the prophetic announcement of judgment is continued in the apocalyptic talk of a world judgment by God, e.g., in the apocalypse of Is 24-27. (Of the relationship of Is 24-27 to Gen 6-9 see J. Lewis, *A Study of the Interpretation of Noah. . . ,* 1968, 8.) Here too it is God who judges and destroys. As in the flood narrative it is a question of humankind as a whole. The corruption of the human race is presumed. The destruction is not definitive; some are saved. The exegesis of Gen 6-9 showed that creation and flood are complementary; this corresponds to the apocalyptic where the creation of a new heaven and a new earth (Is 65:17) follows the apocalyptic world judgment. The correspondence between talk about primeval time and end time in the Old Testament extends even to the very language used. H. Gunkel first drew attention to this in his work *Schöpfung und Chaos in Urzeit und Endzeit* (1896) (see also C. Westermann, *Angang und Ende in der Bibel,* CwH 100, 1969).

The flood narrative derives its specifically biblical meaning from the context, which leads from the flood, across God's destructive action toward his own people (as in Gen 6-9 toward his own creation), to the destruction in the apocalyptic end judgment. It is the same God who resolves to destroy humankind in primeval time and then to preserve it as long as the earth lasts, who announces destruction to his people at the climax of its history and preserves it in a remnant, who at the last judgment at the end of human history is the judge and savior of humanity. This is because this God is *one*. This God was not involved in any history of the gods, in any struggle with other gods. Everything is focused on what takes place between God and his own people. It is the *one* God whom Israel encounters in its history and who is the God and Lord of humankind from its beginning to its end. What is special to the narrative of Gen 6-9 over against many other flood narratives, namely that it tells the story of destruction and salvation through the one God, is but the other side of the broad context in which it takes its place in the Old Testament.

One can, with caution, extend this line still further. The reason for the destruction of humanity by the flood is its sin. The same reason recurs in the prophetic announcement of judgment, where the sin is determined more specifically as disobedience to Yahweh and forgetfulness of his saving acts. Pre-exilic prophecy reaches its goal in the message of Deutero-Isaiah. He bases the salvation of the remnant of Israel on forgiveness and in particular on the servant songs, where the servant undergoes vicarious suffering for the sins of the people. The same motifs recur in the Apocalyptic. The message of Jesus of Nazareth takes on a new aspect when seen in this broad context. The work of forgiveness and redemption, which is directed to the present and the end time, takes its setting in life in the context of the action of God which destroys and saves and which leads from the primeval era across the history of God's people, particularly the prophets of doom and Deutero-Isaiah, to the final event. This perspective gives the work of Jesus Christ for the whole of humankind a broader and firmer base.

The flood narrative has a more general meaning that goes beyond the specifically biblical and is based on its world-wide distribution. This amazing fact, the distribution, is ground for concluding that it was expressing something fundamental for early humanity and its understanding of existence. The story states that people, from the earliest accessible stages of human history, were conscious that they were threatened not only personally, but as a member of the species homo sapiens. This awareness of being threatened complements their awareness of their created state. The creator can take back what he has created. This has been given expression in the narrative of the flood. We can be certain that actual flood disasters gave rise to the narrative; one does not trace the broad distribution of the story back to a "universal" disaster that flooded the whole planet Earth in remote antiquity, but to the real awareness of early humankind that it was threatened. This was linked with experiences of disasters in different places.

The question has been raised whether the biblical flood narratives are talking about a universal or a partial flood. G. von Rad, e.g., writes: "According to the priestly presentation therefore we must understand the flood as a disaster involving the whole cosmos" (p. 128). But P can only have meant the "cosmos" known to him, a flat surface, bounded more or less by the areas described in Gen 10. That would be a partial, not a cosmic disaster in our picture of the world. So too collapses the explanation given for the world-wide distribution of the flood story from the earliest time down to the present, e.g.: "On the one hand the distribution of the story . . . on the other hand its remarkable uniformity (flood caused by rain) require that we assume an actual cosmic experience and a primeval recollection which certainly is often woolly. . . ." (von Rad, p. 124). But if each of the many flood narratives was concerned only with an event corresponding to a limited world picture, then it is impossible that they all have a primeval recollection as their basis. The findings of tradition history accord with this. The traditions of a great flood arose and were handed down not only in very different places but also at different times. The chronological distances are as amazing as the geographical. It is difficult to imagine that flood narratives which are still handed down orally in the 20th century go back to the same event as those which were fixed in writing in the second millennium before Christ.

The universal significance of the flood narrative does not need any support from the assumption of a primeval recollection of a definite event in remote antiquity. What is universal in it is not a particular event in primeval time or the primeval recollection resulting from it. It is the express awareness in all the narratives that the human race is threatened, the background at times being particular experiences of disasters.

As humans gradually settled down to live as separate peoples, they began to think politically, and the predominant threat became political, i.e., there was danger to their existence as a people and as a nation. The possibility that the whole of humankind might be destroyed receded into the background. It was only with the Apocalyptic that the possibility of wholesale extermination returned to the perspective. One can understand then how, in the period when national existence was secure, the flood narrative had no significance even in the Christian church. Right down to the most recent explanations of Genesis, there was no acknowledgement that creation and flood were complementary to each other. Consequently, while creation was always an important part of the teaching of the church, the flood had no significance at all and for all practical purposes disappeared completely from the proclamation. It is possible that in a future which will be even more aware than the present of dangers and threats to humanity as a whole, the narrative of the flood will be heard anew. One can already recognize signs of this.

477

The Later History of the Flood Story

Literature: N. Schmidt, *The Apocalypse of Noah and the Parables of Enoch: Oriental Studies* (1926). Sh. Speigel, "Noah, Daniel, and Job Touching on Canaanite Relics in the Legend of the Jews," *Ginsberg Jubilee Vol.*, AAJR (1945) 305-355. G. Vermes, "La communauté de la Nouvelle Alliance d'après ses écrits récemments découverts," EThL 27 (1951) 70-80. E. Hoskyns-N. Davey, *The Riddle of the NT* (1958). T. Jansma, "Investigation into the Early Syrian Fathers on Genesis. An Approach to the Exegesis of the Nestorian Church to the Comparison of Nestorian and Jewish Exegesis," OTS 12 (1958) 69-181. J.W. Doeve, "Lamech's achterdocht in 1Q Genesis Apocryphon," NTT 15 (1960/1961) 401-415. J.C. Jebram, VT 15 (1965) 167ff. E. Testa, "Noe nuovo Adamo secondo i Santi Padri," RivBib 14 (1966) 509-514. M. Black-A.M. Denis, *Apocalypsis Henochi Graece* (1970). H. Gese, "Die Religion Altsyriens," *Die Religionen der Menschheit* 10, 2 (1970) 1-231; 87. E. Testa, "La figura di Noe secondo i SS. Padri," SBFLA 20 (1970) 138-165.

J.P. Lewis, *A Study of the Interpretation of Noah. . . .* (1969), has presented a comprehensive account of the Jewish and early Christian interpretation of the flood narrative. I refer to it here.

a) *The Narrative as a Whole and in Details.* There are very few references to the flood in the Old Testament outside the primeval story; there are more in the New Testament, and more still in the Apocrypha. Is 54:9f. sets God's promise to Israel in exile that he will turn to her once more side-by-side with his oath (only here) at the end of the flood. The passage indicates that Deutero-Isaiah presumed that his hearers knew of the flood. The New Testament on a number of occasions puts the primeval and final judgments in parallelism, so 2 Peter 3:6f., and Mt 24:37-44: "As were the days of Noah, so will be the coming of the Son of Man. . . ," cf. Lk 17:26f. (Irenaeus resumes this). 1 Peter 3:20f. compares salvation through baptism with the salvation of the eight people in the ark; the water of baptism is described here as the ἀντίτυπος of the waters of the flood.

When one surveys what is said about the flood in the Apocrypha, Pseudepigrapha, Philo, Pseudo-Philo and Josephus, in the rabbinic and early Christian literature (details in J.P. Lewis), the first impression is that there is almost no limit to the number of possible interpretations. They range from mere mention of it as an event in the primeval period to the most abstruse and far-fetched allegorical explanations of almost every tiny detail. The survey shows that in the period from Ezekiel to Origen both Jewish and Christian exegesis were unusually preoccupied with the flood; it is mentioned often and in the most widely differing contexts. It also appears that much of this preoccupation concerned itself with minting the motifs of the narrative into small coins which each used for his own, often limited, ends. There is scarcely any sign of awareness of the monumental dimensions of the story as it concerned the fate of the whole of humankind.

The ethical exhortation, which resumes the corruption of humankind at that time (e.g., exemplified in Gen 6:1-4) as the "moral of the story," is especially popular in both Jewish and Christian exegesis. The Book of Jubilees depicts the flood story in such a way as to trace Jewish customs back to what happened then. By means of florid allegorical exegesis Philo exalts the religious values of the present, introducing Greek thought and ideas uncritically. It is of no concern to him that the same detail is the source of contradictory explanations, e.g., at one time the flood signifies the purification of the soul, at another the power of the evil one. Josephus (Ant. III and IV) and Pseudo-Philo on the other hand merely want to present the story itself, each in his own way. This is also true by and large of the rabbinic interpretation (especially in the Babylonian Talmud and in the Midrash Genesis Rabbah), even when they add another meaning to the plain meaning of the text; rabbinic exegesis presents a varied picture.

b) *The Figure of Noah.* Besides mention in the genealogies (1 Chron 1:4; Lk 3:36) Noah, together with Daniel and Job, is the exemplar of the just man in Ezek 14:14, 20. This exaltation of Noah persists through the whole history of exegesis. So too in the New Testament, Heb 11:7: "By faith Noah constructed ...and became an heir of the righteousness which comes by faith." In 2 Peter 2:5 Noah is described as a "herald of righteousness." Both Jewish and Christian exegesis have made use of the ethical exaltation as the moral of the story, contrasting Noah, the exemplar of righteousness and piety, with corrupt humanity of his time; e.g., Sir 44:17; Tob 4:12; Wis 10:4; TestBenjamin 10:6; the Book of Adam and Eve 3:1.

Early Christian exegesis continues the moral application, contrasting the evil generation of the flood with the righteousness of Noah. The apologists found the knowledge of the flood story in Greek tradition a convenient point of contact. Justin (Apology), like Josephus before him, identified Deucalion with Noah. Noah was much more often a type of Christ. He is explained in this context as the new Adam, the first of a new human race. This explanation is found in many of the fathers of the church. Noah can also be described as a prophet (J.C.H. Lebram, VT 15 [1965] 167ff.). In the Qumran community the "teacher of righteousness" is the new Noah (cf. G. Vermes, 1951).

c) *Changes in Modern Times.* It was only in modern times, when the plain meaning of the text had prevailed again, that the allegorical-typological and the moralizing explanations lost their significance. It was now a question of the historicity of the flood. It was pursued in the context of the history of religions and inquired about the relationship of the many recently recovered flood stories to the biblical story.

But the question of historicity paid no attention to the framework of the story: God's decision to destroy and its reversal. The theological interpretation was then restored fully to its place. The exegetes of the 19th century saw no problem here. The just God exercises judgment over the corrupt human race. F. Delitzsch comments on 8:1: "... with the rising of the waters his justice had become clear, but now his hidden grace came to light and gained the upper hand." When the flood event is assumed into an abstract systematic theology it becomes apparent how inappropriate this is in face of the uniqueness of the decision to destroy and its reversal at the end of the story. Something had to be narrated the like of which never happened again and which becomes quite incomprehensible in the timeless attributes of God.

Our age cannot view an event like the flood in so remote a way as did the theologians of the 19th century. It is no longer possible to see God's righteousness or God's just anger at work in the world-wide disasters that we have experienced and in the almost daily news of further disasters. On the other hand, one can no longer live through these disasters without asking how God's action is related to them or at least how God can permit them. The flood story slowly but surely lost all theological interest as the great process of destruction was blandly subordinated to the attributes of God. But today its theological significance can no longer be neglected. It is the task of those who explain the primeval story of the flood to think through the problem again in a world that has changed. What does it mean for those whose understanding of the world is conditioned by the natural sciences to say that God's action encompasses all reality, disasters included? And can one say that this all encompassing action takes its origin from an assurance to preserve the world of humankind "as long as the earth lasts"?

Noah and His Sons

Literature

W. Volck, "Noah und seine Söhne," RE XIV (1897; 1904³) 140-148.   R. Dussaud, "Cham et Canaan," RHR 59 (1909).   J. Herrmann, "Zu Genesis 9:18-27," ZAW 30 (1910) 127-131.   K. Budde, ZAW 34 (1914) 241-253; ZAW 36 (1916) 1-7.   F. Stähelin, "Der Name Kanaan," *Festschr. J. Wackernagel* (1923) 150-153.   E. Dhorme, "Les peuples issus de Japhet d'après Chapitre X de la Genèse," Syria 13 (1932) 28-49.   A. Reubeni, *Shem, Ham, and Japhet. The People of the Bible, their Racial Connections and Place in History* (Hebr., Engl. Summary) (1932).   E. Lund, "Ein Knotenpunkt in der Urgeschichte. Die Quellenfrage Genesis 9:18-19," ZAW 56 (1938) 34-43.   A. Poebel, JNESt 1 (1942) 247-306.   B. Mazar, "Palestine at the Time of the Middle Kingdom," BEHJ 1 (1946) 37-38, 59.   J.E. Surfelt, "Noah's Curse and Blessing, Gen 9:18-27," CTM 17 (1946) 737-742.   W. Borgeaud, *Museum Helveticum* 4 (1947) 240-249.   H.G. Güterbock, AJA 52 (1948) 123-125.   M. Noth, *A History of Pentateuchal Traditions* (1972).   L. Rost, "Noah der Weinbauer. Bemerkungen zu Genesis 9:18ff.," BHTh 16 (1953) 169-178 = *Das kleine Credo und andere Studien zum Alten Testament* (1965) 44-53.   A. van Selms, "The Canaanites in the Book of Genesis," OTS 12 (1958) 182-213.   J. Heemrood, "Kanaan verflucht," HLa 12 (1959) 129-131.   S. Moscati, *Sulla storia del nome Canaan,* AnBib 12 (= SBO 3) (1959) 266-269.   W. Schottroff, WMANT 30 (1969) 148-150.

Text

9:18 The sons of Noah who went out of the ark were Shem, Ham, and[a] Japheth. And Ham it was who was the father of Canaan.

19 These three[a] were the sons of Noah and the whole earth was populated[b] from them.

20 And Noah as the first[a] to cultivate the soil planted a vineyard.

21 He drank from the wine and became drunk, and lay uncovered[a] in his tent[b].

22 When Ham, the father of Canaan, saw his father's[a] nakedness, he told[b] his brothers outside.

23 But Shem and Japheth took[a] the cloak, put it[b] on the shoulders of each of them, walked backwards and so covered their father's nakedness; their faces were turned away[c] so that they did not see their father's nakedness.

24 When Noah awoke[a] from the effects of the wine and knew what his youngest[b] son had done to him,

25 he said: Cursed be Canaan![a] Slave of slaves shall he be to his brothers[b]!

26 And he said: Blessed be Yahweh[a], the God of Shem, But Canaan shall be his[b] slave.

27 May God enlarge[a] Japheth, that he may dwell in the tents of Shem, and Canaan be his slave.

18a   The Bombergiana (Venice 1524/25) reads וְיִפֶת for וָיֶפֶת.

19a   BrSynt §85b.   **b** נפצה is Ni. of נפץ (= פוץ) as 1 Sam 13:11; Is 33:3; Ges-K §67dd, neglect of doubling; in KBL under נפץ, qal, "to be shattered, to be scattered," in Gen 9:19 "populate."

20a   ויחל used adverbially, "as first." The rendering in BrSynt is not accurate: "and Noah began to be a farmer."

21a   ויתגל on the form, Ges-K §75bb.   **b** בתוך = in, BrSynt §106i; cf. J. van Dijk, "A Neglected Connotation of three Hebrew Verbs," VT 18 (1968) 16-30.

22a   LXX adds ויצא.   **b** The pronominal object is omitted, as is often the case, Ges-K §117f.

23a   The Gk and the Sam have the plural, the singular is possible grammatically, Ges-K §146t, BrSynt §132.   **b** BrSynt §137.   **c** The predicate of the nominal sentence can be replaced by an adverb of place, BrSynt §25b.

24a   On the form Ges-K §70a.   **b** To express the superlative, Ges-K §133g.

25a   Some Gk Mss. replace 'Canaan' by 'Ham', obviously with harmonizing intent.   **b** On the form of the curse, cf. W. Schottroff, *Der Altisraelitische Fluchspruch*, WMANT (1969) 25, 47, 53, 55, 156.

26a   For all passages ברוך יהוה, cf. Schottroff, 165, 167; also J.-P. Audet, "Esquisse historique de genre littéraire de la 'bénédiction' juive et de "l'eucharistie" chrétienne," RB 65 (1958) 371-399.   **b** למו need not be altered; it can be a case of a sing., so Is 44:15.

27a   פתה = to enlarge, to create space, only here. O. Procksch and L. Rost understand it as "to allure, to tempt" (e.g., Ex 22:15). But that is not possible because the verb is never constructed with ל in this sense (cf. J. Hoftijzer OTS 12 [1958] 25). On the form Ges-K §75gg.

Literary Form

On the history of Exegesis, cf. C. Westermann, *Genesis 1-11: Erträge der Forschung* 7 (1972) 92-94.

9:18-27 belong to J and consist of two self-contained units: vv. 18-19 and vv. 20-27. The second unit is a story of Noah and his sons which leads to Noah pronouncing blessings and curses over the sons.

One's first inclination is to classify the unit 9:18-19 as a genealogical detail. But there is nothing either before or after with which it is as such connected. On the other hand v. 19b, which says that the whole of post-diluvial humanity stems from Noah's three sons, is of such import as to make it unlikely that the passage is part of a genealogy. One agrees with H. Gunkel when he writes: "vv. 18 and 19 are clearly the close of J's flood narrative . . . and at the same time the introduction to the family tree of Shem, Ham, and Japheth in Gen 10." This is confirmed as certain because the whole series of flood stories tell that the whole of humankind derives from those saved from the flood. The conclusion is that the story which begins in v. 20 has originally nothing to do with vv. 18-19; however it has a natural link with them because it also deals with Noah and his sons. And further, the words "Ham, who was the father of Canaan" in v. 18 are a subsequent addition to balance the name Canaan in v. 25.

The Narrative 9:20-27:

The story tells of an outrage, v. 22, and its punishment, vv. 24f. as well as of an act of piety, v. 23, and its recognition, vv. 26, 27; The father curses one son and blesses the other two. 9:20-27 then takes its place in the stories of crime and punishment which form a group within the J text of Gen 1-11 (cf. Introduction, 3B). It follows that 9:20-27 belongs to J (against K. Budde, R. Smend, and W. Eichrodt and others) and that it is a unity within J. The passage differs from the other crime and punishment narratives in that (a) God is not the one who punishes, (b) there is an act of piety, acknowledged as such, together with the outrage, (c) the blessing and curse, it seems, define the destinies of peoples. This third point of difference pushes 9:20-27 to the edge of the primeval event, and fits well with the fact that the names of the three sons of Noah are the same as those which are the starting point of the Table of Nations in Gen 10.

Moreover, the occasion for the outrage committed by one of the sons, the drunkenness of his father, is linked with a detail about the history of civilization, namely that Noah the farmer began by cultivating the vine, 9:20. The structure of 9:20-27 is markedly contrived. Four elements come together, each having its own line of tradition:

1) The three sons of Noah (genealogy)
2) The detail about the history of civilization (as in Gen 4:17ff.)
3) The narrative of crime and punishment
4) The curses and the blessings.

The main difficulties, which hitherto have not found a solution that is generally accepted, are due to the coalescence of four so diverse elements in so short a text. One must be particularly careful in the exegesis to take account of each of these elements in itself and then to ask how they came together.

(1) The three sons of Noah, Shem, Ham, and Japheth, are part of a genealogical tradition which is well attested: in J in 9:18-19, Gen 10, as well as in P. The same succession is preserved too in the narrative in 9:20-27, but with a deviation. The same order occurs in vv. 22, 23 with the words "the father of Canaan" added as in v. 18. In the second part of the narrative however the curse is pronounced not over Ham who had committed the outrage but over Canaan. Shem and Japheth are mentioned again in vv. 26 and 27. How is this to be explained?

There is broad agreement in the literary-critical school which solves the problem by eliminating חם אבי in v. 22 so that the text reads: "Then Canaan saw his father's nakedness. . . ." (J. Wellhausen, K. Budde, H. Holzinger, O. Procksch, H. Gunkel, G. von Rad, L. Rost and others). This removes the difficulty at one stroke. It is Canaan who commits the outrage, v. 22, and who incurs the curse, v. 25. This solution seems so convincing that it cannot be countered by tradition criticism. One must conclude then that there are two different traditions about the order of Noah's sons in 9:20-27; together with Shem-Ham-Japheth there would also be Shem-Japheth-Canaan (according to v. 24 he is the youngest son). But this conclusion depends solely on the elimination of the appendage in v. 22, and so on a literary-critical hypothesis. It is natural to concede that the appendage that explains the link between Ham and Canaan is the same in vv. 19 and 22: 19: "And Ham it was who was the father of

Canaan''; 22: ''(Ham) the father of Canaan.'' There is a weightier argument. The name Canaan in v. 25 is the name of the one who incurs his father's curse; it occurs in the pronouncement of a curse. The curse is repeated substantially in the last sentence of both blessings in vv. 26 and 27: ''and Canaan shall be his slave.'' In addition it occurs in the two explanations added in vv. 18 and 22 that describe Ham as the father of Canaan.

One fact emerges very clearly from this. Of its five occurrences, the name Canaan is fixed firmly only in the curse in v. 25. This is the only place where it is genealogy but of a narrative which leads to the curse. On the other hand the last sentence in vv. 26 and 27 repeats what is said in v. 25, and in vv. 18 and 22 the addition reveals a subsequent intent to give balance. The name Canaan therefore is attested with certainty only as an individual name, not as part of the series of the three sons of Noah.

All explanations beginning with the supposition that the basis of the text is two different series of the names of Noah's sons misconstrue the situation. It is not possible to solve the problem of the lack of agreement of the names in vv. 22 and 25 by simply striking out the words ''Ham, the father of. . . .'' as the literary critics would. We must leave the contradiction as it is. The narrative is concerned with an outrage of Ham against his father Noah. The same person who committed the outrage in v. 22 falls under the curse in v. 25. The Yahwist has preserved, together with the story of Ham's outrage, a curse over Canaan which could be resumed because of the genealogical proximity of Canaan to Ham. Those who heard the story knew the descendants of Ham as identical with those of Canaan. Ham, like Canaan, was the forefather; they understood his function in the story in this way, not as an individual. It was only when people no longer understood the identity in function of Ham and Canaan that it became necessary to add ''the father of Canaan'' in v. 22 by way of explanation; and this was appended subsequently in v. 18. It remains an open question whether the further determination of the narrative goes a step beyond this explanation.

(2) The cultural-historical note about the beginning of viticulture in v. 20 is independent of the narrative and serves mainly as its exposé. If v. 20 stood alone, it would be a ''tiny unity'' of cultural-historical interest. As 4:17ff. show, such information was handed down in genealogical form; v. 20 follows very well on vv. 18-19. It is like 5:29, which is also in a genealogy.

(3) The narrative. If one prescinds from the question of the significance of the curse and blessing, then the story is about individuals (so too B. Jacob). The action takes place within the family circle; it is a story of what happens between a father and his sons. The situation is presented in vv. 20-21; one son acts impiously, the other two piously toward their father. The one incurs a father's curse, the others receive the father's blessing.

Where and how does the application to a people enter into this part of the story? B. Jacob comments on v. 22: ''The sin of Canaan is shamelessness, unbridled sexuality. The euphemism for this is 'uncovering of the shame','' thus following the explanation given in almost all commentaries. G. von Rad, like H. Gunkel, sees the narrative as the result of what the immigrant Israelites encountered in Canaan: ''. . . the amazement and abhorence with which the newly arrived Israel encountered the sexual depravity of the Canaanites (cultic prostitution).'' But does the text really say this? Vv. 22-23 contrast the conduct of sons toward their father. Ham's sin does not consist in a general shamelessness or in unbridled sexuality, but in dishonoring his father, while Shem and Japheth conducted themselves with piety. This gentle nuance calls for an important decision. If Ham's sin is "sexual corruption," "unbridled sexuality," there arises at once the well-known question of the sexual corruption of Canaan as is presupposed in Hosea and Lev 18:3. It is obvious in this case that the son of Noah represents the Canaanite people. But if the outrage consists in dishonoring the father, then one can no longer say that the text is speaking about anything specifically to do with the historical Canaanite people. It is much more a question of the obligations of the son to take care of his father who has become heavy with wine, as in the Aqht myth (cf. ANET p. 150, 11.32-33).

, Setting in Life

When we inquire into the origin and setting in life of the passage we must pay particular attention to the parts and their constitutive elements. It has been determined that vv. 18-19 are the end of the Yahwistic flood narrative; the distribution over the earth of those who stem from the sons of the one who was saved is an ancient motif that belongs to the conclusion of the story.

The three sons of Noah originate from and belong to a genealogy. They follow the pattern according to which a sequence of ancestors ends with three brothers (cf. Introduction 2, the genealogies in J). the threefold sequence Shem-Ham-Japheth precedes the narrative; it is an important element in its construction, vv. 22, 23 and 25-27. The note about the progress in civilization, namely that Noah was the first to plant the vine, also belongs to a genealogy and has been handed down in this context, as the parallel notes in 4:17ff. show. The narrative of 9:20-27 passed through many stages before reaching the final form that has come down to us. The narrative itself develops in v. 21 out of the family tree. It belongs to the large group of narratives that grew up as elaborations of a note in the genealogy. The note speaks of something circumstantial (Noah cultivates the vine); the narrative composes a story out of this and shapes it into a drama *(Geschehensbogen)*, vv. 21-25. The effect of the wine is to weaken or impair the faculties of one, and another takes advantage of it. A son dishonors his own father whose faculties are impaired and so incurs the father's curse. The goal is again something circumstantial: the father's curse imposes on the son a state of servitude under his brothers. The narrative belongs to the group of crime and punishment stories characteristic of the primeval event and is close to the family stories of the patriarchal history.

The most difficult question is that of the origin of the blessing and curse. Blessing and curse occur in the primeval event, 3:14f. in the patriarchal stories, Gen 27, in the context of the history of the tribes, Gen 49, and later in the political history. The curse in 9:25 is in the context of the primeval event. However because of the pronouncements, which were added later, first over Shem, who can only mean Israel, and then over Japheth, and this is politically oriented, it takes on political overtones. The son of Noah the first wine grower now becomes the people of Canaan which is enslaved to Israel and Japhet(?). This alone is certain; everything else in these pronouncements remains problematic.

The Yahwist has indicated the many layers by means of the lack of agreement of the names in vv. 22 and 25. One can conjecture that there was an older form of the narrative which told only of the son of Noah the winegrower and which ended with the curse over his son.

Commentary

[9:18-19] These two verses belong to the conclusion of J's flood narrative; salvation began with God's assurance after the sacrifice. There follows now a closing remark that a new humanity takes its origin from the sons of Noah after the flood. There is a whole series of parallels in other flood narratives. Humanity has perished; the conclusion throws a bridge from the one who was saved and his family to humanity rising anew after the flood. It makes good sense that J first gives the names of Noah's sons here (P has already mentioned them in 5:32; 6:10; 7:13). It is only here that they acquire their significance as those who are the source of post-diluvial humanity. J expresses this very well and clearly by the arrangement of vv. 18 and 19 which are almost in rhythmic form: v. 18: 2:2:3; v. 19: 3:3. V. 18 indicates the family tree: "The sons of Noah were Shem, Ham, and Japheth." This is elaborated by a participial clause, "who went out of the ark," which gives the sentence a different character. The elaboration puts the world-shaking event of the flood into the family tree. The three saved from the flood with their father are the subject of what follows.

V. 19 forms a contrast: these three — the whole of humankind takes its origin from them! The meaning of the contrast is this: humanity is conceived here as a unity, in a way different from the creation; humanity in all its variety across the earth, takes its origin from these three who survived the flood. The purpose of the contrast is to underscore the amazing fact that humanity scattered in all its variety throughout the world comes from the one family. The verb "was populated" is also to be understood in this sense. H. Gunkel remarks: "The expression has its setting in the story of the building of the tower." It is found at the conclusion, 11:8 and 9, as well as in 10:18, as a leitmotif going through the texts that follow the flood. In 11:8 and 9 it is in the qal describing God's action of punishment; in Is 33:3 too it describes a momentous event. The verb therefore can have a different echo, corresponding to which is a different concept of the dispersion of humankind over the earth. There is no speculation in 9:19 and 10:18 over the way in which humankind disperses. It is merely a factual record that the whole of humanity dispersed over the world as then known goes back to the family saved from the flood. The remark "And Ham it was who was the father of Canaan" has no significance in the intention of vv. 18-19. It is not intended to put the three sons of Noah, in contrast to the population of the whole earth, in a family relationship to individuals. They are meant to be the three, and this is emphasized at the beginning of v. 19, from whom all beings on earth stem. The juxtaposition of the sentences which express this: "Shem, Ham, and Japheth. These three were. . . ," was destroyed by the addition — as was the rhythm too. We can be certain then that the note which links Ham to Canaan is a subsequent addition. The reason for it must lie outside these verses because in content it adds nothing to vv. 18 and 19; it can only be to balance Ham in v. 22 and Canaan in v. 25.

Literature: Gen 9:20-27: W. Staerk, ZAW 42 (1924) 41-42, 56; "Zur alttestamentlichen Literarkritik," ZAW 42 (1924) 34-74. A. Lods, "La caverne de Lot," RHR 95 (1927) 204-206. C.A. Simpson, "The Book of Genesis. Introduction and Exegesis," IB 1 (1952) 556ff. J. Hempel, ZAW 65 (1953) 138. U. Cassuto, *Blessing and Curse,* EB (B) (1954ff.). J. Hoftijzer, "Some Remarks to the Tale of Noah's Drunkenness," OTS 12 (1958) 22-28. R. Graves-R. Patai, *Hebrew Myths: The Book of Genesis* (1964) 120-122. F.W. Basset, "Noah's Nakedness and the Curse of Canaan. A Case of Incest?," VT 21 (1971) 232-237.

[9:20-27] The structure of the narrative presents no difficulties. It has already been given: exposé, 20-21; conduct of brothers, 22-23; the father's reaction in curse, 25; and blessing, 26, 27, introduced in 24.

Literature: Gen 9:20: Sh. Marenhof, "A Forgotten Root," AJSL 52 (1936) 116-117. H.W. Wolff, EvTh 16 (1956) 363 = ThB 22 (1973²) 280. F.C. Fensham, *The Spirit of the Vine* (1968).

[9:20] The ויחל is used adverbially: Noah was the first to cultivate the vine. The verb יחל (in the primeval story also in 4:26; 6:1; 10:8; 11:6) is characteristic of the primeval event but is used advisedly, generally as called for by the context; it deals with a beginning, the first time something is done. When Noah is described here as a farmer, it does not mean "that Noah was the first farmer" (H. Gunkel, similarly A. Dillmann, J. Skinner), but rather that the cultivation of the soil has taken a further step forward from agriculture to viticulture. It is presumed that Noah is the agricultural heir of his ancestors which is in full accord with J's concept. The advance in civilization is described in a genealogy as in 4:17ff. (see Comm.). Once more the benefits of civilization are traced back to a person, not to the gods (Osiris, Dionysus). The suggestion that Noah may have been originally a Canaanite wine god is certainly not correct. According to A. Dillmann the home of the vine is in east Pontus and Armenia. But this has no necessary link with the place where P has the ark settle, because the tradition of the beginning of viticulture is independent of the flood tradition.

It is important that Gen 9:20 regards viticulture as a step forward in relation to agriculture. This is expressed also in 5:29: "And he named him Noah saying: this one will create relief for us from our work and from the toil of our hands from the ground which God has cursed." In commenting above on these verses we accepted an older form which was later complemented in accordance with 3:17: "He will bring us relief in (from) our work." Viticulture and its produce is regarded as an advance on agriculture. Over and above the toil and labor of the farmer to produce the necessities of life, it yields a product that brings joy and relaxation. The rhythm of work and celebration demands that the celebration be the high point; festivity supercedes daily drudgery. The production of wine opens the way to festal drinking; there is more than the mere prolongation of life from the fruits of the field. One can understand how in Israel the vine and its fruit became the sign of the blessed life in the messianic era: "They shall sit every man under his vine and under his fig tree, and none shall make them afraid" (Mic 4:4; other passages in B. Jacob).

Literature: Gen 9:21: H.J. van Dijk, "A Neglected Connotation of Three Hebrew Verbs," VT 18 (1968) 16-30. J.A. Bailey, "Initiation and the Primal Woman in Gilgamesh and Genesis 2-3," JBL 89 (1970) 137-150, esp. 145. J.P. Brown, "Peace Symbolism in Ancient Military Vocabulary," VT 21 (1971) 1-23; esp. 15, 22.

[9:21] The real action begins in v. 21. It is a series of three acts: Noah drank some of the wine, he became drunk, and he lay uncovered in his tent. The product of the vine made its way from the near east (Asia Minor or Pontus?) in many directions as the word that still accompanies it indicates: יין, voino, οἶνος, vinum, wine. Drunkenness as such was not regarded as reprehensible in antiquity. If a person became drunk at a celebration, it was always good for a story, but no judgment was passed. When F. Delitzsch comments: "Scripture narrates the sins of even the greatest saints," he misunderstands the meaning of the text.

The ancients were well aware of the effects of intoxication. They knew that wine could stupify the senses and weaken the faculties and have other dangerous consequences which could result in one being uncovered without knowing; and this was something disgraceful (see Hab 2:15; and Lam 4:21). In the Ugaritic myth ''The Tale of Aqht'' the dutiful son is described as he ''who takes him by the hand when he is drunk, carries him when he is sated with wine,'' (ANET 150). There is no need to offer the excuse that Noah did not yet know the effects of the wine (O. Procksch and others). Noah lies uncovered in his tent; to be uncovered is a disgrace as Ex 20:26; 2 Sam 6:26; 10:4f. show. J.A. Bailey writes: ''Nakedness in the Old Testament usually refers to the loss of human and social dignity'' p. 145 (see above).

[9:22]   With Noah and his sons living together it was the duty of the sons in such a situation to stand by the father, in this case to cover him, as the citation from Ugarit shows. It was a grave breach of custom when Ham saw his father lying naked in his tent, did not cover him, but left him there and went outside and told his brothers. This is narrated so clearly that it is difficult to understand how exegetes have missed the obvious meaning. H. Gunkel writes: ''According to v. 22 Canaan saw his father's shame and communicated it to his brothers. Both are sinful: he should not have looked and at least should not have spoken of it.'' Gunkel's explanation is within the framework of a Christian individual ethic which holds almost all exegetes captive here. He concludes: ''This cannot be all, because v. 24 presumes that Canaan has done something to him.'' He refers to H. Holzinger who supposes that the son had removed the father's garment completely.

Many exegetes conjecture a grave sin of this sort on the part of Canaan (J. Skinner, G. von Rad, W. Zimmerli, C.A. Simpson and others). H. Winckler thinks it pederasty. F.W. Basset, VT 21 (1971) 232ff. concludes from the idiomatic meaning of the phrase ''to see the shame of someone,'' which refers to sexual intercourse in Lev 18 and 20, that the sin of Noah's son was incest with his mother. This idiomatic usage was no longer understood in the later addition of v. 23. Basset, like H. Gunkel, begins with the argument that v. 24 says that the son had done something to his father. All these conjectures have missed the point. They have not seen that Ham's outrage consists in not covering his father. This is what v. 24 is talking about. Basset's assumption that it is a question of the idiomatic usage is misleading. The narrative makes it perfectly clear that the sentence ''when Ham saw his father's nakedness'' can only be meant literally.

On גגד: L. Schmidt, *Menschlicher Erfolg und Jahwes Initiative. Studien zu Tradition, Interpretation und Historie in Überlieferungen von Gideon, Saul und David,* WMANT 38 (1970).

[9:23]   The behavior of the two other brothers is described here in almost intricate detail compared with the rest of the narrative. The intention is obviously to draw attention to their pious conduct which, significantly, is unfolded in a series of concrete verbs: they took (the cloak) — put it — walked backwards — so covered — were turned away — did not see. F. Delitzsch's explanation shows how differently Westerners can present the event. ''The spirit of their action is reverent, chaste simplicity and adroitness combined with love.'' U. Cassuto notes correctly: ''The style is almost poetic in form and shows signs of parallelism.'' (Cf. also S. Gevirtz, *Patterns in the Early Poetry of Israel* (1963.) H.

Gunkel is reading into the text when he describes the different behavior of the sons in vv. 22 and 23: "The story presents thereby types of peoples" (others similarly). The text hitherto has shown no sign of a history of peoples. J sets the different behavior of the children toward their parents in primeval time and at the very place in the primeval event where for the first time the sons have a role that determines the event further. It is from Noah's sons that the human race branches, 9:19. And this opens the possibility of different attitudes toward parents (Prov 30:17). The reaction of the father shows that this differentiation has its effect in the history of humankind.

According to J. Herrmann, ZAW 30 (1910) 127-131, an older form of the narrative in v. 23 mentioned only Shem. In favor of this is not only the singular of ויקח and שכם, but also that the episode would run more naturally if only one person were involved. Further, where contrasts in behavior are described elsewhere, especially in the patriarchal stories, the event concerns two individuals. השמלה is the garment that one throws over oneself or in which one sleeps, Ex 22:26f.; Deut 24:13.

Literature: Gen 9:24: F. Gaboriau, *Le thème biblique de la connaissance* (1969). J.A. Emerton, "A Consideration of Some Alleged Meanings of ידע in Hebrew," JSSt 15 (1970) 145-180.

[9:24] Noah wakes up from sleep and is sober again. He learns what his younger son has done to him (how, is not important for the narrative) and pronounces a curse over him. The commentaries scarcely give any consideration to the reason why the father reacts in this way. A modern would at least say that the reaction was disproportionate. But it is not the reaction of a moment. It is rather a question of a line of demarcation in human relations that was taken very seriously in the ancient world: the continuity of the life of a group of people depends on the stream of tradition being passed on undisturbed from one generation to another. This was only possible when the elders were respected by the younger, those going by those coming. Respect for elders was a command necessary for the maintenance of the group, and this is difficult for us to understand in our circumstances. That is the reason why Noah cursed the son who mocked him. Noah does not act as an individual in an individual father-son relationship, but as representative of the group who must act in this way in order to preserve its continuity.

This makes clearer the meaning and function of the episode 9:20-27 at this place in J, after the conclusion of the flood and before humankind divided into branches over the earth: before the flood the primeval story told of human failure in the community of marriage and of brotherhood. Immediately after the flood and before humankind begins to divide into peoples, there is the failure of the son in relation to his father. It is a question here of a basic element of historical continuity as one saw it at that time. It depends above all on the fact that something can be passed on in a group from one generation to the next. It is only in this way that progress, cultural growth and the preservation of values is possible. The danger point in this process lies in the transition from one generation to another. It can remain intact only if embedded in a basic attitude of respect toward those becoming old and consequently weak. This is the basis of the narrative in 9:20-27.

Literature: Gen 9:25-27: A.Jirku, "Götter Habiru oder Götter der Habiru?,"

ZAW 44 (1926) 237-242. J. Muilenburg, "A Study in Hebrew Rhetoric: Repetition and Style," VT.S 1 (1953) 97-111. J.M. Robinson, "Heilsgeschichte und Lichtungsgeschichte," EvTh 22 (1962) 113-140. E. Osswald, "Zum Problem der vaticinia ex eventu," ZAW 75 (1963) 27-44. J. Scharbert, "Solidaritätsprinzip," LThK 9 (1964) 864-865. A. van Selms, "Judge Shamgar," VT 14 (1964) 294-309. D. Neiman, "The Date and Circumstances of the Cursing of Canaan," *Biblical Motifs. Origins and Transformations* (1966) 113-134. P. Buis, VT 17 (1967) 478f. H.G. Link, "Segen," TBLNT II 2 (1971) 1119-1127.

Excursus: *The Explanation of the Three Brothers in 9:25-27.*

The narrative up to v. 24 gave no occasion at all to raise the question of peoples and their relations because it deals with individuals. It is only with the effect of the blessing and curse on the future that the possibility arises that the pronouncements over Noah's sons hold also for the peoples represented in them. Two possibilities are indicated: if one takes as one's starting point that the narrative is concerned with the sons of Noah, then one can only understand these three as the ancestors of the whole of humankind. Earlier exegesis was unanimous in this. F. Delitzsch speaks of "the threefold humankind that stems from the three." U. Cassuto still represents this opinion when he says: "The purpose of this narrative is to characterize the three branches of humankind. . . ." The opinion however cannot be sustained because the pronouncements in vv. 25, 26, 27 are obviously not dealing with the "threefold humankind" or "the three branches of humankind." Exegetes must confront the fact that the pronouncements deal only with individual peoples and their relationship to each other, and ask why. G. von Rad, e.g., assumes a subsequent reworking which has destroyed the notion of the unity of the three families of peoples: "The narrative is not talking about the ecumenical scheme of nations, Shem-Ham-Japheth, but about a much older and more limited Palestinian one: Shem, Japheth and Canaan."

The other possibility is to take as one's starting point the etiological meaning of the pronouncements. H. Gunkel writes: "A scholarly explanation of the blessing requires that one ask what present situation does it presume?" "There are very concrete circumstances to which it relates, such as are present to the narrator." The blessing is always the main thing in such narratives, "because it indicates that which still continues to be effective in the present." It is here that Gunkel explains precisely what is meant by an etiological narrative. It can only start from the present situation, i.e., from the situation present to the narrator which the narrative is meant to explain. G. von Rad also classifies 9:18-27 as an etiological story which is to explain why the Canaanites are slaves ("The Beginnings of Historical Writing in Ancient Israel" in *The Problem of the Hexateuch and Other Essays* [1966] 166-204). This explanation has many supporters, e.g., F.W. Basset: "The story seems designed to discredit the Canaanite and justify the Israelite and Philistine hegemony over them." Or W. Schottroff: "There must be an established political situation concerned with the distribution of people and it must be derived from an act of blessing and cursing after the flood." The actual situation from which the narrative is derived is, according to most scholars, the era of David and Solomon, i.e., the time of the the Yahwist. So W. Schottroff: "The distribution of power in the kingdom of David and Solomon, such as it was at the time of J." He draws attention nevertheless to the difficulties to which this explanation gives rise: Israel is equated with Shem only here, and there is no certainty at all as to who is meant by Japheth.

Actually the only thing that is certain among the many indications of a historical situation that could be the starting point of the explanation is the servitude of Canaan (due to the curse), and that is about the only point in which the many variants agree. But even this becomes questionable when one considers vv. 26 and 27 together with v. 25. According to them Canaan is subjected both to Shem (Israel) and Japheth. This cannot apply to the Davidic-Solomonic era if, as many assume, Japheth is to be identified with the Philistines. But there can be no question of any other explanation of Japheth as a people who at this time put Canaan into subjection.

490

Interpretations that begin from a historical political situation divide here. One group eliminates the Japheth pronouncement (J. Herrmann) or tries to explain it in another way (L. Rost). The other maintains that it is impossible that the pronouncement originated in the Davidic-Solomonic era (H. Gunkel). One can only be amazed at the ingenious and fanciful attempts of the first group to submit the Japheth announcement to history. J. Herrmann strikes it out, being of the opinion that vv. 20-27 dealt originally only with Shem and Canaan. L. Rost takes J. Herrmann's end result as his starting point. The two pronouncements on Shem (= Israel) and Canaan originated in the early period of David, perhaps shortly after the transfer of the ark to Jerusalem. Israelite prevalence over the Canaanites is now assured, and that is what these two pronouncements are saying. According to Rost the occasion for the addition of the Japheth pronouncement was the "annexation of the areas listed in 1 Kings 5:9-13 (Eng. 4:24ff.) as Solomon's territory," p. 175; people belonging to Japheth lived here, perhaps at influential levels in society. This explains the dwelling in the tents of Shem. J. Hoftijzer offers a similarly complicated solution: vv. 25 and 26 describe two different phases. The earlier phase, when Israel put Canaan under the yoke, is followed by a later phase, when Israel was put under the yoke by Japheth (who could be the Philistines, the Assyrians, the Babylonians). A. Bertholet too assumes that the Japheth pronouncement is secondary; it was inserted after Alexander the Great.

Because the pronouncements cannot originate in the Davidic-Solomonic era, H. Gunkel concludes that they are earlier. He thinks that it is a question of "relationships between peoples from time immemorial . . . three original peoples are meant." Gunkel thinks that it is precarious to propose hypotheses as to which peoples are meant. He conjectures that Canaan is an earlier and much larger Canaan, that Shem is the still nomadic Aramaic-Hebrew group of peoples, and that Japheth describes the northern and sea peoples of the second millenium. Gunkel's explanation is problematic because his methodological basis collapses when one has to ask, "What contemporary situation do the pronouncements presume?" When he himself explains that the attempt to relate them to historical situations in Israel must be considered a failure, and conjectures that they are linked with events sometime in the 2nd millenium, then the etiological explanation settles nothing.

One has imagined all sorts of different peoples and historical situations. J. Skinner looks to the 14th century and sees in Shem the Ḥabiru (so too J. Herrmann); but was Yahweh (v. 25) the god of the Ḥabiru? A. van Selms sees in the pronouncements "a program of cooperation between the Hebrew invaders from the East and the Pelasgic invaders from the West against the settled population of Canaan." D. Neiman wants to explain them as a battle-cry from the conflicts with the Canaanites in the time of Joshua or Deborah; they grew out of the desire to legitimate the coalition between Israel (Shem) and the sea peoples (Japheth) against Canaan. Others conjecture that Japheth means the Phoenicians (K. Budde) or the Suti or the Amurri (J. Skinner); the description of Canaan as a son of Ham refers to the Egyptian hegemony over Canaan in the 17th or 18th dynasty (A. van Selms).

The sweep of the possibilities suggested here is amazing. The historical situations alleged to explain the pronouncements stretch from about the middle of the 2nd millennium to the period after Alexander the Great. There is no methodological basis for further conjectures, as Gunkel's embarrassment should have already made clear. Only a new methodological approach to the text can help. B. Jacob is the only one, as far as I know, who gives the exegesis a quite different direction when he says: "In the narrative Ham, Canaan, Shem, Japheth are individuals, sons and grandsons of Noah. They must be the same in the curse and the blessing."

Literature: Gen 9:25: S.H. Blank, HUCA 23 (1950/1951) 75. A. Bentzen, *Introduction.* . . . Vol. 1, "Poetry: Patriarchal Words" (1952⁶) 141ff. J. Scharbert, "Leid," HThG II (1963) 37-44.

[9:25] The curse decrees that the son who has dishonored his father is to live in disgrace; it is in the context of a family event. The disgrace is that he must live in servitude to his own brothers. The closest parallel is Gen 27:29: "Be lord of your brothers, and may your mother's sons bow down to you," and 27:40 "and you shall serve your brother." There is also the beginning of the Joseph story where the lordship of a brother over his brothers is a dominating motif. Both parallels belong to the patriarchal history. The curse of servitude under one's brothers is not to be construed primarily as political servitude. It is to be seen in the perspective of the family where it is something unnatural and unheard of for a brother to become a slave of his brothers. The curse can certainly have its effects in the political area; but it is here pre-political, a social matter. Just as in 4:2-16 the punishment is expulsion from the community, so here it is the servitude of a brother to his brothers. The consequence of dishonoring one's father is servitude under one's brothers. The curse upon the son who dishonored his father does not refer to the political status of a particular people among others. It refers rather to the state of servitude of one brother to his brothers which has become possible because of the outrage committed.

Literature: Gen 9:26: R. Kittel, "Segen und Fluch," RE XVIII (1906³) 148-154. F. Schmidtke, "Die Japhetiten der biblischen Völkertafel," BSHT 7 (1926). A. Kuschke, "Die Lagervorstellung der priesterlichen Erzählung: Eine überlieferungsge-schichtliche Studie," ZAW 63 (1951) 74-105. A. Murtonen, VT 9 (1959) 168.

[9:26] The ויאמר at the beginning of v. 25 continues the preceding sequence וידע . . . וייקץ of v. 24 both grammatically and in content. On the contrary the וימאר at the beginning of v. 26 is abrupt and without context. One would expect something like: "But to his son Shem he said," or something similar. The curse of Canaan rises directly out of the narrative and is based on the transition verse, 24. On the contrary the mechanically repeated ויאמר of vv. 26 and 27 is rather loosely tacked on. This is in accord with the context inasmuch as the curse over Canaan (Ham) is necessary for the course of the narrative (as v. 24 shows) whereas the blessing over Shem and Japheth is not. They only did their duty. Their conduct was what was required of sons; it did not call for any commendation. On the other hand it was not necessary that a son do some good deed to gain his father's blessing.

But what does the blessing over Shem consist in? The second of the two sentences repeats the context of the curse of Canaan, and is itself repeated literally at the end of v. 27. The other sentence praises the god of Shem. Apart from the repetition nothing is said about what the blessing over Shem consists in. No definite event is mentioned that gives direction to his future. This is all the more striking because the frequently used formula ברוך יהוה, when it occurs outside the language of cult, always gives as the reason a definite act of Yahweh; e.g., 14:20: "who has delivered your enemies into your hand. . . ," or 24:27: "who has not forsaken his steadfast love and his faithfulness towards my master." (Further passages in B. Jacob and W. Schottroff, 165, 167.) But in all these passages the cry of praise looks back to an event that has just taken place; to this extent it has no meaning in a blessing.

The simple בָּרוּךְ with a subsequent predication of God is a doxology such as, e.g., occurs at the conclusion of the Books of Psalms. The majority of interpreters see here a deliberate subtlety, namely that "the ancestor blesses (praises) the God from whom all good comes over Shem" (H. Gunkel, G. von Rad); but this is to fail to take account of the context. Others understand the sentence in the sense "that Shem's highest good lies in the religion of Yahweh" (O. Procksch); but this is simply read into the text. One cannot avoid the conclusion that the old narrative ended with the curse over Canaan (= Ham) and that the sequence of the three sons of Noah suggested that it be complemented by a blessing over the other two. V. 26 is certainly not an old formula of blessing that was at hand to the narrator. Shem can only mean Israel here because Yahweh is the God of Israel only; nowhere else is Shem used for Israel. The equation is no more than an ad hoc construction; it has no support in the tradition.

The second sentence, which repeats what v. 25 says, also has its difficulties in content, while in form it follows close on the first. No promise was ever made to Israel that Canaan would be its slave. The promise was that it would drive out or destroy the Canaanites but not that it would exercise dominion over them (so correctly B. Jacob). V. 26 then is to be regarded as a secondary development consisting of a doxology to Yahweh, the God of Shem (= Israel), and an adapted form of the curse in v. 25.

Literature: Gen 9:27: I. Lewy, VT 6 (1956) 433. F. Dumermuth, "Zur deuteronomischen Kulttheologie und ihren Voraussetzungen," ZAW 70 (1958) 59-98; esp. 64-65.

[9:27] The blessing over Japheth differs from that over Shem in that a concrete event in the future is announced to Japheth. The first two sentences refer to a historical situation: the expansion of Japheth throughout his own territory and into that of Shem (tents generally mean places of residence). This can only be an originally independent blessing that was part of the tradition and it is the only pronouncement that has anything to do with political events. The explanation of the name by the pronouncement (as, e.g., Gen 49:16; Dan), the announcement of the expansion (e.g., Is 55), and the dwelling in the territories of other people (e.g., Deut 10:6f.) is attested many times. However, it is a dubious procedure to harmonize the pronouncement with that over Shem. The expansion into Shem's territory, whether by conquest or in a friendly way, cannot have arisen in the same context as the blessing over Shem. Yet F. Delitzsch can write: "The language of the New Testament is the language of Javan applied to the tents of Shem." And he supports in this way the interpretation of the Talmud: "It is from this blessing that the Talmud correctly derives its justification of the use of the Greek language in sacred context." There is a political-historical interpretation (e.g., G. von Rad, W. Zimmerli) that goes with the religious: Japheth can only mean the Philistines who together with Israel put Canaan under the yoke. But it is difficult to imagine that the Philistines received a blessing together with Israel which promised them that they would expand into the tents of Shem (Israel). It is no longer possible to know the origin and original meaning of the blessing over Japheth.

It has been shown that each of the three pronouncements is to be judged differently. Only v. 25 belongs originally to the narrative. The consequence of dishonoring the father is a curse which brings servitude under one's brothers. The blessings over Shem and Japheth did not arise together with the narrative but were added in accord with the sequence of three brothers. Shem therefore was referred to Israel, and this occurs nowhere else in the Old Testament, and Yahweh is "blessed," i.e., praised, as the God of Israel. V. 27 is an independent blessing over Japheth. It was only with the addition of vv. 26 and 27 that the curses and blessings of Noah took on the function of indicating the destinies of peoples, and only then that the narrative of vv. 20-27 as a whole was regarded as serving to explain these individual destinies. Understood in this way, 9:20-27 would form no part of the primeval story. One must therefore renounce all attempts to see in the three pronouncements of vv. 25-27 a coherent notion of three peoples or groups of peoples.

Purpose and Thrust

The outrage of Ham and his punishment by the father's curse is to be seen in the context of the narratives of crime and punishment in Gen 2-11. J's intention becomes clear: he wants to speak of one's culpability in the three basic communities of human relationships — between man and woman (2-3), brother and brother (4:2-16), parents and children (9:20-27). A point of contact with 2-3 (B. Jacob has drawn attention to this) is that nakedness is a *leitmotif* in the life together of man and woman; in 9:20-27 it is the exposure of the father before the children that offends the dignity of the paternal state. When the child "exposes" his own parents (Ham's action is meant in this broader sense), the sacred relationship between parents and children is threatened. The father must curse the son who has dishonored him. And so the disgrace of the father causes a state of disgrace, that of servitude under one's brothers.

By contrasting the conduct of the brothers the author is throwing into relief an attitude that is basic to the general well-being of the human community of all peoples, and that took the form of the fourth commandment in Israel. The narrative makes Ham the bearer of the curse and Shem and Japheth the bearers of the blessing. In this way it is saying that, as generation follows generation, human existence can only be healthy where it is acknowledged that a relationship of respect of the new generation to the older is basic to human community. This attitude saw cultural, economic and spiritual progress as possible only where what had already been achieved was passed on carefully from one generation to the next. To dishonor one's fathers threatened not only what was passed on, but progress as well. Blessing and tradition will be considered further in the commentary on Gen 27.

The story of Noah and his sons deals in an indirect way with what we call tradition. Tradition here embraces the preservation of what has been achieved as well as that which makes further progress possible. A basic attitude which is an unconditional presupposition for both is that which has respect for elders in their weakness. This narrative could well have much to say to the coming generations.

The other side of what is narrated here is of fundamental importance for the history of human community: it is announced here for the first time that a brother is to be a slave of his brothers. There breaks into the family structure another social structure that is foreign to it — slavery.

The Table of
the Nations

Literature

S. Bochart, *Geographia sacra seu Phaleg et Canaan* (1646-1651; 1707[4]). J.J. Stähelin, *Kritische Untersuchungen über den Pentatuech, die Bücher Josua, Richter, Samuels und der Könige* (1843). A. Knobel, *Die Völkertafel der Genesis, Ethnographische Untersuchungen* (1850). A. Kuenen, *Gesammelte Abhandlungen zur biblischen Wissenschaft* (1973). H. Winckler, *Geschichte Babyloniens und Assyriens* (1892) Bd. 3; *Die babylonische Kultur* (1902) 8-9. M. Jastrow, "The Hamites and Semites in the Tenth Chapter of Genesis," PAPS 43 (1904) 173-207. S. Poznanski, "Zur Zahl der biblischen Völker," ZAW 24 (1904) 301-308. E. Nestle, "Die schreibunkundigen Völker von Genesis 10," ZAW 25 (1905) 271. S. Krauss, "Zur Zahl der biblischen Völkerschaften," ZAW 26 (1906) 33-48. E. Meyer, *Die Israeliten und ihre Nachbarstämme* (1906). S.D. Peet, "The Three Sons of Noah and the Three Great Races," AAOJ 29 (1908). J.A. Knudtzon, *El-Amarna-Tafeln*, VAB 2 (1915). Th. Arldt, "Die Völkertafeln der Genesis und ihre Bedeutung für die Ethnographie Vorderasiens," WZKM 30 (1917/1918) 264-317. F.C. Burkitt, "Note on the Table of Nations (Genesis X)," JThS 21 (1920) 233-238. A.H. Sayce, "The Tenth Chapter of Genesis," JBL 44 (1925) 193-202. F. Hommel, *Ethnologie und Geographie des Alten Orients* (1926). B. Moritz, "Edomitische Genealogien I," ZAW 44 (1926) 81-93. U. Cassuto, "The Story of Tamar and Judah," *J.M. Simḥoni Memorial Vol.* (1929) 96-97. E. Dhorme, "Les Peuples issus de Jahpet d'après le chapitre X de la Genèse," Syria 13 (1932) 28-49. A. Reubeni, *Shem, Ham and Japheth.* . . . (1932). S. Wagner, *Die Stammtafel des Menschengeschlechtes. Nach der biblischen ur-Überlieferung dargestellt und ethnologisch gedeutet (1. Mos. X)* (1935; 1947[2]). G. Ryckmans, *Les noms propres sud-sémitiques, Bibliothèque du Muséon* 1-3 (1934/1935). W. Mooch, "Die Einheit des Menschengeschlechts," ZKRU 12 (1935) 227-239; 13 (1936) 1-11, 95-103. S. Mowinckel, *The Two Sources.* . . . (1937). L. Rost, *Die Vorstufen von Kirche und Synagoge im Elten Testament*, BWANT 4, 24 (1938). D. Poulet, *Tous les hommes sont-ils fils de Noë?* (1941). A. Lauha, "Zaphon. Der Norden und die Nordvölker im Alten Testament," AAF 49 (1943). Y.M. Grintz, "Hap-Pelištīm bi-Gerār wehap-Pelištīm šel hoph hayyām," *Studies in Memory of M. Schorr* (1945) 96-112. B. Mazar, BEHJ 1 (1946). J. Vosté, "La table ethnographique de Genèse X d'après Mar Išoʿdad de Merw," *Muséon* 59 (1946) 319-332. B.N. Piperow, "Die alte Ethnographie des Orients nach der Bibel: (Exegese) Genesis 10:1-30," JThFUS 25 (1947). J.R. Garcia, EstB 8 (1949) 327-355. G. Hölscher *Drei Erdkarten*, SAH 3 1944/1948 (1949) 35-44. A. Dussaud, *Prélydiens, Hittites et Achéens* (1953) 74-76. C.H. Gordon, *Introduction to Old Testament Times* (1953) 28-32. W. Brandenstein, "Bemerkungen zur Völkertafel in der Genesis," *Festschr. A. Debrunner* (1954) 57-83. J. Simons, "The 'Table of Nations' (Genesis X): Its General Structure and Meaning," OTS 10 (1954) 155-184. D.J. Wiseman, "Genesis 10: Some Archaeological Considerations," JVI 87 (1955) 13-24, 113-118. A. Guillaume, "L'apport de la langue et des traditions Arabes à l'interprétation de l'Ancien Testament," *L'Ancien Testament et L'Orient* (1957) 111-121. G. Ryckmans, "L'Arabie antique et la Bible," *L'Ancien Testament et L'Orient* (1957) 88-109. A.Alt, "Die Deutung der Weltgeschichte im Alten Testament," ZThK 56 (1959) 129-137. J. Simons, *The Geographical . . . Texts of the OT* (1959). F.M.Th. Böhl, "Babel and Bibel, I," JEOL 16 (1959/1962) 103-118. G. Fohrer, ZAW 73 (1961) 1-30. J.C.L. Gibson, "Observations on Some Important Ethnic Terms in the Pentateuch," JNESt 20 (1961) 217-238. H. Junker, "Die Zerstreuung der Völker nach der biblischen Urgeschichte," TThZ 70 (1961) 182-185. M. Noth, "Die Ursprünge des alten Israel im Lichte neuer Quellen," AFLNW 94 (1961), esp. 9f. R.A. Bowman, IDB I (1962) 362-365. E.A. Speiser, "Ethnic Divisions of Man," IDB III (1962). O. Eissfeldt, "Archronische, anachronische und synchronische Elemente in der Genesis," JEOL 17 (1963) 148-164. J.M. Fenasse, "La table des peuples," BTS 52 (1963). A. Kubik, "Die Völkertafel, ihre literarische Struktur und Entstehungszeit," RTK 10 (1963) 45-68. C. Sant, "Links Between the Three Main Divisions. Genealogy and Chronology," MTh 15 (1963) 41-49. J.C.H. Lebram, VT 15 (1965) 193. F. Festorazzi, *La Bibbia e il problema della origine. . . .* (1966). W. Richter, BZ 10 (1966) 96-105. F.J. Los, "The Table of Peoples of the Tenth Chapter of Genesis," *The Mankind Quarterly* 7 (1967) 144-152. K. Koch, VT 19 (1969) 37-81. G.J. Kuiper, "Targum Pseudo-Jonathan: A Study in Genesis 4:7-10:16," Aug. 10 (1970) 533-570. A.F. Rainey, *El Amarna Tablets. Suppl. to J.A. Knudtzon, Die El-Amarna-Tafeln; Alter Orient u. Altes Testament* 8 (1970). M.H. Woodstra, "The Toledot of the Book of Genesis and their Redemptive-Historical Significance," CTJ 5 (1970) 184-189. R.A. Bennett,Jr., "Africa and the Biblical Period," HThR 64 (1971) 483-500. E. Testa, "La dottrina teologica sulla 'generazioni della secessione' (Contributo alla storia della esegesi su Gen 10:1-11:26)," SBFLA 21 (1971) 33-53.

Text

10:1 These are the genealogies of the sons of Noah. "The sons of Noah were"[a]: Shem, Ham[b], and Japheth; . . . and sons were born to them after the flood.

2 The sons of Japheth are: Gomer and Magog and Madai and Javan[a] and Tubal and Meshech[b] and Tiras.

3 The sons of Gomer are: Ashkenaz and Riphath[a] and Togarmah.

4 The sons of Javan are: Elishah[a] and Tarshish, Kittim and "Rhodanim"[b].

5 From these the coastal peoples spread. "These are the sons of Japheth"[a] according to their lands, each[b] with its own language, according to their clans within their nations.

6 The sons of Ham are: Cush and Egypt and Put and Canaan.

7 The sons of Cush are: Seba[a] and Havilah and Sabtah and Ragmah and Sabteca. The sons of Ragmah are: Sheba and Dedan.

8 And Cush begot[a] Nimrod. And he was the first man of might on earth.

9 He was a mighty hunter before Yahweh. And so it is said[a]: Like Nimrod, a mighty hunter before Yahweh.

10 The beginning of his kingdom was Babel and Erech[a] and Akkad and Kalneh[b] in the land of Shinar.

11 From this land he went up to Asshur[a] and built Nineveh and Rehoboth-Ir and Kalah

12 and Resen between Nineveh and Kalah; that is the great city[a].

13 And Egypt begot the Ludim and the Anamim[a] and the Lehabim, and the Naphtuhim[b]

14 and the Pathrusim and the Casluhim[a] and the "Kaphtorim," from whom[b] the Philistines came[c].

15 And Canaan begot Sidon, his first-born, and Heth,
16 and the Jebusites and the Amorites and the Girgashites,
17 and the Hivites and the Arkites and the Sinites[a]
18a and the Arvadites and the Zemarites and the Hamathites.
18b Afterwards the Canaanites spread abroad,
19 so that[a] the territory of the Canaanites extended from Sidon
   toward[b] Gerar as far as Gaza and toward Sodom and Gomorrah
   and Admah and Zeboim[c] as far as Lasha[d].

20 These are the sons of Ham
   according to their clans,   according to their languages
   in their lands,   in their nations.

21 To Shem also[a] sons were born, to him who was the father of all
   the sons of Eber, to the elder brother of Japheth[b].

22 The sons of Shem are: Elam and Asshur and Arpachshad and
   Lud and Aram[a].

23 And the sons of Aram are: Uz[a] and Hul[b] and Gether and Mash[c].

24 And Arpachshad begot[a] Shelah, and Shelah begot Eber.
25 And to Eber two sons were born[a]: the name of one was Peleg,
   because in his days humankind divided itself, and the name of
   his brother was Joktan[b].

26 And Joktan begot Almodad[a] and Sheleph and Hazarmaveth[b]
   and Jerah

27 and Hadoram and Uzal[a] and Diklah
28 and Obal[a] and Abimael and Sheba
29 and Ophir and Havilah and Jobab. All these are the sons of
   Joktan.

30 And their territory extends from Mesha[a] toward Sephar[b] as far as
   the mountains in the east.

31 These are the sons of Shem
   according to their clans,   according to their languages,
   in their lands,   in their nations.

32 These are the clans of the sons of Noah, according to their
   genealogies, in their nations, and from them the nations spread[a]
   on the earth after the flood.

1a With K. Budde add בני נוח (Haplography). **b** some Mss have וחם; the ו is also missing in 1 Chron 1:4.
2a the Gk has καὶ Ελισα after Javan, although it mentions him in v. 4 as a son of Javan. **b** Sam מושך, Gk Μοσοχ.
3a 1 Chron 1:6 reads דיפת; but the versions are as in Gen 10:3.
4a Sam reads אליש. **b** MT has דדנים; 1 Chron 1:7 has ר, also some Mss, Sam and Gk.
5a insert אלה בני יפת following vv. 20 and 31. **b** איש, each, each one, every — severally, Ges-K § 139b.
7a the Gk renders both סבא and שבא by Σαβα.
8a Sam has הליד for ילד.
9a for the use of the imperf., Ges-K § 107g.
10a Gk Ορεχ. **b** Gk Χαλαννη.
11a accus. of place Ges-K § 118d.f.
12a BrSynt § 28biv.
13a Gk Ενεμετιειμ. **b** Gk Νεφθαλιειμ.
14a Gk Χασλωνιειμ. **b** the אשר sentence is to be understood after כפתרים (cf. Amos 9:7). **c** BrSynt § 148.
17a Gk Ασεννναῖον.

19a the Sam differs markedly from MT. **b** Ges-K § 144h. **c** in some Mss
צביים. **d** TgJer and Jerome קלרה = Callirhoë.
21a Ges-K §135h. **b** Gk ἀδελφῷ Ιαφεθ τοῦ μείζονος.
22a Gk (with Mss) adds καὶ Καιναν.
23a Sam (1 Ms) חוץ. **b** Sam חויל; **c** Gk Μοσοχ, so too 1 Chron 1:17.
24a Gk adds here τὸν Καιναν, καὶ Καιναν ἐγέννησεν.
25a Sam and Gk ילדו. **b** Gk Ιεκταν.
26a for explanation of the first syllable, Ges-K §35m. **b** a group of Mss reads חצר
מות.
27a Sam and Gk איזל.
28a Sam and 1 Chron 1:22 עיבל.
30a Gk Μασση. **b** Gk Σωφηρα.
32a Sam and LXX insert איי.

Literary Form

Gen 10 gives a first impression of system and lack of system wonderfully interwoven. This is due to R who has worked two sources together, the systematic
approach of P and the unsystematic of J. P's system is extremely simple and
readily recognizable:

These are the genealogies of the sons of Noah:

The sons of Japheth are. . . .
  The sons . . . are. . . .
  The sons . . . are. . . .
These are the sons of Japheth according. . . .
The sons of Ham are. . . .
  The sons . . . are. . . .
  The sons . . . are. . . .
These are the sons of Ham according. . . .
The sons of Shem are. . . .
  The sons. . . .
These are the sons of Shem according. . . .
These are the clans of the sons of Noah according. . . .
  and from them the nations spread on the earth after the flood.

It is beyond dispute that this is a self-contained system and as such a literary
construction. Here, if anywhere, P's hand is clearly discernible.

The purely literary-critical explanation of Gen 10 confines itself to setting
the contribution of J over against that of P, i.e., to taking out those sentences that
do not fit into P's system. The conclusion generally is that R has made P's system
the ground plan and has passed on P's table of the nations intact, "taking over
from J only bridge passages" (H. Gunkel, ad loc.). This may well be. However,
it is not enough to set P's complete table of the nations against the incomplete
table of J. One must first of all study the structure of the whole that R has
constructed; only then can one make a judgment about the constituent parts.

The first thing that strikes one about R's construction is that in two
identical places, after the concluding phrase "these are the sons of Ham (Shem)"
he has inserted a self-contained passage from J: 10:8-19 (J) before 10:20 (P) and
10:24-30 (J) before 10:31 (P). A corresponding insertion is missing before "these
are the sons of Japheth" v. 5. Apart from these two large insertions, J is virtually
restricted to vv. 1b and 21.

What follows from this? In contrast to the narrative texts, e.g., the flood narrative, R does not try to create a new table of the nations from the two lying before him. Rather, he takes the text of P, which presents a closed system, and expands it in two places with parts of J in such a way that they are clearly recognizable as additions.

	J	P
Introduction	(9:18-19)	10:1a
Japheth		10:2-5
Addition	missing	
Ham		10:6-7
Addition	10:8-19	
Conclusion		10:20
Shem	(21)	10:22-23
Addition	10:24-30	
Conclusion		10:31
Conclusion of the whole		10:32

It is only by separating the parts of the chapter in this way that a second striking characteristic becomes evident; the both additions from J are very much more detailed than the parts of P to which they are added; they also contain more names.

If one removes those verses of P that belong to the pattern, 1a, 5, 20, 31, 32, the following names remain:

Japheth (2-4)	:	7 names of the first generation
		3 + 4 names of the second generation
Ham (6-7)	:	4 names of the first generation
		5 names of the second generation
		2 names of the third generation
Shem (22-23)	:	5 names of the first generation
		4 names of the second generation

The picture that emerges is remarkable because there is no division into branches such as one presumes from 10:1a and 32. There is no increase in numbers; those of the second generation after Noah are approximately the same as those of the third generation. The reason is that on each occasion only one or two descendants of Shem, Ham, and Japheth are named, but not all of them. The traditional form of the genealogy is obviously inadequate. It can present growth and expansion in the family context, but not the division and spread of the nations over the earth as then known. The history of nations cannot be presented as family history.

One can appreciate then all the more P's attempt, albeit with inadequate means, to conceive as a whole the nations known at that time. The genealogy, for all its inadequacy, has the advantage of presenting the nations as a whole in the manner of a family. Its disadvantage is this: between the introductory "the sons . . . are" and the concluding "these are the sons . . . ," only names are in fact listed. No clue at all is given to determine the territory further nor is there any indication of the relationship to each other of the peoples named. The structural sentence: "The sons of A are BCDE," can really say nothing more than that the nations take their origin from the three primal ancestors.

R's achievement is this: by means of the two great additions from J he removes from the whole the impression of a contrived system of a list of names and thereby gives it the appearance of a history of the nations.

To make this clear, we must now look at the structure of the passages from J. It follows a definite pattern, while P merely enumerates.

8-12:	And Cush begot
13-14:	And Egypt begot. . . .
15-19:	And Canaan begot. . . .
	Parallel in the second addition 24-30:
24-25:	And Arpachshad begot. . . .
26-30:	And Joktan begot. . . .

It follows necessarily from this pattern that each time, before the part beginning with "and X begot," there must have stood a sentence that described those in question as descendants of one of the sons of Noah. The structure of the parts makes this conclusion certain; in fact, one of these sentences is preserved at least in part, namely v. 21: "To Shem also sons were born." This is parallel to 10:1b: ". . . and sons were born to them after the flood"; H. Gunkel, and others, therefore rightly ascribe this to J. The both additions in v. 21: "To the father of all the sons of Eber" and "To the elder brother of Japheth" are clearly secondary. The beginning of v. 21: "To Shem also sons were born" was followed originally by the list of these sons; this has been omitted in favor of P's list in v. 22.

We have then two elements of the structure of J's table of the nations; the third is the note on the territory of the nations just mentioned:

30:	"And their territory extends from . . . to. . . ."
[10:	"The beginning of his kingdom was. . . ."]
19:	"so that the territory of the Canaanites extended from . . . to. . . ."

The structure of the table of the nations of J was as follows:

I. To Shem (Ham, and Japheth) sons were born
List of the sons
II. And he . . . begot. . . .
III. Their territories extended from . . . to. . . .

J differs from P mainly in not repeating the pattern each time and by loosening the structure of parts I and II with concrete pieces of information. The other difference, linked with the first, is that the names in J vary continually between names of countries or cities and names of persons. There is further a real genealogy in J. V. 8 runs: "And Cush begot Nimrod, who was . . . who was. . . ." Likewise the begetting of sons is meant literally in 10:1b and 21 ("to Shem also sons were born"). P uses the quite impersonal formula "the sons of Shem are . . . ," v. 22, in place of the phrase "and A begot B."

The third difference is that J presents everything else as a schematically articulated system. The enumeration is interrupted and expanded by different pieces of information (Intro.: 9:19b: from him the whole world was populated):

10:1b:	. . . After the flood
8b-12:	Nimrod and his kingdom
14:	The origin of the Philistines
15:	His first born
18b-19:	Description of the territory of the Canaanites

500

21:       the father of all the sons of Eber
          the elder brother of Japheth
25b: because in his days humankind divided itself
30:       the territory of the sons of Joktan

There remains the task of comparing the names themselves in J and P. Only the names of the sons of Noah conform completely. For the rest, apart from some of the sons of the sons of Noah, agreement is non-existent. The sons of Japheth are completely missing in J; both have Cush, Egypt and Canaan as the sons of Ham, P adding Put. Arpachshad is the only name common to the sons of Shem; J calls him the only son of Shem. One can at least presume a common tradition for the sons of the sons of Noah, but not beyond them. Apart from these, only three names are shared, but in very different contexts: Asshur is a son of Shem in P, but part of Nimrod's conquest in J. Havilah appears in the Ham group as a son of Shem, in J in the Shem group as a son of Joktan; Sheba (שְׁבָא) too appears as a son of Joktan, while in P he is a grandson of Cush. All other names are different. A further difference is that P has far fewer names than J.

	P	J
Sons of Japheth	7 + 7	—
Sons of Ham	4 + 7	3 + 11
Sons of Shem	5 + 4	1 + 17

In addition there are twenty place names in J that are lacking in P.

One can attempt to explain these very peculiar findings only at the conclusion of the study of the individual elements. One result can be established already: because it is essentially a question of listing names, R, when using P as his base, must have omitted the same names occurring in J. This means,

(a) that the original list of the sons of Noah in J was in almost complete agreement with that in P, as appears again with the sons of Ham. We can conclude therefore that the list in J contained the sons of Ham and Shem in the same sequence. The basic number three rules out the likelihood that J did not have a Japheth list. Also ruled out is that J had only Arpachshad as the sons of Shem.

(b) R could only make a selection from the following sequences, i.e., the sequences of the third and fourth generations; and so either P (the sons of Cush, Gomer, Javan, Aram) or J (sons of Egypt, Canaan, Arpachshad) were used. We at least have an explanation then of why there is no parallelism at all in the subordinate sequences.

Setting in Life

The inquiry into the setting in life of the table of the nations has a twofold starting point: (a) the form of the genealogies in Genesis is highly developed and rich in variety (see Intro. 2); (b) the table of the nations is unique and has no parallel either inside or outside the Old Testament. If we look at Gen 10 J and Gen 10 P in the context of the history of the genealogies, we note that the main difference between them is that the structure of J is predominantly verbal (A begot B, to A sons were born), and that of P predominantly nominal (the sons of A are . . .). J still retains by and large the original thrust of the genealogy: descent from persons. P on the contrary is heavily formalized; the genealogy for him is but a

501

form, a long way from the original thrust. With P, only Shem, Ham, and Japheth are clearly personal names; with J many names are entirely or primarily personal.

The genealogies in J are also closer to narrative (see Intro. 2); accordingly, the J-texts in Gen 10 describe more an *event* — how humankind spread over the earth and became the nations that they now are. The P-texts, following the basic line of P, describe rather a *situation* — the state of being nations as a result of the spread of humankind over the earth. P puts the emphasis on what is common to all nations, J on the contrary stresses the different ways in which the different groups have developed.

This difference can explain the origin of the text a step further. The J-text of Gen 10 is close to Gen 4:17-26. This is especially so in 10:8-12; the phrase "he was the first," which has grown out of the genealogy, is the same in both cases. Just as 4:17-26 describes cultural progress in the framework of a genealogy, so does Gen 10-J the spread of peoples. The setting in life of Gen 10-J then is the "pre-historical presentation of history" by means of genealogies, which has been taken from the patriarchal history and applied to the primeval story (Intro. 2).

The origin and development of the text can be explained even more precisely. H. Gunkel has seen that 9:8-19 (J) is both the conclusion of the flood narrative and the introduction to J's table of the nations. This observation of Gunkel's can be taken a step further. J's table of the nations is an extension of this conclusion of the flood narrative. Gen 10 (J) unfolds the sentence of 9:19b: "and the whole earth was populated from them." 9:18, 19 then is to be understood as at the same time the conclusion of Gen 6-9 (J) and the introduction to Gen 10 (J). The explanation is supported by the fact that this concluding motif is a permanent part of the flood tradition. A more common conclusion of the flood narratives is: ". . . and they begot children from whom descend all people who now live on earth," or "all people on earth, yellow, white, brown and red, descend from those saved" (J. Riem, *Die Sintflut in Sage und Wissenschaft*, 1906, 1925[2], pp. 32, 44, 56. See also Comm. on 6:5-8:22, Excursus, The Flood in the History of Religions).

Understanding what is the basic motif of Gen 10 (J), one must distinguish between the extension of the motif by means of the genealogy and elaborations that can no longer be understood. The exegesis will show the following elaborations:

in 10:10	"and Erech and Akkad and Kalneh"
in 11f.:	"and Rehoboth-Ir and Kalah and Resen between Nineveh and Kalah"
in 13b-14:	Eight names (sons of Egypt)
in 17-18a:	Nine names: four Canaanite peoples (tribes) and five Phoenician cities
in 26-30:	Thirteen names: the sons of Joktan.

These elaborations stand out from the context in that they are all mere enumerations and have no grammatical link with the form of the genealogy. One can recognize the origin and setting of some of them: in 10:16-18a nine names have been subsequently assimilated to each other, four of Canaanite peoples (tribes), five of Phoenician cities (see Comm.). In 10:26-30 thirteen names are listed as sons of Joktan, all of which point to the southwest coast of Arabia. Because we know of commercial dealings with Phoenician cities and with South Arabia from the time of Solomon, we presume that the basis of these enumerations are lists from the commercial chancery of the Jerusalem court. These elaborations insert another genre into the genealogies that present the division of the nations after the flood: lists, which preserved information about distant countries and served the practical goal of commerce with these territories.

From the very start P is much more inclined to make lists than J; the genealogical form remains merely external. And so in Gen 10 P no longer allows a clear distinction between a genealogical nucleus and different kinds of elaborations. P's table of the nations is no longer a genealogy of the spread of the nations over the earth, but a compilation of the nations in the form of a list. This is a good example of the great gap between the tradition history of J and P in Gen 10. P has only three names that are clearly personal: Shem, Ham, and Japheth which belong to the tradition history of the flood story: they are also the connecting link between 6-9 (P) and 10 (P). The sons of Japheth however, the nations of the far north, have nothing at all to do with a genealogy of the sons of Noah; this is not possible because they only became known to Israel in the 7th century (the greater number of these names occur also in Ezekiel). The nations in Ezekiel are often named together with commercial products that come from these regions. One presumes therefore that these names too were preserved and handed down in commercial centers. P integrates them perfectly into his presentation in 10:2-3, whereas in J they are obviously elaborations of another nucleus. This holds too for the possible elaborations in 6-7, 20 (sons of Ham), the sons of Cush 7a and the sons of Ragmah 7b; similarly in 22, 23, 31 (sons of Shem) the sons of Aram, 23. Here too these sequences of names are no longer recognizable as elaborations. There is only one place in P where they are, that is in the case of the sons of Javan, v. 4, with the divergent endings: "Kittim and Rhodanim." This reflects the gradual acquisition of information about foreign lands which led to the otherwise perfectly unified and extensive end product, Gen 10 (P).

We can distinguish then two stages in the process of formation of the tables of the nations in Gen 10 which point to two very different places of origin: beginning with a pre-political and pre-national form of life, information about distant peoples has been handed down which has grown out of the narration, in this case out of the conclusion of the flood story. It is still there in the nucleus of the J-text, which is not really a table of the nations, but describes how the descendants of the one saved from the flood populated the earth. The elaborations in J presume a national and differentiated way of life in which the specialized field of commerce needed information about distant lands with whom commercial relations existed. One can no longer distinguish the two in P. What predominates there is information about foreign nations preserved in lists which is in part the result of commercial relations, but was probably collected and preserved in the circles in which the priestly writing originated. The names in J and P are for the most part very different. In J, in addition to geographical information some historical information is added, e.g., in vv. 8-12, which is completely lacking in P. All this points to a considerable gap between the sources of the tradition in J and P.

Literature: Gen 10:1: R. Dussaud, "Cham et Canaan" RHR 59 (1909)). K. Budde, "Eine übersehene Textherstellung (Gen 10:1)," ZAW 30 (1910) 277-280. J. Begrich, "Mabbul . . . ," ThB 21 (1964) 39-54. H. Schmid, *Missionsbate* 46 (1970) 10-17. H. Strauss, ZAW 82 (1970) 91-102.

Commentary

The Table of the Nations is introduced by the toledot-formula of P (Intro. 2).

[**10:1**] "These are the genealogies of the sons of Noah." K. Budde, with a finely attuned sense to the language of P, has recognized that the second בני נח has fallen out by haplography. The reading therefore should be: "The sons of Noah were Shem, Ham, and Japheth." The sentence 1b, "and sons were born to them after the flood," belongs to J and is considered together with v. 8.

Literature: Gen 10:2-5: E. Nestle, "Acht Söhne Japhets in Genesis 10," ZAW 24 (1904) 135-137. E. Robertson, "Notes on Javan," JQR 20 (1908) 466-508, 812-824. F. Schmidtke, "Die Japhetiten der biblischen Völkertafel," BSHT 7 (1926). J. van der Ploeg, "La règle de la Guerre. Tradition et notes," VT 5 (1955) 373-420. A. van Selms, "The Canaanites in the Book of Genesis," OTS 12 (1958) 187-213. G.R. Cardona, "I nomi dei figli di Togarmah secondo il Sepher Yosephon," RS.O 49/50 (1966) 17-28. J.P. Brown, "Literary Contexts of Common Hebrew-Greek Vocabulary," JSSt 13 (1968) 163-191; VT 21 (1971) 1-23. A. Malamat, "The Egyptian Decline in Canaan and the Sea-Peoples," C.II: Judges, *The World History of the Jewish People* I, III (1971) 24-128.

[**10:2-5**] The sons of Japheth (P). Seven sons of Japheth are named; sons of only two of these are named — in all there are fourteen. The "sons" are peoples or countries. The genealogical pattern is only the form of presentation; it is not meant to indicate descent. Only Japheth is a person; he does not stand for a people or a country. The same holds for Shem and Ham; all three are only the names of persons and they are part of the tradition history of the flood. They do not belong to the table of the nations, but act as a connecting link with it.

Japheth: the name agrees phonetically with the Greek Ιαπετός, one of the Titans. He is the son of Ouranos and Gaia and his sons are Atlas, Prometheus and Epimetheus. The sons of Japheth are mostly in the area of Asia Minor and Armenia, and so one presumes a connection between them (so E. Meyer, O. Procksch, F. Schmidtke and others).

The Sons of Japheth: Gomer. This people is also mentioned in the Old Testament in Ezek 38:6 (as one of those in alliance with Gog). The name is attested in cuneiform as Gimirrai and in classical authors as Κιμμέριοι. Their original dwelling place was on the north coast of the Black Sea between the Don and the Danube; there are still echoes of the name in the peninsula of Crimea. Homer knows them there (Od. XI 14). Displaced by the Scythians (their land is later described as the land of the Scythians) they conquer the king of Urartu c. 714 and settle in the area of Lake Van. There is evidence of wars with the Assyrians in the time of Esarhaddon, 681-668. After being defeated by the Assyrians they conquer Gugu of Luddi (Gyges of Lydia) and settle in Cappadocia (which the Armenians describe as Gamir); Herodotus gives an account of this. The Cimmerians are an Indo-European people. In the 6th century they disappear from history. The Persians do not separate the Cimmerians and the Scythians; they become kindred people.

Magog. The name occurs again in Ezek 38:2; 39:6 and is just as uncertain there as it is here (see W. Zimmerli, *Comm.* ad loc.). One can only say that in the passages in Ezekiel Magog occurs with the same groups of peoples; Tubal and Meshech occur there too. The word has been explained as a derivation from the Assyrian *mat Gaga* or *mat Gugu,* i.e., land of . . . , or from the Hebrew as an artificial formation from the personal name Gog with מ indicating place, and with the same meaning. The name is not attested in cuneiform nor can it be supported by Ezek 38:2; 39:6 because it is too uncertain there.

Authors have referred to similar sounding countries like *Gaga(ja)* in the Amarna letters (I 38, H. Gunkel, J. Skinner; a country in the north, an indeterminate place), to a princely tribe *gagi* in the area south of Assyria (L. Dürr) or to the land *(mat-)* of Gugu = Gyges of Lydia. W. Zimmerli thinks that the land of Gyges is most likely (Comm. 942; bibliog. 921f.; E. Meyer, A.H. Sayce and others). Josephus maintains that Magog is a description of the Scythians; F. Delitzsch, F. Schmidtke and many moderns have accepted this. But discussion has to the present yielded no certain conclusion. The name Magog remains uncertain.

Madai. The name is used often in the Old Testament to designate the Medes, Is 13:17, as well as the country of the Medes, 2 Kings 17:6; 18:11; Is 21:2, Jer 25:25; 51:11, 28; it is common too in cuneiform, *ma-da-a-a,* first used in Shalmaneser III (858-824) in northeast Assyria. The Medes took part in the overthrow of the Assyrian empire, 614, 612; their kingdom was founded about the middle of the 7th century. Like the Persians, they are an Indo-European people. They are often mentioned together with the Persians and are finally assumed into the Persian empire. The word Madai in Daniel and Esther designates the Medes and the Persians together. It is uncertain whether the designation Umman-manda, which occurs in cuneiform in the third millennium, refers to the same people. Despite some contestation (A.H. Sayce) and doubt (J. Simons) it can be taken as certain that the word Madai refers to the Medes.

Javan. The explanation of the name as the Ionians is also certain. It refers to the Ionian Greeks on the coast of Asia Minor where they had been advancing since the 8th century. They are mentioned elsewhere in the Old Testament in Ezek 27:13 and Is 66:19. After Alexander the Great the name was extended to all Greeks, Joel 4:8, Zech 9:13; Dan 8:21; 10:20; 11:2, as the Gk and Vg versions show. In Ezek 27:13 Javan is mentioned together with Tubal and Meshech. The name is attested frequently in cuneiform, from the time of Sargon, and is used throughout the whole of the East as far as India to designate the Greeks (Sanskrit, Javana).

Tubal and Meshech are mentioned together in all Old Testament passages where they occur (Ezek 27:13; 32:26; 38:2f.; 39:1; Is 66:19 LXX; Ps 120:5 is an exception), as well as in the cuneiform texts and Herodotus. (S. Bochart, *Geographica sacra,* 1646-1651, has determined them as Assyrian *mushku* and *tabali,* at the time of Tiglath-Pileser I, and then of Sargon; Herodotus, III 94 has Μόσχοι and Τιβαρηνοί). Both settled in eastern Asia Minor: "Tubal's territory is in Cilicia, Meshech's in Phrygia" (W. Zimmerli *Comm.* 652, on Ezek 27:13). Later, probably due to the influx of the Cimmerians, both were driven into the mountain country southeast of the Black Sea. According to Herodotus they belonged to the 19th satrapy of Darius. Both are mentioned together with Javan in Is 66:19. Assyrian inscriptions mentioned them as militarily strong peoples.

Tiras. This people is not mentioned elsewhere in the Old Testament and there is no corresponding name in the cuneiform texts. Egyptian inscriptions from the time of Mer-ne-Ptah (1225-1215) mention the Tw-rw-s (Turusa) who attack Egypt at the end of the 13th century. One of the prisoners of Ramses III is described as belonging to them. They are identified as one of the sea peoples, as the Tyrrhenians (first by F. Tuch) who since the 5th century "live on the islands or peninsulars of the Aegean Sea," (J. Simons), as the far-off Etruscans. Josephus saw them as the Thracians.

Literature: Gen 10:3: A. Goetze, *Kizzuwatna* (1940); on Togarmah, 19-20.   G. Lanczkowski, MDAI 2 (1958).   N. Walker, "The Peshitta Puzzle and its Implications," VT 18 (1968) 268-270.

[10:3]   *The Sons of Gomer.* Why are these three peoples associated with Gomer, i.e., with the Cimmerians, as sons? What is their relationship geographically or historically to him and to each other? These questions must be raised even though we can scarcely expect precise answers to them. They can only be considered when we have found out who these three people are.

Ashkenaz. In Jer 51:27 the kingdoms of Ararat, Minni and Ashkenaz are summoned to war against Babylon. This is the only place where Ashkenaz is mentioned in the Old Testament, and it points in a direction that is certain: the three "enemies from the north" are brought together, like the peoples in Ezek 38:2. Even clearer is the mention of Ararat. Just as Gomer and Ashkenaz belong together in Gen 10, so too do the Gimirrai and Ashkuza (or Ishhuza), in Assyrian inscriptions (first in Esarhaddon), and the Cimmerians and the Scythians in Herodotus (has the ו in Ashkuza been changed into נ?). H. Winckler was first to equate Ashkuza with the Scythians. In favor of this too is the fact that Manna and Ashkuza are mentioned together in Esarhaddon just as are the Minni and the Ashkenazi in Jer 51:27. The Ashkenazi, an Indo-European people, first inhabited southern Europe (to the north of the Black Sea), displaced the Cimmerians before them from this same area and settled around Lake Urmia. First there were wars and then friendly relations with the Assyrians. They took part in the conquest of Nineveh in 612. They probably made incursions as far as Palestine (Scythian raids). "The Scythians replaced the Cimmerians as rulers in the northern part of the Near East" (F. Schmidtke); the old land of the Cimmerians became the land of the Scythians. One can understand then the association with Gomer as the father of the Ashkenazi.

Riphath. The name does not occur again in the Old Testament nor in the cuneiform texts. So far it cannot be explained (U. Cassuto and others). Josephus maintains that the Riphateans are the Paphlagonians (between the Black Sea and Bythinia). This would fit well side-by-side with the Cimmerians and the Scythians but we do not know the reason for this equation by Josephus.

Togarmah. The name occurs in Ezek 27:13f. together with Javan, Tubal, and Meshech; in Ezek 38:3-6 with Gomer, Magog, Tubal, and Meshech. We are sure then of the area. In the Hittite texts of Boghaz-koy, Tagarama is attested as a district and a city (at the time of King Muršiliš II). It probably corresponds to the Assyrian *Til-garimmu* (as F. Delitzsch first suggested), a city on the border of Tabal (= Tubal). According to A. Goetze (*Kleinasien*, KAO 1957², 46) it is to be identified with the *gürün* between the upper courses of the Halys and the Euphrates. Ezek 27:14 mentions commercial dealings between Togarmah and Tyre.

The answers to the questions posed above are: the association of Ashkenaz with Gomer is clear, with Togarmah is possible, with Riphath — no answer.

Literature: Gen 10:4: G. Oppert, *Tarshish und Ophir* (1903).   W.F. Albright, "Mari and Egyptian Excavations of the 20th and 19th Century B.C. Studies in Personal

Names from the Two Sources," BASOR 83 (1941) 21-22, 34. A. Schulten, *Tartessos* (1950²) c. 3. D.R. Jones, "A Fresh Interpretation of Zechariah IX-XI," VT 12 (1962) 241-259; 247f. G. Garbini, "Tarsis e Gen 10, 4," BibOr 6 (1964) 13-19. P. Cintas, Tarsis — Tartessos — Gades," Sem. 16 (1966) 5-37. W. Wifall, "Asshur and Eber, or Asher and Heber? A Commentary on the Last Balaam Oracle Num 24:21-24," ZAW 82 (1970) 110-114. K. Galling, "Der Web der Phöniker nach Tarsis in literarischer und archäologischer Sicht," ZDPV 88 (1972) 140-181.

[**10:4**] *The Sons of Javan.* Four sons of Javan are mentioned. While the first two, Elishah and Tarshish, are the names of peoples in the singular, as is always the case in P's table of the nations, the second two are plural in form, Kittim and Rhodanim, singular as such in Gen 10 (P). The presumption is that it is a set pair of names that was appended here from another context because it filled out the table in this place.

Elishah. The place is mentioned again in Ezek 27:7; it is certainly worth noting that here it is from Elishah that purple is transported to Tyre, the classical source of this material (W. Zimmerli, *Comm.* ad loc.). Earlier there was great uncertainty about the localization of Elishah; now however there is virtual unanimity in equating it with Alashiah of Akkadian and Hittite inscriptions and with Cyprus, the land of copper (the name copper comes from Cyprus). The Amarna letters 34-40 are addressed by a king of Alashiah to the Pharaoh and mention the export of copper. Alashiah is mentioned further in the texts from Mari, Nuzi, and Ugarit (see further W. Zimmerli, *Comm.*; Ezek 27:7). A Ugaritic text mentions it together with Yam(w)an, which corresponds to the association of Elishah with Javan in Gen 10:4.

J. Simons has recently contested the equation Elishah-Alashiah with Cyprus on the ground that Kittim appears in the same sequence and that Κίτιον is Cyprus without any doubt. But the reason is not convincing because, as was noted above, "Kittim and Rhodanim" are originally an independent element in tradition that is appended to fill out the table. Because Kittim, together with Elishah, originally designates a city and then the surrounding country, they can be designations of different areas on Cyprus that were used for the whole island by different groups and (or) at different times. J. Simons holds that all other attempts that have been made hitherto to explain the word are "guesswork." He would suggest Crete, which is otherwise not mentioned.

Tarshish. The name raises considerable difficulties precisely because it occurs so often in the Old Testament. It is mentioned expressly as a far distant place in Is 66:19; Ps 72:10 and particularly in Jonah 1:3; 4:2. From the time of Solomon (1 Kings 10:22) there is constant mention of the ships of Tarshish. It trades in silver, iron, tin, and lead. All this seems to point clearly to Tartessos, the Phoenician colony in Spain, at the mouth of the Guadalquiver. This is the general opinion: "On the basis of what is said in the Old Testament, Tarshish can only be Tartessos in Spain," W. Schmidtke; so too the majority of modern interpreters. J. Simons, and others, object: "A further difficulty is that the map of the world would be extended considerably by this one name." The only cuneiform attestation is an inscription of Esarhaddon: "All kings who live in the midst of the sea, from Cyprus and Javan as far as Tarshish, submit to my feet" (R. Borger, *Die Inschriften Asserhaddons*, 1956, 86). Here too a reference to Tartessos in Spain is unlikely. Finally, the question arises whether the author of the table of the nations, who has such remarkable and precise geographical knowledge, would have described as a son of Javan the well-known Phoenician colony in Spain, Tartessos. One can assume then with E. Speiser *(Comm.)*: "The biblical name may refer to more than one place." W.F. Albright assumes a place on Sardinia with the same name; but that is uncertain.

Kittim and Rhodanim. If these two names are an independent element in tradition and were appended here by way of completion, then they describe two of a kind: they are the two large islands of Cyprus and Rhodes which lie off the south coast of Asia Minor (read Rhodanim instead of Dodanim). There were Greek settlements on both islands so that the designation "sons of Javan" makes sense. Rhodes is mentioned in Homer, Il. II 654f.

Kittim is a Hebrew form of the Greek Κίτιον, a city on Cyprus (in the area of Larnaca?). The name of the city is written as Kt or Ktj in Phoenician inscriptions. It occurs in other places in the Old Testament, Num 24:24; Is 23:1, 12; Jer 2:10; Ezek 27:6; Dan 11:30, but always as the designation of a region or a people, never of a city. The name has been extended from the city to a wider region and then to the whole island. Later, in 1 Macc, it can mean the whole Greek peninsula, and the Vg translates Ezek 27:6 *de insulis Italiae.*

Literature: Gen 10:5: L. Rost, "Die Bezeichnungen für Land und Volk im Alten Testament," *Festschr. O. Procksch* (1934) 137-139. J.R. Kupper, *Les nomades en Mesopotamie. . . .* (1957). F.A. Munch, "Verwandtschaft und Lokalität in der Gruppen-bildung der altisraelitischen Hebräer," KZS 12 (1960) 438-440. E.A. Speiser, " 'People' and 'Nation' of Israel," JBL 79 (1960) 157-163. W.H. Gispen, "Genesis 2:10-14," *Festschr. Th.C. Vriezen* (1966) 115-124; A. Malamat, "Aspects of Tribal Societies in Mari and Israel," *Les Congrès et Colloques de l'Université de Liège* 42 (1967) 129-138.

[10:5a] "From these the coastal peoples spread." The first question is whether the מאלה refers to the "sons of Javan (A. Dillmann) or to all the "sons of Japheth" (U. Cassuto). It can be solved easily by paying attention to the meaning of איים: countries (regions) that border on the sea, and so the coastal areas. This obviously holds for "the sons of Javan," and for Javan itself too, but not for the other "sons of Japheth." So "from these" can only refer to the sons of Javan. There is a further question: Is it intended to suggest that the names of all peoples or lands are not mentioned, but only the most important, and from them many more ramified (so A. Dillmann and U. Cassuto)? But this is rather a reading back into the text. If one takes the expression literally, it merely describes an event. This is confirmed by v. 32 where the same sentence occurs again and refers to all peoples of the earth. The author of the table of the nations is saying thereby that the peoples were subdividing and ramifying throughout the whole time-span from the end of the flood to the present. The sentence does not really suit the style of the rest of the table which shows an even pattern; it is merely an attempt to balance this geographical picture with the time gap. It stands hard by the sons of Javan, because over against the two older domains the "ramification" corresponds closest to the current situation of the author.

[10:5b] V. 5b is a "refrain verse" which recurs after each of the three groups of peoples, vv. 5b, 20, 31. It closes a section in a solemn, monotonous way like the close of each of the days of creation. This threefold repetition is extremely important for P. He very cleverly produces the impression in the listener that the comprehensive variety of names issues each time into something uniform, common to all, and all-embracing. It is this that closes each section and P thereby quietly indicates that the origin of all the peoples of the earth lies in the creator's will and blessing. He is saying that a people is more than a mere conglomeration of persons; it is an articulated part of the human race, and the race exists only in these parts. There are certain basic elements common to all that indicate that they share in the human race — the land, which is the people's living space and provides it with food; the language, which binds all members of the people together and makes meaningful existence and community life possible; the families (clans), which give continuity to the life of the people as generation follows generation. The closing phrase "within their nations" does not add anything new but merely serves as a summary conclusion: within all peoples of the three great groups.

As far as we know this is the first attempt in the history of humankind to conceive and define the basic elements of the entity "people." It arose from the theological impulse to express how the separation of humankind into people is grounded in the will and blessing of the creator.

To summarize what has been said about the sons of Japheth: first, the identification of the names. Of the main group, the seven sons of Japheth, five can be explained with certainty, one (Tiras) is not altogether certain, and one (Magog) is very uncertain. Of the first subgroup, the sons of Gomer, two are certain, one (Riphath) cannot be explained. Of the second subgroup, the four sons of Javan, three are certain while the fourth (Tarshish) is uncertain. That is, of the fourteen names, ten can be explained with certainty, two are probable or uncertain, and no explanation has yet been found for the other two. This result is to be regarded very positively: almost all the peoples whom P associates with Japheth can be identified. The result is confirmed because the majority of the names occur partly in the same grouping in Ezekiel: 38:1ff. Magog, Meshech, Tubal, Gomer, Togarmah; in 38:18 Tarshish; in 27:7 and 12 Elishah and Tarshish; in 27:13f. Javan, Tubal, Meshech and Beth-Togarmah. 38:6 describes this group of people as coming "from the extreme north."

The localization of these peoples is clear. Looking at them from Israel, they are the peoples from the far north, further north than Syria and Assyria, the majority from Asia Minor across to Armenia. Some are further west, how far is uncertain. Some are further east, but these too, seen from Israel, are peoples from the north.

It is possible at the same time to have a fair idea of the period in question. If the majority of these peoples are found also in Ezekiel and partly in the same grouping, then this too must be an indication of an outlook conditioned by a certain period. P and Ezekiel are in any case chronologically close to each other; so the outlook must be that of the 6th century. And when assume, as we must, that Ezekiel and P rest on the same traditions, then the peoples mentioned will have become known in Israel in the 7th century as the peoples of the far north. This coincides with what we know of them from other sources. The majority of them came in contact with the Near East in the 8th century. It is only after this that they can gradually become known in Israel.

A number of these peoples are mentioned in Ezekiel in the context of their commercial products. One can assume then that this was one of the ways that information about them came to Israel.

The conclusion therefore is that J cannot have known the majority of them. His list cannot have had this Japheth-group, but something completely different.

Literature: Gen 10:6-7, 20: B. Luther, ZAW 21 (1901) 1-96. W.R. Smith, *Kinship and Marriage in Early Arabia* (1903²) 24-25. W. Spiegelberg, *Ägyptische Randglossen zum Alten Testament* (1904). F. Stähelin, "Der Name Kanaan," *Festschr. J. Wackernagel* (1923) 150-153. E.F. Sutcliffe, "Chananaeus autem tunc erat in terris (Gen 10:6; 13:7)," VD 6 (1926) 62-64. J.A. Montgomery, *Arabia and the Bible* (1934) c. 3. W.F. Albright, "Dedan," BHTh 16 (1953) 1-12. S. Moscati, AnBib 12 (1959) 266-269. M.C. Astour, JBL 84 (1965) 422-425. F.V. Winnett, "The Arabian Genealogies in Genesis," *Essays in Honor of H.G. May* (1970) 171-196. J. Heller, "Zephanjas Ahnenreihe (Eine redaktionsgeschichtliche Bemerkung zu Zeph. I 1)," VT 21 (1971) 102-104.

[**10:6-7, 20**] *The Sons of Ham (P).* The structure of the second part of P's table of the nations is remarkable in that the peoples descended from Cush in v. 7 do not correspond to the four "sons" of Ham. These latter are listed as the four great people of the south, moving from south to north, and so are easily explained. But, contrary to what one would expect, the groups of peoples who belong to each of these lands do not follow. There are the "sons" of only one of them, Cush; and these, insofar as they can be explained, do not belong to any of the lands mentioned, but to Arabia. Some of these J describes differently and puts in a different order.

The two groups of names in v. 7 are the result of an accretion within the P tradition; each is independent, the five sons of Cush and the two sons of Ragmah. If this is correct, it reflects the gradual growth of information about foreign lands. The first addition is a group of Arabian peoples who have become known through commerce; they are attached to Nubia because they seem to be best suited there. The second is a group that often occurs together, Sheba and Dedan. This is likewise attached because it claims one of the names of the previous group as its father. One must distinguish then in the history of tradition between the main group, the four great peoples of the south, which are fixed and deep in tradition, and the groups that are added, which are but a sample of regions hitherto unknown, but are not yet a fixed tradition. We can explain in this way why Canaan is linked with Ham. The information about the four great peoples of the south reaches far back into the past and is familiar with the link between Canaan and Egypt. This is preserved too in later times.

Cush. The land south of Egypt, Nubia, in Greek, Ethiopia; in Egyptian inscriptions Kos or Kas, also the Assyrian *Kūsū* (with e and i). It is described often in this way in the Old Testament, in detail in Is 11:11 (Lower Egypt, Upper Egypt, Nubia); Jer 13:23 speaks of the dark-skinned Cushites. Nubian princes were the Pharoahs for about half a century from about 715 on.

Misraim. This is the general Semitic designation for Egypt. The ending is generally explained as a dual referring to the both kingdoms of Egypt; but neither the designation nor the form are certain. Is 11:11 and Jer 44:15 restrict it to Lower Egypt, but elsewhere it is always Egypt as a whole. It is called the "land of Ham" in Pss 78:51; 105:23, 27; 106:21, 22. The land of Egypt was known to the Israelites from the earliest times, e.g., Gen 12:10-20.

Put. It occurs in the Old Testament in Nahum 3:9; Jer 46:9; Ezek 30:5; the Greek renders it as Λίβυες in Ezek 27:10 and 38:5, as does the Vg. Josephus too understands it as Lybia. Nahum 3:9 distinguishes it from Lybia (Egypt, Put, the

Lybians). It has been equated therefore with the Egyptian Punt, on the Somali coast, west of the Red Sea (so E. Meyer, H. Gunkel, O. Procksch and others). F. Delitzsch and A. Dillmann have raised objections, adding to the evidence of the translations that of the Greek and Latin writers; so Jerome: "Mauritaniae fluvius usque in praesens Phut dicitur." This river is attested too by Pliny and Josephus I, 6.2, the Χώρα Φούτη. The sequence of the enumeration, moving from south to north, speaks in favor of Lybia, as well as the fact that in the Old Testament Put is often described as a war-like people that provides mercenaries for foreign rulers (Egypt, Nahum 3:9; Tyre, Ezek 27:10; the army of Gog, Ezek 38:5). We know that about Lybia, but not about the Somali coast. J. Simons explains the juxtaposition of Put and Lubim in Nahum 3:9 as a poetic description of Lybia.

Canaan. This is the designation of the land and the people of the lowlands west of the Jordan, especially of the coastal plain, including Phoenicia (it is found as an ancient term by which the Phoenicians describe themselves). In the Amarna tablets it describes Palestine. However, Canaan is used here in a very broad sense (so J. Skinner, J. Simons). It is probably due to a very old tradition that it is ascribed to Ham and not to Shem. See A. van Selms, OTS 12 (1958) 187-213.

[10:7] *The Sons of Cush.* Five sons of Cush and two sons of Ragmah are mentioned. The purpose is to give further information about the distant south. It is certain that the majority of the names describe peoples in Arabia. The association with Cush does not necessarily mean origin or dependence. It is probable that a geographical association is intended.

[10:7a] *Seba.* According to Josephus (Ant. 2,249) this is Meroe, the country (or a city in the country) between the white and the blue Nile. In Ps 72:10 it is, together with Sheba, a country in the far south. It is mentioned in Is 43:3 and 45:14 together with Egypt and Cush. Strabo (16:4, 8, 10) knows Σαβά(ι) on the African coast; Josephus knows it as a city of the Ethiopians. The three names together in Deutero-Isaiah can explain why the series in v. 7 is joined with Cush.

Havilah. Cf. Comm. on Gen 2:11. Havilah occurs in J's table of the nations, 10:29, as a son of Joktan. In 25:18 (the sons of Keturah) it is the eastern border of Ishmaelite Arabs. All that is certain is that a stretch of land in Arabia is meant; the same according to 1 Sam 15:7. Gen 2:11 must refer to a large area. If the word means "sand-land" (according to S. Bochart, many think so; cf. Literature on 10:1-32), it could refer to several regions.

Sabtah. From F. Tuch and A. Dillmann right up to the present (H. Gunkel, J. Skinner, B. Jacob, J. Simons) it is thought likely that this is the old Arabian commercial city of Sabatah or Sabotah in the Hadramaut.

Ragmah. Ezek 27:22 names it together with Sheba as a commercial people (with Tyre). It could be the south Arabian city *Ragmat* mentioned in Minaean and Sabaean inscriptions.

Sabteca. The name has hitherto not been attested elsewhere. O. Procksch considers a foundation of the Nubian Pharoah Shebiktu (Shabataka); so too M.C. Astour, "Sabtah and Sabteca. Ethiopian Pharao Names in Genesis 10," JBL 84 (1965) 422-425.

[10:7b] Two sons of Ragmah are attached, Sheba and Dedan. Both names are also mentioned together in Gen 25:3 (in the genealogy of the sons of Keturah) and Ezek 38:13 (as merchant peoples). This explains why both names are attached; they form an independent element of tradition.

Sheba (Saba), the Sabaeans. 1 Kings 10:1ff. tells the story of the queen of Sheba; Sheba is mentioned in Is 60:6; Jer 6:20; Ezek 27:22; Job 1:15; Ps 72:15. P has made a distinction between שׁבא and סבא (see above). It is a people in southwest Arabia, a rich people and land with extensive commerce. It flourished in the 7th century and was supplanted later by the Minaeans. In Gen 10:28 it is attributed to Joktan. The name spread widely; Sheba had commercial colonies in north Arabia (A. Dillmann, J. Simons) and this perhaps explains why it is mentioned in different genealogical contexts.

Dedan. Is 21:13 speaks of the caravans of Dedan; it is mentioned in Jer 25:23 and 49:8 with Edom and other tribes of Arabia. In Ezek 25:13 it is people on the border of Edom. The name occurs in south Arabic inscriptions.

[10:20]   The conclusion of the sons of Ham tallies with v. 5 (see above).

Literature: Gen 10:22-23: P. Haupt, "Die Etymologie von Aram," ZDMG 61 (1907) 194-195.   J.P. Peters, "The Eldest Son of Shem," HomR 52 (1908) 248-251, 335-339.   F.W. König, *Die Geschichte Elams* (1931).   A. Poebel, "The Name of Elam in Sumerian, Accadian and Hebrew," AJSL 48 (1931) 20-22.   W.F. Albright, "The Biblical Tribe of Massā and Some Congeners," *Studi Orientalistici G. Levi Della Vida I* (1956) 1-14.   B. Mazar, "The Aramaean Empire and its Relations With Israel," BA 25 (1962) 98-120.

[10:22, 23]   *The Sons of Shem.* The structure is the same as with the sons of Ham: the list of the sons of Shem, v. 22, is not followed by any clear subdivision. Four further names are attached to one of the peoples mentioned, namely Aram. The explanation is the same.

Elam. This great people and country lay east of Babylon with Susa as its capital. It is known from the 3rd millennium, toward the end of which it ruled over Babylon. It is not a Semitic people. During its long history it was in constant contact with the Assyrian and Babylonian empires. After the destruction of Susa by Asshurbanipal in the middle of the 7th century it ceased to exist as an independent state. It is mentioned often in the Old Testament; an Elamite king, Ched-or-Laomer appears in Gen 14:1.

Asshur. The ancestral seat lay on the middle Tigris. It achieved its greatest expansion under Asshurbanipal. It is mentioned often in the Old Testament.

Arpachshad. J. Skinner *(Comm.)* has recorded in detail and discussed the many attempts to explain this name. A solution to the problem has not yet emerged (so E.A. Speiser). H. Gunkel and others had already assumed that the name must stand for Babylon, and J. Skinner supported this very strongly. Babylon, he says, cannot be missing from the list. He also alleges in its favor that the three last consonants correspond to the Bab. *kashdu,* the Hebr. Kasdim (= Chaldeans). This is but a conjecture and does not explain the name fully. However, it is certainly correct that Arpachshad stands for Babylon here. It is probable that the clue to understanding it is in 11:10ff. (P) where it appears as a personal name, which agrees with 10:22. P saw in Babylon the oldest and most important representative of the Semitic family of peoples and described it as the firstborn of Shem, 11:10.

Lud. The name gives rise to serious difficulties among the sons of Shem. It is explained for the most part as Lydia in Asia Minor. But a country in this western region does not conform with the other names in the group (so too J. Simons and others). It would certainly belong to the Japheth-peoples. The Ludim mentioned by J in 10:13 are Hamites, and they cannot be meant here. P. Jensen (ThLZ, 1895, 510; DLZ 24, 1899, 939) has conjectured *lubdu*, attested in cuneiform, on the upper reaches of the Tigris; U. Cassuto accepts this as a conjecture. The question must remain open.

Aram. The Arameans are a group of peoples in Syria and Mesopotamia, and are very widely dispersed. They remained nomads for a long time (still in Amos 9:7) and are first mentioned in Assyrian texts in the time of Tiglath-pileser. They appear often in the Old Testament; their country is often called Aram-naharaim, which the Gk usually renders by Mesopotamia. J. Simons deals with it in detail under Aram.

[10:23] *The Sons of Aram.* This group of names has, for all intents and purposes, not yet been explained. Hul and Gether are completely unknown. There is but the faintest indication of what Mash might be — it could be Strabo's Mt. Masius, north of Nisibis. The land of Uz is mentioned in the Old Testament, but its identification is uncertain. According to U. Cassuto and J. Simons it is not the Edomite land of Job 1:1; Lam 4:22 (KBL: "between Edom and Arabia"). In Gen 22:21 Uz is a son of Nahor and corresponds perhaps to the *uṣṣai* in an Assyrian text of Shalmaneser III. It is worth noting that the Aramaic list of J comprises for the most part other names.

[10:31] V. 31 closes the list of the descendants of Shem; it agrees literally with vv. 20 and 5.

[10:32] V. 32 closes P's table of the nations. The first part of the verse merely draws everything together and is a typical concluding formula of P, introduced by אלה. The table of the nations has been concerned with "the clans of the sons of Noah," as they were introduced in 10:1a. The *tōledōt* is resumed from 10:1a and determined further only by "in their nations," which is the real conclusion of the table.

The sentence that follows immediately, "And from them the nations spread on the earth after the flood," does not suit the context very well. The words "from them" cannot refer to the peoples of 32a; the determination of time "after the flood" shows that it can only refer to the sons of Noah. But this is harsh grammatically. The sentence is almost the same as 9:19b (J). It is an ancient element of tradition that is really part of the conclusion of the flood narrative. P has taken it up again into the conclusion of his wide ranging table of the nations so as to link it with its starting point, "after the flood" *(inclusio)*.

The Additions of J in the Table of the Nations.

It has already been said at the beginning that the Yahwistic sections of the table of the nations consist almost exclusively of two self-contained additions that have been inserted each time before the "refrain verses" of P, i.e., before vv. 20 and 31: they are vv. 8-19 and 24-30; in addition there are vv. 1b and 21.

The First Addition 10:1b, 8-19. One can conclude from 10:21: "To Shem also sons were born," that a corresponding sentence is to be added before v. 8 which has fallen out because of P's parallel enumeration in v. 6. The sentence 10:1b (J): ". . . and sons were born to them after the flood," which joins with the names of the three sons in 9:18, 19, would have been followed by something like: "Sons were born to Ham: Cush, Egypt and Canaan." These three names are gleaned from vv. 8, 13, 15.

Literature: Gen 10:8-12: P. Haupt, *Der keilinschriftliche Sintflutbericht . . .* (1881). A. Jeremias, *Isdubar-Nimrod, eine altbabylonische Heldensage* (1891). A. Boissier, ZAW 30 (1910) 35-36. T.T. Haluszczynskyj, *De urbis Babel exordiis ac de primo in terra Sinear regno. Narratio Genesis XI, 1-9; X, 8-12 monumentis babylonico-assyriacis illustrata* (1917). A. Jirku, "Nimrod," OLZ 20 (1917) 169-172. J.W. Rothstein, "Zu Jirkus Aufsatz über Nimrod in OLZ Sp. 169ff.," OLZ 20 (1917) 249-250. F.M.Th. Böhl, "Wie was Nimrod?," NThS 2, 2 (1918). N.D. Leeuwen, "Wie waren Kus en Nimrod?," GThT 22, 1 (1920). J.D. Prince, "A Possible Sumerian Original of the Name Nimrod," JAOS 40 (1920) 201-203. E.G. Kraeling, "The Origin and Real Name of Nimrod," AJSL 38 (1921/1922) 214-220. P. Dhorme, RB 33 (1924) 532-556; 35 (1926) 66-82, 223-239; 532-556. A. Deimel, "Nimrod (Gen 10:8-12)," Or 26 (1927) 76-80. K. Thieme, "Nimrod, Kusch und Babel. Zum universalhistorischen Ertrag der 'Biblischen Urgeschichte'," HJ 74 (1955) 1-11. J. Jelito, "Nimrod," RBL 9 (1956) 5-9. E.A. Speiser, "In Search of Nimrod," ErIs 5 (1958) 32-45. G.E. Wright, *Biblical Archeology* (1962²). P.T. English, "Cushites, Colchians and Khazars," JNESt 18 (1959) 49-53. W. von Soden, "Nimrod," RGG³ IV (1960) 1496-1497. Th.C. Vriezen, "The Edomite Deity Qaus," OTS 14 (1965) 330-353. J. Coppens, "Une nouvelle date pour le document Yahviste," EThL 42 (1966) 567-572. M.E.L. Mallowan, *Nimrod and its Remains* (1966). E. Lipinski, "Nimrod et Assur," RB 73 (1966) 77-93. E. Ullendorff, *Ethiopia and the Bible* (1968). P. Amiet, "Quelques ancêtres du chasseur royal d'Ugarît," UG 6 (1969) 1-8.

[10:8-12] Even those exegetes who do not subscribe to the division into the sources J and P, point out that this passage stands outside the stylistic movement of the table of the nations (e.g., B. Jacob, J. Simons, and U. Cassuto; the latter suggests that we have here a citation from a Nimrod epic). The difference is obvious. While P's table of the nations is strictly an enumeration, vv. 8-12 is closer to a narrative or a report. The text approximates to enumeration only in the series of names in v. 10: "and Erech and Akkad and Kalneh," and in v. 11f.: "And Rehoboth-Ir and Kalah and Resen between Nineveh and Kalah." It is to be noted that both these series are prefixed to a further specification that actually belongs to the name that precedes the series. Most exegetes maintain that the remark at the end of v. 12: "that is the great city," refers to Nineveh. The consequence is that both series of names belong to a later stage and that of the text of vv. 10-11 in its older form did not contain the series.

It is only now that the form of the account is seen clearly. It is found unencumbered in vv. 8 and 9: "The beginning of his kingdom was Babylon in the land of Shinar. From this land he went up to Asshur and built Nineveh, i.e., the great city." It is part of the report which is expressed in 9:19b in this way: "and the whole earth was populated from them (the three sons of Noah)." J reports how this took place while P describes in the table of the nations the situation which came about from the division of the peoples.

The structure of vv. 8-12 shows how the process of populating this part of the earth took place:

8a:	Part of a genealogy
8b:	Elaboration: he was the first (achievements)
9:	Elaboration: the mighty hunter
10:	The beginning of his kingdom
11-12:	The expansion of his kingdom

It is a self-contained episode; the founding of a kingdom is reported, more precisely the origins of the oriental empires. There are three acts: the birth of the lord, the foundation of the kingdom, the expansion. It is essential, first, that the founding of the empires is described as something new, as "progress," and that it took place in the course of the history of humankind; second, that these empires did not arise from the movement of peoples but from the seizure of power by a man (a king); third, that what characterizes this empire is the extension of dominion. The origin and growth of the oriental empires is thus described in the way we know it from history.

One does not comprehend what is essential to this text by confining oneself merely to the names (as distinct from the table of the nations where everything depends on the names). One must look to the pattern which covers the stages of the origin and growth of the empire. Nimrod is not to be pinned down to a historical figure. He is the famous founder of the kingdom on the two rivers and is still spoken of today, v. 9.

[**10:8**] "And Cush begot Nimrod." If Nimrod, about whom there is unanimity, is meant to be an individual, then Cush too cannot be the name of a land or a people, at least not primarily. The enumeration of the names of the sons of Noah comes first in J, 9:18; the enumeration of the three sons of one of Noah's sons follows, but this is not found in J. If an individual is mentioned before and after Cush, then Cush can hardly be a collective. The sentence, "Cush (the Cushites) begot Nimrod (a person)," would scarcely make sense. We have rather a genealogy consisting of three parts:

9:18: the sons of Noah are. . . .
add: Ham (or Shem) begot Cush
10:8: and Cush begot Nimrod, who was. . . .

We have the same stylistic form as in 4:17-26; here too the progress of humanity is described within the framework of a genealogy — humankind expands over the earth.

Nimrod. B. Jacob gives a detailed account of the explanations offered for the name Nimrod and concludes: "But there is no sign at all of a Nimrod or similar name." Likewise J. Skinner and others, and the situation has not changed despite more recent attempts. The name is linked with Marduk, the tutelary god of Babylon (A.H. Sayce, J. Wellhausen); with Nuzi-Maruttash, a king of the Kassite dynasty (P. Haupt, H.W. Hilprecht); as *nu-marad* (man from Marad) with the middle Babylonian city Marad (F. Delitzsch); with the constellation Orion, who appears as a mighty hunter in Greece and later as a hunter translated to the sky; in Syriac the constellation is known as *gabbār;* with Amen-hotep III (1411-1375) who is called *neb-ma-re,* in the Amarna letters Nimmuri (K. Sethe); with Gilgamesh, who is described as a *gibbōr* in the epic, and presented as hunter in sculpture (so many interpreters); with the Babylonian god of war and the hunt, Ninurta (H. Zimmern, KBL); more recently (E.A. Speiser, ErIs 5 [1958] 32-45) with Tukulti-Ninurta I, of the 13th century, the first Assyrian master of Babylon; as Ninos a figure of Greek story. Further details can be found in the commentaries of B. Jacob and J. Skinner.

Nimrod occurs once more in the Old Testament in Mic 5:5: here Asshur is called the land of Nimrod. The passage harmonizes well with Gen 10:8 because here too Nimrod is a founder-figure. Both point back to a legendary tradition (G.

von Rad, ad loc.) in which Nimrod is the founder of the Assyrian-Babylonian and Assyrian kingdoms. What is of particular importance is that the name is current right down to the 10th-8th centuries both in the designation "land of Nimrod" and in the language of 10:9. It is not to be assumed then that this Nimrod can be identified with some historical figure or other. The net result of all these endeavors is that Gen 10:8f. intends the type of a leader of the early period of Mesopotamia, like Gilgamesh of the epic, and that Tukulti-Ninurta (who is certainly not to be identified with Nimrod) became a legendary founder figure (Ninos).

[10:8b]   The agreement between vv. 8-12 and 4:17-26 is even clearer in v. 8b: the same verb החל is there in the same context, 4:26 (passim). It is there too in 9:20 when Noah is the first to cultivate the vine. Nimrod began to be a *gibbōr* on earth; he was the first man of might on earth. "The word expresses the idea of violent, tyrannical power, like the arab. *gabbār*" (J. Skinner). Gilgamesh is portrayed as a mighty lord in exactly the same way (Tablet I, 3-28); dominion and the exercise of power coalesce completely here (H. Gunkel). And Nimrod's dominion is seen as something new, as an epoch making beginning.

[10:9]   It has been acknowledged since A. Dillmann that v. 9 is inserted here as an independent tradition. The sentence is completely self-contained; v. 10 follows immediately on v. 8. But one does not conclude from this that v. 9 is a later addition. It has been inserted by J himself as an independent tradition about Nimrod. Nimrod was a mighty hunter as a proverb, still current, says. גבר has a somewhat different and more general meaning than in v. 8 inasmuch as it can be rendered adjectively. The "לפני י can be given a positive or negative value: with Yahweh's approval or in defiance of Yahweh. B. Jacob rejects a value judgment: "The popular saying in Israel reflects merely the great impression that the person has made. It is a form of the superlative." It is to be noticed that the last four words of 9a coincide with the last four of 9b. It is clear that the whole sentence is shaped out of the proverb. Proverbs of this kind, in which the deeds or conduct of a contemporary are compared with those of a famous figure from the past, are found all over the earth.

The words גבר־ציד, which one can render more accurately "mighty at the hunt," need further explanation. Most commentaries refer to the representations of kings at the hunt both in Egypt and Mesopotamia (cf. K. Galling, BRL, 286-290; IDB "Hunting," with literature and illustrations). The motif is very common; Gilgamesh too is described as hunting the lion. But when B. Jacob, e.g., says: "Hunting was a favorite pastime of the Babylonian kings," then this could be misleading. The hunt certainly became a sport of the kings in later times; but originally such was not at all the case. Behind this lies one of the functions of the king from the early period of the sacral kingship. One of his special duties was to ward off and destroy the wild animals threatening the community. What became a sport and pastime in the high cultures was once a necessity that secured the life of the community. Only now can we understand fully the significance of גבר־ציד: the founder king was a man of might and power because he subdued the wild animals (see the struggle against the monster in the Gilgamesh epic).

Literature: Gen 10:10: J.D. Prince, "Note on Akkad," JBL 25 (1906) 55-57.   S.

Landersdorfer, "Das Land Sin'ar," BZ 11 (1913) 350-363. E.G. Kraeling, "Calneh Genesis 10, 10," JBL 54 (1935) 233-234. W.F. Albright, "The End of 'Calneh in Shinar' (Gen 10:10)," JNESt 3 (1944) 254-255. A.S. Yahuda, "Calneh in Shinar," JBL 65 (1946) 325-337. P. Humbert, "Trois notes . . . ," OH (1955) 196-198. M. Noth, *Die Ursprünge des alten Israel im Lichte neuer Quellen*, AFLNW 94 (1961). C.H. Gordon, "Calneh," IDB I (1962) 490. A. Malamat, "Kingship and Council in Israel and Sumer; A Parallel," JNES 22 (1963) 247-253. R. Giveon, "Toponymes Ouest-Asiatiques à Soleb," VT 14 (1964) 239-255. A. Malamat, "Organs of Statecraft in the Israelite Monarchy," BA 28 (1965) 34-65 = B.A. Reader (1970) 163-198. G. Wallis, "Sinear," BHHW 3 (1966) 1805. J.A. Thompson, "Samaritan Evidence for 'All of them in the Land of Shinar' (Gen 10:10)," JBL 90 (1971) 99-102.

[10:10] It is stated here for the first time that Nimrod was a king and his realm was a kingdom. The verse is saying that Nimrod became a king and founder of a kingdom by means of his mighty deeds, v. 8. The beginning of this kingdom was Babel, i.e., he became master of the city of Babel in the land of Shinar.

Babel: bāb-ilu: "It had predominance since the suppression of the Elamites by Hammurabi (about 2000) and since then was regarded in the whole of the Near East as the first city in the world" (H. Gunkel). It is mentioned very often in the Old Testament; e.g., Gen 11:9; Is 13:1.

Shinar is the whole land of Babylon in the Old Testament. It is not to be equated with Sumer (E.A. Speiser and others), but with Sumer and Akkad together. It corresponds to the southern part of modern Iraq; so BRL; Sum. *Singi-Uri;* Egyp. *Sngr;* Gk Σιγγαρα. In the Old Testament it is found in Gen 11:2; 14:1, 9; Josh 7:21; Is 11:11; Zech 5:11; Dan 1:2 (on the etymology of Shinar see A. Poebel, AJSL 48 [1931] 26). The series of names which has been added mentions three more Babylonian cities: Erech, Akkad, and Kalneh.

Erech, the Babylonian Uruk, today Warka, on the Euphrates, about 125 miles south east of Babylon. It is the city of Gilgamesh and is very old. Already in the 4th millennium the 2nd dynasty of Uruk is mentioned; in the Sumerian King list it is one of the first cities after the flood (see P. Dhorme, RB 35 [1926] 66f. 231f.; S.N. Kramer, IDB II 124).

Akkad, Bab. *Akkada,* Sum. *Agade,* founded by Sargon I (c. 2500) and made the capital, it is situated in the north of Babylonia; the exact place is not known. The name occurs only here in the Old Testament.

Kalneh: no city of this name is known. Consequently W.F. Albright has suggested that it be read as כלנה = all of them (as in Gen 42:36). Likewise E.A. Speiser and J. Skinner. But such an alteration is hazardous, because there is no such formation with כל anywhere else in Genesis 10. A combination such as "all of them in the land. . . ." occurs nowhere else.

Literature: Gen 10:11-12: A.H. Layard, *Nineveh and its Remains* (1849²). K. Bezold, *Ninive und Babylon* (1903²; 1909³). E. Nestle, "Resen, Genesis X 12," ExpT 15 (1904) 476. "Resen in Genesis 10," ZDMG 58 (1905) 158-160. A.H. Sayce, ExpT 21 (1910); 22 (1911) 426-430. O. Schroeder, "Über die Urform des Stadtnamens Nineve," ZAW 35 (1915) 246-248. C.C. Torrey, "'Nineveh' in the Book of Tobit," JBL 41 (1922) 237-245. J. Neusner, "The Conversion of Adiabene to Judaism," JBL 83 (1964) 60-66.

[10:11-12] *The Expansion of Nimrod's Kingdom.* B. Jacob maintains that the translation "from this land he went up to Asshur" is impossible because the verb יצא means only to leave a land. He translates: "From this land Asshur went out. . . ." But by doing so he has to alter the meaning of ראשית in v. 10, which he translates: "And the culmination of his kingdom was Babel and. . . ." This is very unlikely and no one has accepted it. However, Jacob has correctly noted the linguistic difficulty. It would be solved if a verb had fallen out between יצא and אשור.

Many commentaries have pointed out that there is a historical fact behind the verse, namely that Babylonia was the older civilization and influenced the culture in the north. "The whole region, culture and political organization of Assyria were derived from the South-State" (J. Skinner). The sentence at the same time reveals another important fact of the early history of Mesopotamia, that side-by-side with conquest peaceful colonization played an important role. ". . . and he built Nineveh, i.e., the great city." Gen 4:17 also spoke of the building of a city; it (Enoch) follows on agriculture (Cain). 10:11 differs from this. The building of the city is in the context of the expansion of a kingdom of a potentate. J has distinguished clearly two stages in the development of civilization. The difference between J and P in Gen 10 becomes evident here. The J text is concerned with the beginning of the great kingdoms which lie in a much earlier period than P's Japheth peoples. The gap between Gen 10 P and Gen 10 J is considerable.

Nineveh. This is the Assyrian city Ninua (Nina) on the left bank of the Tigris opposite the modern Mosul, "one of the most ancient and influential cities of the land" (H. Gunkel). Sennacherib made it his residence in the 8th century. The appellation "the great city" is found in Jonah 1:2; 3:2, 3; 4:11; Jdt 1:1. Diodorus and Strabo are aware of its great significance, and excavations have confirmed its size.

The series which is added (as in v. 10) mentions three more Assyrian cities: "and Rehoboth-Ir and Kalah and Resen between Nineveh and Kalah."

Rehoboth-Ir: A purely Hebrew designation meaning the "city Piazzas." Some (e.g., U. Cassuto) understand it as a translation of the Assyrian *rēbit Ninā* — a suburb of Nineveh, others as a place close by Nineveh.

Kalah: Ass. Kalḫu or Kalaḫ, south of Nineveh, a foundation of Shalmaneser I (c. 1300); for a long time, right down to Sargon, it was the (royal) residence. Today it is Nimrud (so called after this verse).

Resen. The text describes the location of this place: "between Nineveh and Kalah." The precise spot is not known. Some interpreters conjecture that behind it lies the Ass. *Ris-ini,* "fountain-head," source.

If the assumption that these two series of names in vv. 10 and 11-12 are additions is correct, then it follows that the places that are unknown occur only there.

Literature: Gen 10:13-14: W.M. Müller, "Die Söhne Mizraims, Genesis 10:13-14," OLZ 5 (1903) 471-475.   W. Spiegelberg, "נפתחים (Gen. X 13)," OLZ 9 (1907) 276-279.   W.F. Albright, "Zu Anamin," JPOS 1 (1921) 57, 187-194.   A. Alt, "Zwei neue Philisternamen?," ZAW 47 (1929) 250-251.   G.A. Wainwright, "Caphtor — Cappadocia," VT 6 (1956) 199-210.   Y.M. Grintz, "The Genealogy of 'Mizraim' (Gen 10:13-14) and the Aegean World," *Studies in Early Biblical Ethnology and History* (1969) 72-90.   A. Pelletier, "Σαββατα. Transcription grecque de l'Araméen," VT 22 (1972) 436-447.

[**10:13-14**]   *Mizraim (Egypt).* At first sight vv. 13-14 seem to be dealing with the sons of Mizraim (Egypt), as vv. 8-12 dealt with the sons of Cush. However, it is immediately obvious how different this passage is. Vv. 13-14 are not a real parallel to vv. 8-12; their arrangement is primitive. After the introduction "and Mizraim (Egypt) begot" there is merely a series of names. Right down to the end of v. 14 there is a succession of seven (eight) names linked only by "and." Moreover in J the names of the peoples would not be possible as objects of ילד. In P on the contrary it is possible to say: "The sons of A are B, C, D (peoples)." It is something quite different to say: "Mizraim (Egypt) begot the Ludim. . . ." Such a wooden way of speaking is certainly not to be attributed to J. The solution to the problem is the same as in vv. 8-12. The seven (eight) names of peoples form an independent element of tradition (like the two series in vv. 10 and 11-12). They have been joined rather loosely and not too skillfully to J's introductory sentence (similarly U. Cassuto). This means that if J reported anything about Mizraim (Egypt), it has no longer been preserved. The series of names in vv. 13-14 is part of another stratum; it is an independent, self-contained list.

This list both in its constituent parts and as a whole (i.e., the meaning of the series) remains for the most part unexplained. It is associated with Egypt, as the introduction says, and this is confirmed by one of the two names that can be explained with certainty: Pathrusim (from Patros) means the inhabitants of upper Egypt. A further confirmation is that the Ludim, even though not identified as a people, are mentioned in Jer 46:9 and Ezek 30:5 together with Cush and Put, which indicates the same region. A second identification, though not absolute, is almost so. It is practically certain that Caphtor is a designation for Crete. The list then contains not only parts of the population of Egypt, but also peoples who are contiguous to or have connections with Egypt. The latter is the case with Crete, the former probably with the Lehabim who are almost universally explained as the Lybians, a neighboring people to the northwest of Egypt. The following then are the names, some explained, some not:

> Ludim: not explained, but somewhere in the region of Egypt
> Anamim: not explained
> Lehabim: Lybians, outside Egypt
> Naphtuhim: not explained (the lower Egyptians?)
> Pathrusim: the upper Egyptians
> Casluhim: not explained
> Kaphtorim: the Cretans, outside Egypt

The list as a whole shows no sign of a structure or system though it does reveal something of its origin. One of the names about which there is certainty, Pathrusim, is in the plural here; in other places it is always in the singular as the name of a region (Is 11:11; Jer 44:1, 15; Ezek 30:14; Ps 68:31, with emendation; KBL). The other, Kaphtorim, is out of place in the list. If Crete is assumed into the list because it had contacts with Egypt from earliest times, it would be natural to mention the land, here the island, by name. One cannot meaningfully assert that the whole population of Crete belongs to the Egyptian group of peoples. Moreover there is a third observation: the sentence that has been appended in v. 14, generally regarded as a marginal note, "from whom the Philistines came," refers very probably to the Kaphtorim (see Amos 9:7; Jer 47:4). It is formulated in such a way as if the name of the region, Kaphtor, were in the text.

It is obvious that the plural ending of all seven names is not equally appropriate in each case and the names have been standardized in order to form a list; the list came into being by giving all names the ending -im. The conclusion is that the list is at second hand; names originally of different kinds have been brought into uniformity. One must therefore be even more cautious in explaining them. J. Simons seems to me to be justified in leaving five of the seven unexplained and attributing insufficient probability to the many explanations hitherto attempted (especially in the older commentaries, e.g., F. Delitzsch; A. Dillmann is more cautious; recently U. Cassuto).

Literature: Gen 10:15-19: F.M.Th. Böhl, *Kanaanäer und Hebräer* (1911). F. Schachenmeyer, *Hethiter und Achäer* (1935). J. Simons, "Two Notes on the Problem of the Pentapolis," OTS 5 (1948) 91-117. H.L. Ginsberg, "A Preposition of Interest to Historical Geographers," BASOR 122 (1950/1951) 12-14. J. Nougayrol, *Le Palais royal d'Ugarit IV* (1956), review by H. Cazelles, VT 8 (1958) 103-106. H. Eybers, "Who were the Hivites?," OTWSA.P 2-5 (1959) 6-14. T.C. Mitchell, "The Old Testament Usage of Nesāma," VT 11 (1961) 177-187; 182. H. Donner, "Kallirrhoë. Das Sanatorium Herodes' des Grossen," ZDPV 79 (1963) 59-89. M. Haran, "The Rise and Decline of the Empire of Jeroboam Ben Joash," VT 17 (1967) 266-297. J. van Seters, "The Terms 'Amorite' and 'Hittite' in the Old Testament," VT 22 (1972) 74-81.

[10:15-19] *The Sons of Canaan (J).* Once more it is a question of a text that has been assembled. Vv. 15, 18b, 19 deal with the expansion of the peoples as J presents them. A series of names has been put in between, all of them ending with םי. The break in style between the two parts is obvious and has long been recognized, even if it has not been explained. The literary-critical explanation, namely that it is a matter of a gloss or a secondary addition (J. Wellhausen and others), needs to be modified. Vv. 16-18a represent an independent element of tradition from another context that has been attached to the key word Canaan by way of geographical information. The list is not uniform: the first four names are a series of pre-Israelite peoples in Canaan which occur often in the Old Testament and with many variants (see Synthesis, A. van Selms, OTS 12 (1958) 190, n. 27). The last five are five Phoenician cities which are artificially assimilated to the grammatical form of the preceding names. There is no parallel in the Old Testament to this second series.

While vv. 16-18a is a mere enumeration of names, the rest of the text, vv. 15, 18b, 19 is characterized by verbs:

> And Canaan begot. . . .
> Afterwards the Canaanites spread abroad, so that the territory of the Canaanites extended from . . . to. . . .

It is here that one finds the framework of J's original presentation. It is likely however that something has fallen out between vv. 15 and 18b because of the insertion of the series (J. Skinner has observed that 18b does not follow smoothly on 15). The text is not a constitutive part of a fixed table of the nations, but an account of the spread of humankind over the earth as then known. If one compares it with vv. 8-12 (J), it is clear that J wanted to set side-by-side two different ways in which peoples spread. He sets expansion by growth and migration (15, 18b, 19) over against expansion by conquest on the part of potentates (8-12). The other point of interest in contrast to P is obvious: P is interested in the static situation, in the state of the peoples that comprise humankind as it extends over the known world. J is interested in the process, in the events, in how it came about that peoples spread over the earth. Accordingly P's presentation is characterized by uniformity, by what is common to all (the refrain verses, 5, 20, 31), J's by variety, by what is peculiar to each (15, 18b, 19, in contrast to 8-12). The difference is diminished or obscured by the insertion of vv. 16-18a which in their static intent correspond more to P than to J.

[10:15]   The sentence "and Canaan begot" runs parallel to the formula used in v. 13 (Mizraim) and v. 8 (Cush). J intends the name to represent primarily an individual figure. He is describing the way from the family and its father to the clans and peoples. Canaan therefore was the father of the peoples of Canaan. It is quite possible then that for J, family structures are determinative for the relationships between peoples that arise from them; Sidon as the first-born takes precedence over the other son Heth. This reflects a historical recollection of the precedence of Phoenicia in early times.

Canaan. The name Canaan is used comprehensively in this text (and so in 15, 18b, 19). "This passage lays stress on the fundamental unity between the Phoenician towns and the inhabitants of Palestine proper" (A. van Selms, op. cit., 187). This is of special significance: in the historical books of the Old Testament, where Canaan is the land promised to Israel, Phoenician territory is never reckoned as part of Canaan. The reason is that it never belonged to the land promised to Israel and at no time did Israel claim it. Gen 10:15-19 reflects an outlook that is independent of this. Canaan is not seen here from the point of view of Israel, but as a member of the family of peoples. For further details on the geography and ethnology of Canaan, cf. J. Simons, op. cit.; M. Noth, *The Old Testament World* (1966).

Sidon, the first-born of Canaan, stands for Phoenicia. Sidon is older than Tyre as a leading power in Phoenicia, and so the Phoenicians are called after it not only in the Old Testament, Judg 18:7; 1 Kings 5:20; 16:31 . . . , but also in Homer (Iliad VI, 290f.) and in Assyrian inscriptions. Tyre only became the leading power in the time of David and Solomon (the kingdom of Hiram), and so it is quite certain that J does not intend to describe his contemporary situation but the origin and growth of Canaan. There is probably a Semitic explanation of the name of the city as fishing-city (so Justin); it is widely known for shipping and commerce. The absence of Tyre is to be explained by the fact that Sidon stands for the whole of Phoenicia from the time that it was a leading power. In 1 Kings 16:31 a king of Tyre is referred to as "king of the Sidonians."

Heth is the other son of Canaan. He stands for the Hittites. They are mentioned regularly when the pre-Israelite peoples of Canaan are enumerated (e.g., Gen 15:20; all passages in KBL and A. van Selms, op. cit., 190); what is peculiar here is that Heth is mentioned together with Sidon before the other Canaanite peoples. J. Simons describes them as late Hittites and assumes a connection with the classical Hittite empire which extended as far as the plain between Lebanon and anti-Lebanon; so too KBL; "scattered remains of the Hittite empire." Other scholars (O. Procksch, B. Jacob) see no connection at all. In P too "Hittite" has a rather broad meaning. It can be used to describe the inhabitants of the land where the patriarchs wandered, Gen 23, and where the wives of Esau are described as daughters of Canaan, Gen 26:34; 27:46; 36:2. Similarly too in Ezek 16:3, 45. However, it is to be noted that the Hittites who are named in the Old Testament have Semitic names like Uriah, 2 Sam 11:3. Moreover they are not confined to a region in Palestine but are found in the north and in the south. The meaning attached to Heth in this passage agrees with the Assyrian designation of Palestine as "the land of the Hittites."

[**10:16-17a**]   There follows a series of gentilitial names, first, four Canaanite peoples, and then, grammatically assimilated to them, five Phoenician cities.

Jebusites: the inhabitants of the city of Jerusalem and its environs (Josh 15:8; 18:28; Judg 1:21; 19:10; 2 Sam 5:6-9); according to Ezek 16:3, 45 they are of Amorite and Hittite origin. They are mentioned regularly in the enumerations of the pre-Israelite peoples of Canaan.

Amorites. Amurru had been the early Babylonian designation for the whole of Palestine and Syria from the 3rd millennium. It is an important name and occurs frequently in Assyrian and Egyptian (Amar or Amura) documents. In the Amarna letters it designates the region of Lebanon. In the Old Testament it designates the mountain range of central Palestine as the region where the Amorites settled (Num 13:29; Deut 1:44; Josh 11:3); hence, "the hill country of the Amorites," Deut 1:7, 19, 20. "Amorites" can also mean the pre-Israelite population as a whole, Gen 15:16; 48:22; Josh 10:12; Amos 2:9f. This comprehensive description could still square with the Akkadian "land of the Amurru." The present passage uses "Amorite" only in the narrower sense, as part of the population of Canaan together with the others (so too U. Cassuto). A detailed discussion of the problem is found in J. van Seters, VT 22 (1972) 64-81.

Girgashites. The name occurs only in the lists that are parallel to vv. 16-18a (Gen 15:21; Deut 7:1; Josh 3:10; 24:11; Neh 9:8) and in Phoenician inscriptions; there is too the Ug. proper name *grgs.* An inscription of Ramses II mentions Qarqisha among the followers of the Hittite king. This could be the same name (so A.H. Sayce, U. Cassuto, J. Simons). The region where they lived is unknown. H. Ewald has conjectured a connection with the Γεργεσηνοί near the lake of Gennesareth, Lk. 8:26.

Hivites. A people or tribe probably in central Palestine; they are mentioned in the vicinity of Gibeon (Josh 9:7; 11:19) and Shechem (Gen 34:2). Josh 11:3 speaks of the "Hivites at the foot of Hermon." In the Gk the name is frequently interchanged with the Hittites and the Horites. H. Eybers (see above), supposes that חוי and חרי are transcriptions of the same name and that the Hurrians are meant. J. Simons maintains that this is not proven. H. Eybers cites further literature.

[**10:17b, 18a**]   This closes the Canaanite list of peoples; there follows a series of five Phoenician cities.

Arkites. The city of Ἄρκη, or its inhabitants (Josephus has Ἄρκη ἐν τῷ Λιβάνῳ); Ass. *Arqā;* in the Amarna letters Irqata; in Roman times Caesarea in Lebanon; today *Arqā,* north of Tripoli. The place is mentioned in Egyptian and Akkadian inscriptions. The name occurs only here in the Old Testament.

Sinites. According to Jerome סין was situated in the vicinity of *ʿArqā,* but its exact location was no longer known to him. This name too occurs only here in the Old Testament. It has been attested recently in the texts of Ugarit. H. Cazelles, VT 8 (1958) 103, in his review of J. Nougayrol's *Le Palais Royal D'Ugarit IV,* writes: "We have . . . a surprising amount of information about the Siyannu (the סיני of Gen 10:17 and 1 Chron 1:15) . . . this country severed its links with Ugarit at the time to become independent."

Arvadites. This island city is the most northern of the Phoenician cities and has preserved its name right up to the present day. In cuneiform it is *aruada;* in the Amarna letters *arwada;* it is mentioned in Egyptian in the time of Thutmose III; the Greek form Ἄραδος is found in Herodotus and Strabo. Today it is *Ruad*. It was once a flourishing and significant city. It is mentioned again in the Old Testament in Ezek 27:8, 11.

Zemarites. A Phoenician city south of Arvad; Akk. *ṣimirra,* Amarna letters *ṣumur,* Egypt. *Du-mu-ra;* perhaps preserved in the name *ṣumra* a village near Tripoli. Simirra is mentioned together with Arqa in the Assyrian texts of Tiglath-pileser III. In classical writers it is Simyra.

Hamathites. The well-known city of Hamath on the Orontes, the only inland city of the Phoenician group; the Assyrian province of Hammatu is named after it. In the Seleucid period it was known as Ἐπιφάνεια; today it is *Ḥamah*. The name occurs often in the Old Testament, e.g., Amos 6:2.

The list of the five Phoenician cities in Gen 10:17b, 18 is one of the most reliable documents in the chapter. All the names can be identified with certainty. In contrast to the list of Canaanite peoples in 10:16, 17a, these Phoenician cities have no connection with Israel's claims to Canaan; we have objective information about a neighboring people. We certainly have to do with an originally independent tradition. The question arises whether the list belonged originally to the commercial centers or to the court. Under Solomon commerce was centered around the royal court and we know of his commercial agreements with Hiram of Tyre. We can be certain then that this list of Phoenician cities was drawn up and kept in the court chancery in Jerusalem.

[10:18b-19]   Vv. 18b-19 follow directly on v. 15. A sentence has fallen out after v. 15, something like: "Sons were born to them. . . ." (see above). So the "clans of the Canaanites" are the descendants of the two sons of Canaan, v. 15, who have grown into clans. The verb פוץ occurs also in 11:4, 8, 9 and previously in 9:19. It is a neutral idea with no judgment value attached and describes the natural process of expansion of a group that began with a family and grows from one generation to another. It envisages a peaceful, or at least predominantly peaceful, expansion which presumes a still rather sparse population in Canaan. This is probably an insight that is historically correct. In contrast to Mesopotamia, 10:8-12, and despite the predominance of different powers at different epochs, the expansion and settlement of the different groups that populated Canaan went on for the most part peacefully.

[10:19]   The process begun in v. 18b leads to the final result described in v. 19: the outline of the territory of the Canaanites. The passage is extremely difficult. J. Simons has dealt with it in detail, OTS 5 (1948) 91-117.

גבול is "the territory with legitimately established borders" (B. Jacob). The northern limit is Sidon; two southern limits are given, Gerar and Gaza; the two prepositions have the same meaning (J. Simons). Gerar is six miles SSW of Gaza, and so a direct line from Sidon to Gaza through Gerar is not possible. Gerar, the more southerly, is the real border and "as far as Gaza" is either an additional explanation using the better known place in the vicinity (so J. Simons) or a marginal gloss (H. Gunkel, O. Procksch and others).

The second detail can mean either a line from Sidon to Sodom and its environs or horizontally from Gerar (Gaza) to Sodom. J. Simons, who tries to construct the border lines from the place data, shows that the first is grammatically impossible, and so what is meant is the horizontal line from Gerar (Gaza) to Sodom and the other cities; cf. the three sketches by J. Simons, op. cit. 93. But the difficulty here is that the Negev is cut off. Moreover there is a further difficulty: (a) The assumed location of Sodom and Gomorrah (Adamah and Zeboim) is uncertain: at the northern or southern end of the Dead Sea? Details in J. Simons; (b) The location of Lasha is uncertain. It is equated traditionally with Kallirrhoë, east of the Dead Sea, the health resort of Herod the Great (see H. Donner, ZDPV 79 [1963] 59-89), so too the Jerusalem Targum, Jerome, and J. Simons with many others. H. Donner remarks: "The locale offers no support for the identification of Kallirrhoë with Lasha of Gen 10:19 which has been carried on from Rabbinic tradition."

Now these many difficulties seem to me to make Simons' bland solution impossible; he presumes a perfectly unified text. On the other hand a merely literary-critical solution (as e.g. in H. Gunkel) contributes little. I propose therefore to depart entirely from the border lines from which J. Simons starts. V. 19 does not intend anything more than to give approximate indications of the territory by naming a few places along the border which seem to be important. J gives two border points, one in the SW and one in the SE. The reason is that two traditions lay before him: "From Sidon as far as Gerar and as far as Lasha" — and: "From Sidon as far as Gaza and as far as Sodom and Gomorrah." He combined them so as to preserve both. The only addition is "Adamah and Zeboim" as a parallel to "Sodom and Gomorrah."

Literature: Gen 10:21, 24-30: G. Oppert, *Tarshish und Ophir* (1930). E. Stucken, "Polynesisches Sprachgut in Amerika und Sumer," MVÄG 31 (1926/1927). G. Horsefield, "Sela — Petra," QDAP 7 (1937) 15. O. Eissfeldt, "Ugarit und Alalach," FF 28 (1954) 80-85 = KS III (1966) 270-279. M. Tsevat, VT 4 (1954) 41. S. Rin, "The מות of Grandeur," VT 9 (1959) 324-325. R. Schubart, "Der Babylonische Turm, das Weltmodell der Antike," *Antaios* 2 (1960) 240-248. G. Vajda, "Fragments d'un Commentaire Judéo-Arabe sur le livre d'Isaïe," VT 13 (1963) 208-224. E. Birnbaum, "The Michigan Codex. An Important Hebrew Bible Manuscript Discovered in the University of Michigan Library," VT 17 (1967) 373-415. H. von Wissmann, "Zaabram," PRE XI (1968) 1291-1312. K. Koch, *Die Hebräer* (1969) 37ff. V. Christides, "L'enigme d'Ophir," RB 77 (1970) 240-247. G.R.H. Wright, "Petra. Some Unusual Views," ZDPV 88 (1972) 182-184.

[10:21, 24-30] This second addition from J is preserved only in a number of fragments. The first sentence is already damaged: the names of the sons born to Shem are missing. They have fallen out in favor of P's list of the sons of Shem in v. 22. We cannot say whether J had the same sons as P in v. 22. Only the descendants of Arpachshad are given in vv. 24-30, and these only in one direction. It is to be noted that only personal names are given in vv. 24 and 25 and not one of them can be shown to be the name of a people or a place. The place names only occur in the list of the sons of Joktan, vv. 26-30. This latter, as is the case so often in v. 10, is an originally independent element of tradition that has been appended to the name Joktan.

What then remains of J's own theme in Gen 10, the division of humankind over the inhabited earth? Vv. 24-25 do not deal with it; the verses contain only personal names. When one adverts that the sequence Arpachshad - Shela - Eber - Peleg occurs again in P 11:10-17, while there is no parallel here in J, one concludes that vv. 24-25 (J) belong in context to the genealogy 11:10-32, and so to the line that leads from Shem to Abraham, and not to the division of humanity over the earth. The remark in v. 25b confirms this: "because in his (Peleg's) days humankind divided itself." This remark is very strange and really impossible in the context which as a whole is concerned with the division of humanity over the earth. But it makes a lot of sense if vv. 24-25 are part of the context of 11:10-32.

The conclusion then is that no coherent division of Shem has been retained from J's division of humankind over the earth. Because the division of Japheth is also missing in J, the parts of J that have been retained deal only with the division of "Ham."

[10:21] J. Skinner has seen that the text of v. 21 is not intact. The subject of ילד is missing which becomes obvious when one compares it with the same sentence in 4:26 (where the גם־הוא stands before ילד). To support his argument Skinner points out that nowhere else is the subject of a pual of ילד missing. It is certain then that the passage has been disturbed here, or breaks off incomplete. Two additions have been appended: The first is, "The father of all the sons of Eber." The explanation is that through him some sort of honorific title was conferred on Shem and so אב here can only mean primal ancestor, father, and primogenitor of the tribe (so B. Jacob, U. Cassuto and others). The author of this addition is saying by means of the peculiar formulation that for him, just as for P 11:10ff., Shem was not the physical father of Eber. This signals the collapse of all hypotheses that read out of v. 21 that Shem was the direct physical father of Eber.

The second addition, independent of the first, "the elder brother of Japheth" is also directed to Shem's exaltation. The genealogy of Shem takes third place in Gen 10; this could give a negative impression. The author therefore following the sequence in 9:18, underscores the fact that Shem, not Japheth, is the eldest son of Noah. A further indication that the two sentences are additions is that stylistically they are quite outside the context.

[10:24] Arpachshad appears abruptly at the beginning of this verse. This is the main reason (e.g., in J. Skinner) why most modern interpreters (A. Dillmann, H. Gunkel, O. Procksch, J. Skinner and others) regard the whole of v. 24 as an addition by R who wants to harmonize P and J. But there are two reasons why this is extremely improbable. First, because such an assumption badly underestimates the work of R. We have remarked so far that his work is very meticulous. Where he harmonizes, he does it so adroitly that the reader for the most part does not notice it. If v. 24 is due to R, then by introducing Arpachshad so abruptly, he only creates the difficulty. One should not attribute an error like this to R. The second reason is that no harmonization is necessary if v. 21 does not say that Shem is the direct physical father of Eber.

Something must have fallen out then between vv. 21 and 24. Reasons on either side point this way: the sentence 21a is cut short and the name that begins 24 is not an insertion. It is obvious too what has fallen out—the list of the sons of Shem which is missing in J. R has arranged so that they are in v. 22 (P). One can conclude with certainty that J's list of the sons of Shem between vv. 21 and 24 has fallen out in favor of P's, v. 22. Another question is whether the order of the sons of Shem in J was exactly the same as that in P. One can conjecture that J had only Elam, Aram and Arpachshad. When the Gk has Kenan in addition in v. 24

between Arpachshad and Shelah, then that is a further sign that there were a number of different traditions for the descendants of Shem.

In any case the first sentence of v. 24 refers to the fact that sons were born to Shem, among them Arpachshad. The sequence from Shem, through Arpachshad, Shelah, Eber to Peleg is parallel to 11:10-17 P. The latter clearly means them to be personal names. This must hold likewise for the same names in 10:24-25. All attempts to imagine the names of peoples or places behind Arpachshad, Shelah, Eber, Peleg, Joktan are on the wrong track and so need not be accounted for here. The much discussed question whether עבר could mean the Habiri is also otiose (rejected too by N.A. van Uchelen, *Abraham de Hebreeër*, 1964, ch. IV). There can be no intention of presenting Eber as the eponymous hero of the Israelites because, as U. Cassuto has pointed out, the Israelites are usually called עברים either by non-Israelites or in conversation with non-Israelites (for further details, K. Koch, VT 19 [1969] 37ff.). Neither can he be the progenitor of Israel because many other people outside Israel derive from him. There are echoes of such a meaning only in the late addition 21b.

[10:25] The names of the two sons of Eber are also purely personal names. In the case of Peleg, the explanatory remark demonstrates this; Joktan too has come down as an Arabic personal name. The opinion that the two sons of Eber represent the north and south Semites (J. Skinner and others), or the attempts to explain Peleg as a place name, are without foundation.

The remark: "because in his days the earth divided itself" (the earth = those populating the earth, humankind, as 11:1) only has meaning if Peleg is a personal name. This is an elaboration typical of the J genealogy. In one sentence it ascribes an event to the generation designated by the name (Intro. §2). What is meant is something like what is described in 11:1-9, although one cannot say whether this remark in the genealogy has this or another intent. In any case the sentence is an autonomous witness to an ancient narrative about the division of humanity in the early period, independent of 11:1-9.

The name of the second son of Eber, Joktan, does not occur in 11:10-17 (P). It reflects a separate tradition (of J?). The figure is obviously introduced here merely to act as a link with the list of Arabic tribal names that follows in vv. 26-29. This can be demonstrated with certainty here because Joktan (in the form יקשן) occurs in yet another place in the Old Testament, Gen 25:2f. as a son of Abraham and Keturah and as the father of Sheba and Dedan. Here too Arabic tribes are associated with him. F. Delitzsch comments: "Joktan is also a person among the Arabs; he is the progenitor of all primal Arabic tribes." The identification of this Arabic *el-qaḥṭan* with the Hebr. יקטן is not so certain, as J. Simons insists; but the structural parallel persists.

[10:26-30] *The "Sons" of Joktan.* The introductory words are purely a formality, in contrast to v. 24. The series of the 13 names that now follow are clearly tribes, not personal names. Because of the length of the list the introductory sentence is resumed again in the conclusion: "All these are the sons of Joktan," v. 29b. The names themselves are not in any way adapted to the context (as they are e.g. in 15-18); they are simply names without endings. Nine of the 13 names cannot be identified (so J. Simons). The description of the region in v. 30 remains utterly obscure even today. Nevertheless the group as a whole can be localized with certainty. This is due, remarkably enough, mainly to one single name that has been preserved right up to the present day as the name of a region on the SW coast of Arabia, to the east of Yemen — Hadramaut or Hadramūt, which appears in our text as Hazarmaveth. The name occurs in Sabaean inscriptions, in Strabo 16:4, 2, and Pliny; O. Procksch notes that "the name has been preserved for 3000 years."

Sheba is the second name that is certain in vv. 26-30: "Of the four great Arabian states *saba', ma'in, qatabān* and *ḥadramaut,* Sheba survived all the others and in the course of time took them over" (M. Höfner, BHHW III, 163f.). The mention of Sheba in 10:28 is not a reference to the later Sabaean kingdom: "Sheba was primarily the name of a tribe" (M. Höfner). This is the meaning too in Gen 25:3 where Sheba and Dedan are sons of Joktan who himself is the son of Abraham and Keturah. In the table of the nations, 10:7, Sheba (Seba, see textual note) is one of the sons of Cush together with Dedan (as in 25:3) and Havilah (as in 10:29). All contexts point to the south of Arabia. When the name occurs in the north of Arabia (KBL, J. Simons), then this is probably to be traced back to Sheba's commercial interests; it would have had branches and colonies there (J. Simons). "Sheba" can also be used on occasions to designate the whole Arabian peninsula. Sabaean royal inscriptions have been preserved, but they say nothing as yet about a queen of Sheba, 1 Kings 10.

Ophir and Havilah form a second group. Both are mentioned elsewhere in the Old Testament and both are famous for gold. Ophir occurs often, 1 Kings 9:28; 22:49; Is 13:12; Jer 10:9 (emendation); Ps 45:10; Job 22:24; 28:16; its location is still disputed. East Africa, South Africa, India have been proposed. But what A. Dillmann said in 1882 is still repeated today (e.g., by B. Jacob, J. Skinner): somewhere in South Arabia is most probable. In any case the context of 10:26-29 points clearly in this direction.

Havilah, like Sheba, is one of the sons of Cush, 10:7; both contexts point to South Arabia. Up to the present however there is no proof that either Havilah or Ophir are the names of places or tribes there. Havilah too, like Sheba, can stand for the whole Arabian peninsula (so probably Gen 2:11). If the name is derived from חול = sand, it could easily appear in many places. "Perhaps the name is still preserved in the modern Chaulan in SW Arabia" (H. Ringgren, BHH II, 715). 715).

Sheleph and *Uzal* form a third group: their location is not known, but the names are. The tribal name *šlp* occurs in Sabaean inscriptions and in Arabian geographers (H. Gunkel, J. Skinner, KBL). According to G.R. Driver it has been discovered recently on a piece of pottery at Elat, BASOR 90 (1943) 34. It corresponds to Σαλαπῆνοι mentioned by Ptolemy.

Uzal (the Sam and Gk have a somewhat different form) occurs again in Ezek 27:19: "wrought iron came from Uzal" for barter with Tyre. According to Arabic tradition Uzal (or Azal) was the pre-Islamic name for *Ṣan'a,* the capital of the Yemen (north). S. Cohen, following E. Glaser, sees here the city of Azalla near Medina mentioned in one of Ashurbanipal's campaigns in Arabia, IDB IV, 741.

There remain the names not yet identified: Almodad, Jerah (it is possible that they could be connected with the cult of the moon-god which was widespread in South Arabia), Hadoram, Diklah (Arabic word for the date-palm, refers to a region rich in palms), Obal (missing in many Gk mss.; Abil is used of many areas in Yemen), Abimael (meaning probably: "my father, truly, is God") and Jobab.

[**10:30**]　A. Dillmann comments on v. 30: "It is not possible to explain this verse with certainty because the three names there cannot be determined." The situation has not altered in the meantime; the judgment of J. Simons is similar. Mesha was explained earlier as the territory of Mesene in the Euphrates-Tigris Delta. A. Dillmann, following Gen 25:14, altered it to Massa (North Arabia). For *Sephar,* reference is made to a place called *Isfar* in the south of the Hadramaut. But all this is mere conjecture. Nor can "the mountains of the east," whose place in the sentence is uncertain, be explained.

A survey of what has been explained and what has not been explained in vv. 26-30 shows clearly that this list of South or Southwest Arabian tribes cannot have been composed specifically for the table of the nations because the 13 names cover too samll an area. It is not related to the attempt to name in a single scheme all peoples and lands known at the time. It would have been very much in accord with the intent of Gen 10 (of J as well as of P) to enumerate the four ancient South Arabian states (see above). That the list has not been composed for the context becomes even clearer when so many names from Southwest Arabia are given, and none at all from the rest of Arabia. Dedan at least should have been mentioned; it occurs elsewhere together with names in the list (see above).

We can be certain then that an independent tradition was at hand for 10:26-30. Commerce with South Arabia is mentioned expressly in the time of Solomon. Some of the names occur elsewhere in a commercial context (Ophir, Uzal). The list therefore "is best explained from the time of Solomon when South Arabian commercial shipping played an important role" (O. Procksch; however he takes J as the author). J. Simons too accepts that the list "may be due to their commercial activity." The same original setting in life therefore suggests itself for this list as for the list of the Phoenician cities in 10:17-18: the royal commercial center in Jerusalem where, among other things, there were detailed lists of the cities and regions with which there were commercial dealings.

Purpose and Thrust

The extraordinary significance of the table of the nations has often been underscored. F. Delitzsch, for example, says: "Nowhere is there a survey of the relationship of peoples to each other comparable to the biblical table of the nations, so universal in its horizon and sweep, so utterly comprehensive in its intent." One can parallel this with many similar judgments from more recent times. Basic to the theological understanding of the table of the nations is the question whether its real thrust is in the line of salvation history or of a universal history seen in a theological context. F. Delitzsch writes: "The goal of this great genealogical map of the world is . . . to extract from the medley of peoples the line of promise with the chosen race." G. von Rad on the contrary sees it differently. "In Gen 10 the extremely complex reality in which Israel found itself is represented . . . as God's creation." He refers to Acts 17:26. The chapter traces God's command and blessing from 9:1 just as does Gen 5 from 1:28. It is the most forceful and most heavily underscored statement of the Bible about the effect of God's blessing, which extends over the whole earth and the whole of human history, whereas his saving action is of necessity bound to a people that has been chosen. Only a family tree of the nations, beginning with the one rescued from the annihilation of humanity and conceived as a unity both in time and in space, could say so forcefully that God's blessing, bestowed on his human creature means in reality the history of the whole of humanity, means humanity stretched across the face of the earth "as long as the earth lasts." If P announces the creation, preservation and blessing of humanity in Gen 1 and Gen 9, he "literalizes" it in Gen 10, tracing the lines from the sons of Noah across the whole map of the world as known at that time.

The significance of the table of the nations as a part of the primeval story consists above all in this: the creation of humans (and the blessing that goes with it) is carried on by virtue of its internal and necessary consequence. It means that all people existing in the present, all of them, belong to the human race that God created. But this internal and necessary consequence does not for the most part reach fulfillment. When a person becomes settled a much stronger countercurrent is at work which distinguishes "foreigners" from members of one's own people. This tendency is usually so strong that the distinction between "nationals" and "foreigners" is a judgment value. What is foreign is already instinctively rejected, negatively judged, at least regarded with mistrust. This can be reflected in such expressions as barbarians, savages, pagans, and so on, and can lead one to confine what is truly human to what is found among one's own people and deny it to others. The assertion that all people, even the "foreigners," are created by God becomes threadbare and loses all meaning. "As a rule one does not concern oneself much with foreigners when national or commercial interests are not at stake. Often enough one simply despises them as barbarians and never embraces them in a nobler unity" (A. Dillmann).

But the significance of the table of the nations consists precisely in that the biblical primeval story draws the consequence of humankind's God-created state: "All individuals and peoples are of the same race, the same dignity and the same character" (A. Dillmann). At the beginning of the Torah, more precisely in the transition from the primeval story with its creation and flood to the history of God's people that begins at the end of Gen 11, the line is traced programmatically from the creation of humans to the present. Humanity as it exists today is humanity as created by God. Seventy peoples are mentioned in this chapter (the number emerges with a little assistance); the number indicates at the same time the fullness and the wholeness of the peoples. One thing only is said of them — all of them with all their differences go back to one common origin.

The assertion in Gen 10 that the whole of humankind in all its members is created, preserved and blessed by God comes necessarily into conflict with the threat that some of them — Canaanites, Assyrians, Aramaeans and others — can pose to Israel in the course of her history. What is said of the Canaanites in the Book of Deuteronomy, the oracles against the nations, and much else, seems to stand in absolute opposition to the statement of the table of the nations. It would have little meaning then to underscore the universal assertion of Gen 10 because in reality it was meaningless for the historical Israel. One must first of all acknowledge this contradiction because only then can it become clear that it stems necessarily from the center of the Old Testament (election and first commandment); but clear too that what is peculiar to the Old Testament is that God's history with his people went on through the centuries so that his action on Israel's behalf was of positive significance for other peoples, for humanity, as indicated in Gen 12:3 (J), expressed in Is 45; 42:1-4; Is 19 and other places, and definitively in the New Testament where, in the speech on the Areopagus, the good news which holds for all peoples is brought into relationship with God's primeval action toward them. "And he made from one every nation of men to live on all the face of the earth, having determined allotted periods and the boundaries of their habitation," Acts 17:26.

Genesis 11:1-9

The Tower of Babel

Literature

General: J.J. Stähelin, *Kritische Untersuchungen.* . . see 10:1-32 (1843). H. Hupfeld, *Die Quellen.* . . see 6:5-8:22 (1853) 138, 223. G. Ebers, *Aegypten und die Bücher Mose's. Sachlicher Commentar zu den ägyptischen Stellen in Genesis, Exodus. Bd. I* (1868). O. Gruppe, ZAW 9 (1889) 154. H. Holzinger, *Einleitung in den Hexateuch* (1893) 141-168. H. Gunkel, *Schöpfung und Chaos,* (1895; 1921²) 147. B. Stade, "Beiträge zur Pentateuchkritik. 2.) Der Thurm zu Babel 3.) Die Eiferopferthora," ZAW 15 (1895) 157-178 = Ausgewählte Reden u. Abhandlungen (1899; 1907²) 274-280. F. Loofs, *Die Schöpfungsgeschichte, der Sündenfall und der Turmbau zu Babel: Hefte zur christlichen Welt* 39 (1899). J. Wellhausen, *Die Composition,* (1899³; 1964⁴). O. Happel, "Der Turmbau zu Babel (Gen. 11:1-9)," BZ 1 (1903) 225-231; 2 (1904) 337-350; 3 (1905) 17-31. J. Nikel, *Genesis u. Keilschriftforschung.* . . §8 (1903) 188-200. B.H. Lesêtre, "La Tour de Babel," RPA 2 (1906) 357-363. S.D. Peet, "The Tower of Babel and Confusion of Tongues," AAOJ 24 (1908). A. Schulz, *Doppelberichte im Pentateuch. Ein Beitrag zur Einleitung in das Alte Testament* (1908) 40-45. A. Allgeier, *Über Doppelberichte in der Genesis. Eine kritische Untersuchung und eine principielle Prüfung* (1911) 43-48. R. Smend, *Die Erzählung des Hexateuchs.* . . (1912). S.G. Stevens, "The Tower of Babel; History in Picture," BW 4 (1913) 185-189. V. Zapletal, "Der Turmbau von Babel Genesis 11:1-9," BZ 14 (1917) 301-304. O. Eissfeldt, *Hexateuch-Synopse.* . . , (1922; 1962²). A. van Hoonacker, "De Toren van Babel en de verwarring der Talen," VMAW VI (1923) 128-139. W. Staerk, ZAW 42 (1924) 39-41, 54-56. P. Heinisch, "Der Turmbau von Babel (Gen 11:1-9)," StC 1 (1924/1925) 139-169. K. Budde, "Einheitlichkeit und Erhaltung von Gen 11:1-9," *Festschr. K. Marti*, BZAW 41 (1925) 45-51. J. W. Rothstein, "Die ältere Schicht (J¹) in der jahwistischen Ueberlieferung der Urgeschichte," *Festschr. K. Marti*, BZAW 41 (1925) 238-252. T. Hesse, "Der Turmbau zu Babel," RKZ 83 (1933) 327-329, 337-339. A. Brock-Utne, "Genesis 11:1-9 im Lichte der Kulturgeschichte des Nahen Ostens," ARW 32 (1935) 293-310. J. de Keulenaer, "Losse beschouwingen over den toren van Babel en de Talen-verwarring volgens Gen 11:1-9," CMech 11 (1937) 468-483. O.E. Ravn, "Der Turm zu Babel. Eine exegetische Studie über Genesis 11:1-9," ZDMG 91 (1937) 352-372. J. de Keulenaer, "De historicitate Gen 11:1-9," CMech 12 (1938) 251. W.F. Albright, JBL 58 (1939) 99. P.A.H. de Boer, "Genesis 11:1-9. Een vertaling met aanteekeningen en een opmerking over de beteekenis," NThS 24 (1941) 304-309. J. Chaine, "La Tour de Babel (XI 1-9)," *Mélanges E. Podechard* (1945) 63-69. E.G. Kraeling, "The Earliest Hebrew Flood Story: Gen XI 2-9," JBL 66 (1947) 279-293. B. Piperow, "Die schimarische Zerstreuung der Völker nach der Bibel. Exegese des Berichtes vom Turmbau zu Babel Genesis 11:1-9," JThFUS 24 (1947). M Noth, *A History of Pentateuchal Traditions* (1972). A. Lefèvre, RSR 2 (1949) 408-409. J. Schoneveld, "De betekenis van de Babylonische Tempeltoren," NTT 5 (1950/1951) 321-328. G.F. Baur-A. Mauville, "The Tower of Babel, Gen 11:1-9," *Priestly Studies* 21 (1953) 84-106. N. Hötzel, "Vielheit der Völker und Sprachen Schöpfungstat oder Sündenfolge? Eine Auseinandersetzung mit Gen 11:1-9," ZMR 37 (1953) 308-316. A. Møller, *Exegetische Betrachtungen zu ausgewählten Kapiteln der Bücher Genesis und Exodus, Dansk Tunge* 1 (1953). C. Schedl, *Geschichte des AT.* . . (1956; 1965²) 169-176. B. Gemser, OTS 12 (1958) 1-21. J. de Goitia, "La torre de Babel. Valor simbolico de la narracion de Gen 11:1-9," VyV 17 (1959) 401-418. H. Junker, TThZ 70 (1961) 182ff. M. Noth, *Ursprünge.* . . , (1961) 9. O. Eissfeldt, *Stammessage und Menschheitserzählung in der Genesis. Wahrheit und Dichtung in der Ruth-Erzählung*, SAB 110, 4 (1964-1965). K. Koch, EvTh 26 (1966) 217-239. W. Brueggemann, "David and his Theologian," CBQ 30 (1968) 156-181. K. Koch, Hebräer, VT 19 (1969) 37ff. J.L. Crenshaw, "Popular Questioning of the Justice of God in Ancient Israel," ZAW 82 (1970) 384-395. K.M. Meyer-Abich, "Voraussetzungen und Implikationen der Zukunftsforschung," WPKG 59 (1970) 535-549. R. Schwarzenberger, *Reflexionen Israels über die Anfänge* (1970) 330-332. N. Lohfink, "Die Einheit von Israel und Juda," US 26 (1971) 154-164. R. Mack, "The Main Aspects of Sin in the Old Testament," GBT 4 (1971) 1-8. H.D. Preuss, *Verspottung fremder Religionen im Alten Testament*, BWANT 12 (92) (1971). H. Werner, *Uraspekte menschlichen Lebens nach Texten aus Genesis 2-11*, ExBib (1971).

Motif of "Confusion of Languages": G.L. Bauer, *Hebräische Mythologie.* . . . (1802) 218-227. F. Kaulen, *Die Sprachverwirrung zu Babel. Linguistisch-theologische Untersuchungen über Gen XI 1-9* (1861). L. Reinisch, *Der einheitliche Ursprung der Sprachen der Alten Welt* (1873). A. Hammerschmid, "Die Sprachenverwirrung zu Babel," ThPM 8 (1898) 1-15, 89-101, 228-240. C. Fabani, *L'origine e la moltiplicazione del linguaggio* (1904). M.D. Gibson, "The Confusion of Tongues," ExpT 15 (1904) 473-474. A. Trombetti, *L'unita d'origine del linguaggio* (1905). A. Ludwig, "Die Bibel und die Einheitlichkeit des Ursprungs der Sprache," WZKM 20 (1906) 234-236. G. Geiger, "Zur babylonischen Sprachverwirrung: (1. Mos. 11:1-9). Eine biblische Studie," ThPM 17 (1907) 665-672. A. Trombetti, *Come si fa la critica di un libro con nuovi contributi alla dottrina della monogenesi del linguaggio e alla glottologia generale comparata* (1907). A. Drexel, *Die Frage nach der Einheit des Menschengeschlechtes im Lichte der Sprachforschung. Mit einem kulturgeschichtlichen, einem rassentheoretischen und einem methodisch-kritischen Anhang*, Origines I, IV (1925). L. Bloomfield, *Language* (1933). A. Wadler, *Der Turm von Babel. Urgemeinschaft der Sprachen* (1935). M. Honnorat, *La tour de Babel et la langue primitive de la terre* (1936). J. Perzl, "Die inheit des Menschengeschlechts im Lichte der neueren sprachwissenschaftlichen Forschung," ZKTh 60 (1936) 120-122. L. Turrado, "La confusion de languas cuando la torre de Babel," CuBi 5 (1948) 142-148. A. Borst, *Der Turmbau von Babel. Geschichte der Meinungen über Ursprung und Vielfalt der Sprachen der Völker. 4 Bde.* (1957-1963). W. Zimmerli, see 9:1-17 (1959). G. Rinaldi, "La lingua e le lingue," BibOr 4 (1962) 85-94. S.N. Kramer, "The 'Babel of Tongues.' A Sumerian Version," JAOS 88 = AOS 53 (1968) 108-111. H. Schmökel, "Sprachverwirrung — auf sumerisch," Süddeutsche Ztg 74 (1969).

Motif of "Building a Tower": A. Jeremias, *Das Alte Testament in Lichte des alten Orients.* (1904; 1930⁴) 52-53, 277-287. M. Jastrow, "The Tower of Babel," *Independent* 58 (1907) 822-826. R. Koldewey, *Die Tempel von Babylon und Borsippa* (1911). A. Jeremias, *Handbuch der altorientalischen Geisteskultur*, "Stufentürme" (1913; 1929) 44-47. R. Koldewey, "Der babylonische Turm nach der Tontafel des Anubelschunu," MDOG 59 (1918) 1-38. A. Moberg, *Babel Torn: Een översikt: Acta Universitatis Lundensis* NS 1 (1918). T. Dombart, "Der babylonische Turm," JdI 34 (1919) 40-64; *Der Sakralturm* (1920). E.G. Kraeling, "The Tower of Babel," JAOS 40 (1920) 276-281. J.P. Peters, "The Tower of Babel at Borsippa," JAOS 41 (1921) 157-159. L. Waddell, "Historical Origin and Economic Purpose of the Tower of Babel and the Name 'Shinar' in Babylonian Inscriptions," AsR (1922). T. Dombart, "Der Stand des Babelturmproblems," Klio 21 (1927) 135-174. E. Unger, "Der Turm zu Babel," ZAW 45 (1927) 162-171. H. Gressmann, *The Tower of Babel* (Preface by J. Obermann): The H. Stich Stroock Lectures at the Jewish Institute of Religion, NY (1928). H. Gunkel, "Turmbau," RGG² V (1931) 1325-1326. A. Moberg, "Herodotos and Modern

Reconstructions of the Tower of Babel," MO 25 (1931) 140-164. H.T. Bossert, "Die Darstellung des Turmbaues zu Babel in der bildenden Kunst," MDOG 71 (1932) 15-22. G. Martiny, "Astronomisches zum babylonischen Turm," MDOG 71 (1932) 11-15; "Der Turm zu Babel," FF 10 (1934) 30-31. W. Recken, "Der Turm von Babel," *Kosmos* (1934) 100-103. M. Daisomont, *Nieuws over den toren van Babel?* (1937). G. Martiny, "Etemenanki, der Turm zu Babel," ZDMG 92 (1938) 572-578. T.A. Busink, *De toren van Babel. Zijn vorm en zijn beteekenis* (1938). F. Wetzel-F.H. Weissbach, *Das Hauptheiligtum des Marduk in Babylon*, WVDOG 59 (1938). C.L. Woolley, Ur Excavations. V: *The Ziggurat and its Surroundings* (1939). T.A. Busink, *Sumerische en Babylonische Tempelbouw* (1940). H.J. Lenzen, *Die Entwicklung der Zikurrat von ihren Anfängen bis zur Zeit der III. Dynastie von Ur* (1941). T.A. Busink, "Etemenanki, de toren van Babel," JEOL 10 (1945/1948) 526-536. L.H. Vincent, "Mesopotamian Towers in General," RB 53 (1946) 403-440. H. Heras, "El episodio de la Torre de Babel en las Tradiciones de la India," EstB 7 (1948) 293-325. C. Ziegler, "Archaische Hochtempel in Mesopotamien," FF 24 (1948) 49-54. F. Nardoni, "I construttori de Babele non furono superbi," *L'Ultima R* 3 (1948) 18-23. T.A. Busink, *De babylonische Tempeltoren (Gen 11:1-9)* (1949). A. Romeo, "Torre de Babele," EC 2 (1949) 619-621. A. Parrot, "Ziggurats et Tour de Babel," RB 57 (1950) 449-454; "La Tour de Babel et les Ziggurats," NC 1, 2 (1950) 153-161. J. Prado, "La ciudad y Torre de Babel," EstB 9 (1950) 273-294. H. Quiring, "Sintflut, Stufenturn und erstes Gotteshaus," Saec. 1 (1950) 397-404. J. Heuschen, "De torenbouw van Babel," REcL 39 (1952) 288-294. H. Minkowski, "The Tower of Babel: Fact and Fancy," *The Geographical Magazine* 28 (1955) 390-400. B. van Iersel, "Der Turmbau zu Babel," HLa 9 (1956) 57-61. H. Quiring, "Die 'heilige' Siebenzahl und die Entdeckung des Merkur," Altertum 4 (1958) 208-214. R. Schubart, *Antaios* 2 (1960) 240-248. B.V. Blei, *Der Turm zu Babel*, Diss. Wien (1964). H. Haag, "Turm zu Babel," Bibel-Lexikon (1968²) 1786-1788. W. von Soden, "Etemenanki vor Asarhaddon nach der Erzählung vom Turmbau zu Babel und dem Erra-Mythos," UF 3 (1971) 253-264.

Text

11:1 And (it happened)[a] the whole world had one language[b] and one vocabulary[c].

2 And as they journeyed from the east[a], they found a plain in the land of Shinar and settled there.

3 And they said to each other: Come, let us make bricks and bake them thoroughly![ab] And they used brick for stone and bitumen[c] for mortar.

4 And they said: Come, let us build a city and a tower[a], with its summit touching the heavens[bc]. So we will make a name for ourselves, lest we be scattered over the face of the earth[d].

5 Then Yahweh came down to look at[a] the city and the tower that the sons of man had built.

6 And Yahweh said: See[a]: they are one people and they have all one lanuage, and this is only the beginning[b] of what they will do[c]. Henceforth[d] nothing will be impossible for them in what they propose[e] to do.

7 Come, we will go down and confuse[a] their language there, so that[b] no one understands[c] the language of his neighbor!

8 And Yahweh scattered them from there over the face of the whole earth, and they left off[a] building the city[b].

9 For this reason one called[a] its name Babel[b], because there Yahweh confused the language of the whole world, and from there Yahweh scattered them over the whole earth.

1a Ges-K speaks of the daring sentence construction. However it cannot be explained in purely grammatical terms. The ויהי at the beginning of v. 1 is really the anticipated ויהי

that begins v. 2; the latter is the real beginning of the narrative, while v. 1 is a prelude to it describing the situation. On the construction see too E. König, Syntax §362f. **b** On χεῖλος for שׂפה in Gk, see H.S. Gehman VT 1 (1951) 89: "a non-Greek usage taken over from Hebrew." **c** BrSynt §83a: "The cardinal numbers 1 and 2 agree like adjectives with the noun." So too E.A. Speiser ad loc. Gk καὶ φωνὴ μία πᾶσιν anticipates a לכלם at the end of the verse (cf. BH, Appar.). It is quite possible that the Gk preserves the original text here; the effect would be a smoother rhythmic parallelism.

2a מקדם BrSynt §20b, noun without determining article, particularly frequent in the context of the directions of the heavens. Many recent exegetes (e.g., B. Jacob) translate by "eastwards"; against this is that all ancient versions understand מן as "from" (so too BrSynt).

3ab The *figura etymologica*, Ges-K §117r, by anaology with Akkadian; see Comm. On the cohortative with הבה BrSynt §6a. **c** It is important from the standpoint of the narrator that the Hebrew word for bitumen is used here, and not the Akkadian loan word כפר *(kūprū)* as in 6:14.

4a "city and tower" can be a sort of hendiadys according to E.A. Speiser (see Comm.), and so can mean a city crowned with a tower or a city with a tower. **bc** On the sentence construction, BrSynt §25d. F. Delitzsch: "The ב indicates contact as נגע ב." **d** On the sentence construction Ges-K §107a, 152w.

5a "The original meaning of the ל is most plainly seen in those infinitives with ל which expressly state a purpose (hence as the equivalent of a final clause, e.g., Gen 11:5," Ges-K §114g.

6a On the use of הן BrSynt §4. **b** החלם inf. hiph. of חלל, Ges-K §67w. cf. P.P. Saydon, "The inceptive Imperfect in Hebrew and the Verb hēḥēl 'to begin'," Bib 35 (1954) 43-50. **c** On the construction לעשׂת, I. Soisalon-Soininen, "Der Infinitivus Constructus mit ל im Hebräischen," VT 22 (1972) 82-90. **d** On the use of ועתה H.A.Brongers, "Bemerkungen zum Gebrauch des adverbialen We'attāh im AT," VT 15 (1965) 289-299. **e** On the form without reduplication Ges-K §67dd.

7a The same as on bc. **b** אשׁר in the sense of "so that" Ges-K §107q and 165b; cf. Gen 24:3. **c** שׁמע in the sense of "understand" as Gen 42:23.

8a On חדל D.W. Thomas, "Some Observations on the Root חדל," VT.S 4 (1957) 8-16. **b** Sam and Gk add "and the tower" so as to harmonize.

9a the 3rd pers. sing. masc. can express the indefinite subject, Ges-K §144d, BrSynt §36d; E. König, *Syntax* §324e. **b** Gk has Συγχυσις for בבל. F.M.Th. Böhl, "Die Etymologie von 'Babel', Genesis 11:9," ZAW 36 (1916) 110-113.

Literary Form

The correspondence between the beginning and the end of 11:1-9 is most striking: the whole world had one language, v. 1 — Yahweh confused the language of the whole world, v. 9. The consequence of the event narrated between the beginning and the end is the confusion of the languages. The event is constructed in two parts which are obviously meant to be parallel. In the first part, vv. 2-4, people act and speak, in the second, vv. 5-8, God acts and speaks. The construction corresponds exactly to the framework in vv. 1 and 9: the earlier situation, v. 1, is transferred into the present situation, v. 9, by an action of the people and the intervention of God. It is not that there is an interchange or dialogue between God and the people. The parts stand juxtaposed in two blocks: the decision of the people, vv. 3-4, and its execution (which is not narrated, but presumed in v. 5) and the decision of God, vv. 5-7, and its execution, v. 8. The construction shows that the narrator is not interested in the event as such, but in how the present situation resulted from the earlier. The narrative in the form in which it lies before us is etiological: behind it lies the query about a present situation which is explained by something that happened in the past.

A series of narratives in Gen 1-11 is concerned with the question of how the present situation came about from the earlier. All of them find that the present situation is worse; it is the result of something that has happened in primeval time. In all of them the earlier situation which humanity experienced is not accessible; one concludes to it as something that is the opposite of the present. The event that gave rise to the present is usually presented in the pattern of crime and punishment. All these etiological narratives and motifs are to be carefully distinguished from those in a historical context, as, for example, in Josh 1-9. Gen 1-11 always aims at explaining something that is a part of human existence, something that is always related to human existence as created existence, something incomprehensible in the created state, e.g., the pains suffered by a woman at childbirth. The present situation which is to be explained reaches as far back as the human memory can go and beyond. It is in this beyond, beyond all human experience, that there lies the event that is to explain the present situation; it is a primeval event.

What is peculiar to Gen 1-11 is that the primeval event makes contact with history by means of the name Babel in the land of Shinar. The conclusion to be expected from the structure as presented so far would be a sentence corresponding exactly to 11:1: "But since then the languages of the whole world are confused." Instead, the name of the historical city of Babylon is explained as a witness that God confused languages. The explanation is an addition; the narrative would be complete without it. It is more in accord with the historical etiologies in which the name of a place is often explained by a historical event. Such an element shows that there are different stages in the growth of 11:1-9. It is precisely this, that Gen 11:1-9 hovers between primeval and historical event, that gives the narrative its own peculiar character.

Moreover, the motif of the confusion of languages in the narrative is amalgamated with other motifs. This is clearest in the sequence of v. 7 and v. 8: God decides to confuse the languages of humankind, v. 7. But the execution of the decision consists in something else: the dispersion of humankind over the whole earth. As the narrative moves, this can only mean that the dispersion implies the division of language; but the peculiar discontinuity between vv. 7 and 8, as well as v. 9, shows that the two motifs were originally independent of each other.

While the motif of the confusion of languages belongs only to 11:1-9, that of the dispersion of humankind is already part of the conclusion of the flood narrative. In J, 9:18f., the conclusion of the flood narrative leads directly to the distribution of the descendants of the sons of Noah over the earth. In P the sentence is, in tradition history, the link between 6-9 (J) and 23 (P). As far as concerns 11:1-9 then, the motif of the dispersion links the narrative of the building of the tower with the flood narrative, even though at times it is used differently, while the motif of the confusion of languages belongs only to 11:1-9. On the other hand, non-Israelite parallels show that the motif of the confusion of languages can likewise be linked with the flood narrative (see below).

The motif of the confusion of languages is more determinative for the shaping of the narrative than that of the dispersion. It forms the exposition, v. 1, the etiological conclusion, v. 9a, and determines the reflection and the decision of God in the middle, vv. 6-7. The motif of the dispersion is only integrated into the narrative in v. 8a. God intervenes so as to disperse humankind.

It must be recognized further that the motif (of the dispersion) was assumed into the narrative of the building of the tower. The same motif at the end of the flood narrative has not God, but humans as subject and is neutral in stance (so in 9:19, the same verb here, and 10:25), while in the narrative of the building of the tower it is a punishment or a defensive action of God. It is only now that the motif appended in v. 4 can be understood: "lest we be scattered over the face of the earth." It is only when understood as a punishment that it could be the reason for the building of the tower. Both in 4a and in 9b the motif is, from the point of view of tradition history, secondary; the motif of the confusion of languages alone explains the name Babel, not that of the dispersion. It has no real function in the narrative in vv. 4b and 9b. If the verses were missing the movement of the narrative would not suffer.

There is now the further question of the relationship of these two motifs, confusion of languages and dispersion, to that of the building of a city and (or) a tower. Vv. 2-4 and 5 deal exclusively with the building, apart from the motive appended in v. 4b. That is to say that the first of the two parts is dominated entirely by the motif of the building of the city and (or) tower. This is all the more striking when the motif recedes well into the background in the second part, vv. 5-8. V. 5 follows immediately on vv. 2-4 and is part of the same motif. But God's reflection in v. 6, his decision in v. 7, and its execution in v. 8 contain practically nothing more from the narrative of the building of the tower. The second part of the reflection in v. 6 can relate to it, but it is not mentioned. It is very striking that God's decision and its execution has no relation at all to the tower; only v. 8b "and they left off building the city" comes back to it. And the etiological conclusion explains the name Babel from the other two motifs.

The Question of the Unity

So far it has been a question only of the fact that the narrative has been constructed out of three definite motifs. How is this to be explained? The explanation that has predominated is the literary-critical: its starting point is doublets, especially the twice narrated descent of God in vv. 5 and 7, and its conclusion is that the narrative is the result of two versions that have been worked together.

An account of the history of research on this question is given in C. Westermann, *Genesis 1-11: Erträge der Forschung* 7 (1972) 99-101. G.L. Bauer had already distinguished "a double myth . . . one of the building of the tower . . . the other of the origin of language," *Hebräische Mythologie.* . . . (1802) 2-6; but he did not question the unity of 11:1-9. B. Stade, W. Staerk and H. Gunkel did not regard it as a unity; many more recent exegetes have followed them (J. Skinner, O. Procksch, W. Zimmerli, G. von Rad, G. Wallis and others, further names in Gunkel, p. 94), for the most part with restrictions. H. Gunkel was the first to try to separate the two recensions; subsequent scholarship has concerned itself mainly with his solution. W. Staerk and O. Happel concede that two narratives formed the basis of Gen 11:1-9, but maintain that it is impossible to give a critical separation into sources. K. Budde supported the unity of the narrative with the argument that dispersion and confusion of languages require each other as means and end. P. Heinisch, U. Cassuto and E.A. Speiser argue that city and tower are inseparably linked in the Babylonian building plan — they are a sort of hendiadys. J. Pedersen, U. Cassuto and others argue that a division into two sources would destroy the obvious structure of the narrative.

H. Gunkel distinguishes a city recension, vv. 1, 3a, 4 (part), 5 ("the city"), 6a, 7, 8b, 9a from a tower recension, vv. 2, 3b, 4 (part), 5, 6b, 8a, 9b. He establishes a series of doublets and then starts with the doublet city-tower, which he maintains however is not entirely certain. This forces him to dismember the sentences in vv. 4 and 5 where "city" and "tower" occur together, and to assign the city in the one and the tower in the other each to its respective recension. This almost desperate excision of individual words shows the weakness of the literary-critical analysis. It is to be noted that Gunkel's argument proceeds on purely literary-critical grounds and presumes from the very start two written recensions. There is no form-critical consideration which would have to begin with the narrative as a whole and with the individual components of this whole.

The structural parallel in the two parts, vv. 2-4 and 5-8, favors the unity of the narrative (especially U. Cassuto, who adds a number of other indications of unity). One must certainly agree with H. Gunkel and others that 11:1-9 was not shaped in a single mold and that it shows clear signs of gradual growth. However, the obvious unity of the narrative in its present form permits the conclusion that the three motifs came together and developed in the pre-literary stage.

We must now ask if we can find out anything about the pre-history of the tower narrative or more precisely of the three motifs brought together in it.

Literature: The History of Religions Gen 11:1-9: (See in general the introductory bibliography to the flood, 6:5-8:22): H. Lüken, *Die Traditionen des Menschengeschlechts* (1856; 1869[2]) 307-335. G.A. Smith, *The Chaldean Account of Genesis* (1876) 120-131. O. Gruppe, *Die griechischen Culte und Mythen in ihren Beziehungen zu den orientalischen Religionen*, I (1887) 677-679. H. Winckler-H. Zimmern, *Die Keilinschriften und das Alte Testament* (1903[3]) (=KAT) 616f. A. Gustavs, "Religionsgeschichtliches aus 'Koldewey, Die Tempel von Babylon und Borsippa'," ZAW 32 (1912) 65-68. J.G. Frazer, *Folk-Lore. . . ,* (1923) 143-152. A. Jirku, *Altorientalischer Kommentar zum Alten Testament* (1923) 52-53. S. Thompson, *Motif-Index. . . ,* VI (1932; 1958[2]) 805. H. Baumann, *Schöpfung und Urzeit. . . .* (1936, 1964) 256-260. E. Dhorme, *Les religions de Babylonie et d'Assyrie* (1949) 178-182. A. Parrot, *The Tower of Babel* (1955); — "Mari et l'Ancien Testament," RHPhR 35 (1955) 117-120. E.A. Speiser, "The Cuneiform Background of the Tower of Babel Story," Or 25 (1955); "Word Plays on the Creation Epic's Version of the Founding of Babylon," Or 25 (1955/1956) 317-323. R. Borger, "Die Inschriften Asarhaddons, Königs von Assyrien, §2," AfO.B 9 (1956) 27-41. S.N. Kramer, *Sumerian Literature and the Bible* (1959). St Strelcyn, "Une tradition éthiopienne d'origine juive yéménite concernant l'écriture," RoczOr 23 (1959) 67-72. J.A. Soggin, SMSR 33 (1962) 227-256. J. Politella, "Before Babel. The Puzzle of Ancient Cosmogonies," *Encounter* 29 (1968) 278-289. L Cagni, "L'epopea di Erra," SS 34 (1969). A. Frenz, "Der Turmbau," VT 19 (1969) 183-195. W.G. Lambert, "Destiny and Divine Intervention in Babylon and Israel," OTS 17 (1972) 65-72. L. de Heusch, *Le roi ivre ou l'origine de l'État* (1972).

1. The motif of the dispersion of humankind over the face of the earth occurs not only in the Old Testament, but also in many other places at the conclusion of the flood story. It is frequently linked with the confusion of languages, as shown in the collection of H. Lüken. The Indian story talks of the three sons of the one saved from the flood from whom humanity is dispersed over the earth, p. 315. "The Basques too still possess an old story that language was confused after the flood," p. 317. In the Irish story, "the tower of Conan," the story of the building of the tower is linked with a flood, p. 317; likewise with the

Mexicans, p. 319, and so on. The motifs are found together only rarely in the collection of J.G. Frazer. The two or three motifs are linked in examples cited by J. Riem, *Die Sintflut und Wissenschaft* (1906, 1925[2]), nos. 29, 43, 158, 181, 193, 272: and R. Andree, *Die Flutsagen ethnographisch betractet* (1891) nos. 66, 68. Riem gives an example from the Indians of Columbia, No. 159: "Some people did not perish at this time, they were dispersed round about. Their languages were then confused, because before the flood they all had only one language. After the flood their languages were different." M. Winternitz comments in his collection, MAGW 31 (1901) 305-333: "The flood is the primeval cause of the dispersion of humans over the earth in the stories of the . . . Lithuanians (No. 24), Melanesians (No. 32); see also Nos. 16; 49; 51; 59; 60; 61." The survey shows that the dispersion of humankind over the earth often forms a concluding motif of the flood narrative, as in the Old Testament. It shows at the same time that the dispersion and the confusion of language are closely connected and attract each other, though each can occur independently as well. For the most part the two motifs are not in the context of the building of a tower.

2. The tower stories from Africa (J.G. Frazer 143f., H. Baumann 256f.) show a type that does not end with a dispersion or a confusion of languages. The conclusion is the destruction of the building by the divinity with the frequent addition that the people who tried to climb to heaven perish. This is a standard conclusion in the stories that H. Baumann has collected. There is scarcely an exception: ". . . but the props collapsed and the people died" (256); ". . . the tower burst in two in the middle and buried the workers under its ruins" (258). One case, where the confusion of languages is added, is regarded as due to Christian influence. See too L. de Heusch op. cit.: ". . . a myth . . . where people build an enormous tower to touch heaven and to conquer immortality."

This corresponds to the parallels that A. Frenz quotes from the Veda, handed down in four (five) variants. In each of the variants the god Indra causes the brick-built tower to collapse by pulling out his brick. The consequence is the overthrow of the builders. On one occasion they are killed; in other cases they are changed into spiders. This is an etiological extension. The dispersion and the confusion of languages is completely absent as in the African stories. There is a type like this in the Jewish-Greek tradition, as F. Delitzsch has indicated, *Comm.* p. 264f.: "Men, proud and alienated from God, built a tower so as to reach to heaven; then the gods (God) sent storms that demolished the tower and divided the language of men that had hitherto been one." The confusion of languages is linked here with the building of the tower. The goal of the event is the destruction of the tower.

Many peoples then had a story of the building of a tower that ended with its destruction and was often linked with the annihilation of those who had undertaken to build it. The data provides further information; it demonstrates the independence of the tower narrative on the one hand and on the other the independence of the dispersion and confusion of languages (often linked with the flood narrative). Moreover, the tower narrative while still independent was not etiological. The goal of this older type of narrative was the failure of the attempt to reach heaven by means of a tower. We have here a primeval event that establishes the present state of reality: the definitive separation of the realm of God, the heavens, from that of people.

A further result of the survey is that the two motives in 11:4b: "so we will make a name for ourselves" and "lest we be scattered. . . ," belong to a later stage in the development of the narrative. The original motive is indicated in the sentence "with its summit touching the heavens." In all the tower stories mentioned so far the building is a means to reach the heavens. For example, the second of the versions from the Veda cited by A Frenz reads: "Then the demons . . . laid bricks in layers. 'We will climb up to the heavens' (they said)," p. 184. It is this that arouses the anger of the divinity in all the stories and evokes the counter-measures. A. Frenz says correctly that the stories in the Veda represent a type that is older than the present biblical narrative.

3. All the modern commentaries state that so far no parallel to the biblical narrative is known among Israel's immediate neighbors. There has been no change in the situation insofar as the story as a whole is concerned. However, there is now a Sumerian parallel for one of the motifs — confusion of languages. The text is from the epic of Enmerkar ca. 2000 and has been translated by S.N. Kramer, "Man's Golden Age: A Sumerian Parallel to Genesis 11:1," JAOS 63 (1943) 191-193. It can be complemented by a new discovery "The 'Babel of Tongues': A Sumerian Version," JAOS 88 = AOS 53 (1968) 108-111. The text begins with a description of the "Golden Age" and says in 11. 136-140 that there was nothing at all to threaten the people: ". . . there was no fear, no terror. . . ."; then positively: "In those days . . . the land Martu, resting in security, the whole universe, the people in unison (?), to Enlil in one tongue. . . ." Kramer conjectured a verb "gave praise" in the first translation in 1943. In the new text it is "spoke," and now the continuation is intelligible, 11. 147-155: "Enki, the Lord of wisdom. . . . Changed the speech in their mouths, (brought?) contention into it. Into the speech of man that (until then) had been one" p. 111.

The completed text is no longer merely a parallel to v. 1, but to the motif as a whole, unity of language 11:1, and confusion of language 11:9. In the Sumerian text, the confusion of language was the result of rivalry between the gods Enki and Enlil. In Gen 11:1-9 some sort of rivalry between God and the people has taken its place. The parallel has added significance inasmuch as it comes from an area into which the biblical narrative has transposed the event of the tower. Tradition history shows that the motif of the confusion of language is not necessarily part of the story of the tower, but could belong to a completely different type of narrative, a myth about the gods.

A further parallel to the decision to build a tower, coming from the same area, will be considered in the exegesis of v. 3.

The parallels as a whole show that a series of elements of different origin have been brought together in the composition of Gen 11:1-9. The motif of the dispersion of people over the face of the earth is a concluding motif in Gen 6-9 as well as in extra-biblical narratives. The motif of the confusion of languages occurs in a Sumerian myth about the gods without any connection with the building of a tower. The pre-history of the tower story shows that its goal is neither the dispersion of humanity nor the confusion of language. These two motifs already occur together in conclusions of the flood narrative. One must attend to this background when inquiring into the development and meaning of the biblical story of the tower.

The Structure of the Narrative in J

The parallels from the history of religions show an amazing variety in the history of the motifs. One can now ask by way of conclusion how J put together his narrative from the materials at hand to him. It has become clear by now that the attempt to divide the narrative and its growth into two literary versions cannot be correct. The main reason is that such a division into two strands does not take into account that the point of departure of any explanation must be the three motifs that shape the narrative; in other words, that the building of the tower must be regarded as an independent motive without the other two.

This having been said, it is clear, in broad lines, what J has done. The building of the tower dominates vv. 2-5. It then recedes into the background. God reflects and his plan of counter-action is concerned mainly with confusing the languages, the motif that provides the etiological framework for the narrative in vv. 1 and 8. J has linked this with the motif of the dispersion in such a way that in v. 8 the latter takes the place of God's intervention against the tower to which one can still conclude from the older form of the narrative. J has fixed the motif of the dispersion firmly in the body of the narrative by appending it in v. 4b as an additional motive. This recalls what he has already done in Gen 2-3 where he likewise assumed another motif into the conclusion of the narrative (3:23, the tree of life) and anchored it in the Introduction, 2:9.

This explains the repetition of God's coming down in vv. 5 and 7 which was one of the main arguments for the separation into literary sources: "according to one version Yahweh came down from heaven to find out what people were doing, according to the other, to frustrate their works" (H. Gunkel). Starting from the text it would be more accurate to say: according to the other, to confuse the language of humankind. It is clear then that God's descent in vv. 5 and 7 belongs to the building of the tower (see above: 5 goes with 2-4) and its purpose is a direct intervention; in 7 it belongs to the confusion of language. Another layer of tradition is introduced in v. 6. It makes sense therefore to describe this *other* intervention of God in the same phrases — coming and acting. The repetition then is to be traced back to two layers of tradition that come together in the narrative. J assumed both deliberately into his narrative because each had originally a different meaning and context, and J tends to preserve a number of forms of tradition side-by-side. He achieves this stylistically when he sets into relief God's reflection in v. 6, which for him forms the high point of the narrative, by framing it with similar wording in vv. 5 and 7.

Setting in Life

1. It seems that the question of the setting in life in which the narrative arose can be answered easily because the scene is clearly localized. The event takes place "in the land of Shinar," v. 2, and the conclusion says explicitly that the city concerned was Babylon, v. 9. Most scholars therefore have no doubt that the narrative originated in Babylon (e.g., F.M.Th. Böhl, ZAW 36 [1916] 110-113; E.G. Kraeling, JAOS 40 [1920] 279; H. Gressmann, *The Tower of Babel* [1928] 4; W.F. Albright, JBL 58 [1939] 99, who wants to fix the period in Babylonian history when it arose; A. Parrot, *The Tower of Babel* [1955] 64, "The Babylonian origin is beyond doubt"). How then did the story, in modified form, travel from Babylon to Palestine? "Perhaps an ancient forerunner of Herodotus who visited Babylonia as tradesman . . . brought the story back to Palestine. . . ." E.G.

Kraeling, 281. Other scholars on the contrary have no less doubt that the narrative cannot have originated in Babylon (among others B. Jacob, G. von Rad, U. Cassuto, A. Brock-Utne). Their main argument is that the narrative reveals a polemic against Babylon: God's punitive intervention against the building of the city and the naming, which has a negative accent. U. Cassuto goes furthest when he sees in the story something of a parody, a satire against Babylon. Both extremes — a Babylonian story or an anti-Babylonian story — fall into the same methodological error: they make Babylon the theme or center of the narrative, which it is not.

2. One must likewise reject on methodological grounds another very common approach to Gen 11:1-9 which takes the building as its starting point and is dominated by the question, "Which building was the Tower of Babel?" The question has been discussed in a series of studies. Was it the ziggurat Etemenanki in the temple area, Esagila, in Babylon, or was it the ziggurat Ezida in Borsippa (Birs Nimrud)? Before the excavation one used to refer to Herodotus's description in the context of his presentation of the Zeus-Belos (= Marduk) temple in Babylon, cited by A. Moberg, MO 25 (1931) 140f. For a long time after the excavations, the Tower of Babel was almost universally equated with the Etemenanki (so R. Koldewey and many others). A lively controversy errupted over its reconstruction; cf. A. Moberb; T. Dombart, *Klio* 21 (1927). Other scholars maintained for a variety of reasons that Borsippa was more probable (G. Smith, E.G. Kraeling, J.P. Peters).

But all these scholars who were asking, which is the real Tower of Babel, presumed that the narrative in Gen 11:1-9 was inspired by this building, i.e., by its ruins. The ruins then raised the question, "How did it happen that this mighty tower fell into ruins?" Gen 11:1-9 then would be the etiology of the ruins of the ziggurat in Babylon. But the story cannot be explained in this way. This is not the end of the narrative and 11:8b says that they left off building the city; nothing is said of the tower.

One cannot simply ask then, "Which was the tower of the story in Gen 11:1-9?," without being clear beforehand about what sort of story it is. Does it intend to say something about a definite tower in the city of Babylon (or near by) or not? When one asks, "What does the story say about Babylon?," then it is very little (so too O.E. Ravn at the end of his article ZDMG 91 [1937] 352-372); it knows of the city of Babel in the plain in the land of Shinar. But what it says about the tower does not apply to the ziggurat in Babylon, which in fact did serve to link heaven and earth. The height of the ziggurat was to be understood positively and Gen 11:1-9 shows no awareness of this, nor of the fact that it is a sacred edifice against which the god honored in it would scarcely intervene. This is described in detail by A. Parrot (see Bibl. above). The narrator was probably thinking of a fortress tower when he used מגדל (so O.E. Ravn, p. 359), as in Judg 8:9 and 9:46f.

3. The conclusion is that the story neither had its origin in Babylon nor intended to say anything about a particular tower which might be discovered again some time as one of the ziggurats in or near the city of Babylon. The motif of the building of the tower is independent and stands on its own feet without being tied to any place. The story, which was alive in the oral tradition in Israel, was localized in Babylon in the land of Shinar. Such a localization in one of the

great empires was necessary because the gigantic buildings there were well known (A. Parrot: "33 sacred towers in 27 different cities"). Israel knew of the huge towers in Mesopotamia, especially in the ancient city of Babylon. The material used in construction was also known, 11:3, but the function of these enormous ziggurats was not.

The subject of this narrative is "the sons of man," i.e., humankind. It is a story of primeval event and, as with other such stories in Gen 1-11, it has no fixed place of origin. One can only say that the basic motif is world wide, but that there are no parallels among Israel's immediate neighbors (as with 4:2-16 and 6:1-4). In any case the narrative took shape in Israel and shows that it must have gone through a very long process of tradition history until it acquired its present form. When O. Eissfeldt ascribes 11:1-9 to his L source and gives as the reason: "The narrative of the building of the tower also appears very archaic by its strongly anthropomorphic conception of God," (*Introduction*, p. 196), then this holds for the older form to which one can conclude that it does not hold for the form that has come down to us, which reveals so many clear signs of a gradual development and of reflective formation.

For the literary-critical problem of the position of 11:1-9 within the J tradition, and for its relationship to Gen 10 and Gen 6-9, see the survey of scholarship in C. Westermann, *Erträge*. . . . 7 (1972), which also covers the history of research *in toto*. O. Happel surveys the earlier research, see Bibliog. to 11:1-9, 1903-1905.

Literature: Gen 11:1-3: A.B. Ehrlich, *Randglossen*. . . . (1908). S.N. Kramer, "Man's Golden Age: A Sumerian Parallel to Genesis XI:1," JAOS 63 (1943) 191-194. H.S. Gehman, VT 1 (1951) 89. P. Humbert, *Hommage à W. Vischer* (1960) 68. H.G. Link, TBLNT II 2 (1971) 1119ff.

Commentary

[11:1] The narrator uses a nominal sentence to describe the situation from which the story begins, and which is to be changed into its opposite in the course of the narrative. The ויהי is not really in place here; it does not introduce any event. A comparison with v. 2, where it also occurs at the beginning, shows this. The ויהי is more like our "once upon a time" which introduces the situation at the beginning of the tale. It is just the same in the parallels from the Veda that A. Frenz quotes: "The imperfect of the first sentence KS TB āsan corresponds to our 'once upon a time' which introduces a tale" (op. cit., p. 186). If one wishes to be more precise, then one must say: "There was once a time when. . ."; but that would be too precise. The vague ויהי is to be understood as a formula; it cannot be translated adequately. The description "the whole world had one language. . ." is to be understood from the context of the whole; i.e., it would be misconstrued as an independent self-contained statement. Its function is to explain that the present situation, in which languages are confused or multiple, was not the original. There is experience only of the present situation; there has never been experience of 11:1, i.e., never as far back as the human memory reaches. It is a hypothesis to which one concludes from the unnatural present situation.

It was the common experience of humanity in an early stage that the multiplicity of languages was not natural. This is expressed in the many stories of the confusion of languages spread throughout the world. Their starting point is

that at one time all peoples spoke the same language, as in the Sumerian parallel
that is quoted. It is to be noted that such an experience could only occur in a
small, limited territory, and that "the whole world" could only be the world
known at that time. There must have been circumstances within a confined
language area that were the basis of such experience. We cannot reconstruct
them. One could imagine a small group which for generations, as far back as
memory could go, did not come into contact with people who spoke a different
language. Then revolutionary upheavals brought them face to face with people
who spoke a strange language and they had to deal with them. They now became
aware of how unnatural was a plurality of languages. It was embarrassment at the
fact of the "confusion of languages" that raised the question: Was there a time
when this was not the case, when everyone spoke the same language? It was not a
theoretical question, but the result of social upheaval. It was only the transition
from the small, self-sufficient group to the larger social unities that demanded
constant commerce with those who spoke other languages that gave rise to this
question.

This means the collapse of all those explanations of and reflections on
11:9 that do not take into account this social factor and that raise abstract,
theoretical questions about the "original language" of humankind. F. Delitzsch
discussed the matter in detail. At an earlier stage he thought that Gen 11:1
provided the basis for the derivation of an original language of humankind, and
that the techniques of comparative philology could still demonstrate traces of it in
present-day languages; he later abandoned this. The expression "one language
(lip) and one vocabulary" describes poetically the unity of language by means of
the organ of speech, שׂפה, and the words that proceed from it, דברים. The
repetition serves to emphasize.

Literature: Gen 11:2: S. Landersdorfer. "Das Land Šinʿar," BZ (1913) 350-
363. P. Humbert, "Mythe de création. . . ," RHPhR 16 (1936) 452. E.G. Kraeling
"Miqqedem in Genesis 11:2," JQR 38 (1947/1948) 161-165. J. Simons, *The Geographical and Topographical Texts. . .* , (1959) §236. L. Krinetzki, "'Tal' und 'Ebene'
im Alten Testament," BZ NF 5 (1961) 204-220. Th. Jacobsen, "Shinar," IDB 4 (1962)
332.

[11:2] It is only in v. 2 that the exposé is given; the action begins in v. 3. V. 2
ends with a situation — "and they settled there"; the action now begins. It is to
be noted that the exposé does not really fit the context of talk about primeval
event, because the detachment of a group and its settlement in a place with a
definite name is not "pre-history." 11:2 obviously contains the residue of an
itinerary. 11:1-9 is clearly part of the transition from primeval event to history.
This holds as well for the narrative 11:1-9 as it does for the enumerations in Gen
10. And there is a more obvious point of contact between 10 and 11:1-9, namely
the movements of groups and peoples in 10:11 and 18; and besides, the division
of humankind in 10:25 appears as the explanation of a name in a genealogy.

In Gen 1-9 "man" incorporates humankind before there was any differentiation. The division of humanity begins with the end of the flood and all the
texts that follow immediately are concerned with it either directly or indirectly.
The motif that is the basis of Gen 10 (J and P), namely 9:19, arises directly out of
the flood narrative. 11:1-9 on the contrary is an independent tradition: the division
of humankind is seen from a particular point of view — that of dispersion and
confusion as making life more difficult or as punishment.

The exposé, v. 2, describes the way of life of a group in process of migration; more exactly, a transition from nomadic to sedentary life. It certainly leaves much in the air. The subject of the three verbs remains undefined; it is not mentioned. One cannot without more ado say that the subject of v. 1, כל־הארץ, is also the subject of v. 2. V. 1 is prefaced to the whole by way of explanation, but is not a constitutive part of the event narrated. It is not said who they are who came out of the east; this was left in the air deliberately. Likewise, the very general indication of place "from the east" was not made more precise, again consciously (the use of קדם in 2:8 and 4:16 is similar). The transition from these undefined items to "in the land of Shinar," the first concrete detail, is characteristic of the narrative. The itinerary moves from the distant darkness of primeval time into the clear light where history begins. Many interpreters translate מקדם by "eastwards" (e.g., E.G. Kraeling, B. Jacob); this is possible; but the verb suggests the usual sense in which מן is used: "a meaning which is guaranteed by its origin in Egyptian in the form ḳdm with the same sense," P. Humbert, "Mythe de création. . . ." p. 452.

The itinerary consists of three stages: departure — discovery — settlement. The form of speech of the itinerary, a basic form for descriptions of groups on the move, will be studied in another context (12:4-9). The first and third stages, departure and settlement, occur most frequently in the itineraries and the same verbs as here are used. On the other hand, the middle stage occurs rarely, "they found." It presumes that the group on the move is looking for something. It is difficult to explain the meaning of ימצאו. It is a special designation for the manner of life of the group on the move, on the way to some goal that it does not yet know. The group, on the move and looking for something, undergoes its most important experiences between the poles of seeking and finding; here it has the particular experience of the action of the divinity which promises a goal, shows the way, leads to it.

The migrant group finds a בקעה, a plain in a valley, a "broad sunken valley with flat sides" (KBL). Herodotus says of Babylon, I, 178, 193: ϰέεται ἐν πεδίῳ μεγάλῳ. Cf. L. Krinetzki (1961). A. Parrot (1955) writes: "'a plain'; these two words are enough. They recall at once the endless region which stretches the ochre-colored carpet of its now-abandoned flats for hundreds of kilometres." The word occurs later in the promise of the land to Israel, Deut 8:7; 11:11; also in the context of promise in Is 40:4; 41:18; 63:14. It has the same echo in the present context: the plain in the valley that they discover makes the life of the group possible for a time. It provides water, food, tranquility; they can settle there and stay, as the third verb now says. The location of the plain still remains undefined; it is only said that it is in the land of Shinar, and Shinar means here, as in Gen 10, the whole of Mesopotamia; so Th. Jacobsen, S. Landersdorfer. It is only in v. 9 that it is stated expressly that the plain in question is the one in which the city of Babylon is situated.

The third verb, ישב, always means an action in the context of the itinerary, not a situation. The translation therefore is: they settled there, not they remained there or they lived there. The verb leaves it an open question, how long the group remained in the plain where it settled.

Literature: Gen 11:3: H.A. Frankfort, *Kingship and the Gods. . . ,* (1948; 1962²). J. Fichtner, "Der Begriff des 'Nächsten' im Alten Testament mit einem Ausblick auf Spätjudentum und Neues Testament," JThSB NF 4 (1955) 23-52. M. Held, "The Action-Result (Factitive-Passive) Sequence of Identical Verbs in Biblical Hebrew and Ugaritic," JBL 84 (1965) 272-282. E. Lipinski, "Recherches sur le livre de Zacharie," VT 20 (1970) 31. E. Noort, "Eine weitere Kurzbemerkung zu 1 Samuel XIV 41," VT 21 (1971) 112-116.

Gen 11:4: R.J. Fox, ExpT (1906/1907) 522-524. E. König, *Historisch-kritisches Lehrgebäude der hebräischen Sprache, Bd. II. Historisch-komparative Syntax der hebräischen Sprache* (1907) §362f. P. Riessler, ThQ 93 (1911) 493-504. M. Weber, *Gesammelte Aufsatze . . . III*, (1923) 16, 34. E.A. Speiser, Or 25 (1956) 317-323. L. Kopf, VT 8 (1958) 191. J. Milgrom, "Did Isaiah Prophesy during the Reign of Uzziah?," VT 14 (1964) 164-182; 166. A. Malamat, "Campaigns to the Mediterranean by Iahdunlim and Other Early Mesopotamian Rulers," Ass ST 16 (1965) 365-373. P.J. Calderone, "Dynastic Oracle and Suzerainty Treaty. 2. Samuel 7:8-16," Logos 1 (1966) 1-80; 45. G. Wallis, ZAW 78 (1966) 141, 144. E. Birnbaum, VT 17 (1967) 373-415. T. and D. Thompson, "Some Legal Problems in the Book of Ruth," VT 18 (1968) 79-99; 85. W.W. Hallo, "Antediluvian Cities," JCS 23 (1970/1971) 57-67. B. Margulis, "A Weltbaum in Ugaritic Literature?," JBL 90 (1971) 481-482. H.P Müller, "Mythische Elemente in der jahwistischen Schöpfungserzählung," ZThK 69 (1972) 259-289; 284.

[11:3-4] The action begins with the third verse which narrates the decision of the people to build a city and a tower. The decision has two parts: v. 3a the decision to prepare to build together with, v. 3b, an additional explanation of interest for the history of civilization. It is only in v. 4a that there follows the decision to build a city and a tower linked with the reason for it in v. 4b. The normal narrative method would be to put the decision to build a city and a tower at the beginning; the execution, and this is what v. 3 is talking about, would then follow. This is confirmed by v. 3b which is concerned with execution, not with decision. The execution of the decision is missing completely from vv. 3-4, though presumed in v. 5b. It is possible of course that the decision narrated in vv. 3-4 implies execution; but one expects that a story about the building of the tower will tell about its construction. The reason for the unusual pattern in vv. 3-4 can be that 11:1-9 contains a late, much adapted reshaping of an older and simpler narrative, permeated with further reflection. The emphasis has been shifted from the event to the motifs that give the event its course.

[11:3] "And they said to each other": these words preface a decision which is formulated in the cohortative and introduced by the interjection הבה "come!," (as is also God's decision in v. 7). The same interjection introduces the decision to take measures against the Israelites who were becoming too numerous in Egypt, Ex 1:10. The decision itself is formulated poetically: "Let us brick bricks and burn brands," certainly a traditional and lapidary phrase. This is confirmed by the description of the building of Esagila in Enuma Elish VI 60-62:

> Let its brickwork be fashioned. . . .
> The Annunaki applied the implement;
> For one whole year they moulded bricks.
> When the second year arrived,
> They raised high the head of Esagila toward Apsu.
>
> (ANET, 68f.)

There are three points of contact with Gen 11:3-4: 1. The decision to make bricks; 2. the subsequent building of the tower; 3. the emphasis on the height of the tower, "with its summit touching the heavens" (for heavens as apsu, see E.A. Speiser, Or 25 [1956] 321). In addition the etymological construction נלבנה לבנים has an equivalent in the akk. *ilbinu libittu* and *libittašu iltabnu* (see Speiser, p. 75; so too M. Held, op. cit.). The solemn decision in v. 3 is associated with the preparations to build, specifically with the preparation of bricks; this corresponds to the Enuma Elish passage cited. E.A. Speiser, Comm. p. 76, explains the background: "For the ceremonial and year-long preparation of the sacral bricks and the solemn laying of the first brick were standard practices bound up with the religious architecture of Mesopotamia." The building inscriptions quoted by J.G. Frazer in *Folklore*. . . . ch. 5, illustrate these solemn ceremonial preparations; there are even similar phrases, "laid bricks, I manufactured burnt bricks" and "to raise its turrets to heaven." For the ritual of the preparation of the bricks see also H.A. Frankfort, *Kingship and the Gods*, (1948; 1962²) 272-274.

[11:3b] An explanatory note about the building material is added. The sentence is not part of the decision in v. 3a which is taken up again in v. 4. The explanatory note in 3b is a parenthesis; it is directed to the listener or reader. It is not a comment on the decision but an explanation of the technical way in which it was executed (it is not necessary therefore to transpose the half verse after v. 4, as H. Gunkel proposes). It is important that the narrator indicates in this way that he is informed about the land in which the event takes place; he is familiar with the technique of building. The explanation contrasts the local way of building, stone and mortar, with the foreign, bricks and bitumen. The excavations in Palestine show "that asphalt was never at any time used as the binding material in the construction of walls" K. Galling, BRL 40. B. Jacob remarks on the significance of this way of building for the history of civilization: "This discovery, so rich in its consequences, was one of the most important ever made. By making bricks people liberated themselves from natural stone and its deposits. Civilization, which draws large groups of people together, begins with the brick" (Comm. ad loc.). Also O.E. Ravn, p. 358: "Even today we can still take these beautifully fired bricks in our hand."

[11:4] The beginning of v. 4 shows that the decision was originally concerned with the building enterprise; the first words agree almost literally with the first words of v. 3. The sentences are separated from each other only by the parenthesis in v. 3b; two decisions following directly on each other have a clumsy effect. It is conceivable that v. 4a was the introduction in an earlier version of the narrative. There are three parts:

> "And they said [to each other]:
> Come, let us build a city and a tower,
> with its summit touching the heavens!"

The last of these three lines is the goal to which the decision leads. The rhythm of the language tells us this. The concluding step renders the decision audacious, beyond anything that is normal. It is an expression of the will to greatness, to something "over and above." This being said, there can be nothing further; it cannot be outbid, nor can it be invested with an additional motif. The two sentences that follow in v. 4b draw attention in that two motifs that could be independent of each other are linked together by the conjunction פן. The words "lest we be" do not refer to the preceding motif, "so we will make a name for ourselves," but to the building of the tower. This passage is a particularly clear example of the gradual growth of the narrative. The two motifs in v. 4b have grown together in the course of the narrative tradition and have then been bound together grammatically and logically so that they appear as a single motif. The exegesis must have regard for each motif in itself and enquire into its particular meaning and context.

"City and tower"; v. 5 "the city and the tower"; v. 8 "the city." The narrative speaks twice of "city and tower," once of "city" alone, but not of "tower" alone. The text offers no help to the attempt to divide the narrative into a city recension and a tower recension. Such a separation loses all support if E.A. Speiser's explanation is correct, that we have here the literary device of hendiadys: "The sense . . . is 'city crowned by a tower'," op. cit. 322. Similarly O.E. Ravn: "The tower as a fortification is but a natural complement to the city," op. cit. 366; so too A. Brock-Utne. One can therefore translate v. 4a: "Let us build a city with a tower. . . ." O.E. Ravn has studied מגדל in detail with support from E.G. Kraeling. It describes generally the fortress of a city and is often mentioned together with the walls, e.g., 2 Chron 14:6; Is 2:15; see J. Milgrom VT 14 (1964) 166. It can be applied too to the fortifications as a whole. But the word can also designate a wooden structure (watch tower) in the vineyard, Is 5:2. All usages are colored by the basic notion of size or height: "Migdal means something that is notable for its size," O.E. Ravn op. cit. 359. It is therefore a suitable word to describe the huge Babylonian ziggurats.

"With its summit touching the heavens." E.A. Speiser wants to demonstrate that what lies behind 11:1-9 is not the actual site of one of the great Babylonian buildings, but a literary influence, namely the passage in Enuma Elish, VI 62: "they raised the head of Esagila toward heaven *(mihrit apsi)*," p. 319. The phrase refers primarily to persons, "to elevate" and was then transferred to buildings; it was not used only for the ziggurat of Babylon. There is a parallel phrase that Nabopolassar and Nebuchadnezzar use of the new construction of Etemenanki: "to rival the heavens," p. 319; and another in an Assyrian text of the restoration of the temple Esharra by Esarhaddon: *"ana šamē* = toward heaven" (together in this case with the preparation of bricks). See R. Borger, AfO.B 9 (1956) 27-41, §2. There is perhaps too a Ugaritic parallel, see B. Margulis, JBL 90 (1971) 481f.: "A tree (with) its 'head' in the firma[ment]."

There are therefore in the biblical narrative echoes of the formulas used at the foundation of the city of Babylon in Enuma Elish. But that does not necessarily exclude an actual visual experience of the mighty ziggurats in Babylonia which is reflected in the narrative. It was these buildings that were spoken about in Israel that communicated the impression of reaching to the heavens. It is important for the narrative of 11:1-9 that the phrase "to the heavens" is used in the context of the foundation of the founding of Babylon," E.A. Speiser p. 321. The biblical narrative too is concerned with founding: the transition from the migrant state to the founding of a city, 11:2-3. The parallel Babylonian expression can also show that the phrase in v. 4, "with its summit touching the heavens," is to be considered in its own right without the two motifs added in v. 4b.

The narrative of the building of the tower concentrates on the idea of "size" contained in מגדל; this is what the words "to the heavens" mean. An older type of narrative (see under literary form), in accord with primitive thinking, speaks of reaching to, climbing, storming the heavens. This is saying the same at an earlier cultural level. The high culture of Mesopotamia raises the scaling of the heavens "to rival the heavens" (E.A. Speiser). And it is very significant that this is the only text in the Old Testament presentation of the primeval event, Gen 1-11, where the city of Babylon in the plain of Shinar is the scene of what is happening. J has seen that what he wants to say about human ambition in this narrative is expressed in a unique way in the mighty buildings in the valley of the two great rivers.

[11:4b]   "So we will make a name for ourselves." This second motive is like the first; the "name" is the result of the ambition. The same mode of speech occurs in Is 63:12; Jer 32:20; Neh 9:10. God makes a name for himself by his saving acts on behalf of Israel. In 2 Sam 8:13 David makes a name for himself; in 2 Sam 7:23 with שׂים, God makes a name for Israel. In all these passages someone makes a name for himself (in one place he makes it for another) by means of outstanding deeds; cf. also Gen 6:4. P.J. Calderone, op. cit. p. 45 writes: "*Shem*, 'reputation' is used unrestrictedly with various verbs . . . but with *'śh* it is confined to the king (2 Sam 7:9; 8:13), to Yahweh working wonders in Egypt (Jer 32:20; Is 63:12, 14; Dan 9:15; Neh 9:10; also Josh 7:9 with modification), and to the builders of the tower of Babel (Gen 11:4) who in some way are rebelling against God and trying to be like Him." (See also T. and D. Thompson, op. cit. 1968), p. 85 with further parallels). This usage stands apart therefore from the usual: to give or receive a name. Name can only be understood as fame; a name that draws attention and recognition. It is a question of contemporary and posthumous fame. A famous name is known in a wide circle and lives on.

        J. Calvin comments (*Genesis*, 128): "This is always the way of the world, never to bother about heaven and to look for immortality on earth where everything is transitory." Such an interpretation is possible only because Calvin equates the era of the buiding of the tower with his own. The opposition between a worldly and a spiritual attitude cannot be read back into the narrative. The narrator gives no indication that the intention of making a name for oneself is reprehensible as such. H. Gunkel wants to explain the sentence out of a mentality peculiar to antiquity. "One who is childless erects a monument to himself, 2 Sam 18:18, or sets up a memorial tablet in the temple, Is 56:5." But these two passages are talking about something different. It is not a name won by an outstanding deed, but the ordinary name. The concern that one be remembered after death is part of that community understanding of life that belongs to the family. The individual lives on in his children; the fulfillment of the need of the two examples quoted by Gunkel is based on childlessness. It is something new and very different when a man makes a name (gains fame) by a deed or series of deeds, e.g., Gilgamesh, II 160, "a name that endures — I will set up for myself," or David, 2 Sam 8:13. In both cases it is a king. Name in the sense of fame, name that one makes for oneself by one's deeds, this is only possible in a rather large community. It is the significance of the deeds for the community that gives them recognition and meaning; that is what is meant by the "name." Sir 40:19 brings both together: "Children and the building of a city establish a man's name."

This is to be distinguished further from a community striving after a name (this can only be understood in the sense of fame). The individual achieves it by an outstanding deed, but it presumes the larger political community. The pressure to make a name for oneself could be linked with the transition to sedentary life. The small groups of nomads come into contact with the great and famous empires and cities and want to be like them. But in any case a cause like this cannot belong to the first stage of the origin and growth of the narrative but only to the stage of higher cultural development. The possibility presented in Gen 11:1-9, that a people acquires fame by means of enormous buildings, was well known in the world round about Israel (see the beginning and end of the Gilgamesh Epic). This takes on a fixed expression in the Old Testament: תהלה is used of the fame of a city, Jer 48:2; 49:25; 51:41; cf. Ezek. 26:17. There are two sides to these passages: one can speak positively of the fame of a city or a country. However the danger of presumption, of over-reaching oneself is close at hand. Is 2:12-15 describes this impressively — the prophet proclaims that God overthrows all that is proud and lofty, and this certainly includes presumption.

The third motive is: "lest we be scattered over the face of the earth." F. Delitzsch had already seen that this reason does not harmonize with the preceding motive. It must be considered in its own right because it is quite obvious that it has been added here, the purpose being to anchor one of the conclusions, "and from there Yahweh scattered them over the earth," in the first part of the narrative (see above).

The last section of v. 4 can only be understood in the context of vv. 8a and 9b and will be considered together with them. On the word פוץ, see L. Kopf VT 8 (1958) 191.

[**11:5-9**]   The second part of the narrative: the intervention of Yahweh. The narrative of the event concludes with v. 8; v. 9 contains the etiological conclusion: "for this reason one called. . . ." Vv. 5-9 contain very little action; the narrative imperfect וירד, v. 5, is followed by the long reflection ויאמר, 6-7, and then by ויפץ, v. 8. This section is rendered particularly difficult because the descent of God narrated in v. 5 is followed by a decision to descend yet again in v. 7. A literary-critical analysis offers no solution, as we have seen. The root of the difficulty is that several motifs coalesce which originally do not belong together. V. 5 speaks only of the building that the people had erected and nothing more; v. 6a of the unity of language (also of the unity of the group); v. 6b of the possibility of some further rash deed; v. 7 of the decision to confuse language; v. 8a of the execution (not of the confusion of language, but) of the dispersion; v. 8b of the consequence, the cessation of building. V. 9 draws both themes together as the reason for naming the city: God has confused language — God has dispersed them.

The outline of this complicated picture is easily recognizable: God sees — reflects — decides — intervenes, and the effect of the intervention. It is coherent. The two originally self-contained and independent motifs are woven into this outline of the narrative of the building: (a) from the community of all people in one place to their dispersion over the face of the earth; (b) from a language common to all to the confusion of languages.

Literature: Gen 11:5: H. Hommel, "Das religionsgeschichtliche Problem des 139. Psalms," ZAW 47 (1929) 110-112.   F. Michaeli, *Dieu à l'image de l'homme*, (1950).

[11:5] "Then Yahweh came down to look at. . . ." This sentence, like the corresponding one in v. 7, presumes that God is not among people on earth, but above in heaven. This is something different from Gen 2-3; 4; 6-9. Nevertheless the talk is still that of primeval time inasmuch as God's descent from heaven is not presented as "revelation." Even when God comes down to look at what the people have built and to proceed against it, he is as it were in the same sphere as the people. Nothing happens which corresponds in any way to "revelation"; it is but an intimation of the other dimension to which God belongs. The fact that this is the only place where God descends (11:5 and 7) proves that the talk is still of primeval time. Later, from Gen 12 on, when it is presupposed that God is in heaven or speaks or acts from heaven, it is always a question in some way or another of a revelation. H. Gunkel makes much use of these passages in explaining 11:5 and continues: "This belief, that the divinity lives in heaven, occurs as a remnant of astral religion (or even of meteorological religion) among the peoples round about; to wit in Canaan long before Israel." Let it be said once for all that this element cannot be regarded as a "remnant of astral religion." It occurs across the whole face of the earth and in all conceivable religions, even the primitive. Moreover, the representation of God in heaven (or even God - heaven) is so general and undetermined that it can at times have quite different meanings, varying each time according to context.

Here the descent is meant to be part of God's punitive (more accurately: defensive or preventative) intervention, just as in Ex 3:8 it is part of God's liberating intervention. Strictly speaking no representation of heaven goes with it (11:4 is different). The intervention of God, which is the thrust of the narrative, is the intervention of the descent. The same "descent so as to punish" occurs in a Babylonian text; cf. E.G. Kraeling, JAOS 20 (1920) 279f.: "The descent of the deity for punitive purposes (v. 7) finds an analogy also in a passage of the so-called Kedar-Laomer texts. 'If the king does not speak righteousness, inclines toward wickedness, then his shêdu will descend from Esharra, the temple of all the gods' (Jeremias AT, p. 180)." U. Cassuto, ad loc., mentions a Ugaritic parallel, I K 35-36. The narrator puts emphasis on this "descent of God" as a movement to counterbalance the ascent of the people "to the heavens" by means of their building. By means of this literary device J has succeeded in arranging for the course of the narrative to be governed by two movements, from below to above and from above to below. Many interpreters see it as an expression of mockery: "It deliberately sets the achievements of these people and the regard of God in sharp contrast, full of irony and mockery" H.D. Preuss, BWANT 12 (1971) 51f. Preuss remarks further that this mockery is directed against Babel and its religion. But this is a gross misunderstanding. The narrative is not concerned with Babel and its religion but with humanity. The event described here is of such proportions that mockery and irony are out of place. On the question of the theological importance of this phrase, see the review of F. Michaeli's, *Dieu à l'image de l'homme* (1950) by H. Cazelles, VT 2 (1952) 189-191.

Literature: Gen 11:6: H. Cazelles, Discussion of F. Sierksma, "Quelques remarques. . ." OTS 9 (1951) 136-169, VT 2 (1952) 381. P.P. Saydon, "The Inceptive Imperfect in Hebrew and the Verb hēḥēl 'to begin'," Bib 35 (1954) 43-50. N.P. Bratsiotis, "Der Monolog. . .," ZAW 73 (1961) 30-70 §3a. H.A. Brongers, "Bemerkungen zum Gebrauch des adverbialen we attāh im Alten Testament," VT 15 (1965) 292. A.F. Knight, "The Lord is One," ExpT 78 (1966/1967) 8-10. R. Lapointe, CBQ

32 (1970) 161ff. I. Soisalon-Soininen, "Der Infinitivus Constructus mit ל im Hebräischen," VT 22 (1972) 82-90; 85f.

[11:6] God's first response after looking at the work of the people is not an action but a reflection (cf. N.P. Bratsiotis, who calls 11:6-7 a monologue, p. 33; but it would be more accurate to describe it as a consideration, a reflection. On the theological meaning of such a divine monologue, see R. Lapointe, op. cit.). It is almost completely determined by the motif of the language. God's reflection is not a direct reaction to the people's work that he has come down to look at. It begins rather with a summation of the situation and repeats almost word for word the sentence of the exposé, v. 1. It is only in v. 6b that there is an indirect reaction to the work of the people, "this is only the beginning of what they will do. . . ." This reflection is the basis of a decision to intervene in v. 7. However, it is not an intervention against the work of the people, but against the unity of language. The intervention therefore is directed more against what people may be expected to do in the future (". . . nothing will be impossible for them"), than against the work that they are engaged in now. This rather complicated reflection of God betrays a relatively late stage in the narrative as we have it. It is not concerned with simple facts and conclusions drawn from them. It is colored rather by reflection, by consideration of the possibilities that would now be open to people if all restrictions on information and understanding were set aside and they could consequently act as a self-contained unity: "henceforth nothing will be impossible for them." This must lead to the absolute autonomy of humankind. Hence the limitation which belongs to their created state would be called in question: their position vis-a-vis the creator. Humanity exists only in its state as creature; so its continuation is endangered by the threat of autonomy.

The narrative reaches its climax in the last part of God's reflection: "Nothing will be impossible for them in what they propose to do." The intervention follows on this. The verb בצר III occurs but rarely; it is found again in the niphal only in Job 42:2; in the piel = to make inaccessible in Is 22:10; Jer 51:53. The Job passage is important for the understanding of Gen 11:6. It is the beginning of Job's answer to God's address: "I know that you can do all things, and that no purpose of yours can be thwarted." This verse is of the utmost importance in this place in the structure of the Book of Job. God has put Job in his place; and Job now acknowledges God for what he really is. This is what 42:2 is saying.

The meaning of God's reflection in Gen 11:6 thereby becomes clear; there is the fear that people could become like God (cf. Gen 3:5). The same two verbs (the same roots) occur in Job 42:2 as in Gen 11:6b: זמם and בצר III. When one adds that זמם is a rare word and בצר III very rare, then it looks as if there is a fixed formula behind these two verses. Because the Genesis passage is in a reflective (= interpretative) context, one assumes that Job 42:2 is closer to the fixed formula. It would be a formula of the praise of God: "Nothing that you will is impossible to you." Echoes of the praise of God, known to the listeners, in a reflection of God that is the basis of an intervention against humankind, throw into still sharper relief that it is against human presumption, albeit only feared, that God must intervene.

It is at this climax of the narrative that something further becomes clear: the simple and direct thrust of the story of the building of a tower by people in primeval time, the basic narrative, is that humans were no longer satisfied with the limited state of their existence, but wanted to force their way into the realm of the gods or God. This was worked over and adapted in a later stage but in such a way as to preserve the basic motif, that of people overstepping their limits.

Literature: Gen 11:7: F.M. Cross, Jr., "The Council of Yahweh in Second Isaiah," JNESt 12 (1953) 274-277. H. Bardtke, "Der Traktat der Schreiber (Sopherim)," WZL 3 (1953/1954) 31-49. H. Schmid, ZAW 67 (1955) 172. F. Festorazzi, "I plurali di Gen 1:26, 3:22, 11:7 e l'intima natura del peccato dei progenitori," BeO 5 (1963) 81-86. G.A. Cooke, ZAW 76 (1964) 23. M. Takahashi, "An Oriental's Approach to the Problems of Angelology," ZAW 78 (1966) 343-350.

[**11:7**] The result of the reflection, v. 6, is the decision to confuse the language of the people "so that no one understands the language of his neighbor." On the plural, "we will go down," cf. comments on 1:26 and 3:22. One is not to assume as background remnants of polytheistic talk or the idea of the heavenly court (as do many modern exegetes, like G.A. Cooke, F.M. Cross, H. Schmidt); according to E.A. Speiser the singular in v. 5 speaks against this. Gen 11:7 is one of the thirteen places where the Jewish scribes have altered the text (into the singular); (cf. H. Bardtke, above). The older form, where the decision follows on what the people are doing, shows that this decision is secondary and against the original course of the narrative. The decision of v. 7 is formulated within a mentality that wants to explain the confusion of language. Accordingly it is difficult to present its execution. In fact the confusion of language is the consequence of God's intervention which prevented the people from completing the building, v. 8b. And so the decision, v. 7, and its execution, v. 8, do not harmonize. God carries out his decision to confuse the language of the people, v. 7, while dispersing humanity over the face of the earth, v. 8.

In the older form of the narrative, the dispersion of humanity is a consequence of an intervention of God against the building. The sequence of vv. 7 and 8 shows that the motifs of the confusion of language and the dispersion of humankind have been deliberately joined at a later stage; this is the case again in v. 9b, perhaps too in v. 6a. Plurality of peoples and plurality of languages are seen as belonging together as in P 10:5, 20, 31. Gen 10 (J and P) regards the division of humanity into a plurality of peoples and languages as a consequence of the blessing of God upon those saved from the flood. 11:1-9 regards the repeal of this plurality as endangering humankind. From this point of view the relationship between decision, v. 7, and execution, v. 8, becomes meaningful. Because the two motives extend the old theme of people stepping beyond their limits by building the tower that is to reach to the heavens, the dispersion of humanity (8) can imply the confusion of its languages (7). But if God's decision is directed primarily at the unity of language, then its object is not merely communication in general, but the specific human enterprise aimed at storming the heavens. If there is no longer anything to prevent worldwide mutual communication, then people can undertake ventures that overstep their human limits. C.H. Gordon comments: "The greatest American handbook on linguistic science inadvertently takes the above biblical view of the main function of language; i.e., to make human cooperation possible. C.L. Bloomfield, *Language* (1933) 23-27," *Introduction to Old Testament Times*, (1953) 29, n. 17.

Literature: Gen 11:8: D.W. Thomas, "Some Observations on the Root חדל,"

VT.S 4 (1957) 8-16.   H.D. Preuss, ". . . ich will mit dir sein!," ZAW 80 (1968) 139-173.

[**11:8**]   The execution of the decision, according to v. 7, can only be intended in this way: those dispersed over the face of the earth develop different languages and can no longer understand each other. But instead of this, a quite different consequence is mentioned in v. 8b: they left off building the city. This does not follow naturally. In the older form of the narrative it was: God intervenes against the building — the builders abandon their work — they are dispersed. The present sequence of 8a and 8b is conditioned by the fact that God's intervention consists in the dispersion of humankind. There is no indication at all of the means God used to effect the dispersion; it is constructed out of the motif of dispersion which in its older form had humankind itself as the subject.

> *Literature:* Gen 11:9: E. Pannier, "Babylone," DB (V) I (1895) 1351-1357.   F.M.Th. Böhl, "Die Etymologie von 'Babel', Genesis 11:9," ZAW 36 (1916) 110-113.   R. Koldewey, *Das wiedererstandene Babylon* (1925⁴).   E. Unger, Babylon. *Die heilige Stadt nach der Beschreibung der Babylonier*. Kap. KVIII Der Turm zu Babel (1931; 1970²) 191-200.   I.J. Gelb, "The Name of Babylon," JIAS 1 (1955) 1-4; "Etymologia nominis Babel," Bib 37 (1956) 130.   Th.C. Vriezen, *Jahwe en zijn Stad* (1962).   J. Heller, EvTh 27 (1967) 255.   B.O. Long, *The Problem of Etiological Narrative in the Old Testament*, BZAW 108 (1968) 23-25.   F. Golka, "Zur Erforschung der Ätiologien im Alten Testament," VT 20 (1970) 90-98.

[11:9]   The Etiological Conclusion.

The narrator here steps out of his role as storyteller (the narrative of the event ends with v. 8b) and appends a conclusion which links the event that happened in primeval time with a situation in the present (עַל־כֵּן in the same sense in Gen 2:24) which (present situation) finds its explanation in the event just narrated: the name of the city of Babylon. In Babel (בָּבֶל) Yahweh confused the language of humankind (בלל); this event gave Babel its name.

The following points are to be noted in the explanation of the etiological conclusion:

1. The conclusion is quite independent and the narrative is complete without it.

2. This means that the narrative is not rendered etiological by the conclusion. The narrative as such is etiological inasmuch as its purpose is to explain the plurality of languages (or the fact that people cannot communicate and make themselves understood) as well as the dispersion of humankind over the earth. The explanation of the name of Babel is a situation etiology.

3. The older form of the narrative, which can still be reconstructed, was not etiological. Its thrust was that God prevented the construction of a building that was to reach to the heavens. The etiological conclusion therefore, which explains the name of the city of Babel, is a relatively late accretion in the growth of the narrative. The fact that the narrative does not lead to the founding of a city but to the frustration of the founding of a city is a further sign that it is an accretion. Gen 10:10 has something very different to say about the founding of Babylon.

The fact that the city on the Euphrates is explained by means of a Hebrew verb, בלל, which has only a slight resemblance to Babel, is an indication of the cultural level at which such amateurish "popular etymologies" occur; they are frequent in the early layers of the Old Testament. They cease with the beginning of historical writing. "Even the cuneiform etymology . . . Bab-il = the gate of God is perhaps only a . . . popular etymology" (H. Gunkel ad loc.; J. Heller, op. cit. p. 259 writes: "The biblical explanation by means of the root *bll* in Gen 11:9 contains therefore the third 'stage of development' of the name." For further literature see above).

Purpose and Thrust

The story of the Tower of Babel exercises its own peculiar fascination even today. In the film "Metropolis," which was shown all over the world in the 1920s, the leading actress narrated and explained it with a distinctly social alignment. We can only confirm to our amazement that this aspect is not absent even from the biblical primeval story: the building of a massive structure that presumes definite technical discoveries and mathematical skills, as well as the common will of a group of people who think it necessary to erect the building. It is no exaggeration to say that Gen 11:2-9 in essence anticipates the possibility of a development that would be realized only in the technical age in a way that would affect the whole of humanity. It had its forerunners in the huge buildings of the high cultures throughout the world; and so Gen 11:1-9 must have played this part in one of these great empires.

One must be careful therefore to distinguish between the first founding of a city in 4:17, and the "city with a tower," the great city in 11:4. The city of 4:17 is a requirement of sedentary life and its function is to provide the necessary security and shelter. We find in 11:2 also indication of the transition from nomadic to sedentary life. But with the note "with its summit touching the heavens" the city envisaged takes on a completely new meaning; it serves to present ambition. It is this that is new and other over against 4:17. This is the clue to understanding the different motifs that have come together in 11:1-9. The basic motif, that people want to demonstrate their greatness in a work of their own hands, is illustrated too in a prophetic context:

> You said in your heart,
> I will ascend to heaven;
> above the stars of God
> I will set my throne on high; . . .
> I will ascend above the heights of
>   the clouds,
> I will make myself like the most
>   high.   (Is 14:13-14)

Similarly in Jer 51:53. The motif is the same; in Gen 11:1-9 it is presented as something of which one is capable in primeval time, in Is 14:13f. as taking place in the course of history, in the Babylonian world empire (cf. P. Humbert, "Démesure. . . ," *Homm. à W. Vischer* [1960] 68f.).

It is no mere chance that the motif of Gen 3:5 occurs again in Is 14:13f., "like the most high." It is obvious that J, by putting the two parallel passages 3:5 (subject, the individual person) and 11:4 (subject, humanity) at the beginning and the end of the primeval story, wants to say that human beings, left to their own resources by the creator, are in the gravest danger because of their aspiration to burst their created limits, to acknowledge no longer that they stand before God, but to be like God or to reach to the heavens with their works. This is decisive in J's understanding of humanity. When J prefaces his history of the growth of Israel from Abraham to the taking of the land with an account of primeval events which sets up the relationship not only of Israel but of the world and humankind to God, he is saying something that is of the very essence of his idea of the relationship of a human being to God and of one's created state — humans are to remain within the limits assigned to them. Here alone can their existence find fulfillment. If people overstep them, they put their existence in danger. And J has already seen that the drive to overstep these limits can come from the individual, 3:5, just as from humanity as a group, 11:4. He has set out the significance of this drive in such a way that it is not as such reprehensible or directed against God, but appears as something of an ambitious aspiration that belongs to human beings.

It is this that constitutes the parallel between Gen 3 and 11: aspiration after knowledge ("to know what is good and evil") is not in itself opposed to God anymore than is aspiration after fame by means of a work that embodies ambition. In both places J is saying that this aspiration merely hides within itself the possibility of overstepping the limits and that it is precisely here that human existence is in such great danger. Behind Gen 11:1-9 stands the idea of human ambition which only revealed itself in the course of human history in conjunction with the great achievements of civilization. The monumental buildings of the ancient high cultures are the most immediate and at the same time the most impressive and imposing expression of this ambitious drive whose subject is a number, a group. It is only at a later stage that the idea of ambition, refined still further, is applied to the intellectual accomplishment of an individual person. It is one's ambition that is the basis of the outstanding intellectual achievement of a thinker, a political leader, an artist.

The significance of Gen 11:1-9 consists also in this, that it is a continuation of the beginnings of civilization described in 4:17ff. It adds this drive to raise oneself to the heights of ambition which is so peculiar to and determinative of the whole of the history of humankind. The drive in itself is not condemned, and the narrative says this clearly in 11:6 in the divine reflection which wants to avert in the future a danger that has its seed in these beginnings (so too G. von Rad). God's intervention in Gen 11:1-9 does not consist directly in the consolidation or destruction of the building, but is directed against the goals aimed at. It is "rather of a preventative character" (G. von Rad). Its purpose, as J describes it, is to avert the overstepping of the limits and to throw people back within the limits of their state as creatures. One cannot say then: "The story about the Tower of Babel concludes with God's judgment on humankind; there is no word of grace" (G. von Rad). Rather God's intervention, by effecting the division of humankind into peoples and languages, is the beginning of a way of life that marks the transition from primeval event to history which begins in Gen 12. There will be much talk from now on about the overstepping of the limits which is the concern of 11:1-9, as in Is 13 about Babylon, and Is 2 about Israel itself; but the tower will never reach the heavens.

The principal motif in 11:1-9 is the heritage of an earlier, simpler form of the narrative. Side-by-side with it are the two secondary motifs, which, though they can certainly appear independently of each other, are nevertheless closely connected.

The Unity and the Dispersion of the Human Race

God's intervention in v. 8 consists in the dispersion of humanity over the earth and this is the source of the premonition thereof added to v. 4. The intervention is directed against the work itself in an older form of the narrative. In the present case the dispersion of humanity over the earth is rather in the nature of a punishment by God (more accurately, a preventative measure), so differing from Gen 10 and 9:18f. But one should not play these off against each other nor should one draw literary- critical conclusions. God's intervention in v. 8 is to be understood solely in the context of the principal motif of 11:1-9. Here only one aspect of the event is envisaged and is explained by God's reflection in v. 6b. It is not a question of something that has happened, but of a possibility. The unity of the whole of humankind could make complete emancipation possible, and could burst all restrictions. The ancient story of the tower is but an example of this; it indicates the direction in which humanity could go.

J carries the old motif of the dispersion of humankind further and sees in worldwide historical perspective the threat posed by the unity of humankind which can lead to dehumanization. Understood in this way God's intervention in v. 8, is not really a punishment but a means to ward off from people the threat that is only hinted at in v. 6b. A. Dillmann takes a similar view: ". . . and it is also a salutary restriction on the further development of one's sinful presumption"; B. Jacob writes ". . . a single walled city . . . symbol of concentration, of a herd instinct which feels itself smothered in the pressing mass." The purpose of God's intervention in v. 8 is to guard humanity against a danger that grows with its unity; and so there is no longer any opposition to Gen 10. The human race exists in a plurality of peoples over the earth with an abundance of potential for development in individual peoples, cf. 10:5, 20, 31. This is what humanity is and this is what preserves it in being.

Plurality of Languages is a necessary part of human existence in a plurality of peoples; it is its clearest and most striking characteristic. As such it can become an independent motif that can appear separately and, in the form in which 11:1-9 has come down, be seen in clearer relief than the motif of the plurality of peoples. It forms the framework in vv. 1 and 9, and the theme of God's decision in v. 7 is the confusion of languages (differing from his intervention in v. 8). F. Delitzsch quotes the Sibylline Oracles 3,99f.: "They were all the same in speech and they wanted to climb up to the starry heavens." The motif mirrors a reflection that is found in a number of places in early humanity and is the result of people's experience of the limits set them by being shut up in a single language area. This has obviously been a universal experience. The question which it raised could always be answered by a story about how it happened. But it is equally obvious that the experience of the language barrier — each language area asked: Why don't all people speak our language? — was at the beginning but one of the restrictions, and could only be answered by explaining it as a punishment. This explains how this independent motif became linked with that of the building of the tower.

Primeval time and eschatological time (Urzeit und Endzeit) correspond often in the Old Testament. Attention is therefore turned to the future when these language barriers will be abolished once more. This is so in Zeph 3:5-11 where the speech of all peoples will be changed so that they may all serve the Lord with one accord. This is the context of Acts 2:11 where the good news of the Christ event bursts the language barriers: "We hear them telling in our own tongues the mighty works of God." The talk here is really about the marvel of a new understanding beyond the barriers of language. But this does not in any way alter the plurality and difference of languages. It corresponds to 11:1-9 in that the barriers set to understanding by the variety of languages have also a positive aspect which serves humanity. The barriers remain even after Christ and persevere in face of the work of the Christian mission. The marvel of a new understanding in Acts 2 also corresponds to Gen 11:1-9 in that its purpose is service that renounces its own ambition and fame (11:4).

The Genealogy of Shem

Literature

See Lit. on Gen 5 and 10: E. Bertheau, "Die Zahlen der Genesis in Cap. 5 und Cap. 11," JDTh 23 (1878) 657-682. C.E. Sachau, *The Chronology of Ancient Nations* (1879). A. Dillmann, *Beiträge aus dem Buch der Jubiläen zur Kritik des Pentateuch-Textes*, SAB 29, 3 (1883). G.B.Gray, *Studies in Hebrew Proper Names* (1896) esp. 2ff. F. Hommel, *Die altisraelitische Überlieferung in inschriftlicher Beleuchtung* (1897) 201, 209, 212, 293ff. C.H.W. Johns, *Assyrian Deeds and Documents Recording the Transfer and Property.* III (1898-1923) = AJSL 42 (1926) 170-275. H. Ranke, *Early Babylonian Personal Names: Series D,* Vol III of: *The Babylonian Expedition of the University of Pennsylvania* (1905). K. Tallqvist, *Neubabylonisches Namenbuch* (1905); *Assyrian Personal Names* (1914). Th. Arldt, WZKM (1917-18) 264-317. A. Bertholet, *Kulturgeschichte Israels* (1919; 1920[2]) 136. H. Zimmern, "Die sieben Weisen Babyloniens," ZA 35 (1923) 151-156. D.D. Luckenbill, *Ancient Records of Assyria and Babylonia* (1926-1927). O. Eissfeldt, *Introduction.* . . . (1966) §30, §118. H.G. Güterbock, "Die historische Tradition und ihre literarische Gestaltung bei Babyloniern und Hethitern bis 1200," ZA 42 (1934) 1-91. P. Philippson, *Genealogie als mythische Form: Studien zur Theologie des Hesiod*, SO 7 (1936). Th. Jacobsen, AsSt 11 (1930) 76-85. M. Noth, *A Hist. of Pent. Trad.* (1972). N. Schneider, "Patriarchennamen in zeitgenössischen Keilschrifturkunden," Bib 33 (1952) 516-522. D.J. Wiseman, *Chronicles of Chaldean Kings (626-556 B.C.) in the British Museum* (1956). S. Moscati, *The Semites in Ancient History* (1959). R. de Vaux, "Les patriarches hébreux et les découverts modernes," RB 53 (1946) 328-349. B. Lundman, Rel och Kultur 34-37, (1956). J.C.L. Gibson, "Light from Mari on the Patriarchs," JSSt 7 (1962) 44-62. C.H. Gordon, *Hebrew Origins in the Light of Recent Discovery: Biblical and Other Studies* (1963) 3-14. A.L. Oppenheim, *Ancient Mesopotamia: Portrait of a Dead Civilization* (1964). H.B. Huffmon, *Amorite Personal Names in the Mari Texts* (1965). R. de Vaux, "The Hebrew Patriarchs and History," ThD 12 (1964) 227-240. L.M. Muntingh, "Die historisiteit van die Hebreuse aartsvaderhale in Genesis," SAAWK (1966) 399-406. H. Seebass, *Der Erzvater Israel und die Einführung der Jahweverehrung in Kanaan*, BZAW 98 (1966). H. Cazelles, "Mari et l'Ancien Testament," BFPUL 182 (1967) 73-90. J. Henninger, *Über Lebensraum und Lebensformen der Frühsemiten*, AFLNW 151 (1968). A. Malamat, *(History of the Jewish People),* 1. (in Hebr.) (1969) 9-90. B. Hrouda, "Vorderasien," IB (1971). T.C. Hartman, "Some Thoughts on the Sumerian King List and Genesis 5 and 11b," JBL 91 (1972) 25-32.

Text

11:10 This is the genealogy of Shem: When Shem was 100 years old, he begot Arpachshad, two years[a] after[b] the flood.

11 After Shem begot Arpachshad, he lived another 500 years, and begot sons and daughters[a].

12 When Arpachshad was 35 years old[a], he begot Shelah.

13 After Arpachshad begot Shelah, he lived another 403 years, and begot sons and daughters.

14 When Shelah was 30 years old, he begot Eber.

15 After Shelah begot Eber, he lived another 403 years, and begot sons and daughters.

16 When Eber was 34 years old, he begot Peleg.

17 After Eber begot Peleg, he lived another 430 years, and begot sons and daughters.

18 When Peleg was 30 years old, he begot Reu.

19 After he begot Reu, he lived another 209 years, and begot sons and daughters.

20 When Reu was 32 years old, he begot Serug.

21 After Reu begot Serug, he lived another 207 years, and begot sons and daughters.

22 When Serug was 30 years old, he begot Nahor.

23 After Serug begot Nahor, he lived another 200 years, and begot sons and daughters.

24 When Nahor was 29 years old, he begot Terah.

25 After Nahor begot Terah, he lived another 119 years, and begot sons and daughters.

26 When Terah was 70 years old, he begot Abram, Nahor, and Haran.

10a The dating is in the accus. Ges-K § 118i.   **b** On the use of אחר cf. E. Wiesenberg, "Chronological Data in the Zadokite Fragments," VT 5 (1955) 288.

11a Gk adds וימת, Sam in addition the total life-span, and so right through vv. 13, 15, 17 etc., corresponding to Gen 5.

The differing numbers in MT, Sam, Gk.

		MT		Sam			Gk	
10-11	Shem	100	500	100	500	600	100	500
12-13	Arpachshad	35	403	135	303	438	135	430
	χαιναν	—	—	—	—	—	130	330
14-15	Shelah	30	403	130	303	433	130	330
16-17	Eber	34	430	134	270	404	134	370
18-19	Peleg	30	209	130	109	239	130	209
20-21	Reu	32	207	132	107	239	132	107
22-23	Serug	30	200	130	100	230	130	200
23-25	Nahor	29	119	79	69	149	79	129
26	Terah	70	135	70	75	145	70	135

12a חי is 3rd pers. masc. sing. pf. Qal; cf. 5:5 (P); 3:22 (J).

Literary Form

The genealogy of Shem (P), the title given at the beginning of 11:10, traces itself in nine members from Shem to the three sons of Terah, 11:26, which concludes it. The genealogy of Terah begins in v. 27 with a similar title, though what follows, vv. 27, 31, 32, have a very different form from 11:10-26. The genealogy of Shem is very like that of Adam in Gen 5 (Adam to Noah). It traces itself through ten (nine) generations in such a way that on each occasion the line is represented by one son, the eldest. It is anchored in numbers. The age at which

559

the first son was begotten and the subsequent life-span are given, and there is mention of further unnamed sons and daughters. Missing in 11:10-26 when comparing it with Gen 5 are the total life-span and the sentence "then he died" (the Sam adds both, the Gk the latter only). In the midst of this extensive agreement it is particularly striking that 11:10-26 contain only nine members, not ten like Gen 5.

Despite the great similarity one cannot describe 11:10-26 as a continuation of Gen 5 as do many commentators (A. Dillmann, W. Zimmerli and others). Gen 5 is speaking about the whole human race, 11:10-26 obviously about one branch only. The history of humankind is not taken any further here. The branch that is continued is to be understood only in the light of its goal, Abraham. 11:10-26 traces Abraham back to one of the sons of Noah who were the starting point of humanity after the flood. This branch has only nine members. By omitting the tenth P wants to say that something different is beginning with this as yet unnamed tenth member. He thereby marks the transition from the primeval story to the history of the patriarchs. The title given to the history of the patriarchs, following the scheme hitherto used, is ואלה תלדת תרח. It is the key word יצא = go forth in v. 31, linked with the name of the land of Canaan, that tells what is happening in the history that now begins.

The passage is saying two things: the history of the patriarchs is a continuation of the history of humanity; the history of Abraham grows out of one branch of this history. But at the same time something else is being said: what is happening in this tenth member is something special, something new. This is the reason why the attempt by some exegetes to compare 11:10-26, as corresponding to Gen 5 (see Comm. on ch. 5 and literature), with the Sumerian king lists after the flood, is not convincing. The apparently similar structure, genealogy-flood-genealogy, gave occasion for this. T.C. Hartman (see above) concludes in this way: "In sum, then, apart from the superficial difference in format, namely listing-flood-listing, the Sumerian King-List and Gen 5 and 11B seem to differ significantly enough as to suggest a denial that the Sumerian document served as a source for the latter."

The Numbers: We have the same situation with regard to the numbers as in Gen 5. The Sam and Gk diverge notably from the MT. Both raise the age at which the first son was begotten by one hundred years each time (not with Shem, and it is different with Nahor). The result is that the sum total of the ages of begetting in the nine is 390 in MT, 1040 in Sam, 1270 in Gk (there are ten in Gk which inserts Kainan between Arpachshad and Shelah; cf. J.S. de Vries, IDB I, 581). While Gk and Sam agree here, the Gk overall has a higher life-span than MT and Sam. The difference is so remarkable that it requires an explanation.

The majority of exegetes say that the Sam and the Gk have altered the numbers of the MT. The reason for the alteration was a difficulty that resulted from reconciling the numbers of Gen 11 with those of Gen 5, namely that Noah was still living at the time of Abraham, and Shem at the time of Jacob. This difficulty was met by raising the age at which the first son was begotten and so prolonging the interval between the flood and Abraham by 650 years in the Sam, and by 880 (or 780) years in the Gk. The reason could also be that Sam and Gk thought that the difference between the two intervals of time in Gen 5 and Gen 11 was too great (in Gen 5, 1656 in MT). In both cases, the responsibility for the alteration lies with Sam and Gk which agree in essentials. There is no need to go into the differences between the Gk and the Sam (see table above), even though these numbers have attracted the attention of scholars and new attempts are being made continually to solve the system and the relationship of the three to each other (A. Bosse, MVG 13 [1908] 101-176; S. Euringer BZfr 2 [1909]; S. Makloet, BiLi 24 [1956-1957] 234-236; J. Meysing, RSR 39 [1965] 209-229. A good synthesis in S.E. McEvenue, *The Narrative Style. . . ,* [1971] 55-59).

What is common to all three systems of numbers (and their variants) is that they are subsequent constructions like the numbers in Gen 5. An obvious example is the numbers given for Shem, 100 + 500, so U. Cassuto and E.A. Speiser. One can see here very clearly the intention of P in the remarkable differences between Gen 5 and Gen 11 in the ages of begetting and the life-spans and the subsequent length of the periods. The age of begetting in the case of Shem is 100 years. Then it varies between 35 and 29 (70 in the case of Terah); and Shem lived another 500 years. P is thereby saying that Shem as a son of Noah belongs to the era that closes with Noah. The numbers reveal here that for P Shem belongs in tradition history to the list of the sons of Noah (with which the genealogy of Gen 5, or the flood story, closes), not to the list of the ancestors of Abraham where it stands merely as a link with what has preceded. This leads to a further conclusion: the much lower age of begetting and life-span in Gen 11 over against Gen 5 does not signify for P (at least not primarily) a diminution of life potency, but is conditioned by the different nature of the two series of generations. Only Gen 5 is concerned with humanity in primeval time. 11:10-26 on the contrary speaks merely of the descendants of an individual branch that leads to a historical people; it is the transition to history. The lower numbers are conditioned by the partial character of this transition series. P has indicated the transitional quality by the diminution in the numbers from Shem through those that follow.

P has given a further indication of this by expressly adding "two years after the flood" to the birth of Arpachshad. This note creates considerable chronological difficulties. It stands in contradiction to the previous statement that Shem begot Arpachshad in the 100th year of his life. "Noah began to beget when he was 500 years old in the year of the flood, not two years after it" (B. Jacob ad loc.). Some (e.g., H. Gunkel) explain these discrepancies by saying that they were only meant to be approximations. But this does not hold for P for whom numbers are so important. Other exegetes feel constrained to regard "two years after the flood" as a gloss (A. Dillmann, K. Budde, H. Holzinger, J. Skinner and others); the reason: to begin a new era with Arpachshad (J. Skinner). But it is a dubious procedure to eliminate this note as a gloss because it would have been the glossator who first introduced the difficulty into the text. The *lectio difficilior* is to leave the note in the text. Jewish interpreters (Rashi; B. Jacob in a detailed excursus) tried to explain it by complicated calculations. B. Jacob translates: "A second year after the mabbul." U. Cassuto explains "two years after the flood" as after the rain had stopped. These varied attempts only underline the difficulty.

One must see this together with two other incongruities in the context: in 10:22 Arpachshad was the third son of Shem, in 11:10 he is the eldest. But more important is this: in 10:22 the name occurs in the sequence Elam-Asshur-Arpachshad-Lud-Aram, where Arpachshad must be the name of a people or its land; in 11:10 it is clearly the name of a person. Taking these three incongruities together, the conclusion is that P regards the Arpachshad of 10:22 as different from the one in 11:10. This does not mean that P presumed two individuals with the same name, but that he saw the Arpachshad of 11:10 in the context of a tradition different from that of the one of 10:22. In the former he stands for a corporate unity, in the latter he is merely a member of a genealogical series.

Setting in Life

For the origin of 11:10-26 reference should be made to the general remarks on genealogies in the Introduction §2. What marks 11:10-26 out among the genealogies of Gen 1-11 is its function as the transition from primeval event to the history of the patriarchs. With this end in view P has drawn together many originally independent parts. The extraordinarily schematic character of the composition corresponds to the literary formation. Apart from the additional clause "two years after the flood" in v. 10, every member of the genealogy contains the same sentences in the same order (except v. 26). The composite character of the genealogy is in keeping with the different origin of its parts. The name Shem comes from the list of the three sons of Noah at the conclusion of J's flood narrative 9:18, in P's descendants of Noah 6:10, and is taken up again in 10:1.

The series Shem-Arpachshad is also primeval and is common to J, 10:21, 24, and P, 10:22. The series Serug-Nahor-Terah is of a different kind and origin. All three names are attested as place names, all three point to the area around Haran in northern Mesopotamia, which is mentioned in v. 31 as a place where the clan of Terah settled for a while. There is a tradition here of identification of the names of persons and places which is to be distinguished carefully from the identification of the names of persons, places and peoples in Gen 10. The process of tradition in which the place names in the region of Haran became the names of the forefathers of Abraham does not belong to the primeval story but to the history of the patriarchs.

Only the context of the history of the patriarchs can explain how these names of Abraham's forefathers carry a real recollection of the wanderings and halts of Abraham's ancestors. They were not preserved in the form of itineraries but of genealogical lists.

The names Shelah, Eber and Peleg form another self-contained group. We can go just a step further in the explanation of their origin. They occur in J in 10:(21), 24, 25 where they are not part of the division of the peoples over the earth, but are a foreign body, because they belong to the partial line that traces itself from Shem to Abraham. Agreeing with P, these three names follow Shem and Arpachshad:

	J	P
Shem	10:21	11:10
Arpachshad	24	10-12
Shelah	24	12-15
Eber	24	14-17
Peleg	25	16-19

P may have taken over the group from J or, more likely, there is an older tradition behind both. This is as far as the explanation can go. P has taken up this series, part of the tradition at hand to him, in a similar way and has combined it with other elements, as he did in Gen 5 (P) with an older list from 4:17ff. (J).

562

There remain the names that occur only in 11:10-26 (P), Reu and Serug. Neither is found elsewhere in the Old Testament. It can be demonstrated with certainty that Serug is a place name and as such belongs to the group Serug-Nahor-Terah; Reu remains the only name that does not belong to any group.

Literature: (cf. Lit. for Gen 5 & 10). Gen 11:10-17: E. Wiesenberg, "Chronological Data in the Zadokite Fragments," VT 5 (1955) 284-308. G. Fohrer, "Tradition und Interpretation im Alten Testament," ZAW 73 (1961) 1-30. J. Lindblom, ZAW 75 (1963) 263-288.

Commentary

[11:10-17] On Gen 11:10-17, see Comm. on names in Gen 10; cf. Table in notes on Text of 11:10-26.

Literature: Gen 11:18-21: G. Morawe, "Peleg," BHH III, 1411. F. van Trigt, *Die Geschichte der Patriarchen. Genesis 11: 17-50:26* (1963).

[11:18-21] *Reu:* The name is unknown and occurs only here (and in 1 Chron 1:25). There may be a connection with the personal name רעואל Ex 2:18; Num 10:29 (father-in-law of Moses) and Gen 36:4, 10, 13, 17 (son of Esau); רעו could be an abbreviation of this name. It has been conjectured that it sounds like the name of a god or that it is a place name. F. Hommel (see above) would see in it an Aramaean tribe, Ruʿûâ.

[11:20-23] *Serug:* Exegetes universally equate this name with the Akk. place name Sarugi near Haran (N. Schneider, Bib 33 [1952] 516-522; ZAW 40 [1922/23] 153), a city and region between Haran and Carchemish. It is mentioned by Arabian geographers, Syrian writers and in Assyrian inscriptions. R. de Vaux writes: "It is Saroug, which was an important Christian center and which is called today Serudj, half way between Haran and the Euphrates," (ThD 12 [1964] 230). C.H.W. Johns had already adduced the cuneiform attestation for Serug and Nahor in "An Assyrian Doomsday Book," Ass. Bibl 17 (1901) 72. According to N. Schneider, see above, it occurs once too as a personal name in the third period of Ur.

Literature: Gen 11:22-24: A.S. Yahuda, *Die Sprache. . . ,* (1929) I, 278-279. I.J. Gelb-P.M. Purves-A.A. MacRae, *Nuzi Personal Names* (1943). E. Bilgiç, "Die Ortsnamen der kappadokischen Urkunden," AfO 15 (1945/1951) 23. L. Hicks, "Nahor," IDB (1962) 497-498. A. Malamat, "Mari," BA 34 (1971) 2-22.

[11:22-24] In P Nahor is the grandfather and the brother of Abraham, in J only the brother. According to Gen 22:20-24 Nahor is an important Aramaean tribe whose descendants are enumerated. According to Gen 27:43; 28:10; 29:4 the family of Nahor lives in Haran, while 24:10 speaks of the "city of Nahor." H. Gunkel writes: "It is perhaps related to the Mesopotamian proper names *Na-ḥa-ra-a-u, Na-ḥa-ra-u* . . . and the place name *Til-Nahiri.*" This would fit, as *Til-Nahiri* is situated close to Haran. The name has now been found in the Mari texts, 19th and 18th centuries, in a form identical with the biblical name: "As we now know from the Mari records, there was in the patriarchal age a city by the name of Nahur located in the region of Haran." (E.A. Speiser; likewise U. Cassuto, R. de Vaux; also *Archives Royales de Mari XV,* p. 130; E. Bilgiç writes: ". . . Nahur is to be found not far from Haran. Nahur occurs frequently in the Mari Texts; it is the residence of the viceroy of the king of Mari. . . ."; N. Schneider has shown that *Na-ha-ru-um* is an Akkadian personal name which he equates with the biblical Nahor.)

Literature: Gen 11:24-26: P. Jensen, "Hittiter und Armenier," ZA 6 (1894) 70, 154.   E.G. Kraeling, "Terach," ZAW 40 (1922/1923) 153-154.   F. Bork, ZAW 47 (1929) 206-222.   C. Virolleaud, *La légende de Keret, roi Sidonien: Mission de Ras Shamra* 2 (1936).   R. Dussaud, *Les découvertes de Ras Shamra (Ugarit) et l'Ancien Testament* (1937; 1941²) 81.   W.F. Albright, "Was the Patriarch Terah a Canaanite Moon-God?," BASOR 71 (1938) 35-40.   C.H. Gordon, "TRH, TN and NKR in the Ras Shamra Tablets," JBL 57 (1938) 407-410.   P. Joüon, "Trois noms de personnages bibliques à la lumière des Textes d'Ugarit (Ras Shamra)," דנאל יששכר תרח: Bib 19 (1938) 280-285.   R. de Langhe, *Les textes de Ras Shamra-Ugarit* I, II (1945).

[11:24-26] *Terah:* E.G. Kraeling compares this name with that of the Aramaean city Til-sa-turahi north of Haran, which Shalmaneser II took in 854 (so too O. Procksch; likewise U. Cassuto, R. de Vaux). It is a Semitic name, Ass. *tarhu* or *turahu* = Ibex. Accordingly W.R. Smith explains it in terms of a totem as the name of a clan that calls itself after the Ibex. It occurs also as a personal name in Safaitic inscriptions, W.F. Albright, JPOS 1 (1920-21) 78. Against the suggestion that it may be the name of a god, cf. W.F. Albright, bibliog. above. A. Virolleaud and R. Dussaud thought that they could find the name Terah in the Keret epic. P. Joüon agrees with them. C.H. Gordon supports the contrary view and concludes: "There is no valid evidence pointing to the mention of Terah in any Ras Shamra text published so far." Likewise R. de Langhe (for all references see Lit. above).

The result of this is surprising. The three names Serug, Nahor and Terah (E.G. Kraeling includes Peleg and Reu also) are all attested as place names, and all three are in the neighborhood of Haran (so too J. Simons commenting on Arpachshad and J.C.L. Gibson, JSSt 7 [1962] 54). The occurrence of Nahur as a place name in the Mari Texts has drawn attention to these findings. What does one conclude from this?

1. The findings confirm the composite character of the genealogical series of 11:10-26. the last three names come from an originally independent group in which the personal name is identical with a place name, and these place names point to a particular region in the neighborhood of Haran in North Mesopotamia.

2. At the same time the composite character of the passage confirms it as a transition piece. The first two names, Shem and Arpachshad, obviously belong to the primeval event (9:18 J; 10:1 P; 10:22 P); the last three just as clearly belong to the history of the patriarchs inasmuch as they speak of the place from which the clan of Terah began its wandering. In between lies the Shelah-Eber-Peleg group which cannot be determined any further and which is attested in J, 10:21, 24, 25. There remains the name Reu, which cannot be assigned with certainty to any of the three groups. We can assume then that it was P himself who shaped the genealogy of 11:10-26 out of these different components so as to create a transition passage from the primeval story to the history of the patriarchs.

3. As for the last part of the series, the group Serug-Nahor-Terah, the question arises of their relationship to each other as personal names and as place names. The text certainly intends them to be personal names. They describe the family of Abraham, v. 26, and Abraham is never a place name; it is a purely personal name. The name of his father Terah is therefore a personal name too, as are also the names of his brothers Nahor and Haran. This is the case in J, vv. 28-30, and in Josh 24:2.

It would be possible to connect the personal names with the place names in that the city is named after its founder as in 4:17. But this possibility has no support here because the names Serug-Nahor-Terah belong to the transition to the history of the patriarchs, and the patriarchs as semi-nomads are not founders of cities.

Gen 24:10 hints at another possibility: Abraham's servant sets off for the city of Nahor (or the city, Nahor?). It can well be that semi-nomadic life identified places and persons because tradition there attached itself to persons rather than to place names. It is quite possible that with this as starting point there was a gradual process of identification of place names and personal names, and that this would offer an explanation of the names of the Shelah-Nahor-Peleg group. But this must remain a mere possibility; others are conceivable. Only a survey of the relationship between place names and personal names in the whole of the patriarchal history can lead to a conclusive judgment.

Literature: Gen 11:26: M.A. Beek, "Haran," BHH II, 647. J.H. Breasted, "The Earliest Occurrence of the Name of Abram," AJSL 21 (1905) 22-36. M. Berthoud, "Où fut Charan de Térach et d'Abram?," RThPh 37 (1905) 294-301. A. Vuilleumier, "Quelques réflexions au sujet de l'article de M. Berthoud," RThPh 37 (1905) 302-321. S.H. Langdon, "The Name Abraham in Babylonian," ExpT 21 (1910) 88-90. W.F. Albright, "The Names Shaddai and Abraham," JBL 54 (1933) 173-193. F.M. Bauer, *Abram, Son of Terah* (1948). I.J. Gelb, "The Early History of the West Semitic Peoples," JCS 15 (1961). C.H. Gordon, "Haran" (Place), IDB (1962) 524. L. Hicks, "Abraham," IDB (1962) 14-21. G. Sauer, "Bemerkungen zu den 1965 edierten ugaritischen Texten," ZDMG 116 (1966) 235-241.

[11:26] The genealogical list issues in three names as does the list in Gen 5 in the three sons of Noah. In the language of the genealogies this means that the vertical line of ancestors has its goal in the horizontal line of a simultaneously living group which as a group derives from these ancestors. The trio at the end of the genealogy is the basis of the interconnection or relationship of the group or the totality signified in the three names. The three sons of Noah at the end of the flood narrative signify humanity represented in its three fathers, Gen 10. In 11:26 the same number 3 signifies a totality of a completely different kind — the clan that derives from Terah (and his forefathers). It is the totality that is envisaged and it is this that colors the whole of the patriarchal history. This becomes clear at the end of the Abraham cycle in Gen 24 where Abraham's servant sues for a wife for the patriarch's son in the "city (of) Nahor." It becomes clear likewise in the middle of the Jacob-Esau cycle when Jacob flees from his brother Esau to his brother Laban (in the same place), and takes from there Leah and Rachel as wives.

This confirms that the purpose of the genealogical list in 11:10-26 is to serve as a transition to the patriarchal history. At the same time the framework is traced within which this history is to be played out.

Purpose and Thrust

11:10-26 has, within the priestly work as a whole, the important function of a transition from the primeval story to the patriarchal history. God's blessing and its effect embraces both. When the creation blessing is repeated after the flood it becomes the linchpin that clamps together on the one hand humanity as it advances chronologically, Gen 5, and geographically, Gen 10, and on the other, the clan of Abraham as it forms itself out of one branch of those blessed after the flood. One of the sons of Noah is the father of one of the three branches of the peoples of the earth. The same son is at the same time the father of a branch which represents not a group of peoples, but leads to a "tiny unity," a clan, with which God will make a covenant. The significance of this transition for P is to be judged from what an earlier Israelite tradition could say: the ancestors of Abraham mentioned in the genealogy "served other gods," Josh 24:2. By means of the genealogy in 11:10-26, P succeeds in pointing out that even Abraham's ancestors, who served other gods, lived from the power of God's blessing, God who created heaven and earth and who by creating and preserving humanity in the primeval event blessed all people.

One can understand then why 11:10-26 has no parallel in J (apart from the group Shelah-Eber-Peleg). J had no need of such a transition piece to secure theologically the passage from the primeval event to the patriarchal history. In his view the patriarchal history can follow the division of the people in both its aspects (10 and 11:1-9) without a transition. However, we can recognize a very important parallel between the views of J and P in that both of them, though in very different ways, see the continuity between the primeval story and the patriarchal history in the effectiveness of God's blessing. P, at a much later stage of theological reflection, has applied the idea of blessing to God's work at creation, to his work in the primeval event; and so he can fashion a transition for it to the patriarchal history. J introduces the idea only in the patriarchal history and, by means of it, likewise fashions, from the other side, a clamp between the primeval event and the patriarchal history in his prologue 12:1-3. This is a convincing example that there can be basic agreement in intent in different theological frameworks and systems.

The patriarchal history begins with 11:27-32 (11:27, 31f. P; 28-39 J). The exegesis of vv. 27-31 will be found at the beginning of the second volume.

The Formation and Theological Meaning of the Primeval Story

Literature

1. *Surveys (History of Research):* L. Diestel, *Geschichte des Alten Testaments in der christlichen Kirche* (1869). T.K. Cheyne, *Founders of Old Testament Criticism* (1893). H. Holzinger, *Einleitung in den Hexateuch* (1893). C.A. Simpson, *Pentateuchal Criticism* (1914; 1924[2], repr. 1948). B. Jacob, *Quellenscheidung und Exegese im Pentateuch* (1916). A. Lods, *Jean Astruc et la critique biblique au XVIIIe siècle* (1924). W. Baumgartner, "Der Kampf um das Deuteronomium," ThR 1 (1929) 7-25; "Wellhausen und der heutige Stand der alttestamentlichen Wissenschaft," ThR 2 (1930) 287-307. J. Pedersen, "Die Auffassung vom Alten Testament," ZAW 49 (1931) 161-181. P. Humbert, "Die neuere Genesisforschung," ThR 6 (1934) 147-160, 207-228. H.S. Nyberg, "Das textkritische Problem des Alten Testaments am Hoseabuch demonstriert," ZAW 52 (1934) 241-254. W. Baumgartner, "Alttestamentliche Einleitung und Literaturgeschichte," ThR 8 (1936) 179-222. J. Coppens, *Histoire critique des livres de l'Ancien Testament* (1938; 1942[2]). I. Engnell, *Traditionshistorische Einleitung zum Alten Testament* (1940). W. Baumgartner, "Die Auslegung des Alten Testaments im Streit der Gegenwart," SThU 11 (1941) 17-38 = W. Baumgartner, "Zum Alten Testament und seiner Umwelt" (1959) 179-207. U. Cassuto, *The Documentary Hypothesis and the Composition of the Pentateuch* (1942; 1961[2]). A. Bea, "Neuere Probleme und Arbeiten zur biblischen Urgeschichte," Bib 25 (1944) 70-87. C.A. Simpson, *The Early Traditions of Israel. A Critical Analysis of the Pre-Deuteronomic Narrative of the Hexateuch* (1948). O. Eissfeldt, "Die neueste Phase der Entwicklung der Pentateuch-Kritik," ThR 18 (1950). H.H. Rowley, *The Growth of the Old Testament* (1950). C. North, "Pentateuchal Criticism," H.H. Rowley (ed.) *The OT and Modern Study* (1951) 48-83. F. Hesse, "Die moderne Pentateuchforshcung," ELKZ 7 (1953) 164-167. R. de Vaux, "Reflections on the Present State of Pentateuchal Criticism" in *The Bible and the Ancient Near East* (1953; 1972) 31-47. J.A. Lewy, *The Growth of the Pentateuch. A Literary, Sociological, and Biographical Approach* (1955). M.S.Seale, "The Glosses in the Book of Genesis and the JE Theory," ExpT 67 (1955/1956) 333-335. H.J. Kraus, *Geschichte der historisch-kritischen Erforschung des Alten Testaments von der Reformation bis zur Gegenwart* (1956; 1969[2]). O. Eissfeldt, *Die Genesis der Genesis. Vom Werdegang des 1. Buches der Bibel* (1958; 1961[2]). Y. Kaufmann, *The Religion of Israel. From Its Beginnings to the Babylonian Exile* (1960). M.H. Segal, "The Composition of the Pentateuch – A Fresh Examination," ScrHie (1961) 68-114. D.N. Freedman, "Pentateuch," IDB III (1962) 711-727. H. Cazelles, "Pentateuque," DBS VII (1964; 1966[2]) 687-858. S. Mowinckel, *Erwägungen zur Pentateuchquellenfrage* (1964). Th.C. Vriezen, "Twenty Five Years of the Old Testamentic Study in the Netherlands," OTS 14 (1965). F.V. Winnett, "Re-Examining the Foundations," JBL 84 (1965) 1-19. O. Eissfeldt, "Sechs Jahrzehnte alttestamentliche Wis-

senschaft," VT.S 15 (1966) 1-13; "Erwägungen zur Pentateuchquellenfrage," OLZ 61 (1966) 213-218.   R. Rendtorff, "Literarkritik und Traditionsgeschichte," EvTh 27 (1967) 138-153.   O. Kaiser, *Introduction to the Old Testament* (1970²; 1975).   H.W. Wolff, *Bibel AT,* ThTh 7 (1970).   D.A. Knight, *The Traditions of Israel,* SBL Dissertation Series 9 (1973).

2. *Hexateuch – Pentateuch:* J.J. Astruc, *Conjectures. . . ,* (1753).   J.S. Vater, *Commentar über den Pentateuch III* (1805).   W.M.L. de Wette, *Kritik der israelitischen Geschichte I* (1807).   J.J. Stähelin, *Kritische Untersuchungen über den Pentateuch. . .* (1843).   K.H. Graf, "Die sogenannte Grundschrift des Pentateuchs," AWEAT 1 (1869) 466-477.   Th. Nöldeke, *Untersuchungen zur Kritik des Alten Testaments* (1869) 1-144.   E. Riehm, *Studien und Kritiken. Die sogenannte Grundschrift des Pentateuch* (1872).   A. Kuenen, *An Historical-Critical Inquiry into the Origin and Composition of the Hexateuch* (1886).   J. Wellhausen, *Die Composition des Hexateuch und der historischen Bücher des AT* (1889; 1963⁴).   C. Cornill, "Beiträge zur Pentateuchkritik," ZAW 11 (1891) 1-34.   B. Stade, "Beiträge zur Pentateuchkritik," ZAW 15 (1895) 157-266.   J. Dahse, *Textkritische Bedenken gegen des Ausgangspunkt der heutigen Pentateuchkritik,* ARW (1903).   J. Wellhausen, *Prolegomena to the History. . .* (1957).   B.D. Eerdmans, *Alttestamentliche Studien I-IV* (1908-1912).   H. Holzinger, "Nachprüfung von B.D. Eerdmans, Die Komposition der Genesis (Alttestamentliche Studien I)," ZAW 30 (1910) 245-258; 31 (1911) 44-68.   H.A.M. Wiener, *Essays in Pentateuchal Criticism* (1910).   J. Dahse, *Textkritische Materialien zur Hexateuchfrage* (1912).   W. Möller, *Wider den Bann der Quellenscheidung. Anleitung zu einer neuen Erfassung des Pentateuch-Problems* (1912).   R. Smend, *Die Erzählung des Hexateuch, auf ihre Quellen untersucht* (1912).   G. Hölscher, "Der Hexateuch," ThR 16 (1913) 287-293.   D. Hoffmann, *Die wichtigsten Instanzen gegen die Graf-Wellhausensche Hypothese* (1916).   O. Eissfeldt, "Die Schichten des Hexateuch als vornehmste Quelle für den Aufriss einer israelitisch-jüdischen Kulturgeschichte," KS I (1962) 33-43.   E. Naville, *La haute critique dans le Pentateuque. Réponse à M. le Professeur Humbert* (1921).   O. Eissfeldt, *Hexateuch-Synopse* (1922; 1962²).   J. Benzinger, *Beiträge zur Quellenscheidung im AT* (1924).   M. Löhr, *Untersuchungen zum Hexateuchproblem,* I BZAW 38 (1924).   W. Möller, *Die Einheit und Echtheit der fünf Bücher Mosis* (1931).   A. Bea, *Institutiones Biblicae, II: De Pentateucho* (1933²).   P. Volz-W. Rudolph, *Der Elohist als Erzähler. Ein Irrweg der Pentateuch-Kritik?* BZAW 63 (1933).   U. Cassuto, *La questione della Genesi* (1934).   G. von Rad, *The Problem of the Hexateuch and other Essays* (1938; 1966).   R.H. Pfeiffer, *Introduction to the OT* (1941); Amer. 1948²; Brit. 1953²).   I. Engnell, *Gamla Testament. En traditionshistoriske inledening, I* (1945).   A. Bea, "Il problema del Pentateuco e della storia primordiale," Civ.Cat. (1948) 116-127.   M. Noth, *A History of Pentateuchal Traditions (1948; 1966₃).*   O. Eissfeldt, *Die ältesten Traditionen Israels. Ein kritischer Bericht über C.A. Simpson's The Early Traditions of Israel,* BZAW 71 (1950).   L. Rost, "Der geschichtliche Ort der Pentateuchquellen," ZThK 53 (1956) 1-10.   F. Dornseiff, "Die Verfasser des Pentateuch," Altertum 5 (1959) 205-213.   H. Cazelles, "The Torah (Pentateuch)," in A. Robert-A. Feuillet (edd.) *Introduction to the Old Testament* (1968) 67-166.   I. Engnell, *Critical Essays on the Old Testament* (1970).

3. *Yahwist (and Elohist):* B. Luther, "Die Persönlichkeit des Jahwisten," in E. Meyer, *Die Israeliten und ihre Nachbarstämme* (1906; 1967²) 105-173.   H. Holzinger-R. Smend, "JE in den geschichtlichen Büchern des AT," ZAW 39 (1921) 181-217.   E. von Lehmann, *La pensée du Jahviste,* SM 3 (1927).   H. Hellbardt, *Der Elohist als selbständige Geschichtsquelle,* ThBl (1933);   *Der Jahwist in der biblischen Urgeschichte,* Diss. (1935).   G. Hölscher, *Geschichtsschreibung in Israel. Untersuchungen zum Jahwisten und Elohisten,* SNVAO (1952).   M.L. Henry, *Jahwist und Priesterschrift. Zwei Glaubenszeugnisse des Alten Testaments* (1960).   H.W. Wolff, "The Kerygma of the Yahwist," Interp 20 (1966) 131-158.   R. Kilian, "Der heilsgeschichtliche Aspekt in der elohistischen Geschichtstradition," ThGl 56 (1966) 369-384.

4. *The Priestly Writing:* O. Fischer, "Die Chronologie des Priesterkodex. . . ," ZAW 31 (1911) 241-255.   A. Jepsen, ZAW 47 (1929) 251-255.   G. von Rad, *Die Priesterschrift im Hexateuch, eine literarische Untersuchung,* BWANT 65 (1934).   F.X.

Kortleitner, *Quo tempore codex sacerdotalis existerit* (1935). B. Luther, "Ḳāhāl und ʿedāh als Hilfsmittel der Quellenscheidung im Priesterkodex und in der Chronik," ZAW 56 (1938) 44-63. P. Humbert, "Die literarische Zweiheit des Priester-Codex in der Genesis," ZAW 58 (1940/1941) 30-57. E. Auerbach, "Die babylonische Datierung im Pentateuch und das Alter des Priester-Codex," VT 2 (1952) 334-342. J. Hempel, "Priester-kodex," RE 22 (1954) 1943-1967. Y. Kaufmann, "Der Kalender und das Alter des Priesterkodex," VT 4 (1954) 307-313. R. Borchert, *Stil und Aufbau der priesterlichen Erzählung* (1957). A.S. Kapelrud, "The Date of the Priestly Code (P)," ASTI 3 (1964) 58-64. J.G. Vink, "The Date and Origin of the Priestly Code in the OT," OTS 16 (1969) 1-144. S.E. McEvenue, *The Narrative Style.* . . . (1971).

5. *Genesis:* J.G. Eichhorn, "Über Mosis Nachrichten. . . ," (1779; 1799²). K.D. Ilgen, *Die Urkunden.* . . (1798). F. Bleek, *De libri Geneseos origine (Ergänzungshypothese)* (1836). E. Böhmer, *Das erste Buch der Thora* (1862). E. Schrader, *Studien zur Kritik.* . . , (1863; 1921²). B.W. Bacon, *The Genesis of the Genesis, a Study of the Doc. Sources in Accordance with the Results of Critical Science Illustrating the Presence of Bibles within the Bible* (1893). W.H. Green, *The Unity of the Book of Genesis* (1895). E. Sievers, *Hebräische Genesis: Metrische Studien II* (1904). A.R. Gordon, *The Early Traditions of Genesis* (1907). J. Dahse, *Wie erklärt sich der gegenwärtige Zustand der Genesis?* (Skizze einer neuen Pentateuch-hypothese) (1913). A. von Hoonacker, "The Literary Origin. . . ," Exp 8 (1916) 259-299. E. Naville, *The Unity of Genesis* (1915). W. Eichrodt, *Die Quellen der Genesis von neuem untersucht*, BZAW 31 (1916). A. Lods, "Le rôle de la tradition orale dans la formation des récits de l'Ancien Testament," BHR 88 (1923). W. Staerk, "Zur alttestamentlichen Literarkritik. . . ," ZAW 42 (1924) 34ff. S. Mowinckel, "The Two Sources. . . ," ANVAO II (1937) 1-84. C.A. Simpson, "The Book of Genesis, Introduction and Exegesis," IB I (1952). S. Mowinckel, "Before Abraham was. . ." (The genus litterarium of Genesis 1-11)" CBQ 15 (1953) 131-140. S.R. Külling, *Zur Datierung der 'Genesis-P-Stücke', namentlich des Kapitels XVII* (1964).

Pentateuchal Research

The significance of the first eleven chapters of the Bible is that they bring God into relationship with everything that is. They are not only an introduction to the history of the people of God that begins in Gen 12, but also put it into a perspective that embraces all that exists, from the stars to the grass and the trees, from the one man whom God asks "Where are you?" to the most distant peoples of the then known world. What is presented then in Gen 1-11 is not intended primarily as a sequence of happenings that is to be continued in the sequence of events beginning in Gen 12. It is rather a series of happenings narrated one after the other, beginning with the creation of heaven and earth up to the Tower of Babel and the genealogy annexed to it, which intends to present by means of this succession the plenitude and breadth of being precisely as created being.

Exegetical method must be in accord with the universal outlook of the primeval story. The exegesis of Gen 1-11 has shown that a one-track method is inadequate. The text is so polymorphic, so many-sided and has so many layers that one must approach it accordingly. The lines of approach however can be reduced to two, each of which takes the text as handed down as its starting point. The first line leads from the present text to the first written records out of which it took shape in a gradual process of literary formation. This is the literary-critical or literary-historical method with its different stages. The direction that it takes is from the first written records as starting point to the present text as end point. The second line takes the present text as its starting point and pushes back step-by-step across the different stages of the oral tradition to the formation of the smallest units, i.e., to the individual narratives, genealogies, and so on. This is the method of form criticism and tradition history. However, the framework within which the questions are placed must be expanded in accordance with the universal outlook of the primeval story, because the motifs of the primeval event are found throughout the whole of humankind.

The conclusion of a commentary on the primeval story requires a synthesis of its formation and theological significance.

The result of the present state of Pentateuchal research is that the documentary hypothesis (I) is in need of a revision that must affect primarily the criteria for separation into sources (II). Tradition history in the pre-literary stage (III) is presented in its broad lines in the introduction to this commentary; it can now be put on a methodological basis. Tradition history in the written stage (IV) gives a picture, modified in many points, of the literary works of J and P and of R. From this comes the theological significance of the primeval story (V), the peculiarity (1) and principal features (2) of the talk about God, and finally the significance of the primeval event in the whole of the Old Testament (3).

We must now deal with a question that was left open in the Introduction, namely the written stage of the tradition of the text of Genesis. It can only be treated in the context of the question of the formation of the Pentateuch. It is not possible to discuss the problem of the Pentateuch extensively here, and there are many accounts of the history of Pentateuchal research (see Lit. above, 1. Surveys). We will only outline the present state of the question as seen by five scholars: C. North, R. de Vaux, H. Cazelles, S. Mowinckel, O. Kaiser. Comparing their conclusions, one is amazed at the agreement. They are at one that the Graf-Wellhausen hypothesis, which was the result of the research of the period to the end of the 19th century, still prevails in its essentials among the majority of scholars; i.e., that the Pentateuch (or Hexateuch or Tetrateuch) was formed by working together a number of written sources, the oldest of which is J (or a strand in J), the youngest P (e.g., C. North p. 48). Furthermore, all are agreed that both the older and the more recent challenges to the separation into sources have not succeeded. But all have definite reservations: it is no longer permissible to accept the classical theory of four sources without any restriction as was done by and large round about 1900, when it was regarded as *the* solution.

C. North (1951) reduces the present state of scholarship to two basic problems: the one is that of the historical character of the accounts in the Pentateuch, the other is the question of the value of the Pentateuch as a source for the history of religions. He agrees with J. Pedersen and I. Engnell that the Pentateuch is not a historical account in the modern sense of the word, p. 74. It is rather a history of tradition, i.e., history interpreted, which North describes as salvation history (or sacred history) and which H. Cazelles underscores even more strongly. North is here in opposition to C.A. Simpson (1948) who is of the opinion that history can be reconstructed directly from the sources of the Pentateuch, p. 75 n. 1. There is a modification here: Simpson, who gives a detailed and careful account of the history of research, still stands, methodologically, with Wellhausen who wanted to derive a chronological framework for the history of Israel directly from the separation into sources. But Wellhausen is here the heir of a century of Pentateuchal research that preceded him. K.D. Ilgen had already set the goal of achieving, by means of the dating of the sources, a "critically justified history of Israel, its civil constitution, its worship, its morality and religion, its language and culture," *Die Urkunden*. . . . (1798) XV. More recent research is opposed to this in that it does not permit direct historical conclusions; it permits only conclusions about the history of traditions which interpret historical events.

The second problem is whether a religious-historical development can be read out of the chronological sequence of the sources. Here North concedes to the Nordic critics J. Pedersen and I. Engnell that the attempt to construct a rectilinear development of the religion of Israel, as Wellhausen had done in masterful wise, must be abandoned. However, he criticizes them because they see the traditions too much "without dimensional depth" (p. 77, *flächenhaft*) and in the question of chronological succession that necessarily accompanies this, they have no convincing criteria and their judgments are arbitrary. The formation of the Pentateuch from sources or layers is still valid for a history of the development of the religion of Israel. However, the criteria must be more objective and any rigid a priori schema must be abandoned.

North asks in conclusion, what are we to say about the sources or documents. "It seems quite clear that if we bury the 'documents', we shall have to resurrect them — or something very like them," p. 77. This holds too for the present state of research. North's reason is that, even giving full weight to the importance of oral tradition (H.S. Nyberg, I. Engnell), nothing has altered. The formation of the Pentateuch is a literary process and must be judged by literary criteria. One must agree with North. No answer has yet been given to the question about the criteria for judging when the oral stage of the tradition came into existence.

R. de Vaux (1953, 1972) agrees in his summing up with the two points made by North. He agrees too that the Pentateuch is not the product of a scribe at his desk, and that consequently one must concede an essential part to oral tradition in the formation of the Pentateuch (I. Engnell; H. Gunkel established this). But like North, de Vaux insists that despite this the literary stage retains its importance. He refers to the literary traditions both inside and outside the Old Testament. In the Old Testament itself there are references to books from which information has been taken. De Vaux also maintains that a tradition-history exegesis is necessary. But he stays with the essentials of the classical source theory; the Pentateuch is the result of four great streams of tradition (J E D P) that were formed, developed and preserved in different milieux, probably at sanctuaries. However, two modifications are to be made with regard to the classical theory: the traditions have remained alive and assimilated new material; they have an extensive pre-history that must be taken into account.

H. Cazelles (1964, 1966) has given the most detailed account of Pentateuchal research in recent times and has come to grips with a great deal of literature. His view of the state of the question, 736ff., differs markedly from those of North and de Vaux. He considers that Pentateuchal research has entered a new stage because of the results of archaeological research. The Pentateuch can no longer be regarded as an isolated document. It is much more part of the life of a community or people, and this in turn must be seen in the context of the history of the peoples of the Ancient Near East with their political, social and religious developments, p. 748. One must recognize that the history of law, codices, covenant treaties, the historiography of the Ancient Near East are prerequisites for Pentateuchal research, 752-768.

Cazelles deals in detail with the Yahwistic, Elohistic, Deuteronomic and Priestly work (768-844) and returns in the closing section (855-858) to his point of departure: the texts of the Pentateuch can no longer be regarded as the product of the intellectual or literary activity of a single person. They have deep roots in the life of the people of Israel, and the life of Israel is part of the broader history of the peoples of the Ancient Near East. Literary-critical research has not thereby lost its value; rather it is extended by attention to the whole life of Israel and of its surrounding world.

The work of literary criticism however has undergone no notable alteration either in its method or its results. It is here that Cazelles' work differs decisively from that of North and de Vaux; he sees no challenge in the more recent works that attack the source theory. In the section "La théorie documentaire" (737-747) he takes as his point of departure the classical results of the separation of sources (cited according to H.H. Rowley 1950) which remain for him undisturbed. He deals with the attacks on the source theory, rejecting them each time in the usual manner.

At no stage in this section does Cazelles indicate that he thinks that the conclusion of the Nordic or Jewish scholars should give occasion for revision of the classical Pentateuchal criticism. He maintains that the great majority of studies on the Pentateuch hold to the source division and is convinced that all attacks on it have been dismissed in recent times. He mentions H. Gunkel's thesis only in passing (767, 792) and cautions against it. He does not see Gunkel's work as significant for the history of Pentateuchal research.

S. Mowinckel in his study *Erwägungen zur Pentateuchquellenfrage* (1964) is closer to North and de Vaux than Cazelles, though he differs from them in some important points. He brings into clearer focus the form-critical and traditio-historical approach to the Pentateuch begun with H. Gunkel.

After an account of the history of research, there follow detailed treatments of P, J, and E under the question: "Was there an Elohist?" He retains in its broad lines the accepted view that P and J are separate writings and grew up separately. Nevertheless he links throughout features of the traditio-historical approach with the purely historical. In his discussion of an Elohistic work he comes to the conclusion that there are not sufficient reasons for an E source parallel to J from Genesis to Numbers (112). One reason that has led him to this is the growing conviction, the result of the traditio-historical approach, that unevenness and contradictions have lost their probative power (59). Mowinckel here revokes explicitly his earlier attempt to find an E source in Gen 1-11, *The Two Sources*. . . . (1937).

Mowinckel differs from Cazelles in that he does not look for the change in the situation merely in the new knowledge that archaeological research has contributed. He sees it as well in the results and method of form-criticism, which presupposes an oral process of formation of many texts, and in the traditio-historical method. He differs from North and de Vaux in that it is precisely this new methodology, which both have indeed acknowledged but have not yet applied, that leads to an acceptance of one of the conclusions of those who contest the classical source theory, namely that there is no independent literary document E.

The most recent account of *O. Kaiser* (1969, 1972, 1975) synthesizes briefly the history of research from the beginnings to the present. He distinguishes a pre-critical, philological and critical period and under the last the old documentary hypothesis, the fragment hypothesis, the supplementary hypothesis, the new documentary hypothesis, and the "newest documentary hypothesis." Then, without speaking of a new period or a new hypothesis, he adds the form-critical and traditio-historical method which "not only presuppose the results of literary criticism, but in their turn can contribute a clarification of the literary-critical evidence" (42). Form-criticism determines the literary type of the individual narrative and its setting in life; tradition history leads "necessarily to the question of the origin of the various larger units" (42). Kaiser mentions H. Gunkel, and H. Gressmann as the pioneers of the traditio-historical method, as well as A. Alt, G. von Rad and M. Noth, but not J. Pedersen and I. Engnell.

One gains the impression that these two new tools have left literary criticism completely unscathed. There is nothing to indicate that they could compel a thorough re-examination of the literary-critical method.

In a final paragraph, "attacks upon the documentary hypothesis," p. 42, Kaiser first mentions scholars like P. Volz, W. Rudolph and S. Mowinckel who have contested an independent Elohistic source, but who remain basically with a documentary hypothesis. He then expounds I. Engnell's thesis with a brief mention of J. Pedersen. He raises the same critical objections as does North. It is surprising that Kaiser makes no reference in this paragraph to the objections of U. Cassuto, B. Jacob, Y. Kaufmann and N.H. Segal, whereas Cazelles' survey in 1964 deals with Cassuto's arguments in detail. But one cannot give an adequate account of the present state of Pentateuchal research if one does not take into account Cassuto's radical attack on all source division, which goes much further than

J. Pedersen and I. Engnell, and the discussion it aroused.

If one compares Kaiser's account of the history of scholarship with the other four, one will come to the conclusion that his and Cazelles' assumption, however differently based, that the documentary hypothesis continues unshaken and unaltered and has only been supplemented in more recent times, does not correspond accurately to the present situation. One must say rather with North and de Vaux that the documentary hypothesis has not on the whole remained unshaken, but is undergoing a process of revision and fresh critical examination. The reason why such an examination is necessary is that the key word "traditio-historical," which has won the approval of almost all scholars, has been taken up by I. Engnell as a war cry against the source hypothesis, whereas Kaiser, taking his stand with A. Alt, G. von Rad and M. Noth, understands it as a supplement that leaves the source hypothesis untouched.

But Kaiser is forward-looking in another point of his account. In §7 he deals with "the growth of the Pentateuchal narrative at its pre-literary stage," after giving attention to the method of form criticism as applied to literary types of Israelite narrative and law. He says correctly at the beginning, "we necessarily enter into an entirely hypothetical area." Nevertheless he is convinced that the study of the pre-literary stage must precede the study of the literary stage of the growth of the Pentateuch. Other scholars too have recognized this, in particular O. Eissfeldt who, though a strict adherent of the source hypothesis, adds to his account of the written stage a section "the pre-history of the narrative threads" (*Die Genesis der Genesis* pp. 41-55), where he shows that a treatment of the pre-literary types of the Pentateuch embraces much more than the mere two considered by Kaiser, "narrative" and "law."

The prior study of the pre-literary stage carries within it a consequence for the source division. There is the possibility that certain data in the text that hitherto provided arguments for a literary-critical division are to be explained from the pre-literary stage and so lose their probative value for the literary stage. (W. Staerk goes beyond H. Gunkel; he opposes and rejects Gunkel's literary-critical division into J^1 and J^2, alleging that Gunkel "remains bogged down in the dogmatic of source criticism," because the inconsistencies, e.g., in Gen 11:1-9, are due not to literary sources but to the process of tradition history.) P. Volz also goes beyond Gunkel in the same way. There must be a thorough and fresh study of the classical arguments for source division from the point of view of tradition history where an oral stage has preceded the literary stage.

The end result of the study of the more recent surveys of Pentateuchal scholarship is that the last stage of the source theory, the "newest documentary hypothesis" (O. Kaiser, p. 40), is followed by a stage in which the documentary hypothesis is in process of revision; this is where we are now. The revision is conditioned by the fact that our knowledge of the early history of Israel and its surrounding world is far more extensive than at the high point of the documentary hypothesis. It is further conditioned by the realization that the written stage of the formation of the Pentateuch was preceded by an oral stage (H. Gunkel and H. Gressmann on the one side, J. Pedersen and I. Engnell on the other), which presupposes corresponding methods of study (form-critical, traditio-historical). In between lies a transitional stage when it was thought that either the traditio-historical method was to take the place of the literary-critical (I. Engnell; in a different way U. Cassuto), or that the two methods were to be used side-by-side in such a way that the work of form-criticism and tradition-history presupposes literary criticism (H. Gunkel, M. Noth, O. Kaiser and many others).

There are some further works to be added that have not been mentioned in the preceding surveys: *F.V. Winnett* (1965) takes as his starting point that the principles of literary criticism are in need of thorough revision. In opposition to many who want to divide the Yahwistic text of Gen 1-11 into two sources, he comes to the same conclusion as

W. Staerk: "The primeval history, after the P-additions have been removed, gives the impression of being the work of a single, creative mind," p. 2. "The author derived his material from oral sources . . . these materials have fused in his mind into a new creation," p. 3. It is only with Gen 12-50 that Winnett develops his further theories about J.

M.S. Seale (1955) wants to prove the literary unity of Genesis by means of the peculiar style of the author who deliberately used explanatory and repetitive glosses throughout.

D.N. Freedman (1962) lays emphasis on the use of the two methods together; form-criticism and tradition-history have made important contributions to the study of the Pentateuch, but have not made literary criticism unnecessary. The archaeological discoveries are indispensable for Pentateuchal scholarship, especially for the historical background. (Freedman's presentation of the position and further direction of Pentateuchal studies is close to mine.)

R. Rendtorff (1967) wants to stimulate and encourage the discussion between Nordic (especially I. Engnell), and German scholarship. He shows that the purely literary-critical method that Engnell and others attacked has scarcely any representatives now in German scholarship (one could say the same with regard to U. Cassuto). He refers then to the traditio-historical suggestions already made by H. Gunkel and H. Gressmann. This was subsequently continued by G. von Rad and M. Noth. (Noth's position is rather more subtle, see below III.) As Rendtorff sees it, the difference is that the Scandinavian tradition-history fixes its attention wholly on the present text, while the German "history of traditions" aims to include the complete process of the tradition. Rendtorff has been more radical in recent years, especially as a result of his discussion with Israelite scholars. He has gone so far as to put in question the whole theory of sources (unpublished theses).

J.A. Lewy (1955) represents a new supplementary hypothesis. He wants to prove "that the Pentateuch began with one basic document . . . which was enlarged, revised, and annotated over a long period," p. 9. The "proto-Pentateuch" was composed at the time of David by Nathan for the education of Solomon, then it was revised often and edited anew. Large parts of the Pentateuch are older than Amos and Isaiah.

H.W. Wolff (1970) emphasizes, among other criteria, the theological individuality of the written sources: "Differences in arrangement . . . make possible association with a source," p. 47, particularly different ideas of God. It is only "the inner coherence of the narrative and . . . an original kerygmatic purpose" that can give proof of a continuous independent source. ("Zur Thematik der elohistischen Fragmente," EvTh 29 [1969] 60 = H.W. Wolff, *Ges. Stud. z. AT,* ThB 22, [1973²] 402-417.)

I. Toward a Revision of the Documentary Hypothesis

(The following reflections can only point the direction that Pentateuchal research will take in the future. The exegesis of Gen 1-11 in the present volume is the basis. Only what follows therefrom can really make any reasonable claim. It is not possible here to make a decision about the problem of E.)

Both defenders and contesters of the "documentary hypothesis" were under the influence of its all-determining fascination because it was *the* explanation of the Pentateuch for a long period and could only be applauded or rejected. The formation of the Pentateuch was, in the hypothesis, identical with its literary formation. In the formation of a literary work that can be traced back to an author, one knows the period and place in which it arose together with the historical situation and the cultural outlook. One can say that the science of biblical introduction grew out of this procedure. Its ancestors are the humanists who raised the question of authorship in the context of the classical literature of Greece and Rome. When several authors (J E D P and others) took the place of the one author Moses the situation was not basically altered. One should not delude oneself over this.

The meaning of the traditio-historical explanation of the Pentateuch is this: The Pentateuch is now seen to be the result of a centuries-long process of the formation of tradition instead of a scribal composition. The formation of the book is one stage among others in this process. It implies the hypothesis that the book arose from working together several originally independent documents. But because this is only one stage among others, neither acceptance nor rejection of the documentary hypothesis can explain the formation of the Pentateuch as a whole. The documentary hypothesis is no longer the key that opens the whole of the Pentateuch. The authors who gave the Pentateuch its written form differ from the classical authors in that they are as much mediators of tradition as they are authors.

The fact that an oral stage of tradition preceded the written is not enough on which to base a traditio-historical explanation. J. Wellhausen, A. Dillmann and others could say this without it having any influence on their exegetical method. They had not seen the methodological relevance of taking over older traditions. They understood the traditions as "raw material" which the author worked over and handled like the potter handles the clay. They did not see that the old traditions, e.g., the flood narrative, had a life and history of their own before the biblical author took them over, and that he had great respect for them and wanted them to live on in his work. He did not regard them as "raw material" but as the word of the fathers which he had to pass on. The stage that preceded the fixation in writing claims the same basic importance for the formation of a Pentateuchal text as does the writing stage. The crucial point is that the written version is the result of an unbroken line from its beginnings in word of mouth, through many stages of oral tradition, right up to its fixation in writing. The individual passage passes thereby through contexts that were already there before its insertion into the written whole. The traditio-historical method therefore requires an explanation that has equal regard for both the oral and the written stages of the formation of the Pentateuch.

It seems to me particularly important for the present state of scholarship that those who strongly contest the documentary hypothesis, like B. Jacob and U. Cassuto, agree in this point with its defenders. Cassuto too, just like H. Gunkel, admits that there was an older tradition of the flood story at hand to P in Gen 6-9 to which he gave the form he thought appropriate. There is broad agreement then that one has to reckon with two stages of formation in the texts of Genesis.

The result of these considerations is that the exegesis of the Pentateuch, and indeed of Genesis, has from the very outset to deal with several stages of the formation of the text. The final form of the text was fashioned according to literary principles and laws, the individual sections, in any case in part, according to those of oral tradition. Two possibilities are thereby excluded for the exegesis: first, the alternative, either the traditio-historical method (e.g., I. Engnell) or the literary-critical (e.g., H. Cazelles); exegesis must rather make use of both and, in some way or other, link them together. There is a second possibility that is excluded: one cannot add the two methods together mechanically, as it were applying first one method to the text and then the other (e.g., M. Noth). If one takes as one's point of departure that the path from the individual passage, e.g., the individual narrative, to the final literary product, Gen 1-11, is very varied and sinuous, then one must bring the two methods into relationship with each other, the one constantly supplementing and correcting the other.

II. The Criteria for Source Division

A striking facet of more recent Pentateuchal study is this: When source division was at its height (e.g., in H. Holzinger's *Einleitung in den Hexateuch,* 1893) a long catalogue of criteria was set up for assigning a text to one of the sources. This gradually became smaller and smaller until it reached zero point in U. Cassuto's study, *The Documentary Hypothesis* (1961). Some scholars to be sure, who still adhered to the classical division into sources without modification, also retained this catalogue intact; an example is H. Cazelles' great work on the Pentateuch where he took over the criteria from H.H. Rowley (1950). However, the majority of scholars who defend the source theory have been more cautious in this regard. Typical is the reserved judgment of M. Noth who held that the only criterion that carries any weight is the "fact of the multiple occurrence of the same narrative elements in different settings." De Vaux holds that the criteria of doubling and of the variation of the designations for God are as cogent as ever (1972, pp. 37-40). O. Kaiser summarizes: "The supporters of classical Pentateuchal criticism can . . . point to . . . the basic literary-critical criteria of the evidence of continuous doublets, to which differences of linguistic usage, style and *Tendenz* correspond," p. 43. What was at the beginning the "basic criterion" is omitted here: incongruities and contradictions, of which Mowinckel says that they have lost their probative power in the traditio-critical method.

Recent Pentateuchal research on the whole shows that one has to treat the classical criteria for source division with much greater caution and that without exception they have lost their certainty. The reason for this is the different approach that has been taken in the last decades. As far as I know there has been no study in recent years of the criteria for source division that asks, "How are they to be applied today?," except that of U. Cassuto. He examines the "five pillars" that support the construction of the source theory, asks if they are tenable and is finally convinced that they are now all in ruins. They are: 1. the use of the names for God, 2. the difference in style and language, 3. contradictions and different points of view, 4. doublets and repetitions, 5. the composite character of individual passages (op. cit. 14; similarly H. Cazelles following H.H. Rowley, *The Growth* . . . [1950]; here there is the additional criterion of anachronism).

Before dealing with these criteria individually, something must be said about the modification that has been introduced in the application of these criteria with the recognition of an oral pre-history of the texts.

Gunkel's thesis, "Genesis is a collection of stories" (H. Gressmann: Moses-Stories), first served as an antithesis to the hitherto existing explanation. As such it had great value which remains uncontested to the present. However, it was not able to explain the formation of the Pentateuch or of Genesis as a whole, but only a stage of the process. Genesis in the form in which it has come down to us is not a collection of stories. One cannot describe P as a "collection of stories." It all too clearly bears the stamp of the scribe. Gunkel himself sees this: "P is a genuine writer, he has erected a unified building of his own out of the building stones that have come down to him,'' §6, 5. Gunkel nowhere describes P as a collector. But J too presents a coherent and comprehensive event (W. Staerk has rightly made this objection against Gunkel, and G. von Rad has carried it further).

Gunkel's thesis was certainly suited to draw attention to the fact that the individual narratives originally had their own life, but not to explain the formation of Genesis as a whole. He did not ask the question about the consequences for the literary work and for the source division when it is recognized that the "smallest units" first had a life of their own which followed laws different from those of a written text. The questions raised by literary criticism, form-criticism and tradition-history must still be brought into a methodological relationship to each other. How little this exercise has been realized is shown, e.g., by the relationship of M. Noth's *A History of Pentateuchal Traditions* to the introduction to Gunkel's commentary on Genesis. Gunkel's new approach is that he set into relief the importance of the pre-literary history of the individual narrative. Noth has scarcely taken this up. He certainly speaks of the history of tradition, but means by it in essence the history of the "themes" (i.e., according to von Rad, the themes that shape the Pentateuch as a whole). The history of the "smallest units," on which Gunkel put all the emphasis, scarcely plays any role for him. Noth and Gunkel however agree that the work of literary criticism remains apart, untouched by the methods of form-criticism and tradition-history. Here the critical question arises: can literary-criticism go on simply as before in the face of form-criticism and tradition-history?

1. Style and Language.

One presumes that a writer has a recognizable style; not so a "collector" (H. Gunkel). The criterion of style is of a different kind for P and Deuteronomy than for J and E. With P (and Deuteronomy) the argument is clear. The parts of the Pentateuch attributed to P show a unified style that can be demonstrated by a series of stylistic characteristics. But there can be no clear argument for J (and E) if they are not works of writers in the same way as P. The essentials of the stylistic characteristics of P have long since been established. Already in 1869 Th. Nöldeke had made a study of the style of the priestly passages and had achieved a high degree of certainty in determining them. S.E. McEvenue in his work (1971) has articulated these stylistic characteristics with far greater precision and refinement for a series of P texts. Even the most radical opponents of all source division do not contest that these characteristics are there. But the task is not, as it is almost always understood, to compare the style of P with that of J (and E), but only to set out the obvious differences between J (and E) and the conciseness of P. It is only in this way that the question about style can come to a certain, clear conclusion. There is a series of texts in the Pentateuch, and in Genesis, which in their rigid conciseness of style, overall demonstrable, differ from a series of texts in which these characteristics are missing. The result is a certain and clear argument for the literary unity of this series, the P layer. As for J (and E) this argument has proved nothing more than that they do not belong to P.

If the argument from style is set within these limits, then it is not invalidated even by U. Cassuto.

The argument from language and usage is often linked with that from style (the use of different designations for God will be treated separately). The constant use of a particular word for a particular theme can under certain circumstances reveal the usage of a writer, though not always and never by itself. The difference in the use of individual words or phrases can under certain conditions be an additional argument for the division of sources, but it cannot be used solely and as something absolutely certain in itself (as by eliminating a verse). There is a further consideration. H. Gunkel has made the important discovery that many old narratives contain words that occur only, or almost only, in them, e.g., גפר in Gen 6:14. These special words that belong to the old stories themselves cannot be attributed to the language of J or P. It becomes still clearer then that the use of a particular word cannot be claimed *eo ipso* as in itself a certain criterion that it belongs to a particular source.

One must agree then with the basic assertion of P. Volz and W. Rudolph that one is not justified methodologically in separating J and E merely on the basis of linguistic usage. One must concede also to U. Cassuto that usage alone is not a reliable support for source division. Cassuto exaggerates only when he contests the possibility of differences in usage between P and the old sources. One cannot expect any certain results from a mechanical comparison of the usage in different sources. The argument of different usage can be employed together with other criteria when asking about the literary relationship, and then only with the greatest prudence. One must agree too with M.S. Seale (1955) that two same words used for the same thing must be considered apart from source division, and that at times they admit of very different explanations.

2. The Different Names for God.

From the time of J. Astruc and B. Witter the different names for God have been the main argument for source division, as shown by the still regular use of "Yahwist" and "Elohist." Even today many exegetes regard them as standard (e.g., R. de Vaux, A. Bentzen, R.H. Pfeiffer; see also O. Eissfeldt, *Intro.* . . p. 182f.; G. Fohrer, *Intro.* . . p. 146f.; A. Weiser, *Intro.* . . pp. 74ff.; O. Kaiser, *Intro.* . . p. 78f.; H.W. Wolff, *Bibel AT,*ThTh 7 [1970] 47; O. Keel-M. Küchler, *Synoptische Texte II,* p. 17f.); but many have contested its probative value (from J. Dahse and B.D. Eerdmans to U. Cassuto). That it is no longer completely convincing is clear, e.g., in M. Noth.

The starting point for doubt about the reliability of this criterion has obviously been its mechanical application; i.e., every passage before Ex 3 and 6 where "Yahweh" occurs must be attributed to the Yahwist, and where "Elohim" occurs, to E or P. In face of this mechanical application which consciously or unconsciously depends on a purely literary view of the formation of the text, those who contest any source division readily point to the exceptions where it fails (especially U. Cassuto). However, none of the attempts to explain the variation in the name for God in another way have so far led to any convincing result. The alternative as such cannot be pursued further here.

It follows from Gunkel's approach first that the criterion of the names for God must have greater significance for P than for the older levels. Then, if P is a writer in the proper sense, one who shaped his own work to the last detail, he must consider the use of the names for God to be important. Moreover P knows of a different use before and after the revelation to Moses in Ex 6:3. When therefore in Gen 1-11, Elohim is used throughout those passages which for reasons of style are attributed to P, then the argument from the use of the name for God is added to that of style. The reasoning of U. Cassuto and the still more dubious reasoning of M.H. Segal does not get around this fact. Segal thinks that Ex 6:3 is not concerned with the revelation of the name but only with its meaning. But it is difficult to conceive that the same writer who has the name of Yahweh first revealed to Moses, also uses it in Genesis. And further, one can scarcely imagine that the same writer could have said in Gen 4:26: "It was then that people began to call on the name of Yahweh," while the sentence was comprehensible and meaningful in J. The criterion of the different names for God in Gen 1-11, taken with the two passages Gen 4:26 and Ex 6:3, has retained its full force despite all opposition. The name for God is not as stringent a criterion for J as it is for P; it has long been generally recognized that in certain circumstances J deliberately uses "Elohim" (e.g., in Gen 3:1-7). It is only a mechanical application of the criterion that is excluded.

The study of the use of the names for God must first of all establish and survey the fact throughout the whole of the Pentateuch or Genesis without regard for the conclusions of source divisions (so F. Delitzsch in the Intro. to his commentary). At the same time it is indispensable to compare the different uses of the names for God in the whole of the Old Testament outside the Pentateuch (one must agree here with U. Cassuto and M.H. Segal, who have carried out the comparison in broad lines, but who have come to different conclusions). The comparison shows, among other things, that variation in the name for God is certainly possible in a literary unity. When the oracle of Balaam says, "How can I curse whom El has not cursed? How can I denounce whom Yahweh has not denounced?," Num 23:8, no one will want to assign the two halves of the verse to two authors. On the other hand the "Elohistic Psalter" shows that the change of the original name for God in the text can be due to redaction.

A further sequel to Gunkel's approach is that the use of the name for God must always be referred to and explained out of the whole unit. The following are the consequences for the primeval story in Gen 1-11: The first survey shows that the variation in the names for God does not suffice to establish a separation between literary layers. In Gen 4:17-24; 9:18-24; 10:1-32 (except v. 9); 11:10-32, there is no name for God. In 6:5-8:22 Yhwh and Elohim intermingle in such a way that this text must be excluded. Obvious units with different names for God are the following:

Gen	1:1-2:4a; 5:2-32; 9:1-17	:	*elohim*
	2:4b-3:24	:	*yhwh elohim*
	4:1-16; 6:1-4; 11:1-9	:	*yhwh*

This does not offer any certain basis for source division. However it shows clearly that the variation in the name for God is not arbitrary, nor is it conditioned by each immediate context (U. Cassuto has tried in vain to prove this). The name varies with the variation of the unit. An exception is 3:1b-5 where the use of Elohim is conditioned by the material. This means that the variation in the name for God must have something to do with the conception of the textual units as a whole. The variations are due to those who narrated or passed on or wrote the texts as unities. If then God is designated as Elohim throughout Gen 1:1-2:4a and as *yhwh elohim*, 2:4b-3:24 (the exception in 3:1b-5 is conditioned by the material), this can only be explained from the conception of those who at any given time have spoken or written the whole textual unit. But this has not yet proved the existence of two literary layers or sources in Gen 1-11. It has proved that two different voices are being heard through the two different names for God.

The question now arises of the position of the larger units in Gen 1-11 where the names for God are different. The self contained creation account 1:1-2:4a uses Elohim. The next clearly recognizable unit that uses only Elohim is 5:1-32; Elohim occurs here only in vv. 1, 2 (twice) and no more. But 5:1-32 is indisputably a unit. One is justified then in saying that the text unit 5:1-32, like 1:1-2:4a, uses Elohim. The two units form a unity in content; the blessing that the creator confers on his human creature is fulfilled in the series of generations presented in 5:1-32. This homogeneity in content is confirmed by vv. 1-2 which take up 1:27-28 almost literally, while 5:1-32 show no sign of any link with 2:4b-3:24. The language coincides with the content and the style. Because of the agreement of these three criteria, it is highly probable that Gen 1 and 5 belong together as a literary unit.

Gen 4:1-16; 6:1-4; 11:1-9 use only the name Yahweh. They are three textual units. The choice of the name for God belongs to the one who planned them as wholes. All three are narratives of crime and punishment (Intro. §3B), none of which uses the name Elohim in Gen 1-11. This demonstrates that the use of Yahweh is coterminus with the conception and the content of a group of several texts. 2:4b-3:24, which uses *yhwh elohim,* also belongs to this group.

We have seen so far that (1) the name for God varies with the textual units, and (b) homogeneous groups of texts differ from each other in the different names they use for God. The block 6:5-8:22 does not conform to this. The names *yhwh* and *elohim* apparently vary at will. This would mean, following the principles used hitherto, that the criterion of different names for God fails utterly. However, it is striking that the conclusion of the flood narrative in 9:1-17 uses Elohim without exception. But this fact alone is not sufficient for a division into sources in 6-9. The flood narrative is one of the cases where a single criterion is not enough. But if it can be established that there is a continuous doubling throughout 6:5-8:22, i.e., two complete narratives side-by-side, and if the differences in the numbers used in various places confirm the juxtaposition, then what was said about the variation of the name for God in complete units holds also for 6:5-9:17. I have demonstrated in the commentary that there are two narratives here that have been worked into one in masterly fashion. It has been shown above that 1:1-2:4a and 5:1-32 are homogeneous in content; the same can be demonstrated for 9:1-17 and 1:1-2:4a. The blessing conferred by God on his creatures in 1:28 is repeated almost word for word in 9:1, and the statement that a human being is created in the image of God in 1:26 recurrs in both 5:1-2 and 9:1-6. Both are mentioned in Gen 1-11 only in textual units that form a stylistic unity and use only Elohim for the name of God

One must grant to those who contest the source theory that the variation in the name for God, taken in itself and used mechanically, cannot demonstrate difference in authorship. The variation is significant for determining different sources or layers only when it is referred to textual units. It points to those who conceived these units. It is with them that the criterion is mainly concerned in Gen 1-11. Consequently it stands in immediate relationship to differences in style and content that have to do with the object of the unit. We have dealt only with texts in Gen 1-11 where the criterion can be clearly applied. Let it be emphasized that only certain of the texts in Gen 1-11 can be assigned to different sources or layers on the basis of this criterion.

3. The Criterion of Contradictions and Discrepancies.

One must use this criterion with particular caution. One can say from the beginning that it can no longer be applied as an absolute criterion (so S. Mowinckel), that it has been proved untenable in very many cases (P. Volz, W. Rudolph, B. Jacob, U. Cassuto, M.H. Segal), and that it has meaning only in relation to other criteria.

Classical literary criticism used it recklessly and never tired of discovering new incongruities or contradictions so as to postulate a new source. One can speak here of a false trail that Pentateuchal criticism took which relied on a purely literary formation of Genesis. One must agree very much with the critics of source division in this case.

From A.B. Witter and J.J. Astruç up to O. Eissfeldt *(Die Genesis der Genesis)* scholars took as their starting point defects that they noticed: disruptive unevenness, "repetitions, contradictions, breaks and sutures" (O. Eissfeldt 4). What was disrupted was a "smooth narrative flow," and it was just this that source criticism sought to restore by dividing into sources or layers. This smooth narrative flow was presumed for the whole Pentateuch, and of course for Genesis. It was held that Gen 1-50 was a continuous narrative. One must ask of this approach: When defects and disruptions were observed in the context, should not that have raised the question whether Gen 1-50 was really a coherent narrative? This notion, consciously or unconsciously, presupposed an author who told a continuous story from Gen 1 to Gen 50. But neither Gen 1-50 nor Gen 1-11 and Gen 12-50 are internally coherent narratives; they are another genre.

The problems of this approach, which a scholarship that relies solely on literary criticism has not overcome even today, appear where it applies the same criteria to the whole complex Gen 1-11 as to an individual narrative, like Gen 11:1-9. Captivated by the notion of an author, it was not seen that whereas Gen 11:1-9 was a narrative and to be judged as such, Gen 1-11 could not be described and judged as a narrative in the same way. It was only with the traditio-historical approach that it gradually became clear that an individual narrative and a composition like Gen 1-11 are two entities each of its own kind and must be judged accordingly.

When it is recognized that J is neither a writer who composes his own coherent story, nor a mere collector who gathers stories and puts them in order, but that his work includes both collecting and his own contribution, then the question of the setting and the function of the individual text in the composition takes priority. The succession of individual narratives in 2-11 (J) was till then widely regarded as a mere chronological succession. Conclusions were then drawn from the standpoint of a smoother self-contained time sequence to the incongruities in the present sequence. And so another question now arises instead: What is the purpose of the composition, which can have had a quite different point of view from that of chronological sequence? The exegesis has shown that the relationship of the creation narrative to the flood narrative is not primarily that of chronological succession but of complementarity. The argument had been advanced early that 4:17-26 (J) could not possibly belong to the same source as Gen 6-8 (J), because the reason behind it would lose all meaning if all perished in the flood. The argument collapses when it is recognized that 4:17-26 arose independently of Gen 6-8 and was not taken up by J under the aspect of chronological succession. There collapses too the main foothold for dividing J into two literary streams within Gen 1-11 (K. Budde, J. Wellhausen, H. Gunkel, C.A. Simpson, R. Smend, W. Eichrodt, O. Eissfeldt, R.H. Pfeiffer, G. Fohrer; contrary, in particular, W. Staerk). All other arguments that aim at confirming such a division of sources within J are likewise untenable, as, e.g., H. Gunkel's analysis of 11:1-9 into two literary variants.

Exegetes (F. Delitzsch and others) have for a long time read into the series of crime and punishment narratives in Gen 2-11 (J) an intensification of sin. This carried with it the tacit presupposition that the purpose was primarily the chronological succession of the narratives. This "mounting avalanche of sins" collapses if J's intention was to present the main types of transgression. It is important for the history of scholarship that S. Mowinckel, who looked for a literary layer E together with J in Gen 1-11, later expressly renounced this attempt.

There are inconsistencies everywhere in the individual units in Genesis. They belong to the nature of the text. An example is the detail about the year of birth of Arpachshad "two years after the flood" in P 11:10, which does not agree with the information given in the preceding P passage (see Comm.). The only intelligible explanation is traditio-historical. The inconsistency is to be traced back to different traditions that P has worked together.

On the other hand such inconsistencies or contradictions in other situations can also be signs of different literary layers, always of course together with other criteria. This is the case with the numbers in the two flood narratives of J and P. The different numbers of animals that went into the ark, and the dates of the flood, can only belong to two different narratives. One has only to read the very contrived explanation by B. Jacob, E. Nielsen or U. Cassuto to confirm that there are two literary strands to the flood narrative.

4. The Criterion of Doublets and Repetitions.

Following the many objections of B. Jacob, E. Nielsen, U. Cassuto, M.H. Segal and others, this criterion too must be determined more exactly. It is no longer permissible to use it absolutely, i.e., one cannot conclude to two literary sources from the mere occurrence of doublets.

The question of doublets in Genesis has entered a new stage with the traditio-historical method. It has shown with certainty in a number of places that the final literary shape of the text reveals that there were several narratives at hand to the author who worked them together. This is the case in Gen 1 where an "action-account" and a "word-account" have been established. It is also the case in Gen 2-3 where the author has woven a story about the tree of life with one about the "tree in the middle of the garden." It is so too with the flood narrative which comprises not only two literary patterns, but reveals several more ancient ones in the background.

A new situation has arisen over against the method of literary-critical research; variants of one and the same story are not exceptions but the rule. Most, if not all, stories in Genesis existed in several, often many, variants before their written redaction. But one must also admit that there were very different possibilities of dealing with them open to the one who gave them written form, be he J or P. One cannot in principle exclude that variants may be passed on juxtaposed as well as woven together into one. U. Cassuto is right when he refers to Livy and Dante who constantly assumed several variants of the same story into their work. One must of course take into consideration the different levels of cultural development; nevertheless one cannot exclude *a priori* that J and P have taken several variants of the same story into their work. One cannot therefore agree with M. Noth when he regards the doublets an absolute criterion for source division.

The doublets too can only be used as a criterion for source division in the context of and in relation to other criteria. This should be clear from Gen 1-3.

Source criticism distinguished two creation accounts from the very beginning; J. Wellhausen separated the older J, Gen 2 from the later P, 1:1-2:4a. Gen 1 and Gen 2 were generally regarded as doublets and as such referred to different sources. It has been shown in the Commentary that this is not so. Once again it is the traditio-historical approach that corrects the literary-critical (cf. Comm. 1:1-2:4a, literary form). Gen 1 is a narrative of the creation of the world, a cosmogony, which has resumed an account of the creation of human beings. Gen 2 on the contrary is a narrative of the creation of humanity. Both belong to separate streams of tradition. It can be demonstrated that 1:26-30 (Comm. ad loc.) was originally independent and was later joined to the creation of the world by P. Consequently, and in opposition to the common opinion, it is not Gen 1 but Gen 1:26-30 that is the parallel to 2:4b-24. The creation of human beings in 1:26-30 has become part of the creation of the world, while in 2:4b-24 it is an independent narrative; there are here two different stages of the tradition of talk about the creation.

This is confirmed by the same situation in Mesopotamia. The Sumerian myths had independent stories of the creation of humans. The later Akkadian epic Enuma Elish combines the creation of the world and the creation of humans as does P. The matter is therefore much more complicated than hitherto imagined. The doublets go back not to the written, but to the oral stage. In the oral pre-history however the situation is different, as already shown. If 1:26-30 is a doublet of Gen 2 in the strict sense, then theoretically the creation of the world in Gen 1 and the creation of humans in Gen 2 could belong to the same literary layer. The real doublet, 1:26-30 and Gen 2, alone would not suffice for a division into sources. It has weight only together with the other criteria. In Gen 6-9 on the other hand one can conclude with certainty to two sources from the way in which two complete, or almost complete, flood stories are worked together.

The doublets or doublings within a self-contained text are a quite different case. They must be carefully distinguished from the doubling of two or more complete stories and judged differently.

One of the best known of these doublets is that of the trees in the garden of Eden. The explanation is that both trees belonged originally to two different narratives, and that J wove the narrative of the tree of life with his own of the "tree in the middle of the garden." This is to reject a twofold literary strand that many exegetes have derived from this doubling (e.g., J. Begrich). The same holds for 11:2-9 (cf. Comm. ad loc.). The conclusion therefore is the following: doublings within a self-contained text insofar as they are confined to a single part of the text and do not with other doublings give a clearly recognizable continuous event (as in 6-9), are not a sufficient argument for literary division.

Finally, mention must be made of a third kind of doubling that has nothing to do with the two preceding: stylistic repetition within a narrative. Repetition has long been recognized as a particularly important and frequent device of the priestly style. Reference should be made to S.E. McEvenue who has made a careful study of it. However, one must not conclude that the older sources could not have used this stylistic device and that the repetitions found there must be a sign of different sources. It is much more likely that here too repetition was deliberate. Repetition as such can never be a sign of different sources.

5. *Theological Differences and Varieties of Viewpoint.*

This has been hitherto a particularly weighty argument for source division. It was thought that the most important difference between J and P was that they have a very different theology and world view. A decisive argument for the existence of an independent source E in Genesis was thought to be the way in which the revelation of God diverged from J. But this argument too can no longer lay claim to absolute validity. Once we recognize the original independence of the individual units and the independent paths of tradition that they followed before being inserted into the written work, we can use this argument only together with others and with the greatest discretion.

The exegesis of Gen 1 has shown that P has worked over an older creation account. One can certainly still speak of a theology of P, but one must proceed with great caution and reservation. One cannot allege every sentence that occurs in the literary work of P as a crown witness for a theology peculiar to P alone. All Old Testament writers, be they J, P, the author of the succession narrative, the Deuteronomist or the Chronicler, are theologians in a basically different way from the theologians of the 19th and 20th centuries. The decisive difference is that none of them ever presumes to be a "creator" of his own theology. All of them, without exception, are first and foremost mediators of tradition. They propose what their ancestors have said. However substantial and individual an impression they have given to what came down to them, they are never mere givers, but always at the same time receivers. Consequently we cannot fit all these writers into a theology of their own as clearly as we might like.

The greatest caution is required with the older layers. It has always been taken as self-evident that the theologian J had the idea that God formed human beings out of clay or earth with his hands. One was quick then to speak of J's anthropomorphic idea of God. But it is extremely unlikely that this was J's own idea. On the contrary it is certain that he took it over. At that time and still hundreds of years later it was a well-minted and widespread idea, and one can no longer say that it is characteristic of the theologian J. We are in need of a thorough reorientation here. With every single theological, ideological, or ethical trait we must put the question, "Is this characteristic of the theologian J or rather of the tradition at hand to him?" It follows then that only those traits that can be clearly identified right throughout the whole work of a writer can be characterized as peculiar to him (so too H.W. Wolff, above), and that from the outset one has to reckon with a number of traits that do not quite fit into this picture. One must be particularly cautious about assigning passages to another source by means of this criterion.

III. Tradition History in the Pre-Literary Stage

The examination of the criteria for source division has shown that a whole series of phenomena, which one hitherto ascribed to the literary stage, go back into the history of the text before it was fixed in writing in the literary work. So the question arises of the tradition history in the pre-literary stage. H. Gunkel was the first to carry through the methodological distinction between these two stages in the introduction to his commentary on Genesis, §4, "History or Tradition of the Stories of Genesis in Oral Tradition." This was crucial to the new approach over against the purely literary-critical method. Gunkel demonstrated in his introductory paragraph that the object of the oral stage of tradition was not the literary work and its literary components, but the individual story. In this he differs from the subsequent conceptions of the formation of Genesis of O. Eissfeldt and M. Noth. Eissfeldt to be sure recognizes a "pre-history of the narrative threads" (*Die Genesis der Genesis* 41-56), but in practice presents the "material at hand" as pieces merely to be added together. He knows nothing of a tradition history of the individual stories. For him they have no life of their own but enter into the history of the tradition only when they become a constitutive part of a written work.

Noth's relationship to Gunkel's new approach is more complicated. At the beginning of his work he attributes great importance to the oral stage of tradition and follows Gunkel. But his attention is directed, as appears later, not to the individual stories but to the great themes of the tradition that were handed down in the cult before the literary elaboration. He is as little interested as Eissfeldt in the individual life of the narratives, in their types, or in their individual histories before they were inserted into the written work. Noth's conception of the growth of Genesis is much closer to Wellhausen's than to Gunkel's and is practically unaffected by the introduction to Gunkel's commentary. Some scholars expressly reject Gunkel's new approach, e.g., R. Smend, W. Eichrodt, H. Cazelles.

A careful examination of the individual steps that Gunkel takes in this paragraph reveals the first traces of an outline of the tradition history in the pre-literary stage; but they still remain tentative and vague. Gunkel starts by distinguishing between the oral and the written stage of the tradition. "When the stories were put into writing, they were already very old and had a long history behind them. By the very nature of the process the origin of the story recedes steadily from the gaze of the scholar and goes back into primeval time." Gunkel goes here to the heart of the matter. The student of a text that has a purely written origin can give all his attention to the time, place and circumstances of the process of formation, i.e., he can approach the problem with the best criteria that contemporary scholarship can put at his disposal. But in the case of a text that has been formed in oral tradition all this is missing. A fixed point of formation "recedes steadily from the gaze of the scholar." The scholar has to do not with a point of origin but with a line, the path of the tradition. There is a fixed point here too; however it is not the beginning but the end: the fixation in writing. What is the starting point in literary-critical study is the end point in the study of the pre-literary stage.

We can be certain therefore of the *first step*. The first question to be put arises from the end point, the fixation in writing. Did the texts that are united in the written corpus follow a common path of tradition, or did different parts follow different paths? Gunkel had also put this question; but it is not clear that he considers it the decisive question from which one must begin and on which all further procedure depends. The problem has long since been solved for the Pentateuch. The texts that begin with Exodus have a history separate from the Genesis texts. We can be equally certain of the answer for the text of Genesis 1-50: chs. 1-11 have a history separate from chs. 12-50 (the Masoretes and the Midrash already understood Gen 1-11 and 12-50 as two books, cf. L. Blau, *Studien zum Althebräischen Buchwesen und zur biblischen Literaturgeschichte*, 1902). This is the first important gain for the history of the oral tradition stage. If the primeval story and the patriarchal history have each gone their different ways before they were fixed in writing, then there was at this stage no "Genesis." There were two streams of tradition, each absolutely independent. The course of each must be studied separately (so too J. Pedersen and I. Engnell).

One must go back likewise beyond the first parting of the ways of the traditions of 1-11 and 12-50. Can one distinguish within these two great complexes further groups of texts that have been handed down each in its own particular way? It is generally acknowledged that in 12-50, the Joseph narrative, 37-50, represents an independent tradition that has a completely different character than 12-36. Moreover it is quite obvious that Gen 12-25 (Abraham) and Gen 25-36 (Jacob-Esau) has each had its own pre-history. On the other hand it is not clear that this is the case in Gen 1-11, namely that there are particular groups of traditions. The problem here must obviously be approached in a different way.

In the *second step* one must prescind from the sequence of the texts in the written form and ask about the history of each individual textual unit. In this way the form-critical question is integrated into the traditio-historical proceeding from a textual unit as belonging to a group of similar texts (genre). It is to be noted here that the form-critical method cannot be applied in the same way to prose texts as to psalms, prophetic utterances or wisdom sayings. With prose texts one must rather develop a methodology out of the nature of the theme. I have tried to do this in "Arten der Erzählung in der Genesis," ThB 24 (1964) 9-91.

(a) Considering the textual data as a whole, one must distinguish between those individual texts that belong to the written stage and those that precede it. In Gen 12-50 one must distinguish from the narratives proper texts which, formulated as speeches by God, are constructions of the writer, as Gen 12:1-3, or texts which (also formulated as speeches by God) have obviously been added later to an already existing narrative, as Gen 22:15-18; many of the promises are like this (cf. J. Hoftijzer, C. Westermann).

(b) When it is no longer possible to distinguish clearly between the oral and written formation of individual texts, the question turns to the textual units and asks if they reveal anything about the way they have been handed down before they were inserted into the written work. When the question is put in this way it quickly becomes obvious that the course of such a tradition reveals itself more clearly if a homogeneous group of texts are taken together. In Gen 1-11 there is an immediate distinction between narrative and numerative texts.

The genealogies appear as an independent literary form whose history and original function (setting in life) remain to be shown. They are a standard example of the way in which tradition history works because their insertion into the literary stage furnishes information about the preceding oral stage. The differences between the genealogies of J and P show that those taken up into J are closer to their original form and function, while those taken up into P show signs of considerable literary adaptation to the form and thrust of the whole priestly work. In order to elaborate the history of these genealogies, they must be seen in relationship to those in the rest of the Old Testament. One sees then, among other things, that the genealogies in the patriarchal history are, from the point of view of tradition history, older than those in the primeval story; they originate in the community life of the clan and their function is to pass on its "history" in a succession of ancestors. The scope of the question must be broadened so as to prove this with certainty; there must be a study of the genealogies among Israel's neighbors and predecessors. This belongs to the third step.

The narrative texts of Gen 1-11, like those of Gen 12-50, reveal particular groups that point to different paths of tradition. The methodological term "parallel" presupposes as normal that one text is parallel to another. It is normal in oral tradition that a narrative is handed down in a number of variants (e.g., Gen 1-3). In Gen 1-11 the one group is that of the creation narratives (to which the flood narrative is close), the other is that of the narratives of crime and punishment. Both have obvious connections with each other, but each is to be considered in itself. One can conclude from the differences between 1:1-2:4a (P) and 2-3 that, in the oral stage of tradition, each followed a particular path, that of the creation of the world and that of the creation of human beings. Here too the scope of the question must be broadened to prove the thesis with greater certainty.

The *third step* is to broaden the scope of the question. It is a necessary result of the abundance of parallels from the history of religions, particularly to the texts of Gen 1-11, but not only this. Archaeological discoveries have called for a thorough revision of our view of partiarchal stories (A. Alt, W.F. Albright, R. de Vaux and others). But while extending the scope of the question beyond the borders of Israel and the books of the Old Testament it is indispensable to examine the methodology. However, it is not a matter of another method, that of the school of the history of religions. It is much more a matter of broadening the scope of the question. It is not the methodology that requires this, but the object under consideration; i.e., the fact that there are creation and flood stories, genealogies and collections of family laws, both outside Israel and among its predecessors that offer a comparison.

Neither is it a matter of broadening the scope of the question so that it can be related directly to the method of literary criticism, as do H. Cazelles and a number of other scholars. On the contrary the non-Israelite texts cannot be compared in a two-dimensional way with those of the Old Testament; they must be seen each in the context of its own tradition. A comparison is only profitable when it takes as its starting point the principles of tradition history indicated here (cf. C. Westermann, "Sinn und Grenze religionsgeschichtlicher Parallelen im AT," ThLZ 90 [1965] 489-496). Such a comparison cannot stop for example with the question: Is the biblical flood narrative dependent on the Babylonian or vice versa? The comparison must take into account the tradition history on both sides, both within the Bible and outside it. One comes then from a point by point comparison to a perspective that must view the extra-biblical comparative text in its own context so as to be able to use it as a comparison with the biblical context. For example, the creation of the world through the divine word occurs in both P and in the theology of Memphis (Intro. §3, A, III the types of creation, 4). The significance of the comparison in the history of accounts of creation is that in both cases creation through the word is a late stage that interprets anew or corrects the older accounts.

The consequence of seeing the extra-Israelite parallels in the context of their own tradition history is that there are texts in the high cultures of the near east that show characteristics that are not to be explained from the mythical-polytheistic thought pattern of these cultures, but have been taken over from a pre-mythical way of thinking. Consequently the explanation usually alleged, that the Old Testament has demythologized the mythological notions of the surrounding world, is no longer sufficient of itself. Demythologizing certainly retains its importance, e.g., in the creation of the heavenly bodies; but it is no longer to the point to say that all texts from Israel's surrounding world are exclusively mythological. We have rather to deal with a pre-history of biblical texts that have a mythical and pre-mythical stage.

This methodological consideration coincides with the fact that whole primeval motifs reach beyond the high cultures of the near east to a pre-history and so to the early cultures. There are cases too where there are parallels only in the early cultures, e.g., the narrative of the tower in Gen 11:1-9. The explanation of this complicated text can be advanced substantially by a comparison with parallels from the early cultures. H. Gunkel foresaw this development in his Introduction, §3, 2a.

We have here a very obvious difference from the purely literary-critical method. Literary authorship requires unconditionally a demonstrable literary-critical path from the "original" to the copies or versions or variants. It is not possible to demonstrate this step-by-step when comparing Old Testament texts with parallels from the early cultures. The fact, e.g., that stories about the building of a tower or about a flood occur in early cultures, far apart and with no relationship to each other, has, in the present state of scholarship, not yet been fully explained. However, this much may be said: the narratives of the primeval event in Gen 1-11 express a self-understanding of human beings in their world in early times that goes back beyond the differentiation of cultures and so shows striking common characteristics.

The method of tradition history starts from the end point, i.e., from the insertion of the old narratives into the written works (J and P). From there it inquires about the particular paths along which the individual blocks were handed down. The conclusion for Gen 1-11 is that the writers of J and P took over texts that link Israel's understanding of the person and the world with that of humanity both in the high cultures and in the early cultures. This common heritage that Israel takes over from its pre-history is joined to specifically Israelite traditions by the written works of J and P. It is only when equal importance is given to both, to the taking over of the heritage and to the new shape that it takes in the specifically Israelite context, that we can understand what these texts want to say. It is obvious that the written stage of tradition too takes on new aspects from this pre-history; the work of J and P must be seen against the background of what has preceded them.

IV. Tradition History in the Literary Stage: J and P

The Yahwistic and the Priestly Work. Preliminary note. It is not possible here to take account of these two works as wholes. Our attention will be restricted essentially to J and P in the primeval story, though this single part of the work can only be understood and qualified from the whole. We must take the risk of this fragmentary survey, in such wise that an overall presentation that takes its stand thereon can be corrected and rendered more exact by the individual parts.

The most important aspect of the traditio-historical approach for J and P is that what is characteristic of both cannot be drawn simply from those texts that are attributed to each. It is necessary first of all to set in relief the relationship of J and P to the traditions that were at hand to them; their setting in life in the course of tradition must be studied. What is characteristic of J and P lies as much in what they receive as in what they give. It is important to see how far they have impressed themselves independently on each individual text, and how far they are receivers.

The thrust of tradition history is not to cut up a unity into its constitutive parts, but to study a unity, a whole, the path of tradition that it followed from the origin of the individual part to the final form of the whole. Its purpose is not to analyze but to find contexts. To distinguish between J and P here serves to make two steps or stages along the path of the tradition clearer than otherwise would be possible. At the end it will be seen that the work of the redactor in putting J and P together acquires its own independent significance, and that the theological meaning of this synthesis only reveals itself if it is recognized that R is putting together in his own way two independent stages of tradition and thereby presenting a third stage.

1. The Yahwist in Genesis 1-11

(a) *References to the Work as a Whole:* Gen 2-11 contain no references to the formation of the work or its author, with one exception, 4:17-26, where the obvious interest in the cultural achievements points to the era of David and Solomon; this has disappeared completely in P. If J intends to show that the foundations of the present civilization were laid in primeval time and stand in the context of the creation of human beings, then this favors the era of David and Solomon where such interest is attested; likewise the international breadth of cultural creativity which corresponds to the origin and growth in primeval time.

The primeval story is a constitutive part of a complete work that stretches from the beginning of the history of Israel as a settled people in Palestine back to the creation, to the beginning of humankind. The motives that directed this conception can only be gathered from the complete work. J had predecessors in Mesopotamia (the Atrahasis epic) who prefaced primeval event to historical event as well as synthesizing the main motifs of the primeval event. The Yahwistic work is the first of such breadth in Israel. In contrast to the Mesopotamian conception, it is the first, as far as we know, in the history of the world to bring together a historical whole that compasses several quite different epochs. The primeval story does not move immediately into political history (the kingship) as do the Mesopotamian works, but is separated from it by two epochs: the patriarchal period (Gen 12-50), and the period of wandering groups, gradually consolidating themselves (Exodus to settlement in the land), and which gave themselves a political shape only after settlement in the land.

This conception, which corresponds well to our modern understanding of history, is what characterizes the Yahwistic work. Such a broad view, surveying extensive and different epochs, is only possible from the era of David and Solomon on. It is still most likely that there is reflected here a gradual awareness of belonging to the community of nations such as they were at this epoch. Israel knows that it is one of the "families of the earth," Gen 12:3, a part of humankind. The historical work of the Yahwist presents this membership of the race by showing the way from the beginning of humankind, through the patriarchal period, to the settlement in the land destined for Israel. What is peculiar to J's plan is that membership of the human race from the beginning is not such as to lead directly to an actualization of the primeval event in cult; the medium by which it is related to the present is history. The primeval myths have been detached from their original setting in life and become part of a historical work divided into epochs (G. von Rad in particular has pointed this out).

It is precisely because of this relationship of the primeval event to history that there are continual echoes of individual motifs therefrom in later parts of the Yahwistic work: the many-sided phenomenon of human community, the puzzle of human transgression, language in the fullness of its potential, the relationship of humans to the animals and so on.

(b) *The Composition of Gen 2-11 in J:* Gen 1-11 in both J and P consists of narrative and numerative texts (Intro. §3); the numerative texts prevail in P, the narrative in J. The genealogies are traced from Adam to Abraham and make it possible to arrange the primeval texts in a chronological order that is continued in the succession of generations of the patriarchs. J and P coincide in structure: creation-genealogy-flood-genealogy. In addition the narratives of crime and punishment are special to J, three before and two after the flood narrative which forms the center piece in both P and J. It is this group of narratives that makes up the peculiar contribution of the Yahwistic primeval story. They reveal a deliberate arrangement on J's part. By means of a number of narratives of the same type J wants to show how multiform is human transgression. In one series, Gen 3; 4; 9, the individual is the transgressor, in the other, 6:11, it is a plurality. In the first, Gen 3 and 4 are deliberately related to each other by the object of the transgression: against God (3), against a brother (4). There are parallels too between 2:18-24 and 6:1-4, between 6:1-4 and 11:1-9.

The work of J underwent subsequent additions and insertions, as 10:8-12 shows; but this can only be demonstrated from the work as a whole.

(c) *The Textual Units in Gen 2-11: The Enumeration*. The genealogies and a piece of information, 2:10-14, inserted into the creation story, belong to the numerative texts in 2-11 (J). The genealogies of J exhibit a great variety and are close to narrative; they contain many elaborations. Nevertheless they remain close to the early form in the patriarchal stories, and differ notably from the later systematic and abstract form of P.

The Narrative: Narrative predominates in 2-11 (J). But J is not the source of any of them. They all have a long history behind them, and this must be borne in mind when judging the Yahwistic work. We can no longer simply identify style, vocabulary, motifs and intention with those of the writer and author J; but we certainly encounter the work of J where he is recognizable as the one who shapes, links and fashions into a whole the narratives that have come down to him. It is precisely here that the most notable difference to P appears — the tendency of J is to preserve, that of P to reshape. This can be seen inasmuch as J, while shaping and collecting, remains a narrator. All texts that are not numerative are really narrative, while in P the two narrative texts of Gen 1 and 6-9 are not pure narratives. This fact shows that J is very close to the tradition and method of narrative, and that it was still alive at his time. In addition, there are plenty of etiological motifs in J, while they are no longer there in P.

(d) *The work of J on the traditions at hand to him:* In the narrative of the primeval event J takes over and passes on texts which did not originate from Israel's meeting with Yahweh who saved it out of Egypt, but which circulated before and beyond Israel. Their universal extension corresponds to their universal object. It is J's intention to link what is common to the history of humankind with the particular traditions of the people of Israel.

The starting point is that there were plenty of such narratives about the primeval event and that a great assortment of them were at hand to J. The Yahwist in general has to choose from a number of variants which he forms into a whole. He can do this in a variety of ways. The narrative at hand to him remains unaltered in its main lines. J is saying here that his contribution consists in small additions, omissions and formulations, as in Gen 6-9 (J). He can shape a coherent, self-contained narrative out of two independent narratives (2:4b-3:24). He can allow a variant to speak within a narrative by resuming one of its disparate motifs and linking it with the narrative he has selected, so again in 2:4b-3:24; 11:1-9, and often with minor motifs. It is here that J's tendency to preserve is in evidence.

One must distinguish among the narratives taken up into Gen 1-11 those that have a recognizable pre-history in the high cultures of the Near East and those that have not. It is striking that the former is the case with the two narratives assumed by P, while the latter is the case with what is special to J, i.e., with the narratives of crime and punishment; there are parallels to these only in primitive cultures. This special material in Gen 1-11 presupposes a pre-history that is relatively unaffected by the surrounding high cultures. It must be assumed that here J is in contact with an oral tradition whose origin and course can no longer be traced. The different pre-history (Gen 6-9, Mesopotamian; 6:1-4 probably Canaanite; the others unknown) points to a long and complicated process. J is dealing with narratives that must have already gone through several stages of tradition. One can distinguish in the flood story a pre-mythical and a mythical stage, in 6:1-4 a myth, an etiological narrative and the form given it by J.

What J has done with the narratives in detail: in Gen 2:4b-3:24 J has united two originally independent narratives into one and thereby linked with one another the two motifs of the creation of human beings and of human limitation. If the goal of the narrative of the creation of humans that J chose is the community of man and woman, then J reveals that his intention is to present the primeval event of crime and punishment as one that affects humankind in this very community. J's way of working reveals itself in the subtle and carefully worked out technique with which he has put the two narratives together. Moreover he has inserted additions in Gen 3 that bring some particular aspects of human existence into partnership with the basic event. The original independence of the motif of the tree of life is still to be proved. As in 11:1-9 he inserts the variants by adding them to the conclusion. But this elaboration of the narrative ending is anchored in the narrative itself by way of preparation. Exactly the same technique in Gen 3; 4; 11 is of itself a sufficiently weighty argument for the same hand in each case.

4:2-16 reveals J's work above all in that the structure of the second part follows closely that of 3:14-19. J wants to underscore the parallel here: the crime against the brother is put with that against God, the relationship of brother to brother with that of man and woman. The deliberate parallel is particularly obvious in the question addressed to Adam and to Cain. In the pronouncement of punishment, 4:11, a variant is worked over in 11b and 12a. In 6:1-4 J is able to present something typically human by mythical allusion. He is speaking about humankind in Gen 2-11, and so he can say that even the mythical has its significance for the history of humankind. But Yahweh sets a limit to people's attempt to outbid themselves, and this is presented by a mythical event. The relationship of Gen 6:1-4 to 11:1-9 is clear, and also its reference back to 3:5. What J wants to say to his own generation occurs again later in the accusations of the prophets, especially in Is 14. J is bound to the material at hand in Gen 6-9, and almost the same arrangement is apparent in J and P. Nevertheless J has given expression to his own view of the flood in a number of details. In the introductory part 6:5-8 he has elaborated the ancient core, vv. 5a, 6a, by an addition, vv. 6, 7c, and an underlining v. 5b. By means of the words: "God was sorry. . . ." he links the introduction to the flood story with the creation of humans. The conclusion of the flood narrative, 8:20-22, refers back to the beginning, 6:5-8. The incomprehensible, that God will destroy his own creation, finds a resolution in God's new decision to leave the earth, *'adāmah,* to man, *'ādām,* despite his inclination to evil. In this way J expresses his understanding of the link between creation and flood. In 9:20-27 J adds to the two basic relationships of man to woman and brother to brother, Gen 3 and 4, that of parents to children, which now passes over into history in curse and blessing. 11:1-9, which stands on the threshold between primeval event and history, only becomes comprehensible from an older stage of the narrative where the goal of the tower was to mount to the heavens. Two variants were linked with this original narrative theme, the goal of one being the dispersion of humankind, of the other the confusion of languages.

There are united then in each of these narratives several levels of formation, several lines of narration, several originally independent motifs. The traditio-historical approach to these narratives in Gen 2-11 reveals an abundance of primeval motifs from which J has made a choice and fashioned his own artistic whole. J's way of working becomes apparent: he is receiver and preserver, he coins anew and reshapes.

(e) *God, the World and the Person in J: J's Understanding of Human Nature.* J's primeval story is dominated by his interest in human beings, their potential and their limits (G. von Rad). The narrative of the creation of human beings and their expulsion from the garden 2:4b-3:24 is sufficient proof of this. There are also other texts that reveal this lively interest in people. One is quite justified in speaking about a "humanism" (G. von Rad). But it is too limited a view to regard this as original to J; J is an heir. These traditions about humanity go back to the primitive cultures prior to differentiation into particular political and religious traditions. J gives them new meaning by prefacing them to the historical traditions and so making them part of a historical work. The creation narrative and the genealogies deal with humankind and its potential, those of crime and punishment with its limits.

For J, a human being created by God is not the absolute individual, but is a person in the context of one's actual existence: a person in community, one who has to provide for oneself, a person with a task. A person detached from these three factors is not a true person. Moreover it means that the dynamic power to grow conferred on a person is articulated into these three factors, as the genealogies in Gen 4 show. In Gen 2 the people receive the commission to work the ground. Gen 4 sees the rise of those two forms of life that are basic to the history of humankind — agriculture and cattle breeding. Cultural achievements grow and ramify, and the history of civilization, anchored in the commission given by God, is an important part of the history of humankind.

J is interested in the concrete and hence in variety; this affects his approach to the limitation of humanity. He is obviously concerned with people's all-round ability to defy their human state and so to act against the will of their creator. We have pointed out above the deliberate arrangement of the transgressions according to subject and object. J is not aware of an abstract notion of sin according to which individual transgressions would be but manifestations of the one sin, nor of a notion of the fall, which only appeared in late Judaism.

Suffering, death, and a variety of deficiencies are part of the limitation of human existence. The correlative of transgression is punishment which always affects existence in some way for the worse. What is typical of J is that this worsening occurs in a variety of ways. God's punishment is never mechanical; it is characteristic of J that when he elaborates the punishment imposed upon man and woman in 3:14-19, each is different. Each of these varied deficiencies in human life gives rise to questions. One of the answers is to point out that the primeval cause is a transgression or a crime. Not that the answer can satisfy the question. What happened was primeval event, and this is no longer historically demonstrable.

The created state of humans consists in much more than has been mentioned so far. J deals with the basic functions of speech and with the phenomenon of shame in Gen 2-3, of the positive and negative aspects of envy in Gen 4; he sees both as psychosomatic. The sequence of Gen 4 on Gen 3 makes it clear that humanity is not only Adam and Eve, but also Cain and Abel. He mentions the two basic forms of economic and social life, agriculture and cattle keeping, and knows that the division of labor belongs to work itself.

J's understanding of the World, Time and History: J's understanding of history reveals itself in his overall thinking. For him, history does not begin only with the formation of the political system and state, but with the origin of the human race. This is the basis of his comprehensive conception of history: it embraces the social (starting from the family), the economic, the cultural, the religious. This is because, as he sees it, humankind's origin is created origin. But the creator is lord of his creation (Gen 6-9) and so participates in all that happens. God's creation remains in God's hand. Because everything that happens in the history of humanity grows out of creation, the linear idea of history is not sufficient for J. History is time extending into the future; but this time consists in cyclic rhythms.

The world is that which subsists in time; its subsistence is in the rhythms of day and night, summer and winter. This subsistence takes its stand on the promise of God, 8:20-22. God's action is as much concerned in cyclic time as in linear time. J, in contrast to P, has no well-defined world concept. The world of which he speaks is the world of humanity. His creation narrative belongs to the tradition of the creation of human beings; whatever is experienced of the world has to do with human beings. The animals, for example, are not important because of their kinds and species, but because of their significance for and relationship to people.

J's understanding of God and Worship: One should not presuppose an abstract or theoretical idea of God in J; God is not an object of thought and speculation, but he who acts and speaks. God has to do with what happens, and what happens has to do with God. It is essential to J's understanding of God that God as creator has to do with all that happens. His is not a "theology" in the later sense of a specialized area with a specialized vocabulary. It is here that he differs most markedly from P. For J, God is not concerned with the individual, isolated person, but with the person in every aspect of one's life. J does not understand religion in the sense of a specialized area of events that has to do only with the relationship between God and the individual (piety) or the group (cult) — it is different with P. When J speaks of God, he means all that happens, and he cannot speak of what is happening without at the same time speaking explicitly or implicitly of God.

This is the reason why, according to J, the beginning of the cult coincides with the beginning of humankind or with the beginning of civilization, 4:26. When he says there, "It was then that people began to call on the name of Yahweh," he cannot mean the God of Israel; he means calling on God as significant for all humankind. It is similar when J presupposes sacrifice and the distinction between clean and unclean for the whole of human history. God the creator is also he who preserves and sustains his creation.

God's punishment goes together with preservation. Human beings are created with the capacity to act against God, their creator, and thereby to betray their human existence. When they "will be like God," they put themselves in danger. God's punishment, which thrusts people back within their limits, preserves their humanity. People's works too can endanger them by outbidding them. This is the reason why J speaks of the advances in civilization in low key, though they are based on a commission from God. Increase in power like the means to power is a threat not only to the oppressed but also to the oppressor. But punishment must confine life and can be the cause of suffering. This is the crisis point in the confrontation between the creator and the creature. The revolt of humans can take on such proportions that "God is sorry" that he created them. The consequent decision to destroy brings about an incomprehensible contrast to creation. Whereas the mythological presentation traces this back to a conflict between the gods, J transposes it into God himself. God's regret in face of his creation is a warning that his regret then over the general apostasy and his decision to destroy will recur in the case of his own people. But the decision to destroy humanity is balanced at the end of the flood story by the promise to preserve it, despite its inclination to evil, "as long as the earth lasts."

2. The Priestly Writing in Genesis 1-11

(a) *References to the work as a whole:* The primeval story in P is related to the work as a whole much more rigorously and distinctly than in J. This is a clear indication that P must be later than J. The work as a whole is held together by two pins that penetrate even to the primeval story: one is theological, the other expresses P's understanding of history. The theological pin consists in the thesis that everything that happens does so at the command of God, and that everything that exists owes its existence to this command. The basic motif of the creation account, creation through the word (more accurately, command) of God, is for P the basic motif of all history. The historical pin is closely linked with the theological. Where God commands and creates through command, there is order; there is articulation in what God has commanded and so order. The seven-day pattern is meant to be an articulated whole that moves to a goal. The week of creation corresponds to the ordered whole of history that moves to a goal. History is divided into epochs that are marked as *toledot;* as such they were anchored in the *toledot* of the heavens and the earth, 2:4a.

(b) *The composition of 1-11 in P:* the arrangement of Gen 1-11 (P) is simple; it is done in blocks: creation-genealogy-flood-genealogy. It is very systematic. The variety of J's primeval event is missing; all is reduced to what is absolutely essential. All that remains in P of the numerous events in J are the creation and the flood; their relationship to each other emerges very clearly from this. Apart from these two events, P's primeval story contains only genealogies which, consequently, have greater significance for him than for J. The genealogy gives direction to the whole of P: the creation is designated as *toledot* in 2:4a, and the flood is inserted into the genealogy of Noah.

The arrangement in J is according to concrete events; that in P is abstract and theoretical and follows a well thought out system of numbers that corresponds to the predominance of the genealogy. But the arrangement can only be understood from the overall plan and structure of the whole work of which it is a carefully planned part. It leads in two steps from the creation, 1:1-2:4a, to the flood, 6-9 P, by means of the genealogy in Gen 5, and by means of the genealogy in Gen 10 from the flood to the broad horizons of the history of the nations as the setting where the history of God's people takes place, to which Gen 11 (from Noah to Abraham) is the second step in the transition. Because of this systematization, worked out with precise dates, P's primeval story is, more obviously than J's, the prologue to the history of the people of God which begins at the end of Gen 11 with Abraham.

(c) *The textual units in P, Gen 1-11. The Enumeration:* The genealogies in P lead in an unbroken sequence from Adam to Abraham. In J they are like a winding track, in P like a paved street. They stand in direct relationship to their basic theological framework. The blessing conferred by God on his creatures: ''be fruitful and multiply,'' is effective in the succession of generations listed in the genealogies. A human being is a creature that continues in time by virtue of the blessing.

The conception of the priestly writing is universal, even though its idea of the universal is different from J's. This is shown by prefixing 5:1-3 to the ten-part genealogy of Gen 5: the history of humankind takes its beginning from the blessing of the creator. Gen 5 and 10 are related to each other in that the genealogy of Gen 5 presents the growth of humankind as it moves through history, and that in Gen 10 as it moves across the world. The recurring caption *toledot,* which articulates the whole, says at the same time that all *toledot* stand in the perspective of the *toledot* of Adam. P illustrates the third stage in tradition in the adaptation of the genealogies: the oldest stage is the function of the genealogy in the clan; J demonstrates the second stage by applying it to the primeval story; in the third stage the priestly writing uses it as a means to relate the primeval story to history as the genealogy conceives it.

P makes deep inroads into the stock of the genealogies coming down to him. First, he combines smaller units of tradition and forms them into a sequence of ten. Second, he adds the dates (the life-spans of individuals) which make possible a continuous numbering; they belong originally to the genre of the chronicles composed in the royal courts.

The narrative: the priestly writing differs from J in using only two narratives in Gen 1-11, and even they are no longer simply narratives. However, P agrees with J first in that he narrates or reports the primeval event and does not speak of it didactically; second that the two narratives that P has, J also has. Both narratives in P, 1:1-2:4a and 6-9, are firmly inserted into the whole work by means of deep inroads into the material that has come down. Nevertheless, having regard for the time gap between J and P, it must be acknowledged that P inclines to preserve material as well as to reshape it. The narratives in P serve to teach and are very close to teaching. One must therefore appreciate even more the fact that P preserves what has come down by not teaching about the primeval beginning (like the pre-Socratics) but by telling the story of primeval time.

(d) *The work of P on the traditions at hand to him. The Creation Narrative:* P constructed a series of events out of the sentence, "God created the world through his word." He unfolded the elements of the command and related them to an older presentation in which God acted. One must distinguish P's own contribution from the material handed down in each individual work of each day, so as to put the priestly creation account into perspective: older and traditional presentations of creation speak as P presents creation. P does not want to have the first word or the last word; he wants to be but one voice in a long series of voices.

The individual works move in the direction of an abstract conception of creation. The three works of separation at the beginning point to an understanding of the world in the categories of time and space; ancient notions take on a new meaning here. The creation of the plants and animals according to their kinds introduces priestly wisdom into the creation description that is new to the traditional material. The ancient notion that the earth brings forth plants takes on a new aspect. The division of the works of creation into periods also points in the direction of a scientific comprehension of the world.

The flood narrative: The construction of the flood narrative, and particularly the sweeping perspective of the closing part, Gen 9, shows P's real intention, namely, to throw the whole weight on the theological significance. It is not the flood as an event in primeval time that is the important thing, but the consequences of it for God and his people. Gen 9 reveals the transition from narration of an event to static, conceptual speech. While P is bound completely to the tradition at hand in the actual story of the flood, he speaks for the most part independently in Gen 9. A long speech by God is more suited stylistically to one of the persons acting than to the genre of flood story. It is much more a means of theological interpretation. The transference of emphasis from event to speeches is also an indication of a cultural change. Where speeches begin to predominate, a specifically theoretical interest is presupposed on the part of the listeners. The completely theological direction here reveals the particular interest of the worshiping community, to which the priestly writing is addressed.

This interest can be made more precise. God's speech in Gen 9 is directed to Noah. The flood narrative is inserted into the genealogy of Noah, 9:28-29. A narrative about Noah comes out of the flood narrative. P shifts the accent from God's judgment over the whole of humankind, from which one was saved, to this one and his piety. For the sake of the pious man the human race survives the catastrophe.

Traditional material at hand: The presupposition in what has been said is that P is relying on traditional material at hand in Gen 1 and 6-9. A distinction is to be made between traditional units of whole narratives *(Vorlage)*, and material that consists of individual elements *(Vorgegebenes)*. We are dealing with a traditional unit *(Vorlage)* when we diagnose an "action-account" and a "command-account" in Gen 1 (W.H. Schmidt and others). We presuppose a traditional unit for Gen 6-9, as was demonstrated in the excursus to 7:11b. In neither case is it possible to reconstruct the traditional unit. It is to be assumed that the older narratives did not come down in a single, fixed form, but in variants. The doublets 9:14f. and 16 could point to such variants, as also the two sentences in 9:11.

Individual motifs in tradition *(Vorgegebenes)* are to be distinguished from

596

traditional units *(Vorlage)*. The motif of creation by the word in Gen 1 is the peculiar expression of the theology of P; but as a motif it is an element at P's disposal, as the theology of Memphis and the Akkadian hymns show. The sentence in 6:13a is probably an echo of a similar sentence from the prophecy of judgment, Amos 8:2. This reveals the systematic thinking of P which links primeval event and history.

Style and terminology: For the characteristics of P's style I refer to the studies of S.E. McEvenue and Th. Nöldeke. The narrative style predominates in J; P moves over into a static, conceptual style. The genealogies dominate the whole of P's chapters 1-11, and one of the two narratives, 1:1-2:4a, is very close in style to the genealogies. The other narrative, 6-9, is much more like a report with its dates and abundance of other numerical details. In 7:1-3 for example P reports everything in the minutest detail, while J is content to describe what is happening. J's arrangement of sentences in 7:1-3 is determined by the chain of verbs, while in P numerative substantives predominate. J narrates the end of the flood, 8:3, while P fixes it with numerical details (see also 8:13a,b). It is to be noted that the numbers in P do not derive from the narrative, as is the case with the few numerical details in J; the system of numbers is constructed with reference to the end of the flood.

A striking difference in style between J and P is that P adds long speeches by God to the event which serve to explain it theologically.

The terminology: P's static, conceptual presentation takes on a theological aspect because theological ideas are prominent in P, whereas J's spoken narrative style does not need them. J as good as does without theological ideas, whereas they are essential and indispensable for P. This is so for the idea of the image and likeness of God, of blessing, for the theologically impressed creation term ברא, for תולדת and for ברית. While J tells a story of fratricide, P proclaims the law that forbids murder. The language of P stands apart from that of J both chronologically and in content by making use of a theological, conceptual vocabulary for the stories of the primeval event.

(e) *God, the World and the Person in P: P's understanding of humanity.* The person is important for P not from the empirical, observable point of view, but from that of systematic theology. There is no sign in P of J's lively interest in the variety and many-sidedness of the human. His interest in the person is strictly theological. God created the person to be his counterpart, 1:26, and P restricts his talk about the person to this with disciplined severity. Everything else that is to be said of the person as God's creature is to be subordinated to it. However, it is to be noted that, despite this shifting of accent, P's understanding of humanity is not basically different from J's. In addition to the basic specification of origin from God (reinforced in P by creation in the image and likeness of God), there are in Gen 1, as in Gen 2, the same three precisions that are part of it: 1. the person is created for community, 1:27b, 2. the person is provided with the necessary means of life, 1:29, and 3. the person receives a commission with regard to the rest of creation, 1:26b, 28b. The difference is that J is concerned further with all three.

The difference between P and J is particularly evident in the judgment passed on human cultural work. P includes cultural work and human attributes together under the idea of dominion over the rest of creation (or over the earth), and this stands in the context of the blessing conferred by God and its inherent dynamism. He says no more of this. The reason for this difference is that P is addressing a cultic community that is no longer interested directly in political, cultural, and social events. This accords with P's exclusive interest in one's relationship to God that leads to an alternative of the pious and the godless. But this is not to be made absolute: God did not create pious and godless, Jews and pagans, but human beings; the verse about the image and likeness of God has universal meaning. Every person is from God — this sentence takes absolute precedence to any alternative between peoples. But the alternative is there in the flood narrative — no explanation or reason is given: humanity is corrupt and Noah is the one "just man." P here is speaking into his own time. Noah is the pious one who has remained blameless amidst the corruption of his age. P arrives at this alternative out of the contemporary situation in which the Jewish community is struggling for its existence. One can understand why any interest in the variety of human transgressions retreats and is spoken of no more.

Understanding of the world, time and history: P has a distinct, reflective idea of the world as a whole with regard to both space and time (and so reveals itself as the later work). He is closer to modern thinking here than is J, and his world view is far more extensive. Spatially P knows the earth as a part of the cosmos; he deliberately demythologizes the heavenly bodies and they become constitutive parts of the world. P is aware of the extraordinary extension of the inhabited world, as the table of nations in Gen 10 shows. The same Gen 10, especially the sentences that conclude the three parts, shows that chronologically P understands world history as the history of the nations, whom he is the first to define comprehensively. The inflated numbers in the genealogy in Gen 5 are an indication that P assumes that the history of humankind extends far back into a distant past.

P makes a statement that is basic for his understanding of history when he presents the primeval story in the form of genealogies. Constitutive of the genealogies are the constants, the same continuous succession of begetting, birth and death, and the variables, the names and the numbers. This holds also for the history of humankind in all its stages and forms. History is only made by the association and interplay of events that take place within these constants and variables. In contrast to the western view, P does not see history as consisting solely in historically demonstrable changes and incidents that are brought into a single, linear course of events. Rather there are at work too in every event elements of the permanent that are always and everywhere the same and common to all people. All history takes its origin from creation and the blessing. The other important view point is the division of history into periods; but this is inseparably linked with P's understanding of God and worship.

P's understanding of God and worship: For P creation and history stand very close to each other. The creation narrative contains as introduction and conclusion two elements that are likewise introduction and conclusion for history. World history as a whole and its subdivisions corresponds to the creation event as a whole and its subdivisions. It has already been shown that the constitutive parts of the divine command shape the creation account. But the same command is the foundation of all that happens. In Gen 6-9 the scheme of command and execution is for the first time followed through in a carefully worked out pattern. The beginning (something like Gilg. XI) is modified so that the building of the ark becomes part of the divine commission. God's word of command alone is what matters. P has put special emphasis on 7:13-16a; this is the climax because Noah obeys God's word. It makes preservation possible and leads to the covenant. 8:15-19 again has the same construction as 6:13-21, commission and execution. The event of the flood begins and ends with a commission to Noah which he executes. This emphasis on the scheme "command and execution" has a far reaching theological significance. It is a question of the salvation of Noah. Salvation is determined in the command of God. God's acts of saving and commanding are not yet separated; salvation is introduced in the command of God. The act of command embraces also the act of saving, as the command, "be fruitful. . . ," embraces the blessing.

The scheme "command and execution" dominates the following historical epochs: the patriarchal history, Gen 17, the Exodus event, Ex 6, and the Sinai event, Ex 24:15b-18, which is followed in 25:1ff. by the commission to construct the holy place, the goal of all preceding commands and commissions. The command or the commission of God which P always speaks of together with its execution, is to be distinguished from the ordinance or law that sets a limit to human activity.

The sequence of the days of creation reaches its conclusion and goal in the seventh day which God sanctifies and blesses. What is being said here is that all time is directed toward the holy time, and it is this that dominates the whole of the priestly work. The dating of the flood event corresponds to the seven-day scheme of creation; it leads to the date (8:13) dominated by the number "one." The basis of the Sabbath and the new year is laid in the primeval event. Both consequently are significant not only for the cult of the Jewish people, but for the whole of humankind. At every stage in the primeval history of P there are signs of its relationship to the whole.

All that has been said so far gives us to understand that the determining characteristic of this God is majesty. It is in accordance with the structure of the priestly work that the idea כבוד first occurs where the glory of God is revealed at the holy place; but implicitly it is the God of majesty who speaks and acts in 1-11. Over and against this majestic God is the attitude of humans, the unreserved respect for what God has commanded, trustful obedience as exemplified in Noah.

Worship in P: It remains only to add to what has been said already about worship something of the way in which P's understanding of worship differs most markedly from J's. Worship in P is bound utterly with revelation. Worship only becomes possible through the revelation of the glory of God at the holy place, Sinai, before Moses and the Israelites. According to P then there can be neither sacrifice nor distinction between clean and unclean beforehand; he omits both in the flood narrative. P understands cult as something very particular, and so it begins only with the revelation to Israel. For J the cult is part of the history of humankind from the very beginning and so he can speak of the sacrifice of Cain, Abel, and Noah without embarrassment. There is a fundamental difference here that those who contest the division into sources cannot explain away.

However the understanding of God in P has also a universal aspect, though in a different way from J; it is not empirical, but theological and reflective. It is that everything that happens from the creation on is related to the origin of the worship in the temple at Jerusalem in a way that can only be hinted at but not explained.

3. The Work of the Redactor

The biblical primeval story has come down to us from the hands of the redactor who has given it its present form. The significance of his work is that the form that he impressed on it has been effective right down to the present day. R's synthesis has taken the floor and remained in possession. It is a construct of texts that has its own independence and its own individual contribution to make over and above those of J and P. R wants to preserve several points of view of one and the same event and pass them on (cf. especially Gen 6-9). This accords with the way in which both J and P handled the traditions that came to them. They too wanted to preserve points of view that need not be in complete agreement with their own. But R's attitude to tradition is more profound and thoroughgoing. He has to do with complete works which he unites, works which themselves are in many ways very different, even opposed, in their apprehension of the matter they present. R created out of these a new, coherent and self-contained narrative. But this was only possible because R shared with J and P a basic attitude to reality and event. Many voices can hand down event and reality, and in the process each voice retains its own pitch and key. This is the secret of tradition; tradition has many voices insofar as it is concerned with reality and event.

All this of course presupposes that the individual voices with their different pitches and keys are basically in concord about the same thing. J, P, and R and the primeval event are the classical example. Despite all differences and even contradictions, what they share in common stands out. For example R, by combining J and P, creates a new tension between creation of the world and creation of humans and allows it to be developed further. When different voices in different keys, counterpoised and in harmony, can be heard and preserved, then the presumption is that they have a profound, firm and unshakable sharing in common. This is the reason why one can speak of a theological meaning of the primeval story as a whole.

V. The Theological Meaning of the Primeval Story

Preliminary Note: The presupposition of this concluding section is that one can investigate the theological meaning of Gen 1-11 as a whole. It has been shown in the commentary that one is not justified exegetically in extracting Gen 1-3, "creation and fall." Christian tradition as a whole has been dominated by an interpretation that has confined the theological meaning to Gen 1-3. This has not only deprived Gen 4-11 of their importance, but has also distorted the meaning of Gen 1-3. To mention only the three most important points: the narrative texts and the numerative text of Gen 1-11 belong together and mutually interpret each other; creation and flood are complementary; the revolt against God in Gen 3 and that against a brother in Gen 4 belong together. One can only arrive at the theological meaning of the primeval story when one reads Gen 1-11 as a whole in the synthesis that R has put together.

1. God-Talk in the Primeval Story

(a) *The concept of theology:* The God of whom Gen 1-11 speaks is concerned with humankind as a whole and the world as a whole. The fact that this God is the creator of humankind and the world means that God as a being is related to these wholes, to humankind, and to the world, but our ideas of religion and theology have by definition a particular character. We know only a plurality of religions and theologies; a religion or a theology of humanity is not in the realm of our experience. Talk of creator and creation, and beyond of primeval event, transcends our ideas of religion and theology. This accords with the fact that the motifs of primeval event have a universal character and virtually cover the whole of the earth. Our idea of religion on the contrary looks to the particular and to the traditions peculiar to each.

(b) *The object of theology:* The identification of the creator with the God whom Israel met in its history is the reason why the primeval event has been pre-fixed to history. The natural consequence of this is an assimilation that becomes more marked in the course of the tradition history. The assimilation of primeval event to history is much further advanced in P than in J, and even more so in Deutero-Isaiah. One can understand then why modern exegetes begin with Deutero-Isaiah when they want to come to grips with the specifically theological meaning of "creation faith" (G. von Rad, "The Theological Problem of the Old Testament Doctrine of Creation" [1936] in *The Problem of the Hexateuch. . .* [1966] 131-143).

Once one has recognized the tendency to even out one will ask about the specific meaning of the primeval event at the point where the assimilation begins; and it is here that the difference in the primeval talk emerges even more strongly. What is peculiar to it is that the world and humankind stand over against God. The keynote is comprehensive talk about reality. There is no attempt to talk about God and his particular acts. This, from the viewpoint of the Old Testament, is what the history, played out between God and Israel, is all about. This history begins with the encounter with the saving God at the exodus from Egypt which determines all that follows and gives rise to a continuous historical exchange. There is no sign of this in the God-human relationship in the primeval story, nor is there any sign of the separation of the spheres of existence that makes up the historical state. Every area of existence is related alike directly to God. There is no separation between the sacred and the profane, i.e., there is no religious area of existence. Consequently there is no such thing as revelation. In the primeval event it occurs neither as an encounter in history (Epiphany) nor as an encounter with the holy one (Theophany). God and his people are not at such a distance from each other that God has to reveal himself (see comments on P). If the primeval event is not to be understood as revelation, if there is nothing in the texts that stems from revelation or understands itself as such, then the old controversy between *revelatio generalis* and *revelatio specialis* is no more.

Nor is there that permanent relationship that results from such revelation. There is no election or covenant, and these are of the very essence of a special relationship to God (ברית in Gen 9 means merely a "solemn assurance"). The relationship in the primeval event is not described as faith, and nowhere in the rest of the Old Testament is the relationship to the creator called "faith in the creator" or "creation-faith." Nor does the person break some such permanent relationship; there can be no apostasy to other gods because this presupposes differentiation into peoples. "Sin" certainly plays an important role in the primeval event, but it is misleading to construe this into some sort of general notion. The crimes and transgressions mentioned in the texts of Gen 1-11 are always something belonging to a specific human being, things that can and do happen wherever a person is.

2. The main characteristics of the God-talk in the Primeval Story.

There is nothing in the primeval event that is determinative of a particular relationship to God. What is peculiar to the primeval relationship to God consists then in something over and above all other relationships of God to his people and to the world, whatever they may be. This is the reason why what is said in the primeval event relates to the present differently than does God's history with his people. Statements about humans in a particular, circumscribed history are only accessible to us across the chasm of history, i.e., by means of the two questions: What happened at that time? and What does it mean for us? Statements about humankind and the world as a whole, on the other hand, relate differently to our present situation. In Gen 4:2-16, the question is not: What does it mean for us today that Cain at that time murdered his brother?, but: Is humanity really such as presented here? Likewise it is wrong to ask: What does it mean for us today that Eve at that time ate the forbidden fruit in the garden? The question is rather: Is human nature really such as presented here?

By pre-fixing Gen 1-11 to the Pentateuch and by making it part of the Bible, it is being said that people, in the particular history that begins in Gen 12, remain such as they are said to be in Gen 1-11. Primeval event goes along with the particular history of God with his people. What was said about humanity in Gen 1-11 is valid for humanity henceforth. The unchangeable in the person and one's world constantly recurs in the narratives and reports of the different epochs of history. Certain elements never alter; a person needs nourishment, 1:28; 2:8, and community, 2; a person transgresses and retains the impulse to go beyond one's limits.

(a) *Creation as comprehensive talk about reality:* In the creation declaration, people for the first time conceptualized the origin of humankind and the world as a whole. To speak of the creator is to speak of the whole. No one experiences and "knows" humankind as a whole or the world as a whole. They are not empirically accessible. It is only when seen in their source and origin, only when seen as creation, that they can be spoken of and conceptualized as a whole. Everything that is included in the world and humankind must therefore share in this origin from the creator. In the primeval story both J and P, each in a different way, are concerned to compass the whole in what they have to say.

This concept of the world and humanity as a whole, stemming from talk about creator and creation, has, in Greek thought, been detached from the creator and become ontology; the pre-Socratics mark the transition. The idea of the whole and of "origin from" has remained. But the personal act of creating has been transformed into a neutral causality, and "origin from" . . . into being. From the pre-Socratics right up to the present, ontology has been coined out of talk about the creator. The idea of the whole or of being can never deny that this is its source. There is ontology only because people once understood their world as creation.

The priestly writing is concerned to present the world that God has created in its wholeness. This concern is already clear in the first sentence; systematic thinking that envisages the whole is developed to perfection in Gen 1. The existence of the world is conceived of in the categories of time and space; living things, plants and animals, are conceived of in their species as an articulated whole. The same concern is apparent in Gen 5 and 10 where humanity's continuation through time and across space is likewise presented as a whole. The intention is unmistakable: to bring the work of the creator into relationship with everything in heaven and on earth. To unfold what is meant by "creator of heaven and earth" P has to outline all those areas that later became the object of the natural sciences. J stresses the totality of human existence; P is the systematizer, J is the empiricist. The relationship of the person to God, the exchange between creature and creator is, in J, so intimately linked with life-cycles and vital functions that it cannot be detached from them. All people at all times and in all places are included as well as all that is specifically human and common to all, such as has become later the object of the human sciences — anthropology in its various forms, sociology and psychology, linguistics and ethics. When J speaks of the human being he includes every aspect and every manifestation of the human in all its length and breadth. It would have been impossible to have coined the idea of the "human" had it not been preceded by the all-embracing idea of "humanity" in the conception of the creation of the human being (C. Westermann, 'adam', THAT I, [1971] 41-57).

It is only when one takes this perspective and sees how comprehensively J speaks of humanity and P of the world that one can gauge the skill and the achievement of the redactor. He has united two very different world-views into a whole and has allowed each to speak for itself. It is this combination that has made the biblical primeval story effective through the millennia. This concern to speak comprehensively brings the primeval talk about humanity and the world into a very natural affinity with the sciences, and it is not by chance that J and P are impressed with signs of the basic divisions of the sciences into the natural and the human. There is no need for any conflict between the biblical account of creation and the scientific study of the world and humanity; we are on the threshold of a new dialogue between the two. Such a dialogue is meaningful because each of the natural sciences can only address itself to a restricted area, whereas the biblical primeval story speaks of the whole.

(b) *Maintenance and preservation:* In order to make clear the proper meaning of the creation declaration, one must take as one's starting point that each individual creation narrative, each creation myth or each simple sentence that makes a statement about creation, is not directed primarily to saying something about an event in the past, but is spoken to and into the present. We can say this because we have established that the primary motif of the creation narratives was not a question about the origin, but about the world and humanity under threat in the present. The creation question arose out of the reflection on the present and so the link between the origin and the present must be obvious. The primeval story gives witness to it in two ways: (1) The person was not created by God as an individual being, but in community which opens the future to all people; both J and P present the creation of humans in this way. P uses the idea of blessing and its universal dynamism (Table of the Nations). The effect of the creator's blessing is experienced throughout the whole of the history of humankind: it is at work in birth, growth, maturity, the decrease in vitality and in dying. Death in this context is a necessary part of life and has a positive meaning. The existence of the individual in one's life-span from birth to death is identical with one's created state; God has created the person to fill out this life-span. (2) The continuation of the human race across the millennia of human history is not a mechanical process. Just as the individual, so too the human race is in danger. Experience of catastrophes is part of the experience of reality. Accordingly saving and preservation are also part of human existence. The narrative of humankind in danger, the flood, complements the creation narrative. Its goal is "stabilization" of the world "as long as the world lasts" 8:22. This is the other way in which the work of the creator affects the present: the creator holds the world of humanity in his hands. The point of reference of the human world is the creator; the creator is the source and confirmation of its stability. This indicates at the same time that humankind and its world is moving toward a goal that lies hidden in the will of the creator.

(c) *Created in the image of God:* The most striking statement of the primeval story, over and above God being the creator, preserver and sustainer of creation, is that God created human beings in his image. According to the explanation given in the commentary the sentence means that God created humanity to be his counterpart so that something can happen between God and the individual. J presents in narrative form what P expresses by means of the idea of the image and likeness of God; he has the creation of humanity lead to an exchange between God and human beings. There is to be added to the remarks on 1:26ff. the meaning of this statement on primeval event which is common to P and J. The sentence intends to give an explanation: If one can say of all people that they are creatures of God, one can also say of them that they are created in the image of God. To be in the image and likeness of God means that human dignity cannot be abrogated by distinctions between groups or sorts of people, that it is inherent in the will of the creator, and that it embraces all. This implies the most stringent political-social rider imaginable: all classifications of people carry their own limitations. Dissimilarities cannot thereby be abolished, but neither can they be absolutized.

The image and likeness of God includes what we call responsibility. It makes possible the question that God directs to the man: "Adam, where are you?" "Where is your brother Abel?" It is the same question that the judge of the world puts in Mt 25. Both statements, in primeval event and in end event, embrace the history of the human race. Human beings are responsible; this is later called conscience in some cultures. But the word conscience does not reflect adequately what the primeval story intends. It belongs to human beings, created as God's counterparts, not only that they can be called to account, that they are responsible, but that human beings can question where there is no one in the realm of creation who can give them an answer. Humans can ask after the meaning of their existence with the question "why?"; it is an expression of the complaint directed to God. This question about meaning is universal; it is not bound to any particular religion, it rings out even where religion is rejected.

(d) *Punishment of the "Evil One" and tolerance of evil:* Gen 1-11 says further that God punishes people. There is no human existence without the potential to transgress and to overstep the appointed limits; there was never humanity "before the fall." God puts limits to human potential. J describes the many and different transgressions of people and the corresponding reactions of God; he is not as schematic as P. God's punishment is directed at the person as a responsible creature and so is expressly "human." In Gen 3 and 4 it is far removed from the "curse of the evil deed," from the "realm of the deed that brings its own fate'' (K. Koch), where the evil deed itself is effective. This pre-theological notion, which rests on magical thinking, can certainly sound through, as it does in Gen 4:10; but the personal notion predominates, namely that God demands the brother's blood, 4:9. It is only this that makes possible the response, that the doer come forward. This is of the utmost importance for the whole history of humankind, because it has remained the basis for all legal procedure right up to the present day — the accused must have the freedom to reply to the accusation.

The second characteristic is the limiting function of such punishment. Gen 3 with the "will to be like God" and the motif of the tree of life deals with this, as do also 6:1-4 and 11:1-9. This motif must have been particularly important for J. But one must attend carefully to the nuances: one's striving for something lofty is not condemned as such; but it is precisely here that one's human condition is in gravest danger. It is here that it is said of God that he preserves one's humanity in his restrictive punishment. It is necessary for J to speak of God here: it is not people as transgressors, but people as idealists — humans in their highest aspirations who need God to restrict them so that they remain human.

The third characteristic of punishment in the primeval story is that it is not based on a set of fixed principles. God is not the just judge; his punishment is not in the service of justice (in the sense of a principle), but in the service of life. Humanity must be destroyed because it is corrupt; a new humanity is preserved in Noah which is not merely a "good" humanity. J has underscored this inconsequence rather crassly. A touch of forgiveness always follows on the punishment; the punishment is always in the service of life. The statement that concludes the flood narrative is closely related to this. It speaks of another attitude of God to human wickedness. God is not only opposed to it as the one who punishes; he can also tolerate and suffer it even without intervening. The decision never to destroy the world of humanity again because of its wickedness presupposes that "the imagination of a person's heart is evil from one's youth," 8:21, i.e., God's blessing and its effect is firmly assured "as long as the earth remains," and it makes no distinction between the good and the wicked (Mt 5:45). No political, social, theological or ecclesiastical adaptation can in any way alter the fact that a person grows up with an inclination to evil and that the creator will suffer it and not change it.

3. *The primeval event in the Old Testament as a whole.* In conclusion we consider the meaning for the Old Testament as a whole of what the primeval event has said of God and his relationship to people and to the world. The meaning lies in the pre-fixing of the primeval story to the history. Talk about God in Gen 1-11 thereby has a share in talk about God in the rest of the Pentateuch and the other parts of the Old Testament. The God who delivered Israel out of Egypt, whom Israel encountered in its history, is at the same time the God who created heaven and earth and humankind. So Israel's experience of the saving God is put into a broad, comprehensive perspective. As creator, God stands in a relationship to people outside Israel throughout the whole of the history of humankind, in a relationship to the whole world, all of whose being and powers he has created and sustained. It is no longer possible to construct a theology of the Old Testament exclusively from "salvation history," from the relationship of God to his

people, and subordinate the universal aspect to it. The universal and the particular aspects of God's action should be left each to itself, and their peculiar ways of speaking not be confused. Three consequences follow from this:

(a) The attempt to interpret Gen 1-11 in terms of salvation history only must be abandoned, because the object of salvation history is the people of God, whereas the object of the primeval event is humankind and the world. A theology of the Old Testament that follows a single line, that brings everything under one and the same idea (salvation, faith, revelation, promise, sin, etc.) is not feasible.

(b) The question arises, Where and how does God's universal action continue after his history with his people begins? How does it continue to speak in, with, and under the influence of the account of God's dealing with his people, retain its own voice and acquire its significance? One looks for this in the many and varied links between the two aspects in the talk about God's action after the history begins, and one must be careful to allow both to be seen in their reciprocal effects.

(c) It is only in this way that one can see the significance of the complementarity of creation and flood for the whole of the Old Testament. The creator holds his creation in his hands; he can destroy it again. The assurance that he will sustain the human world at the end of the flood is a pointer to the end of the world. Talk about the end of the world is taken up again in the Apocalyptic; there God's particular action merges again into a universal. Apocalyptic is concerned once more with the world and humanity. The circle is thereby closed. Talk of the end of the world in the Apocalyptic presupposes that God's action toward humankind and the world has not been interrupted during the salvation history. At the end as at the beginning, the world and humankind are in God's hands. God's universal action has always remained the broader perspective of his action toward his people. The Bible can only speak of the end of the world and humankind because God is the creator of them both.

It is only in this broader context that the work of Jesus Christ can be seen in its full significance as God's action in the "middle of the time." When the New Testament conceives this action in the context of beginning and end (Jn 1:1-14; Rev 1:8), it is pointing to the universal perspective which determines God's action as creator of the world and humankind in the primeval story, and in which both beginning and end are included.

Abbreviations

The abbreviations, with very few exceptions, follow S. Schwertner, *Internationales Abkürzungsverzeichnis für Theologie und Grenzgebiete* (Berlin/New York: de Gruyter) 1974.

AAB	Annuaire de l'académie r. de Belgique. Brussels
AAF	Archives de l'art francais. Paris
AAJR—TS.AAJR	Texts and Studies. American Academy for Jewish Research. New York
AAOJ	American antiquarian and oriental journal. Chicago
ABR	Australian Biblical Review. Melbourne
ACQ	American Church Quarterly. Pelham, N.Y.
ACR	Australasian Catholic Record. Manly, N.S.W.
ADAJ	Annual of the Department of Antiquities of Jordan. Amman
AFLNW	Arbeitsgemeindschaft für Forschung des Landes Nordrhein-Westfalen
AfO	Archiv für Orientforschung. Graz.
AION	Annali del'istituto universitario orientale de Napoli. Naples
AJA	American Journal of Archaeology. Princeton, N.J.
AJSL	American Journal of Semitic Languages and Literatures. Chicago
AJT JR	American Journal of Theology. Chicago
AKM	Abhandlungen für die Kunde des Morgenlandes. Leipzig
ALBO	Analecta Lovaniensia Biblica et Orientalia. Louvain
ALGM	*Ausführliches Lexicon der griechischen und römischen Mythologie.* ed. Wilhelm Heinrich Roscher. Leipzig
Altertum	Altertum. Berlin
ALUOS	Annual of Leeds University Oriental Society. Leiden
AnBib	Analecta Biblica. Rome
AncB	Anchor Bible. New York
ANET	*Ancient Near Eastern Texts Relating to the Old Testament.* ed. J. B. Pritchard
Ang.	Angelicum. Rome
Antaios	Antaios
Anton.	Antonianum. Rome
ANVAO	Avhandlinger i norske videnskaps-akademi i Oslo.
AO	Der alte Orient. Leipzig
AOH	Acta Orientalia Academiae Scientiarum Hungaricae. Budapest
AOT	Altorientalische Texte zum Alten Testament. Tübingen 1909, 1926².

APPP	Abhandlungen zur Philosophie und Pädagogik. Bonn
ArOr	Archiv Orientalni. Prague
ArtAs	Artibus Asiae. Ascona
ARW	Archiv für Religionswissenschaft. Leipzig
AS	Assyriological Studies. Chicago
AsR	Asian Review. London
AssBibl	Assyriologische Bibliothek. Leipzig
AsSt	Asiatische Studien. Bern
AStE	Annuario di Studi Ebraici. Rome
ASTI	Annual of the Swedish Theological Institute (in Jerusalem). Leiden
ATA	Alttestamentliche Abhandlungen. Munich
AThR	Anglican Theological Review. New York
Aug.	Augustinianum. Rome
AUSS	Andrews University Seminary Studies. Berrien Springs, Mich.
AVTRW	Aufsätze und Vorträge zur Theologie und Religionswissenschaft. Berlin
AWEAT	Archiv für Wissenschaftliche Erforschung des Alten Testaments. Halle
AWR	Aus der Welt der Religion. Giessen
AzTh	Arbeiten zur Theologie. Stuttgart
BA	Biblical Archaeologist. New Haven, Conn.
Bab.	Babyloniaca. Paris
BASOR	Bulletin of the American Schools of Oriental Research. New Haven, Conn.
BBB	Bonner Biblische Beiträge. Bonn
BEHJ	Bulletin des études historiques juives.
BenM	Benediktinische Monatsschrift. Beuron
BeO	Bibbia e Oriente. Milan
BetM	Bet(h) Mikra. Jerusalem
BEvTh	Beiträge zur Evangelische Theologie. Munich
BEThL	Bibliotheca Ephemeridum Theologicarum Loveniensium. Louvain
BFPUL	Bibliothèque de la faculté de philosophie et lettres de l'université de Liège. Liège
BHH	Biblisch-historisches Handwörterbuch. Göttingen
BHR	Bibliothèque d'humanisme et renaissance. Geneva
BHTh	Beiträge zur historischen Theologie. Tübingen
Bib	Biblica. Rome
BibOr	Biblica et Orientalia. Rome
BibSac	Bibliotheca Sacra and Theological Review. Andover, Mass.
BSTR	
Bijdr.	Bijdragen. Tijdschrift voor philosophie en theologie. Nijmegen
BiKi	Bibel und Kirche. Stuttgart
BiLe	Bibel und Leben. Düsseldorf
BiLi	Bibel und Liturgie. Klosterneuberg b. Wien
BRL	Bodleian Library Record. Oxford
BrSynt	C. Brockelmann, *Hebräische Syntax*, 1956.
BSHT	Breslauer Studien zur Historischen Theologie. Breslau
BSt	Biblische Studien. Neukirchen
BTS	Bible et Terre Sainte. Paris
Burg	Burgense. Burgos
BVC	Bible et Vie Chrétienne. Paris
BW	Biblical World. Chicago
BWANT	Beiträge zur Wissenschaft vom Alten und neuen Testament. Stuttgart
BWAT	Beiträge zur Wissenschaft vom Alten Testament. Stuttgart
BZ	Biblische Zeitschrift. Paderborn

Abbreviations

BZAW	Beihefte zur Zeitschrift für die Alttestamentliche Wissenschaft. Berlin
BZfr	Biblische Zeitfragen. Münster
BZNW	Beihefte zur Zeitschrift für die Neutestamentliche Wissenschaft. Berlin
CAB	Cahiers d'archéologie biblique. Neuchatel
Cath.	Catholicisme. Paris
CBG	Collationes Brugenses et Gandavenses. Ghent
CBQ	Catholic Biblical Quarterly. Washington
CBrug	Collationes Brugenses. Bruges
CD	*Church Dogmatics* I/1 — IV/4, Karl Barth, (1936-1969).
ChW	Christliche Welt. Gotha
CiFe	Ciencià y Fe. Buenos Aires
CivCatt	Civiltà Cattolica. Rome
CleR	Clergy Review. London
CMech	Collectanea Mechliniensia. Malines
CNFI	Christian News from Israel. Jerusalem
ConQ	Congregational Quarterly. London
CoTh	Collectanea Theologica. Warsaw
CQ	Classical Quarterly. London
CQR	Church Quarterly Review. London
CTJ	Calvin Theological Journal. Grand Rapids, Mich.
CTM	Concordia Theological Monthly. St. Louis, Mo.
CTom	Ciencia Tomista. Salamanca
CuBi	Cultura Biblica. Madrid
CuW	Christentum und Wissenshaft. Leipzig
CwH	Calwer Hefte zur Förderung biblischen Glaubens und christlichen Lebens. Stuttgart
DB(H)	*Dictionary of the Bible.* ed. James Hastings. Edinburgh
DBS	Dictionnaire de la Bible. Supplement. Paris
DB(V)	Dictionnaire de la Bible. ed. F. Vigouroux. Paris
DTh ThR	Deutsche Theologie. Stuttgart
DThC	Dictionnaire de Théologie Catholique. Paris
DTT	Dansk Teologisk Tidsskrift. Copenhagen
DViv	Dieu Vivant. Paris
EB(B)	Encyclopaedia Biblica. ed. Institutum Bialik et Museum Antiquitatum Iudaicarum. Jerusalem
EBrit	Encyclopaedia Britannica. Edinburgh
EC	Enciclopedia Cattolica. Vatican City
EHPhR	Études d'Histoire et de philosophie religieusses. Paris
EKL	Evangelisches Kirchenlexicon. Göttingen
ELKZ	Evangelisch-lutherische Kirchenzeitung. Munich
Encounter	Encounter. Indianapolis, Ind.
EPAPS	Early Proceedings of the American Philosophical Society. Philadelphia
Er	Eranos. Göteborg.
ERE	*Encyclopaedia of Religion and Ethics.* ed. James Hastings. Edinburgh
Erls	Eretz-Israel. Jerusalem
ErJb	Eranos-Jahrbuch. Zürich
EstB	Estudios Biblicos. Madrid
ET(Expt)	Expository Times. Edinburgh
EtCl	Études Classiques. Namur
EThL	Emphemerides Theologicae Louvanienses. Louvain
ETR	Études Théologiques et Religieuses. Montpellier
EvErz	Evangelische Erziehung. Frankfurt

EvTh	Evangelische Theologie. Munich
ExBib	Exempla Biblica. Göttingen
Exp.	Expositor. London
FF	Frate Francesco. Parma
FFC	Folklore Fellows Communications. London
Folkl.	Folklore. London
FRLANT	Forschungen zur Religion und Literatur des Alten und Neuen Testaments. Göttingen
FuH	Fuldäer Hefte. Berlin
GBT	Ghana Bulletin of Theology. Accra
Ges-K	*Gesenius' Hebrew Grammar* (ed. E. Kautzsch. Eng. trans. from 28th German ed. by A. E. Cowley) 1910².
GlDei	Gloria Dei. Graz
GordR	Gordon Review. Boston
Gr.	Gregorianum. Rome
GThT	Gereformeerd Theologisch Tijdschrift. Aalten
GuW	Glaube und Wissen. Munich
Hebr.	Hebraica. Chicago
HibJ	Hibbert Journal. London
HJ	Historisches Jahrbuch der Görres-Gesellschaft. Munich
HK	Handkommentar zum Alten Testament. Göttingen
HLa	Heilig Land. Nijmegen
HomR	Homiletic Review. New York
HT	History Today. London
HThG	Handbuch Theologischer Grundbegriffe. Munich
HThR	Harvard Theological Review. Cambridge, Mass.
HTS	Hervormde Teologiese Studies. Pretoria
HUCA	Hebrew Union College Annual. Cincinnati
IB	*Introduction à la Bible* (edd. A. Robert-A. Feuillet). Paris
IDB	Interpreter's Dictionary of the Bible. New York
Interp.	Interpretation. Richmond, Virg.
Iraq	Iraq. British School of Archaeology. London
IThQ	Irish Theological Quarterly. Maynooth
JA	Journal Asiatique. Paris
JAOS	Journal of the American Oriental Society. Baltimore, Md.
JBL	Journal of Biblical Literature. Philadelphia
JBW	Jahrbuch der Biblischen Wissenschaft.
JCS	Journal of Cuneiform Studies. New Haven, Conn.
JdI	Jahrbuch des (k.) deutschen archäologischen Instituts. Berlin
JDTh	Jahrbücher für deutsche Theologie. Stuttgart
JEOL	Jaarbericht van het vooraziatisch-egyptisch genootschap 'Ex Oriente Lux'. Leiden
JIAS	Journal of the Institute of Asiatic Studies.
JJS	Journal of Jewish Studies. London
JMUES	Journal of the Manchester University Egyptian and Oriental Society. Manchester
JNES	Journal of Near Eastern Studies. Chicago
JQR	Jewish Quarterly Review. London
JRAS	Journal of the Royal Asiatic Society of Great Britain and Ireland. London
JSOR	Journal of the Society of Oriental Research. Toronto
JSSt	Journal of Semitic Studies. Manchester
JThFUS	Jahrbuch der theologischen Fakultät der Universität Sophia. Tokyo

Abbreviations

JThS	Journal of Theological Studies. Oxford
JThSB	Jahrbuch der theologischen Schule Bethel. Bethel
Jud.	Judaica. Zürich
JVI	Journal of the Victoria Institute. London
Kairos	Kairos. Zeitschrift für Religions-wissenschaft und Theologie. Salzburg
Kath.	Der Katholik. Strasbourg
KBL	Köhler, Ludwig und Walter Baumgartner. *Lexicon in Veteris Testamenti Libros*. Leiden
KEH	Kurzgefasstes Exegetisches Handbuch. Leipzig
KHC	Kurzer Hand-Commentar zum Alten Testament. Tübingen
KKZ	Katholische Kirchenzeitung. Salzburg
Klio	Klio. Leipzig
KrR	Křest'anská Revue. Prague
KS	Kleine Schriften. Tübingen
KuD	Kerygma und Dogma. Göttingen
KVR	Kleine Vandenhoeck-Reihe. Göttingen
LR	Lutherische Rundschau. Stuttgart
LSSt	Leipziger Semitistische Studien. Leipzig
LThK	Lexikon für Theologie und Kirche. Freiburg
Lum.	Lumen. Vitoria
MAB.L	Mémoires de l'Académie R. de Belgique. Classe des lettres et des sciences morales et politiques. Brussels
Man.	Manuscripta. St. Louis, Mo.
MAGW	Mitteilungen der anthropologischen Gesellschaft in Wien. Vienna
Mar.	Marianum. Ephemerides Mariologiae. Rome
MDAI	Mitteilungen des deutschen archäologischen Instituts. Munich
MDOG	Mitteilungen der deutschen Orientgesellschaft. Berlin
MGWJ	Monatsschrift für Geschichte und Wissenschaft de Judentums. Breslau
MIOF	Mitteilungen des Instituts für Orientforschung. Berlin
MO	Monde Orientale. Uppsala
MRP	Magazin für Religionsphilosophie, Exegese und Kirchengeschichte. Helmstädt
MTh	Melita Theologica. La Valetta
MVÄG	Mitteilungen der vorderasiatisch-ägyptischen Gesellschaft. Leipzig
MVG	Mitteilungen zur vaterländischen Geschichte. St. Gallen
MythBibl.	Mythologische Bibliothek. Leipzig
NC	Nouvelle Clio. Revue Menuelle de la découverte historique. Brussels
NCent	Nineteenth Century and After. London
NKZ	Neue Kirchliche Zeitschrift. Erlangen
NRTh	Nouvelle Revue Théologique. Louvain
NThS	Nieuwe Theologisch Tijdschrift. Haarlem
NTT	Norsk Teologisk Tidsskrift. Oslo
Numen	Numen. Leiden
Numen(Suppl)	Numen (Supplements). Leiden
NZSTh	Neue Zeitschrift für systematische Theologie. Berlin
OLZ	Orientalische Literaturzeitung. Berlin
Or.	Orientalia. Rome
ORPB	Oberrheinisches Pastoralblatt. Freiburg im B.
OSCU	Oriental Studies of the Columbia University. New York
OstKSt	Ostkirchliche Studien. Würzburg
OTS	Oudtestamentische Studien. Leiden

OTSt	Old Testament Studies. Edinburgh
OTWSA.P	Ou Testamentiese Werkgemeenskap in Suid-Afrika. Papers read at . . . Pretoria
Paid.	Paideuma. Frankfurt
PAPS	Proceedings of the American Philosophical Society. Philadelphia
PBl	Pastoralblätter für Homelitek, Katechetik und Seelsorge. Stuttgart
PenCath	Pensée Catholique. Paris
PEQ	Palestine Exploration Quarterly. London
PRE	Paulys Real-Encyclopädie der classischen Altertumswissenschaft. Stuttgart
Protest.	Protestantesimo. Rome
PSBA	Proceedings of the Society of Biblical Archaeology. London
PTh	Pastoraltheologie. Göttingen
QDAP	Quarterly of the Department of Antiquities in Palestine. London
RA	Revue d'Assyriologie et d'Archéologie Orientale. Paris
RAC	Reallexikon für Antike und Christentum. Stuttgart
RB	Revue Biblique. Paris
RBL	Ruch Biblijny i Liturgiczny. Cracow
RCB	Revista de Cultura Biblica. Rio de Janeiro
RE	Realencyklopädie für protestantische Theologie und Kirche. Gotha
REB	Revista eclesiástica Brasileira. Petrópolis
REcL	Revue Ecclesiastique de Liège. Liege
Refor.	Reformation. Berlin
RevBib	Revista Biblica. Buenos Aires
REJ	Revue des Etudes Juives. Paris
RGG	Religion in Geschichte und Gegenwart. Tübingen
RHPhR	Revue d'Histoire et de Philosophie Religieuses. Strasbourg
RHR	Revue de l'Histoire des Religions. Paris
RivBib	Rivista Biblica. Rome
RKZ	Reformierte Kirchenzeitung. Freudenberg
RLA	Reallexikon für Assyriologie. Berlin
RLV	Reallexikon der Vorgeschichte. Berlin
RoB	Religion och Bibel. Stockholm
RoczOr	Rocznik orientalistyczny. Warsaw
RPA	Revue Practique d'Apologètique. Paris
RR	Review of Religion. New York
RSO	Rivista degli Studi Orientali. Rome
RSPhTh	Revue des Sciences Philosophiques et Théologiques. Paris
RSR	Recherches de Science Religieuse. Paris
RThPh	Revue de Theologie et de Philosophie. Lausanne
RTK	Roczniki Teologigczno-kanoniczne. Lublin
RVV	Religionsgeschichtliche Versuche und Vorarbeiten. Giessen
SAAWK	Suid-Afrikaanse Akademie vir Wetenskap en Kuns.
Saec.	Saeculum. Munich
Sal.	Salesianum. Turin
SAOC	Studies in Ancient Oriental Civilization. Chicago
SAVK	Schweizerisches Archiv für Volkskunde. Basel
SBFLA	Studii Biblici Franciscani Liber Annuus. Jerusalem
SBO	Studia Biblica et Orientalia. Roma
SBS	Stuttgarter Bibelstudien. Stuttgart
SBT	Studies in Biblical Theology. London
ScC	Scuola Cattolica. Milan
Schol.	Scholastik. Freiburg im B.
ScrHie	Scripta Hierosolymitana. Jerusalem

Abbreviations

Scrip.	Scripture. Edinburgh
ScrVict	Scriptorium Victoriense. Victoria
SEÅ	Svensk Exegetisk Årsbok. Lund
SEAJT	South East Asia Journal of Theology. Singapore
Sef.	Sefarad. Madrid
Sem.	Semitica. Paris
SGV	Sammlung gemeinverständlicher Vorträge und Schriften. Tübingen
SKG	Schriften der Königsberger Gelehrten Gesellschaft. Halle
SKZ	Schweizerische Kirchenzeitung. Lucern
SMSR	Studi e Materiali di Storia delle Religione. Rome
SNVAO	Skrifter utgitt av det norske videnskaps-akademi i Oslo.
SS	Studi Semitici. Rome
SSN	Studia Semitica Neerlandica. Assen
SSO	Studia Semitica et Orientalia. Glasgow
StANT	Studia Antoniana. Rome
StC	Studia Catholica. Nijmegen
StGen	Studium Generale. Berlin
StHell	Studia Hellenistica. Louvain
SThU	Schweizerische Theologische Umschau. Berne
StOr	Studia Orientalia. Helsinki
StTh	Studia Theologica. Lund
Studiën	Studiën. 's-Hertogenbosch
StZ	Stimmen der Zeit. Freiburg im B.
SvTK	Svensk Teologisk Kvartalskrift. Lund
Syr.	Syria. Paris
Tarb.	Tarbiz. Jerusalem
TB	Theologische Bücherei. Munich
TBTL	Tyndale Biblical Theology Lecture. London
TEH	Theologische Existenz Heute. Munich
Textus	Textus. Jerusalem
ThA	Theologische Arbeiten. Berlin
THAT	*Theologisches Handwörterbuch zum Alten Testament.* edd. E. Jenni/ C. Westermann. Munich/Zürich
ThBl	Theologische Blätter. Leipzig
ThD	Theology Digest. St. Mary's, Kansas
ThGl	Theologie und Glaube. Paderborn
ThLZ	Theologische Literaturzeitung. Leipzig
Thought	Thought. New York
ThPh	Theologie und Philosophie. Freiburg im B.
ThPM	Theologisch-Praktische Monatsschrift. Passau
ThPQ	Theologisch/Praktische Quartalschrift. Linz
ThQ	Theologische Quartalschrift. Tübingen
ThR	Theologische Rundschau. Tübingen
ThSt(B)	Theologische Studien. Ed. K. Barth. Zurich
ThSt(U)	Theologische Studien. Utrecht
ThT	Theologisch Tijdschrift. Leiden
ThTh	Themen der Theologie. Stuttgart
ThViat	Theologia Viatorum. Berlin
ThW	Theologische Wissenschaft. Stuttgart
ThWAT	*Theologisches Wörterbuch zum Alten testament.* edd. G. J. Botterweek/H. Ringgren. Stuttgart (English. *Theological Dictionary of the Old Testament* I, 1974ff.)
ThWNT	*Theologisches Wörterbuch zum Neuen Testament.* ed. G. Kittel. Stuttgart (in English trans.)

ThZ	Theologische Zeitschrift. Basel
TS	Theological Studies. Woodstock, Md.
TOTL	Tyndale Old Testament Lecture. London
TS.AAJR	Texts and Studies. American Academy for Jewish Research. New York
TThQ	Tübinger Theologische Quartalschrift. Stuttgart
TThSt	Trierer Theologische Studien. Trier
TThZ	Trierer Theologische Zeitschrift. Trier
TTK	Tidsskrift for Teologi og Kirke. Oslo
TynB	Tyndale Bulletin. London
UÄA	Urkunden des ägyptischen Altertums. Leipzig
UF	Ugarit-Forschungen. Neukirchen.
Ug.	Ugaritica. Paris
US	Una Sancta. Meitingen
UUÅ	Uppsala Universitets Årsskrift. Uppsala
UVB	Uruk. Vorläufiger Bericht.
VAA(EK)	Veröffentlichungen der Arbeitsgemeinschaft für das Archiv- und Bibliothekswesen in der evangelischen Kirche. Neustadt
VAB	Vorderasiatische Bibliothek. Leipzig
VD	Verbum Domini. Rome
VF	Verkündigung und Forschung. Munich
VigChr	Vigiliae Christianae. Amsterdam
VMAW	Verslagen en mededeelingen der k. akademie van wetenschappen. Amsterdam
VT	Vetus Testamentum. Leiden
VT.S	Vetus Testamentum. Supplements. Lieden
VyV	Verdad y Vida. Madrid
WiWei	Wissenschaft und Weisheit. Freiburg im B.
WO	Welt des Orients. Göttingen
WPKG	Wissenschaft und Praxis in Kirche und Gesellschaft. Göttingen
WThJ	Westminster Theological Journal. Philadelphia
WVDOG	Wissenschaftliche Veröffentlichungen der deutschen Orientgesellschaft. Leipzig
WZKM	Wiener Zeitschrift für die Kunde des Morgenlandes. Vienna
WZ(L)	Wissenschaftliche Zeitschrift der Karl-Marx-Universität. Leipzig.
YOS	Yale Oriental Series. New Haven, Conn.
ZA n.f.	Zeitschrift für Assyriologie. Leipzig
ZÄS	Zeitschrift für ägyptische Sprache und Altertumskunde. Berlin
ZAW	Zeitschrift für die alttestamentliche Wissenschaft. Berlin
ZBK	Zürcher Bibelkommentare. Zurich
ZDMG	Zeitschrift der deutschen morgenländischen Gesellschaft. Wiesbaden
ZDPV	Zeitschrift des deutschen Palästina-Vereins. Wiesbaden
ZE	Zeitschrift für Ethnologie. Braunschweig
ZEvRU	Zeitschrift für den evangelische Religionsunterricht. Berlin
ZKG	Zeitschrift für Kirchengeschichte. Stuttgart
ZKRU	Zeitschrift für den Katholischen Religionsunterricht an höheren Schulen. Düsseldorf
ZKTh	Zeitschrift für katholische Theologie. Vienna
ZMR	Zeitschrift für Missionskunde und Religionswissenschaft. Berlin
ZNW	Zeitschrift für die neutestamentliche Wissenschaft. Berlin
ZRGG	Zeitschrift für Religions- und Geistesgeschichte. Cologne.
ZThK	Zeitschrift für Theologie und Kirche. Tübingen

Index of Hebrew Words

(exclusive of proper names peculiar to genealogies)

Index of Hebrew Words

Index of Biblical References

Index of Biblical References

41			30	198	32	
1	294	10			10ff.	55
42			2	312	14	410
36	517		13	130	34	224
43			15	126	33	
11	294		28	224	19	341
21	369	12			34	
44			12	101	10	99
9f.	311		17	436	21	173
23	369		41	294, 436	35	
45			51	436	1-3	173
7	423	13			2	170
46			17	369	35	170
9	327, 357	14			36	
30	231		16,21	433	1,4,7	170
47		15			39	
27	140		5,8	105	3	117
48			16	290	32-43	170
4	140		21	46, 334	40	
22	522	16			33f.	170
49	485		15	162		
16	493		29f.	173	**Leviticus**	
23	422	18			1	
25	105		4	227	9	454
33	170	19			5	
50			1,2a	172, 437	2	136
20	423		12b	467	6	
			17b	311	10	463
Exodus	8	20			7	
1- 18	2		9,11	170, 172f.	34	463
1-3	64		17	249	9	
1			18	308	22f.	140
7	136, 140		26	488	10	
10	545	21			17	463
21	369		23-25	467	11	
2			28-32	466	3-5	125
2	166	22			10	136
3,5	420		5	265	14	126
18	563		26f.	489	19f.	137
24	441	23			20f.	136
3	42, 339, 578		12	173	22,29	126
8	550		18f.	464	29	126, 136
4		24			39	162
11	202		15b-18	172, 599	41f.	136
24ff.	313		25ff.	424	46	136
5			25-27	412f.	12	
1	101		25	170	2-7	160
6	42, 339, 578, 599		1f.	111, 451, 599	15	
3	578f.	29			33	160
14	327		18,25,41	454	16	
28	198, 224	31			20	170
7			6	162	18	488
9,12	138		12-17	173	3	485
28	136		12-14	171	20	488
9			14	170	22	
5	130		16	162, 474	5	136
25	202		17	173	23	
27	231	32-34		67	19,21	436

Index of Biblical References

Index of Biblical References

Index of Biblical References

Index of Subjects

Index of Names

633